Microsoft Windows XP

SERVICE PACK 2 EDITION

Complete Concepts and Techniques

Microsoft Windows XP

SERVICE PACK 2 EDITION

Complete Concepts and Techniques

Gary B. Shelly
Thomas J. Cashman
Steven G. Forsythe

Shelly Cashman Series®
An imprint of Course Technology, Cengage Learning

Australia • Brazil • Japan • Korea • Mexico • Singapore • Spain • United Kingdom • United States

COURSE TECHNOLOGY
CENGAGE Learning™

Microsoft Windows XP
Complete Concepts and Techniques, Service Pack 2 Edition

Gary B. Shelly
Thomas J. Cashman
Steven G. Forsythe

Managing Editor: Alexandra Arnold

Senior Acquisitions Editor: Dana Merk

Senior Product Manager: Karen Stevens

Product Manager: Reed Cotter

Associate Product Manager: Selena Coppock

Print Buyer: Laura Burns

Production Editor: Jennifer Goguen

Quality Assurance: Alex White, Shawn Day

Copy Editor: Marilyn Martin, Foxxe Editorial

Proofreader: Lori Silfen, Christine Clark

Composition: GEX Publishing Services

ISBN-13: 978-0-619-25496-4

ISBN-10: 0-619-25496-3

Course Technology
25 Thomson Place
Boston, Massachusetts 02210
USA

Cengage Learning is a leading provider of customized learning solutions with office locations around the globe, including Singapore, the United Kingdom, Australia, Mexico, Brazil, and Japan. Locate your local office at: **international.cengage.com/region**

Cengage Learning products are represented in Canada by Nelson Education, Ltd.

For your lifelong learning solutions, visit **course.cengage.com**

Purchase any of our products at your local college store or at our preferred online store **www.ichapters.com**

PHOTO CREDITS: *Project 1, pages WIN 1.04-05* Bill Gates, Courtesy of Microsoft Corporation; *Project 3, pages WIN 3.02-03* sport car, sunset, and road, Courtesy of Art Today; computer, Courtesy of PhotoDisc, Inc; moon landing, Courtesy of Nova Development; other images, Courtesy of Art Today; *Project 4 pages WIN 4.02-03* Golf, flying toasters, little girl, Courtesy of Nova Development; *Project 5 pages WIN 5.02-03* Timepunch clock, man looking at watch, clock at angle, profile of man, blocks of gold, monitor, green timepunch clock, scale, Courtesy of PhotoDisc, Inc; *Project 6 pages WIN 6.02-03* Icons, clouds and grass, papers, Courtesy of Art Today.

Printed in the United States of America
7 8 9 10 09 08

Microsoft Windows XP

SERVICE PACK 2 EDITION

Complete Concepts and Techniques

Contents

3 PROJECT THREE

File, Document, and Folder Management and Windows XP Explorer

4 PROJECT FOUR

Modifying Your Desktop Work Environment

5 PROJECT FIVE

Customizing Your Computer Using Control Panel

6 PROJECT SIX

Advanced File and Web Searching

APPENDIX A

APPENDIX B

Preface

The Shelly Cashman Series® offers the finest textbooks in computer education. We are proud of the fact that our *Microsoft Windows 3.1, Microsoft Windows 95, Microsoft Windows 98,* and *Microsoft Windows 2000* textbooks have been so well received by instructors and students. The *Microsoft Windows XP* books continue with the innovation, quality, and reliability found in these previous editions. This Service Pack 2 Edition includes the following enhancements:

- Updated throughout for Service Pack 2
- All new appendix on Windows XP Service Pack 2 security features
- Tear-off quick reference Windows XP CourseCard, providing Windows skills at your fingertips

In our *Windows XP* books, you will find an educationally sound and easy-to-follow pedagogy that combines a step-by-step approach with corresponding screens. The Other Ways and More About features offer in-depth knowledge of Windows XP. The project openers provide a fascinating perspective on the subject covered in the project. The Shelly Cashman Series *Microsoft Windows XP* textbooks will make your computer operating system class exciting and dynamic and one that your students will remember as one of their better educational experiences.

Features of Microsoft Windows XP

Microsoft Windows XP is the most significant upgrade since the introduction of Windows 95. The enhancements to Windows XP include: (1) a new look and feel to the user interface; (2) increased reliability and security; (3) increased performance to run programs faster; (4) the ability to create multiple user accounts and easily switch between accounts: (5) a redesigned Start menu and Control Panel; (6) a more comprehensive Help and Support system; (7) increased emphasis on the use of digital media; (8) an easy-to-install home or small office network; and (9) new versions of Windows Media Player, Movie Maker, Internet Explorer, and Windows Messenger. The Service Pack 2 update to Windows XP offers additional security features.

You can upgrade from your current Windows operating system to either Windows XP Professional or Windows XP Home Edition. Windows XP Professional includes all the features of Windows XP Home Edition, plus extra features for business and power users. For more information about the new features of Windows XP and the differences between Windows XP Professional and Windows XP Home Edition, see Appendix A. For more information on the enhancements provided by the Service Pack 2 installation, see Appendix B.

Windows XP and the Figures in This Book

The figures in this book were created using Windows XP Professional. If you plan to step through the projects in this book, you may notice subtle differences between the images on your desktop and the corresponding figure in the book. These differences may be due to the Windows version from which you upgraded; the Internet connection used; or the version of Windows XP installed on the computer. For example, the commands on the Start menu in Home Edition may be different from those in Professional; a button or tab in a dialog box may be different; or a default setting may be different. Although the vast majority of the steps in this book work with both Home Edition and Professional, any steps that do not work with Home Edition are identified.

Objectives of This Textbook

Microsoft Windows XP: Complete Concepts and Techniques, Service Pack 2 Edition is intended for a six- to ten-week, two-unit course that covers Windows XP. No computer experience is assumed. The objectives of this book are:

- To teach the fundamentals and skills necessary to use Windows XP adequately
- To provide a knowledge base for Windows XP upon which students can build
- To expose students to real-world examples and procedures that will prepare them to be skilled users of Windows XP
- To encourage independent study and help those who are working alone

Other Ways

1. Click Switch to Classic View, double-click Keyboard icon, drag Repeat rate slider
2. Click Start button, click Help and Support, click Index button, type `keyboards`, double-click adjusting repeat rate and repeat delay, click Keyboard link, drag Repeat delay slider

The Shelly Cashman Approach

Features of the Shelly Cashman Series *Microsoft Windows XP* books include:

- Project Orientation: Related topics are presented using a project orientation that establishes a strong foundation on which students can confidently learn more advanced topics.
- Screen-by-Screen, Step-by-Step Instructions: Each task required to complete a project is identified throughout the development of the project. Then, steps to accomplish the task are specified and are accompanied by screen shots.
- Thoroughly Tested Projects: Every screen in the textbook is correct because it is produced by the author only after performing a step, which results in unprecedented quality.
- Two-Page Project Openers: Each project begins with a two-page opener that sets the tone for the project by describing an interesting aspect of Windows XP.
- Other Ways Boxes for Reference: Microsoft Windows XP provides a variety of ways to carry out a given task. The Other Ways boxes displayed at the end of most of the step-by-step sequences specify the other ways to do the task completed in the steps. Thus, the steps and the Other Ways box make a comprehensive reference unit.
- More About Feature: These marginal annotations provide background information about the topics covered, adding interest and depth to learning.

More About

Locating All Files and Folders

The Search Companion is the easiest way to locate a file or folder. Windows Explorer provides a quick way to view files and folders, My Computer provides a simpler view of folders, and My Network Places provides a view of computers, files and folders, printers, and other network resources.

Organization of This Textbook

Microsoft Windows XP: Complete Concepts and Techniques, Service Pack 2 Edition provides detailed instruction on how to use Windows XP. The material is divided into six projects and an appendix:

Project 1 – Fundamentals of Using Microsoft Windows XP In Project 1, students learn about user interfaces and Microsoft Windows XP. Topics include launching Microsoft Windows XP; logging on to the computer; using the Start menu; adding icons to the desktop; maximizing and minimizing windows; moving, sizing, and scrolling windows; launching an application program; using Windows Help and Support; logging off from the computer; and turning off the computer.

Project 2 – Working on the Windows XP Desktop In Project 2, students work on the Windows XP desktop. Topics include creating a document on the desktop by launching an application; creating and naming a document on the desktop; opening, saving, printing, and closing a document on the desktop; storing documents in the My Documents folder; opening, modifying, and printing documents within a folder; creating shortcuts on the Start menu and desktop; copying a folder onto a disk; deleting documents, shortcuts, and folders; working with and switching between user accounts; and changing the user password and picture.

Project 3 – File, Document, and Folder Management and Windows XP Explorer
In Project 3, students manage open windows on the desktop and learn to use Windows XP Explorer. Topics include using the My Computer window; changing the format of icons in a window; displaying drive and folder contents; opening a document and launching an application program from a window; cascading and tiling open windows; launching Windows XP Explorer; displaying files, folders, and drive and folder contents in Explorer; expanding a drive or folder; launching an application from Explorer; copying, moving, renaming, and deleting files and folders; displaying object properties; organizing and storing files in the My Pictures folder; viewing pictures in filmstrip view and as a slide show; sharing folders and e-mailing pictures; finding files and folders; and using the Run command.

Project 4 – Modifying Your Desktop Work Environment In Project 4, students modify desktop properties, display Web content on the desktop, customize the taskbar, customize folders, and change folder options. Topics include changing the desktop environment; desktop themes and appearance; screen savers; adding active desktop items to the desktop; customizing the taskbar; adding a toolbar to the taskbar; adding a shortcut icon to a toolbar; using the Address toolbar to display Web pages; customizing the Start menu and notification area; changing folder options; and working with underlined icons.

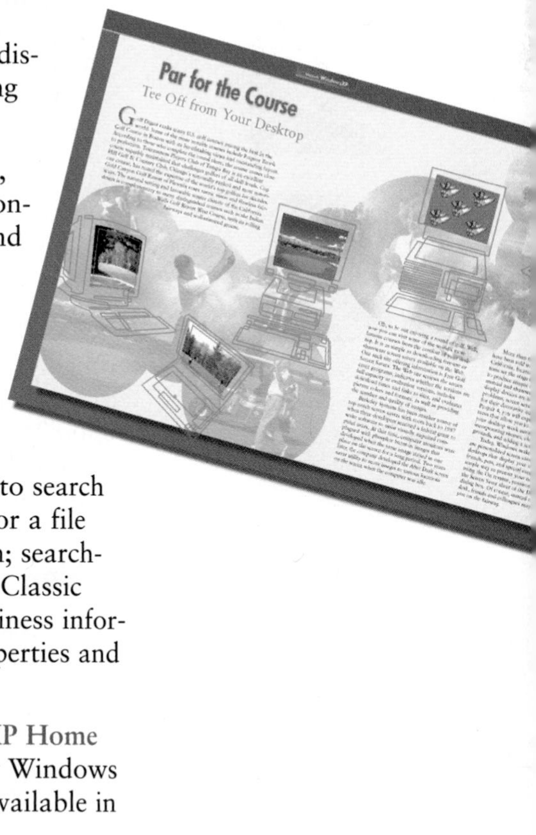

Project 5 – Customizing Your Computer Using Control Panel In Project 5, students customize the Windows XP environment using the tasks in the Control Panel folder. Topics include customizing the keyboard, mouse, date, and time; customizing the computer for physically challenged people; viewing user accounts and privileges; adding a hardware device and printer; using Troubleshooters to solve hardware problems; viewing hardware properties; and adding and removing a software program.

Project 6 – Advanced File and Web Searching In Project 6, students search for files on the computer and Web pages on the Internet. Topics include specifying a beginning point of a search; using Search Companion to search for all files and folders, digital media files, and document files; searching for a file based on the date, file type, or a word or phrase in the file; saving a search; searching for picture, music, and video files; changing a search preference; using Classic Internet Search to search for Web pages, mailing addresses, maps, and business information; restoring a deleted file using the Recycle Bin; and viewing the properties and emptying the contents of the Recycle Bin.

Appendix A – New Features of Windows XP Professional and Windows XP Home Edition Appendix A at the back of this book provides a listing of the new Windows XP features including a comparison that identifies whether the feature is available in both editions.

Appendix B -- Windows XP Service Pack 2 Security Features Appendix B at the back of the book provides students with an understanding of the new security features offered in Service Pack 2, including Windows Security Center.

Windows XP CourseCard – This highly visual, four-color, six-sided CourseCard on Windows XP allows you quick access to tips and tricks long after your class is complete.

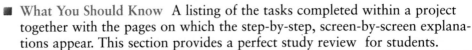

End-of-Project Student Activities

A notable strength of the Shelly Cashman Series *Microsoft Windows XP* textbooks is the extensive student activities at the end of each project. Well-structured student activities can make the difference between students merely participating in a class and students retaining the information they learn. These activities include:

- What You Should Know A listing of the tasks completed within a project together with the pages on which the step-by-step, screen-by-screen explanations appear. This section provides a perfect study review for students.
- Learn It Online Every project features a Learn It Online page comprised of ten exercises. These exercises utilize the Web to offer project-related reinforcement activities that will help students gain confidence in their Windows XP abilities. These exercises include True/False, Multiple Choice, Short Answer, Flash Cards, Practice Test, Learning Games, Tips and Tricks, Newsgroup usage, Expanding Your Horizons, and Search Sleuth.
- Use Help Users of Windows XP must know how to use Help and Support. This book contains extensive Help activities. These exercises alone distinguish the Shelly Cashman Series from any other set of Windows XP instructional materials.
- In the Lab These assignments require students to make use of the knowledge gained in the project to solve problems on a computer.
- Cases and Places Unique case studies allow students to apply their knowledge to real-world situations. These case studies provide subjects for research papers based on information gained from a resource such as the Internet.

Shelly Cashman Series Teaching Tools

Two categories of ancillary material accompany this textbook: Teaching Tools (ISBN 0-7895-6597-8) and Online Content. These ancillaries are available to adopters through your Course Technology representative or by calling one of the following telephone numbers: Colleges and Universities, 1-800-648-7450; High Schools, 1-800-824-5179; Private Career Colleges, 1-800-648-7450; Canada, 1-800-268-2222; Corporations with IT Training Centers, 1-800-648-7450; and Government Agencies, Health-Care Organizations, and Correctional Facilities, 1-800-477-3692.

Teaching Tools

The Teaching Tools for this textbook include both teaching and testing aids. The contents of the Teaching Tools CD-ROM are listed below.

- Instructor's Manual The Instructor's Manual is made up of Microsoft Word files that include lecture notes, solutions to laboratory assignments, and a large test bank. The files allow you to modify the lecture notes or generate quizzes and exams from the test bank using your own word processing software. Where appropriate, solutions to laboratory assignments are embedded as icons.
- Figures in the Book Illustrations for every screen in the textbook are available. Use this ancillary to create a slide show from the illustrations for lecture or to print transparencies for use in lecture with an overhead projector.
- ExamView ExamView is a state-of-the-art test builder that is easy to use. ExamView enables you to quickly create printed tests, Internet tests, and computer (LAN-based) tests. You can enter your own test questions or use the test bank that accompanies ExamView. The test bank is the same as the one described in the Instructor's Manual section.

- Course Syllabus Any instructor who has been assigned a course at the last minute knows how difficult it is to come up with a course syllabus. For this reason, sample syllabi are included that can be customized easily to a course.
- Project Reinforcement True/false, multiple choice, and short answer questions help students gain confidence in their abilities.
- Interactive Labs Eighteen completely updated, hands-on Interactive Labs that take students from ten to fifteen minutes each to step through help solidify and reinforce mouse and keyboard usage and computer concepts. Student assessment is available.
- PowerPoint Presentation This lecture ancillary contains a PowerPoint presentation for each project in the textbook. You also may make these PowerPoint presentations available to students on the network for project review, or to be printed for classroom distribution.

Online Content

If you use Blackboard or WebCT, a free test bank for this textbook is available in a simple, ready-to-use format. Visit the Instructor Resource Center for this textbook at course.com to download the test bank, or contact your local sales representative for details.

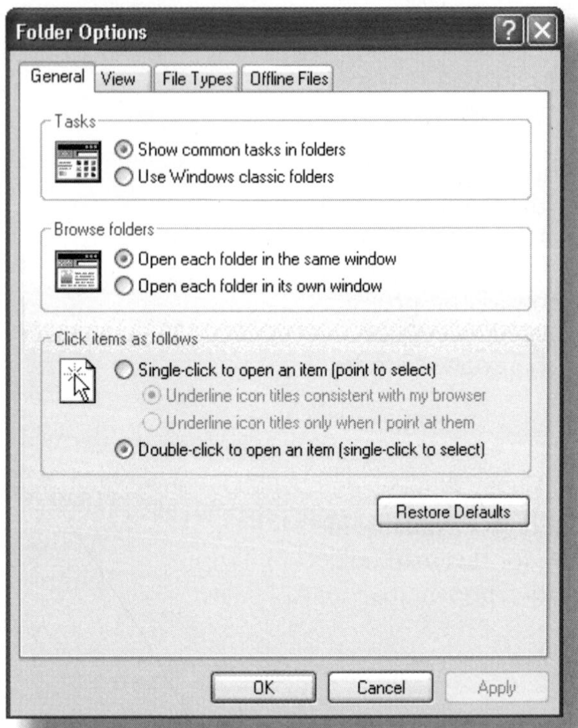

FIGURE 1

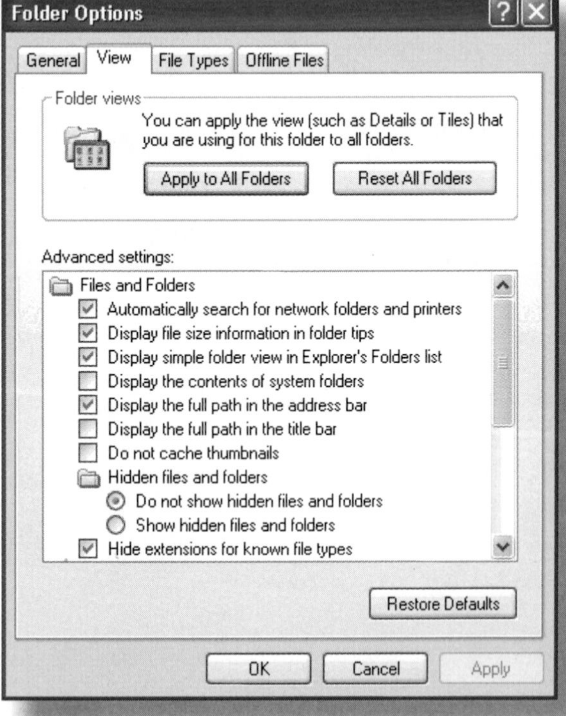

FIGURE 2

Instructions for Restoring the Default Folder Options Settings

The projects and assignments in this textbook are presented using the default folder options settings, as chosen by Microsoft. To ensure your success in completing the projects and assignments, you must install the Windows XP operating system on your computer and restore the folder option settings. The following steps illustrate how to restore the default folder option settings.

1. Click the Start button on the taskbar and then click the My Computer command on the Start menu.
2. Click Tools on the My Computer menu bar.
3. Click the Folder Options command on the Tools menu to display the Folder Options dialog box (Figure 1).
4. If necessary, click the General tab in the Folder Options dialog box to display the General sheet.
5. On a piece of paper, write down the name of each folder option that is selected in the General sheet in the Folder Options dialog box.
6. Click the Restore Defaults button in the General sheet.
7. Click the View tab to display the View sheet (Figure 2).
8. On a piece of paper, write down the name of each advanced setting that is selected in the View sheet in the Folder Options dialog box.
9. Click the Restore Defaults button in the View sheet.
10. Click the OK button in the Folder Options dialog box.
11. Click the Close button in the My Computer window.

As a result of restoring the default folder option settings, you can perform the steps and assignments in each project of this book. If, after finishing the steps and assignments, you must restore the folder options to their original settings, perform steps 1 through 4 above, click the option button of each setting you wrote down in step 5, perform step 7 above, click the check box and option button of each setting you wrote down in step 8, and then perform step 10 and step 11.

Shelly Cashman Series – Traditionally Bound Textbooks

The Shelly Cashman Series presents the following computer subjects in a variety of traditionally bound textbooks. For more information, see your Course Technology representative or call 1-800-648-7450. For Shelly Cashman Series information, visit Shelly Cashman Series at **scseries.com**

COMPUTERS	
Computers	Discovering Computers 2006: A Gateway to Information, Complete Discovering Computers 2006: A Gateway to Information, Introductory Discovering Computers 2006: A Gateway to Information, Brief Discovering Computers: Fundamentals, Second Edition Teachers Discovering Computers: Integrating Technology in the Classroom, Third Edition Essential Introduction to Computers, Sixth Edition (40-page)
WINDOWS APPLICATIONS	
Microsoft Office	Microsoft Office 2003: Essential Concepts and Techniques (5 projects) Microsoft Office 2003: Brief Concepts and Techniques (9 projects) Microsoft Office 2003: Introductory Concepts and Techniques, Second Edition (15 projects) Microsoft Office 2003: Advanced Concepts and Techniques (12 projects) Microsoft Office 2003: Post Advanced Concepts and Techniques (11 projects) Microsoft Office XP: Essential Concepts and Techniques (5 projects) Microsoft Office XP: Brief Concepts and Techniques (9 projects) Microsoft Office XP: Introductory Concepts and Techniques, Windows XP Edition (15 projects) Microsoft Office XP: Introductory Concepts and Techniques, Enhanced Edition (15 projects) Microsoft Office XP: Advanced Concepts and Techniques (11 projects) Microsoft Office XP: Post Advanced Concepts and Techniques (11 projects)
Integration	Teachers Discovering and Integrating Microsoft Office: Essential Concepts and Techniques, Second Edition Integrating Microsoft Office XP Applications and the World Wide Web: Essential Concepts and Techniques
PIM	Microsoft Outlook 2002: Essential Concepts and Techniques • Microsoft Office Outlook 2003: Introductory Concepts and Techniques
Microsoft Works	Microsoft Works 6: Complete Concepts and Techniques[1] • Microsoft Works 2000: Complete Concepts and Techniques[1]
Microsoft Windows	Microsoft Windows XP: Comprehensive Concepts and Techniques[2] Microsoft Windows XP: Brief Concepts and Techniques Microsoft Windows 2000: Comprehensive Concepts and Techniques[2] Microsoft Windows 2000: Brief Concepts and Techniques Microsoft Windows 98: Comprehensive Concepts and Techniques[2] Microsoft Windows 98: Essential Concepts and Techniques Introduction to Microsoft Windows NT Workstation 4
Notebook Organizer	Microsoft Office OneNote 2003: Introductory Concepts and Techniques
Word Processing	Microsoft Office Word 2003: Comprehensive Concepts and Techniques[2] • Microsoft Word 2002: Comprehensive Concepts and Techniques[2]
Spreadsheets	Microsoft Office Excel 2003: Comprehensive Concepts and Techniques[2] • Microsoft Excel 2002: Comprehensive Concepts and Techniques[2]
Database	Microsoft Office Access 2003: Comprehensive Concepts and Techniques[2] • Microsoft Access 2002: Comprehensive Concepts and Techniques[2]
Presentation Graphics	Microsoft Office PowerPoint 2003: Comprehensive Concepts and Techniques[2] • Microsoft PowerPoint 2002: Comprehensive Concepts and Techniques[2]
Desktop Publishing	Microsoft Office Publisher 2003: Comprehensive Concepts and Techniques[2] • Microsoft Publisher 2002: Comprehensive Concepts and Techniques[1]
PROGRAMMING	
Programming	Microsoft Visual Basic .NET: Comprehensive Concepts and Techniques[2] • Microsoft Visual Basic 6: Complete Concepts and Techniques[1] • Java Programming: Comprehensive Concepts and Techniques, Second Edition[2] • Structured COBOL Programming, Second Edition • Understanding and Troubleshooting Your PC • Programming Fundamentals Using Microsoft Visual Basic .NET
INTERNET	
Concepts	Discovering the Internet: Brief Concepts and Techniques • Discovering the Internet: Complete Concepts and Techniques
Browser	Microsoft Internet Explorer 6: Introductory Concepts and Techniques, Windows XP Edition • Microsoft Internet Explorer 5: An Introduction • Netscape Navigator 6: An Introduction
Web Page Creation	Web Design: Introductory Concepts and Techniques • HTML: Comprehensive Concepts and Techniques, Third Edition[2] • Microsoft Office FrontPage 2003: Comprehensive Concepts and Techniques[2] • Microsoft FrontPage 2002: Comprehensive Concepts and Techniques[2] • Microsoft FrontPage 2002: Essential Concepts and Techniques • JavaScript: Complete Concepts and Techniques, Second Edition[1] • Macromedia Dreamweaver MX: Comprehensive Concepts and Techniques[2]
SYSTEMS ANALYSIS	
Systems Analysis	Systems Analysis and Design, Sixth Edition
DATA COMMUNICATIONS	
Data Communications	Business Data Communications: Introductory Concepts and Techniques, Fourth Edition

[1]Also available as an Introductory Edition, which is a shortened version of the complete book, [2]Also available as an Introductory Edition and as a Complete Edition, which are shortened versions of the comprehensive book.

XP

Microsoft

WINDOWS

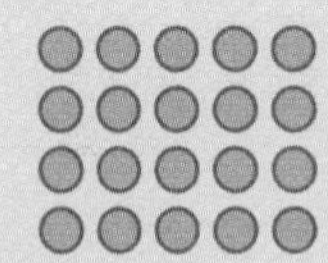

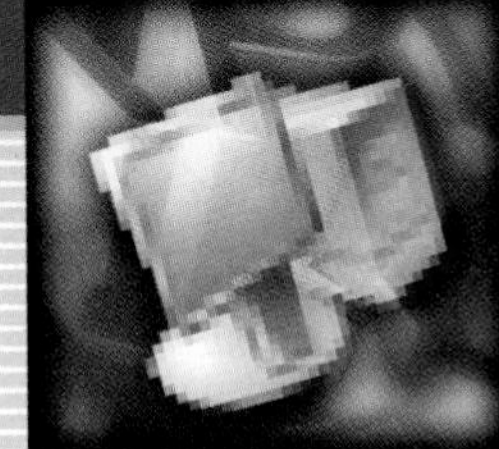

Microsoft Windows XP

PROJECT

Fundamentals of Using Microsoft Windows XP

OBJECTIVES

You will have mastered the material in this project when you can:

- Describe Microsoft Windows XP and Windows XP Service Pack 2
- Explain operating system, server, workstation, and user interface
- Log on to the computer
- Perform the basic mouse operations: point, click, right-click, double-click, drag, and right-drag
- Identify the objects on the desktop
- Display the Start menu
- Identify the My Computer and My Documents windows
- Add and remove a desktop icon
- Open, minimize, maximize, restore, and close a window
- Move and size a window on the desktop
- Scroll in a window
- Understand keyboard shortcut notation
- Launch an application program
- Use Windows XP Help and Support
- Log off from the computer and turn off the computer

Windows XP

Fast at Any Speed

Publicized as the fastest Windows operating system yet, Windows XP continues the momentum with quicker startup, better performance, and a new, simplified visual appearance. Innovative products continue to evolve under the leadership and guidance of Bill Gates, Microsoft's chairman and chief software architect.

Bill Gates's computing efforts began when he was in grade school, when he and classmate, Paul Allen, learned the BASIC programming language from a manual and programmed a mainframe computer using a Teletype terminal they purchased with the proceeds from a rummage sale. In high school, their thirst for more computing power continued. Gates and Allen wrote custom programs for local businesses during the summer and split their $5,000 salaries between cash and computer time. They also debugged software problems at local businesses in return for computer use.

By the time Gates was a sophomore in high school, he was teaching his computer skills to his classmates at the request of one of his teachers. In 1972, Gates and Allen read an article in Electronics magazine about Intel's first microprocessor chip.

Start
1972
1975
1980
1985
1990
1995
2001
Bill Gates
File Edit View Help

They requested a manual from Intel, developed a device that experimented with pushing the chip to its limits, and formed the Traf-O-Data company; an endeavor that ultimately would lead to the formation of something much larger.

In 1973, Gates entered Harvard and Allen landed a programming job with Honeywell. They continued to communicate and scheme about the power of computers.

Then, in 1975, the Altair 8800 computer showed up on the cover of Popular Electronics. This computer was about the size of the Traf-O-Data device and contained a new Intel computer chip. At that point, they knew they were going into business. Gates left Harvard and Allen left Honeywell.

When they formed Microsoft in 1975, the company had three programmers, one product, and revenues of $16,000. The founders had no business plan, no capital, and no financial backing, but they did have a product - a form of the BASIC programming language tailored for the first microcomputer.

IBM approached Microsoft in 1980 and asked the company to provide an operating system for its new IBM personal computer. The deadline? Three months. Gates purchased the core of a suitable operating system, dubbed Q-DOS (Quick and Dirty Operating System). Microsoft's version, MS-DOS, would become the international standard for IBM and IBM-compatible personal computers. Riding the meteoric rise in sales of IBM-compatible computers and attendant sales of MS-DOS, Microsoft continued to improve its software stream of revisions. At a significant branch of the family tree, Windows made its debut, providing an intuitive graphical user interface (GUI). Similarly, Windows 95, Windows 98, Windows NT, Windows 2000, and Windows Millennium provided further advances.

The Microsoft Windows XP operating system family (Windows XP Professional, Windows XP Home Edition, Windows XP Media Center Edition, Windows XP Table PC Edition, and Windows XP 64-Bit Edition) sets high standards for efficiency and stability and provides advanced productivity and support tools. Appendix A at the back of this book provides a table of new features and compares the two editions. As you complete the projects in this book, you will gain the skills you need to work in the Windows XP environment and see for yourself how its advanced functionality can make your job easier.

Microsoft Windows XP

Fundamentals of Using Microsoft Windows XP

PROJECT

CASE PERSPECTIVE

After weeks of planning, your organization finally installed Microsoft Windows XP on all workstations. As the computer trainer for the upcoming in-house seminar, you realize you should know more about Microsoft Windows XP but have had little time to learn. Since installing Windows XP, many employees have come to you with questions. You have taken the time to answer their questions by sitting down with them at their computers and searching for the answers using the Microsoft Help and Support feature.

From their questions, you determine that you should customize the seminar to cover the basics of Windows XP, including basic mouse operations, working with windows, launching an application, and searching for answers to their questions using Windows XP Help and Support. Your goal is to become familiar with Microsoft Windows XP in order to teach the seminar effectively to the participants.

Introduction

An **operating system** is the set of computer instructions, called a computer program, that controls the allocation of computer hardware such as memory, disk devices, printers, and CD-ROM and DVD drives, and provides the capability for you to communicate with the computer. The most popular and widely used operating system is **Microsoft Windows**. **Microsoft Windows XP**, the newest version of Microsoft Windows, allows you to easily communicate with and control your computer.

Microsoft Windows XP Operating Systems Editions

The Microsoft Windows XP operating systems consist of Microsoft Windows XP Professional, Microsoft Windows XP Home Edition, Microsoft Windows XP Media Center Edition, Microsoft Windows XP Tablet PC Edition, and Microsoft Windows XP 64-Bit Edition.

Microsoft Windows XP Professional is the operating system designed for businesses of all sizes and for advanced home computing. Windows XP is called a **32-bit operating system** because it uses 32 bits for addressing and other purposes, which means the operating system can perform tasks faster than older operating systems. In business, Windows XP Professional is commonly used on computer workstations and portable computers. A **workstation** is a computer connected to a server. A **server** is a computer that controls access to the hardware and software on a network and provides a centralized storage area for programs, data, and information. Figure 1-1 illustrates a simple computer network consisting of a server and three computers (called workstations) and a laser printer connected to the server.

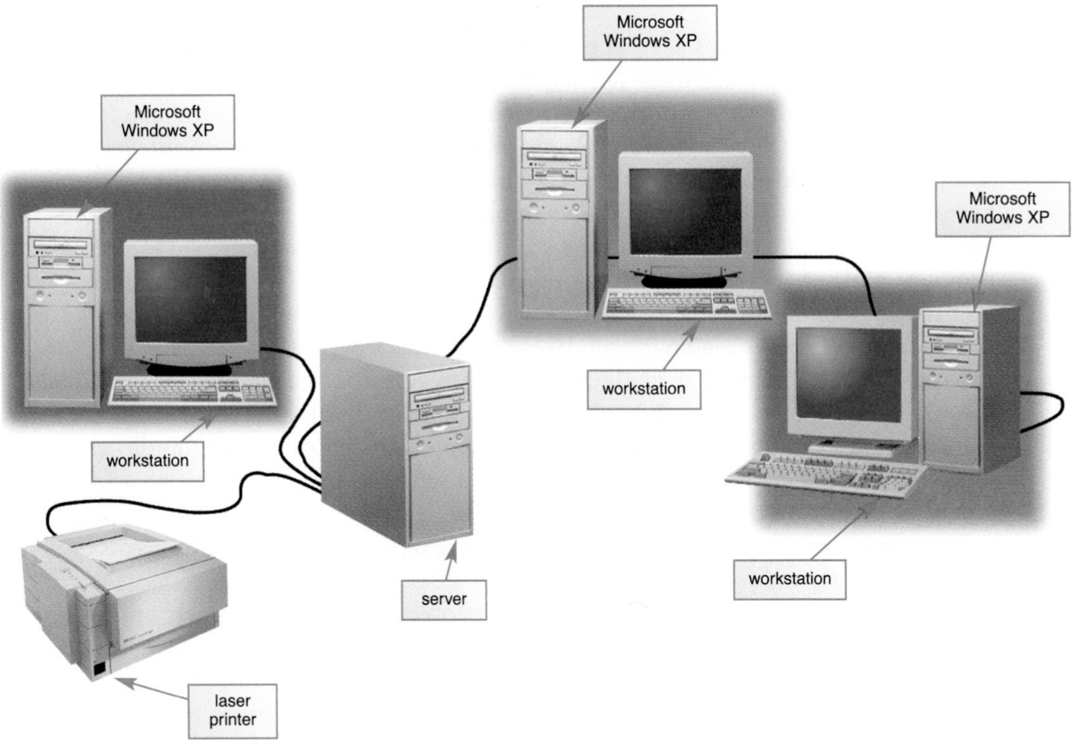

FIGURE 1-1

Microsoft Windows XP Home Edition is designed for entertainment and home use. Home Edition allows you to establish in the home a network of computers that share a single Internet connection, share a device such as a printer or a scanner, share files and folders, and play multi-computer games.

Microsoft Windows XP Media Center Edition is designed for use with a Media Center PC. A **Media Center PC** is a home entertainment desktop personal computer that includes a mid- to high-end processor, large capacity hard disk, CD and DVD drives, a remote control, and advanced graphics and audio capabilities. **Microsoft Windows XP Tablet PC Edition** is designed for use on a special type of notebook computer, called a Tablet PC. A **Tablet PC** allows you to write on the device's screen using a digital pen and convert the handwriting into characters the Tablet PC can process. A **Windows XP 64-Bit Edition** is also available for individuals solving complex scientific problems, developing high-performance design and engineering applications, or creating 3-D animations.

> **More About**
>
> **Microsoft Windows XP**
>
> Microsoft Windows XP combines the best features of Microsoft Windows 98 with the power and reliability of Microsoft Windows 2000. Windows 98, designed for use on personal computers, is the most popular operating system for personal computers. Windows 2000, designed for use on a computer network, is the most widely used business version of Windows.

Windows XP Service Pack 2

Periodically, Microsoft releases a free update to the Windows XP operating system. These updates, referred to as **service packs**, contain fixes and enhancements to the operating system. In August 2004, Microsoft released the Windows XP Service Pack 2 (SP2). **Windows XP Service Pack 2** contains advanced security features that protect a computer against viruses, worms, and hackers. For more information about Windows XP Service Pack 2, see the More About on page WIN 1.08.

Microsoft Windows XP Professional

Microsoft Windows XP (called **Windows XP** for the rest of the book) is an operating system that performs every function necessary for you to communicate with and use the computer.

More About

Microsoft Windows XP

A vast amount of information about Microsoft Windows XP is available on the Internet. For additional information about Microsoft Windows XP, launch the Internet Explorer browser (see pages WIN 1.45 and WIN 1.46), type `www.scsite.com/winxp/more.htm` in the Address box in the Microsoft Internet Explorer window, and then press the ENTER key.

Microsoft Windows XP Service Pack 2

A table summarizing the new features contained in the Windows XP Service Pack 2 is available on the Internet. For additional information about Windows XP Service Pack 2, visit the Windows XP More About Web Page (www.scsite.com/winxp/more.htm) and then click Windows XP Service Pack 2.

More About

The Windows XP Interface

Some older interfaces, called command-line interfaces, required that you type keywords (special words, phrases, or codes the computer understands) or press special keys on the keyboard to communicate with the interface. Today, graphical user interfaces incorporate colorful graphics, use of the mouse, and Web browser-like features, making today's interfaces user-friendly.

Windows XP includes several **application programs** (Internet Explorer, Windows Media Player, Windows Movie Maker, Windows Messenger, and Outlook Express developed by Microsoft Corporation), which are programs that perform an application-related function such as word processing. **Microsoft Internet Explorer 6** integrates the Windows XP desktop and the Internet. The **Internet** is a worldwide group of connected computer networks that allows public access to information on thousands of subjects and gives users the ability to use this information, send messages, and obtain products and services. Internet Explorer allows you to work with programs and files in a similar fashion, whether they are located on the computer, a local network, or the Internet. **Windows Media Player 10** lets you create and play CDs, watch DVDs, listen to radio stations all over the world, and search for and organize digital media files. **Windows Movie Maker 5.1** can transfer recorded audio and video from analog camcorders or digital video cameras to the computer, import existing audio and video files to use in the movies you make, and send the finished movie to a friend by e-mail or post it on the World Wide Web.

Windows Messenger 4.7 is an instant-messaging program that allows you to view who is currently online, send an instant message or a file to a business associate or friend, have a conversation with a group of people, or invite someone to play a game. **Outlook Express 6** is an e-mail program that lets you exchange mail with friends and colleagues, trade ideas and information in a newsgroup, manage multiple mail and news accounts, and add stationery or a personal signature to messages. To use the application programs that can be executed under Windows XP, you must know about the Windows XP user interface.

This book demonstrates how to use Microsoft Windows XP to control the computer and communicate with other computers on a network. In Project 1, you will learn about Windows XP and how to use the Windows XP user interface.

What Is a User Interface?

A **user interface** is the combination of hardware and software that you use to communicate with and control the computer. Through the user interface, you are able to make selections on the computer, request information from the computer, and respond to messages displayed by the computer. Thus, a user interface provides the means for dialogue between you and the computer.

Hardware and software together form the user interface. Among the hardware devices associated with a user interface are the monitor, keyboard, and mouse (Figure 1-2). The **monitor** displays messages and provides information. You respond by entering data in the form of a command or other response using the **keyboard** or **mouse**. Among the responses available to you are responses that specify which application program to run, what document to open, when to print, and where to store data for future use.

The computer software associated with the user interface consists of the programs that engage you in dialogue (Figure 1-2). The computer software determines the messages you receive, the manner in which you should respond, and the actions that occur based on your responses.

The goal of an effective user interface is to be **user-friendly**, which means the software can be used easily by individuals with limited training. Research studies have indicated that the use of graphics can play an important role in aiding users to interact effectively with a computer. A **graphical user interface**, or **GUI** (pronounced gooey), is a user interface that displays graphics in addition to text when it communicates with the user.

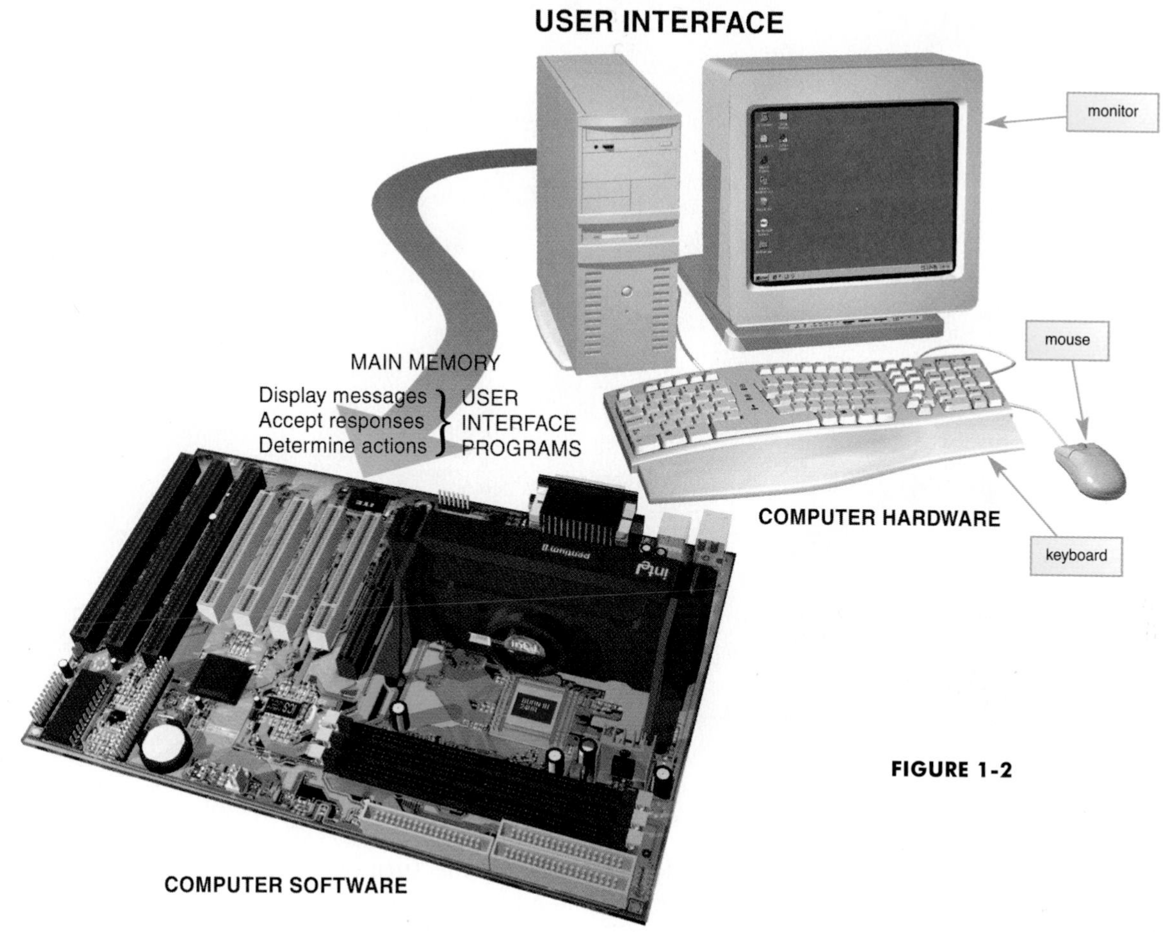

FIGURE 1-2

The Windows XP graphical user interface was designed carefully to be easier to set up, simpler to learn, faster and more powerful, and better integrated with the Internet than previous versions of Microsoft Windows.

Launching Microsoft Windows XP

When you turn on the computer, an introductory black screen consisting of the Microsoft Windows XP logo, progress bar, copyright messages (Copyright © Microsoft Corporation), and the word, Microsoft, displays. The progress bar indicates the progress of launching the Windows XP operating system. After approximately one minute, the Welcome screen displays (Figure 1-3 on the next page).

The **Welcome screen** shows the names of every computer user on the computer. On the left side of the Welcome screen, the Microsoft XP logo and the instructions, To begin, click your user name, display. On the right side of the Welcome screen is a list of the **user icons** and **user names** for all authorized computer users (Annie Meyer, Brad Wilson, and Guest). Clicking the user icon or user name begins the process of logging on to the computer. The list of user icons and names on the Welcome screen on your computer may be different.

More About

User Names and Passwords

A unique user name identifies each user. In the past, users often entered a variation of their name as the user name. For example, Brad Wilson might have chosen bradwilson or bwilson. Today, most Windows XP users use their first and last name as the user name. A password is a combination of characters that allows you access to certain computer resources on the network. Passwords should be kept confidential.

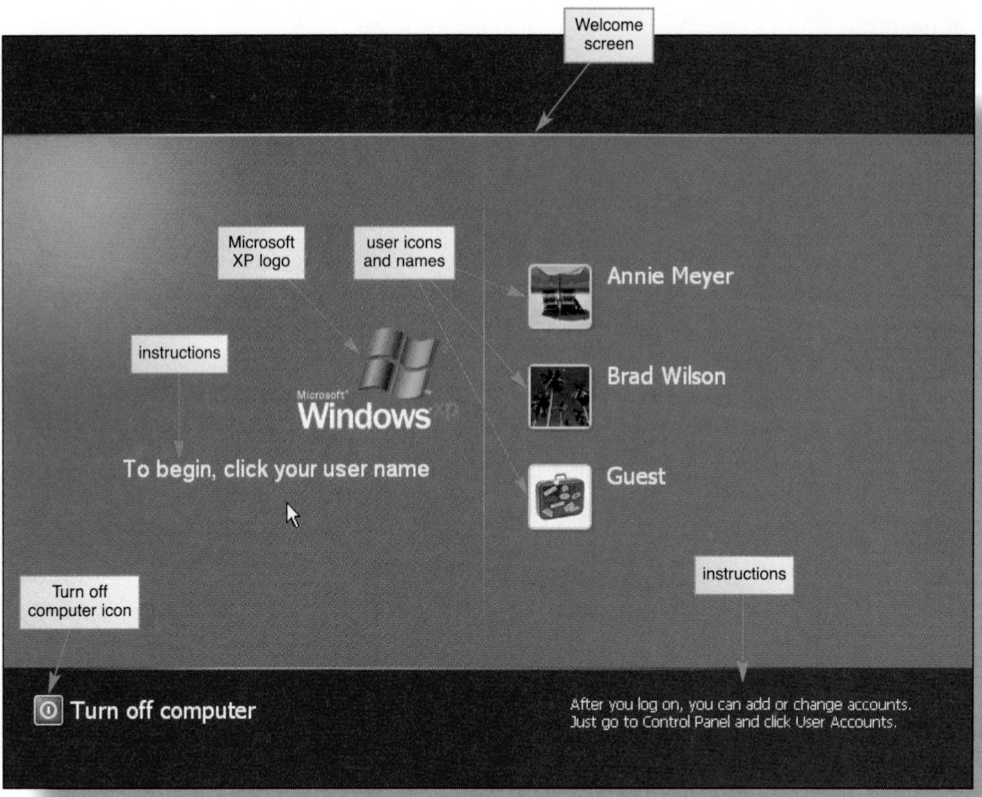

FIGURE 1-3

Microsoft Mice

For additional information about Microsoft Mice, launch the Internet Explorer browser (see pages WIN 1.45 and WIN 1.46), type `www.scsite.com/winxp/more.htm` in the Address box in the Microsoft Internet Explorer window, and then press the ENTER key.

At the bottom of the Welcome screen are the Turn off computer icon and the instructions, After you log on, you can add or change accounts. Just go to Control Panel and click User Accounts. Clicking the Turn off computer icon initiates the process of shutting down the computer. The **Control Panel** allows you to create a new user, change or remove an existing user, and change user information. The user information that can be changed consists of the user icon and user name, user password, and account type (Administrator, Limited account, and Guest account).

The Windows XP User Interface

The Windows XP user interface provides the means for dialogue between you and the computer. Part of this dialogue involves requesting information from the computer and responding to messages displayed by the computer. You can request information and respond to messages by using either the mouse or the keyboard.

More About

Buttons

Buttons are an integral part of Windows XP. When you point to them, their function displays in a ToolTip. When you click them, they appear to recess on the screen to mimic what would happen if you pushed an actual button. All buttons in Windows XP operate in the same manner.

A **mouse** is a pointing device used with Windows XP that may be attached to the computer by a cable. Although not required to use Windows XP, Windows XP supports the use of the **Microsoft IntelliMouse** (Figure 1-4). The IntelliMouse contains three buttons, the primary mouse button, the secondary mouse button, and the wheel button between the primary and secondary mouse buttons. Typically, the **primary mouse button** is the left mouse button and the **secondary mouse button** is the right mouse button although Windows XP allows you to switch them. In this book, the left mouse button is the primary mouse button and the right mouse button is the secondary mouse button. The functions the **wheel button** and wheel perform depend on the software application being used. If the mouse is not an IntelliMouse, it will not have a wheel button between the primary and secondary mouse buttons.

Using the mouse, you can perform the following operations: (1) point; (2) click; (3) right-click; (4) double-click; (5) drag; and (6) right-drag. These operations are demonstrated on the following pages.

Many common tasks, such as logging on to the computer, are performed by pointing to an item and then clicking the item. **Point** means you move the mouse across a flat surface until the mouse pointer rests on the item of choice. As you move the mouse across a flat surface, the IntelliEye optical sensor on the underside of the mouse senses the movement of the mouse (Figure 1-5), and the mouse pointer moves across the desktop in the same direction.

More About

The Mouse

The mouse, though invented in the 1960s, was not used widely until the Apple Macintosh computer became available in 1984. Even then, some highbrows called mouse users "wimps." Today, the mouse is an indispensable tool for every computer user.

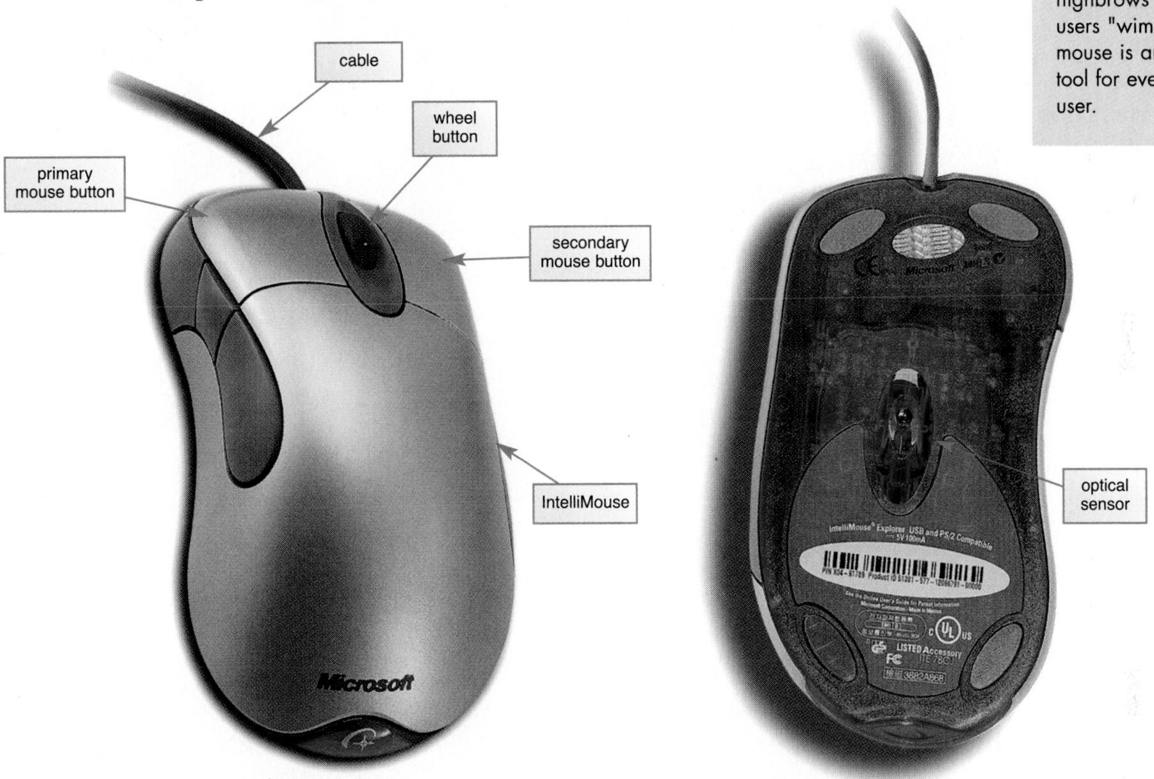

FIGURE 1-4

FIGURE 1-5

Click means you press and release the primary mouse button, which in this book is the left mouse button. In most cases, you must point to an item before you click.

Logging On to the Computer

After launching Windows XP but before working with Windows XP, you must log on to the computer. Logging on to the computer opens your user account and makes the computer available for use. In the steps on the next page, the Brad Wilson icon and the Next button are used to log on to the computer and enter a password.

Note: In a school environment, you will want to log on to the computer by pointing to and clicking *your user icon* on the Welcome screen and typing *your password* in the text box instead of the password shown in the steps.

Perform the steps on the next page to log on to the computer by pointing to and clicking your user icon on the Welcome screen, typing your password, and then pointing to and clicking the Next button.

More About

Logging on to the Computer

If, after logging on to the computer, you leave the computer unattended for twelve or more minutes, the Welcome screen will display and you will have to log on to the computer again to gain access to your account.

Note: Use your icon to log on to the computer instead of Brad Wilson's icon.

To Log On to the Computer

1 Point to the Brad Wilson icon (or your icon) on the Welcome screen by moving the mouse across a flat surface until the mouse pointer rests on the icon.

Pointing to the Brad Wilson icon displays a yellow border on the icon and dims the other user icons and names (Figure 1-6).

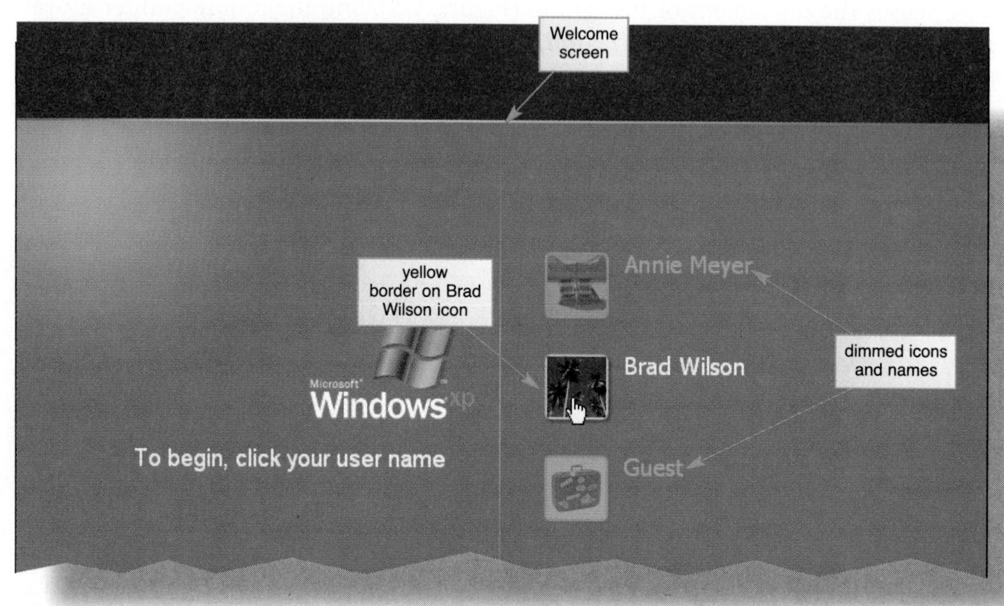

FIGURE 1-6

2 Click the Brad Wilson icon by pressing and releasing the left mouse button, type `lakers` **(or your password) in the Type your password text box, and then point to the Next button.**

Windows XP highlights the Brad Wilson icon and name, displays the Type your password text box containing a series of bullets (••••••) and an insertion point, and the Next and Help buttons (Figure 1-7). A ***text box*** *is a rectangular area in which you can enter text. The bullets in the text box hide the password entered by the user.*

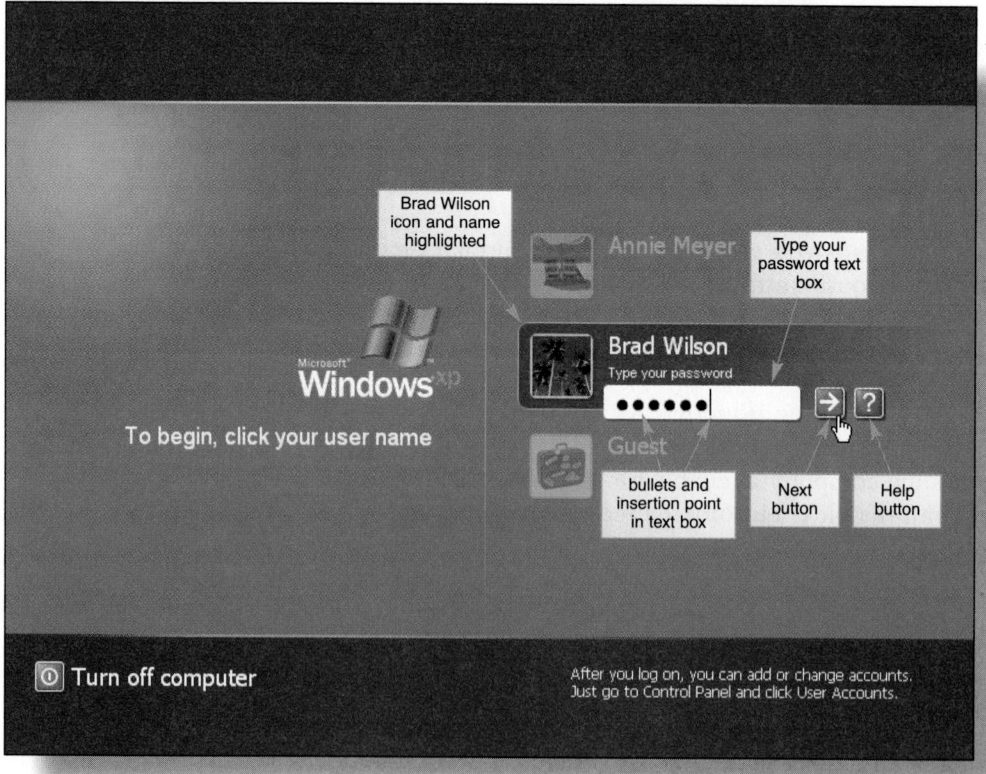

FIGURE 1-7

3 Click the Next button.

The contents of the Welcome screen change to contain the word, Welcome, on the left side of the screen and the user name, user icon, and message, Loading your personal settings..., on the right side. This screen displays momentarily while the user is logged on the computer and then several items display on a background called the ***desktop*** *(Figure 1-8). The background design of the desktop is Bliss, but your computer may display a different design.*

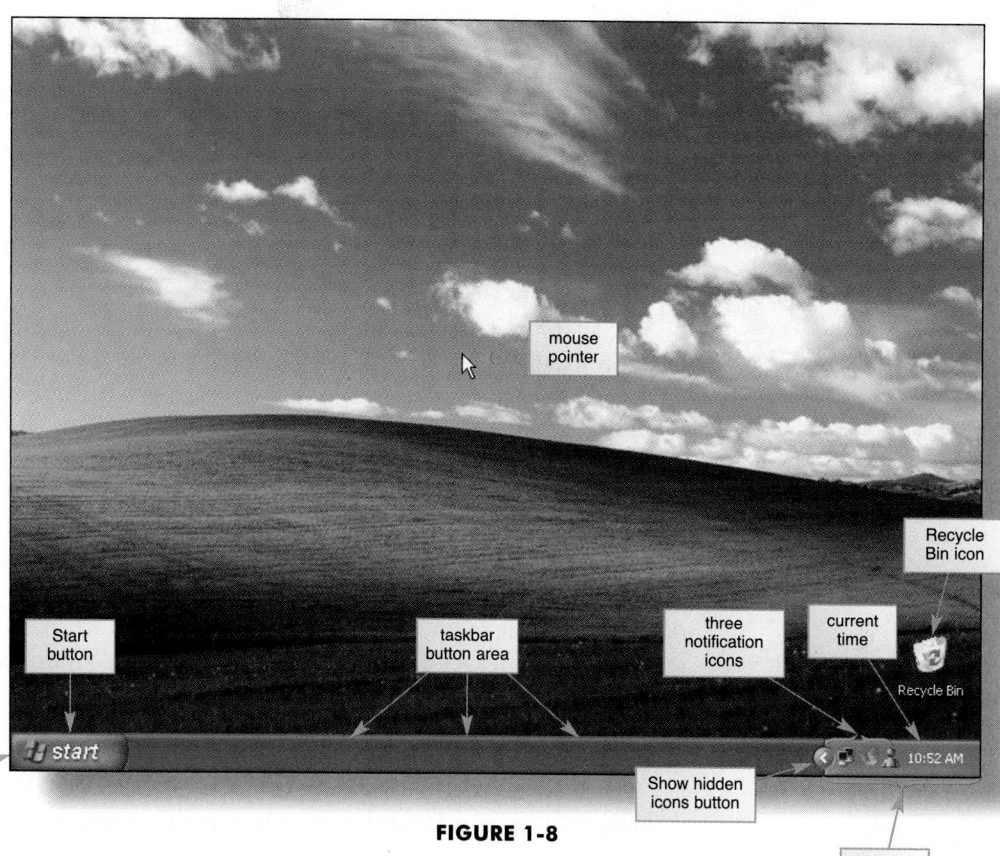

FIGURE 1-8

The items on the desktop in Figure 1-8 include the Recycle Bin icon and its name in the lower-right corner of the desktop and the taskbar at the bottom of the desktop. The Recycle Bin icon (**Recycle Bin**) allows you to discard unneeded objects. Your computer's desktop may contain more, fewer, or different icons because you can customize the desktop of the computer.

The **taskbar** shown at the bottom of the screen in Figure 1-8 contains the Start button, taskbar button area, and notification area. The **Start button** allows you to launch a program quickly, find or open a document, change the computer's settings, obtain Help, shut down the computer, and perform many more tasks. The **taskbar button area** contains buttons to indicate which windows are open on the desktop. In Figure 1-8, no windows display on the desktop and no buttons display in the taskbar button area.

The **notification area** contains the Show hidden icons button, three notification icons, and the current time. The **Show hidden icons button** indicates that one or more inactive icons are hidden from view in the notification area. The three **notification icons** in the notification area provide quick access to programs on the computer. Other icons that provide information about the status of the computer display temporarily in the notification area. For example, the Printer icon displays when a document is sent to the printer and is removed when printing is complete. The notification area on your desktop may contain more, fewer, or different icons because the contents of the notification area can change.

In the center of the desktop is the mouse pointer. On the desktop, the **mouse pointer** is the shape of a block arrow. The mouse pointer allows you to point to objects on the desktop and may change shape when it points to different objects. A shadow may display behind the mouse pointer to make the mouse pointer display in a three-dimensional form.

More About

The Contents of the Desktop

Because Windows XP can be easily customized, your desktop may not resemble the desktop in Figure 1-8. For example, a different background design may display on the desktop when computer manufacturers want to highlight their company name or logo. In a school environment, the computer administrator may change the background design.

More About

The Notification Area

The Show hidden icons button displays on the left edge of the notification area if one or more inactive icons are hidden from view in the notification area. Clicking the Show hidden icons button displays the hidden icons in the notification area and replaces the Show hidden icons button with the Hide button. Moving the mouse pointer off the Hide button removes, or hides, the inactive icons in the notification area and redisplays the Show hidden icons button.

When you click an object, such as the Brad Wilson icon or the Next button in Figure 1-7 on page WIN 1.12, you must point to the object before you click. In the steps that follow, the instruction that directs you to point to a particular item and then click is, Click the particular item. For example, Click the Next button means point to the Next button and then click.

The Windows XP Desktop

Nearly every item on the Windows XP desktop is considered an object. Even the desktop itself is an object. Every **object** has properties. The **properties** of an object are unique to that specific object and may affect what can be done to the object or what the object does. For example, a property of an object may be the color of the object, such as the color of the desktop. You will learn more about properties in Project 3 of this book.

The Windows XP desktop and the objects on the desktop emulate a work area in an office. You may think of the Windows desktop as an electronic version of the top of your desk. You can place objects on the desktop, move the objects around on the desktop, look at them and then put them aside, and so on. In Project 1, you will learn how to interact and communicate with the Windows XP desktop.

Displaying the Start Menu

The **Start menu** allows you to easily access the most useful items on the computer. A **menu** is a list of related commands and the **commands** on a menu perform a specific action, such as searching for files or obtaining Help. The Start menu contains commands that allow you to connect to and browse the Internet, launch an e-mail program, launch application programs, store and search for documents, customize the computer, and obtain Help on thousands of topics. Perform the following steps to display the Start menu.

Steps To Display the Start Menu

1 Point to the Start button on the taskbar.

The mouse pointer on the Start button causes the color of the Start button to change to light green and displays a ToolTip (Click here to begin) (Figure 1-9). The ToolTip provides instructions for using the Start button.

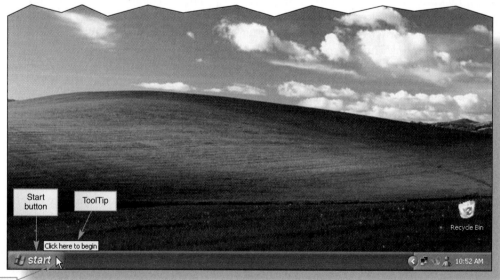

FIGURE 1-9

2 Click the Start button.

The Start menu displays (Figure 1-10). The color of the Start button changes to dark green, and the Start button is recessed. The top section of the Start menu contains the user icon and name (Brad Wilson), the middle section contains two columns of commands, and the bottom section contains two commands (Log Off and Turn Off Computer). The commands on the Start menu on your computer may be different.

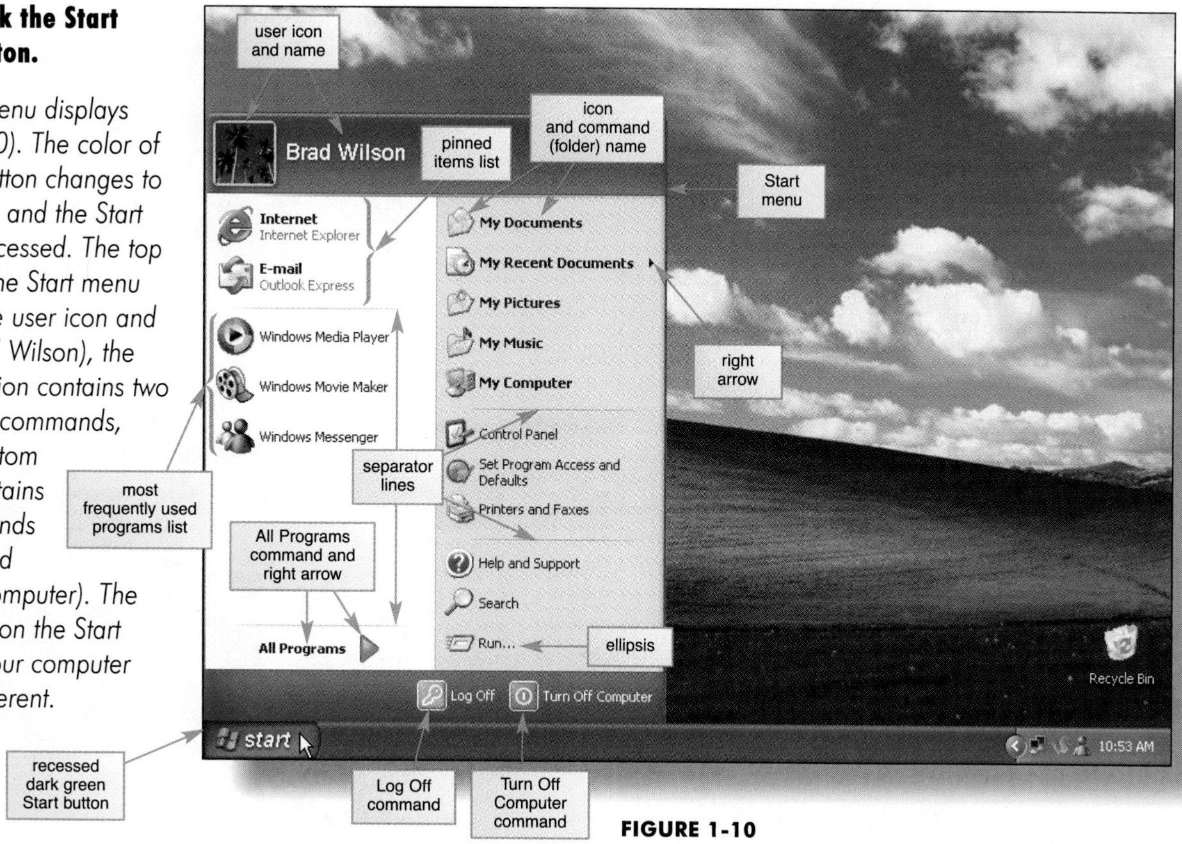

FIGURE 1-10

3 Point to All Programs on the Start menu.

When you point to All Programs, Windows XP highlights the All Programs command on the Start menu by displaying the All Programs command name in white text on a blue background and displays the All Programs submenu (Figure 1-11). A ***submenu*** *is a menu that displays when you point to a command followed by a right arrow. Whenever you point to a command on a menu or submenu, the command name is highlighted.*

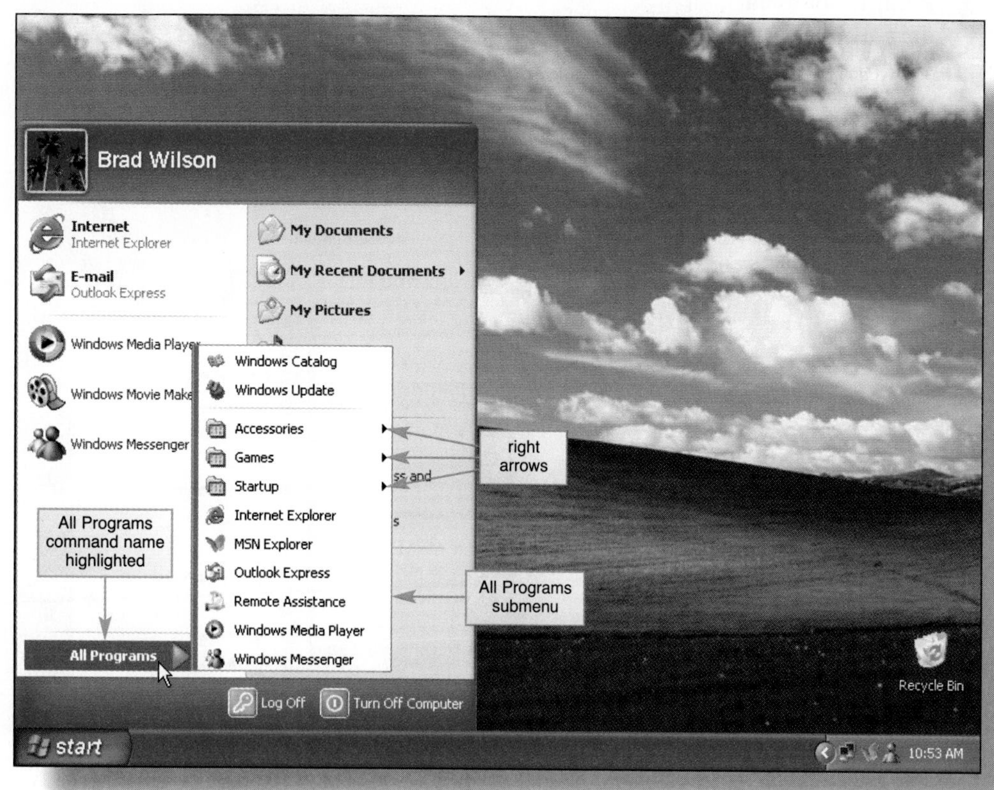

FIGURE 1-11

4 Point to Accessories on the All Programs submenu.

When you point to Accessories, Windows XP highlights the Accessories command on the All Programs submenu and displays the **Accessories submenu** *(Figure 1-12). To launch an application from the Accessories submenu, click the command on the submenu containing the application name. For example, to launch Notepad you would click the Notepad command on the Accessories submenu.*

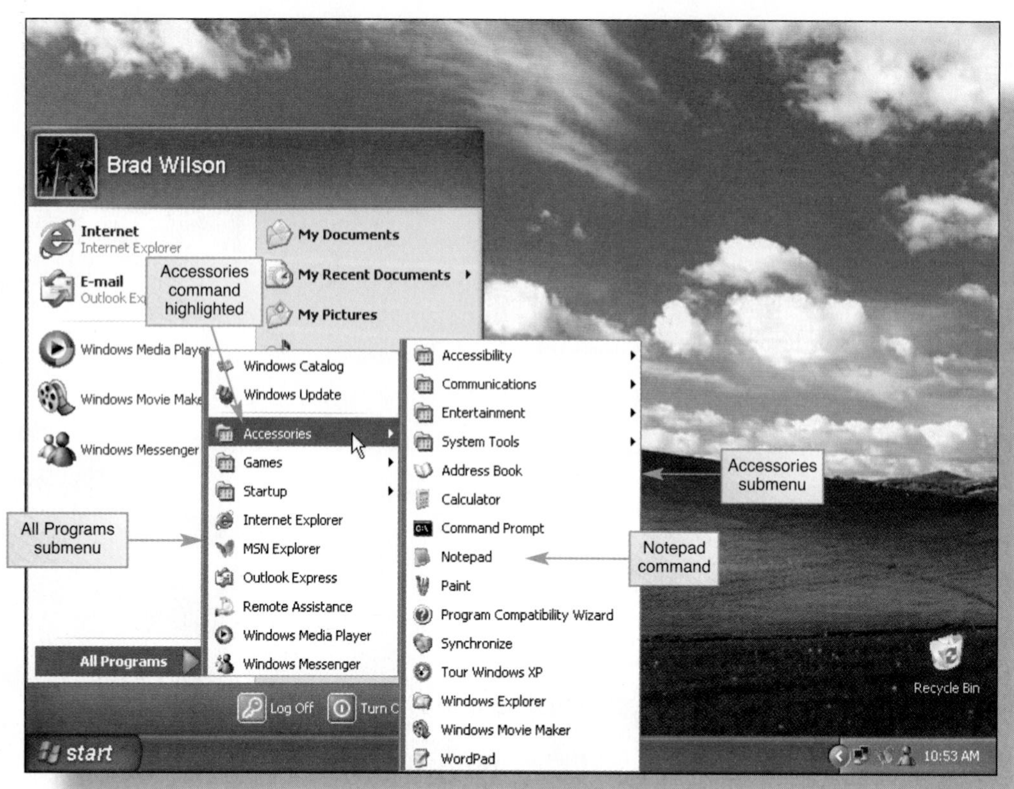

FIGURE 1-12

5 Point to an open area of the desktop (Figure 1-13).

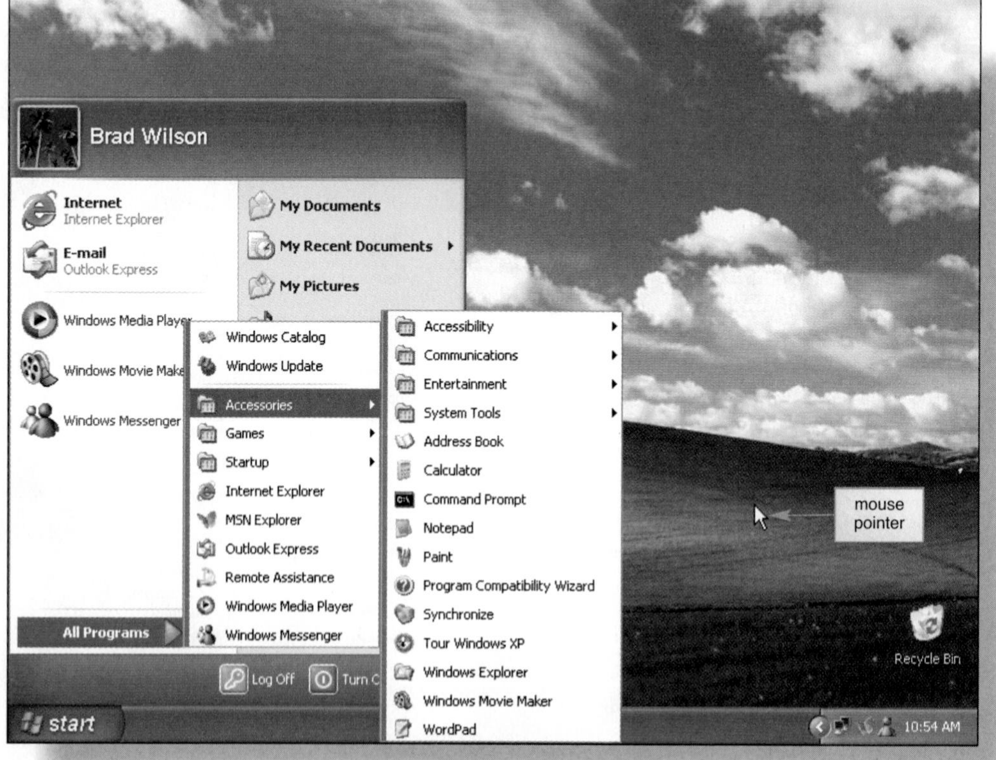

FIGURE 1-13

6 Click the open area.

The Start menu, Accessories submenu, and All Programs submenu close, and the recessed dark green Start button changes to its original light green color (Figure 1-14). The mouse pointer points to the desktop. To close any menu, click an open area of the desktop except the menu itself.

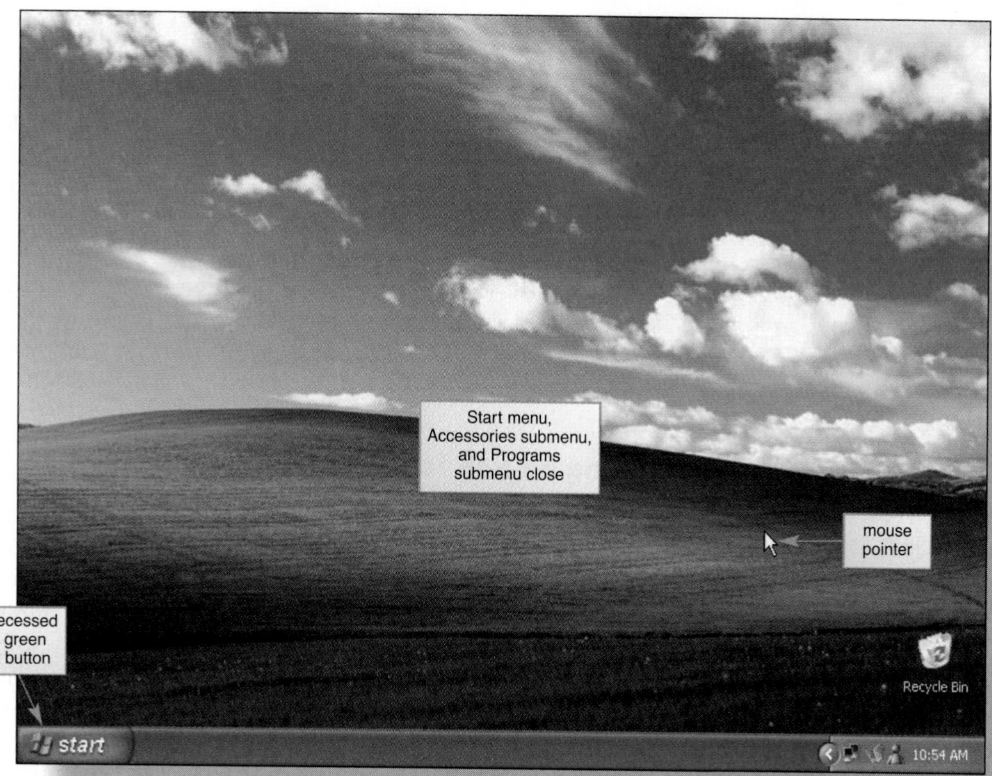

FIGURE 1-14

Other Ways

1. Press CTRL+ESC
2. Press WINDOWS (WINDOWS key on Microsoft Natural keyboard)

The middle section of the Start menu shown in Figure 1-10 on page WIN 1.15 consists of two columns of commands. Each command is identified by a unique icon and name. Commands may represent an application program, folder, or operation.

The list of commands above the separator line at the top of the left column, called the **pinned items list**, consists of the default Web browser program (Internet Explorer) and default e-mail program (Outlook Express). The list of commands below the separator line, called the **most frequently used programs list**, contains the most frequently used programs. Programs are added to the list when you use them. Currently, three programs (Windows Media Player, Windows Movie Maker, and Windows Messenger) display in the list.

The most frequently used programs list can contain up to six programs. If the list contains less than six programs when you start a new program, the program name is added to the list. If the list contains six names when you start a program that is not on the list, Windows XP replaces a less frequently used program with the new program. The All Programs command displays below the separator line at the bottom of the left column.

A list of commands to access various folders displays above the separator line at the top of the right column (My Documents, My Recent Documents, My Pictures, My Music, and My Computer). If the computer is connected to a network, the My Network Places command may display below the My Computer command. Below the separator line are other commands. They are commands to customize the computer (Control Panel), specifies which programs are accessible from the Start menu, desktop and other locations (Set Program Access and Defaults), and add printers and fax printers to the computer (Printers and Faxes). Below the separator line at the bottom of the right column are commands to obtain Help (Help and Support), search for documents and folders (Search), and launch programs (Run).

More About

The Start Menu

The Start menu has finally been redesigned! The Start menu is larger, more colorful, easier to use, and is truly the starting point for using Windows XP. In addition, the Start menu changes to suit the work habits of the user. Commands to access the Internet and an e-mail program, and a constantly changing list of frequently used application commands display prominently on the Start menu. Hooray for innovation!

A **right arrow** following a command in the Start menu indicates that pointing to the command will display a submenu. The All Programs command is followed by a green right arrow and the My Recent Documents if present is followed by a smaller black arrow. One command (Run) is followed by an **ellipsis** (...) to indicate more information is required to execute the command.

Windows XP provides a number of ways in which to accomplish a particular task. In the remainder of this book, a single set of steps will illustrate how to accomplish a task. Those steps may not be the only way in which the task can be completed. If you can perform the same task using other means, the Other Ways box specifies the methods. In each case, the method shown in the steps is the preferred method, but it is important for you to be aware of all the techniques you can use.

More About

Desktop Icons

In the past, rows and rows of icons could be seen on Windows desktops. That was the past! Today, the Windows XP desktop contains only the Recycle Bin icon. The Recycle Bin icon, the lone desktop icon, vigilantly waits to dispose of your trash. Yes, the word of the day at Microsoft is uncluttered.

Adding an Icon to the Desktop

Although the Windows XP desktop may contain only the Recycle Bin icon (see Figure 1-8 on page WIN 1.13), you may want to add additional icons to the desktop. For example, you may want to add the My Computer icon to the desktop so you can view the contents of the computer. One method to view the contents of the computer is to click the My Computer command on the Start menu to open the My Computer window. If you use My Computer frequently, you may want to place the My Computer icon on the desktop where it is easier to find.

One method of adding the My Computer icon to the desktop is to right-click the My Computer command on the Start menu. **Right-click** means you press and release the secondary mouse button, which in this book is the right mouse button. As directed when using the primary mouse button to click an object, normally you will point to the object before you right-click it. Perform the following steps to add the My Computer icon to the desktop.

To Add an Icon to the Desktop

Click the Start button.

The Start menu displays and the Start button is recessed (Figure 1-15). The My Computer command displays on the Start menu.

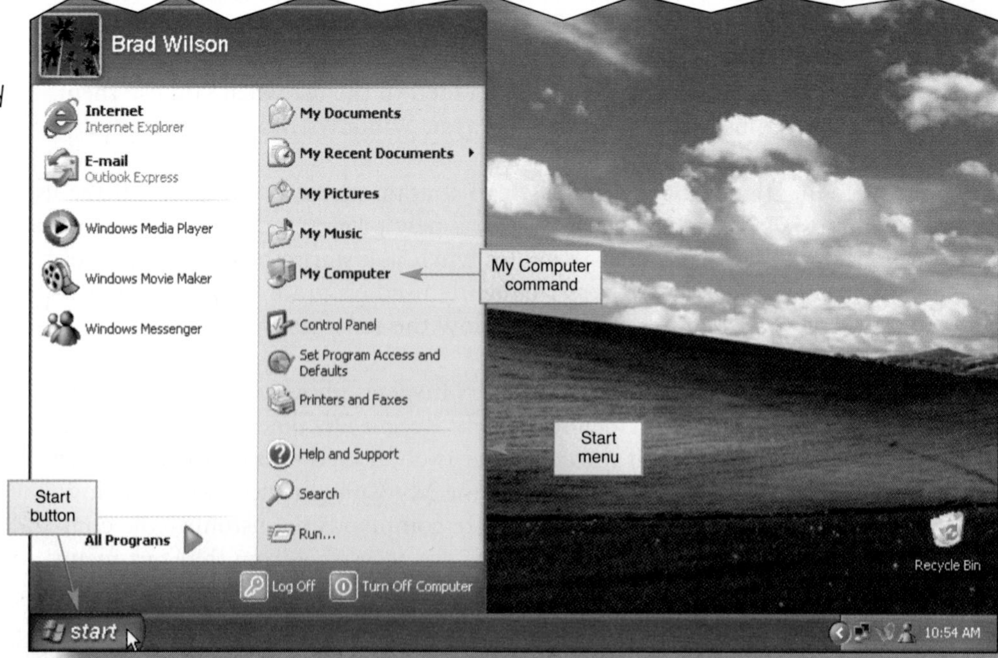

FIGURE 1-15

2 Point to My Computer on the Start menu and then press and release the right mouse button.

Windows XP highlights the My Computer command and displays a shortcut menu containing nine commands (Figure 1-16). Right-clicking an object, such as the My Computer command, displays a **shortcut menu** *that contains commands specifically for use with that object.*

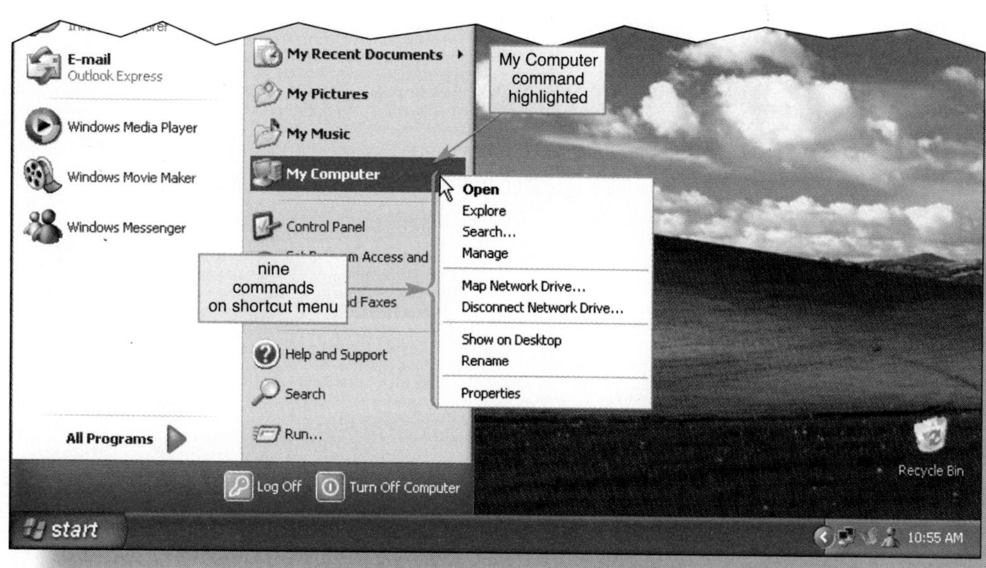

FIGURE 1-16

3 Point to Show on Desktop on the shortcut menu.

When you point to Show on Desktop, Windows XP highlights the Show on Desktop command (Figure 1-17).

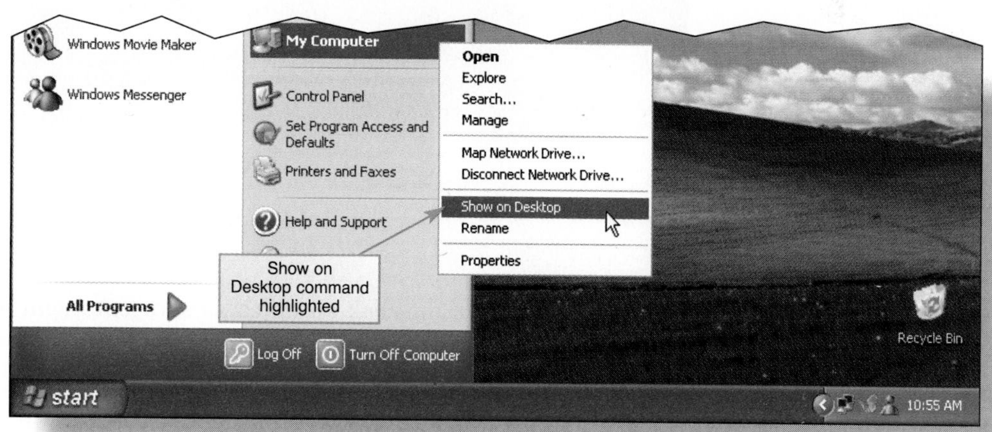

FIGURE 1-17

4 Click Show on Desktop.

The shortcut menu closes and the My Computer icon displays on the desktop (Figure 1-18). The Start menu remains on the desktop.

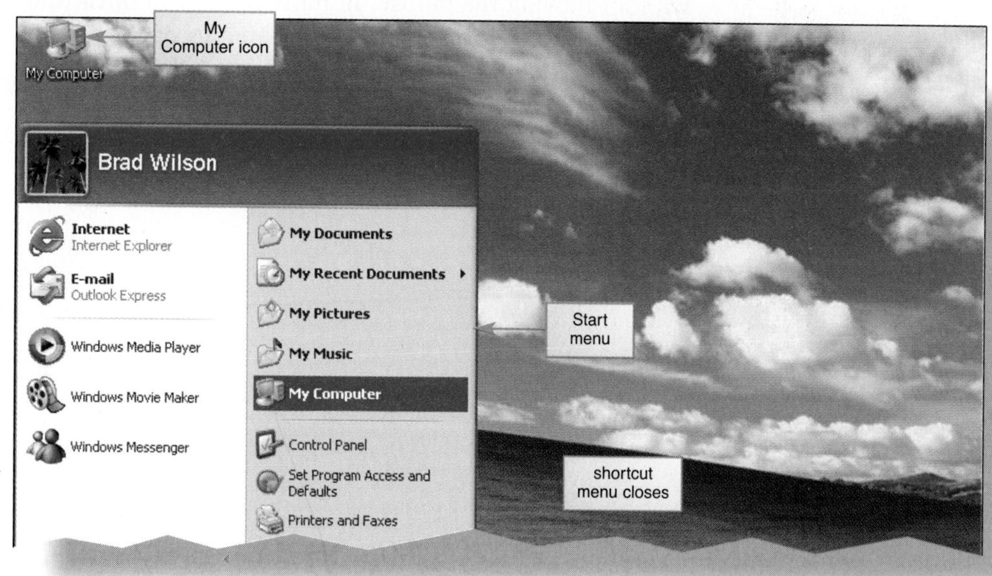

FIGURE 1-18

5 Click an open area on the desktop to close the Start menu.

The Start menu closes (Figure 1-19). The My Computer icon and mouse pointer remain on the desktop.

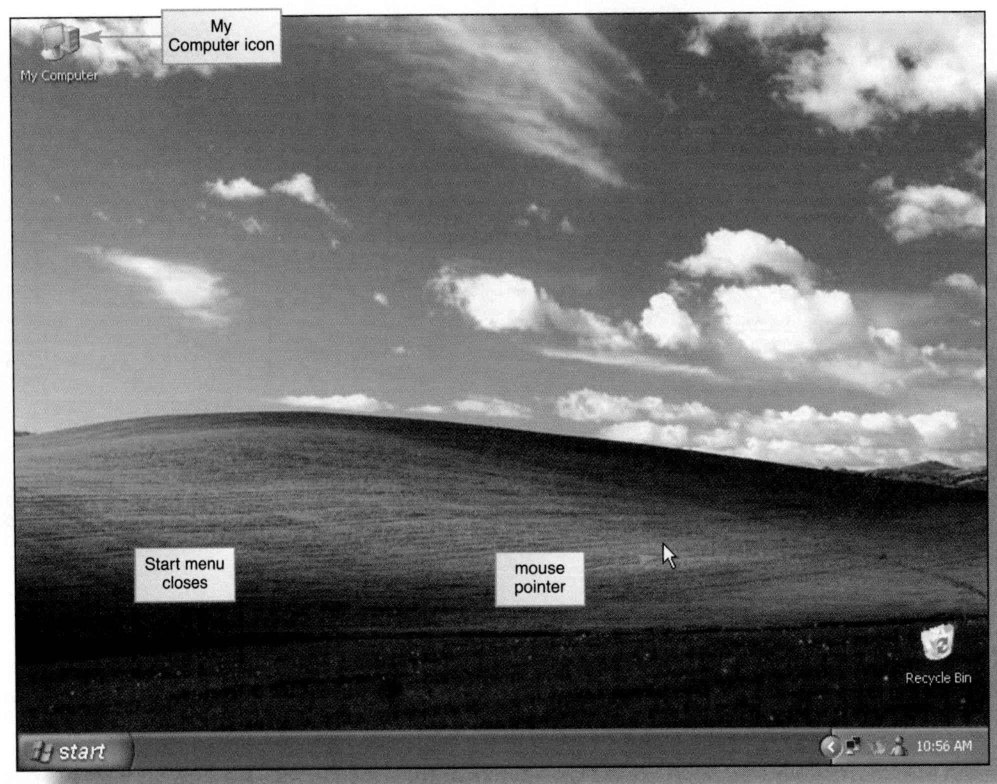

FIGURE 1-19

Other Ways

1. On Quick Launch toolbar right-drag icon to desktop, click Create Shortcuts Here
2. Right-click desktop, point to New, click Shortcut, type item location, click Next button, type shortcut name, click Finish
3. Right-click desktop, click Properties, click Desktop tab, click Customize Desktop, click icon title, click OK button, click OK button

Whenever you right-click an object, a shortcut menu will display. As you will see, the use of shortcut menus speeds up your work and adds flexibility to your interaction with the computer.

Opening a Window Using a Desktop Icon

Double-click means you quickly press and release the left mouse button twice without moving the mouse. In most cases, you must point to an item before you double-click. Perform the following step to open the My Computer window by double-clicking the My Computer icon on the desktop.

More About

The Right Mouse Button

The earliest versions of Microsoft Windows made little use of the right mouse button. In Windows XP, the right mouse button makes it easy to display a list of commands for an object (called a shortcut menu) and to copy and move objects on the desktop.

Steps To Open a Window Using a Desktop Icon

1 Point to the My Computer icon on the desktop and then double-click by quickly pressing and releasing the left mouse button twice without moving the mouse.

The My Computer window opens and the recessed dark blue My Computer button displays in the taskbar button area (Figure 1-20). The My Computer window allows you to view the contents of the computer.

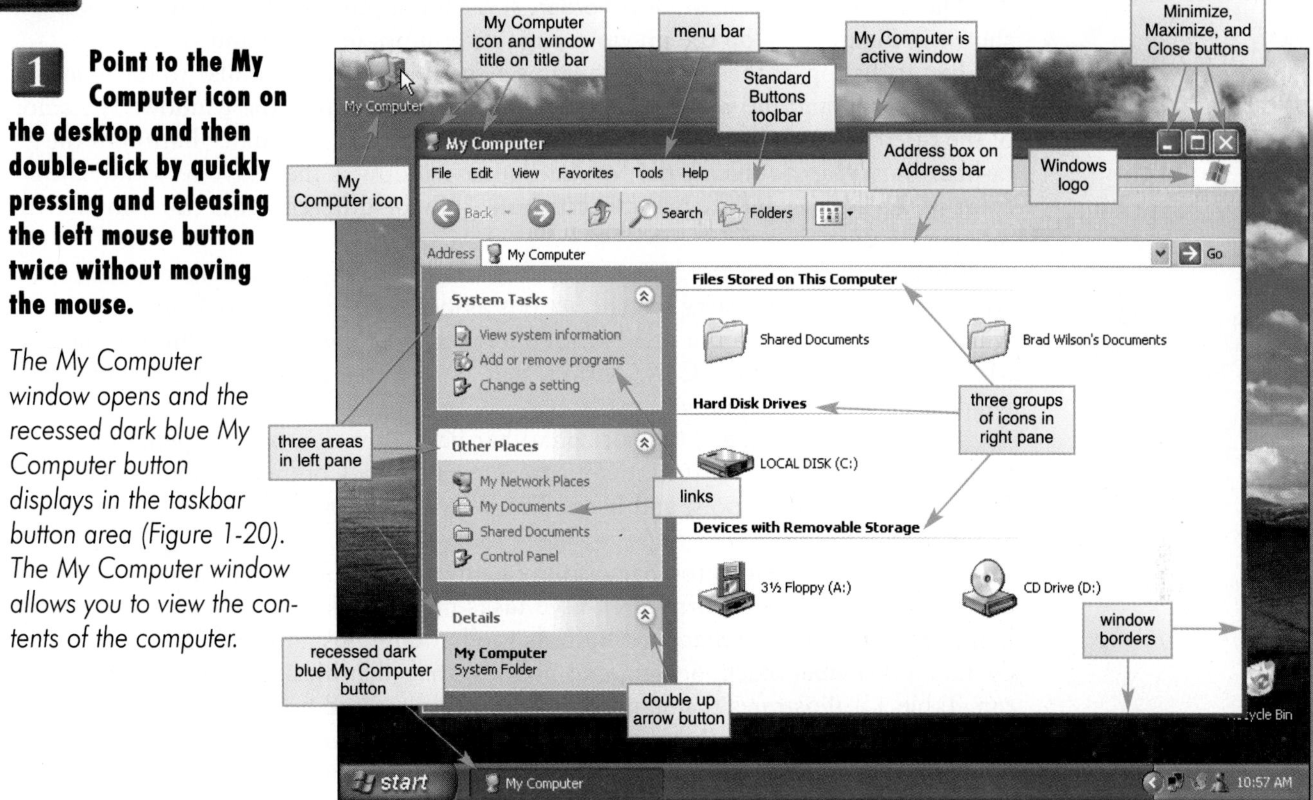

FIGURE 1-20

The My Computer window, the only open window, is the active window. The **active window** is the window you currently are using or that currently is selected. Whenever you click an object that opens a window, such as the My Computer icon, Windows XP will open the window; and a recessed dark blue button in the taskbar button area will identify the open window. The recessed dark blue button identifies the active window. The contents of the My Computer window on your computer may be different from the contents of the My Computer window shown in Figure 1-20.

Other Ways

1. Right-click desktop icon, click Open
2. Press WINDOWS+E (WINDOWS key on Microsoft Natural keyboard)

Double-Clicking Errors

While double-clicking an object, you easily can click once instead of twice. When you click an object such as the My Computer icon once, the icon becomes the active icon and the icon is dimmed. To open the My Computer window after clicking the My Computer icon once, double-click the My Computer icon as if you had not clicked the icon at all.

Another possible error is moving the mouse after you click the first time and before you click the second time. In most cases when you do this, the icon will be dimmed the same as if you had clicked it just one time.

A third possible error is moving the mouse while you are pressing the mouse button. In this case, the icon might actually move on the screen because you have inadvertently dragged it. To open the My Computer window after dragging it accidentally, double-click the icon as if you had not clicked it at all.

More About

Double-Clicking

Double-clicking is the most difficult mouse skill to learn. Many people have a tendency to move the mouse before they click a second time, even when they do not want to move the mouse. You should find, however, that with a little practice, double-clicking becomes quite natural.

The My Computer Window

The Contents of the My Computer Window

Because windows are easily customized, your My Computer window may not resemble the window in Figure 1-20 on page WIN 1.21. For example, different toolbars may display below the menu bar, icons may display smaller, grouping of icons may not display, and different areas may display in the left pane of the window.

The thin blue line, or **window border**, surrounding the My Computer window shown in Figure 1-20 on the previous page determines its shape and size. The **title bar** at the top of the window contains a small icon that is similar to the icon on the desktop and the **window title** (My Computer) identifies the window. The color of the title bar (dark blue) and the recessed dark blue My Computer button in the taskbar button area indicate the My Computer window is the active window. The color of the active window on your computer may be different from the color shown in Figure 1-20.

Clicking the icon at the left on the title bar will display the **System menu**, which contains commands to carry out the actions associated with the My Computer window. At the right on the title bar are three buttons, the Minimize button, the Maximize button, and the Close button, that can be used to specify the size of the window or close the window.

The **menu bar**, which is the horizontal bar below the title bar of a window (Figure 1-20), contains a list of menu names for the My Computer window: File, Edit, View, Favorites, Tools, and Help. The Windows logo displays on the far right of the menu bar.

The Standard buttons toolbar displays below the menu bar. The **Standard Buttons toolbar** allows you to perform often-used tasks more quickly than using the menu bar. Each button on the Standard Buttons toolbar contains an icon. Three buttons contain a **text label** (Back, Search, and Folders) that identifies the function of the button. Table 1-1 illustrates the Standard Buttons toolbar and briefly describes the function of each button. Each button will be explained in detail as it is used. The buttons on the Standard Buttons toolbar on your computer may be different.

Table 1-1 Standard Buttons Toolbar

BUTTON	*FUNCTION*
Back	Displays the previous window (provided it was displayed just previously). To go back more than one window, click the Back button arrow and then click a window title on the list.
	Displays the next window. To go forward more than one window, click the Forward button arrow and then click a window title on the list.
	Displays the drive or folder containing the currently selected drive or folder in the hierarchy of drives and folders on the computer in the right pane.
Search	Displays the Search Companion in the Search Companions area.
Folders	Displays the hierarchy of drives and folders on the computer in the Folders area.
	Displays a list of views.

Below the Standard Buttons toolbar is the Address bar. The **Address bar** allows you to launch an application, display a document, open another window, and search for information on the Internet. The Address bar shown in Figure 1-20 contains the Address box which includes the My Computer icon, window title, down arrow, and the Go button.

The area below the Address bar is divided into two panes. The System Tasks, Other Places, and Details areas display in the left pane. A title identifies each area. A button displays to the right of the title in each area to indicate whether the area is expanded or collapsed. A button identified by a **double up arrow** indicates the area is expanded. A button identified by a **double down arrow** indicates the area is collapsed. When you click the double up arrow button, the area collapses and only the title and the double down arrow button display. When you click the double down arrow button, the area expands and the entire contents of the area are visible.

All three areas in the left pane are expanded. The **System Tasks area** contains a title (System Tasks) and three tasks (View system information, Add or remove programs, and Change a setting) associated with the My Computer window. The **Other Places area** contains a title (Other Places) and links to four folders (My Network Places, My Documents, Shared Documents, and Control Panel) associated with the My Computer folder. The **Details area** contains a title (Details), the window title (My Computer), and the folder type (System Folder) of the My Computer window. Clicking the double up arrow collapses the area and leaves only the title and double down arrow button.

Pointing to a task in the System Tasks area or a folder name in the Other Places area underlines the task or folder name and displays the task or folder name in light blue. Underlined text, such as the task and folder names, is referred to as a **hyperlink**, or simply a **link**. Pointing to a link changes the mouse pointer to a hand icon, and clicking a link displays information associated with the link. For example, clicking the Add or remove programs task in the System Tasks area allows you to install or remove application programs and clicking the My Documents folder in the Other Places area opens the My Documents window.

The right pane of the My Computer window contains three groups of icons. The top group, Files Stored on This Computer, contains the Shared Documents and Brad Wilson's Documents icons. A title to the right of each icon identifies the folder names. The **Shared Documents folder** contains documents and folders that are available (shared) to other computer users on the network, and Brad Wilson's Documents contains his personal documents.

The middle group, Hard Disk Drives, contains the LOCAL DISK (C:) drive icon. A title to the right of the icon identifies the drive name, LOCAL DISK (C:). The bottom group, Devices with Removable Storage, contains the 3½ Floppy (A:) and CD Drive (D:) icons and labels. The three icons in the Hard Disk Drives and Devices with Removable Storage sections, called **drive icons**, represent a hard disk drive, 3½ floppy drive, and a Compact Disc drive. The number of groups in the right pane and the icons in the groups on your computer may be different.

Clicking a drive or folder icon selects the icon in the right pane and displays details about the drive or folder in the areas in the left pane. Double-clicking a drive or folder icon allows you to display the contents of the corresponding drive or folder in the right pane and information about the drive or folder in the areas in the left pane. You may find more, fewer, or different drive and folder icons in the My Computer window on your computer.

More About

My Computer

While the trade press and media once poked fun at the My Computer name, Microsoft continues to expand the concept. Windows XP now showcases the My Computer, My Documents, My Pictures, and My Music names by placing them on the Start menu. In addition, the new My Videos folder also was added to the operating system. Microsoft contends that beginners find these names easier to understand.

Minimizing a Window

Two buttons on the title bar of a window, the Minimize button and the Maximize button, allow you to control the way a window displays or does not display on the desktop. When you click the **Minimize button** (Figure 1-20 on page WIN 1.21), the My Computer window no longer displays on the desktop and the recessed dark blue My Computer button in the taskbar button area changes to a non-recessed medium blue button. A minimized window still is open but does not display on the screen. To minimize and then redisplay the My Computer window, complete the steps on the next page.

More About

Minimizing Windows

Windows management on the Windows XP desktop is important in order to keep the desktop uncluttered. You will find yourself frequently minimizing windows and then later reopening them with a click of a button in the taskbar button area.

Steps To Minimize and Redisplay a Window

1 Point to the Minimize button on the title bar of the My Computer window.

The mouse pointer points to the Minimize button on the My Computer window title bar, the color of the Minimize button changes to light blue, a ToolTip displays below the Minimize button, and the recessed dark blue My Computer button displays on the taskbar (Figure 1-21).

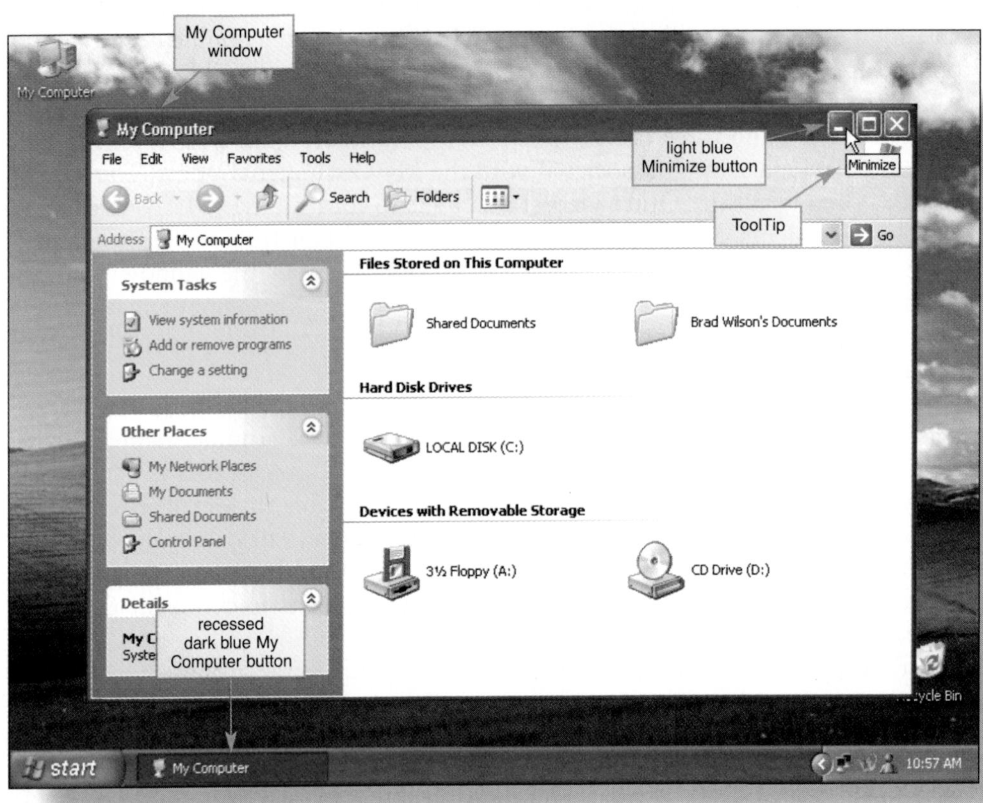

FIGURE 1-21

2 Click the Minimize button.

When you minimize the My Computer window, Windows XP removes the My Computer window from the desktop, the My Computer button changes to a non-recessed button, and the color of the button changes to medium blue (Figure 1-22).

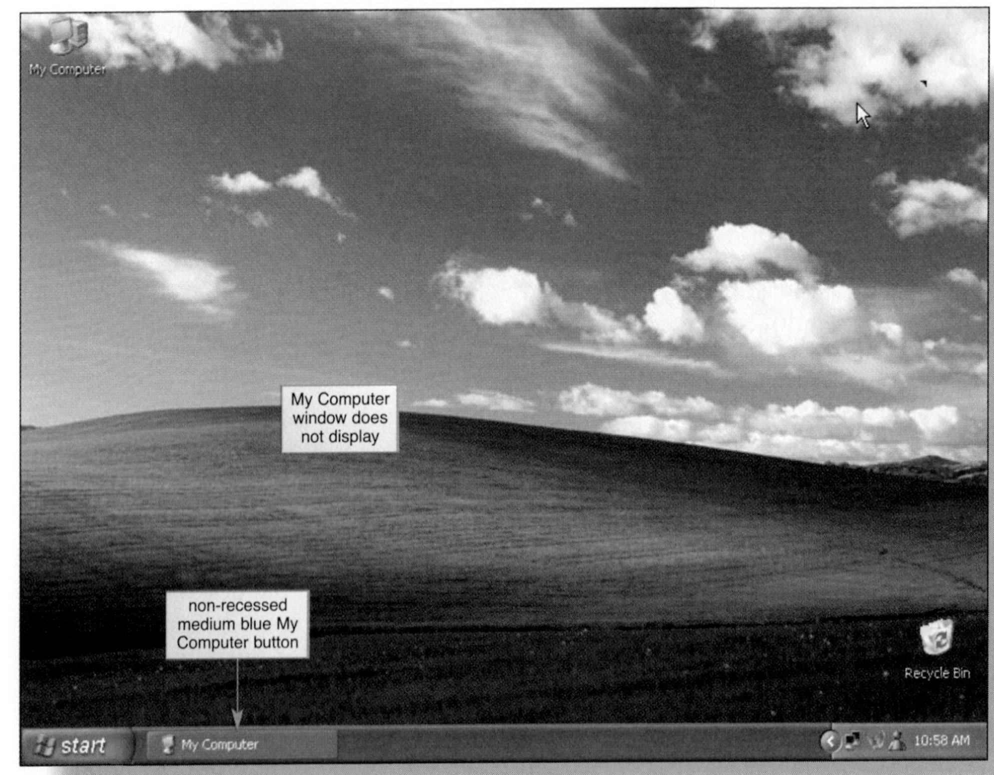

FIGURE 1-22

3 Click the My Computer button in the taskbar button area.

The My Computer window displays in the same place and size as it was before being minimized and the My Computer button on the taskbar is recessed (Figure 1-23). With the mouse pointer pointing to the My Computer button, the color of the button is medium blue. Moving the mouse pointer off the button changes the color to dark blue. The My Computer window is the active window because it contains the dark blue title bar.

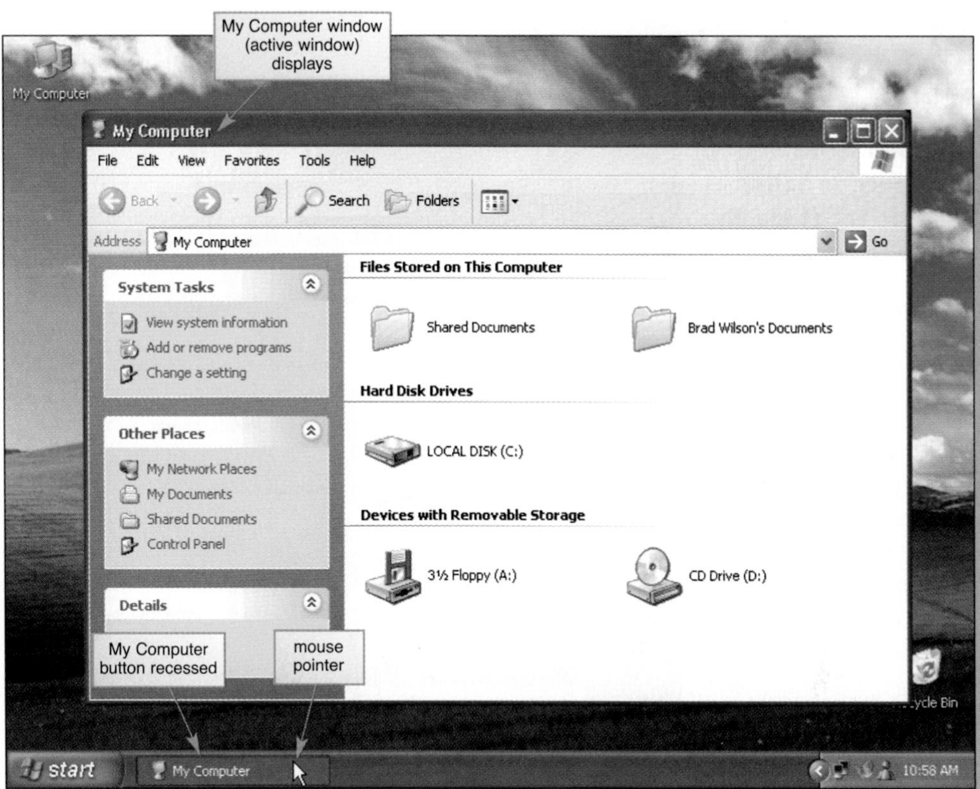

FIGURE 1-23

Whenever a window is minimized, it does not display on the desktop but a non-recessed dark blue button for the window does display in the taskbar button area. Whenever you want a minimized window to display and be the active window, click its button in the taskbar button area.

As you point to many objects when you work with Windows XP, such as a button or command, Windows XP displays a ToolTip. A **ToolTip** is a short on-screen note associated with the object to which you are pointing. ToolTips display on the desktop for approximately five seconds. Examples of ToolTips are shown in Figure 1-9 on page WIN 1.14, Figure 1-21 on page WIN 1.24, and Figures 1-24, 1-26, and 1-28 on the following pages. To reduce clutter on the screen, the ToolTips will not be shown on the remaining screens in this book.

Other Ways

1. Click icon on left side of title bar, click Minimize, in taskbar button area click taskbar button
2. Right-click title bar, click Minimize, on taskbar button area click taskbar button
3. Press WINDOWS+M (WINDOWS key on Microsoft Natural keyboard), press WINDOWS+SHIFT+M

Maximizing and Restoring a Window

Sometimes when information displays in a window, the information is not completely visible. One method of displaying the entire contents of a window is to enlarge the window using the **Maximize button**. The Maximize button maximizes a window so the window fills the entire screen, making it easier to see the contents of the window. When a window is maximized, the **Restore Down button** replaces the Maximize button on the title bar. Clicking the Restore Down button will return the window to its size before maximizing. To maximize and restore the My Computer window, complete the steps on the next page.

More About

Maximizing Windows

Many application programs run in a maximized window by default. Often you will find that you want to work with maximized windows to better view the contents of the window. Did you know that double-clicking the title bar also maximizes a window?

To Maximize and Restore a Window

1 Point to the Maximize button on the title bar of the My Computer window.

The mouse pointer points to the Maximize button on the My Computer window title bar and the color of the Maximize button changes to light blue (Figure 1-24). A ToolTip identifying the button name displays below the Maximize button.

FIGURE 1-24

2 Click the Maximize button.

The My Computer window expands so it and the taskbar fill the desktop (Figure 1-25). The Restore Down button replaces the Maximize button, the My Computer button in the taskbar button area does not change, and the My Computer window still is the active window.

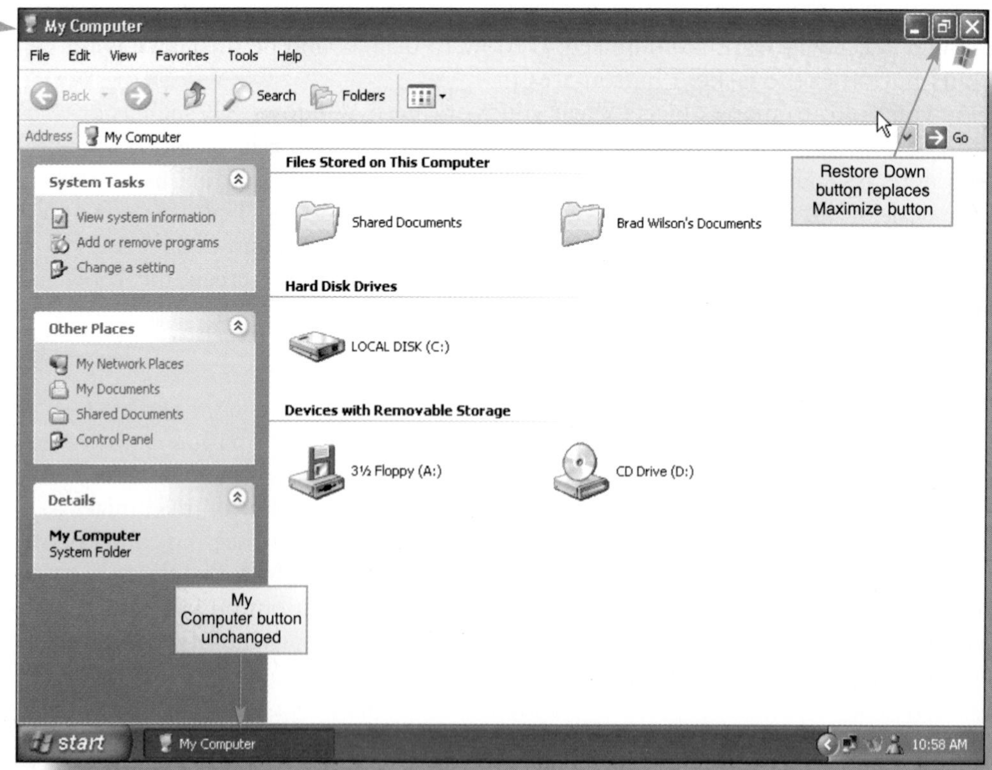

FIGURE 1-25

3 Point to the Restore Down button on the title bar of the My Computer window.

The mouse pointer points to the Restore Down button on the My Computer window title bar and the color of the Restore Down button changes to light blue (Figure 1-26). A ToolTip displays below the Restore Down button identifying it.

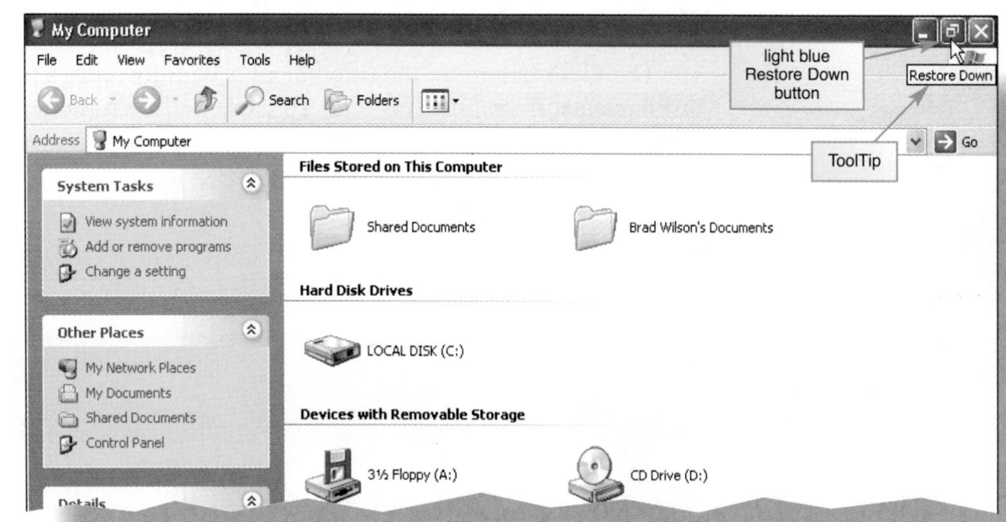

FIGURE 1-26

4 Click the Restore Down button.

The My Computer window returns to the size and position it occupied before being maximized (Figure 1-27). The My Computer button does not change. The Maximize button replaces the Restore Down button.

FIGURE 1-27

When a window is maximized, such as in Figure 1-25, you also can minimize the window by clicking the Minimize button. If, after minimizing the window, you click its button in the taskbar button area, the window will return to its maximized size.

Other Ways

1. Click icon on left side of title bar, click Maximize, click icon on left of title bar, click Restore
2. Right-click title bar, click Maximize, right-click title bar, click Restore
3. Double-click title bar, double-click title bar

Closing a Window

The **Close button** on the title bar of a window closes the window and removes the taskbar button from the taskbar. To close and then reopen the My Computer window, complete the following steps.

Steps To Close a Window

1 Point to the Close button on the title bar of the My Computer window.

The mouse pointer points to the Close button on the My Computer window title bar and the color of the Close button changes to light red (Figure 1-28). A ToolTip displays below the Close button.

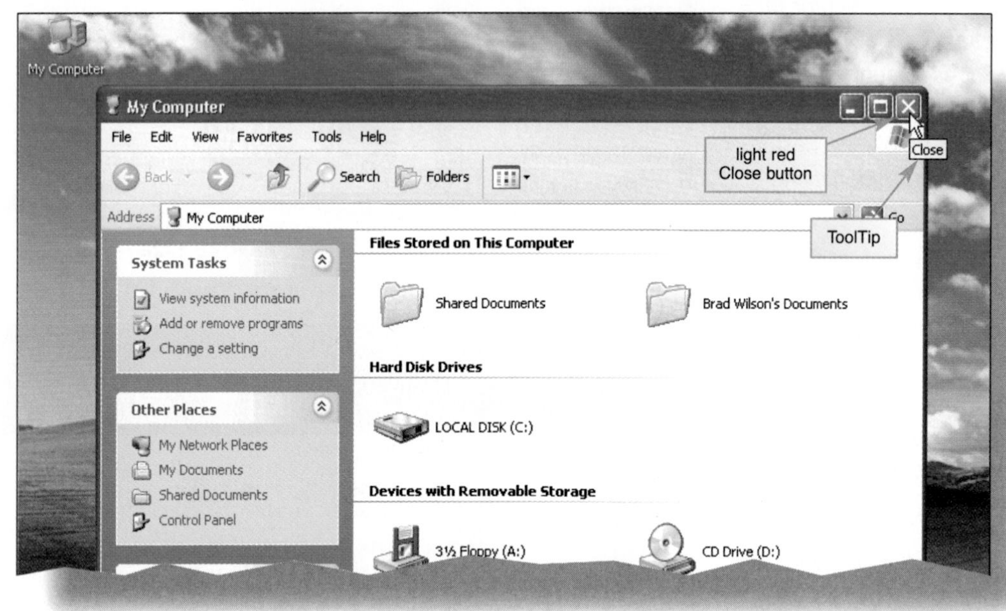

FIGURE 1-28

2 Click the Close button.

The My Computer window closes and the My Computer button no longer displays in the taskbar button area (Figure 1-29).

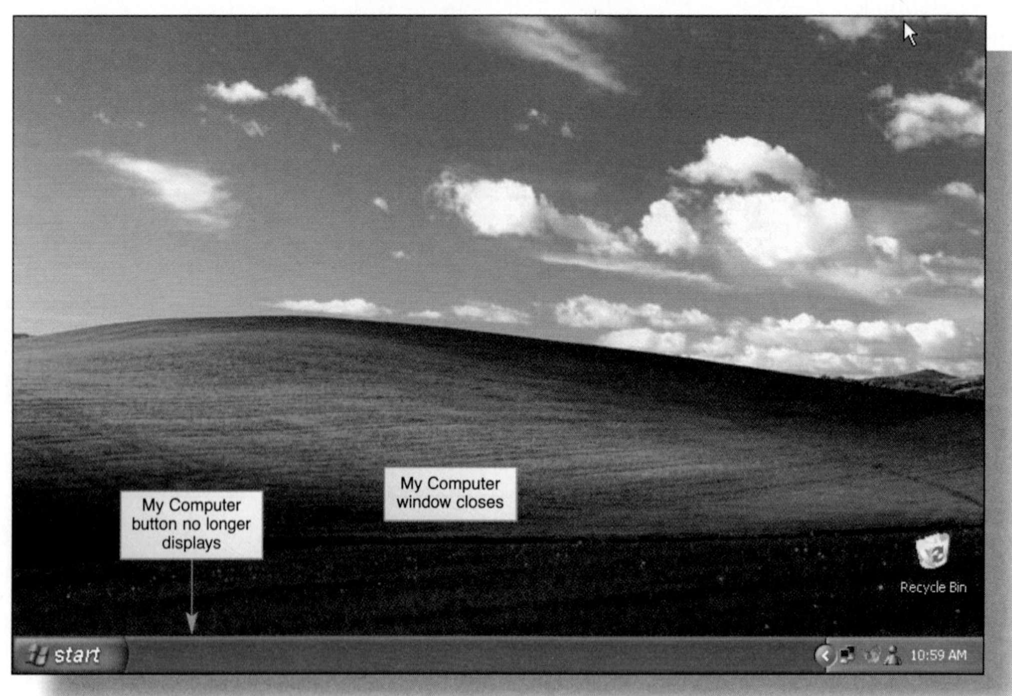

FIGURE 1-29

Other Ways

1. Click icon on left side of title bar, click Close
2. Right-click title bar, click Close
3. Press ALT+F4

Opening a Window Using the Start Menu

Previously, you opened the My Computer window by double-clicking the My Computer icon on the desktop. Another method of opening a window and viewing the contents of the window is to click a command on the Start menu. Perform the following steps to open the My Documents window using the My Documents command on the Start menu.

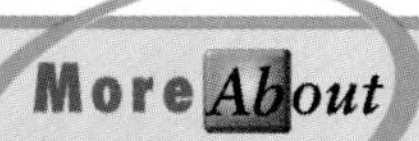

Opening a Window

Although the preferred method of opening a window in previous Windows versions was to double-click a desktop icon, the redesigned Start menu now makes it easier to open those windows.

To Open a Window Using the Start Menu

1 Click the Start button on the taskbar and then point to the My Documents command on the Start menu.

The Start menu displays, the Start button is recessed on the taskbar, the color of the button changes to dark green, and the mouse pointer points to the highlighted My Documents command on the Start menu (Figure 1-30).

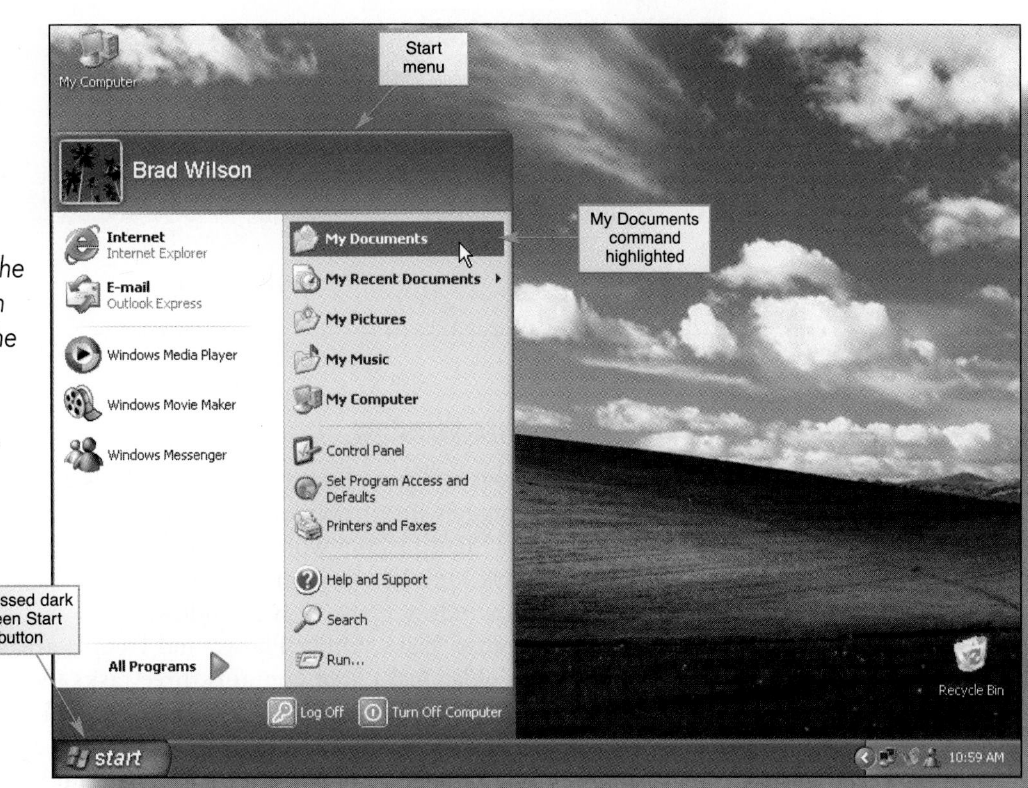

FIGURE 1-30

2 Click My Documents on the Start menu.

The My Documents window opens, the recessed dark blue My Documents button displays in the taskbar button area, and the My Documents window is the active window (Figure 1-31). You may find more, fewer, or different folder icons in the right pane on your computer.

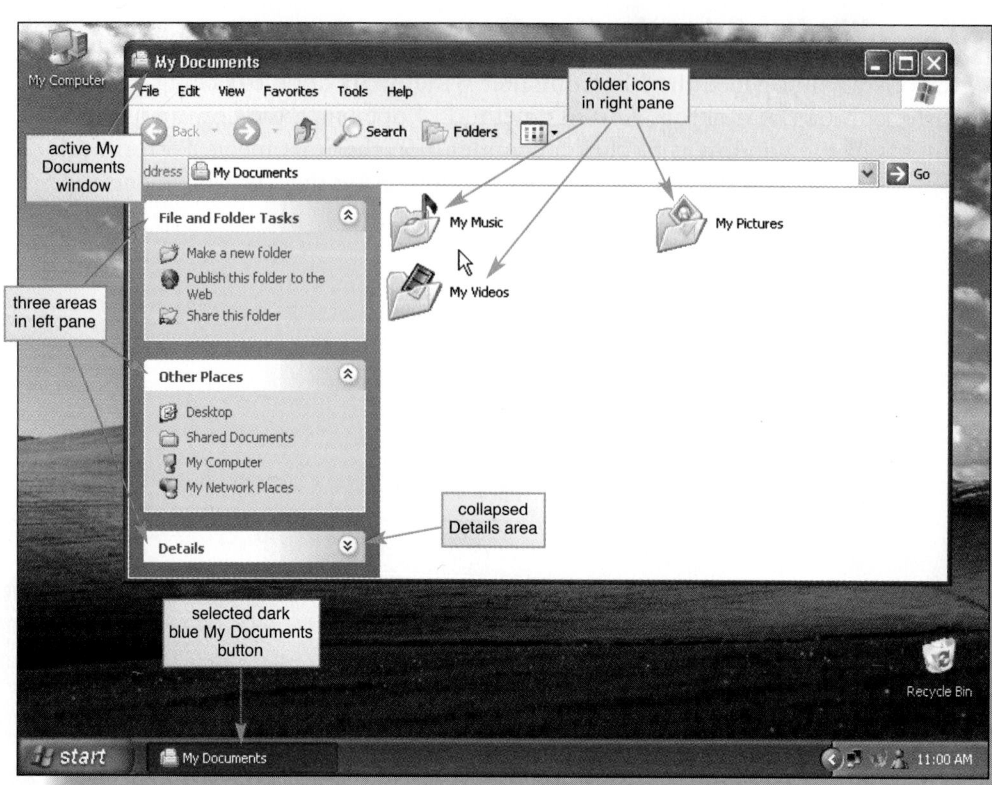

FIGURE 1-31

Other Ways

1. Click Start button, right-click My Documents, click open

The My Documents Window

The **My Documents window** shown in Figure 1-31 is a central location for the storage and management of documents. The title bar at the top of the My Documents window identifies the window and the color of the title bar (dark blue) and the recessed dark blue My Documents button in the taskbar button area indicate the My Documents window is the active window.

The File and Folder Tasks, Other Places, and Details areas display in the left pane. The **File and Folder Tasks area** contains three tasks (Make a new folder, Publish this folder to the Web, and Share this folder). The **Other Places area** contains links to four folders (Desktop, Shared Documents, My Computer, and My Network Places). The **Details area** is collapsed and only the title and a double down arrow button display in the area.

The right pane of the My Documents window contains the My Music, My Pictures, and My Videos folders. Clicking a folder icon in the right pane highlights the icon in the right pane and changes the files and folder tasks in the File and Folder Tasks area in the left pane. Double-clicking a folder icon displays the contents of the corresponding folder in the right pane, adds another area to the folder (My Music Tasks area, My Pictures Tasks area, or My Videos Tasks area) in the left pane, and changes the file and folder information in the left pane.

More About

Dragging

Dragging is the second-most difficult skill to learn with a mouse. You may want to practice dragging a few times so you will be comfortable with it. Do not let dragging become a drag — PRACTICE!!

Moving a Window by Dragging

Drag means you point to an item, hold down the left mouse button, move the item to the desired location, and then release the left mouse button. You can move any open window to another location on the desktop by pointing to the title bar of the window and then dragging the window. To drag the My Documents window to the center of the desktop, perform the following steps.

Steps To Move a Window by Dragging

1 Point to the My Documents window title bar (Figure 1-32).

FIGURE 1-32

2 Hold down the left mouse button, move the mouse down so the window moves to the center of the desktop, and then release the left mouse button.

As you drag the My Documents window, the window moves across the desktop. When you release the left mouse button, the window displays in its new location on the desktop (Figure 1-33).

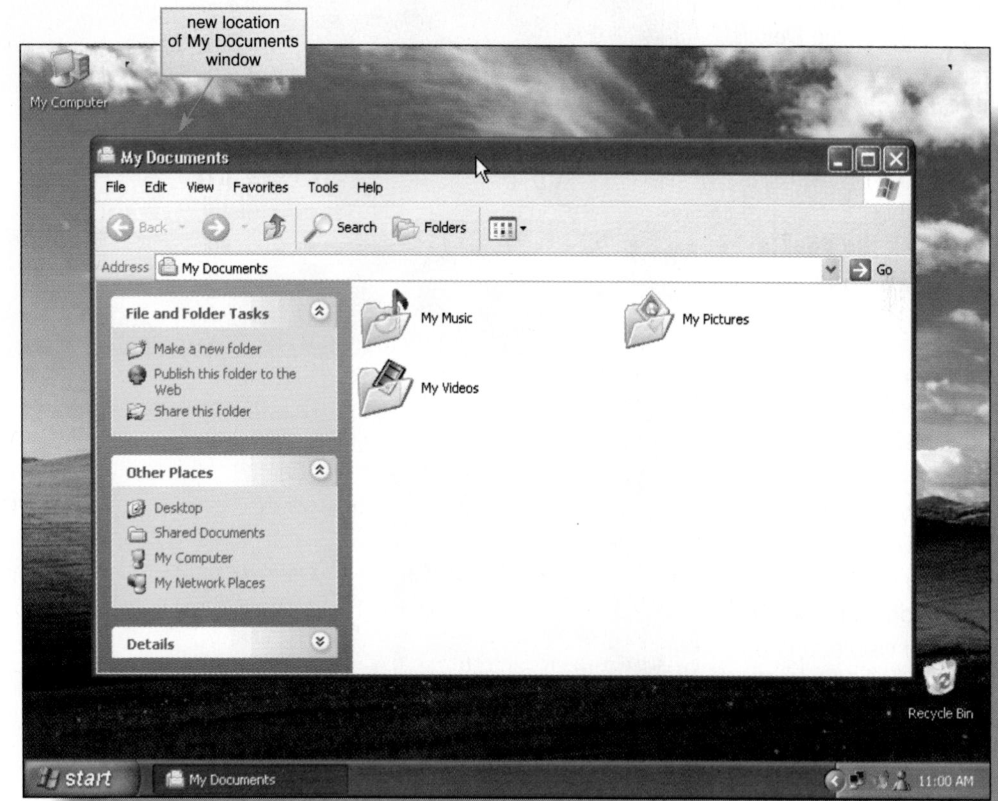

FIGURE 1-33

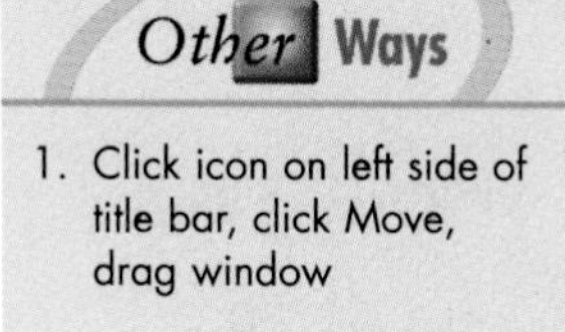

1. Click icon on left side of title bar, click Move, drag window

Expanding an Area

The Details area in the My Documents window is collapsed and a double down arrow button displays to the right of the Details title (Figure 1-34). Clicking the button or the area title expands the Details area and reveals the window title (My Documents) and folder type (System Folder) in the Details area. Similarly, clicking the double up arrow button or the area title collapses the area so only the area title and double down arrow button display in the area. Perform the following steps to expand the Details area in the left pane of the My Documents window.

Steps To Expand an Area

1 Point to the double down arrow button in the Details area.

The mouse pointer changes to a hand icon and points to the double down arrow button in the Details area and the color of the Details title and button changes to light blue (Figure 1-34).

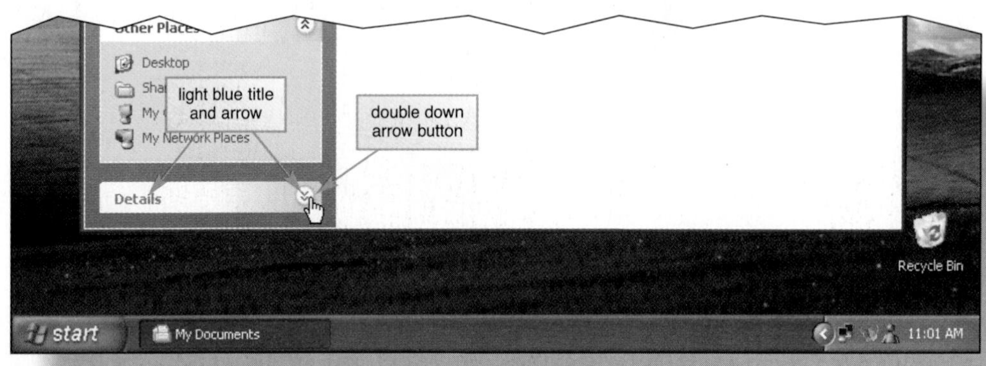

FIGURE 1-34

2 Click the double down arrow button.

The Details area expands, the window title (My Documents) and folder type (System Folder) display in the area, the double down arrow on the button changes to a double up arrow, a portion of the left pane is not visible, and a scroll bar displays in the area (Figure 1-35).

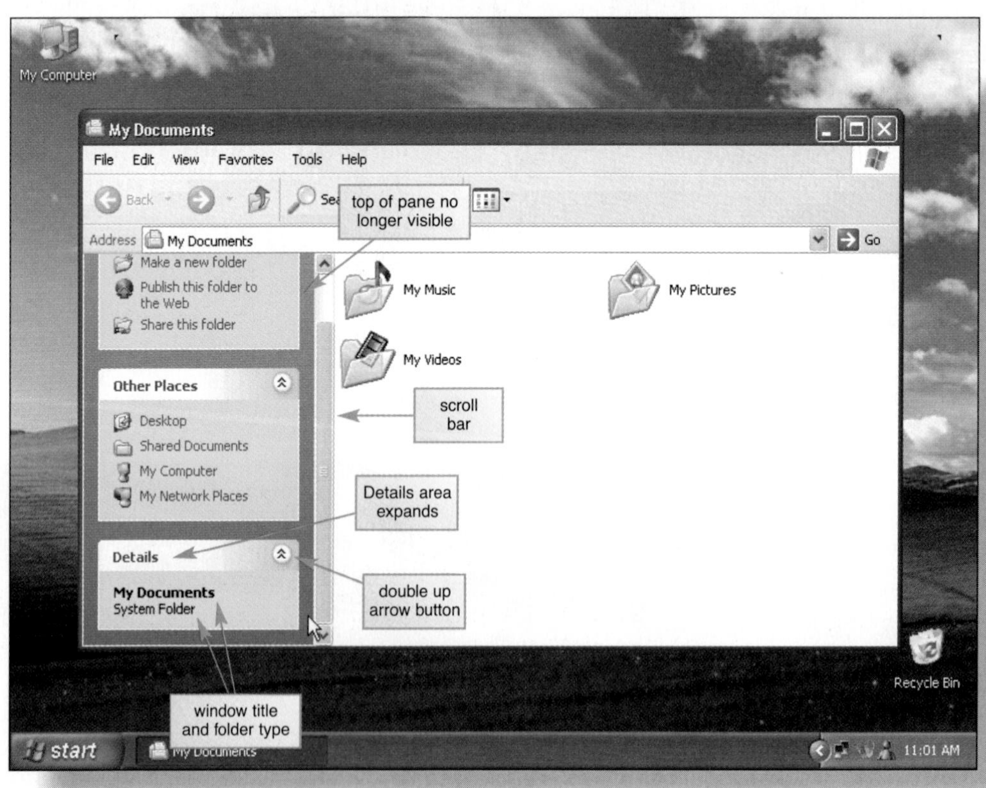

FIGURE 1-35

1. Click area title

A **scroll bar** is a bar that displays when the contents of a pane or window are not completely visible. A vertical scroll bar contains an **up scroll arrow**, a **down scroll arrow**, and a **scroll box** that enable you to view areas that currently are not visible. A vertical scroll bar displays along the right side of the left pane in the My Documents window shown in Figure 1-35. In some cases, the vertical scroll bar also may display along the right side of the right pane in a window.

More About

Window Sizing

Windows XP remembers the size of the window when you close the window. When you reopen the window, it will display in the same size as when you closed it.

Scrolling in a Window

Previously, the My Documents window was maximized to display information that was not completely visible in the My Documents window. Another method of viewing information that is not visible in a window is to use the scroll bar.

Scrolling can be accomplished in three ways: (1) click the scroll arrows; (2) click the scroll bar; and (3) drag the scroll box. On the following pages, you will use the scroll bar to scroll the contents of the left pane of the My Documents window. Perform the following steps to scroll the left pane using the scroll arrows.

More About

Scrolling

Most people will either maximize a window or size it so all the objects in the window are visible to avoid scrolling because scrolling takes time. It is more efficient not to have to scroll in a window.

Steps To Scroll Using Scroll Arrows

1 Point to the up scroll arrow on the vertical scroll bar.

The color of the up scroll arrow changes to light blue (Figure 1-36).

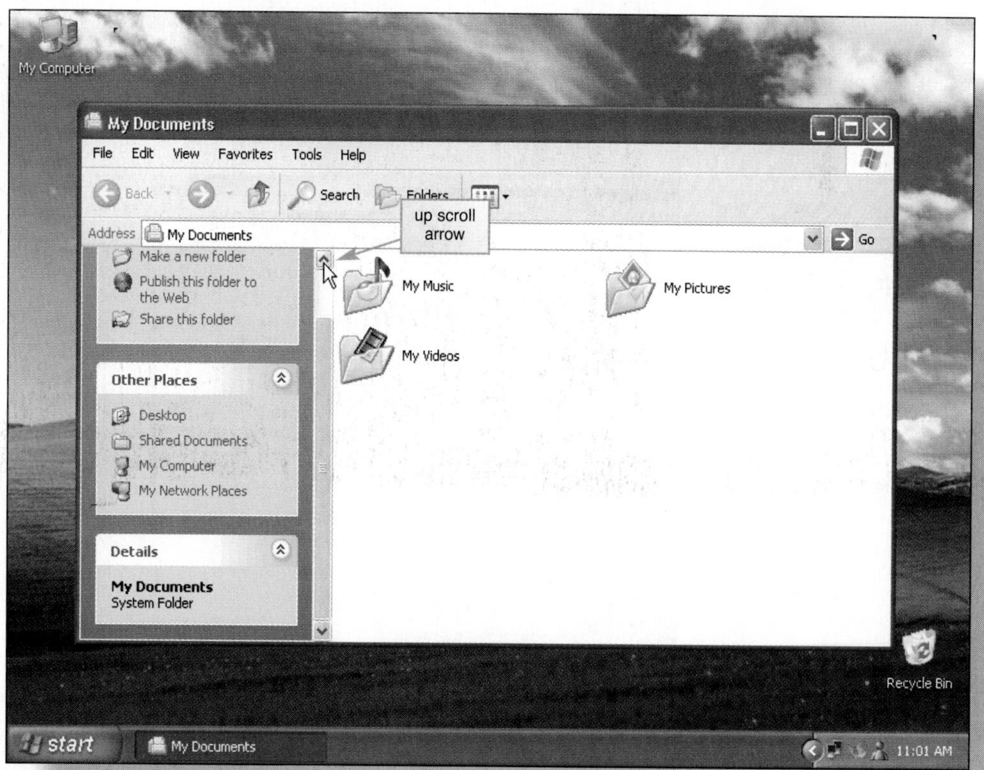

FIGURE 1-36

2 Click the up scroll arrow two times.

The left pane scrolls down (the contents in the left pane move up) and displays a portion of the text in the File and Folder Tasks area at the top of the pane that previously was not visible (Figure 1-37). Because the size of the left pane does not change when you scroll, the contents in the left pane will change, as seen in the difference between Figure 1-36 on the previous page and Figure 1-37.

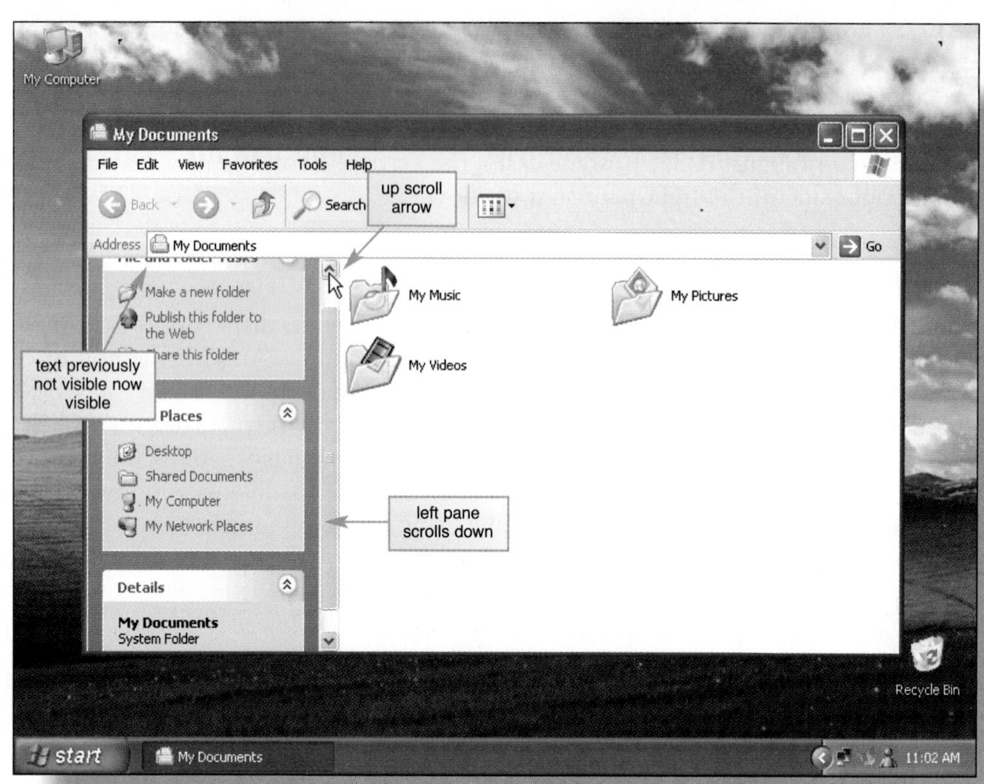

FIGURE 1-37

3 Click the up scroll arrow three more times.

The scroll box moves to the top of the scroll bar and the remaining text in the File and Folder Tasks area displays (Figure 1-38).

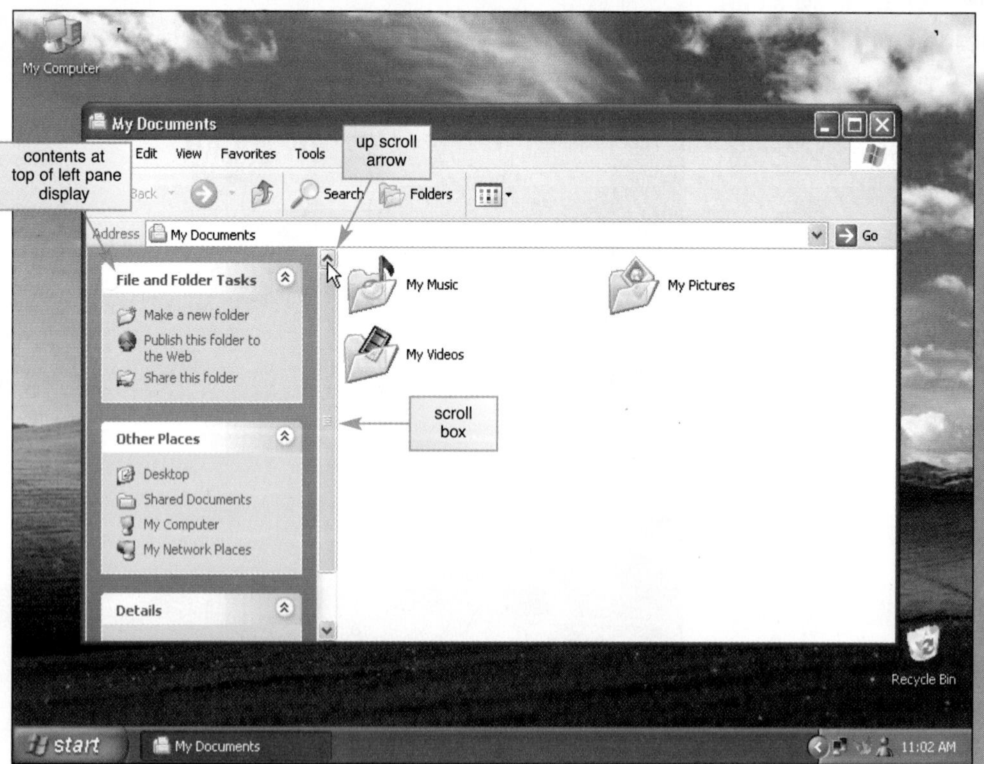

FIGURE 1-38

You can scroll continuously using scroll arrows by pointing to the up or down scroll arrow and holding down the left mouse button. The area being scrolled continues to scroll until you release the left mouse button or you reach the top or bottom of the area.

The Scroll Bar

In many application programs, clicking the scroll bar will move the window a full screen's worth of information up or down. You can step through a word processing document screen by screen, for example, by clicking the scroll bar.

Scrolling by Clicking the Scroll Bar

You also can scroll by clicking the scroll bar itself. To scroll to the top of the left pane by clicking the scroll bar, complete the following steps.

To Scroll Using the Scroll Bar

1 Point to the scroll bar below the scroll box (Figure 1-39).

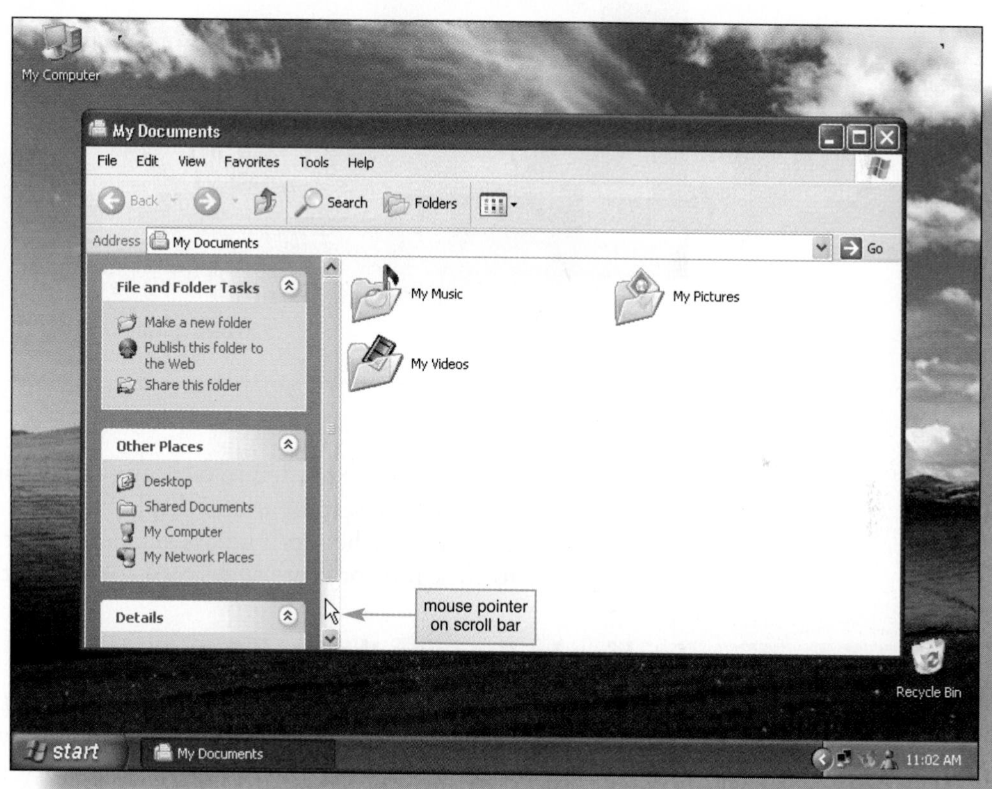

FIGURE 1-39

2 Click the scroll bar one time.

The scroll box moves to the bottom of the scroll bar and the bottom of the left pane displays (Figure 1-40).

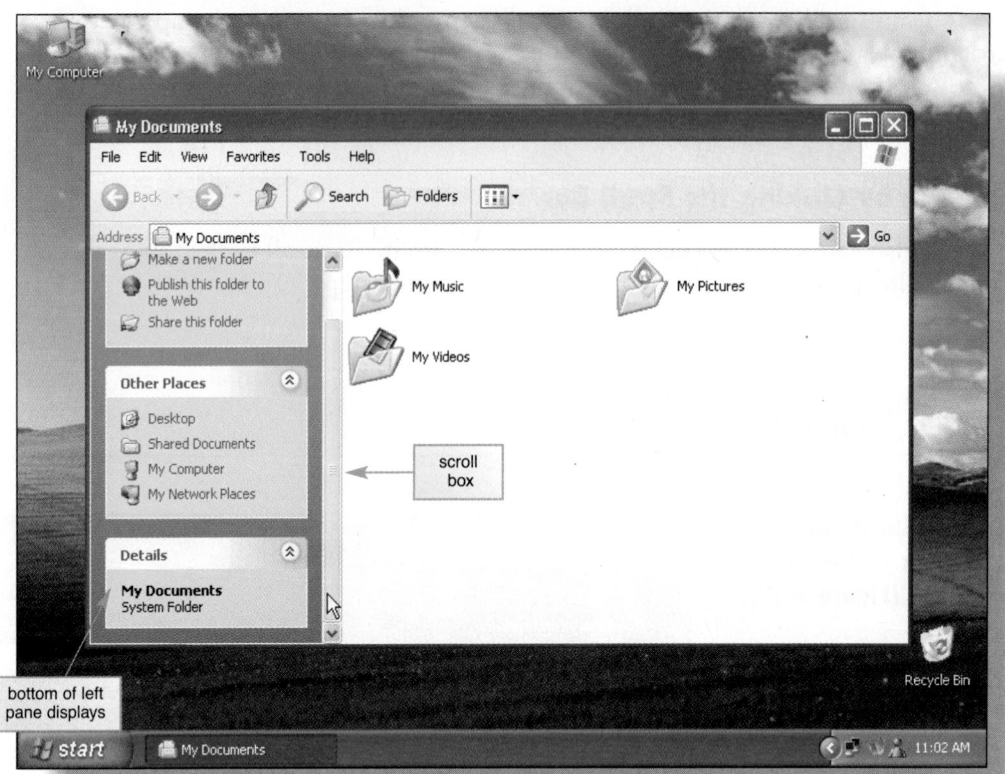

FIGURE 1-40

In the previous steps, you needed to click the scroll bar one time to move the scroll box to the top of the scroll bar and display the contents at the top of the left pane. In those cases where the scroll box is small and more contents are not visible, you may have to click four or more times to scroll to the top.

> **More About**
>
> **The Scroll Box**
>
> Dragging the scroll box is the most efficient technique to scroll long distances. In many application programs, such as Microsoft Word, as you scroll using the scroll box, the page number of the document displays next to the scroll box.

Scrolling by Dragging the Scroll Box

The third way in which you can scroll is by dragging the scroll box. To view the contents of the left pane of the My Documents window by dragging the scroll box, complete the following step.

Steps To Scroll by Dragging the Scroll Box

1 With the mouse pointer pointing to the scroll box on the scroll bar, drag the scroll box up the scroll bar until the scroll box is about halfway up the scroll bar.

As you drag the scroll box up the vertical scroll bar, additional parts of the left pane become visible (Figure 1-41). Notice that the information in the left pane moves as you drag the scroll box.

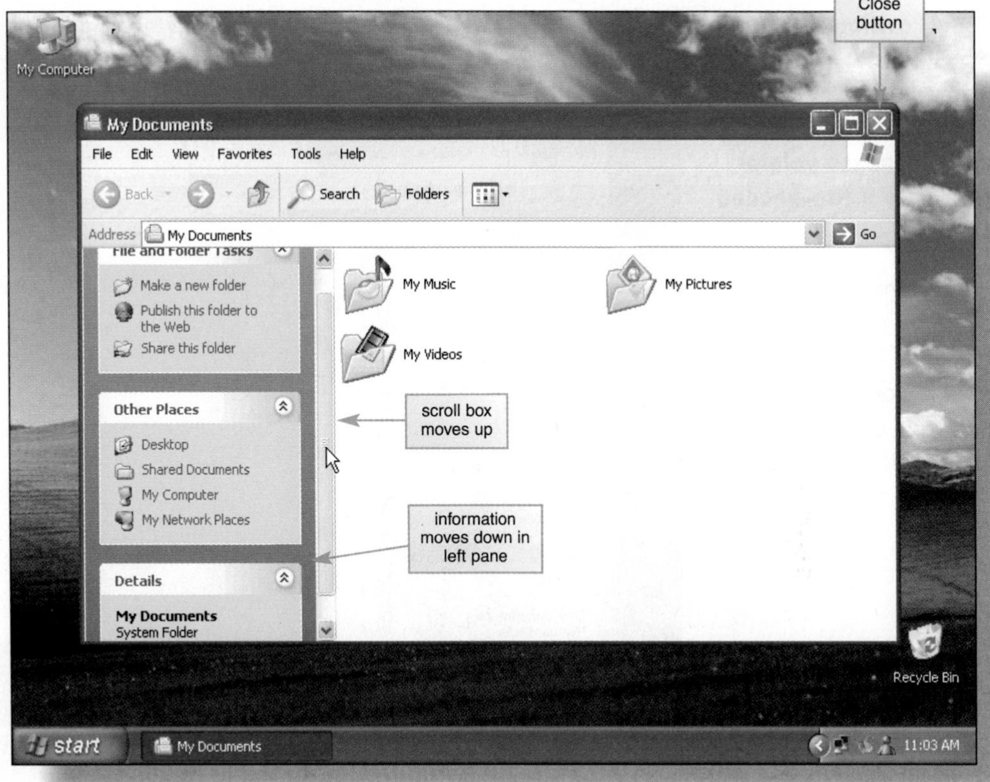

FIGURE 1-41

In previous examples, a vertical scroll bar displays in the left pane of the My Documents window. In addition, a sole vertical scroll bar may display in the right pane of a window or together with a scroll bar in the left pane of the window. In either case, the scroll arrows and scroll box allow you to view the contents of a window that currently are not visible. Being able to view the contents of a window by scrolling is an important Windows XP skill because in many cases the entire contents of a window are not visible.

More About

Scrolling Guidelines

General scrolling guidelines: (1) To scroll short distances (line by line), click the scroll arrows; (2) To scroll one screen at a time, click the scroll bar; and (3) To scroll long distances, drag the scroll box.

Sizing a Window by Dragging

As previously mentioned, sometimes when information displays in a window, the information is not completely visible. A third method to display information that is not visible is to change the size of the window by dragging the window. For example, you can drag the border of a window to change the size of the window. To change the size of the My Documents window, perform the steps on the next page.

Steps To Size a Window by Dragging

1 Position the mouse pointer over the bottom border of the My Documents window until the mouse pointer changes to a two-headed arrow.

When the mouse pointer is on top of the bottom border of the My Documents window, the pointer changes to a two-headed arrow (Figure 1-42).

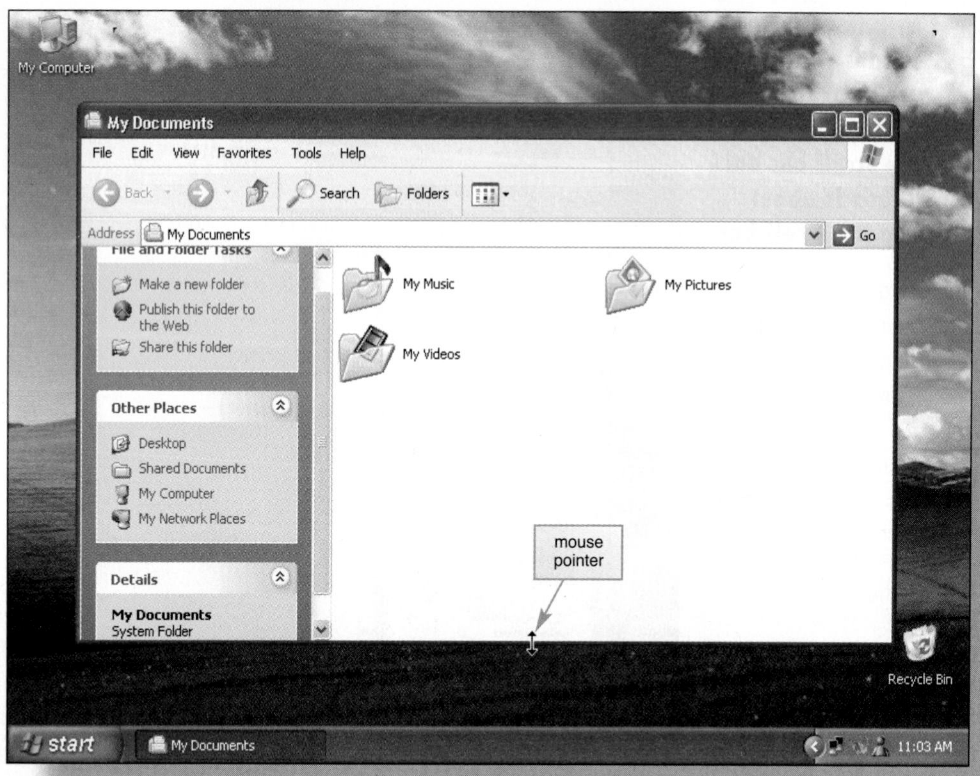

FIGURE 1-42

2 Drag the bottom border downward until the entire Details area is visible in the My Documents window.

As you drag the bottom border, the My Documents window, vertical scroll bar, and scroll box change size. After dragging, the Details area is visible and the vertical scroll bar is no longer visible (Figure 1-43).

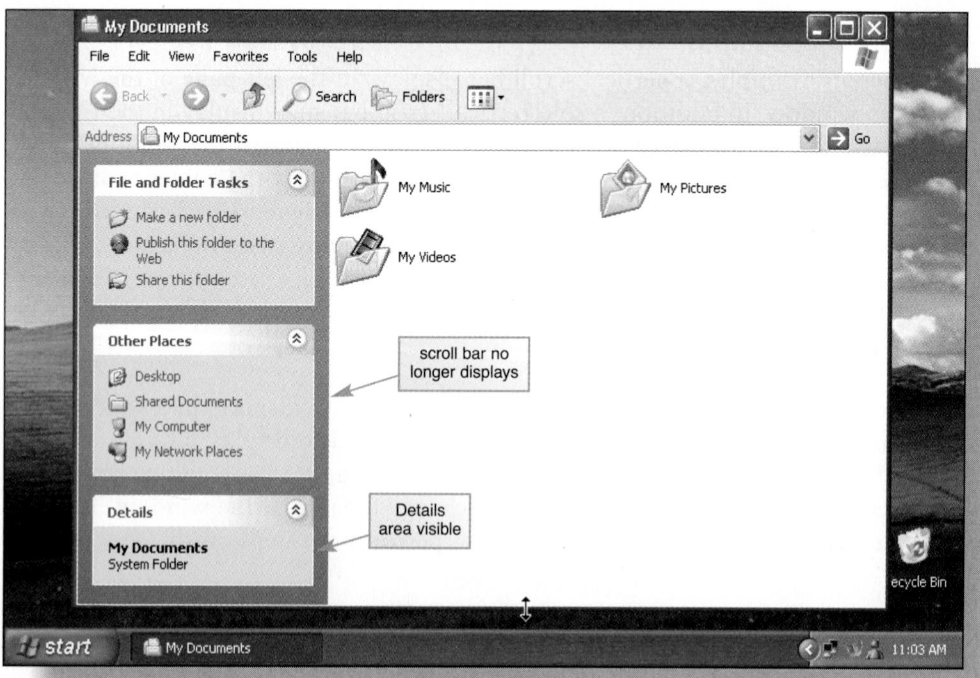

FIGURE 1-43

In addition to dragging the bottom border of a window, you also can drag the other borders (left, right, and top) and any window corner. If you drag a vertical border (left or right), you can move the border left or right. If you drag a horizontal border (top or bottom), you can move the border of the window up or down. If you drag a corner, you can move the corner up, down, left or right.

Collapsing an Area

The Details area in the My Documents window is expanded and a double up arrow button displays to the right of the Details title (Figure 1-43). Clicking the button or the area title collapses the Details area and removes the window title (My Documents) and folder type (System Folder) from the Details area. Perform the following steps to collapse the Details area in the My Documents window.

Steps To Collapse an Area

1 Point to the double up arrow button in the Details area.

The mouse pointer changes to a hand icon, points to the double up arrow button in the Details area, and the color of the Details title and button changes to light blue (Figure 1-44).

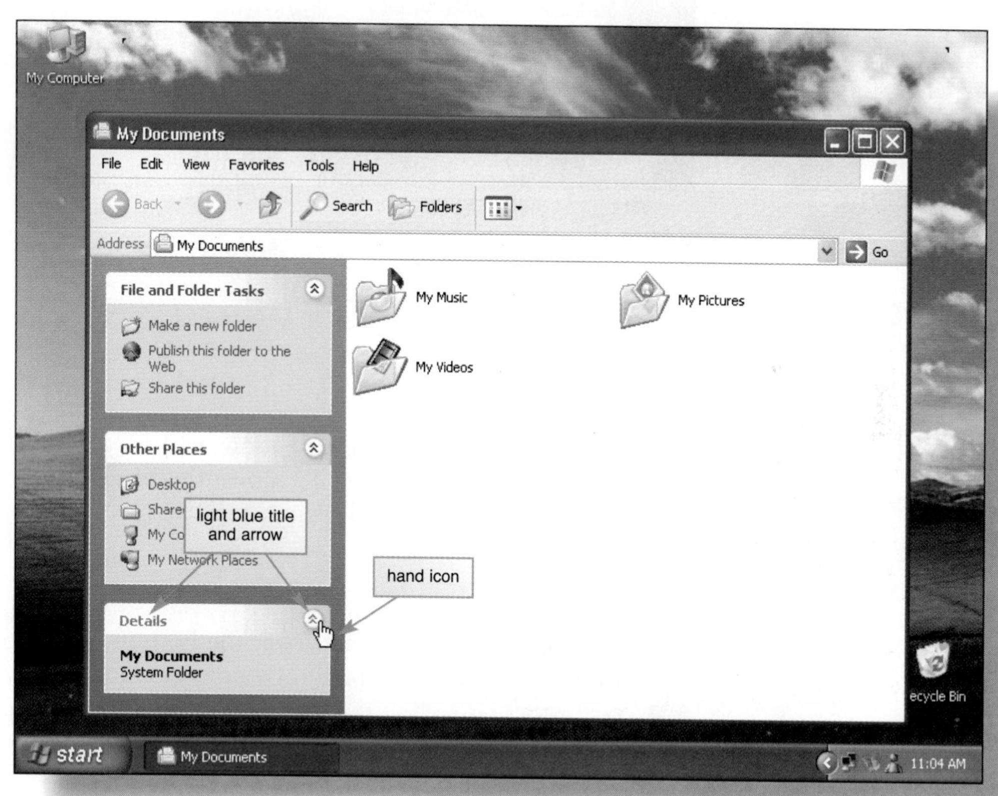

FIGURE 1-44

2 **Click the double up arrow button.**

The Details area collapses and only the Details title and the double down arrow button display (Figure 1-45).

FIGURE 1-45

Other Ways

1. Click area title

Resizing a Window

After moving and resizing a window, you may wish to return the window to approximately its original size. To return the My Documents window to about its original size, complete the following steps.

TO RESIZE A WINDOW

1. Position the mouse pointer over the bottom border of the My Documents window border until the mouse pointer changes to a two-headed arrow.
2. Drag the bottom border of the My Documents window up until the window is the same size as shown in Figure 1-31 on page WIN 1.30 and then release the mouse button.

The My Documents window is approximately the same size as it was before you made it smaller.

Closing a Window

After you have completed work in a window, normally you will close the window. To close the My Documents window, complete the following steps.

TO CLOSE A WINDOW

1. Point to the Close button on the right of the title bar in the My Documents window (see Figure 1-45).
2. Click the Close button.

The My Documents window closes and the desktop contains no open windows (Figure 1-46). Because the My Documents window is closed, the My Documents button no longer displays in the taskbar button area.

FIGURE 1-46

Deleting a Desktop Icon by Right-Dragging

The My Computer icon remains on the desktop. In many cases after you have placed an icon on the desktop, you will want to delete the icon. Although Windows XP has many ways to delete desktop icons, one method of removing the My Computer icon from the desktop is to right-drag the My Computer icon to the Recycle Bin icon on the desktop. **Right-drag** means you point to an item, hold down the right mouse button, move the item to the desired location, and then release the right mouse button. When you right-drag an object, a shortcut menu displays. The shortcut menu contains commands specifically for use with the object being dragged.

When you delete an icon from the desktop, Windows XP places the item in the **Recycle Bin**, which is an area on the hard disk that contains all the items you have deleted not only from the desktop but also from the hard disk. When the Recycle Bin becomes full, you can empty it. Up until the time you empty the Recycle Bin, you can recover deleted items from the Recycle Bin. To delete the My Computer icon by right-dragging the icon to the Recycle Bin icon, perform the steps on the next page.

More About

Right-Dragging

Right-dragging was not available on some earlier versions of Windows, so you might find people familiar with Windows not even considering right-dragging. Because it always produces a shortcut menu, right-dragging is the safest way to drag.

Steps To Delete a Desktop Icon by Right-Dragging

1 Point to the My Computer icon on the desktop (Figure 1-47).

FIGURE 1-47

2 Hold down the right mouse button, drag the My Computer icon over the Recycle Bin icon on the desktop, and then release the right mouse button.

The My Computer icon displays on the desktop as you drag the icon. When you release the right mouse button, the My Computer icon no longer displays and a shortcut menu displays on the desktop (Figure 1-48). The shortcut menu contains the bolded Move Here command and the Cancel command.

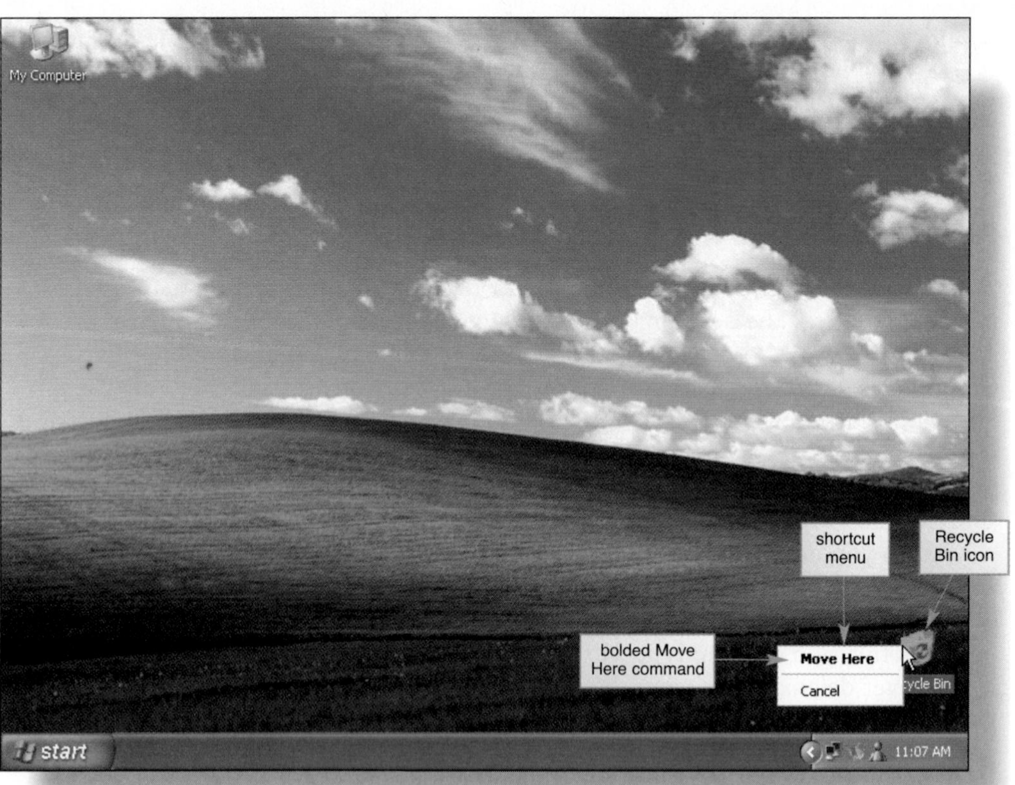

FIGURE 1-48

3 Point to Move Here on the shortcut menu.

The Move Here command is highlighted (Figure 1-49).

FIGURE 1-49

4 Click Move Here and then point to the Yes button in the Confirm Delete dialog box.

The shortcut menu no longer displays on the desktop and the Confirm Delete dialog box displays on the desktop (Figure 1-50). A ***dialog box*** *displays whenever Windows XP needs to supply information to you or wants you to enter information or select among several options. The Confirm Delete dialog box contains a question, a message, and the Yes and No buttons.*

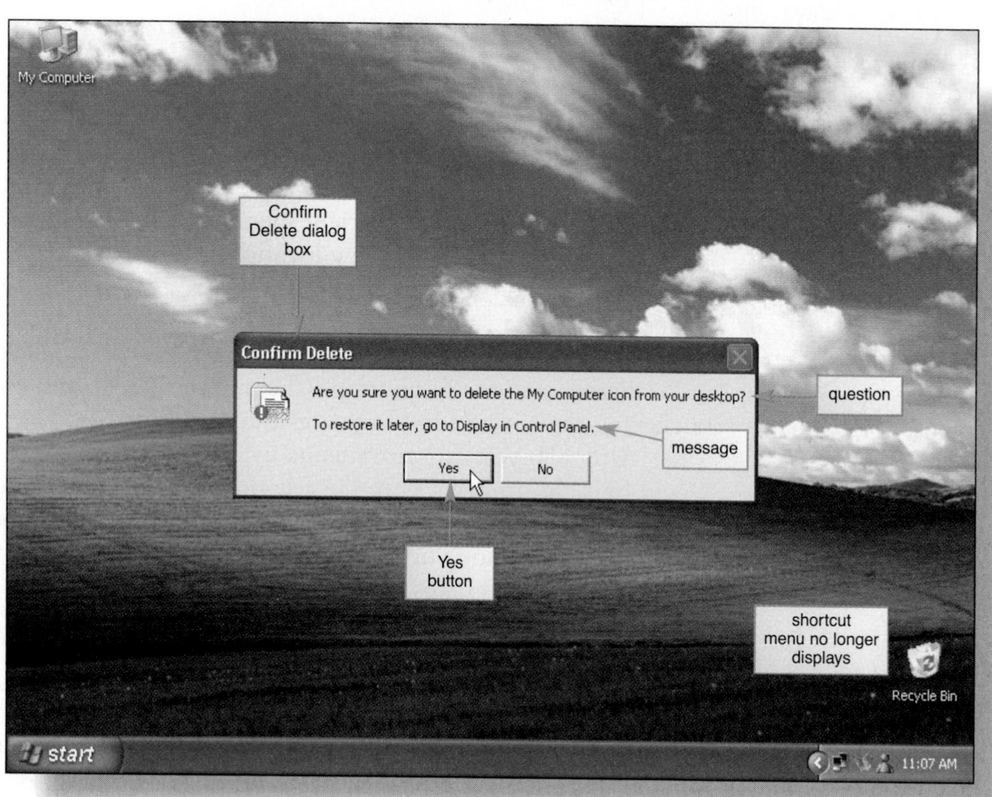

FIGURE 1-50

5 Click the Yes button.

The Confirm Delete dialog box closes and the My Computer icon no longer displays on the desktop (Figure 1-51). The My Computer icon now is contained in the Recycle Bin.

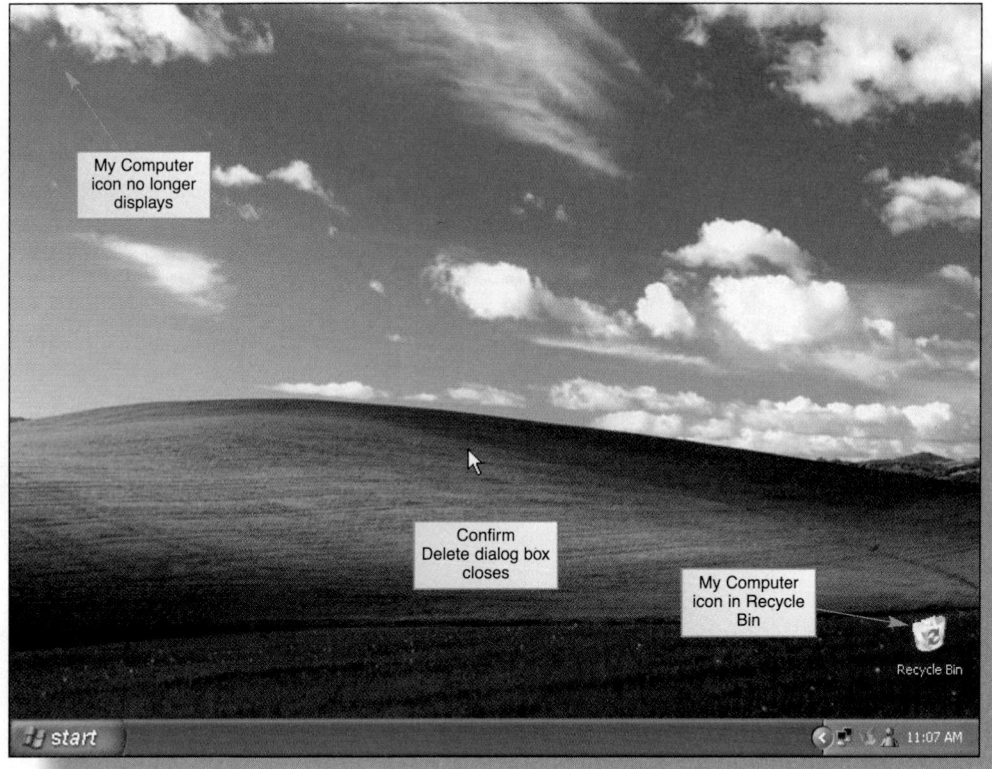

FIGURE 1-51

Other Ways

1. Drag icon to Recycle Bin, click Yes button
2. Right-click icon, click Delete, click Yes button

In Figure 1-48 on page WIN 1.42, the My Computer icon remains in its original location on the desktop and the shortcut menu contains two commands, Move Here and Cancel. The **Move Here command** in bold (dark) font identifies what would happen if you were to drag the My Computer icon with the left mouse button. If you click Move Here on the shortcut menu shown, Windows XP will move the icon from its current location to the new location. If you click Cancel, the operation will be terminated and the **Cancel command** will reset anything you have done during the operation.

In Figure 1-50 on the previous page, the Confirm Delete dialog box contains the Yes button and the No button. Clicking the Yes button completes the operation and clicking the No button terminates the operation.

Although you can move icons by dragging with the primary (left) mouse button and by right-dragging with the secondary (right) mouse button, it is strongly suggested you right-drag because a menu displays and, in most cases, you can specify the exact operation you want to occur. When you drag using the left mouse button, a default operation takes place and that operation may not be the operation you intended to perform.

Summary of Mouse and Windows Operations

You have seen how to use the mouse to point, click, right-click, double-click, drag, and right-drag in order to accomplish certain tasks on the desktop. The use of a mouse is an important skill when using Windows XP. In addition, you have learned how to move around and use windows on the Windows XP desktop.

The Keyboard and Keyboard Shortcuts

The **keyboard** is an input device on which you manually key in, or type, data. Figure 1-52 shows the Microsoft Office keyboard designed specifically for use with Microsoft Office and the Internet. The Single Touch pad along the left side of the keyboard contains keys to browse the Internet, copy and paste text, and switch between applications. A scroll wheel allows you to quickly move within a document window. The Hot Keys along the top of the keyboard allow you to launch a Web browser or e-mail program, play multi-media, and adjust the system volume.

> **More About**
>
> **The Microsoft Office Keyboard**
>
> When using the Single Touch pad, Microsoft Office users place their left hand on the pad and their right hand on the mouse. These hand positions allow them to get more work done in less time. They also report that when using Hot Keys they can increase productivity because they do not have to take their hand off the keyboard as frequently to use a mouse.

FIGURE 1-52

Many tasks you accomplish with a mouse also can be accomplished using a keyboard. To perform tasks using the keyboard, you must understand the notation used to identify which keys to press. This notation is used throughout Windows XP to identify a **keyboard shortcut.**

Keyboard shortcuts consist of (1) pressing a single key (such as press the ENTER key); or (2) pressing and holding down one key and pressing a second key, as shown by two key names separated by a plus sign (such as press CTRL+ESC). For example, to obtain Help about Windows XP, you can press the F1 key and to display the Start menu, hold down the CTRL key and then press the ESC key (press CTRL+ESC).

Often, computer users will use keyboard shortcuts for operations they perform frequently. For example, many users find pressing the F1 key to launch Windows XP Help and Support easier than using the Start menu as shown later in this project. As a user, you probably will find the combination of keyboard and mouse operations that particularly suit you, but it is strongly recommended that generally you use the mouse.

> **More About**
>
> **Microsoft Keyboards**
>
> For additional information about Microsoft keyboards, launch the Internet Explorer browser (see pages WIN 1.45 and WIN 1.46), type `http://www.scsite.com/winxp/more.htm` in the Address box in the Microsoft Internet Explorer window, and then press the ENTER key.

Launching an Application Program

One of the basic tasks you can perform using Windows XP is to launch an application program. A **program** is a set of computer instructions that carries out a task on the computer. An **application program** is a program that allows you to accomplish a specific task for which that program is designed. For example, a **word processing program** is an application program that allows you to create written documents; a

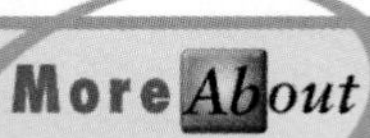

Application Programs

Several application programs (Internet Explorer, Movie Maker, Media Player, and Windows Messenger) are part of Windows XP. Most application programs, however, such as Microsoft Office and Microsoft Access must be purchased separately from Windows XP.

presentation graphics program is an application program that allows you to create graphic presentations for display on a computer; and a **Web browser program** is an application program that allows you to search for and display Web pages.

The **default Web browser program** (Internet Explorer) displays in the pinned items list on the Start menu shown in Figure 1-10 on page WIN 1.15. Because the default **Web browser** is selected during the installation of the Windows XP operating system, the default Web browser on your computer may be different. In addition, you can easily select another Web browser as the default Web browser. Another frequently used Web browser program is **MSN Explorer**.

Launching an Application Using the Start Menu

The most common activity performed on a computer is running an application program to accomplish tasks using the computer. You can launch an application program by using the Start menu. To illustrate the use of the Start menu to launch an application program, the default Web browser program (Internet Explorer) will be launched. Perform the following steps to launch Internet Explorer using the Internet command on the Start menu.

To Launch a Program Using the Start Menu

1 Click the Start button on the taskbar and then point to Internet on the pinned items list on the Start menu.

The Start menu displays (Figure 1-53). The pinned items list on the Start menu contains the **Internet command** *to launch the default Web browser program and the name of the default Web browser program (Internet Explorer). The default Web browser program on your computer may be different.*

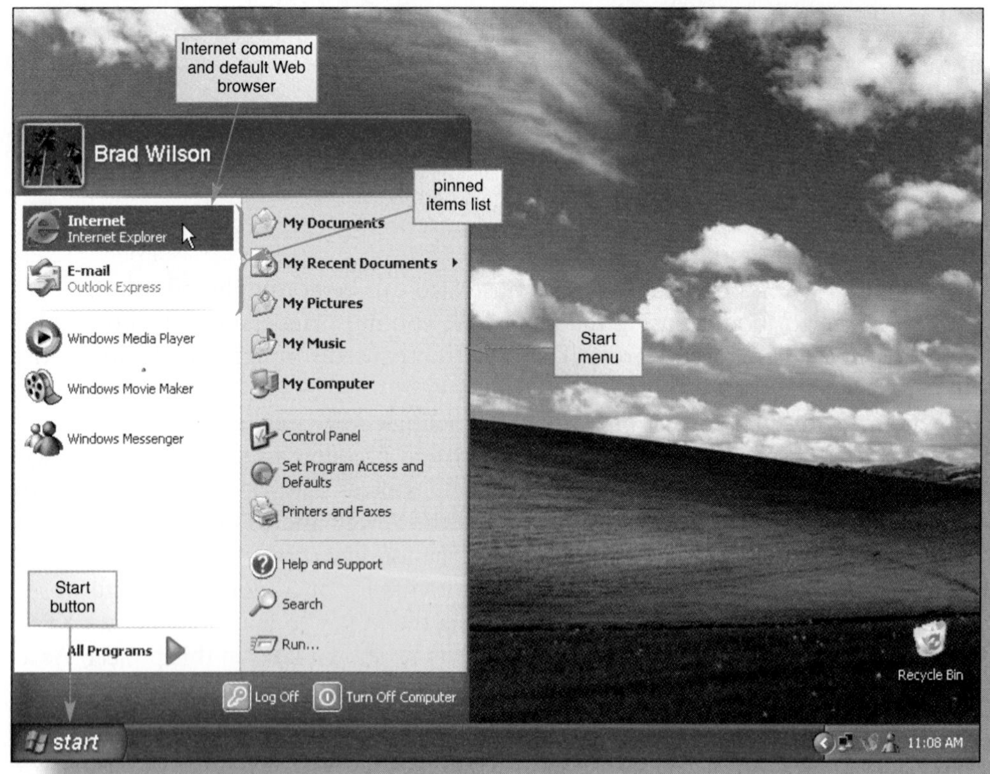

FIGURE 1-53

2 Click Internet.

Windows XP launches the Internet Explorer program by displaying the Welcome to MSN.com – Microsoft Internet Explorer window, displaying the MSN home page in the window, and adding a recessed button on the taskbar (Figure 1-54). The URL for the Web page displays in the Address bar. Because you can select the default Web browser and the Web page to display when you launch the Web browser, the Web page that displays on your desktop may be different.

3 Click the Close button in the Microsoft Internet Explorer window.

The Microsoft Internet Explorer window closes.

FIGURE 1-54

Any computer connected to the Internet that contains Web pages you can reference is called a **Web site**. The **MSN.com Web site**, one of millions of Web sites around the world, is stored on a computer operated by Microsoft Corporation and can be accessed using a Web browser. The Welcome to MSN.com **Web page** shown in Figure 1-54 is the first Web page you see when you access the MSN.com Web site and is, therefore, referred to as a **home page**, or **start page.** The Web page that displays on your computer may be different.

After you have launched a Web browser, you can use the program to search for and display additional Web pages located on different Web sites around the world.

Other Ways

1. Click Start button, in most frequently used program list click Internet Explorer
2. Click Start button, point to All Programs, click Internet Explorer
3. On Quick Launch toolbar, click Internet Explorer icon
4. Press CTRL+ESC, press I

Using Windows Help and Support

One of the more powerful Windows XP features is Help and Support. Help and Support is available when using Windows XP or when using any application program running under Windows XP. This feature is designed to assist you in using Windows XP or the various application programs.

Windows XP Help and Support

If you purchased an operating system or application program nine years ago, you received at least one, and more often several, thick technical manuals that explained the software. With Windows XP, you receive a lightweight manual with only 34 pages. The Help and Support feature of Windows XP replaces reams and reams of printed pages in hard-to-understand technical manuals.

Help and Support brings together the Help features that were available in previous versions of Windows (Search, Index, and Favorites) with the online Help features found on the Microsoft Web site. Help and Support includes access to articles in the Microsoft Knowledge Base, communication with Windows XP newsgroups, and troubleshooting solutions.

Help and Support also includes tools that allow you to view general information about the computer, update changes to the operating system, restore the computer to a previous state without losing data files, and permit an individual at another computer to connect to your computer and walk you through the solution to a problem.

Launching Help and Support

Before you can access the Help and Support Center services, you must launch Help and Support. One method of launching Help and Support uses the Start menu. To launch Help and Support, complete the following steps.

To Launch Help and Support

1 Click the Start button on the taskbar and then point to Help and Support on the Start menu.

Windows XP displays the Start menu and highlights the Help and Support command (Figure 1-55).

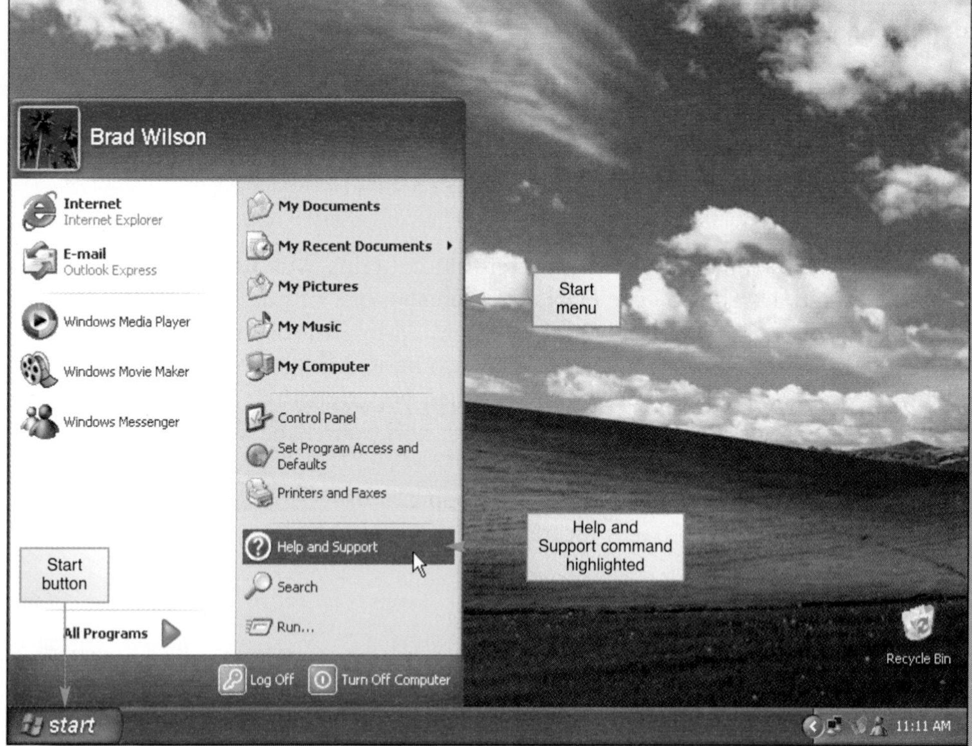

FIGURE 1-55

2 Click Help and Support and then click the Maximize button on the Help and Support Center title bar.

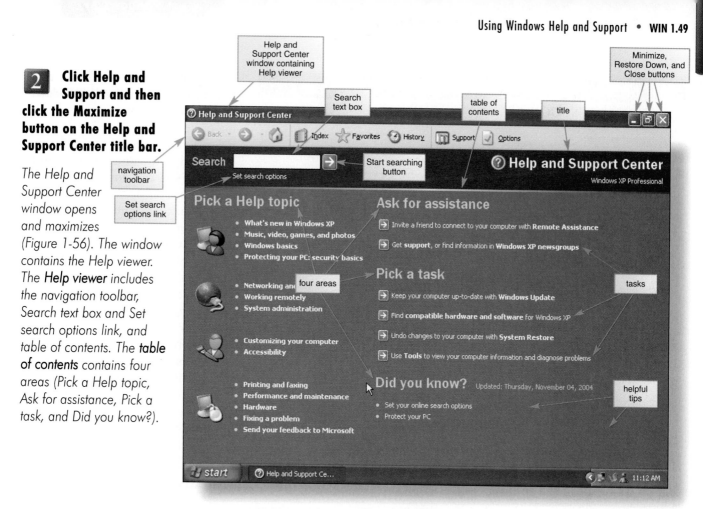

*The Help and Support Center window opens and maximizes (Figure 1-56). The window contains the Help viewer. The **Help viewer** includes the navigation toolbar, Search text box and Set search options link, and table of contents. The **table of contents** contains four areas (Pick a Help topic, Ask for assistance, Pick a task, and Did you know?).*

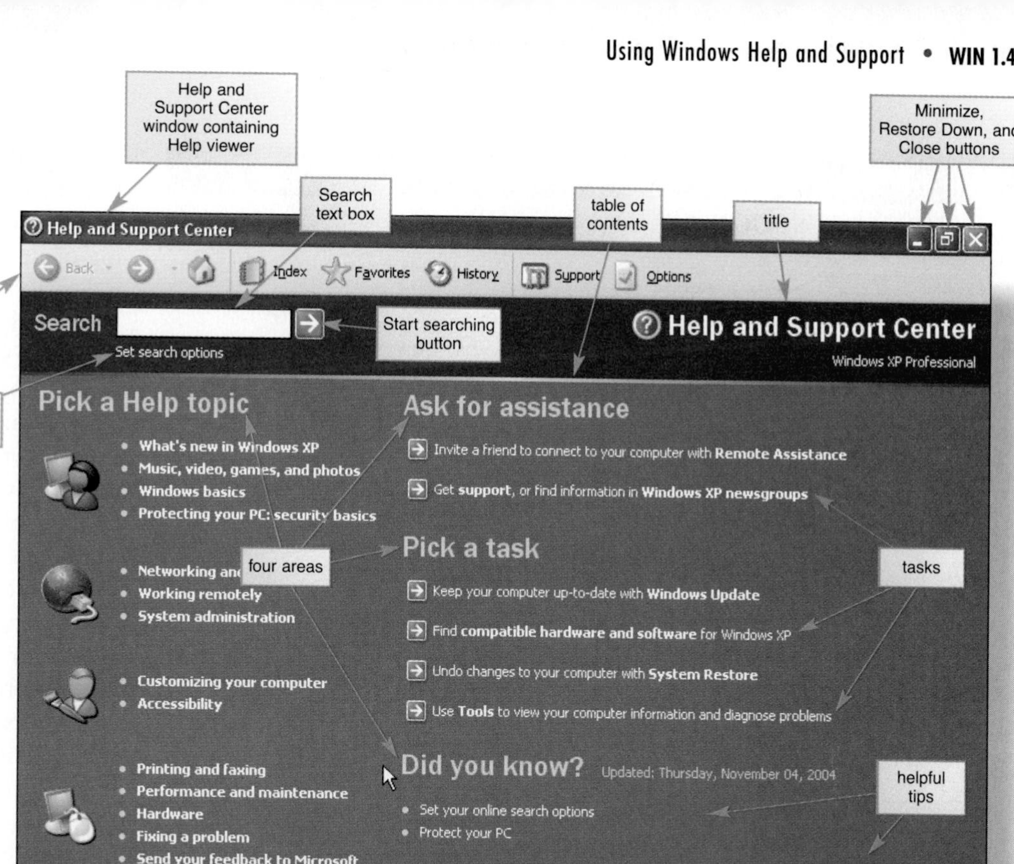

FIGURE 1-56

The Help and Support Center title bar shown in Figure 1-56 contains a Minimize button, Restore Down button, and Close button. You can minimize or restore the Help and Support Center window as needed and also close the Help and Support Center window.

The navigation toolbar displays below the title bar. The **navigation toolbar** allows you to navigate through Help topics and pages, browse and save Help topics and pages, view previously saved Help topics and pages, get online support for questions and problems, and customize the Help viewer. An icon identifies each button on the **navigation toolbar**. Six buttons contain a text label (Back, Index, Favorites, History, Support, and Options). Table 1-2 on the next page illustrates the navigation toolbar and briefly describes the functions of each button. The buttons on the navigation toolbar on your computer may be different.

The area below the navigation toolbar contains the Search text box and Start searching button used to search for Help, the Set search options link to set the criteria for searching the Help and Support Center, and the window's title (Help and Support Center).

The **table of contents** contains four areas. The **Pick a Help topic area** contains four category groups. A unique icon identifies each group. Clicking a category in a group displays a list of subcategories and Help topics related to the category.

The **Ask for assistance area** contains two tasks. The first task (**Remote Assistance**) allows another individual at another computer to connect and control your computer while helping to solve a problem. The second task (**Windows XP newsgroups**) allows you to obtain Help from product support experts or discuss your questions with other Windows XP users in newsgroups.

Other Ways

1. Press F1
2. Press CTRL+ESC, press H
3. Press WINDOWS+F1 (WINDOWS key on Microsoft Natural keyboard)

More About

The Table of Contents

The table of contents in Windows XP resembles the Contents sheet in previous versions of Windows. To display the Contents sheet you had to click the Contents tab in the Help window. Now, the table of contents displays in a prominent position and contains links to online Help and Support topics.

Table 1-2 Help Toolbar	
BUTTON	FUNCTION
Back	Displays the previous Help topic or page (provided it was displayed just previously). To go back more than one topic or page, click the Back button arrow and then click a topic or page title on the Back button list.
Forward	Displays the next Help topic or page. To go forward more than one topic or page, click the Forward button arrow and then click a topic name or page title on the list.
Home	Displays the Help and Support Center home page.
Index	Displays an index of Help topics.
Favorites	Displays a list of previously saved Help topics or pages.
History	Displays a list of Help topics and pages read during the current session.
Support	Displays a list of online support options for getting Help.
Options	Displays a list of options to customize the Help and Support Center.

The **Pick a task area** contains four tasks. The first task (**Windows Update**) allows you to access a catalog of items such as device drivers, security fixes, critical updates, the latest Help files, and Internet products that you can download to keep your computer up-to-date. The second task (**compatible hardware and software**) allows you to search for hardware and software that is compatible with Windows XP. The third task (**System Restore**) allows you to store the current state of your computer and restore your computer to that state without losing important information. The fourth task (**Tools**) contains a collection of fifteen helpful tools to keep your computer running smoothly. The **Did you know? area** is updated daily with helpful tips for using Windows XP.

Browsing for Help Topics in the Table of Contents

After launching Help and Support, the next step is to find the Help topic in which you are interested. Assume you want to know more about finding information using the Help and Support Center. Perform the following steps to use the table of contents to find a Help topic that describes how to find what you need in the Help and Support Center.

Steps To Browse for Help Topics in the Table of Contents

1 Point to Windows basics in the Pick a Help topic area.

The mouse pointer changes to a hand icon when positioned on the Windows basics category and the category is underlined (Figure 1-57).

Windows basic category underlined

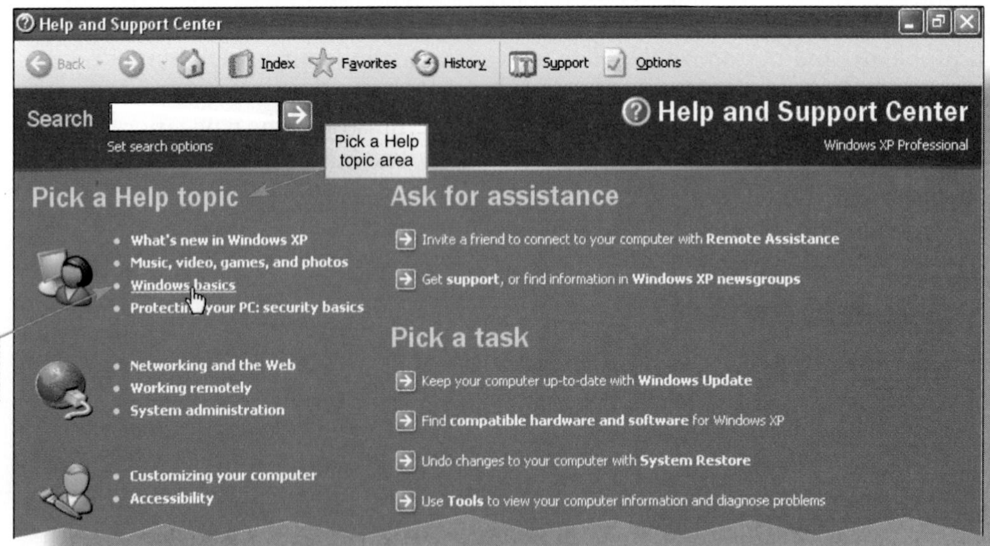

FIGURE 1-57

2 Click Windows basics and then point to Tips for using Help.

The navigation pane and topic pane display in the Help and Support Center window (Figure 1-58). The Windows basics area in the navigation pane contains five categories and the underlined Tips for using Help category. The See Also area contains four Help topics. The topic pane contains the Help and Support toolbar and the Windows basics page.

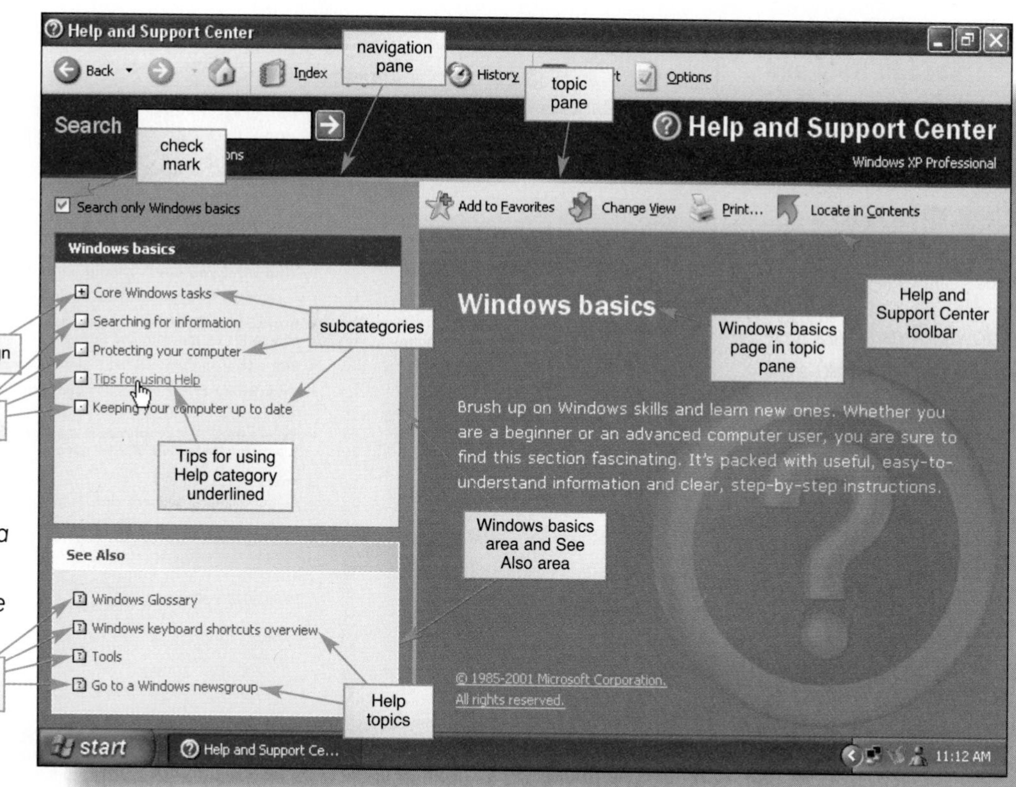

FIGURE 1-58

3 Click Tips for using Help and then point to Find what you need in Help and Support Center in the topic pane.

Windows XP highlights the Tips for using Help category in the Windows basics area, displays the Tips for using Help page in the topic pane, and underlines the Find what you need in Help and Support Center task (Figure 1-59). The Add to Favorites button and Print button on the Help and Support Center toolbar are dimmed to indicate the page cannot be added to the favorites list or printed.

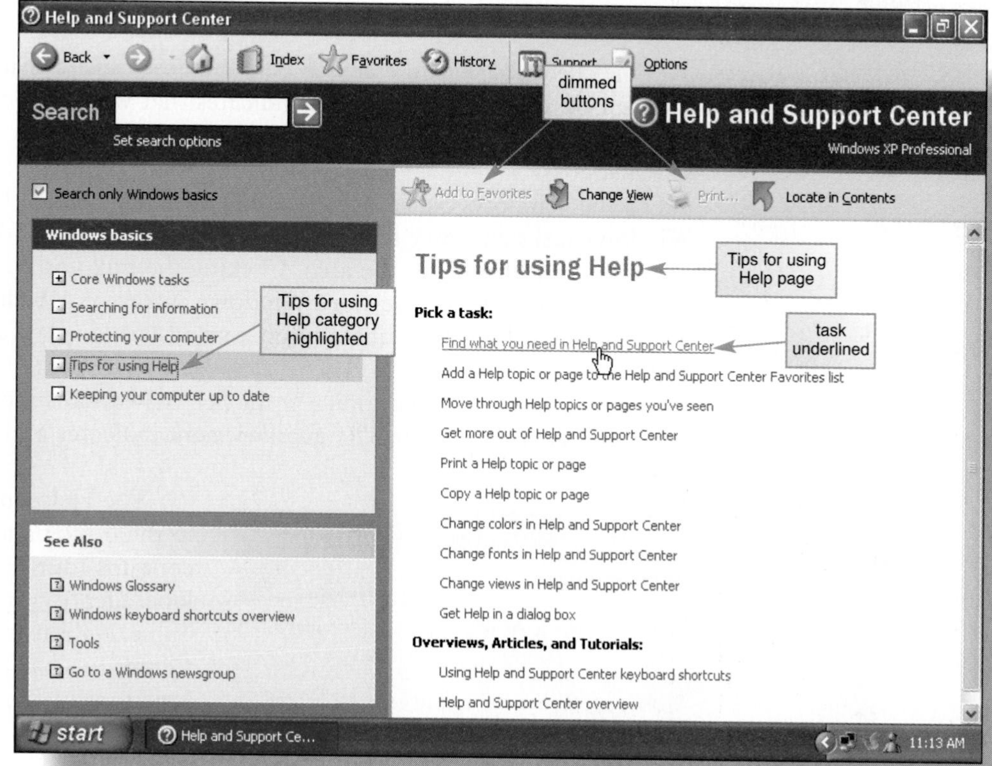

FIGURE 1-59

4 Click Find what you need in Help and Support Center and then read the information in the To find what you need in Help and Support Center topic in the topic pane.

Windows XP removes the dotted rectangle surrounding the Tips for using Help category in the Windows basics area and displays the To find what you need in Help and Support Center topic in the topic pane (Figure 1-60). Clicking the Related Topics link displays a list of related Help topics.

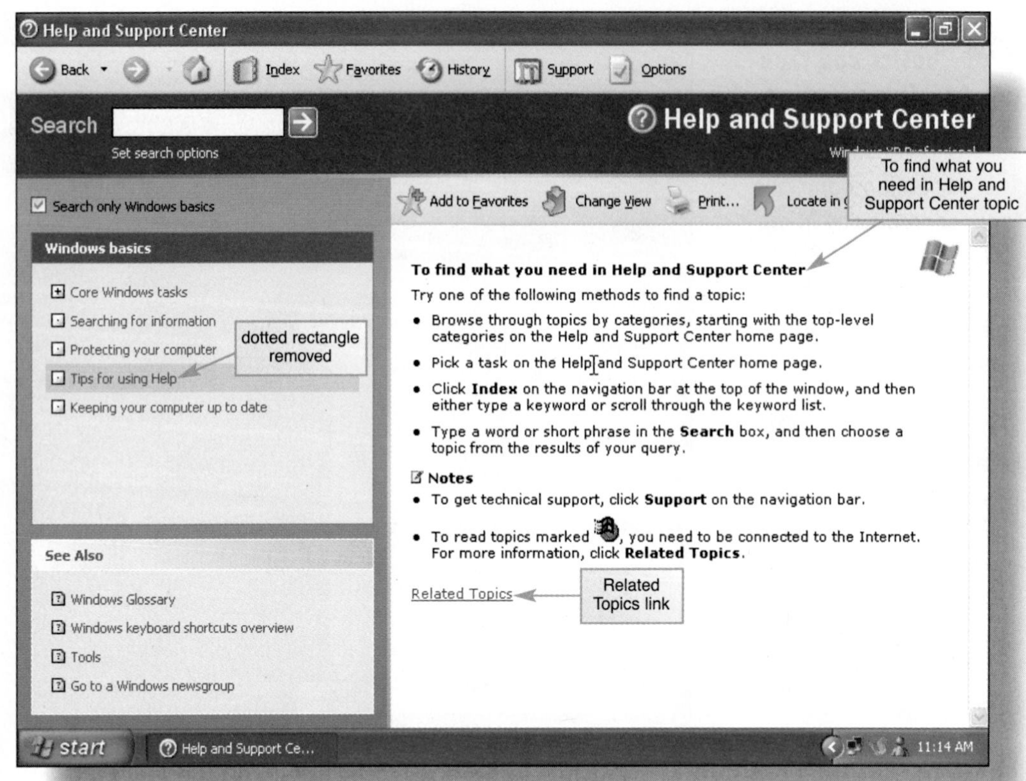

FIGURE 1-60

Other Ways

1. Press TAB until category or topic is highlighted, press ENTER, repeat for each category or topic

The check mark in the **Search only Windows basics check box** shown in Figure 1-58 on the previous page indicates that when searching for a Help topic using the Search text box, only the topics in the Windows basics category will be searched.

In the Windows basics area, the **plus sign** in the small box to the left of the Core Windows tasks category indicates the category contains subcategories but the subcategories do not display in the area. Clicking the box with the plus sign displays a list of subcategories below the Core Windows category. A **bullet** in a small box indicates a category. Clicking the bullet within a small box displays a list of tasks in the topic pane.

Each of the four Help topics in the See Also area is identified by a question mark in a document icon. The **question mark** indicates a Help topic without further subdivision.

The Help and Support Center toolbar in the topic pane shown in Figure 1-58 contains four buttons. An icon and text label identify each button on the toolbar. Table 1-3 illustrates the Help and Support Center toolbar and briefly describes the functions of the buttons.

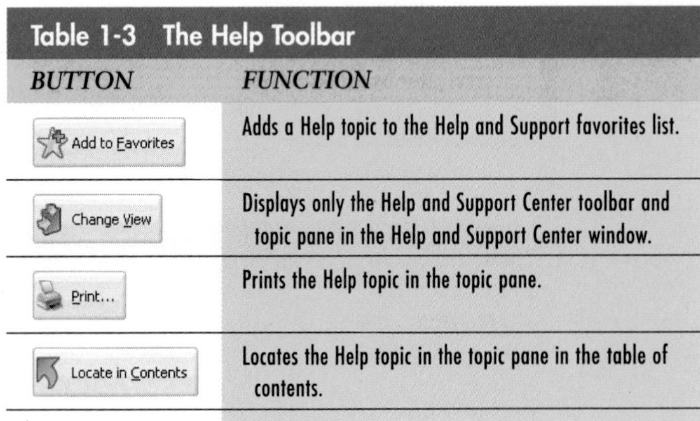

Table 1-3 The Help Toolbar

BUTTON	FUNCTION
Add to Favorites	Adds a Help topic to the Help and Support favorites list.
Change View	Displays only the Help and Support Center toolbar and topic pane in the Help and Support Center window.
Print...	Prints the Help topic in the topic pane.
Locate in Contents	Locates the Help topic in the topic pane in the table of contents.

Bookmarking a Help Topic

After using the table of contents to browse for a Help topic by category, you may want to **bookmark**, or save, the resulting Help topic for easy retrieval in the future. Assume you want to bookmark the To find what you need in Help and Support Center topic you found (Figure 1-60) and return to this page in the future. Perform the following steps to use the Add to Favorites button on the Help and Support Center toolbar to bookmark this topic.

Steps To Bookmark a Help Topic

1 Click the Add to Favorites button on the Help and Support Center toolbar and then point to the OK button in the Help and Support Center dialog box.

The Help and Support Center dialog box displays (Figure 1-61). The dialog box contains a message, and the OK button.

2 Click the OK button.

The Help and Support Center dialog box closes. Although not visible, the To find what you need in Help Support Center name is added to the Help and Support Center favorites list.

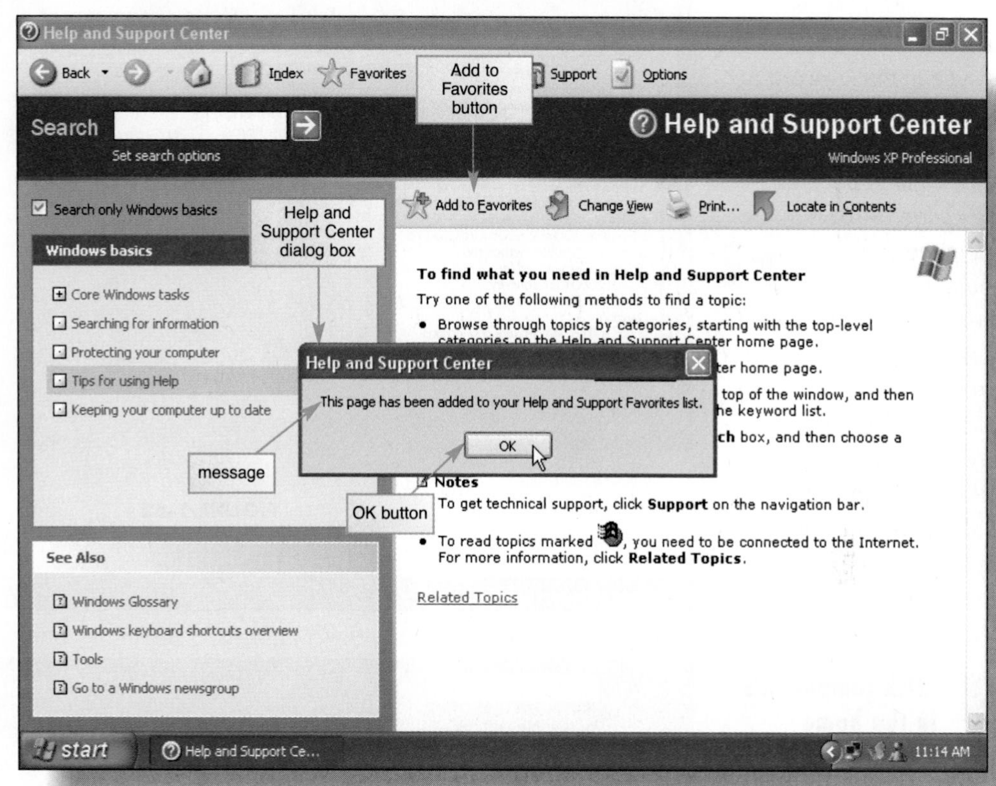

FIGURE 1-61

Other Ways

1. Press SHIFT+F10, press A

In the future, if you want to return to a favorite Help topic, click the Favorites button on the **navigation toolbar**, click the topic name in the Favorites area, and then click the Display button. The topic will display in the topic pane of the Help and Support Center window. The steps to display a topic are illustrated later in this project.

Using the Help and Support Center Index

A second method of finding answers to your questions about Windows XP is to use the Help and Support Center Index. The **Help and Support Center Index** contains a list of index entries, each of which references one or more Help topics. Assume you want more information about home networking. Perform the steps on the next page to learn more about home networking.

Steps To Search for Help Topics Using the Index

1 Click the Index button on the navigation toolbar, type home networking **in the Type in the keyword to find text box, and then point to components in the home network in the list box.**

The Index area, containing the Type in the keyword to find text box, list box, and Display button, displays in the navigation pane and the Index page displays in the topic pane (Figure 1-62). When you type an entry in the text box, the list of index entries in the list box automatically scrolls and the entry you type (home networking) is highlighted in the list. Several entries display indented below the home networking entry.

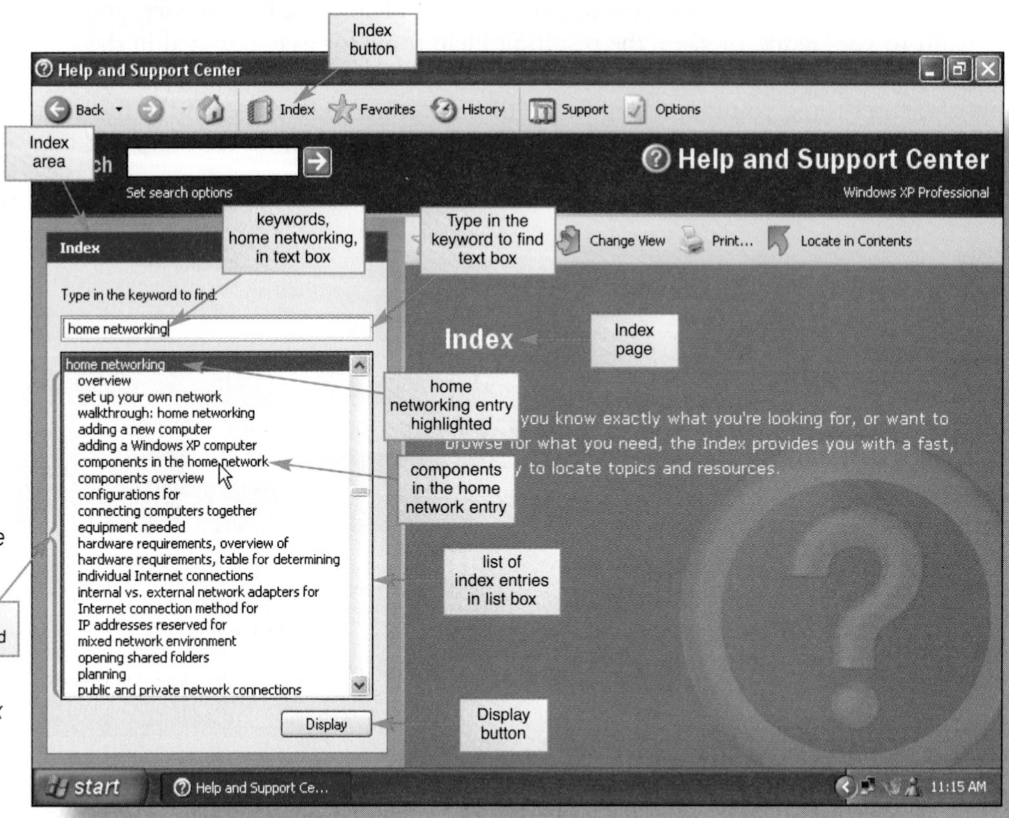

FIGURE 1-62

2 Click components in the home network in the list box and then point to the Display button.

Windows XP displays the components in the home network entry in the text box and highlights the components in the home network entry in the list box (Figure 1-63). The yellow outline surrounding the Display button indicates the button is recessed.

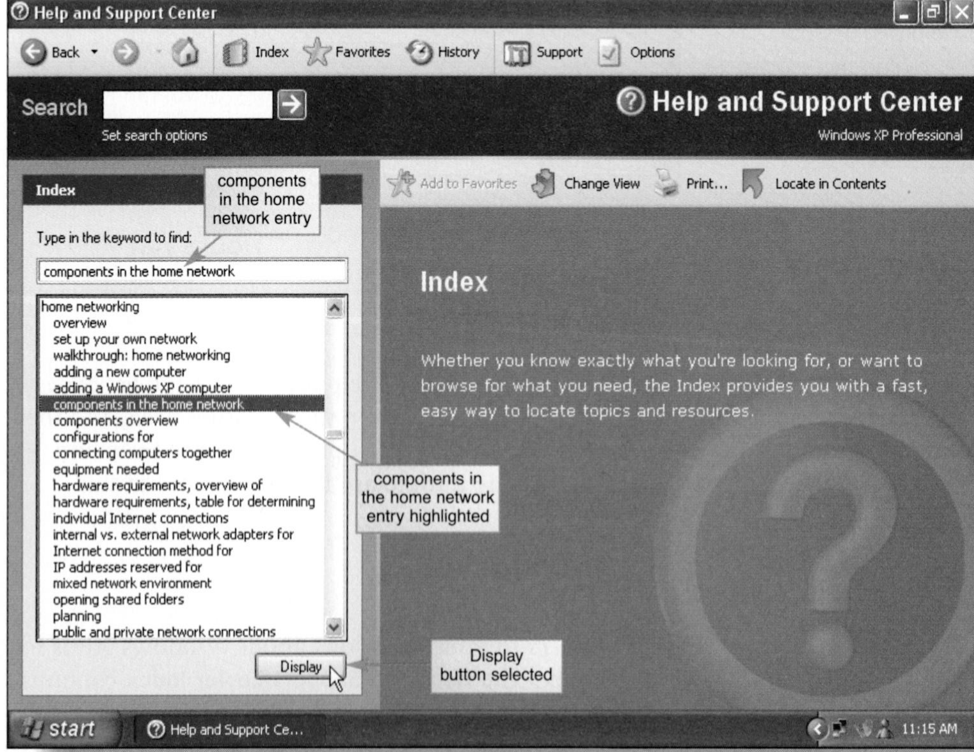

FIGURE 1-63

3 Click the Display button.

The Home and small office networking tools overview topic displays in the topic pane (Figure 1-64). The topic contains an overview of home and small office networking tools. Additional information is available by using the vertical scroll bar in the topic pane.

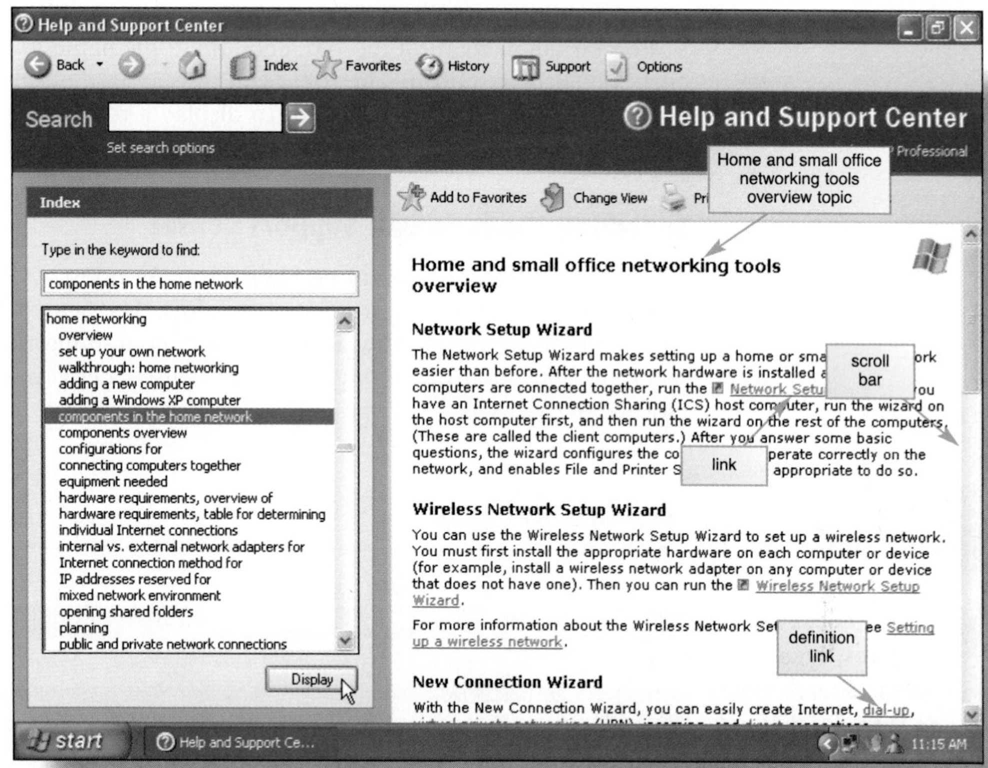

FIGURE 1-64

In Figure 1-64, the Network Setup Wizard link, Wireless Network Setup Wizard link, and Setting up a wireless network link are underlined and displayed in blue font and the dial-up link is underlined and displayed in green font to indicate that clicking the link will display its definition. To remove the definition, click anywhere off the definition. Although not visible in Figure 1-64, other links, such as the Related Topics link, display at the bottom of the page, underlined, and in blue font. Clicking the Related Topics link displays a pop-up window that contains topics related to the home or small office network overview.

Other Ways

1. Press ALT+N, type keyword, press DOWN ARROW until topic is highlighted, press ALT+D (or ENTER)

Bookmarking a Help Topic

After using the Index sheet to search for and display a Help topic, assume you want to bookmark the Home and small office networking tools overview topic and return to this topic in the future (see Figure 1-64). Perform the following steps to bookmark this topic.

TO BOOKMARK A HELP TOPIC

1. Click the Add to Favorites button on the Help and Support Center toolbar.
2. Click the OK button in the Help and Support Center dialog box.

The Home and small office networking tools overview name is added to the Help and Support favorites list (Figure 1-64).

More About

The Index

The Index probably is the best source of information in Windows Help and Support because you can enter the subject in which you are interested. Sometimes, however, you will have to be creative to discover the index entry that answers your question because the most obvious entry will not always lead to your answer.

In the future, if you want to return to a favorite Help topic, click the Favorites button on the navigation toolbar, click the topic name in the Favorites area, and then click the Display button. The topic will display in the topic pane of the Help and Support Center window. The steps to display a topic are illustrated later in this project.

Searching the Help and Support Center

A third method of obtaining Help about Windows XP is to use the Search text box in the Help and Support Center window. The Search text box allows you to enter a keyword and display all Help topics containing the keyword. Assume you want more information about computer viruses. Perform the following steps to learn more about viruses.

Steps To Search the Help and Support Center

1 **Click the Search text box, type** `virus` **in the Search text box, and then point to the Start searching button.**

The Search text box contains the word, virus, and the insertion point (Figure 1-65).

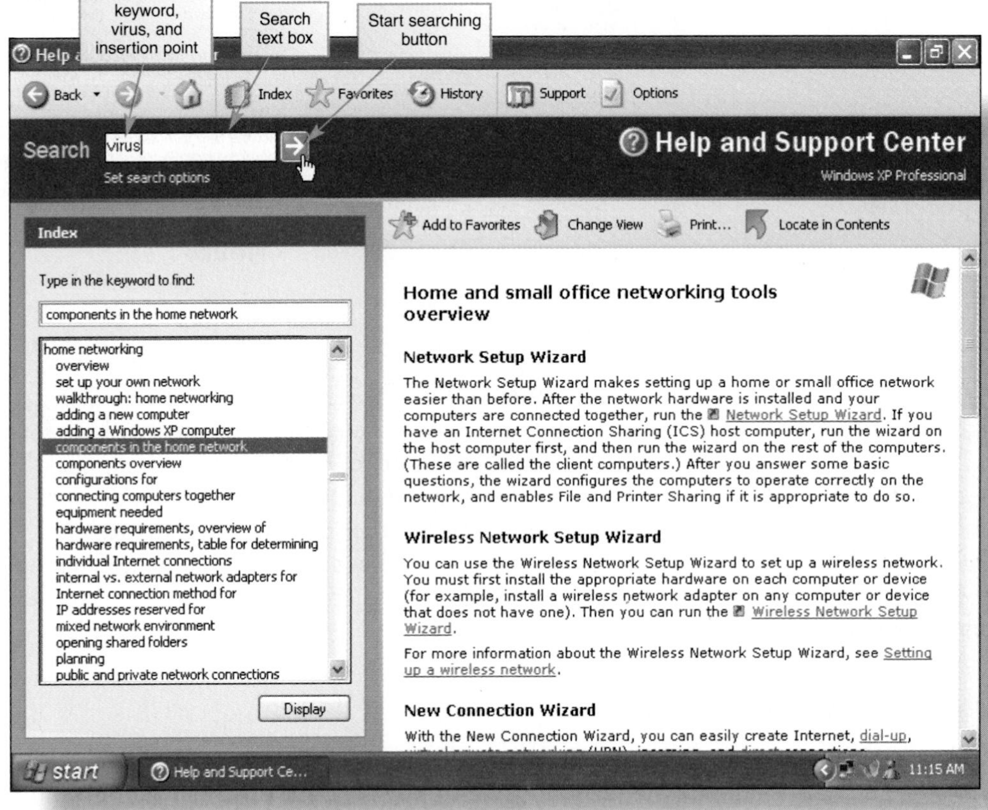

FIGURE 1-65

2 **Click the Start Searching button and then point to the Help protect against viruses and Trojan horses link in the Suggested Topics list box.**

The Search Results area in the navigation pane indicates 30 entries contain the word, virus (Figure 1-66). Several entries display below the Suggested Topics header, fifteen entries can be viewed by clicking the Full-text Search Matches header, and 0 entries can be viewed by clicking the Microsoft Knowledge Base header. The Help protect against viruses and Trojan horses link is underlined. The Browse the search results page displays in the topic pane.

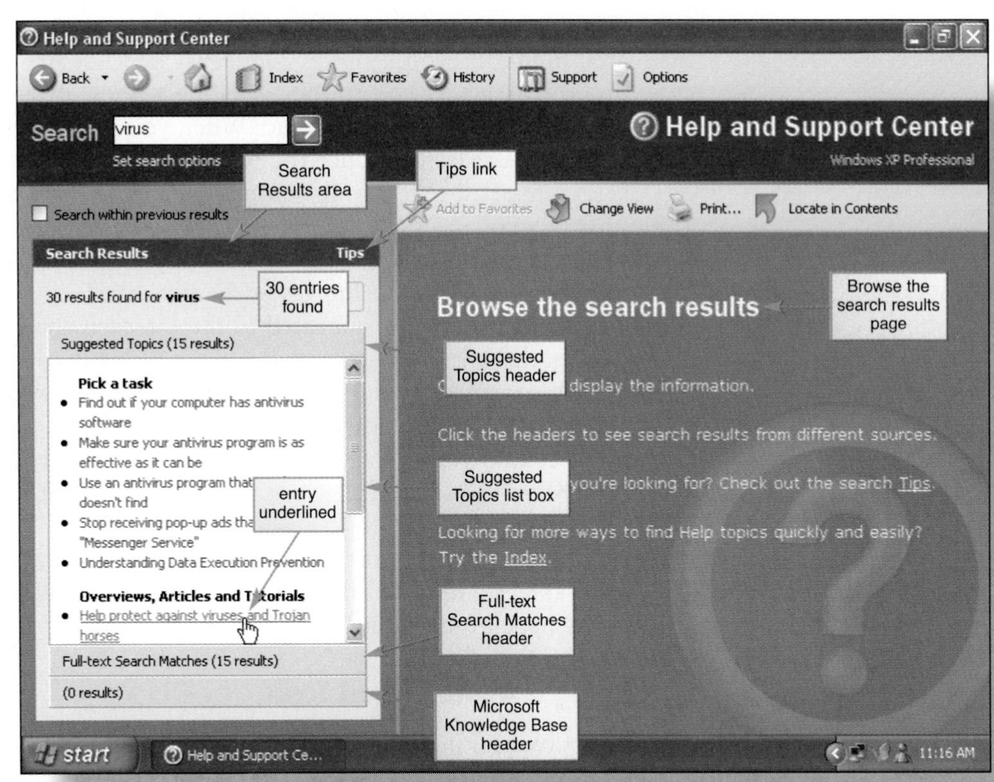

FIGURE 1-66

3 **Click Help protect against viruses and Trojan horses in the Suggested Topics list box.**

The Protecting against viruses and Trojan horses topic, which contains information about viruses, displays in the topic pane (Figure 1-67). Each occurrence of the keyword, virus, is highlighted and the Trojan horses link displays in green font and is underlined. Clicking the Trojan horses link displays its definition.

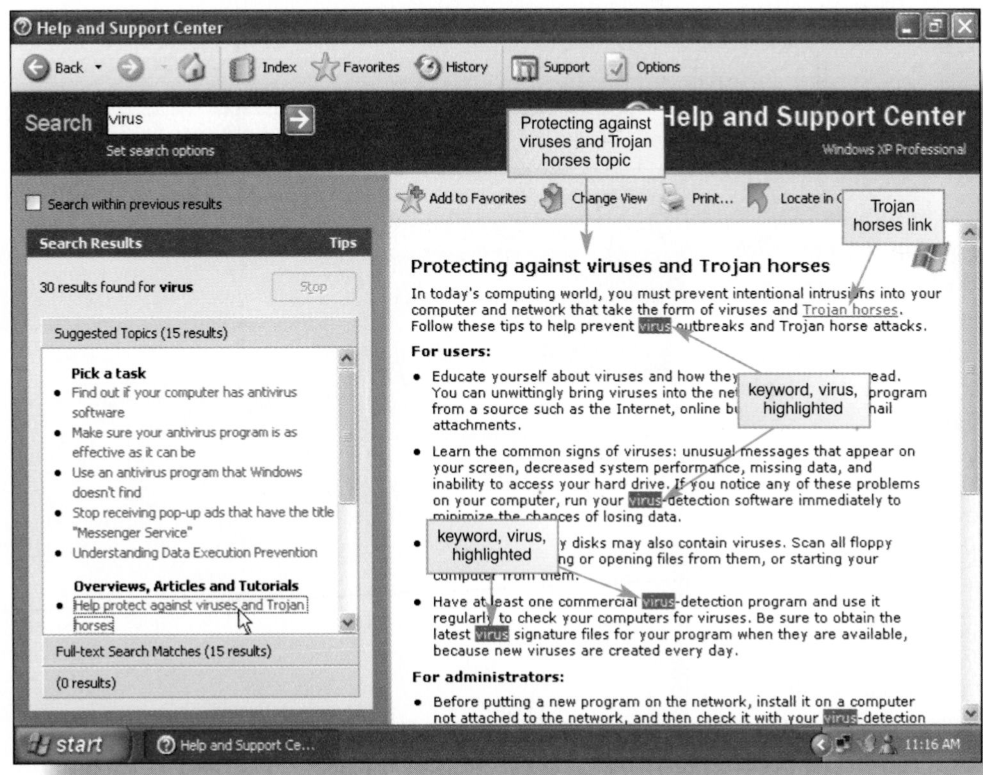

FIGURE 1-67

1. Press ALT+S, type keyword, press ENTER

In Figure 1-66 on the previous page, the Suggested Topics header indicates that the search found fifteen results. A **Suggested Topics search** matches the keyword you enter in the Search text box to the terms the author of the Help topic or page defines as keywords for that particular topic. When you perform a Suggested Topics search, the results of the search produce the best match to your keyword.

Clicking the Full-text Search Matches header at the bottom of the Suggested Topics list box collapses the Suggested Topics list box and displays the Full-text Search Matches list box. The **Full-text Search** provides matches that are often not as relevant as the results of the Suggested Topics search.

When the computer is connected to the Internet, the Help and Support Center also searches the Microsoft Knowledge Base Web site for topics or articles that are relevant to the keyword you enter. The **Microsoft Knowledge Base** is a source of technical support information and self-help tools for Microsoft products. Clicking the Microsoft Knowledge Base header displays the Microsoft Knowledge Base list box in the Search Results area. Currently, the Microsoft Knowledge Base list box contains 0 results.

The Tips link displays at the right side of the Search Results area. Clicking the Tips link displays additional tips for searching in the Help and Support Center Search Tips page in the topic pane.

The Favorites List

The idea for a Favorites list came from surfing the Web. When you find an interesting Web page, you add it to your favorites list, making it possible to return to the page easily in the future. In Help and Support, you find a helpful topic and add it to your favorites list.

Displaying a Bookmarked Topic

After bookmarking the To find what you need in Help and Support Center and Home and small office networking tools overview topic, you can display either topic in the topic pane by clicking the appropriate name in the favorites list. Assume that you want to display the Find what you need in Help and Support Center topic. Perform the following steps to display the topic.

Steps To Display a Bookmarked Topic

1 Click the Favorites button on the navigation toolbar, click Find what you need in Help and Support Center in the Favorites area and, then point to the Display button.

The Favorites area contains the favorites list (Figure 1-68). Two topic names display in the favorites list and the Favorites page displays in the topic pane. The Rename, Remove, and Display buttons display below the Favorites area.

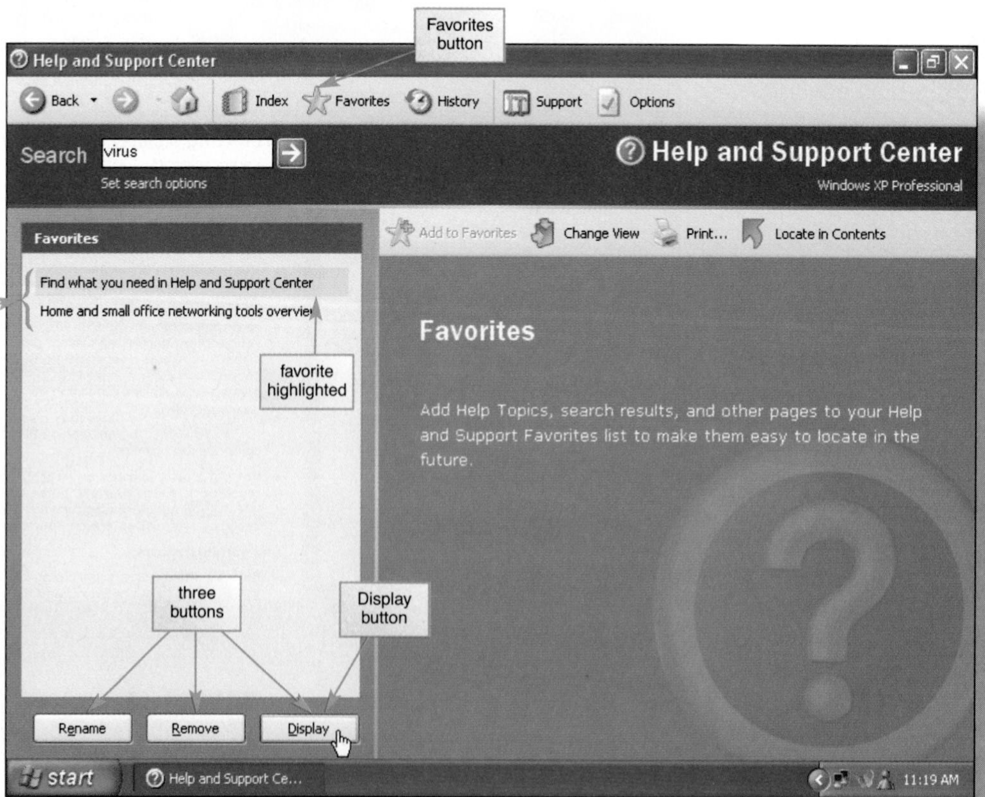

FIGURE 1-68

2 Click the Display button in the Favorites area.

The Find what you need in Help and Support Center topic remains highlighted in the favorites list and the To find what you need in Help and Support Center topic displays in the topic pane (Figure 1-69).

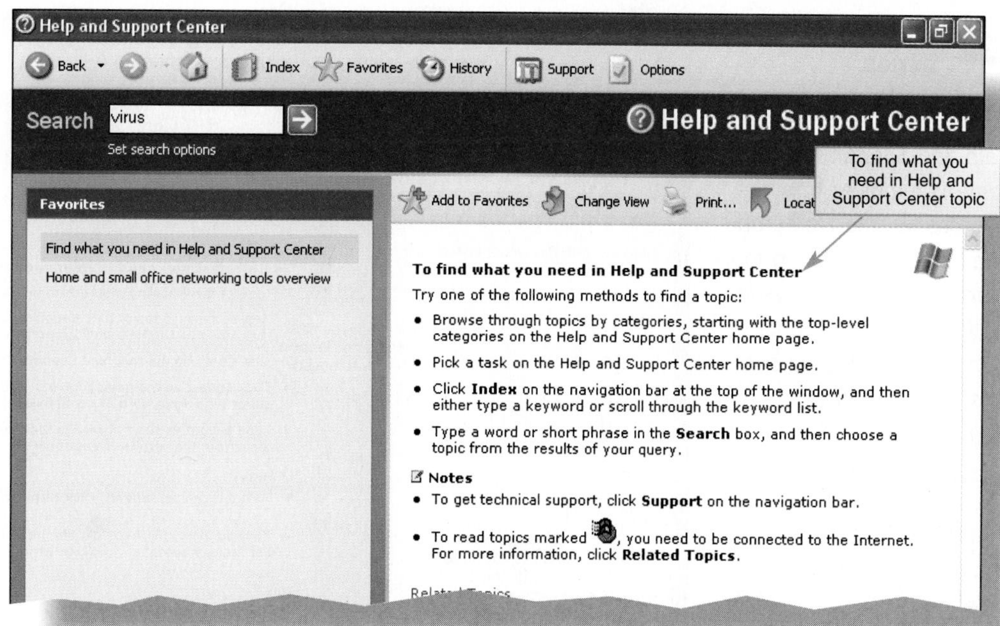

FIGURE 1-69

Other Ways

1. Press ALT+A, press TAB key until favorite is highlighted, press ENTER, press ALT+D

Removing a Bookmark

In addition to viewing a Help topic in the favorites list, you also may want to remove a Help topic. Assume that you want to remove the Find what you need in Help and Support Center and Home and small office networking tools overview topics from the list of favorites. Perform the following steps to remove the two topics.

To Remove a Bookmark

1 Point to the Remove button.

The favorites list contains two topic names (Figure 1-70). The Find what you need in Help and Support Center name is highlighted and the Remove button is recessed.

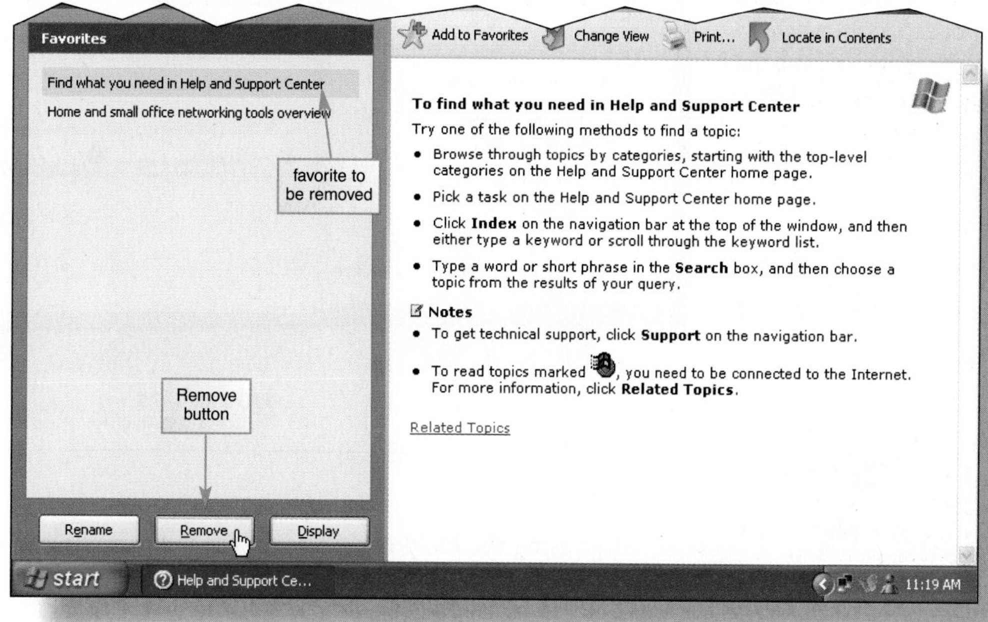

FIGURE 1-70

2 Click the Remove button.

The Find what you need in Help and Support Center name is removed from the favorites list, the Home and small office networking tools overview name displays in the list, and the Rename, Remove, and Display buttons are dimmed (Figure 1-71).

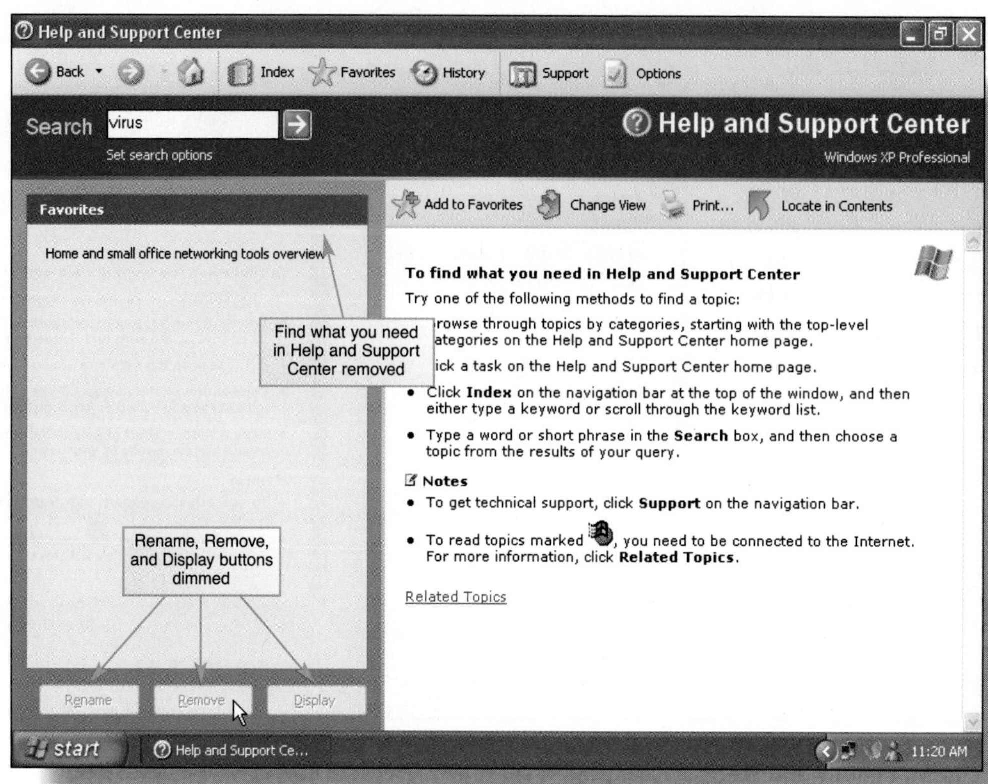

FIGURE 1-71

3 Click Home and small office networking components overview in the favorites list and then click the Remove button.

The Home and small office networking tools overview name is removed from the favorites list (Figure 1-72).

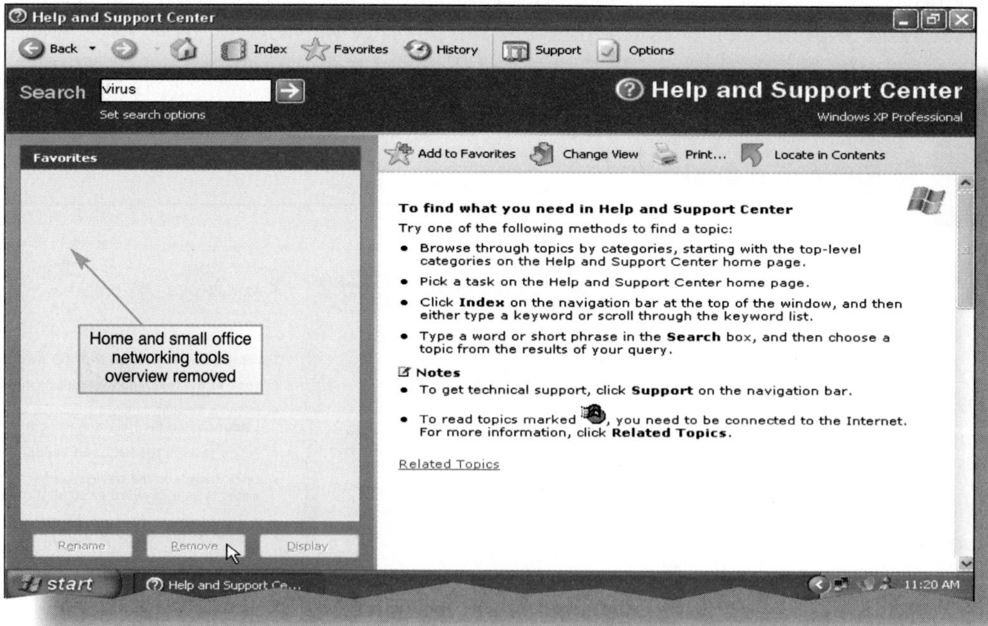

FIGURE 1-72

Other Ways

1. Press TAB key to highlight favorite, press ENTER, press TAB to highlight remove button, press ENTER

After using the Help and Support Center, normally you will close the Help and Support Center. To close the Help and Support Center, complete the following step.

TO CLOSE THE HELP AND SUPPORT CENTER

1 Click the Close button on the title bar of the Help and Support Center window.

Windows XP closes the Help and Support Center window.

Logging Off the Computer

Some users of Windows XP have turned off their computers without following the log off procedure only to find data they thought they had stored on disk was lost. Because of the way Windows XP writes data on the disk, it is important you log off the computer so you do not lose your work.

Logging Off and Turning Off the Computer

After completing your work with Windows XP, you should close your user account by logging off from the computer. Logging off from the computer closes any open applications, allows you to save any unsaved documents, ends the Windows XP session, and makes the computer available for other users. Perform the following steps to log off from the computer.

To Log Off from the Computer

1 **Click the Start button on the taskbar and then point to Log Off on the Start menu.**

Windows XP displays the Start menu and highlights the Log Off command (Figure 1-73).

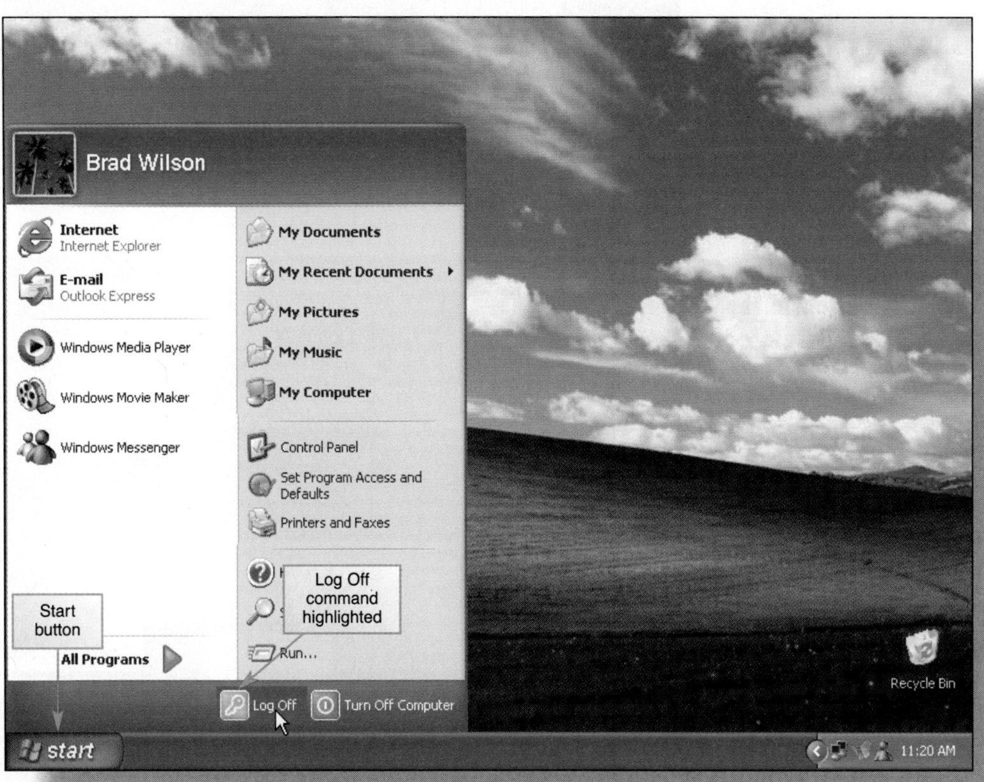

FIGURE 1-73

2 Click Log Off.

The Log Off Windows dialog box displays (Figure 1-74). The dialog box contains three buttons (Switch User, Log Off, and Cancel). The buttons allow you to perform different operations, such as allowing another user to log on while your programs and files remain open (Switch User), close your programs and end your Windows session (Log Off), and canceling the process of logging off (Cancel).

FIGURE 1-74

3 Point to the Log Off button in the Log Off Windows dialog box.

Pointing to the Log Off button changes the color of the button to light orange and displays the Log Off balloon (Figure 1-75). The balloon contains the balloon name, Log Off, and the text, Closes your programs and ends your Windows session.

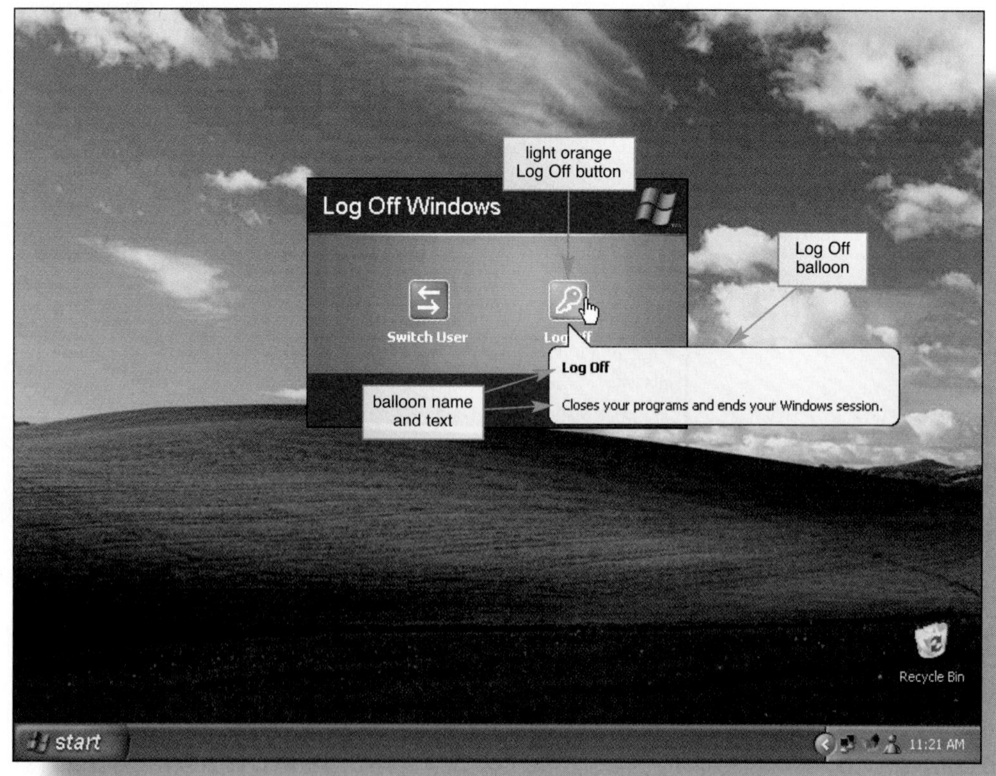

FIGURE 1-75

Click the Log Off button.

Windows XP logs off from the computer and displays the Welcome screen (Figure 1-76). A message displays below the Brad Wilson name on the Welcome screen to indicate the user has unread e-mail messages.

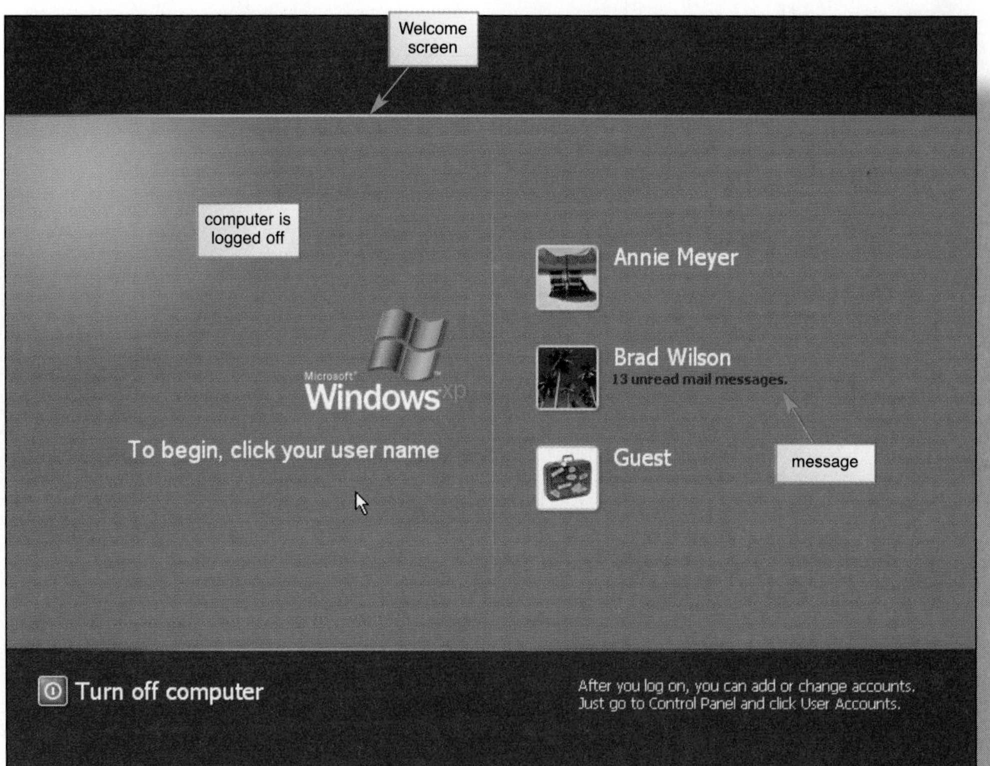

FIGURE 1-76

1. Press CTRL+ESC, press L, press L

While Windows XP is logging off, a blue screen containing the word, Welcome, displays on the desktop and the messages, Logging off..., and Saving your settings..., display on the screen momentarily. The blue screen closes and the Welcome screen (Figure 1-76) displays on the desktop. At this point, another user can log on.

If you accidentally click Log Off on the Start menu as shown in Figure 1-73 on page WIN 1.61 and you do not want to log off, click the Cancel button in the Log Off Windows dialog box to return to normal Windows XP operation.

After logging off, you also may want to turn off the computer using the **Turn Off Computer link** on the Welcome screen. Turning off the computer shuts down Windows XP so you can turn off the power to the computer. Many computers turn the power off automatically. If you are sure you want to turn off the computer, perform the steps on the next page. If you are not sure about turning off the computer, read the steps on the next page without actually performing them.

Steps To Turn Off the Computer

1 Point to the Turn off computer link on the Welcome screen.

Pointing to the Turn off computer link underlines the Turn off computer link (Figure 1-77).

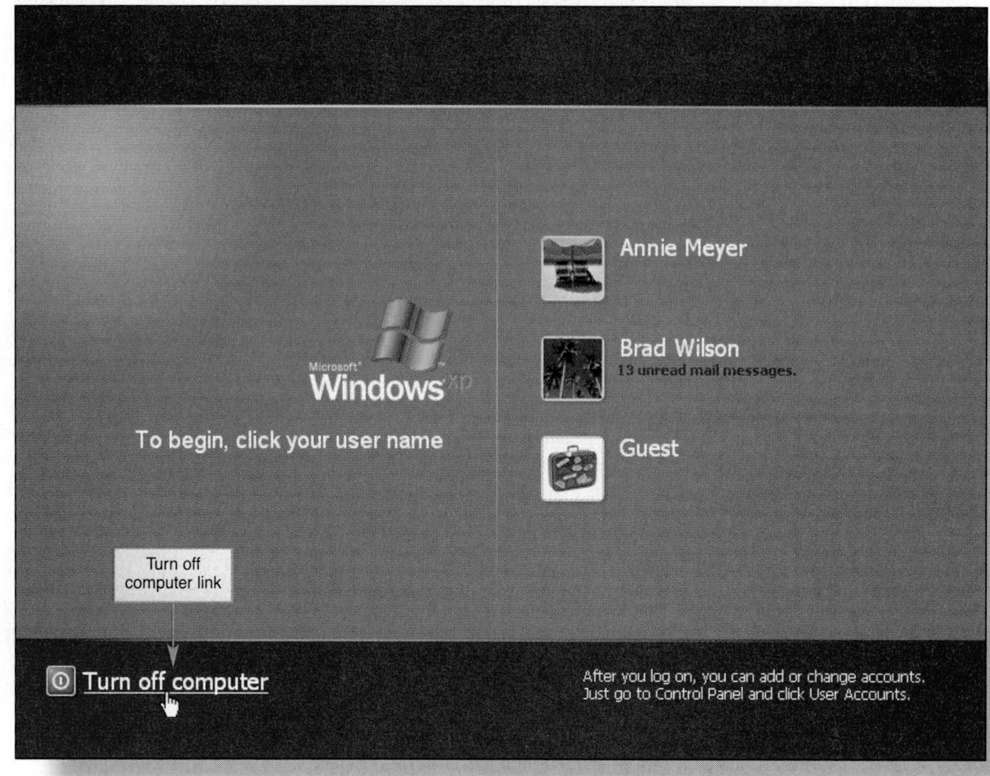

FIGURE 1-77

2 Click Turn off computer.

The Welcome screen darkens and the Turn off computer dialog box displays (Figure 1-78). The dialog box contains four buttons (Stand By, Turn Off, Restart, and Cancel). The buttons allow you to perform different operations, such as placing the computer in stand by mode (Stand By), shutting down Windows XP (Turn Off), restarting the computer (Restart), and canceling the process of shutting down Windows XP (Cancel).

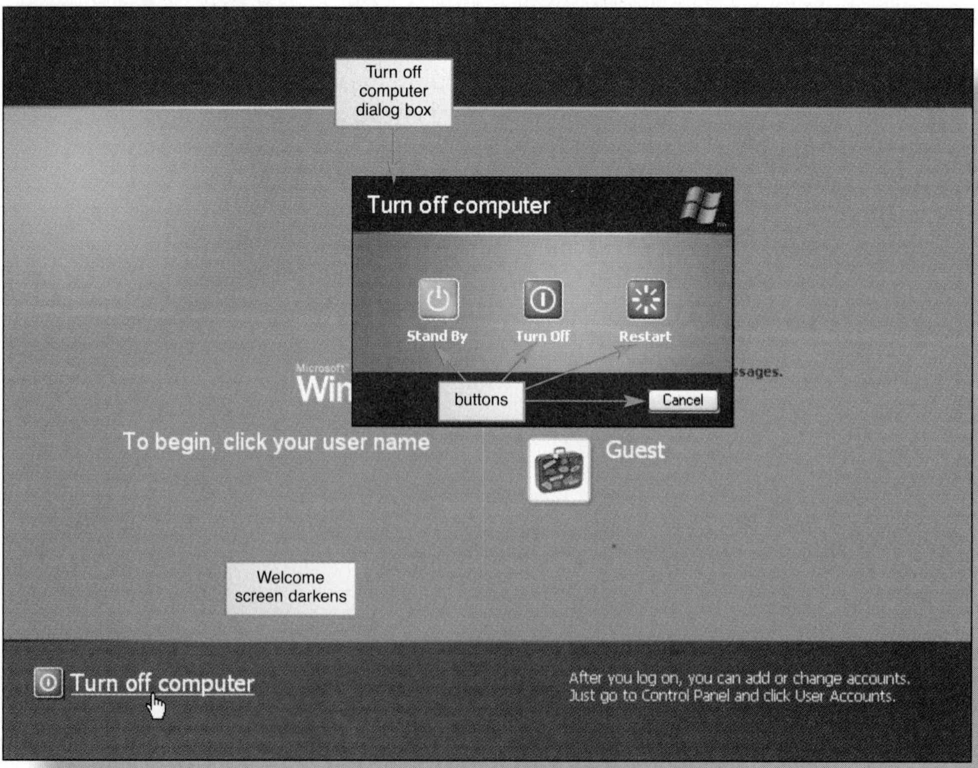

FIGURE 1-78

3 Point to the Turn Off button in the Turn off computer dialog box.

The color of the Turn Off button changes to light red and the Turn Off balloon displays (Figure 1-79). The balloon contains the balloon name, Turn Off, and the text, Shuts down Windows so that you can safely turn off the computer.

4 Click the Turn Off button.

Windows XP is shut down.

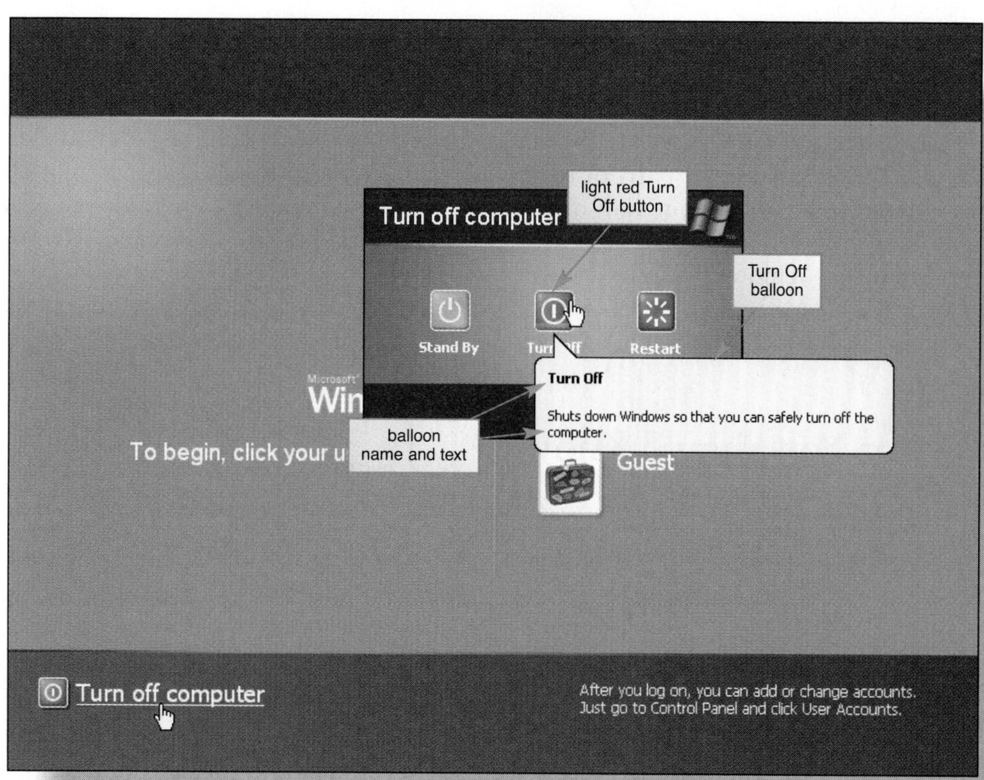

FIGURE 1-79

Other Ways

1. Press CTRL+ESC, press U, use ARROW KEYS to select Turn Off, press ENTER
2. Press ALT+F4, use ARROW KEYS to select Turn Off, press ENTER

While Windows XP is shutting down, a blue screen containing the word, Welcome, displays on the desktop and the message, Windows is shutting down..., display momentarily. At this point you can turn off the computer. When shutting down Windows XP, you should never turn off the computer before these messages display.

If you accidentally click Turn off computer on the Welcome screen as shown in Figure 1-77 and you do not want to shut down Windows XP, click the Cancel button in the Turn off computer dialog box in Figure 1-78 to return to normal Windows XP operation.

CASE PERSPECTIVE SUMMARY

While continuing to answer questions about Windows XP in the workplace, you spent nearly every free moment in the two weeks prior to the seminar learning about the newly installed operating system. Then, the daily training sessions kept you busy for the following three months. You taught 35 workshops and trained all of the 324 employees in the company. Your supervisor, who attended the Windows XP seminar, complimented your success by giving you a sizable pay raise and time off to attend the annual Comdex computer convention in Las Vegas, Nevada.

Project Summary

Project 1 illustrated the Microsoft Windows XP graphical user interface. You launched Windows XP, logged on to the computer, learned the parts of the desktop, and learned to point, click, right-click, double-click, drag, and right-drag. You opened, minimized, maximized, restored, and closed a Windows XP window, as well as learned how to launch an application. Using the table of contents, Index, Search, and Favorites, you obtained Help about Microsoft Windows XP and bookmarked important Help topics. You logged off from the computer using the Log Off Command on the Start menu and then shut down Windows XP using the Turn off computer link on the Welcome screen.

What You Should Know

Having completed this project, you now should be able to perform the following tasks:

- Add an Icon to the Desktop *(WIN 1.18)*
- Bookmark a Help Topic *(WIN 1.53, WIN 1.55)*
- Browse for Help Topics in the Table of Contents *(WIN 1.50)*
- Close a Window *(WIN 1.28, WIN 1.41)*
- Close the Help and Support Center *(WIN 1.61)*
- Collapse an Area *(WIN 1.39)*
- Delete a Desktop Icon by Right-Dragging *(WIN 1.42)*
- Display a Bookmarked Topic *(WIN 1.58)*
- Display the Start Menu *(WIN 1.14)*
- Expand an Area *(WIN 1.32)*
- Launch a Program Using the Start Menu *(WIN 1.46)*
- Launch Help and Support *(WIN 1.48)*
- Log Off from the Computer *(WIN 1.61)*
- Log On to the Computer *(WIN 1.12)*
- Maximize and Restore a Window *(WIN 1.26)*
- Minimize and Redisplay a Window *(WIN 1.24)*
- Move a Window by Dragging *(WIN 1.31)*
- Open a Window Using a Desktop Icon *(WIN 1.21)*
- Open a Window Using the Start Menu *(WIN 1.29)*
- Remove a Bookmark *(WIN 1.59)*
- Resize a Window *(WIN 1.40)*
- Scroll by Dragging the Scroll Box *(WIN 1.37)*
- Scroll Using Scroll Arrows *(WIN 1.33)*
- Scroll Using the Scroll Bar *(WIN 1.35)*
- Search for Help Topics Using the Index *(WIN 1.54)*
- Search the Help and Support Center *(WIN 1.56)*
- Size a Window by Dragging *(WIN 1.38)*
- Turn Off the Computer *(WIN 1.64)*

Learn It Online

Instructions: To complete the Learn It Online exercises, launch your Web browser using the steps on pages WIN 1.46 and WIN 1.47, click the Address box, enter `scsite.com/winxp/exs.htm`, and then press the ENTER key. When the Windows XP Learn It Online page displays, follow the instructions in the exercises below.

1 Project Reinforcement TF, MC, and SA

Below Windows XP Project 1, click the Project Reinforcement link. Print the quiz by clicking Print on the File menu. Answer each question. Write your first and last name at the top of each page, and then hand in the printout to your instructor.

2 Flash Cards

Below Windows XP Project 1, click the Flash Cards link. When Flash Cards displays, read the instructions. Type 20 (or a number specified by your instructor) in the Number of Playing Cards text box, type your name in the Name text box, and then click the Flip Card button. When the flash card displays, read the question and then click the Answer box arrow to select an answer. Flip through Flash Cards. Click Print on the File menu to print the last flash card if your score is 15 (75%) correct or greater and then hand it in to your instructor. If your score is less than 15 (75%) correct, then redo this exercise by clicking the Replay button.

3 Practice Test

Below Windows XP Project 1, click the Practice Test link. Answer each question, enter your first and last name at the bottom of the page, and then click the Grade Test button. When the graded practice test displays on your screen, click Print on the File menu to print a hard copy. Continue to take practice tests until you score 80% or better. Hand in a printout of the final practice test to your instructor.

4 Who Wants to Be a Computer Genius?

Below Windows XP Project 1, click the Computer Genius link. Read the instructions, enter your first and last name at the bottom of the page, and then click the Play button. Hand in a printout of your score to your instructor.

5 Wheel of Terms

Below Windows XP Project 1, click the Wheel of Terms link. Read the instructions, and then enter your first and last name and your school name. Click the Play button. Hand in a printout of your score to your instructor.

6 Crossword Puzzle Challenge

Below Windows XP Project 1, click the Crossword Puzzle Challenge link. Read the instructions, and then enter your first and last name. Click the Play button. Work the crossword puzzle. When you are finished, click the Submit button. When the crossword puzzle redisplays, click the Print button. Hand in the printout.

7 Tips and Tricks

Below Windows XP Project 1, click the Tips and Tricks link. Click a topic that pertains to Project 1. Right-click the information and then click Print on the shortcut menu. Construct a brief example of what the information relates to in Windows XP to confirm that you understand how to use the tip or trick. Hand in the example and printed information.

8 Newsgroups

Below Windows XP Project 1, click the Newsgroups link. Click a topic that pertains to Project 1. Print three comments. Hand in the comments to your instructor.

9 Expanding Your Horizons

Below Windows XP Project 1, click the Expanding Your Horizons link. Click a topic that pertains to Project 1. Print the information. Construct a brief example of what the information relates to in Windows XP to confirm that you understand the contents of the article. Hand in the example and printed information to your instructor.

10 Search Sleuth

Below Windows XP Project 1, click the Search Sleuth link. To search for a term that pertains to this project, select a term below the Project 1 title and then use the Google search engine at google.com (or any major search engine) to display and print two Web pages that present information on the term. Hand in the printouts to your instructor.

1 Using the Help and Support Center

Instructions: Use Help and Support Center and a computer to perform the following tasks.

Part 1: ***Using the Question Mark Button***

1. If necessary, launch Microsoft Windows XP and log on to the computer.
2. Right-click an open area of the desktop to display a shortcut menu.
3. Click Properties on the shortcut menu to display the Display Properties dialog box.
4. Click the Desktop tab in the Display Properties dialog box.
5. Click the Help button on the title bar. The mouse pointer changes to a block arrow with a question mark (Figure 1-80).

FIGURE 1-80

6. Click the list box in the Desktop sheet. A pop-up window displays explaining the list box. Read the information in the pop-up window and summarize the function of the list box.

   ____

7. Click an open area of the Desktop sheet to remove the pop-up window.
8. Click the Help button on the title bar and then click the Customize Desktop button. A pop-up window displays explaining what happens when you click this button. Read the information in the pop-up window and summarize the function of the button.

   ____

9. Click an open area in the Desktop sheet to remove the pop-up window.
10. Click the Help button on the title bar and then click the monitor icon in the Desktop sheet. A pop-up window displays explaining the function of the monitor. Read the information in the pop-up window and summarize the function of the monitor. .

    ____

11. Click an open area in the Desktop sheet to remove the pop-up window.
12. Click the Help button on the title bar and then click the Cancel button. A pop-up window displays explaining what happens when you click the button. Read the information in the pop-up window and summarize the function of the Cancel button.

____

13. Click an open area in the Desktop sheet to remove the pop-up window.
14. Click the Cancel button in the Display Properties dialog box.

Part 2: ***Finding What's New in Windows XP***

1. Click the Start button and then click Help and Support on the Start menu.
2. Click the Maximize button on the Help and Support Center title bar.
3. Click What's new in Windows XP in the navigation pane.
4. Click What's new topics in the navigation pane. Ten topics display in the topic pane (Figure 1-81).
5. Click What's new on your desktop in the topic pane.
6. Click Start menu (or the plus sign in the small box preceding Start menu) to expand the entry. Read the information about the Start menu.
7. Click the Using the Start menu link.

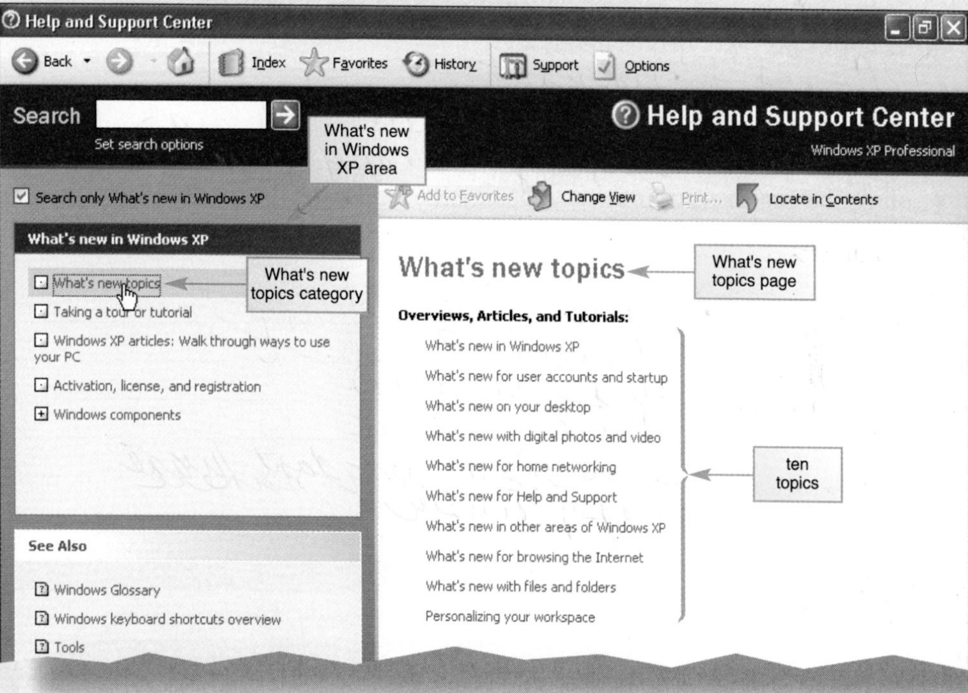

FIGURE 1-81

8. Click the Print button on the Help and Support toolbar to print the topic. Click the Print button in the Print dialog box.
9. Scroll the topic pane to display the Related Topics link. Click the Related Topics link to display a pop-up window containing three related topics. List the three topics.

whats new
about account
what new - file folders

10. Click Display a program at the top of the Start menu in the pop-up window.
11. Click the Print button on the Help and Support toolbar to print the topic. Click the Print button in the Print dialog box.

(continued)

Using the Help and Support Center *(continued)*

Part 3: ***Viewing Windows XP Articles***

1. Click Windows XP articles: Walk through ways to use your PC in the What's new in Windows XP area in the navigation pane. A list of overviews, articles, and tutorials displays in the topic pane (Figure 1-82).
2. Click Walkthrough: Making music in the topic pane. Read the Making music article in the topic pane. List four ways in which you can use Windows XP musically.

   Play Music, Create Playlist, Internet radio
   Create CD's

3. Click Play music in the Making Music area. Scroll to display the Display details about a CD area. List the three steps to display details about a CD.

   Connect to Internet
   Insert CD into CDRom
   when displayed copy from CD

4. Scroll to the top of the window to display the Making Music area.
5. Click Create CDs in the Making Music area. Scroll to display the steps to burn your own CD. List the six steps to burn a CD.

   open windows
   insert Blank CD
   click copy CD
   choose playlist
   Clear those you dont want
   Copy music

6. Read other articles of interest to you in the Making music area.
7. Click the Close button in the Help and Support Center window.

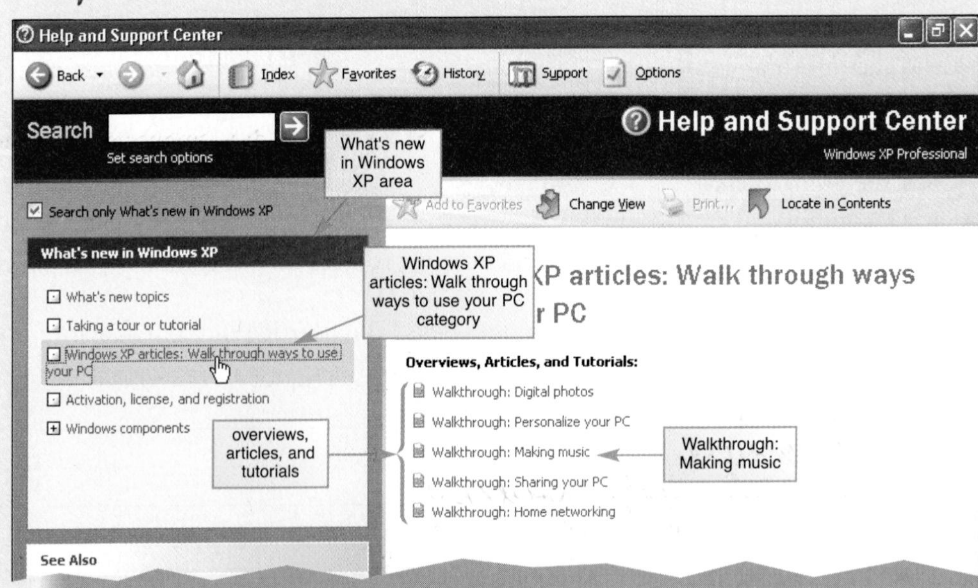

FIGURE 1-82

Use Help

2 Using Windows Help and Support to Obtain Help

Instructions: Use Help and Support Center and a computer to perform the following tasks.

1. Find Help about Help and Support Center keyboard shortcuts by exploring the Windows keyboard shortcuts overview in the Accessibility category in the table of contents.
   a. What general keyboard shortcut is used to display the Start menu?
   CTRL + ESCp WINDOW SIGN
   b. What general keyboard shortcut is used to display the shortcut menu for an active window?
   shift F10
   c. What general keyboard shortcut is used to view the properties for a selected item?
   ALT + Enter
   d. What dialog box keyboard shortcut is used to move backward through options?
   CTRL - Left ARROW
   e. What dialog box keyboard shortcut is used to display Help?
   shift F10
   f. What natural keyboard shortcut is used to display or hide the Start menu?
   Ctrl + ESCp (WINDOW)
   g. What natural keyboard shortcut is used to open the My Computer window?
   WINDOW + E
2. Use the Help Index feature to answer the following questions in the spaces provided.
   a. How do you reduce computer screen flicker?
   advance preformance and maint. Tools
   b. What dialog box do you use to change the appearance of the mouse pointer?
   customize computer
   c. How do you minimize all windows?
   maintaining your computer
   d. What is a server?
   My computer Information - General a computer that provides shared
3. Use the Search text box in the Help and Support Center window to answer the following questions in the spaces provided.
   a. How can you reduce all open windows on the desktop to taskbar buttons?
   click [icon] on the taskbar
   b. How do you launch a program using the Run command?
   secondary Logon
   c. What are the steps to add a toolbar to the taskbar?
   Right click on whatever you want
   d. What wizard do you use to remove unwanted desktop icons?
   Right click Drag
   e. Close the Help and Support Center window.

(continued)

Use Help

Using Windows Help and Support to Obtain Help *(continued)*

4. The tools to solve a problem while using Windows XP are called **troubleshooters.** Use the Help and Support Center to find the list of troubleshooters. Answer the following questions in the spaces provided.
   a. What problems do the home and small office networking troubleshooter allow you to resolve?

   b. List five Windows XP troubleshooters.

5. Use the Help and Support Center to obtain information about software licensing and product activation. Answer the following questions in the spaces provided.
   a. What is software piracy?

   b. What are the five types of software piracy?

   c. Why should I be concerned about it?

   d. What is an EULA (end user licensing agreement)?

   e. Can you legally make a second copy of an operating system (Windows XP) for use at home, work, or on a portable computer?

   f. What is Windows Product Activation?

6. Search using the keyword, glossary, to find the Glossary and then find the definition for the following terms. Write the definitions in the spaces provided.
   a. maximize

   b. My Documents

   c. title bar

   d. linked object

   e. server

7. Close the Help and Support Center window.

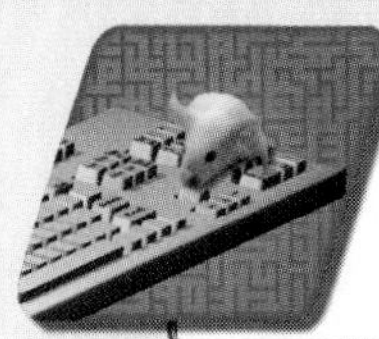

In the Lab

1 Improving Your Mouse Skills

Instructions: Use a computer to perform the following tasks.

1. If necessary, launch Microsoft Windows XP and log on to the computer.
2. Click the Start button on the taskbar, point to All Programs on the Start menu, point to Games on the Program submenu, and then click Solitaire on the Games submenu.
3. Click the Maximize button in the Solitaire window (Figure 1-83).
4. Click Help on the Solitaire menu bar and then click Contents. If the Contents sheet does not display, click the Contents tab.
5. Read the Solitaire overview.
6. Click Solitaire in the Contents sheet. Click and read the three Help topics (Play Solitaire, Change game options, and Choose a scoring system).
7. After reviewing the Help topics, close the Solitaire window.
8. Play the game of Solitaire.
9. Click the Close button on the Solitaire title bar to close the game.

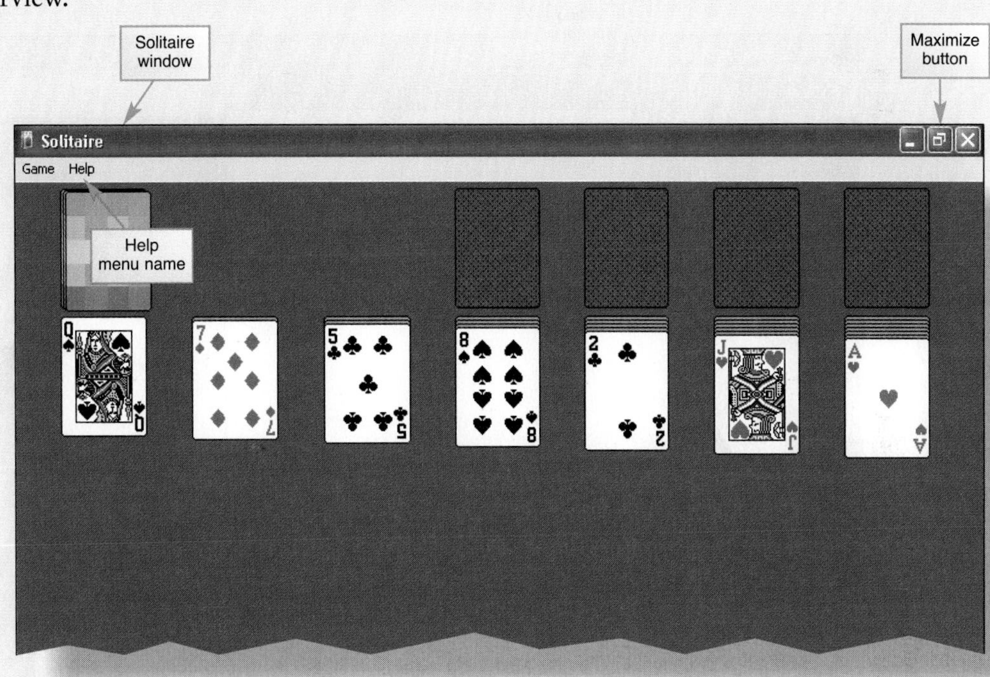

FIGURE 1-83

2 Taking the Windows XP Tour

Instructions: Use a computer to perform the following tasks.

Part 1: *Launching the Windows XP Tour*

1. If necessary, launch Microsoft Windows XP and log on to the computer.
2. Click the Start button and then click Help and Support on the Start menu.
3. Click the Maximize button on the Help and Support Center title bar.
4. Click What's new in Windows XP in the navigation pane.

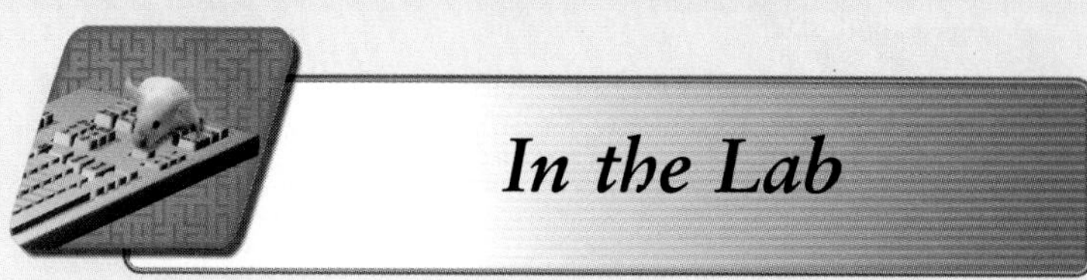

Taking the Windows XP Tour *(continued)*

5. Click Taking a tour or tutorial in the navigation pane. The Taking a tour or tutorial page displays in the topic pane.
6. Click Take the Windows XP tour in the topic pane. The Windows XP Tour window dialog box displays (Figure 1-84).
7. If your computer does not have speakers or earphones, proceed to Step 8 below. If your computer has speakers or earphones, follow the steps in Part 2.
8. If your computer does not have speakers or earphones, follow the steps in Part 3.

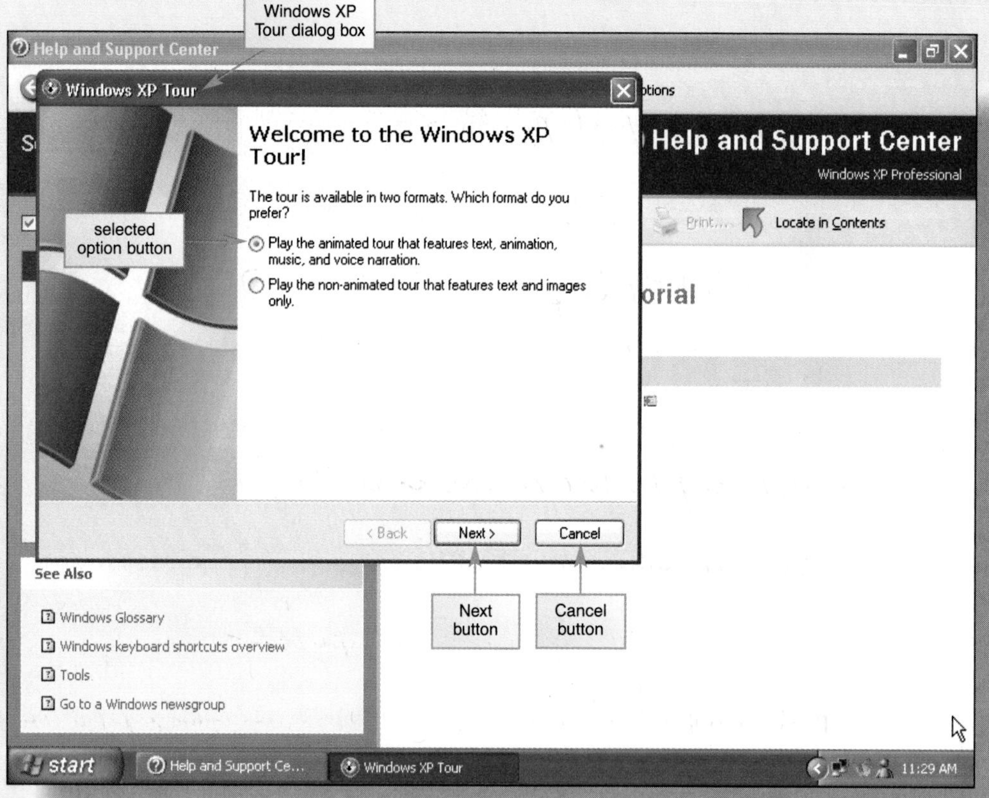

FIGURE 1-84

Part 2: ***Taking the Windows XP Tour with Sound and Animation***

1. Verify that the Play the animated tour that features text, animation, music, and voice narration button is recessed in the Windows XP Tour dialog box and then click the Next button.
2. Listen to the voice narration of the introduction to the Windows XP tour.
3. Click the gray Windows XP Basics button and answer the following questions.
   a. What is the narrow band at the bottom of the desktop called? Task Bar
   b. What identifies a shortcut icon? right click
   c. What icons display on the desktop the first time you launch Windows? Welcome

In the Lab

d. What is contained in the notification area? messages

e. How does Windows keep the taskbar tidy? cookies

f. What does a right-facing arrow on a Start menu command signify? ________

g. In which folders are text, image, and music files placed? MY DOCUMENTS, my music INTENNE

h. What does the Restore Down button do? takes IT down to the

i. What appears when a program needs some information from you before it can complete a command? Dialog box

j. What do you use to set up user accounts? ________

k. Where do you go when you want to interrupt your Windows session and let someone else use the computer? DOWNSIZE, SAVE, off.

4. Click the Skip Intro button in the lower corner of the desktop to skip the introduction to the Windows XP tour.
5. If available, click the Best for Business button and listen to the narration.
6. Click the red Safe and Easy Personal Computing button and listen to the narration.
7. Click the green Unlock the World of Digital Media button and listen to the narration.
8. Click the blue The Connected Home and Office button and listen to the narration.
9. Click the red Exit Tour button on the desktop to exit the Windows XP tour.
10. Click the Close button in the Help and Support center window.
11. You have completed this lab assignment.

***Part 3:** Taking the Windows XP Tour without Sound or Animation*

1. Click the Play the non-animated tour that features text and images only button in the Windows XP Tour dialog box and then click the Next button.
2. Click the Start Here button to read about the basics of the Windows XP operating system.
3. Scroll the Windows XP Basics window and read the paragraph below the Windows Desktop heading. Click the Next button to display the next topic.
4. Scroll the Windows XP Basics window and read the paragraphs below the Icons heading. Answer the following questions.
   a. What icon displays on the desktop the first time you launch Windows? welcome
   b. Does deleting a shortcut icon affect the actual program or file? No
5. Click the Next button to display the next topic. Scroll the Windows XP Basics window and read the paragraphs below the Taskbar heading. Answer the following question.
   a. Where is the notification area located? window
6. Click the Next button to display the next topic. Scroll the Windows XP Basics window and read the paragraphs below the Start Menu heading. Answer the following question.
   a. What does a right-facing arrow mean? Help
7. Click the Next button to display the next topic. Scroll the Windows XP Basics window and read the paragraph, below the Files and Folder heading. Answer the following question.
   a. In which folders are text, image, and music files placed? my pictures / media player

(continued)

In the Lab

Taking the Windows XP Tour *(continued)*

8. Click the Next button to display the next topic. Scroll the Windows XP Basics window and read the paragraphs below the Windows heading. Answer the following question.
   a. What displays if a program needs some information from you before it can complete a command? mill ask ______
9. Click the Next button to display the next topic. Scroll the Windows XP Basics window and read the paragraphs below the Control Panel heading. Answer the following questions.
   a. What Windows feature do you use to customize computer settings? ______
   b. Where is this feature located? ______
10. Click the Next button to display the next topic. Scroll the Windows XP Basics window and read the paragraphs below the Ending Your Session heading. Answer the following question.
    a. What do you do when you want to interrupt your Windows session and let someone else use the computer? ______
11. Click the Next button repeatedly to display the topics in the remaining sections of the Windows XP tour.
12. Click the Close button in the window to end the tour.
13. Click the Close button in the Help and Support Center window.
14. You have completed this lab assignment.

3 Launching and Using the Internet Explorer Application

Instructions: Perform the following steps to launch the Internet Explorer application.

Part 1: *Launching the Internet Explorer Application*

1. If necessary, launch Microsoft Windows XP and log on to the computer.
2. If necessary, connect to the Internet.
3. Click the Start button and then click Internet in the pinned items list on the Start menu. Maximize the Microsoft Internet Explorer window.
4. If the Address bar does not display below the Standard Buttons toolbar in the Microsoft Internet Explorer window, click View on the menu bar, point to Toolbars, and then click Address bar on the Toolbars submenu.

Part 2: *Entering a URL in the Address Bar*

1. Click the URL in the Address bar to highlight the URL.
2. Type `www.microsoft.com` in the Address bar and then press the ENTER key.
3. Answer the following questions.
   a. What URL displays in the Address bar? ______
   b. What window title displays on the title bar? ______

______

In the Lab

4. If necessary, scroll the Web page to view the contents of the Web page. List five links (underlined text) that are shown on this Web page.
   ____
   ____
5. Click any link on the Web page. What link did you click? ______________________________
6. Describe the Web page that displayed when you clicked the link? ______________________________
   ____
7. Click the Print button on the Standard Buttons toolbar to print the Web page.

Part 3: ***Entering a URL in the Address Bar***

1. Click the URL in the Address bar to highlight the URL.
2. Type `www.disney.com` in the Address bar and then press the ENTER key.
3. What window title displays on the title bar? ______________________________
4. Scroll the Web page to view the contents of the Web page. Do any graphic images display on the Web page?
   ____
5. Pointing to an image on a Web page and having the mouse pointer change to a hand indicates the image is a link. Does the Web page include an image that is a link? ______________________________
   If so, describe the image. ______________________________
6. Click the image to display another Web page. What window title displays on the title bar?
   ____
7. Click the Print button on the Standard Buttons toolbar to print the Web page.

Part 4: ***Displaying Previously Displayed Web Pages***

1. Click the Back button on the Standard Buttons toolbar. What Web page displays?
   ____
2. Click the Back button on the Standard Buttons toolbar twice. What Web page displays?
   ____
3. Click the Forward button on the Standard Buttons toolbar. What Web page displays?
   ____

Part 5: ***Entering a URL in the Address Bar***

1. Click the URL in the Address bar to highlight the URL.
2. Type `www.scsite.com` in the Address bar and then press the ENTER key.
3. Scroll the Web page to display the Operating Systems link.
4. Click the Operating Systems link.
5. Click the textbook title of your Windows XP textbook.
6. Click the Steve's Cool Web Sites link on the Web page.
7. Click any links that are of interest to you. Which link did you like the best? ______________________________
8. Use the Back button or Forward button to display the Web site you like the best.
9. Click the Print button on the Standard Buttons toolbar to print the Web page.
10. Click the Close button on the Microsoft Internet Explorer title bar.

In the Lab

4 Launching an Application

Instructions: Perform the following steps to launch the Notepad application using the Start menu and create the homework list shown in Figure 1-85. **Notepad** is a popular application program available with Windows XP that allows you to create, save, and print simple text documents.

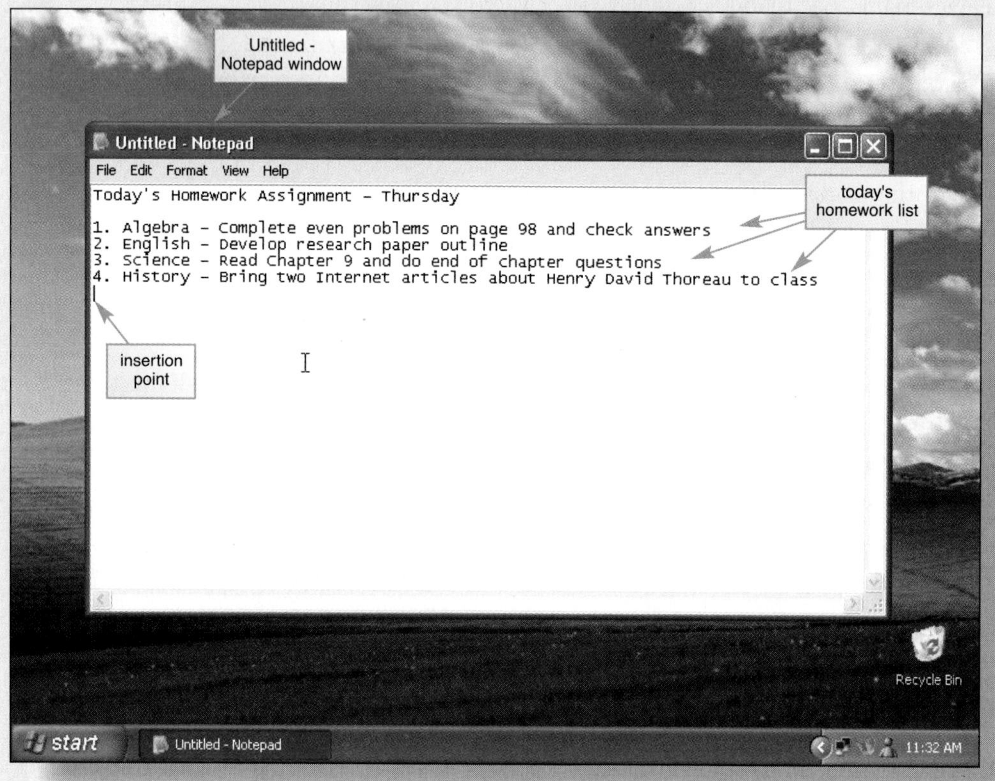

FIGURE 1-85

Part 1: Launching the Notepad Application

1. If necessary, launch Microsoft Windows XP and log on to the computer.
2. Click the Start button.
3. Point to All Programs on the Start menu, point to Accessories on the All Programs submenu, and click Notepad on the Accessories submenu. The Untitled - Notepad window displays and an insertion point (flashing vertical line) displays in the blank area below the menu bar.

In the Lab

Part 2: ***Creating a Document Using Notepad***

1. Type `Today's Homework Assignments - Thursday` and then press the ENTER key twice.
2. Type `1. Algebra - Complete even problems on page 98 and check answers` and then press the ENTER key.
3. Type `2. English - Develop research paper outline` and then press the ENTER key.
4. Type `3. Science - Read chapter 9 and do end of chapter questions` and then press the ENTER key.
5. Type `4. History - Bring two Internet articles about Henry David Thoreau to class` and then press the ENTER key.

Part 3: ***Printing the Today's Homework Document***

1. Click File on the menu bar and then click Print. Click the Print button in the Print dialog box to print the document.
2. Retrieve the printed Today's Homework list from the printer.

Part 4: ***Closing the Notepad Window***

1. Click the Close button on the Notepad title bar.
2. Click the No button in the Notepad dialog box to not save the Today's Homework document.

Cases and Places

The difficulty of these case studies varies:
◗ are the least difficult; ◗◗ are more difficult; and ◗◗◗ are the most difficult.

1 ◗ Using Search in Help and Support, and the keyword, walkthroughs, find the tutorial on Digital photos. In a brief report, summarize the steps to send a photo by e-mail and process your photos on the Web. Include a description of Microsoft Picture IT!

2 ◗ Technical support is an important consideration when installing and using an operating system or an application software program. The ability to obtain a valid answer to a question at the moment you have the question can be the difference between a frustrating incident and a positive experience. Using XP Help and Support, the Internet, or another research facility, write a brief report on the options that are available for obtaining Help and technical support while using Windows XP.

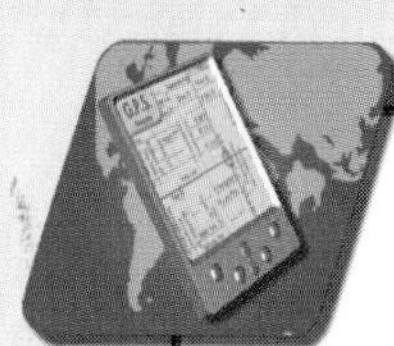

Cases and Places

3 ▶ The Windows XP operating system can be installed only on computers found in the Windows XP hardware compatibility list. Locate three older personal computers. Look for them in your school's computer lab, at a local business, or in your house. Use Help and Support and the Internet to find the Microsoft Web page that contains the Windows XP hardware compatibility list. Check each computer against the list and write a brief report summarizing your results.

4 ▶▶ Early personal computer operating systems were adequate, but they were not user-friendly and had few advanced features. Over the past several years, however, personal computer operating systems have become increasingly easy to use, and some now offer features once available only on mainframe computers. Using the Internet, a library, or other research facility, write a brief report on three personal computer operating systems. Describe the systems, pointing out their similarities and differences. Discuss the advantages and disadvantages of each. Finally, tell which operating system you would purchase and explain why.

5 ▶▶ Microsoft's decision to make Internet Explorer, Media Player, and Movie Maker part of the Windows XP operating system caused many legal concerns for Microsoft. Using the Internet, computer magazines and newspapers, or other resources, prepare a brief report on these legal problems. Explain the arguments for and against combining these applications and the operating system. Identify the key players on both sides of the legal battle and summarize the final decision. Did the legal process or final decision affect the release date and contents of Windows XP? Do you think computer users benefited from this decision? Explain your answers.

6 ▶▶▶ In addition to Windows XP, Microsoft also sells the Windows 98 operating system. Some say Windows XP will replace Windows 98 in the future. Using the Internet, computer magazines, or other resources, prepare a brief report comparing and contrasting the operating systems. How do their graphical user interfaces compare? What features and commands are shared by both operating systems? Does either operating system have features or commands that the other operating system does not have? Explain whether you think Windows XP will replace Windows 98.

7 ▶▶▶ Because of the many important tasks an operating system performs, most businesses put a great deal of thought into choosing an operating system. Interview a person at a local business about the operating system it uses with its computers. Based on the interview, write a brief report on why the business chose that operating system, how satisfied it is with it, and under what circumstances it might consider switching to a different operating system.

Microsoft Windows XP

PROJECT

Working on the Windows XP Desktop

OBJECTIVES

You will have mastered the material in this project when you can:

- Launch an application, create a text document, and save the document on the desktop
- Create, name, and save a text document directly on the desktop
- Move documents to the My Documents folder
- Arrange objects in the My Documents folder in groups
- Create and name a folder in the My Documents folder
- Move documents into a folder
- Add and delete a shortcut on the Start menu
- Open a document using a shortcut on the Start menu
- Create and delete a shortcut on the desktop
- Open a folder using a desktop shortcut
- Modify and print documents in a folder
- Open, modify, and delete multiple documents
- Understand taskbar button grouping
- Minimize all open windows
- Copy a folder onto a floppy disk
- Open a folder stored on a floppy disk
- Delete multiple files and folders
- Understand user accounts and user account types
- Change a password and picture
- Switch between user accounts

Conquering Clutter

Organizing Desktop Documents

Many people live in a state of clutter chaos. Entire businesses, including The Container Store, revolve around the theme of finding thousands of storage solutions for curing our home office, laundry room, and closet clutter. Organization experts make their livings helping clutterbugs make order of their disorder. George Carlin's popular monologue discusses our need to find more and more places to store all our stuff. Experts believe that keeping organized can improve health by reducing stress.

Microsoft Windows XP can be regarded as a type of clutter conqueror. With thousands of hardware devices and software products available for desktop and notebook computers, users need to manage these resources easily and quickly. One of Windows XP's impressive features is the ease with which users can create and access documents and files on the desktop.

In Project 2, you will organize the lives of two computer users by developing and updating their daily reminder lists. You will create folders, use shortcuts, open and modify multiple documents, and manage user accounts.

Windows has come a long way since Bill Gates announced plans to add graphical capabilities to the IBM personal computer in 1983. The Microsoft chairman took this step to help current personal computer users work

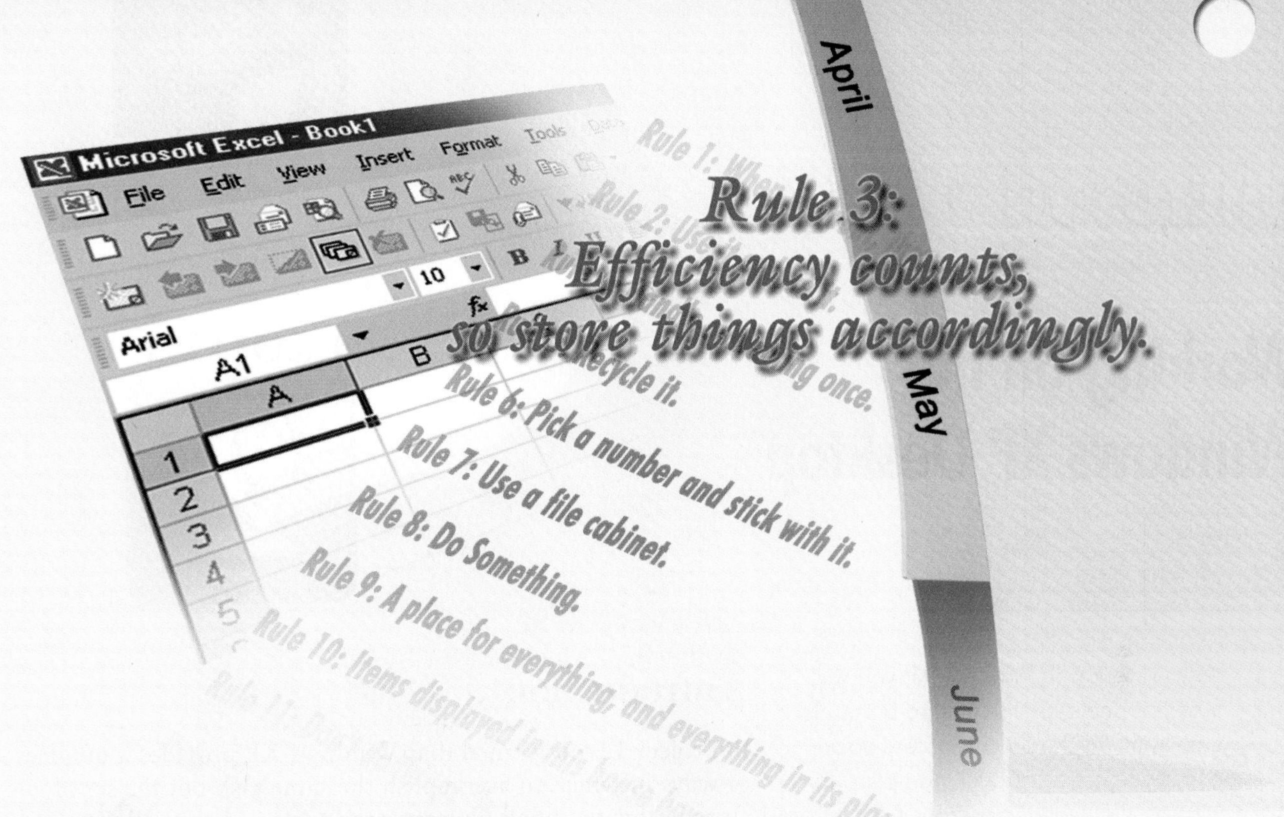

more effectively and, of course, to entice others to buy systems. More than three million computers were sold that year.

Gates's graphical intentions were fueled by work being done at Xerox's Palo Alto Research Center in California. He saw researchers there using an invention they called a mouse to move a pointer instead of using arrow keys on the keyboard to move a cursor.

Then, working with Apple, Microsoft developed software for the Macintosh computer. Combining its original innovations with those of Xerox, Microsoft created the graphical user interface and experimented with the use of various icons and fonts to make the screen user-friendly. In addition, Microsoft introduced Word and Excel for the Macintosh platform. When the Mac was released in 1984, it became a success among users, particularly students.

Microsoft's next step was to develop these applications for the IBM-PC and IBM-compatible computers. The company's innovations resulted in the release of Windows 3.1 in 1992, which sold three million copies within two months; Windows 95, a major upgrade to the Windows operating system; and Windows 98, boasting global sales of ten million copies within the first six months. Other Windows releases including Windows NT and Windows 2000 were received with equal enthusiasm among the millions of Windows users worldwide.

Gates has indicated that Microsoft will continue to release new Windows versions every two or three years, evident in the recent release of Windows XP. He is convinced that individuals will want to take advantage of user interface enhancements and innovations that make computing easier, more reliable, faster, and integrated with the Internet.

Working on the Windows desktop in this project, you will find out for yourself how these features can save time, help you work efficiently, and ultimately reduce computer clutter.

Microsoft Windows XP

Working on the Windows XP Desktop

PROJECT

CASE PERSPECTIVE

As you work with Windows XP, you will find that one essential feature is the ease with which you can access documents you use constantly. You also will find that working with multiple documents at the same time is vital. The company where you work has placed you in charge of developing the text documents to keep track of the daily reminders. As you begin the assignment, you discover that reminders seem to change constantly. You realize that if you could work on the Windows XP desktop and store all documents in the My Documents folder, you would save a great deal of time. In this project, you will learn the skills that are essential to your success and gain the knowledge required to work efficiently on the Windows XP desktop.

Introduction

In Project 1, you learned that Windows XP provides a number of ways in which to accomplish the same task but the set of steps in this textbook illustrates the preferred method. The capability of accomplishing a task in a variety of ways is one of Windows XP's more powerful features.

In Project 2, you will learn two methods of creating documents on the desktop. You also will discover the intuitive nature of the Windows XP desktop and the My Documents folder by creating a folder in the My Documents folder, storing documents in this folder, and then moving the folder from the My Documents folder onto a floppy disk. In addition, you will learn about user accounts, changing the information in those accounts, and switching between user accounts.

Assume each morning you create two daily reminders lists: one for Mr. Sanchez and one for Ms. Pearson. Mr. Sanchez and Ms. Pearson review the lists throughout the day. You must update the lists as reminders are added during the day. In addition, Mr. Sanchez and Ms. Pearson must be able to view, add, and delete reminders on either list. You decide to use **Notepad**, a popular application program available with Windows XP, to create the daily reminders lists. The finished documents are shown in Figure 2-1.

The name of each document displays at the top of the printed page, the text of the document (the daily reminders) displays below the document name, and a page number displays at the bottom of the page. The first printed document contains a list of Monday's reminders for Mr. Sanchez. The second printed document contains a list of Monday's reminders for Ms. Pearson. The following sections illustrate two methods of creating these documents.

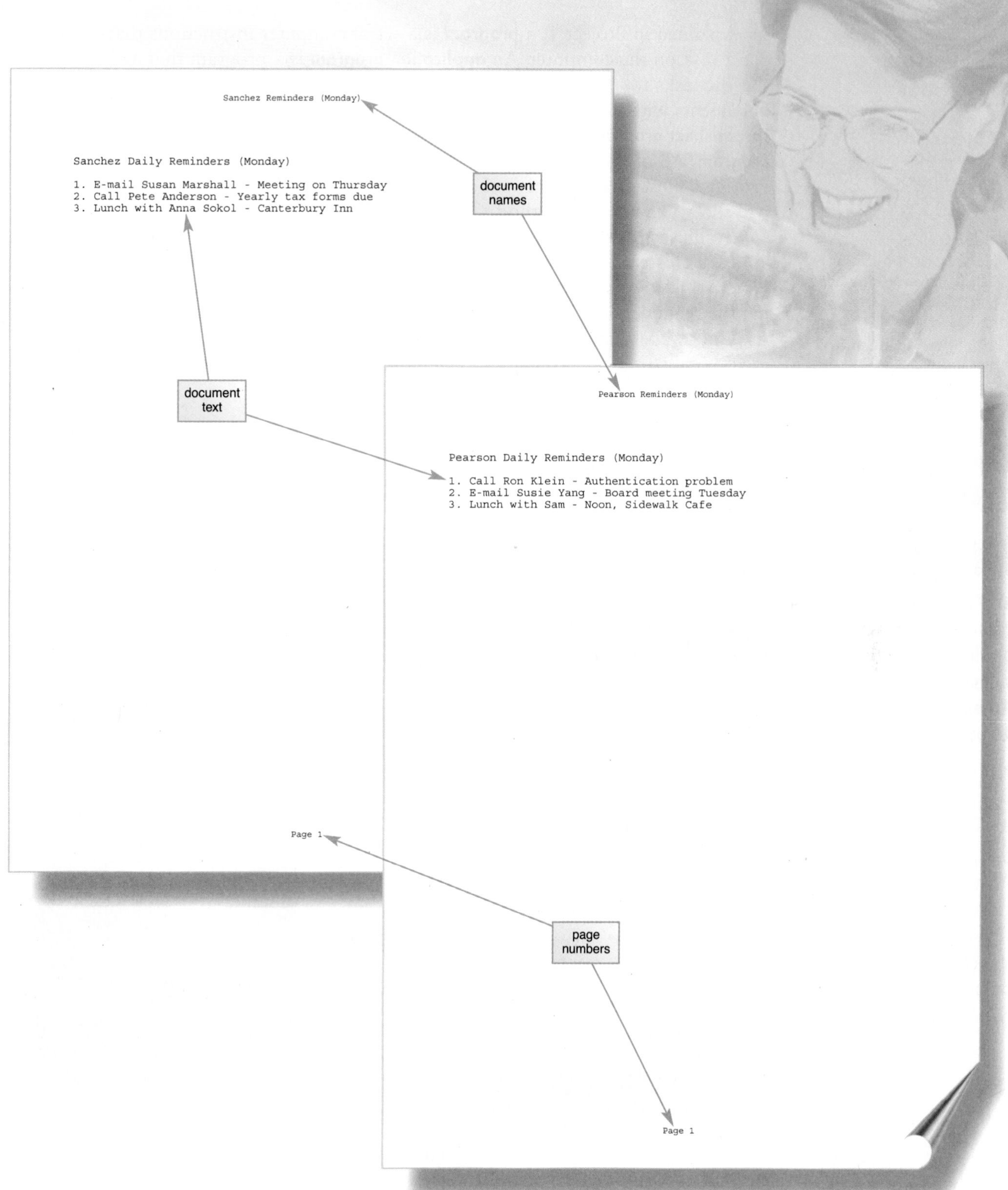
Sanchez Reminders (Monday)
Sanchez Daily Reminders (Monday)
1. E-mail Susan Marshall - Meeting on Thursday
2. Call Pete Anderson - Yearly tax forms due
3. Lunch with Anna Sokol - Canterbury Inn
Page 1
document names
document text
Pearson Reminders (Monday)
Pearson Daily Reminders (Monday)
1. Call Ron Klein - Authentication problem
2. E-mail Susie Yang - Board meeting Tuesday
3. Lunch with Sam - Noon, Sidewalk Cafe
Page 1
page numbers

FIGURE 2-1

Creating a Document by Launching an Application Program

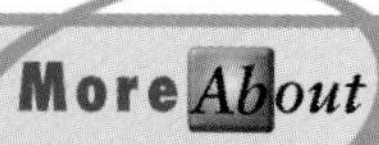

Application Programs

Several application programs (Internet Explorer, Movie Maker, Media Player, and Windows Messenger) are part of Windows XP. Many application programs, such as Microsoft Office, however, must be purchased separately from Windows XP.

As explained in Project 1, a **program** is a set of computer instructions that carries out a task on the computer. An **application program** is a program that accomplishes specific tasks for which the program is designed. For example, you create written documents with a **word processing program**, spreadsheets and charts with a **spreadsheet program**, and graphics presentations with a **presentation graphics program**. All of these applications display on your computer as you use them. Project 1 illustrated one method of starting an application program. This project will show you another method.

To illustrate how to use an application program to create a written document, you will create the document that contains the daily reminders for Mr. Sanchez using Notepad. You will create the document by launching the Notepad application, typing the reminders for Mr. Sanchez, and then saving the document on the desktop. In Windows terminology, opening an application program and then creating a document is called the **application-centric approach**. Perform the following steps to launch Notepad and enter the reminders for Mr. Sanchez.

Steps To Launch a Program and Create a Document

1 Click the Start button. Point to All Programs on the Start menu. Point to Accessories on the All Programs submenu. Point to Notepad on the Accessories submenu.

The Start menu, All Programs submenu, and Accessories submenu display (Figure 2-2). The Accessories submenu contains the highlighted Notepad command to launch the Notepad program.

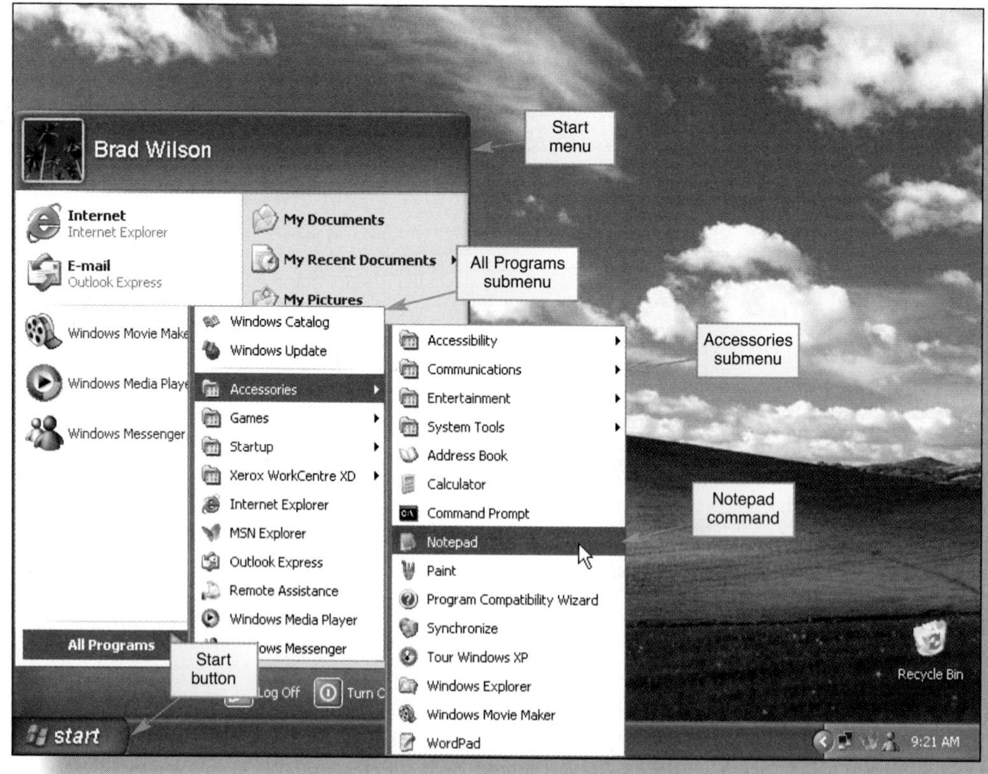

FIGURE 2-2

2 **Click Notepad. Type** `Sanchez Daily Reminders (Monday)` **and then press the ENTER key twice. Type** `1. E-mail Susan Marshall - Meeting on Thursday` **and then press the ENTER key. Type** `2. Call Pete Anderson - Yearly tax forms due` **and then press the ENTER key. Type** `3. Lunch with Anna Sokol - Canterbury Inn` **and then press the ENTER key.**

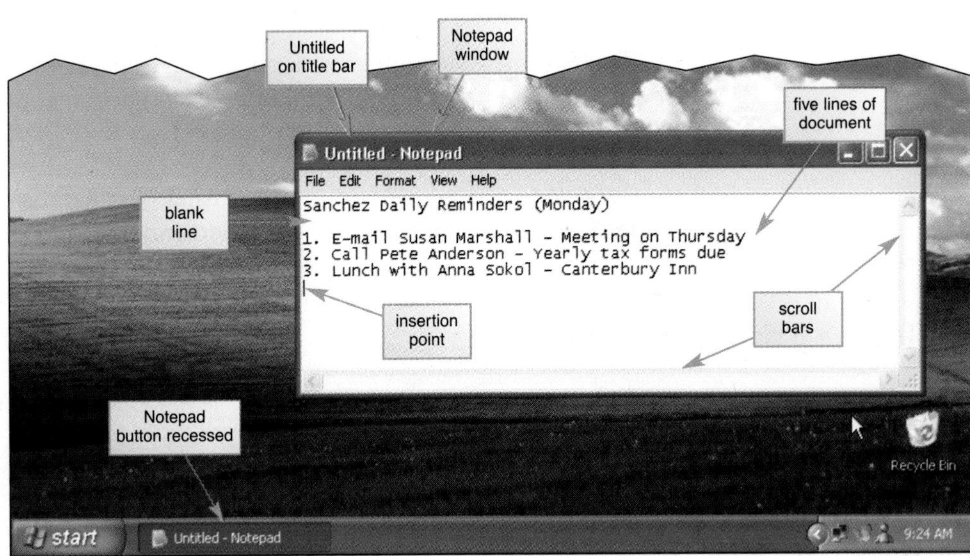

FIGURE 2-3

The Notepad program launches, the text of the document is entered, and a recessed Notepad button displays in the taskbar button area (Figure 2-3).

Other Ways

1. Right-click desktop, point to New, click Text Document, double-click New Text Document icon, enter text
2. Click Start button, click Run, type `Notepad`, click OK button, enter text
3. Press CTRL+ESC, press R (first letter of command name) type `Notepad`, press ENTER key, enter text

In Figure 2-3, the word, Untitled, in the title bar (Untitled - Notepad) and on the Notepad button indicates the document has not been saved on disk. The area below the menu bar contains the five lines of the document including the blank line, a line containing an insertion point, and two scroll bars. The **insertion point** is a flashing vertical line that indicates the point at which text typed on the keyboard will display. The scroll bars do not contain scroll boxes, indicating the document is not large enough to require scrolling.

Although not visible when you begin typing the Sanchez Daily Reminders (Monday) document in Figure 2-3, the Notepad command is added to the most frequently used programs list on the Start menu (see Figure 2-20 on page WIN 2.18).

Saving a Document on the Desktop

When you create a document using a program such as Notepad, the document is stored in the main memory (RAM) of the computer. If you close the program without saving the document or if the computer accidentally loses electrical power, the document will be lost. To protect against the accidental loss of a document and to allow you to modify the document easily in the future, you can save the document on disk (hard disk or floppy disk) or on the desktop. When you save a document on the desktop, a document icon displays on the desktop and the document is stored on the hard disk.

When you save a document, you must assign a file name to the document. All documents are identified by a **file name**. A file name should be descriptive of the saved file. Examples of file names are Sanchez Reminders (Monday), Office Supplies List, and Automobile Maintenance. A file name can contain up to 255 characters, including spaces. Any uppercase or lowercase character is valid when creating a file name, except a backslash (\), slash (/), colon (:), asterisk (*), question mark (?), quotation mark ("), less than symbol (<), greater than symbol (>), or vertical bar (|). File names cannot be CON, AUX, COM1, COM2, COM3, COM4, LPT1, LPT2, LPT3, PRN, or NUL.

More About

Saving a Document

Many computer users can tell at least one horror story of working on their computers for a long period of time and then losing the work because of a power failure or software problem. Be Warned: Save and save often to protect the work you have completed on your computer.

To associate a document with an application, Windows XP assigns an extension of a period and up to three characters to each document. All documents created using the Notepad program are text documents and are saved with the .txt extension.

To save the document you created using Notepad on the desktop using the file name, Sanchez Reminders (Monday), perform the following steps.

Steps To Save a Document on the Desktop

1 Click File on the menu bar and then point to Save As.

The File menu opens in the Notepad window (Figure 2-4). The ellipsis (...) following the Save As command indicates Windows XP requires more information to carry out the command and will open a dialog box when you click Save As.

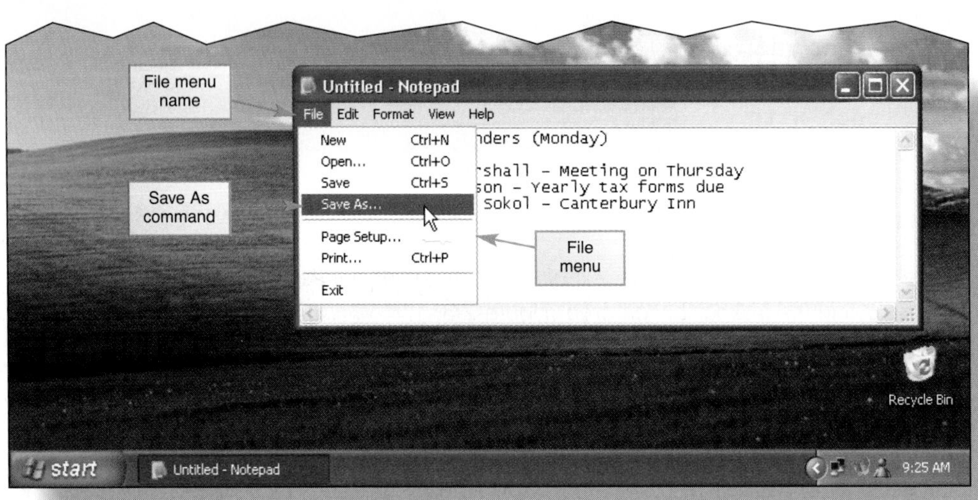

FIGURE 2-4

2 Click Save As. Type `Sanchez Reminders (Monday)` **in the File name text box. Point to the Desktop icon on the Shortcut bar.**

The Save As dialog box displays (Figure 2-5). The My Documents entry in the Save in box and the selected My Documents button on the Shortcut bar indicate the file will be saved in the My Documents folder. The File name text box contains the document name. When you save this document, Notepad will add the .txt extension to the file name automatically. Pointing to the Desktop icon on the Shortcut bar displays a three-dimensional button.

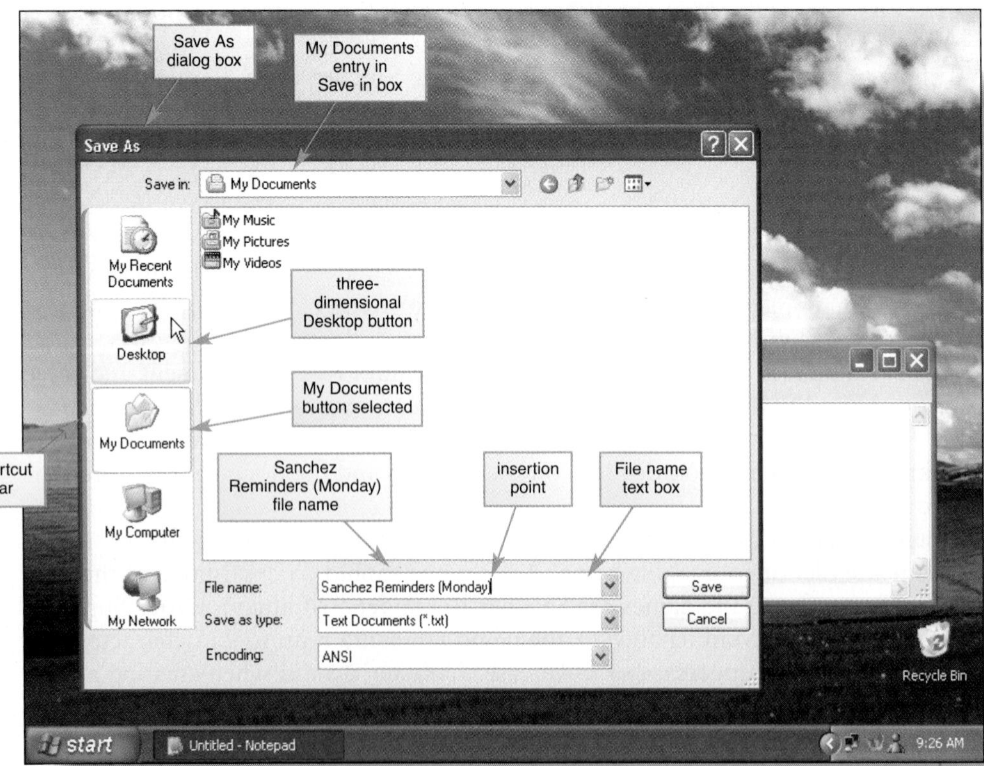

FIGURE 2-5

3 Click the Desktop button and then point to the Save button in the Save As dialog box.

The Desktop entry displays in the Save in box, the names of three folders display in the list, and the Shortcut bar contains the selected Desktop button (Figure 2-6).

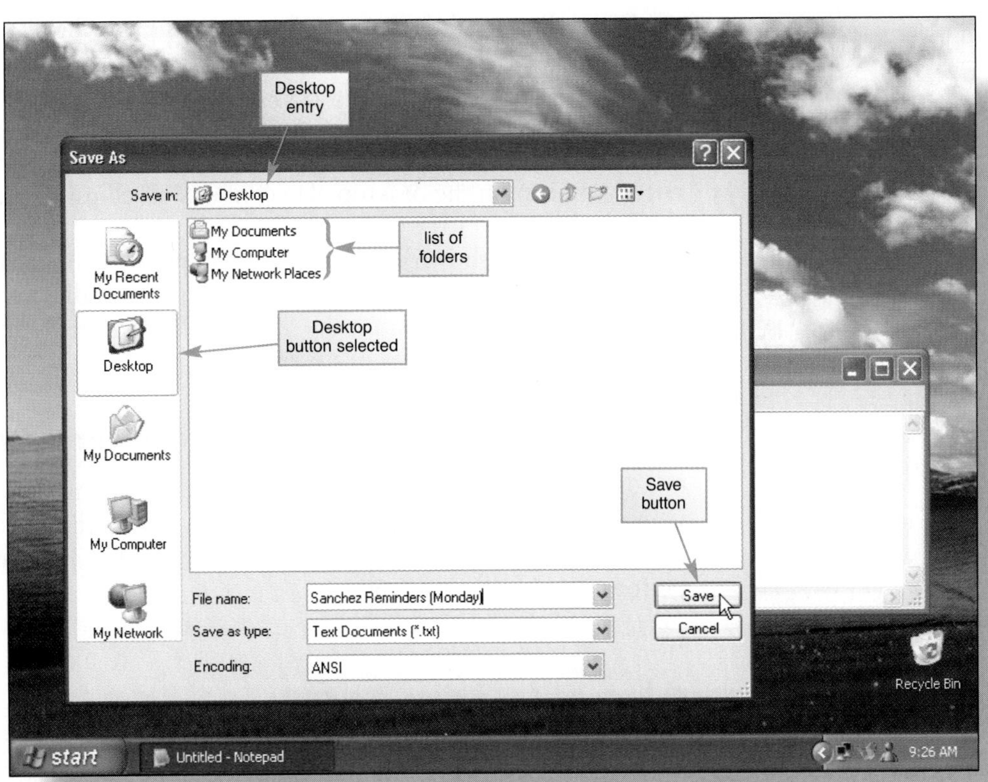

FIGURE 2-6

4 Click the Save button.

Windows XP saves the Sanchez Reminders (Monday) document on the desktop and closes the Save As dialog box. The Sanchez Reminders (Monday) document icon displays on the desktop, and the file name becomes part of the Notepad window title and the button name in the taskbar button area. The ellipses indicate part of the file name is not shown (Figure 2-7).

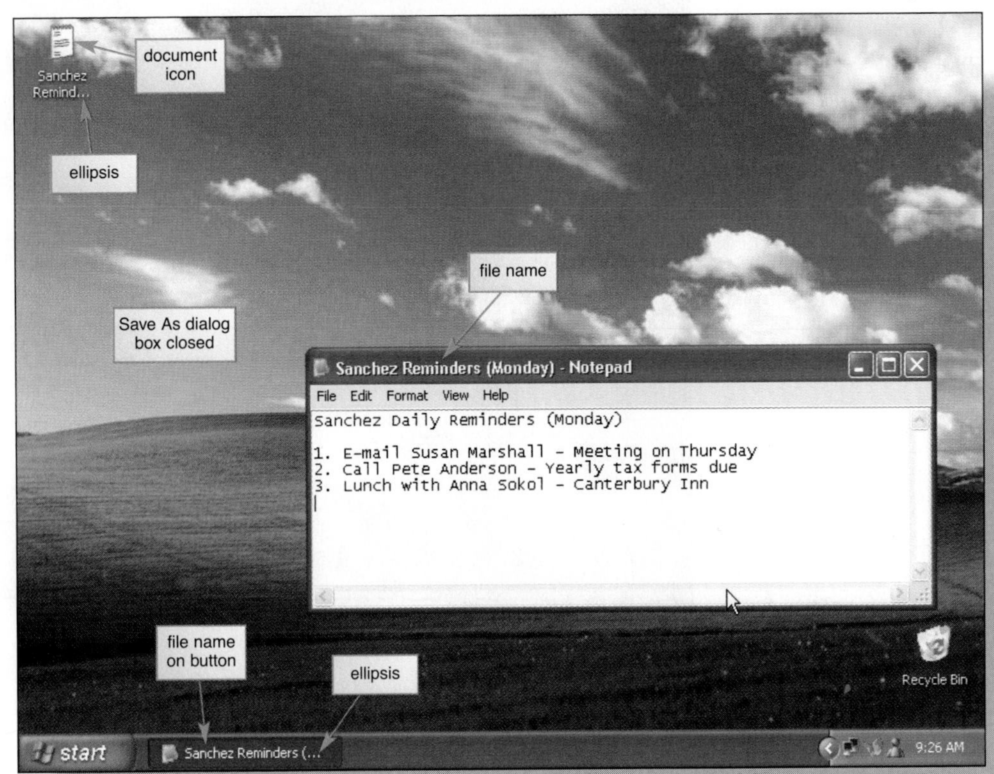

FIGURE 2-7

Menus

After clicking a menu name on the menu bar, point to another menu name on the menu bar to open that menu. To close a menu without carrying out a command, click anywhere on the desktop except on the menu.

Depending on the computer's settings, the Sanchez Reminders (Monday) icon may display along the left side of the desktop or at another location on the desktop.

In Figure 2-7 on the previous page, the file name on the button in the taskbar button area contains an ellipsis (...) to indicate the entire button name does not fit on the button. To display the entire button name, point to the button. The file name on the document icon on the desktop also contains an ellipsis. To display the entire icon name, point to the icon.

The method shown in the previous steps for saving a file on the desktop can be used to save a file on a floppy disk or on the hard disk of the computer by clicking the My Computer button on the Shortcut bar and then double-clicking 3½ Floppy (A:) or LOCAL DISK (C:) in the list box.

Printing a Document from an Application Program

Quite often, after creating a document and saving it, you will want to print it. One method of printing a document displayed on the desktop is to print it directly from an application program. To print the Sanchez Reminders (Monday) document, perform the following steps.

To Print a Document from an Application Program

1 Click File on the menu bar and then point to Print.

The File menu, containing the highlighted Print command, displays (Figure 2-8).

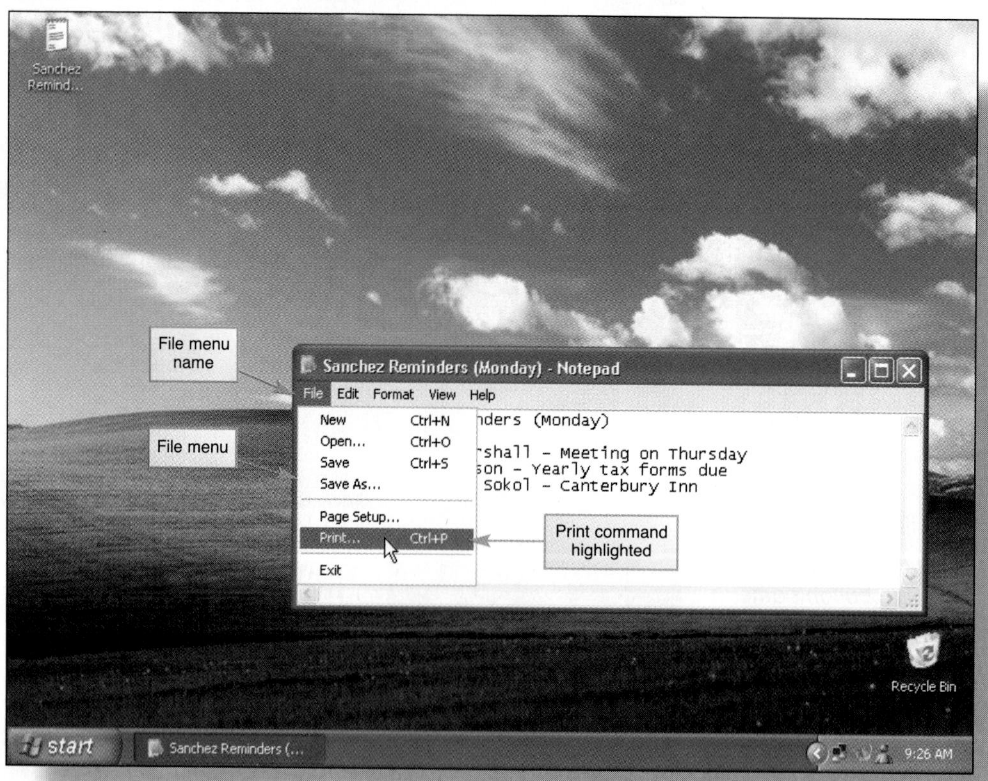

FIGURE 2-8

2 Click Print. Point to the Print button in the Print dialog box.

The Print dialog box, containing the General sheet, displays (Figure 2-9). The selected All option button and the value 1 in the Number of copies text box indicate one copy of all pages will print.

3 Click the Print button.

The Sanchez Reminders (Monday) document prints.

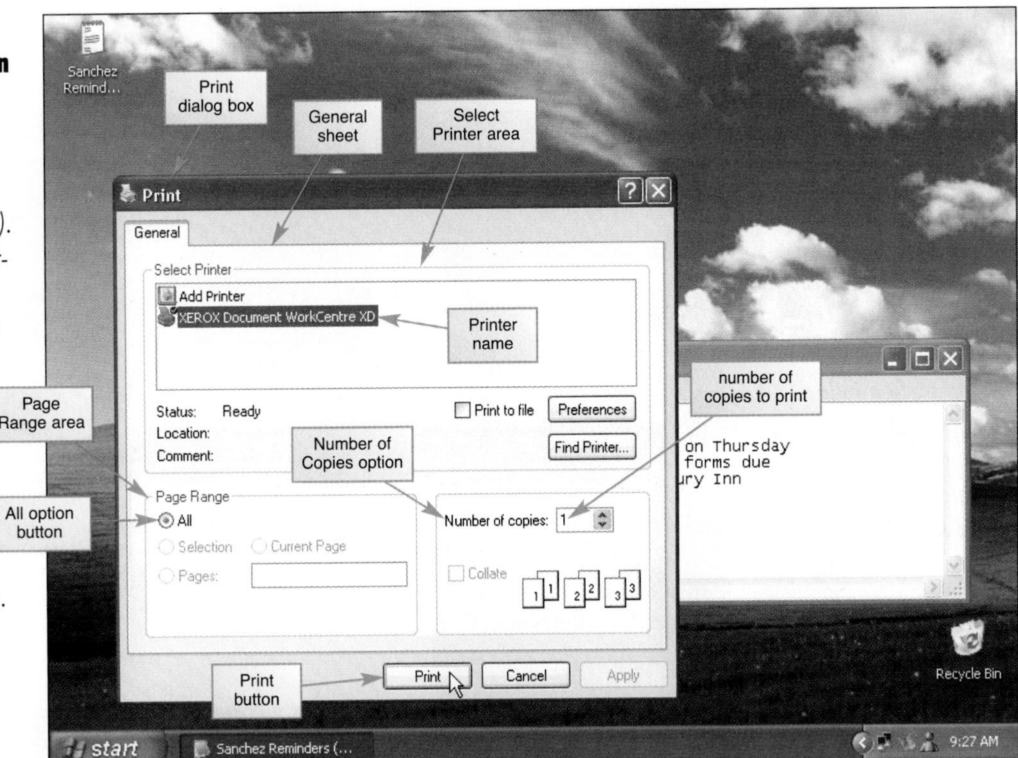

FIGURE 2-9

In Figure 2-9, the General sheet in the Printer dialog box contains the Select Printer, Page Range, and copies areas. The highlighted printer icon in the Select Printer area indicates that, in this case, the XEROX Document WorkCentre XD printer is ready to print the document. The Page Range area contains four option buttons. The option buttons give you the choice of printing all pages of a document (All), selected parts of a document (Selection), current page (Current Page), or selected pages of a document (Pages). The selected All option button indicates all pages of a document will print. The value 1 in the Number of copies box indicates one copy of the document will print.

Other Ways

1. Right-click document icon, click Print
2. Press ALT+F, press P, press TAB key repeatedly to select Print button, press P

Closing a Document

After creating, saving, and printing the Sanchez Reminders (Monday) document, the use of the document is complete. Perform the steps on the next page to close the Notepad window containing the document.

More About

Printing

Printing is and will remain an important output form for documents. Many sophisticated application programs, however, are extending the printing capability to include transmitting faxes, sending e-mail, and even posting documents on Web pages of the World Wide Web.

To Close a Document

1. **Point to the Close button on the Notepad title bar (Figure 2-10).**

2. **Click the Close button.**

The Sanchez Reminders (Monday) - Notepad window closes and the Sanchez Reminders (Monday) - Notepad button no longer displays on the taskbar.

FIGURE 2-10

Other Ways

1. On title bar double-click Notepad icon
2. On title bar click Notepad icon, click Close
3. On File menu click Exit
4. Press ALT+F, press X; or press ALT+F4

More About

Document-Centric

The document-centric concept will progress to the point where you neither know nor care what application was used to create a document. For example, when you include a hyperlink to a Web page in a document, you will not care how the page was created. Only the content of the page is of interest.

After completing the reminders list for Mr. Sanchez, the next step is to create a similar list for Ms. Pearson.

Creating and Naming a Document on the Desktop

Opening an application program and then creating a document (**application-centric approach**) was the method used to create the first document. Although the same method could be used to create the document for Ms. Pearson, another method, which is easier and more straightforward, is to create the new document on the Windows XP desktop without first starting an application program. Instead of launching a program to create and modify a document, you create a blank document directly on the desktop and then use the Notepad program to enter data into the document. This method, called the **document-centric approach**, will be used to create the document that contains the reminders for Ms. Pearson.

To create a blank document directly on the desktop, perform the following steps.

Steps To Create a Blank Document on the Desktop

1 Right-click an open area on the desktop, point to New on the shortcut menu, and then point to Text Document on the New submenu.

The shortcut menu and New submenu display (Figure 2-11).

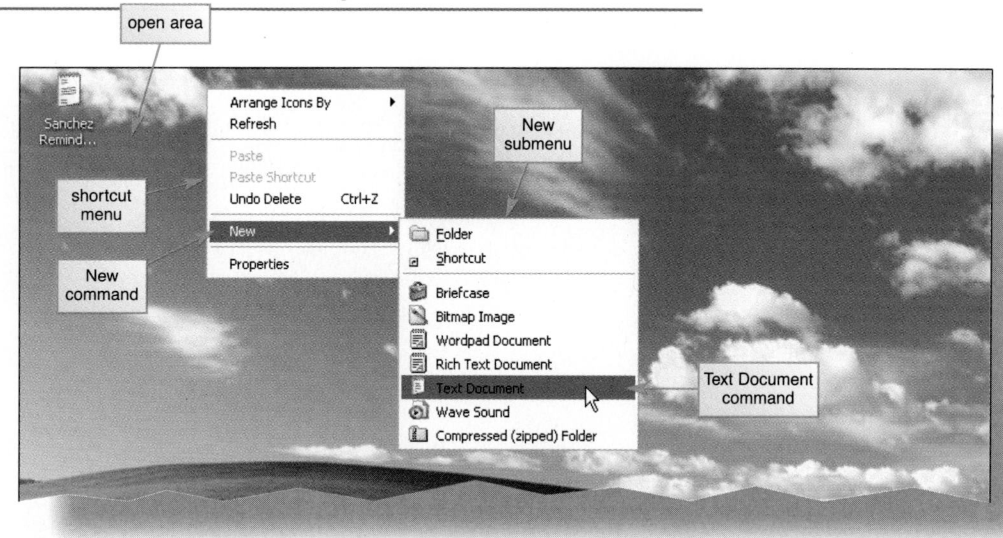

FIGURE 2-11

2 Click Text Document.

The shortcut menu and New submenu close, a blank text document with the default name, New Text Document, is created and its icon displays on the desktop (Figure 2-12). The ***icon title text box*** *below the icon contains the highlighted default file name followed by an insertion point. Whenever highlighted text displays in a text box, any characters you type will replace the highlighted text.*

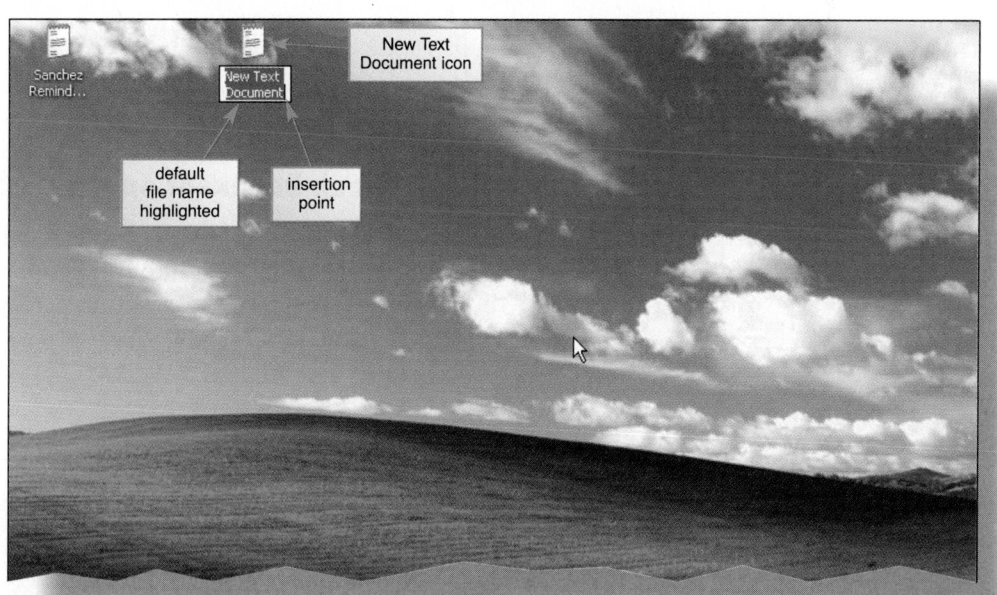

FIGURE 2-12

A blank document has been created on the desktop to contain the daily reminders for Ms. Pearson. The icon may display on the desktop where you right-clicked the desktop or along the left side of the desktop, depending on the computer's settings.

Naming a Document

After you create a blank document on the desktop, normally you will name the document so it is easily identifiable. In Figure 2-12, the default file name (New Text Document) is highlighted and the insertion point is blinking, so you can type the new name. To give the name, Pearson Reminders (Monday), to the document you just created, complete the step on the next page.

More About

Creating Blank Documents on the Desktop

The phrase, creating a document on the desktop, may be confusing. The document you actually create contains no data. It is blank. In effect, you are placing a blank piece of paper with a name on your desktop. The document has little value until you add text or other data to it.

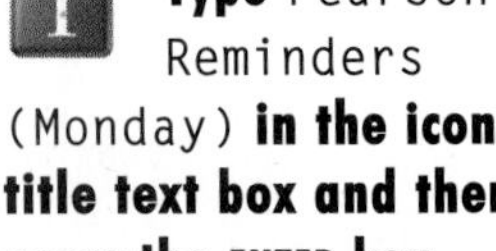

To Name a Document on the Desktop

1 **Type** `Pearson Reminders (Monday)` **in the icon title text box and then press the ENTER key.**

The file name, Pearson Reminders (Monday), displays in the icon title text box, replacing the default name (Figure 2-13). The Pearson Reminders (Monday) icon is selected.

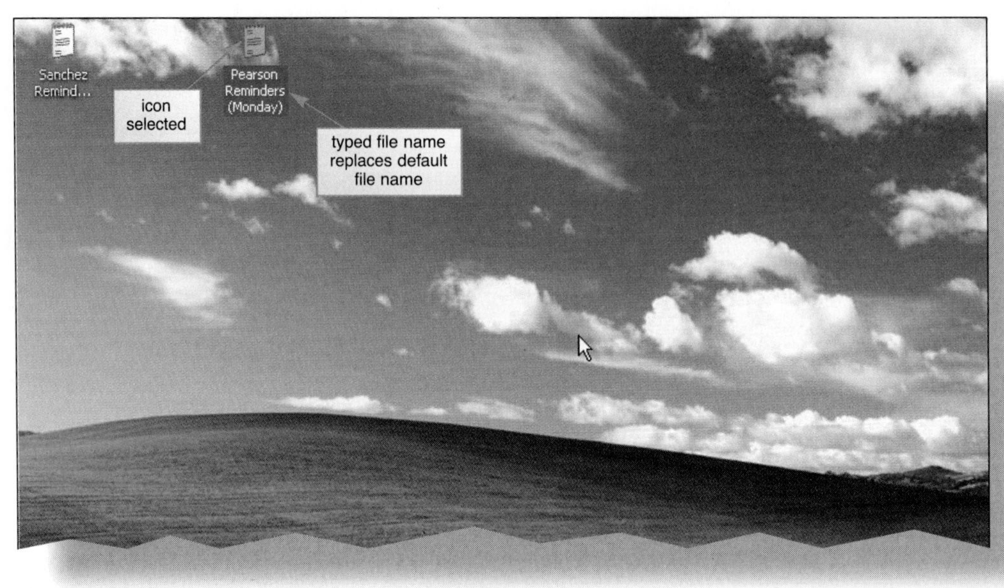

FIGURE 2-13

Other Ways

1. Right-click icon, on shortcut menu click Rename, type file name, press ENTER
2. Click icon to select icon, press F2, type file name, press ENTER

Entering Data into a Blank Document on the Desktop

Although you have created the Pearson Reminders (Monday) document, the document contains no data. To enter data into the blank document, you must open the document. To open a document on the desktop, perform the following steps.

To Open a Document on the Desktop

1 **Point to the Pearson Reminders (Monday) icon on the desktop.**

Although not visible in Figure 2-14, a ToolTip indicates the file is a text file (Type: Text Document), was modified (created) on 10/15/2006 at 9:29 AM, and contains no text (Size: 0 bytes) (Figure 2-14).

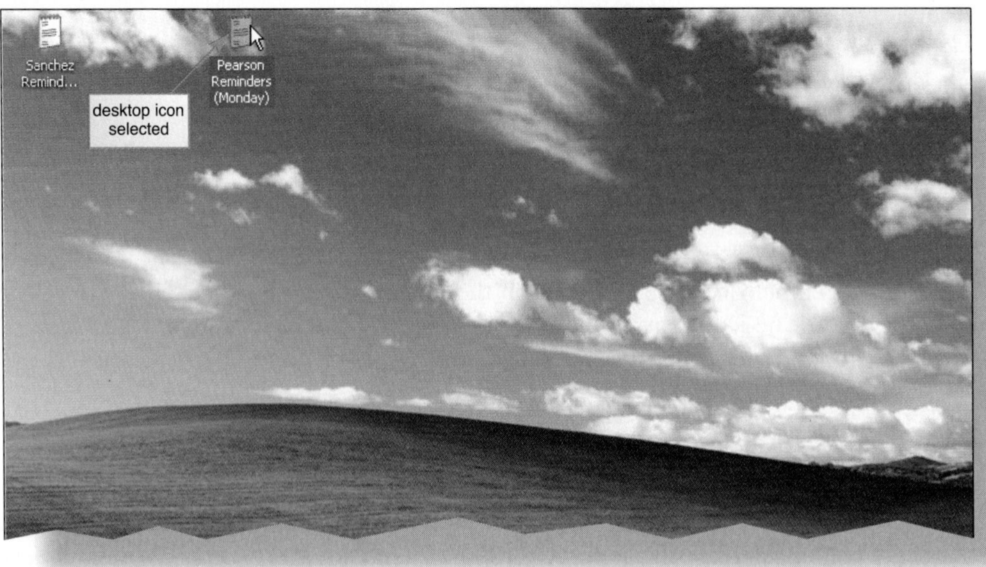

FIGURE 2-14

2 Double-click the Pearson Reminders (Monday) icon.

The Notepad window opens and the Pearson Reminders (Monday) document displays in the Notepad window (Figure 2-15). The document contains no text. The insertion point is located at the beginning of the first line of the document.

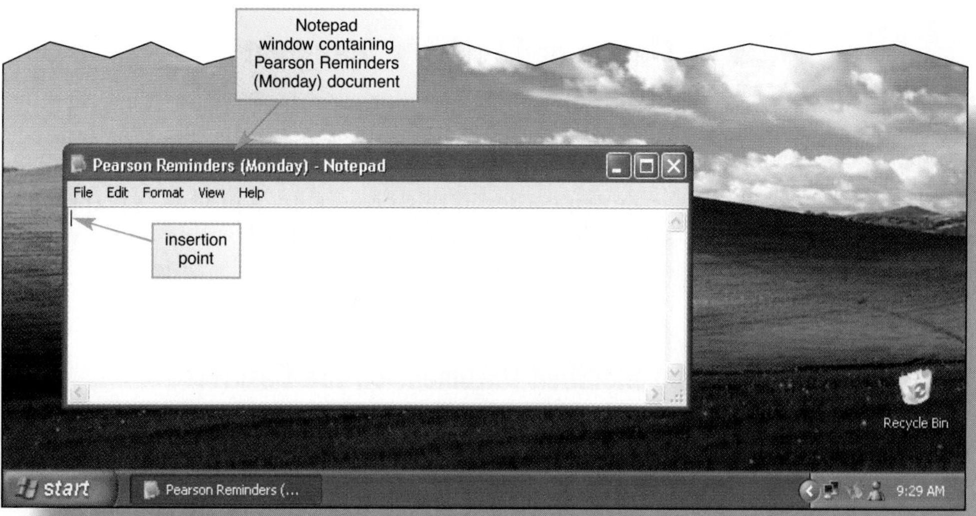

FIGURE 2-15

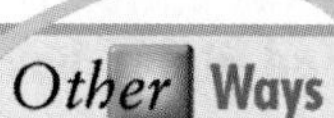

1. Right-click icon, on shortcut menu click Open
2. Click icon to select icon, press ENTER

After the document is open, you can enter the required data by typing the text (the daily reminders) in the document. To enter the text for the Pearson Reminders (Monday) document, perform the following step.

Steps To Enter Data into a Blank Document on the Desktop

1 Type `Pearson Daily Reminders (Monday)` **and then press the ENTER key twice. Type** `1. Call Ron Klein - Authentication problem` **and then press the ENTER key. Type** `2. E-mail Susie Yang - Board meeting Tuesday` **and then press the ENTER key. Type** `3. Lunch with Sam - Noon, Sidewalk Cafe` **and then press the ENTER key.**

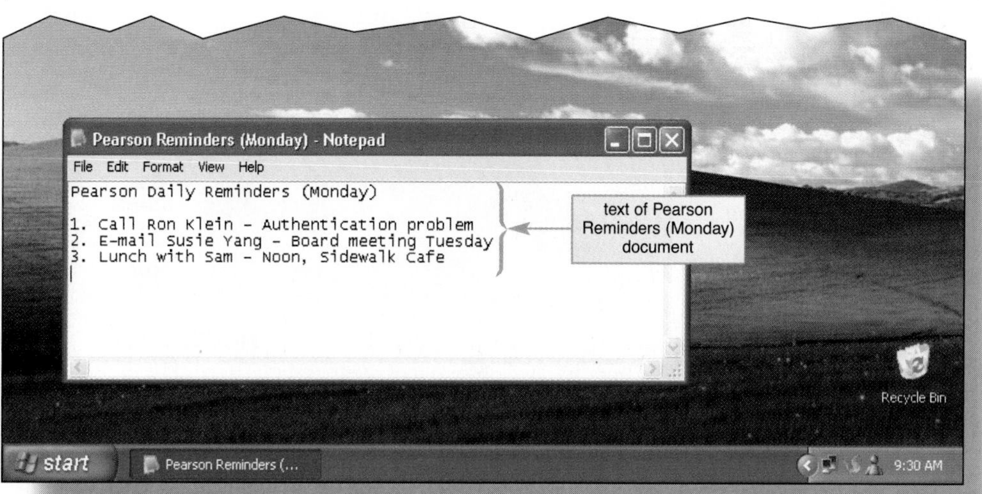

FIGURE 2-16

The text for Pearson Reminders (Monday) displays in the document (Figure 2-16).

You can type as many words and lines as necessary for the document. Entering text into the Pearson Reminders (Monday) document modifies the document, which results in the need to save the document.

Saving a Document

If you make many changes to a document, you should save the document while you are working on it. To save the document, click File on the menu bar and then click Save.

Closing and Saving a Document

After entering the text into the Pearson Reminders (Monday) document, you will close and save the document so the text you entered will remain part of the document. You accomplish this by using the Save As command on the File menu as shown earlier in this project. In Windows XP applications, you can close and save a document in one procedure. To close and save the Pearson Reminders (Monday) document, complete the following steps.

Steps To Close and Save a Modified Document on the Desktop

1 Click the Close button on the Notepad title bar. Point to the Yes button in the Notepad dialog box.

Because you changed the Pearson Reminders (Monday) document, Windows XP displays the Notepad dialog box asking if you want to save the changes you made to the document (Figure 2-17).

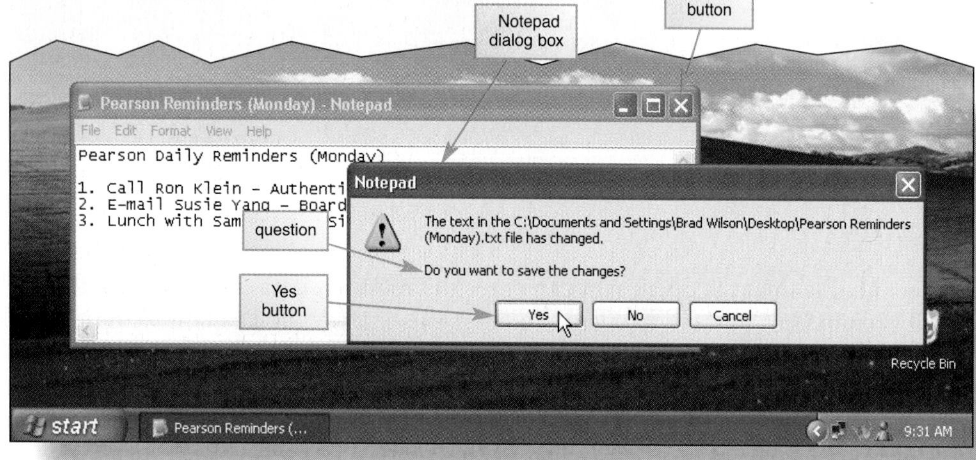

FIGURE 2-17

2 Click the Yes button.

The Notepad dialog box and Notepad window close and the modified Pearson Reminders (Monday) document is saved on the desktop (Figure 2-18).

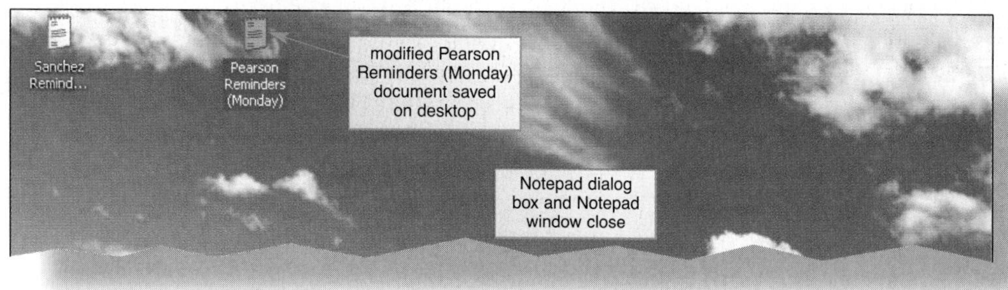

FIGURE 2-18

3 Click an open area of the desktop to deselect the Pearson Reminders (Monday) document on the desktop.

Other Ways

1. On File menu click Save As, click Save button, click Yes button, click Close button
2. On title bar click Notepad icon, click Close, click Yes button
3. On title bar double-click Notepad icon, click Yes button
4. Press ALT+F, press S, press ALT+F, press X

In most Windows XP application programs, if you attempt to close the program without saving the document, a dialog box displays asking if you want to save the document before closing the program. This is the way in which Windows XP ensures you accidentally do not lose changes made to a document.

After saving and closing the Pearson Reminders (Monday) document, the second document is complete.

Storing Documents in the My Documents Folder

After creating documents on the desktop, you can perform several operations on the documents. You can modify and save the documents, print one or both documents, create a folder on the desktop to contain the documents and move the documents to the folder, or store the documents in the My Documents folder. The **My Documents folder** is a central location for storing and managing documents and folders. Having a single storage location for documents makes it easier to make a copy of the documents so that they are not accidentally lost or damaged.

The following sections illustrate how to move the documents on the desktop to the My Documents folder, open the My Documents folder, arrange the icons in the My Documents folder, create a new folder in the My Documents folder, and then move the documents into the new folder.

More About

My Documents

Windows XP creates a unique My Documents folder for each computer user. From an administrative position, this process makes it easier to back up important files and folders in each computer user's My Documents folder.

Moving Multiple Documents to the My Documents Folder

After creating the Sanchez Reminders (Monday) and Pearson Reminders (Monday) documents, you should move the documents from the desktop to the My Documents folder. Prior to moving the two documents, the documents must be selected. Perform the following steps to select the Sanchez Reminders (Monday) and Pearson Reminders (Monday) documents and move the documents from the desktop to the My Documents folder.

Steps To Move Multiple Documents to the My Documents Folder

1 Click the Sanchez icon on the desktop. While holding down the SHIFT key, click the Pearson Reminders (Monday) icon on the desktop, and then release the SHIFT key.

Both icons are selected (Figure 2-19). The mouse pointer points to the Pearson Reminders (Monday) icon on the desktop.

FIGURE 2-19

2 Drag the Pearson Reminders (Monday) icon onto the Start button on the taskbar. Do not release the left mouse button.

When you drag the icon onto the Start button, the Start menu displays and the Pearson Reminders (Monday) icon on the Start button appears dimmed (Figure 2-20). The two icons on the desktop are no longer dimmed.

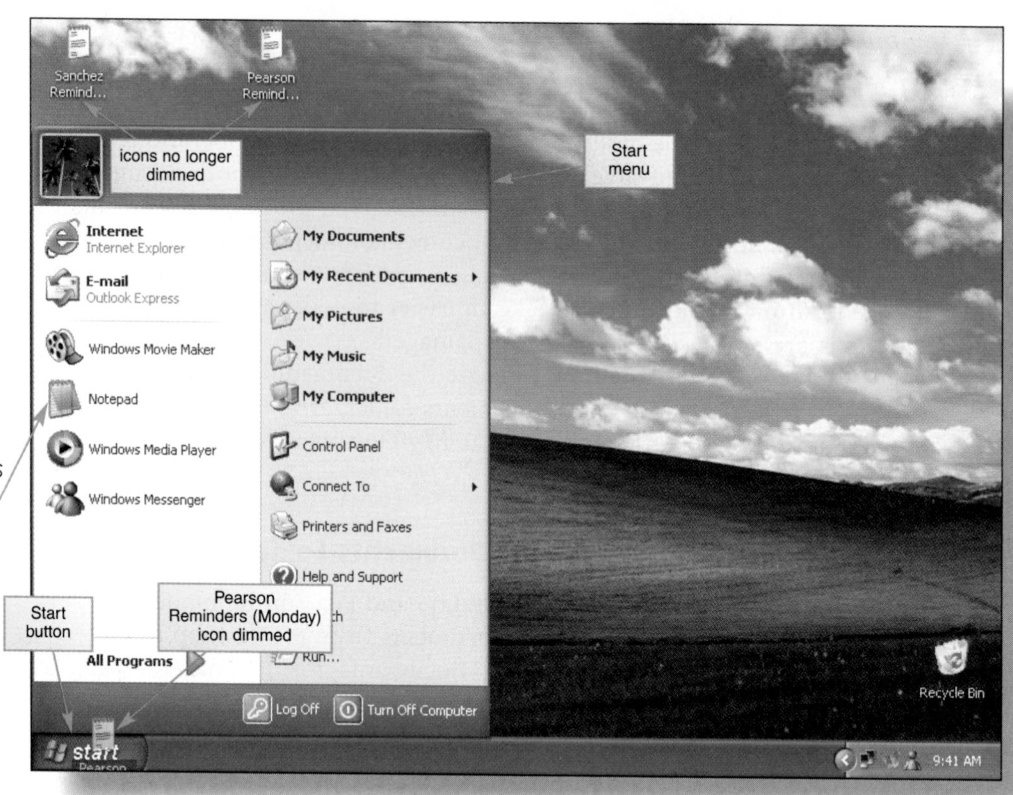

FIGURE 2-20

3 Drag the Pearson Reminders (Monday) icon onto the My Documents command on the Start menu. Do not release the left mouse button.

When you drag the icon onto the My Documents command, the Pearson and Sanchez Reminders (Monday) icon remain dimmed and the My Documents command is highlighted (Figure 2-21).

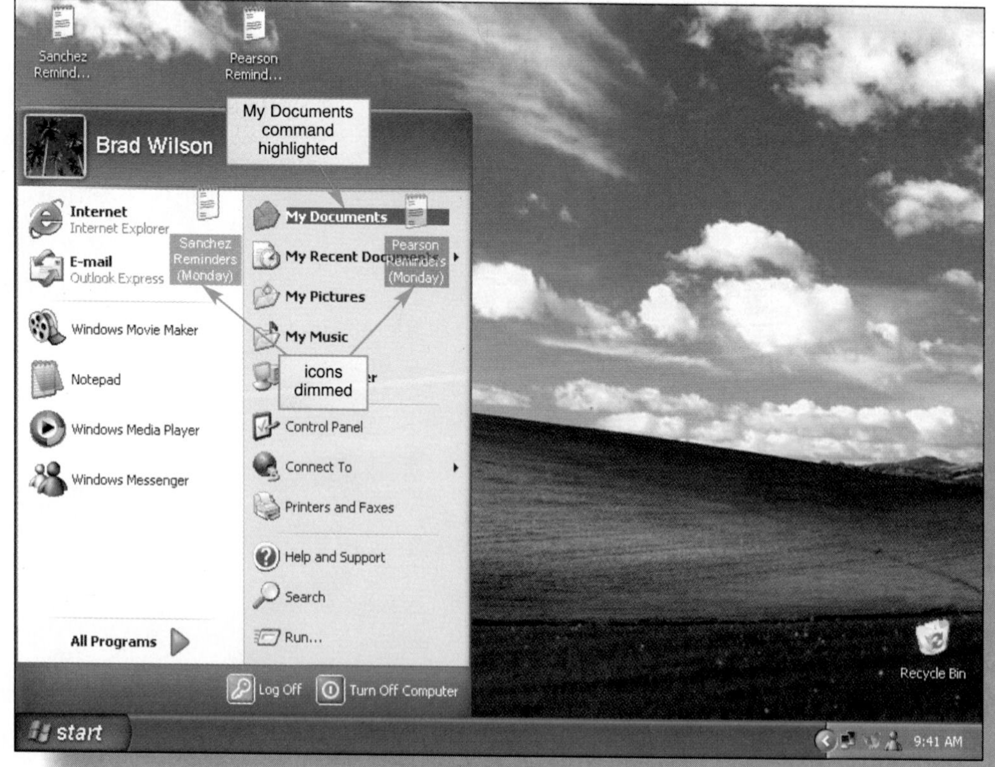

FIGURE 2-21

4 Release the left mouse button.

When you release the left mouse button, the Start menu remains on the desktop, the My Documents command remains highlighted, the Sanchez Reminders (Monday) and Pearson Reminders (Monday) icons are removed from the desktop, and the documents are moved to the My Documents folder (Figure 2-22).

5 Click an open area of the desktop to remove the Start menu.

The Start menu no longer displays on the desktop.

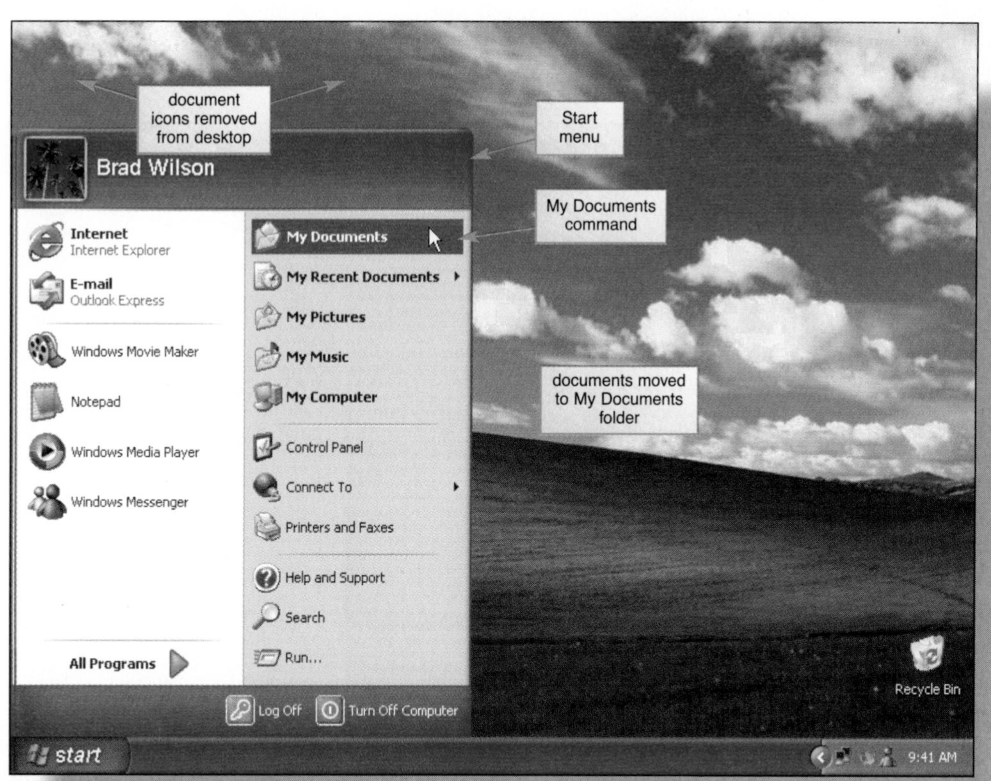

FIGURE 2-22

When the Start menu displays in Figure 2-20, the Notepad command displays in the most frequently used programs list. Although not visible until dragging the Pearson Daily Reminders (Monday) onto the Start button in Figure 2-20, the command was placed on the Start menu when the Notepad program was used in Figure 2-3 on page WIN 2.07 to create the Sanchez Reminders (Monday) document.

Opening the My Documents Folder

After moving the Sanchez Reminders (Monday) and Pearson Reminders (Monday) documents from the desktop to the My Documents folder, you may want to verify that the documents have been moved properly by opening the My Documents folder. Perform the step on the next page to open the My Documents folder.

Other Ways

1. Click Start button, click My Documents, select documents, drag icons to My Documents window
2. Select document icons, right-drag icons to Start button and then to My Documents, click Move Here

More About

The My Document Folders

The My Documents folder contains three folders: My Pictures, My Music, and My Videos. Windows XP creates, in the My Documents folder, a unique My Documents, My Pictures, and My Music folder for each computer user. When you display the Start menu, your personal My Documents, My Pictures, and My Music folders display on the menu.

To Open the My Documents Folder

1 Click the Start button. Click My Documents on the Start menu.

The Sanchez Reminders (Monday) and Pearson Reminders (Monday) icons display in the right pane of the My Documents window (Figure 2-23). The document name, file type (Text Document), and file size (1 KB) of each document display to the right of its icon.

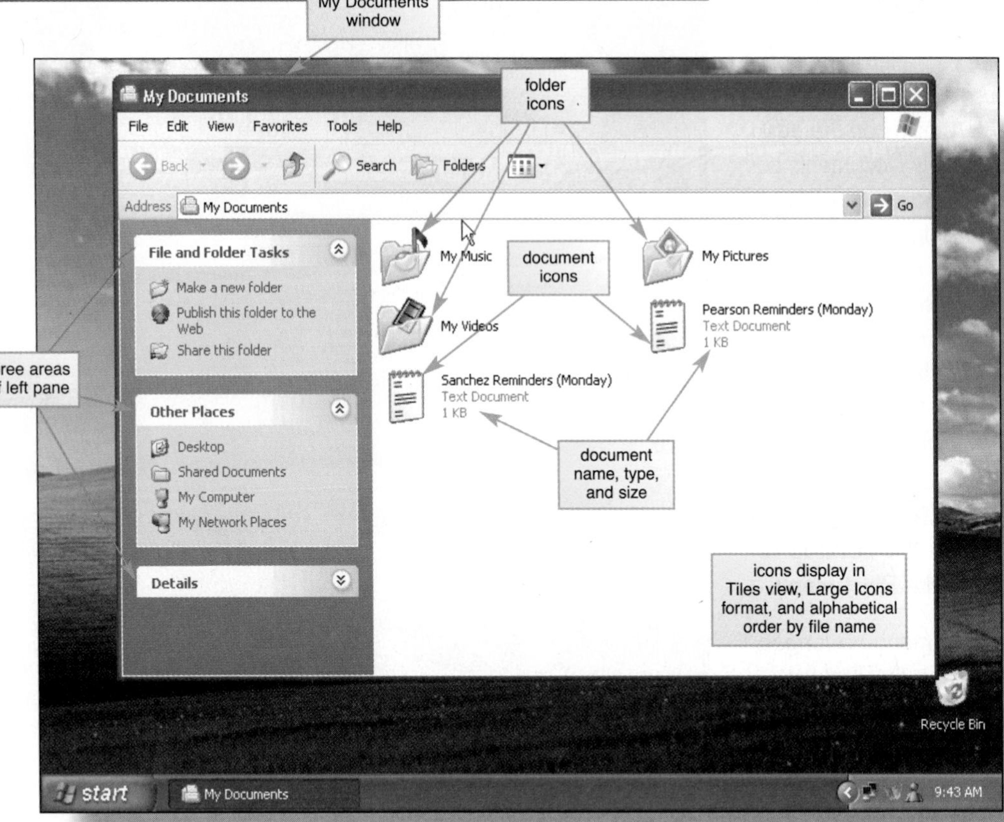

FIGURE 2-23

Other Ways

1. Press CTRL+ESC, press M, press ENTER

The right pane of the My Documents window also contains the My Music, My Pictures, and My Videos folder icons. The left pane contains the File and Folder Tasks area, Other Places area, and collapsed Details area. The File and Folder Tasks are tasks designed for working with folders.

Arranging the Icons in the My Documents Window

The icons in the My Documents window shown in Figure 2-23 display in Tiles view using a format called Large Icons. **Tiles view** displays the files and folders as tiles, which consist of an icon and icon description. The **Large Icons format** refers to the large size of the icons. In addition, the icons are arranged in alphabetical order based upon file name.

There are other methods of sequencing and arranging the icons in a window. A more practical arrangement is to display the icons in groups based upon file type. This arrangement places files of the same type (File Folder, Text Documents, Microsoft Word, Microsoft Excel, and so on) in separate groups. When a window contains many icons, this layout makes it faster and easier to find a particular file or folder.

Currently, the icons in the right pane of the My Documents window in Figure 2-23 are not grouped and display in alphabetical order by file name. Grouping the icons by file type is a two-step process. First, the icons are arranged in groups using the Show in Groups command. Then, the icons are arranged by file type using the Type command. Complete the following steps to display the icons in the My Documents window in groups.

Steps To Arrange the Icons in a Folder in Groups

1 Click View on the menu bar, point to Arrange Icons by on the View menu, and then point to Show in Groups on the Arrange Icons by submenu.

The View menu and Arrange Icons by submenu display (Figure 2-24). The five views (Thumbnails, Tiles, Icons, List, and Details) display on the View menu. A bullet preceding the Tiles command indicates Tiles is the current view. A bullet preceding the Name command indicates the icons are arranged by file name. A check mark preceding the Auto Arrange command indicates Windows XP will arrange all icons automatically when you click Show in Groups.

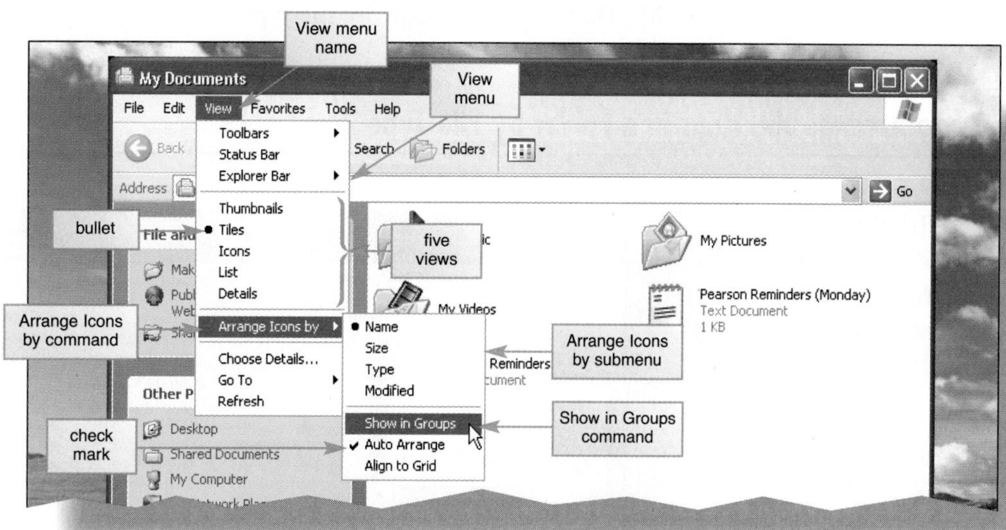

FIGURE 2-24

2 Click Show in Groups.

The icons in the My Documents window are arranged in three groups and each group consists of icons beginning with the same letter of the alphabet (Figure 2-25). A single letter heading identifies each group.

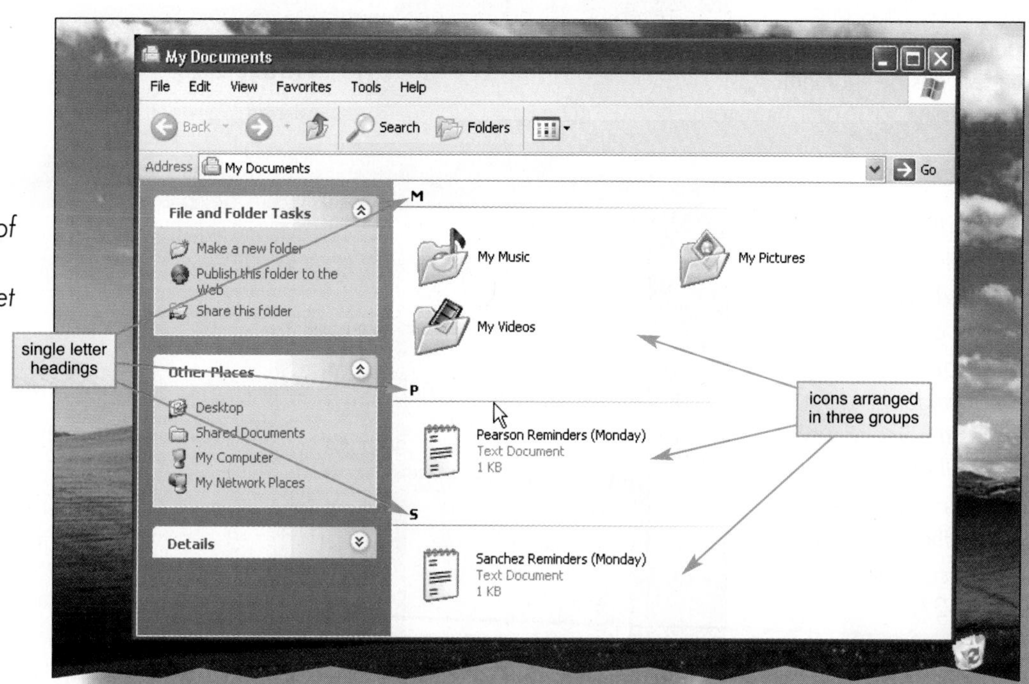

FIGURE 2-25

Other Ways

1. Right-click right pane, point to Arrange Icons By, click Show in Groups

After grouping the icons in the My Documents window, the icons should be arranged by file type. Complete the following steps to arrange the icons in the My Documents window by file type.

Steps To Arrange the Icons in a Folder by File Type

1 Click View on the menu bar, point to Arrange Icons by on the View menu, and then point to Type.

The View menu and Arrange Icons by submenu display (Figure 2-26). A bullet preceding the Name command indicates the icons remain arranged by file name. A check mark preceding the Show in Groups command indicates the icons are arranged in groups. The four ways to arrange icons (Name, Size, Type, and Modified) display on the Arrange Icons by submenu.

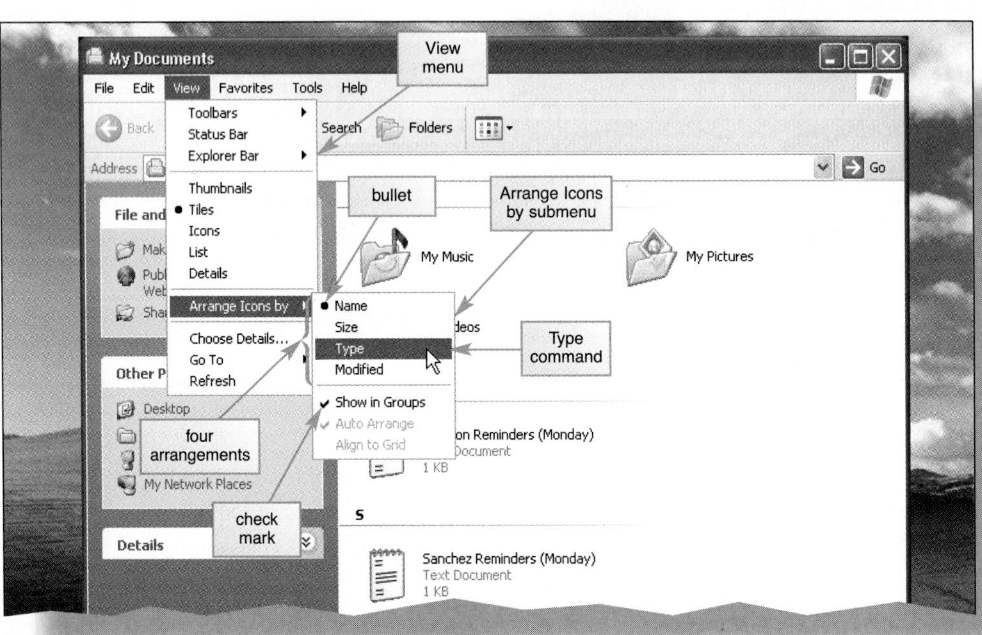

FIGURE 2-26

2 Click Type.

The icons in the My Documents window are rearranged into two groups and each group contains icons of the same file type. The File Folder heading identifies the first group of icons as file folders and the Text Document heading identifies the second group as text document icons (Figure 2-27).

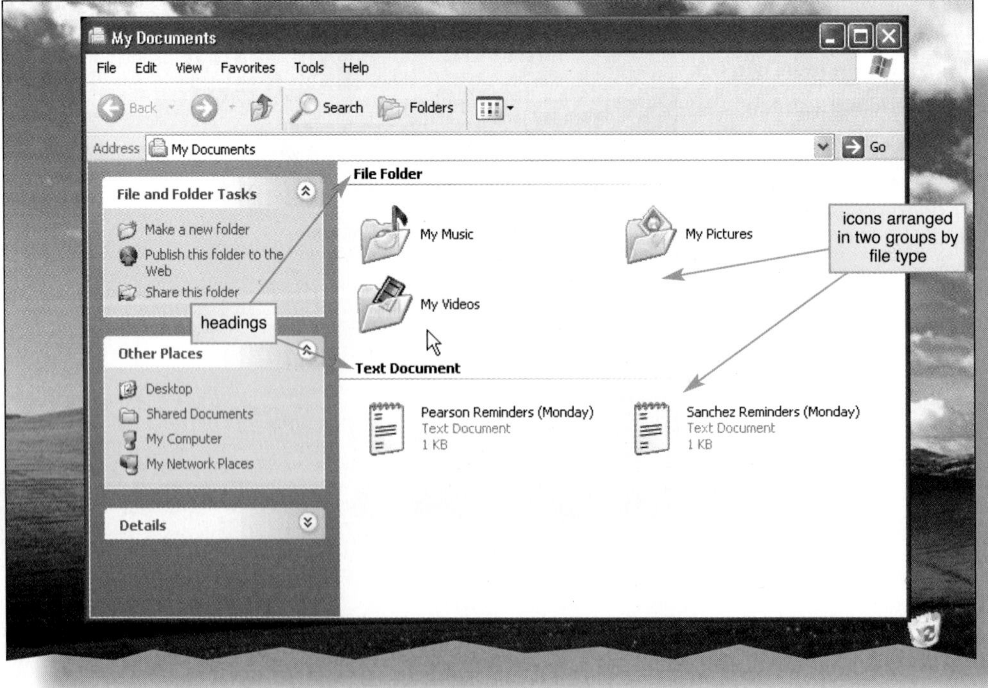

FIGURE 2-27

1. Right-click right pane, point to Arrange Icons By, click Type
2. Press ALT+V, press I, press T

The File Folder group shown in Figure 2-27 contains three folder icons (My Music, My Pictures, and My Videos) and the Text Document group contains two document icons [Sanchez Reminders (Monday) and Pearson Reminders (Monday)]. Although not visible in Figure 2-27, a bullet no longer precedes the Name command but now precedes the Type command on the Arrange Icons by submenu.

Creating a Folder in the My Documents Folder

After moving the Sanchez Reminders (Monday) and Pearson Reminders (Monday) documents to the My Documents folder, you will want to keep the two related documents together so you can find and reference them easily among other text documents that may be stored in the My Documents folder.

Windows XP allows you to place one or more documents into a folder in much the same manner as you might take a document written on a piece of paper and place it in a file folder. To place a document in a folder, you first must create the folder. To create and name a folder in the My Documents folder for the Sanchez Reminders (Monday) and Pearson Reminders (Monday) documents, complete the following steps.

To Create and Name a Folder in the My Documents Folder

1 Point to Make a new folder in the File and Folder Tasks area of the My Documents window.

Pointing to the Make a new folder task displays a hand icon and selects the task (Figure 2-28). Clicking the Make a new folder task will create a folder in the File Folder group using the default folder name, New Folder.

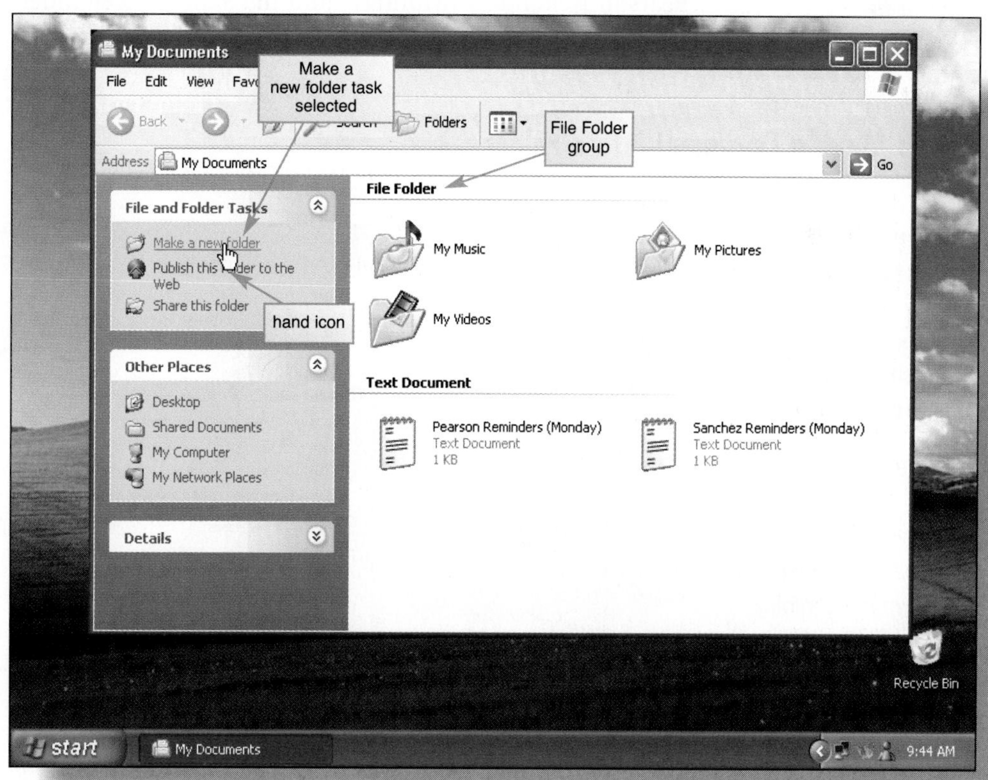

FIGURE 2-28

2 Click Make a new folder. Type `Daily Reminders` **in the icon title text box and then press the ENTER key.**

The File and Folder Tasks area contains tasks designed for working with folders and the selected Daily Reminders folder icon displays in the File Folder group (Figure 2-29). The folder name, Daily Reminders, displays in the icon title text box.

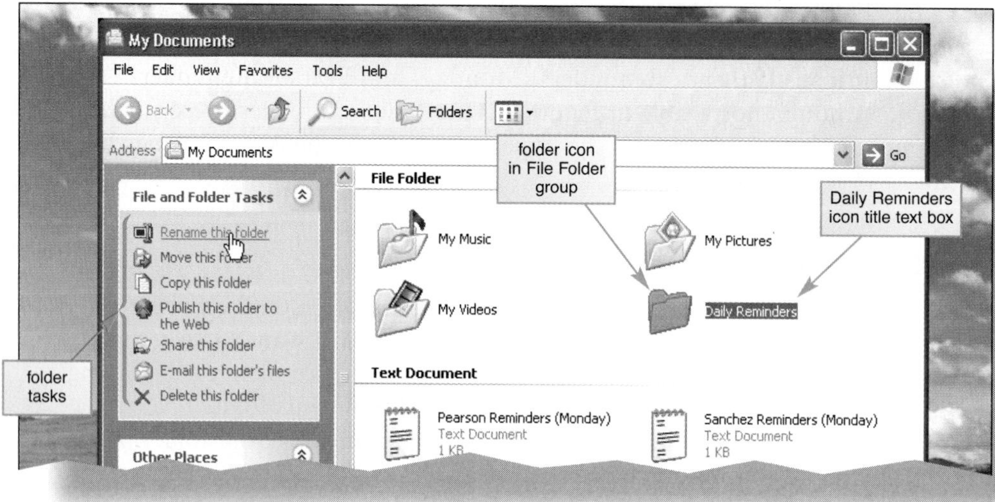

FIGURE 2-29

Other Ways

1. On File menu point to New, click Folder, type file name, press ENTER
2. Press ALT+F, press W, press F, type file name, press ENTER

Moving Documents into a Folder

After you create a folder in the My Documents folder, the next step is to move documents into the folder. For the Daily Reminders folder, you should move the Pearson Reminders (Monday) and the Sanchez Reminders (Monday) documents into the folder. To accomplish this, complete the following steps.

Steps To Move a Document into a Folder

1 Right-drag the Sanchez Reminders (Monday) icon onto the Daily Reminders folder icon. Point to Move Here on the shortcut menu.

The dimmed Sanchez Reminders (Monday) icon displays over the dimmed Daily Reminders folder icon, a shortcut menu containing the highlighted Move Here command displays, and the Sanchez Reminders (Monday) icon still displays in the Text Document group (Figure 2-30). The contents of the File and Folder Tasks area changes to contain tasks designed specifically for working with files.

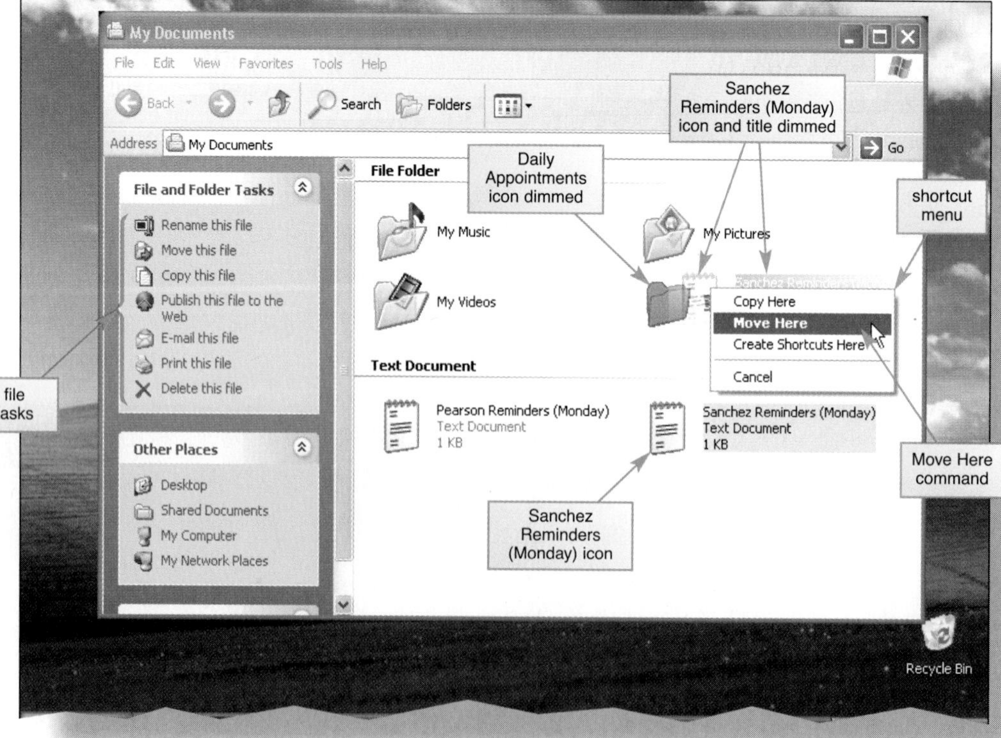

FIGURE 2-30

2 Click Move Here.

The Sanchez Reminders (Monday) document is moved into the Daily Reminders folder and the Sanchez Reminders (Monday) icon no longer displays in the Text Document group (Figure 2-31). The File and Folder Tasks area contains tasks designed for working with folders.

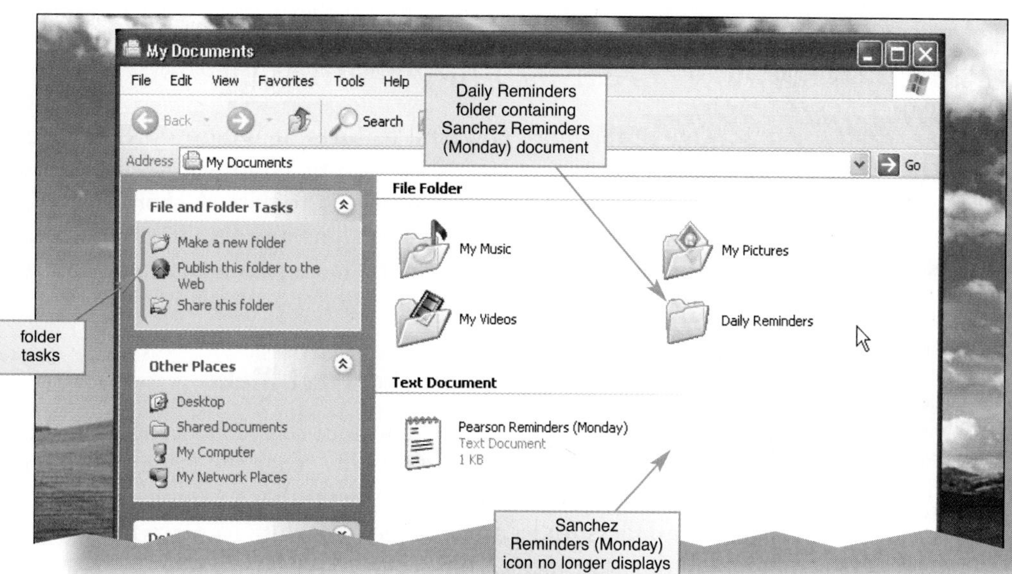

FIGURE 2-31

3 Right-drag the Pearson Reminders (Monday) icon onto the Daily Reminders icon. Click Move Here on the shortcut menu. Point to the Close button in the My Documents window.

The Pearson Reminders (Monday) document is moved into the Daily Reminders folder and the Pearson Reminders (Monday) icon and Text Document group no longer display in the My Documents window. The icons no longer display in folder name order (Figure 2-32).

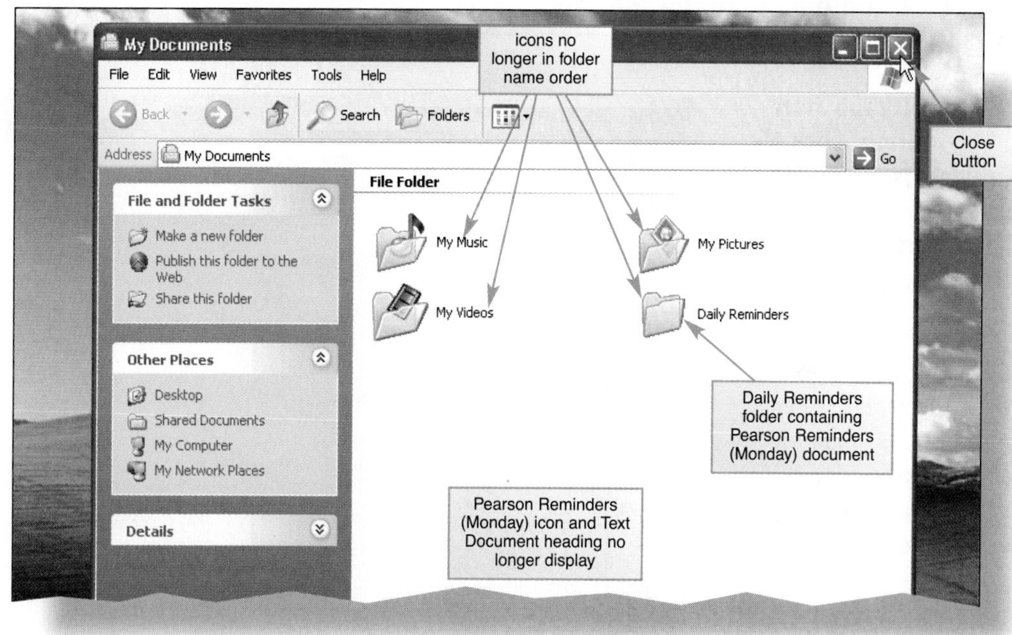

FIGURE 2-32

4 Click the Close button.

The My Documents window closes.

Other Ways

1. Drag document icon onto folder icon
2. Right-click document icon, click Cut, right-click folder icon, click Paste
3. Click document icon, in left pane click Move this file, in Move Items dialog box click My Documents, click folder name, click Move button

The next time you open the My Documents folder, the icons in the File Folder group will display in alphabetical order by folder name (see Figure 2-33 on the next page).

The ability to organize documents and files within a folder allows you to keep the My Documents folder organized when using Windows XP. Project 3 will discuss how to organize the files on the floppy and hard drives.

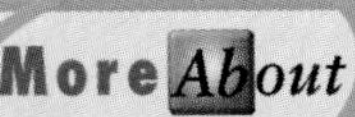

Shortcut Icons

A shortcut icon is a pointer to the location of a document or application on the hard drive. The shortcut icon is not the actual document or application. When you delete a shortcut icon, you delete the shortcut icon but do not delete the document or application. They remain on the hard drive.

Creating Folder Shortcuts

One of the more powerful features of Windows XP is its capability of being easily customized. One way to customize Windows XP is to use shortcuts to launch application programs and open files or folders. A **shortcut** is a link to any object on the computer or on a network, such as a program, file, folder, disk drive, Web page, printer, or another computer. Placing a shortcut to a folder on the Start menu or on the desktop can make it easier to locate and open the folder.

Adding a Shortcut on the Start Menu

You can add a folder shortcut to the Start menu that displays when you click the Start button. You do not actually place the folder on the menu, instead you place a shortcut to the folder on the menu. For example, you may want to open the Daily Reminders folder from the Start menu. To place the Daily Reminders folder shortcut on the Start menu, complete the following steps.

Steps To Add a Shortcut on the Start Menu

1 **Click the Start button. Click My Documents on the Start menu. Point to the Daily Reminders icon in the My Documents window.**

The My Documents window opens (Figure 2-33). The Daily Reminders folder icon displays in the My Documents window. Opening the My Documents window causes the icons in the right pane to display in order by folder name.

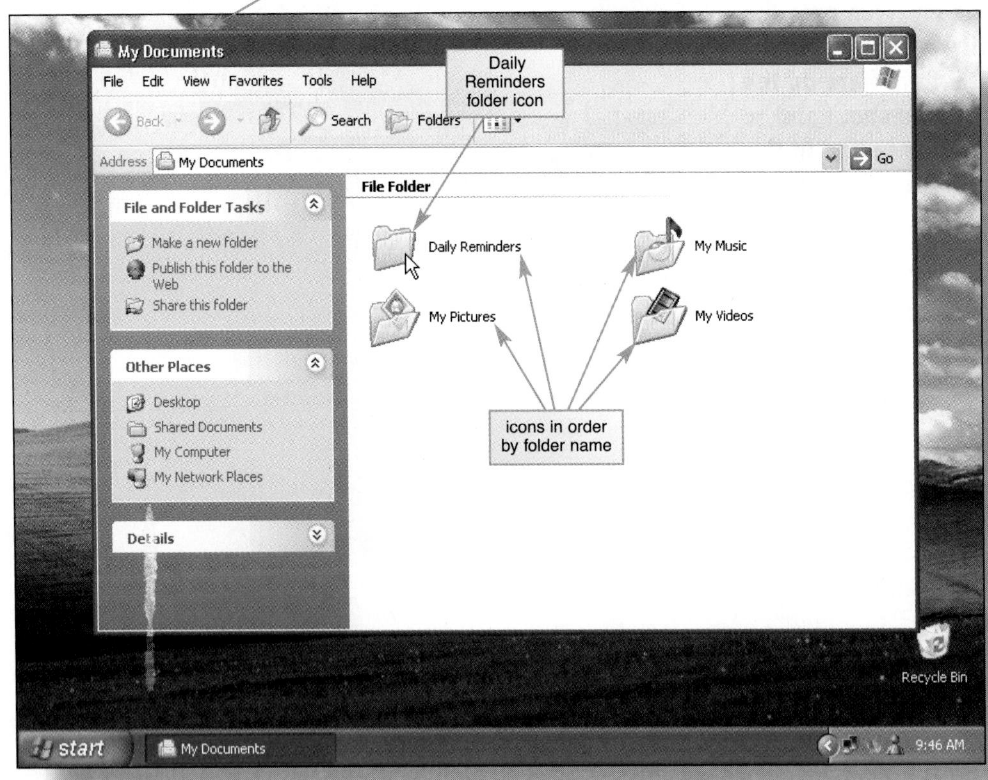

FIGURE 2-33

2 Drag the Daily Reminders icon onto the Start button. Do not release the left mouse button.

When you drag the icon onto the Start button, the Start menu displays on top of the My Documents window, and the Daily Reminders tile is dimmed (Figure 2-34).

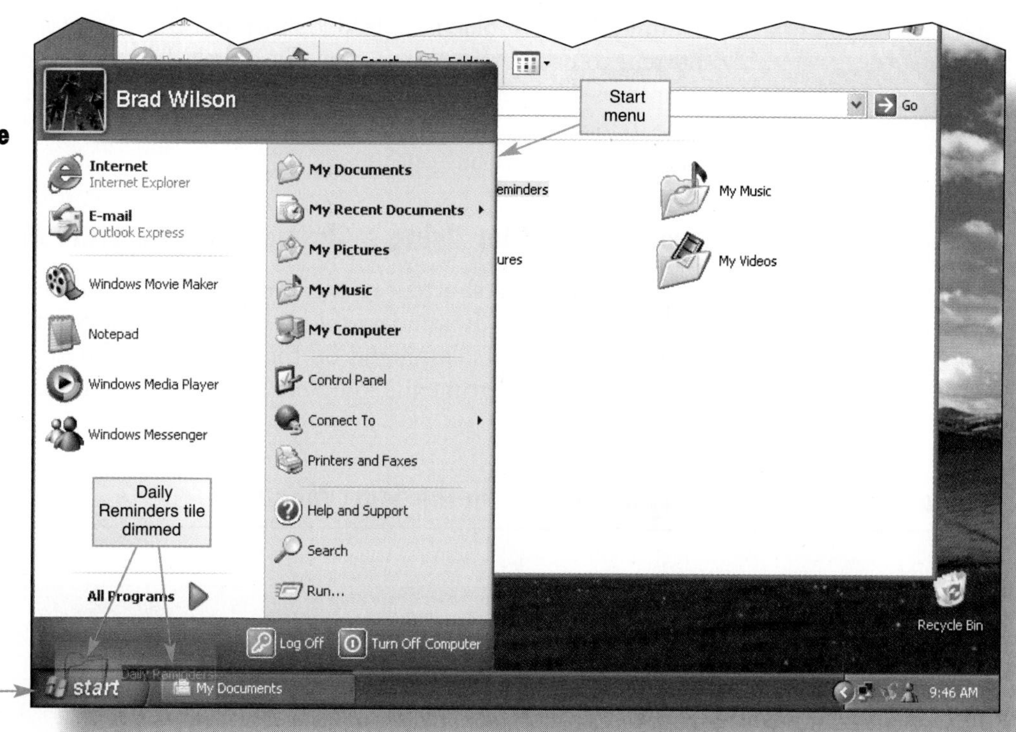

FIGURE 2-34

3 Release the left mouse button.

When you release the mouse button, the Daily Reminders shortcut displays in the pinned items list on the Start menu (Figure 2-35). Although not completely visible, the Daily Reminders icon and name remain in the File Folder group in the My Documents window.

4 Click an open area of the desktop to close the Start menu. Click the Close button in the My Documents window.

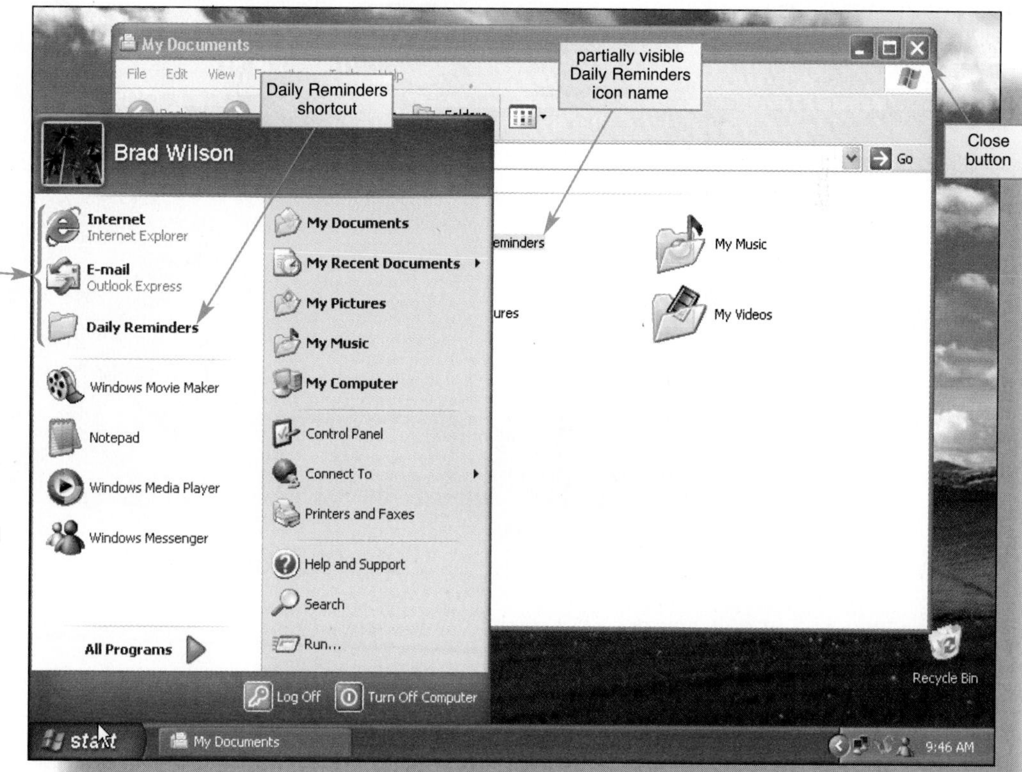

FIGURE 2-35

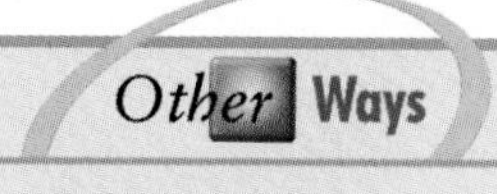

1. Right-drag folder icon onto Start button

In addition to placing a folder shortcut on the Start menu, you also can place a shortcut to other items (programs, files, disk drives, Web pages, printers, or other computers) on the Start menu in a similar manner. To place a shortcut for one of these items on the desktop, you display its icon on the desktop and then drag the icon onto the Start button.

Opening a Folder Using a Shortcut on the Start Menu

After placing a shortcut to the Daily Reminders folder on the Start menu, you can open the Daily Reminders folder by clicking the Start button and then clicking the Daily Reminders command on the Start menu. To open the Daily Reminders folder from the Start menu, complete the following steps.

To Open a Folder Using a Shortcut on the Start Menu

1 Click the Start button. Point to Daily Reminders in the pinned items list.

The Start menu displays and the highlighted Daily Reminders shortcut displays on the Start menu (Figure 2-36).

FIGURE 2-36

2 Click Daily Reminders. Point to the Close button in the Daily Reminders window.

The Start menu closes and the Daily Reminders window displays on the desktop (Figure 2-37). The Pearson Reminders (Monday) and Sanchez Reminders (Monday) documents display in the Daily Reminders window. The location of the Daily Reminders folder displays in the Address box.

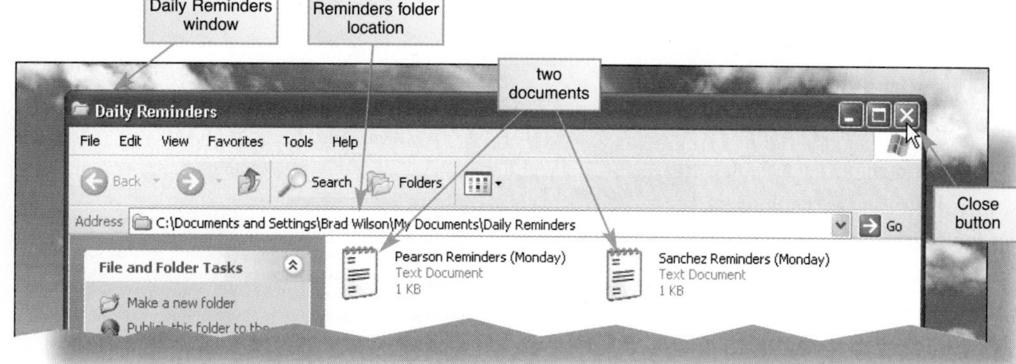

FIGURE 2-37

3 Click the Close button in the Daily Reminders window.

The window closes.

Other Ways

1. Click Start button, press D (first letter of folder name), press ENTER
2. Press CTRL+ESC, press D (first letter of folder name), press ENTER

After opening the Daily Reminders window, double-clicking either icon in the right pane launches Notepad and displays the associated document in the Notepad window.

Removing a Shortcut from the Start Menu

Just as you can add shortcuts to the Start menu, you also can remove them. To remove the Daily Reminders shortcut from the Start menu, complete the following steps.

More About

Removing Shortcuts

Remember: When you remove a shortcut, you remove only the shortcut and its reference to the file or folder. The file or folder itself is stored elsewhere on the hard disk and is not removed.

Steps To Remove a Shortcut from the Start Menu

1 Click the Start button. Right-click Daily Reminders on the Start menu and then point to Remove from This List on the shortcut menu.

The Start menu displays, the highlighted Daily Reminders command displays on the Start menu, a shortcut menu displays, and the highlighted Remove from This List command displays on the shortcut menu (Figure 2-38).

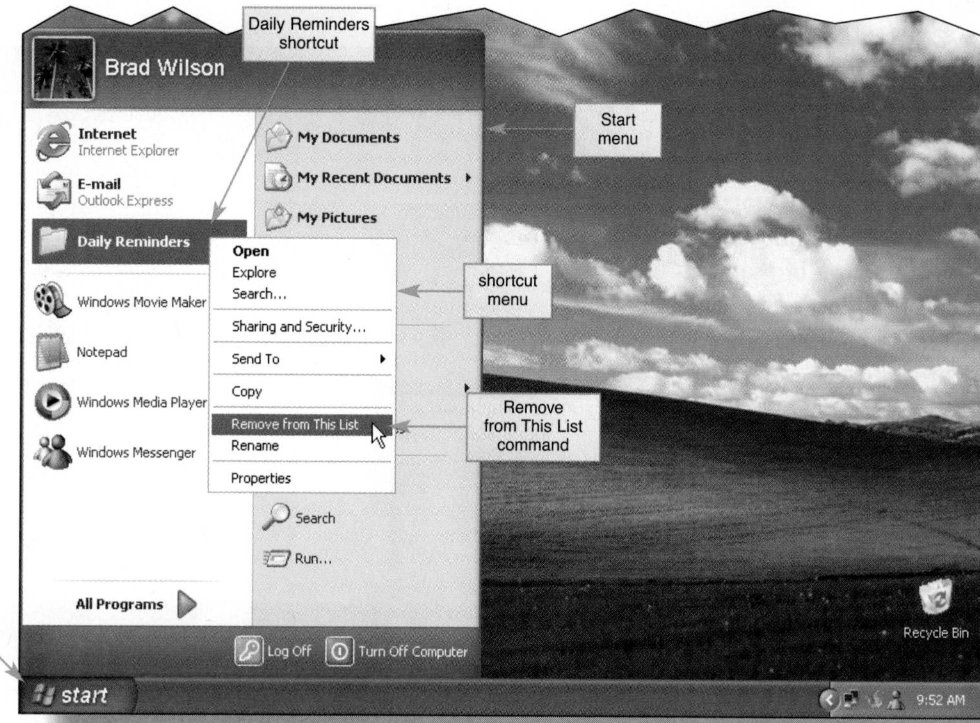

FIGURE 2-38

2 **Click Remove from This List.**

The Daily Reminders shortcut no longer displays on the Start menu (Figure 2-39).

3 **Click an open area of the desktop to close the Start menu.**

The Start menu closes.

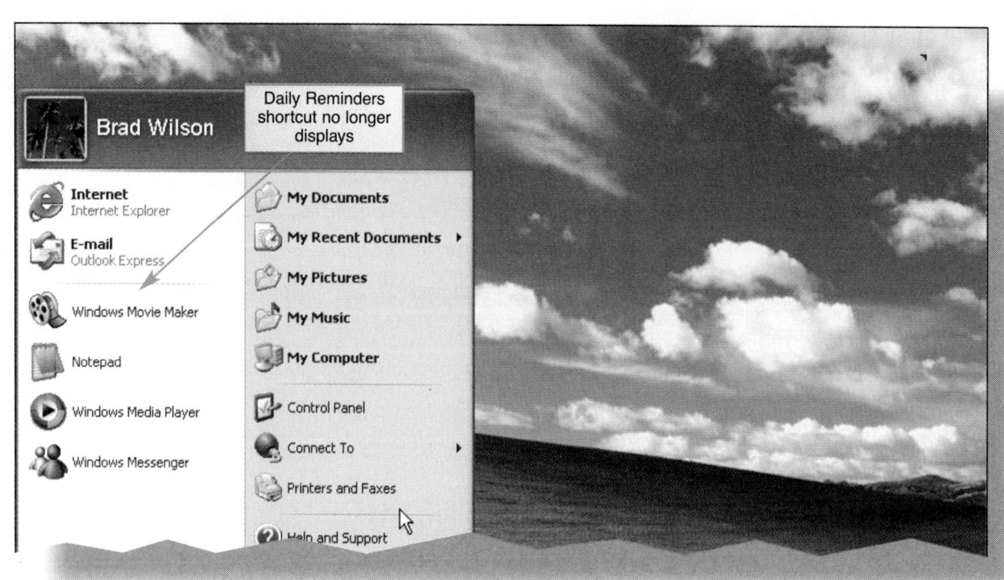

FIGURE 2-39

The capability of adding shortcuts to and removing them from the Start menu provides great flexibility when customizing Windows XP.

Creating a Shortcut on the Desktop

You also can create shortcuts directly on the desktop. To create a shortcut for the Daily Reminders folder on the desktop, complete the following steps.

Steps To Create a Shortcut on the Desktop

1 **Click the Start button. Click My Documents on the Start menu. Right-drag the Daily Reminders icon from the My Documents window into an open area of the desktop. Point to Create Shortcuts Here on the shortcut menu.**

The My Documents window displays, the My Documents icon is right-dragged to the desktop, a shortcut menu displays, and Create Shortcuts Here command is highlighted (Figure 2-40).

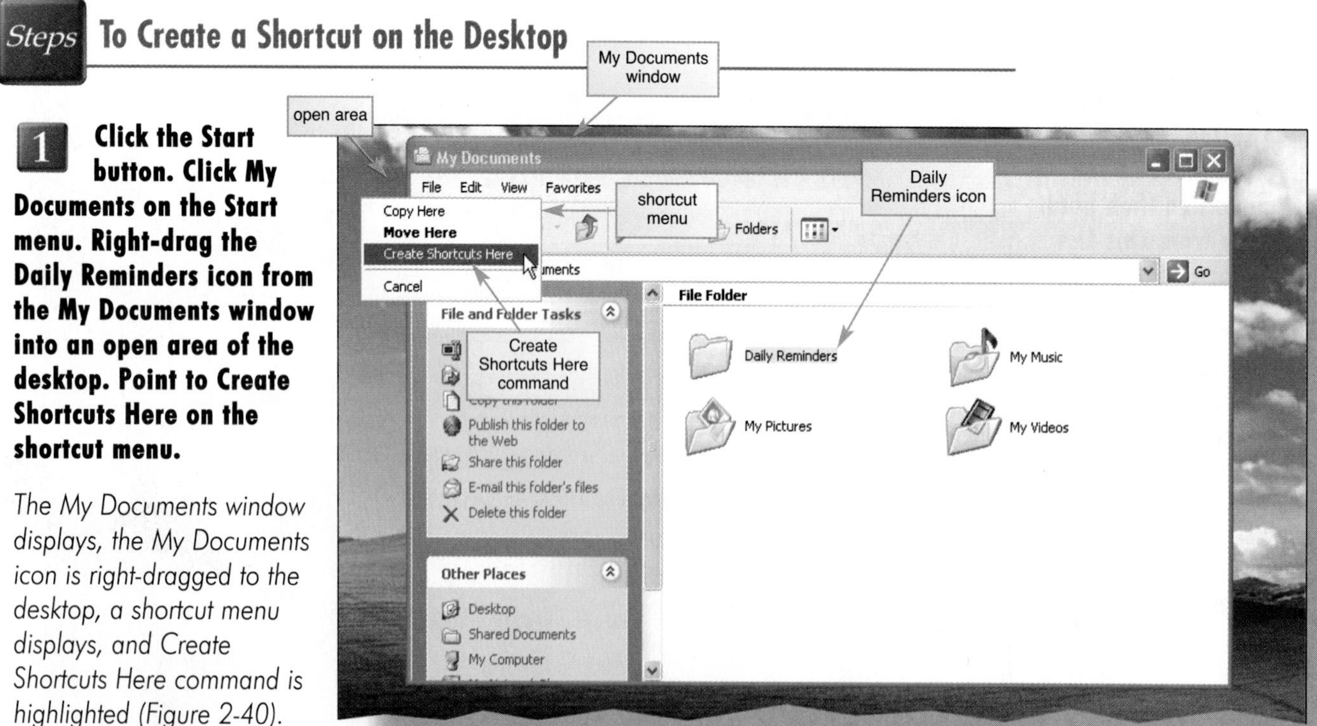

FIGURE 2-40

2 Click Create Shortcuts Here. Point to the Close button in the My Documents window.

Windows XP creates a shortcut on the desktop (Figure 2-41). The shortcut is identified with an icon name (Shortcut to Daily Reminders) and a small arrow in the bottom-left corner of the icon. The shortcut may display on the desktop where you dragged it or along the left side of the desktop, depending on the computer's settings.

3 Click the Close button in the My Documents window.

The My Documents window closes.

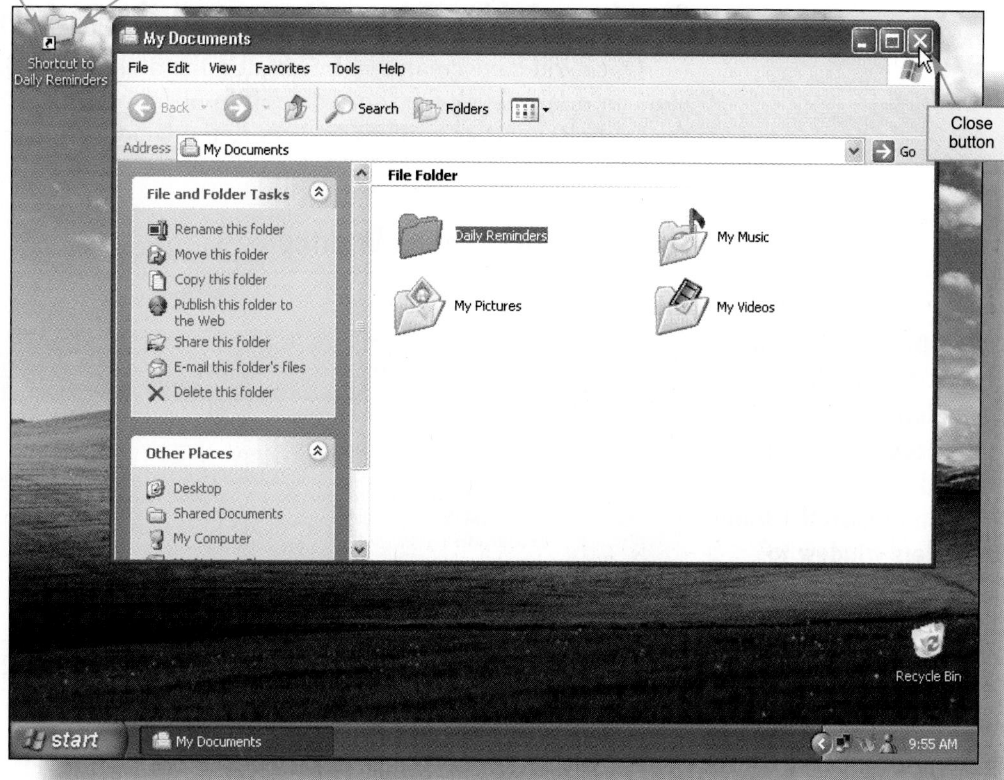

FIGURE 2-41

Other Ways

1. Right-click folder icon, on shortcut menu point to Send To, on Sent To submenu click Desktop (create shortcut)

Shortcuts are quite useful because they can reference programs, files, disk drives, Web pages, printers, and other computers. You can store a document in the My Documents folder on the computer's hard disk and then create a shortcut to the folder on the desktop. In that manner, you can open the document from the desktop but the document remains stored in the My Documents folder on the computer's hard disk.

Opening and Modifying Documents within a Folder

You can modify a document stored in the Daily Reminders folder by opening the My Documents folder, opening the Daily Reminders folder containing the document, and then opening the document you want to modify or, you can double-click the shortcut icon on the desktop to open the Daily Reminders folder and then modify the document.

Assume that you received more information about the daily reminders for Mr. Sanchez. An Internet meeting with the sales department in the western United States has been scheduled for 3:00 p.m. and the sales department must be notified of the meeting. To add this item to the schedule, first you must open the Daily Reminders folder that contains the Sanchez Reminders (Monday) document.

More About

Working with Documents

To modify a document, you open the document instead of an application program and then open the document as you did previously in this project. Does this feel more natural? Research has indicated that people feel more at home working with documents directly instead of dealing with application programs and then documents.

Opening a Folder Using a Shortcut on the Desktop

Once you have created a shortcut on the desktop for the Daily Reminders folder, you can double-click the shortcut icon to open the Daily Reminders window. To open the Daily Reminders window and resize the window, complete the following step.

Steps To Open a Folder Using a Shortcut on the Desktop

1 Double-click the Shortcut to Daily Reminders folder icon on the desktop. Move and resize the Daily Reminders window to resemble the window shown in Figure 2-42.

The Daily Reminders window opens and the recessed Daily Reminders button displays in the taskbar button area (Figure 2-42). The Shortcut to Daily Reminders folder icon remains on the desktop. Each of the document icons displays in the Daily Reminders window, indicating the documents are contained within the Daily Reminders folder.

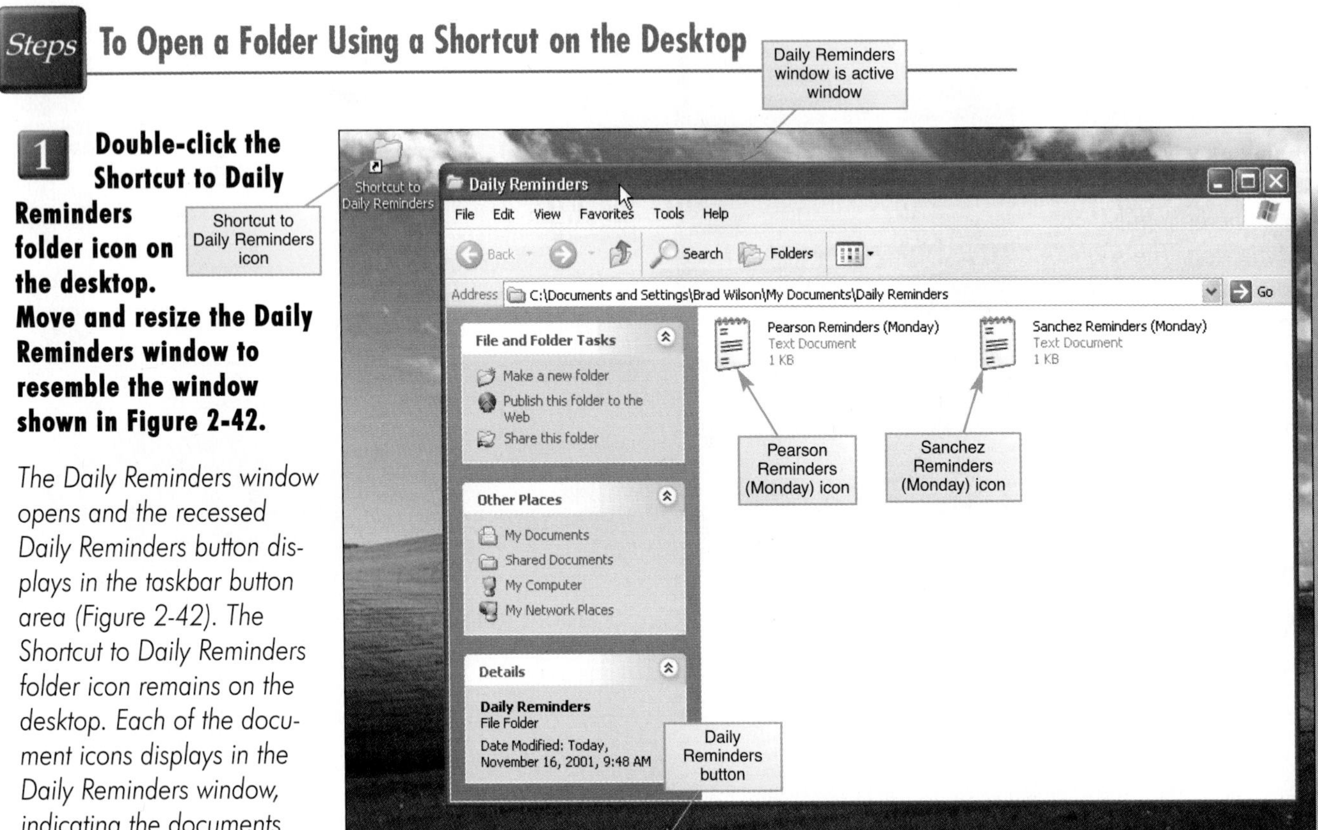

FIGURE 2-42

Other Ways

1. Right-click shortcut icon on desktop, click Open

In Figure 2-42, the dark blue Daily Reminders title bar and recessed button in the taskbar button area indicate the Daily Reminders window is the active window.

Opening and Modifying a Document Stored in a Folder

After opening the Daily Reminders folder, you must open the document you want to modify. To open the Sanchez Reminders (Monday) document and enter the text about the Internet meeting, complete the following steps.

To Open and Modify a Document in a Folder

1 Double-click the Sanchez Reminders (Monday) icon in the Daily Reminders window.

Notepad launches, the Sanchez Reminders (Monday) document displays in the Notepad window, and the Sanchez Reminders (Monday) - Notepad button displays in the taskbar button area (Figure 2-43). The active Notepad window and the inactive folder window now are open.

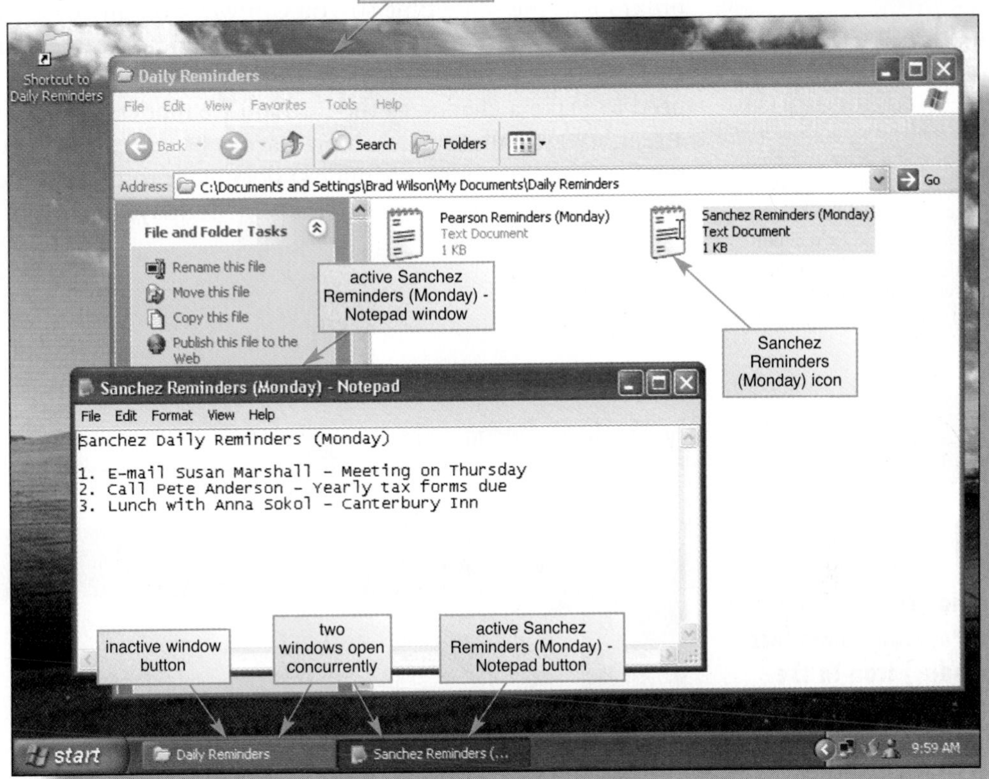

FIGURE 2-43

2 Press the DOWN ARROW key five times to move the insertion point to the end of the document. Type `4. Notify Sales - NetMeeting at 3:00 p.m.` **and then press the ENTER key.**

The insertion point moves to the end of the document and the entry is added to the document (Figure 2-44).

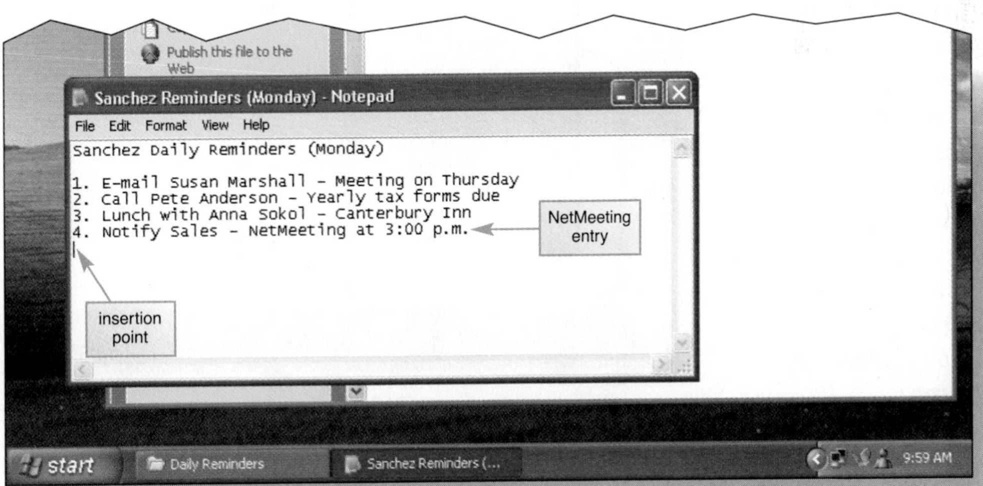

FIGURE 2-44

Other Ways

1. Right-click document icon, on shortcut menu click Open, enter text
2. Click document icon to select icon, press ENTER key, enter text

Opening Windows

In addition to clicking the taskbar button of an inactive window to make that window the active window, you may click any open area of the window. Many people routinely click the title bar of a window to activate the window.

Opening Multiple Documents

Windows XP allows you to open more than one document and application program at the same time so you can work on any desired document. The concept of multiple programs running at the same time is called **multitasking**. To illustrate two documents and an application program open at the same time, assume you need to make a change to the Pearson Reminders (Monday) document to include a reminder to talk to Dan about Carol's birthday party. You do not have to close the Sanchez Reminders (Monday) document to do this. Complete the following steps to open the Pearson Reminders (Monday) document and make changes.

Steps To Open and Modify Multiple Documents

1 Click the Daily Reminders button on the taskbar. Point to the Pearson Reminders (Monday) icon in the Daily Reminders window.

The Daily Reminders window now displays on top of the Sanchez Reminders (Monday) window and becomes the active window, denoted by the dark blue title bar (Figure 2-45). The Sanchez Reminders (Monday) window becomes the inactive window, the Daily Reminders button is recessed, and the Sanchez Reminders (Monday) - Notepad button is not recessed.

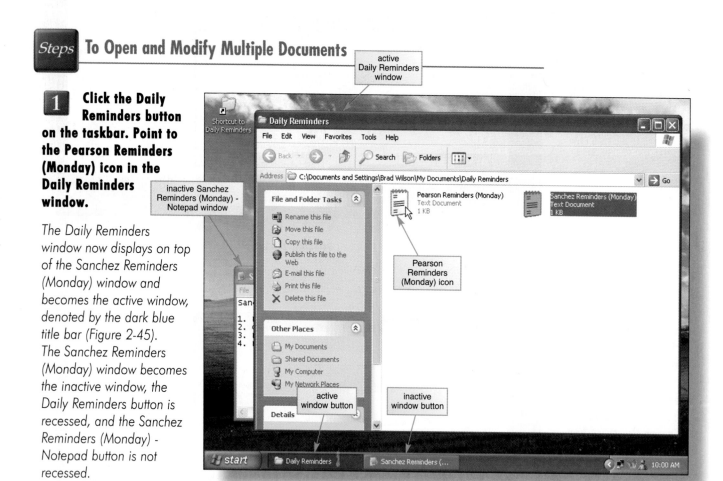

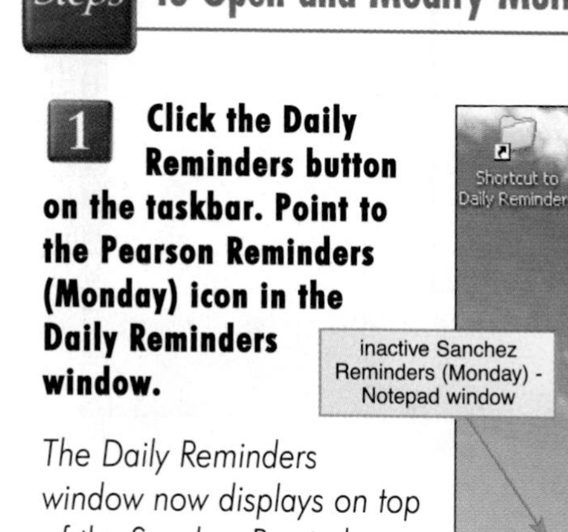

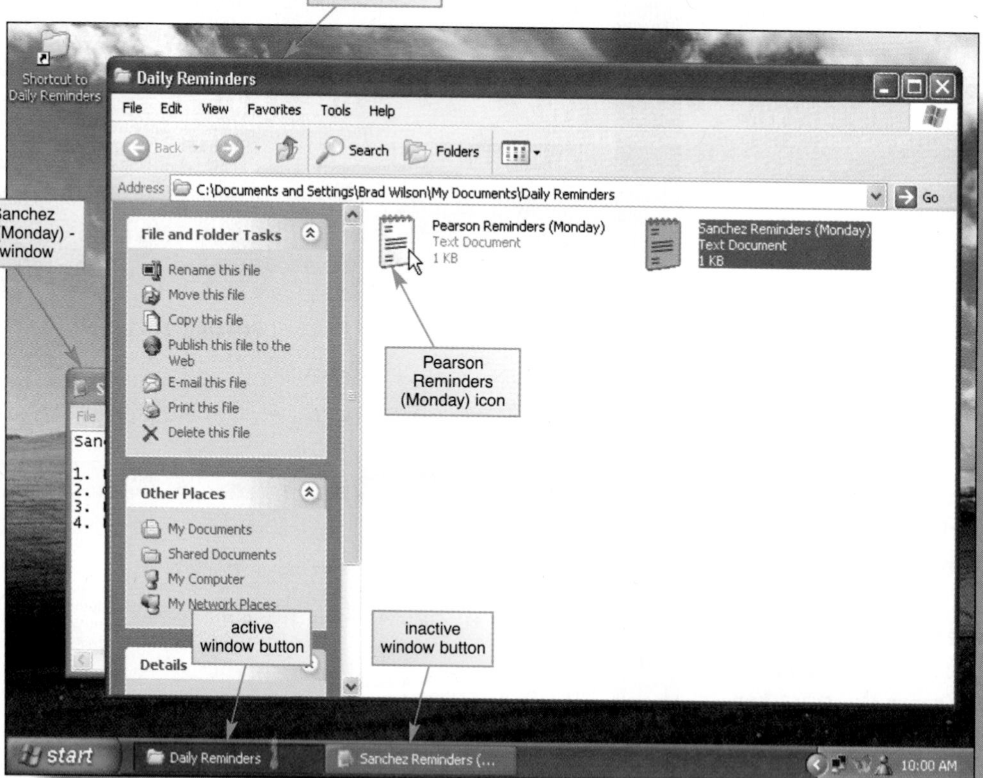

FIGURE 2-45

2 Double-click the Pearson Reminders (Monday) icon. Press the DOWN ARROW key five times to move the insertion point to the end of the document in the Notepad window. Type `4. Call Dan - Birthday party for Carol` **and then press the ENTER key.**

The Pearson Reminders (Monday) - Notepad window opens on top of the other two open windows, the recessed Pearson Reminders (Monday) - Notepad button displays in the taskbar button area, and the insertion point moves to the end of the document (Figure 2-46).

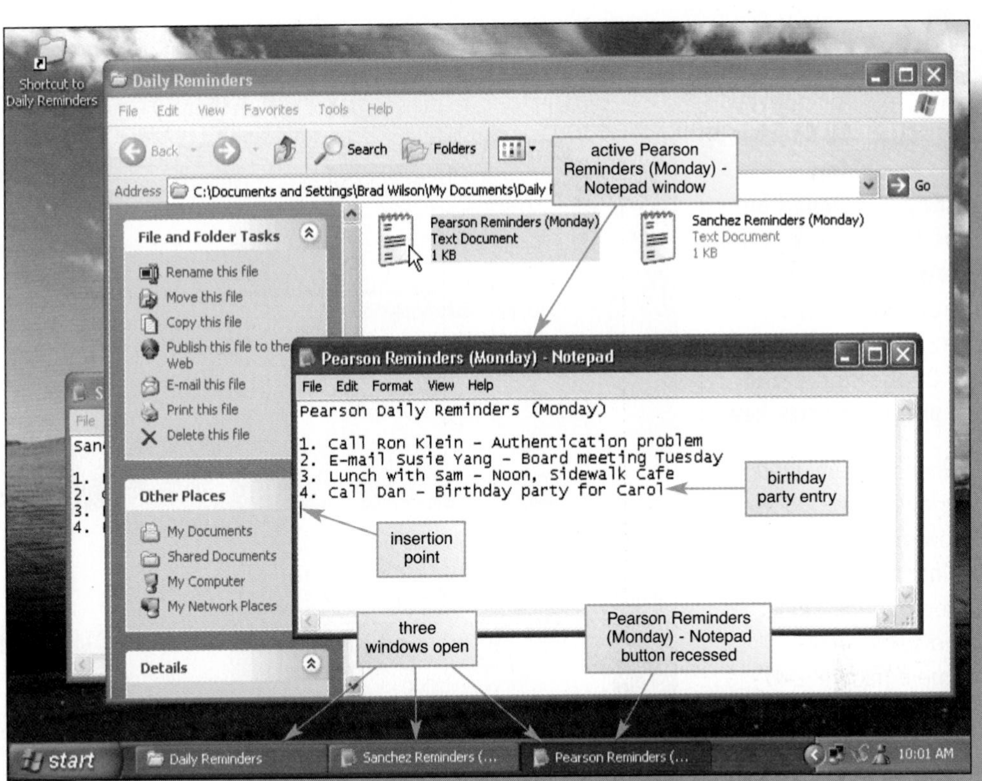

FIGURE 2-46

Other Ways

1. Right-click document icon, on shortcut menu click Open, enter text
2. Click document icon to select icon, press ENTER, enter text

After you have modified the Pearson Reminders (Monday) document, you receive information that a dinner meeting with Art Perez has been scheduled for Mr. Sanchez for 7:00 p.m. at The Crab House. You are directed to add this entry to Mr. Sanchez's reminders. To do this, you must open the Sanchez Reminders (Monday) - Notepad inactive window. To open an inactive window and modify the document, complete the step on the next page.

To Open an Inactive Window

1 Click the Sanchez Reminders (Monday) - Notepad button on the taskbar. When the window opens, type `5. Dinner with Art Perez - 7:00 p.m., The Crab House` **and then press the ENTER key.**

The Sanchez Reminders (Monday) - Notepad window displays on top of the other windows on the desktop and the dinner entry displays in the document (Figure 2-47).

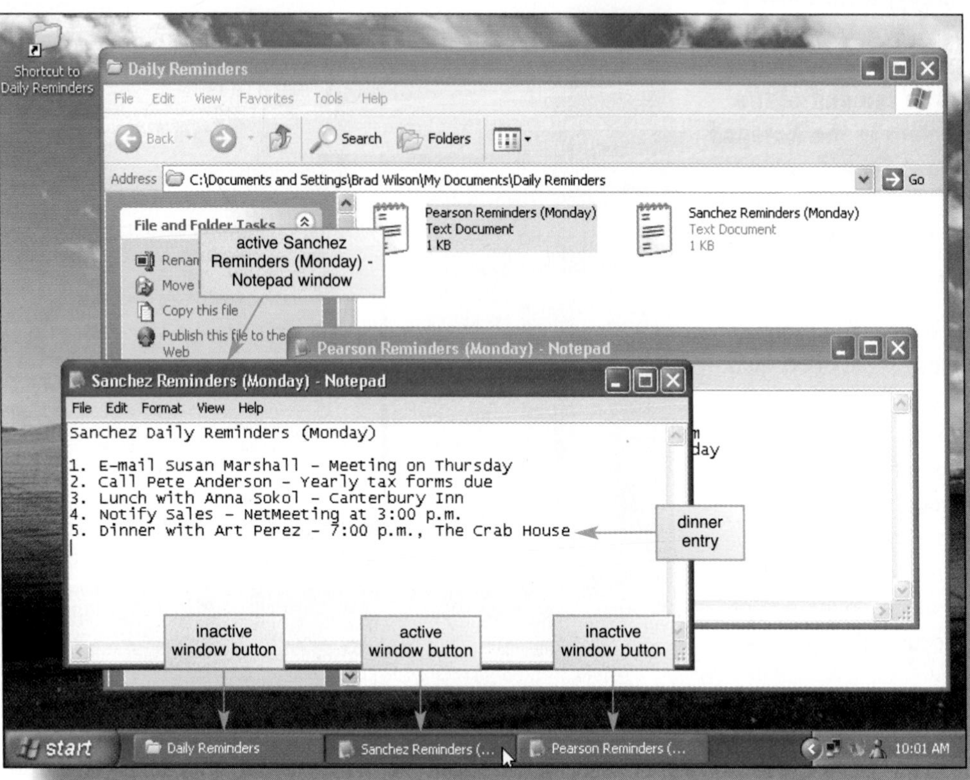

FIGURE 2-47

Other Ways

1. Press ALT+TAB until name of window displays, release keys
2. If visible, click title bar of window

Taskbar Button Grouping

In Figure 2-47, two text documents windows [Sanchez Reminders (Monday) - Notepad and Pearson Reminders (Monday) - Notepad] and one folder window (Daily Reminders) are open on the desktop and three buttons display in the taskbar button area. If you open additional text document windows on the desktop, the taskbar would quickly become overcrowded with buttons. To maintain an uncluttered taskbar, Windows XP uses **taskbar button grouping** to display a single button on the taskbar for multiple documents opened by the same application program.

Figure 2-48 illustrates the taskbar if three additional text documents, Anderson Reminders (Monday) - Notepad, Yang Reminders (Monday) - Notepad, and McCormick Reminders (Monday) are opened on the desktop. When the fifth text document is opened, a single button replaces the five Notepad icons on the taskbar. The button contains a program icon (Notepad icon), the number of Notepad documents (5), program name (Notepad), and a down arrow. The down arrow indicates several documents are open.

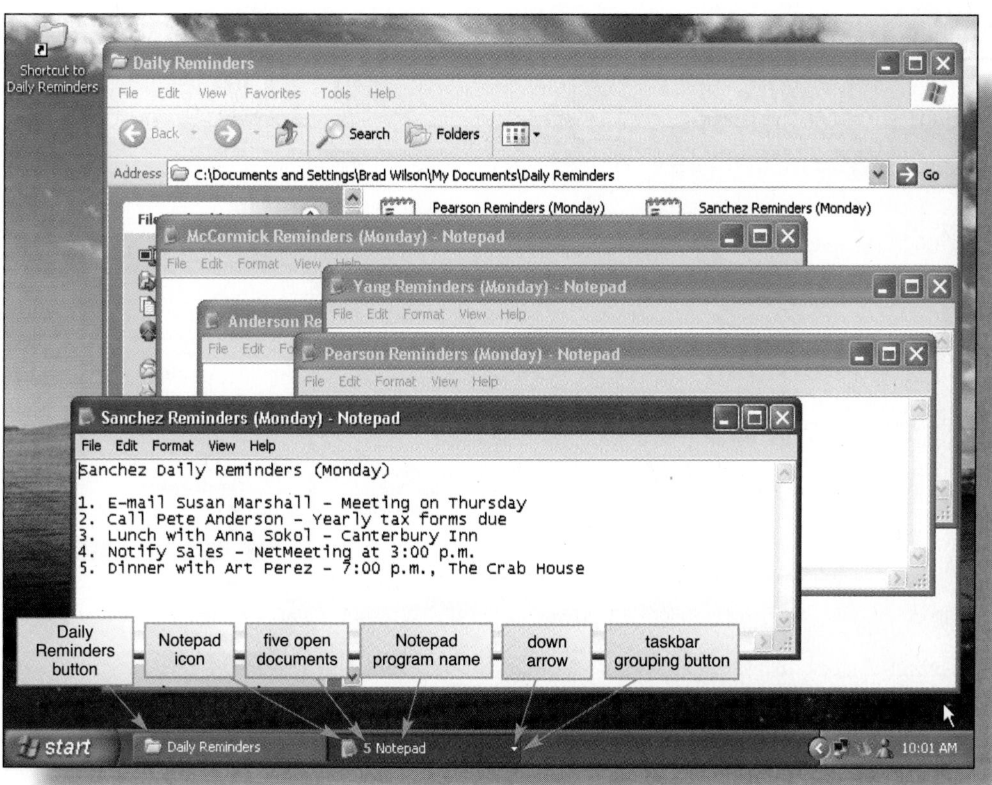

FIGURE 2-48

The Notepad button provides access to all five text documents. To access any of the Notepad documents, click the taskbar grouping button to display a list of documents and then click a document name in the list. To perform the same operation (cascade, tile, minimize, and close) on all documents, right-click the Notepad button and click the appropriate command on the shortcut menu. For example, right-click the Notepad button and then click Minimize Group on the shortcut menu to minimize all open text document windows. Another method to minimize all open windows is shown in the following section.

Minimizing All Open Windows

As shown previously, Windows XP allows you to open multiple windows on the desktop and work in any of the open windows by clicking the appropriate button in the taskbar button area. If additional windows are opened and a taskbar grouping button does not display on the taskbar, too many windows or a single maximized window can still limit the view of the objects on the desktop. To allow you to view the desktop easily without closing the windows on the desktop, you can use the Show the Desktop command to minimize all open windows. The **Show the Desktop command** makes the desktop visible by minimizing all open windows on the desktop.

Currently, the Sanchez Reminders (Monday) - Notepad, Daily Reminders, and Pearson Reminders (Monday) - Notepad windows are open on the desktop. A button for each window displays in the taskbar button area (see Figure 2-47). A recessed button displays for the active Sanchez Reminders (Monday) - Notepad window and non-recessed buttons display for the remaining inactive windows. To minimize the open windows and remove the clutter on the desktop, perform the steps on the next page.

To Minimize All Open Windows

1 Right-click an open area of the taskbar and then point to Show the Desktop.

A shortcut menu displays and the Show the Desktop command is highlighted (Figure 2-49). A check mark precedes the Lock the taskbar command to indicate the taskbar is locked and cannot be moved to another location on the desktop.

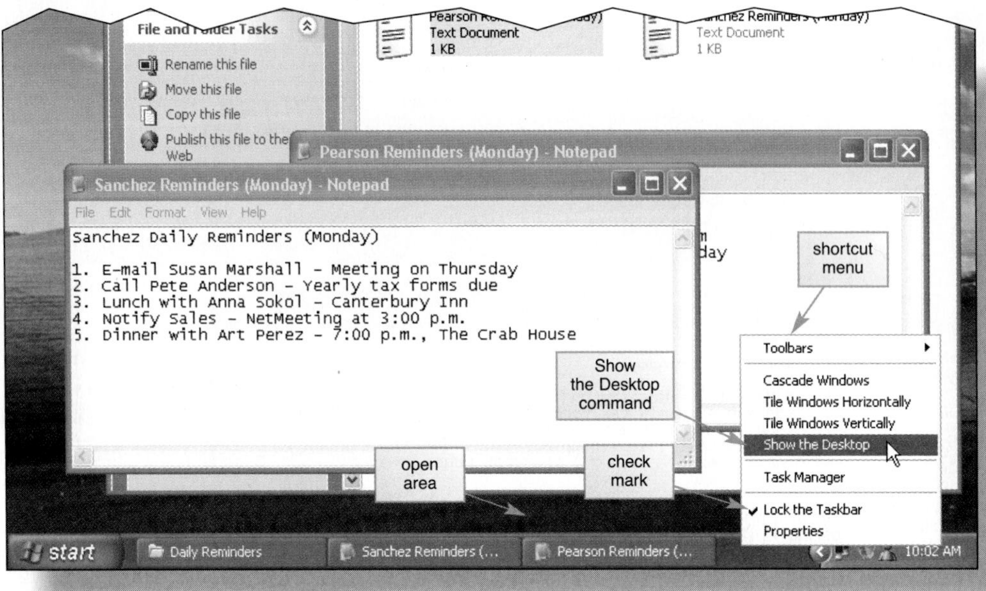

FIGURE 2-49

2 Click Show the Desktop.

Windows XP minimizes all three open windows (Figure 2-50). A non-recessed button for each minimized window displays in the taskbar button area.

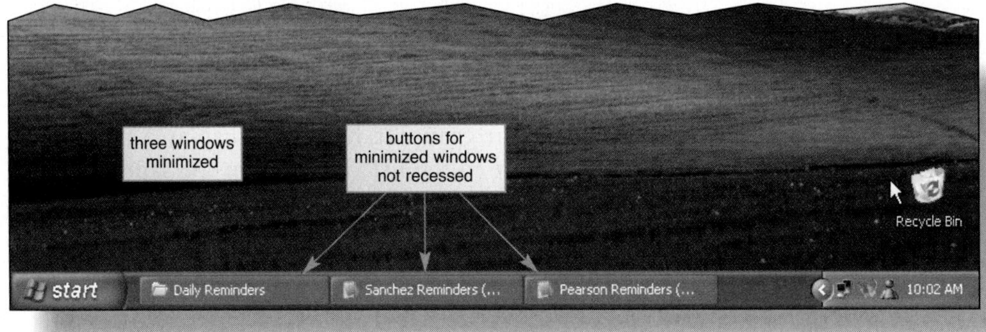

FIGURE 2-50

Other Ways

1. Click the Minimize button on each window
2. On Quick Launch toolbar click Show Desktop icon
3. Right-click taskbar grouping button, click Minimize Group

To open any of the minimized windows and be able to work in that window, click the corresponding button in the taskbar button area. To open all three windows and return the desktop to the way it looked before clicking the Show the Desktop command (see Figure 2-49), right-click an open area of the taskbar and then click the Show Open Windows command.

More About

Closing Windows

The choice of how to close windows is yours. In most cases, you will want to choose the method that causes the least amount of work.

Closing Multiple Windows

When you have finished working with multiple windows, close them. If the windows are open on the desktop, you can click the Close button on the title bar of each open window to close them. Regardless of whether the windows are open on the desktop or the windows are minimized using the Show the Desktop command, you also can close the windows using the buttons in the taskbar button area.

To close the Sanchez Reminders (Monday) - Notepad and Pearson Reminders (Monday) - Notepad windows from the taskbar, complete the following steps.

Steps To Close Open Windows and Save Changes from the Taskbar

1 Right-click the Sanchez Reminders (Monday) - Notepad button on the taskbar. Point to Close.

A shortcut menu displays containing a variety of commands for the window associated with the button that was clicked (Figure 2-51).

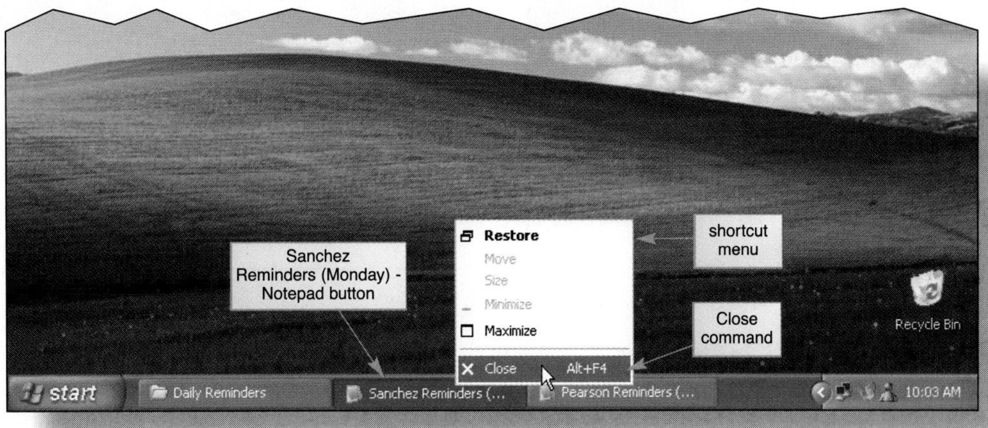

FIGURE 2-51

2 Click Close. Point to the Yes button in the Notepad dialog box.

The Notepad dialog box displays asking if you want to save the changes (Figure 2-52).

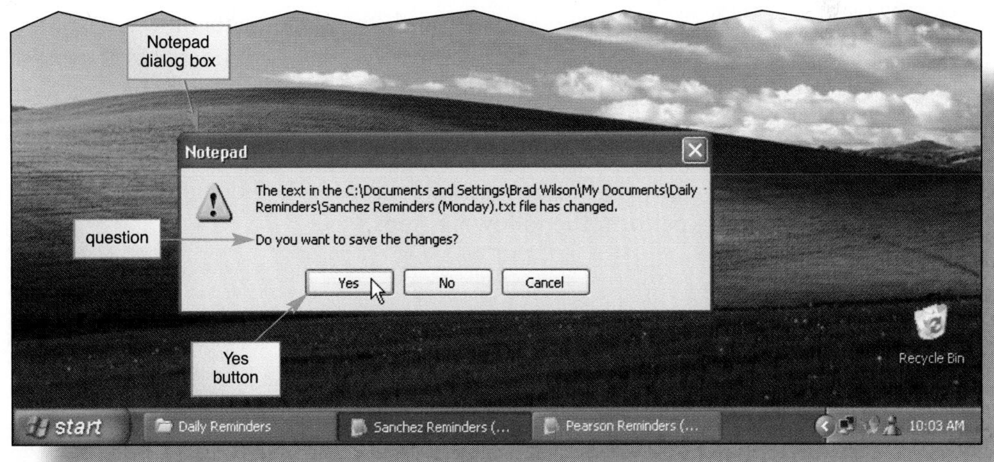

FIGURE 2-52

3 Click the Yes button. Right-click the Pearson Reminders (Monday) - Notepad button on the taskbar. Point to Close.

A shortcut menu displays (Figure 2-53). The modified Sanchez Reminders (Monday) document is saved in the Daily Reminders folder and its button no longer displays in the taskbar button area.

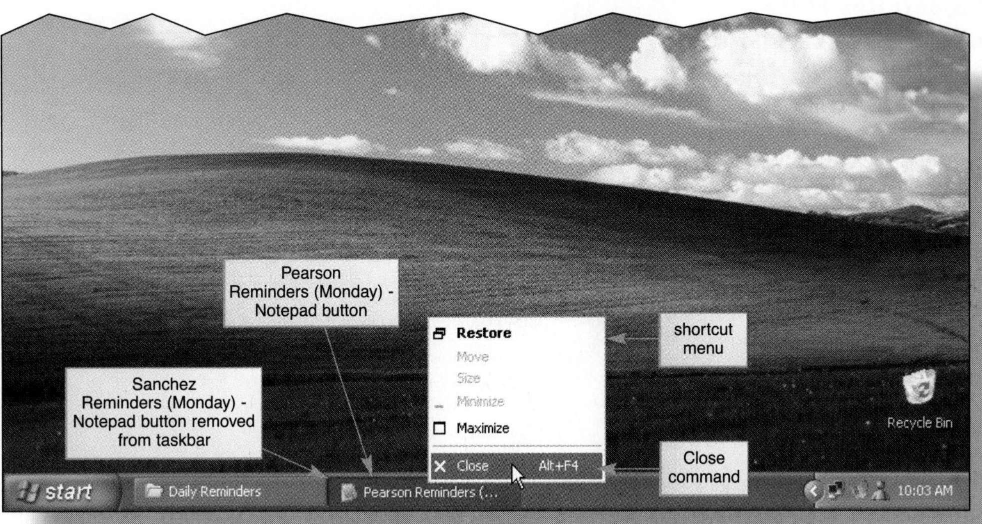

FIGURE 2-53

4 **Click Close. When the Notepad dialog box displays asking if you want to save the changes, click the Yes button.**

Only the Daily Reminders button remains in the taskbar button area (Figure 2-54).

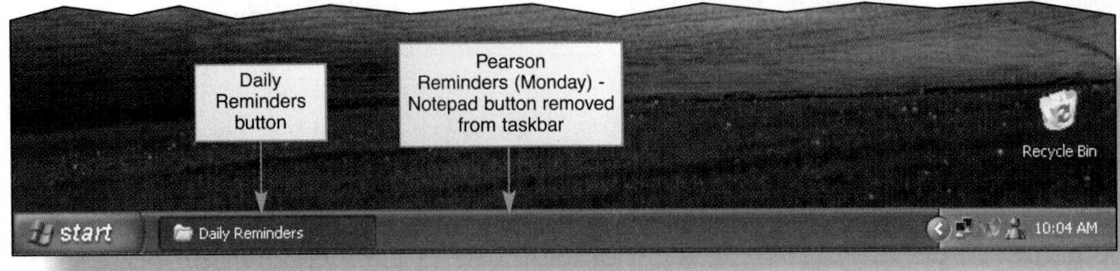

FIGURE 2-54

Other Ways

1. Click taskbar button, on File menu click Save, click Close button
2. Click taskbar button, on title bar click Close button, click Yes button
3. Click taskbar button, on File menu click Exit, click Yes button

The capability of Windows XP to process multiple documents at the same time and perform multitasking with multiple programs running at the same time is a primary feature of the operating system.

Printing a Document from within a Folder

After you modify and save documents on the desktop, print them so you have an updated hard copy of the Sanchez Reminders (Monday) and the Pearson Reminders (Monday) documents. Earlier in this project, you used the Print command on the File menu to print an open document. You also can print multiple documents from a folder without opening the documents. To print both the Sanchez Reminders (Monday) and the Pearson Reminders (Monday) documents from the Daily Reminders folder, perform the following steps.

Steps To Print Multiple Documents from within a Folder

1 **Click the Daily Reminders button on the taskbar. Click the Pearson Reminders (Monday) icon in the Daily Reminders folder to select the icon. While holding down the SHIFT key, click the Sanchez Reminders (Monday) icon, and then release the SHIFT key.**

Both icons are selected (Figure 2-55). The File and Folder Tasks area contains tasks designed specifically for working with selected items.

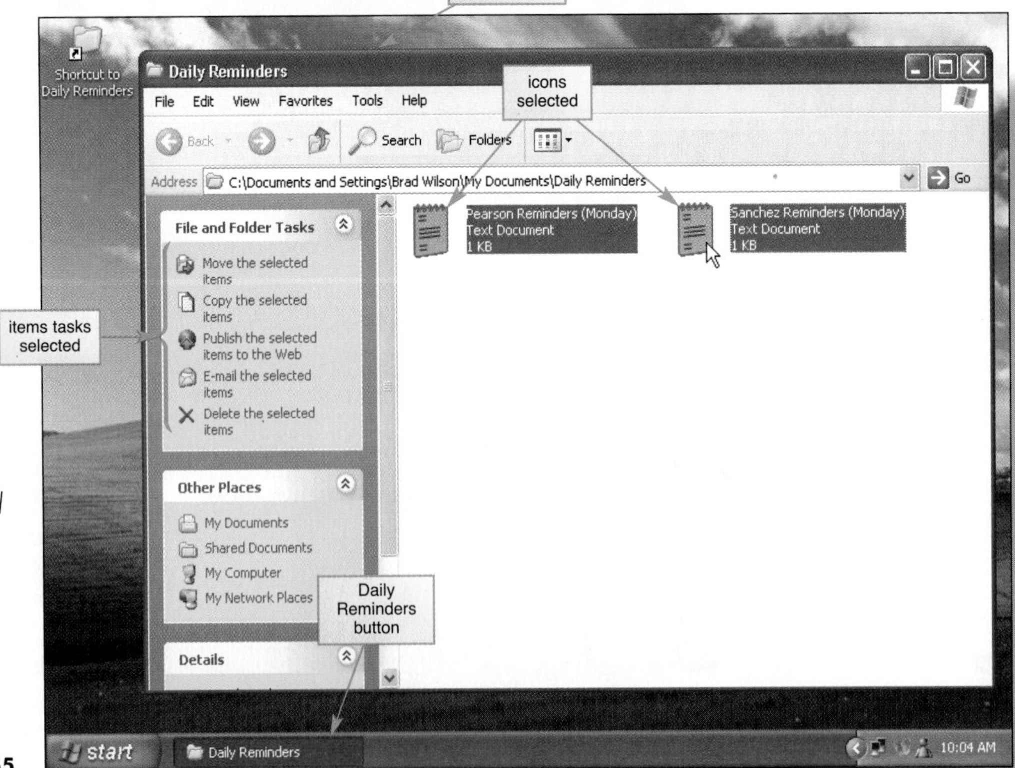

FIGURE 2-55

2 Right-click the Sanchez Reminders (Monday) icon. Point to Print on the shortcut menu.

A shortcut menu, containing the Print command, displays (Figure 2-56).

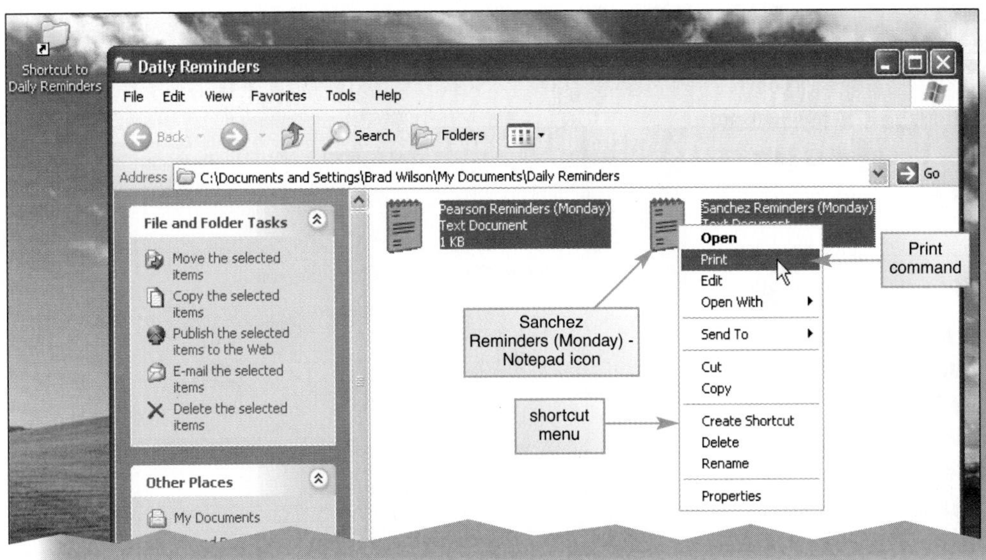

FIGURE 2-56

3 Click Print.

The modified documents print as shown in Figure 2-57.

4 Click the Close button in the Daily Reminders window.

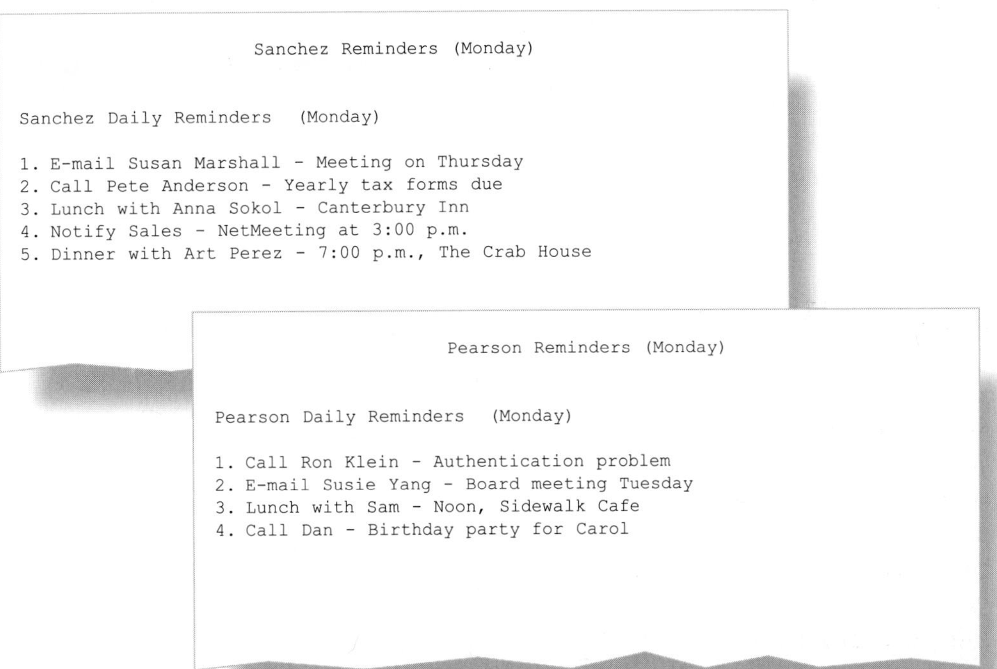

Sanchez Reminders (Monday)

Sanchez Daily Reminders (Monday)

1. E-mail Susan Marshall - Meeting on Thursday
2. Call Pete Anderson - Yearly tax forms due
3. Lunch with Anna Sokol - Canterbury Inn
4. Notify Sales - NetMeeting at 3:00 p.m.
5. Dinner with Art Perez - 7:00 p.m., The Crab House

Pearson Reminders (Monday)

Pearson Daily Reminders (Monday)

1. Call Ron Klein - Authentication problem
2. E-mail Susie Yang - Board meeting Tuesday
3. Lunch with Sam - Noon, Sidewalk Cafe
4. Call Dan - Birthday party for Carol

FIGURE 2-57

1. Select document icons, on File menu click Print

Copying a Folder onto a Floppy Disk

A shortcut on the desktop is useful when you are using one or more documents within the folder frequently. It is a good policy to make a copy of a folder and the documents within the folder so if the folder or its contents are accidentally lost or damaged, you do not lose work. This is referred to as making a **backup** of the files and folders. To make a backup of the Daily Reminders folder on a floppy disk in drive A of the computer, complete the steps on the next page.

Steps To Copy a Folder onto a Floppy Disk

1 Insert a formatted floppy disk into drive A.

2 Click the Start button. Click My Documents on the Start menu. Right-click the Daily Reminders icon in the My Documents window. Point to Send To on the shortcut menu. Point to 3½ Floppy (A:) on the Send To submenu.

The My Documents window displays, a shortcut menu displays, and the Send To submenu displays (Figure 2-58). The 3½ Floppy (A:) command is highlighted on the Send To submenu.

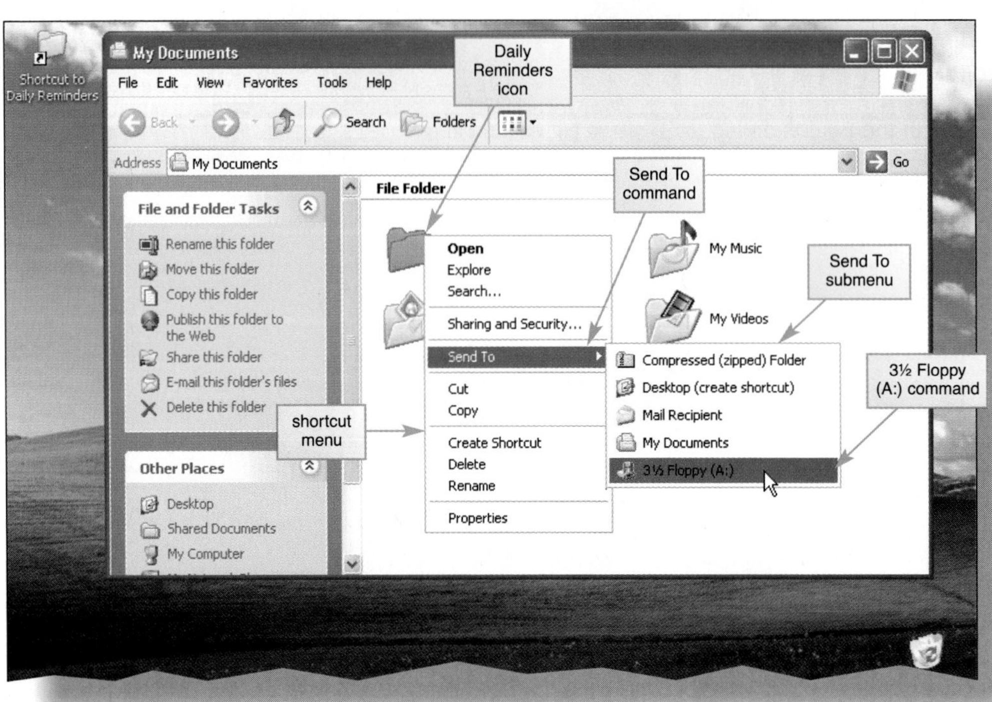

FIGURE 2-58

3 Click 3½ Floppy (A:).

While the Daily Reminders folder and the documents within the folder are being copied, the Copying dialog box displays (Figure 2-59).

4 Click the Close button in the My Documents window.

The My Documents window closes.

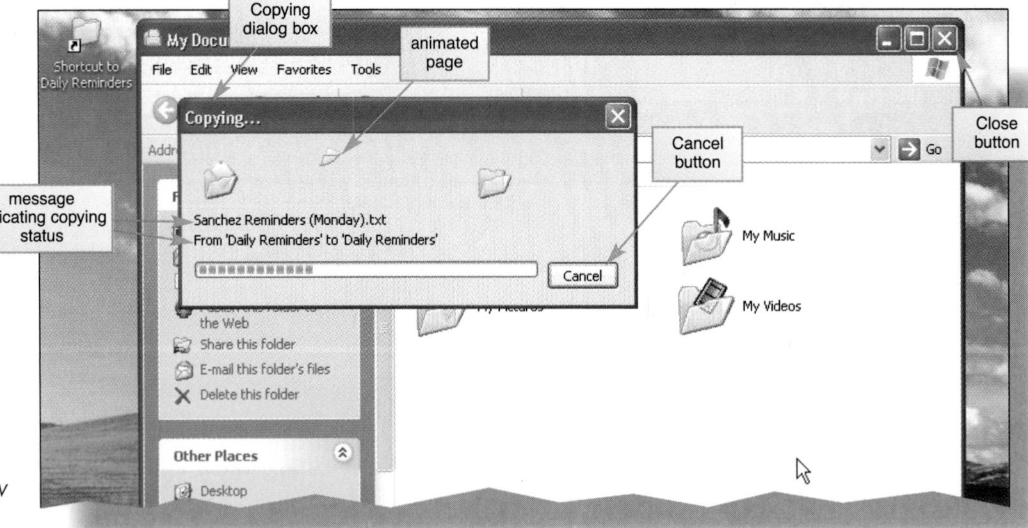

FIGURE 2-59

Other Ways

1. Select folder icon, in left pane click Copy this folder, click 3½ Floppy (A:), click Copy button
2. Select folder icon, on File menu point to Send To, click 3½ Floppy (A:)

In Figure 2-59, a message explains which folders and files are being copied, and animated pages fly from one folder to the other folder in the dialog box. After the folder and all documents have been copied, the Copying dialog box closes. When the copying process is complete, the Daily Reminders folder and the documents in the folder are stored both in the My Documents folder and on the floppy disk in drive A. If you want to stop the copying process, click the Cancel button in the Copying dialog box.

As mentioned earlier, it is a good policy to make a copy of a folder and the documents within the folder so if the folder or its contents are accidentally lost or damaged, you do not lose work. In addition to backing up the Daily Appointments folder on a floppy disk, it is important to back up the entire contents of the My Documents folder on a second hard drive or removable drive. To back up the contents of the My Documents folder, click the Start button to display the Start menu, right-click the My Documents command to display a shortcut menu, click Send To on the shortcut menu, and then click the location of the backup drive.

More About

The Send To Command

Commands can easily be added to and removed from the Send To submenu. To view the steps to accomplish this, launch Help and Support, click the Index button, type send to, click adding destinations to Send To menu, and then click the Display button.

Opening a Folder on a Floppy Disk

After copying a folder onto a floppy disk, you may wish to verify that the folder has been copied properly onto the floppy disk or, you may wish to open a document stored in the folder directly from the floppy disk. To open a folder stored on a floppy disk, complete the following steps.

More About

USB Flash Drive

Instead of storing a folder on a floppy disk, you may want to use a USB flash drive. A ***USB flash drive*** plugs into a USB port on either the front or back of a computer, is small and lightweight enough be to transported on a keychain or in a pocket, and costs less than twenty dollars. USB flash drives are ideal for students who work on both a school computer and home computer.

Steps To Open a Folder Stored on a Floppy Disk

1 Click the Start button and then click My Computer. Point to the 3½ Floppy (A:) icon in the My Computer window.

The My Computer window opens and the My Computer button is recessed (Figure 2-60). Notice the Back and Forward buttons on the Standard Buttons toolbar appear dimmed and are unavailable. When the buttons are not dimmed, you can click the buttons to display the previously displayed windows.

FIGURE 2-60

2 Double-click 3½ Floppy (A:). Point to the Daily Reminders icon in the 3½ Floppy (A:) window.

The 3½ Floppy (A:) window opens in the same window as the My Computer window was displayed and the 3½ Floppy (A:) button replaces the My Computer button in the taskbar button area (Figure 2-61). Because the My Computer window was opened before opening the 3½ Floppy (A:) window, the Back button on the Standard Buttons toolbar no longer is dimmed and is available for use.

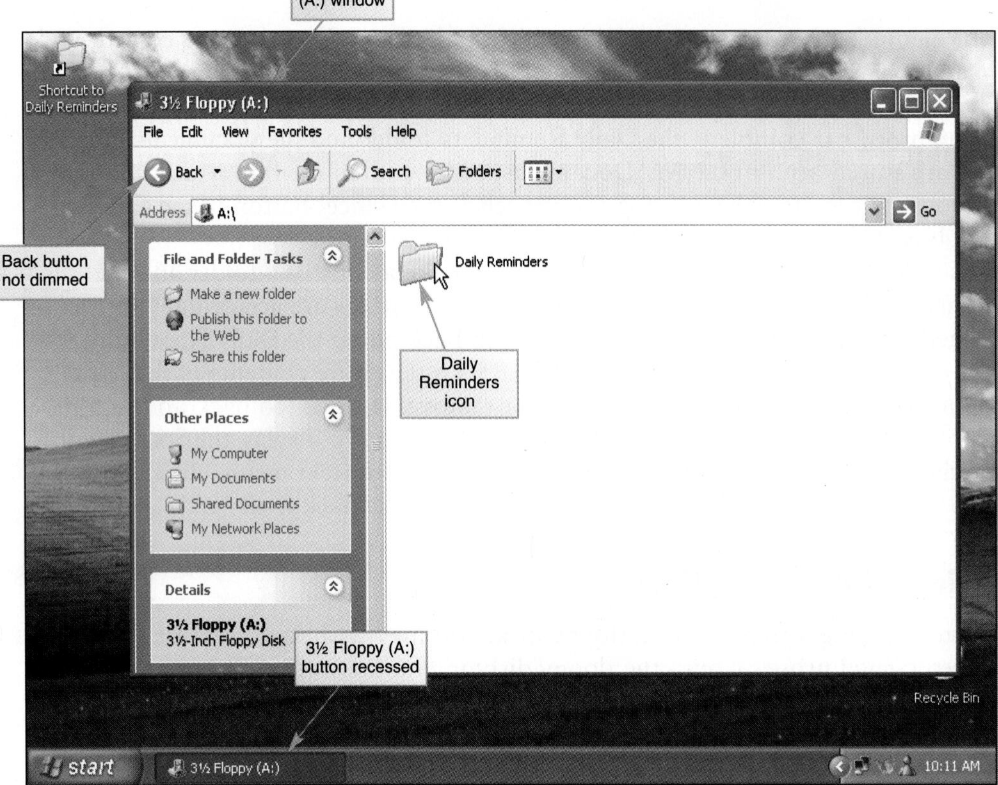

FIGURE 2-61

3 Double-click the Daily Reminders icon. Point to the Close button on the Daily Reminders title bar.

The Daily Reminders window opens in the same window as 3½ Floppy (A:) was displayed (Figure 2-62). The Daily Reminders button replaces the 3½ Floppy (A:) button.

4 Click the Close button. Remove the floppy disk from drive A.

The Daily Reminders window closes and the Daily Reminders button no longer displays in the taskbar button area.

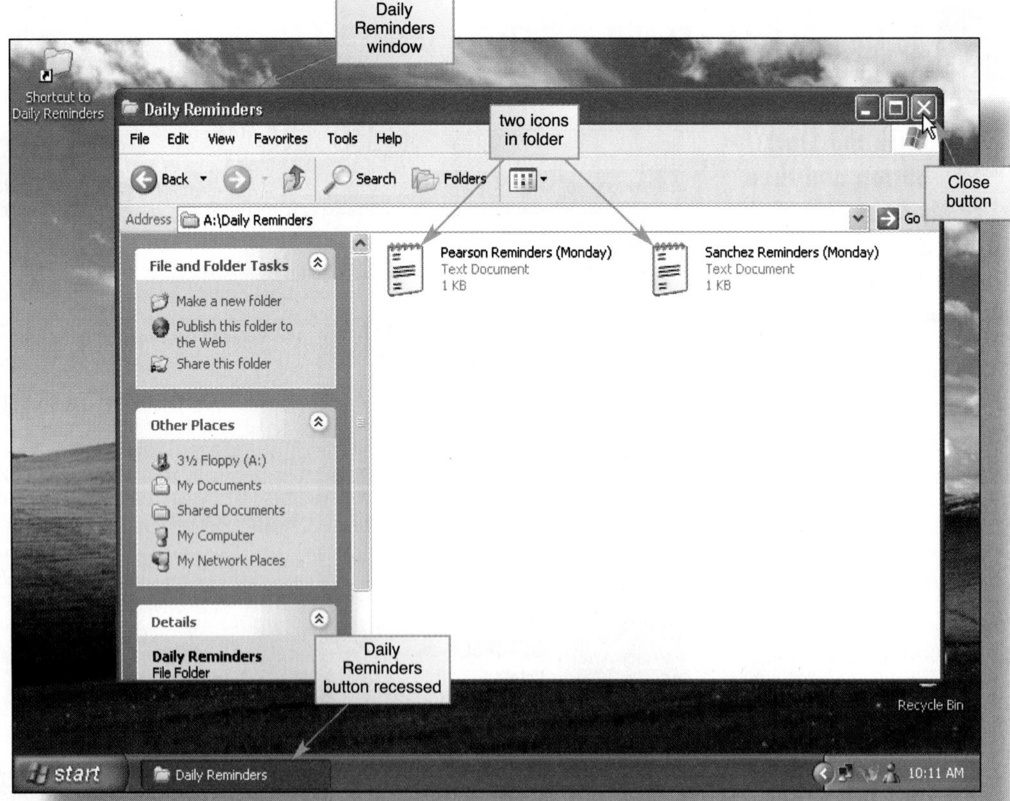

FIGURE 2-62

If you wish to open one of the documents in the folder stored on the floppy disk in drive A as shown in Figure 2-62, double-click the document icon.

Other Ways

1. Click Start button, click My Computer, double-click 3½ Floppy (A:), right-click folder icon, on shortcut menu click Open
2. Click Start button, click My Computer, double-click 3½ Floppy (A:), select folder icon, on File menu click Open

Deleting Shortcuts, Files, and Folders

In many cases after you have worked with files and folders in the My Documents window, you will want to delete the files and folders. Windows XP offers four different techniques to perform this operation: (1) right-drag the object to the Recycle Bin; (2) drag the object to the Recycle Bin; (3) click a task in the File and Folder Tasks area; and (4) right-click the object and then click Delete on the shortcut menu. The steps in this section will demonstrate the first three methods.

It is important to realize what you are doing when you delete a file or folder. Always be extremely cautious when deleting anything. When you **delete a shortcut** from the desktop, you delete only the shortcut icon and its reference to the file or folder. The file or folder itself is stored elsewhere on the hard disk and is not deleted. When you **delete the icon** for a file or folder (not a shortcut), the actual file or folder is deleted.

When you delete a file or folder from the desktop, Windows XP places these items in the **Recycle Bin**, which is an area on the hard disk that contains all the items you have deleted not only from the desktop but from the hard disk as well. When the Recycle Bin becomes full, empty it. Up until the time you empty the Recycle Bin, you can recover deleted files and application programs. Even though you have this safety net, you should be extremely cautious whenever you delete anything from the desktop or hard disk.

At the end of the week, you no longer have a need for the Sanchez Reminders (Monday) and Pearson Reminders (Monday) documents or the Daily Reminders folder. You decide you can delete them safely from the My Documents folder. To accomplish this, you must delete the two files and the folder in which the documents are stored. In addition, the shortcut to the Daily Reminders folder on the desktop should be deleted. To delete the shortcut, complete the following steps.

Steps To Delete a Shortcut from the Desktop

1 Right-drag the Shortcut to Daily Reminders icon onto the Recycle Bin icon on the desktop. Point to Move Here on the shortcut menu.

As you right-drag the Shortcut to Daily Reminders icon to the Recycle Bin, the shortcut icon and the Recycle Bin icon appear dimmed. After right-dragging, the Shortcut to Daily Reminders icon on the desktop is no longer dimmed, a shortcut menu with two commands displays, and the Recycle Bin icon is dimmed (Figure 2-63).

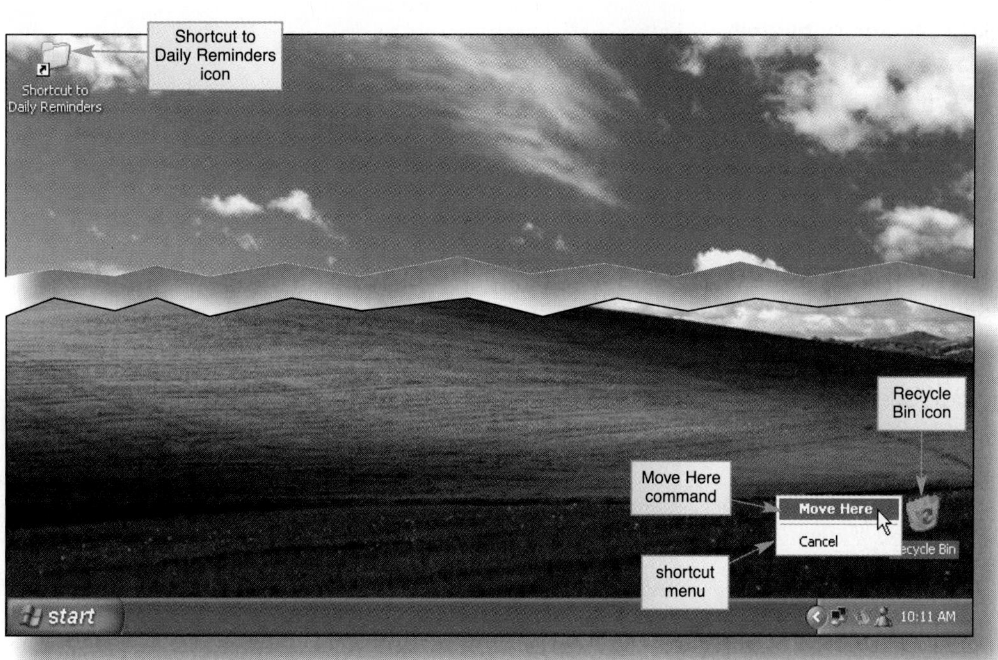

FIGURE 2-63

2 Click Move Here.

The Shortcut to Daily Reminders icon no longer displays on the desktop (Figure 2-64). The icon now is in the Recycle Bin.

FIGURE 2-64

Other Ways

1. Drag shortcut icon to Recycle Bin
2. Right-click shortcut icon, on shortcut menu click Delete, click Yes button

As noted previously, you can recover an object you have moved to the Recycle Bin from the desktop or the hard disk. To do so, double-click the Recycle Bin icon to open the Recycle Bin window, click the object you want to restore, and then click Restore this item in the Recycle Bin Tasks area of the Recycle Bin window.

Deleting Multiple Files

You can delete several files at one time. You decide to delete both the Sanchez Reminders (Monday) and the Pearson Reminders (Monday) documents. To do so, complete the following steps.

Steps To Delete Multiple Files from a Folder

1 Click the Start menu. Click My Documents. Double-click the Daily Reminders icon in the My Documents folder. Place the mouse pointer below and to the right of the two document icons in the Daily Reminders window. Drag through until both icons are selected. Point to Delete the selected items in the Daily Reminders window.

The Daily Reminders window opens and the Sanchez Reminders (Monday) and Pearson Reminders (Monday) icons are selected (Figure 2-65). The Delete the selected items task in the File and Folder Tasks area is underlined.

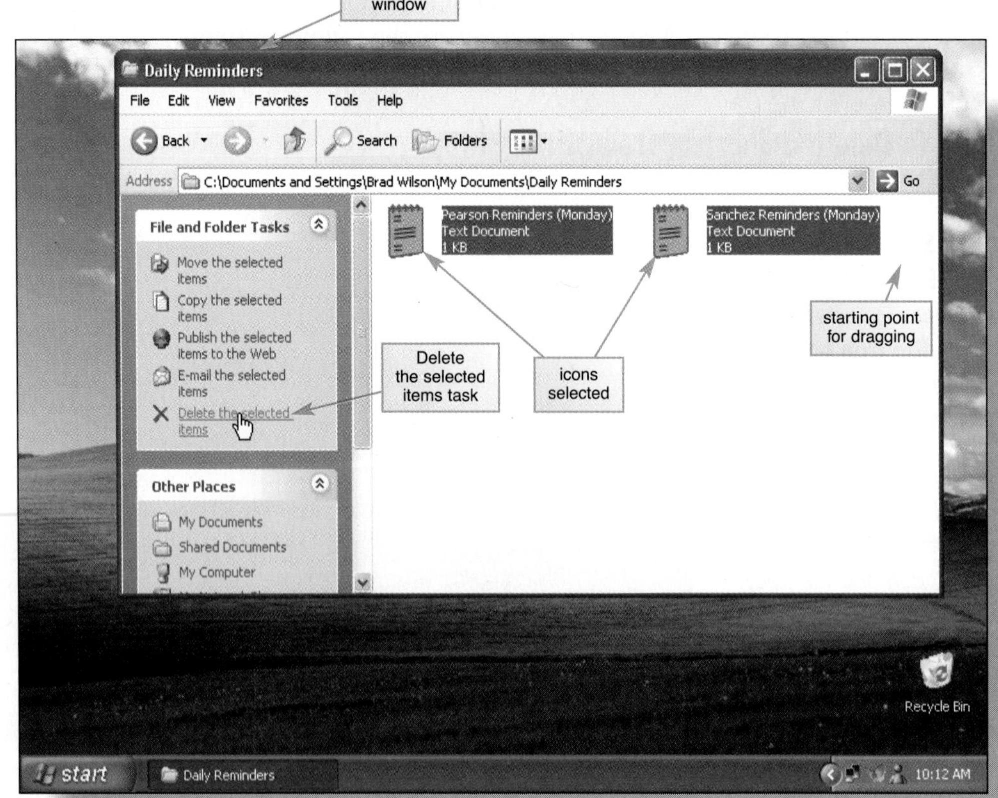

FIGURE 2-65

2 Click Delete the selected items. Point to the Yes button in the Confirm Multiple File Delete dialog box.

The Confirm Multiple File Delete dialog box displays (Figure 2-66). This dialog box ensures that you really want to delete the files. On some computers, this dialog box will not display because a special option has been chosen that specifies not to show this dialog box. If the dialog box does not display on your computer, the files were placed directly in the Recycle Bin.

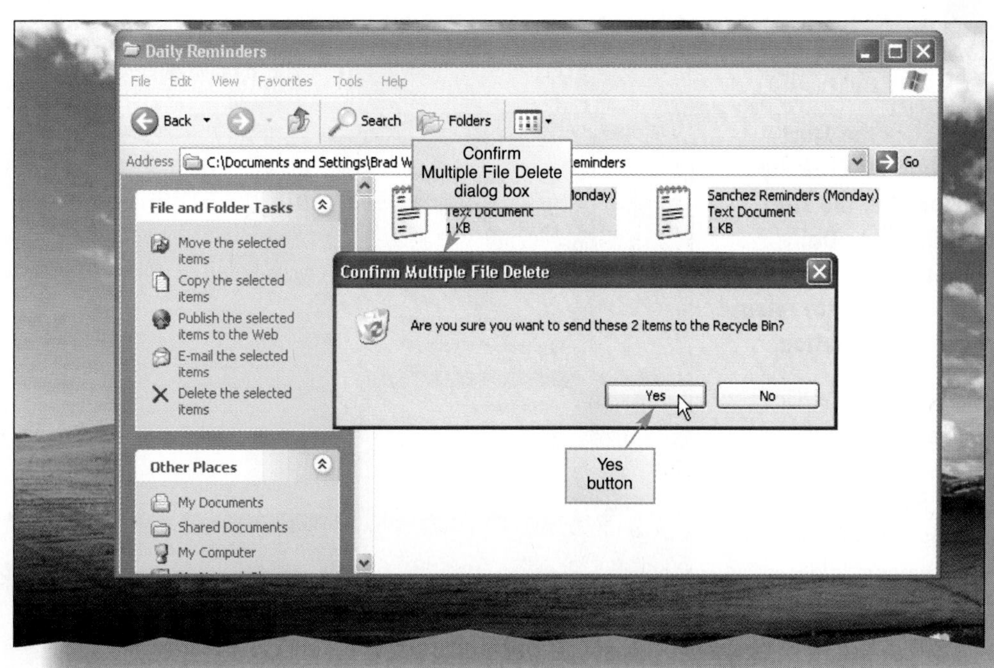

FIGURE 2-66

3 Click the Yes button. Point to the Close button in the Daily Reminders window.

The two files are removed from the right pane of the Daily Reminders window and placed in the Recycle Bin (Figure 2-67).

4 Click the Close button.

The Daily Reminders window closes.

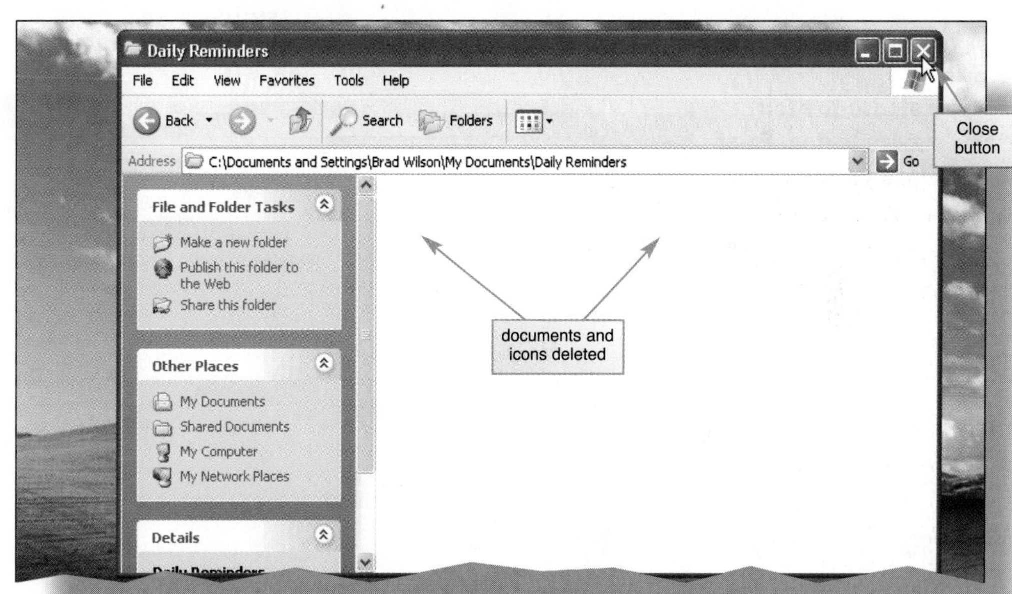

FIGURE 2-67

Deleting a Folder from the My Documents Folder

You also can delete folders in the My Documents folder. To delete the Daily Reminders folder, complete the steps on the next page.

Other Ways

1. Click first document icon, hold down CTRL key, click other icon, release CTRL key, right-click either icon, on shortcut menu click Delete, click Yes button
2. Select two icons, on File menu click Delete, click Yes button

To Delete a Folder from the My Documents Folder

1 Click the Start button. Click My Documents on the Start menu. Drag the Daily Reminders icon to the Recycle Bin. Do not release the left mouse button.

When you drag the Daily Reminders icon in the My Documents folder to the Recycle Bin icon, the Daily Reminders icon in the My Documents folder is selected and a dimmed Daily Reminders icon displays on the Recycle Bin icon (Figure 2-68).

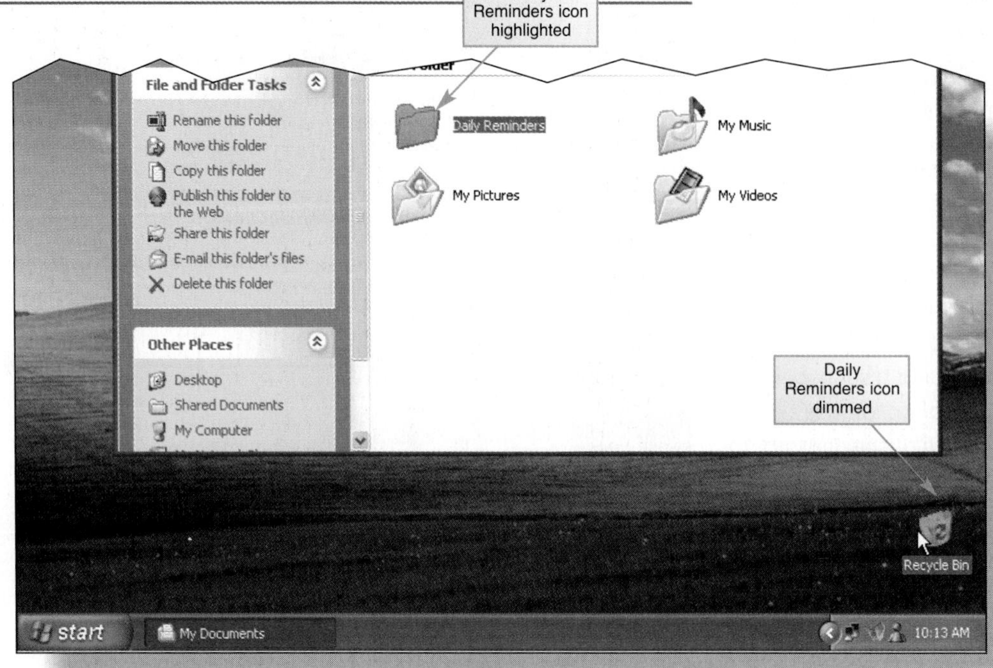

FIGURE 2-68

2 Release the left mouse button. Point to the Close button in the My Documents window.

When you release the left mouse button, the dimmed tile no longer displays on the Recycle Bin icon and the Daily Reminders folder is moved to the Recycle Bin (Figure 2-69). The Daily Reminders folder icon no longer displays in the My Documents folder and the remaining folder icons in the My Documents folder are rearranged.

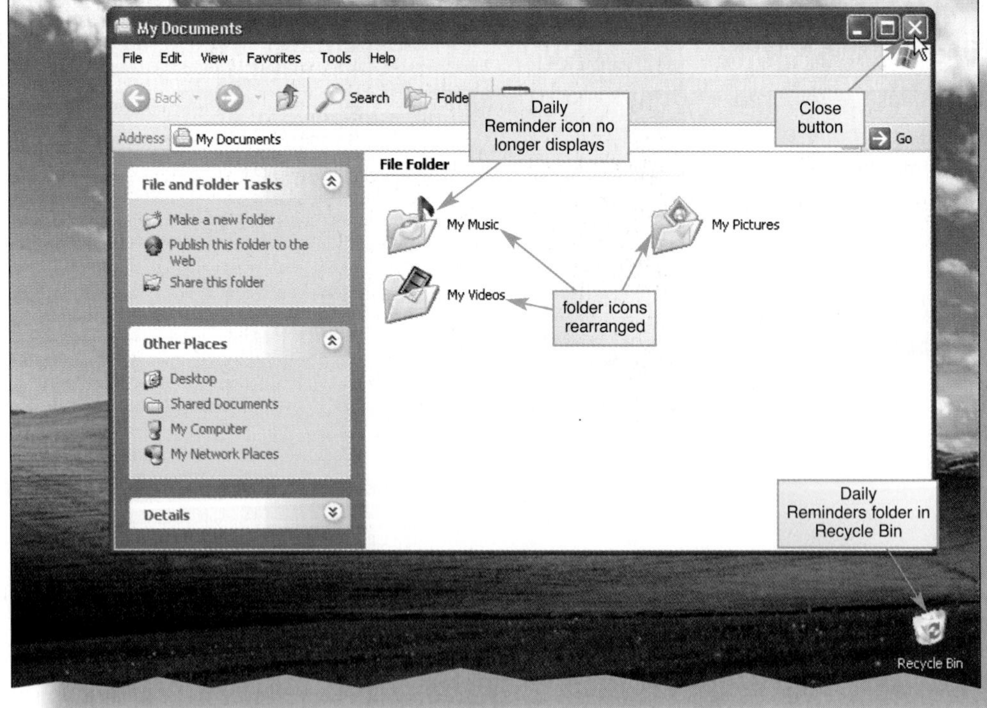

FIGURE 2-69

3 Click the Close button.

The My Documents window closes.

Other Ways

1. Right-drag folder icon to Recycle Bin, click Move Here

In summary, you have used three different methods to delete an object from the My Documents folder: (1) right-drag the object to the Recycle Bin; (2) click a task in the File and Folders Tasks area; and (3) drag the object to the Recycle Bin.

It is important to understand that when you delete a folder icon, you are deleting the folder and its contents from the computer. Therefore, you must be extremely cautious when deleting files.

If after deleting an icon from the desktop you wish to return the icon immediately to the desktop, you can right-click the desktop and then click the Undo Delete command on the shortcut menu. For example, if you delete the Shortcut to Daily Reminders icon from the desktop, right-click the desktop and click Undo Delete on the shortcut menu. Windows XP will retrieve the deleted icon from the Recycle Bin and place it again on the desktop. In addition, you can press CTRL+Z to undo the last operation performed. You also can return multiple deleted icons to the desktop in a similar fashion.

Working with User Accounts

The **computer administrator** is the person responsible for setting up and managing a computer or network of computers, assigning passwords and permissions to computer users, and helping computer users with computer or networking problems. The administrator creates a user account for each new computer user.

A **user account** is a collection of all the information Windows XP needs to know about a computer user. This information includes user name, password, picture, workgroups in which the user has membership, and rights and permissions the user has for accessing a computer or computer network. User accounts make it possible for each user to quickly log on to the computer, use a password to keep information confidential and computer settings protected, customize Windows XP, store files in a unique My Documents folder, maintain a personal list of favorite Web sites, and allow other users access to the computer without having to close any open programs.

Each user who logs on to the computer has certain privileges, or **permissions**, based upon the account type assigned to the user by the computer administrator. The three types of Windows XP accounts are Administrator, Limited, and Guest. Each account grants different permissions to the computer user. Table 2-1 lists the account types and permissions.

Table 2-1 User Account Types

ACCOUNT TYPES	PERMISSIONS
Administrator	Sets up and manages computers and networks, assigns passwords and permissions, and helps users with computer or networking problems.
Limited	Provides limited access to the computer for a user who has a user account on the computer. Limited users can change their picture and create, change, or remove a password.
Guest	Provides access to the computer for any user who does not have a user account on the computer.

The user account type assigned by the computer administrator depends upon whether the computer you use is part of a domain, workgroup, or stand-alone computer. A **domain** is a group of computers that are part of a network and share common rules, procedures, and centralized user accounts. A **workgroup** is a simple grouping of computers intended to help users find such things as printers and shared folders within that group.

Most new users are assigned limited accounts. A limited account allows you to create or change a password, change the picture associated with the account, and set up the account to use .NET Passport. **.NET Passport** is a Microsoft service that allows you to create and remember only one user name and password and then use the passport to access computers and Internet sites that support .NET Passport. Microsoft protects the passport information with encryption technology and strict privacy policies so that you are totally in charge of the information in the passport. The following sections illustrate how to change a password, change a picture, and switch between user accounts.

More About

Passwords

If your password is ever rejected while logging on changing your password, or removing your password, make sure the CAPS LOCK key is not on.

Passwords

As a limited user, you can create a new password for an account if no password exists or change the current password if a password exists. A **password** is a security measure used to restrict access to user accounts, computer networks, and computer resources. A password is a string of characters that must be provided before a user can gain access to a computer. A password can be made up of letters, numbers, or symbols. Passwords are case-sensitive, which means lalakers is not the same as LALakers or LALAKERS.

Password Reset Disks

After changing a password or entering a new password, you should create a password reset disk and keep it in a safe place. If you forget your password, the password can be reset using the information on the password reset disk. For more information, search Help and Support using the keywords, password reset disk.

When designing a password, design the password so that others have difficulty guessing the password. As a general rule, make passwords at least seven characters long and include at least two uppercase letters, lowercase letters, or numbers. For example, LALakers is eight characters long and contains three uppercase letters (LAL) and five lowercase letter (akers). When possible, use random characters. The more random the sequence of characters, the more secure the password. For example, sHiP2sHoRe contains random uppercase and lowercase characters.

If it is difficult for you to remember a password because you use multiple passwords or do not use an account frequently, always enter a **password hint** when creating or changing a password. If you forget the password, clicking the Help button on the Welcome screen (see Figure 1-7 on page WIN 1.12) will display the password hint. Remember that anyone is able to see the hint by clicking the Help button, so keep the hint vague enough that other people cannot guess the password.

Changing a Password

The Brad Wilson account is a limited account that already has a password. As such, the only changes allowed to the account are changing the password, removing the password, changing the picture, and setting up the account to use .NET Passport.

In the following steps, the password for Brad Wilson is changed. If you are sure you want to change the password for your account, perform the following steps using your account instead of the Brad Wilson account. If you are not sure about changing the password, read the following steps without actually performing them.

Steps To Change a Password

1 Click the Start button. Point to Control Panel on the Start menu.

The highlighted Control Panel command displays on the Start menu (Figure 2-70). Control Panel allows you access to the user accounts to change a password, remove a password, and change a picture.

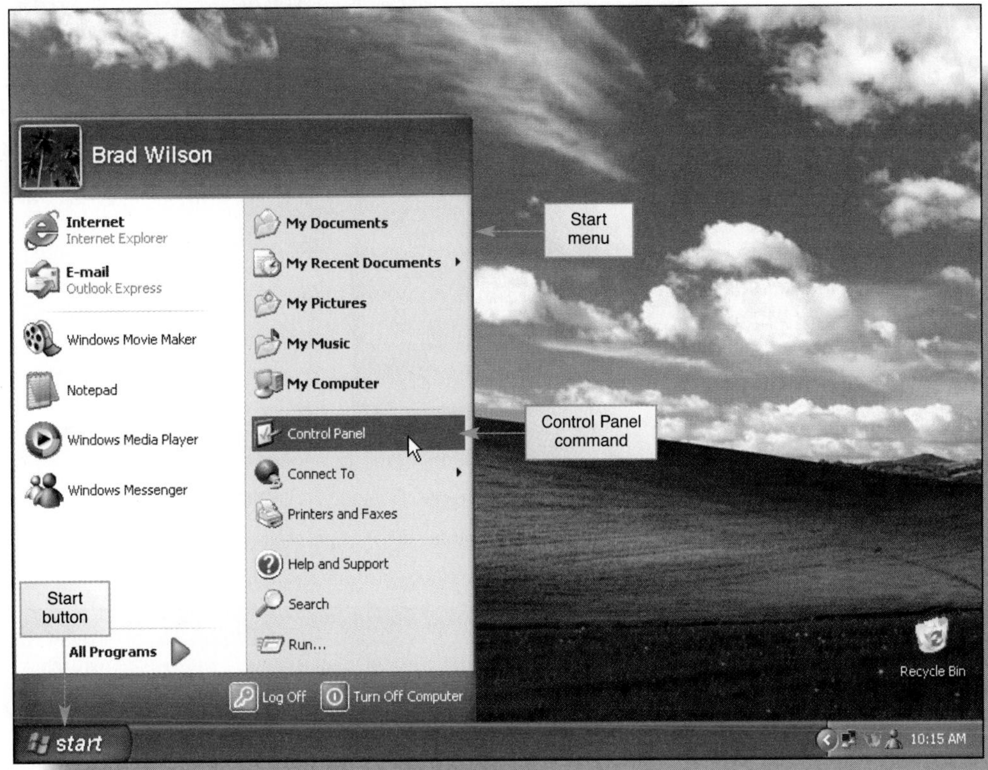

FIGURE 2-70

2 Click Control Panel. Point to User Accounts in the Control Panel window.

The Control Panel window opens and the hand pointer points to the underlined User Accounts category (Figure 2-71).

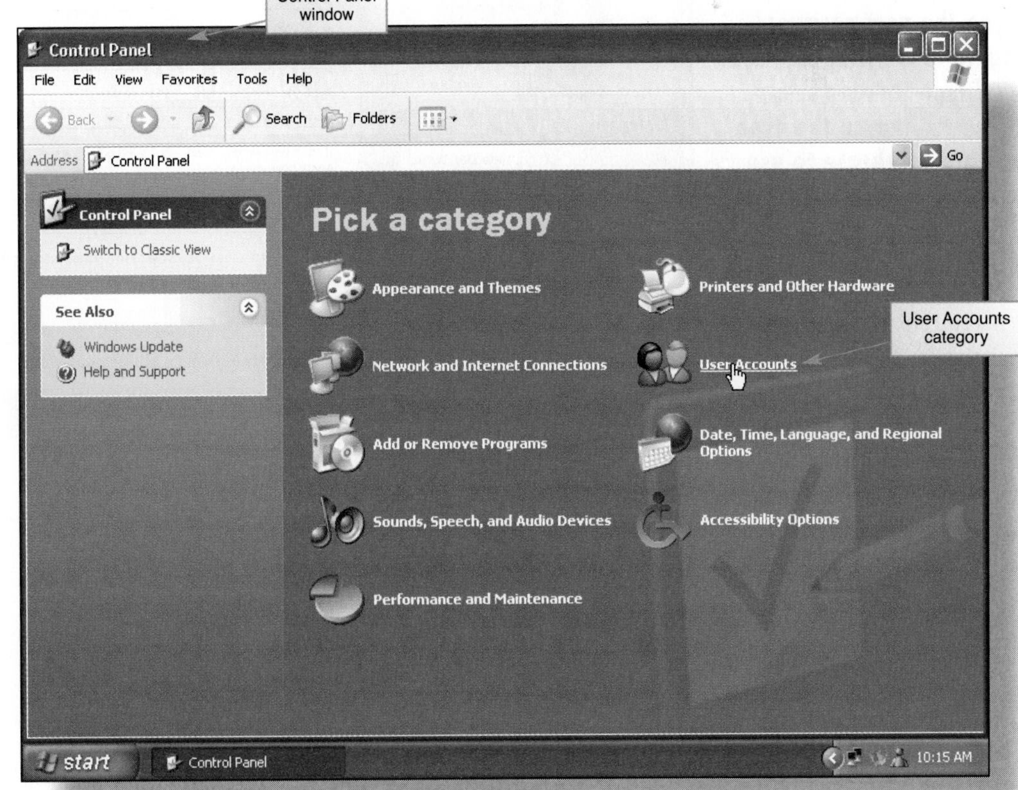

FIGURE 2-71

3 **Click User Accounts. Point to Change my password in the User Accounts window.**

The User Accounts window displays and the hand pointer points to the underlined Change my password task (Figure 2-72). The left pane of the User Accounts window contains the Related Tasks area and Learn About area. The right pane contains four tasks and information (user picture, account name, account type, and password protection status) about Brad Wilson's account.

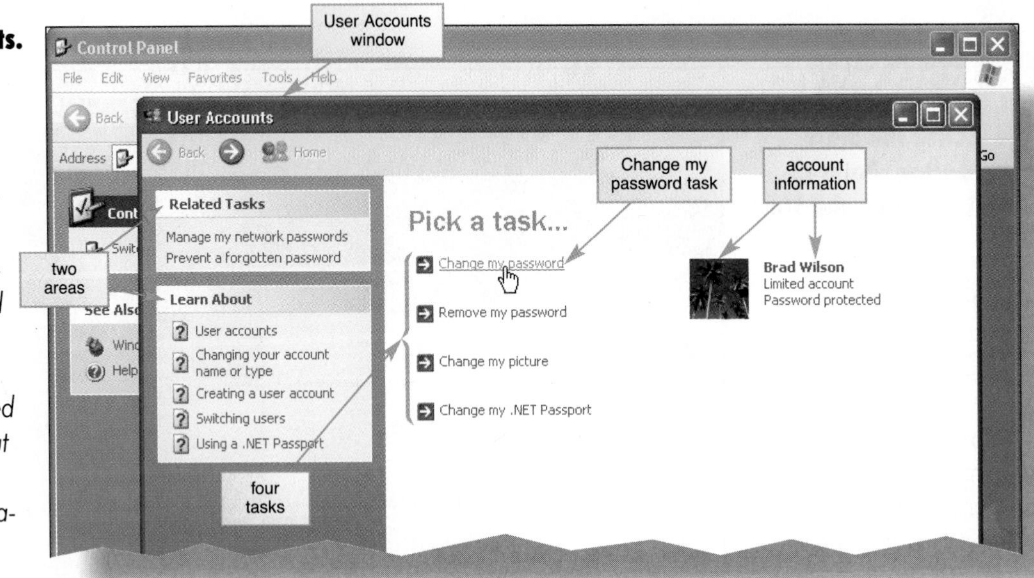

FIGURE 2-72

4 **Click Change my password. Type** `lakers` **in the Type your current password text box, type** `#1LakersFan` **in the Type a new password text box, and type** `#1LakersFan` **in the Type the new password again to confirm text box, and type** `Brad is a Lakers fan` **in the Type a word or phrase to use as a password hint text box. Point to the Change Password button.**

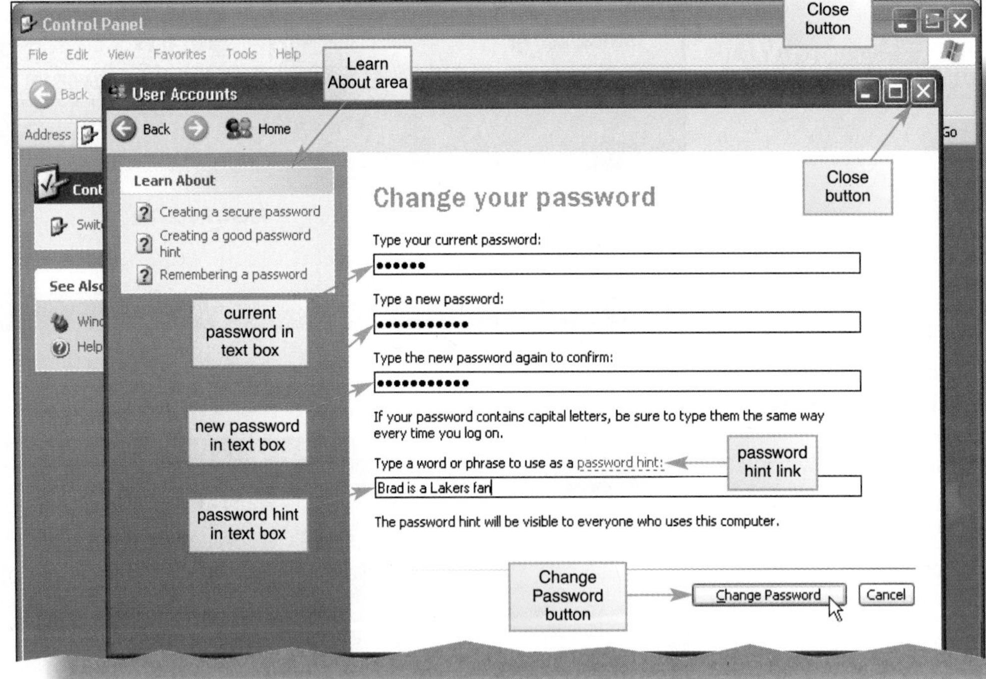

FIGURE 2-73

The current password, new password, and password hint are entered into the four text boxes in the right pane (Figure 2-73). The bullets in the text boxes hide the passwords entered by the user. The left pane changes to contain only the Learn About area. The password hint link and Change Password button display in the right pane.

5 **Click the Change Password button. Click the Close button in the User Accounts window. Click the Close button in the Control Panel window.**

The new password replaces the old password, the password hint is recorded, and the User Accounts and Control Panel windows close.

Changing a User Picture

In addition to changing the password, you also can change the picture associated with a user account. In the steps below, the dirt bike picture replaces the palm tree picture for the Brad Wilson account.

If you are sure you want to change the picture for your account, perform the following steps using your account instead of the Brad Wilson account. If you are not sure about changing the picture, read the following steps without actually performing them.

Steps To Change a User Picture

1 Click the Start button. Click Control Panel. Click User Accounts. Point to Change my picture in the User Accounts window.

The User Accounts window displays and the hand pointer points to the underlined Change my picture task (Figure 2-74).

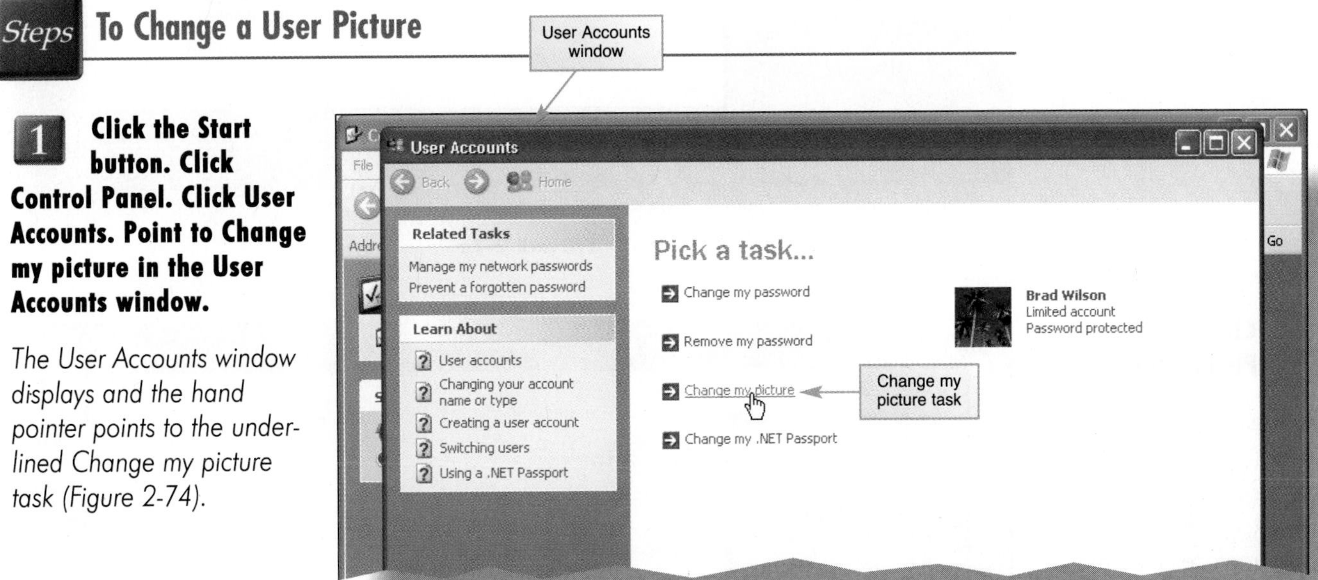

FIGURE 2-74

2 Click Change my picture. Point to the dirt bike picture in the list box.

The right pane contains a definition link (Welcome screen) and a list box containing a dirt bike picture and vertical scroll bar (Figure 2-75). The Browse for more pictures link allows you to view the pictures in the My Pictures folder and the Change Picture button is dimmed. The left pane contains three areas. The pictures in the right pane on your computer may be arranged in a different order.

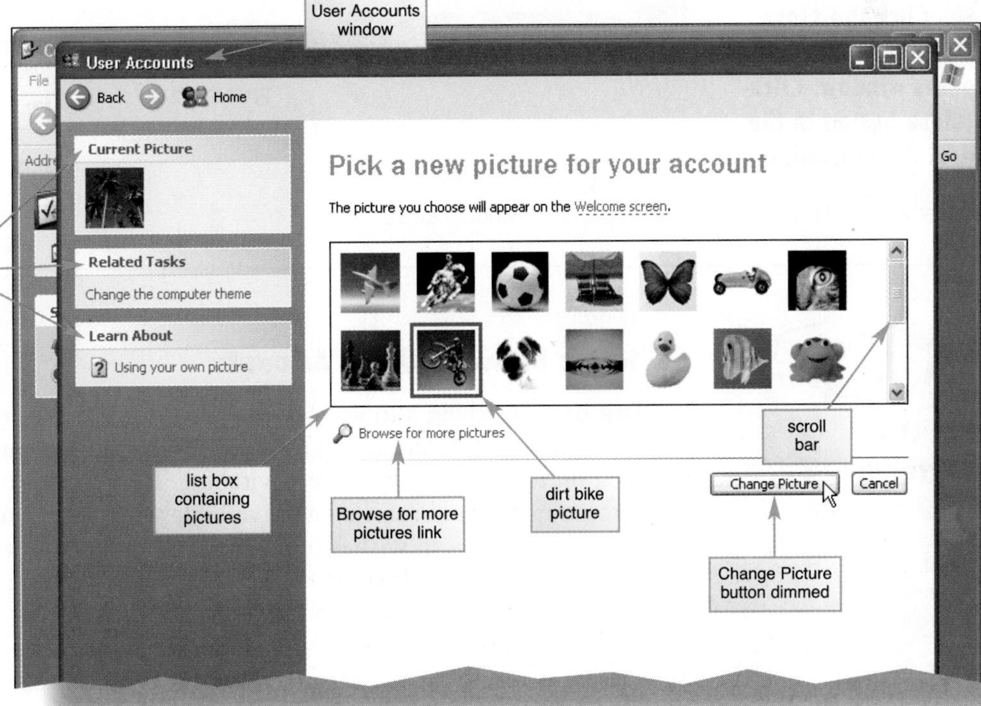

FIGURE 2-75

3 Click the dirt bike picture. Point to the Change Picture button.

The dirt bike picture is selected in the list box and the Change Picture button is no longer dimmed (Figure 2-76).

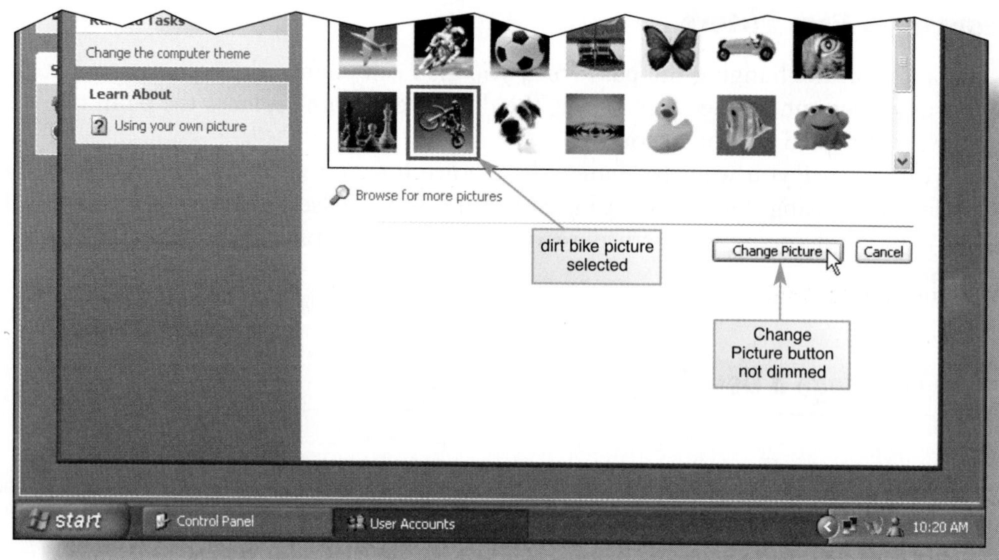

FIGURE 2-76

4 Click the Change Picture button.

The User Accounts window displays as it did in Figure 2-74 on the previous page except the dirt bike picture replaces the palm tree picture in the right pane (Figure 2-77).

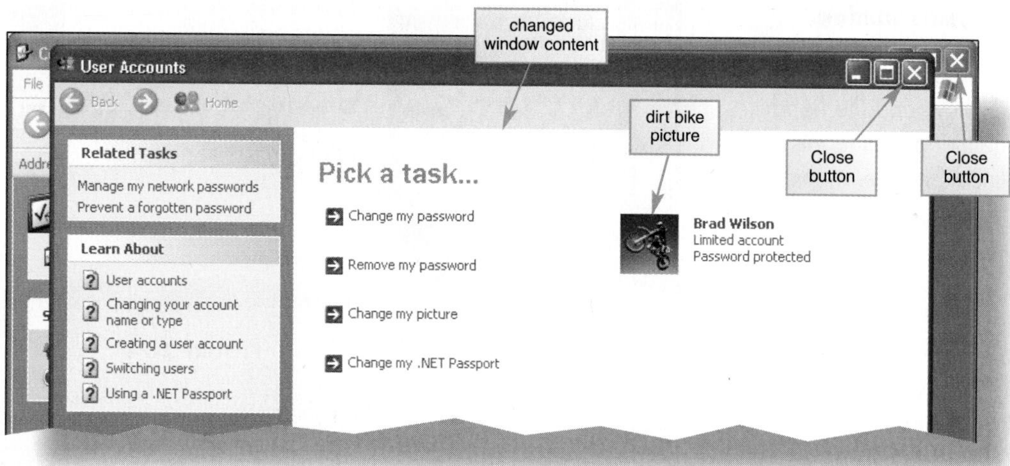

FIGURE 2-77

5 Click the Close button in the User Accounts window. Click the Close button in the Control Panel window.

The User Accounts window and Control Panel window close.

Fast User Switching

Fast User Switching is available on stand-alone computers and on computers connected to a workgroup but is not available if the computer is part of a domain.

Switching between Users Accounts

Fast User Switching allows you to switch from one user account to another user account quickly without having to log off from the computer before switching and then log on to the computer after switching. In addition, documents that are open and programs that are running are available when you switch back to your account. Assume another person wishes to use your computer for a few moments. To accommodate that person, perform the following steps to switch from the Brad Wilson account to the Guest account.

If you are sure you want to switch to the Guest account, perform the following steps using your account instead of the Brad Wilson account. If you are not sure about switching or a Guest account is not available on your computer, read the steps on the next page without actually performing them.

Steps To Switch between User Accounts

1 Click the Start button. Point to the Log Off button on the Start menu.

The Start menu displays and the Log Off button is selected (Figure 2-78).

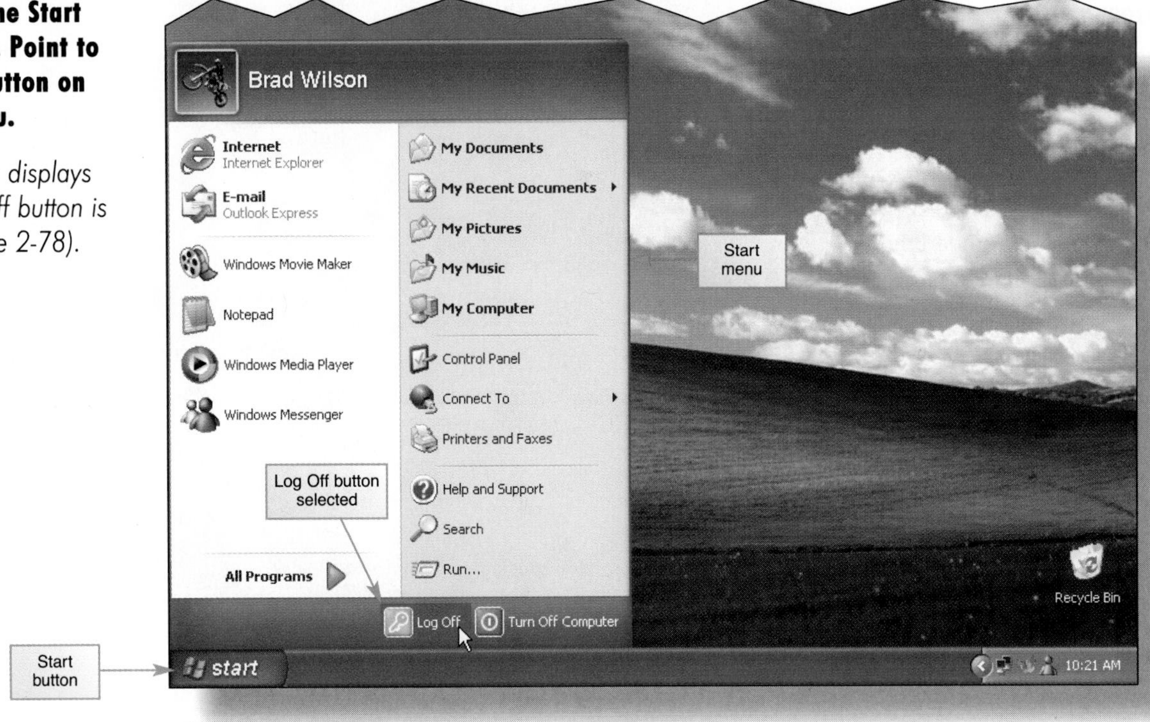

FIGURE 2-78

2 Click the Log Off button. Point to the Switch User button in the Log Off Windows dialog box.

The Log Off Windows dialog box displays (Figure 2-79). The Switch User button is selected and the Switch User balloon displays.

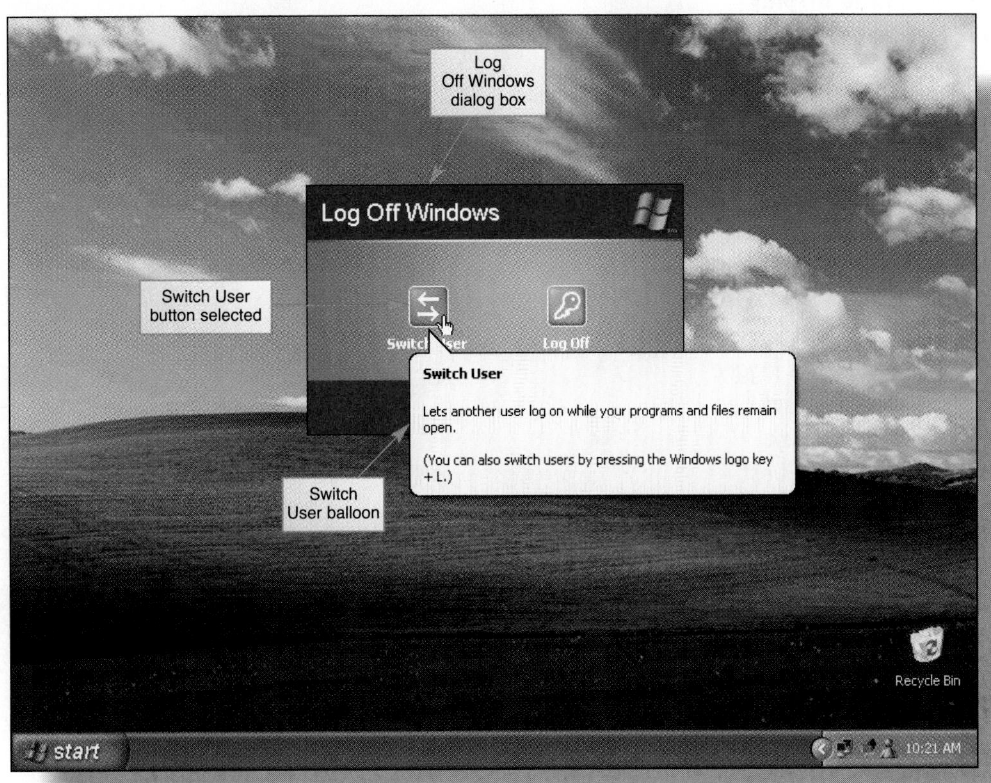

FIGURE 2-79

3 Click the Switch User button. Point to Guest on the Welcome screen.

The Welcome screen displays (Figure 2-80). The Guest icon is selected and the other icons are dimmed. The dirt bike picture displays to the left of the Brad Wilson name and the message, Logged on, displays below the name to indicate the user remains logged on to the computer. Other messages may display below the icons on your computer.

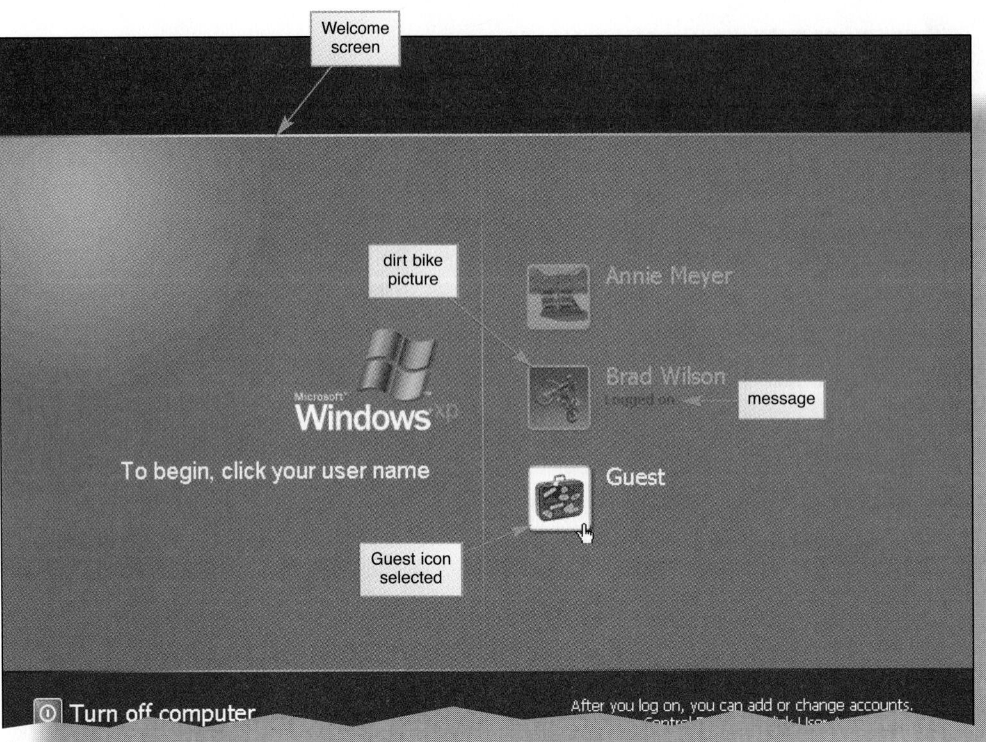

FIGURE 2-80

4 Click the Guest icon. Click the Start button to display the Start menu.

The Welcome screen changes to contain the word, Welcome, on the left side of the screen and the user name, user icon, and message, Loading your personal settings..., on the right side. This screen displays momentarily while the user is logged on to the computer and then the Start menu displays (Figure 2-81). The Guest icon and name display at the top of the Start menu, indicating the Guest account is available for use.

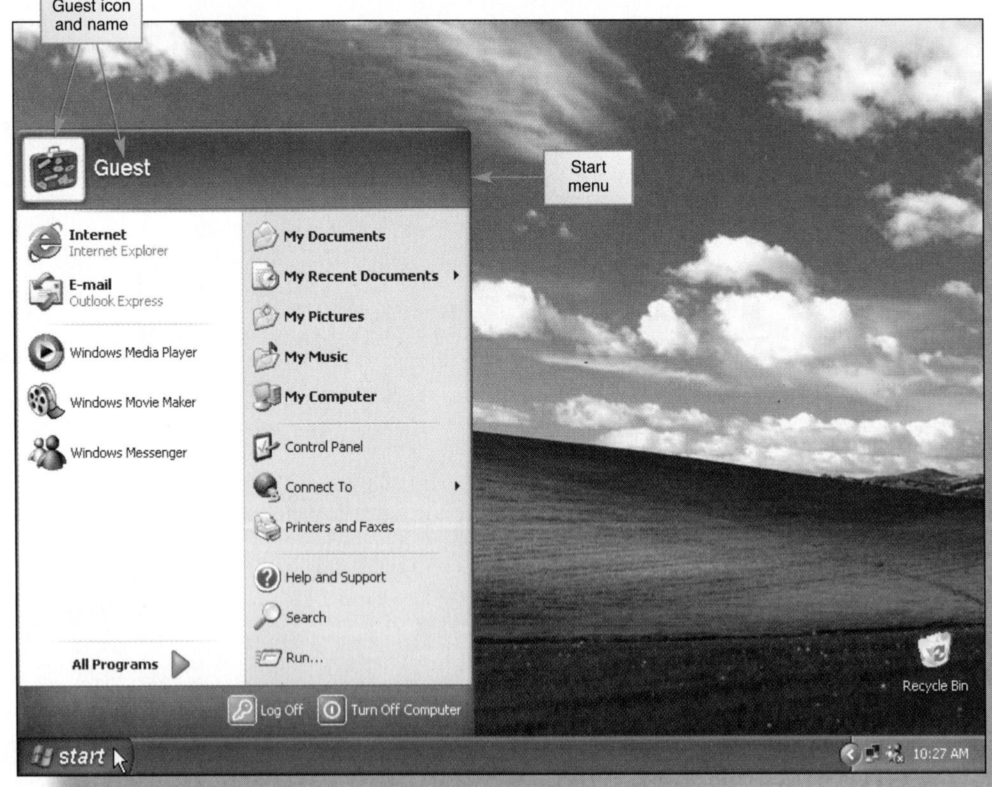

FIGURE 2-81

5 Click an open area of the desktop to remove the Start menu.

The Start menu closes.

After clicking the Guest icon in the Welcome screen in Figure 2-80 to log the Guest account on to the computer, two users (Guest and Brad Wilson) are logged on to the computer. At this point, the other person can use the Guest account to access the computer.

Logging Off from the Computer and Turning Off the Computer

After the other person has completed work on the computer, he or she should log off the Guest account from the computer. Logging off closes any open applications and ends the Windows XP guest session.

If you switched to the Guest account in Steps 1 through 5 on the previous page, perform the steps below to log off the Guest account from the computer. If you did not perform Steps 1 through 5, read the following steps without actually performing them.

TO LOG OFF THE GUEST ACCOUNT FROM THE COMPUTER

1. Click the Start button on the taskbar.
2. Click Log Off on the Start menu.
3. Click the Log Off button in the Log Off Windows dialog box.

Windows XP logs off the Guest account from the computer and displays the Welcome screen (Figure 2-82). A message below the Brad Wilson name on the Welcome screen indicates the Brad Wilson account is logged on. No message displays below the Guest icon.

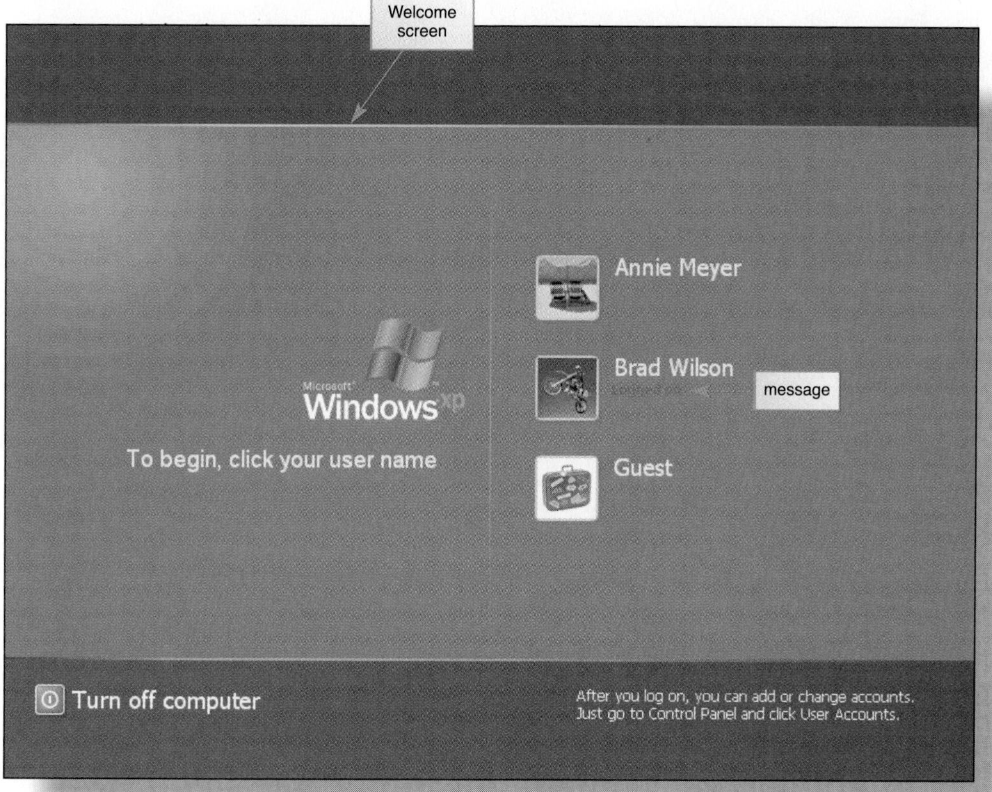

FIGURE 2-82

After logging off the Guest account from the computer, you also decide to log off from the computer. Perform the following steps to log off from the computer.

TO LOG OFF FROM THE COMPUTER

1. Click the Brad Wilson icon on the Welcome screen. If necessary, enter a password.
2. Click the Start button on the taskbar.
3. Click Log Off on the Start menu.
4. Click the Log Off button in the Log Off Windows dialog box.

Windows XP logs off from the computer and displays the Welcome screen (Figure 2-83). No message displays below the Brad Wilson name.

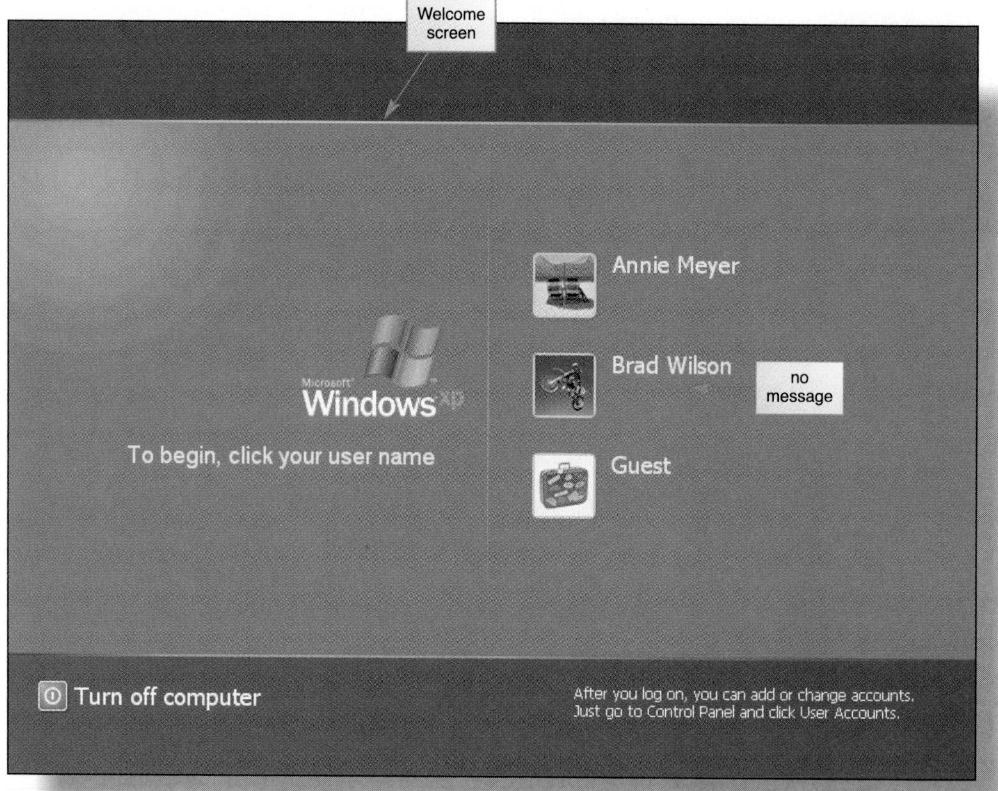

FIGURE 2-83

If you are sure you want to turn off the computer, perform the following steps. If you are not sure about turning off the computer, read the following steps without actually performing them.

TO TURN OFF THE COMPUTER

1. Click the Turn off computer button on the Welcome screen.
2. Click the Turn Off button on the Turn off computer dialog box.
3. If necessary, click the Yes button in the Windows dialog box.

Windows XP logs off from the computer and shuts down Windows XP.

CASE PERSPECTIVE SUMMARY

After creating the Monday daily reminder documents for Mr. Sanchez and Ms. Pearson, you receive an e-mail message from Mr. Sanchez thanking you for the document and stating how easy it is to view and change his reminders. Ms. Pearson stopped by your office to inform you that she showed her daily reminders document to other employees in her department and they also were interested in having them. Your supervisor, after hearing from Mr. Sanchez and Ms. Pearson, complimented your work and placed you in charge of developing a reminders system for the entire company.

Project Summary

In this project you created two text documents on the desktop. You used the application-centric approach for one and document-centric approach for the other. You then moved these documents to the My Documents folder. You modified and printed the documents in the My Documents folder, created a folder in the My Documents folder, placed documents in the folder, and copied the new folder onto a floppy disk in drive A. You worked with multiple documents open at the same time. You placed a document shortcut on both the Start menu and desktop. Using various methods, you deleted shortcuts, documents, and a folder. Finally, you learned about taskbar button grouping, user accounts, and how to change the password, password hint, and picture.

What You Should Know

Having completed this project, you now should be able to perform the following tasks:

- Add a Shortcut on the Start Menu *(WIN 2.26)*
- Arrange the Icons in a Folder by File Type *(WIN 2.22)*
- Arrange the Icons in a Folder in Groups *(WIN 2.21)*
- Change a Password *(WIN 2.51)*
- Change a User Picture *(WIN 2.53)*
- Close a Document *(WIN 2.12)*
- Close and Save a Modified Document on the Desktop *(WIN 2.16)*
- Close Open Windows and Save Changes from the Taskbar *(WIN 2.39)*
- Copy a Folder onto a Floppy Disk *(WIN 2.42)*
- Create a Blank Document on the Desktop *(WIN 2.13)*
- Create a Shortcut on the Desktop *(WIN 2.30)*
- Create and Name a Folder in the My Documents Folder *(WIN 2.23)*
- Delete a Folder from the My Documents Folder *(WIN 2.48)*
- Delete a Shortcut from the Desktop *(WIN 2.45)*
- Delete Multiple Files from a Folder *(WIN 2.46)*
- Enter Data into a Blank Document on the Desktop *(WIN 2.15)*
- Launch a Program and Create a Document *(WIN 2.06)*
- Log Off from the Computer *(WIN 2.58)*
- Log Off the Guest Account from the Computer *(WIN 2.57)*
- Minimize All Open Windows *(WIN 2.38)*
- Move a Document into a Folder *(WIN 2.24)*
- Move Multiple Documents to the My Documents Folder *(WIN 2.17)*
- Name a Document on the Desktop *(WIN 2.14)*
- Open a Document on the Desktop *(WIN 2.14)*
- Open a Folder Stored on a Floppy Disk *(WIN 2.43)*
- Open a Folder Using a Shortcut on the Desktop *(WIN 2.32)*
- Open a Folder Using a Shortcut on the Start Menu *(WIN 2.28)*
- Open an Inactive Window *(WIN 2.36)*
- Open and Modify a Document in a Folder *(WIN 2.33)*
- Open and Modify Multiple Documents *(WIN 2.34)*
- Open the My Documents Folder *(WIN 2.20)*
- Print a Document from an Application Program *(WIN 2.10)*
- Print Multiple Documents from within a Folder *(WIN 2.40)*
- Remove a Shortcut from the Start Menu *(WIN 2.29)*
- Save a Document on the Desktop *(WIN 2.08)*
- Switch between User Accounts *(WIN 2.55)*
- Turn Off the Computer *(WIN 2.58)*

Learn It Online

Instructions: To complete the Learn It Online exercises, launch your Web browser using the steps on pages WIN 1.46 and WIN 1.47, click the Address box, enter `scsite.com/winxp/exs.htm`, and then press the ENTER key. When the Windows XP Learn It Online page displays, follow the instructions in the exercises below.

1 Project Reinforcement TF, MC, and SA

Below Windows XP Project 2, click the Project Reinforcement link. Print the quiz by clicking Print on the File menu. Answer each question. Write your first and last name at the top of each page, and then hand in the printout to your instructor.

2 Flash Cards

Below Windows XP Project 2, click the Flash Cards link. When Flash Cards displays, read the instructions. Type 20 (or a number specified by your instructor) in the Number of Playing Cards text box, type your name in the Name text box, and then click the Flip Card button. When the flash card displays, read the question and then click the Answer box arrow to select an answer. Flip through Flash Cards. Click Print on the File menu to print the last flash card if your score is 15 (75%) correct or greater and then hand it in to your instructor. If your score is less than 15 (75%) correct, then redo this exercise by clicking the Replay button.

3 Practice Test

Below Windows XP Project 2, click the Practice Test link. Answer each question, enter your first and last name at the bottom of the page, and then click the Grade Test button. When the graded practice test displays on your screen, click Print on the File menu to print a hard copy. Continue to take practice tests until you score 80% or better. Hand in a printout of the final practice test to your instructor.

4 Who Wants to Be a Computer Genius?

Below Windows XP Project 2, click the Computer Genius link. Read the instructions, enter your first and last name at the bottom of the page, and then click the Play button. Hand in a printout of your score to your instructor.

5 Wheel of Terms

Below Windows XP Project 2, click the Wheel of Terms link. Read the instructions, and then enter your first and last name and your school name. Click the Play button. Hand in a printout of your score to your instructor.

6 Crossword Puzzle Challenge

Below Windows XP Project 2, click the Crossword Puzzle Challenge link. Read the instructions, and then enter your first and last name. Click the Play button. Work the crossword puzzle. When you are finished, click the Submit button. When the crossword puzzle redisplays, click the Print button. Hand in the printout.

7 Tips and Tricks

Below Windows XP Project 2, click the Tips and Tricks link. Click a topic that pertains to Project 2. Right-click the information and then click Print on the shortcut menu. Construct a brief example of what the information relates to in Windows XP to confirm that you understand how to use the tip or trick. Hand in the example and printed information.

8 Newsgroups

Below Windows XP Project 2, click the Newsgroups link. Click a topic that pertains to Project 2. Print three comments. Hand in the comments to your instructor.

9 Expanding Your Horizons

Below Windows XP Project 2, click the Expanding Your Horizons link. Click a topic that pertains to Project 2. Print the information. Construct a brief example of what the information relates to in Windows XP to confirm that you understand the contents of the article. Hand in the example and printed information to your instructor.

10 Search Sleuth

Below Windows XP Project 2, click the Search Sleuth link. To search for a term that pertains to this project, select a term below the Project 2 title and then use the Google search engine at google.com (or any major search engine) to display and print two Web pages that present information on the term. Hand in the printouts to your instructor.

Use Help

1 Finding Terms and Definitions in the Windows XP Glossary

Instructions: Use a computer and Windows Help and Support to perform the following tasks.

Part 1: Creating a Document on the Desktop

1. If necessary, launch Microsoft Windows XP and log on to the computer.
2. Create a text document on the desktop. Name the document, Windows Definitions.
3. Double-click the Windows Definitions document icon to open the document. Maximize the Windows Definitions - Notepad window.

Part 2: Launching Windows Help and Support and Using the Glossary

1. Click the Start button on the taskbar.
2. Click Help and Support on the Start menu.
3. Click the Index button on the navigation toolbar.
4. Type `glossary` in the Type in the keyword to find text box in the Index area.
5. Click the Display button in the Index area to display the Glossary in the topic pane (Figure 2-84).

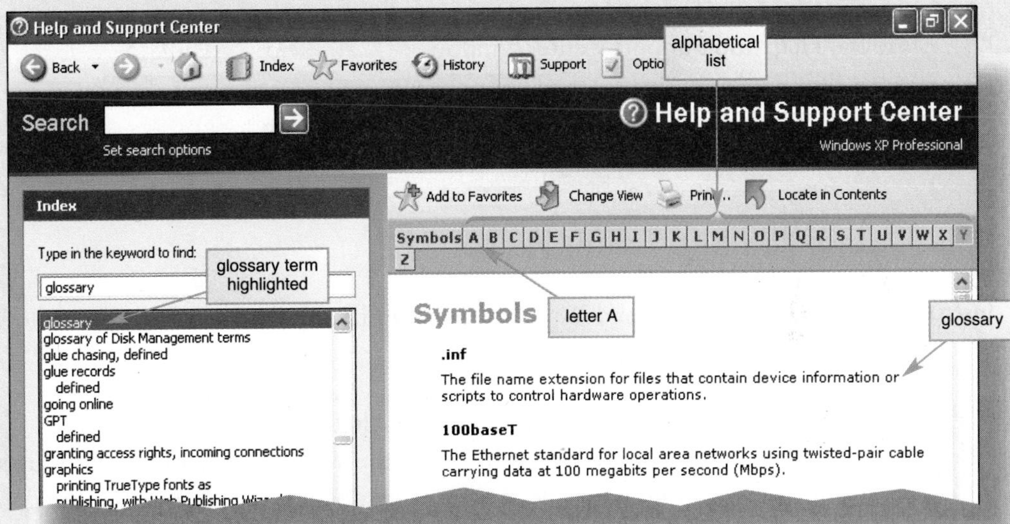

FIGURE 2-84

Part 3: Copying a Term and Its Definition from the Glossary to the Notepad Window

1. Click the first letter (A) in the alphabetical list. A list of the terms beginning with the letter A and their definitions displays.
2. Scroll the window to make the term, active, and its definition visible.
3. Drag through the term and its definition to highlight it.
4. Right-click the highlighted definition to display a shortcut menu.
5. Click Copy.
6. Click the Windows Definitions button in the taskbar button area to display the Windows Definitions - Notepad window.
7. Right-click the text area of the Notepad window to display a shortcut menu.
8. Click Paste. The term and definition display in the window.
9. Position the insertion point between any two words at the right side of the window and then press the ENTER key to move the text to the right of the insertion point to the next line in the document. Repeat this procedure until the entire definition is visible in the window.

(continued)

Finding Terms and Definitions in the Windows XP Glossary *(continued)*

10. Insert a blank line in the document following the definition.
11. Click File on the menu bar and then click Save to save the document.
12. Click the Help and Support Center button in the taskbar button area to display the Help and Support Center window.

***Part 4:** Copying Other Terms and Their Definitions to the Notepad Window*

1. Using the procedure shown previously in Part 3, copy the following terms and their definitions from the Glossary to the Notepad window: boot, drive, and password. The definition for each term should be visible in the Notepad window.
2. Click File on the menu bar and then click Save to save the document.
3. Click File on the menu bar and then click Print to print the document.
4. Click the Print button in the Print dialog box.
5. Close the Windows Definitions - Notepad window.
6. Close the Help and Support Center window.
7. Insert a floppy disk in drive A and copy the Windows Definitions document on the desktop onto the disk.
8. Delete the Windows Definitions document on the desktop.

2 Finding File and Folder Help

Instructions: Use a computer and Windows Help and Support to perform the following tasks.

***Part 1:** Creating a Document on the Desktop*

1. If necessary, launch Microsoft Windows XP and log on to the computer.
2. Create a text document on the desktop. Name the document Working with Files and Folders.
3. Double-click the Working with Files and Folders document icon to open the document. Maximize the Working with Files and Folders - Notepad window.

***Part 2:** Launching Windows Help and Support*

1. Click the Start button on the taskbar.
2. Click Help and Support on the Start menu.
3. Click Windows basics in the Pick a Help topic area.
4. Click Core Windows tasks in the Windows basics area.
5. Click Working with files and folders in the Windows basics area. The Working with files and folders page displays in the topic pane (Figure 2-85).
6. Click Open a file or folder on the Working with files and folders page.

***Part 3:** Copying a Set of Steps to the Notepad Window*

1. Drag through the heading (To open a file or folder) and the two steps below the heading to highlight them.
2. Right-click the highlighted text to display a shortcut menu.
3. Click Copy on the shortcut menu.

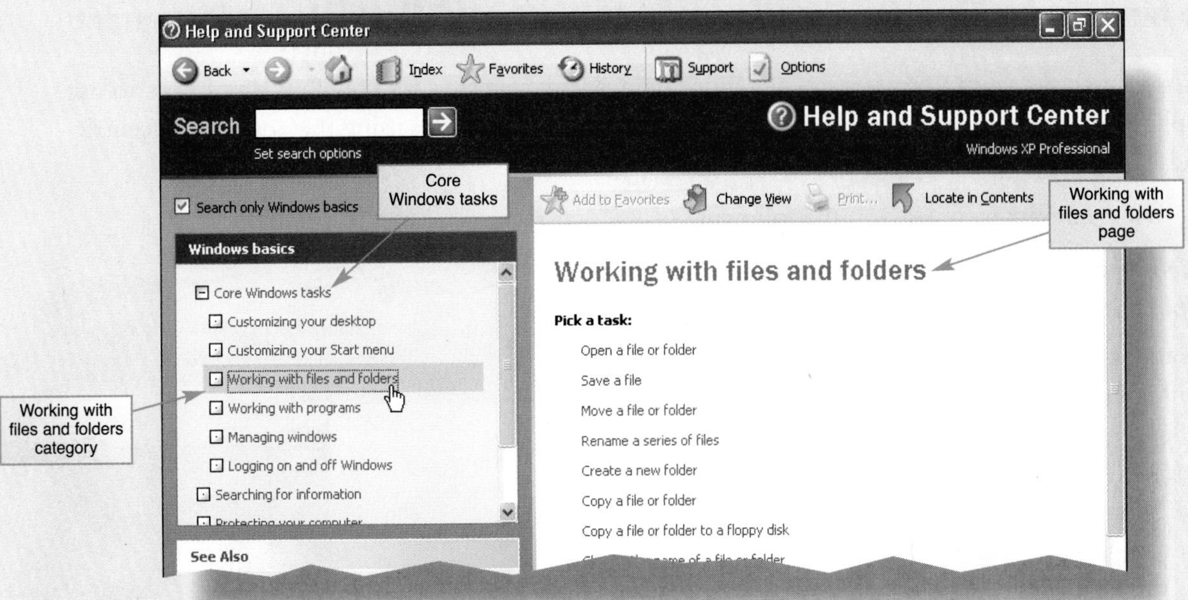

FIGURE 2-85

4. Click the Working with Files and Folders button in the taskbar button area to display the Working with Files and Folders - Notepad window.
5. Right-click the text area of the Notepad window to display a shortcut menu.
6. Click Paste. The heading and steps display in the window.
7. Insert a blank line following the heading.
8. Number and single-space the steps in the Notepad window. Remove any text that is not part of the steps.
9. Insert a blank line following the steps.
10. Click File on the menu bar and then click Save to save the document.
11. Click the Help and Support Center button in the taskbar button area to display the Help and Support Center window.
12. Click the Back button on the navigation toolbar.

Part 4: Copying Other Headings and Steps to the Notepad Window

1. Using the procedure previously shown in Part 3, copy the following headings and steps to the Notepad window: Move a file or folder, Create a new folder, and Copy a file or folder.
2. Click File on the menu bar and then click Save to save the document.
3. Click File on the menu bar, click Print on the File menu, and then click the Print button to print the document.
4. Close the Working with Files and Folders - Notepad window.
5. Close the Help and Support Center window.
6. Insert a floppy disk in drive A and copy the Working with Files and Folders document on the desktop to the disk.
7. Delete the Working with Files and Folders document on the desktop.

In the Lab

1 Launching an Application, Creating a Document, and Modifying a Document

Problem: Your boss asks you to create a list of vendor names and Web sites for company employees to use to order supplies and services. You create the vendor list shown in Figure 2-86 using the application-centric approach and Notepad.

Instructions: Use a computer to perform the following tasks.

Part 1: ***Launching the Notepad Application***

1. If necessary, launch Microsoft Windows XP and log on to the computer.
2. Click the Start button.
3. Point to All Programs on the Start menu.
4. Point to Accessories on the All Programs submenu.
5. Click Notepad on the Accessories submenu.
6. Enter the text shown in Figure 2-86.

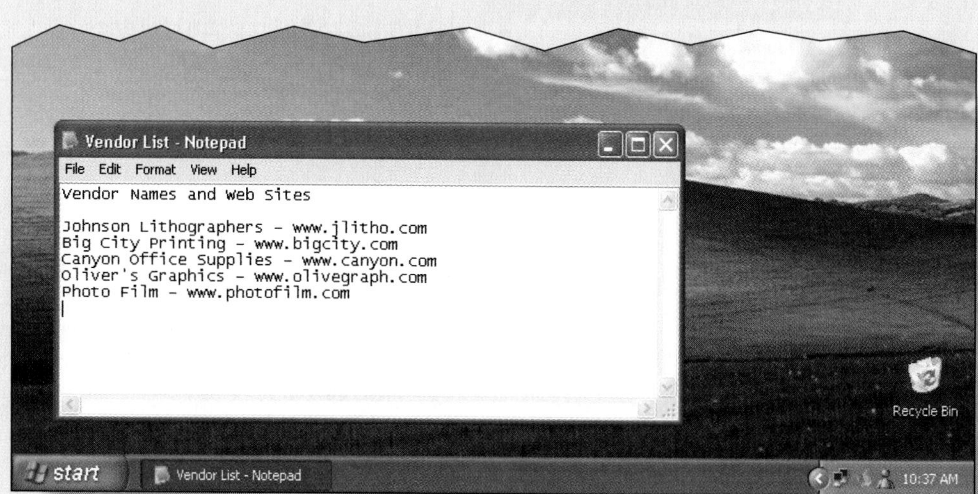

FIGURE 2-86

Part 2: ***Saving the Document on the Desktop***

1. Click File on the menu bar and then click Save As to display the Save As dialog box.
2. Type `Vendor List` in the File name text box.
3. Click the Desktop button on the Shortcut bar.
4. Click the Save button in the Save As dialog box to save the Vendor List document.
5. Click the Close button on the Notepad title bar.

Part 3: ***Moving the Document to the My Documents Folder and Printing the Document***

1. Drag the Vendor List icon onto the Start button. Do not release the left mouse button.
2. Drag the Vendor list icon onto the My Documents command on the Start menu. Do not release the left mouse button.
3. Release the left mouse button to move the Vendor List document to the My Documents folder.
4. Click My Documents.
5. Click the Vendor List icon in the My Documents window and then click Print this file to print the document.
6. Click the Close button in the My Documents window.

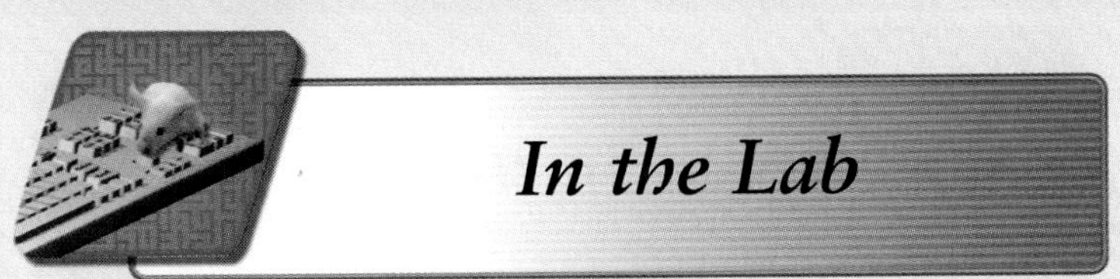

***Part 4:* Modifying and Saving a Document**

1. Click the Start button and click My Documents on the Start menu.
2. Double-click the Vendor List icon.
3. Press the DOWN ARROW key seven times.
4. Type `Kelly's Camera - www.kellyscamera.com` and then press the ENTER key.
5. Click File on the menu bar and then click Save.
6. Click File on the menu bar, click Print on the File menu, and then click the Print button.
7. Click the Close button on the Notepad title bar.

***Part 5:* Moving the Document onto a Floppy Disk**

1. Insert a formatted floppy disk in drive A of your computer.
2. Click the Vendor List icon in the My Documents window and then click Move this file in the File and Folder Tasks area.
3. Click 3½ Floppy (A:) in the Move Items dialog box.
4. Click the Move button.
5. Close the My Documents window.
6. Remove the floppy disk from drive A.

2 Creating, Saving, and Printing the Windows XP Professional Seminar Announcement and Schedule Documents

Problem: A two-day Windows XP Professional seminar will be offered to all teachers at your school. You have been put in charge of developing two text documents for the seminar. One document announces the seminar and will be sent to all teachers. The other document contains the schedule for the seminar. You prepare the documents shown in Figures 2-87 and 2-88 on the next page using Notepad.

Instructions: Use a computer to perform the following tasks.

***Part 1:* Creating the Windows XP Professional Seminar Announcement Document**

1. If necessary, launch Microsoft Windows XP and log on to the computer.
2. Create a blank text document on the desktop. Name the document Windows XP Professional Seminar Announcement.
3. Enter the text shown in Figure 2-87.
4. Save the document on the desktop.
5. Print the document.
6. Close the document.
7. Move the document to the My Documents folder.
8. Create a folder in the My Documents folder called Windows XP Seminar Documents.
9. Place the Windows XP Professional Seminar Announcement document in the Windows XP Seminar Documents folder.

(continued)

In the Lab

Creating, Saving, and Printing the Windows XP Professional Seminar Announcement and Schedule Documents *(continued)*

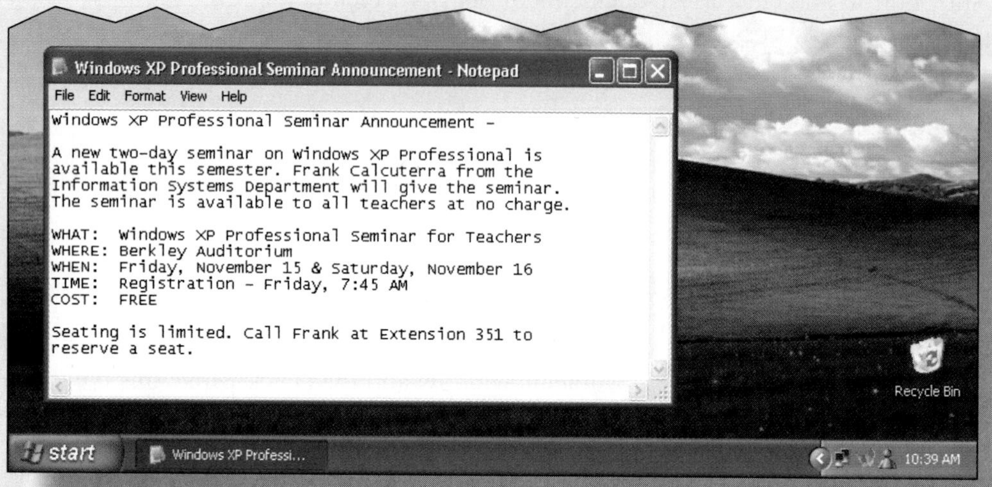

FIGURE 2-87

Part 2: Creating the Windows XP Professional Seminar Schedule Document

1. Create a blank text document on the desktop. Name the document Windows XP Professional Seminar Schedule.
2. Enter the text shown in Figure 2-88.
3. Save the document on the desktop.
4. Print the document.
5. Close the document.
6. Move the Windows XP Professional Seminar Schedule document to the My Documents folder.
7. Place the Windows XP Professional Seminar Schedule document in the Windows XP Seminar Documents folder.
8. Move the Windows XP Seminar Documents folder to a floppy disk.

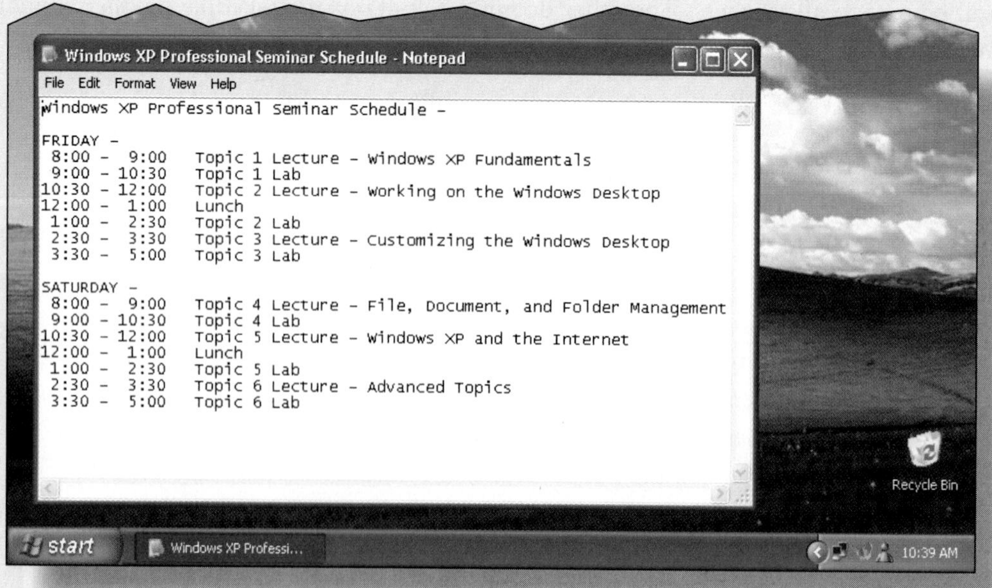

FIGURE 2-88

In the Lab

3 Changing the User Picture

Problem: A fellow student asks you to show him how to change the user picture on his account and prove to his instructor that he made the change. You decide to capture an image of the Start menu containing the current picture, make the change to the picture, and capture another image of the Start menu to confirm the change was made.

Instructions: Use a computer to perform the following tasks.

Part 1: ***Launching the Paint Program***

1. If necessary, launch Microsoft Windows XP and log on to the computer.
2. Click the Start button, point to All Programs on the Start menu, point to Accessories on the All Programs submenu, and then click Paint on the Accessories submenu.
3. Minimize the Paint window.

Part 2: Printing the Old User Picture

1. Click the Start button to display the Start menu.
2. Click the PRINT SCREEN key on the keyboard to place an image of the desktop on the **Clipboard**, which is a temporary Windows storage area. Close the Start menu.
3. Click the Paint button on the taskbar to display the Paint window. Maximize the Paint window.
4. Click Edit on the menu bar and then click Paste to copy the image from the Clipboard to the Paint window.
5. Save the document on the desktop using the file name, Old User Picture.
6. Print the document.
7. Minimize the Paint window.

Part 3: Changing the User Picture

1. Click the Start button. Click Control Panel. Click User Accounts in the Control Panel window.
2. Click Change my picture in the User Accounts window.
3. Click the duck picture in the list box.
4. Click the Change Picture button.
5. Click the Close button in the User Accounts window.
6. Click the Close button in the Control Panel window.

Part 4: Printing the New User Picture

1. Click the Start button to display the Start menu.
2. Click the PRINT SCREEN key on the keyboard to capture and place an image of the desktop on the Clipboard.
3. Click the Paint button to display the Paint window.
4. Click Edit on the menu bar and then click Paste on the Edit menu to display the image in the Paint window.
5. Click File on the menu bar, click Print on the File menu, and then click the Print button to print the image.
6. Use the Save As command to save the document on the desktop using the file name, New User Picture.
7. Close the Paint window.

(continued)

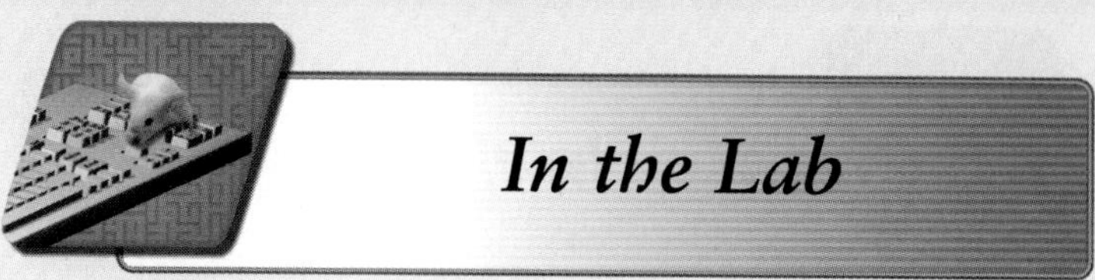

Changing the User Picture *(continued)*

Part 5: Changing the New User Picture to the Old User Picture

1. Click the Start button. Click Control Panel. Click User Accounts in the Control Panel window.
2. Click Change my picture in the User Accounts window.
3. Select the user picture in the list box identified by the Old User Picture document you printed in Part 2, Step 2.
4. Click the Change Picture button.
5. Click the Close button in the User Accounts window.
6. Click the Close button in the Control Panel window.

Part 6: Deleting the Paint Documents

1. Delete the Old User Picture document on the desktop.
2. Delete the New User Picture document on the desktop.

4 Creating, Saving, and Printing Automobile Information Documents

Problem: For eight months, you have accumulated data about your 2005 Dodge Viper automobile. Some of the information is written on pieces of paper, while the rest is in the form of receipts. You have decided to organize this information using your computer. You create the documents shown in Figures 2-89 and 2-90, and Figures 2-91 and 2-92 on page WIN 2.70 using the document-centric approach and Notepad.

Instructions: Use a computer to perform the following tasks.

Part 1: Creating the Automobile Information Document

1. If necessary, launch Microsoft Windows XP and log on to the computer.
2. Create a text document on the desktop. Name the document Automobile Information.
3. Enter the text shown in Figure 2-89.

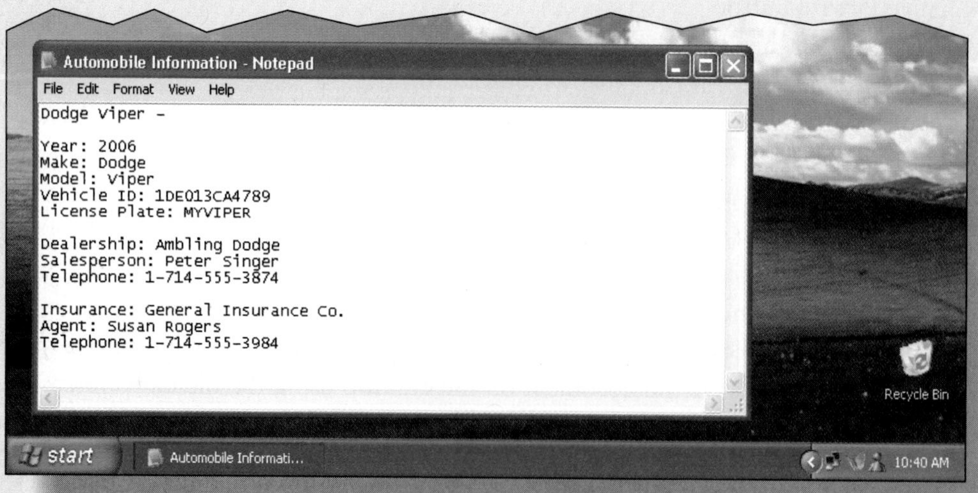

FIGURE 2-89

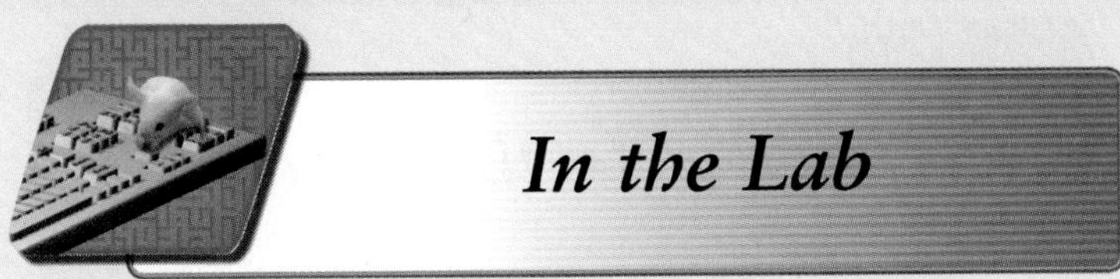

In the Lab

4. Move the document in the My Documents folder.
5. Print the document.
6. Create a folder in the My Documents folder called Automobile Documents.
7. Place the Automobile Information document in the Automobile Documents folder.

***Part 2:** Other Automobile Documents*

1. Create the Phone Numbers document (Figure 2-90), the Automobile Gas Mileage document (Figure 2-91 on the next page), and the Automobile Maintenance document on the desktop (Figure 2-92 on the next page).
2. Move each document in the My Documents folder.
3. Print each document.
4. Place each document in the Automobile Documents folder.
5. Move the Automobile Documents folder to a floppy disk.

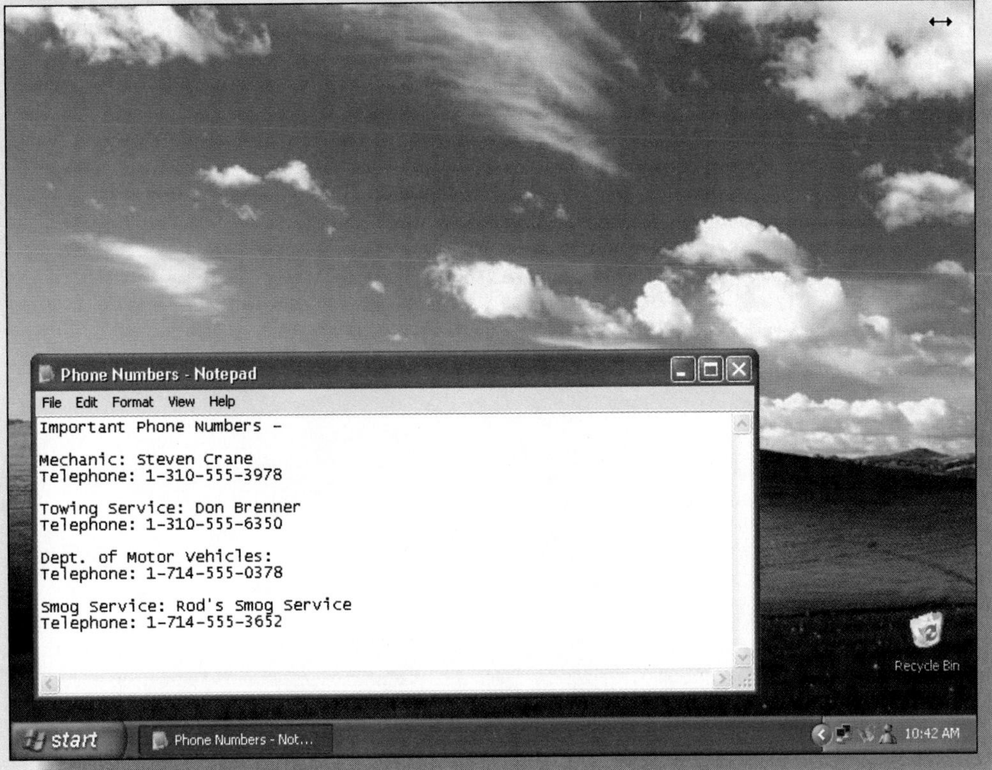

FIGURE 2-90

(continued)

In the Lab

Creating, Saving, and Printing Automobile Information Documents *(continued)*

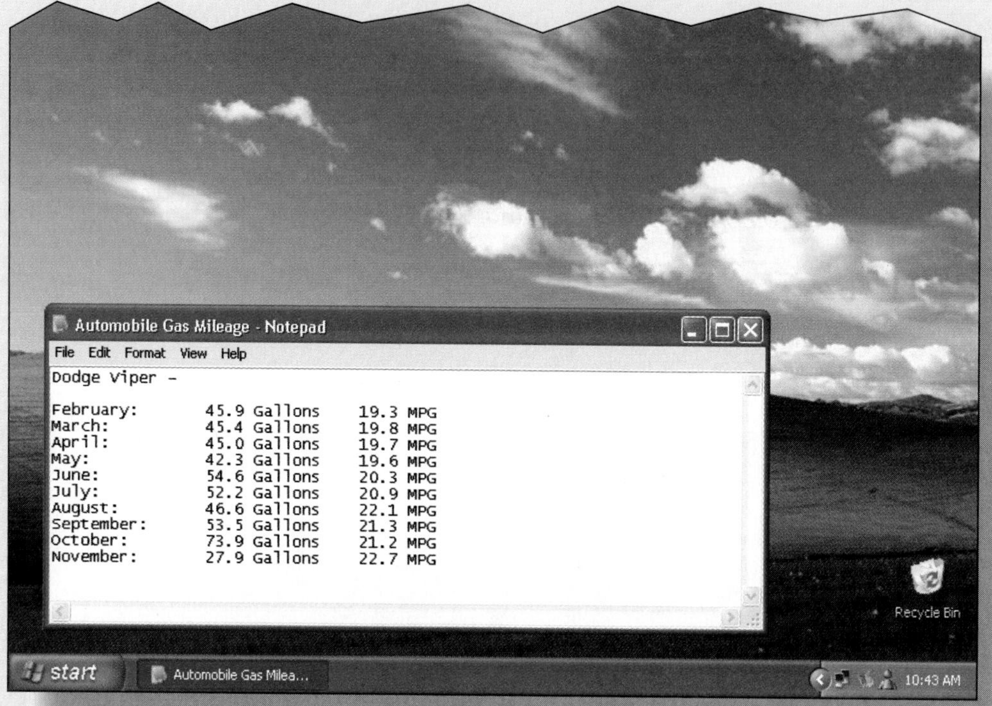

FIGURE 2-91

FIGURE 2-92

Cases and Places

The difficulty of these case studies varies:
▸ are the least difficult; ▸▸ are more difficult; and ▸▸▸ are the most difficult.

1 ▸ A friend owns a chain of fast-food restaurants and approaches you with questions about installing the new Windows XP Professional operating system on several computers. Because the current operating system on each computer is not the same, your friend asks you to prepare a list of operating systems from which you can and cannot upgrade to Windows XP Professional. You prepare the list shown in Figure 2-93. Use Notepad to prepare the list. Use the concepts and techniques presented in this project to start Notepad and create, save, and print the document.

```
                    Supported Upgrade Paths to Windows XP Professional

You can upgrade to Windows XP Professional from these operating systems:
        Windows 98
        Windows 98 SE
        Windows ME
        Windows NT 4.0 Workstation
        Windows 2000 Professional
        Windows XP Home Edition

You cannot upgrade to Windows XP Professional from these operating systems:
        Windows 3.1
        Any Evaluation Version
        Any Server Version
        Windows 95
        Windows NT 3.51 Workstation
        Versions of Windows NT prior to version 3.51
        BackOffice Small Business Server
        Non-Microsoft operating systems
```

FIGURE 2-93

2 ▸ Your employer is concerned that some people in the company are not thoroughly researching purchases of office supplies. She has prepared a list of steps she would like everyone to follow when purchasing office supplies (Figure 2-94). Your employer asks you to use WordPad to prepare a copy of this list and post it in every department. Use the concepts and techniques presented in this project to create a WordPad document on the desktop. Save and print the document. After you have printed one copy of the document, try experimenting with different WordPad features to make the list more eye-catching. If you like your changes, save and print a revised copy of the document. If WordPad is not available on your computer, use Notepad.

```
                    Requests for Office Supplies

1. Determine your department's need for office supplies
2. Identify at least two Internet sites that sell the office supplies you need
3. Obtain prices for the office supplies from their Web site
4. Submit your results to Nancy Bradford for review
```

FIGURE 2-94

3 ▸▸ Prepare a brief report on the document-centric approach versus the application-centric approach when you create a document. Explain what each approach means to the computer user, summarize the advantages and disadvantages of each approach, and indicate which approach you prefer and why. Do you think one approach will be more popular in the future? Will future operating systems emphasize one approach over the other? Support your opinions with information from computer magazines, articles on the Internet, and other resources.

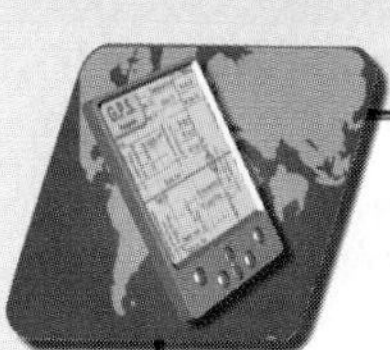

Cases and Places

4 ▶▶ Retraining employees can be an expensive task for a business of any size. Many Windows XP users believe the Windows XP operating system is an intuitive operating system and is easy to learn and thereby, reduces retraining costs. Using the Internet, current computer magazines, or other resources, research this topic and write a brief report summarizing your findings. Include and explain those features that you think make the Windows XP operating system an easy-to-use operating system.

5 ▶▶▶ Microsoft Corporation offers many ways to obtain information about its software products. The Microsoft Web site (www.microsoft.com) contains helpful information about Microsoft products. Products include operating systems (Windows 95, Windows 98, Windows 2000, and Windows XP), application software (Office, Word, Excel, Access, PowerPoint, NetMeeting, Encarta, and Outlook Express), and an online service (MSN). Using any two operating systems, any four application programs, and the online service just mentioned, write a brief report summarizing each product's function. Write a single paragraph about each product.

6 ▶▶▶ Choosing an operating system is an important decision for most businesses. Locate three local businesses: one that uses Windows 98, one that uses Windows 2000, and one that uses Windows XP. Interview a person at each business about their operating system. Based on your interviews, write a brief report on why each business chose that operating system, how satisfied they are with it, and under what circumstances they might consider switching to a different operating system.

7 ▶▶▶ Registering for classes can be a daunting task for incoming college freshmen. As someone who has gone through the process, prepare a guide for students who are about to register for the first time next semester. Your guide should be two or more documents, include a calendar or schedule of key dates and times, a description of the registration procedure, and suggestions for how students can make registration easier. Give the documents suitable names and save them in a folder on the Windows XP desktop. Print each document.

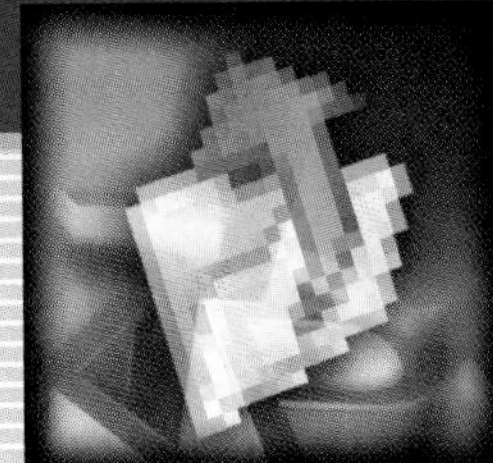

Microsoft Windows XP

PROJECT 3

File, Document, and Folder Management and Windows XP Explorer

OBJECTIVES

You will have mastered the material in this project when you can:

- Display icons in various views in a window
- View the contents of a drive and folder
- Open a document and application program from a window
- Cascade and tile open windows on the desktop
- Copy, move, and delete files from open windows
- Launch Windows XP Explorer
- Expand drives and folders in Explorer
- Display files and folders in Explorer
- Display the contents of drives and folders in Explorer
- Launch an application program from Explorer
- Close folder expansions
- Copy, rename, and delete files in Explorer
- Close Explorer
- Display drive and folder properties
- View bitmap images in a filmstrip and as a slide show
- E-mail files and share folders
- Find files and folders using Search on the Start menu
- Use the Run command

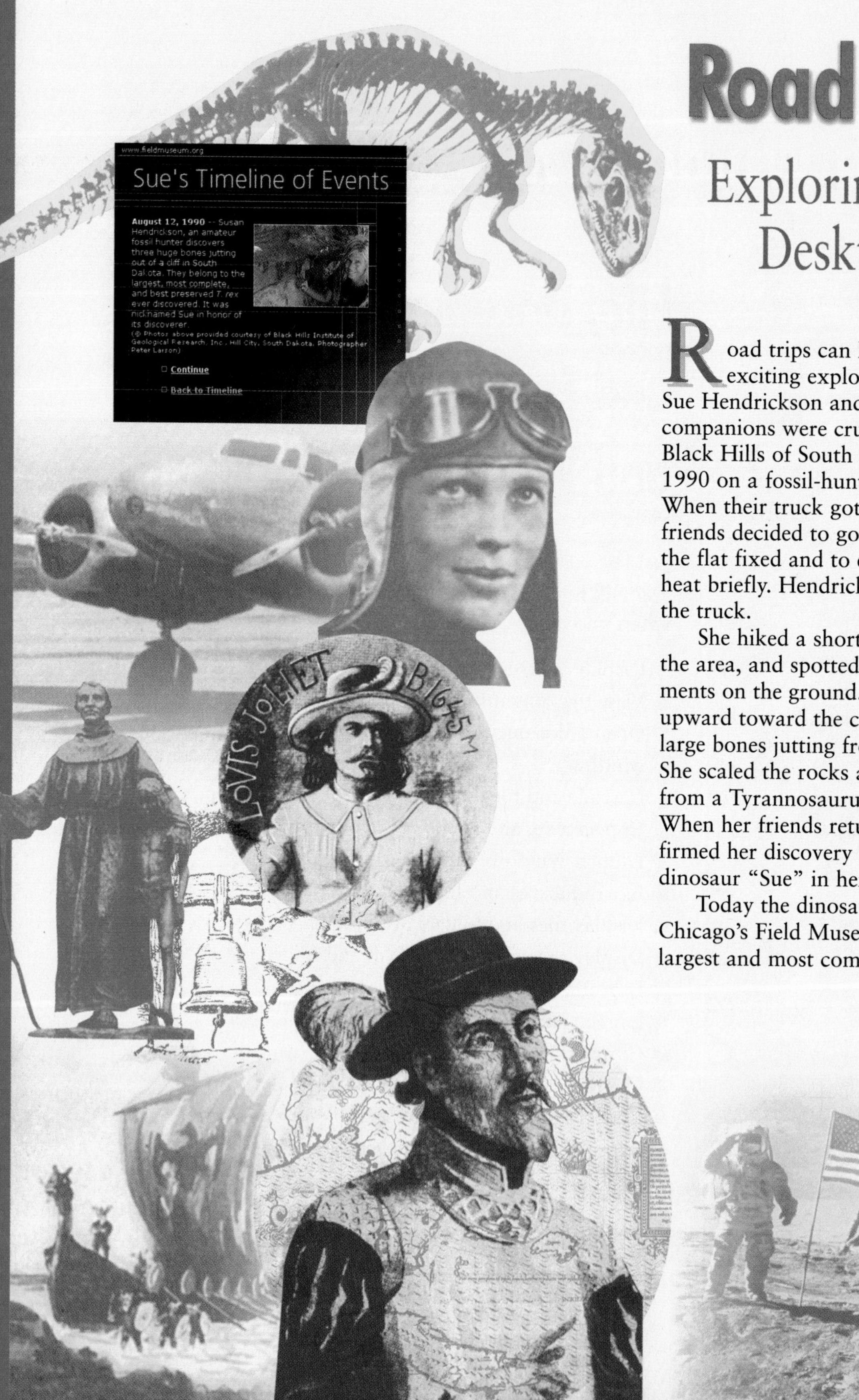
www.fieldmuseum.org
Sue's Timeline of Events
August 12, 1990 -- Susan Hendrickson, an amateur fossil hunter discovers three huge bones jutting out of a cliff in South Dakota. They belong to the largest, most complete, and best preserved T. rex ever discovered. It was nicknamed Sue in honor of its discoverer.
(© Photos above provided courtesy of Black Hills Institute of Geological Research, Inc., Hill City, South Dakota. Photographer Peter Larson)
Continue
Back to Timeline
LOVIS JOLIET B1645M

Road Trip

Exploring the Desktop

Road trips can lead to some exciting explorations. Scientist Sue Hendrickson and her traveling companions were cruising through the Black Hills of South Dakota in August 1990 on a fossil-hunting expedition. When their truck got a flat tire, her friends decided to go into town to get the flat fixed and to escape the summer heat briefly. Hendrickson stayed with the truck.

She hiked a short distance, scanned the area, and spotted some bone fragments on the ground. Then, she gazed upward toward the cliffs and located large bones jutting from the cliff walls. She scaled the rocks and saw the bones from a Tyrannosaurus rex dinosaur. When her friends returned, they confirmed her discovery and named the dinosaur "Sue" in her honor.

Today the dinosaur, Sue, resides in Chicago's Field Museum. She is the largest and most complete preserved

T. rex ever found. The more than 200 fossilized bones in the skeleton stand 13 feet high and 42 feet long. Scientists estimate that Sue weighed seven tons when alive and that she could eat 500 pounds of meat and bones in one bite.

Hendrickson joins the ranks of great explorers throughout the world. After Christopher Columbus's return to Spain from the famous 1492 voyage across the Atlantic, other European explorers began navigating to North America. These great adventurers from Portugal, Spain, Italy, France, and England ventured farther with each voyage. In 1497, John Cabot explored the coasts of Labrador, Newfoundland, and New England. Juan Ponce de León discovered Florida and part of the Yucatán Peninsula in the early 1500s. Hernán Cortés invaded Mexico in 1519 and then conquered the Aztecs.

Every age has produced explorers with an insatiable thirst for knowing what lies over the next hill: Sir Edmund Hillary, Junípero Serra, Louis Joliet, Amelia Earhart, Vasco Nuñez de Balboa, Sir Walter Raleigh, and Leif Ericsson. In the latter half of the twentieth century, Neil Armstrong and Buzz Aldrin led the way to the moon, Jacques Cousteau explored the wonders beneath the sea, and Robert Ballard discovered the resting place of the Titanic.

The increasing power and versatility of modern personal computers have given people the means to embark on these and other grand individual adventures. In this project, you will examine files, documents, and folders on your computer in a variety of ways. The application program provided with the operating system, Windows XP Explorer, and the My Computer window offer two major ways for you to work with files and documents. They allow you to view hardware components on the computer and computer resources on a network, as well as search for computers on a network and map and access network drives.

As a desktop explorer of the twenty-first century, you have the tools to navigate computer and network resources at the click of a mouse button using the best of the Windows operating systems developed to date. Fasten your seat belt and get ready to embark on an exciting road trip using Windows XP Explorer and the My Computer window.

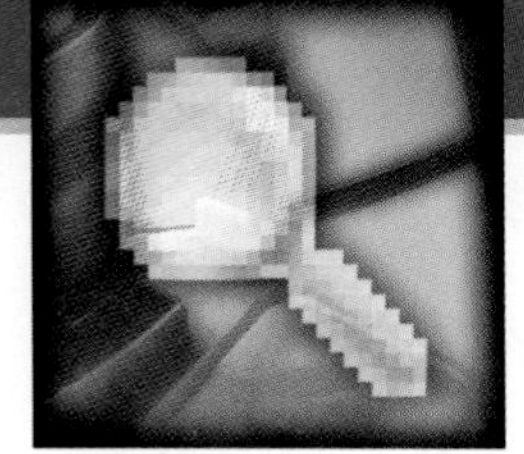

Microsoft Windows XP

File, Document, and Folder Management and Windows XP Explorer

PROJECT

CASE PERSPECTIVE

Your organization has decided to upgrade the operating system on each computer in the office to Windows XP Professional. The new computer administrator believes that to use Windows XP effectively, users must be able to control and manage windows on the Windows XP desktop and to locate files on the computer. An understanding of these skills will be critical for the successful implementation of Windows XP. Everyone is excited about the change, but those who have little computer experience are apprehensive about the new operating system. Your boss asks you to teach a class that emphasizes managing windows, using Windows XP Explorer, and working with files and folders for employees who are not experienced Windows users. Your goal in this project is to become competent using these features of Windows XP so that you can teach the class.

Introduction

In Project 2, you used Windows XP to create documents on the desktop and work with documents and folders in the My Documents folder. Windows XP also allows you to examine the files and folders on the computer in a variety of other ways, enabling you to use the easiest and most accessible manner while working on the computer. The My Computer window and Windows XP Explorer, which is an application program provided with Windows XP, are two major ways for you to work with files and documents. In addition, the My Pictures window allows you to organize and share picture files, e-mail picture files, and view picture files in filmstrip view and as a slideshow. This project will illustrate how to accomplish tasks using these tools as supplied by Windows XP.

My Computer Window

As noted in previous projects, the My Computer command displays on the Start menu. Selecting the **My Computer command** displays a window that contains all the hardware components on the computer (i.e., disk drives, CD-ROM drives, and DVD drives) and two document folders (Shared Documents and Brad Wilson's Documents). To open and maximize the My Computer window and view the components of the computer, complete the following steps.

Steps To Open and Maximize the My Computer Window

1 Click the Start button. Point to My Computer on the Start menu.

The Start Menu displays and the My Computer command displays on the Start menu (Figure 3-1).

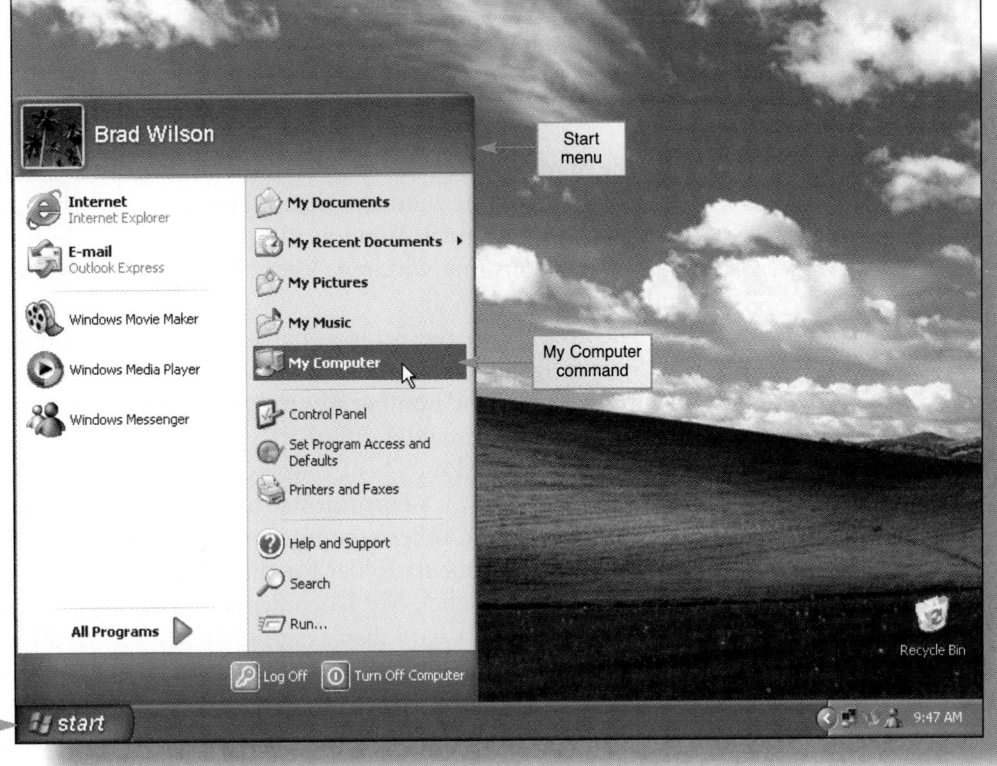

FIGURE 3-1

2 **Click My Computer. Click the Maximize button in the My Computer window.**

Windows XP opens and maximizes the My Computer window (Figure 3-2).

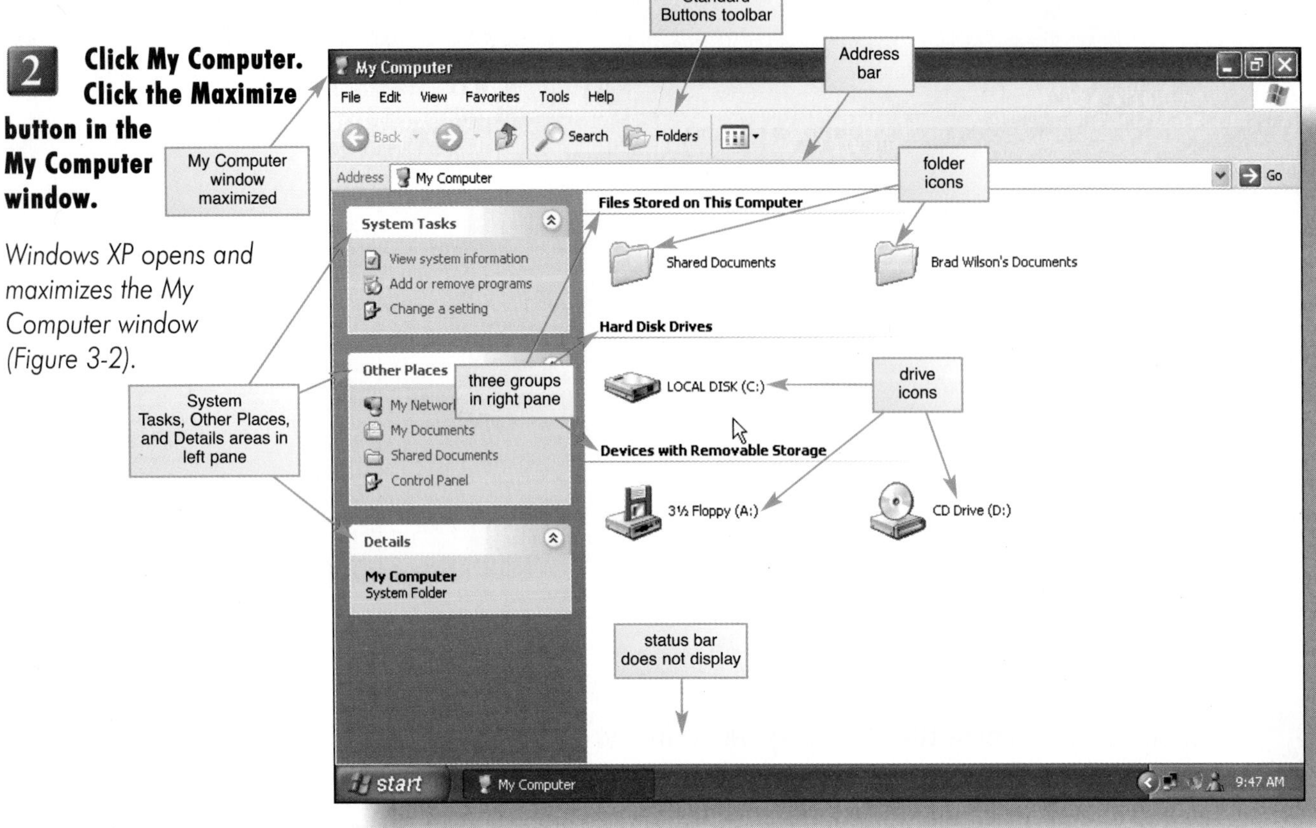

FIGURE 3-2

Other Ways

1. Click Start button, right-click My Computer command, click Open
2. Press WINDOWS+E (WINDOWS key on Microsoft Natural keyboard)

The Standard Buttons toolbar shown in Figure 3-2 contains buttons you can use to navigate between windows (Back, Forward, and Up), search for files and folders (Search button), launch Windows Explorer (Folders button), and change the appearance of the icons in a window (Views button). The Address bar displays below the Standard Buttons toolbar.

The area below the Address bar is divided into two panes. The **left pane** contains the System Tasks, Other Places, and Details areas. The **right pane** contains three groups of icons. The number of groups in the right pane and the icons in the groups on your computer may be different.

The Files Stored on This Computer group contains the Shared Documents folder icon and Brad Wilson's Documents folder icon. The **Shared Documents folder** allows sharing folders with other computer users. The **Brad Wilson's Documents folder** is the personal My Documents folder for the computer user, Brad Wilson. This folder also displays when you click My Documents on the Start menu. Double-clicking the Brad Wilson's Documents icon displays the My Music, My Pictures, and My Videos folders for Brad Wilson. The Brad Wilson's Documents folder may not display on your computer.

The Hard Disk Drives group contains the **LOCAL DISK (C:) icon** that represents the hard disk on the computer. The **hard disk** is where you can store files, documents, and folders. Storing data on a hard disk often is more convenient than storing it on a floppy disk in drive A because using a hard disk is faster, and generally more storage room is available on the hard disk. A computer always will have at least one hard disk drive, normally designated as drive C. On the computer represented by the My Computer window in Figure 3-2, the icon consists of an image of a hard disk and a **disk label**, or title, LOCAL DISK (C:). The label is not required.

The Devices with Removable Storage group contains the 3½ Floppy (A:) and CD Drive (D:) icons. The **3½ Floppy (A:) icon** represents a floppy disk drive and consists of an image of a floppy disk on top of a floppy disk drive. The label for this drive is 3½ Floppy (A:).

The **CD Drive (D:) icon** represents a CD-ROM drive and the label for the drive is CD Drive (D:). The icon consists of an image of a CD-ROM disc on top of an image of a CD-ROM drive because the drive does not currently contain a CD-ROM. If you insert a CD-ROM in the drive, such as an **audio CD** containing music, Windows XP displays a cross and musical note on top of an image of a CD-ROM disc and changes the label to contain the artist's name.

Icons

In many cases, you may not recognize a particular icon because hundreds of icons are developed by software vendors to represent their products. Each icon is supposed to be unique and eye-catching. You can purchase thousands of icons on CD-ROM that you can use to represent documents you create.

The Status Bar

The **status bar** displays at the bottom of the window and contains information about the documents, folders, and programs in a window. The default option for displaying the status bar prevents the status bar from displaying in the My Computer window in Figure 3-2 and other windows. Perform the following steps to display the status bar and view information about the contents of the My Computer window.

Steps To Display the Status Bar in a Window

1 Click View on the menu bar and then point to Status Bar.

The highlighted Status Bar command displays on the View menu (Figure 3-3).

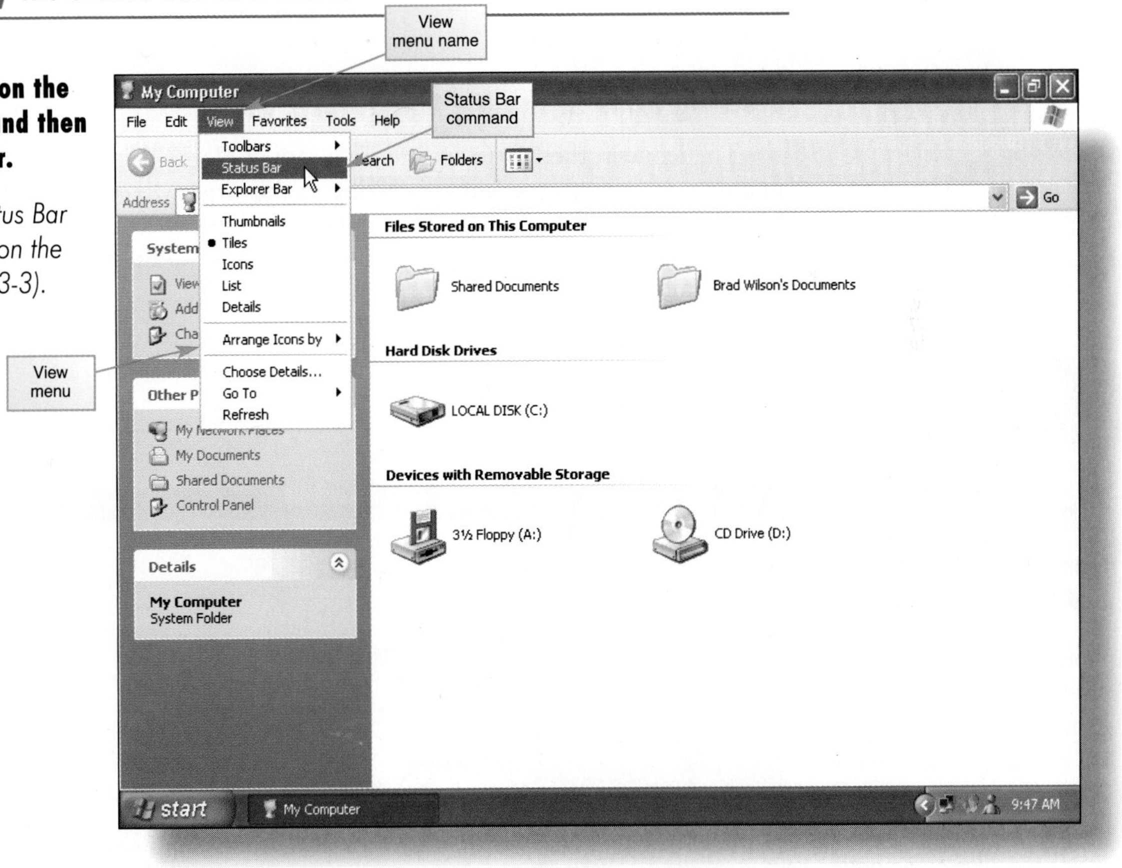

View menu name

Status Bar command

View menu

FIGURE 3-3

2 Click Status Bar.

The status bar at the bottom of the My Computer window indicates the right pane contains five objects (Figure 3-4). The My Computer icon and window title display at the right side of the status bar.

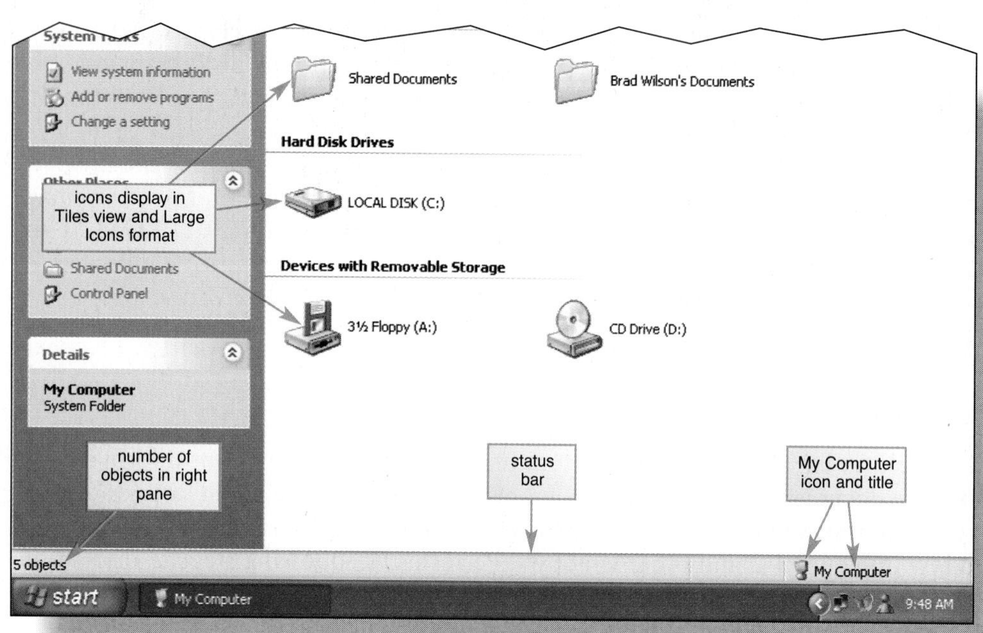

FIGURE 3-4

Viewing Icons in the My Computer Window

The icons in the My Computer window in Figure 3-4 display in Tiles view and in a format called **Large Icons**, referring to the large size of icons. Other formats, however, are available to display the icons in the My Computer window. Complete the following steps to display the icons in the My Computer window in Icons, List, and Details view.

Steps To Change the Format of the Icons in a Window

1 Click the Views button on the Standard Buttons toolbar and then point to Icons.

Windows XP opens the Views button menu containing the Thumbnails, Tiles, Icons, List, and Details commands (Figure 3-5). A bullet precedes the Tiles command to indicate the icons in the right pane display in Tiles view.

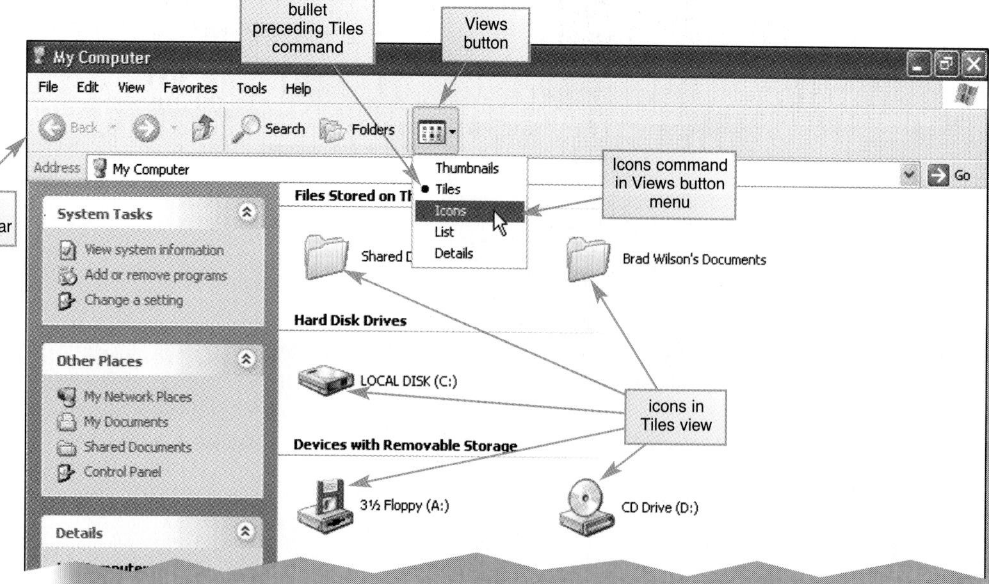

FIGURE 3-5

2 Click Icons.

The icons display in Icons view using the ***Medium Icons*** *format (Figure 3-6). The* ***Icons view*** *displays the icon titles below the icons. The icons remain in groups based upon file type.*

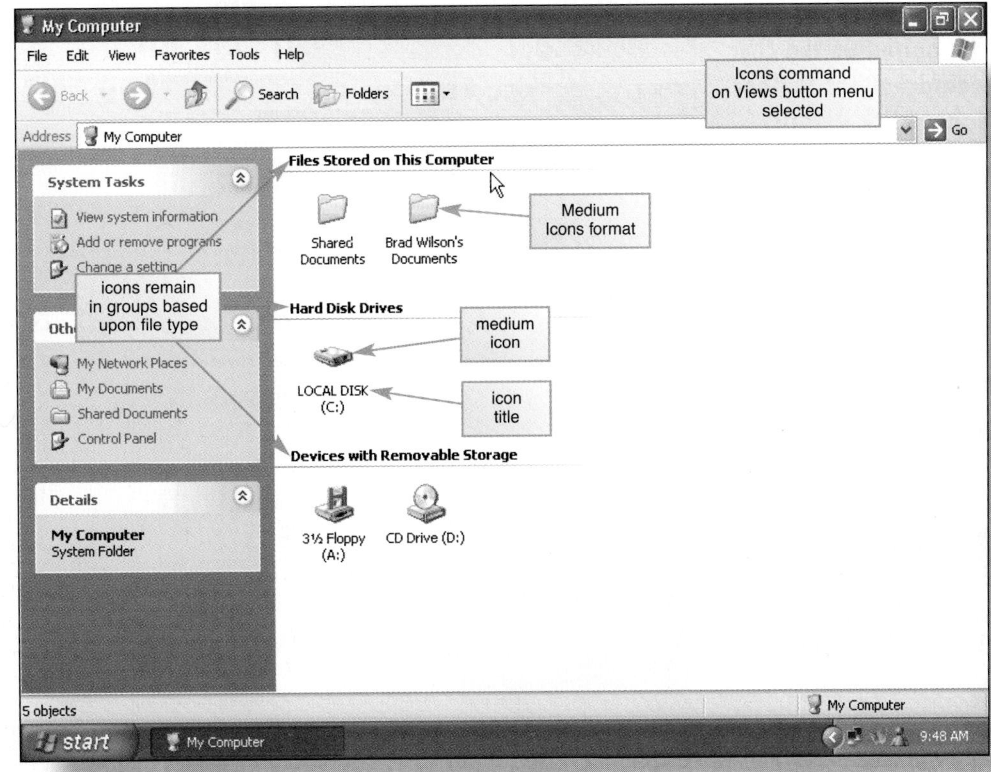

FIGURE 3-6

3 Click the Views button on the Standard Buttons toolbar and then click List.

The icons display in List view using the ***Small Icons format*** *(Figure 3-7). The* ***List view*** *places the drive and folder icons in a list. The icons display in order by file name and are no longer arranged in groups.*

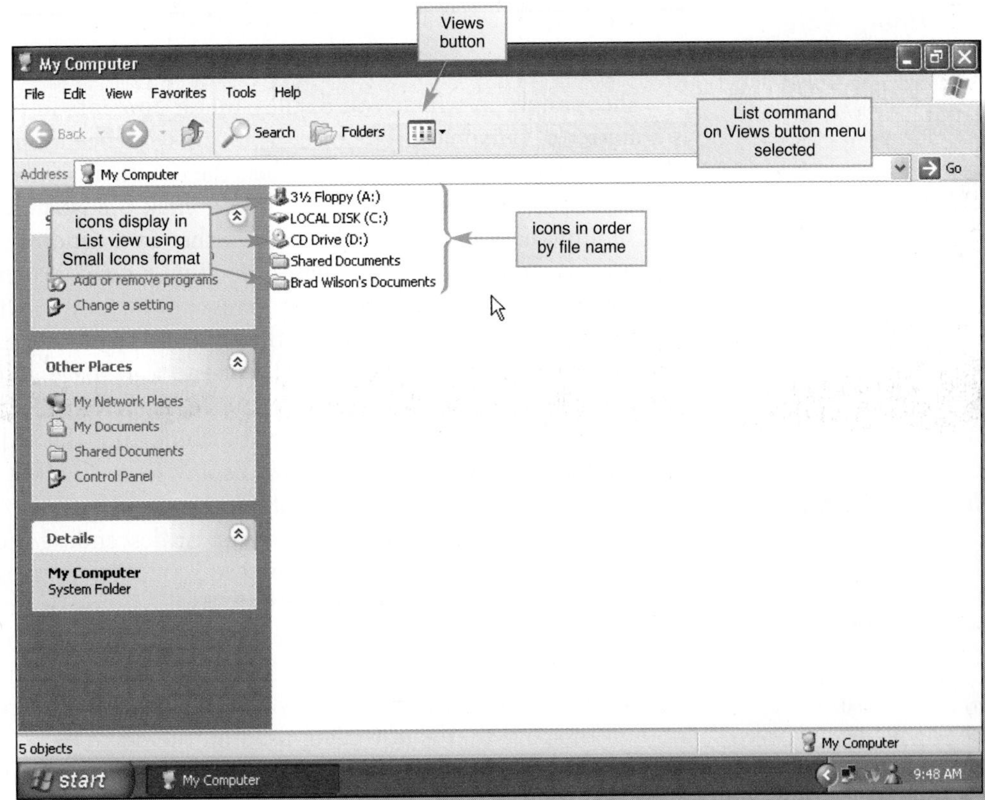

FIGURE 3-7

4 **Click the Views button on the Standard Buttons toolbar and then click Details.**

The icons display in a list in Details view using the Small Icons format (Figure 3-8). The ***Details view*** *provides detailed information about each drive or folder. The icons display in groups based on file type.*

5 **Click the Views button on the Standard Buttons toolbar and then click Tiles.**

The icons in the My Computer window return to Tiles view using the Large Icons format.

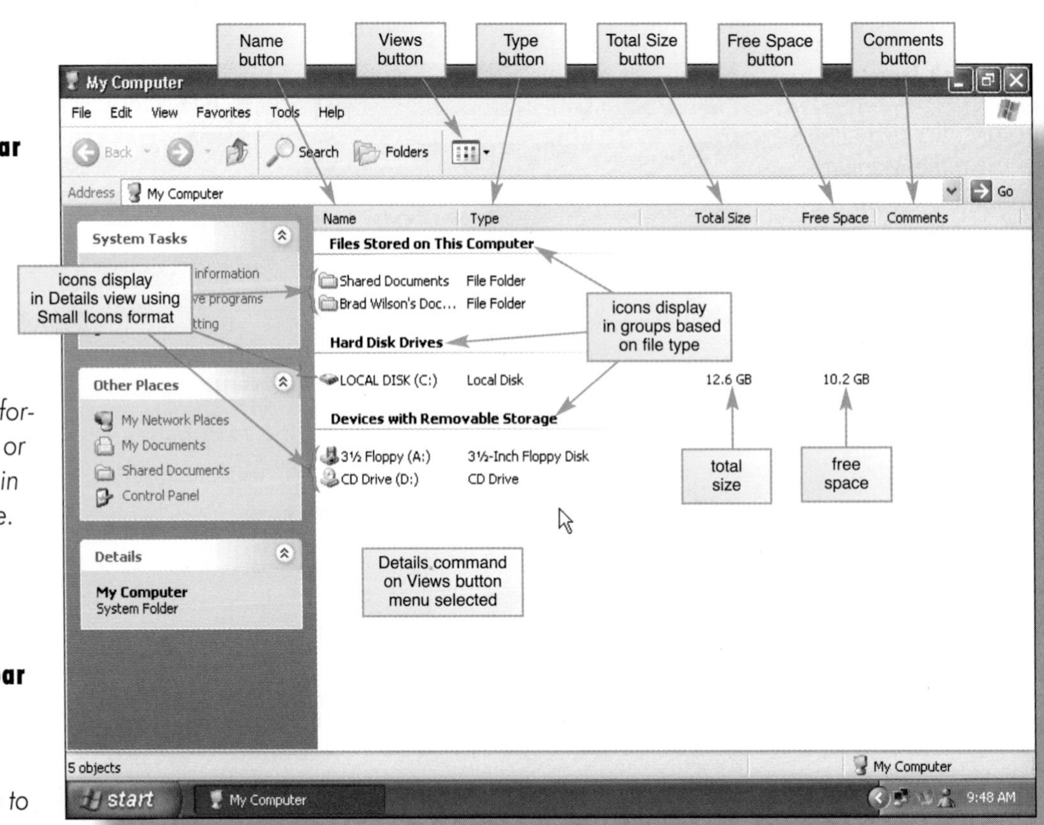

FIGURE 3-8

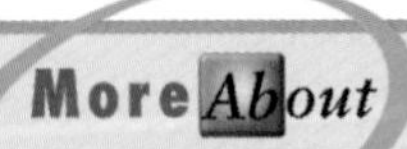

Other Ways

1. Right-click open area in My Computer window, point to View, click icon format
2. On View menu click icon format
3. Press ALT+V, select icon format

More About

Viewing Icons

You can display icons in most windows in Thumbnails view, Tiles view, Icons view, List view, or Details view. Filmstrip view is available in the My Pictures window. You can view pictures as a slide presentation in the My Pictures window, any subfolder in the My Pictures window, or any folder customized as a pictures folder.

The manner in which you display folder contents in the My Computer window is a matter of personal preference. You can sequence the icons shown in the My Computer window in Figure 3-8 when the detailed information displays by using the buttons below the Address bar. If you click the **Name button**, the items will display in alphabetical sequence by name either in ascending or descending sequence. If you click the Name button again, the alphabetical sequence reverses.

If you click the **Type button**, the items will display in alphabetical sequence by type. Although only one entry has the total size and free space values displayed, you also can sequence the icons by total size and free space. Clicking the **Total Size button** causes the items to display in size sequence, from smallest to largest or from largest to smallest. By clicking the Total Size button again, the sequence reverses. Clicking the **Free Space button** causes items to display from smallest to largest based on free space. If you click the **Comments button**, the items will display in alphabetical sequence by comment either in ascending or descending sequence. If you click the Comments button again, the alphabetical sequence reverses.

In Figure 3-8, the Type column tells you the type of object used for each icon. The first two objects are File Folder types. The last three objects are storage media (Local Disk, 3½-Inch Floppy Disk, and CD Drive, respectively). The Total Size column states the size of the Local Disk (12.6 GB) and the Free Space column states the amount of space that is not being used on the disk (10.2 GB). The values for the total size and free space may be different on your computer.

The Windows XP default setting for viewing the icons is the Tiles view. When you close a window, Windows XP remembers the format of the icons in the window and uses that format to display the icons the next time you open the window.

For example, if you close the My Computer window displaying in the Details view as shown in Figure 3-8 and then open the window again, the icons in the window will still display in Details view.

Viewing the Contents of Drives and Folders

In addition to viewing the contents of My Computer, you can view the contents of drives and folders. In previous projects, you have seen both windows for folders and windows for drives. In fact, the contents of any folder or drive on a computer can display in a window.

The default option for opening drive and folder windows, called the **Open each folder in the same window option**, uses the active window to display the contents of a newly opened drive or folder. Because only one window displays on the desktop at a time, this option eliminates the clutter of multiple windows on the desktop. To illustrate the Open each folder in the same window option and view the contents of drive C, complete the following step.

Steps To View the Contents of a Drive

1 Double-click the LOCAL DISK (C:) icon in the My Computer window. If the right pane of the LOCAL DISK (C:) window contains messages indicating the contents of the folder are hidden and should not be modified, click the Show the contents of this folder link.

The maximized LOCAL DISK (C:) window opens in the same window as My Computer was displayed and the LOCAL DISK (C:) button replaces the My Computer button on the taskbar (Figure 3-9). The files and folders in the LOCAL DISK (C:) folder display in Tiles view in the right pane, the contents of the left pane change, and the status bar indicates 21 objects plus 8 hidden objects occupy 328 kilobytes.

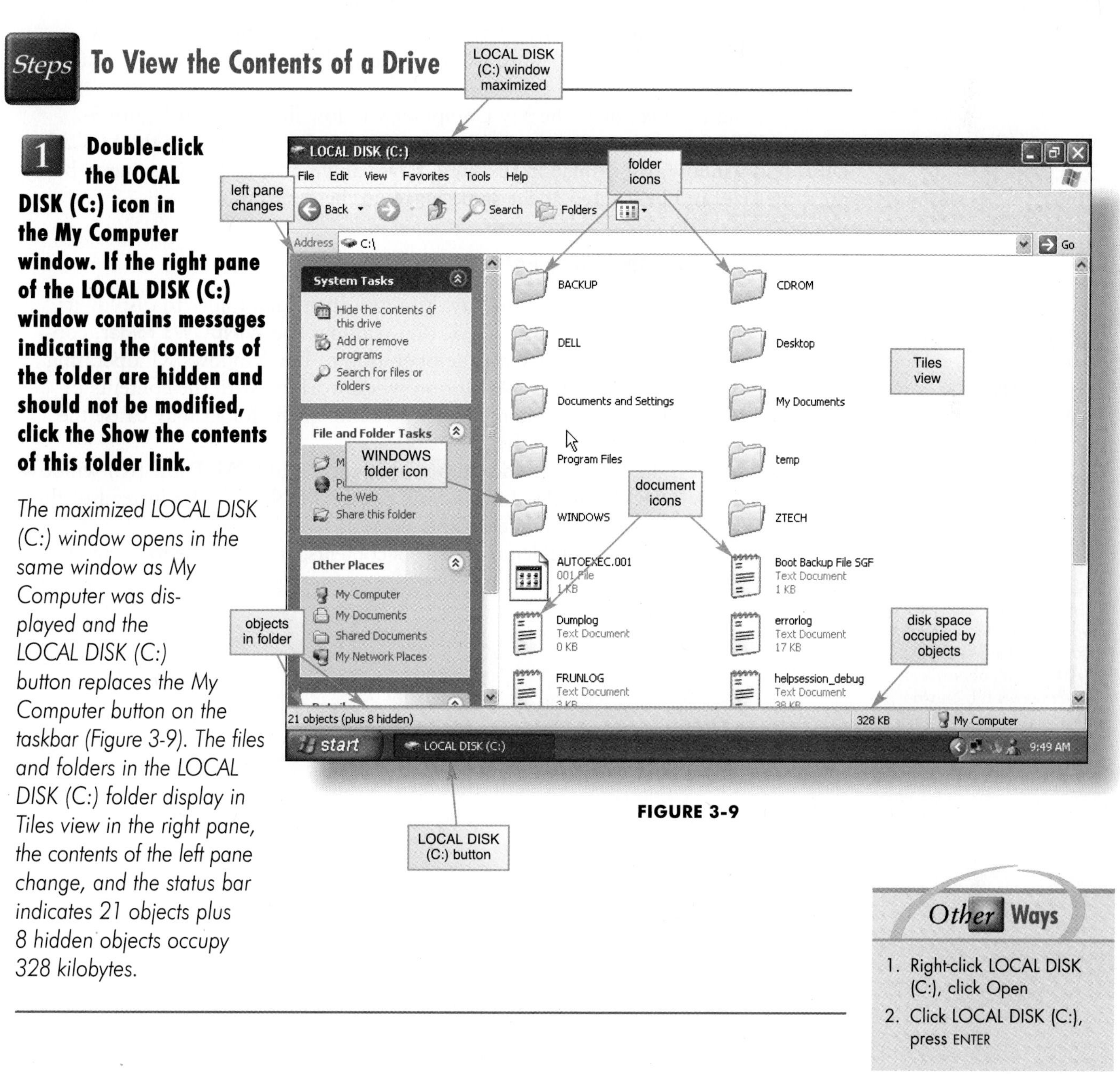

FIGURE 3-9

Other Ways

1. Right-click LOCAL DISK (C:), click Open
2. Click LOCAL DISK (C:), press ENTER

A yellow folder icon represents each folder in the LOCAL DISK (C:) window. Application programs and documents are represented by icons unique to the application program or to the documents the application program opens.

The contents of the LOCAL DISK (C:) window you display on your computer can differ from the contents shown in Figure 3-9 on the previous page because each computer has its own folders, application programs, and documents. The manner in which you interact with and control the programs and documents in Windows XP is the same, however, regardless of the actual programs or documents.

The status bar in Figure 3-9 contains information about the folders, programs, and documents displaying in the window. Twenty-one objects (folders, programs, and documents) and eight hidden files display in the window. Storing a file as a **hidden file**, meaning the name of the file does not display when you use My Computer or Windows Explorer and cannot be found using the Search command, prevents the file from being deleted accidentally.

More About

Hidden Files

The status bar may or may not indicate a folder contains a hidden file. Hidden files usually are placed on your hard disk by software vendors such as Microsoft and often are critical to the operation of the software. Rarely will you designate a file as hidden. You should almost never delete a hidden file.

The designation, 328 KB, on the status bar indicates the objects in the window consume 328 kilobytes of memory on the hard drive. This number does not include the contents of any of the folders displayed in Figure 3-9. Recall from Figure 3-8 on page WIN 3.10 that the entire drive C, which is 12.6 gigabytes in size, has 10.2 gigabytes free. Therefore, more storage space is being used on drive C than 328 kilobytes.

If you did not maximize the My Computer window illustrated in Figure 3-2 on page WIN 3.06 before double-clicking the LOCAL DISK (C:) icon, the LOCAL DISK (C:) window will display in the same physical window as My Computer, be the same size, and be located at the same place on the desktop.

Viewing the Contents of a Folder

In Figure 3-9, 10 folder icons display. You can open each folder to display its contents. One folder in the LOCAL DISK (C:) window, the **WINDOWS folder**, contains programs and files necessary for the operation of the Windows XP operating system. As such, you should exercise caution when working with the contents of the WINDOWS folder because changing the contents of the folder may cause the programs to stop working correctly.

The WINDOWS Folder

The WINDOWS folder displays in the LOCAL DISK (C:) window if the computer was upgraded to Windows XP from Windows 98 or Windows ME. The WINNT folder displays if the computer was upgraded to Windows XP from Windows 2000. WINNT is an abbreviation for Windows NT, an older operating system designed for business networks.

In some cases, the WINNT folder may display in the LOCAL DISK (C:) window instead of the WINDOWS folder. In this case, use the WINNT folder instead of the WINDOWS folder for the remainder of this project.

To open the WINDOWS folder and view its contents, complete the following steps.

Steps To View the Contents of a Folder

1 Point to the WINDOWS icon in the My Computer window (Figure 3-10).

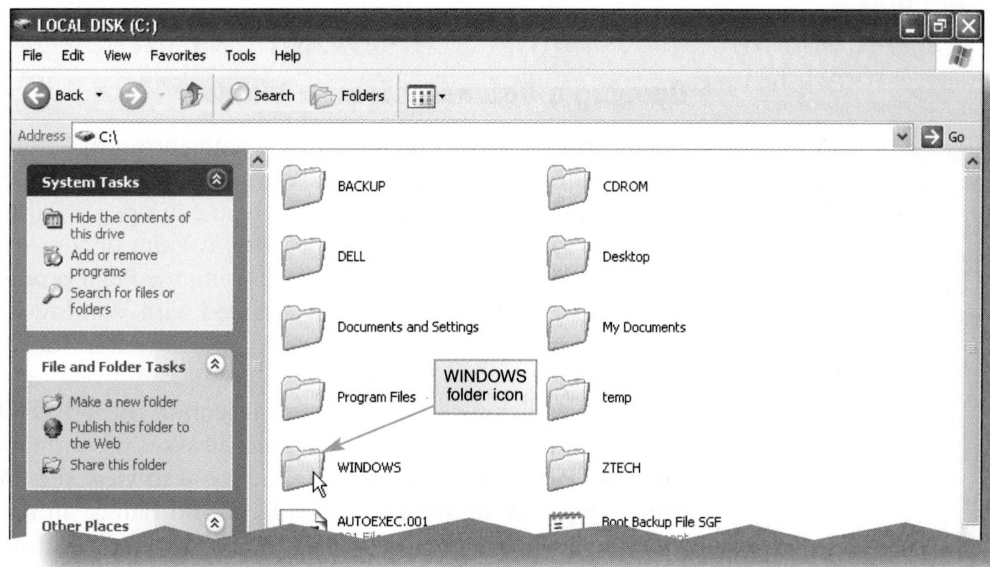

FIGURE 3-10

2 Double-click the WINDOWS icon. If the right pane of the WINDOWS window contains messages indicating the contents of the folder are hidden and should not be modified, click the Show the contents of this folder link.

The maximized WINDOWS window opens in the same window as LOCAL DISK (C:) was displayed and the WINDOWS button replaces the LOCAL DISK (C:) button on the taskbar (Figure 3-11). The contents of the Other Places area in the left pane change (see Figure 3-9 on page WIN 3.11). The files and folders in the WINDOWS folder display in Icons view in the right pane and the status bar indicates 115 objects and 2 hidden objects consume 6.35 megabytes of storage.

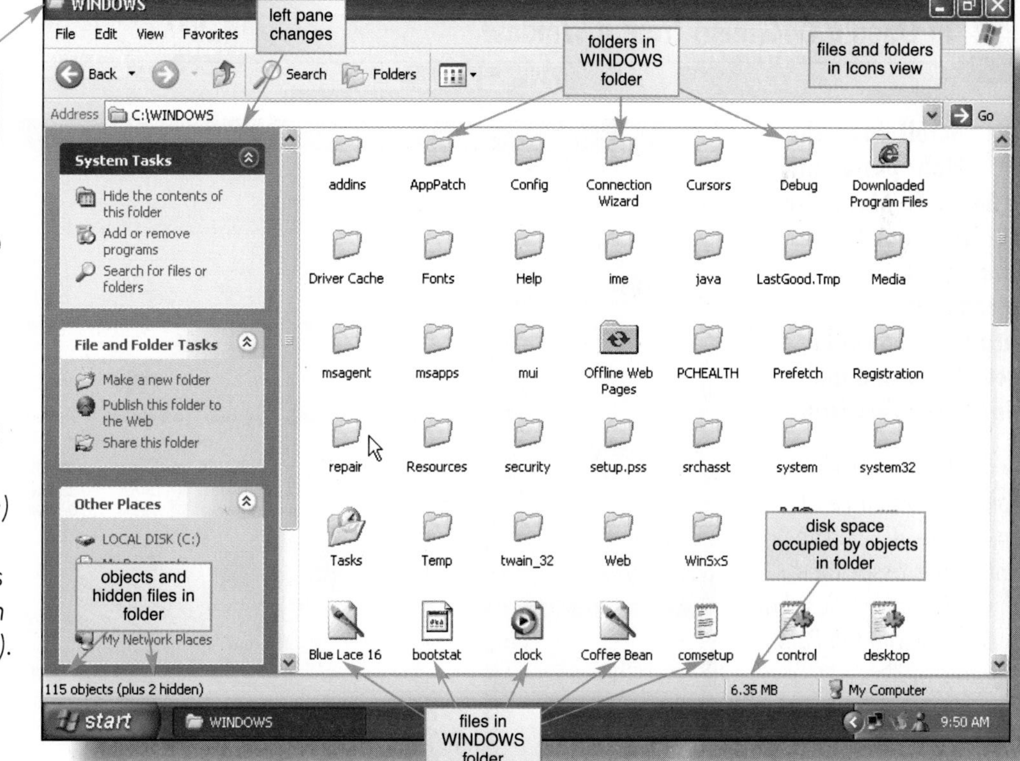

FIGURE 3-11

Other Ways

1. Right-click WINDOWS icon, click Open
2. Click WINDOWS icon, press ENTER

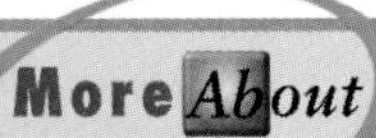

The Paint Program

An image with color usually has more impact than one without color. The Paint program allows you to create black and white or color images. To learn about the Paint program, click the Start button, point to All Programs, point to Accessories, and click Paint. Click Help on the untitled - Paint menu bar and click Help topics.

The majority of objects shown in Figure 3-11 on the previous page are folder icons. As you can see, folder icons always display first in the window. As with every window you will see in the steps illustrated in this book, the contents of the windows on your computer may be different.

Opening a Document from a Window

In Project 2, you created a text document on the desktop and then opened the document by double-clicking the document icon on the desktop. In addition to opening a text document on the desktop, you can open a Paint document located in a folder by following a similar procedure. A Paint document contains a graphics image, called a **bitmap image**, and is created using the **Paint program** (called MSPAINT), which is an application program supplied with Windows XP. Several Paint documents are included with Windows XP and stored in the WINDOWS folder on the hard drive.

Double-clicking a Paint document icon in the WINDOWS folder opens the Windows Picture and Fax Viewer and displays the bitmap image in the viewer. The **Windows Picture and Fax Viewer** allows you to view the image in the document, view other images in the same folder, enlarge and reduce an image, rotate and print an image, copy and delete an image, and display a slide show of images. To open the document containing the Santa Fe Stucco image and view the Santa Fe Stucco image using the Windows Picture and Fax Viewer, complete the following steps.

Steps To Open a Document from a Window

1 Scroll down the right pane until the Santa Fe Stucco icon displays. Point to the Santa Fe Stucco icon. If the computer does not contain the Santa Fe Stucco icon, find and point to another icon.

The right pane scrolls to display the Santa Fe Stucco icon (Figure 3-12). The Paint icon *is associated with all document files that are created with the Paint program.*

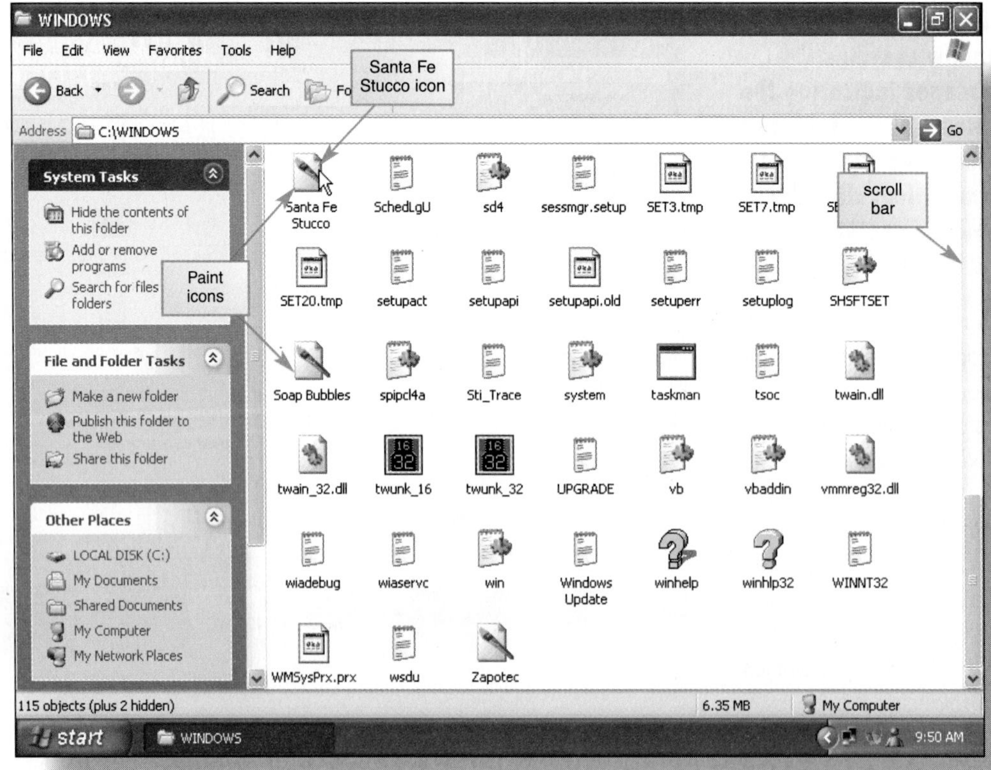

FIGURE 3-12

2 Double-click the Santa Fe Stucco icon. If the Santa Fe Stucco - Windows Picture and Fax Viewer window is maximized, click the Restore Down button and then size the window to the size shown in Figure 3-13.

Windows XP launches the Windows Picture and Fax Viewer. The Santa Fe Stucco - Windows Picture and Fax Viewer window displays on top of the WINDOWS window and the recessed Santa Fe Stucco - Windows Picture and Fax Viewer button displays in the taskbar button area (Figure 3-13). The status bar contains the image dimensions (256 × 256), file type (Bitmap Image), and file size (64.2 KB) of the Santa Fe Stucco image.

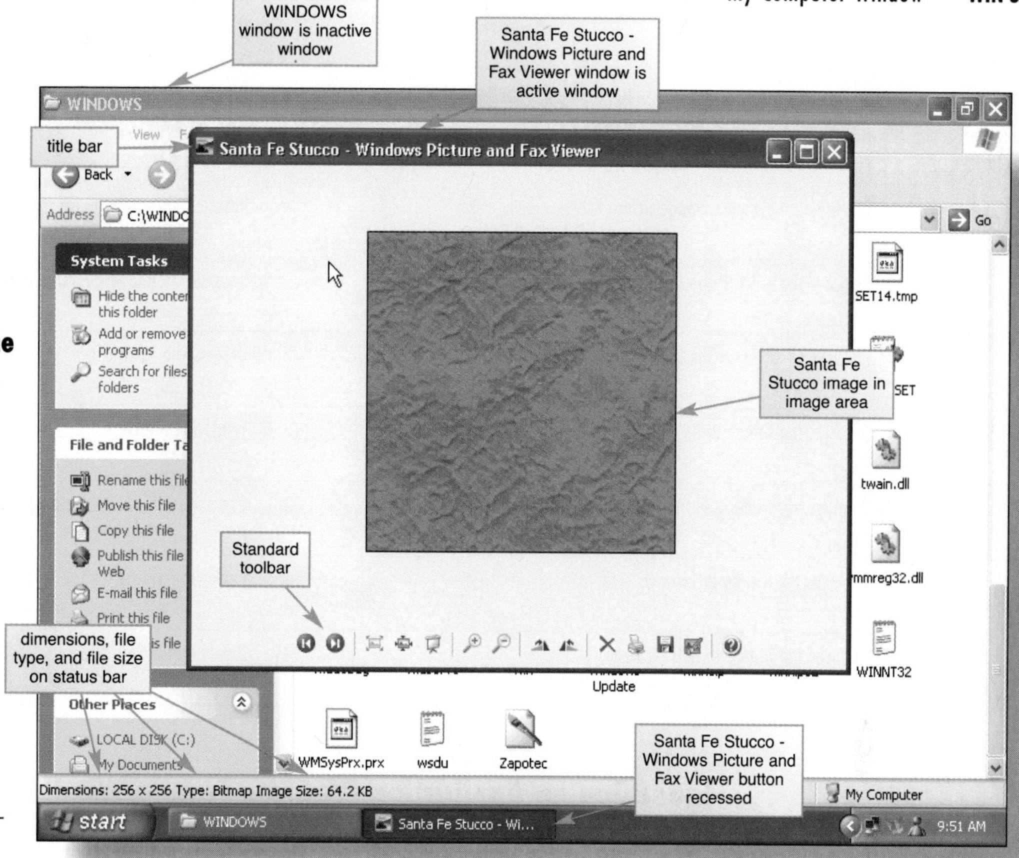

FIGURE 3-13

Other Ways

1. Right-click icon, point to Open With, click Windows Picture and Fax Viewer
2. Click document icon, press ENTER

The Santa Fe Stucco - Windows Picture and Fax Viewer window shown in Figure 3-13 displays on top of the WINDOWS window and is the active window. The WINDOWS window is the inactive window. Currently, a document window and an application window are open on the desktop. The Santa Fe Stucco - Windows Picture and Fax Viewer consists of a title bar, an image area, and the Standard toolbar. The Santa Fe Stucco image displays in the image area.

The **Standard toolbar** allows you to perform a variety of operations on the image in the viewer. Each button on the Standard toolbar contains an icon. Table 3-1 on the next page illustrates the Standard toolbar and briefly describes the function of each button.

More About

Windows Picture and Fax Viewer

You can elect to display Paint documents in either Windows Picture and Fax Viewer or the Paint program. To view a bitmap image using the Paint program, right-click its icon, point to Open With on the shortcut menu, and then click Paint.

Table 3-1 Standard Toolbar

BUTTON	FUNCTION	BUTTON	FUNCTION
	Displays the previous image in the folder.		Rotates the image by 90 degrees clockwise.
	Displays the next image in the folder.		Rotates the image by 90 degrees counter-clockwise.
	Reduces or enlarges the image to fit into the window's current size.		Deletes the image.
	Displays the image in its actual size.		Prints the image.
	Displays each image in the folder in a slide show.		Copies the image to another location.
	Enlarges the image to twice its size.		Closes the viewer and allows editing of the image in Paint program.
	Reduces the image to half its size.		Displays the Help file.

Launching an Application Program from a Window

In addition to opening a document from a window, you also can launch an application program from a window. To launch the Notepad application program, complete the following steps.

Steps To Launch an Application Program from a Window

1 Click the WINDOWS button in the taskbar button area. Scroll until the notepad icon displays in the window. Point to the notepad icon.

The active WINDOWS window displays on top of the Santa Fe Stucco - Windows Picture and Fax Viewer window and its button is recessed in the taskbar button area (Figure 3-14). The notepad icon displays in the right pane.

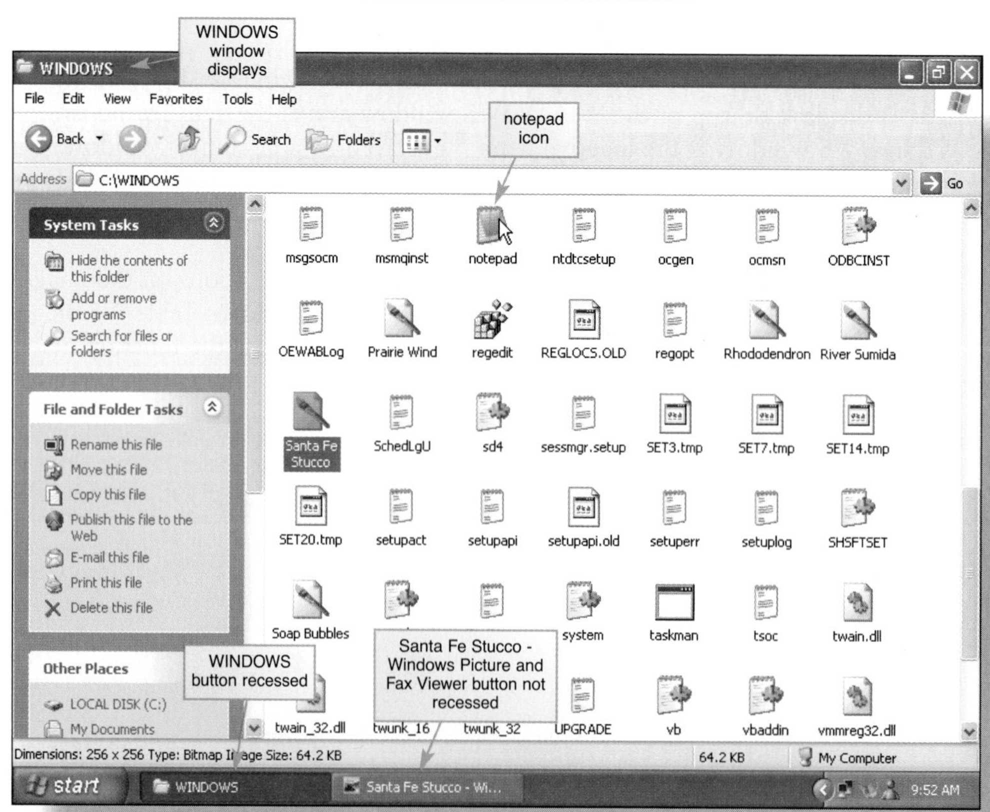

FIGURE 3-14

2 Double-click the notepad icon.

Windows XP launches the Notepad application program (Figure 3-15). The Untitled - Notepad button in the taskbar button area is recessed, indicating the window is active. Three windows now are open on the desktop. Although the Santa Fe Stucco - Windows Picture and Fax Viewer window is not visible on the desktop, its button displays in the taskbar button area.

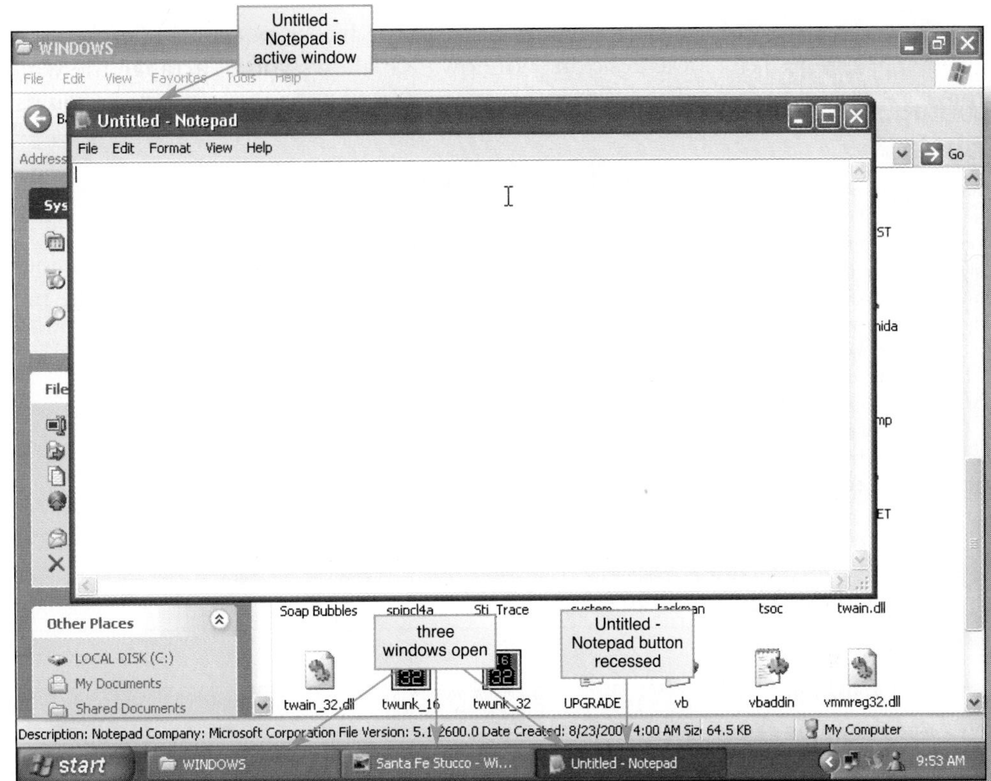

FIGURE 3-15

As shown in Figure 3-15, whenever you click a button for an open window in the taskbar button area, the window displays and becomes the active window. Windows XP also provides another method to switch between windows. If you hold down the ALT key and then press the TAB key, a box showing an icon for each open window displays on the screen, together with the name of the open window. If you continue to hold down the ALT key, each time you press the TAB key, the name of the next open window will display and the associated icon in the box will be highlighted by a colored square. When you release the TAB key, the window associated with the highlighted icon will become the active window.

In this section, you have opened the My Computer window, the LOCAL DISK (C:) window, a folder window (WINDOWS), a document window (Santa Fe Stucco - Windows Picture and Fax Viewer), and an application program window (Untitled - Notepad).

Other Ways

1. Click WINDOWS button on taskbar or press ALT+TAB until WINDOWS displays in box on screen, right-click notepad icon, click Open
2. Click WINDOWS button on taskbar or press ALT+TAB until WINDOWS displays in box on screen, click notepad icon, press ENTER

Managing Open Windows

In Figure 3-15, three windows are open. Windows XP allows you to open many more windows, depending on the amount of RAM you have on the computer. As you can see in Figure 3-15, however, many open windows on the desktop can cause clutter and become difficult to use. Therefore, Windows XP provides some tools with which to manage open windows. You already have used one tool - maximizing a window. When you maximize a window, it occupies the entire screen and cannot be confused with other open windows.

More About

ALT+TAB

In Windows 3.1, an older version of Windows, the most convenient way to switch between open windows was pressing the ALT+TAB keys. Microsoft discovered that most users did not know about this method, so they solved the problem by placing the buttons of open windows on the taskbar.

Managing Windows

Multiple windows open on the desktop intimidate some users. To reduce anxiety, maximize the window in which you wish to work. If you want to switch to another open window, click its button on the taskbar and then maximize it. Many people find working with one window maximized is easier.

In some cases, however, it is important for multiple windows to display on the desktop. Windows XP allows you to arrange the windows in specific ways. The following sections describe the ways in which you can manage open windows.

Cascading Windows

One way to organize windows on the desktop is to **cascade** them, which means they display on top of each other in an organized manner. To cascade the open windows on the desktop shown in Figure 3-15 on the previous page, complete the following steps.

To Cascade Open Windows

1 Right-click an open area on the taskbar. Point to Cascade Windows on the shortcut menu.

Right-clicking the taskbar causes the Untitled - Notepad window to no longer be the active window, and a shortcut menu displays (Figure 3-16). The commands on the menu apply to the open windows on the desktop.

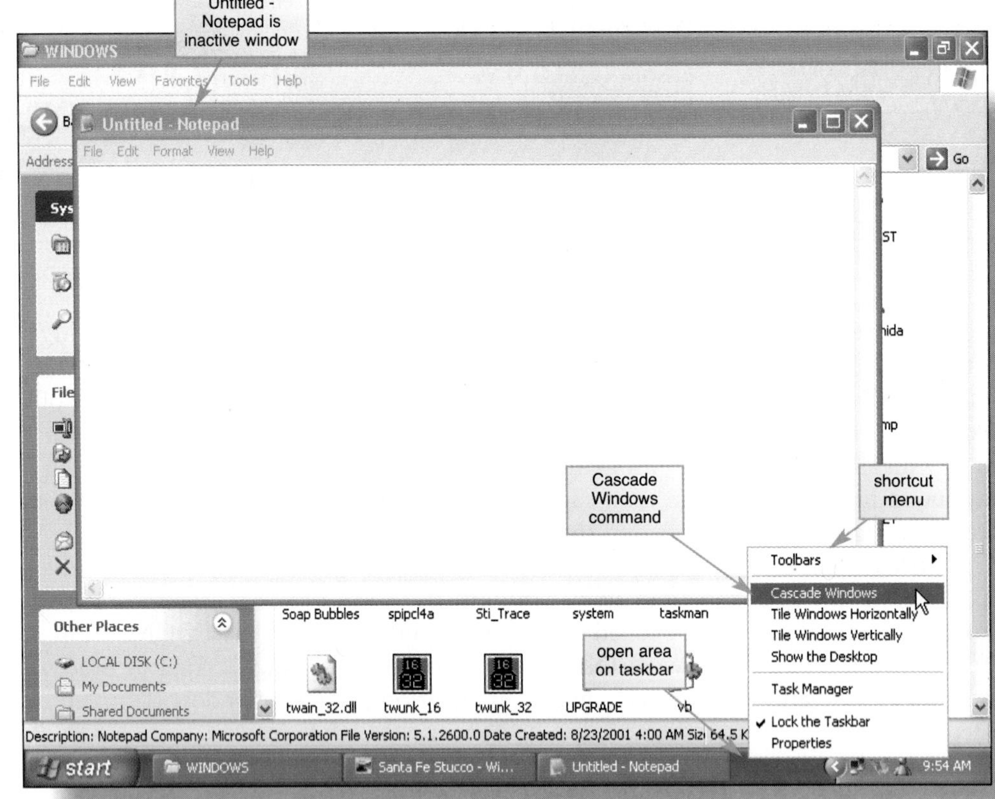

FIGURE 3-16

2 Click Cascade Windows.

The open windows display cascaded on the desktop (Figure 3-17). You can see the title bar of each window and the top two windows move slightly to the right. None of the windows is the active window (all light blue title bars and no recessed buttons).

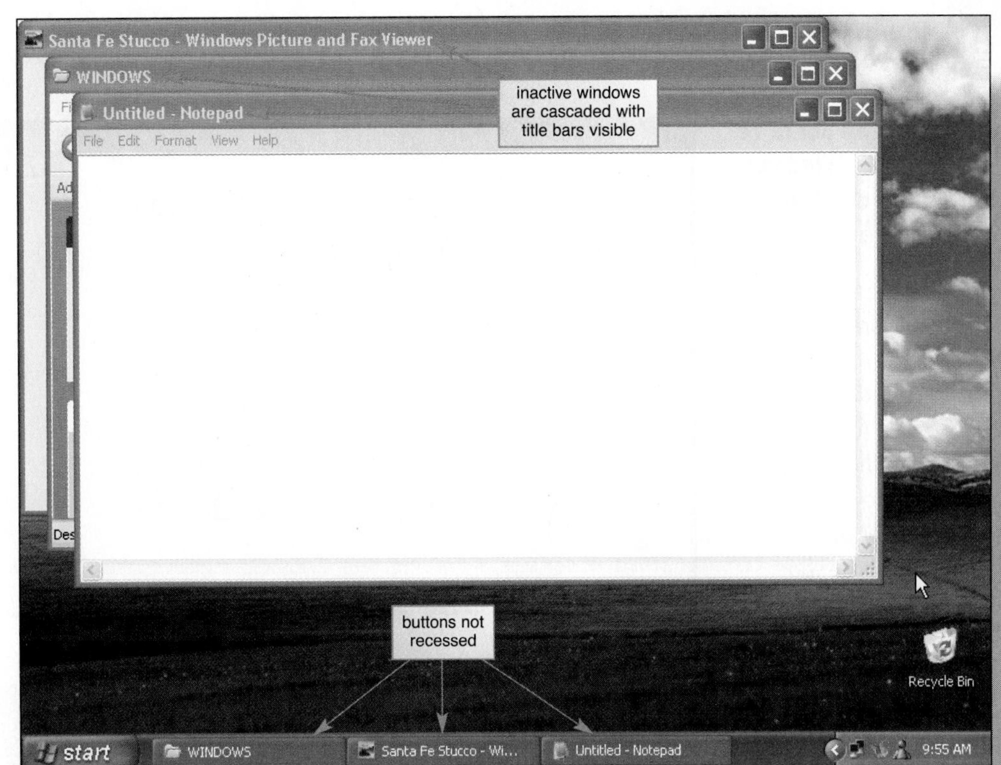

FIGURE 3-17

1. Right-click open area on taskbar, press S, press ENTER

Windows XP cascades only windows that are open. Windows that are minimized or closed will not be cascaded on the desktop. When you cascade the open windows, the windows are resized for cascading. In Figure 3-17, all windows have been resized to be the same size.

Making a Window the Active Window

When windows are cascaded as shown in Figure 3-17, they are arranged so you can see them easily, but you must make one of the windows the active window in order to work in the window. To make the Santa Fe Stucco - Windows Picture and Fax Viewer window the active window, complete the step on the next page.

Steps To Make a Window the Active Window

1 Click the Santa Fe Stucco - Windows Picture and Fax Viewer window title bar.

The Santa Fe Stucco - Windows Picture and Fax Viewer window moves to the top of the desktop indicating it is active (dark blue title bar) and the Santa Fe Stucco - Windows Picture and Fax Viewer button is recessed in the taskbar button area (Figure 3-18).

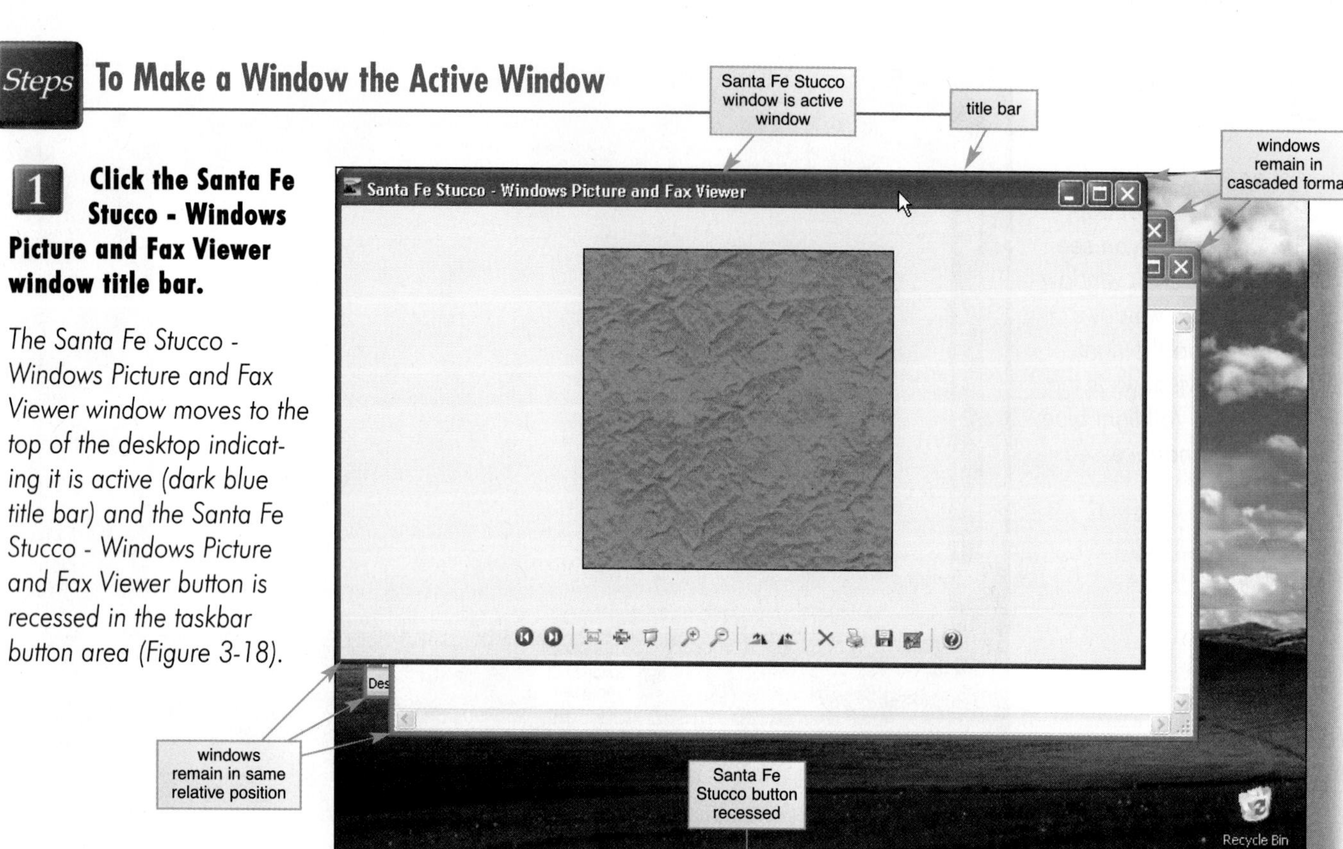

FIGURE 3-18

Other Ways

1. Click Santa Fe Stucco - Windows Picture and Fax Viewer button in taskbar button area
2. Press ALT+TAB until Santa Fe Stucco - Windows Picture and Fax Viewer displays in box, release ALT key
3. Click anywhere in window to make it active

The size of the Santa Fe Stucco - Windows Picture and Fax Viewer window shown in Figure 3-18 does not change and the other windows remain in a cascaded format. The Santa Fe Stucco - Windows Picture and Fax Viewer window title bar remains just above the WINDOWS title bar, which is in the same relative position as it was when it was not the active window (see Figure 3-17 on the previous page).

To make a window the active window, you click the title bar of the window. You also can make a window active by clicking its button in the taskbar button area, or you can click anywhere in the window that you want to become active. You do not necessarily have to click the title bar of the window.

Undo Cascaded Windows

Sometimes after you have cascaded the windows, you may want to undo the cascade operation and return the windows to their size and location before cascading. To undo the previous cascading, complete the following steps.

Steps To Undo Cascading

1 **Right-click an open area on the taskbar. Point to Undo Cascade on the shortcut menu (Figure 3-19).**

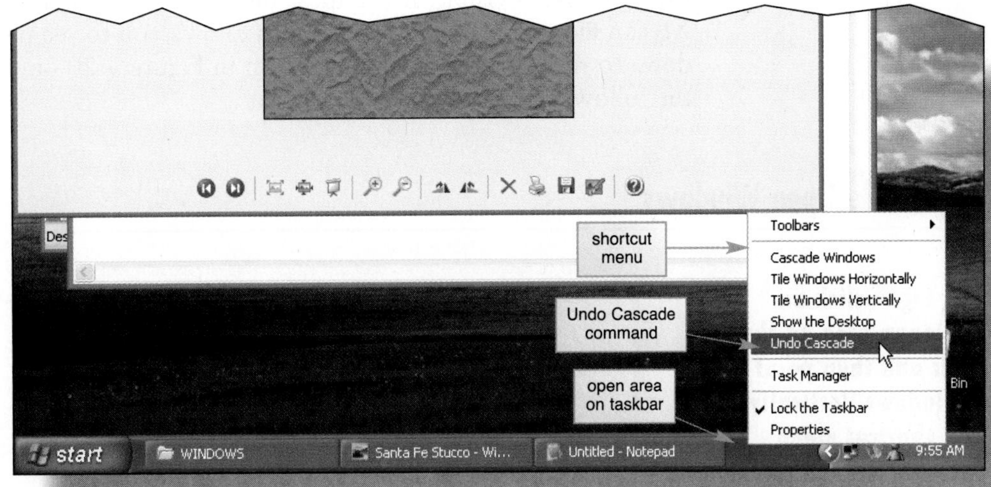

FIGURE 3-19

2 **Click Undo Cascade.**

The Santa Fe Stucco - Windows Picture and Fax Viewer window displays on top of the other windows on the desktop (Figure 3-20). Although not visible, the windows on the desktop display as if they had never been cascaded. The difference is that the maximized WINDOWS window is the active window. The Santa Fe Stucco - Windows Picture and Fax Viewer window remains on top instead of placing Notepad on top as it was before the windows were cascaded (see Figure 3-16 on page WIN 3.18 for the desktop prior to cascading).

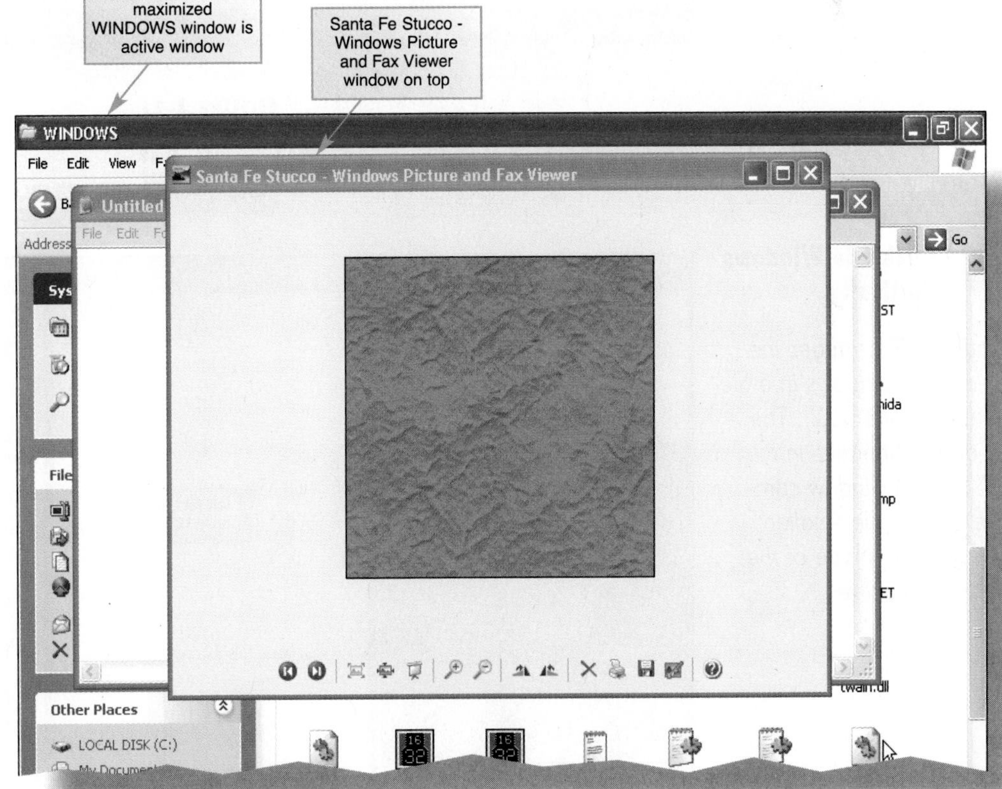

FIGURE 3-20

Other Ways

1. Right-click open area on taskbar, press U
2. Press CTRL+Z

Tiling Open Windows

While cascading arranges the windows on the desktop so each of the title bars in the windows is visible, it is impossible to see the contents of each window. Windows XP can **tile** the open windows, which allows you to see partial contents of each window. To tile the open windows shown in Figure 3-20 on the previous page, complete the following steps.

Steps To Tile Open Windows

1 Right-click an open area on the taskbar and then point to Tile Windows Vertically on the shortcut menu (Figure 3-21).

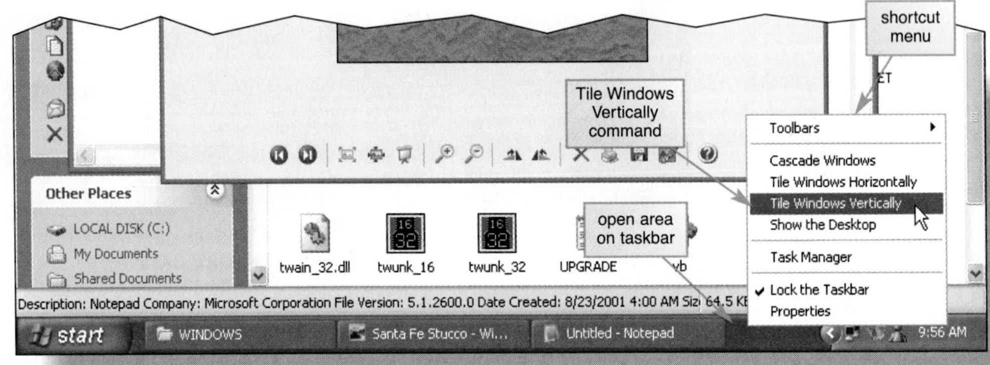

FIGURE 3-21

2 Click Tile Windows Vertically.

Windows XP arranges the three open windows in a tile format (Figure 3-22). The left and right panes in the WINDOWS window combine to fit in the smaller tiled window. None of the windows is active.

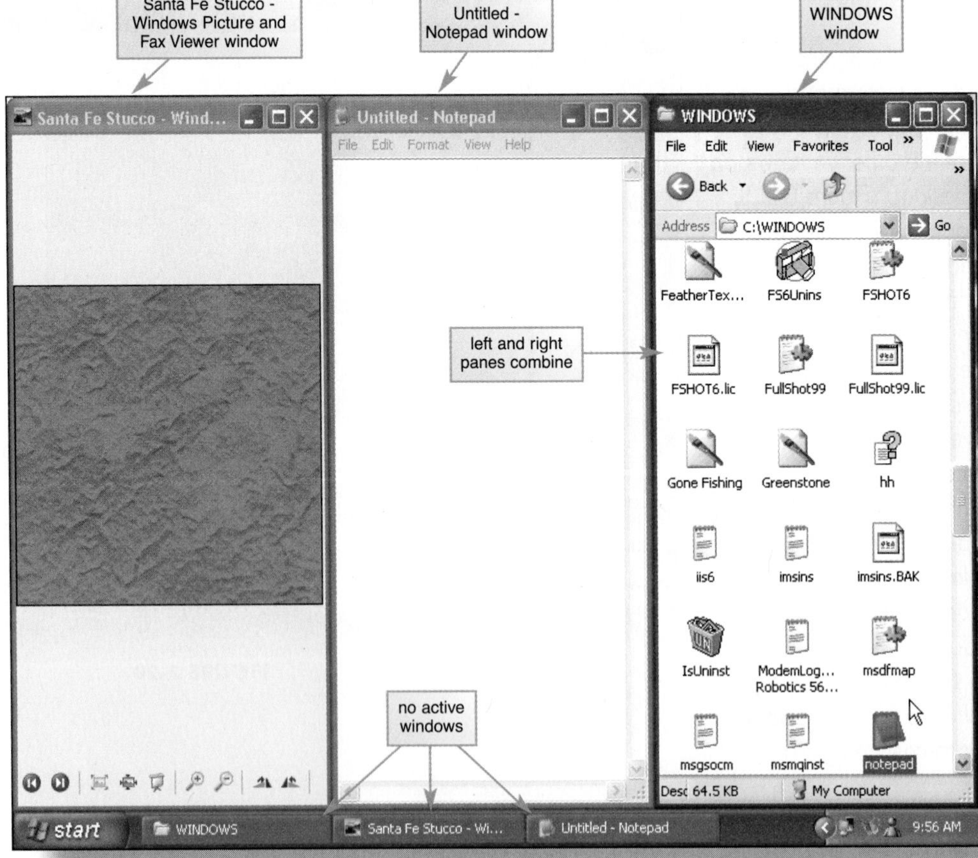

FIGURE 3-22

Other Ways

1. Right-click open area on taskbar, press E

While the windows shown in Figure 3-22 are arranged so you can view all of them, it is likely that the size of each one is not useful to work in. You can undo the tiling operation if you want to return the windows to the size and position they occupied before tiling. If you want to work in a particular window, you may want to click the Maximize button in that window to maximize the window.

To undo the tiling operation and return the windows to the format shown in Figure 3-20 on page WIN 3.21, complete the following steps.

Steps To Undo Tiling

1 Right-click an open area on the taskbar. Point to Undo Tile (Figure 3-23).

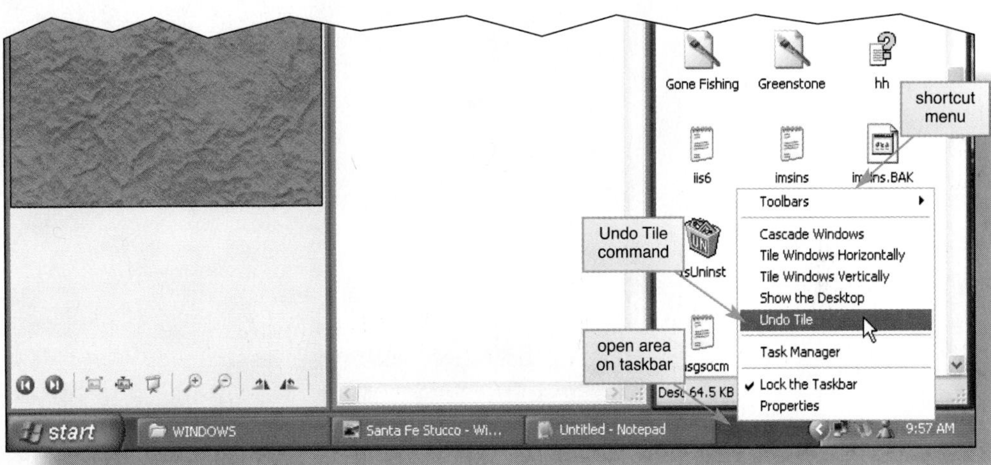

FIGURE 3-23

2 Click Undo Tile.

The windows no longer are tiled and display as if they had never been tiled (Figure 3-24).

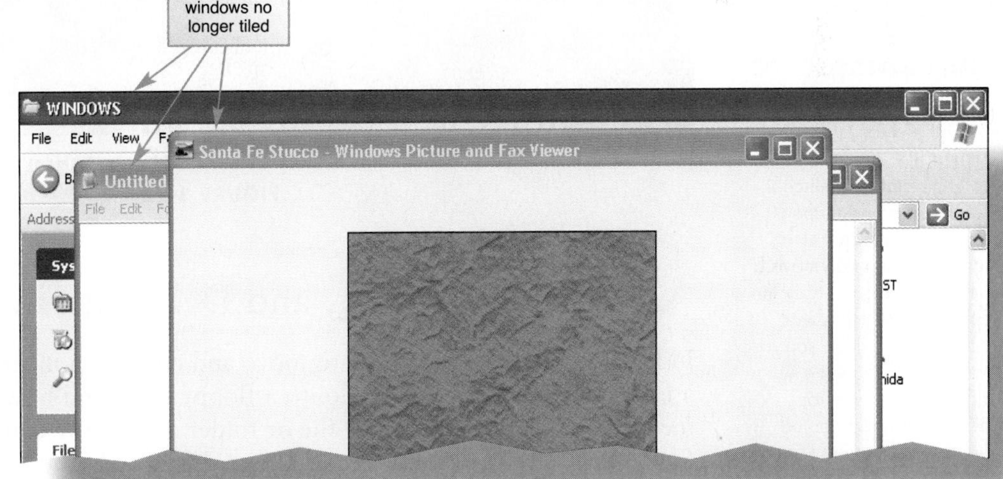

FIGURE 3-24

Other Ways

1. Right-click open area on taskbar, press U
2. Press CTRL+Z

Closing Windows

When you have finished working with windows, normally you should close the windows so the desktop remains uncluttered. To close the three open windows, complete the steps on the next page.

TO CLOSE OPEN WINDOWS

1. Click the Close button in the Santa Fe Stucco - Windows Picture and Fax Viewer window.
2. Click the Close button in the Untitled - Notepad window.
3. Click the Close button in the WINDOWS window.

All the windows are closed and the buttons no longer display in the taskbar button area (Figure 3-25).

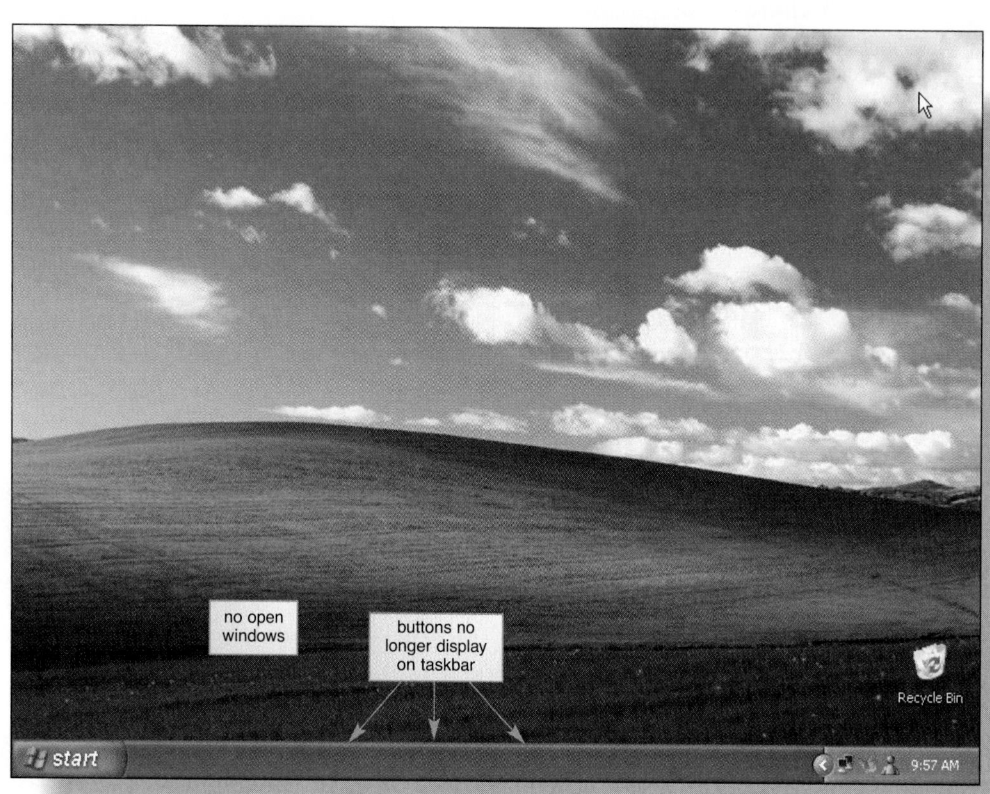

FIGURE 3-25

More About

Copying and Moving

Are copying and moving the same? No! When you copy a file, it is located in both the place to which it was copied and in the place from which it was copied. When you move a file, it is located in only the location to which it was moved. You will be sorry you did not know the difference if a file you thought you had copied was moved instead.

Copying, Moving, and Deleting Files in Windows

In Project 2, you learned how to move and copy document files on the desktop to a folder, how to copy a folder onto a floppy disk, and how to delete files. Another method you can use to copy a file or folder is the **copy and paste method**. To copy a file from one folder to another folder or drive, open the window containing the file, right-click the file to copy, and click the Copy command on the shortcut menu to place a copy of the file in a storage area of the computer called the **Clipboard**. Then, open the folder or drive window that you want the file to be copied to, right-click an open area of the window, and click Paste on the shortcut menu to copy the file from the Clipboard to the window. The following section explains in detail how to perform these tasks.

Copying Files Between Folders

Assume you want to copy three files, Coffee Bean, Gone Fishing, and Greenstone, from the WINDOWS folder to the My Pictures folder. To copy from a folder, the folder window must be open on the desktop. To open the WINDOWS folder window and display the icons for the files you want to copy, complete the following steps.

TO VIEW THE CONTENTS OF A FOLDER

1. Click the Start button on the taskbar.
2. Click My Computer on the Start menu.
3. Double-click the LOCAL DISK (C:) icon in the My Computer window.
4. Double-click the WINDOWS icon in the LOCAL DISK (C:) window.
5. Scroll down the right pane of the WINDOWS window until the icons for the Coffee Bean, Gone Fishing, and Greenstone files are visible in the right pane. If one or more of these icons is not available in the WINDOWS window on your computer, display any other icons.

The Coffee Bean, Gone Fishing, and Greenstone icons are visible in the WINDOWS window (Figure 3-26).

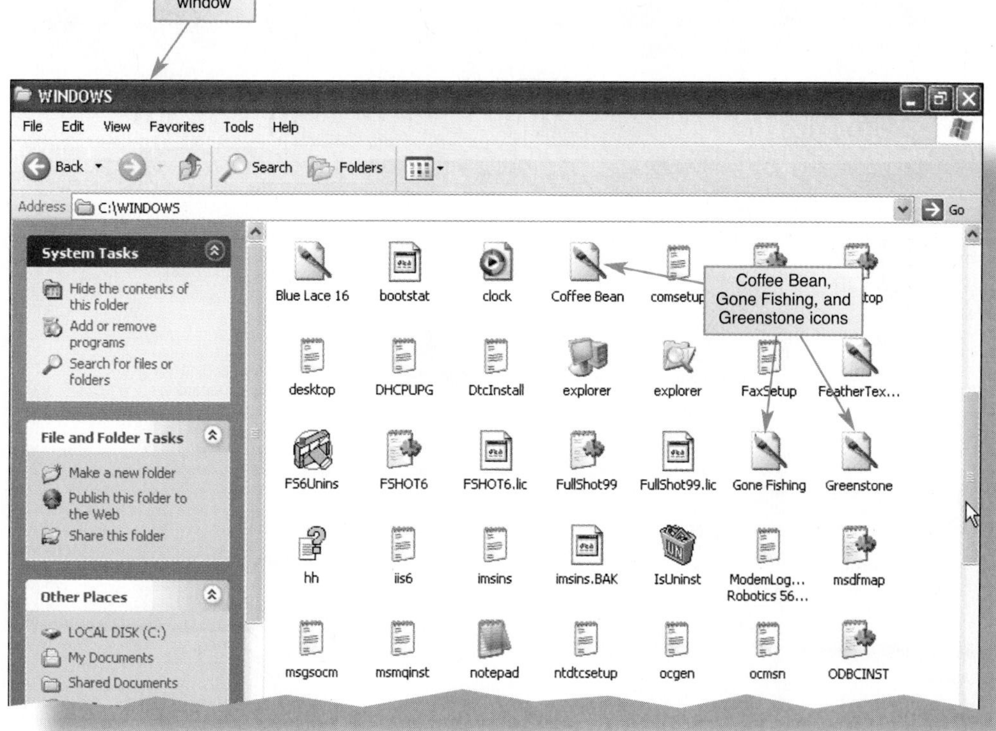

FIGURE 3-26

Once you have opened the folder window and the icons for the files to be copied are visible, you can select the files and then copy them. To copy the Coffee Bean, Gone Fishing, and Greenstone files from the WINDOWS folder to the My Pictures folder, complete the steps on the next page.

Steps To Copy Files to the My Pictures Folder

1 Hold down the CTRL key and then click the Coffee Bean, Gone Fishing, and Greenstone icons. Release the CTRL key. Right-click any highlighted icon and then point to the Copy command on the shortcut menu.

The selected Coffee Bean, Gone Fishing, and Greenstone icons and a shortcut menu display (Figure 3-27). The File and Folder Tasks area contains tasks specifically designed for working with selected items.

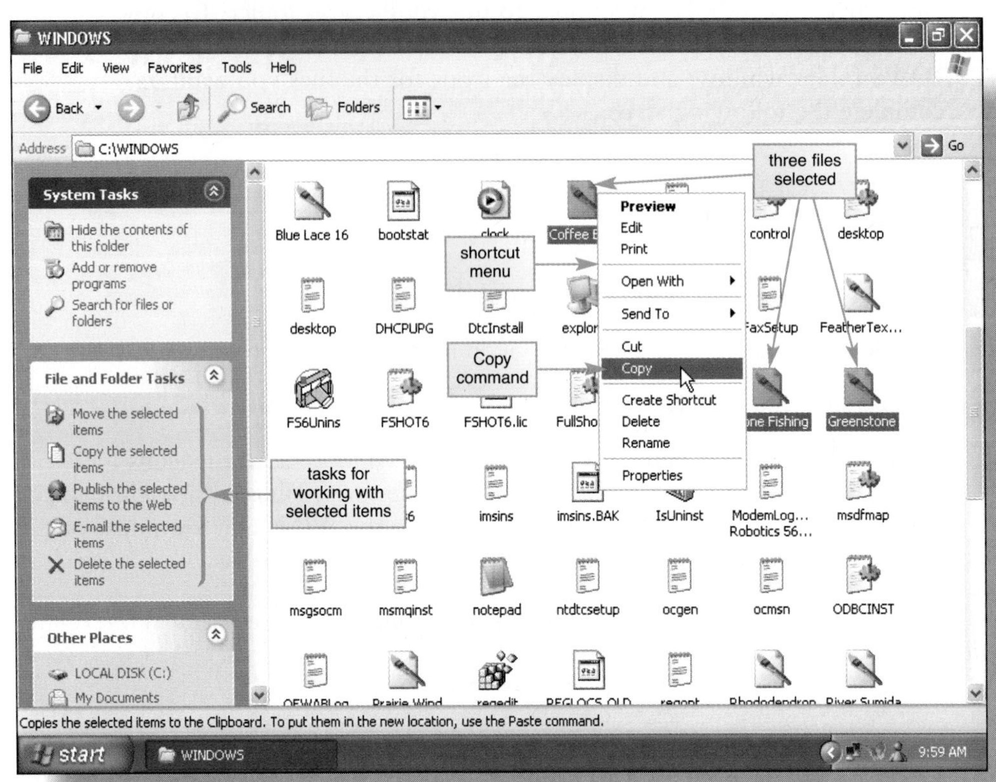

FIGURE 3-27

2 Click Copy. Scroll the left pane to display the Other Places area. Point to My Documents in the Other Places area.

Windows XP copies the three files to the Clipboard, and the Other Places area is fully visible (Figure 3-28).

FIGURE 3-28

3 Click My Documents and then point to the My Pictures icon in the right pane.

The My Documents window opens in the same window as WINDOWS was displayed and the My Music, My Pictures, and My Videos icons display in the My Documents window (Figure 3-29).

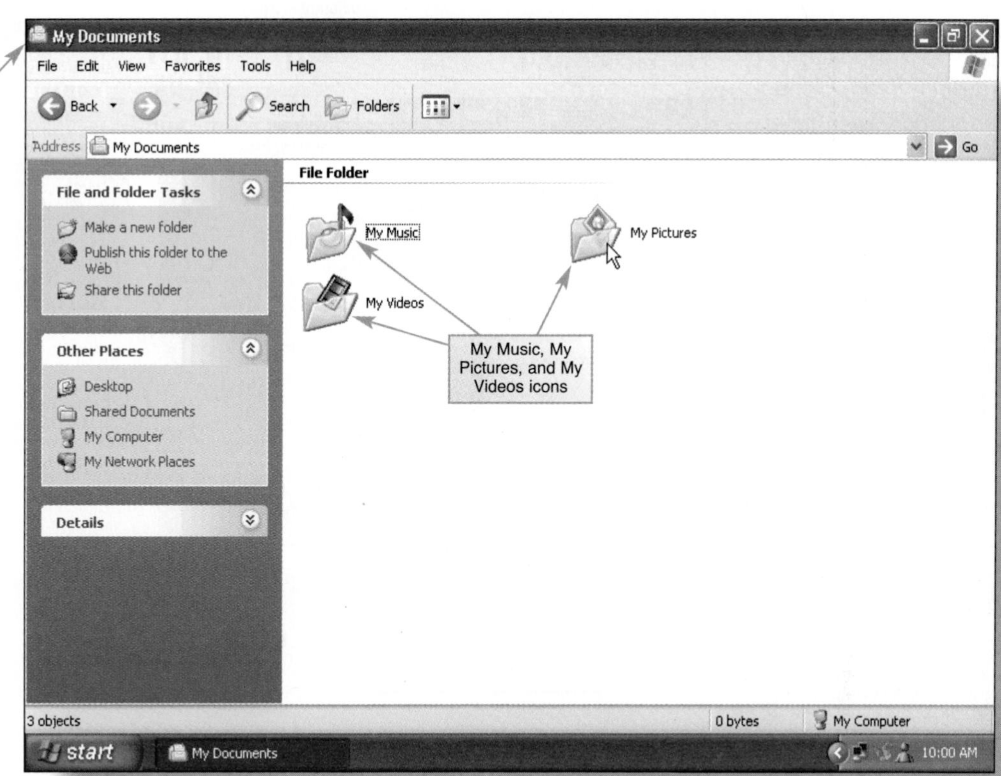

FIGURE 3-29

4 Double-click the My Pictures icon. Right-click an open area of the My Pictures window and then point to Paste on the shortcut menu.

The My Pictures window and a shortcut menu display (Figure 3-30). The Sample Pictures icon displays in the right pane, and the Address box contains the location of the My Pictures folder (C:\Documents and Settings\Brad Wilson\My Documents\My Pictures) on drive C. The Sample Pictures icon may not display and the location of the My Pictures folder may be different on your computer.

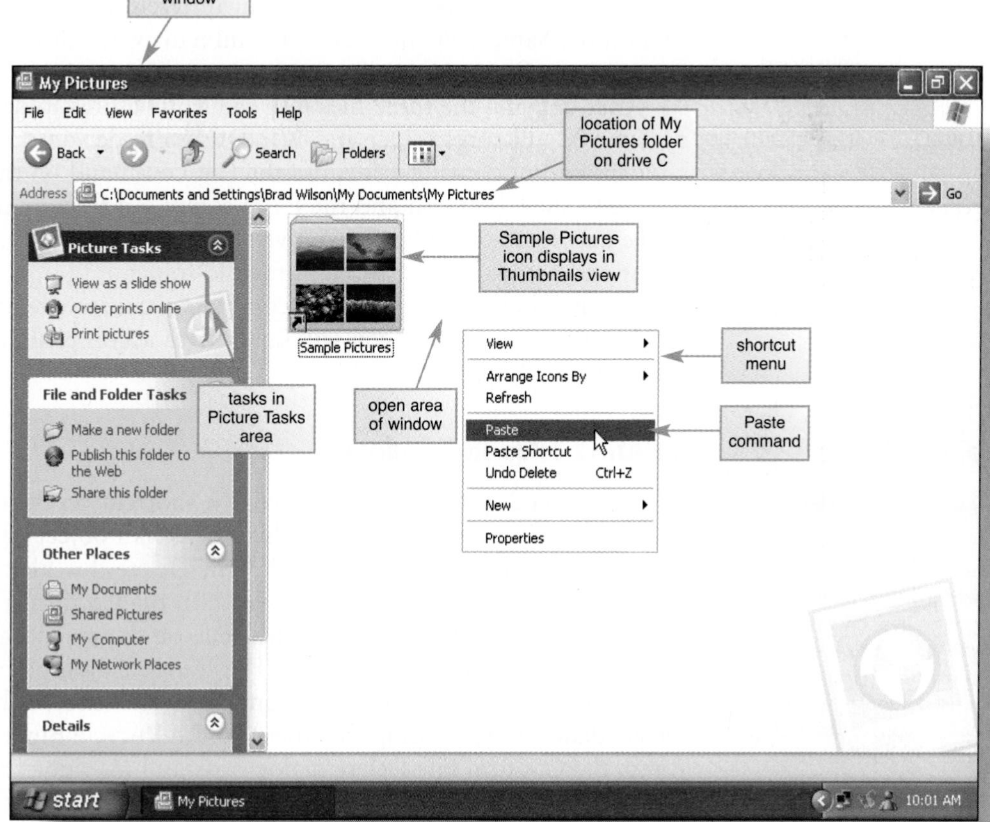

FIGURE 3-30

5 Click Paste.

The Coffee Bean, Gone Fishing, and Greenstone files are copied from the WINDOWS folder to the My Pictures folder (Figure 3-31).

6 Click the Close button to close the My Pictures window.

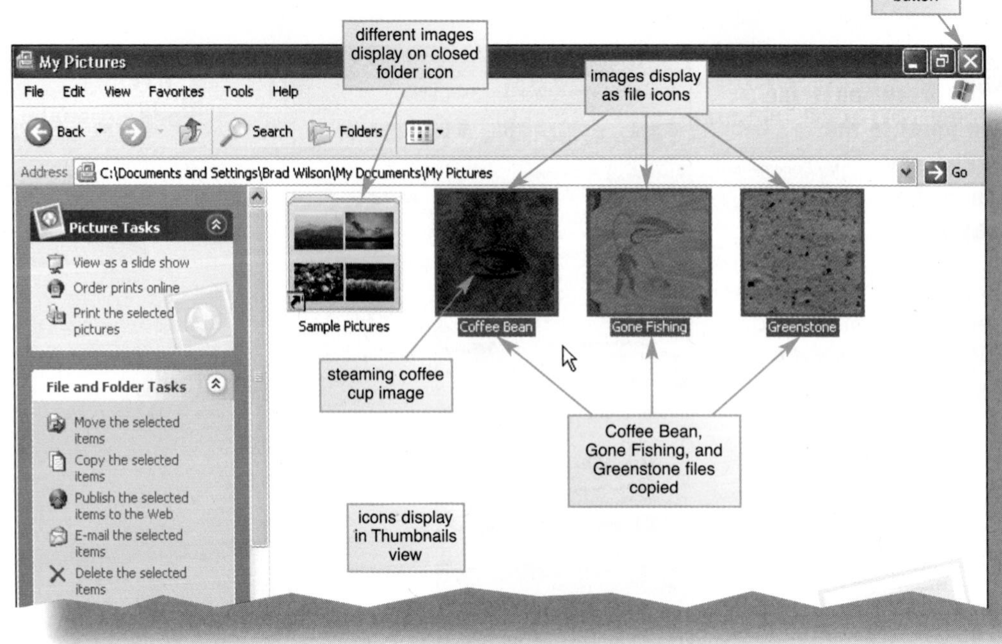

FIGURE 3-31

Other Ways

1. Select file icons, on Edit menu click Copy, display window to contain file, on Edit menu click Paste
2. Select file icons, on Edit menu click Copy To Folder, click plus sign to left of My Documents, click My Pictures, click Copy button
3. Select file icons, in File and Folder Tasks area click Copy the selected items, click plus sign to left of My Documents, click My Pictures, click Copy button
4. Select file icons, press CTRL+C, display window to contain file, press CTRL+V

In Figure 3-31, the Sample Pictures, Coffee Bean, Gone Fishing, and Greenstone icons display in Thumbnails view in the My Pictures window. In **Thumbnails view,** the image stored in a file displays as its icon and up to four images stored in a folder display on the folder icon. In Figure 3-31, the image of a steaming cup of coffee displays on the Coffee Bean icon and four different images display on the closed folder icon on the Sample Pictures icon. Thumbnails view allows you to quickly identify the contents of a file or folder by viewing its icon.

After copying the three files into the My Pictures folder, the files are stored in both the My Pictures folder and WINDOWS folder on drive C. If you want to move a file instead of copying a file, use the Cut command on the shortcut menu to move the file to the Clipboard and the Paste command to copy the file from the Clipboard to the new location. When the move is complete, the files are moved into the new folder and are no longer stored in the old folder.

Moving and copying files is a common occurrence when working in Windows XP. Later in this project, you will see how to accomplish these same tasks using Windows XP Explorer.

More About

Deleting Files

Someone proposed that the Delete command be removed from operating systems after an employee, who thought he knew what he was doing, deleted an entire database, which cost the company millions of dollars to replace. You should regard the Delete command as something to be used with extreme caution.

Deleting Files in Windows

In Project 2, you saw how to delete a shortcut on the desktop, a file in a folder, and a folder. To review, the methods to delete an object (shortcut, file, or folder) are: (1) click the object to be deleted, click the Delete this file task in the File and Folder Tasks area, and then click the Yes button in the Confirm File Delete dialog box; (2) click the object to be deleted, click File on the menu bar, click Delete, and then click the Yes button in the Confirm File Delete dialog box; (3) right-click the object, click Delete on the shortcut menu, and then click the Yes button in the Confirm File Delete dialog box; (4) drag the object to the Recycle Bin and then click the Yes button in the Confirm File Delete dialog box; and (5) right-drag the object to the Recycle Bin, click Move Here on the shortcut menu, and then click the Yes button in the Confirm File Delete dialog box.

Copying, moving, and deleting shortcuts, folders, and files is an important part of using Windows XP. In addition, the ability to manage windows on the Windows XP desktop can make the difference between an organized approach to dealing with multiple windows and a disorganized, confusing mess of windows on the desktop.

The My Computer Window

The title of the window in Figure 3-33 on the next page is My Computer. In previous versions of Windows, the window title was Exploring – My Computer, the Folders button did not display on the Standard Buttons toolbar, and you had to launch Explorer by right-clicking the My Computer icon on the desktop. In fact, if you click the Folders button on the Standard Buttons toolbar, the Folders pane is removed from the window, making it identical to the My Computer window in Figure 3-2 on page WIN 3.06.

Windows XP Explorer

Windows XP Explorer is another program that is part of Windows XP. It allows you to view the contents of the computer, including drives, folders, and files, in a hierarchical format. In Explorer, you also can move, copy, and delete files in much the same manner as you can when working with open windows.

Launching Windows XP Explorer

As with many other operations, Windows XP offers a variety of ways to launch Explorer. To launch Explorer using the Folders button in the My Computer window, complete the following steps.

Steps To Launch Windows Explorer

1 **Click the Start button and then click My Computer on the Start menu. Maximize the My Computer window. Point to the Folders button on the Standard Buttons toolbar.**

The maximized My Computer window displays (Figure 3-32). Pointing to the Folders button on the Standard Buttons toolbar displays a three-dimensional button.

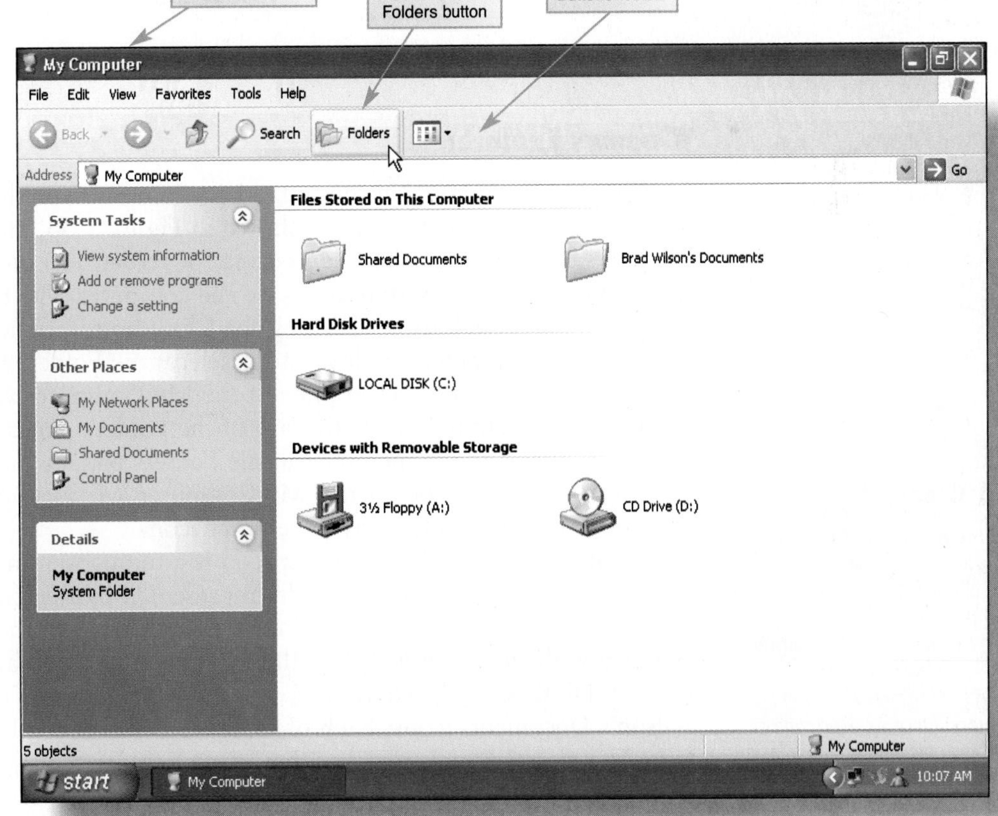

FIGURE 3-32

2 Click the Folders button.

The Folders pane displays in place of the left pane in the My Computer window (Figure 3-33).

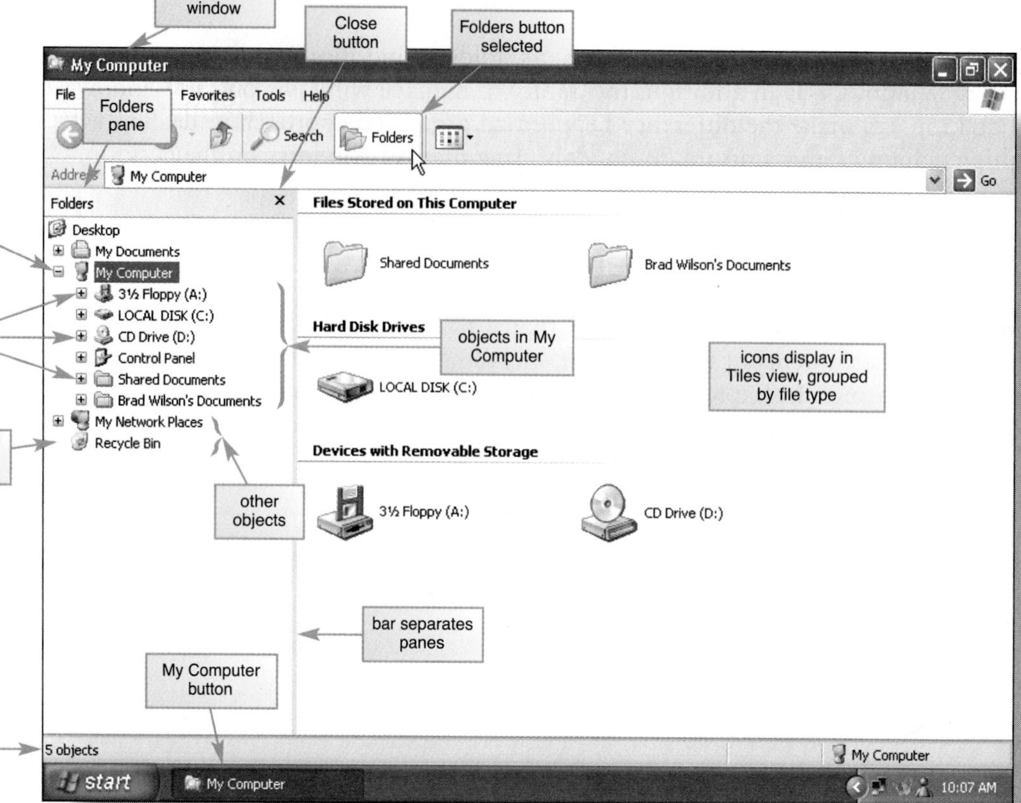

FIGURE 3-33

Other Ways

1. Click Start button, right-click My Computer, click Explorer
2. Right-click Start button or any desktop icon, click Explore on shortcut menu
3. Click Start button, point to All Programs, point to Accessories, click Windows Explorer

More About

A Hierarchy

One definition of hierarchy in Merriam Webster's Collegiate Dictionary is a division of angels. While no one would argue angels have anything to do with Windows XP, some preach that working with a hierarchical structure is less secular (of or relating to the worldly) and more spiritual (of or relating to supernatural phenomena) than the straightforward showing of files in windows. What do you think?

Windows Explorer

Clicking the Folders button in the My Computer window selects the Folders button, displays the Folders pane shown in Figure 3-33, and allows you to use Windows XP Explorer. The **Folders pane** (or **Folder bar**) displays the **hierarchical structure** of files, folders, and drives on the computer. The title bar contains a title (Folders) and Close button. Clicking the Close button removes the Folders pane from the My Computer window and deselects the Folders button. A bar separates the Folders pane and the right pane of the My Computer window. You can drag the bar left or right to change the size of the Folders pane.

The top level of the hierarchy in the Folders pane is the Desktop. Below the Desktop are the My Documents, My Computer, My Network Places, and Recycle Bin icons. Your computer may have other icons.

To the left of the My Computer icon is a minus sign in a small box. The **minus sign** indicates that the drive or folder represented by the icon next to it, in this case My Computer, contains additional folders or drives and these folders or drives display below the icon. Thus, below the My Computer icon are the 3½ Floppy (A:), LOCAL DISK (C:), CD Drive (D:), Control Panel, Shared Documents, and Brad Wilson's Documents icons. Each of these icons has a small box with a plus sign next to it. The **plus sign** indicates that the drive or folder represented by the icon has more folders within it but the folders do not display in the Folders pane. As you will see shortly, clicking the box with the plus sign will display the folders within the drive or folder represented by the icon. If an item contains no folders, such as Recycle Bin, no hierarchy exists and no small box displays next to the icon.

The right pane in the My Computer window illustrated in Figure 3-33 contains three groups of icons. The Files Stored on This Computer group contains the Shared Documents icon and Brad Wilson's Documents icon. The Hard Disk Drives group contains the LOCAL DISK (C:) icon. The Devices with Removable Storage group contains the 3½ Floppy (A:) and CD Drive (D:) icons. A message on the left of the status bar located at the bottom of the window indicates the right pane contains five objects.

Windows XP Explorer displays the drives and folders on the computer in hierarchical structure in the Folders pane. This arrangement allows you to move and copy files and folders using only the Folders pane and the contents of the right pane.

Expanding Drives and Folders

Explorer displays the hierarchy of items in the Folders pane and the contents of drives and folders in the right pane. To expand a drive or folder in the Folders pane, click the plus sign in a small box to the left of the drive or folder icon. Clicking the plus sign expands the hierarchy in the Folders pane. The contents of the right pane remain the same. To expand a folder, complete the following steps.

To Expand a Folder

1 **Point to the plus sign in the small box to the left of the My Documents icon in the Folders pane (Figure 3-34).**

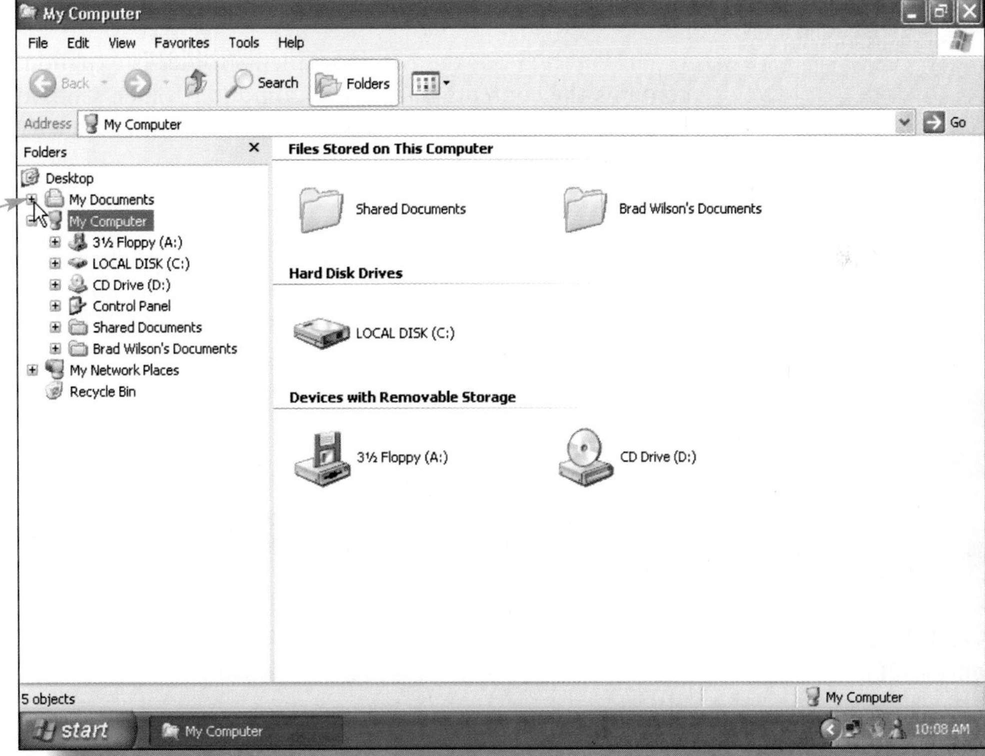

FIGURE 3-34

2 Click the plus sign.

The hierarchy below the My Documents icon expands to display the My Music folder, My Pictures folder, and My Videos folder (Figure 3-35). The minus sign to the left of the My Documents folder indicates the folder is expanded. No sign to the left of the My Music, My Pictures, and My Videos folders indicates the folders contain no additional folders.

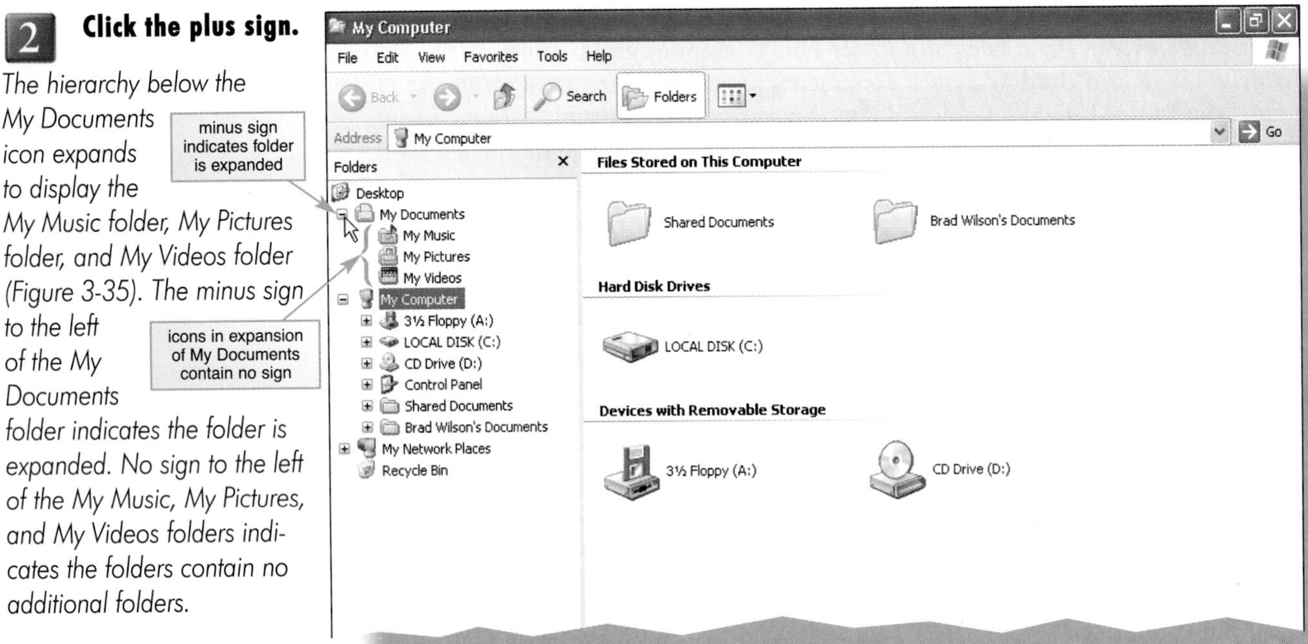

FIGURE 3-35

Other Ways

1. Click folder icon in Folders pane
2. Select folder to expand using ARROW keys, press PLUS on numeric keyboard
3. Select folder to expand, press RIGHT ARROW

In Figure 3-35, the My Documents folder is expanded and the right pane still contains the contents of the My Computer folder. Clicking the plus sign next to a folder icon expands the hierarchy but does not change the contents of the right pane.

Expanding a Drive

When a plus sign in a small box displays to the left of a drive icon in the Folders pane, you can expand the drive to show all the folders it contains. To expand drive C and view the folders on drive C, complete the following steps.

Steps To Expand a Drive

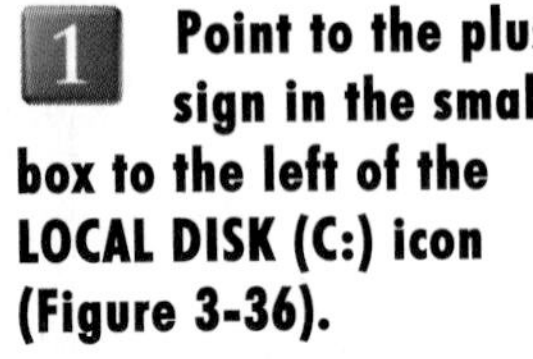

1 Point to the plus sign in the small box to the left of the LOCAL DISK (C:) icon (Figure 3-36).

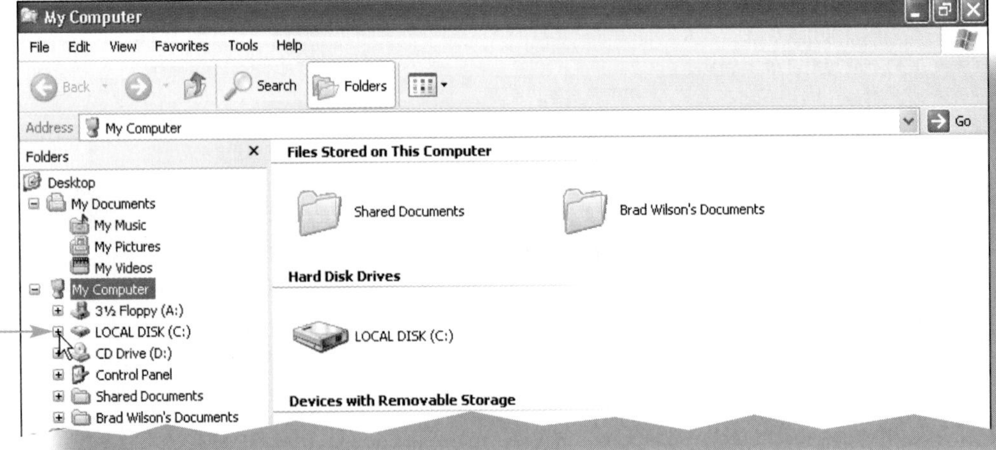

FIGURE 3-36

2 Click the plus sign.

The hierarchy below the LOCAL DISK (C:) icon expands to display folders contained on LOCAL DISK (C:) (Figure 3-37). The folders are indented below the LOCAL DISK (C:) icon and the minus sign to the left of the LOCAL DISK (C:) icon indicates the drive has been expanded. A folder with a plus sign contains more folders.

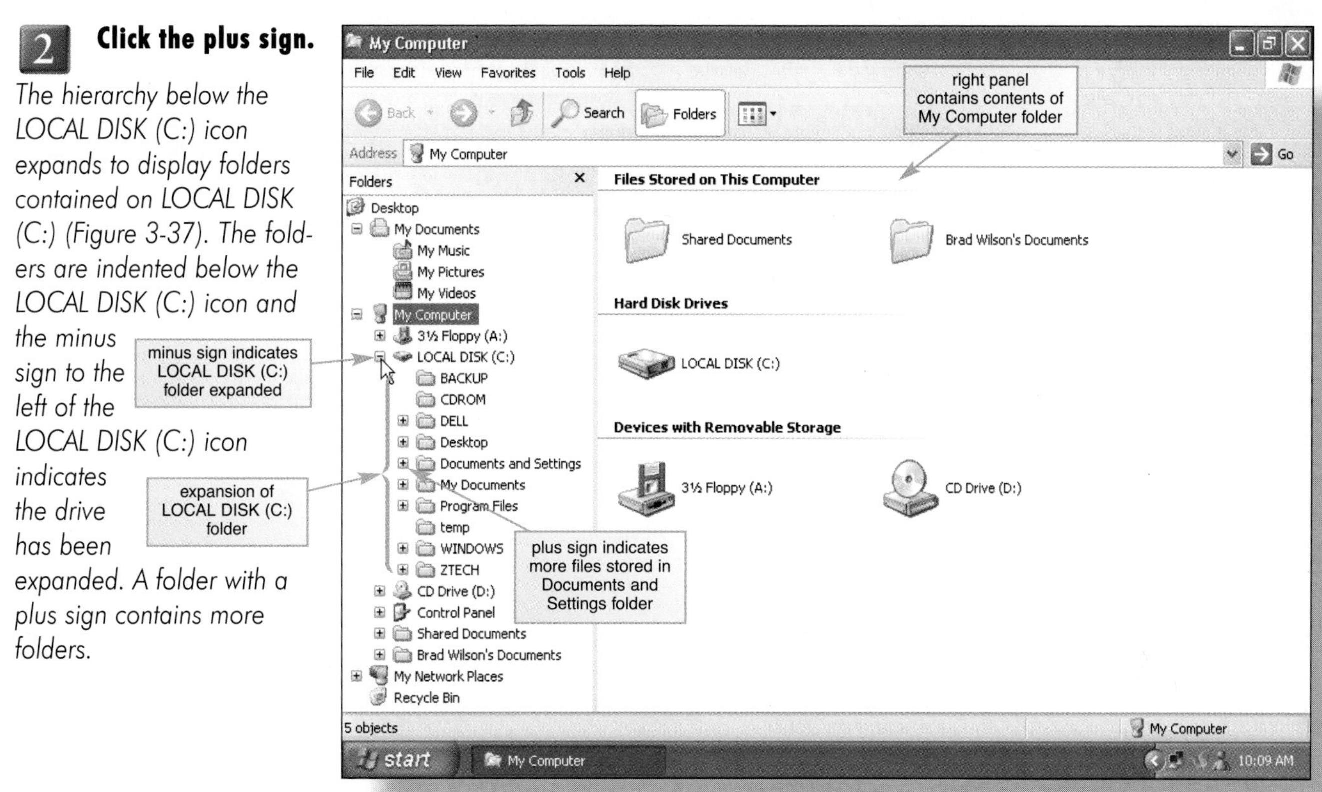

FIGURE 3-37

Other Ways

1. Click drive icon in Folders pane
2. Select drive to expand using ARROW keys, press PLUS on numeric keyboard
3. Select drive to expand, press RIGHT ARROW

In Figure 3-37, the LOCAL DISK (C:) drive is expanded and the right pane still contains the contents of the My Computer folder. Clicking the plus sign next to a drive icon expands the hierarchy but does not change the contents of the right pane.

When a drive is expanded, the folders contained within the expanded drive display in the Folders pane. You can continue this expansion to view further levels of the hierarchy.

Displaying Files and Folders in Windows XP Explorer

You can display files and folders in the right pane in several different views. Currently, the files and folders in the My Computer folder display in Tiles view using Large Icons format and are grouped based upon file type. Other folders may display in a different view. The manner in which you display drive or folder contents in the right pane is a matter of personal preference.

Displaying Drive and Folder Contents

Explorer displays the hierarchy of items in the Folders pane and the contents of drives and folders in the right pane. To display the contents of a drive or folder in the right pane, click the drive or folder icon in the Folders pane. Clicking the icon displays the contents of the drive or folder in the right pane and expands the hierarchy in the Folders pane. Perform the step on the next page to display the contents of the Shared Documents folder.

Steps To Display the Contents of a Folder

1 Click the Shared Documents icon in the Folders pane.

The selected Shared Documents name displays in the Folders pane, the hierarchy below the Shared Documents icon expands, and the right pane contains the contents of the Shared Documents folder (Figure 3-38). The window title changes to Shared Documents, the Shared Documents button replaces the My Computer button on the taskbar, and the status bar indicates two objects display in the right pane.

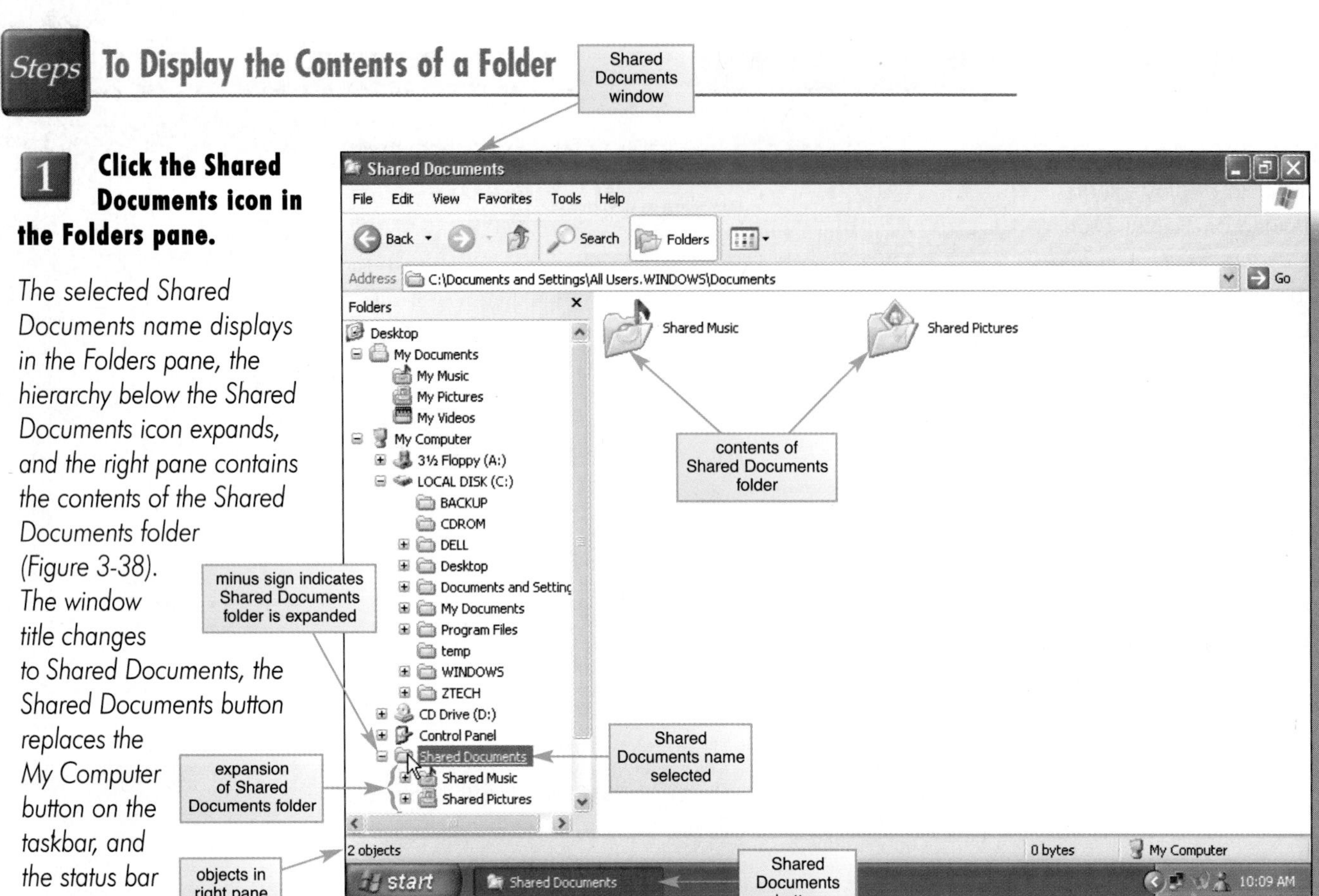

FIGURE 3-38

Other Ways

1. Right-click Shared Documents icon, click Explore

Whenever files or folders display in the right pane of a window, you can display the contents of a file or folder by double-clicking the icon of the file or folder.

In Figure 3-38, you clicked the Shared Documents icon in the Folders pane and the contents of the Shared Documents folder displayed in the right pane and the hierarchy below the Shared Documents icon expanded. If you click an icon of an expanded drive or folder, the contents of the drive or folder display in the right pane. The hierarchy below the icon will not expand because it is already expanded. To display the contents of the expanded LOCAL DISK (C:) drive, complete the following step.

Steps To Display the Contents of an Expanded Drive

1 Click the LOCAL DISK (C:) icon in the Folders pane.

The LOCAL DISK (C:) entry is selected in the Folders pane, the expanded Shared Documents folder collapses, and the contents of the LOCAL DISK (C:) folder display in the right pane (Figure 3-39). Notice that all the folder icons display first and then the file icons display. The status bar indicates 21 objects and 8 hidden objects occupy 328 kilobytes and the amount of space that is not being used on the disk is 10.1 gigabytes.

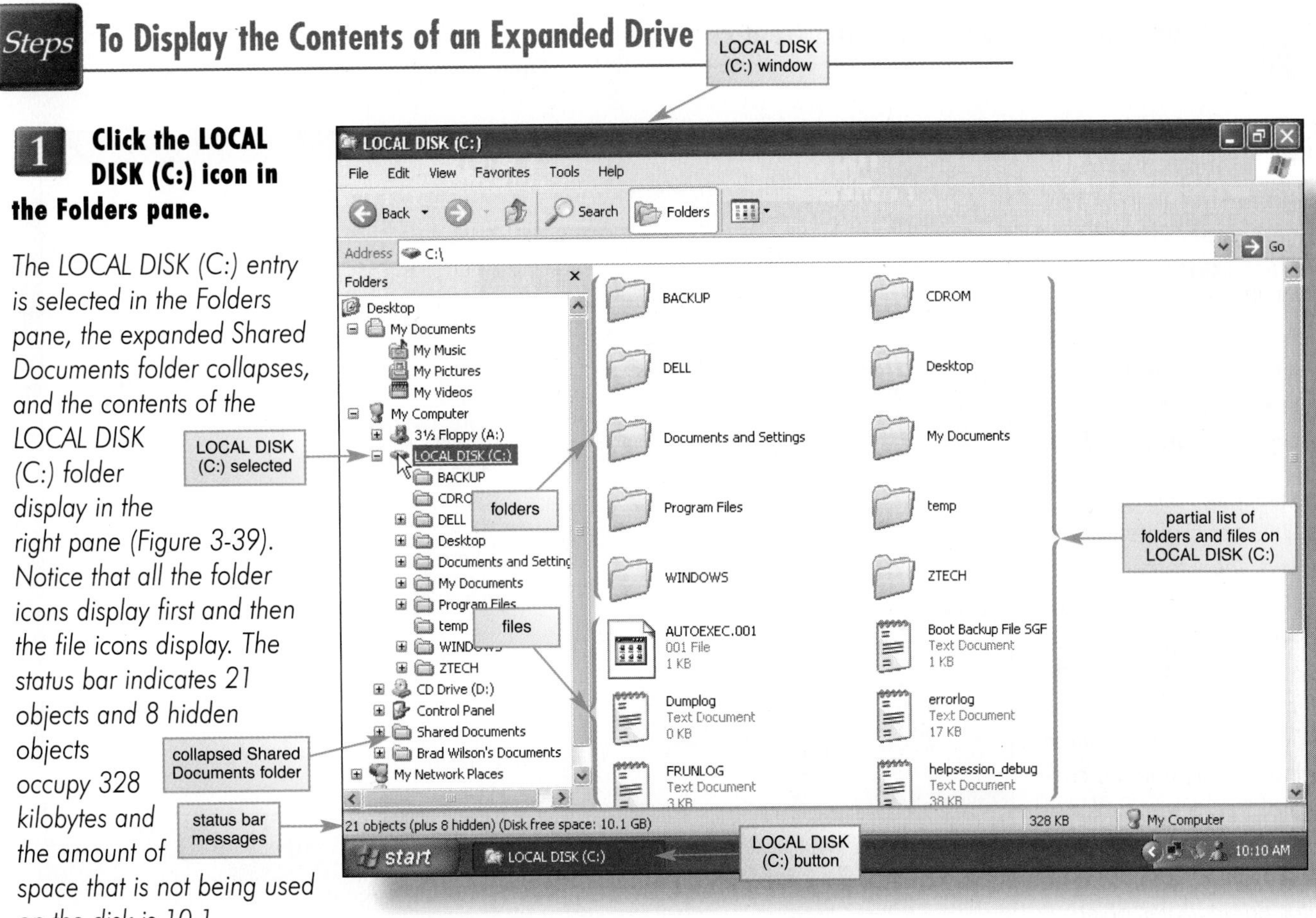

FIGURE 3-39

Other Ways

1. Double-click LOCAL DISK (C:) icon in right pane
2. Press DOWN ARROW to select LOCAL DISK (C:) icon in Folders pane
3. Press TAB to select any drive icon in right pane, press DOWN ARROW or RIGHT ARROW to select LOCAL DISK (C:) icon, press ENTER

Launching an Application Program from Explorer

You can launch an application program from the right pane of a window using the same techniques you used earlier in this project for launching an application program from an open window (see Figure 3-14 on page WIN 3.16 and Figure 3-15 on page WIN 3.17). To launch the Internet Explorer program stored in the Program Files folder, complete the steps on the next page.

Steps To Launch an Application Program from Explorer

1 **Click the plus sign to the left of the Program Files icon in the Folders pane. Click the Internet Explorer icon in the Folders pane. Point to the IEXPLORE (Internet Explorer) icon in the right pane of the Internet Explorer window.**

The Program Files folder and Internet Explorer folder expand, the Internet Explorer folder is selected, the window title changes to Internet Explorer, the Internet Explorer button replaces the LOCAL DISK (C:) button on the taskbar, and the contents of the Internet Explorer folder display in the right pane (Figure 3-40). The status bar indicates objects 6 and 1 hidden object consume 124 kilobytes on drive C.

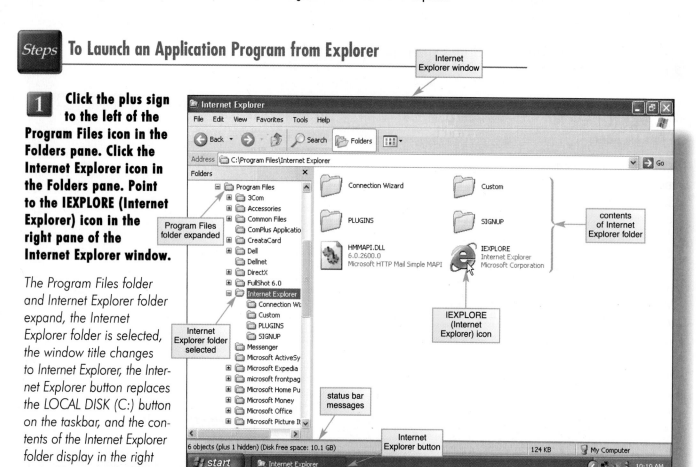

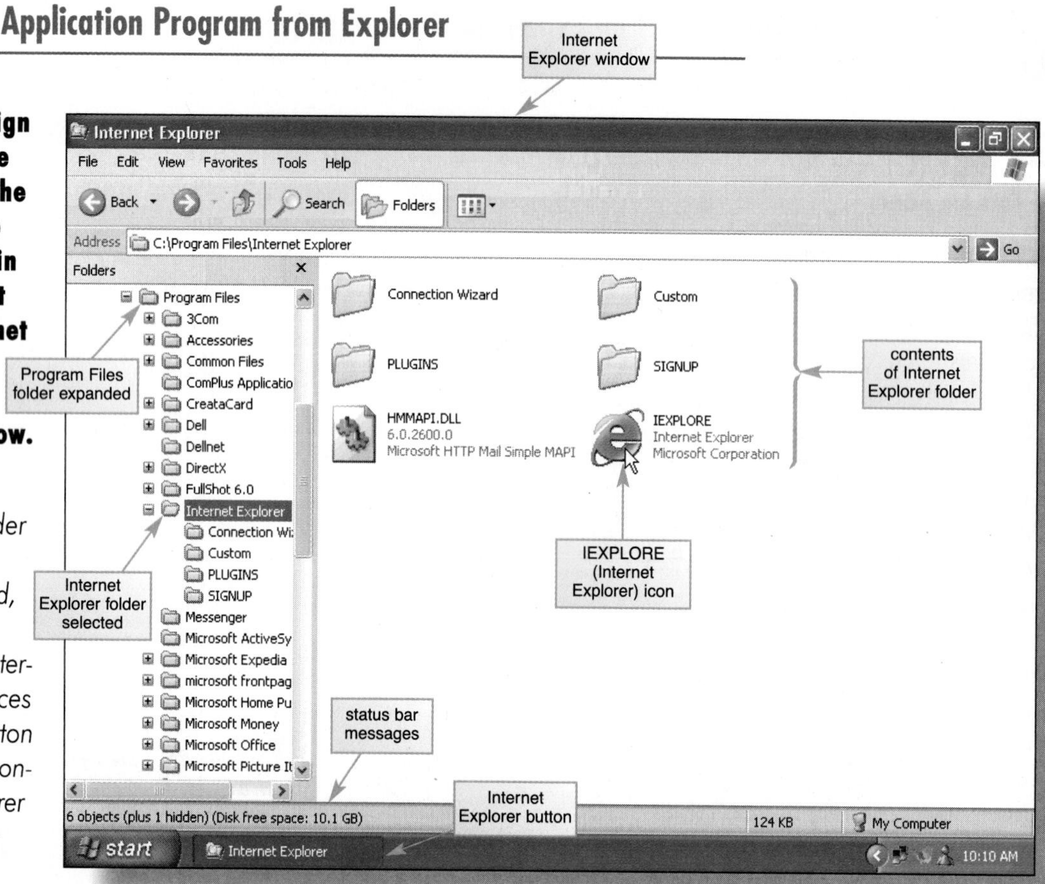

Internet Explorer window

Program Files folder expanded

contents of Internet Explorer folder

IEXPLORE (Internet Explorer) icon

Internet Explorer folder selected

status bar messages

Internet Explorer button

FIGURE 3-40

2 **Double-click the IEXPLORE icon.**

Windows XP launches the Internet Explorer program. The Welcome to MSN.com - Microsoft Internet Explorer window, containing the MSN page, displays (Figure 3-41). Because Web pages are modified frequently, the Web page that displays on your desktop may be different from the Web page shown in Figure 3-41. The URL for the Web page displays in the Address bar.

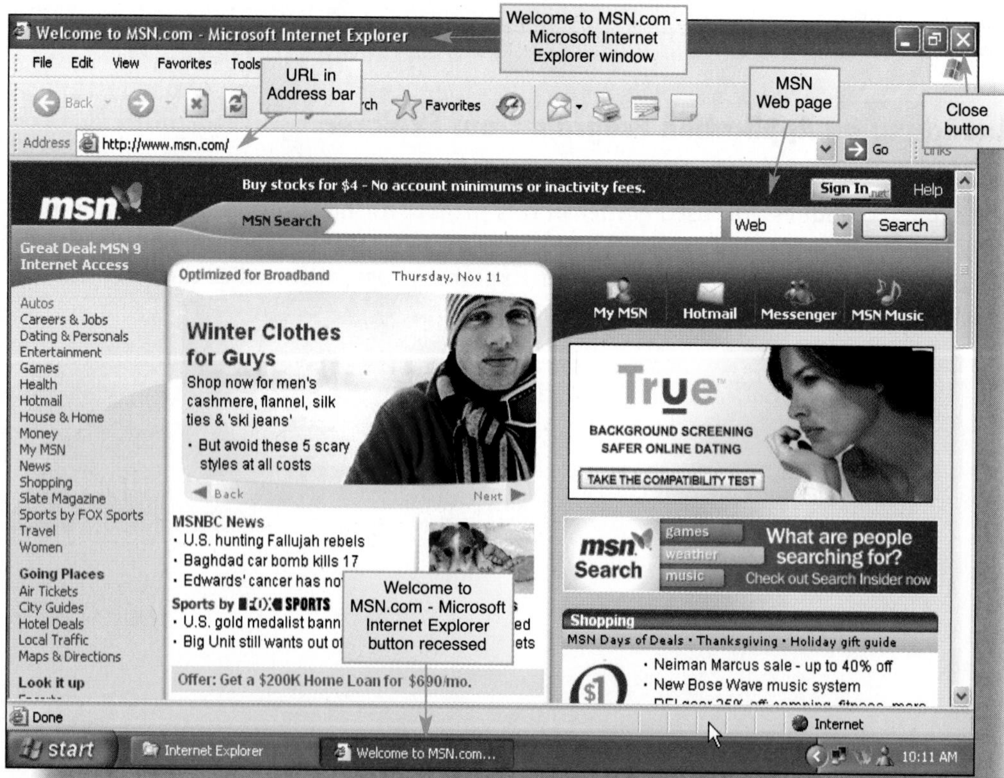

FIGURE 3-41

You can use the Internet Explorer program for any purpose you want, just as if you had launched it from the Start menu. When you are finished with the Internet Explorer program, you should quit the program. To quit the Internet Explorer program, complete the following step.

Thumbnails View

The contents of the My Pictures window in Figure 3-46 on page WIN 3.40 displays in Thumbnails view. In Thumbnails view, the image contained in a file displays as its icon and up to four images from a folder can display on a folder icon. The images on the folder icon are the last four images modified. In addition, you can choose a picture to identify a folder that does not have to be a picture contained in the folder.

TO QUIT AN APPLICATION PROGRAM

1. Click the Close button on the Welcome to MSN.com - Microsoft Internet Explorer title bar.

The Welcome to MSN.com - Microsoft Internet Explorer window closes.

Closing Folder Expansions

Sometimes, after you have completed work with expanded folders, you will want to close the expansions while still leaving the Explorer window open. To close the expanded folders shown in Figure 3-40, complete the following steps.

To Close Expanded Folders

1. Click the minus sign to the left of the Internet Explorer icon.

The expansion of the Internet Explorer folder closes and the minus sign changes to a plus sign (Figure 3-42). The contents of the right pane do not change.

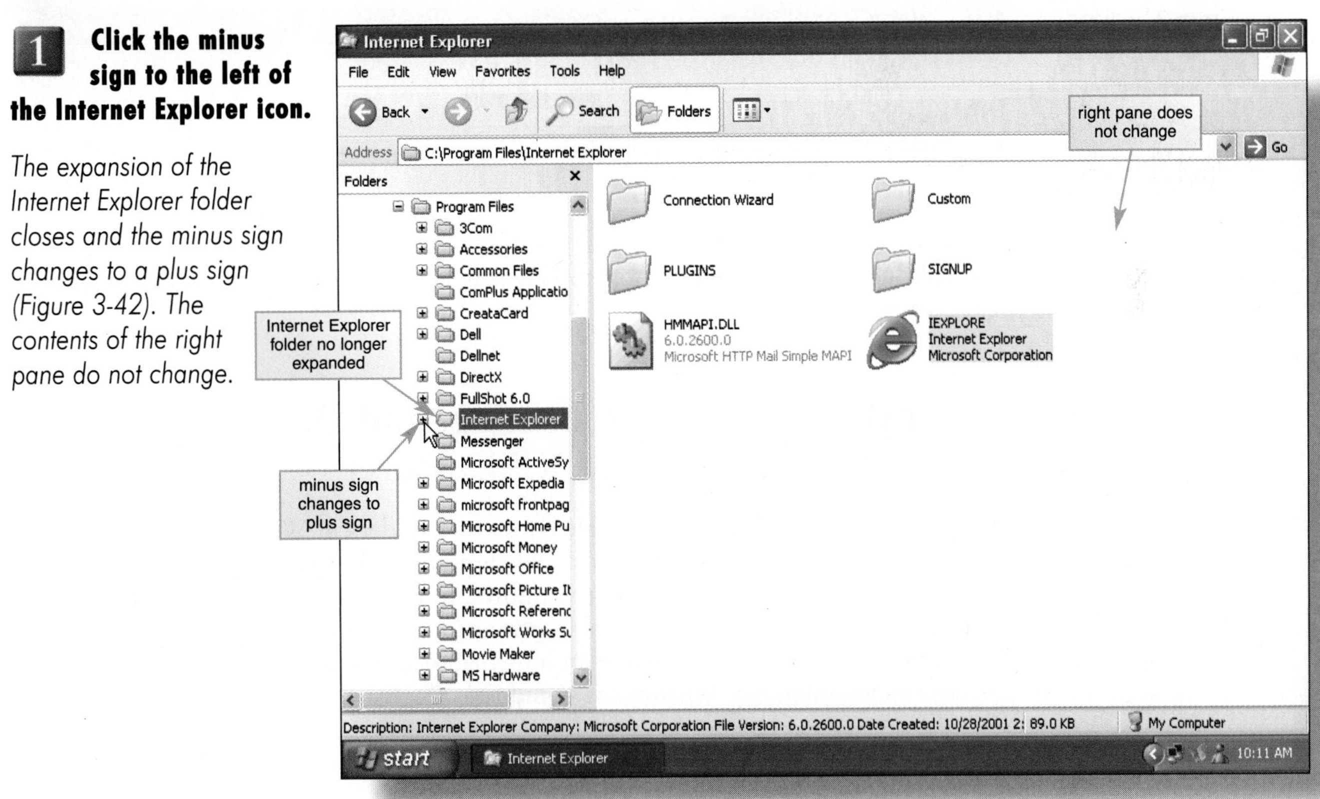

FIGURE 3-42

2 Click the minus sign to the left of the Program Files icon.

The expansion of the Program Files folder closes, the minus sign changes to a plus sign, the window title changes to Program Files, the Program Files button replaces the Internet Explorer button on the taskbar, and the right pane contains the files and folders in the Program Files folder (Figure 3-43).

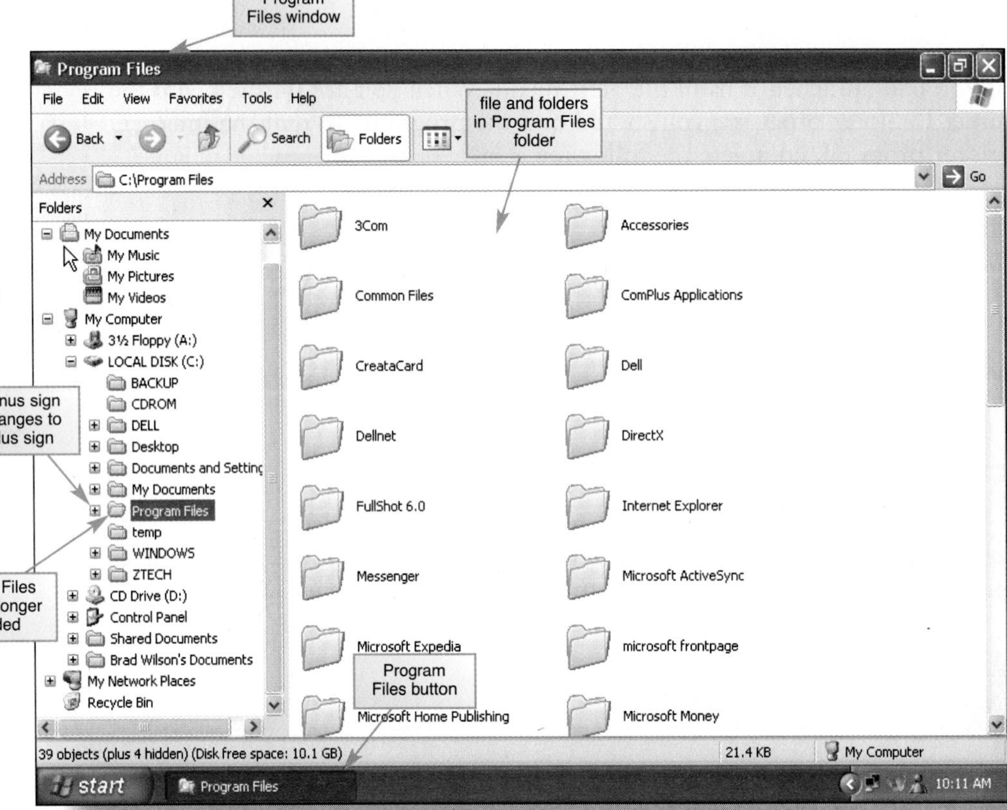

FIGURE 3-43

Other Ways

1. Click expanded folder icon, press MINUS SIGN on numeric keypad
2. Click expanded folder icon, press LEFT ARROW

Moving through the Folders pane and right pane is an important skill because you will find that you use Explorer to perform a significant amount of file maintenance on the computer.

Copying, Moving, Renaming, and Deleting Files and Folders in Windows XP Explorer

You can copy, move, rename, and delete files and folders in Windows XP Explorer using essentially the same techniques as when working in folder windows. Whether you perform these activities in folder windows, in Explorer, or in a combination of the two is a personal preference. It is important for you to understand the techniques used in both cases so you can make an informed decision about how you want to perform file maintenance when using Windows XP.

Copying Files in Windows XP Explorer

In previous examples of copying files, you used the copy and paste method to copy a document file from a folder to another folder. Although you could use the copy and paste method to copy files in Windows XP Explorer, another method of copying a file is to right-drag a file (or folder) icon from the right pane to a folder or drive icon in the Folders pane. To copy the Prairie Wind file from the WINDOWS folder to the My Documents folder, complete the following steps.

Steps To Copy a File in Explorer by Right-Dragging

1 Click the WINDOWS icon in the Folders pane. Scroll the right pane to display the Prairie Wind icon. If the Prairie Wind file is not available, display another icon. Scroll the Folders pane to display the expanded My Documents entry.

The contents of the WINDOWS folder, including the Prairie Wind icon, display in the right pane and the My Pictures folder displays in the expanded My Documents folder in the Folders pane (Figure 3-44).

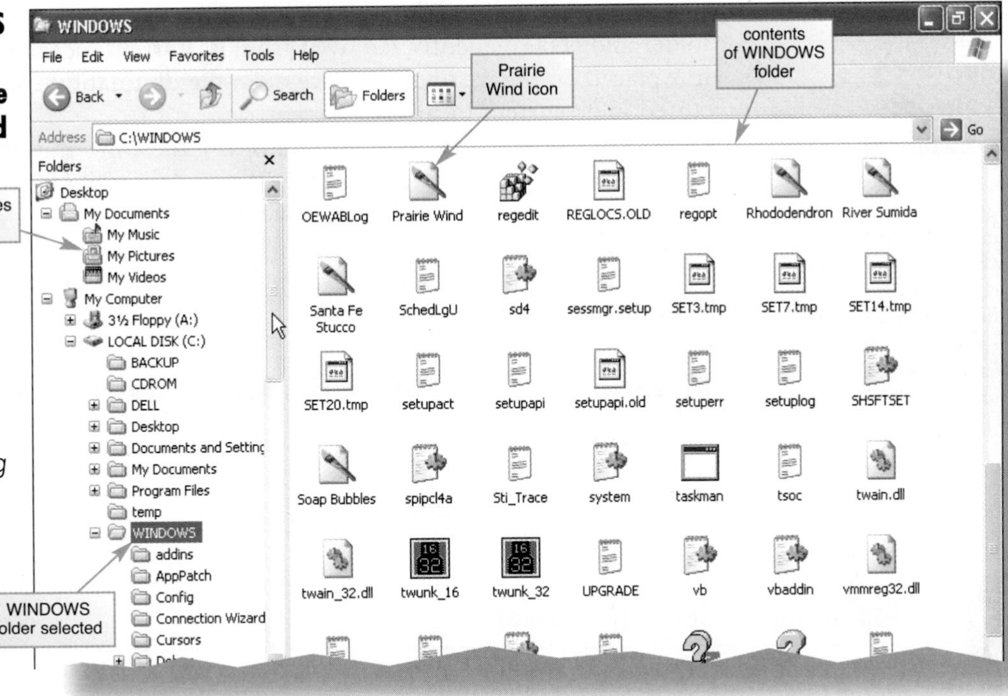

FIGURE 3-44

2 Right-drag the Prairie Wind icon onto the top of the My Pictures icon. Point to Copy Here on the shortcut menu.

The dimmed image of the Prairie Wind icon displays as you right-drag the icon onto the top of the My Pictures icon, a shortcut menu displays, and the dimmed image no longer displays (Figure 3-45).

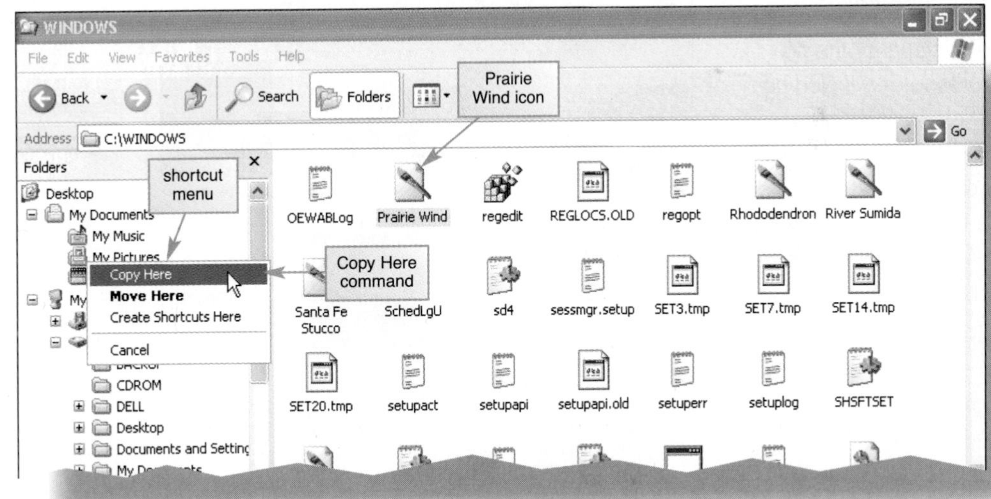

FIGURE 3-45

3 Click Copy Here.

The Prairie Wind file is copied to the My Pictures folder.

Other Ways

1. Right-click file to copy, click Copy, right-click My Pictures icon, click Paste
2. Click file to copy, on Edit menu click Copy, click My Pictures icon, on Edit menu click Paste
3. Select file to copy, press CTRL+C, select My Pictures icon, press CTRL+V

You can move files using the techniques just discussed except that you click **Move Here** instead of Copy Here on the shortcut menu (see Figure 3-45 on the previous page). The difference between a move and a copy, as mentioned previously, is that when you move a file, it is placed on the destination drive or in the destination folder and is permanently removed from its current location. When a file is copied, it is placed on the destination drive or in the destination folder as well as remaining stored in its current location.

In general, you should right-drag or use the copy and paste method to copy or move a file instead of dragging a file. If you drag a file from one folder to another on the same drive, Windows XP moves the file. If you drag a file from one folder to another folder on a different drive, Windows XP copies the file. Because of the different ways this is handled, it is strongly suggested you right-drag or use copy and paste when moving or copying files.

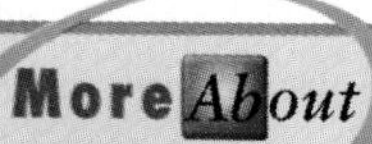

Launching Programs in Explorer

Usually, people find starting application programs from the Start menu or from a window easier and more intuitive than starting programs from Explorer. In most cases, you will not be launching programs from Explorer.

Displaying the Contents of the My Pictures Folder

After copying a file, you might want to examine the folder or drive where the file was copied to ensure it was copied properly. To see the contents of the My Pictures folder, complete the following step.

To Display the Contents of a Folder

1 Click the My Pictures icon in the Folders pane.

The contents of the My Pictures folder, including the Prairie Wind file, display in the right pane (Figure 3-46). If additional files or folders display in the My Pictures folder, their icons and titles also display.

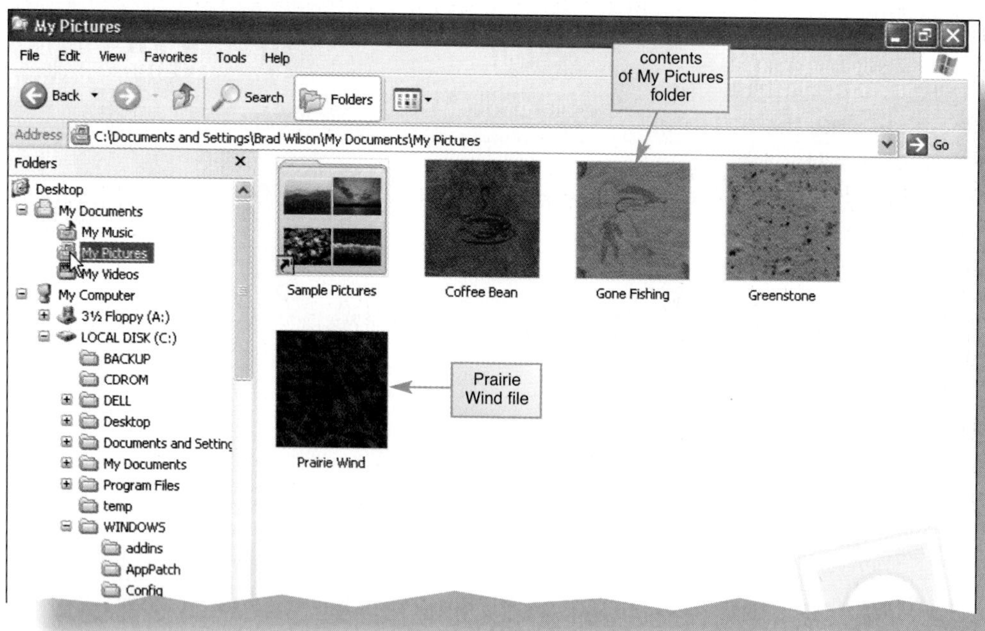

FIGURE 3-46

Renaming Files and Folders

In some circumstances, you may want to **rename** a file or a folder. This could occur when you want to distinguish a file in one folder or drive from a copy, or if you decide you need a better name to identify a file. To change the name of the Prairie Wind file in the My Pictures folder to Blue Prairie Wind, complete the following steps.

Steps To Rename a File

1 **Right-click the Prairie Wind icon in the right pane and then point to Rename on the shortcut menu.**

The selected Prairie Wind icon and a shortcut menu display (Figure 3-47).

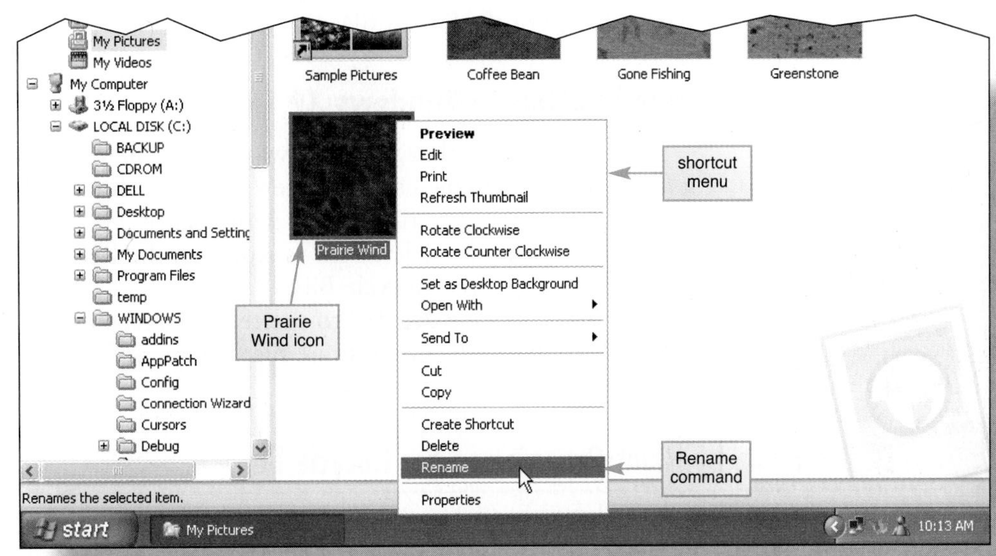

FIGURE 3-47

2 **Click Rename. Type** `Blue Prairie Wind` **and then press the ENTER key.**

The file is renamed Blue Prairie Wind (Figure 3-48). Notice that the file in the My Pictures folder is renamed, but the original file in the WINDOWS folder in drive C is not renamed.

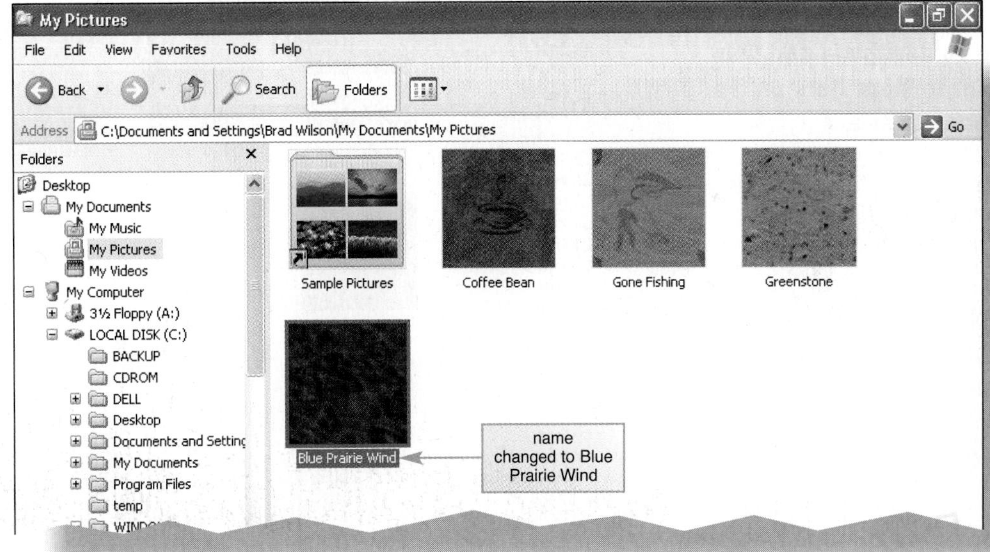

FIGURE 3-48

Renaming files by the method shown above also can be accomplished in other windows. For example, if you open the My Computer window and then open the My Music window, you can rename any file stored in the My Music window using the technique just presented.

Use caution when renaming files on the hard disk. If you inadvertently rename a file that is associated with certain programs, the programs may not be able to find the file and, therefore, may not execute properly.

Other Ways

1. Right-click icon, press M, type name, press ENTER
2. Click icon, press F2, type name, press ENTER
3. Click icon, on File menu click Rename, type name, press ENTER
4. Select icon, press ALT+F, press M, type name, press ENTER

If you change a file name for which a shortcut exists on a menu, in a folder, or on the desktop, Windows XP will update the shortcut link so the shortcut points to the renamed file. The name of the shortcut, however, does not change to reflect the name change of the linked file.

Deleting Files in Windows XP Explorer

A final function that you may want to use in Windows XP Explorer is to delete a file. Exercise extreme caution when deleting a file or files. When you delete a file from a floppy disk, the file is gone permanently once you delete it. If you delete a file from a hard disk, the deleted file is stored in the Recycle Bin where you can recover it until you empty the Recycle Bin.

Assume you have decided to delete the Greenstone file from the My Pictures window. To delete the Greenstone file, complete the following steps.

Steps To Delete a File by Right-Dragging to the Recycle Bin

1 Scroll the Folders pane to display the Recycle Bin icon. Right-drag the Greenstone icon to the Recycle Bin icon in the Folders pane and then point to Move Here on the shortcut menu.

The Greenstone icon in the right pane is right-dragged to the Recycle Bin icon in the Folders pane and a shortcut menu displays (Figure 3-49). The Move Here command is highlighted on the shortcut menu.

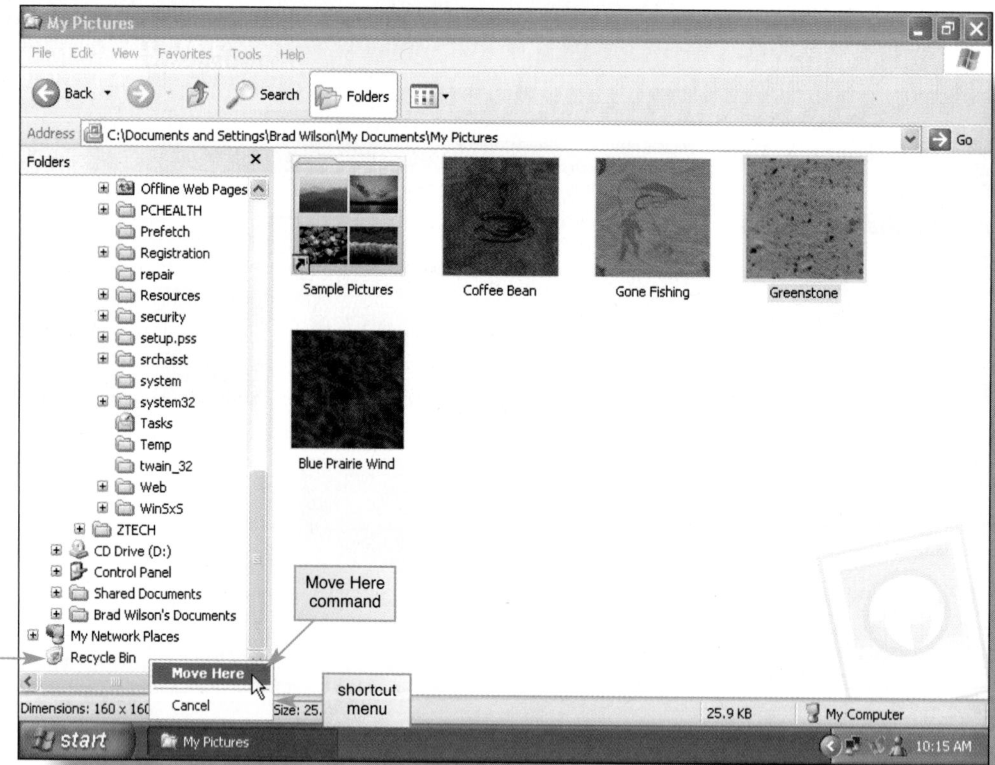

FIGURE 3-49

2 Click Move Here.

The Greenstone icon is removed from the right pane and moved to the Recycle Bin (Figure 3-50). The icons in the right pane are rearranged and the Blue Prairie Wind icon displays in the location the Greenstone icon occupied before being deleted. If you wish to terminate the deleting process before it is complete, you can click the Cancel button on the shortcut menu.

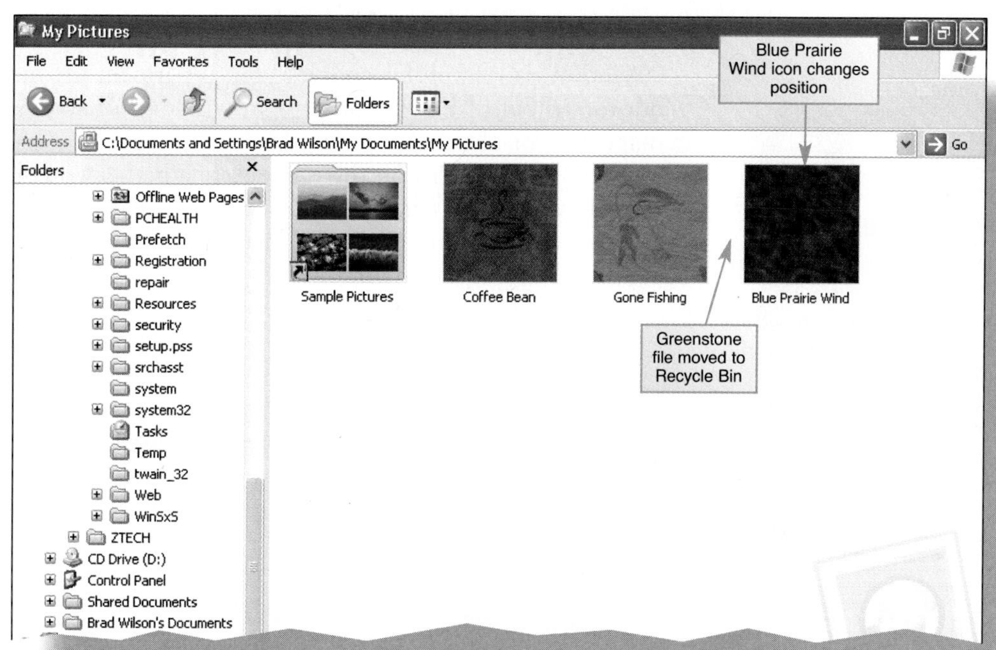

FIGURE 3-50

You can use the methods just specified to delete folders on a floppy disk or a hard disk. Again, you should use extreme caution when deleting files and folders to ensure you do not delete something you may not be able to recover.

Other Ways

1. Drag icon to Recycle Bin
2. Right-click icon, click Delete, click Yes button
3. Click icon, on File menu click Delete, click Yes button
4. Select icon, press ALT+F, press D, press Y

Removing the Status Bar

Earlier in this project, you displayed the status bar to view information about the folders, programs, and documents in the My Computer window. To return the My Computer window to its original state, the status bar should be removed by performing the following steps.

TO REMOVE THE STATUS BAR

1. Click View on the menu bar.
2. Click Status Bar on the View menu.

The status bar no longer displays in the My Computer window.

More About

Deleting Files

This is your last warning! Be EXTREMELY careful when deleting files. Hours of work can be lost with one click of a button. If you are going to delete files or folders from your hard disk, make a backup of those files to ensure that if you inadvertently delete something you need, you will be able to recover the file.

Closing Windows XP Explorer

When you have finished working with Windows Explorer, normally you will close the Explorer window by closing the Folders pane. To close the Folders pane, complete the step below.

TO CLOSE THE EXPLORING WINDOW

1. Click the Close button on the My Pictures window title bar.

Windows XP closes the Exploring window.

Summary of Windows XP Explorer

Windows XP Explorer enables you to perform file maintenance in a single window without displaying additional windows or worrying about window management on the desktop. In addition, it provides a hierarchical view of all drives, folders, and files on the computer. Whether you choose to use Explorer or the My Computer window to perform file maintenance is a personal choice. You may find that some tasks are easier using Explorer and others are easier using the My Computer window.

Properties

The Properties dialog box allows you to customize not only your desktop and working environment, but also to troubleshoot problems with a device as well as defragment and backup a drive. Right-click/Properties is a sequence you should become familiar with in Windows XP.

Properties of Objects

Every object in Windows XP has **properties**, which describe the object. In some cases, you can change the properties of an object. Each drive, folder, file, and program in Windows XP is an object. In the following section, the properties of objects will be shown.

Drive Properties

Each drive on the computer has properties. To display the properties for the hard disk, complete the following steps.

Steps To Display Hard Disk Properties

1 Click the Start button and then click My Computer on the Start menu. Right-click the LOCAL DISK (C:) icon in the right pane of the My Computer window and then point to Properties on the shortcut menu.

Windows XP opens the My Computer window and displays a shortcut menu (Figure 3-51).

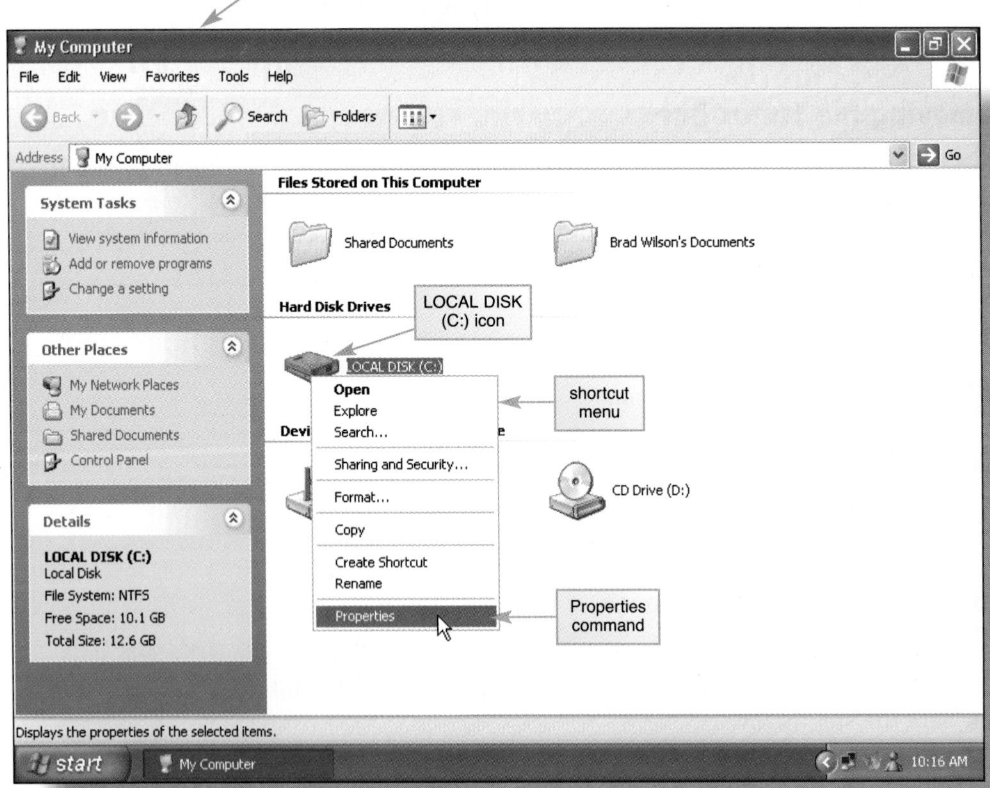

FIGURE 3-51

2 Click Properties and then point to the Cancel button.

The LOCAL DISK (C:) Properties dialog box displays (Figure 3-52). The text box at the top of the General sheet allows you to type a new hard drive label, and the drive type (LOCAL DISK) and File system (NTFS) display. The used space on the drive (dark blue box) and free space (magenta box) display. The total capacity of the disk is specified along with a pie chart.

3 Click the Cancel button.

The LOCAL DISK (C:) Properties dialog box closes.

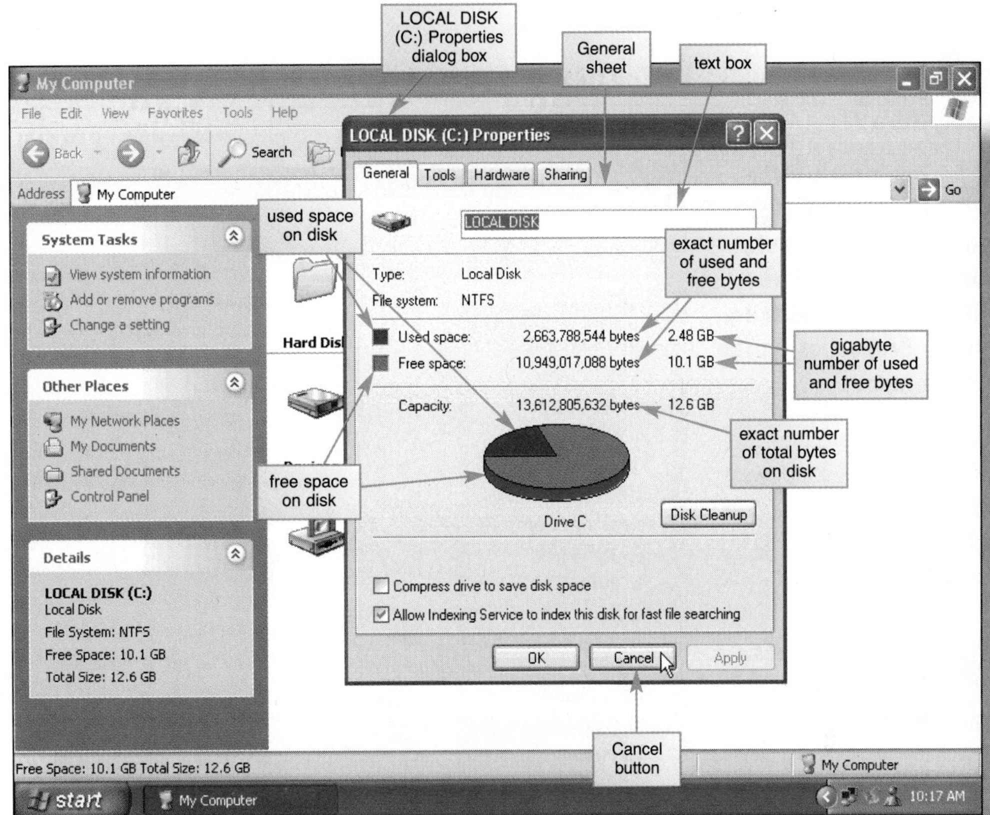

FIGURE 3-52

Other Ways

1. Click drive icon, on File menu click Properties, click Cancel button
2. Select drive icon, press ALT+ENTER, press ESC

The **Tools sheet** in the LOCAL DISK (C:) Properties dialog box shown in Figure 3-52, accessible by clicking the Tools tab, allows you to check errors, defragment, or back up the hard drive. The **Hardware sheet**, accessible by clicking the Hardware tab, allows you to view a list of all disk drives, troubleshoot disk drives that are not working properly, and display the properties of each disk drive. The **Sharing sheet**, accessible by clicking the Sharing tab, allows you to share the contents of a hard disk with other computer users. However, to protect a computer from unauthorized access, sharing the hard disk is not recommended. Other tabs may display in the LOCAL DISK (C:) properties dialog box on your computer.

In Figure 3-52, you might think the number of bytes specified for used space and for free space do not correspond with the gigabyte specification shown, but in fact they do. A **gigabyte of RAM**, or disk space, is not exactly one billion characters, or bytes. Because addresses are calculated on a computer using the binary number system, a gigabyte of RAM or disk space actually is 1,073,741,824 bytes, which is equal to 2^{30}. In Figure 3-52, if you multiply 2.19 by 1,073,741,824, the answer is just less than 2,361,698,816, which is shown as the total number of bytes of used space on the hard drive. Therefore, 2.20 GB is the closest estimate, expressed as gigabytes, for the total amount of used space on the hard drive.

Properties of a Folder

Folders also have properties. To display the properties of the WINDOWS folder, complete the steps on the next page.

To Display Folder Properties

1 Double-click the LOCAL DISK (C:) icon in the My Computer window. Right-click the WINDOWS icon and then point to Properties on the shortcut menu.

Windows XP opens the LOCAL DISK (C:) window and displays a shortcut menu containing the Properties command (Figure 3-53).

2 Click Properties. Point to the Cancel button.

The WINDOWS Properties dialog box displays (Figure 3-54). The WINDOWS folder name displays in a text box. The type, File Folder, is specified. The location of the folder (C:\) is shown. The size in megabytes and actual bytes displays. The WINDOWS folder contains 6,162 files and 261 folders. The date and time the file was created and the file attributes display. These values and the tabs in the dialog box may be different on your computer.

3 Click the Cancel button. Close the LOCAL DISK (C:) window.

The WINDOWS Properties dialog box and the LOCAL DISK (C:) window close.

Other Ways

1. Click folder icon, on File menu click Properties, click Cancel button

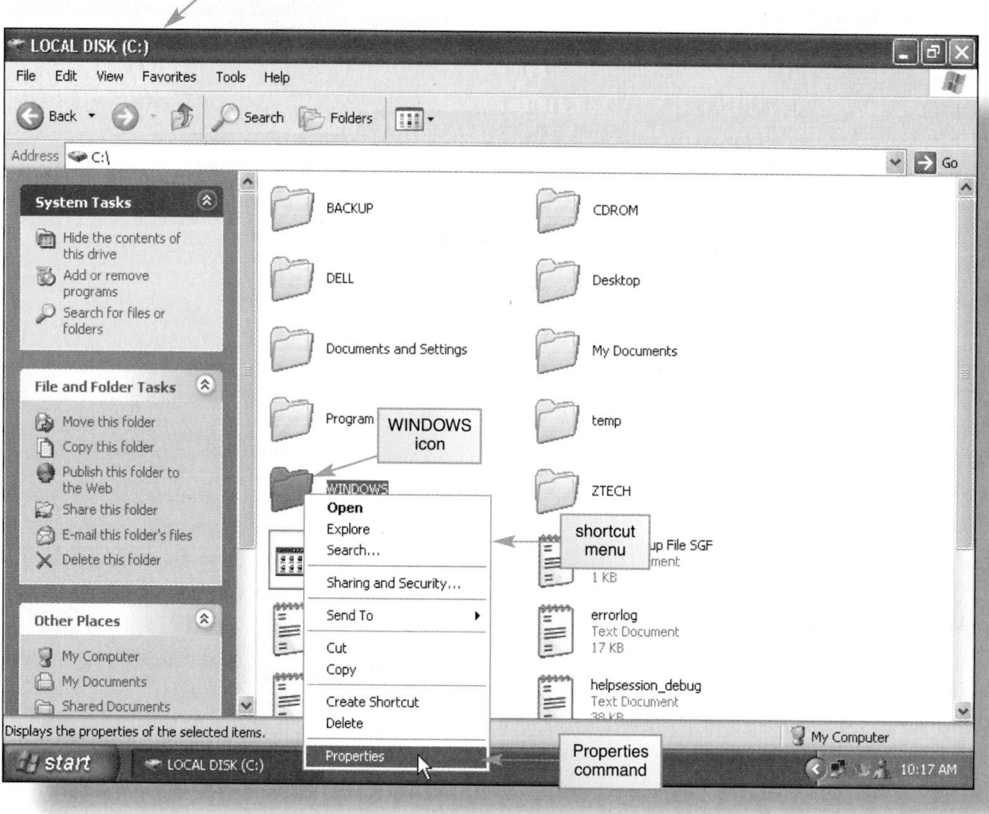

FIGURE 3-53

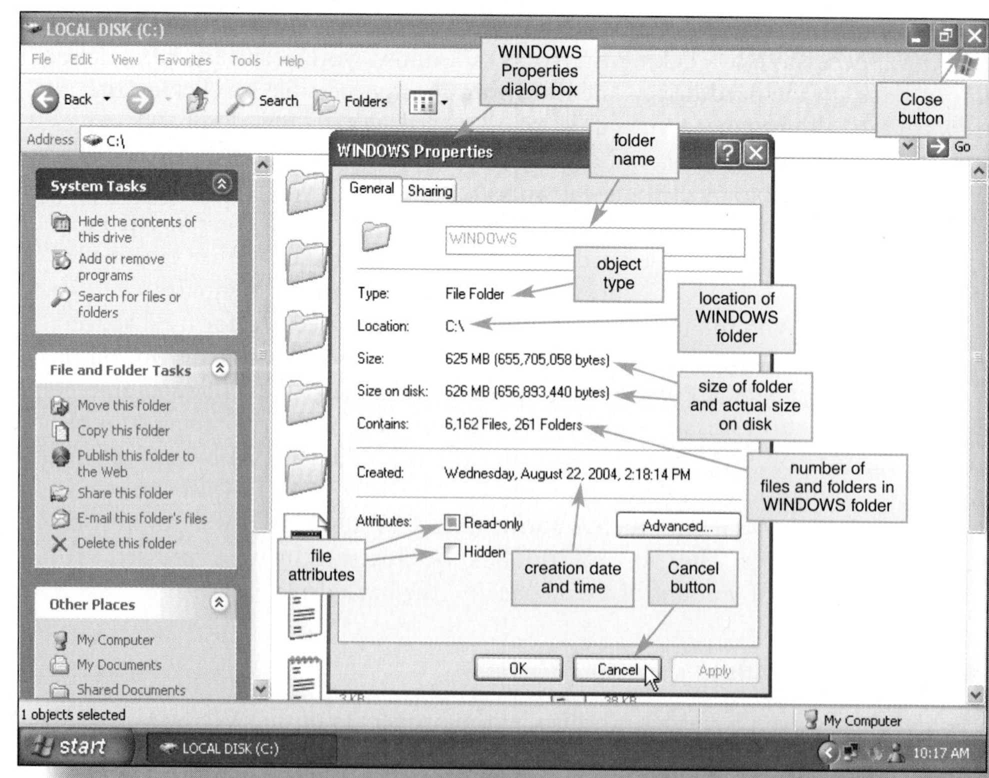

FIGURE 3-54

In the examples of drive and folder properties, you opened windows, right-clicked the object, and then clicked Properties on the shortcut menu. These same steps can be performed in Windows XP Explorer. If you have Explorer open and want to display the properties of drive C, right-click the drive C icon and then click Properties on the shortcut menu.

Files and programs also have properties, although these properties are different from the properties of a hard disk and the properties of a folder.

My Pictures Window

You can organize and share pictures with others on the computer or the Internet using the My Pictures folder. When you save pictures from a digital camera, scanner, or hard drive, Windows stores the pictures in the My Pictures folder. Tasks associated with this folder allow you to view the pictures as a slide show or filmstrip, share pictures with others, e-mail pictures to friends, print pictures, publish pictures to the Internet, and order prints of a picture from the Internet.

The My Pictures window shown in Figure 3-55 has three files containing bitmap images (Coffee Bean, Gone Fishing, and Blue Prairie Wind). When several related documents display in a window, you may wish to create a folder to contain the files and move the files into the folder so you can find and reference them easily among other files that may be stored in the My Pictures folder.

More About

My Pictures

You can organize the photos in the My Pictures window in photo album folders designed to store a small number of related photos. This capability is useful if you want to keep pictures of special events or pictures that you need for a specific purpose separate from other pictures. For more information about making a photo album, search Help and Support using the keywords, photo album.

Creating a Folder in the My Pictures Folder

To reduce clutter in the My Pictures folder and to better organize the files in the My Picture folder, create a folder in the My Pictures window and then move the Coffee Bean, Gone Fishing, and Blue Prairie Wind files into the folder. Perform the following steps to create the Bitmap Images folder in the My Pictures folder.

Steps To Create a Folder in the My Pictures Folder

1 Click the Start button. Click My Pictures on the Start menu. Point to Make a new folder in the File and Folder Tasks area.

The My Pictures window displays (Figure 3-55). The Make a new folder task is underlined in the File and Folder Tasks area and the icons in the right pane display in Thumbnails view.

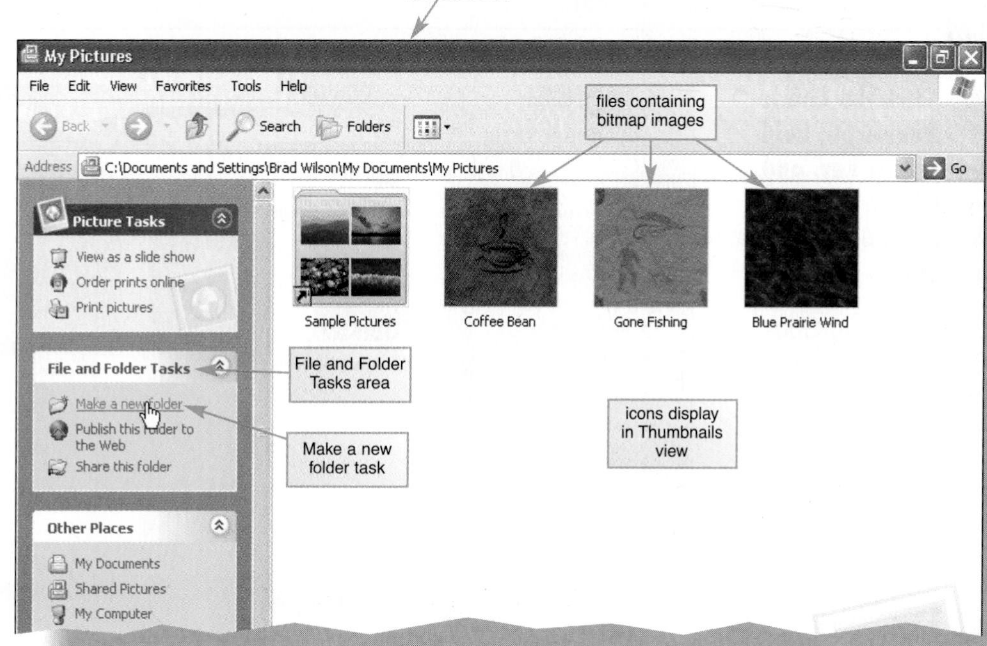

FIGURE 3-55

2 Click Make a new folder, type `Bitmap Images` **in the icon title text box, and then press the ENTER key.**

The Bitmap Images folder is created in the My Pictures folder and the highlighted Bitmap Images icon displays in the right pane (Figure 3-56). An open folder icon identifies the Bitmap Images folder.

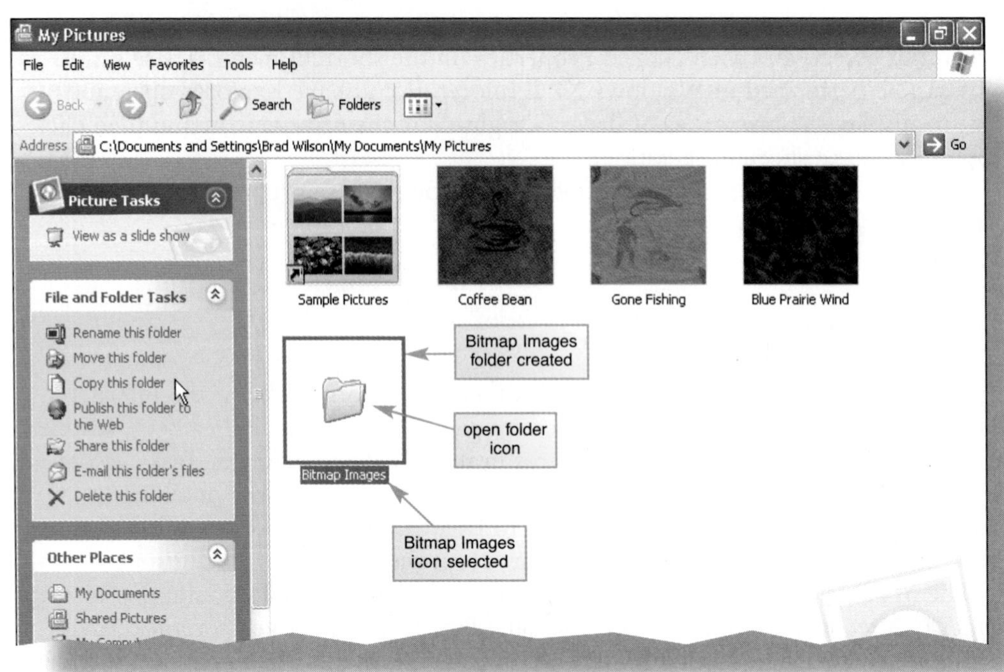

FIGURE 3-56

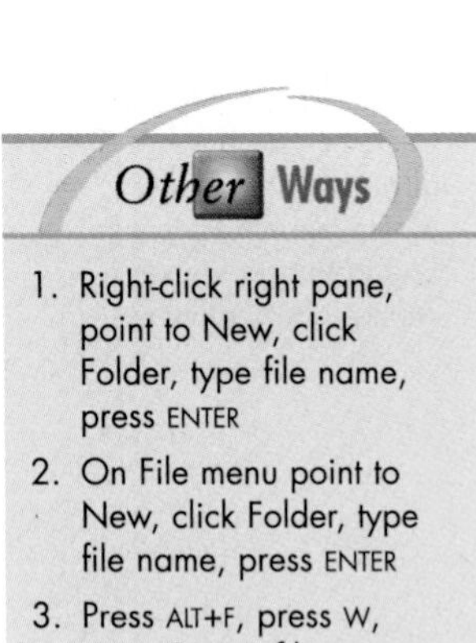

Other Ways

1. Right-click right pane, point to New, click Folder, type file name, press ENTER
2. On File menu point to New, click Folder, type file name, press ENTER
3. Press ALT+F, press W, press F, type file name, press ENTER

Moving Files into the Bitmap Images Folder

After you create the Bitmap Images folder in the My Pictures folder, the next step is to move the three files containing bitmap images into the folder. Perform the following steps to move the Coffee Bean, Gone Fishing, and Blue Prairie Wind files into the Bitmap Images folder.

Steps To Move a File into a Folder

1 Click the Coffee Bean icon, hold down the CTRL key, and then click the Gone Fishing and Blue Prairie Wind icons.

The Coffee Bean, Gone Fishing, and Blue Prairie Wind icons are selected (Figure 3-57).

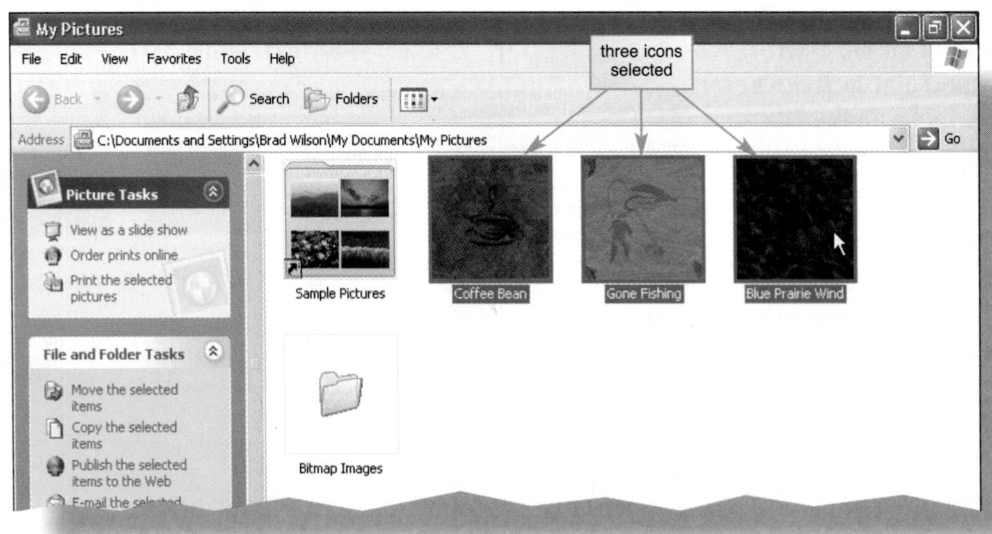

FIGURE 3-57

2 Right-drag the Blue Prairie Wind icon to the Bitmap Images folder icon. Click Move Here on the shortcut menu.

The Coffee Bean, Gone Fishing, and Blue Prairie Wind icons are moved into the Bitmap Images folder (Figure 3-58).

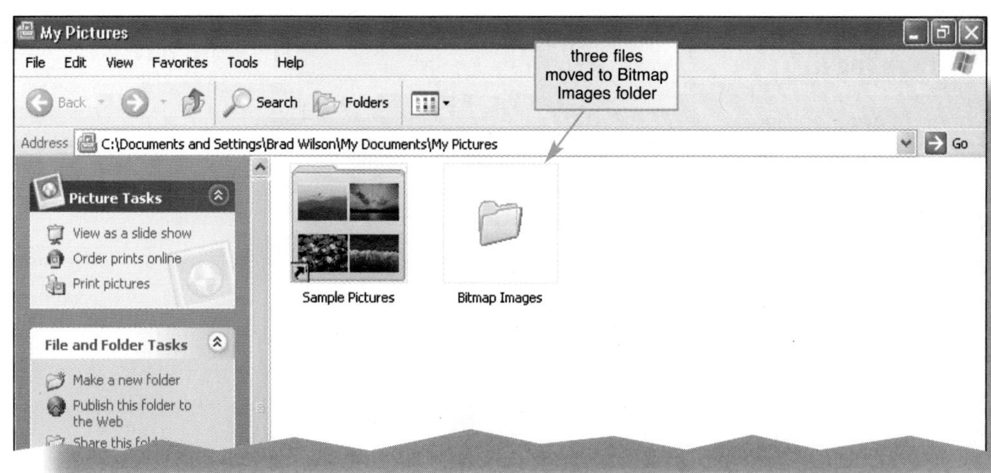

FIGURE 3-58

Other Ways

1. Drag icon to folder icon
2. Right-click icon, click Cut, right-click folder icon, click Paste
3. Click icon, in left pane click Move this file, in Move Items dialog box click My Documents, click My Pictures, click folder name, click Move button

Refreshing the Image on a Folder

After creating the Bitmap Images folder in the My Pictures folder and moving the three files into the folder, an open folder icon displays on the Bitmap Images folder. To replace the folder icon with the bitmap images of the three files stored in the Bitmap Images folder (Blue Prairie Wind, Coffee Bean, and Gone Fishing), the folder icon on the folder must be refreshed. Complete the following steps to refresh the image on the Bitmap Images folder.

Steps To Refresh the Image on a Folder

1 Right-click the Bitmap Images icon and point to Refresh Thumbnail on the shortcut menu.

A shortcut menu displays and the Refresh Thumbnail command is highlighted (Figure 3-59).

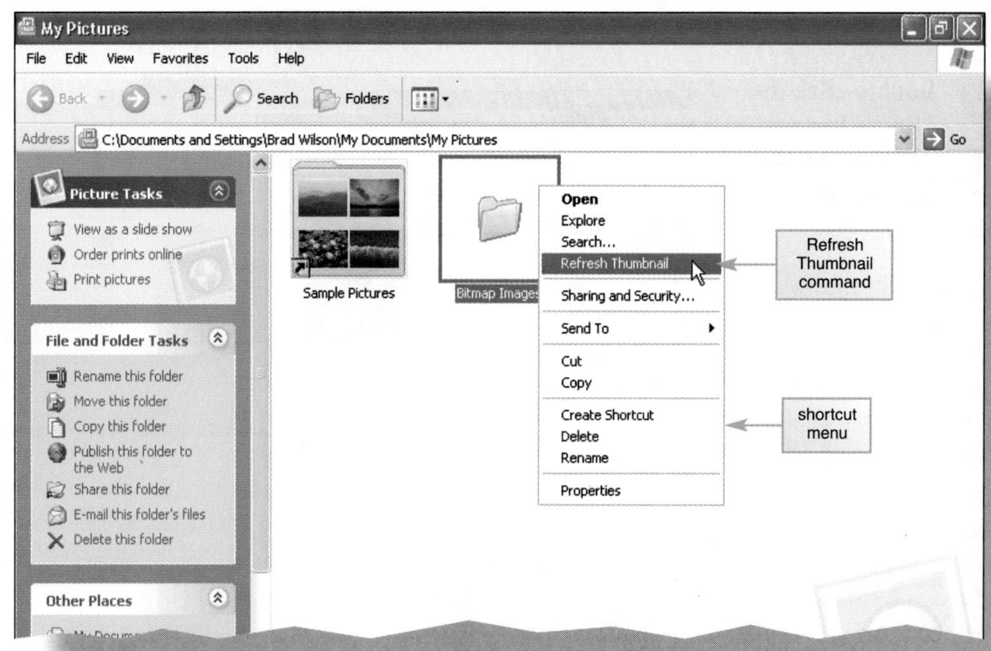

FIGURE 3-59

2 Click Refresh Thumbnail.

The open folder icon on the Bitmap Images folder changes to a larger closed folder icon and the bitmap images contained in the three files in the Bitmap Images folder display on the closed folder icon (Figure 3-60). The Bitmap Images icon is selected.

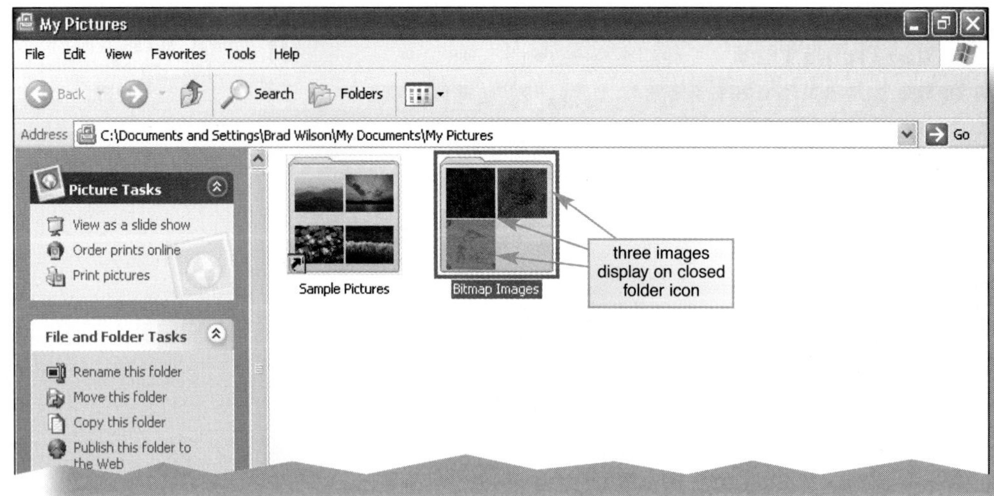

FIGURE 3-60

Other Ways

1. Select folder icon, on menu bar click File, click Refresh Thumbnail

View Images in Filmstrip View or as a Slide Show

You can view the images in a folder in Filmstrip view or as a slide show. **Filmstrip view** displays the images in the folder in a row, allows you to view each image separately, and rotate each image clockwise or counter-clockwise.

Slide Show displays each image in the folder as part of a slide show and allows you to view the next or previous slide, rotate a slide clockwise or counter-clockwise, pause the slide show, and exit the slide show. Perform the following steps to view the images in the Bitmap Images folder in Filmstrip view.

To View Bitmap Images in Filmstrip View

1 Double-click the Bitmap Images icon. Click View on the menu bar and then point to Filmstrip.

The Bitmap Images window opens in the same window as My Pictures was displayed, the View menu displays, and the Filmstrip command is highlighted (Figure 3-61). A bullet precedes the Thumbnails command to indicate the icons in the window display in Thumbnails view.

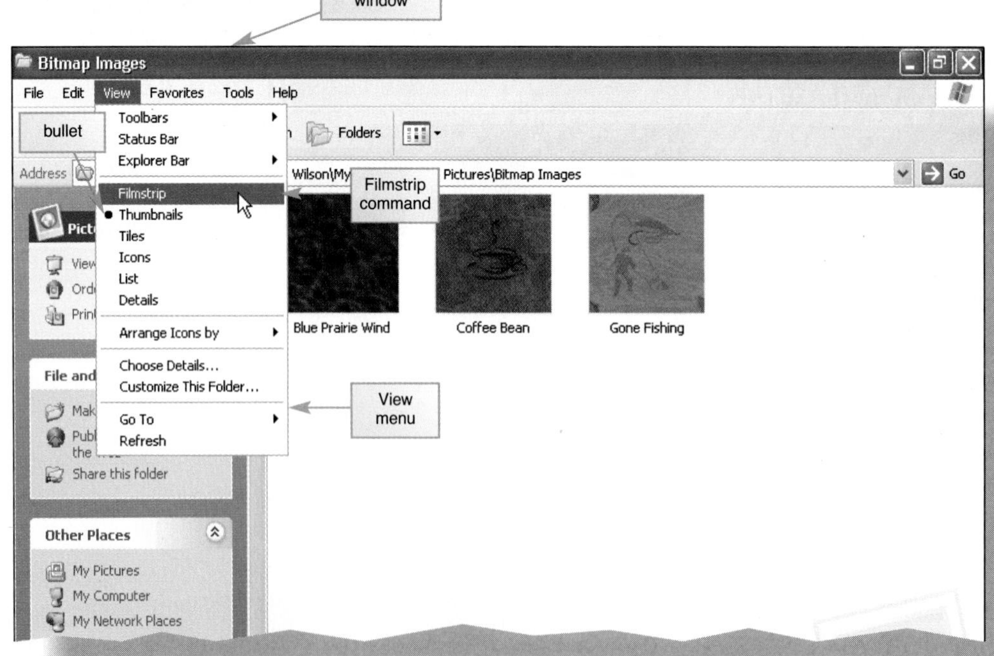

FIGURE 3-61

2 **Click Filmstrip.**

The three files in the Bitmap Images folder (Blue Prairie Wind, Coffee Bean, and Gone Fishing) display in Filmstrip view (Figure 3-62). The images contained in the three files display in a row, an enlarged version of the first image in the row (Blue Prairie Wind) and the Filmstrip toolbar display above the row.

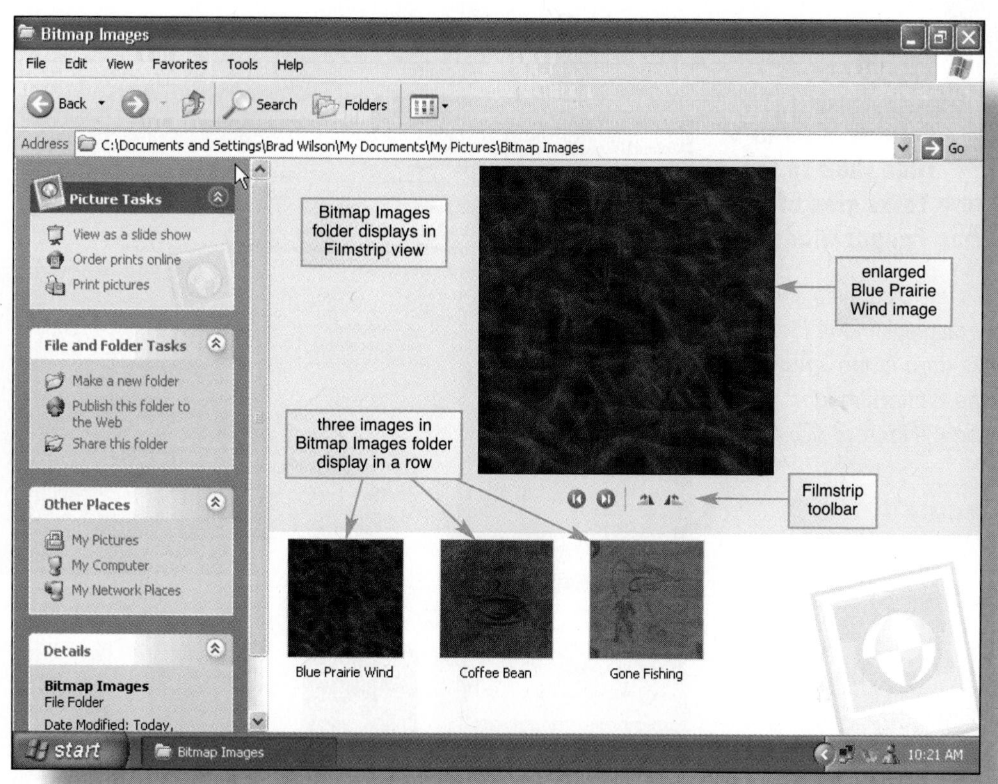

FIGURE 3-62

1. Right-click open area in right pane, point to View, click Filmstrip
2. Press ALT+V, press P

Clicking an image in Filmstrip view displays the image above the row of images in the right pane. Double-clicking an image displays the image in the Windows Picture and Fax Viewer that allows you to edit, print, or save the image in another folder.

The four buttons on the **Filmstrip toolbar** illustrated in Figure 3-62 allow you to scroll through the images and rotate an image clockwise or counter-clockwise. Table 3-2 illustrates the Filmstrip toolbar and briefly describes the function of each button.

Table 3-2 Filmstrip Toolbar

BUTTON	*FUNCTION*
[Previous Image button]	Go to previous image in the filmstrip.
[Next Image button]	Go to next image in the filmstrip.
[Rotate Clockwise button]	Rotates image by 90 degrees clockwise.
[Rotate Counterclockwise button]	Rotates image by 90 degrees counter-clockwise.

Viewing the Images in the My Pictures Folder as a Slide Show

The images in the My Pictures folder also can be viewed as a slide show. Perform the steps on the next page to view the images in the My Pictures folder as a slide show.

Steps To View Images as a Slide Show

1 Point to View as a slide show in the Picture Tasks area of the Bitmap Images window.

The View as a slide show task displays in the Picture Tasks area in the left pane of the Bitmap Images window (Figure 3-63).

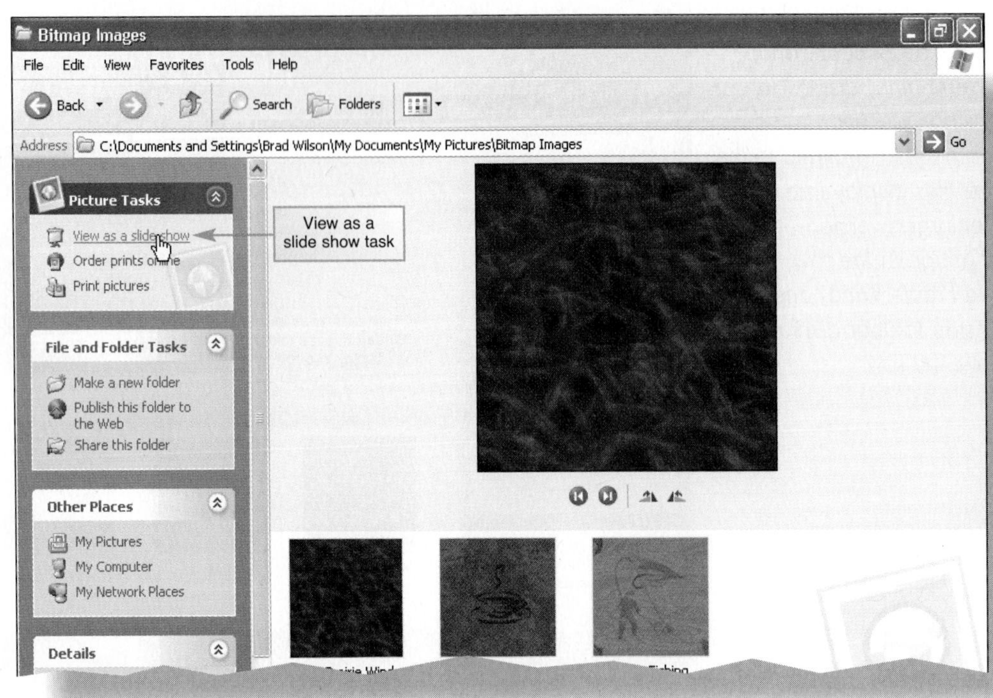

FIGURE 3-63

2 Click View as a Slide Show. Move the mouse to display the Slide Show toolbar.

A black screen displays and the images in the Bitmap Images folder display individually on the screen (Figure 3-64). Currently, the Gone Fishing image displays on the screen. When you move the mouse, the mouse pointer and Slide Show toolbar display.

3 Click the Close the window button on the Slide Show toolbar to end the slide show.

The slide show terminates.

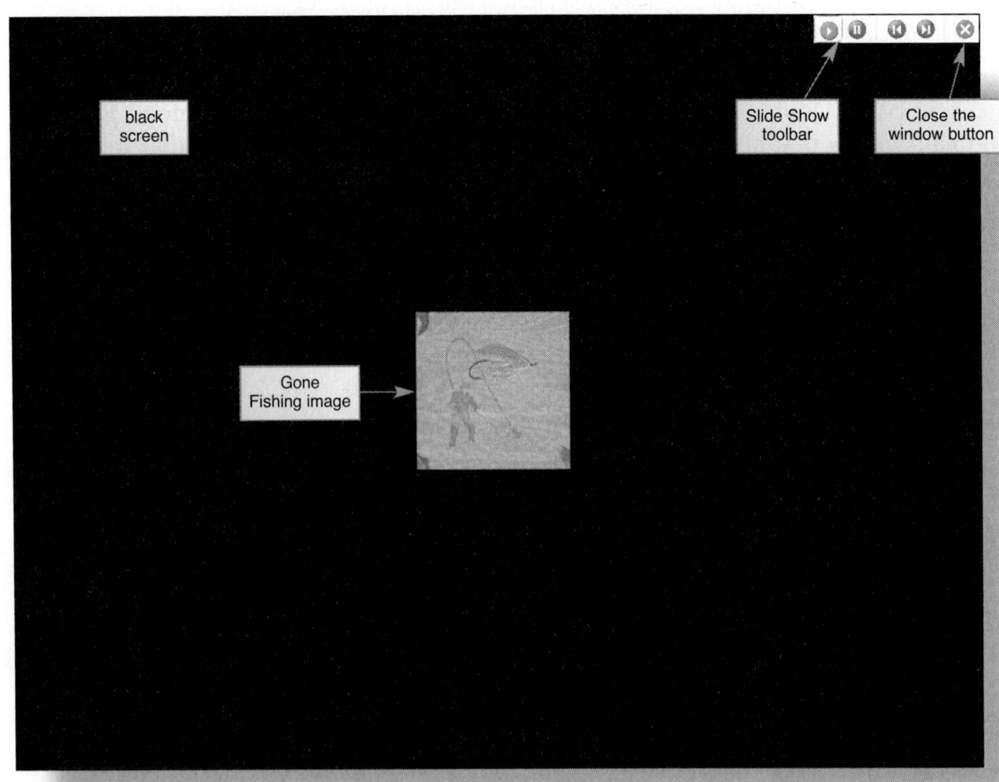

FIGURE 3-64

In Figure 3-64, you can use the buttons on the **Slide Show toolbar** to start the slide show, pause the slide show, display the next or previous slide, and close the slide show. Table 3-3 illustrates the Slide Show toolbar and briefly describes the function of each button.

Table 3-3 Slide Show Toolbar

BUTTON	*FUNCTION*
	Start the slide show.
	Pause the slide show.
	Display previous picture.
	Display next picture.
	Close the slide show.

Changing the View and Displaying the My Pictures Window

Previously, you displayed the Bitmap Images window and viewed the images in the window in Slide Show view. Perform the following steps to reset the view in the Bitmap Images window to Thumbnails and display the My Pictures window.

TO VIEW ICONS IN THUMBNAILS VIEW AND DISPLAY THE MY PICTURES WINDOW

1. Click View on the menu bar and then click Thumbnails.
2. Click My Pictures in the Other Places area in the left pane.

The Bitmap Images window displays in Thumbnails view and the My Pictures window displays on the desktop.

Sharing a Folder

After creating the Bitmap Images folder in the My Pictures folder and moving the bitmap images files into the folder, you may wish to share the contents of the folder with other users on the same computer. To accomplish this, you must copy the Bitmap Images folder to the Shared Pictures folder. The **Shared Documents folder** allows the sharing of folders with other computer users. The Shared Documents folder contains the Shared Music folder and Shared Pictures folder. The **Shared Music folder** allows you to share music files and the **Shared Pictures folder** allows you to share picture files. Perform the steps on the next page to share the Bitmap Images folder.

More About

Sharing Pictures

Moving or copying a file or folder to the Shared Pictures folder makes it available to everyone who uses your computer. If you want to share pictures with a computer user on another computer, consider e-mailing the picture instead of sharing the picture. If you are connected to a network domain, the Shared Documents, Shared Pictures, and Shared Music folders are not available.

Steps To Share a Folder

1 Right-click the Bitmap Images icon in the right pane of the My Pictures window. Point to Copy on the shortcut menu.

A shortcut menu containing the highlighted Copy command displays in the right pane of the My Pictures window (Figure 3-65). The Shared Pictures entry displays in the Other Places area in the left pane.

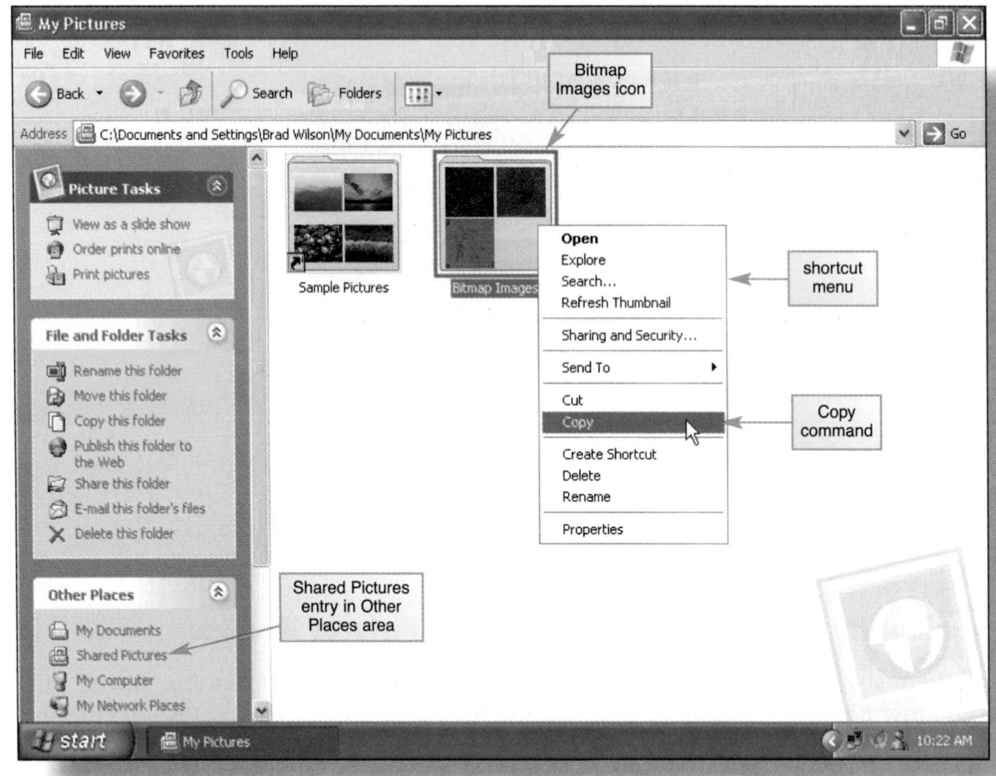

FIGURE 3-65

2 Click Copy. Point to Shared Pictures in the Other Places area.

Windows XP removes the shortcut menu and places a copy of the Bitmap Images folder on the Clipboard (Figure 3-66).

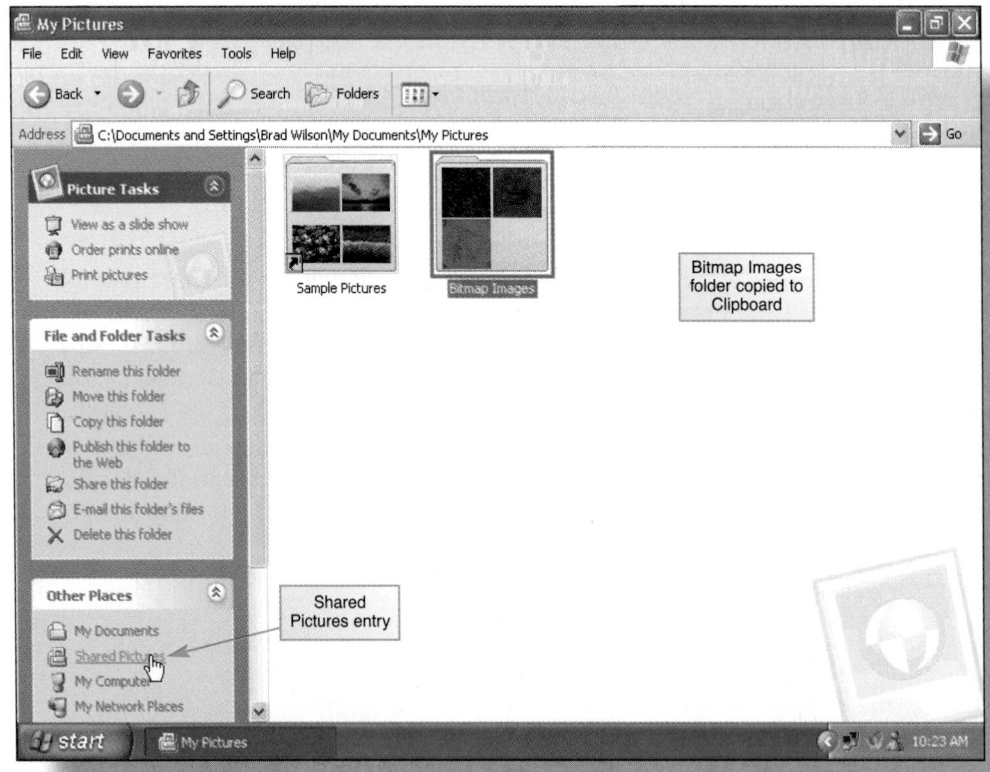

FIGURE 3-66

3 Click Shared Pictures. Right-click an open area of the Shared Pictures window and then point to Paste on the shortcut menu.

The Shared Pictures window and a shortcut menu display (Figure 3-67). The highlighted Paste command displays on the shortcut menu.

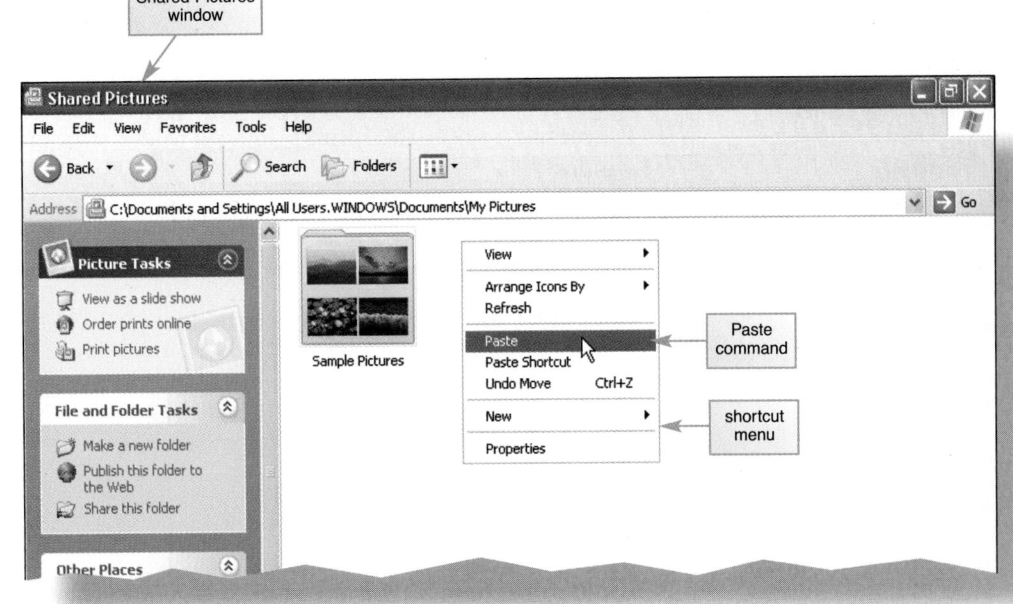

FIGURE 3-67

4 Click Paste on the shortcut menu.

Windows XP copies the Bitmap Images folder to the Shared Pictures window (Figure 3-68).

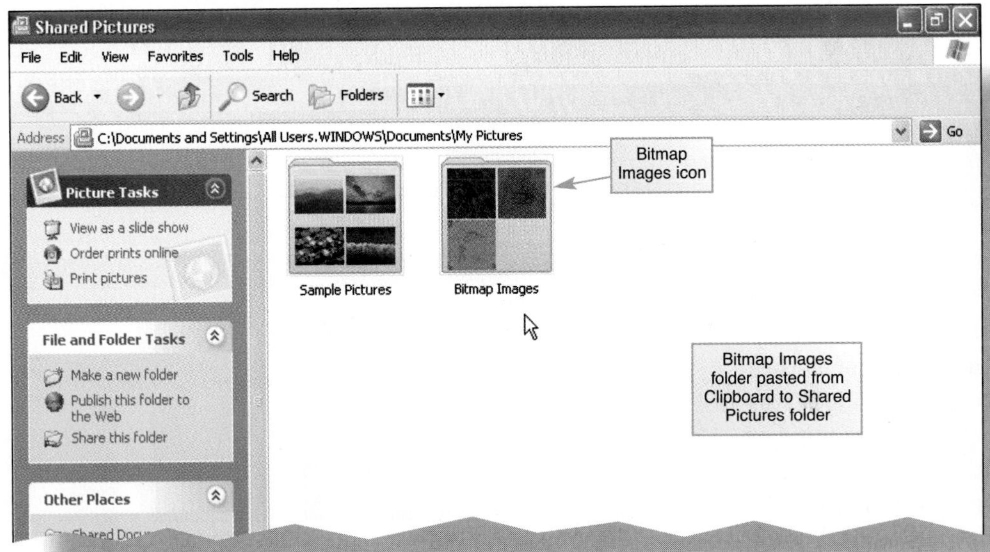

FIGURE 3-68

Other Ways

1. Select folder icon, in File and Folder Tasks area click Copy this folder, click Shared Documents, click Shared Pictures, click Copy button
2. In Windows Explorer, right-drag folder icon to Shared Pictures folder in Folders pane, click Copy Here
3. Select folder icon, on Edit menu click Copy, click Shared Pictures, on Edit menu click Paste

The images in the Bitmap Images folder are available to all users on the computer. Another user can access the Bitmap Images folder by clicking the Start button, clicking My Pictures on the Start menu, clicking Shared Pictures in the Other Places area in the My Pictures window, and then double-clicking the Bitmap Images folder in the Shared Pictures window.

Removing Sharing from a Folder

The original Bitmap Images folder remains in the My Pictures folder and a copy of the folder is placed in the Shared Pictures folder. To remove sharing from the Bitmap Images folder and remove the Bitmap Images folder from the Shared Pictures folder, perform the steps on the next page.

More About

E-Mailing Pictures

E-mailing a picture is an alternative to sharing a picture using the Shared Pictures folder. If you have too many pictures to e-mail or if you wish to send the same pictures to a large number of people, consider using the Publish them to the Web feature. You can publish the pictures to a Web site and e-mail each person the address of the Web site. For more information, search Help and Support using the keywords, publishing to the Web.

TO REMOVE SHARING FROM A FOLDER

1. If necessary, select the Bitmap Images folder icon in the Shared Pictures window.
2. Click Delete this folder in the File and Folder Tasks area.
3. Click the Yes button in the Confirm Folder Delete dialog box.
4. Click the Close button in the Shared Pictures window.

Windows XP removes the Bitmap Images folder from the Shared Pictures window, which no longer allows the folder to be shared by other computer users, and closes the Shared Pictures window.

E-Mailing a Picture

Electronic mail (**e-mail**) has become an important means of exchanging messages and files between business associates and friends. Windows XP allows you to e-mail files, folders, and pictures. E-mailing large images can be time-consuming and often results in the file not reaching its destination. As a result, Windows XP allows you to reduce the size of an image at the time you send it. Perform the following steps to e-mail an image to a friend.

Steps To E-Mail a Picture

1 Click the Start button, click My Pictures on the Start menu, and double-click the Bitmap Images icon in the My Pictures window. Click the Gone Fishing icon to select the icon. Point to E-mail this file in the File and Folder Tasks area.

The Bitmap Images window displays and the Gone Fishing icon is selected (Figure 3-69). The E-mail this file task is underlined in the File and Folder Tasks area.

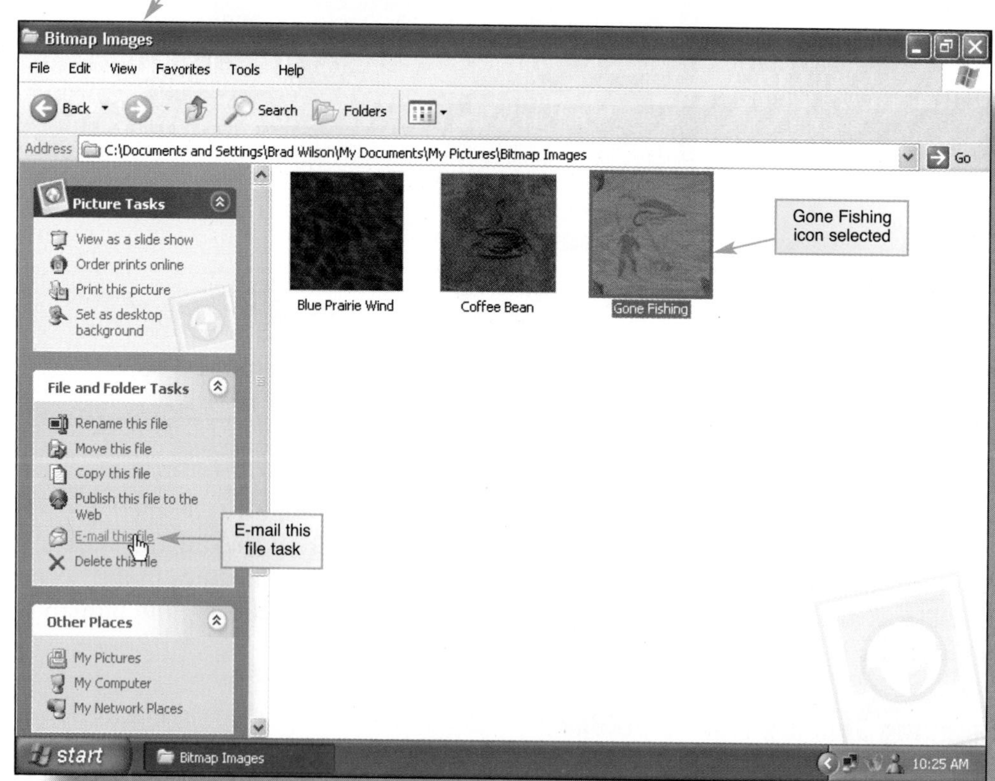

FIGURE 3-69

2 Click E-mail this file. Point to the OK button in the Send Pictures via E-Mail dialog box.

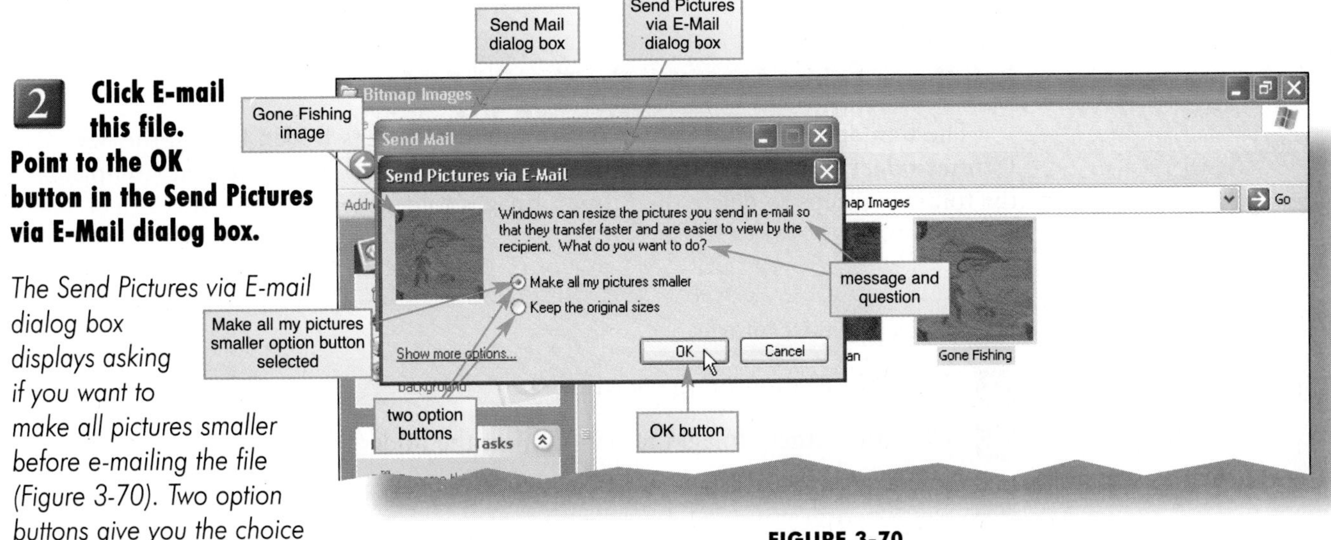

FIGURE 3-70

The Send Pictures via E-mail dialog box displays asking if you want to make all pictures smaller before e-mailing the file (Figure 3-70). Two option buttons give you the choice of making the pictures smaller or keeping the original sizes. The Make all my pictures smaller option button is selected. The Gone Fishing image displays in the dialog box and the Send Mail dialog box displays behind the Send Pictures via E-mail dialog box.

3 Click the OK button. Type `StevenForsythe@msn.com` **in the To text box. Select the message in the message area, type** `I thought you might like this picture for your collection.` **in the message area, and then point to the Send button on the toolbar.**

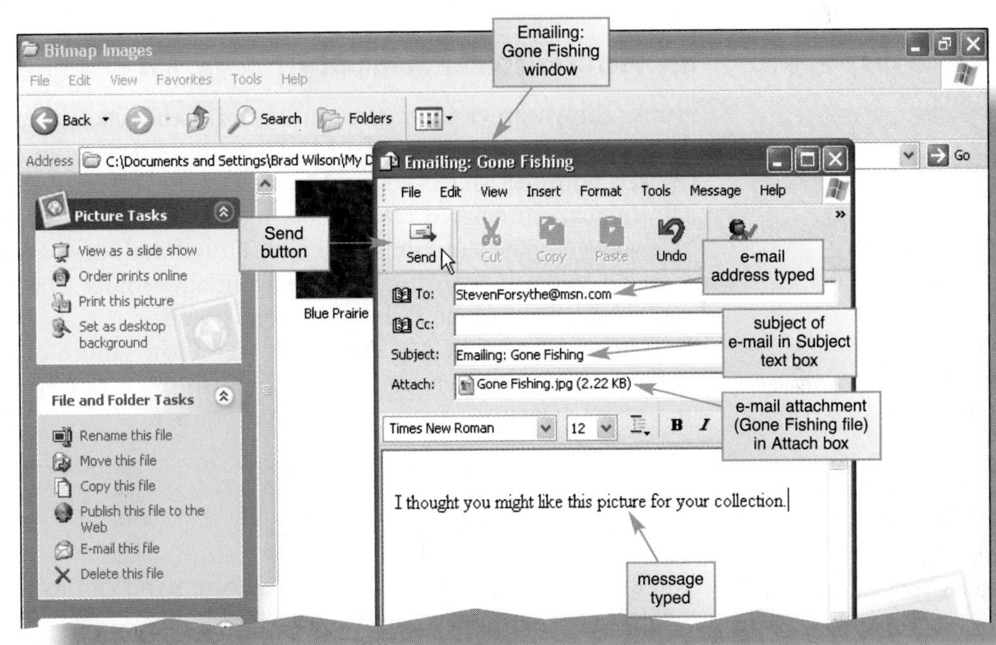

FIGURE 3-71

The Send Mail dialog box displays momentarily and then the Emailing: Gone Fishing window displays (Figure 3-71). The e-mail address and message are typed and the subject (Emailing: Gone Fishing) and attachment, Gone Fishing.jpg (2.22 KB) are automatically added to the Subject text box and Attach box.

4 Click the Send button.

The Send Mail dialog box displays momentarily as the e-mail message is sent and then the Emailing: Gone Fishing window closes. The dialog box on your computer may be different.

5 Click the Close button in the Bitmap Images window.

The Bitmap Images window closes.

Deleting a Folder from the My Pictures Folder

The Bitmap Images folder remains in the My Pictures folder. Return the My Pictures folder to its original state by deleting the Bitmap Images folder. Complete the following steps to delete the Bitmap Images folder.

TO DELETE A FOLDER FROM THE MY PICTURES FOLDER

1. Click the Start button.
2. Click My Pictures on the Start menu.
3. Click the Bitmap Images folder to select the folder.
4. Click Delete this folder in the File and Folder Tasks area.
5. Click the Yes button in the Confirm Folder Delete dialog box.
6. Click the Close button in the My Pictures window.

The Bitmap Images folder is removed from the My Pictures folder and the My Pictures window closes.

My Pictures Folder Summary

As shown previously, you can organize and share pictures with other computer users on a computer using the My Pictures folder. In this section, you viewed and worked with the folders in the My Documents folder (My Music, My Pictures, and My Videos) and Shared Documents folder (Shared Music and Shared Pictures). You viewed images in Filmstrip view, Thumbnail view, and as a slide show. You shared a folder by copying the Bitmap Images folder to the Shared Pictures folder and e-mailed the Gone Fishing file to a friend.

Other tasks in the My Pictures folder allow you to create photo albums to organize small numbers of pictures, publish pictures to a Web site on the Internet, and order prints of a picture from the Internet.

> **More About**
>
> **Find**
>
> Some would argue that Search is the handiest Windows XP tool. If an application program is not represented on the Start menu, many people use Search to display the icon in the Search Results window and then double-click the icon to launch the program.

Finding Files or Folders

You know the location of files you use often and can locate the folder that contains them. In some cases, however, you may know you have a certain file on the computer but you have no idea in what folder it is located. To search every folder manually on the computer to find the file would be time-consuming and almost impossible. Fortunately, Windows XP provides Search Companion.

Search Companion allows you to search for files and folders, pictures and music files, people, computers on a network, and information on the Internet. You can search a computer or other computers on a network. Search Companion allows you to search for files and folders by name, type, or size. You can search for a file based on when you last worked on the file or search for files containing specific text. You also can choose to search with the help of an animated character.

Searching for a File by Name

If you know the name or partial name of a file, you can use Search Companion to locate the file. For example, you know a file named Soap Bubbles exists somewhere on the computer. You want to open the file to see what the image looks like. To search for the file, complete the following steps.

Steps To Search for a File by Name

1 Click the Start button on the taskbar. Point to Search on the Start menu.

The Start menu and highlighted Search command display (Figure 3-72).

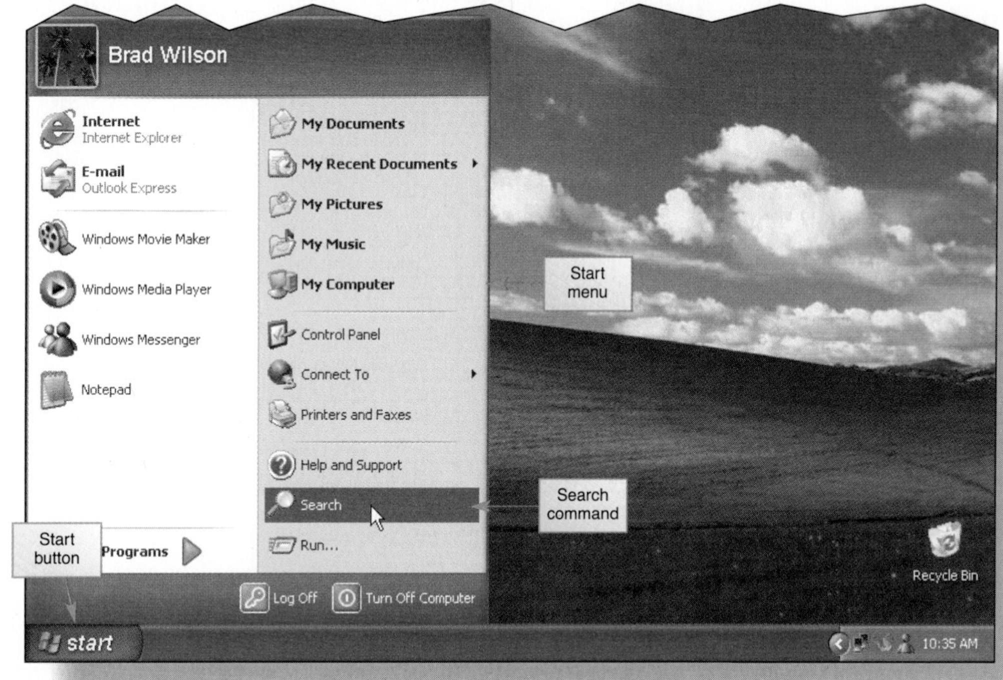

FIGURE 3-72

2 Click the Search command. Maximize the Search Results window. Point to All files and folders in the Search Companion balloon.

The Search Companion pane displays in the Search Results window (Figure 3-73). The pane contains the Search Companion balloon and an animated dog named Rover. The ***Search Companion pane*** *(or* ***Search bar****) allows you to search for pictures, music, and video files; documents; all files and folders; computers or people; and to search on the Internet. The right pane contains a message about starting a search.*

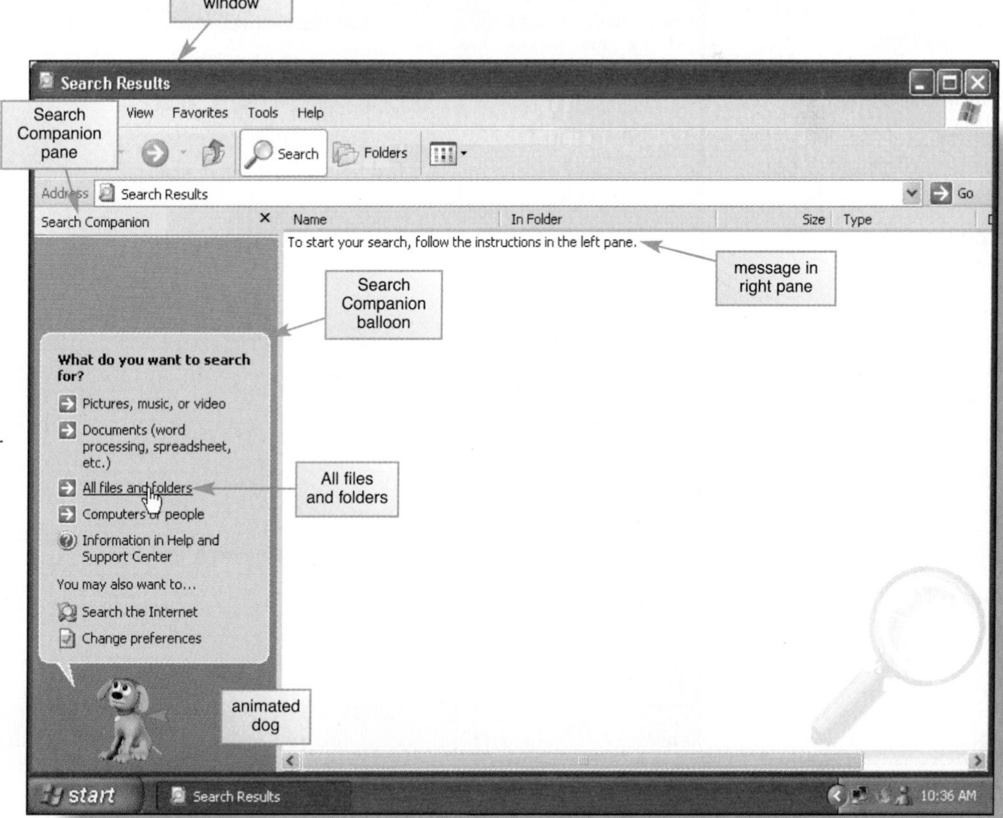

FIGURE 3-73

3 Click All files and folders. Type `soap bubbles` **in the All or part of the file name text box. Point to the Search button.**

The contents of the Search Companion balloon change (Figure 3-74). The keywords, soap bubbles, display in the All or part of the file name text box. The Local Hard Drives (C:) entry in the Look in list box indicates all of LOCAL DISK (C:) will be searched.

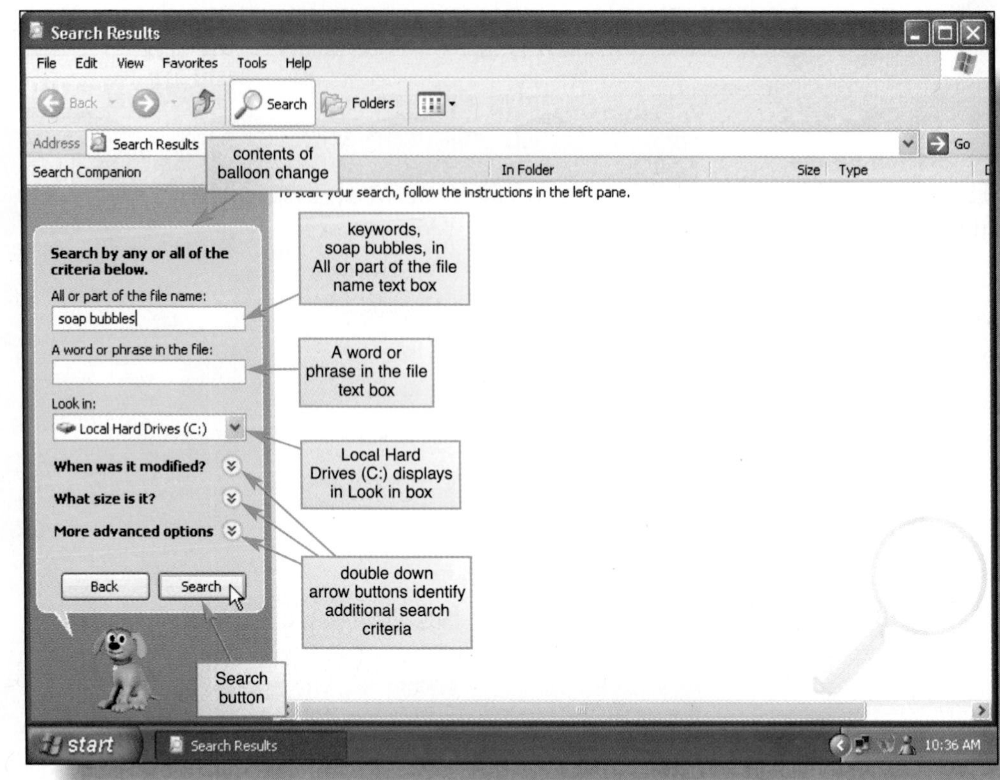

FIGURE 3-74

4 Click the Search button.

While the search continues, a message, locations being searched, a progress bar, and a Stop button display in the balloon (Figure 3-75).

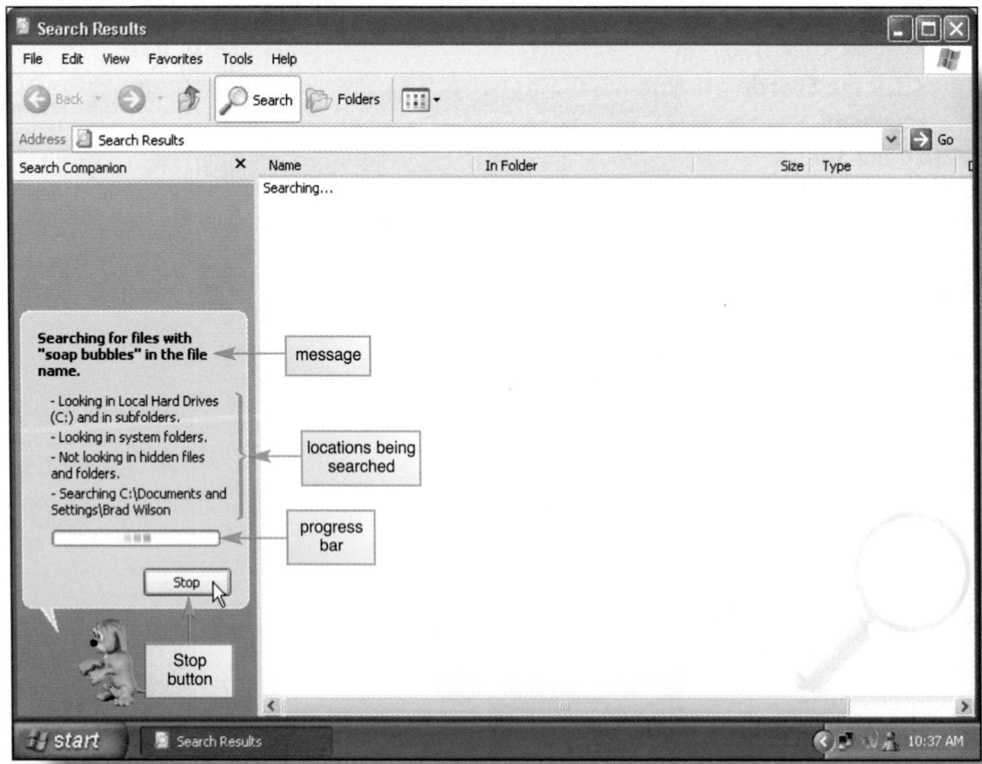

FIGURE 3-75

5 When the Search is complete, point to Yes, finished searching.

Windows XP searches drive C for files and folders with the term, soap, or the term, bubbles, in their names (Figure 3-76). One file is found and the right pane displays the file name (Soap Bubbles), folder location (C:\WINDOWS), file size (65 KB), file type (Bitmap Image), and modification date (7/25/2006). The modification date is partially visible in the right pane.

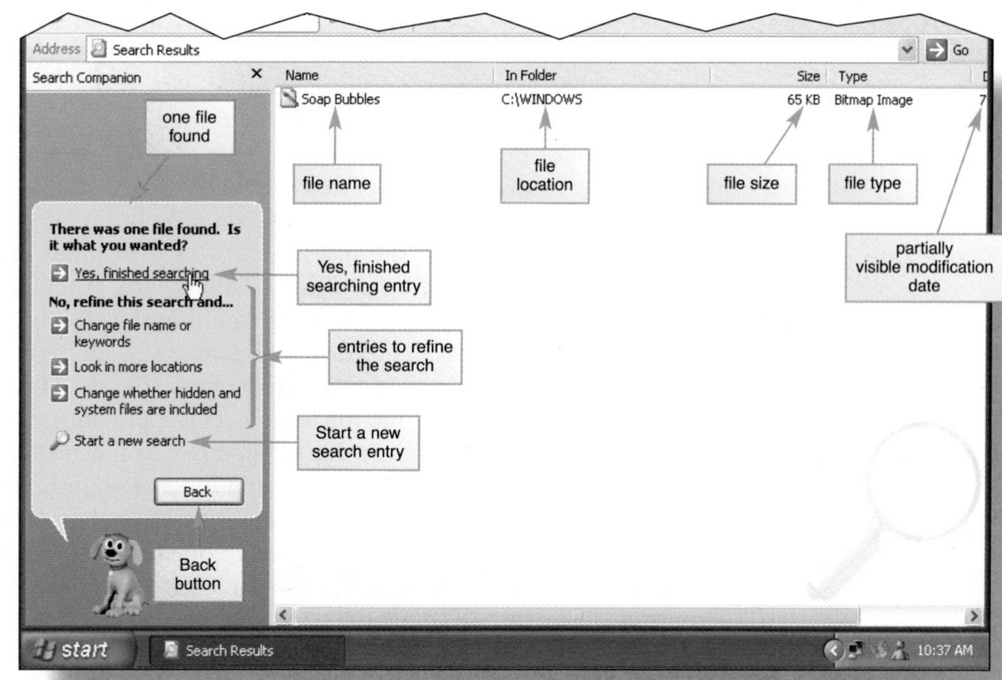

FIGURE 3-76

6 Click Yes, finished searching.

The Other Places area and Details area display in the left pane of the Search Results window and the search results continue to display in the right pane (Figure 3-77).

7 Click the Close button on the Search Results window title bar.

The Search Results window closes.

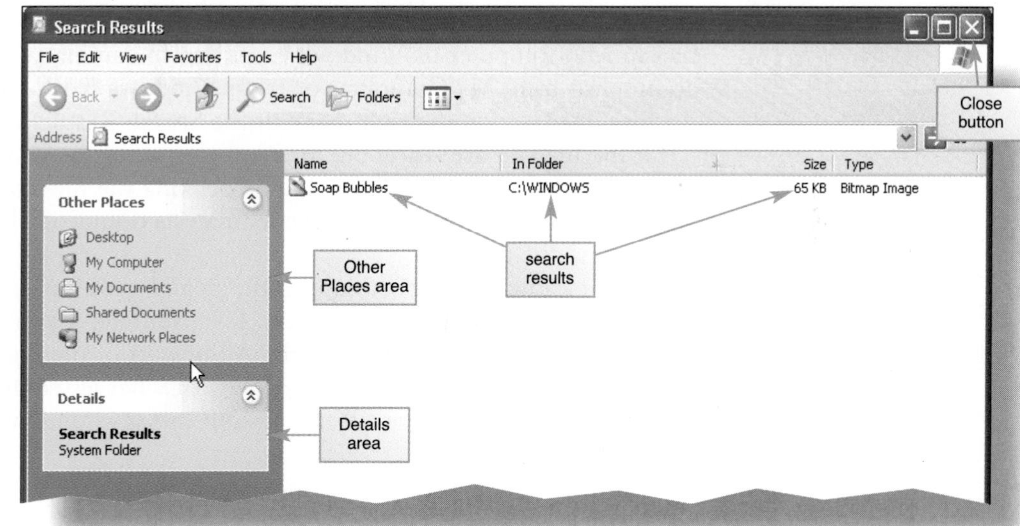

FIGURE 3-77

Other Ways

1. On Standard Buttons toolbar click Search button, select search criteria, click Search button
2. Right-click Start button, click Search, select search criteria, click Search button

In Figure 3-74 on page WIN 3.60, the A word or phrase in the file text box allows you to search for a word or phrase in a file. You may use three additional criteria when searching for all files and folders: modification date, file size, and advanced options. These criteria are identified by double down arrow buttons at the bottom of the balloon shown in Figure 3-74. Searching by modification date allows you to display all files that were created or modified within the last week, past month, past year, or on a specific date. Searching by file size allows you to search for files based on file size in kilobytes. Advanced options allow you to search system folders, hidden files or folders, subfolders, and tape backup, and perform case-sensitive searches. If no files are found in the search, a message (Search is complete. There are no results to display.) displays in the right pane of the Search Results window. In this case, you may want to check the file name you entered or examine a different drive to continue the search on the previous page.

If the search results were not satisfactory as illustrated in Figure 3-76 on the prevoius page, you can refine the search by changing the file name or keywords, looking in more locations, or changing whether hidden and system files are included in the search. To refine the search, select one of the three entries at the bottom of the balloon. To start a new search, click the Start a new search entry. Clicking the Back button starts the search again.

In the right pane of the Search Results window shown in Figure 3-77 on the previous page, after the search is complete you can work with the files found in any manner desired. For example, you can open the file by double-clicking the file icon, or by right-clicking the file icon and then clicking Open on the shortcut menu. You can print the file by right-clicking the file icon and then clicking Print on the shortcut menu. You can copy or move the file with the same method as shown for files in My Computer or Windows Explorer. In summary, any operation you can accomplish from My Computer or from Windows Explorer can be performed on the files displayed in the right pane of the Search Results window.

If the file you are searching for is an executable program file, such as Notepad, you can launch the program by double-clicking the file icon in the right pane of the Search Results window in the same manner as double-clicking the file icon in a window on the desktop.

If you know only a portion of a file's name, you can use an asterisk in the name to represent the remaining characters. For example, if you know a file starts with the letters MSP, you can type `msp*` in the All or part of the file name text box. All files that begin with the letters msp, regardless of what letters follow, will display.

The Search capability of Windows XP can save time when you need to locate a file on the computer.

Run Command

You have seen how to launch programs by double-clicking the program icons in a window, and by clicking the commands on the All Programs submenu or other submenus. Windows XP also offers the **Run command**, located on the Start menu, to launch programs. The Run command is useful when you want to launch an application program quickly. To use the Run command to launch the Notepad program, complete the following steps.

More About

Run

You often will use the Run command with programs stored on a floppy disk that you run one time but do not save on your hard disk. Run has its origins in text-based operating systems, such as MS-DOS, where the only way to cause a program to execute was to type the name of the program and then press the ENTER key.

To Launch an Application Program Using the Run Command

1 Click the Start button on the taskbar and then point to Run.

Windows XP displays the Start menu containing the highlighted Run command (Figure 3-78).

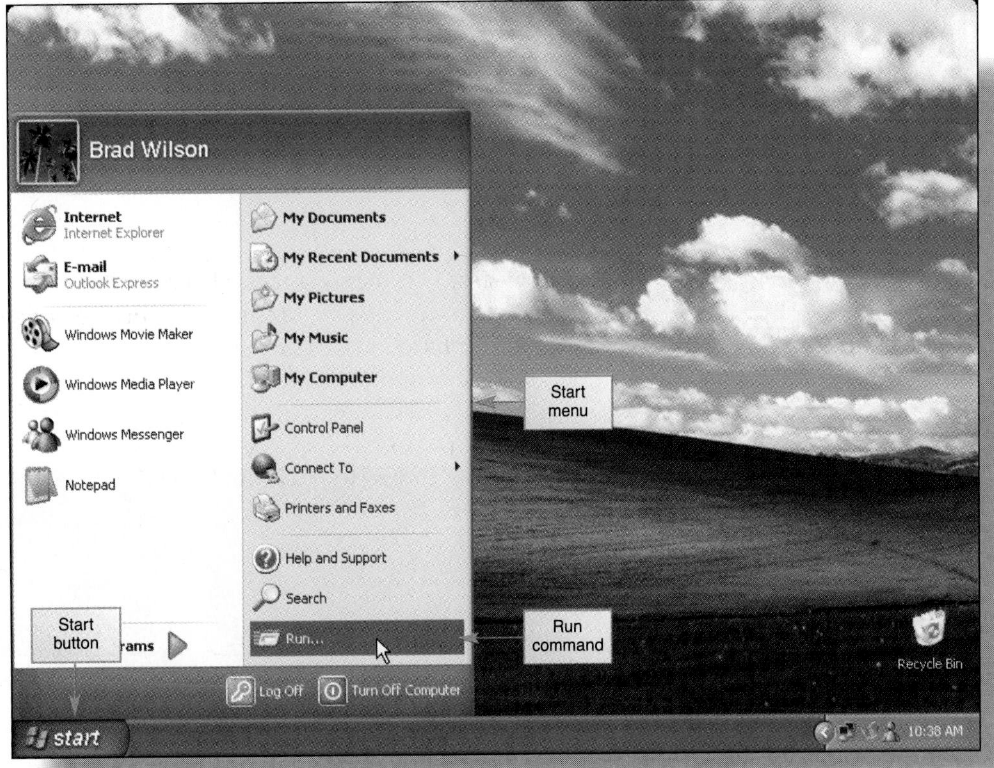

FIGURE 3-78

2 Click Run. Type `notepad` in the Open box in the Run dialog box and then point to the OK button.

The Run dialog box displays (Figure 3-79). The entry, notepad, displays in the Open box.

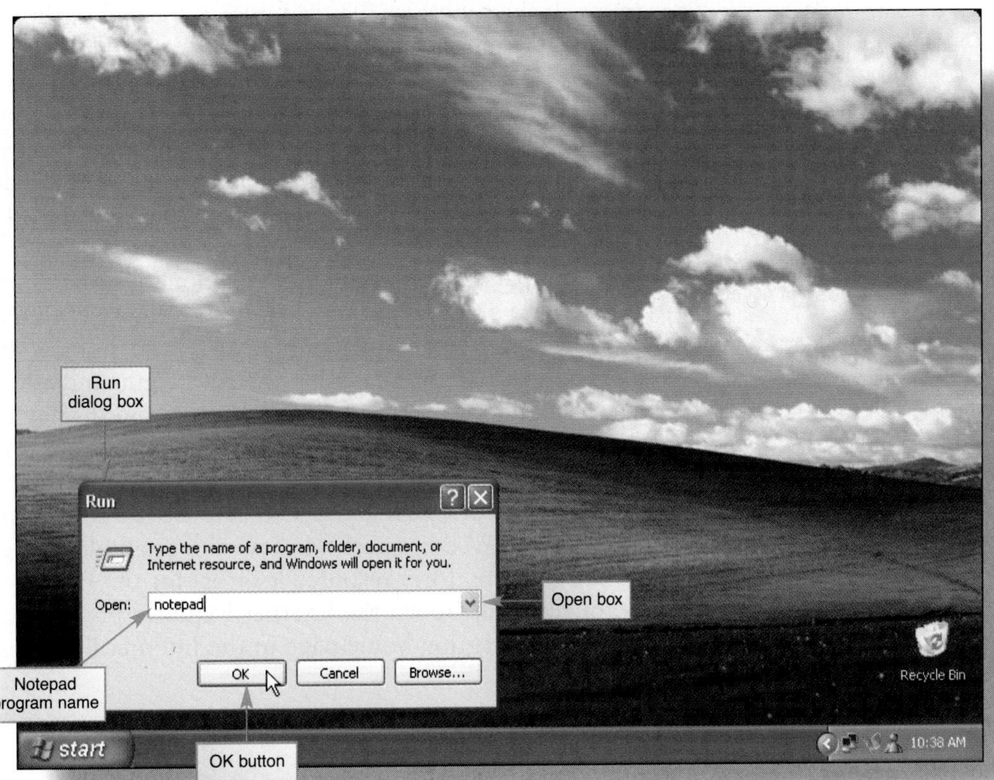

FIGURE 3-79

3 Click the OK button.

Windows XP launches the Notepad program (Figure 3-80). You now can use the Notepad program.

4 Click the Close button on the Untitled - Notepad window title bar.

The Notepad window closes.

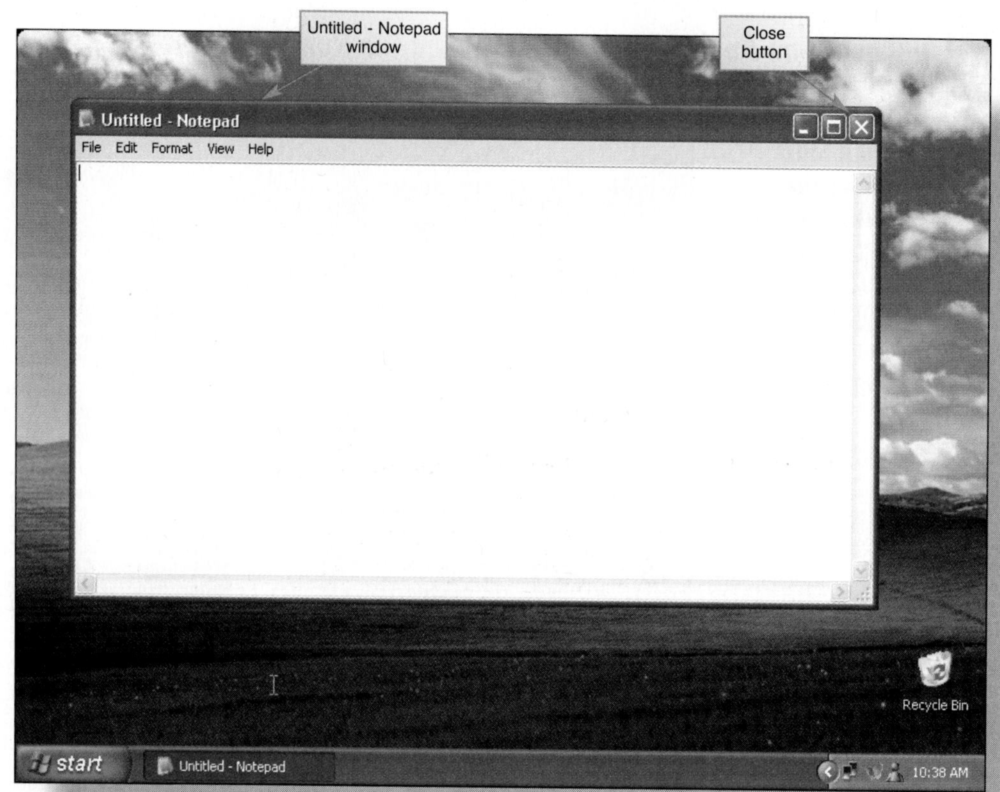

FIGURE 3-80

Other Ways

1. Press CTRL+ESC, press R, type program name, press ENTER
2. Press WINDOWS+R, type program name, press ENTER

More About

Paths

Paths are left over from MS-DOS and the manner in which you had to identify where a file was stored for access. To access a file on your hard drive, you merely need to open a window or, in Explorer, open the folder to access the file. However, you will have to understand and use paths to locate computers on a network.

You can use the Run command to open folders and files as well as executable programs. If the program, file, or folder is located in the WINDOWS folder, you simply type the name of the program, file, or folder. If the file is located elsewhere, you must type the path for the file. A **path** is the means of navigation to a specific location on a computer or network. To specify a path, you must type the drive letter, followed by a colon (:) and a backslash (\). Then type the name of the folders and subfolders that contain the file. A backslash should precede each folder name. After all the folder names have been typed, type the file name. The file name should be preceded by a backslash.

For example, the path name for the Gone Fishing bitmap image file stored in the WINDOWS folder on drive C is: C:\WINDOWS\GONE FISHING.BMP. The file extension (.bmp) identifies the file as a bitmap image file. File extensions must be specified in a path name. Using the Run command and this path name, you can launch the Windows Picture and Fax Viewer and display the Gone Fishing image in the Gone Fishing - Windows Picture and Fax Viewer window.

Although the Run command is extremely useful when launching programs and opening files or folders, you also can use the Run command to display a Web page in the Web browser window. For example, using the Run command and typing the URL (uniform resource locator) for the Federal Bureau of Investigation (www.fbi.gov) will launch the Internet Explorer program and display the Federal Bureau of Investigation home page in the Internet Explorer window.

Logging Off and Turning Off the Computer

After completing your work with Windows XP, you should close your user account by logging off from the computer. Perform the following steps to log off from the computer.

TO LOG OFF FROM THE COMPUTER

1. Click the Start button on the taskbar.
2. Click Log Off on the Start menu.
3. Click the Log Off button in the Log Off Windows dialog box.

Windows XP logs off from the computer and displays the Welcome screen.

After logging off, you also may want to turn off the computer. If you are sure you want to turn off the computer, perform the following steps. If you are not sure about turning off the computer, read the following steps without actually performing them.

TO TURN OFF THE COMPUTER

1. Click the Turn off computer link on the Welcome screen.
2. Click the Turn Off button in the Turn off computer dialog box.

Windows XP is shut down.

CASE PERSPECTIVE SUMMARY

The computer administrator emphasized the importance of users being able to control and manage windows on the Windows XP desktop, and their effective use of Windows XP Explorer. With those words in mind, you developed a one-hour class for employees with little computer experience and offered the classes during normal business hours, on alternating weeknights, and on Saturday mornings. The computer administrator was pleased with the results and recommended you for a newly developed position in his department.

Project Summary

In this project, you viewed icons in windows in different formats. After opening a document and launching an application program, you learned to manage windows on the desktop. Next, you saw how to copy, move, and delete files from an open window. You gained knowledge of Windows XP Explorer, both in how to display files, folders, and drives, and how to copy, move, rename, and delete files. You worked with files and folders in the My Pictures folder, viewed images in Filmstrip view and as a slide show, shared a folder with other computer users, and e-mailed a picture to a friend. Finally, you learned about the Search and Run commands.

What You Should Know

Having completed this project, you now should be able to perform the following tasks:

- Cascade Open Windows *(WIN 3.18)*
- Change the Format of the Icons in a Window *(WIN 3.08)*
- Close Expanded Folders *(WIN 3.37)*
- Close Open Windows *(WIN 3.24)*
- Close the Exploring Window *(WIN 3.43)*
- Copy a File in Explorer by Right-Dragging *(WIN 3.39)*
- Copy Files to the My Pictures Folder *(WIN 3.26)*
- Create a Folder in the My Pictures Folder *(WIN 3.47)*
- Delete a File by Right-Dragging to the Recycle Bin *(WIN 3.42)*
- Delete a Folder from the My Pictures Folder *(WIN 3.58)*
- Display Folder Properties *(WIN 3.46)*
- Display Hard Disk Properties *(WIN 3.44)*
- Display the Contents of a Folder *(WIN 3.34, WIN 3.40)*
- Display the Contents of an Expanded Drive *(WIN 3.35)*
- Display the Status Bar in a Window *(WIN 3.07)*
- E-Mail a Picture *(WIN 3.56)*
- Expand a Drive *(WIN 3.32)*
- Expand a Folder *(WIN 3.31)*
- Launch an Application Program from a Window *(WIN 3.16)*
- Launch an Application Program from Explorer *(WIN 3.36)*
- Launch an Application Program Using the Run Command *(WIN 3.63)*
- Launch Windows Explorer *(WIN 3.29)*
- Log Off from the Computer *(WIN 3.65)*
- Make a Window the Active Window *(WIN 3.20)*
- Move a File into a Folder *(WIN 3.48)*
- Open a Document from a Window *(WIN 3.14)*
- Open and Maximize the My Computer Window *(WIN 3.05)*
- Quit an Application Program *(WIN 3.37)*
- Refresh the Image on a Folder *(WIN 3.49)*
- Remove Sharing from a Folder *(WIN 3.56)*
- Remove the Status Bar *(WIN 3.43)*
- Rename a File *(WIN 3.41)*
- Search for a File by Name *(WIN 3.59)*
- Share a Folder *(WIN 3.54)*
- Tile Open Windows *(WIN 3.22)*
- Turn Off the Computer *(WIN 3.65)*
- Undo Cascading *(WIN 3.21)*
- Undo Tiling *(WIN 3.23)*
- View Bitmap Images in Filmstrip View *(WIN 3.50)*
- View Icons in Thumbnails View and Display the My Pictures Window (WIN 3.53)
- View Images as a Slide Show (WIN 3.52)
- View the Contents of a Drive *(WIN 3.11)*
- View the Contents of a Folder *(WIN 3.13, WIN 3.25)*

Learn It Online

Instructions: To complete the Learn It Online exercises, launch your Web browser using the steps on pages WIN 1.46 and WIN 1.47, click the Address box, enter `scsite.com/winxp/exs.htm`, and then press the ENTER key. When the Windows XP Learn It Online page displays, follow the instructions in the exercises below.

1 Project Reinforcement TF, MC, and SA

Below Windows XP Project 3, click the Project Reinforcement link. Print the quiz by clicking Print on the File menu. Answer each question. Write your first and last name at the top of each page, and then hand in the printout to your instructor.

2 Flash Cards

Below Windows XP Project 3, click the Flash Cards link. When Flash Cards displays, read the instructions. Type 20 (or a number specified by your instructor) in the Number of Playing Cards text box, type your name in the Name text box, and then click the Flip Card button. When the flash card displays, read the question and then click the Answer box arrow to select an answer. Flip through Flash Cards. Click Print on the File menu to print the last flash card if your score is 15 (75%) correct or greater and then hand it in to your instructor. If your score is less than 15 (75%) correct, then redo this exercise by clicking the Replay button.

3 Practice Test

Below Windows XP Project 3, click the Practice Test link. Answer each question, enter your first and last name at the bottom of the page, and then click the Grade Test button. When the graded practice test displays on your screen, click Print on the File menu to print a hard copy. Continue to take practice tests until you score 80% or better. Hand in a printout of the final practice test to your instructor.

4 Who Wants to Be a Computer Genius?

Below Windows XP Project 3, click the Computer Genius link. Read the instructions, enter your first and last name at the bottom of the page, and then click the Play button. Hand in a printout of your score to your instructor.

5 Wheel of Terms

Below Windows XP Project 3, click the Wheel of Terms link. Read the instructions, and then enter your first and last name and your school name. Click the Play button. Hand in a printout of your score to your instructor.

6 Crossword Puzzle Challenge

Below Windows XP Project 3, click the Crossword Puzzle Challenge link. Read the instructions, and then enter your first and last name. Click the Play button. Work the crossword puzzle. When you are finished, click the Submit button. When the crossword puzzle redisplays, click the Print button. Hand in the printout.

7 Tips and Tricks

Below Windows XP Project 3, click the Tips and Tricks link. Click a topic that pertains to Project 3. Right-click the information and then click Print on the shortcut menu. Construct a brief example of what the information relates to in Windows XP to confirm that you understand how to use the tip or trick. Hand in the example and printed information.

8 Newsgroups

Below Windows XP Project 3, click the Newsgroups link. Click a topic that pertains to Project 3. Print three comments. Hand in the comments to your instructor.

9 Expanding Your Horizons

Below Windows XP Project 3, click the Expanding Your Horizons link. Click a topic that pertains to Project 3. Print the information. Construct a brief example of what the information relates to in Windows XP to confirm that you understand the contents of the article. Hand in the example and printed information to your instructor.

10 Search Sleuth

Below Windows XP Project 3, click the Search Sleuth link. To search for a term that pertains to this project, select a term below the Project 3 title and then use the Google search engine at google.com (or any major search engine) to display and print two Web pages that present information on the term. Hand in the printouts to your instructor.

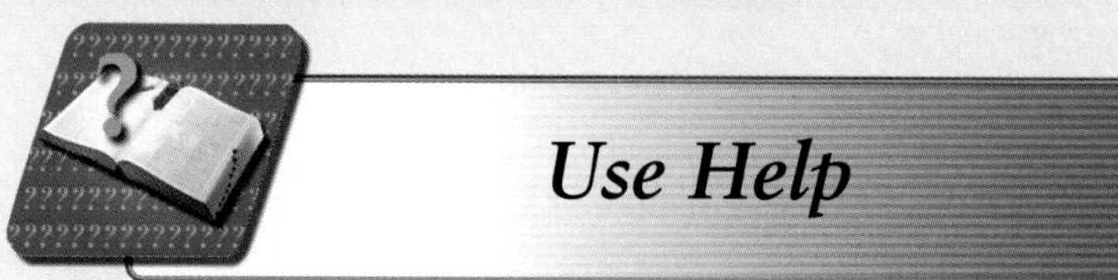

1 Using Windows Help and Support

Instructions: Use Windows Help and Support to perform the following tasks.

1. If necessary, launch Microsoft Windows XP and log on to the computer.
2. Answer the following questions about paths using information from this project.
   a. What is a path? DRIVE, means of Location (Drive)
   b. How do you specify a path? Drive Letter : (colon) Backslash then type the Folder Looking For
   c. Specify the path for a file named Nelson's Math Notes that is stored in the Math Files folder within the My Documents folder in drive C of the computer.
   C:\ WINDOWS \ My DOCUMENTS
3. Launch Windows Help and Support. In the Help and Support Center window, click the Index button, and then type `windows explorer` in the Type in the keyword to find text box. Answer the following questions about Windows Explorer.
   a. What method is recommended for copying a file or folder?
   ___
   b. What dialog box can be used to add the My Documents icon to the desktop?
   ___
   c. What keyboard shortcuts are used to perform the following tasks?
   Copy a file ___ Paste a file ___
   Rename a file ___ Search for a file ___
   Collapse a folder in Explorer ___
4. You recently wrote a business letter to a friend explaining how to install Microsoft Windows XP Professional. You want to see what else you said in the letter, but you cannot remember the name of the file or where you stored the file on the computer. You decide to check Windows Help and Support to determine the locations you could check to find a lost file instead of using the Search command to find the file. List the first two locations suggested by Windows Help and Support. Write those locations in the spaces provided.
   Location 1: WINDOWS
   Location 2: ___
5. You and your brother each have a computer in your bedroom. A printer is attached to your computer. Your brother, whose computer does not have a printer, would like to print some of his more colorful images using the printer attached to your computer. You have heard that for a reasonable cost you can create a home network to connect the two computers. Then, your brother can print documents stored on his computer on the printer connected to your computer. Using Windows Help and Support, determine what equipment is needed to connect two computers in an Ethernet network. Print the Help pages that document your answer.
6. The Windows XP Professional operating system is installed on your computer and the computer is connected to a network. You read in a computer magazine that Windows XP has tools designed for working with files stored on your computer and files stored on the network. You are unsure whether you should use My Briefcase or Offline Files to work with the files on your computer. Using Windows Help, learn about the difference between My Briefcase and Offline Files. Print the Help pages that explain My Briefcase and Offline Files.

In the Lab

1 File and Program Properties

Problem: You want to demonstrate to a friend how to display the properties of a bitmap image, display the image using the Paint program instead of the Windows Picture and Fax Viewer program, and print the image. The **Paint program** is an application program supplied with Windows XP to display bitmap images. You also want to demonstrate how to display the properties of an application program.

Instructions: Use a computer to perform the following tasks and answer the questions.

***Part 1:** Displaying File Properties*

1. If necessary, launch Microsoft Windows XP and log on to the computer.
2. Click the Start button and then click My Computer on the Start menu.
3. Double-click the LOCAL DISK (C:) icon. If necessary, click Show the contents of this folder.
4. Double-click the WINDOWS icon. If necessary, click the Show the contents of this folder link.
5. Scroll until the Soap Bubbles icon is visible. If the Soap Bubbles icon is not available on your computer, find the icon of another bitmap image file.
6. Right-click the Soap Bubbles icon. Click Properties on the shortcut menu. Answer the following questions about the Soap Bubbles file.
   a. What type of file is Soap Bubbles? BITMAT Image
   b. What program is used to open the Soap Bubbles image? WINDOWS
   c. What is the path for the location of the Soap Bubbles file? C
   d. What is the size (in bytes) of the Soap Bubbles file? 64.4KB
   e. When was the file created? Aug-4-
   f. When was the file last modified? 7-16-09
   g. When was the file last accessed? 7-16-09

***Part 2:** Using the Paint Program to Display a Bitmap Image*

1. Click the Change button in the Soap Bubbles Properties dialog box. Answer the following questions.
   a. What is the name of the dialog box that displays? Soap Bubbles Properties
   b. Which program is used to open the Soap Bubbles file? WINDOWS
   c. Which other program is recommended to open the file? _____
   d. List the other programs you can use to open the file?
   Desktop,
2. Click the Paint icon in the Open With dialog box.
3. Click the OK button in the Open With dialog box.
4. Click the OK button in the Soap Bubbles Properties dialog box.
5. Double-click the Soap Bubbles icon to launch the Paint program and display the Soap Bubbles image in the Soap Bubbles – Paint window (Figure 3-81 on the next page).

(continued)

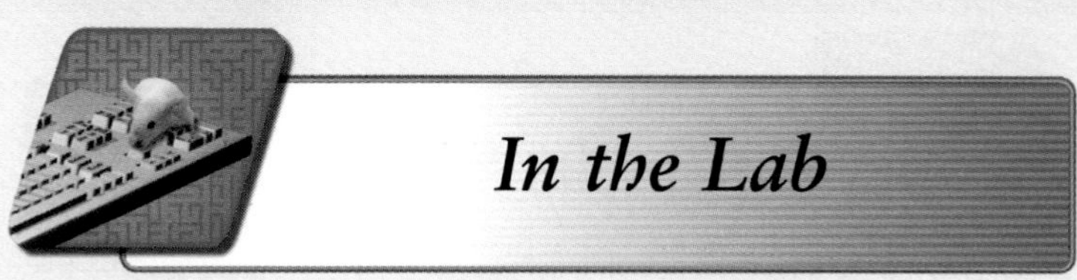

File and Program Properties *(continued)*

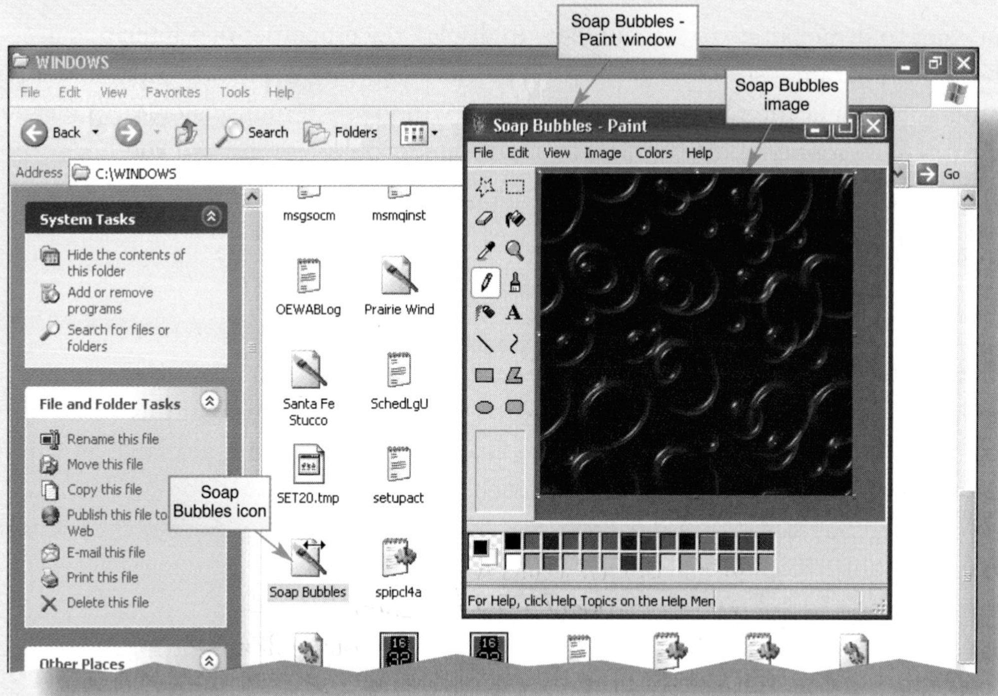

FIGURE 3-81

6. Print the Soap Bubbles image by clicking File on the menu bar, clicking Print on the File menu, and then clicking the Print button in the Print dialog box.
7. Click the Close button in the Soap Bubbles – Paint window.

Part 3: *Resetting the Program Selection in the Open With Dialog Box*

1. Right-click the Soap Bubbles icon. Click Properties on the shortcut menu. Answer the following question.
   a. What program is used to open the Soap Bubbles image? C:\ WINDOWS
2. Click the Change button in the Soap Bubbles Properties dialog box.
3. If necessary, click the Windows Picture and Fax Viewer icon in the Open With dialog box to select the icon.
4. Click the OK button in the Open With dialog box.
5. Click the OK button in the Soap Bubbles Properties dialog box.

Part 4: *Displaying Program Properties*

1. Scroll the right pane of the WINDOWS window until the notepad icon displays.
2. Right-click the notepad icon. Click Properties on the shortcut menu. Answer the following questions.
   a. What type of file is notepad? Application
   b. What is the file's description? notepad
   c. What is the path of the notepad file? C:\ WINDOWS
   d. What size is the notepad file when stored on disk? 67.5 69.120 Bytes
3. Click the Cancel button in the notepad Properties dialog box.
4. Close the WINDOWS window.

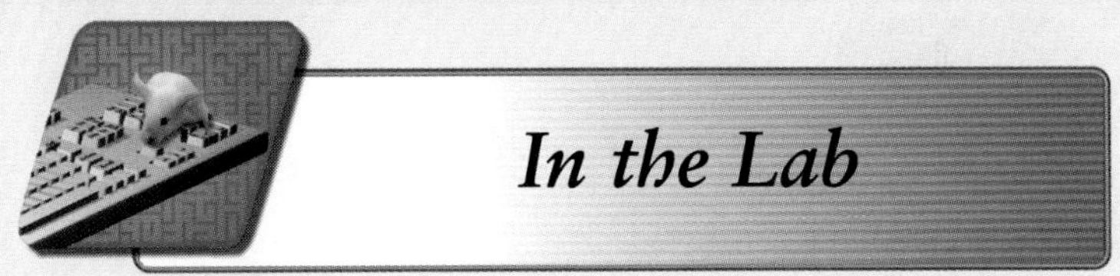

2 My Computer

Problem: You want to use the Paint program to design a happy birthday image for a friend and then e-mail the message to the friend. The Paint program is an application program supplied with Windows XP to create bitmap images. The file name of the Paint program is mspaint, but you do not know the location of the program on the hard drive. So, you decide to use Search to find the mspaint file on the hard drive.

Instructions: Use a computer to perform the following tasks and answer the questions.

Part 1: *Searching for the Paint Program*

1. If necessary, launch Microsoft Windows XP and log on to the computer.
2. Click the Start button on the taskbar. Click Search on the Start menu. Maximize the Search Results window.
3. Click All files and folders in the Search companion balloon. Type `mspaint` in the All or part of the file name text box.
4. Click the Search button. When the Search is complete, click Yes, finished searching.

Part 2: *Creating a Bitmap Image*

1. Double-click the mspaint icon in the Search Results window to launch Paint and display the untitled – Paint window. ***Hint:*** The file type of the Paint program is Application.
2. Click View on the menu bar, point to Zoom, and then click Custom to display the Custom Zoom dialog box.
3. Click the 200% button in the dialog box and then click the OK button to enlarge the image area in the Paint window (Figure 3-82).

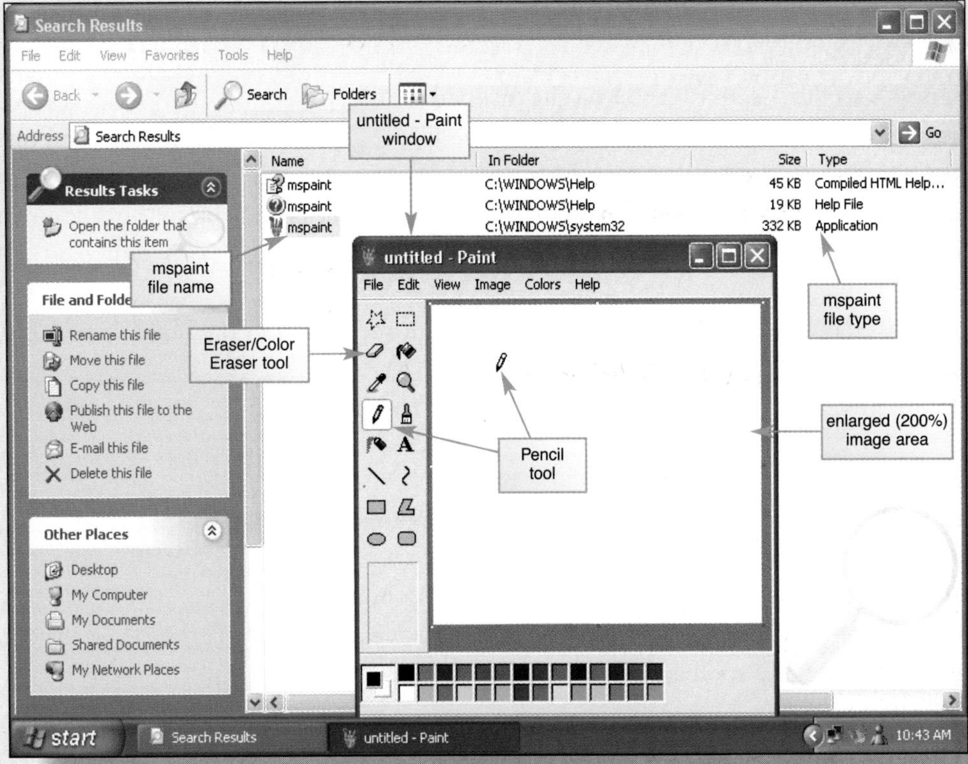

FIGURE 3-82

(continued)

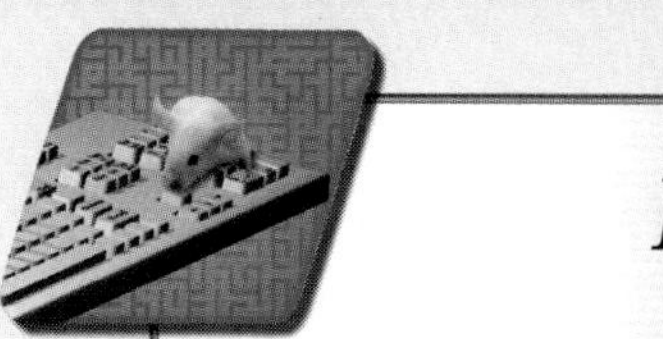

In the Lab

My Computer *(continued)*

4. Use the Pencil tool shown in Figure 3-82 on the previous page to write the message, Happy Birthday Stephen, in the Untitled – Paint window. ***Hint:*** Hold the left mouse button down to write and release the left mouse button to stop writing. If you make a mistake and want to start over, click File on the menu bar, click New on the File menu, and then click the No button in the Paint dialog box.
5. Click File on the menu bar and then click Save As. When the Save As dialog box displays, type `Happy Birthday` in the File name text box, and then click the Save button in the Save As dialog box to save the file in the My Pictures folder.
6. Print the image.
7. Click the Close button in the Happy Birthday - Paint window.
8. Click the Close button in the Search Results window.

Part 3: ***Displaying, Editing, and Saving the Happy Birthday File***

1. Click the Start button and then click My Pictures on the Start menu. Answer the following questions.
   a. Is the Happy Birthday file in the My Pictures folder? yes ____________________
   b. What displays on the Happy Birthday icon? Happy Birthday ____________________
2. Double-click the Happy Birthday icon to display the Happy Birthday image in the Happy Birthday - Windows Picture and Fax Viewer window.
3. In the Happy Birthday - Windows Picture and Fax Viewer window, click the second button from the right on the Standard toolbar to display the Happy Birthday file in the Paint window.
4. Right-click the taskbar and click Tile Windows Horizontally on the shortcut menu. Fill in the blank line below.
   a. Describe the desktop. ____________________
5. Click the Happy Birthday – Paint button on the taskbar.
6. Click the Eraser/Color Eraser tool in the Tool Box (see Figure 3-82) and then use the tool to erase the name, Stephen. ***Hint:*** Hold the left mouse button down to erase and release the left mouse button to stop erasing.
7. Click the Pencil tool (see Figure 3-82) and write the name, Steven, in the Happy Birthday - Paint window.
8. Save the modified image using the Save command on the File menu.
9. Print the modified image.
10. Right-click the taskbar and click Undo Tile on the shortcut menu. Fill in the blank line below.
    a. Describe the desktop. my pictures / file menu ____________________
11. Close the Happy Birthday - Paint window.

Part 4: ***E-Mail the Happy Birthday Image***

1. Click the Happy Birthday icon in the My Pictures window to select the icon.
2. Click E-mail this file in the File and Folder Tasks area.
3. Click the OK button in the Send Pictures via E-Mail dialog box.
4. Type `StevenForsythe@msn.com` in the To text box. Type `Have a happy birthday!` in the message area.
5. Click the Send button on the toolbar.

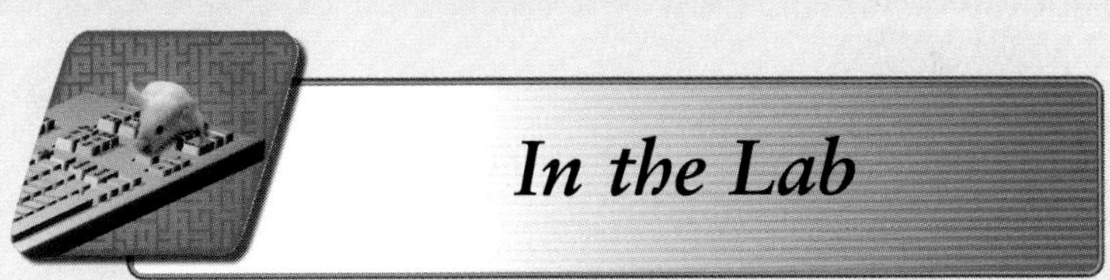

Part 5: ***Deleting the Happy Birthday Image***

1. Click the Happy Birthday icon to select the file.
2. Click Delete this file in the File and Folder Tasks area.
3. Click the Yes button in the Confirm File Delete dialog box.
4. Click the Close button in the My Pictures window.

3 Windows Explorer

Problem: A classmate informs you that the Internet is a great source of photos, pictures, and images. You decide to launch the Internet Explorer program, search for well-known candy and drink logos on the Internet, and save them in a folder. A **logo** is an image that identifies businesses, government agencies, products, and other entities. In addition, you want to print the logos, share the logos with other computer users, and e-mail them to a friend.

Instructions: Use a computer to perform the following tasks and answer the questions.

Part 1: ***Launching the Internet Explorer Program***

1. If necessary, launch Microsoft Windows XP and log on to the computer.
2. Click the Start button and then click My Computer on the Start menu.
3. Click the Folders button on the Standard Buttons toolbar.
4. Expand the LOCAL DISK (C:) folder.
5. Expand the Program Files folder.
6. Display the contents of the Internet Explorer folder.
7. Double-click the IEXPLORE icon to launch Internet Explorer and display the Microsoft Internet Explorer window.

Part 2: ***Finding and Saving Logo Images***

1. Type `www.jellybelly.com` in the Address bar in the Microsoft Internet Explorer window and click the Go button.
2. Find the jelly belly logo, right-click the jelly belly logo, click Save Picture As on the shortcut menu, type `Jelly Belly logo` in the File name box in the Save Picture dialog box, and then click the Save button to save the logo in the My Pictures folder.
3. Repeat Steps 1 and 2 above but type `www.snapple.com` and use the file name, Snapple logo, to save the Snapple logo in the My Pictures folder.
4. Repeat Steps 1 and 2 above but type `www.gatorade.com` and use the file name, Gatorade logo, to save the Gatorade logo in the My Pictures folder.
5. Repeat Steps 1 and 2 above but type `www.jollyrancherfruitchews.com` and the file name, Jolly Rancher logo, to save the Jolly Rancher logo in the My Pictures folder.
6. Close the Microsoft Internet Explorer window.

(continued)

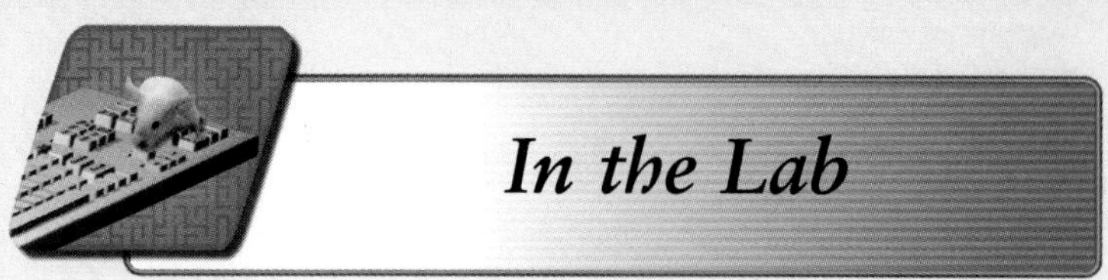

Windows Explorer *(continued)*

7. Click the Start button and click My Pictures. The Jelly Belly logo, Snapple logo, Gatorade logo, and Jolly Rancher logo display in the My Pictures window (Figure 3-83). The logos in the My Pictures window on your computer may be different from the logos shown in Figure 3-83 because businesses may change their logos.

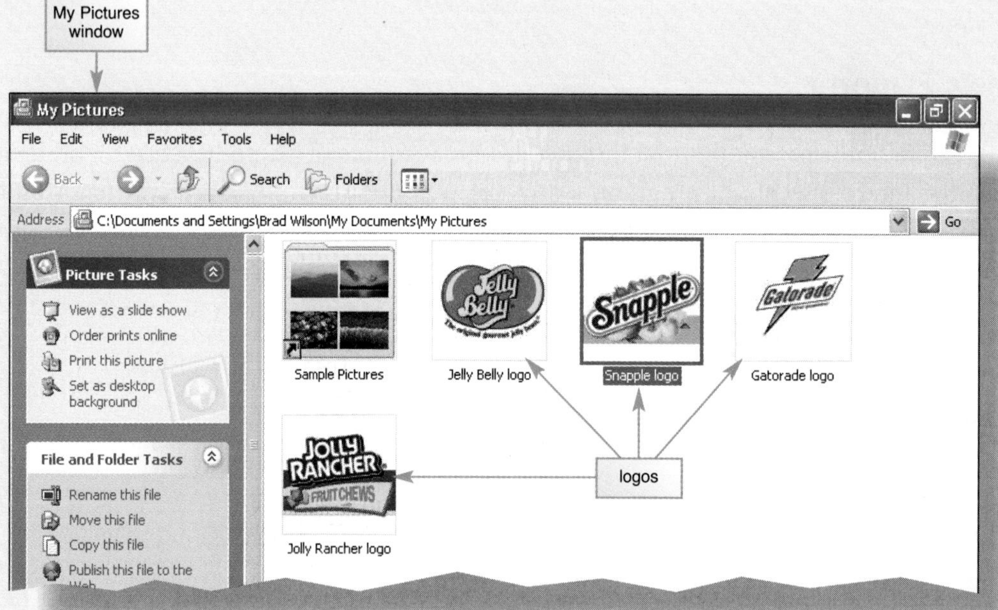

FIGURE 3-83

Part 3: *Displaying File Properties*

1. Right-click each logo file in the My Pictures window, click Properties, answer the question about the logo below, and then close the Properties dialog box.
   a. What type of file is the Jelly Belly logo file? My pictures C: Documents
   b. What type of file is the Snapple logo file? "
   c. What type of file is the Gatorade logo file? "
   d. What type of file is the Jolly Rancher logo file? "
2. Click an open area of the My Pictures window to deselect the Jolly Rancher logo file.

Part 4: *Creating the Candy and Drink Logo Folder in the My Pictures Folder*

1. Click Make a new folder in the File and Folder Tasks area, type `Candy and Drink Logos` in the icon title text box, and then press the ENTER key.
2. Click the Gatorade logo icon, hold down the CTRL key, and then click the Jelly Belly logo, Jolly Rancher logo, and Snapple logo icons.
3. Right-drag the Gatorade logo icon to the Candy and Drink Logos icon and then click Move Here on the shortcut menu.
4. Refresh the thumbnail image on the Candy and Drink Logos folder.

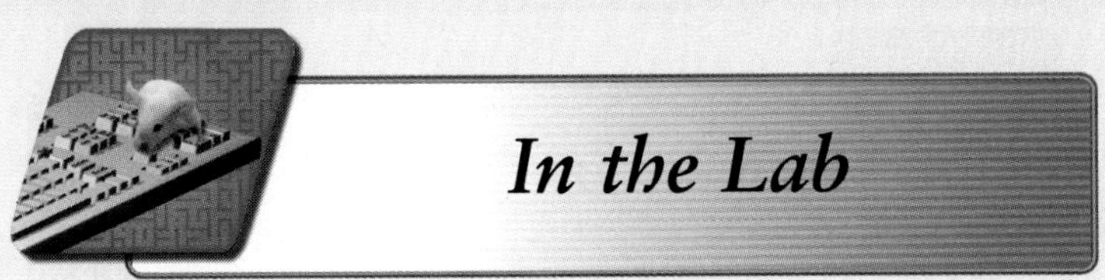

In the Lab

Part 5:* *Printing the Logo Images

1. Click Print pictures in the Picture Tasks area to start the Photo Printing Wizard.
2. Click the Next button in the Photo Printing Wizard window.
3. Verify that a check mark displays in the upper-right corner of each logo. Click the Next button.
4. Verify that the correct printer is being used. Click the Next button.
5. Scroll the Available layouts box to display the 3.5 x 5 in. Prints area. Click the image in the area to select the image. Click the Next button to print the images.
6. Click the Finish button in the Photo Printing Wizard window.

Part 6:* *Sharing the Candy and Drink Logos Folder

1. Right-click the Candy and Drink Logos icon in the My Pictures window. Click Copy on the shortcut menu.
2. Click Shared Pictures in the Other Places area.
3. Right-click an open area of the Shared Pictures window and then click Paste on the shortcut menu.

Part 7:* *E-mail the Files in the Candy and Drink Logos Folder

1. Click the Back button on the Standard Buttons toolbar to display the My Pictures window.
2. If necessary, click the Candy and Drink Logos icon to select the icon.
3. Click E-mail this folder's files in the File and Folder Tasks area.
4. Click the OK button in the Send Pictures via E-Mail dialog box.
5. Type `StevenForsythe@msn.com` in the To text box. Type `I searched the Internet to find these logos. I thought you might like to see them.` in the message area.
6. Click the Send button on the toolbar.

Part 8:* *Removing Sharing from the Candy and Drink Logos Folder

1. Click Shared Pictures in the Other Places area.
2. Select the Candy and Drink Logos icon in the Shared Pictures window.
3. Click Delete this folder in the File and Folder Tasks area.
4. Click the Yes button in the Confirm Folder Delete dialog box.

Part 9:* *Moving the Candy and Drink Logos Folder to a 3½ Floppy (A:) disk

1. Insert a formatted floppy disk in drive A of the computer.
2. Click My Pictures in the Other Places area.
3. Select the Candy and Drink Logos icon in the My Pictures window.
4. Click Move this folder in the File and Folder Tasks area.
5. Click 3½ Floppy (A:) in the Move Items dialog box.
6. Click the Move button in the Move Items dialog box.
7. Click the Close button in the My Pictures window.
8. Remove the floppy disk from drive A of the computer.

In the Lab

4 Using Search to Find Files

Problem: You know that searching is an important feature of Windows XP. You decide to use Search to find the Feather Texture and River Sumida files and also to search for all bitmap images on the hard drive. You will store the files in a folder in the My Pictures folder, print the images, and e-mail them to a friend.

Instructions: Use a computer to perform the following tasks and answer the questions.

Part 1: *Searching for Files in the Search Results Window*

1. If necessary, launch Microsoft Windows XP and log on to the computer.
2. Click the Start button on the taskbar and then click Search on the Start menu. Maximize the Search Results window.
3. Click All files and folders in the Search companion balloon. Type `feather texture` in the All or part of the file name text box. Click the Search button. When the search is complete, click Yes, finished searching in the Search Companion balloon.
4. Click the Feature Texture icon to select the icon. Click Copy this file in the File and Folder Tasks area. Click My Documents in the Copy Items dialog box. Click My Pictures in the Copy Items dialog box. Click the Copy button to copy the image to the My Pictures folder.
5. Click the Close button in the Search Results window.

Part 2: *Searching for Files from Another Window*

1. Click the Start button on the taskbar and then click My Computer on the Start menu.
2. Click the Search button on the Standard Buttons toolbar.
3. Click All files and folders in the Search companion balloon. Type `river sumida` in the All or part of the file name text box. Click the Look in box arrow and then click Local Hard Drives (C:). Click the Search button. When the search is complete, click Yes, finished searching in the Search Companion balloon.
4. Click the River Sumida icon to select the icon. Click Copy this file in the File and Folder Tasks area. Click My Documents in the Copy Items dialog box. Click My Pictures in the Copy Items dialog box. Click the Copy button to copy the image to the My Pictures folder.
5. Click the Close button in the Search Results window.

Part 3: *Searching for Groups of Files*

1. Click the Start button on the taskbar and then click Search on the Start menu. Maximize the Search Results window.
2. Click All files and folders in the Search companion balloon. Click the More advanced options button in the Search Companion balloon (Figure 3-84).

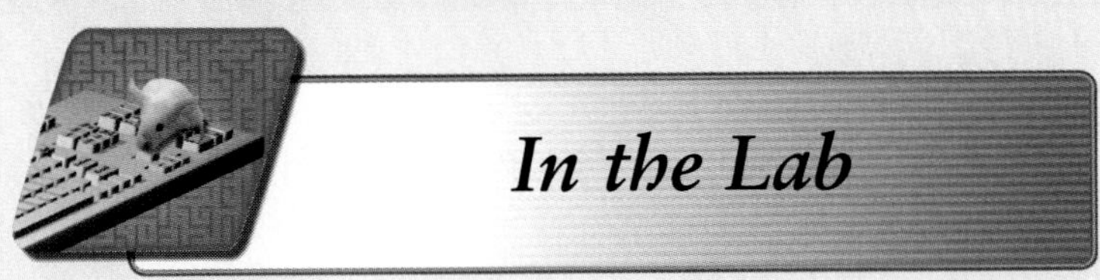

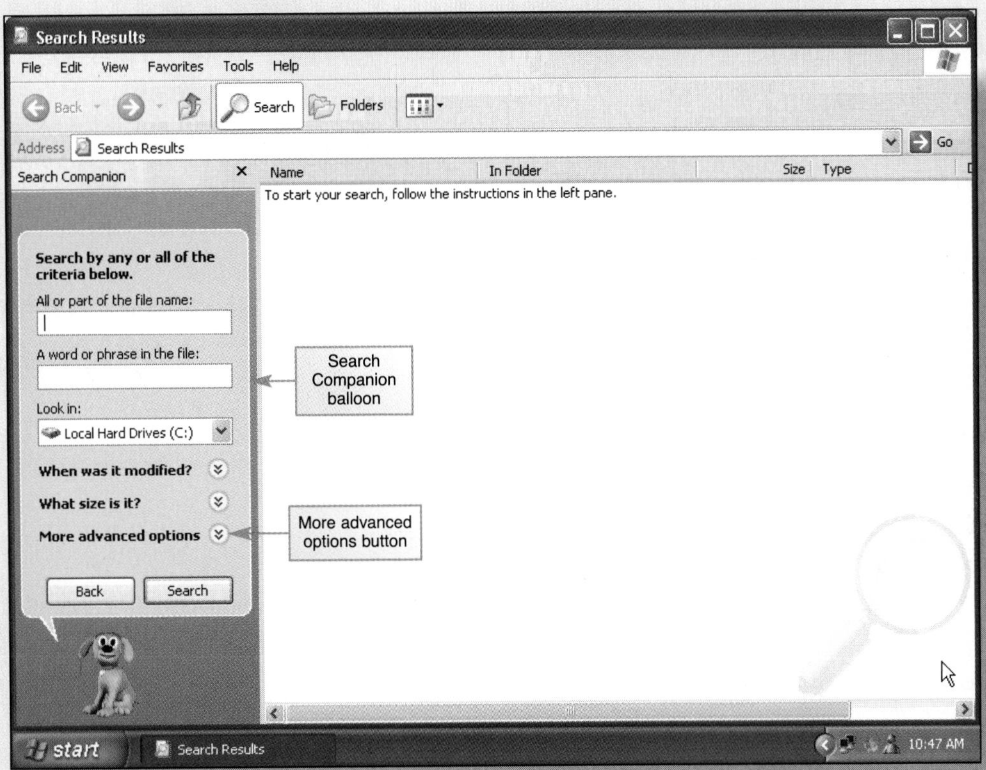

FIGURE 3-84

3. Click (All Files and Folders) in the Type of file list box. Click Bitmap Image in the list box. Click the Search button to search for all bitmap image files on the hard drive. Answer the following question.
   a. How many files were found? NO RESULTS
4. When the search is complete, click Yes, finished searching in the Search Companion balloon.
5. Click the Name button to display the file names in alphabetical order. In the alphabetical list, click the Windows XP icon to select the icon. If the Windows XP icon does not display, select another icon.
6. Click Copy this file in the File and Folder Tasks area. Click My Documents in the Copy Items dialog box. Click My Pictures in the Copy Items dialog box. Click the Copy button to copy the image to the My Pictures folder.

Part 4: ***Creating the Background Images Folder in the My Pictures Folder***

1. Click My Documents in the Other Places area. Double-click the My Pictures icon in the right pane.
2. Click Make a new folder in the File and Folder Tasks area, type `Background Images` in the icon title text box, and then press the ENTER key.
3. Click the River Sumida icon, hold down the CTRL key, and then click the Feature Texture and Windows XP icons.
4. Right-drag the River Sumida icon to the Background Images folder icon and then click Move Here on the shortcut menu.
5. Refresh the thumbnail image on the Background Images folder.

(continued)

In the Lab

Using Search to Find Files *(continued)*

Part 5: ***Printing the Images***

1. Click Print pictures in the Picture Tasks area to start the Photo Printing Wizard.
2. Click the Next button in the Photo Printing Wizard dialog box.
3. Verify that a check mark displays in the upper-right corner of each logo. Click the Next button.
4. Verify that the correct printer is being used. Click the Next button.
5. Scroll the Available layouts box to display the 3.5 × 5 in. Prints area. Click the image in the area to select the image. Click the Next button to print the images.
6. Click the Finish button in the Photo Printing Wizard dialog box.

Part 6: ***E-mail the Files in the Background Images Folder***

1. If necessary, click the Background Images icon to select the icon.
2. Click E-mail this folder's files in the File and Folder Tasks area.
3. Click the OK button in the Send Pictures via E-Mail dialog box.
4. Type `StevenForsythe@msn.com` in the To text box. Type `I searched the Internet to find these background images. I thought you might like to see them.` in the message area.
5. Click the Send button on the toolbar.

Part 7: ***Moving the Background Images Folder to a 3½ Floppy (A:) Disk***

1. Insert a formatted floppy disk in drive A of the computer.
2. Click My Pictures in the Other Places area.
3. Select the Background Images icon in the My Pictures window.
4. Click Move this folder in the File and Folder Tasks area.
5. Click 3½ Floppy (A:) in the Move Items dialog box.
6. Click the Move button in the Move Items dialog box.
7. Click the Close button in the My Pictures window.
8. Remove the floppy disk from drive A of the computer.

Cases and Places

The difficulty of these case studies varies:
▸ are the least difficult; ▸▸ are more difficult; and ▸▸▸ are the most difficult.

1 ▸ Your seven-year old brother cannot get enough of the graphics that display on computers. Lately, he has been hounding you to show him all the graphics images that are available on your computer. You have finally agreed to show him. Using techniques you learned in this project, display the icons for all the graphics image files that are stored on your computer. ***Hint***: Graphics files on Windows XP computers contain file extensions of .bmp, .pcx, .tif, or .gif. Once you have found the graphics files, display them and then print the three you like best.

2 ▸ Your employer suspects that someone has used your computer during off-hours for non-company business. She has asked you to search your computer for all files that have been created or modified during the last 10 days. When you find the files, determine if any are Notepad files or Paint files that you did not create or modify. Summarize the number and date they were created or modified in a brief report to your employer.

3 ▸▸ Backing up files is an important way to protect data and ensure it is not lost or destroyed accidentally. File backup on a personal computer can use a variety of devices and techniques. Using the Internet, a library, personal computer magazines, and other resources, determine the types of devices used to store backed up data, schedules, methods, and techniques for backing up data, and the consequences of not backing up data. Write a brief report of your findings.

4 ▸▸ A hard disk must be maintained to be used most efficiently. This maintenance includes deleting old files, defragmenting a disk so it does not waste space, and from time to time, finding and attempting to correct disk failures. Using the Internet, a library, Windows XP Help and Support, and other research facilities, determine the maintenance that should be performed on hard disks. This includes the type of maintenance, when it should be performed, how long it takes to perform the maintenance, and the risks of not performing the maintenance. Write a brief report on the information you obtain.

5 ▸▸▸ A file system is the overall structure in which files are named, stored, and organized. Windows XP supports three file systems: FAT, FAT32, and NTFS. You must choose a file system when you install Windows XP, a new hard disk, or format an existing hard disk or floppy disk. Before deciding which file system is right for you, research the three file systems to understand the benefits and limitations of each system. Write a brief report comparing the three file systems. Discuss the benefits and limitations of each system.

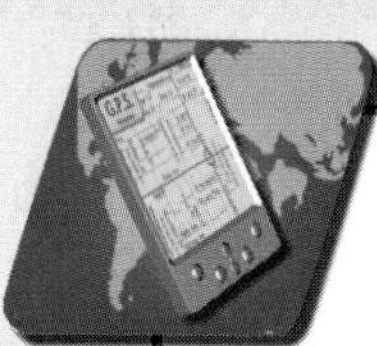

Cases and Places

6 ▶▶▶ The computer resources (RAM, hard drive space, microprocessor chip, and so on) required to run operating systems increase. Visit a computer retail store and/or the Microsoft Web site (www.microsoft.com) to review the minimum hardware requirements for the following Microsoft operating systems: Windows 98, Windows ME, Windows 2000, and Windows XP Professional. Using Microsoft Excel or another method of comparing the operating systems that you design, list the minimum hardware requirements for each operating system. Summarize your findings in a report that includes the minimum hardware requirements for each operating system, summarizes the trend in hardware requirements and computer resources, and comments on whether the minimum hardware requirements are realistic.

7 ▶▶▶ Data stored on disk is one of a company's most valuable assets. If that data were to be stolen, lost, or compromised so it could not be accessed, the company could go out of business. Therefore, companies go to great lengths to protect their data. Visit a company or business in your area. Find out how it protects its data against viruses, unauthorized access, and even against such natural disasters as fire and floods. Prepare a brief report that describes the company's procedures. In your report, point out any areas where you find the company has not protected its data adequately.

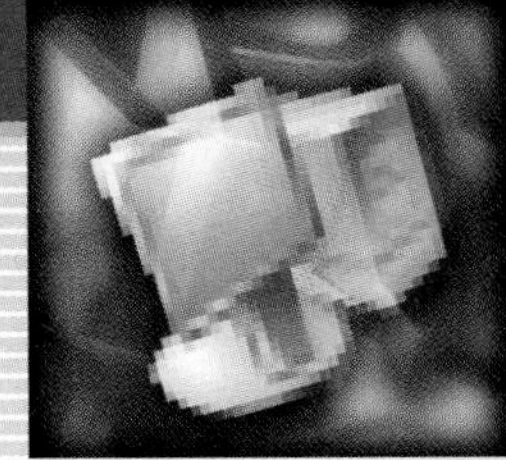

Microsoft Windows XP

PROJECT

Modifying Your Desktop Work Environment

OBJECTIVES

You will have mastered the material in this project when you can:

- Change the desktop work environment
- Select, create, save, and delete a desktop theme
- Change the desktop background
- Add icons to the desktop
- Change the font size and screen saver
- Add and remove an Active Desktop item
- Unlock, move, hide, and resize the taskbar
- Add, resize, and remove a toolbar on the taskbar
- Add and remove a shortcut on a toolbar
- Launch an application from a toolbar
- Use the Address toolbar to display folder content
- Use the Address toolbar to search the Internet
- Customize the Start menu and notification area
- Select a folder option and restore default folder options
- Open a folder in its own window
- Select an icon by pointing
- Open an icon by single-clicking
- Select and copy multiple files when the icons are underlined

Par for the Course

Tee Off from Your Desktop

Golf Digest ranks many U.S. golf courses among the best in the world. Some of the more notable courses include Poquoy Brook Golf Course in Boston with its breathtaking views and outstanding layout. According to those who complete the round there, the course comes close to perfection. Tournament Players Club of Tampa Bay is an excellent course superbly maintained that challenges golfers of all skill levels. Cog Hill Golf & Country Club, Chicago's nationally ranked and most notorious course, has tested the expertise of the world's top golfers for decades. Gold Canyon Golf Resort of Phoenix touts scenic vistas and flawless fairways. The natural setting and favorable winter climate of the California desert is complementary to many distinguished courses such as the Indian Wells Golf Resort West Course, with its rolling fairways and well-trimmed greens.

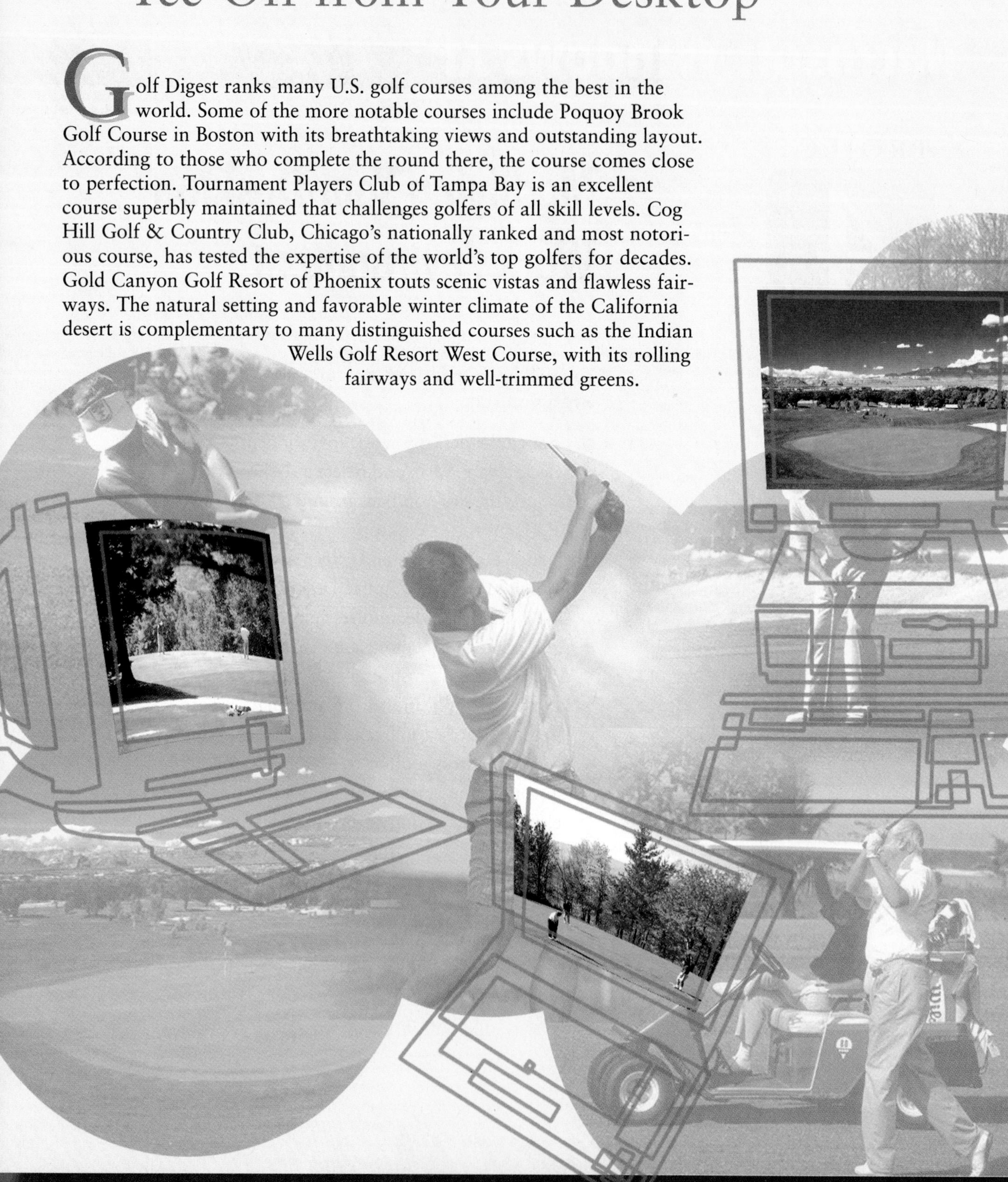

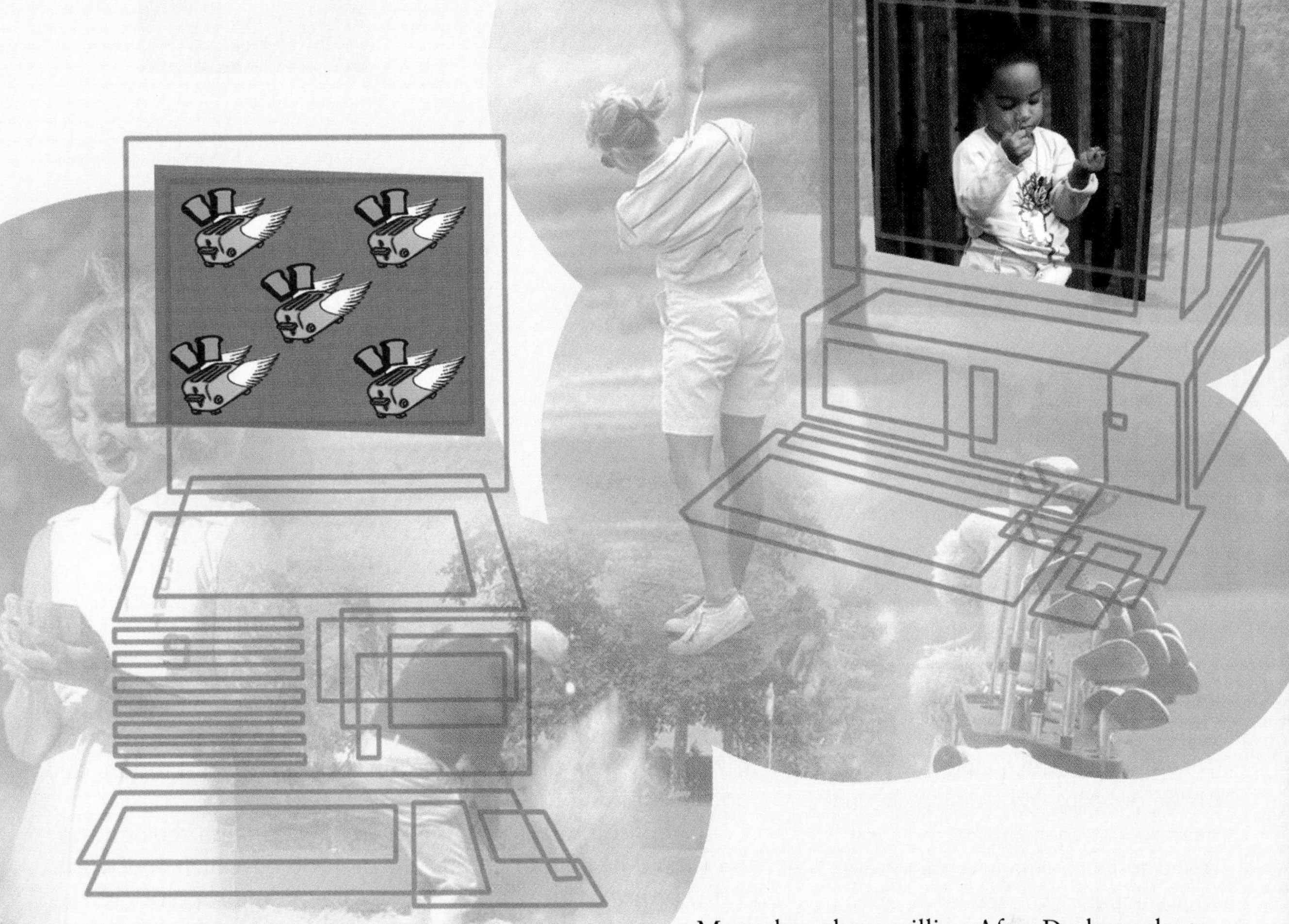

Oh, to be out enjoying a round of golf. Well, now you can visit some of the world's more famous courses from the comfort of your desktop. It is as simple as downloading free-use or shareware screen savers available on the Web. One such site offering information is Free Golf Screen Savers. The Web site reviews the screen saver programs, indicates whether the versions are full-capacity or evaluation versions, includes download times and links to sites, and evaluates picture colors and formats, as well as providing the number and quality of images.

Berkeley Systems has been another source of top-notch screen savers with roots back to 1987 when three developers received a federal grant to write software to assist visually impaired computer users. At that time, computer monitors were plagued with phosphor burnt-in images that developed when the same image stayed in one place on the screen for a long period. Two years later, the company developed the After Dark screen saver utility to move images to various locations on the screen when the computer was idle.

More than three million After Dark products have been sold worldwide. Named after a Berkeley, California, location, the designers at Berkeley Systems set the stage for many other manufacturers to produce unique screen savers, both in the commercial and shareware markets. Although modern display devices are not susceptible to these earlier problems, screen savers have gained in popularity for their decorative and entertainment value. In Project 4, you will explore the Windows XP features that allow you to modify and customize your desktop work environment, which include incorporating themes, changing desktop backgrounds, and adding a screen saver.

Today, Windows makes it easy for you to create personalized screen savers and customized desktops that display your own photos of family, friends, pets, and special events. It also includes a simple way to protect your computer from access using the On resume, password protect option in the Screen Saver sheet of the Display Properties dialog box. Of course, instead of away from your desk, friends and colleagues may expect to find you on the fairway.

Microsoft Windows XP

Modifying Your Desktop Work Environment

PROJECT

CASE PERSPECTIVE

Since installing Windows XP on your computer, you have spent most of your time learning to communicate with Windows XP, launching programs and creating documents, exploring Windows Help and Support, working on the desktop, and learning file and desktop management. Because you spend so much time interacting with your computer, the manner in which you interact with the desktop and the objects on the desktop are important to you. You want to modify your desktop display properties, including changing a desktop theme you find undesirable, personalizing the objects on the desktop (Start menu, taskbar, toolbars, notification area, and folder windows), and changing the folder options. Your assignment in this project is to customize your desktop work environment to suit your needs.

Introduction

In Project 1, you worked with objects on the desktop. In Project 2, you worked with documents on the desktop, minimized open windows on the desktop, and created shortcuts on the desktop. In Project 3, you managed the windows on the desktop by cascading and tiling the windows.

In addition to learning about and working on the desktop, you should be able to modify the desktop on which you work. In this project, you will learn more about the properties of the desktop, select and create a desktop theme, modify the desktop by changing the desktop background, add icons to the desktop, modify the size of text used on menus and icons, modify the desktop appearance, change the screen saver on the desktop, and then add an Active Desktop item to the desktop. You will customize the taskbar by changing the position of the taskbar, hiding the taskbar, adding a toolbar to the taskbar, and adding a shortcut to a toolbar. Finally, you will learn how to change the appearance of a folder and the desktop by changing folder options.

Changing the Desktop Work Environment

Windows XP provides a variety of methods to modify the desktop on which you work. As mentioned in Project 1, most items on the desktop, including the desktop itself, are considered objects. Every object in Windows XP has **properties**, which describe the object. In many cases, you can change an object's properties to fit your needs.

Desktop Properties

A beginning point for modifying the desktop work environment is to change the properties of the desktop. These properties include the choice of a desktop theme and background, settings that determine size and color of the items on the desktop, the appearance of open windows on the desktop, a screen saver, and the Active Desktop items. To change the desktop properties, you must open the Display Properties dialog box. Complete the following steps to open the Display Properties dialog box.

More About

The Desktop

You may be surprised at the many different preferences people have for their computer desktops. Some like quiet, cool colors while others like bright, glittery schemes. There is no single correct way; so preferences are an individual matter. That is why Microsoft and other operating system designers offer the capability of customizing your computer desktop.

To Open the Display Properties Dialog Box

1 Right-click an open area of the desktop. Point to Properties on the shortcut menu.

A shortcut menu containing the highlighted Properties command displays (Figure 4-1).

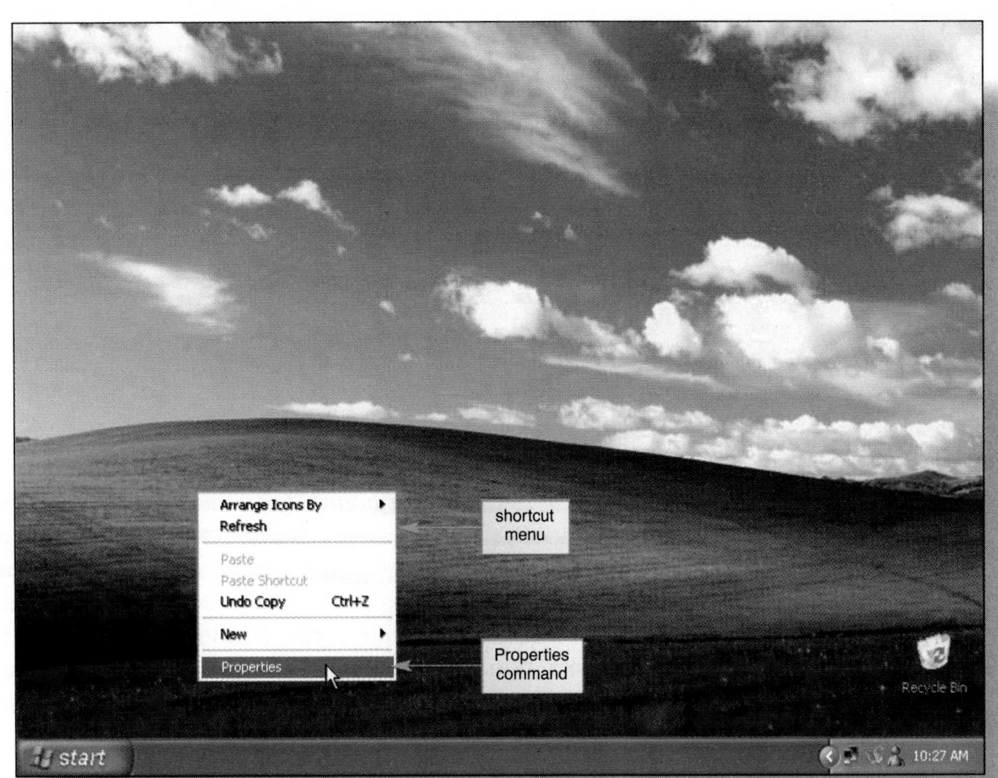

FIGURE 4-1

2 Click Properties.

The Display Properties dialog box and the Themes sheet display (Figure 4-2).

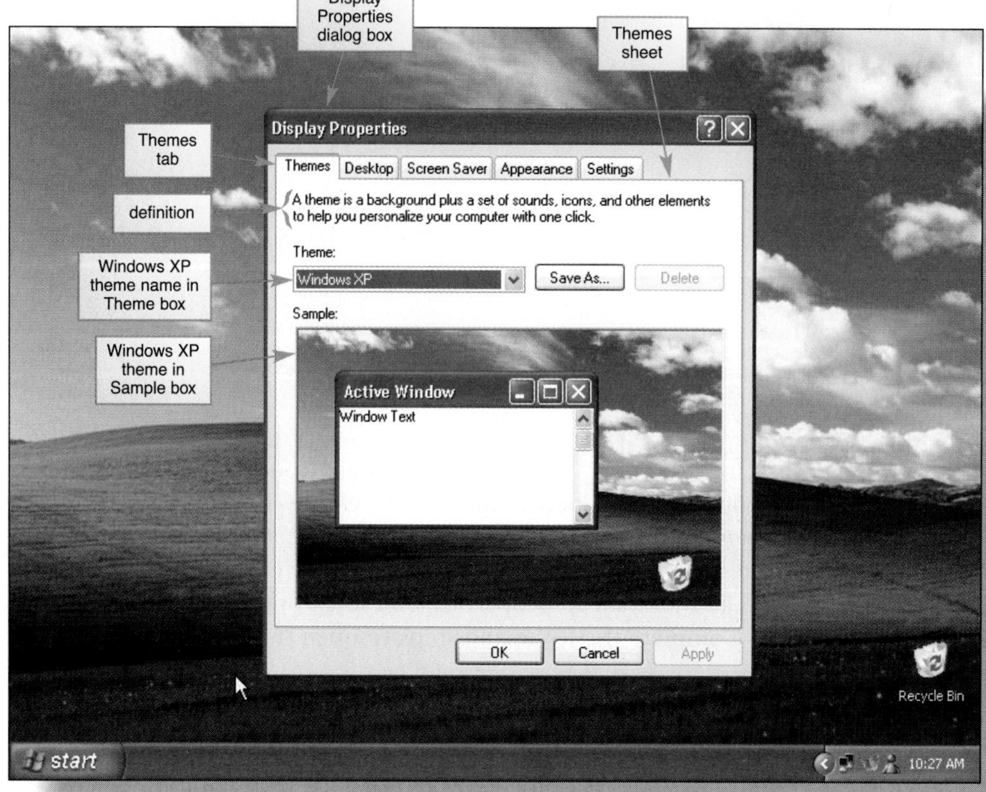

FIGURE 4-2

Other Ways

1. Click Start button, click Control Panel, click Appearance and Themes, click Display icon (or a task)
2. Click Start button, click My Computer, click Change a setting, click Appearance and Themes, click Display icon or a task

In Figure 4-2, the Themes sheet in the Display Properties dialog box contains a definition of desktop theme, Theme box, and sample desktop. Currently, the Theme box contains the highlighted Windows XP theme name, and a sample of how the Windows XP theme looks on the desktop displays in the Sample box. The desktop theme affects the overall look of the desktop, including the background, screen saver, icons, windows, mouse pointers, and sounds.

Desktop Themes

One method of changing the appearance of the desktop on which you work is to change the desktop theme. A **desktop theme** is a set of graphic elements that give the desktop a unified and distinctive look. In addition to determining the look of the various graphic elements on the desktop, a desktop theme also can define the sounds associated with events such as opening or closing a program. Unless modified, the **Windows XP desktop theme** displays when you launch Windows XP. The set of graphic elements that comprise the Windows XP desktop theme include the Bliss background, Windows XP screen saver, Windows XP style windows and buttons, Blue color scheme, Normal font size, 800 x 600 pixel screen resolution, and Medium (16 bit) color quality.

If you wish to change the desktop appearance, you can select another desktop theme or create a new desktop theme by modifying an existing desktop theme and saving it with a new name. In addition, you can restore the traditional Windows Classic look of the Windows desktop by selecting the Windows Classic desktop theme. The **Windows Classic desktop theme** displays the familiar desktop found on computers with a previous version of the Microsoft Windows operating system (Windows 98, Windows 2000, and so on).

More About

The Windows XP Desktop Theme

Windows XP (Modified) may display in the Theme box in Figure 4-2 on your computer because Microsoft Corporation replaced the original Windows XP background with the Bliss background prior to the release of the retail version of Windows XP. This resulted in the word, modified, being added to the Windows XP theme name.

Selecting a Desktop Theme

One method of changing the desktop appearance is to select another desktop theme. To change the appearance of the desktop by selecting the Windows Classic desktop theme, complete the following steps.

Steps To Select a New Desktop Theme

1 On a separate piece of paper, write down the desktop theme name that displays in the Theme box on the desktop on your computer.

2 Click the Theme box arrow in the Display Properties dialog box. Point to Windows Classic in the Theme list.

The Theme list displays with the Windows Classic desktop theme name highlighted (Figure 4-3). The desktop themes in the Theme box may be different on your computer.

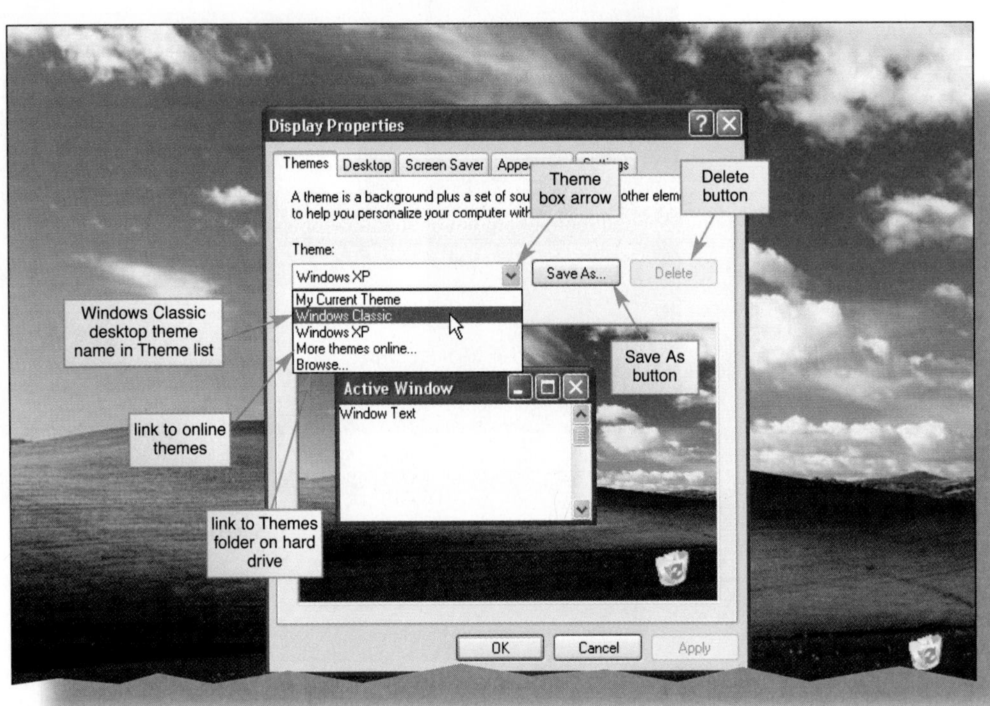

FIGURE 4-3

3 Click Windows Classic. Point to the Apply button.

The Windows Classic desktop theme name displays in the Theme box and a sample of the Windows Classic desktop theme displays in the Sample box (Figure 4-4). The Sample box displays an open window (Active Window) on a solid blue background. The window displays with square corners that are typical of the Windows Classic desktop and a sample of the fonts and colors that display on the title bar, menu bar, and display area.

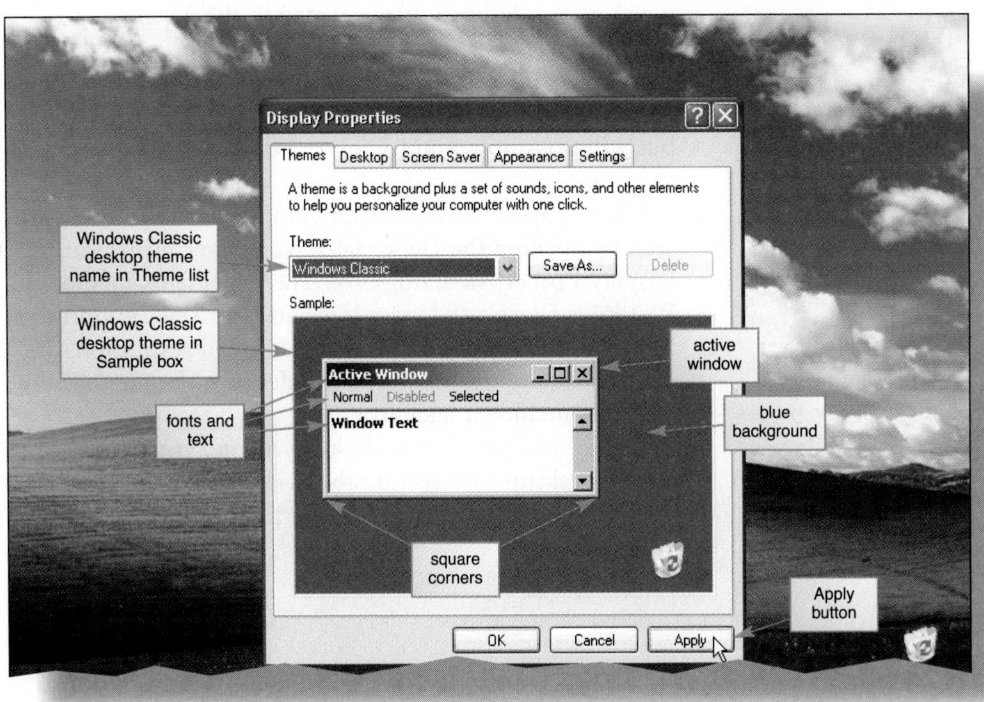

FIGURE 4-4

4 **Click the Apply button.**

The Please Wait screen displays momentarily while the desktop darkens and then the Windows Classic desktop theme is applied to the desktop (Figure 4-5). The Display Properties dialog box displays with the colors and fonts of the Windows Classic desktop theme.

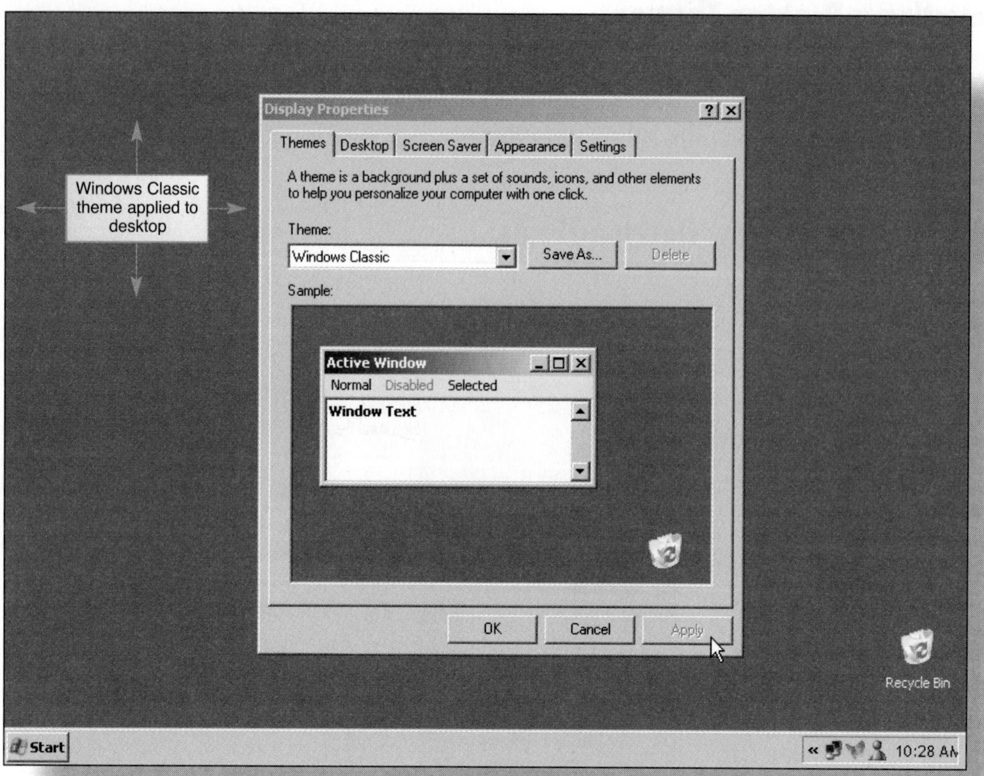

FIGURE 4-5

Desktop Themes

Microsoft introduced desktop themes in Windows 95 as a way to save color schemes, fonts and font sizes, sounds, and other interface elements. In Windows XP, desktop themes are an integral part of the Control Panel and additional themes are available on the Microsoft Plus! for Windows XP Web site.

When you click the Theme box arrow in Figure 4-3 on the previous page, a list of desktop themes displays, plus a link (More themes online) to the Microsoft Plus! for Windows XP Web site that contains additional desktop themes and a link (Browse) to the C:\Program Files\Plus!\Themes folder on the hard drive that contains many of the desktop themes listed in the Theme list.

The Save As button in the Display Properties dialog box allows you to save the desktop theme in the Themes box with a new name. The Delete button allows you to delete a desktop theme you have created or installed from a CD-ROM or the Web, but will not allow you to delete a desktop theme included with the Windows XP software.

The graphic elements that comprise the Windows Classic desktop theme can be seen by clicking the Desktop, Screen Saver, Appearance, and Settings tabs in the Display Properties dialog box. These elements include the Windows XP screen saver, Windows Classic style windows and buttons, Windows Standard color scheme, Normal font size, 800 x 600 pixel screen resolution, and Medium (16 bit) color quality. Unlike the Windows XP desktop theme, the Windows Classic desktop theme does not include a background.

After selecting a new desktop theme, you should revert to the original settings on the desktop by selecting the original Windows XP desktop theme. Perform the following steps to reset the desktop theme.

TO RESET THE DESKTOP THEME

1. Click the Theme box arrow in the Display Properties dialog box.
2. Click the desktop theme name in the Theme list you wrote down in Step 1 on page WIN 4.07.
3. Click the Apply button.

Windows XP displays the desktop theme name from Step 1 on page WIN 4.07 in the Theme box and displays the desktop theme in the Sample box and on the desktop (Figure 4-6).

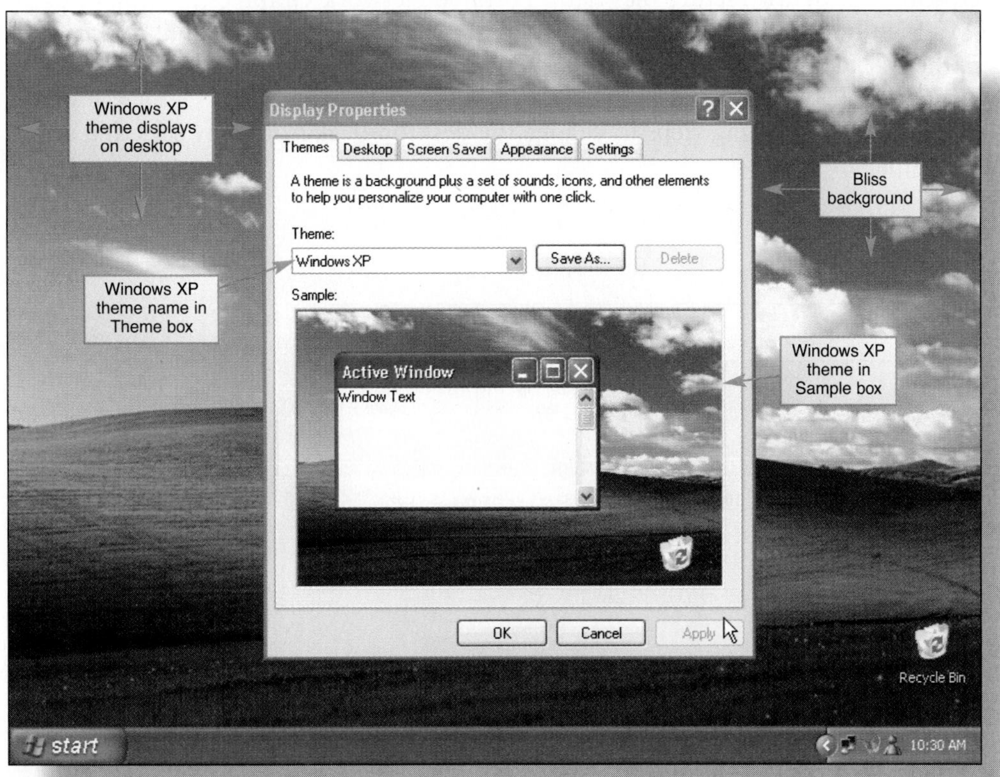

FIGURE 4-6

Creating a Desktop Theme

As mentioned earlier, you can change the desktop appearance of a computer by selecting another desktop theme or creating a new desktop theme by modifying an existing desktop theme and saving it with a new name. You modify an existing desktop theme by changing the graphic elements that comprise the desktop theme. The elements of a desktop theme include a background, screen saver, windows and buttons style, color scheme, font size, screen resolution, and color quality.

In the following sections, you will create a new desktop theme by modifying several of the Windows XP desktop theme elements and then saving the new desktop theme using a unique desktop theme name.

Changing the Desktop Background

One of the elements of a desktop theme is the desktop background. A **desktop background** is any pattern, picture, or wallpaper that can display on the desktop. The **Bliss background** (green grassy hills and white clouds on a blue sky), which is the desktop background for the Windows XP desktop theme, displays on the desktop and in the Sample box in the Display Properties dialog box shown in Figure 4-6 on the previous page.

You can change the desktop background by adding an image (pattern or picture) or wallpaper to the desktop. You can select from a list of images or wallpapers available with Windows XP or use a bitmap file (.bmp), GIF file (.gif), JPEG file (.jpg), Microsoft PhotoDraw Picture file (.dib), Portable Network Graphics file (.png), or HTML file (.htm) as a background. You can use a photograph you took, a picture from the My Pictures folder or WINDOWS folder, or a graphic image you found on a Web page as a background.

Perform the following steps to change the desktop background by selecting the Azul wallpaper.

To Change the Desktop Background

1 Click the Desktop tab in the Display Properties dialog box. Point to Azul in the Background list box.

The Desktop sheet displays (Figure 4-7). The Bliss background displays on the desktop and in the preview monitor, the highlighted Bliss name displays in the Background list, the Apply button is dimmed, and the word, Stretch, displays in the Position box.

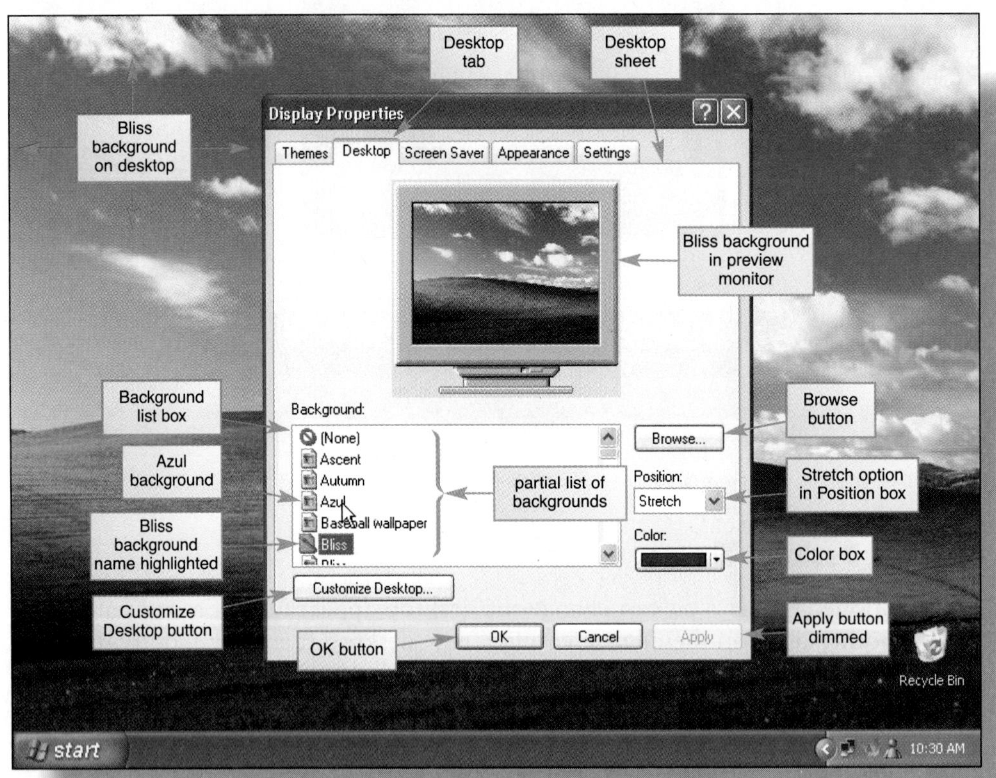

FIGURE 4-7

2 Click Azul. If Azul is not in the Background list on your computer, click another desktop background name. Click the Apply button.

Clicking the Azul name in the Background list highlights the name in the list box, displays the Azul background in the preview monitor, and causes the Apply button to no longer be dimmed. Clicking the Apply button displays the Azul background on the desktop and dims the Apply button (Figure 4-8).

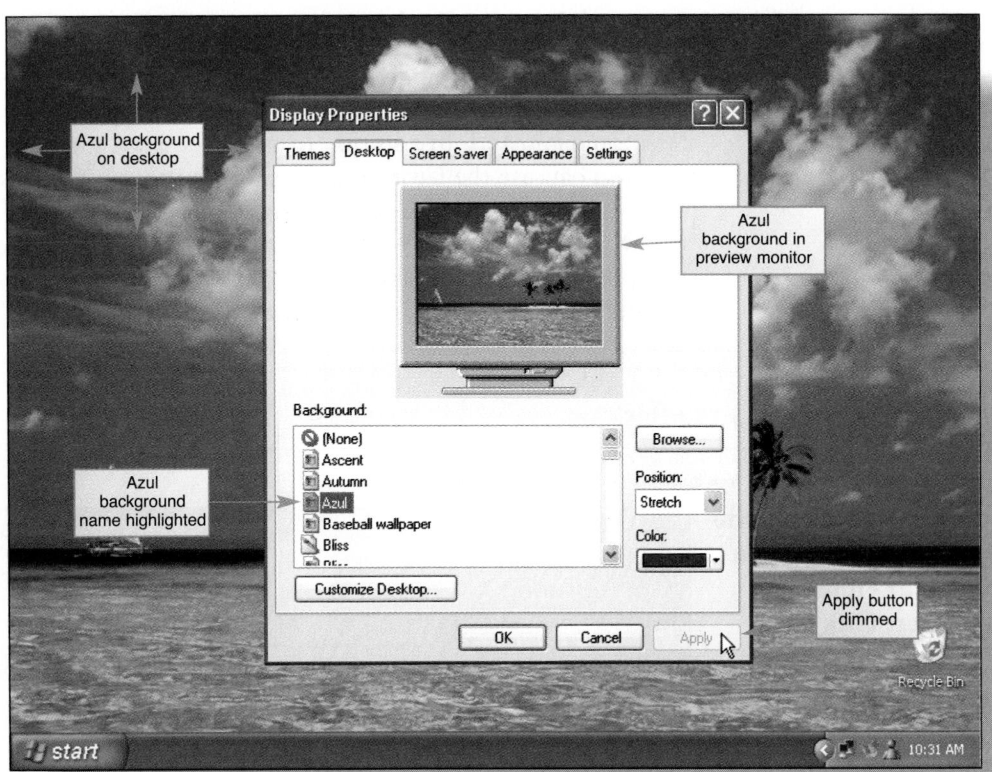

FIGURE 4-8

Other Ways

1. Press TAB until any background desktop name in Background list box is highlighted, press UP or DOWN ARROW until background name is highlighted, press TAB until Apply button is selected, press ALT+A (or ENTER)

The Desktop sheet illustrated in Figure 4-7 contains the preview monitor, Background list box, Position box, Color box, and several buttons (Browse, Customize Desktop, OK, Cancel, and Apply). The Background list box contains a partial list of the available backgrounds (images and wallpapers) you can use to decorate the desktop. The preview monitor displays the background associated with the highlighted background name in the Background list box.

When you select a background name in the Background list box and click the Apply button, the background displays on the desktop as centered, tiled, or stretched, depending on the setting in the Position box. The **Center setting** displays an image in the center of the desktop. The **Tile setting**, designed for use with small images, repeats an image across the desktop until the image covers the entire desktop. The **Stretch setting** enlarges an image to fill the desktop. In Figure 4-8, the Azul background displays on the desktop and the Display Properties dialog box remains open. This allows you to see the effect of the change and to make another change, if you desire. Clicking the OK button in the dialog box displays the Azul background on the desktop and closes the Display Properties dialog box.

The **Browse button** in the Display Properties dialog box allows you to view the background files in the Themes folder on the hard drive and to search for background files on other drives or in other folders. The **Color button** allows you to select a color from a color palette to use on the desktop or create a new color. The **Customize Desktop button** allows you to display the default icon for My Documents, My Computer, My Network Places, and Internet Explorer on the desktop and change the icons; control how often unused desktop icons are removed from the desktop; and display objects or Web pages on the desktop.

More About

The Desktop Background

When you work with Windows XP and do not maximize a window, the desktop background is the single most dominant feature of the computer screen. You should choose the background carefully because your choice can affect your mood, the ease of using your computer, and even others who work nearby.

Customizing the Desktop Items

In Project 1, you added the My Computer icon to the desktop by right-clicking the My Computer command on the Start menu and then clicking the Show on Desktop command. In addition to using the Start menu to add an icon to the desktop, you can use the Customize Desktop button in the Desktop sheet (see Figure 4-7 on page WIN 4.10). The Customize Desktop button allows you to display the My Documents icon, My Computer icon, My Network Places icon, and Internet Explorer icon on the desktop. Perform the following steps to add the My Documents, My Computer, and Internet Explorer icons to the desktop.

Steps To Add Icons to the Desktop

1 Click the Customize Desktop button in the Display Properties dialog box. Click My Documents, My Computer, and Internet Explorer in the Desktop icons area in the Desktop Items dialog box. Point to the OK button in the Desktop Items dialog box.

The Desktop Items dialog box displays (Figure 4-9). The dialog box contains the General and Web tabs, Desktop icons area, Icons list box, and Desktop cleanup area. A check mark displays in the My Documents, My Computer, and Internet Explorer check boxes in the Desktop icons area.

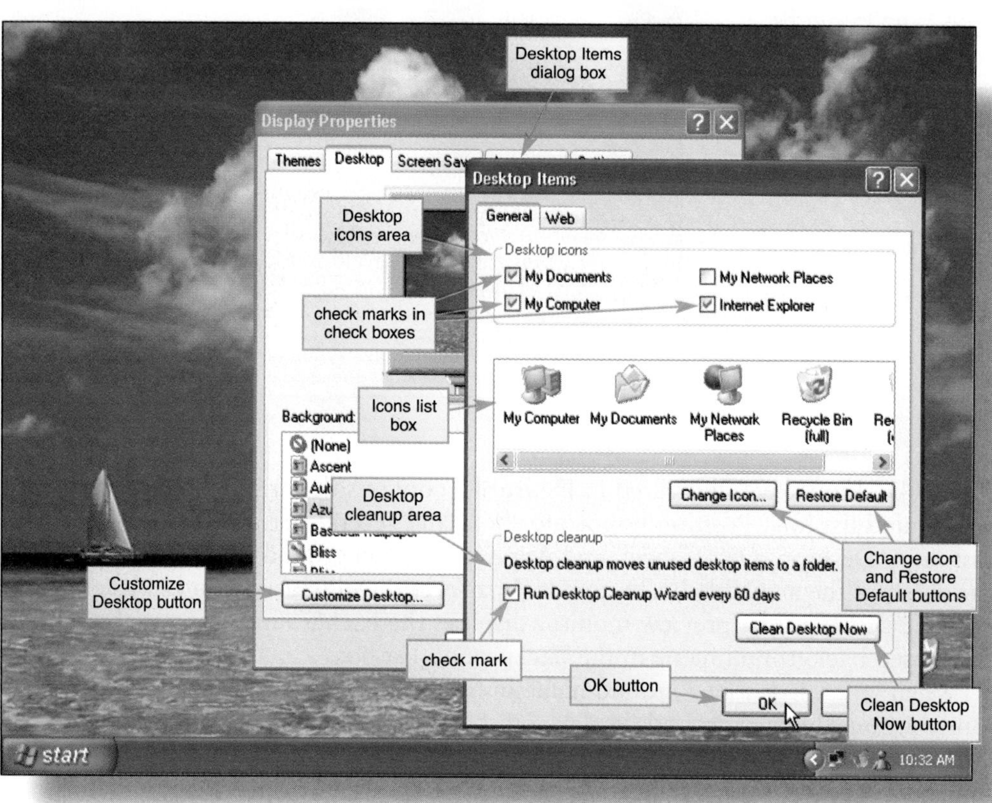

FIGURE 4-9

2 **Click the OK button in the Desktop Items dialog box. Click the Apply button in the Display Properties dialog box.**

Clicking the OK button closes the Desktop Items dialog box. Clicking the Apply button displays the My Documents, My Computer, and Internet Explorer icons along the left side of the desktop and dims the Apply button (Figure 4-10).

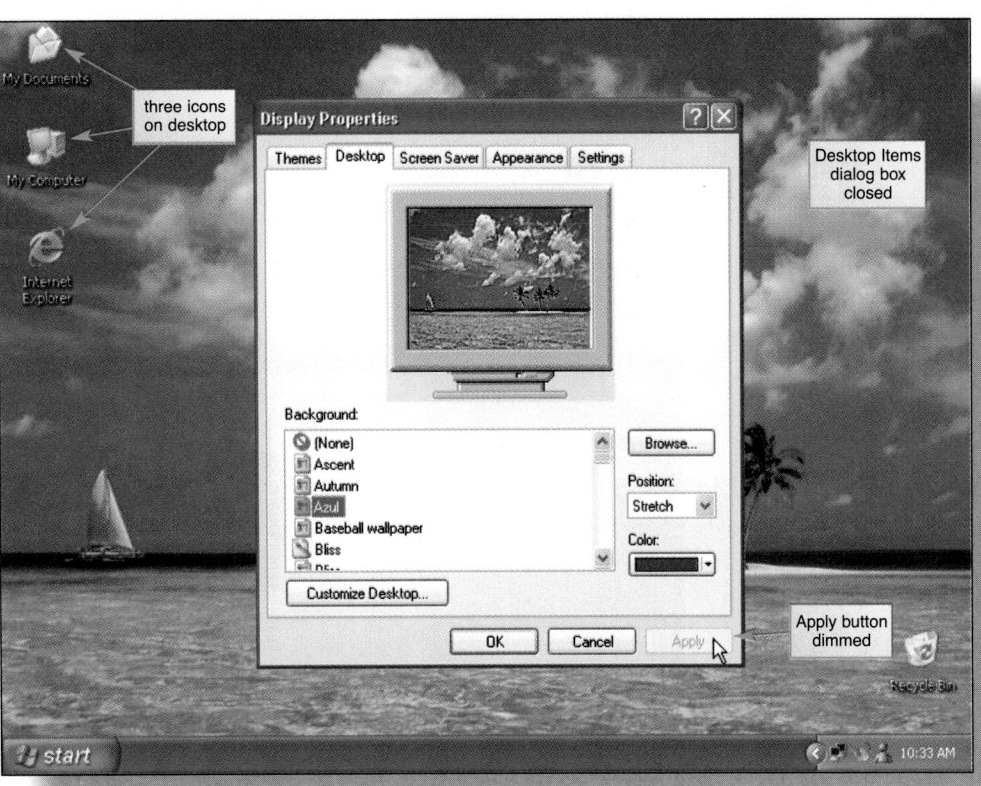

FIGURE 4-10

In Figure 4-9, the Icons list box contains the My Computer, My Documents, My Network Places, Recycle Bin (full), and Recycle Bin (empty) desktop icons. Clicking the **Change Icon button** allows you to change the icon for each of the desktop items in the Icons list box. Clicking the **Restore Default button** restores the Windows default icon for the selected desktop item.

The Desktop cleanup area allows you to move unwanted desktop icons to the Unused Desktop folder on the hard drive by clicking the Clean Desktop Now button. The check mark in the Run Desktop Cleanup Wizard every 60 days check box causes the **Desktop Cleanup wizard** to remove desktop icons automatically from the desktop if the icons have not been used in the previous sixty days.

Changing the Screen Saver

Another element of a desktop theme that you can modify is the screen saver. A **screen saver** is a moving picture or pattern that displays on the monitor when you have not used the mouse or keyboard for a specified period of time. Originally, screen savers were designed to prevent the problem of **ghosting** (a dim version of an image permanently etched on the monitor because the same image is displayed for a long time) by continually changing the image on the monitor. Today's screen savers are animations, designs, and other entertaining or fascinating activities that display on the screen after a period of time has passed without any computer activity. You determine how long this interval should be. It stops execution when you press a key on the keyboard or move the mouse.

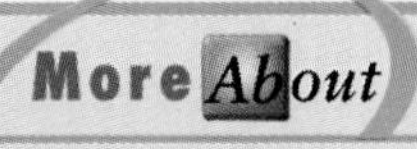

Screen Savers

Berkeley Software, developers of After Dark screen saver software, has created innovative screen savers that play music, act out stories and animations, and thoroughly entertain, while at the same time generating millions of dollars in revenue. Screen savers today vary from cartoons to ever-changing masterpieces of art.

Windows XP provides a variety of screen savers from which you can choose. To change the screen saver, complete the following steps.

Steps To Change the Screen Saver

1 Click the Screen Saver tab in the Display Properties dialog box. Point to the Screen Saver box arrow.

The Screen Saver sheet displays and contains a preview monitor, Screen saver area, and Monitor power area (Figure 4-11). The highlighted Windows XP screen saver name displays in the Screen saver box and the preview monitor shows how the Windows XP screen saver will display. The Monitor power area may or may not display in the dialog box on your computer.

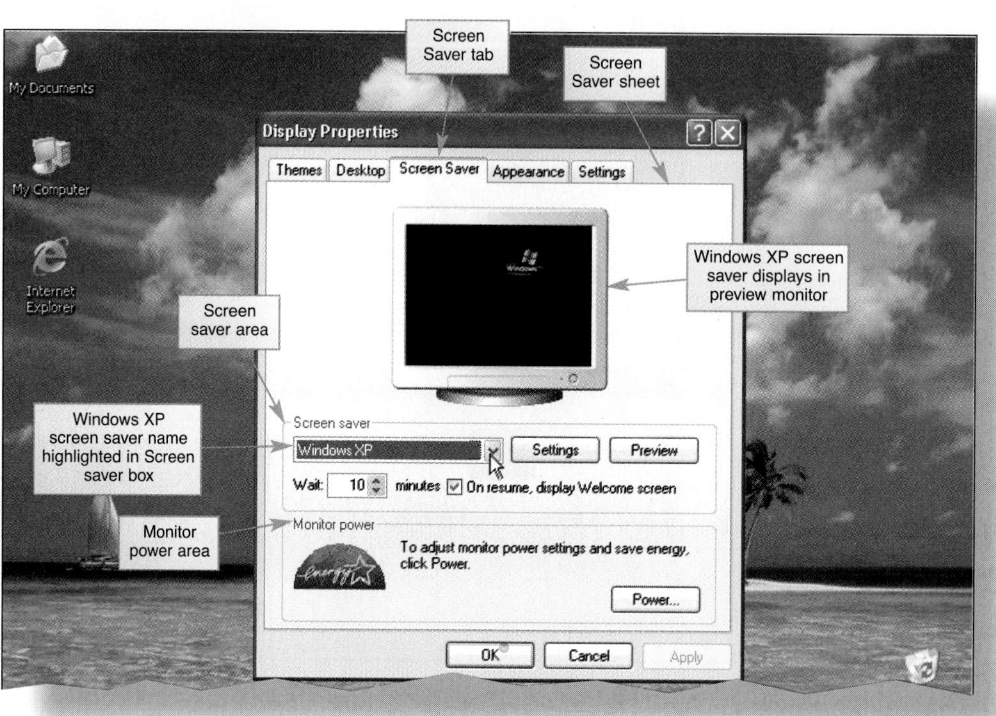

FIGURE 4-11

2 Click the Screen Saver box arrow. Point to 3D FlowerBox in the Screen saver list.

A list of screen savers displays in the Screen saver list (Figure 4-12). Your computer may contain more or fewer screen savers than display in Figure 4-12.

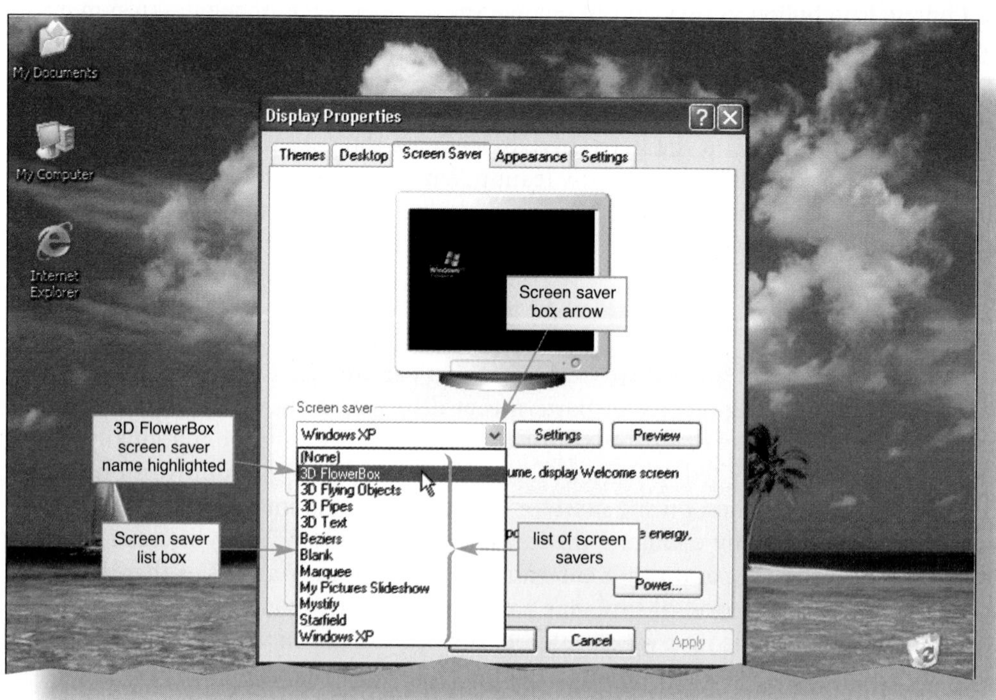

FIGURE 4-12

3 Click 3D FlowerBox.

The 3D FlowerBox screen saver displays in the preview monitor and the 3D FlowerBox name displays in the Screen saver box, indicating it is the selected screen saver (Figure 4-13).

4 Select other screen savers in the Screen saver list to view them.

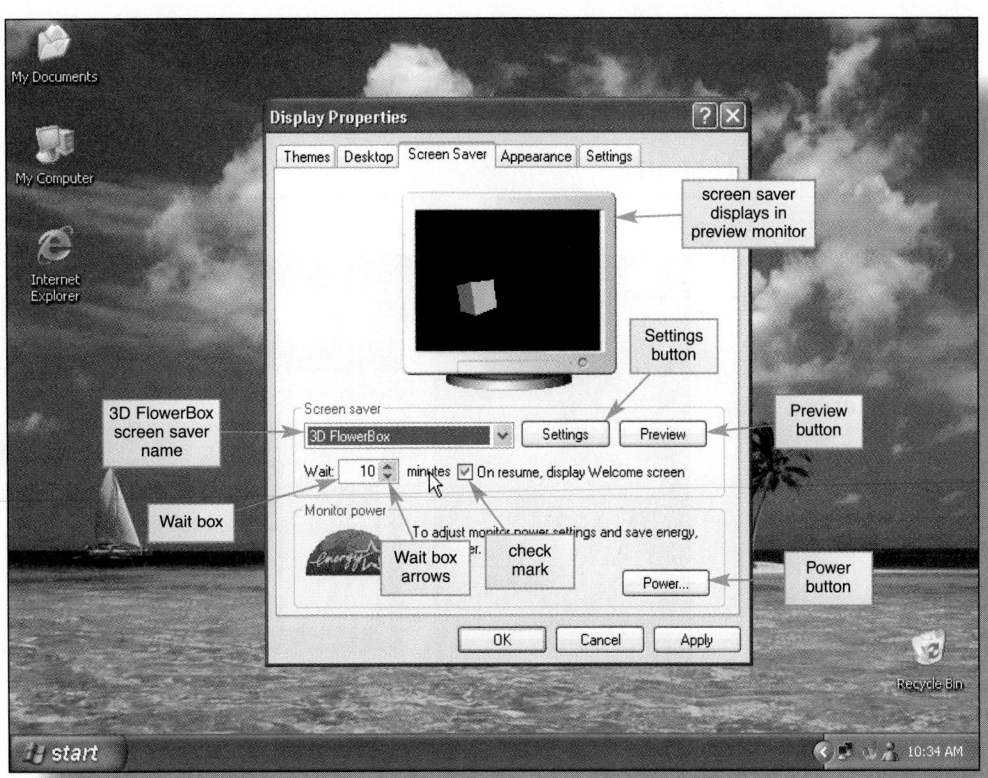

FIGURE 4-13

Other Ways

1. Press TAB until any tab is selected, use RIGHT ARROW to select Screen Saver tab, press TAB to select current screen saver, press UP ARROW or DOWN ARROW to select screen saver

Clicking the **Settings button** in the Screen saver area allows you to change the color, shape, complexity, and size of the image that displays in the 3D FlowerBox screen saver. If you click the **Preview button**, Windows XP displays the screen saver on the entire screen. To stop the preview of the screen saver, move the mouse or press a key on the keyboard. To set the number of minutes of computer inactivity to wait until the screen saver displays, click the Wait box up or down arrow. The number of minutes to wait is set at ten. The check box to the right of the Wait box contains a check mark to indicate the Welcome screen will display when you resume using the computer after the screen saver has started running. If a password is required, you will have to type the password.

Clicking the **Power button** in the Monitor power area allows you to select a power scheme and select the number of minutes or hours of inactivity that you want to elapse before the monitor or hard disk turns off and the system standby or system hibernation turn on.

Changing the Desktop Appearance

Another element of a desktop theme that you can modify is the desktop appearance. **Desktop appearances** include the visual styles of the desktop theme, color scheme for the currently selected visual styles, and the font size options that are available for the currently selected color scheme. The Appearance sheet in the Display Properties dialog box allows you to change the desktop appearances.

To change the font size for the currently selected color scheme (Windows XP), perform the following steps.

Steps To Change the Font Size

1 Click the Appearance tab in the Display Properties dialog box. Point to the Font size box arrow.

The Appearance sheet displays in the Display Properties dialog box (Figure 4-14). The Preview pane illustrates how the current settings look on the desktop. The Windows and buttons box contains the highlighted Windows XP style name, the Color Scheme box contains the Default (blue) color scheme name, and the Font size box contains the Normal font size name.

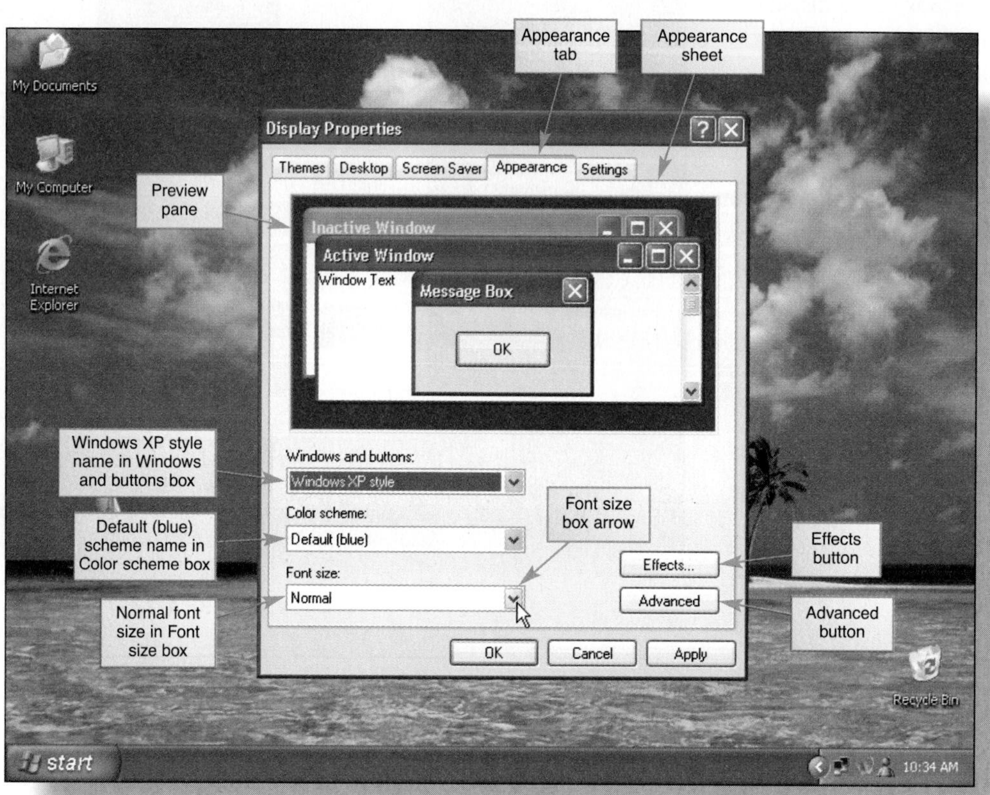

FIGURE 4-14

2 Click the Font size box arrow. Point to Large Fonts in the Font size list.

The Font size list, containing the highlighted Large Fonts entry, displays (Figure 4-15). The Font size list contains the font sizes (Normal, Large Fonts, and Extra Large Fonts) you can apply to the currently selected Default (blue) color scheme.

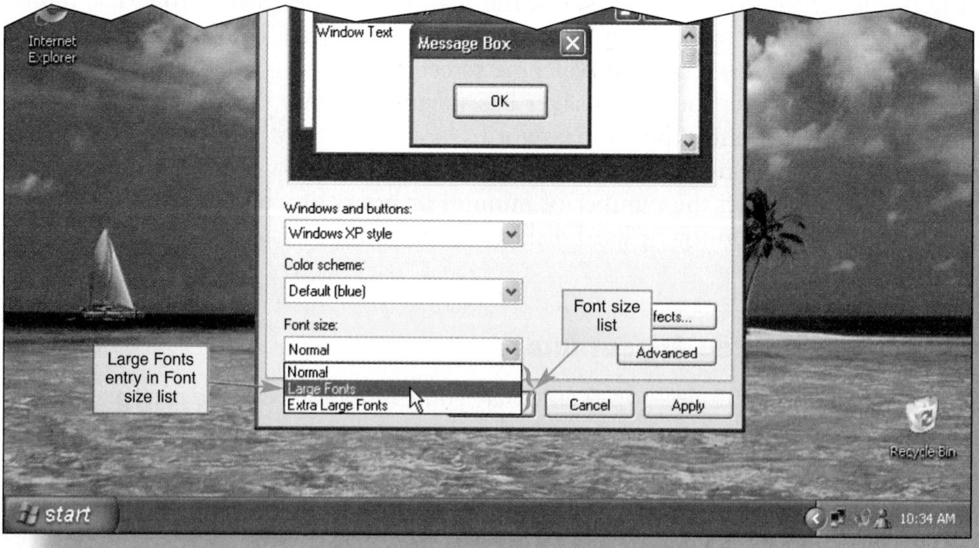

FIGURE 4-15

3 Click Large Fonts. Click the Apply button.

When you click Large Fonts, the size of the text in the Preview pane becomes larger. When you click the Apply button, the font size of all text on the desktop becomes larger and the Apply button is dimmed (Figure 4-16).

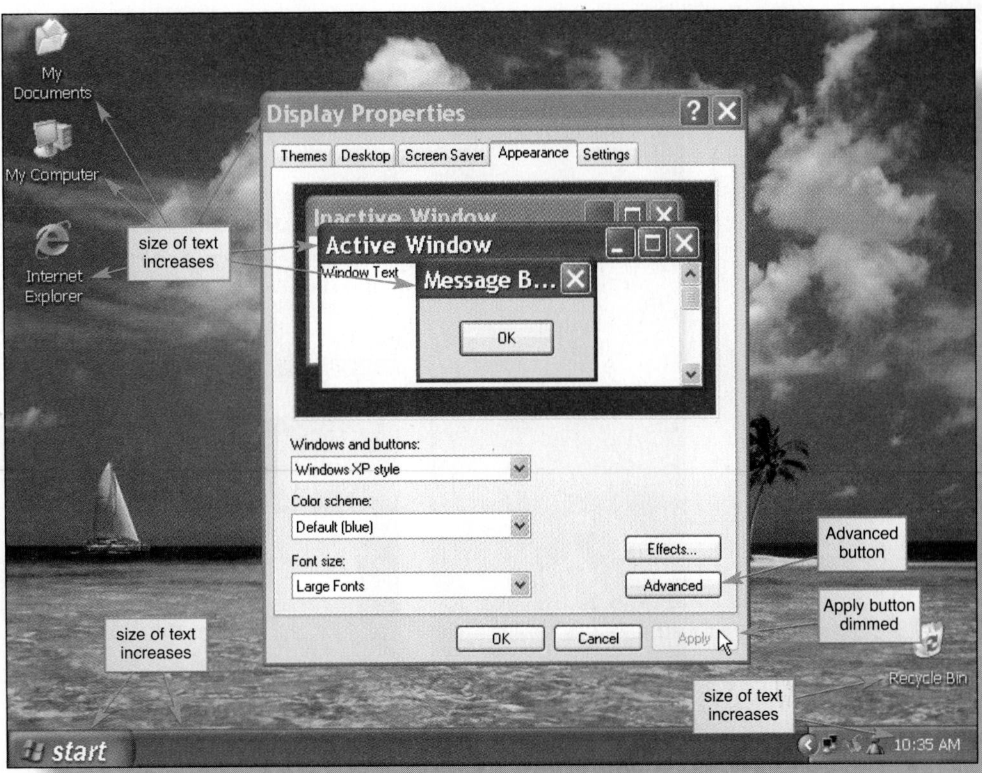

FIGURE 4-16

In Figure 4-14, the Appearance sheet contains the Effects button and Advanced button. The **Effects button** allows you to set the visual effects for menus, icons, and fonts. Among the visual effects you can set for menus, lists, and ToolTips are the **transition effects** (Fade and Scroll). The **Fade effect** allows menus, lists, and ToolTips to fade-in when you open them and dissolve when you close them. The **Scroll effect** allows menus, lists, and ToolTips to slide in and out. Other visual effects include smoothing the edges of screen fonts to improve the readability of large screen fonts; using large icons to represent files, folders, and shortcuts on the desktop; showing a slight shadow on a menu to give the menu a three-dimensional look; displaying window content as you move or size a window; and whether to suppress keyboard shortcuts (underlined characters in menu items) on menus.

The Advanced button in the Appearance sheet is best used when the Windows Classic desktop theme is selected. The **Advanced button** allows you to customize the look of windows, menus, fonts, and icons by changing the font size, font attributes, and color of individual elements of the desktop, such as the active title bar, inactive title bar, scroll bar, and window borders.

Saving the Desktop Theme

After creating a new desktop theme by modifying the Windows XP desktop theme, you should save the new desktop theme. When you save a desktop theme, you must assign a descriptive name to the desktop theme. If you modify the desktop and do not save the new desktop theme, the changes will be lost when you select another desktop theme. Desktop themes are saved automatically in the My Documents folder. Perform the steps on the next page to save the desktop theme using your first and last names.

Other Ways

1. Press TAB until any tab is selected, press RIGHT ARROW until Appearance sheet displays, press TAB until Font Size box is selected, press UP ARROW or DOWN ARROW to select font size, press ALT+A (or ENTER)

More About

Customizing the Color Scheme

To create a customized color scheme, click the Advanced button in the Appearance sheet in Figure 4-16. Select a screen element in the preview pane or a desktop item in the Item box and then select the desired color, font, and font size. Repeat for all screen elements or desktop items. Click the OK button to make the changes.

Steps To Save a Desktop Theme

1 **Click the Themes tab in the Display Properties dialog box. Point to the Save As button in the Themes sheet.**

The Themes sheet displays (Figure 4-17).

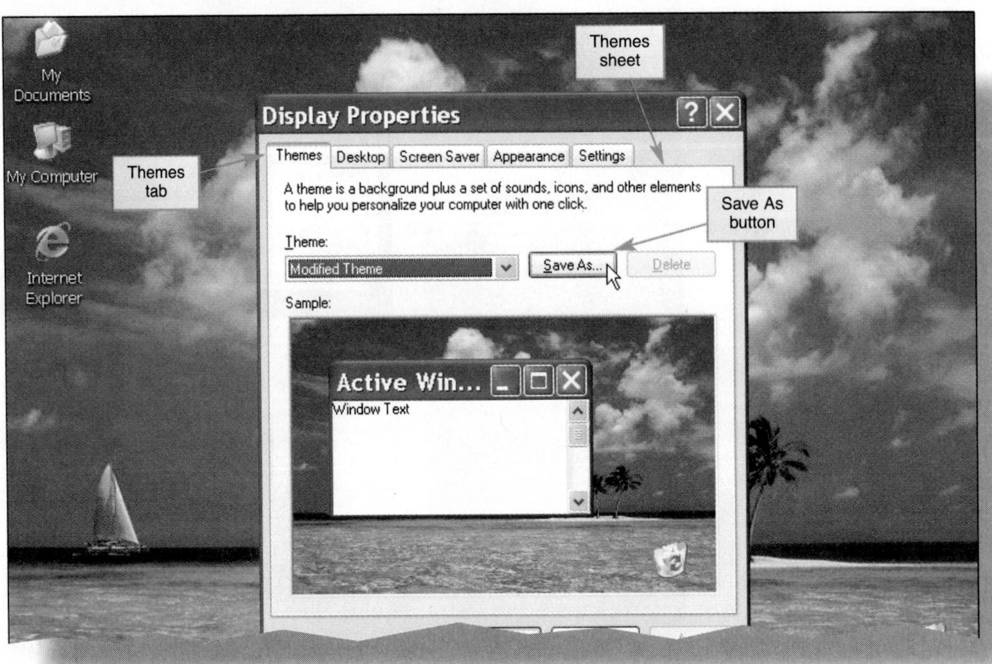

FIGURE 4-17

2 **Click the Save As button. Type** `Desktop Theme of` **in the File name box, press the SPACEBAR, type your first name, press the SPACEBAR, and then type your last name. Point to the Save button.**

The Save As dialog box displays and the file name, Desktop Theme of Brad Wilson, displays in the File name box (Figure 4-18).

3 **Click the Save button. Click the OK button in the Display Properties dialog box.**

The desktop theme is saved in the My Documents folder, the Display Properties dialog box closes, and the new desktop theme displays on the desktop.

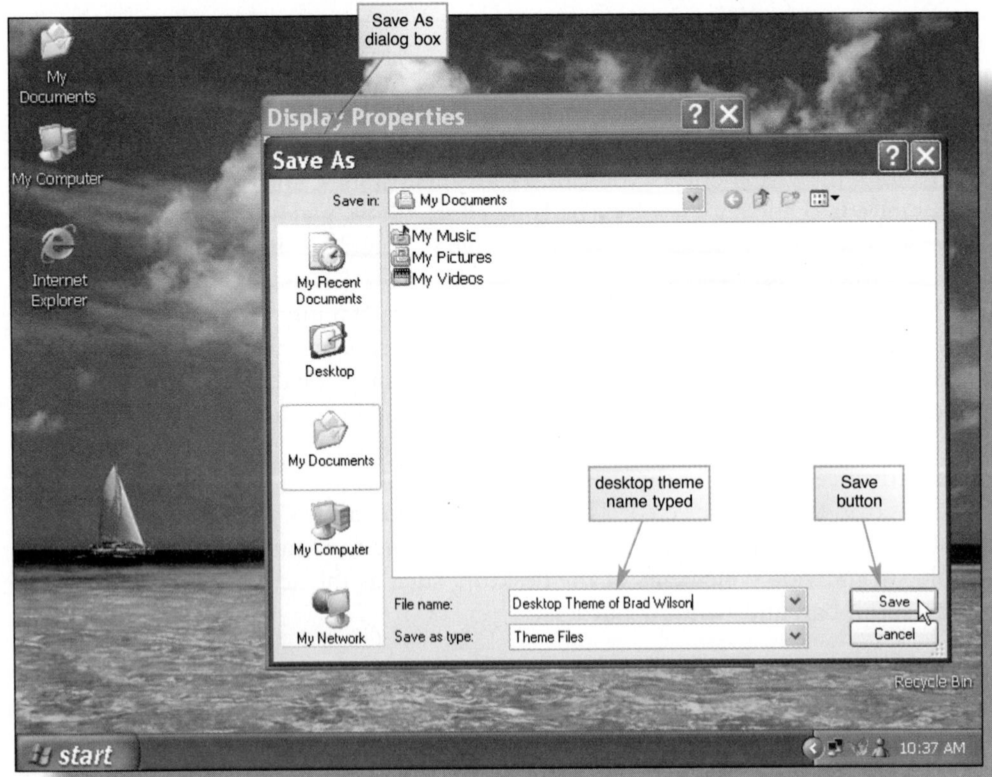

FIGURE 4-18

When you save the desktop theme in Step 3, the items that are saved include the background, position, color, and desktop icons on the Desktop tab; screen saver on the Screen Saver tab; and windows, buttons, color scheme, font size, and all features changed using the Advanced button on the Appearance tab. The mouse pointer scheme and sound scheme also are saved if you made changes to them.

More About

Saving a Desktop Theme

If you modify a desktop theme without saving it, your changes are saved with the name, *Previous theme name (Modified)*. Your modified theme, however, will be lost if you select a different theme. New themes are saved in the My Documents folder.

Deleting a Desktop Theme

After you have finished using the new desktop theme you created and saved, you should remove it. Perform the following steps to remove the desktop theme you created earlier in this project from the desktop.

TO DELETE A DESKTOP THEME

1. Right-click an open area of the desktop and then click Properties on the shortcut menu.
2. Verify the name of the desktop theme you created earlier displays in the Theme box.
3. Click the Delete button.
4. Click the Theme box arrow in the Themes sheet.
5. Click the desktop theme name in the Theme list you wrote down in Step 1 on page WIN 4.07.
6. Click the OK button.

The desktop theme is deleted from the My Documents folder, the Display Properties dialog box closes, and the original desktop theme displays on the desktop.

The My Documents, My Computer, and Internet Explorer icons remain on the desktop. You will use one of these icons, the My Computer icon, later in this project and then you will delete all three icons at the end of this project.

Displaying Web Content on the Desktop

Windows XP allows you to display Web pages from the Internet directly on the desktop and update the content of the pages automatically. Examples of this constantly changing content, referred to as **active content**, can be a weather map, a constantly updating stock market ticker of stock quotes, fast-breaking news stories from a favorite online newspaper, the latest sports scores, or a favorite Web page. When the desktop displays active content, the desktop is referred to as the **Active Desktop™**.

One method of displaying active content on the desktop is to add an Active Desktop item. An **Active Desktop item** displays active content from a Web page directly on the desktop and updates the content periodically. Once on the desktop, you can move and resize the item and specify how often you want to update the active content.

In the process of adding an Active Desktop item to the desktop, you create a connection between the Web site containing the active content and the Internet Explorer browser. This connection, called a **channel**, links the Internet Explorer browser to the Web site, allowing Internet Explorer to determine if the content of the Web site has changed and deliver the updated content to the desktop.

When you create a channel, you have the choice of being notified when new content is available or having the updated content delivered automatically to the desktop. Perform the steps on the next page to add the CBS SportsLine™ item to the desktop.

Steps To Add an Active Desktop Item to the Desktop

1 Right-click an open area on the desktop, click Properties on the shortcut menu, click the Desktop tab in the Display Properties dialog box, and then point to the Customize Desktop button.

The Desktop sheet displays in the Display Properties dialog box (Figure 4-19). The Customize Desktop button displays at the bottom of the dialog box.

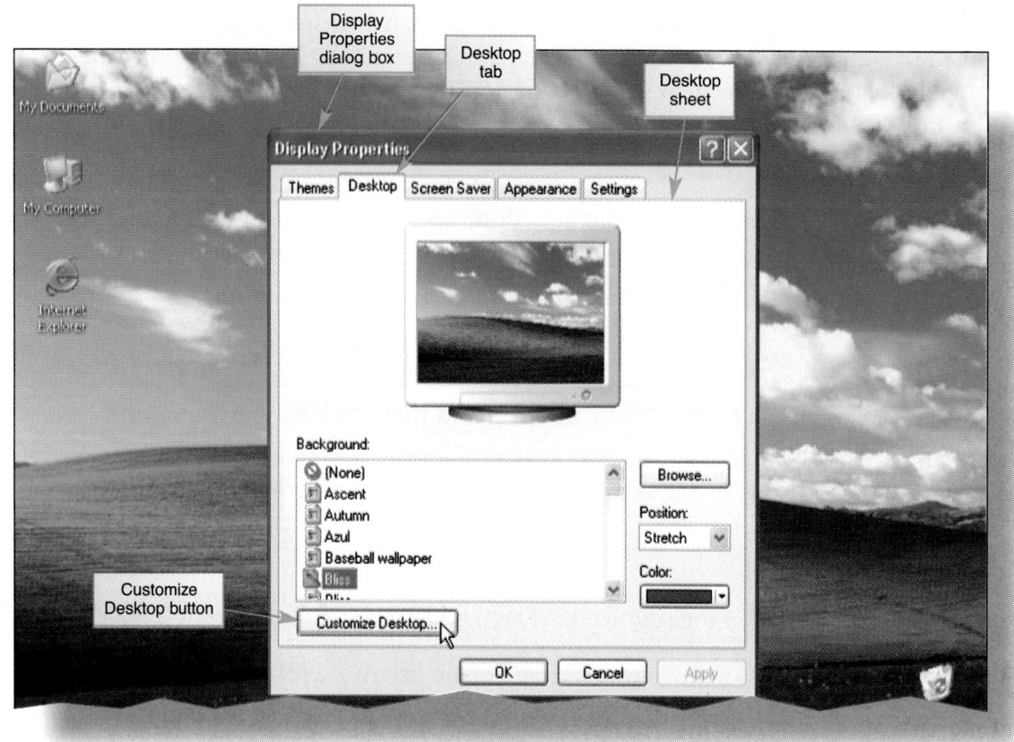

FIGURE 4-19

2 Click the Customize Desktop button. Click the Web tab in the Desktop Items dialog box. Point to the New button.

The Web sheet displays in the Desktop Items dialog box (Figure 4-20). The Web sheet contains instructions to display a Web page on the desktop and the highlighted My Current Home Page entry displays in the Web pages list box.

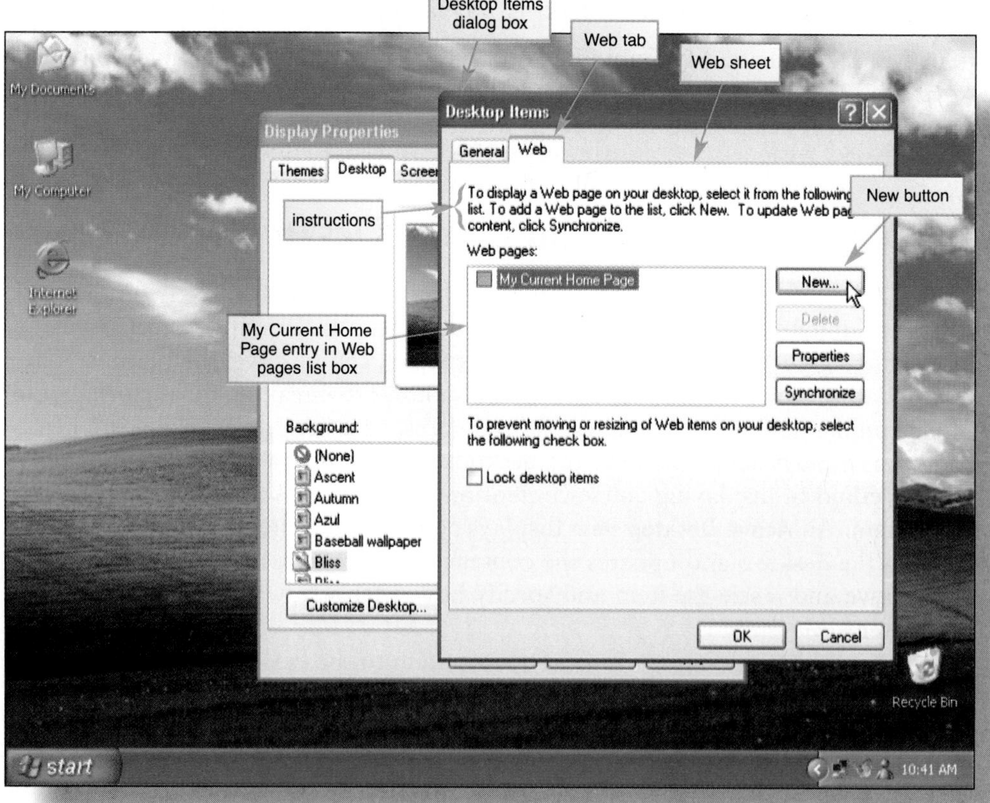

FIGURE 4-20

3 Click the New button. Point to the Visit Gallery button.

The New Desktop Item wizard starts and displays the New Desktop Item dialog box (Figure 4-21). Messages in the dialog box indicate you can add live Web content, a Web page, or pictures to the desktop. Clicking the Visit Gallery button allows you to visit the Internet Explorer 4.0 Active Desktop Gallery *and add a new desktop item.*

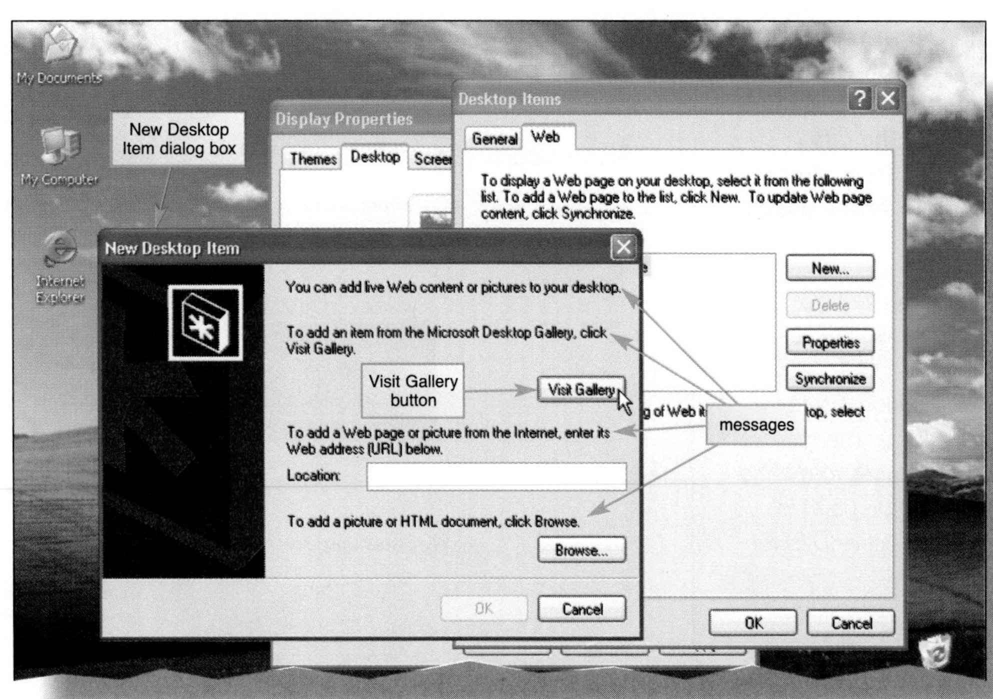

FIGURE 4-21

4 Click the Visit Gallery button. Click the Maximize button in the Internet Explorer 4.0 Desktop Gallery - Microsoft Internet Explorer window.

Windows XP launches Internet Explorer and displays the maximized Internet Explorer 4.0 Desktop Gallery window (Figure 4-22). The gallery contains four active desktop items (Microsoft Investor Ticker, CBS SportsLine, Weather Map from MSNBC, and J-Track Satellite Tracking). Only the Microsoft Investor Ticker item is visible in the window.

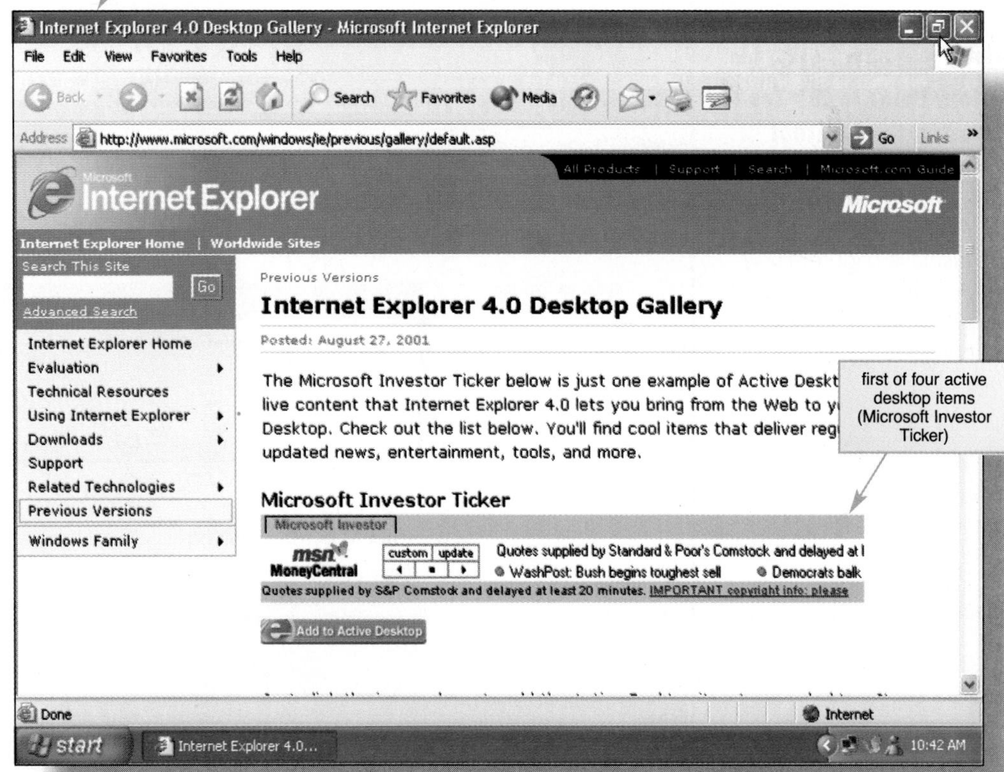

FIGURE 4-22

5 Scroll the Internet Explorer 4.0 Desktop Gallery window to display the CBS SportsLine item. Point to the Add to Active Desktop button.

A sample of the CBS SportsLine desktop item and the Add to Active Desktop button display (Figure 4-23). The mouse pointer changes to a hand icon when you point to the Add to Active Desktop button.

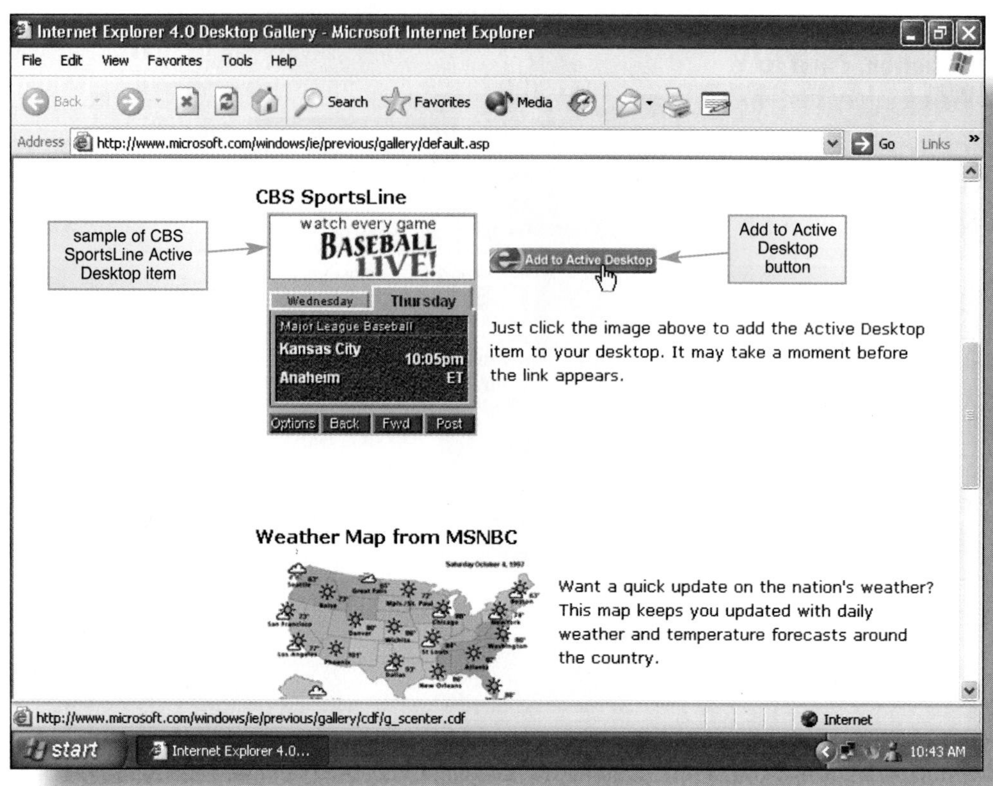

FIGURE 4-23

6 Click the Add to Active Desktop button. Point to the Yes button in the Internet Explorer dialog box.

The Internet Explorer dialog box displays (Figure 4-24). A question asks if you want to add an Active Desktop item to your desktop.

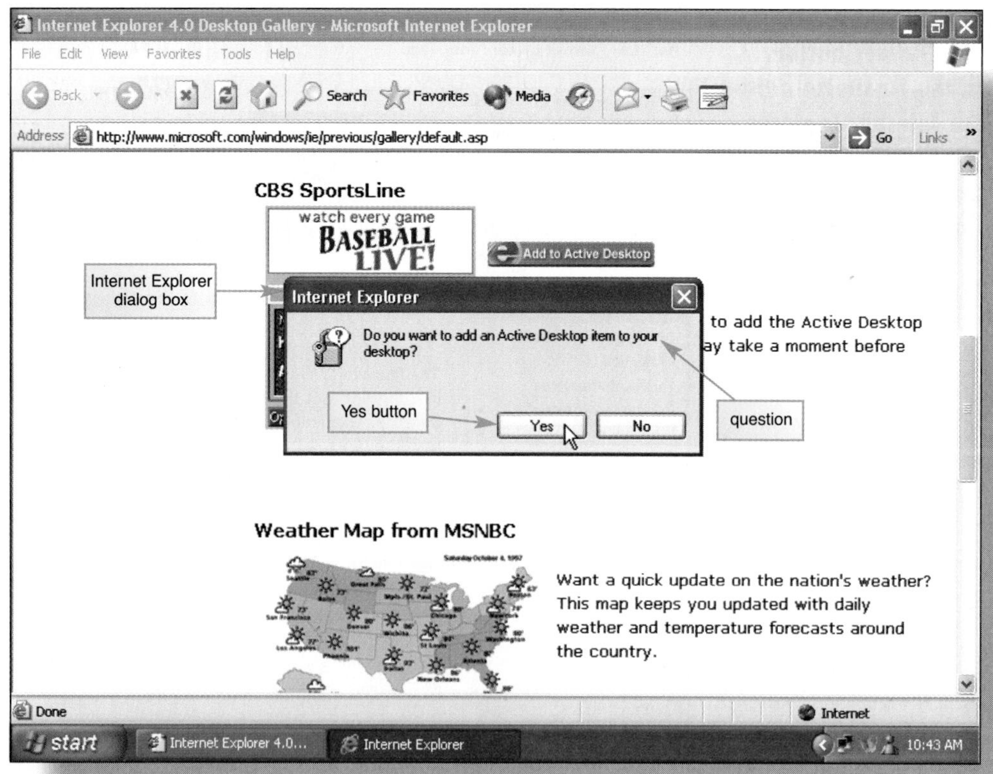

FIGURE 4-24

7 Click the Yes button. Point to the OK button in the Add item to Active Desktop(TM) dialog box.

The Add item to Active Desktop(TM) dialog box displays (Figure 4-25). The dialog box contains a message that indicates you have chosen to make a channel available offline and add the CBS SportsLine desktop item to the Active Desktop.

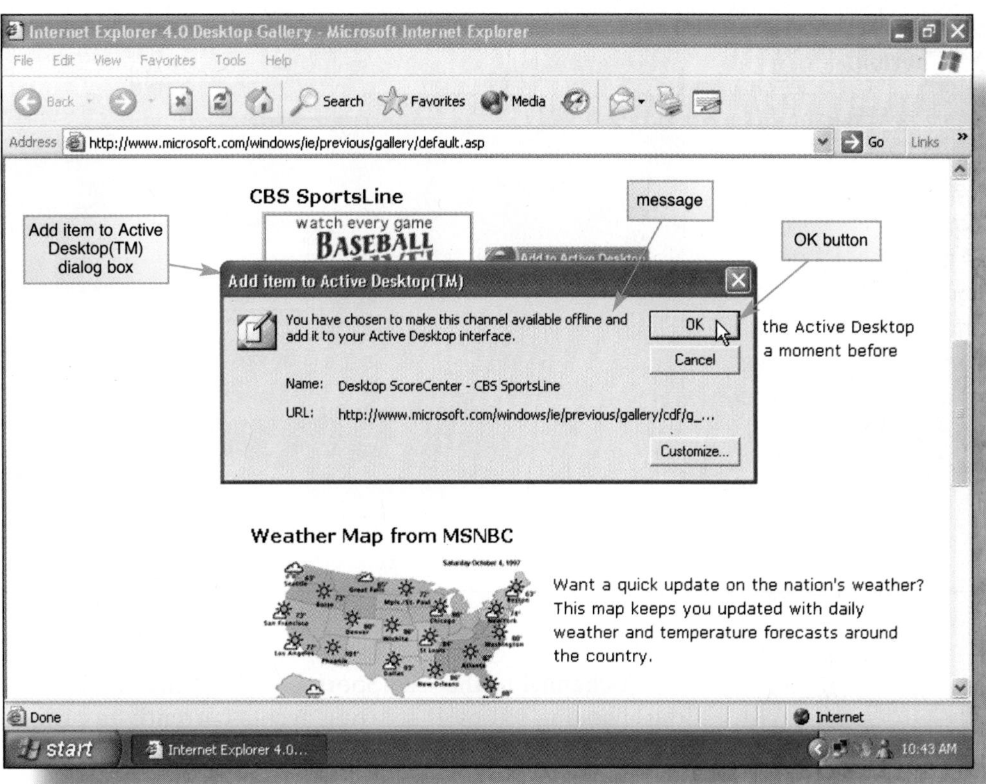

FIGURE 4-25

8 Click the OK button. Point to the Close button in the Internet Explorer 4.0 Desktop Gallery window.

The Synchronizing dialog box displays momentarily while the channel to the CBS SportsLine Web site is established. After the channel is established, the Synchronizing dialog box closes and you can view the CBS SportsLine desktop item by clicking the Close button in the Internet Explorer 4.0 Desktop Gallery window (Figure 4-26).

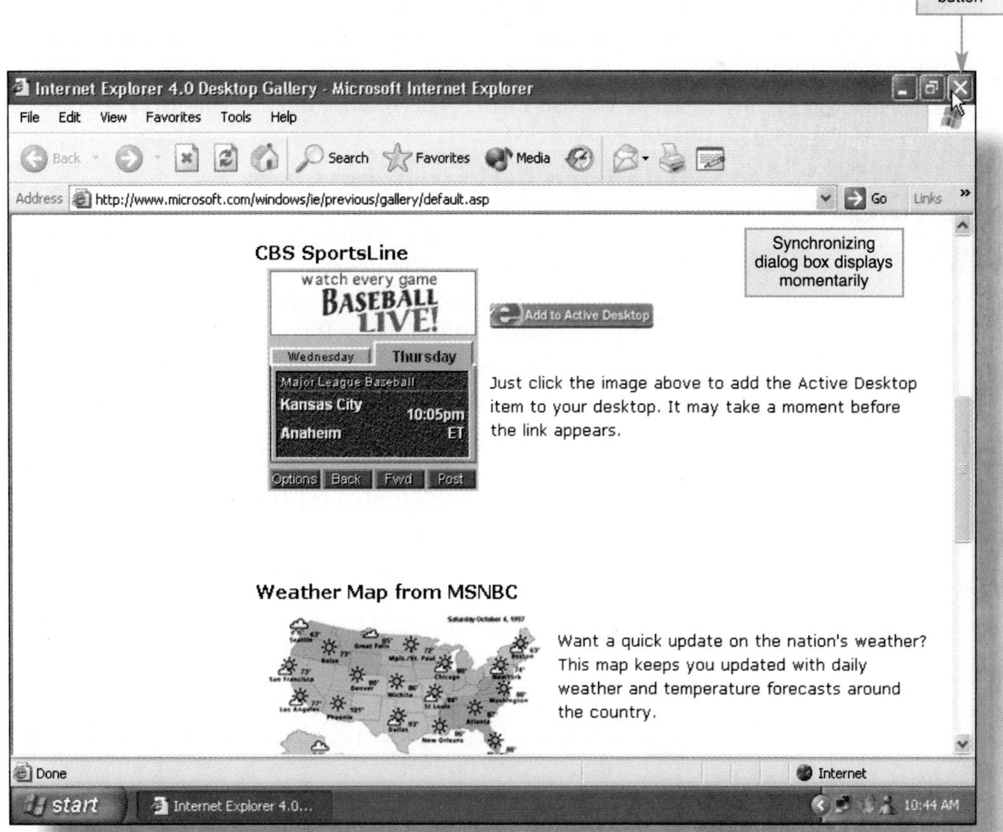

FIGURE 4-26

9 **Click the Close button.**

The Internet Explorer 4.0 Desktop Gallery window closes and the CBS SportsLine item is visible on the Active Desktop (Figure 4-27). The updated sports scores that display toward the bottom of the item change approximately every four seconds.

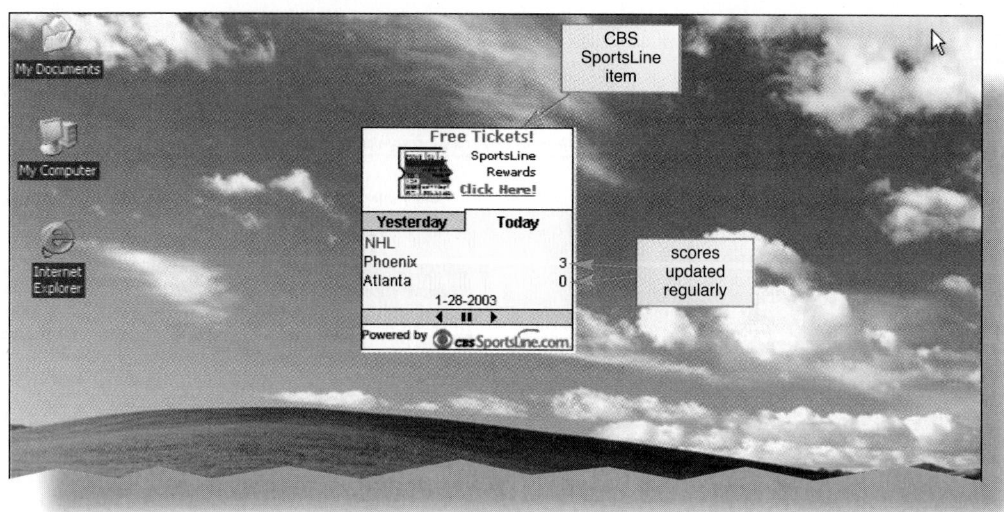

FIGURE 4-27

The Active Desktop™

After adding an Active Desktop item to the desktop, you can move and resize the item. To move it, point to the desktop item name displayed at the top of the item and then drag the gray bar that displays to a new position on the desktop. Point anywhere off the gray bar to remove the gray bar.

A channel to the CBS SportsLine Web site is established. This allows you to view the changing scores of sporting events currently in progress, view the game times of sporting events yet to be played, and obtain additional information about the sporting event that currently displays. Unless you change the schedule, updates are performed according to the schedule set by the Web site's publisher.

After adding the CBS SportsLine desktop item to the desktop, you may want to obtain additional information about a sporting event that displays in the Active Desktop item. To accomplish this, click the score summary on the CBS SportsLine desktop item, maximize the Microsoft Internet Explorer window, and then scroll the window to read the information about the sporting event. When you finish, click the Close button in the Microsoft Internet Explorer window to close the window.

Deleting a Desktop Item

When you no longer wish to view a desktop item on the desktop, you can remove the item from the desktop by pointing to the top edge of the item and then clicking the Close button in the upper-right corner. When a desktop item is removed from the desktop, Windows XP continues to update the item. To prevent further updates and permanently delete the item, perform the following steps.

TO DELETE PERMANENTLY A DESKTOP ITEM

1. Right-click an open area on the desktop and then click Properties on the shortcut menu.
2. Click the Desktop tab in the Display Properties dialog box.
3. Click the Customize Desktop button.
4. Click the Web tab in the Desktop Items dialog box.
5. Click the Desktop ScoreCenter – CBS SportsLine entry in the Web pages list box.
6. Click the Delete button.
7. Click the Yes button in the Active Desktop Item dialog box.

8 Click the OK button in the Desktop Items dialog box.

9 Click the OK button in the Display Properties dialog box.

The CBS SportsLine desktop item is deleted permanently and no longer displays on the desktop.

If after removing a desktop item from the desktop, you wish to return the item to the desktop, follow the steps illustrated on pages WIN 4.20 through WIN 4.24 to return the item.

Desktop Properties Summary

In the previous sections, you customized the desktop work environment by changing the properties of the desktop. These properties included the choice of a desktop theme and desktop background, adding icons to the desktop, changing the screen saver, changing the size of font on the desktop, and displaying Web content on the desktop.

Customizing the Taskbar

Another method of modifying the desktop work environment is to customize the taskbar at the bottom of the desktop. For example, you can move, resize, and hide the taskbar; add toolbars to the taskbar; change the appearance of the taskbar; and change the taskbar properties. The steps in the next sections will illustrate how to customize the taskbar and the toolbars on the taskbar.

Unlocking the Taskbar

By default, the taskbar is locked into position at the bottom of the desktop. **Locking the taskbar** prevents the taskbar from being moved to another location on the desktop and also locks the size and position of any toolbars displayed on the taskbar. Prior to moving or resizing the taskbar, you must unlock the taskbar. After moving or resizing, you may want to lock the taskbar in its new location so that you do not accidentally change the size and position of the taskbar. Perform the following steps to unlock the taskbar.

To Unlock the Taskbar

1 **Right-click an open area of the taskbar. Point to Lock the Taskbar on the shortcut menu.**

A shortcut menu containing the highlighted Lock the Taskbar command displays on the desktop (Figure 4-28). A check mark preceding the Lock the Taskbar command indicates the taskbar is locked.

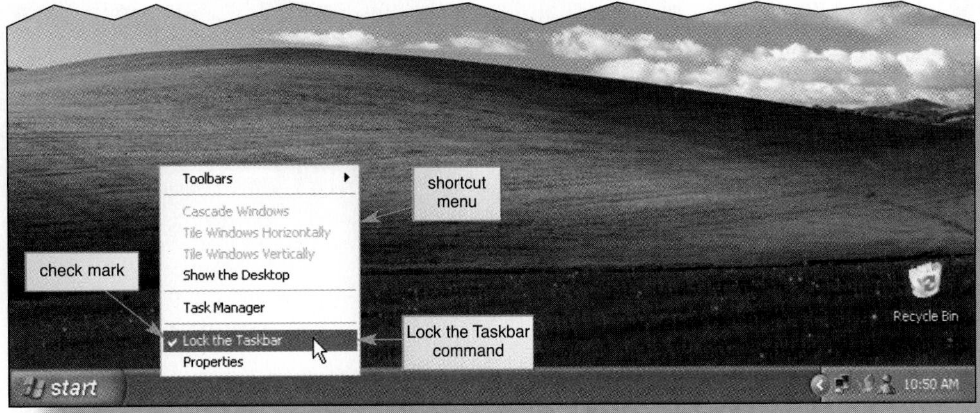

FIGURE 4-28

2 Click Lock the Taskbar.

The shortcut menu closes, the taskbar is unlocked, a small border displays along the top edge of the taskbar, and a dotted vertical bar displays to the right of the Start button (Figure 4-29). Although not visible, the check mark to the left of the Lock the Taskbar command on the shortcut menu no longer displays, which indicates the taskbar is unlocked.

FIGURE 4-29

Other Ways

1. Right-click open area of taskbar, click Properties, click Lock the Taskbar, click OK button
2. Right-click Start button, click Properties, click Taskbar tab, click Lock the Taskbar, click OK button

The small border along the top edge of the taskbar and the dotted vertical bar display because the taskbar is unlocked. If the taskbar is locked, the border and dotted vertical bar do not display. The small border allows you to change the size of the taskbar by dragging the border up or down. The **dotted vertical bar** defines the left edge of the taskbar buttons area. Other dotted vertical bars will display on the taskbar as toolbars are added to the taskbar.

Moving the Taskbar

By default, the taskbar is docked at the bottom edge of the desktop, but it can be moved to any of the four edges of the desktop by dragging. To move the taskbar to the top, left, and right edge of the desktop and then back to the bottom, complete the following steps.

Steps To Move the Taskbar

1 Point to an open area on the taskbar (Figure 4-30).

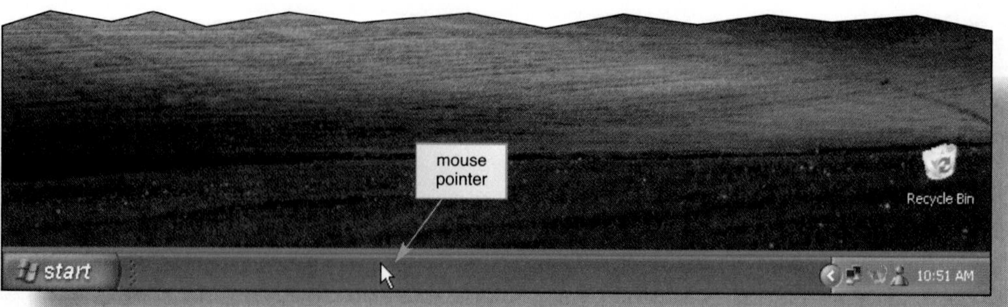

FIGURE 4-30

2 Drag the taskbar to the top of the desktop.

As you drag the taskbar toward the top of the desktop, the taskbar remains at the bottom until the mouse pointer approaches the center of the desktop. Then the taskbar moves to the top of the desktop, displaying on top of any icons on the desktop. When you release the mouse button, the icons on the desktop move below the taskbar, which is docked at the top edge of the desktop (Figure 4-31).

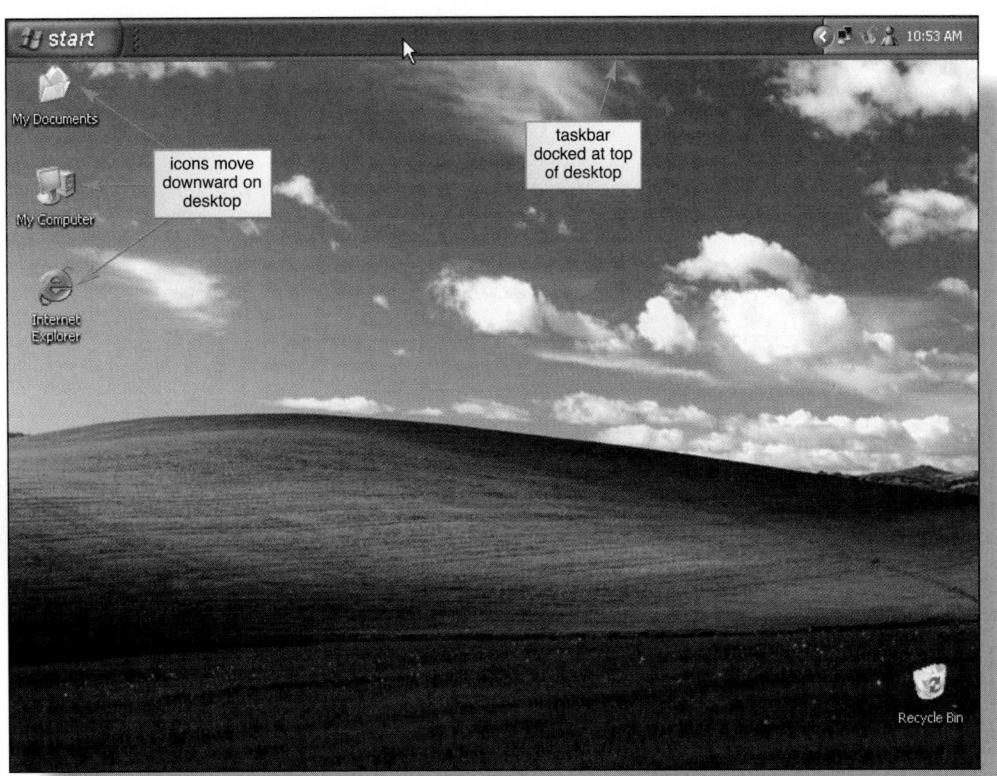

FIGURE 4-31

3 Drag the taskbar to the left and then the right side of the desktop. Drag the taskbar back to the bottom of the desktop.

The placement of the taskbar is an individual preference, but the default for Windows XP is on the bottom edge. Most people prefer to use this default position.

Locking the Taskbar

In the previous two sections, you unlocked the taskbar and then moved the taskbar to the left, right, and top edges of the desktop and then back to its original location at the bottom of the desktop. After moving the taskbar, you may want to lock the taskbar so the position of the taskbar is fixed and cannot be changed. Perform the steps on the next page to lock the taskbar.

TO LOCK THE TASKBAR

1. Right-click an open area of the taskbar.
2. Click Lock the Taskbar on the shortcut menu.

The taskbar is locked, and the small border along the top edge and the dotted vertical bar on the taskbar no longer display (Figure 4-32). Although not visible, a check mark precedes the Lock the Taskbar command on the shortcut menu.

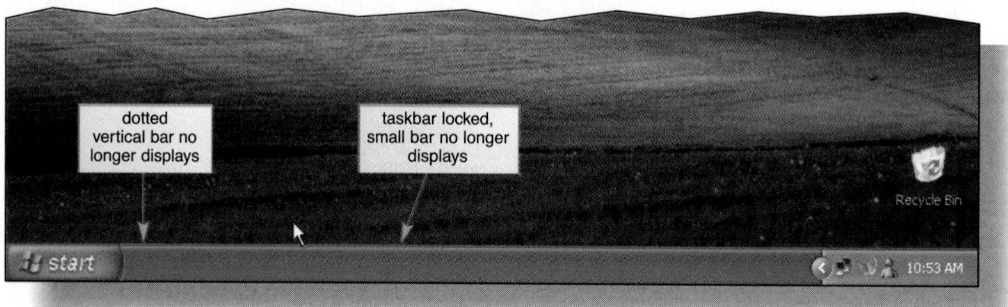

FIGURE 4-32

More About

Hiding the Taskbar

In addition to pointing to the top edge of the hidden taskbar to display the taskbar, you can display the taskbar at any time by pressing the WINDOWS key or pressing CTRL+ESC.

Hiding the Taskbar

Another way to customize the taskbar is to hide the taskbar so that only its top edge is visible at the bottom of the desktop. After hiding the taskbar, pointing to the top edge displays the taskbar on the desktop. The taskbar remains on the desktop as long as the mouse pointer points to the taskbar. The taskbar does not have to be unlocked to hide and redisplay the taskbar. Complete the following steps to hide and then redisplay the taskbar.

Steps To Hide and Redisplay the Taskbar

1. **Right-click an open area on the taskbar. Point to Properties on the shortcut menu.**

A shortcut menu, containing the highlighted Properties command, displays (Figure 4-33).

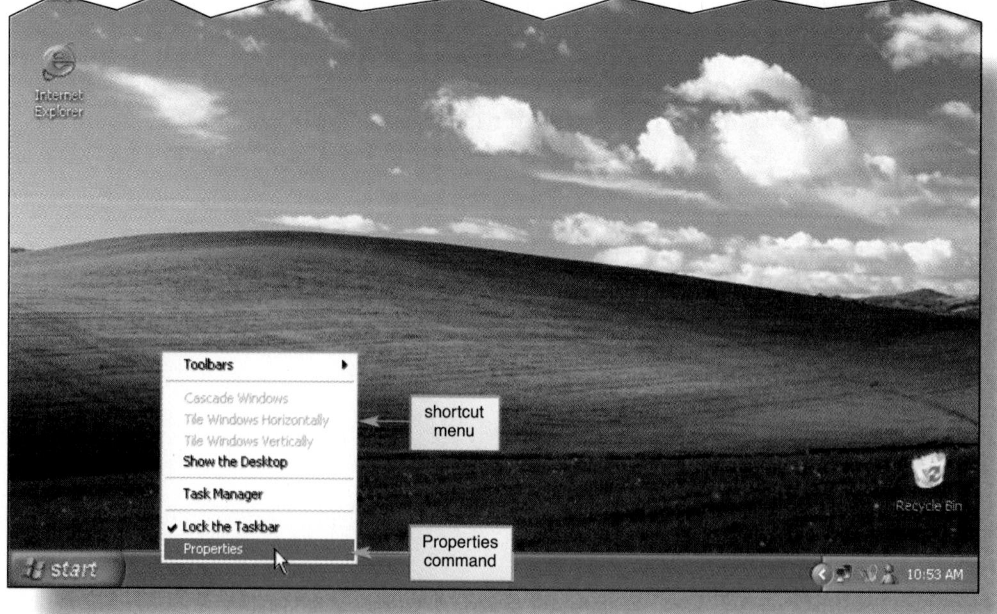

FIGURE 4-33

2 Click Properties. Point to Auto-hide the taskbar.

The Taskbar and Start Menu Properties dialog box and Taskbar sheet display (Figure 4-34). The Taskbar appearance area contains a preview pane containing a portion of a taskbar. The Apply button at the bottom of the dialog box is dimmed.

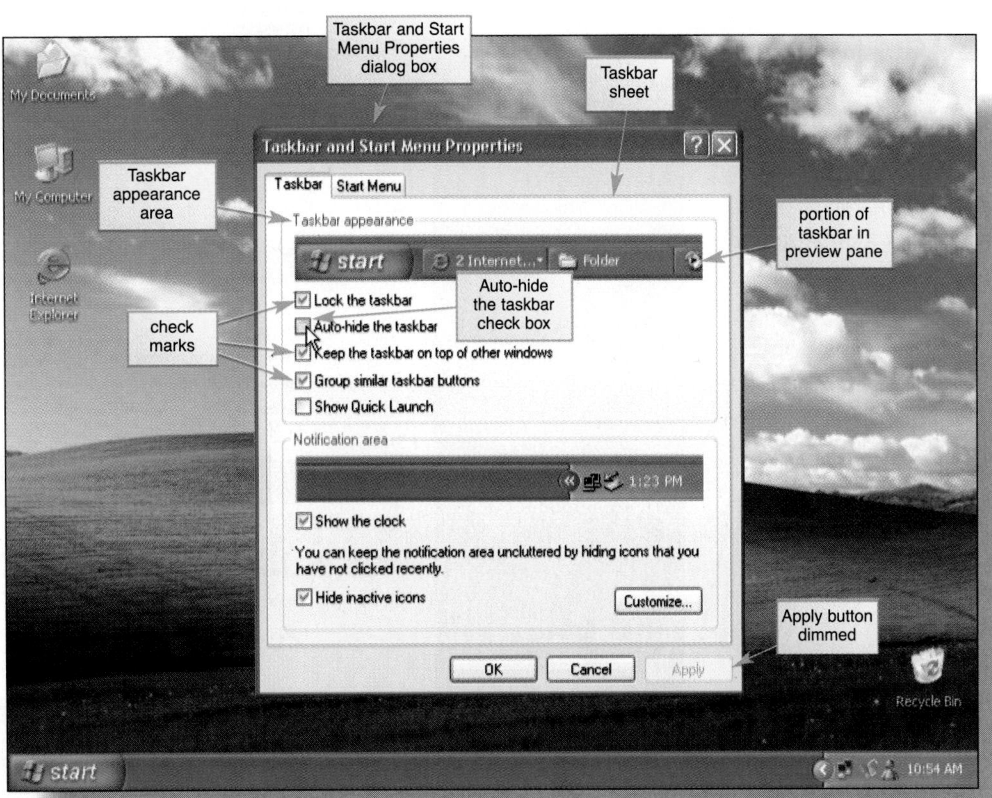

FIGURE 4-34

3 Click Auto-hide the taskbar. Point to the Apply button.

A check mark displays in the Auto-hide the taskbar check box, an outline of the taskbar displays in the preview pane, and the Apply button is no longer dimmed (Figure 4-35).

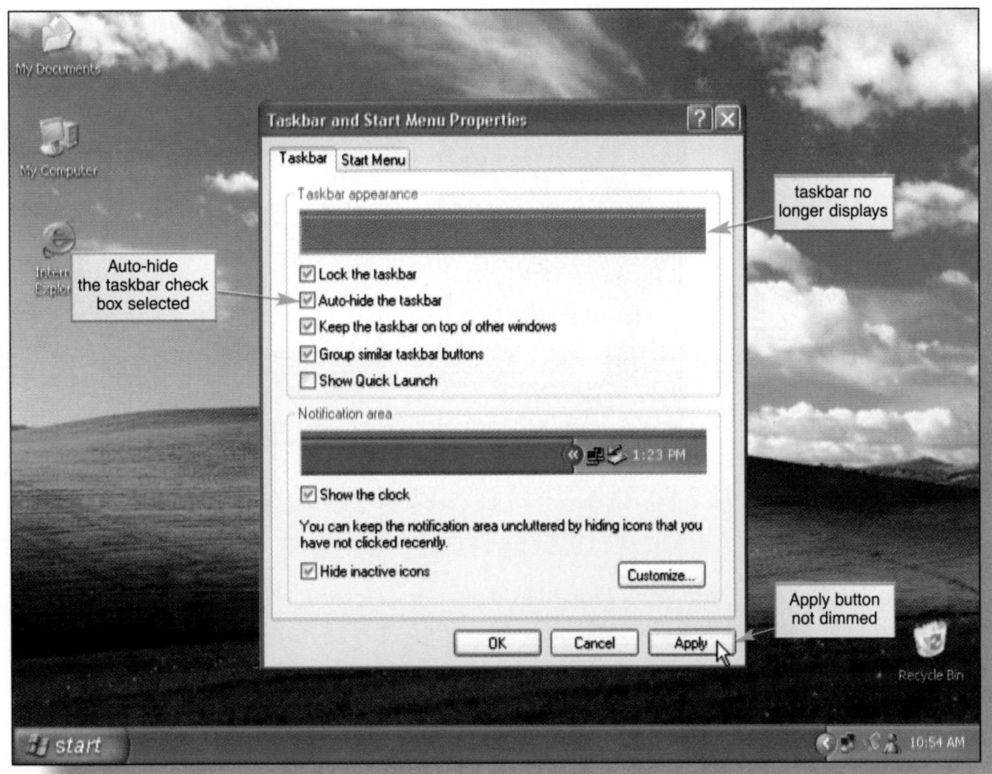

FIGURE 4-35

4 Click the Apply button.

The Apply button dims, the top edge (thin blue horizontal line) of the taskbar displays at the bottom of the desktop, and the Taskbar and Start Menu Properties dialog box remains open (Figure 4-36). Clicking the OK button instead of the Apply button hides the taskbar and closes the dialog box.

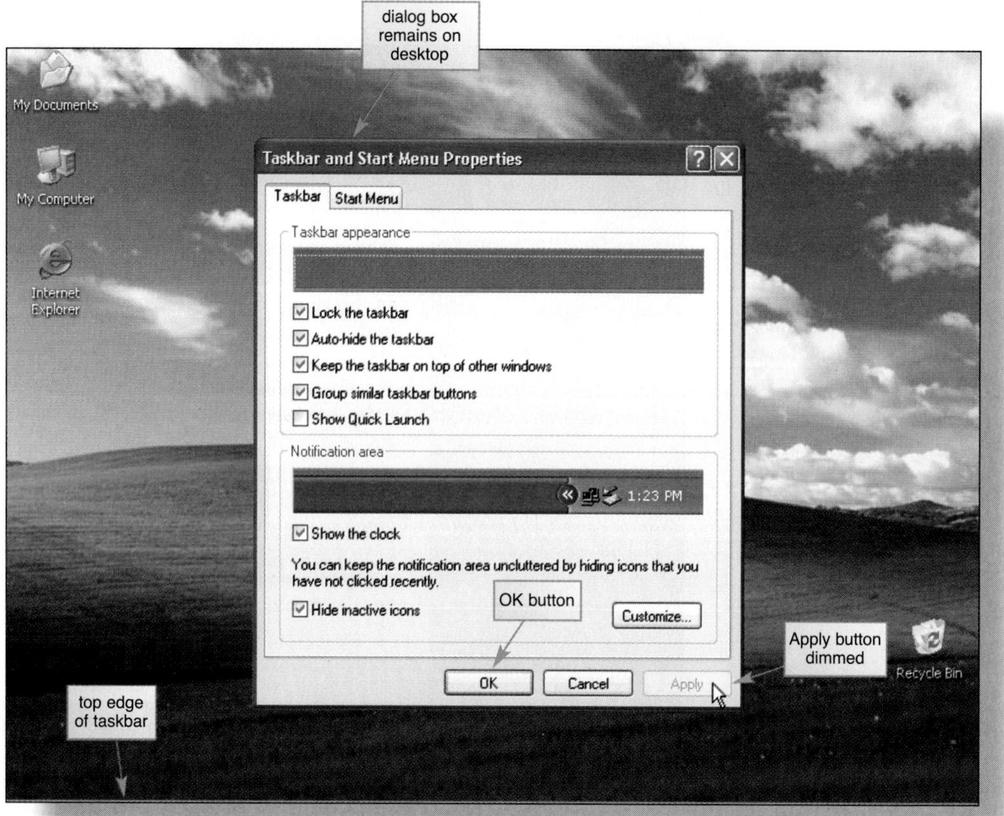

FIGURE 4-36

5 Point to the top edge (thin horizontal line) of the taskbar to display the taskbar again.

When the mouse pointer points to the top edge of the taskbar, the taskbar displays again (Figure 4-37). The taskbar remains on the desktop as long as the mouse pointer points to the taskbar.

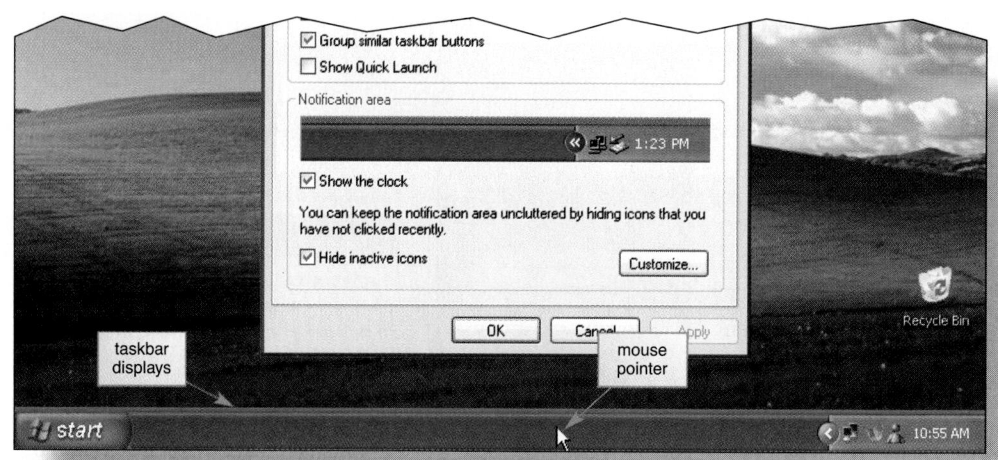

FIGURE 4-37

6 Click Auto-hide the taskbar. Click the OK button.

Clicking the Auto-hide the taskbar check box removes the check mark and redisplays the taskbar on the desktop. Clicking the OK button in the Taskbar and Start Menu Properties dialog box closes the dialog box. The desktop displays as shown before hiding the taskbar.

Other Ways

1. Right-click open area of taskbar, click Properties on shortcut menu, click Auto-hide the taskbar, click OK button
2. Right-click Start button, click Properties, click Taskbar tab, click Auto-hide the taskbar, click OK button

By default, the Lock the taskbar, Keep the taskbar on top of other windows, and Group similar taskbar buttons check boxes contain check marks in the Taskbar sheet in Figure 4-34 on page WIN 4.29. The Auto-hide the taskbar and Show Quick Launch check boxes do not contain check marks.

The **Keep the taskbar on top of other windows check box** allows you to change whether the taskbar displays on top of any other objects on the desktop. A check mark in this check box causes the taskbar to display on top of all objects on the desktop. The **Group similar taskbar buttons check box** turns on the taskbar button grouping feature to display a single button on the taskbar for multiple documents opened by the same application program (see Figure 2-48 on page WIN 2.37). The taskbar button grouping feature is activated when the width of the taskbar buttons on the taskbar decrease to a certain width. The **Show Quick Launch check box** allows you to display the Quick Launch toolbar on the taskbar. The **Quick Launch toolbar** is a toolbar you can customize that allows you to launch a program by clicking an icon on the toolbar and is explained later in this project.

Working with Toolbars on the Taskbar

As shown earlier, one method of modifying the desktop work environment is to customize the taskbar by moving and hiding the taskbar. You also can customize the taskbar by adding and removing a toolbar, moving and resizing a toolbar, and placing a shortcut on a toolbar. The following sections illustrate how to perform these operations.

Adding the Quick Launch Toolbar to the Taskbar

Windows XP provides four toolbars you can add to the taskbar. The **Address toolbar** allows you to search for a Web page, launch an application program, open a document, and open a folder. The **Links toolbar** allows you to go to selected Web sites without first having to launch the Internet Explorer browser. The **Desktop toolbar** contains copies of all the icons currently displayed on the desktop.

The **Quick Launch toolbar** contains icons that allow you to launch the Web browser, view the icons on the desktop, and launch Windows Media Player. **Windows Media Player** is an application included with Windows XP that lets you create and play CDs, watch DVDs, listen to Internet radio stations, and search for and organize digital media files. Perform the steps on the next page to add the Quick Launch toolbar to the taskbar.

More About

The Quick Launch Toolbar

By default, the Quick Launch Toolbar does not display on the taskbar in Windows XP. In Windows 98, Windows 98 SE, Windows ME, and Windows 2000, the Quick Launch Toolbar displayed on the taskbar and contained four icons (Launch Internet Explorer Browser, Launch Outlook Express, Show Desktop, and View Channels).

Steps To Add a Toolbar to the Taskbar

1 Right-click an open area of the taskbar. Point to Toolbars on the shortcut menu. Point to Quick Launch on the Toolbars submenu.

A shortcut menu and the Toolbars submenu display (Figure 4-38). The Toolbars and Quick Launch commands are highlighted and four toolbar names display on the Toolbars submenu. A check mark preceding a toolbar name indicates the toolbar displays on the taskbar. Currently, no check marks display on the Toolbars submenu and no toolbars display on the taskbar.

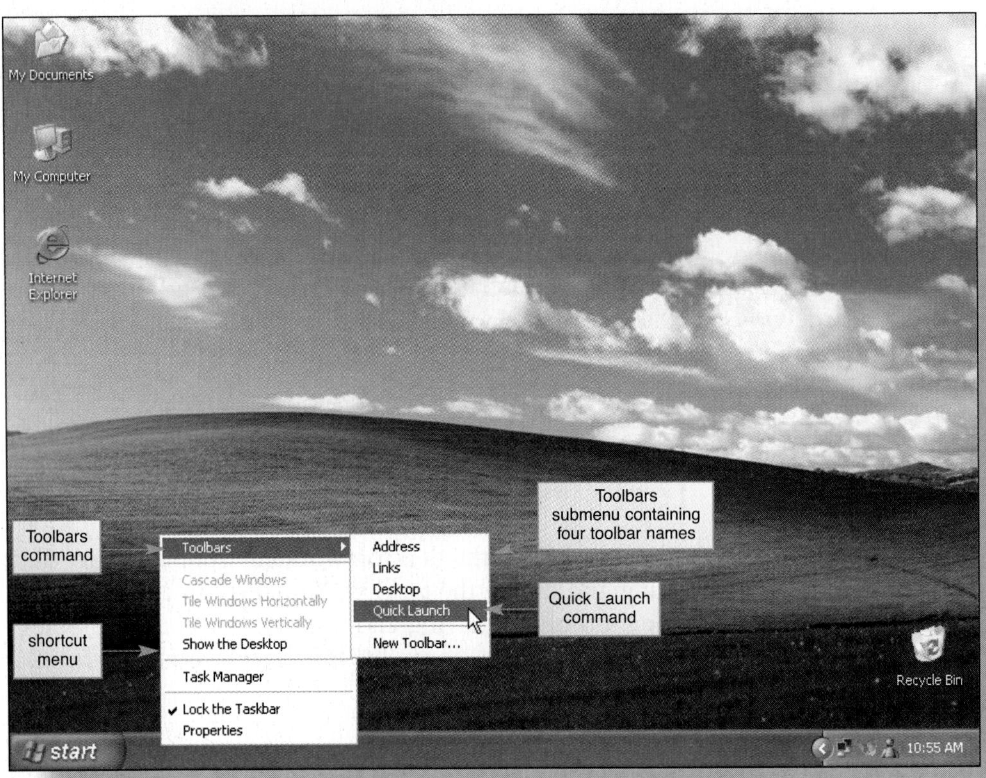

FIGURE 4-38

2 Click Quick Launch.

The Quick Launch toolbar displays on the taskbar (Figure 4-39). By default, the Quick Launch toolbar contains the Launch Internet Explorer Browser icon, Show Desktop icon, and Windows Media Player icon. Although not visible, a check mark precedes the Quick Launch command on the Toolbars submenu to indicate the Quick Launch toolbar displays on the taskbar.

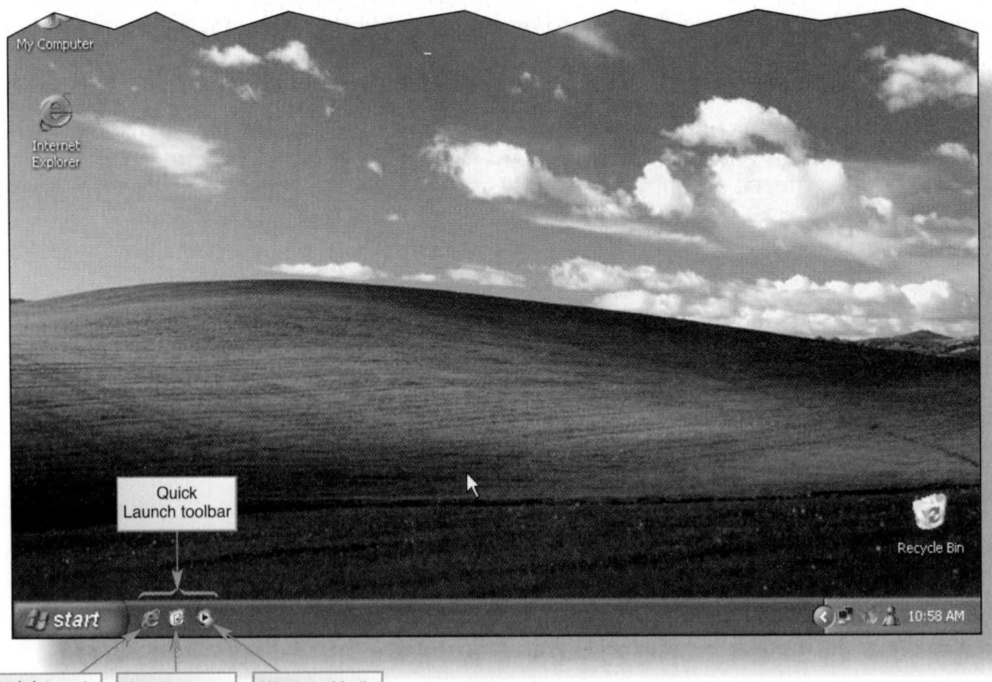

FIGURE 4-39

In the previous steps, the taskbar was locked when the Quick Launch toolbar was added to the taskbar. As a result, the small border that displays along the top edge of the taskbar and the dotted vertical bar that defines the left edge of the taskbar buttons area (see Figure 4-29 on page WIN 4.26) when the taskbar is unlocked, do not display. In addition, a dotted vertical bar that defines the left edge of the Quick Launch toolbar also is not visible.

In addition to adding one of the four toolbars shown in Figure 4-38 to the taskbar, you also can create a custom toolbar and add it to the taskbar. For example, you might create a Current Projects toolbar containing the icons for all the applications and documents with which you currently are working.

More About

Adding a Toolbar to the Taskbar

After adding a toolbar to the taskbar, you can move the toolbar to the *desktop* by dragging the toolbar from the taskbar to an open area of the desktop. A box with the toolbar name on the title bar displays on the desktop. You can move and resize the box to your preference and remove the toolbar from the desktop by clicking the Close button.

Adding a Toolbar to a Folder Window

In addition to adding a toolbar to a taskbar, you also can add a toolbar to a folder window, such as the My Computer or My Documents windows. Windows XP allows three toolbars (Standard Buttons, Address Bar, and Links) to display in a folder window. By default, the Standard Buttons and Address toolbars display in a folder window. To add the third toolbar (Links), open the folder window, display the View menu, point to Toolbars on the View menu, and then click Links on the Toolbars submenu.

Placing a Shortcut on the Quick Launch Toolbar

In Project 2, a **shortcut** was defined as a link to any object on the computer or a network, such as a program, file, folder, disk drive, Web page, printer, or another computer. Two icons on the Quick Launch toolbar (Launch Internet Explorer Browser and Windows Media Player) are shortcuts to application programs. In addition, all the icons on the Links toolbar are shortcuts to Web sites.

After adding the Quick Launch toolbar to the taskbar, you can use the icons on the toolbar to launch Internet Explorer, view the icons currently displayed on the desktop, and launch Windows Media Player. You may want to place additional shortcut icons on the Quick Launch toolbar to launch other applications. For example, you may want to add a shortcut icon for Help and Support on the Quick Launch toolbar to make it easier to launch the Help and Support program. Perform the steps on the next page to place a shortcut icon to the Help and Support program on the Quick Launch toolbar.

Steps To Place a Shortcut on a Toolbar

1 Click the Start button. Point to Help and Support on the Start menu.

The Start menu, containing the Help and Support command, displays (Figure 4-40).

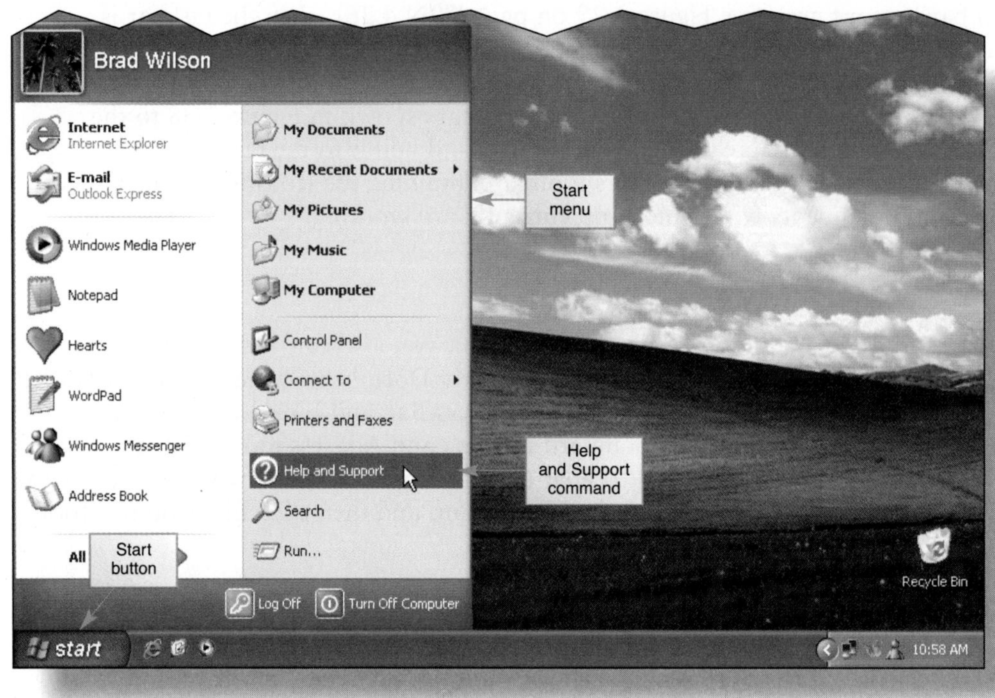

FIGURE 4-40

2 Hold down the right mouse button and right-drag the Help and Support command to the Quick Launch toolbar until a vertical divider line displays. Without releasing the right mouse button, position the vertical divider line to the right of the Show Desktop icon on the toolbar.

When you right-drag the Help and Support command onto the Quick Launch toolbar, a dimmed image of the Help and Support command displays on the taskbar. When you position the command to the right of the Show Desktop icon, a vertical divider line displays to the right of the Show Desktop icon (Figure 4-41).

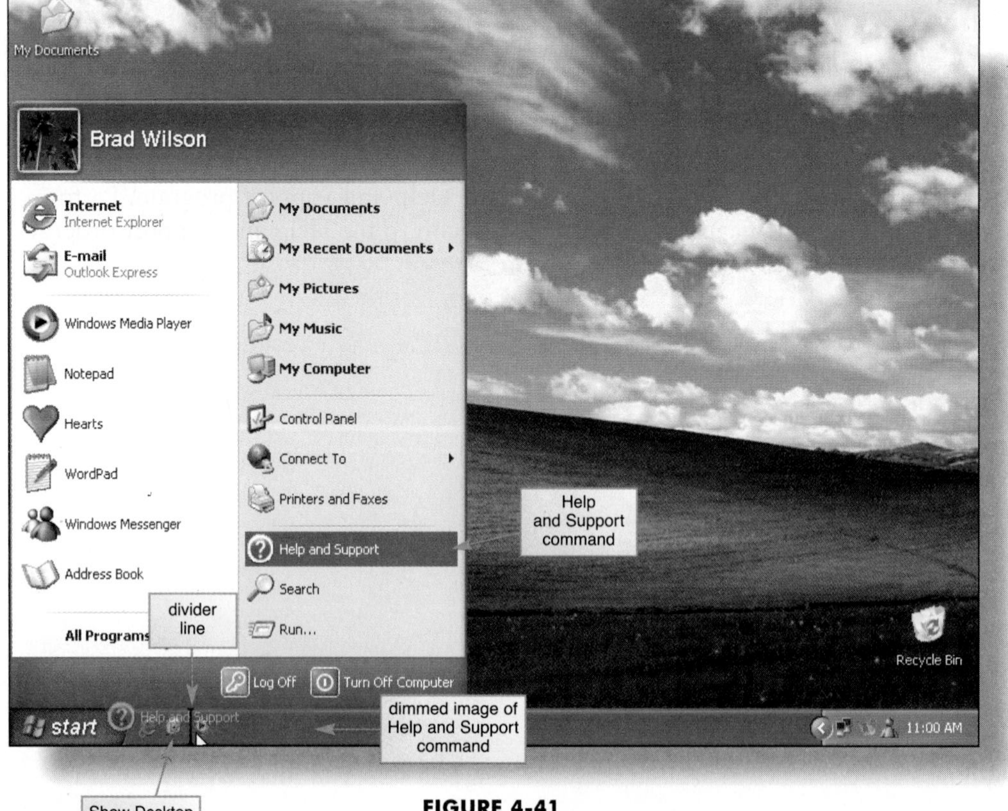

FIGURE 4-41

3 Release the right mouse button. Point to Create Shortcuts Here on the shortcut menu.

When you release the right mouse button, the Start menu closes, (Figure 4-42). The highlighted Create Shortcuts Here command displays on the shortcut menu and the vertical divider line remains on the Quick Launch toolbar.

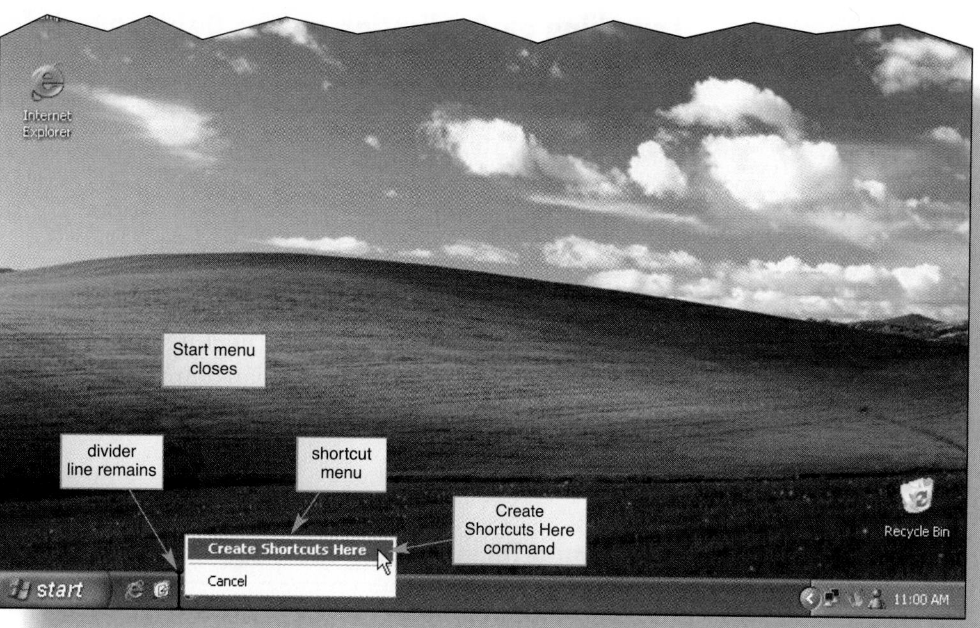

FIGURE 4-42

4 Click Create Shortcuts Here.

The vertical divider line and shortcut menu no longer display and the Help and Support icon, identified by a question mark in a circle, displays to the right of the Show Desktop icon (Figure 4-43). A double chevron (>>) displays to the right of the Help and Support icon and the Windows Media Player icon is hidden from view.

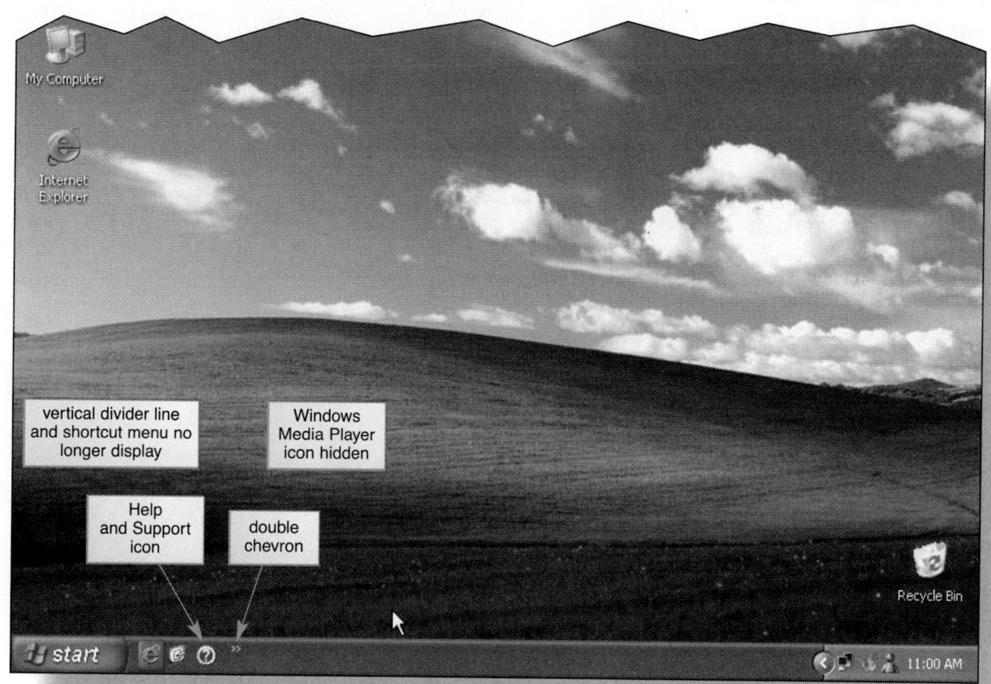

FIGURE 4-43

1. Drag command to Quick Launch toolbar, click open area of desktop to remove Start menu

After placing the Help and Support icon on the Quick Launch toolbar, you can launch Help and Support by clicking the Help and Support icon on the toolbar.

Launching an Application on the Quick Launch Toolbar

If the application you want to launch has an icon on the Quick Launch toolbar, clicking its icon launches the application and opens its window on the desktop. If an icon is hidden from view, such as Windows Media Player in Figure 4-43 on the previous page, and a double chevron displays, several methods allow you to view the hidden icon and launch the associated application.

One method of viewing a hidden icon and launching the associated application is to click the double chevron on the Quick Launch toolbar. Clicking the double chevron displays a box above the taskbar that contains the application names associated with any hidden icons on the Quick Launch toolbar. Clicking an application name in the box launches the associated application. Perform the following steps to launch Windows Media Player using the double chevron on the Quick Launch toolbar.

To Launch an Application on a Toolbar Using the Double Chevron

1 Click the double chevron on the Quick Launch toolbar. Point to Windows Media Player in the box.

Windows XP indents the double chevron icon and displays a box containing the highlighted Windows Media Player command above the taskbar (Figure 4-44).

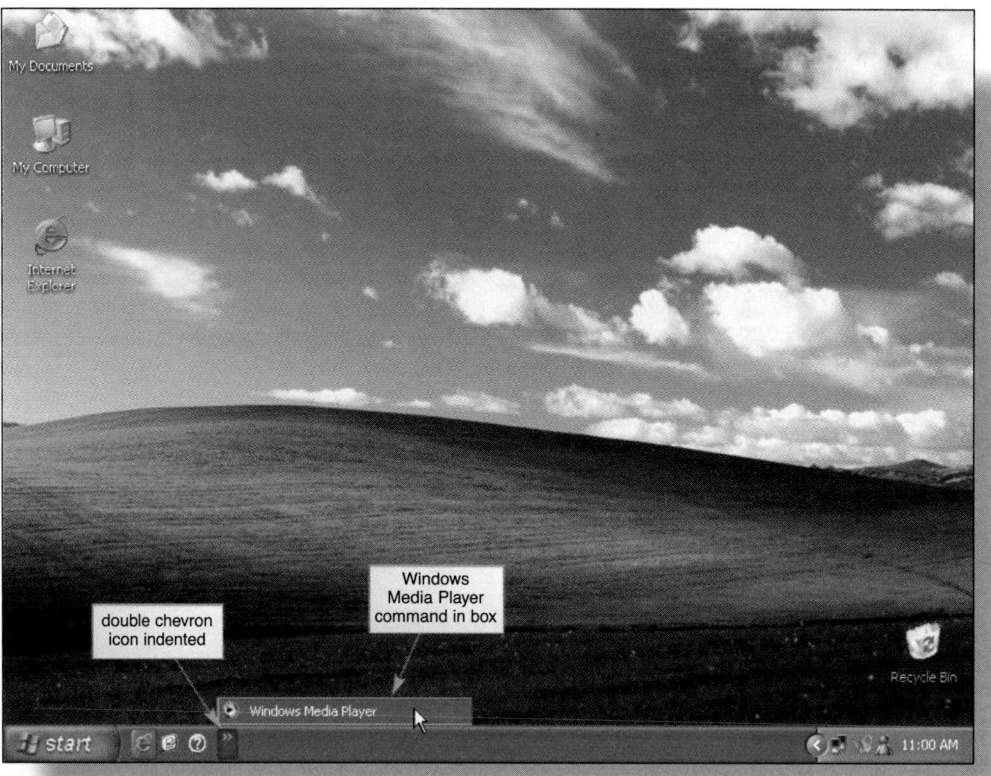

FIGURE 4-44

2 Click Windows Media Player.

Windows XP launches the Windows Media Player program and displays the Windows Media Player window (Figure 4-45). The Windows Media Player button displays on the taskbar.

3 Click the Close button to close the media player.

The Windows Media Player closes.

FIGURE 4-45

Unlocking the Taskbar

Although you can add a toolbar to the taskbar, place a shortcut icon on a toolbar, and launch an application from a toolbar when the taskbar is locked, you cannot resize the taskbar or a toolbar on the taskbar until you unlock the taskbar. In the following sections, additional methods of launching an application from the Quick Launch toolbar will be demonstrated. In the process, the taskbar and the Quick Launch toolbar will be resized to display the hidden Windows Media Player icon on the Quick Launch toolbar and launch the associated application. Before you can resize the taskbar or resize a toolbar on the taskbar, you must unlock the taskbar. Perform the following steps to unlock the taskbar.

TO UNLOCK THE TASKBAR

1. Right-click an open area of the taskbar to display a shortcut menu.
2. Click Lock the Taskbar on the shortcut menu.

The taskbar is unlocked, a small border displays along the top edge of the taskbar, and a dotted vertical bar displays to the right of the Start button and to the right of the Quick Launch toolbar (Figure 4-46). Although not visible, a check mark precedes the Lock the Taskbar command on the shortcut menu.

FIGURE 4-46

Resizing the Taskbar

A second method of viewing a hidden icon on the Quick Launch toolbar and launching its application is to resize the taskbar. After unlocking the taskbar, you may resize the taskbar by dragging the top border of the taskbar upward toward the top of the desktop. As you drag the top border, the sizes of the areas on the taskbar (Start button, Quick Launch toolbar, and notification area) increase. The increased size of the Quick Launch toolbar allows the previously hidden Windows Media Player icon to display on the Quick Launch toolbar. Perform the following steps to resize the taskbar.

To Resize the Taskbar

1. **Point to the top edge of the taskbar until a two-headed arrow displays.**

When the mouse pointer points to the top edge of the taskbar, it changes to a two-headed arrow (Figure 4-47).

FIGURE 4-47

2 Drag the top edge of the taskbar toward the top of the desktop until the taskbar on your desktop resembles the taskbar shown in Figure 4-48.

Windows XP resizes the taskbar (Figure 4-48). The Start button displays along the top edge of the resized taskbar, the icons on the Quick Launch toolbar display in two rows, and the notification area contains a column of notification icons and an expanded date and time entry.

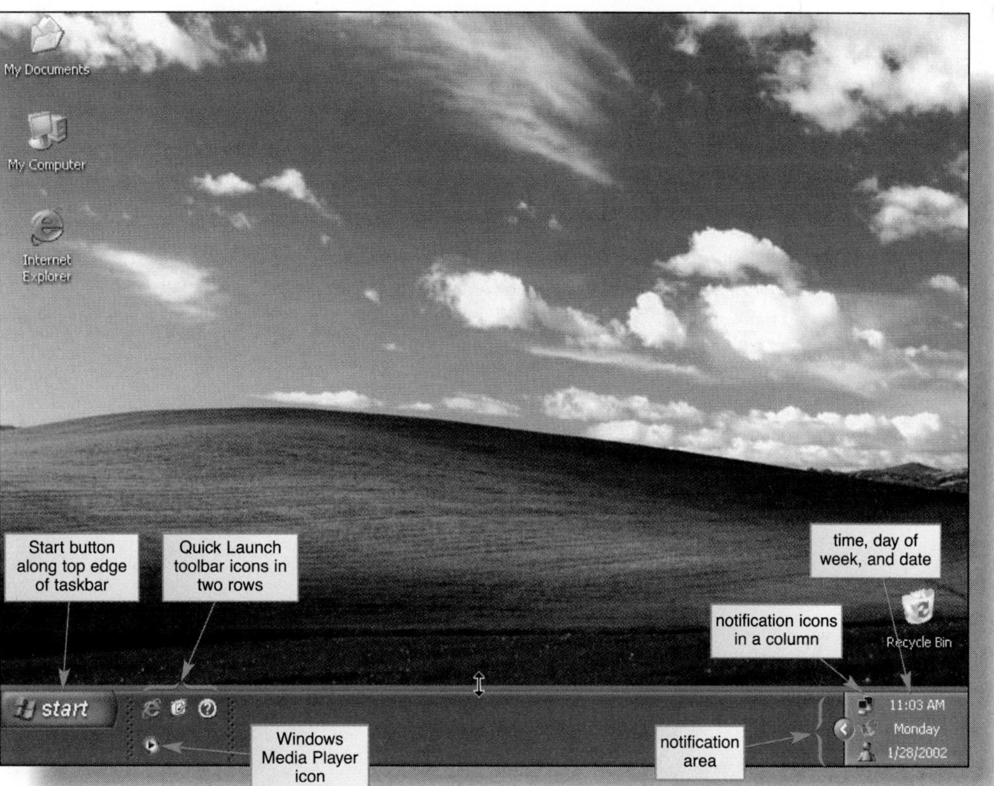

FIGURE 4-48

After resizing the taskbar, you can launch the Windows Media Player application by clicking its icon on the enlarged Quick Launch toolbar.

Returning the Taskbar to Its Original Location on the Desktop

After completing work with the Windows Media Player, you may wish to return the taskbar to its original size by performing the following steps.

TO RETURN THE TASKBAR TO ITS ORIGINAL LOCATION

1. Point to the top edge of the taskbar until a two-headed arrow displays.
2. Drag the top edge of the taskbar downward until the taskbar on your desktop resembles the taskbar shown in Figure 4-47.

Windows XP returns the taskbar to its original location on the desktop.

Resizing the Quick Launch Toolbar

A third method of viewing a hidden icon on the Quick Launch toolbar and launching its application is to resize the toolbar. The taskbar must be unlocked prior to resizing a toolbar.

You resize the Quick Launch toolbar by dragging the dotted vertical bar to the right of the Quick Launch toolbar to the right along the taskbar until the Windows Media Player icon displays on the toolbar. Perform the steps on the next page to resize the Quick Launch toolbar by dragging the dotted vertical bar.

Steps To Resize a Toolbar

1 Point to the dotted vertical bar to the right of the Quick Launch toolbar until a double-headed arrow displays (Figure 4-49).

FIGURE 4-49

2 Drag the vertical bar to the right along the taskbar until the Windows Media Player icon displays on the Quick Launch toolbar.

The Windows Media Player icon displays on the Quick Launch toolbar (Figure 4-50).

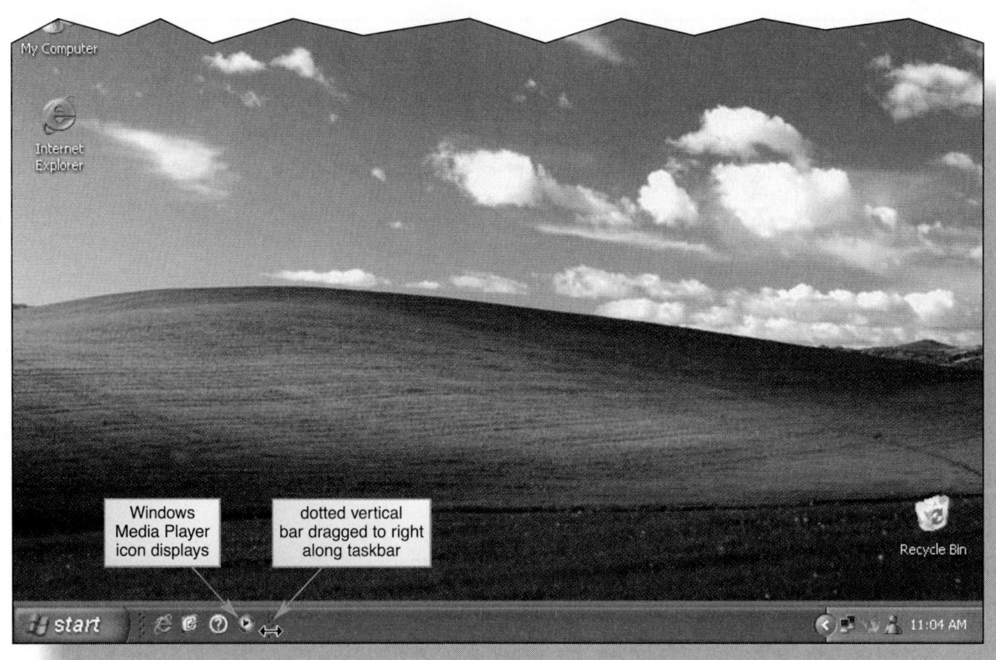

FIGURE 4-50

After resizing the Quick Launch toolbar, the Windows Media Player icon displays on the toolbar, and you can launch the Windows Media Player application by clicking its icon on the Quick Launch toolbar.

Removing a Shortcut from a Toolbar and Resizing a Toolbar

In the previous sections, you placed a shortcut on the Quick Launch toolbar and resized the Quick Launch toolbar. Perform the following steps to remove the Help and Support shortcut from the Quick Launch toolbar and resize the Quick Launch toolbar.

TO REMOVE A SHORTCUT FROM A TOOLBAR AND RESIZE A TOOLBAR

1. Right-click the Help and Support icon on the Quick Launch toolbar to display a shortcut menu.
2. Click Delete on the shortcut menu.
3. Click the Yes button in the Confirm File Delete dialog box.
4. Drag the dotted vertical bar to the right of the Quick Launch toolbar to the left along the taskbar to return the Quick Launch toolbar to its original size.

Windows XP removes the Help and Support icon and double chevron from the Quick Launch toolbar and returns the Quick Launch toolbar to its original size.

The taskbar remains unlocked so that the Address toolbar can be added to the taskbar and used to search the Internet in the following sections.

Adding the Address Toolbar to the Taskbar

In addition to adding the Quick Launch toolbar to the taskbar, you can add three other toolbars (Address toolbar, Links toolbar, and Desktop toolbar) to the taskbar. Each of these toolbars is added to the taskbar using the same procedure used to add the Quick Launch toolbar (see page WIN 4.32). The function of the Address toolbar is multi-faceted: it allows you to search for a Web page, launch an application program, open a document, and open a folder. Perform the following steps to add the Address toolbar to the taskbar.

TO ADD A TOOLBAR TO THE TASKBAR

1. Right-click an open area of the taskbar, point to Toolbars on the shortcut menu, and then point to Address on the Toolbars submenu.
2. Click Address.

A dotted vertical bar and the Address toolbar title display at the right end of the taskbar (Figure 4-51).

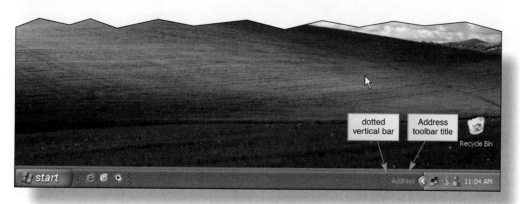

FIGURE 4-51

More About

Toolbar Titles

You can change the appearance of a toolbar by removing the toolbar title. Right-click the toolbar to display a shortcut menu and then click Show Title to remove or display the toolbar title.

Expanding a Toolbar on the Taskbar

When you add the Address, Links, or Desktop toolbar to the taskbar, the toolbars display in a collapsed form with only the dotted vertical bar and toolbar title displaying on the taskbar. You can use two methods to expand the toolbar. One method is to point to the dotted vertical bar and drag the bar to the left along the taskbar until the toolbar is the desired size. A second method is to point to the dotted vertical bar and double-click the bar to display the toolbar at its maximum size. Perform the following steps to expand the Address toolbar by double-clicking its dotted vertical bar.

Steps To Expand a Toolbar

1 Point to the dotted vertical bar to the left of the Address title to display a two-headed arrow.

Pointing to the dotted vertical bar displays a two-headed arrow that allows you to change the size of the toolbar by moving the bar to the left along the taskbar (Figure 4-52).

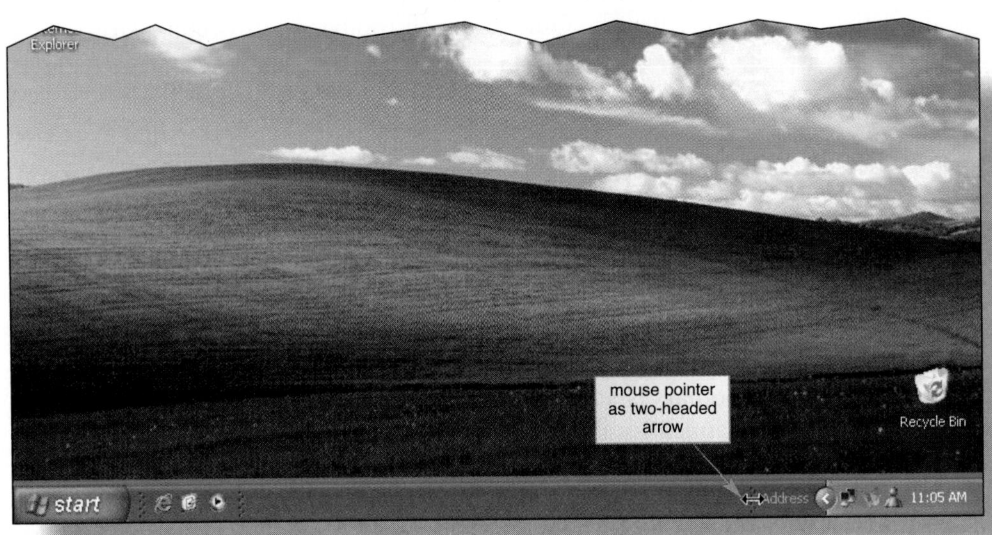

FIGURE 4-52

2 Double-click the dotted vertical bar.

The Address toolbar expands to contain the Address box and Go button (Figure 4-53). The Address box contains an insertion point and the Address box arrow.

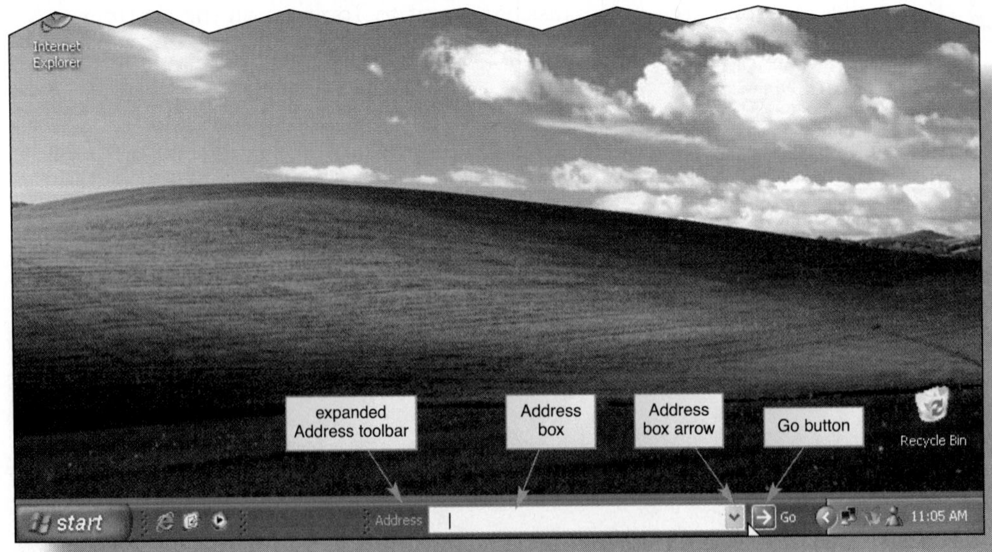

FIGURE 4-53

After expanding the Address toolbar, you can use the Address box to type an address (URL) and display the associated Web page, type an application program name to launch a program, type a folder location (path) to open a folder, type a document name to launch an application and display the document in the application window, or type a keyword or phrase (search inquiry) to display all links to Web pages containing the keyword or phrase. The following sections illustrate these operations.

Locking the Taskbar

After expanding the Address toolbar, you may want to lock the taskbar to keep the Address toolbar in its current position. Perform the following steps to lock the taskbar.

TO LOCK THE TASKBAR

1. Right-click an open area of the taskbar.
2. Click Lock the Taskbar on the shortcut menu.

The taskbar is locked, and the small border along the top edge of the taskbar and the dotted vertical bars on the taskbar no longer display. Although not visible, a check mark precedes the Lock the Taskbar command on the shortcut menu.

Using the Address Toolbar to Display the Contents of a Folder

To display the contents of a folder using the Address toolbar, you must type the path of the folder in the Address box and then click the Go button. A **path** is the means of navigating to a specific location on a computer. To specify a path to a folder on a computer you must type the drive letter, followed by a colon (:), a backslash (\), and the folder name. For example, the path for the WINDOWS folder on drive C is: C:\WINDOWS.

On some computers, the WINDOWS folder does not exist and the path for the WINDOWS folder will cause an error message to display when you perform the following steps. In this case, use the path for the WINNT folder (C:\WINNT) for the remainder of this project.

Perform the following steps to display the contents of the WINDOWS (or WINNT) folder.

To Display the Contents of a Folder Using the Address Toolbar

1. **Type** `c:\windows` **in the Address box. Point to the Go button in the Address toolbar.**

The path of the WINDOWS folder (c:\windows) displays in the Address box (Figure 4-54).

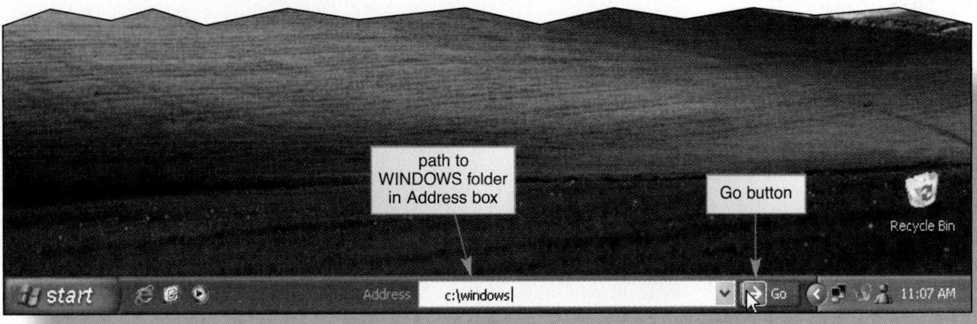

FIGURE 4-54

2 Click the Go button. Maximize the WINDOWS window.

A folder icon and the WINDOWS path (c:\windows) display in the Address box and the contents of the WINDOWS folder displays in the right pane of the WINDOWS window (Figure 4-55). The files and folder in the WINDOWS folder may be different on your computer

3 Click the Close button.

The WINDOWS window closes.

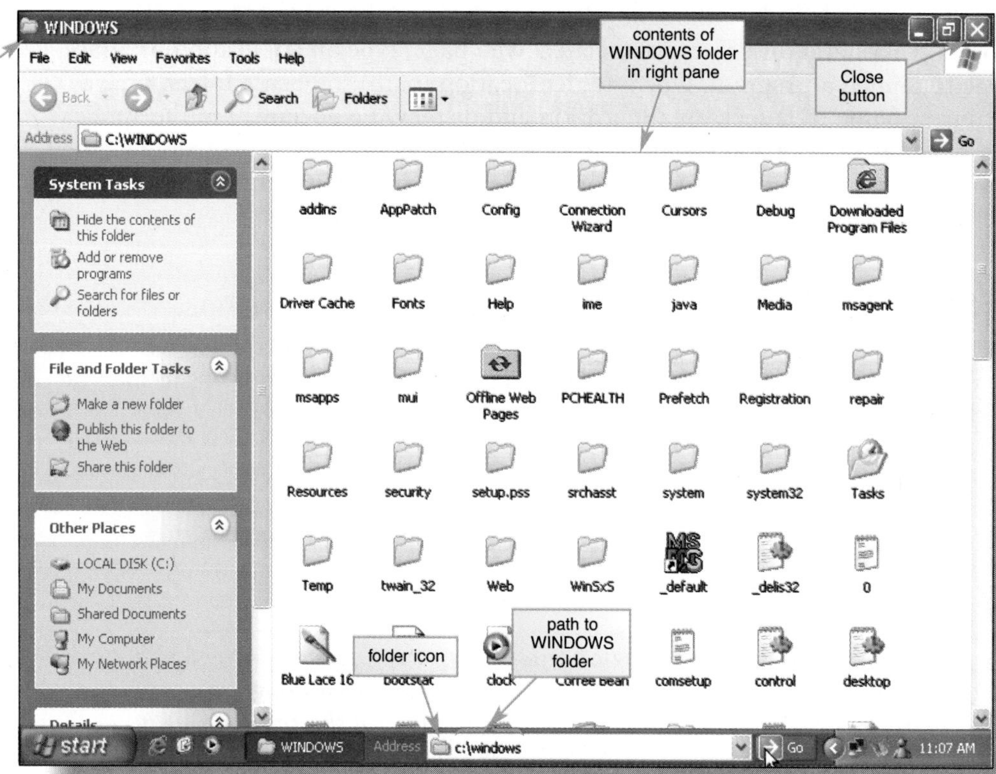

FIGURE 4-55

Other Ways

1. Click Address box arrow, click path in Address list
2. Click Address box, type path until Address list box displays, click path in Address list

Using the Address Toolbar to Display a Web Page

To search for and display a Web page using the Address toolbar, you must type an address, or Uniform Resource Locator (URL), and then click the Go button. A unique URL identifies each Web page in a Web site. For example, the URL for the Microsoft Web page is www.microsoft.com. Perform the following steps to type the URL of the Microsoft Web page in the Address box, launch the Internet Explorer browser, and display the Microsoft Web page in a window.

Steps To Display a Web Page Using the Address Toolbar

1 Click the Address box, type `www.microsoft.com` **in the Address box, and then point to the Go button.**

The URL for the Microsoft Web page displays in the Address box (Figure 4-56).

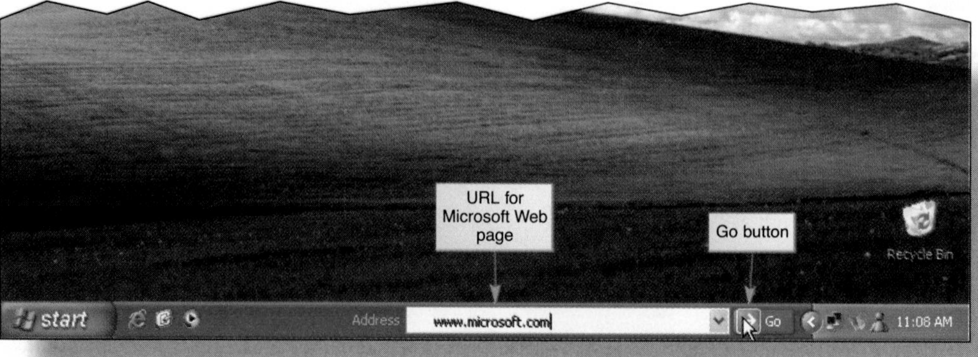

FIGURE 4-56

2 Click the Go button.

The Internet Explorer Web browser launches and the Microsoft Web page displays in the Microsoft Corporation Web Site window (Figure 4-57). The URL for the Microsoft Web page displays in the Address box on the taskbar and the actual URL displays in the Address box in the Microsoft Corporation window. The Microsoft Internet Explorer window may display on your computer.

Click the Close button.

The Microsoft Corporate Web Site window closes.

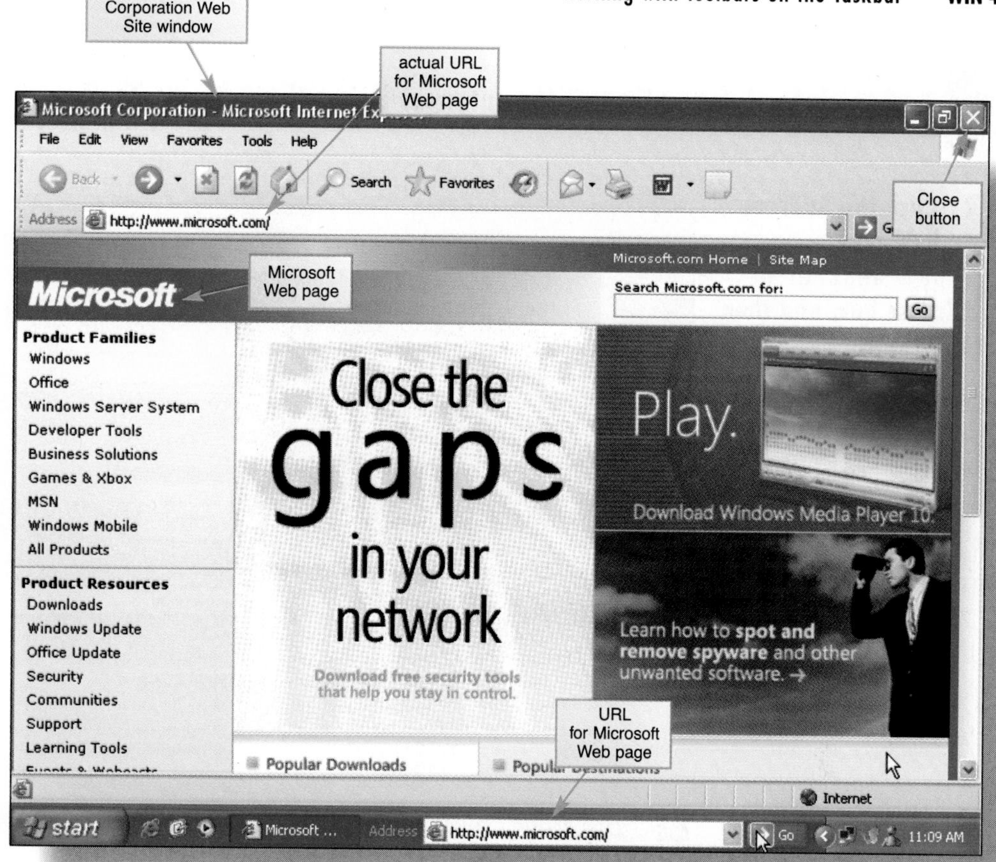

FIGURE 4-57

Other Ways

1. Click Address box arrow, click URL in Address list
2. Click Address box, type URL until Address list box displays, click URL in Address list

Using the Address Toolbar to Search for Information on the Internet

To search for information on the Internet using the Address toolbar, you must type a keyword or phrase and then click the Go button. For example, you might enter the phrase, national weather, to search for and display the links of all Web pages containing the phrase, national weather.

Perform the steps on the next page to type the phrase, national weather, in the Address box and display all links to Web pages containing the phrase, national weather.

Steps To Search for Information on the Internet Using the Address Toolbar

1 Click the Address box, type `national weather` **in the Address box, and then point to the Go button.**

The phrase, national weather, displays in the Address box (Figure 4-58).

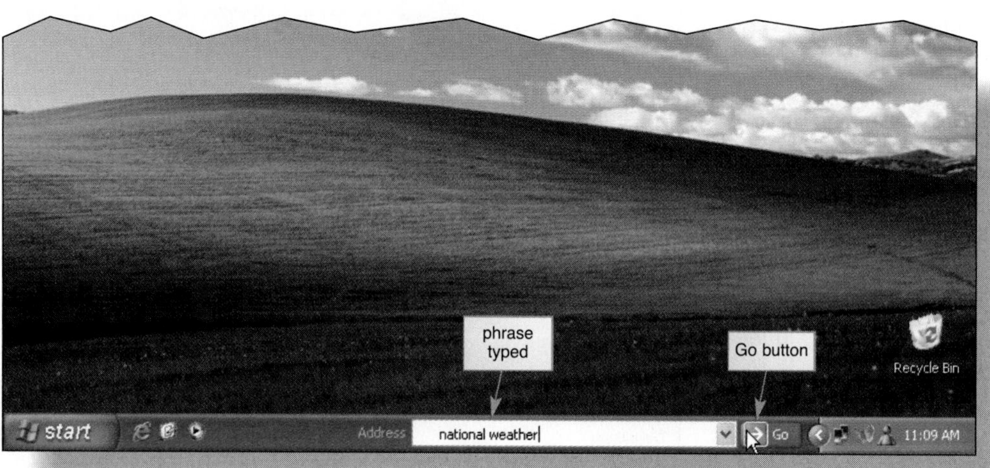

FIGURE 4-58

2 Click the Go button. Scroll the MSN Search window to view the web sites. Point to the Close button in the MSN Search window.

A list of web sites containing the phrase, national weather, display in the MSN Search window (Figure 4-59). The Internet Explorer icon and search inquiry display in the Address box on the taskbar, and the actual Web page URL and search inquiry display in the address box of the MSN Search window. The Microsoft Internet Explorer window may display on your computer.

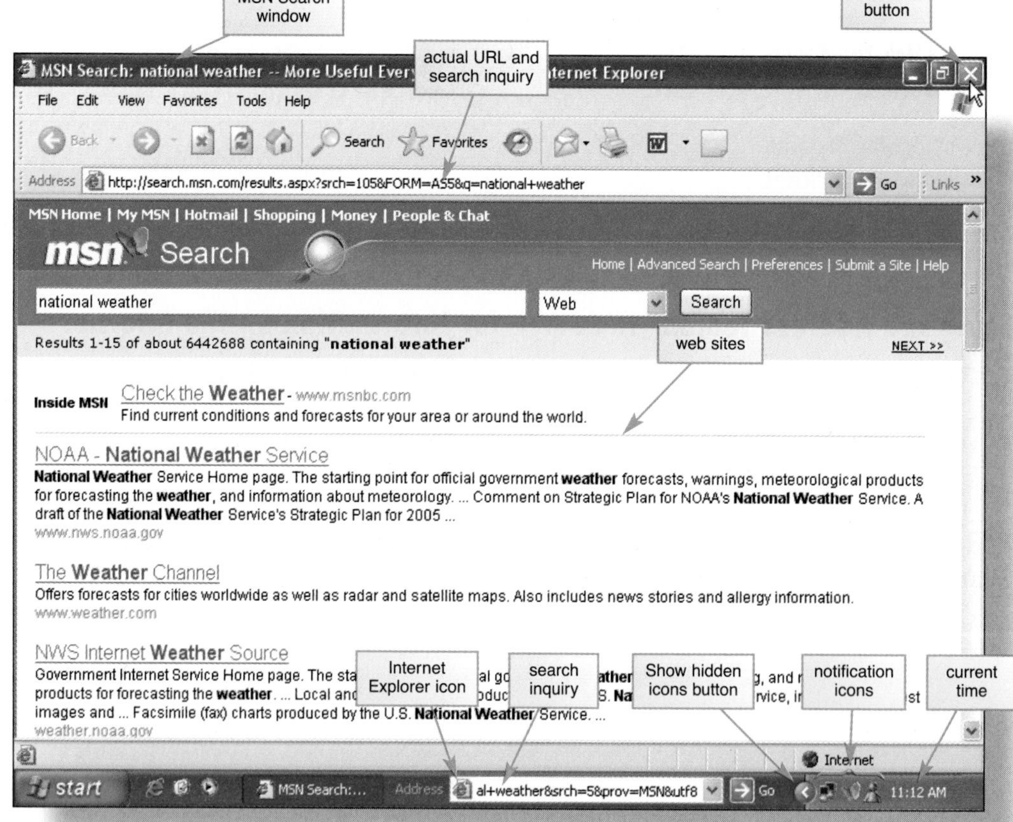

FIGURE 4-59

3 Click the Close button.

The MSN Search window closes.

In addition to using the Address toolbar to display a Web page, display the contents of a folder, and search for information on the Internet, you also can use the Address toolbar to launch a program and open a document. To launch an application, such as Notepad, you type the application name (Notepad) in the Address box and then click the Go button. The Untitled - Notepad window will display on the desktop. To display a document, such as the Greenstone.bmp document, you type the document name (Greenstone.bmp) in the Address box and then click the Go button. The Greenstone.bmp document will display in the Greenstone – Windows Picture and Fax Viewer window.

More About

The Address Toolbar

Search engines that process search requests have their own rules for entering a search inquiry. On some, you may have to place the word AND between two words to find Web pages containing both words. With other search engines, you select a check box (Any of the words, All the words, and so on) to perform a search. To learn the rules for a search engine, look for a Tips or Help link and then click the link.

Removing a Toolbar

When you no longer want a toolbar on the taskbar, you can remove the toolbar. Perform the following steps to remove the Quick Launch toolbar and Address toolbar from the taskbar.

TO REMOVE A TOOLBAR FROM THE TASKBAR

1. Right-click an open area on the taskbar.
2. Point to Toolbars on the shortcut menu.
3. Click Quick Launch on the Toolbars submenu.
4. Right-click an open area on the taskbar.
5. Point to Toolbars on the shortcut menu.
6. Click Address on the Toolbars submenu.

Windows XP removes the Quick Launch toolbar and Address toolbar from the taskbar, rearranges the contents of the taskbar, and removes the check mark preceding the Quick Launch and Address commands on the Toolbars submenu.

Customizing the Notification Area

Another method of modifying the desktop work environment is to customize the notification area. The notification area displays the time and also can contain shortcuts that provide quick access to programs, such as MSN Messenger and Volume Control. Other shortcuts display in the notification area to provide information about the status of activities. For example, the Printer icon displays when a document is sent to the printer and is removed when printing is complete.

Currently, the notification area in Figure 4-59 contains the Show hidden icons button, three notification icons, and the current time. The contents of the notification area may be different on your computer. You can customize the notification area by removing the clock, hiding inactive icons, and setting the notification behavior for the items in the notification area. By default, the clock displays and inactive icons are hidden from view. Perform the steps on the next page to set the notification behavior for the Brad Wilson is signed in item.

To Set the Notification Behavior of a Notification Item

1 Right-click an open area in the notification area and then click Properties on the shortcut menu. Point to the Customize button.

The Taskbar and Start Menu Properties dialog box and Taskbar sheet display (Figure 4-60). Check marks display in the Show the clock check box and Hide inactive icons check box in the Notification area to indicate the clock displays and all inactive icons will be hidden. The Customize button allows you to customize the behavior of items in the notification area.

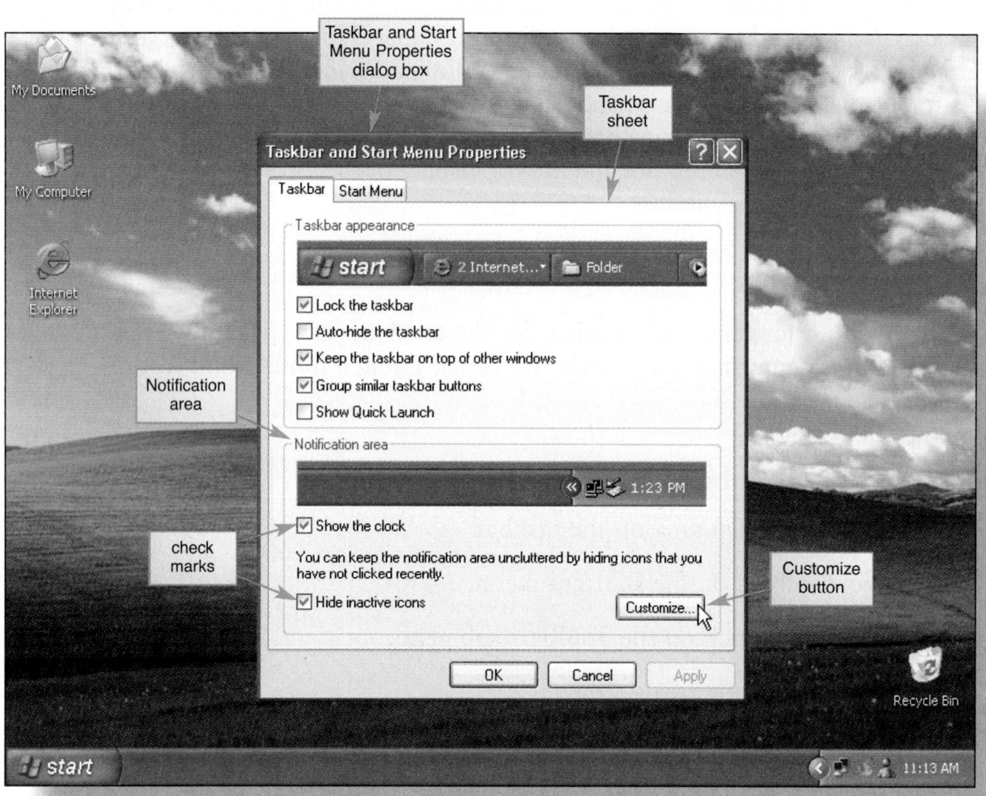

FIGURE 4-60

2 Click the Customize button. Click the behavior to the right of the Brad Wilson is signed in item and then point to the Behavior box arrow.

The Customize Notifications dialog box displays and the Behavior box containing the Hide when inactive behavior displays to the right of the Brad Wilson is signed in item (Figure 4-61). The dialog box contains a list of current and past items and their behaviors. The Hide when inactive behavior displays to the right of all items in the lists. The items in the Customize Notifications dialog box may be different on your computer.

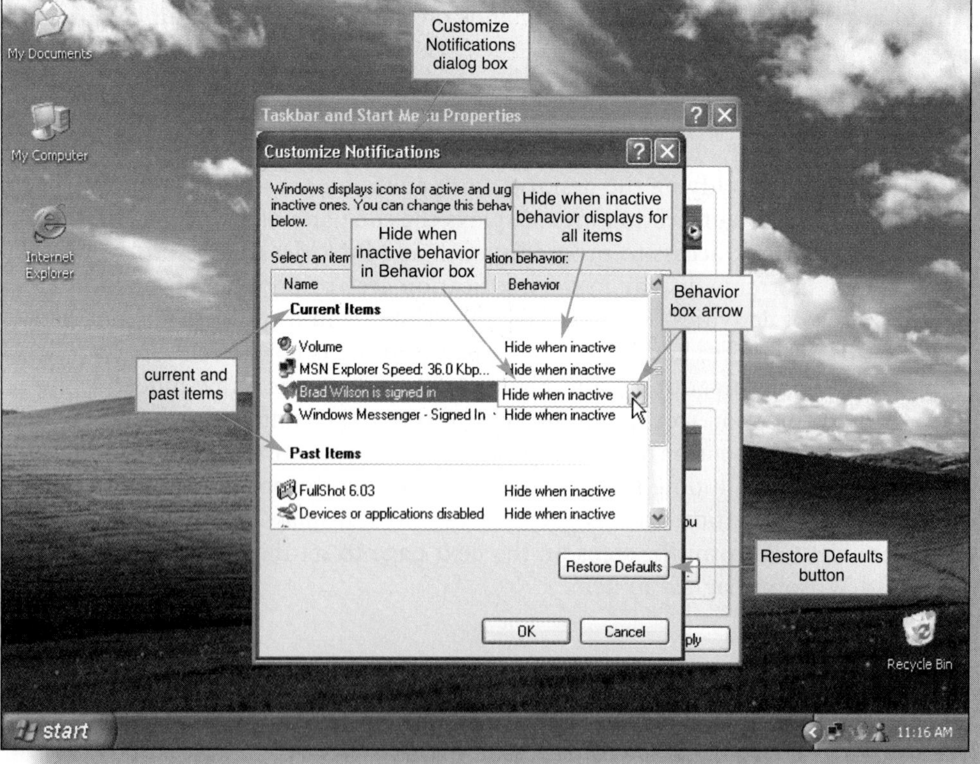

FIGURE 4-61

3 Click the Behavior box arrow. Click Always hide in the Behavior list. Point to the OK button in the Customize Notifications dialog box.

The Always hide behavior is highlighted in the Behavior box (Figure 4-62).

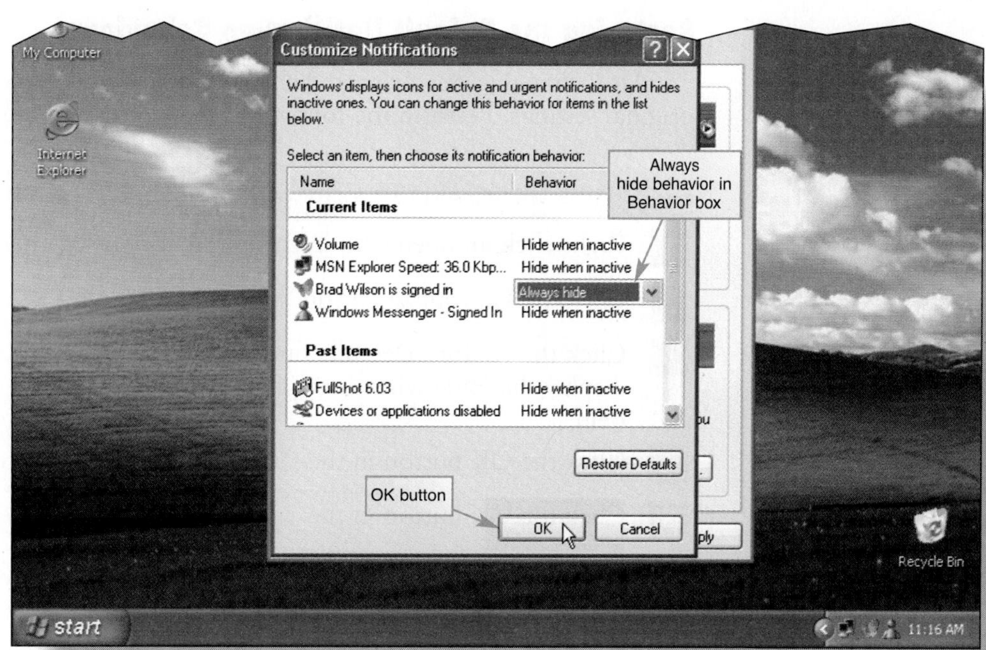

FIGURE 4-62

4 Click the OK button in the Customize Notifications dialog box. Click the OK button in the Taskbar and Start Menu Properties dialog box.

Clicking the OK button in the Customize Notifications dialog box removes the Brad Wilson is signed in icon from the notification area and closes the Customize Notifications dialog box (Figure 4-63). Clicking the OK button in the Taskbar and Start Menu Properties dialog box closes the dialog box.

FIGURE 4-63

The Restore Defaults button in the Customize Notifications dialog box in Figure 4-61 restores the default notification behaviors.

To view the hidden icons in the notification area, click the Show hidden icons button in the notification area. The hidden icons display as long as the mouse pointer points to the notification area.

Restoring the Default Notification Behaviors

After changing one or more behaviors, you should restore the behaviors to their original settings. Perform the following steps to restore the original behaviors.

TO RESTORE THE DEFAULT NOTIFICATION BEHAVIORS

1. Right-click an open area in the notification area and then click Properties.
2. Click the Customize button.
3. Click the Restore Defaults button in the Customize Notifications dialog box to display the Hide when inactive behavior to the right of each current or past item.
4. Click the OK button in the Customize Notifications dialog box.
5. Click the OK button in the Taskbar and Start Menu Properties dialog box.

The default notification behaviors for each current and past item in the Customize Notifications dialog box are restored.

Customizing the Start Menu

Another method of modifying the desktop work environment is to modify the appearance of the Start menu. In Project 2, you customized the Start menu by adding a shortcut to the Daily Reminders folder on the Start menu (see pages WIN 2.26 and WIN 2.27). In addition to adding a shortcut, you may wish to select a different menu style (Windows XP or Windows Classic), choose to display smaller or larger icons on the Start menu, select a larger number of menu items to display in the frequently used programs list, and select another application program as the default Web browser program and Electronic mail program.

Selecting an Icon Size for Programs on the Start Menu

By default, large icons display preceding each command in the pinned item list and most frequently used programs list on the Start menu (see Figure 4-40 on page WIN 4.34). Displaying smaller icons on the Start menu allows more commands to display in the most frequently used programs list. Perform the following steps to display smaller icons on the Start menu and view the smaller icons on the Start menu.

To Display Smaller Icons on the Start Menu

1 Right-click the Start button and point to Properties on the shortcut menu.

A shortcut menu containing the highlighted Properties command displays (Figure 4-64).

FIGURE 4-64

2 Click Properties. Point to the Customize button in the Start Menu sheet.

The Taskbar and Start Menu Properties dialog box and the Start Menu sheet display (Figure 4-65). By default, the Start menu button is selected and the Windows XP Start menu displays in the preview pane. Clicking the Classic Start menu button displays the Windows Classic Start menu.

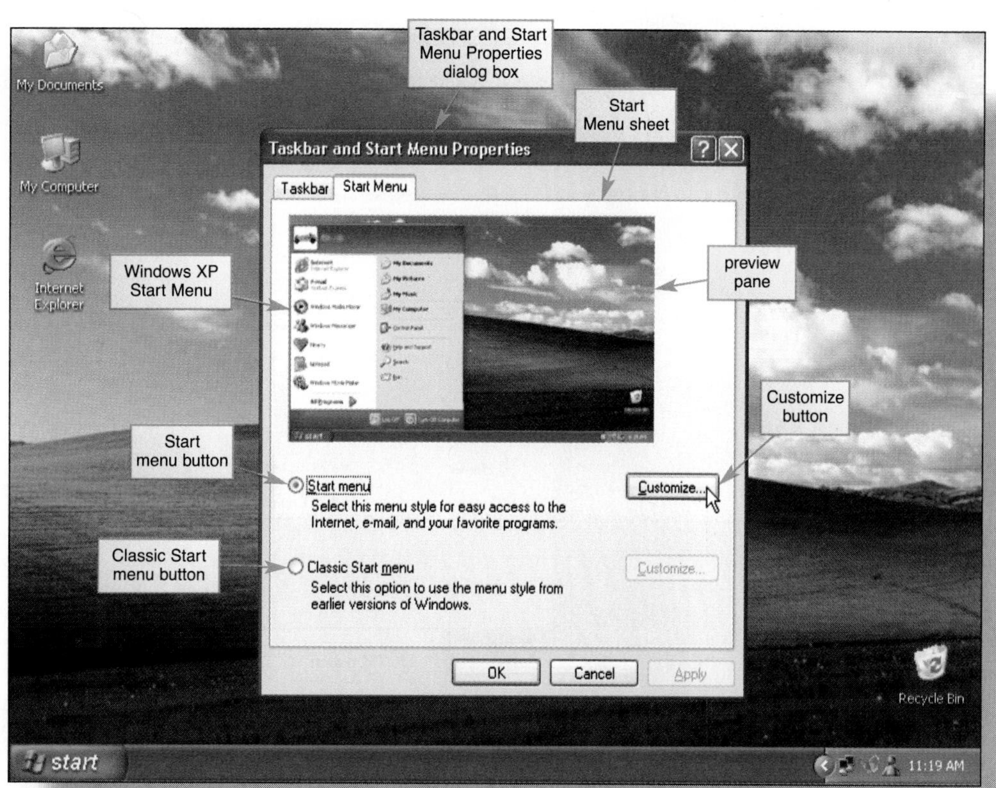

FIGURE 4-65

3 Click the Customize button. Point to Small icons in the Select an icon size for programs area.

The Customize Start Menu dialog box and the General sheet display (Figure 4-66). The Large icons button is selected in the Select an icon size for programs area and pointing to the Small icons option button highlights the option button.

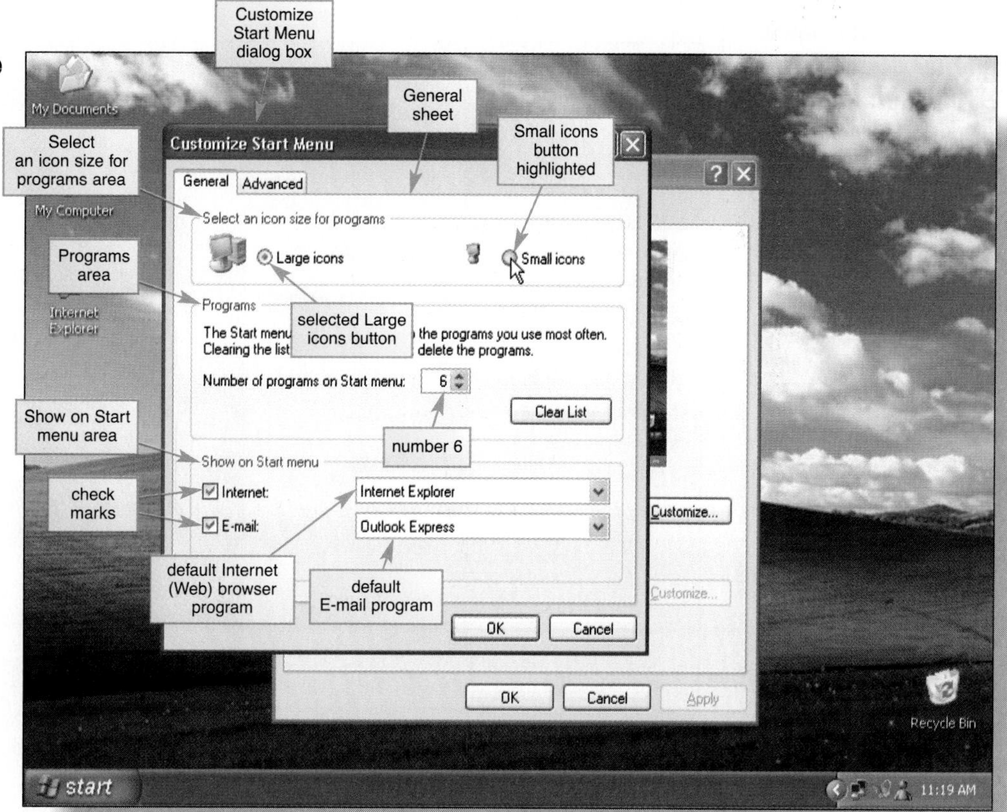

FIGURE 4-66

4 Click Small icons. Point to the OK button in the Customize Start Menu dialog box.

The Small icons button is selected (Figure 4-67).

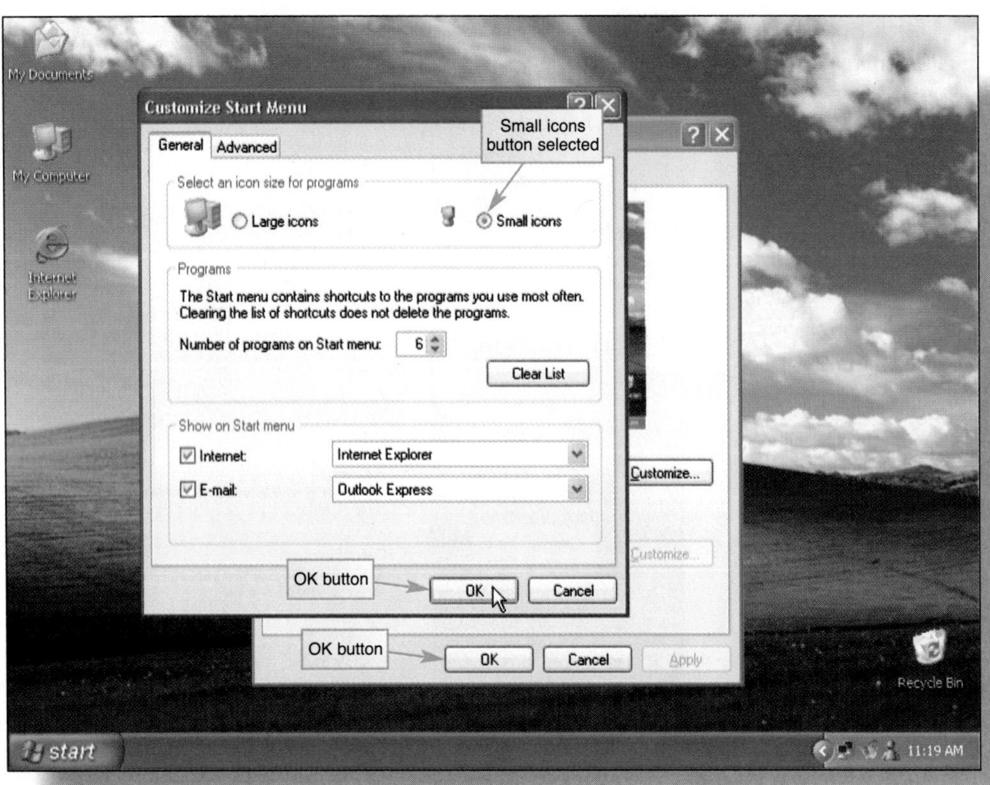

FIGURE 4-67

5 Click the OK button in the Customize Start Menu dialog box. Click the OK button in the Taskbar and Start Menu Properties dialog box. Click the Start button to display the Start menu.

The Customize Start Menu dialog box and Taskbar and Start Menu Properties dialog box close and the Start menu displays (Figure 4-68). Small icons precede the commands in the pinned items list and most frequently used programs list and six programs display in the most frequently used programs list.

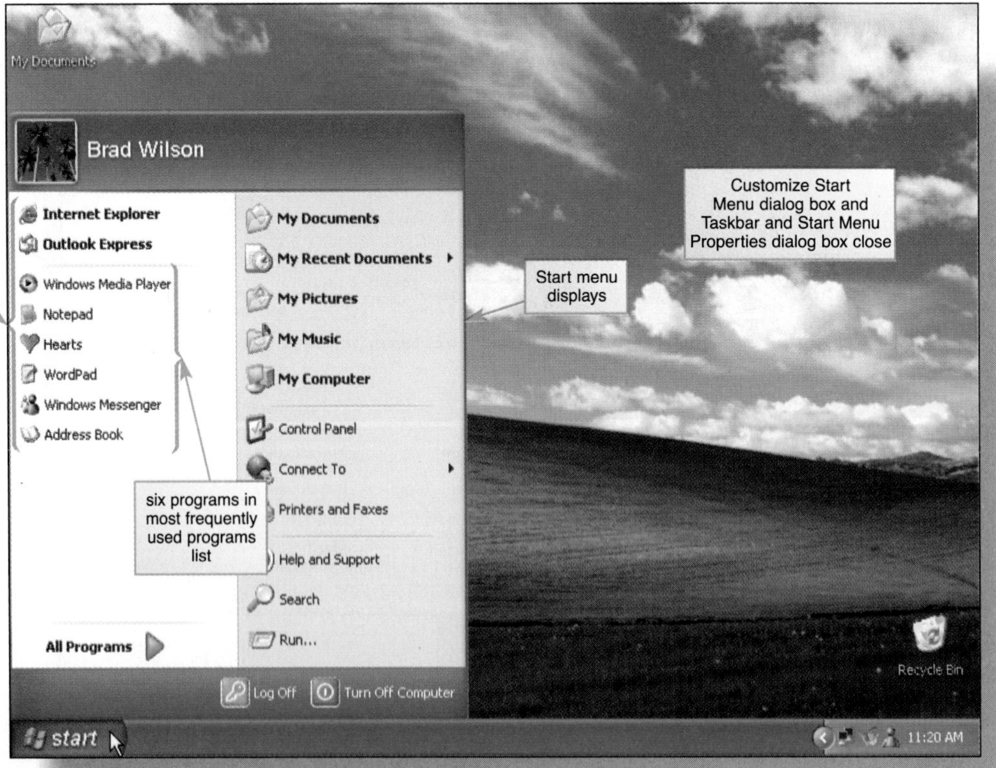

FIGURE 4-68

6 Click an open area of the desktop to close the Start menu.

The Start menu closes.

In Figure 4-66 on page WIN 4.51, the General sheet contains the Select an icon size for programs area, Programs area, and Show on Start menu area. The Large icons button is selected in the Select an icon size for programs area, and the number 6 displays in the Number of programs on Start menu box in the Programs area. The check mark in the Internet check box and the Internet Explorer entry in the Internet box indicate the default Web browser program is Internet Explorer. The check mark in the E-mail check box and the Outlook Express entry in the E-mail box indicate the default E-mail program is Outlook Express.

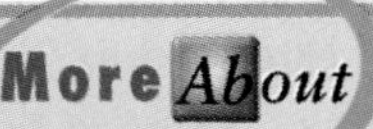

Taskbar Properties

You can change other Start menu properties using the Advanced tab in the Customize Start Menu dialog box. To review these properties, click the Advanced tab, click the Help button (identified by a question mark) on the title bar, and then click each button and check box in the dialog box.

Setting the Maximum Number of Programs in the Most Frequently Used Programs List

By default, the maximum number of programs that display in the most frequently used programs list on the Start menu is six. Increasing this number allows more commands to display in the most frequently used programs list. Perform the following steps to set the maximum number of programs that display in the most frequently used programs list to nine and view the most frequently used programs list on the Start menu.

To Set the Maximum Number of Most Frequently Used Programs

1 Right-click the Start button, click Properties, click the Customize button in the Taskbar and Start Menu Properties dialog box, and then point to the Number of programs on Start menu box up arrow.

Clicking Properties displays the Taskbar and Start Menu Properties dialog box. Clicking the Customize button displays the Customize Start Menu dialog box on top of the Taskbar and Start Menu Properties dialog box (Figure 4-69). The number 6 displays in the Number of programs on Start menu box.

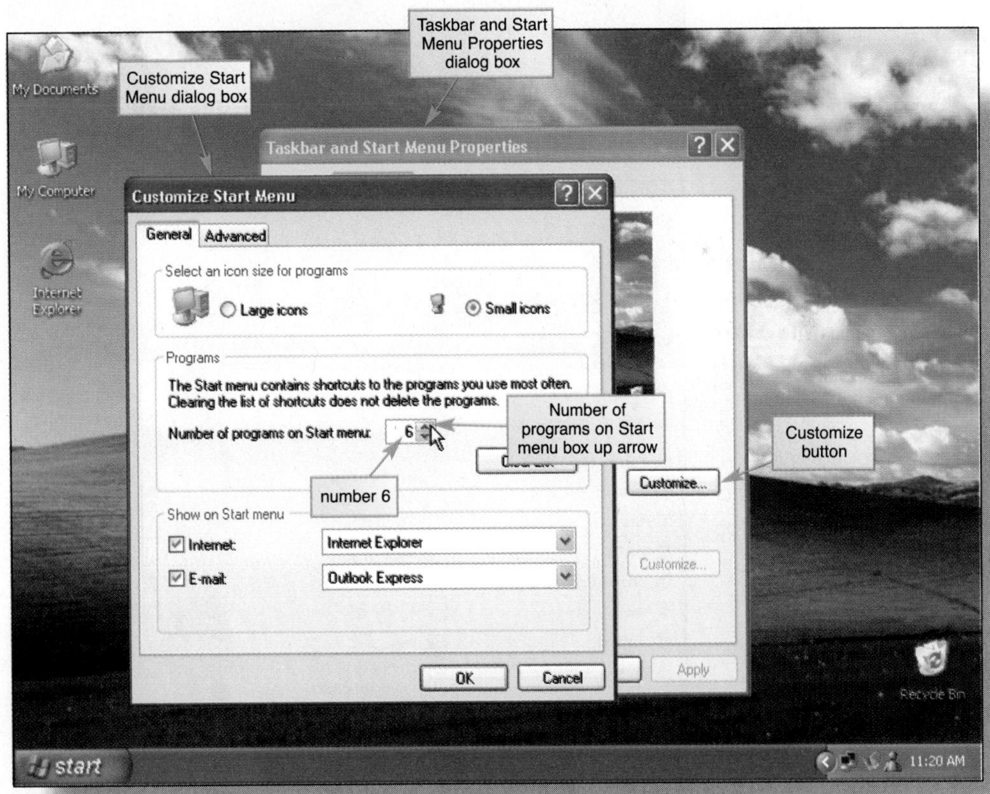

FIGURE 4-69

2 Click the Number of programs on Start menu box up arrow until the number 9 displays. Point to the OK button in the Customize Start Menu dialog box.

The number 9 displays in the Number of programs on Start menu box (Figure 4-70).

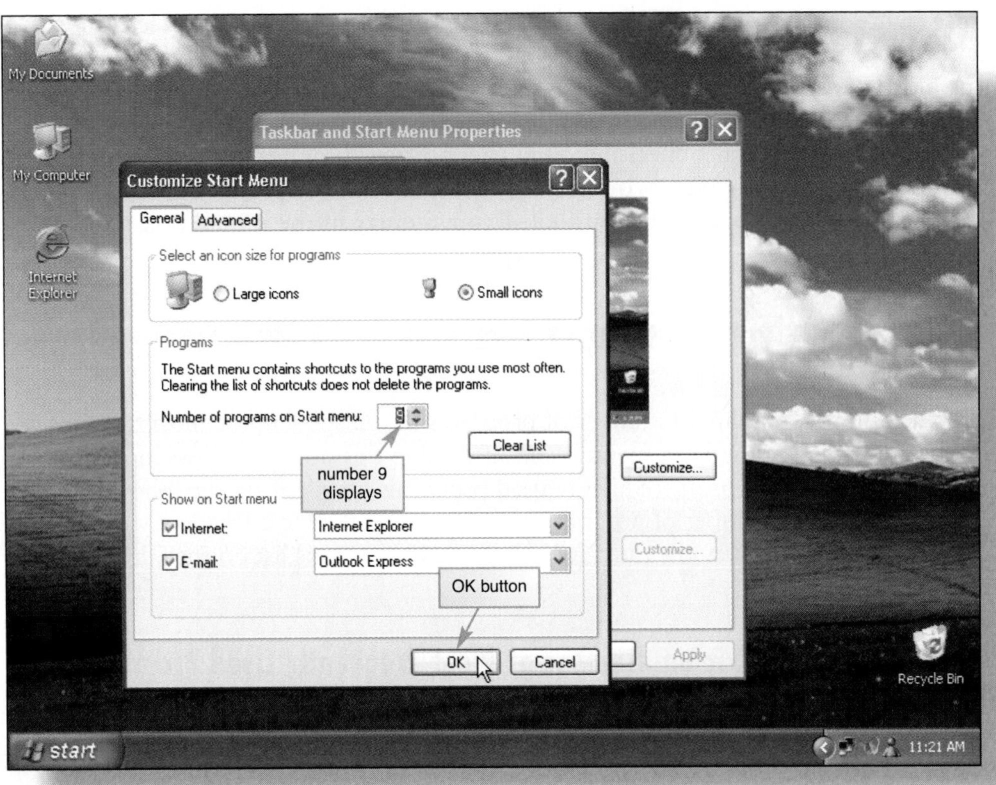

FIGURE 4-70

3 Click the OK button. Click the OK button in the Taskbar and Start Menu Properties dialog box. Click the Start button to display the Start menu.

The Customize Start Menu dialog box and Taskbar and Start Menu Properties dialog box close and the Start menu displays (Figure 4-71). Nine programs display in the most frequently used programs list.

FIGURE 4-71

4 Click an open area of the desktop to close the Start menu.

The Start menu closes.

Resetting the Icon Size and Number of Programs on the Start Menu

After changing the icon size and number of programs settings, you should revert to the original settings by resetting the icon size to large icons and the number of programs to six. Perform the following steps to reset the settings.

TO RESET THE ICON SIZE AND NUMBER OF PROGRAMS

1. Right-click the Start button and click Properties.
2. Click the Customize button in the Taskbar and Start Menu Properties dialog box.
3. Click Large icons in the Select an icon size for programs area in the Customize Start Menu dialog box.
4. Click the Number of programs on Start menu box down arrow until the number 6 displays.
5. Click the OK button in the Customize Start Menu dialog box.
6. Click the OK button in the Taskbar and Start Menu Properties dialog box.

The Large icons button is selected in the Select an icon size for programs area and the number 6 displays in the Number of programs on Start menu box.

Selecting the Default Web Browser or E-mail Program

The default Web browser program and the default E-mail program in Figure 4-66 on page WIN 4.51 are Internet Explorer and Outlook Express, respectively. You can change either of these defaults by clicking either the Internet box arrow or the E-mail box arrow to display the list of available Web browser programs and E-mail programs and then selecting a program name. The list of Web browser programs may include Internet Explorer and MSN and the list of E-mail programs may include Outlook Express, Microsoft Office Outlook, Hotmail, and MSN.

Changing Folder Options

In the previous sections, you modified the desktop work environment by changing the desktop properties, customizing toolbars and the taskbar, customizing the Start menu, and customizing the notification area. In addition to these changes, you also can make changes to folders, windows, and the desktop by changing folder options. **Folder options** allows you to specify how you open and work with icons and windows on the desktop and how you work with files and folders on the desktop.

Displaying the Folder Options Dialog Box

The following sections demonstrate how to customize folders, windows, and the desktop by changing folder options in the Folder Options dialog box. You can display the Folder Options dialog box by opening any folder, clicking Tools on the menu bar, and then clicking the Folder Options command. Complete the steps on the next page to open the My Computer folder and then display the Folder Options dialog box.

Steps To Display the Folder Options Dialog Box

1 Click the Start button, click My Computer icon on the Start menu, click Tools on the My Computer menu bar, and then point to Folder Options.

The My Computer window and Tools menu display (Figure 4-72). The highlighted Folder Options command displays on the Tools menu.

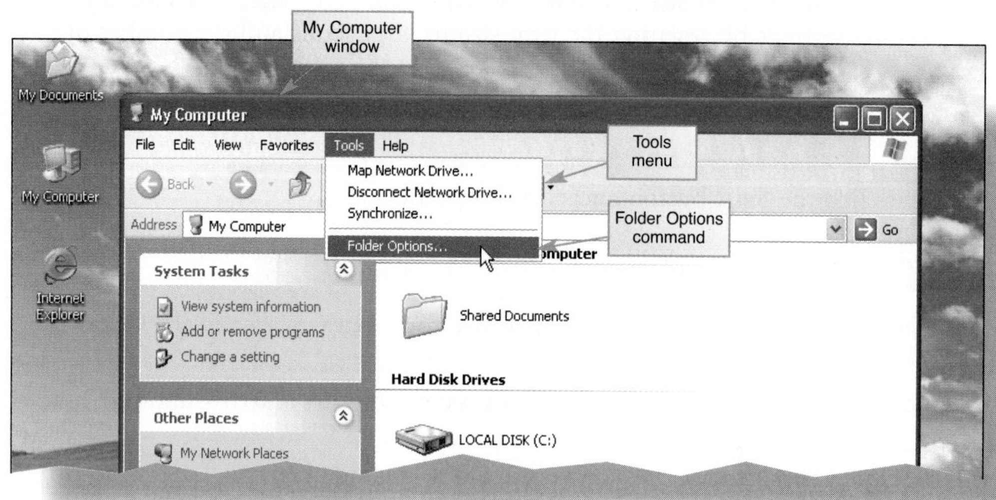

FIGURE 4-72

2 Click Folder Options.

The Folder Options dialog box displays on top of the My Computer window (Figure 4-73). The General sheet displays in the dialog box.

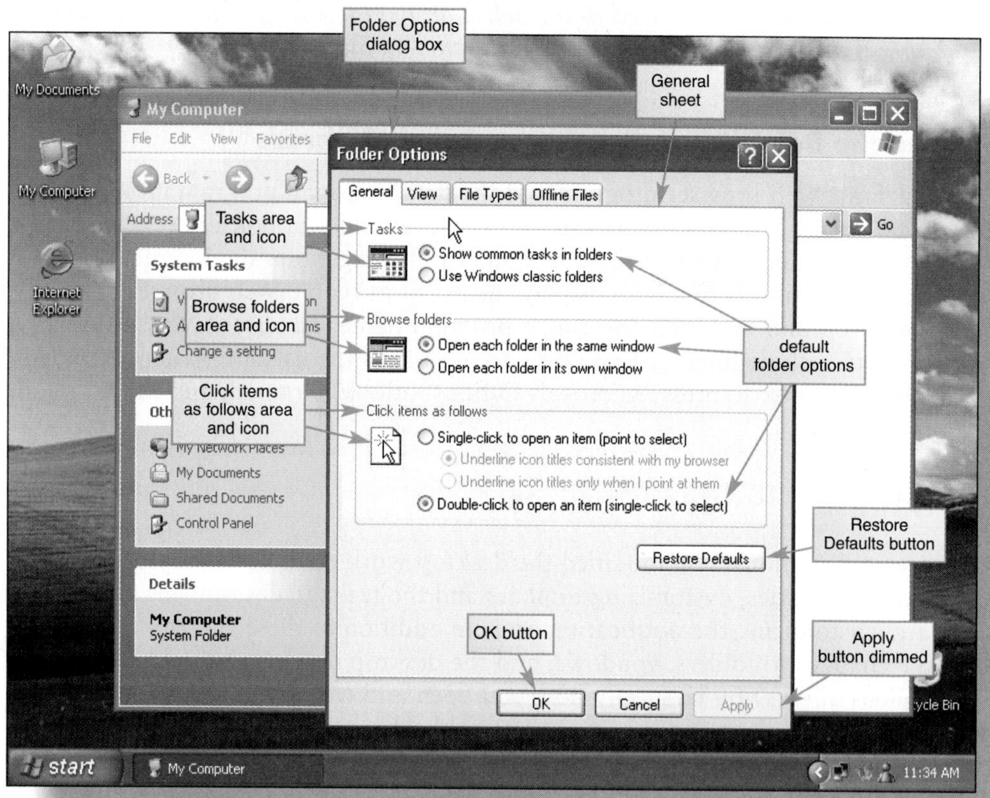

FIGURE 4-73

1. Press ALT+T, press O

In Figure 4-73, the General sheet contains the Tasks, Browse folders, and Click items as follows areas. Each area contains an icon and option button that allow you to change a folder option. Each area also contains a selected option button (color green) indicating the default folder option. A **default folder option** is an option selected by Microsoft Corporation when designing the Windows XP software.

Below the three areas are the Restore Defaults, OK, Cancel, and Apply buttons. The **Restore Defaults button** restores the default folder options, the **OK button** turns on a folder option and closes the dialog box, the **Apply button** turns on a folder option without closing the dialog box, and the **Cancel button** cancels any changes made to the folder options.

The following sections illustrate how to select a folder option in the Folder Options dialog box, how to turn on the folder option, and the results of turning on the folder option.

Displaying Folders as Windows Classic Folders

In previous projects, double-clicking a folder icon caused a folder window to open and display with a left and right pane. The **Show common tasks in folders option** causes all folders to display with a left pane and right pane. The various areas in the left pane contain common tasks that you may perform from within the folder and useful information about the folder. The right pane contains icons or groups of icons that allow you to display the files and folders contained in the folder. The Show common tasks in folders option button is selected, indicating it is the default folder option button.

The **Use Windows classic folders option** causes all folders to look and function like Windows classic folders. **Windows classic folders** display without a left and right pane, and only icons or groupings of icons display in the area below the Address toolbar in the folder window. Perform the following steps to turn on the Use Windows classic folders option.

To Turn On the Use Windows Classic Folders Option

1 Click Use Windows classic folders in the Tasks area and then point to the OK button.

Windows XP selects the Use Windows classic folders option button and changes the icon in the Tasks area to reflect the new selection (Figure 4-74).

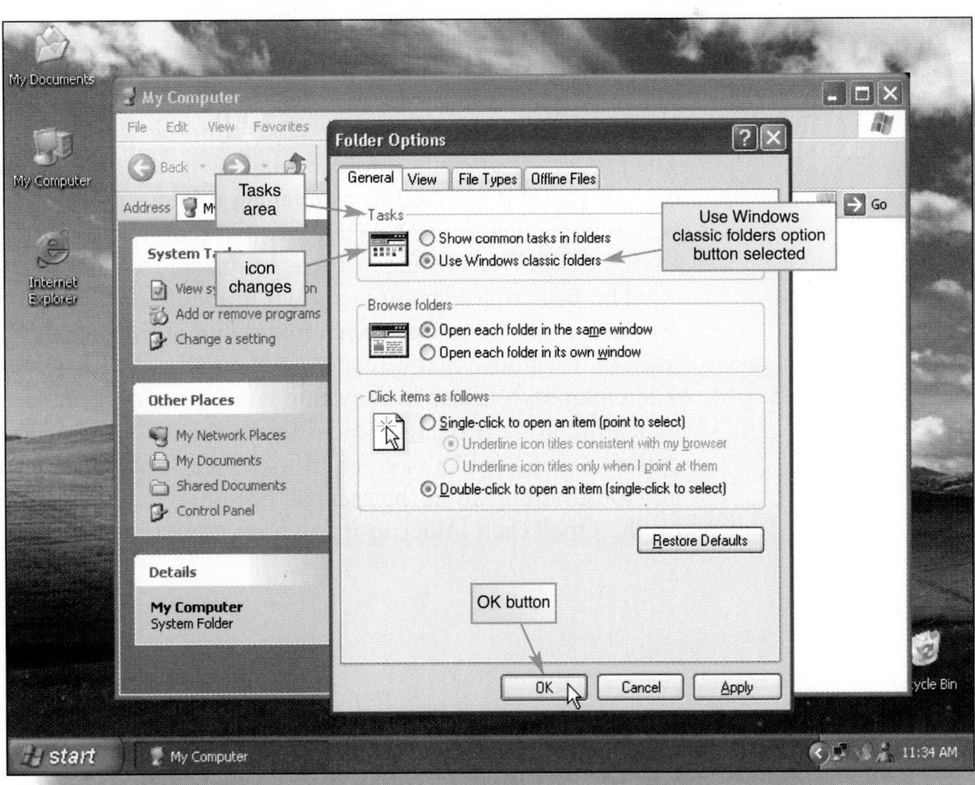

FIGURE 4-74

2 Click the OK button.

Windows XP turns on the Use Windows classic folders option, closes the Folder Options dialog box, and displays the My Computer window as a Windows classic folder (Figure 4-75). The My Computer window does not contain a left and right pane. All folders you open in the future will now display as Windows classic folders.

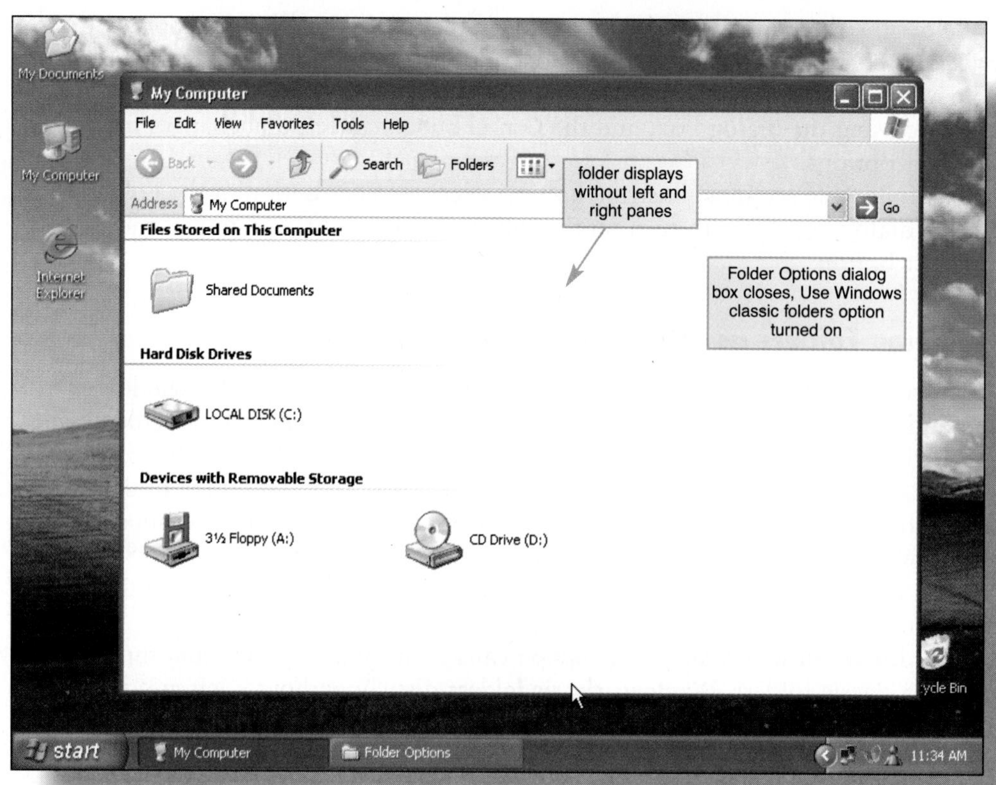

FIGURE 4-75

Opening a Folder in Its Own Window

In previous projects, each time you double-clicked an icon in an open window, the new window opened in the same window where the old window was displayed. The process of opening a folder window in the same window as the previously opened folder is referred to as **opening a folder in the same window**. For example, if you double-click the LOCAL DISK (C:) icon in the open My Computer window, the LOCAL DISK (C:) window opens in the same window as the My Computer window.

The Browse folders area shown in Figure 4-73 on page WIN 4.56 contains two option buttons. The **Open each folder in the same window option** causes a folder to open in a window that already is open and a single button to display on the taskbar. The Open each folder in the same window option button is selected in Figure 4-73, indicating it is the default folder option. The **Open each folder in its own window option** causes a folder to open in its own window, resulting in another open window and another button in the taskbar button area. Perform the following steps to turn on the Open each folder in its own window option.

Steps To Turn On the Open Each Folder in Its Own Window Option

1 Click Tools on the My Computer menu bar, click Folder Options, and then point to Open each folder in its own window in the Browse folders area in the Folder Options dialog box.

The Folder Options dialog box displays (Figure 4-76). The selected Open each folder in the same window option button displays in the Browse folders area and the Open each folder in its own window option button is highlighted.

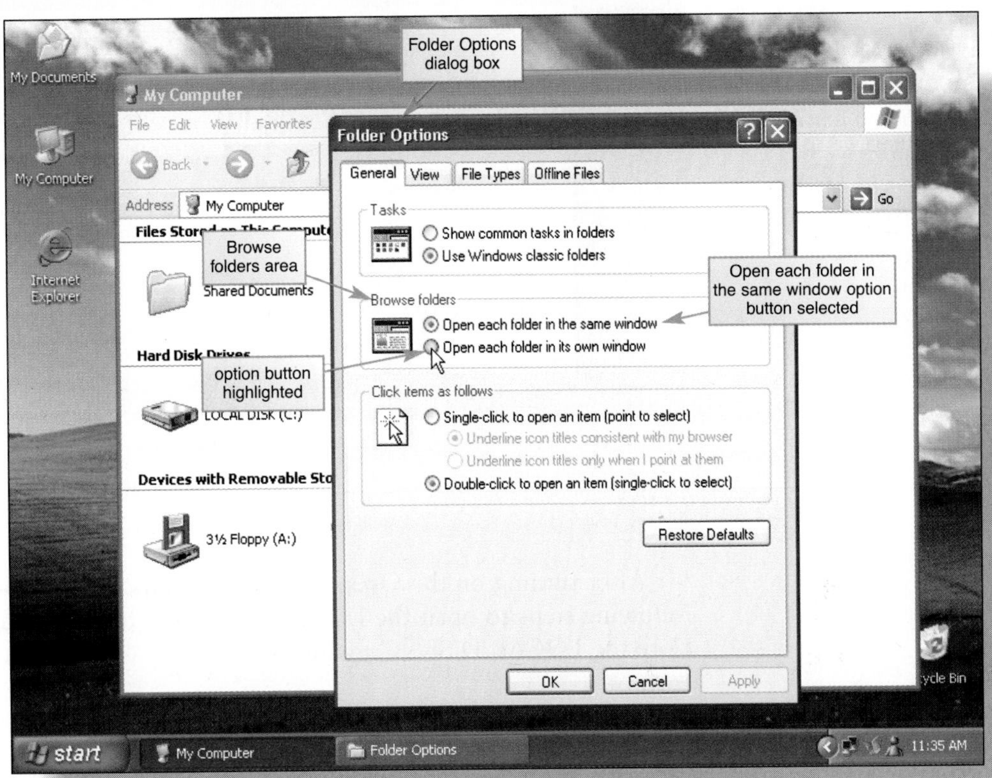

FIGURE 4-76

2 Click Open each folder in its own window. Point to the OK button.

Windows XP selects the Open each folder in its own window option button and the icon in the Browse folders area changes to reflect the selection of the folder option (Figure 4-77).

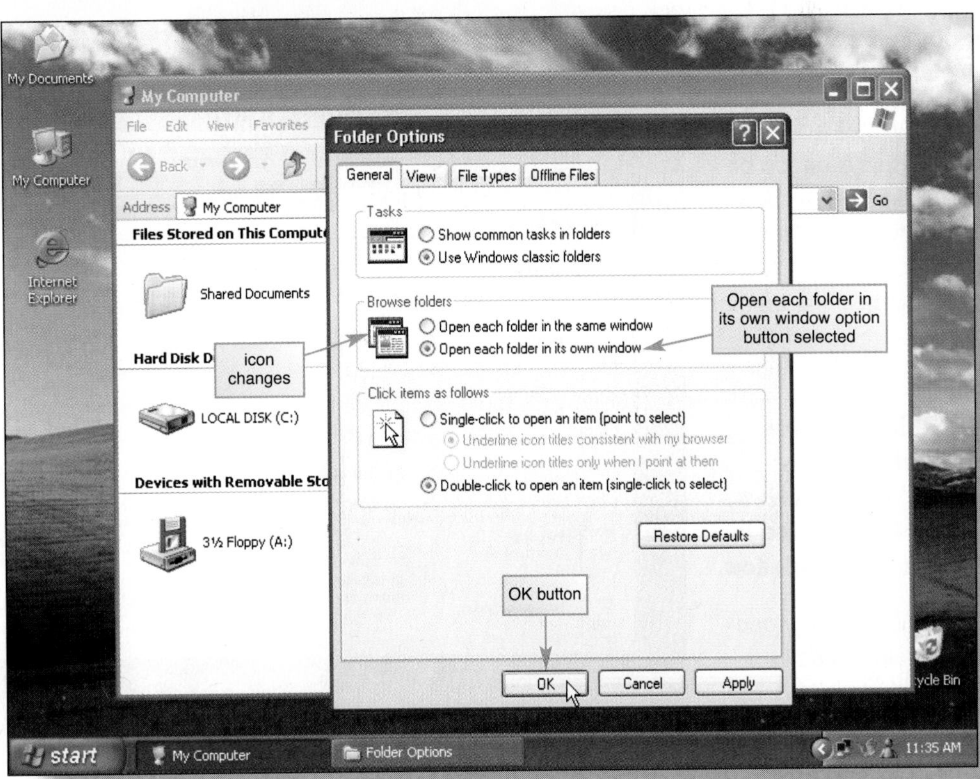

FIGURE 4-77

3 Click the OK button.

The Open each folder in its own window option is turned on and the Folder Options dialog box closes (Figure 4-78).

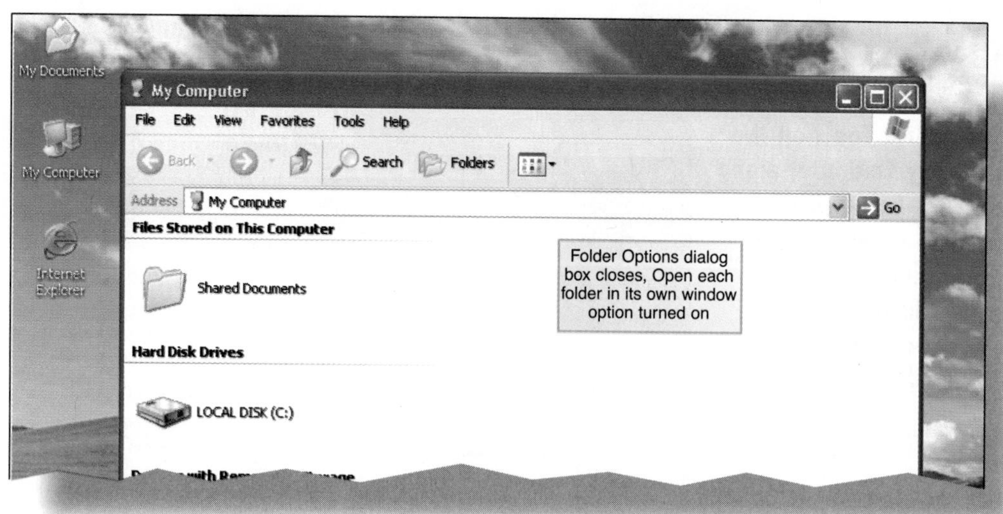

FIGURE 4-78

After turning on the Open each folder in its own window option, perform the following steps to open the LOCAL DISK (C:) folder in its own window and then close the LOCAL DISK (C:) window.

Steps To Open a Folder in Its Own Window

1 Double-click the LOCAL DISK (C:) icon in the My Computer window.

The LOCAL DISK (C:) window displays on top of the My Computer window and the My Computer button and LOCAL DISK (C:) button display in the taskbar button area (Figure 4-79).

2 Click the Close button in the LOCAL DISK (C:) window. Click the Close button in the My Computer window.

The LOCAL DISK (C:) and My Computer windows close.

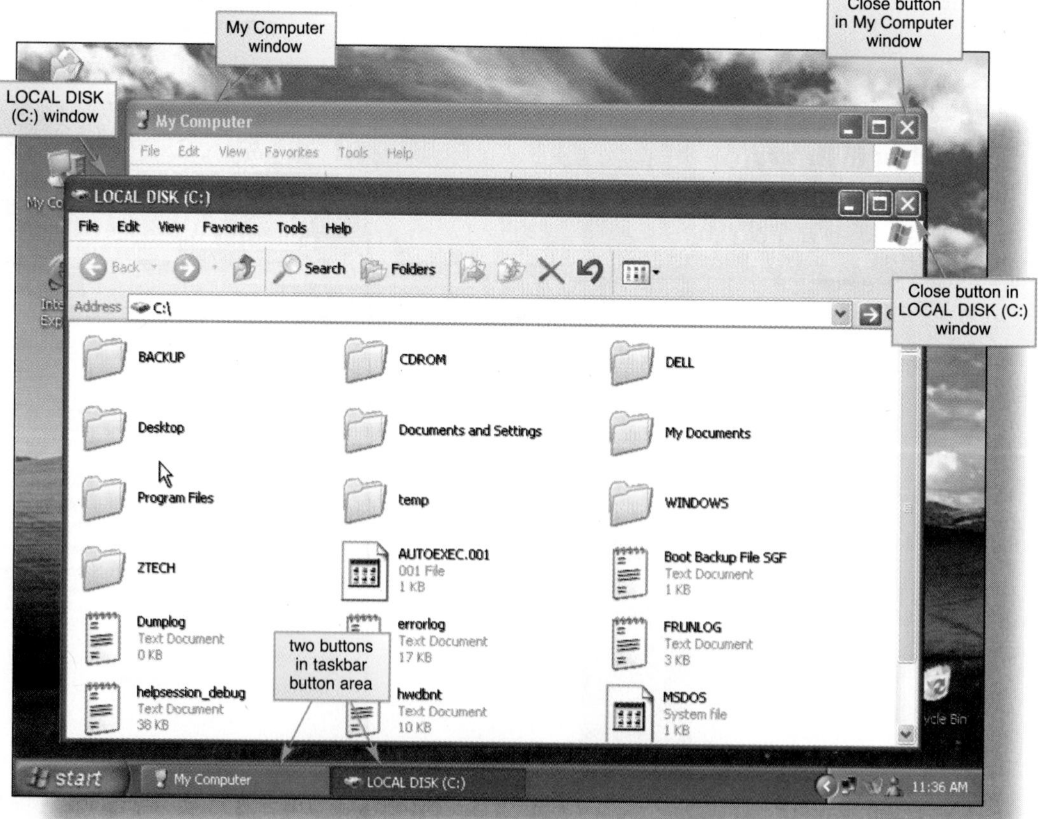

FIGURE 4-79

Restoring the Folder Options to the Default Folder Options

After changing one or more folder options, you can restore the default folder options you changed by clicking the appropriate option button and then clicking the OK button or Apply button. In addition, you can restore all the folder options to the default folder options by clicking the **Restore Defaults button** in the Folder Options dialog box and then clicking the OK button. Perform the following steps to restore the two previously changed folder options to their default folder options.

Steps To Restore the Folder Options to the Default Folder Options

1 Click the Start button, click My Computer on the Start menu, click Tools on the My Computer menu bar, click Folder Options, and then point to the Restore Defaults button in the Folder Options dialog box.

The My Computer window and Folder Options dialog box display (Figure 4-80).

FIGURE 4-80

2 Click the Restore Defaults button. Point to the OK button in the Folder Options dialog box.

The Show common tasks in folders and Open each folder in the same window option buttons are selected (Figure 4-81).

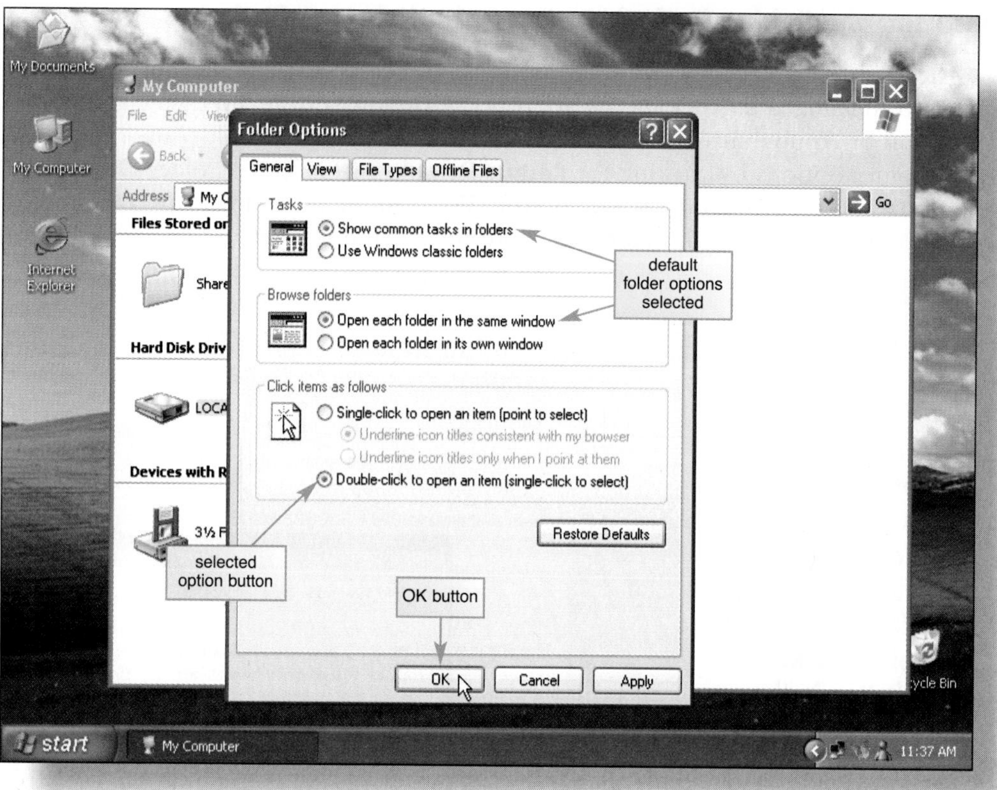

FIGURE 4-81

3 Click the OK button.

Each folder option that previously was changed is restored to its default setting, the Folder Options dialog box closes, and the Show common tasks in folders and Open each folder in the same window folder options are turned on (Figure 4-82). The My Computer window displays with a left and right pane, and now each folder will open in the same window.

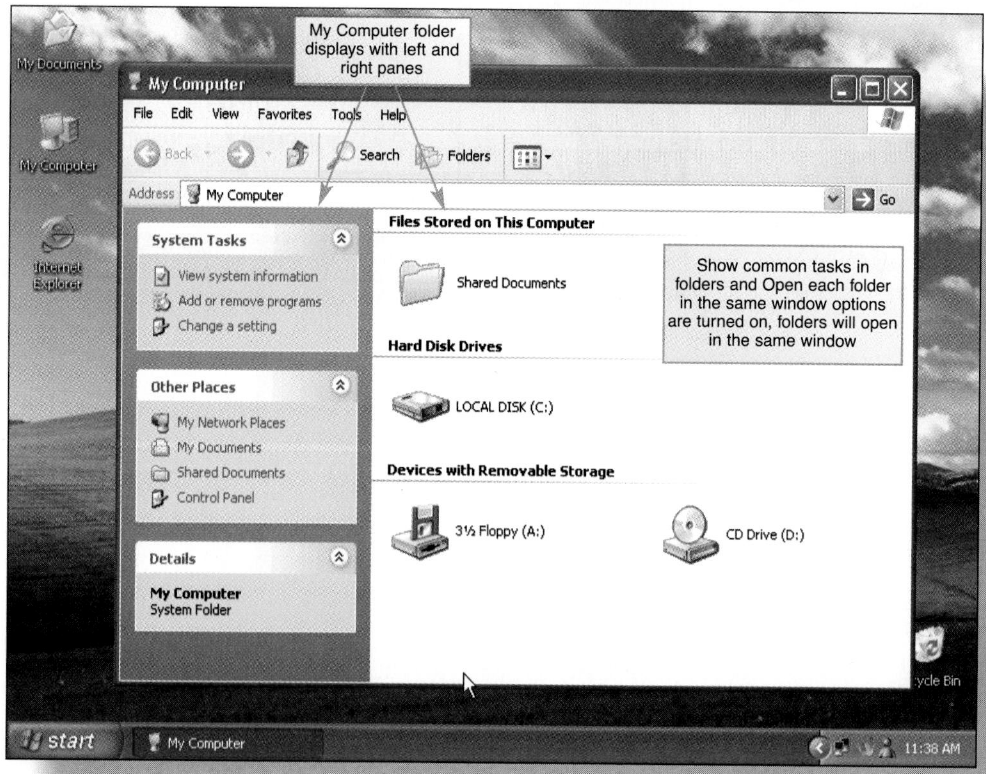

FIGURE 4-82

Opening an Item by Single-Clicking

In previous projects, you double-clicked an icon in a folder or on the desktop to open its window and single-clicked an icon to select the icon. The Click items as follows area in the Folder Options dialog box allows you to choose to single-click or double-click an icon to open its window. You also can choose single-click or point to an icon to select an icon.

The Click items as follows area contains the Single-click to open an item (point to select) option button and the Double-click to open an item (single-click to select) option button. These two option buttons affect the manner in which you select and open items in a folder and on the desktop. In Figure 4-81, the Double-click to open an item (single-click to select) option button is selected, indicating it is the default folder option. As a result, you double-click an icon in a folder or on the desktop to open an item and display its window, and single-click an icon to select the icon.

When you turn on the Single-click to open an item (point to select) option, you single click an icon in a folder or on the desktop to open the item, just as you would click a link on a Web page. After turning on this folder option, you can turn on one of two additional options (Underline icon titles consistent with my browser and Underline icon titles only when I point at them). If you turn on the Underline icon titles consistent with my browser option, icon titles in a folder or on the desktop are underlined. You point to an icon to select the icon, and you single-click an icon to open its window. If you turn on the Underline icon titles only when I point at them option, icon titles in a folder or on the desktop are underlined only when you point to an icon, and you single-click the icon to open its window.

Perform the following steps to turn on the Single-click to open an item (point to select) and Underline icon titles consistent with my browser folder options.

Steps To Turn On the Single-Click to Open an Item (Point to Select) Option

1 Click Tools on the My Computer menu bar, click Folder Options, and then point to Single-click to open an item (point to select) in the Click items as follows area.

The Folder Options dialog box displays (Figure 4-83). The Double-click to open an item (single-click to select) option button is selected in the Click items as follows area and the Single-click to open an item (point to select) is highlighted.

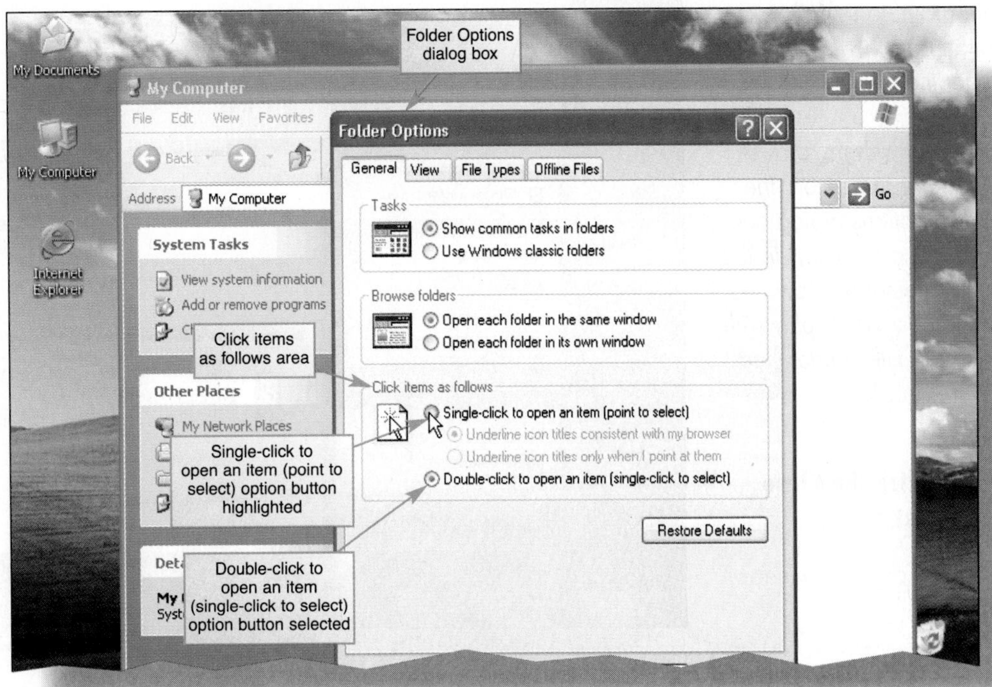

FIGURE 4-83

2 Click Single-click to open an item (point to select). If necessary, click Underline icon titles consistent with my browser. Point to the OK button.

Windows XP changes the icon in the Click items as follows area to reflect the selections and selects the Single-click to open an item (point to select) option button and Underline icon titles consistent with my browser option button (Figure 4-84).

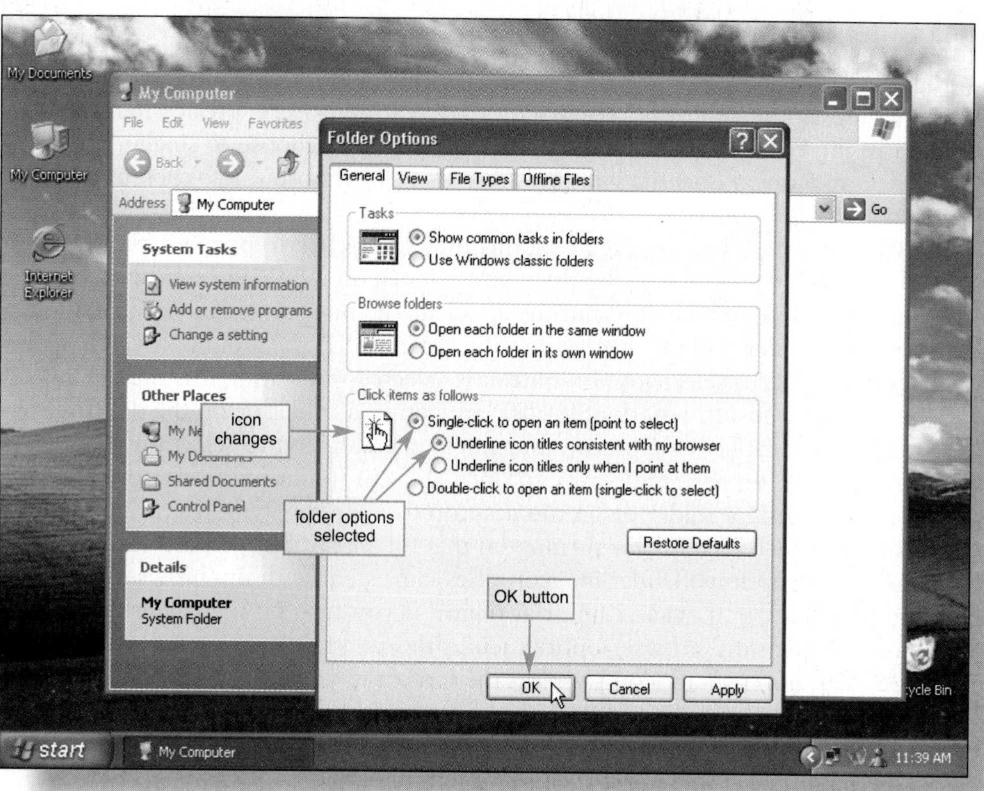

FIGURE 4-84

3 Click the OK button.

The Single-click to open an item (point to select) option and Underline icon titles consistent with my browser option are turned on, the Folder Options dialog box closes, and the icons in the My Computer window and on the desktop display with their icon titles underlined (Figure 4-85).

4 Click the Close button.

The My Computer window closes.

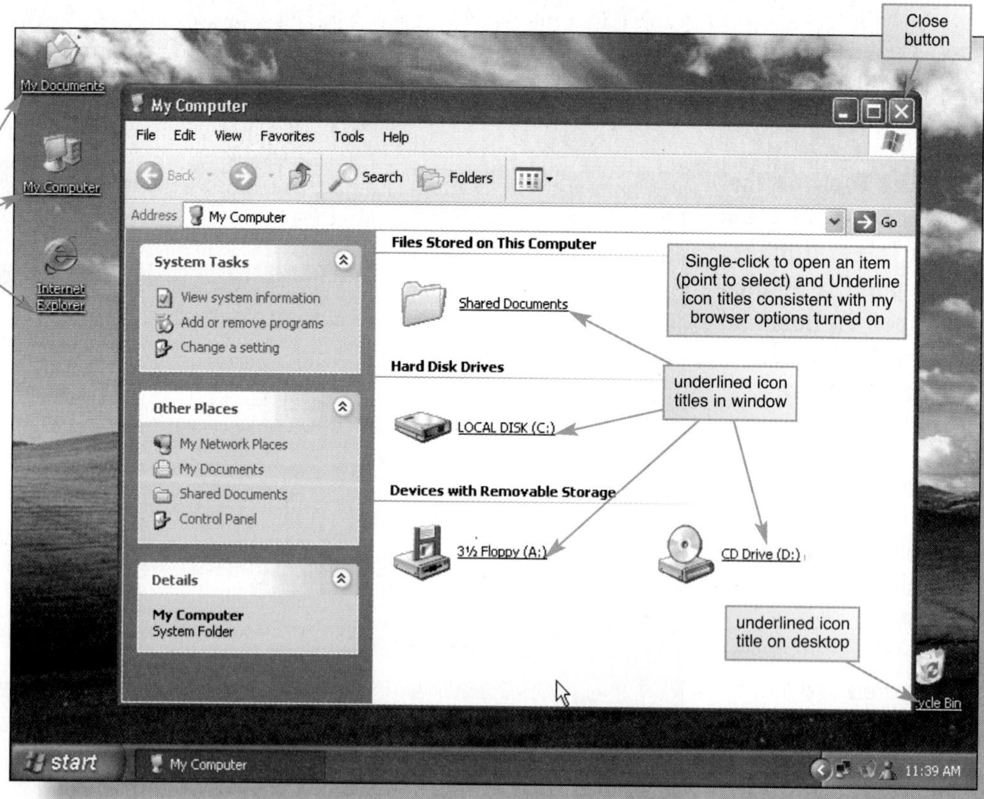

FIGURE 4-85

After turning on the Single-click to open an item (point to select) option, if you select the Underline icon titles only when I point at them option button instead of the Underline icon titles consistent with my browser option button and then click the OK button, the icon titles on the desktop and in all folders will not be underlined. Only when you point to an icon does its icon title display underlined.

Working with Underlined Icons on the Desktop and in Folders

In the previous section, you selected the Single-click to open an item (point to select) option button, selected the Underline icon titles consistent with my browser option button, and then clicked the OK button to turn on the options. As a result, the titles of all icons on the desktop are underlined and the icon titles of the icons in any open folder window and any folder window you open in the future will be underlined.

Several differences are apparent when working with icons and windows after turning on these folder options. To understand these differences, the following sections present steps so that you can practice the techniques for selecting a single icon, opening a folder window, and selecting and copying multiple files. The My Computer icon on the desktop, which was placed on the desktop on pages WIN 4.12 and WIN 4.13, will be used.

Selecting Icons on the Desktop and Opening Windows

After turning on the Single-click to open an item (point to select) and Underline icon titles consistent with my browser options, you point to an icon to select it and single-click the icon to open its window. Perform the following steps to select the My Computer icon on the desktop and open the My Computer window.

Steps To Select an Icon on the Desktop and Open Its Window

1 Point to the My Computer icon on the desktop.

*When you point to the My Computer icon, the mouse pointer changes to a hand (indicating you are pointing to a link) and the My Computer icon is selected (Figure 4-86). In Windows XP terminology, pointing to an object that results in the selection of that object is referred to as **hovering**.*

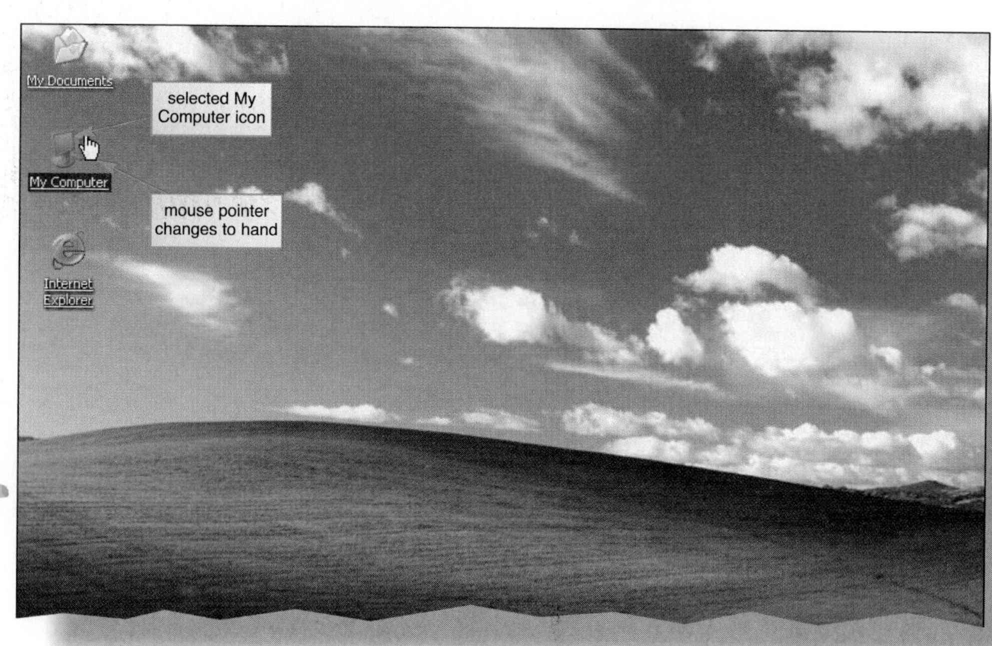

FIGURE 4-86

2 Click the My Computer icon.

The My Computer window displays, the recessed My Computer button displays in the taskbar button area, and the title of each icon in the My Computer window is underlined (Figure 4-87).

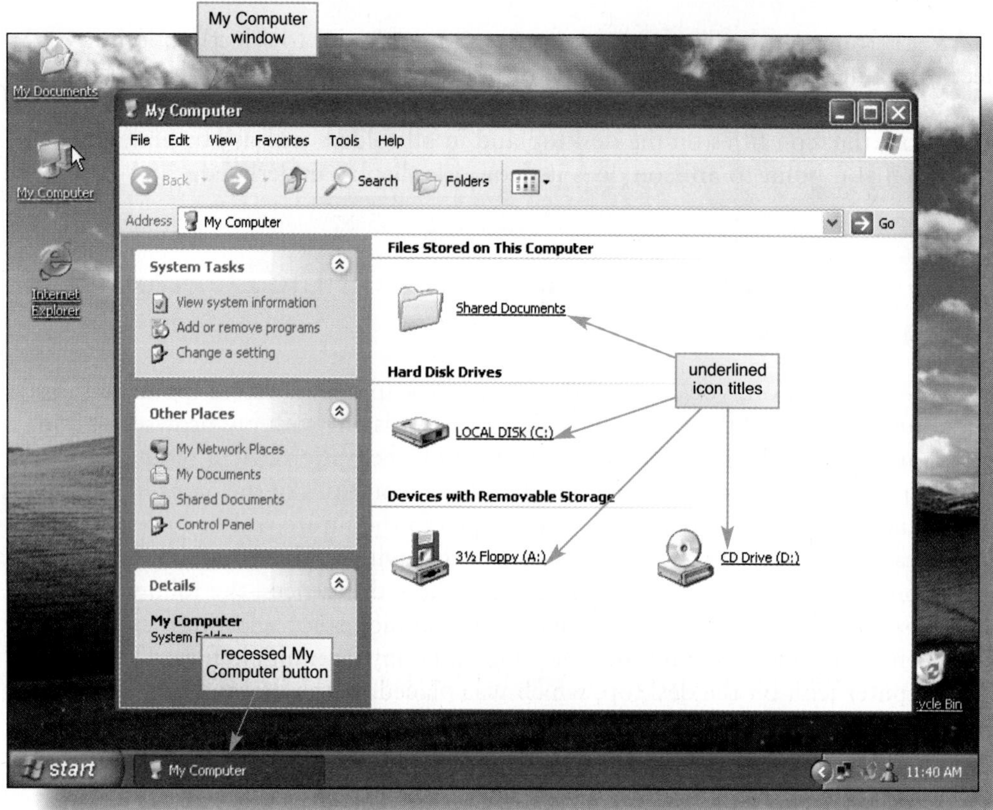

FIGURE 4-87

Other Ways

1. Right-click icon, click Open on shortcut menu
2. Point to icon, press ENTER

Selecting an Icon in a Folder Window

When you point to an icon in a folder window, Windows XP selects the icon. Perform the following steps to select the LOCAL DISK (C:) icon in the My Computer window and then open the LOCAL DISK (C:) window.

To Select an Icon in a Folder and Open Its Window

1 Point to the LOCAL DISK (C:) icon in the My Computer window.

When you point to the LOCAL DISK (C:) icon, the mouse pointer changes to a hand (indicating you are pointing to a link), and the LOCAL DISK (C:) icon is selected (Figure 4-88).

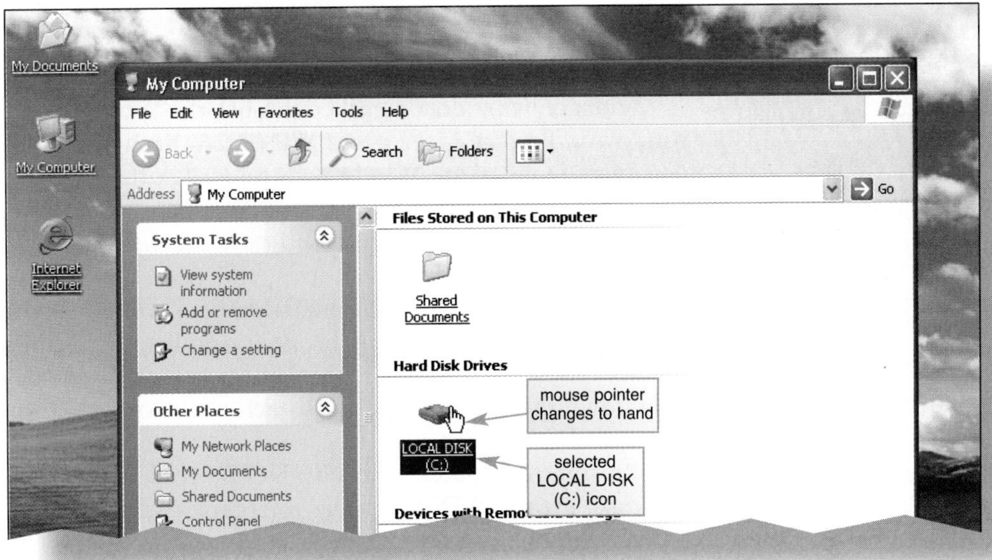

FIGURE 4-88

2 Click the LOCAL DISK (C:) icon.

The LOCAL DISK (C:) window opens in the same window as the My Computer window displays, and a single button displays in the taskbar button area (Figure 4-89).

3 Click the Close button in the LOCAL DISK (C:) window.

The LOCAL DISK (C:) window closes.

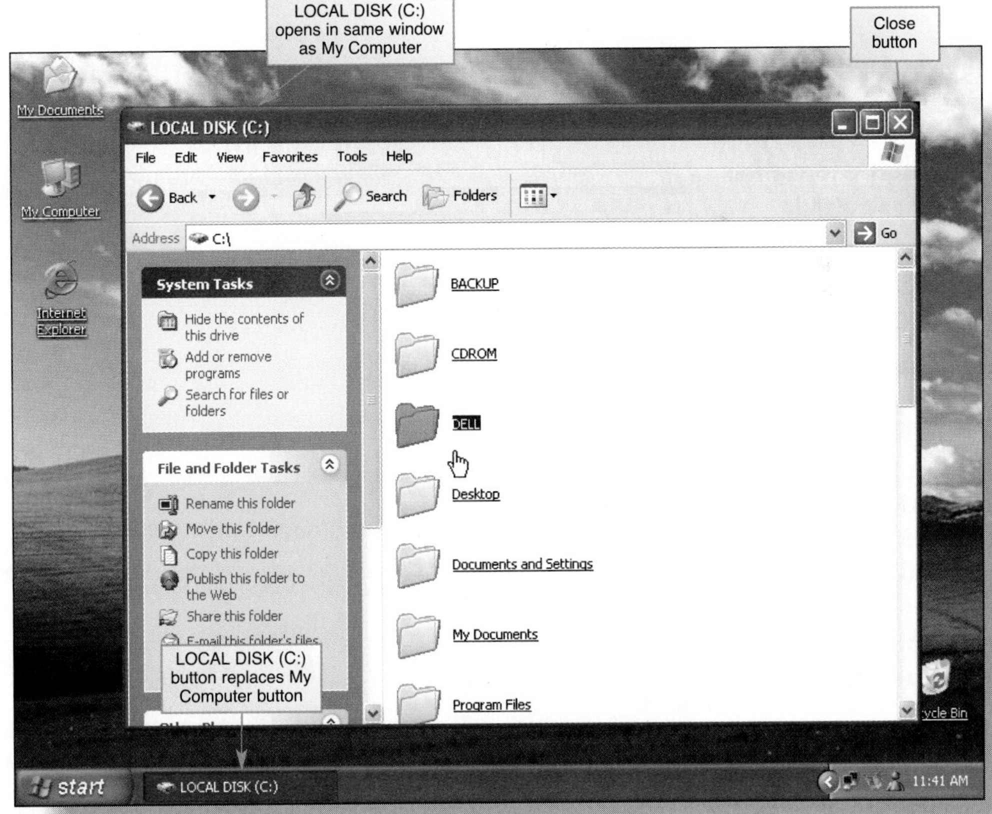

FIGURE 4-89

Other Ways

1. Right-click icon, click Open on shortcut menu
2. Point to icon, press ENTER

Whether an icon is located on the desktop or in a folder window, the manner in which you select an icon and open its window are the same. Point to an icon to select the icon and click the icon to open its window.

More About

Shortcut Menus

Until now, clicking a command on a shortcut menu caused the submenu to display to the right of the shortcut menu. When there is not enough room to the right of the shortcut menu, the submenu will display to the left of the shortcut menu. In Figure 4-91, the Send To submenu displays to the left of the shortcut menu.

Selecting Multiple Files and Copying Files

When copying document icons from the WINDOWS folder to the My Pictures window in Project 3 (see pages WIN 3.26 through WIN 3.38), you selected three document icons in the WINDOWS folder (Coffee Bean, Gone Fishing, and Greenstone) and used the Copy and Paste commands to copy the files to the My Pictures folder. The technique used to select the multiple files was to hold down the CTRL key, click each document icon, and release the CTRL key.

After turning on the Single-click to open an item (point to select) and Underline icon titles consistent with my browser options, the technique to select multiple files is slightly different. To select multiple files you point to one of the document icons, hold down the CTRL key, point to each of the other document icons you wish to select, and release the CTRL key.

On some computers, the WINDOWS folder does not exist on the hard disk. In this case, use the WINNT folder to complete the following steps.

Perform the following steps to select and copy the Coffee Bean, Gone Fishing, and Greenstone files in the WINDOWS folder onto the floppy disk in drive A using the Send To command.

Steps To Select and Copy Multiple Files

1 Insert a formatted floppy disk in drive A.

2 Click the My Computer icon on the desktop, click the LOCAL DISK (C:) icon, and then click the WINDOWS icon. Maximize the WINDOWS window and then scroll down until the icons for the Coffee Bean, Gone Fishing, and Greenstone files are visible.

The maximized WINDOWS window displays and the Coffee Bean, Gone Fishing, and Greenstone icons are visible in the WINDOWS window (Figure 4-90).

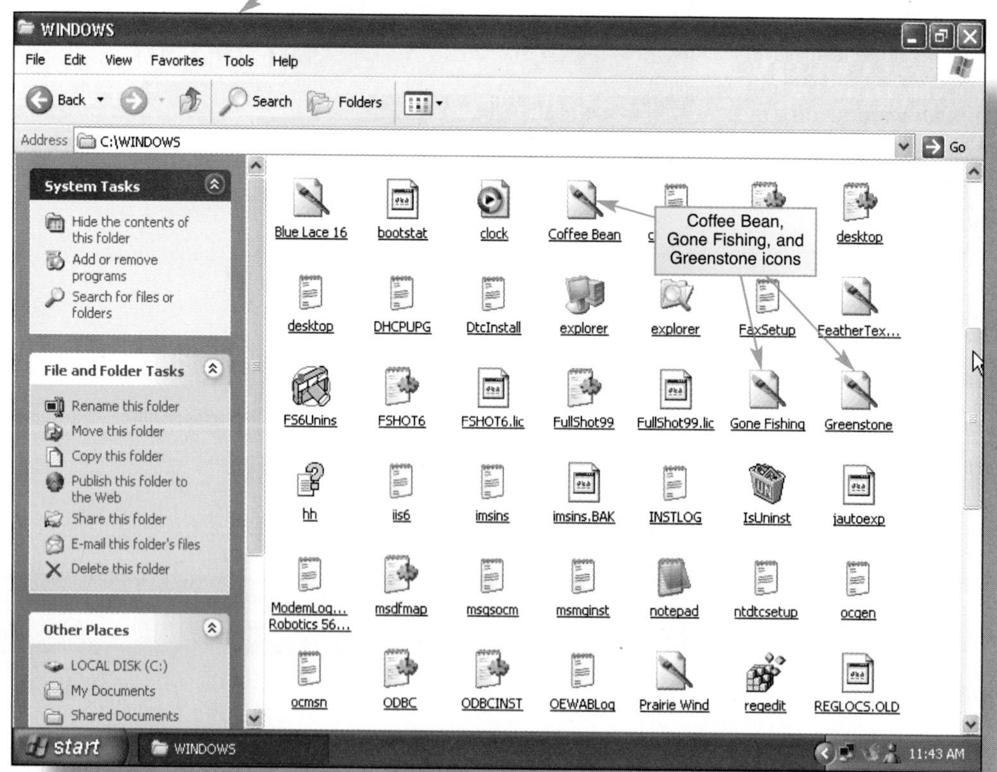

FIGURE 4-90

3 Hold down the CTRL key and then point to the Coffee Bean icon, Gone Fishing icon, and Greenstone icon. Release the CTRL key. Right-click the Gone Fishing icon, point to Send To on the shortcut menu, and then point to 3½ Floppy (A:) on the Send To submenu.

Windows XP selects the Coffee Bean, Gone Fishing, and Greenstone icons and displays a shortcut menu and the Send To submenu (Figure 4-91).

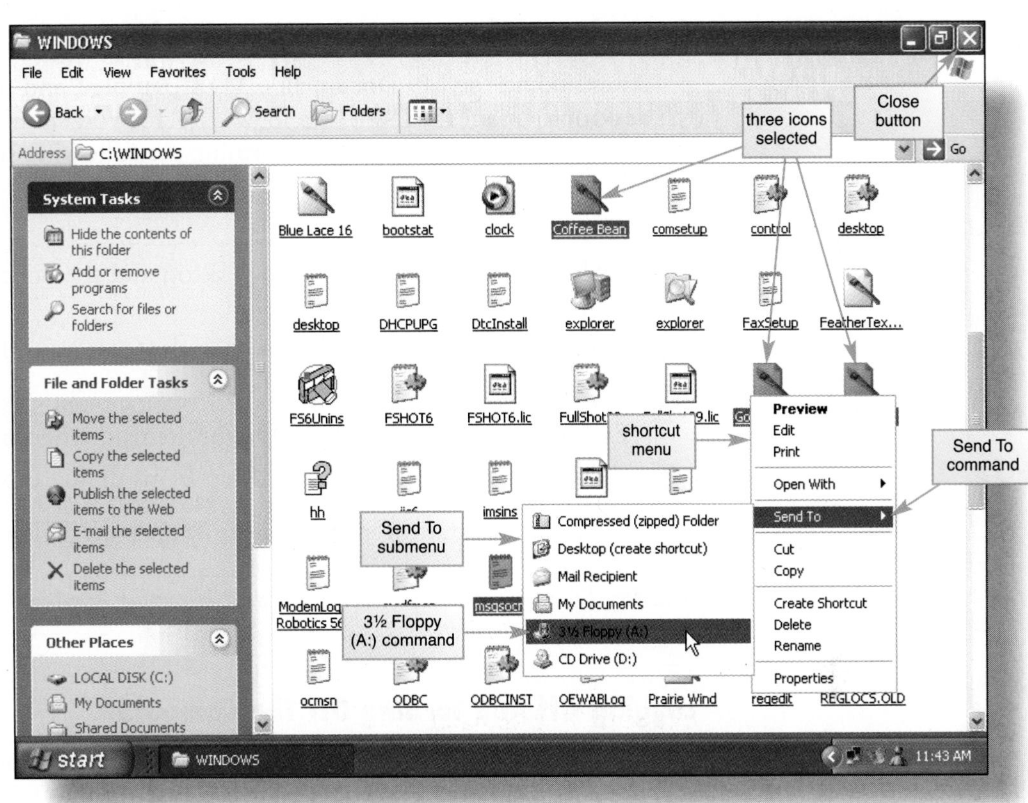

FIGURE 4-91

4 Click 3½ Floppy (A:). Click the Close button in the WINDOWS window.

The Copying dialog box displays while copying the three files to the floppy disk in drive A. The WINDOWS window closes.

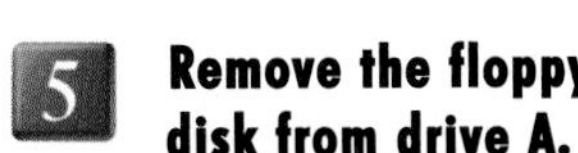

5 Remove the floppy disk from drive A.

Other Ways

1. Select icons of files to copy, on Edit menu click Copy, display 3½ Floppy (A:) window, on Edit menu click Paste
2. Select icons of files to copy, on Edit menu click Copy To Folder, click plus sign to left of My Computer icon, click 3½ Floppy (A:), click Copy button
3. Select icons of files to copy, right-click an icon, click Copy on shortcut menu, display 3½ Floppy (A:) window, right-click open area in 3½ Floppy (A:) window, click Paste on shortcut menu
4. Select icons of files to copy, press CTRL+C, display 3½ Floppy (A:) window, press CTRL+V

Restoring the Folder Options

After making changes to folder options, you should restore the folder options to the default folder options by performing the following steps.

TO RESTORE THE FOLDER OPTIONS TO THE DEFAULT FOLDER OPTIONS

1. Click the My Computer icon on the desktop.
2. Click Tools on the My Computer menu bar.
3. Click the Folder Options icon on the Tools menu.
4. Click the Restore Defaults button in the Folder Options dialog box.
5. Click the OK button in the Folder Options dialog box.
6. Click the Close button in the My Computer window.

The default folder options are restored and the My Computer window closes.

Removing Desktop Icons from the Desktop

After adding the My Documents, My Computer, and Internet Explorer icons to the desktop on pages WIN 4.12 and WIN 4.13, you should remove any desktop icons placed on the desktop by performing the following steps.

TO REMOVE DESKTOP ICONS

1. Right-click an open area of the desktop and then click Properties on the shortcut menu.
2. Click the Desktop tab and then click the Customize Desktop button.
3. Remove the check marks from the My Documents, My Computer, and Internet Explorer check boxes in the Desktop Items dialog box.
4. Click the OK button in the Desktop Items dialog box.
5. Click the OK button in the Display Properties dialog box.

The My Documents, My Computer, and Internet Explorer icons are removed from the desktop.

Logging Off And Turning Off The Computer

After completing your work with Windows XP, you should close your user account by logging off from the computer. Perform the following steps to log off from the computer.

TO LOG OFF FROM THE COMPUTER

1. Click the Start button.
2. Click Log Off on the Start menu.
3. Click the Log Off button in the Log Off Windows dialog box.

Windows XP logs off from the computer and displays the Welcome screen.

After logging off, you also may want to turn off the computer. If you are sure you want to turn off the computer, perform the following steps. If you are not sure about turning off the computer, read the following steps without actually performing them.

TO TURN OFF THE COMPUTER

1. Click the Turn off computer link on the Welcome screen.
2. Click the Turn Off button in the Turn off computer dialog box.

Windows XP is shut down.

CASE PERSPECTIVE SUMMARY

There was certainly much more to Windows XP than just launching programs, performing file and desktop management, and using Windows Help and Support. While learning about features to customize the desktop and work environment, you realized the importance of customizing the computer to fit your personal needs. As a result, you created a new desktop theme to enhance the appearance of the desktop and selected a screen saver to display while the computer was not being used. You personalized the taskbar and selected folder options best suited to the manner in which you interact with folders and the desktop. The computer suddenly became more user friendly, an expression of yourself, and easier to use.

Project Summary

In this project, you modified desktop properties by selecting a desktop theme, creating a new desktop theme, and changing the font size and screen saver. You personalized the taskbar by moving, resizing, and hiding the taskbar; adding toolbars to the taskbar; and adding a shortcut icon to a toolbar. You customized the Start menu by changing the size of icons on the Start menu and customized the notification area by changing the behaviors of items. Finally, you selected and turned on folder options, viewed the results of turning on folder options, and restored folder options.

What You Should Know

Having completed this project, you now should be able to perform the following tasks:

- Add a Toolbar to the Taskbar *(WIN 4.32, WIN 4.41)*
- Add an Active Desktop Item to the Desktop *(WIN 4.20)*
- Add Icons to the Desktop *(WIN 4.12)*
- Change the Desktop Background *(WIN 4.10)*
- Change the Font Size *(WIN 4.16)*
- Change the Screen Saver *(WIN 4.14)*
- Delete a Desktop Theme *(WIN 4.19)*
- Delete Permanently a Desktop Item *(WIN 4.24)*
- Display a Web Page Using the Address Toolbar *(WIN 4.44)*
- Display Smaller Icons on the Start Menu *(WIN 4.50)*
- Display the Contents of a Folder Using the Address Toolbar *(WIN 4.43)*
- Display the Folder Options Dialog Box *(WIN 4.56)*
- Expand a Toolbar *(WIN 4.42)*
- Hide and Redisplay the Taskbar *(WIN 4.28)*
- Launch an Application on a Toolbar Using the Double Chevron *(WIN 4.36)*
- Lock the Taskbar *(WIN 4.28, WIN 4.43)*
- Log Off from the Computer *(WIN 4.70)*
- Move the Taskbar *(WIN 4.26)*
- Open a Folder in Its Own Window *(WIN 4.60)*
- Open the Display Properties Dialog Box *(WIN 4.05)*
- Place a Shortcut on a Toolbar *(WIN 4.34)*
- Remove a Shortcut from a Toolbar and Resize a Toolbar *(WIN 4.41)*
- Remove a Toolbar from the Taskbar *(WIN 4.47)*
- Remove Desktop Icons *(WIN 4.70)*
- Reset the Desktop Theme *(WIN 4.09)*
- Reset the Icon Size and Number of Programs *(WIN 4.55)*
- Resize a Toolbar *(WIN 4.40)*
- Resize the Taskbar *(WIN 4.38)*
- Restore the Default Notification Behaviors *(WIN 4.50)*
- Restore the Folder Options to the Default Folder Options *(WIN 4.61, WIN 4.69)*
- Return the Taskbar to Its Original Location *(WIN 4.39)*
- Save a Desktop Theme *(WIN 4.18)*
- Search for Information on the Internet Using the Address Toolbar *(WIN 4.46)*
- Select a New Desktop Theme *(WIN 4.07)*
- Select an Icon in a Folder and Open Its Window *(WIN 4.67)*
- Select an Icon on the Desktop and Open Its Window *(WIN 4.65)*
- Select and Copy Multiple Files *(WIN 4.68)*
- Set the Maximum Number of Most Frequently Used Programs *(WIN 4.53)*
- Set the Notification Behavior of a Notification Item *(WIN 4.48)*
- Turn Off the Computer *(WIN 4.70)*
- Turn On the Open Each Folder in Its Own Window Option *(WIN 4.59)*
- Turn On the Single-Click to Open an Item (Point to Select) Option *(WIN 4.63)*
- Turn On the Use Windows Classic Folders Option *(WIN 4.57)*
- Unlock the Taskbar *(WIN 4.25, 4.38)*

Learn It Online

Instructions: To complete the Learn It Online exercises, launch your Web browser using the steps on pages WIN 1.46 and WIN 1.47, click the Address box, enter `scsite.com/winxp/exs.htm`, and then press the ENTER key. When the Windows XP Learn It Online page displays, follow the instructions in the exercises below.

1 Project Reinforcement TF, MC, and SA

Below Windows XP Project 4, click the Project Reinforcement link. Print the quiz by clicking Print on the File menu. Answer each question. Write your first and last name at the top of each page, and then hand in the printout to your instructor.

2 Flash Cards

Below Windows XP Project 4, click the Flash Cards link. When Flash Cards displays, read the instructions. Type `20` (or a number specified by your instructor) in the Number of Playing Cards text box, type your name in the Name text box, and then click the Flip Card button. When the flash card displays, read the question and then click the Answer box arrow to select an answer. Flip through Flash Cards. Click Print on the File menu to print the last flash card if your score is 15 (75%) correct or greater and then hand it in to your instructor. If your score is less than 15 (75%) correct, then redo this exercise by clicking the Replay button.

3 Practice Test

Below Windows XP Project 4, click the Practice Test link. Answer each question, enter your first and last name at the bottom of the page, and then click the Grade Test button. When the graded practice test displays on your screen, click Print on the File menu to print a hard copy. Continue to take practice tests until you score 80% or better. Hand in a printout of the final practice test to your instructor.

4 Who Wants to Be a Computer Genius?

Below Windows XP Project 4, click the Computer Genius link. Read the instructions, enter your first and last name at the bottom of the page, and then click the Play button. Hand in a printout of your score to your instructor.

5 Wheel of Terms

Below Windows XP Project 4, click the Wheel of Terms link. Read the instructions, and then enter your first and last name and your school name. Click the Play button. Hand in a printout of your score to your instructor.

6 Crossword Puzzle Challenge

Below Windows XP Project 4, click the Crossword Puzzle Challenge link. Read the instructions, and then enter your first and last name. Click the Play button. Work the crossword puzzle. When you are finished, click the Submit button. When the crossword puzzle redisplays, click the Print button. Hand in the printout.

7 Tips and Tricks

Below Windows XP Project 4, click the Tips and Tricks link. Click a topic that pertains to Project 4. Right-click the information and then click Print on the shortcut menu. Construct a brief example of what the information relates to in Windows XP to confirm that you understand how to use the tip or trick. Hand in the example and printed information.

8 Newsgroups

Below Windows XP Project 4, click the Newsgroups link. Click a topic that pertains to Project 4. Print three comments. Hand in the comments to your instructor.

9 Expanding Your Horizons

Below Windows XP Project 4, click the Articles for Microsoft Windows XP link. Click a topic that pertains to Project 4. Print the information. Construct a brief example of what the information relates to in Windows XP to confirm that you understand the contents of the article. Hand in the example and printed information to your instructor.

10 Search Sleuth

Below Windows XP Project 4, click the Search Sleuth link. To search for a term that pertains to this project, select a term below the Project 4 title and then use the Google search engine at google.com (or any major search engine) to display and print two Web pages that present information on the term. Hand in the printouts to your instructor.

Use Help

1 Using Windows Help and Support

Instructions: Use Windows Help and Support and a computer to perform the following tasks. Answer all questions in the spaces provided.

1. If necessary, launch Microsoft Windows XP and log on to the computer.
2. Right-click the desktop and then click Properties on the shortcut menu to display the Display Properties dialog box.
3. Click the Screen Saver tab.
4. Answer the following questions about energy management using the Question Mark button in the Display Properties dialog box.
   a. What is the Energy Star™ program? to adjust monitor power settings And save energy click power
   b. Who administers the Energy Star™ program? ______
   c. What dialog box does the Power button open? ______
5. Click the Power button.
6. Answer the following questions about energy management using the Question Mark button in the Power Options Properties dialog box.
   a. What power scheme displays in the Power schemes area? Portable / laptop
   b. What does the entry in the Turn off monitor box indicate? pluged in or battery
   c. What does the entry in the Turn off hard disks box indicate? what time off when pluged or using batteries
   d. What does the entry in the System standby box indicate? minutes when using plug or battery
   e. What does the entry in the System hibernates box indicate? Same
7. Click the Cancel button in the Power Options Properties dialog box.
8. Click the Cancel button in the Display Properties dialog box.
9. Click the Start menu button, click My Computer on the Start menu, click Tools on the menu bar, and then click Folder Options.
10. Click the View tab in the Folder Options dialog box.
11. Answer the following questions about the advanced settings. If necessary, use the Question Mark button in the Folder Options dialog box.
    a. What does the Reset All Folders button do? resets all folders
    b. How many advanced settings are active? 9
    c. Which setting is active for hidden files and folders (a selected option button indicates an active setting)? Do not show hidden folders
    d. What does the Restore Defaults button do? Takes screen back to my computer
12. Click the Cancel button in the Folder Options dialog box. Click the Close button in the My Computer window.

In the Lab

1 Creating and Saving a Desktop Theme

Problem: A friend, who owns a tropical fish store, showed you the creative desktop theme she created for the computers in her store. The desktop looked like an aquarium. You own a travel agency and want to create a unique desktop theme for the computers in your agency. Currently, the Windows XP desktop theme displays on the desktop.

Instructions: Use a computer to perform the following tasks and answer the questions.

Part 1: Select the Windows XP Desktop Theme

1. If necessary, launch Microsoft Windows XP and log on to the computer.
2. Right-click the desktop and then click Properties on the shortcut menu to open the Display Properties dialog box.
3. In the space provided, write down the desktop theme name that displays in the Theme box on the desktop of your computer. WINDOW CLASSIC (modified)
4. If necessary, click the Theme box arrow, click the Windows XP desktop theme name in the Theme list, and click the Apply button to apply the Windows XP desktop theme to the desktop.

Part 2: Change the Desktop Background

1. Click the Desktop tab.
2. Scroll the Background list box to display Tulips wallpaper and then click Tulips wallpaper. If the Tulips wallpaper is not available, select another background and use this background for the remainder of this assignment.
3. Click the Apply button to apply the Tulips wallpaper to the desktop.

Part 3: Add Icons to the Desktop

1. Click the Customize Desktop button to display the Desktop Items dialog box.
2. Click My Documents and My Computer in the Desktop icons area.
3. Click the OK button in the Desktop Items dialog box.
4. Click the Apply button in the Display Properties dialog box to display the icons on the desktop.

Part 4: Change the Screen Saver

1. Click the Screen Saver tab.
2. Click the Screen Saver box arrow and then click 3D Flying Objects in the Screen Saver list.
3. Click the Preview button to display the screen saver on the desktop. Move the mouse to remove the screen saver.

Part 5: Change the Color Scheme

1. Click the Appearance tab.
2. Click the Color scheme box arrow and then click Silver in the Color scheme list.
3. Click the Apply button in the Display Properties dialog box to change the color scheme (Figure 4-92).

In the Lab

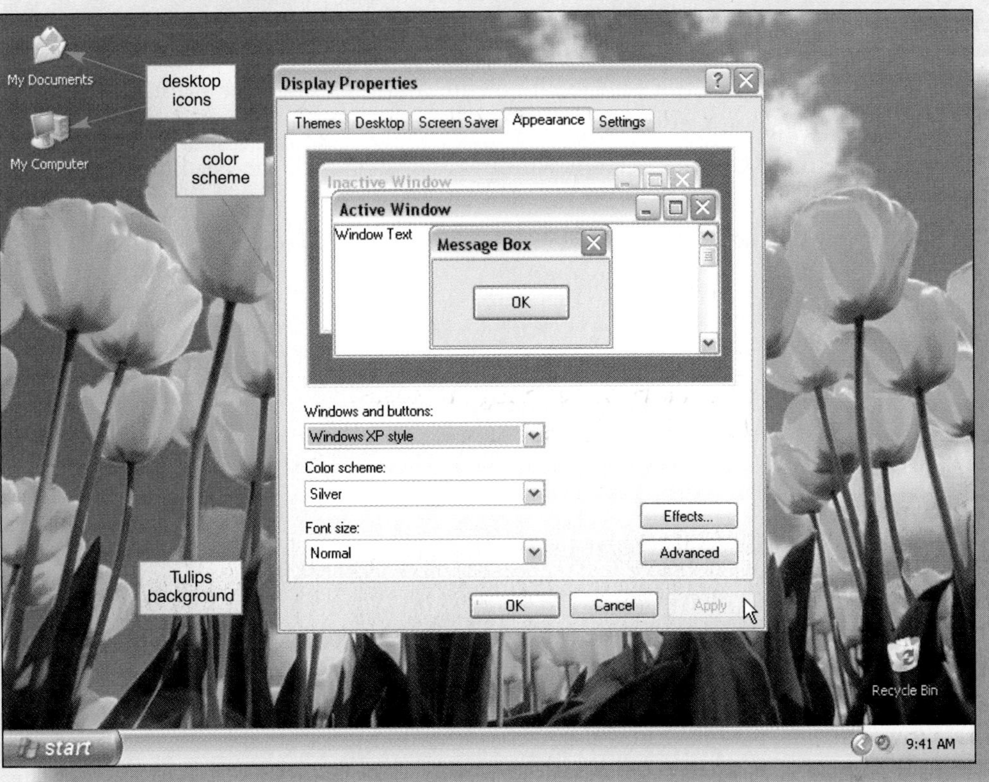

FIGURE 4-92

Part 6: ***Save the Desktop Theme***

1. Click the Themes tab in the Display Properties dialog box.
2. Click the Save As button.
3. Type `Tulip Festival for` in the File name box, press the SPACEBAR, type your first name, press the SPACEBAR, and then type your last name.
4. Click the Save button to save the Travel Agency desktop theme.
5. Click the OK button in the Display Properties dialog box.

Part 7: ***Printing the Desktop***

1. Double-click the My Computer icon on the desktop to display the My Computer window. Resize the My Computer window so that the My Computer window and the desktop icons (My Computer and My Documents) are visible on the desktop.
2. Click the PRINT SCREEN key on the keyboard to place an image of the desktop on the **Clipboard**, which is a temporary Windows storage area.
3. Click the Start button, point to All Programs, point to Accessories, and then click Paint.
4. Maximize the Untitled – Paint window.
5. Click Edit on the menu bar and then click Paste on the Edit menu to copy the image from the Clipboard to the Paint window.

(continued)

In the Lab

Creating and Saving a Desktop Theme *(continued)*

6. Click File on the menu bar, click Print on the File menu, and then click the Print button in the Print dialog box to print the Paint document.
7. Click the Close button in the Untitled – Paint window and then click the No button in the Paint dialog box to quit the Paint program.
8. Click the Close button in the My Computer window to close the window.

Part 8:* *Deleting the Desktop Theme

1. Right-click an open area of the desktop and then click Properties on the shortcut menu.
2. Verify that the name of the desktop theme (Tulip Festival for...) you created earlier displays in the Theme box.
3. Click the Delete button.
4. Click the Theme box arrow.
5. Click the desktop theme name in the Theme list you wrote down in Step 3 of Part 1 on page WIN 4.75.
6. Click the OK button in the Display Properties dialog box.

Part 9:* *Deleting the Icons on the Desktop

1. Right-click an open area of the desktop and then click Properties on the shortcut menu.
2. Click the Desktop tab and then click the Customize Desktop button.
3. Remove the check marks from the My Documents and My Computer check boxes in the Desktop Items dialog box.
4. Click the OK button in the Desktop Items dialog box.
5. Click the OK button in the Display Properties dialog box.
6. Hand in the printed Paint document illustrating your desktop theme to your instructor.

2 Adding an Active Desktop Item to the Desktop

Problem: A fellow employee asks you to show him how to add a desktop item to the desktop, reposition the item on the desktop, and then remove the desktop item. You decide to use the MSNBC Weather desktop item to show him.

Instructions: Use a computer to perform the following tasks and answer the questions.

Part 1:* *Adding an Active Desktop Item to the Desktop

1. If necessary, launch Microsoft Windows XP and log on to the computer.
2. Right-click an open area on the desktop and then click Properties on the shortcut menu.
3. Click the Desktop tab in the Display Properties dialog box.
4. Click the Customize Desktop button.
5. Click the Web tab in the Desktop Items dialog box.
6. Click the New button in the Web sheet.

In the Lab

7. Click the Visit Gallery button in the New Desktop Item dialog box.
8. Click the Maximize button in the Internet Explorer 4.0 Desktop Gallery – Microsoft Internet Explorer window.
9. Scroll the Internet Explorer 4.0 Desktop Gallery window to display the Weather Map from the MSNBC™ item.
10. Click the Add to Active Desktop button.
11. Point to the Yes button in the Internet Explorer dialog box.
12. Click the OK button in the Add item to the Active Desktop(TM) dialog box.
13. Click the Close button in the Internet Explorer 4.0 Desktop Gallery window.

Part 2: ***Sizing the Desktop Item***

1. Size the desktop item so that the entire United States map is visible. To size the item, point to a border or corner to change the mouse pointer to a double-headed arrow and drag the border or corner (Figure 4-93).

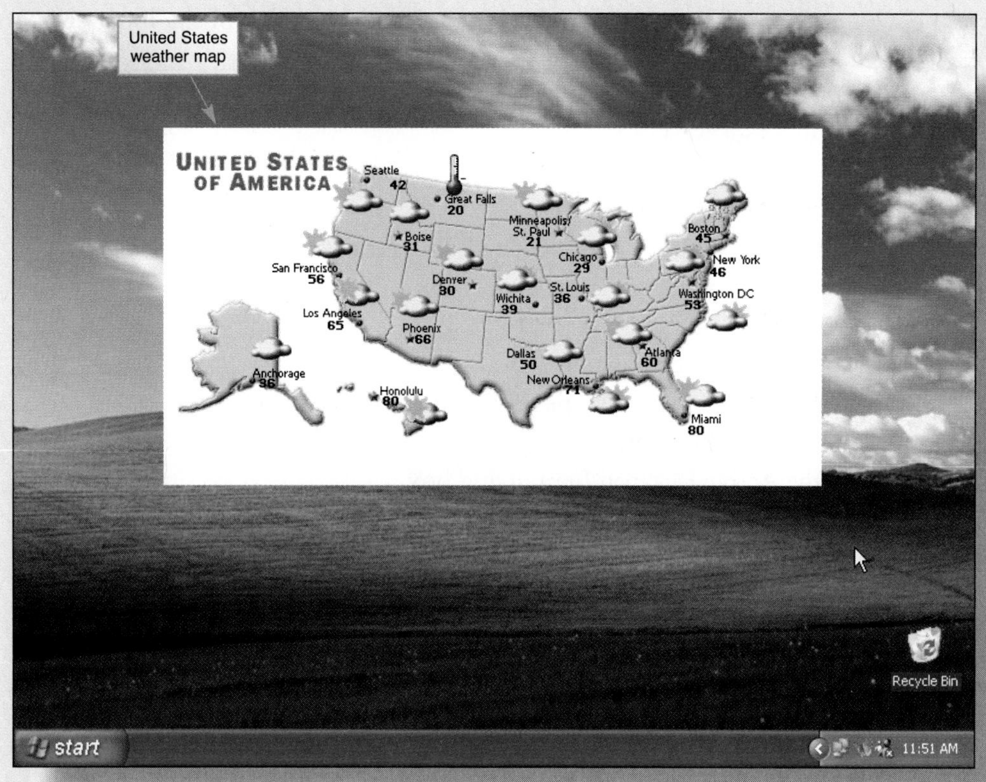

FIGURE 4-93

Part 3: ***Checking the Weather***

1. Click San Francisco on the map. Maximize the Weather Page window. Answer the following questions in the spaces provided.
   a. What are the current temperature, visibility, and humidity in San Francisco?
   54F 10 miles 94%

(continued)

In the Lab

Adding an Active Desktop Item to the Desktop *(continued)*

b. What is the weather forecast for the next four days in San Francisco?

Hi 64 - L 54, Hi 66 L-54 Hi 80 L=54 Hi 87 - Lo 54

c. What are the high and low temperatures for tomorrow in San Francisco?

Hi 64 Lo 54

2. Click the Print button on the Standard Buttons toolbar to print the map.
3. Close the Weather Page window.
4. Click Anchorage on the map. Maximize the Weather Page window. Answer the following questions in the spaces provided.

a. What are the UV index and visibility in Anchorage?

on paper

b. Is snow predicted for Anchorage? If so, which day(s) might it snow?

on paper

c. What are the high and low temperatures in Anchorage for the last day of the forecast?

on paper

5. Click the Print button on the Standard Buttons toolbar to print the map.
6. Close the Weather Page window.

Part 4: ***Removing a Desktop Item from the Desktop***

1. Right-click an open area on the desktop and then click Properties on the shortcut menu.
2. Click the Desktop tab in the Display Properties dialog box.
3. Click the Customize Desktop button.
4. Click the Web tab in the Desktop Items dialog box.
5. Click the MSNBC Weather entry in the Web pages list box.
6. Click the Delete button in the Web sheet.
7. Click the Yes button in the Active Desktop Item dialog box.
8. Click the OK button in the Desktop Items dialog box.
9. Click the OK button in the Display Properties dialog box.
10. Hand in the printed weather map to your instructor.

3 Using the Address Toolbar to Search the Internet

Problem: You decide to use your newly acquired Internet searching skills to earn money during the summer vacation. You take a part-time job in the Information Technology department to assist an instructor doing research on searching techniques. You decide to use the Address toolbar as a means of searching the Internet.

Instructions: Use a computer to perform the following tasks and answer the questions.

Part 1: ***Unlocking the Taskbar and Adding the Address Toolbar to the Taskbar***

1. If necessary, launch Microsoft Windows XP and log on to the computer.
2. Right-click an open area of the taskbar.

In the Lab

3. Click Lock the Taskbar on the shortcut menu to unlock the taskbar.
4. Right-click an open area of the taskbar, point to Toolbars, and then click Address.
5. Double-click the dotted vertical bar to the left of the Address title.

Part 2: ***Locking the Taskbar***

1. Right-click an open area of the taskbar.
2. Click Lock the Taskbar on the shortcut menu to lock the taskbar (Figure 4-94).

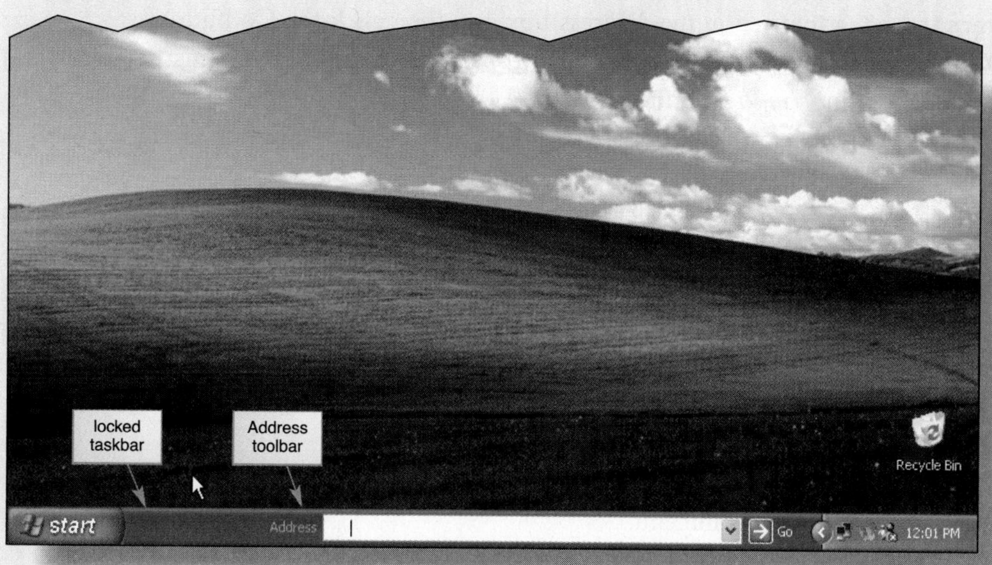

FIGURE 4-94

Part 3: ***Using the Address Toolbar to Display Folder Content***

1. Type `c:\windows` (or `c:\winnt`) in the Address box and then click the Go button.
   a. What folder displays on the desktop? ____________________
2. Type `my documents` in the Address box and then click the Go button.
   a. What folder displays on the desktop? ____________________
3. Type `my documents\my pictures` in the Address box and then click the Go button.
   a. What folder displays on the desktop? ____________________
   b. What object displays to the left of the Address toolbar? ____________________
4. Click the object.
   a. What displays above the object? ____________________
5. Close all open windows.

Part 4: ***Using the Address Toolbar to Display a Web Page***

1. Type `www.microsoft.com` in the Address box and then click the Go button. Print the Web page using the Print button.
2. Type `www.kellybluebook.com` in the Address box and then click the Go button. Print the Web page using the Print button.

(continued)

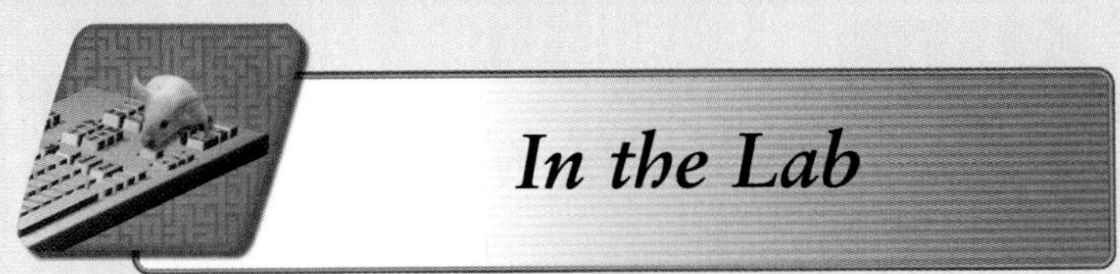

In the Lab

Using the Address Toolbar to Search the Internet *(continued)*

3. Type www.espn.com in the Address box and then click the Go button. Print the Web page using the Print button.
4. Type www.yahoo.com in the Address box and then click the Go button. Print the Web page using the Print button.

Part 5: Using the Address Toolbar to Search for Information

1. Type university of michigan in the Address box and then click the Go button.
2. A list of Web sites may display. If so, click an appropriate link to display the associated Web page.
3. Print the Web page using the Print button.
4. Type stem cell research in the Address box and then click the Go button. Print the Web page using the Print button.
5. A list of Web sites may display. If so, click an appropriate link to display the associated Web page.
6. Print the Web page using the Print button.
7. Type statue of liberty in the Address box and then click the Go button.
8. A list of Web sites may display. If so, click an appropriate link to display the associated Web page.
9. Print the Web page using the Print button.

Part 6: Removing the Address Toolbar on the Taskbar

1. Right-click an open area of the taskbar and then point to Toolbars on the shortcut menu.
2. Click Address on the Toolbars submenu.
3. Close all open windows.
4. Hand in the printed Web pages to your instructor.

4 Working with Folder Options

Problem: You recently took an operating system course at school. The instructor spent an entire hour demonstrating how to change folder options, but there was no time left at the end of the class to practice in the computer lab. You want to practice changing folder options on your home computer.

Instructions: Use a computer to perform the following tasks and answer the questions.

Part 1: Recording the Current Folder Options

1. If necessary, launch Microsoft Windows XP and log on to the computer.
2. Click the Start button and then click My Computer.
3. Click Tools on the My Computer menu bar and then click Folder Options.
4. In the space provided, record which option buttons in the Folder Options dialog box are selected.
show common folder (tasks) open each folder in same window. Underline icon titles consistent with my browser
5. Click the Cancel button in the Folder Options dialog box.
6. Click the Close button in the My Computer window.

In the Lab

Part 2: ***Displaying Icons on the Desktop***

1. Right-click an open area of the desktop and then click Properties.
2. Click the Desktop tab in the Display Properties dialog box.
3. Click the Customize Desktop button in the Display Properties dialog box.
4. Click My Documents and My Computers in the Desktop Items dialog box.
5. Click the OK button in the Desktop Items dialog box.
6. Click the OK button in the Display Properties dialog box.

Part 3: ***Turning on the Open Each Folder in Its Own Window Option***

1. Double-click the My Documents icon on the desktop.
2. Click Tools on the My Documents menu bar and then click Folder Options.
3. Click Open each folder in its own window in the Browse folders area.
4. Click the OK button in the Folder Options dialog box.

Part 4: ***Opening Each Folder in Its Own Window***

1. Double-click the My Pictures icon in the My Documents window.
   a. Does the My Pictures window open in its own window? yes
2. Click the Close button in the My Pictures window.
3. Click the Close button in the My Documents window.

Part 5: ***Turning on the Single-click to Open an Item (Point to Select) Option***

1. Double-click the My Documents icon on the desktop.
2. Click Tools on the My Documents menu bar and then click Folder Options.
3. Click Single-click to open an item (point to select) in the Click items as follows area.
4. If necessary, click Underline icon titles consistent with my browser in the Browse folders area.
5. Click the OK button in the Folder Options dialog box.
6. Click the Close button in the My Documents window.

Part 6: ***Opening a Folder by Single-Clicking***

1. Click the My Documents icon on the desktop.
2. Click the My Pictures icon in the My Documents window.
   a. Does the My Pictures window open in its own window? yes
3. Click the Close button in the My Pictures window.
4. Click the Close button in the My Documents window.

Part 7: ***Opening Multiple Windows on the Desktop***

1. Click the My Computer icon on the desktop, click the LOCAL DISK (C:) icon in the My Computer window, and then click the WINDOWS (or WINNT) icon in the LOCAL DISK (C:) window.
   a. How many windows are open on the desktop? 3 WINDOWS

(continued)

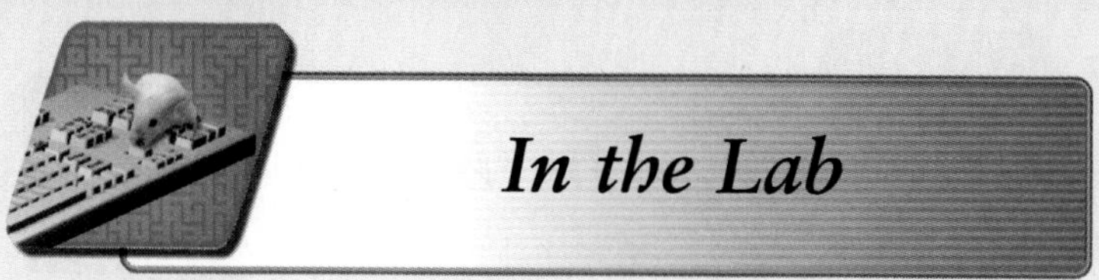

Working with Folder Options *(continued)*

2. Move and Resize the windows on the desktop to make the title bar of each window visible (Figure 4-95).

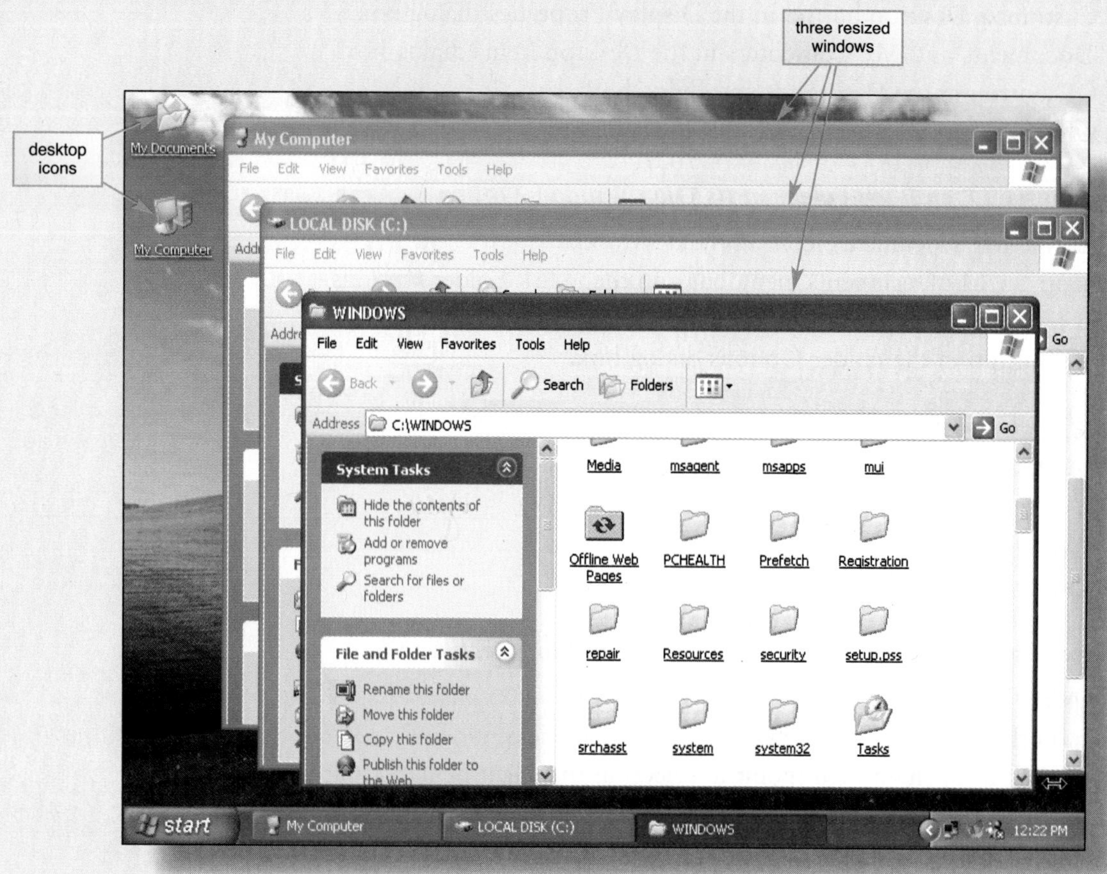

FIGURE 4-95

Part 8: Printing the Desktop

1. Click the PRINT SCREEN key on the keyboard to place an image of the desktop on the Clipboard, which is a temporary Windows storage area.
2. Click the Start button, point to All Programs on the Start menu, point to Accessories on the All Programs submenu, and then click Paint on the Accessories submenu.
3. Maximize the Untitled – Paint window.
4. Click Edit on the menu bar and then click Paste on the Edit menu to copy the image from the Clipboard to the Paint window.
5. Click File on the menu bar, click Print on the File menu, and then click the Print button in the Print dialog box to print the Paint document.
6. Click the Close button in the Untitled – Paint window and then click the No button in the Paint dialog box to quit the Paint program.

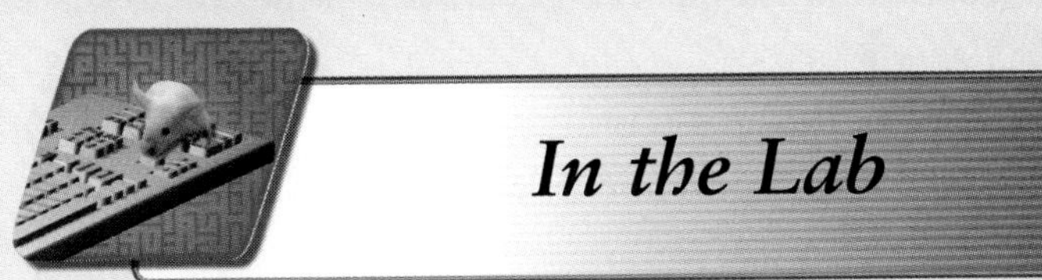

In the Lab

***Part 9:** Selecting and Copying Multiple Files*

1. Insert a formatted floppy disk in drive A.
2. Maximize the WINDOWS window.
3. Scroll down until the icons for the Prairie Wind, River Sumida, and Santa Fe Stucco files are visible.
4. Hold the CTRL key and then point to the Prairie Wind icon, River Sumida icon, and Santa Fe Stucco icon. Release the CTRL key.
5. Right-click the Prairie Wind icon, point to Send To on the shortcut menu, and then click 3½ Floppy (A:) on the Send To submenu.
6. Click the Close button in the WINDOWS window.
7. Click the Close button in the LOCAL DISK (C:) window.
8. Click the Close button in the My Computer window.
9. Remove the floppy disk from drive A.

***Part 10:** Removing the Icons on the Desktop*

1. Right-click an open area of the desktop and then click Properties on the shortcut menu.
2. Click the Desktop tab and then click the Customize Desktop button on the Desktop sheet.
3. Remove the check marks from the My Computer and My Documents check boxes in the Desktop Items dialog box.
4. Click the OK button in the Desktop Items dialog box.
5. Click the OK button in the Display Properties dialog box.

***Part 11:** Resetting the Folder Options*

1. Click the Start button, click My Computer, click Tools on the menu bar, and then click Folder Options on the Tools menu.
2. Click the option buttons in the Folder Options dialog box that correspond to the settings you recorded in Step 4 of Part 1 on page WIN 4.81 and then click the OK button.
3. Click the Close button in the My Computer window.
4. Hand in the printed Paint document illustrating the open windows on the desktop to your instructor.

5 Using the Desktop Properties Dialog Box

Problem: Your boss appoints you to design a desktop that all employees within your company will use. Experiment with all the options in the Display Properties dialog box until you have decided on the perfect desktop theme, background, desktop icons, Active Desktop items, screen saver, color scheme, and font size. Write down all settings. Make sure after this exercise that you reset the computer to its original settings before you made the changes.

Cases and Places

The difficulty of these case studies varies:
▶ are the least difficult; ▶▶ are more difficult; and ▶▶▶ are the most difficult.

1 ▶ Although several screen savers are included with Windows XP, many more are available at local retail computer stores for purchase, and various organizations give them away. In the past, the Anaheim Angels baseball team and Edison International teamed up to give away a free Angels screen saver. The screen saver contained player information, a season schedule, the dates and times of the next games, fun facts and sports trivia, energy-saving facts and tips, and links to the Angels Web page. Locate five free screen savers. In a brief report, describe each screen saver, state the source from which you can obtain the screen saver, and the contents of the screen saver.

2 ▶ In Project 3, you copied multiple files from a folder onto a floppy disk. You used the My Computer window and Windows Explorer and the cut and paste and right-drag methods to copy the files. In this project, you copied multiple files after turning on the Single-click to open an item (point to select) and the Underline icon titles consistent with my browser options. Turn on these folder options and experiment with file copying. Prepare a brief report comparing the process of copying files before and after selecting these folder options. In your opinion, do these folder options make it easier to copy files?

3 ▶▶ Colors, patterns, and the arrangement of the workplace can have a significant effect on worker productivity. These factors might draw attention to some objects, de-emphasize others, speed the completion of tasks, or even promote desirable moods and attitudes. Visit the Internet, a library, or other research facility to find out how colors, patterns, and arrangements can impact a work environment. Using what you have learned, together with the concepts and techniques presented in this project, create the Windows XP desktop that you think would help you work most efficiently. Write a brief report describing your desktop and explaining why you feel it would enhance your productivity.

4 ▶▶ Microsoft's Beta Testing Program allows computer users to preview copies of Windows XP Professional, called beta copies, before releasing the operating system for sale to the public. Using the Internet, Windows Help and Support, computer articles, and your own opinions, find out as much information as you can about Microsoft's Beta Testing Program and then write a brief report stating your findings.

5 ▶▶▶ The taskbar is a central part of the Windows XP desktop. As such, it is important to organize the taskbar and the toolbars on the taskbar to best fit your individual needs. Interview a friend, relative, teacher, businessperson, or other individual to determine which activities he or she performs from his or her desktop. Based on your interview, design the taskbar and toolbars to meet the individual's needs and customize the taskbar. Write a brief report summarizing your experience.

Cases and Places

6 ▶▶▶ In this project, you typed a keyword or phrase in the Address toolbar to search for information on the Internet. In addition, you can perform advanced searches using compound search criteria in which the words, AND, OR, NOT, and NEAR, control how individual keywords are used. You also can specify which keywords are more important and cause multiple keywords to be considered as a single search item. Using the Internet, Windows Help and Support, computer articles, and your own opinions, find out as much information as you can about advanced searches and then summarize your findings in a brief report.

7 ▶▶▶ A key component of Windows XP is the capability of customizing the desktop or computer screen to suit the user. Do other operating systems offer the same capability? Visit a computer vendor and try another operating system. Find out what changes you can make to the computer screen and how these alterations are accomplished. Prepare a brief report comparing the operating system you tried to Windows XP. Contrast the general look of the screens, the ways they are customized, and their potential effects on users. Finally, on the basis of screen appearance alone, tell which operating system you prefer and why.

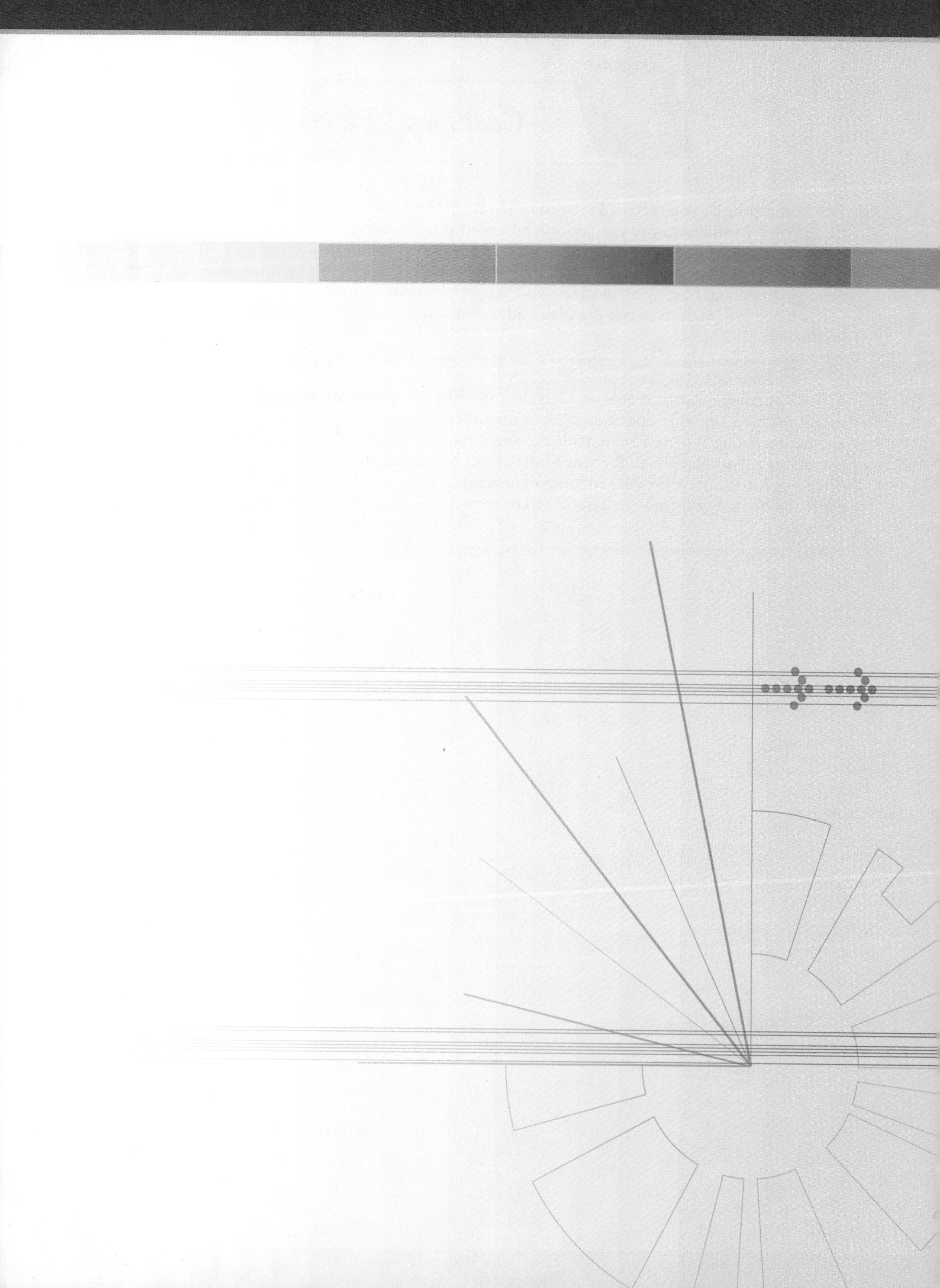

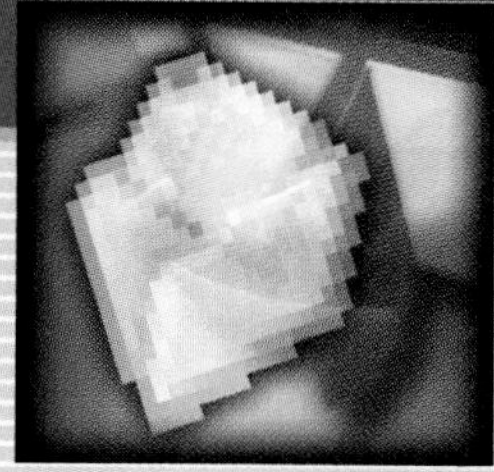

Microsoft Windows XP

PROJECT

Customizing Your Computer Using Control Panel

OBJECTIVES

You will have mastered the material in this project when you can:

- Open the Control Panel window
- Switch to Classic view
- Adjust the keyboard repeat delay, keyboard repeat rate, and cursor blink rate
- Change the mouse button configuration and mouse pointer scheme
- Adjust the double-click speed and pointer speed and display pointer trails
- Turn on ClickLock and Snap To
- Turn on accessibility features
- Turn on MouseKeys and High Contrast
- Explain account privileges and view account information
- Change the date, time, and time zone
- View the date and time format
- Add and remove a hardware device
- Add and remove a printer
- Solve a hardware problem using a troubleshooter
- View hardware properties
- Add and remove a program

Saving Time

Worth Its Weight In Gold

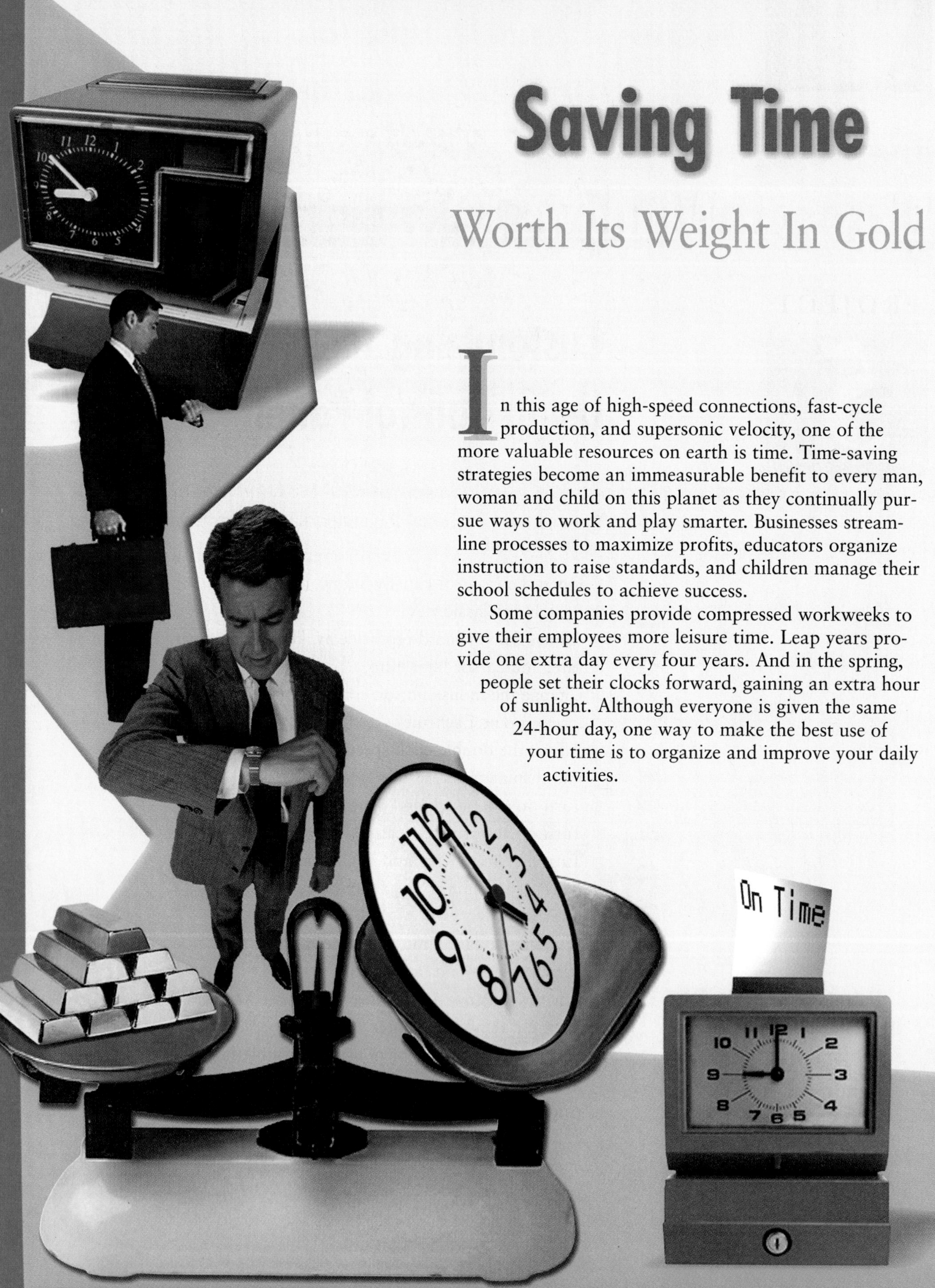

In this age of high-speed connections, fast-cycle production, and supersonic velocity, one of the more valuable resources on earth is time. Time-saving strategies become an immeasurable benefit to every man, woman and child on this planet as they continually pursue ways to work and play smarter. Businesses streamline processes to maximize profits, educators organize instruction to raise standards, and children manage their school schedules to achieve success.

Some companies provide compressed workweeks to give their employees more leisure time. Leap years provide one extra day every four years. And in the spring, people set their clocks forward, gaining an extra hour of sunlight. Although everyone is given the same 24-hour day, one way to make the best use of your time is to organize and improve your daily activities.

Technology offers valuable time-saving resources to customize your environment. By linking people electronically, high-tech industries have found they can provide services and products to help individuals better manage their lives. For example, if you are looking for a new job, many online employment resources such as Monster can help you post your resume and search job listings. At these Web sites, you can create custom search agents that automatically send you notification via e-mail about job opportunities that match your criteria.

You may need a new car to help you get to your job. Every automobile manufacturer now has a presence on the Web. You can view the exteriors and interiors of particular models, watch videos, choose options, examine performance statistics, and check sample total costs and monthly payments. Once you decide on an ideal vehicle, Web sites such as Edmunds Car Buying Guide provide new and used car pricing so you can comparison shop before you buy. To save you more time, you can log on to the nearest virtual or actual car lot. Most dealers have Web sites, so you can check inventory without setting foot in a showroom.

If you own a home or intend to build or remodel one, home improvement software packages allow you to design a new home, deck, kitchen, or bathroom and see three-dimensional views of your creations. By planting virtual perennials and ornamental grasses and installing sprinklers, lights, and a brick walkway, you can visualize your landscaping dreams.

The ability to customize can dramatically streamline your life. As you explore the concepts in this textbook, you will learn that Windows XP offers a myriad of opportunities to make your desktop more efficient. You can resize and tile windows, copy, rename, and delete files and folders, create shortcuts, customize the taskbar, and arrange icons. In Project 5, you will use the Control Panel to customize the keyboard, mouse, and desktop, add a printer, and view hardware properties. These changes allow you to tailor your computer working conditions to your liking.

Imagine the return on being able to gain just a couple hours a day using time wisely. So, plan your day, customize your environment, increase your productivity, and find that saving time is worth its weight in gold.

Microsoft Windows XP

Customizing Your Computer Using Control Panel

PROJECT

CASE PERSPECTIVE

Your parents gave you a new computer and subscriptions to a few computer magazines for Christmas. Since then, you have spent most of your time reading magazines, learning to communicate with Windows XP Professional, launching programs and creating documents, exploring Windows Help and Support, learning file and desktop management, and working on and modifying the desktop.

After reading several magazine articles about customizing a computer, you decide to customize your computer using the Control Panel. You purchase a camera, printer, and tax preparation program. You would like to learn how to add the hardware devices and install the software program. Your goal is to customize the Windows XP environment using the Control Panel and to add the new hardware and software.

Introduction

In Project 4, you modified desktop properties by creating a new desktop theme, personalizing the taskbar, and customizing folder options. The desktop and the items on the desktop are objects. Every object in Windows XP has properties, which describe the object. In Project 4, you customized the manner in which you interacted with the Windows XP environment by changing the properties of objects.

The **Control Panel window** contains categories that allow you to change the properties of an object and thus customize the Windows XP environment. In Project 5, you will use Control Panel to customize the mouse, keyboard, date and time, and time zone. In addition, you will learn how to add a new hardware device to the computer, add a software program, make the computer more usable for physically challenged people, add a printer to the computer, use a troubleshooter to solve a hardware problem, and view the hardware properties of the hardware devices attached to the computer.

You will not be able to perform some tasks in this project unless you have administrative privileges. **Administrative privileges** are granted to all users who have an Administrator account and temporarily can be given to other users, when they obtain permission. If you are working on a computer that is not connected to a network (a standalone computer), the default user account has administrative privileges. The three tasks that require administrative privileges in this project are: changing the date and time, adding new hardware, and adding a software program. Each task that requires administrative privileges is noted in the paragraph above the corresponding steps. In each case, if you do not have administrative privileges, you should read the steps instead of performing them.

The Control Panel Window

To use the Control Panel to change an object's properties, click the Start button, click Control Panel on the Start menu, and then click a category in the Control Panel window. Perform the following steps to open the Control Panel window and view the categories in the window.

To Open the Control Panel Window

1 Click the Start button and then point to Control Panel on the Start menu.

The Start menu and highlighted Control Panel command display (Figure 5-1).

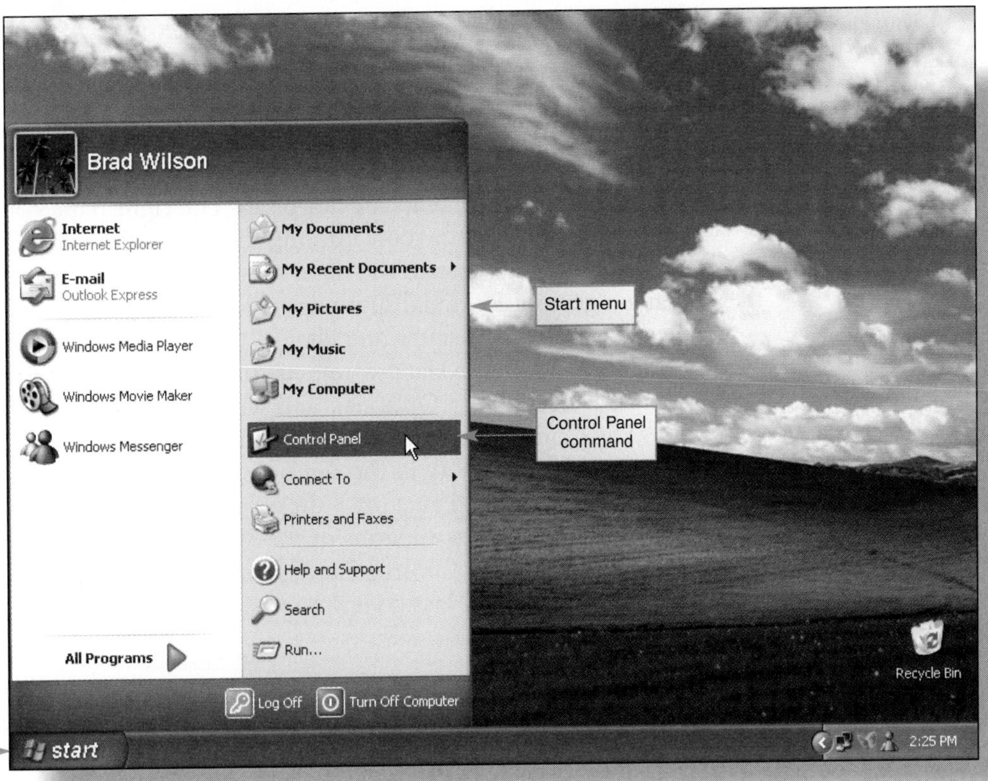

FIGURE 5-1

2 **Click Control Panel.**

The Control Panel window displays (Figure 5-2).

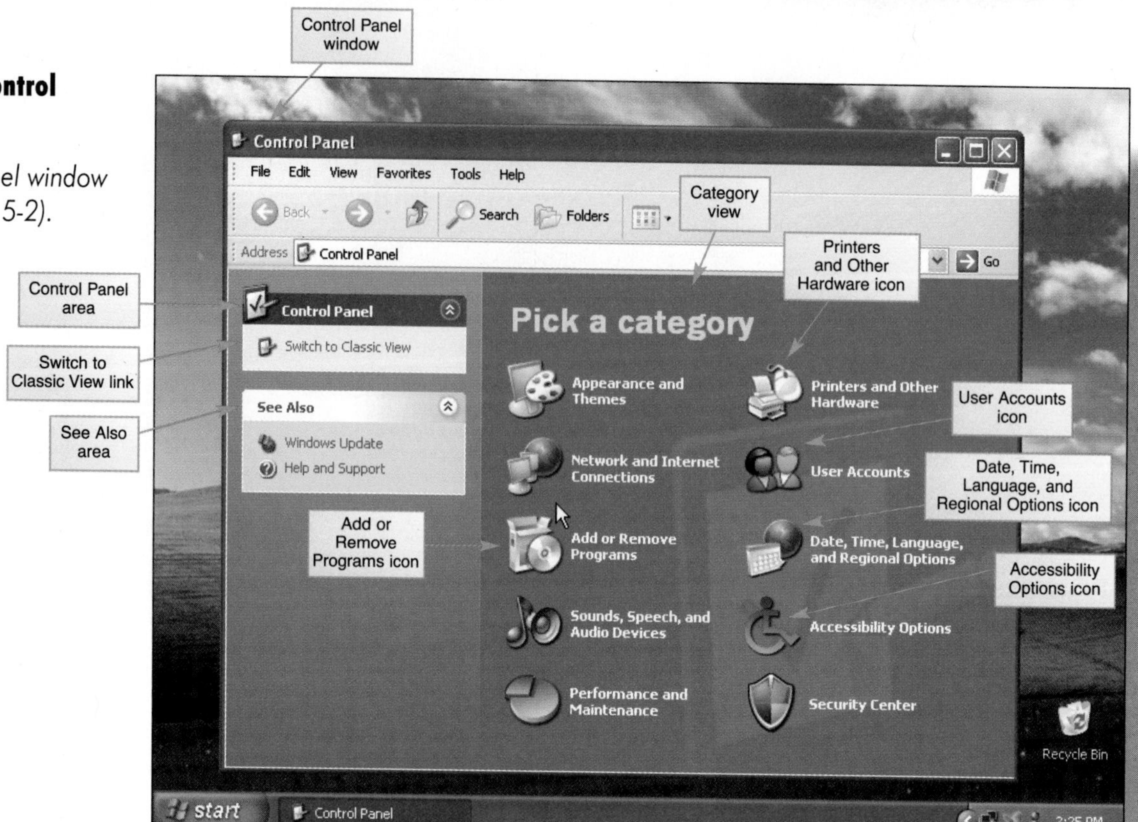

FIGURE 5-2

The Control Panel window is divided into two panes. The Control Panel and See Also areas display in the left pane. The right pane contains ten categories, each identified by a unique icon. Among the categories in the Control Panel window are the categories to change the date, time, language, and regional settings (Date, Time, Language, and Regional Options); add or remove a program (Add or Remove Programs); add a printer and change the properties of the mouse and keyboard (Printers and Other Hardware); customize the computer for physically challenged people (Accessibility Options); and work with user accounts (User Accounts).

The Control Panel window is said to display in **Category view** because of the ten categories that display in the right pane of the window. The Switch to Classic View link in the Control Panel area allows you to display the popular **Classic view** that was common in previous versions of the Windows operating system. The Classic view displays individual Control Panel icons instead of categories. Perform the following steps to switch to Classic view and back to Category view.

Steps To Switch to Classic View and Back to Category View

1 Click Switch to Classic View in the Control Panel area. Maximize the Control Panel window.

The Switch to Category View link replaces the Switch to Classic View link in the Control Panel area and thirty-one icons display in the right pane of the maximized Control Panel window (Figure 5-3). These icons are referred to as Control Panel icons.

2 Click Switch to Category View. Restore the Control Panel window.

The Switch to Classic View link replaces the Switch to Category View link in the restored Control Panel area of the Control Panel window and displays as previously shown in Figure 5-2.

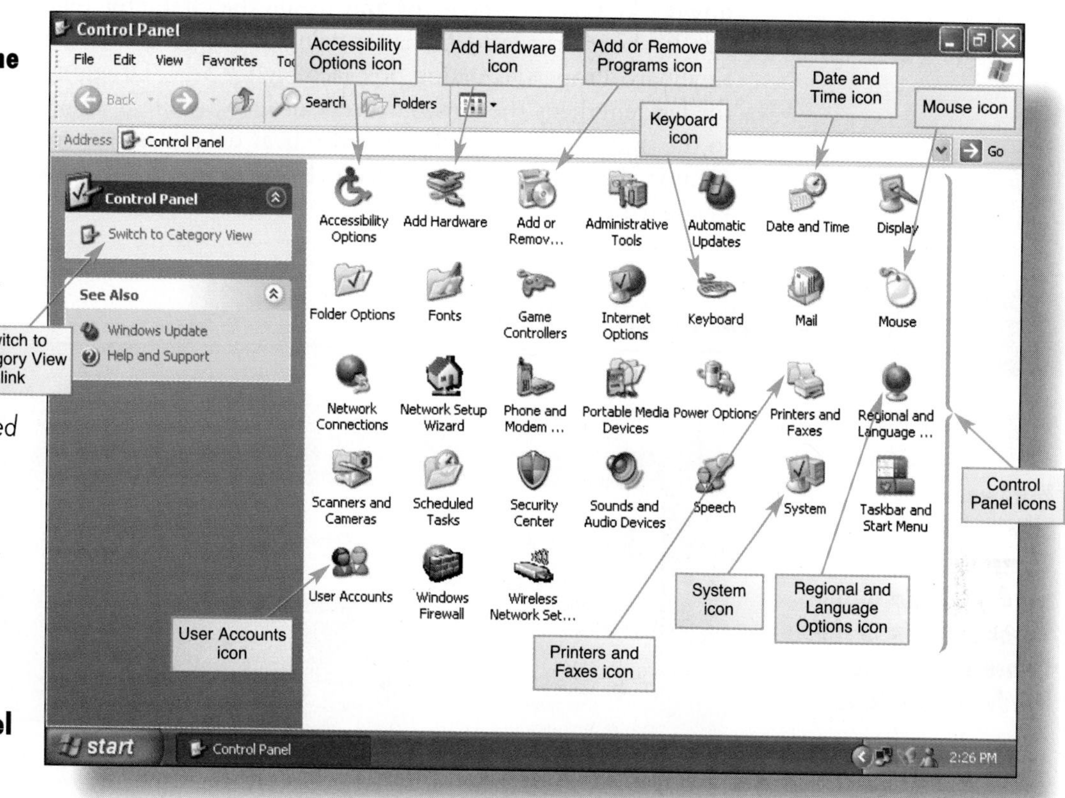

FIGURE 5-3

Among the Control Panel icons shown in Figure 5-3 are the icons to change the properties of the keyboard (Keyboard), the mouse (Mouse), and the date and time (Date and Time). Other icons allow you to add or remove hardware (Add Hardware), add or remove a program (Add or Remove Programs), work with printers and faxes (Printers and Faxes), customize the computer for physically challenged people (Accessibility Options), change regional settings (Regional and Language Options), view hardware properties (System), and work with user accounts (User Accounts).

Customizing

Computer users learn to customize their computers in a variety of ways. Some customize their computers based upon their prior use of a computer, a magazine article they read, or the recommendation of a friend. The purpose of Control Panel is to allow computer users to customize their computers based on their needs and preferences.

Customizing the Keyboard

Windows XP allows you to customize the way you use the keyboard by changing its properties. Among the properties you can change are the keyboard repeat delay, keyboard repeat rate, and cursor (or insertion point) blink rate. Clicking the Printers and Other Hardware category in the Control Panel window in Figure 5-2 and then clicking the Keyboard icon displays the Keyboard Properties dialog box that allows you to change these properties.

Adjusting the Keyboard Repeat Delay

The **keyboard repeat delay** is the amount of time that elapses between holding down a key on the keyboard and seeing the character repeated across the screen. The keyboard repeat delay is set using the Repeat delay slider and text box in the Keyboard Properties dialog box (see Figure 5-5). Dragging the Repeat delay slider to the left lengthens the keyboard repeat delay, while dragging the Repeat delay slider to the right shortens the keyboard repeat delay. Use the text box to test the adjustment in the keyboard repeat delay. Perform the following steps to adjust the keyboard repeat delay.

To Adjust the Keyboard Repeat Delay

1 Click the Printers and Other Hardware icon in the Control Panel window. Point to the Keyboard icon in the Printers and Other Hardware window.

The Printers and Other Hardware window opens in the same window as the Control Panel window displays (Figure 5-4). The contents of the left panel change and six Control Panel icons, including the Mouse and Keyboard icons, display in the or pick a Control Panel icon area in the right pane. The Keyboard icon is selected.

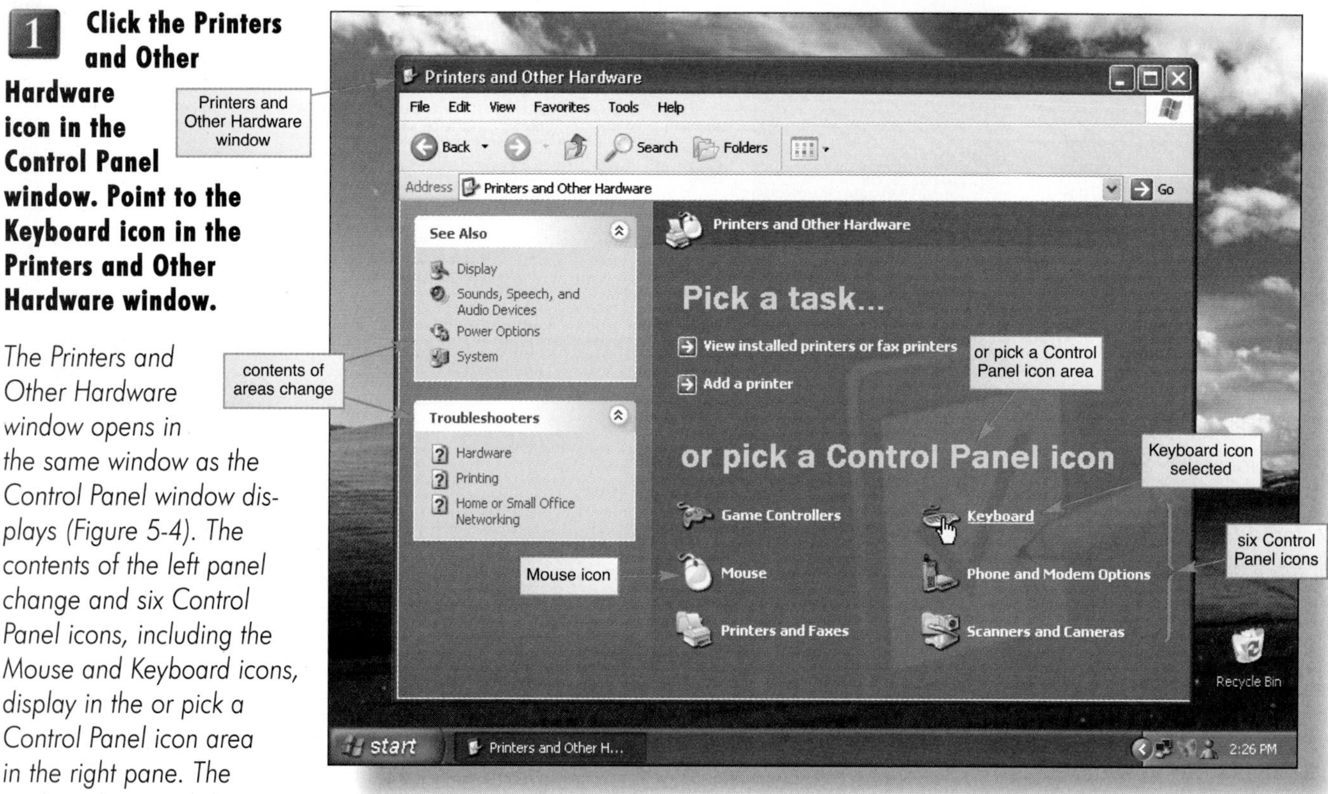

FIGURE 5-4

2 Click the Keyboard icon. Point to the Repeat delay slider in the Character repeat area in the Keyboard Properties dialog box.

The Keyboard Properties dialog box and Speed sheet display (Figure 5-5). The Character repeat area contains the Repeat delay slide and slider and text box.

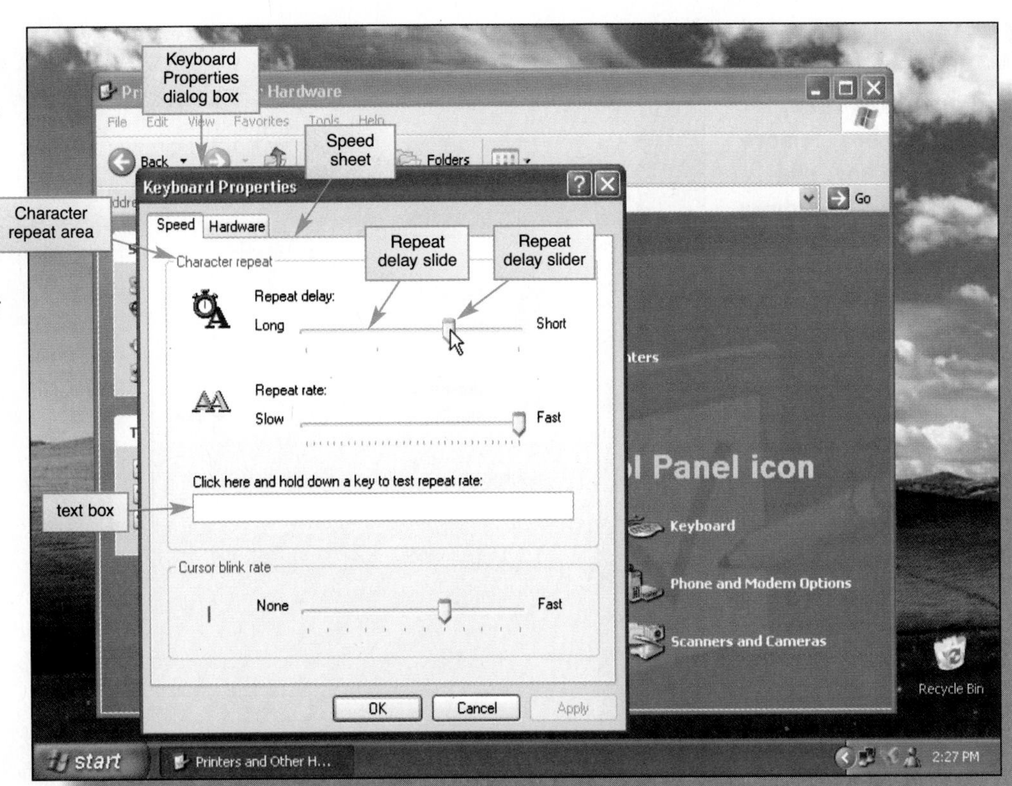

FIGURE 5-5

3 Drag the Repeat delay slider to the left end of the slide, click the text box, and then press and hold down the lowercase X key on the keyboard to test the repeat delay.

The slider is located at the left end of the Repeat delay slide (Figure 5-6). The first x character displays in the text box. After a long delay, the remaining x's display for as long as you hold down the X key.

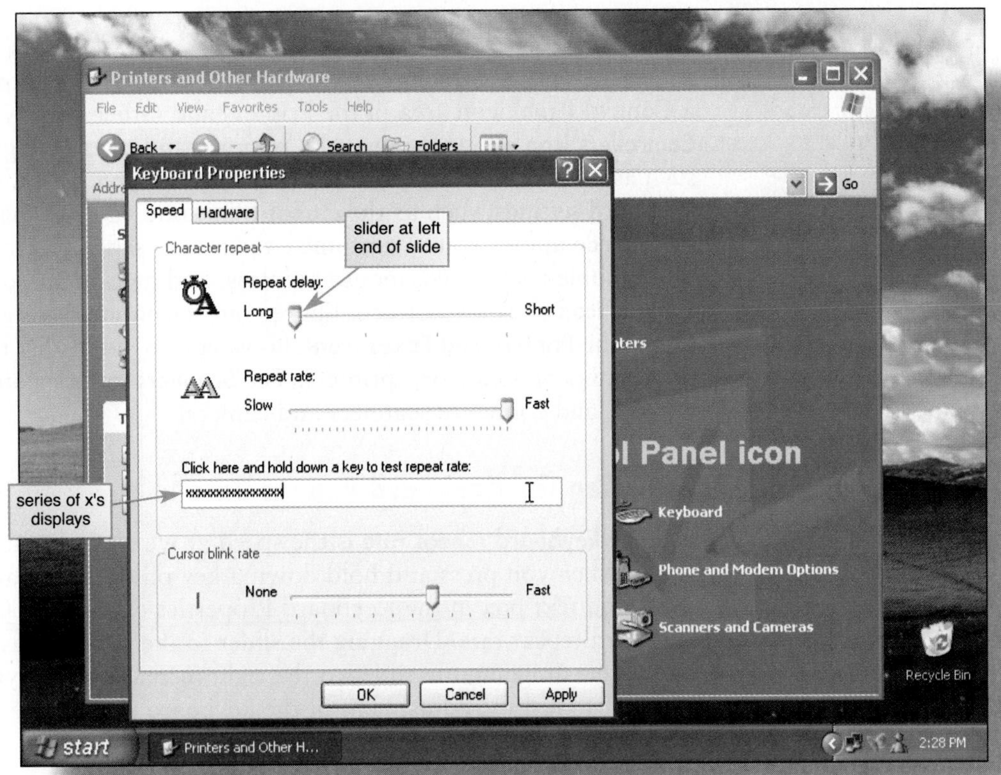

FIGURE 5-6

4 **Drag the Repeat delay slider to the right end of the slide, click the text box, remove the x's in the box, and then press and hold down the X key to test the repeat delay.**

The slider is located at the right end of the Repeat delay slide (Figure 5-7). The first x character displays in the text box. After a short delay, the remaining x's display for as long as you hold down the X key.

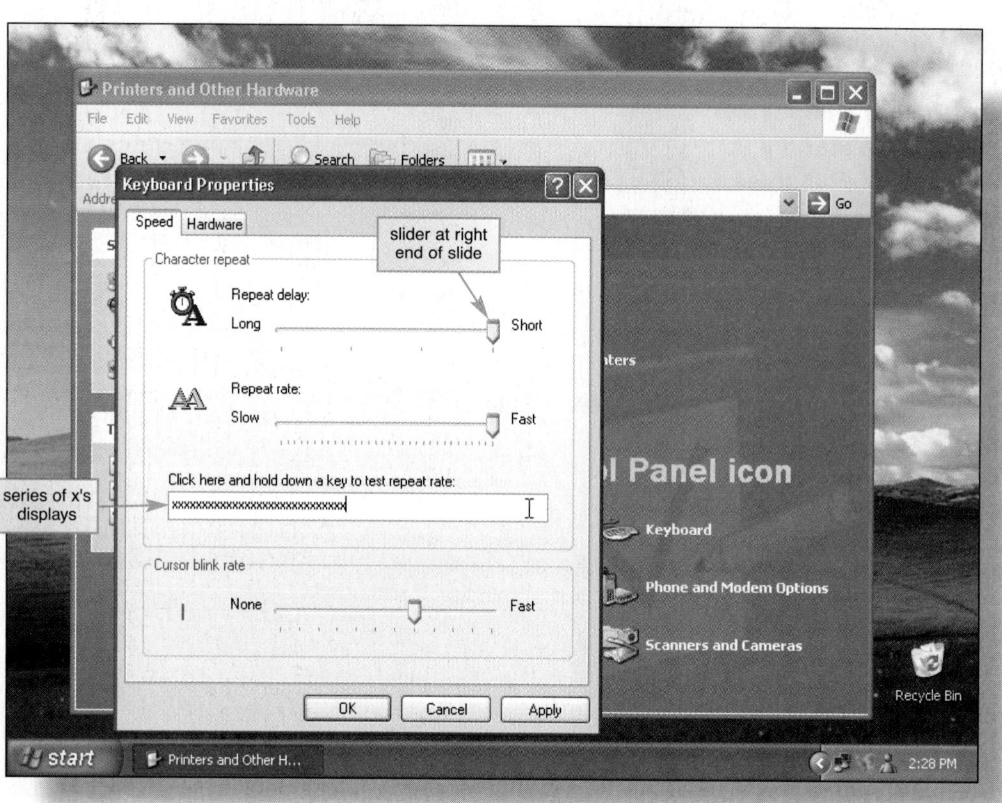

FIGURE 5-7

5 **Experiment with the Repeat delay slider until you find the best keyboard repeat delay for you.**

Other Ways

1. Click Switch to Classic View, double-click Keyboard icon, drag Repeat delay slider
2. Click Start button, click Help and Support, click Index button, type `keyboards`, double-click adjusting repeat rate and repeat delay, click Keyboard link, drag Repeat delay slider

In Figure 5-4 on page WIN 5.08, six Control Panel icons display in the or pick a Control Panel icon area in the Printers and Other Hardware window. The **Game Controllers icon** allows you to add, remove, and configure game controller hardware such as gamepads and joysticks. The **Keyboard icon** allows you to customize the keyboard settings, such as the cursor blink rate and the character repeat rate. The **Mouse icon** allows you to customize the mouse settings, such as the button configuration, double-click speed, mouse pointers, and motion speed. The **Phone and Modem Options icon** allows you to configure your telephone dialing rules and modem settings. The **Printers and Faxes icon** allows you to view a list of installed printers and fax printers and add new printers. The **Scanners and Cameras icon** allows you to add, remove, and configure scanners and cameras.

Adjusting the Keyboard Repeat Rate

The **keyboard repeat rate** is the speed at which a character repeats across the screen when you press and hold down a key on the keyboard. Use the Repeat rate slider and text box in the Keyboard Properties dialog box (see Figure 5-8) to set the keyboard repeat rate. Dragging the slider to the left decreases the keyboard repeat rate, while dragging the slider to the right increases the keyboard repeat rate. Use the text box to test the adjustment of the keyboard repeat rate. Perform the following steps to adjust the keyboard repeat rate.

Steps To Adjust the Keyboard Repeat Rate

1 Point to the Repeat rate slider in the Character repeat area.

The Repeat rate slide and slider display in the Character repeat area (Figure 5-8). The x's remain in the text box from adjusting the keyboard repeat delay.

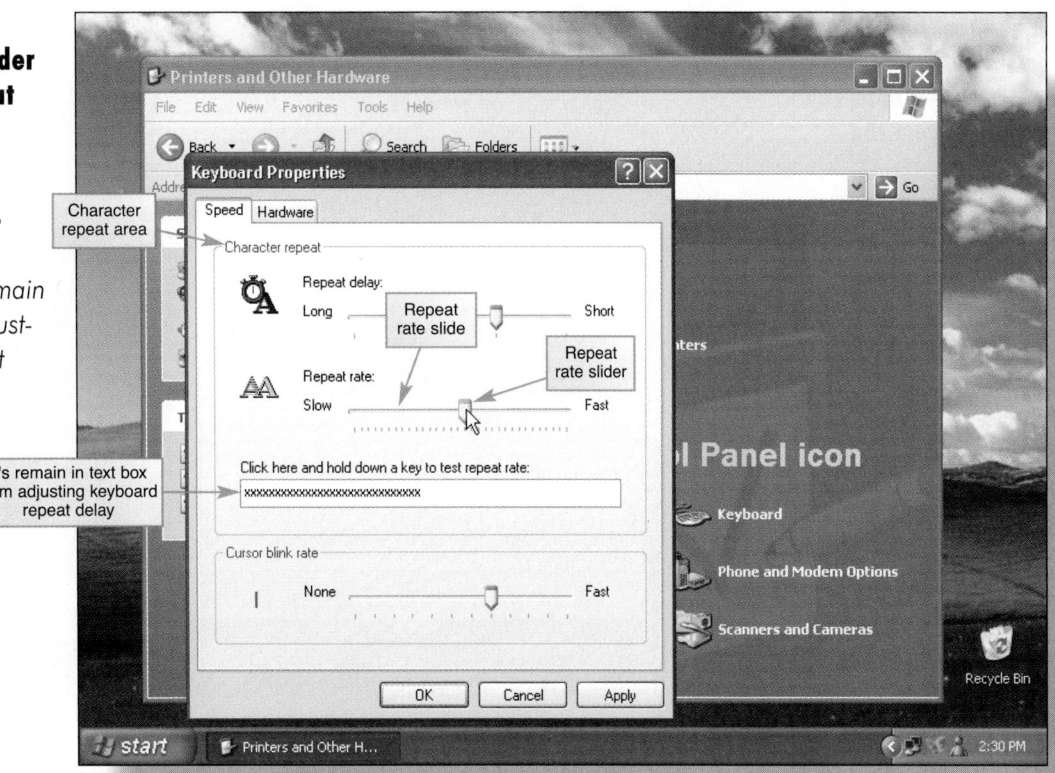

FIGURE 5-8

2 Drag the Repeat rate slider to the left end of the slide, click the text box, remove the x's, and then press and hold down the Z key to test the repeat rate.

The Repeat rate slider is located at the left end of the Repeat rate slide (Figure 5-9). The z character repeats slowly across the text box for as long as you hold down the Z key.

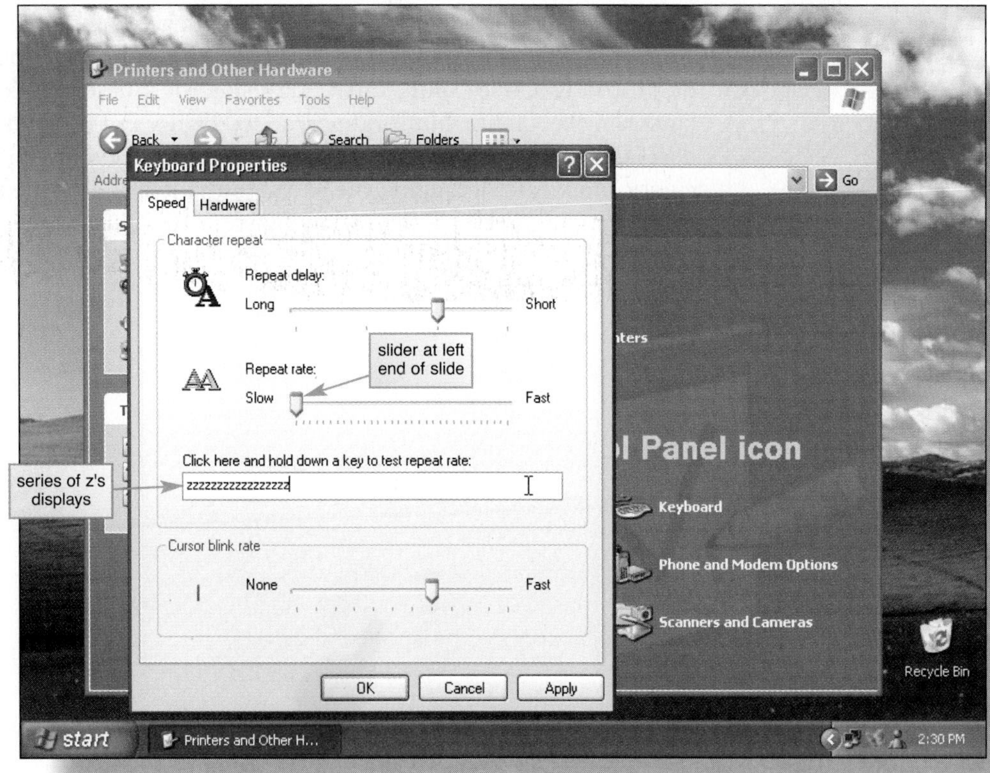

FIGURE 5-9

3 Drag the Repeat rate slider to the right end of the slide, click the text box, remove the z's in the box, and then press and hold down the Z key to test the repeat rate.

The Repeat rate slider is located at the right end of the Repeat rate slide and the z character repeats quickly across the text box for as long as you hold down the Z key (Figure 5-10).

4 Experiment with the Repeat rate slider until you find the best keyboard repeat rate for you.

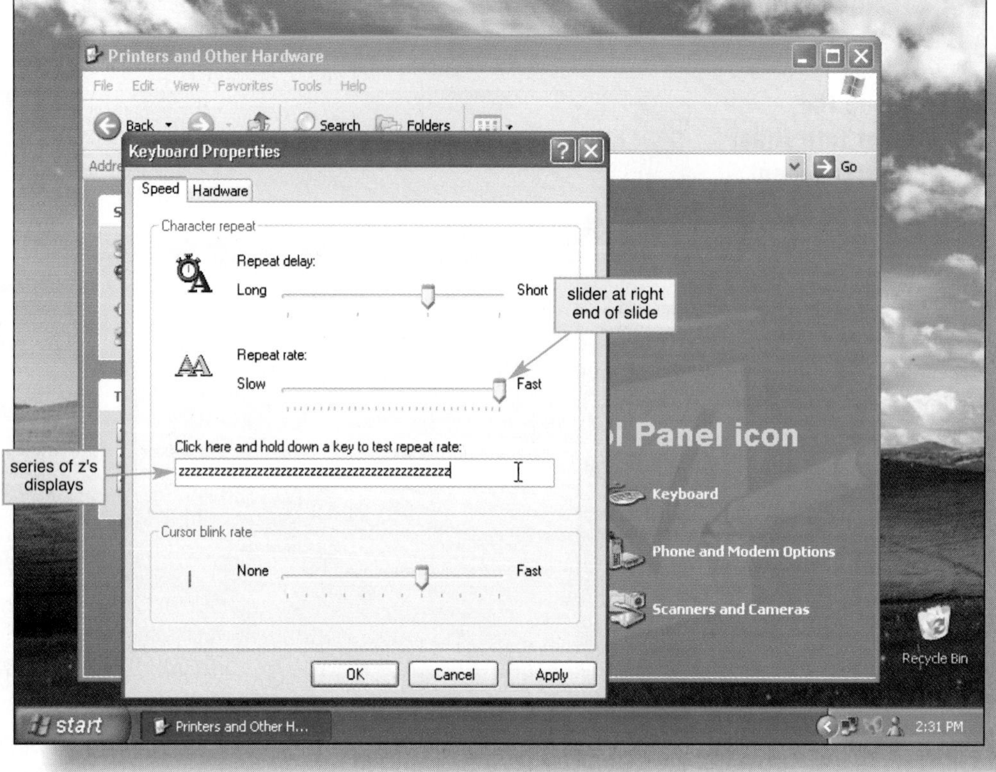

FIGURE 5-10

Other Ways

1. Click Switch to Classic View, double-click Keyboard icon, drag Repeat rate slider
2. Click Start button, click Help and Support, click Index button, type `keyboards`, double-click adjusting repeat rate and repeat delay, click Keyboard link, drag Repeat delay slider

Adjusting the Cursor Blink Rate

The **cursor blink rate** is the speed at which the cursor (insertion point) blinks. Adjusting the cursor blink rate can make it easier to see the insertion point on the desktop. The cursor blink rate is set using the Cursor blink rate slider and a blinking cursor in the Cursor blink rate area (see Figure 5-11). Dragging the slider to the left decreases the cursor blink rate, while dragging the slider to the right increases the cursor blink rate. Dragging the slider to the left end of the slide stops the cursor from blinking. Perform the following steps to adjust the cursor blink rate.

To Adjust the Cursor Blink Rate

1 Point to the Cursor blink rate slider in the Cursor blink rate area.

The Cursor blink rate slide and slider display in the Cursor blink rate area (Figure 5-11). The blinking cursor displays to the left of the Cursor blink rate slide.

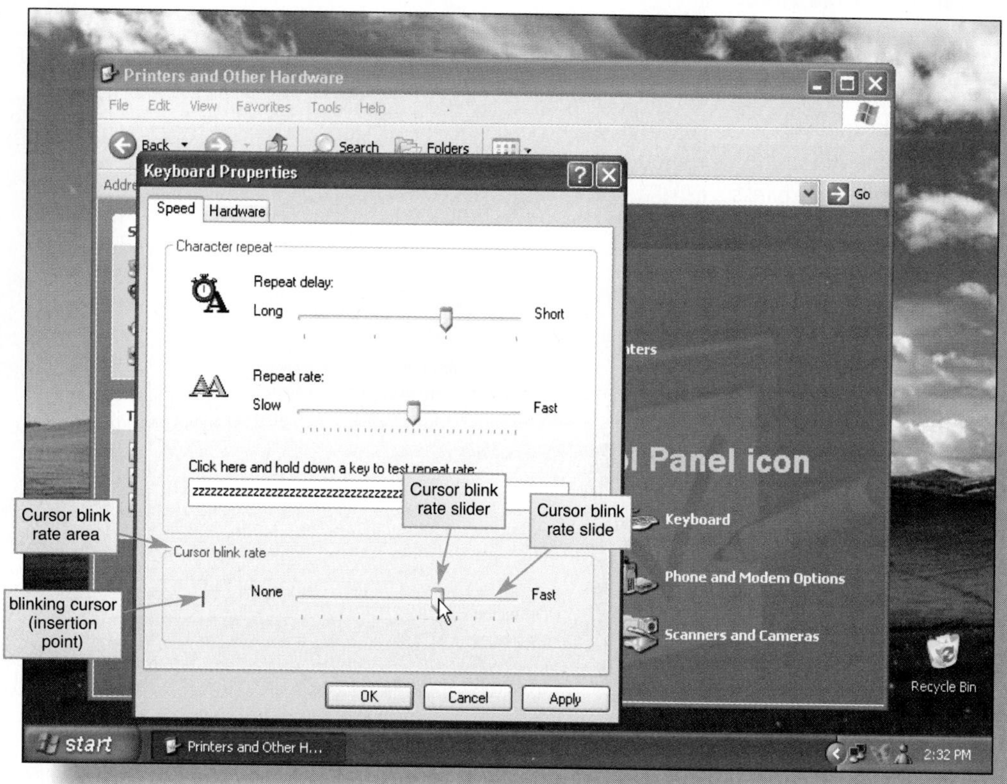

FIGURE 5-11

2 Drag the Cursor blink rate slider to the left along the slide until the slider displays in the position shown in Figure 5-12.

The slider is located at the second setting from the left end of the Cursor blink rate slide (Figure 5-12). The blinking cursor to the left of the Cursor blink rate slide blinks slowly. Moving the slider to the left end of the slide (first setting) stops the cursor's blinking.

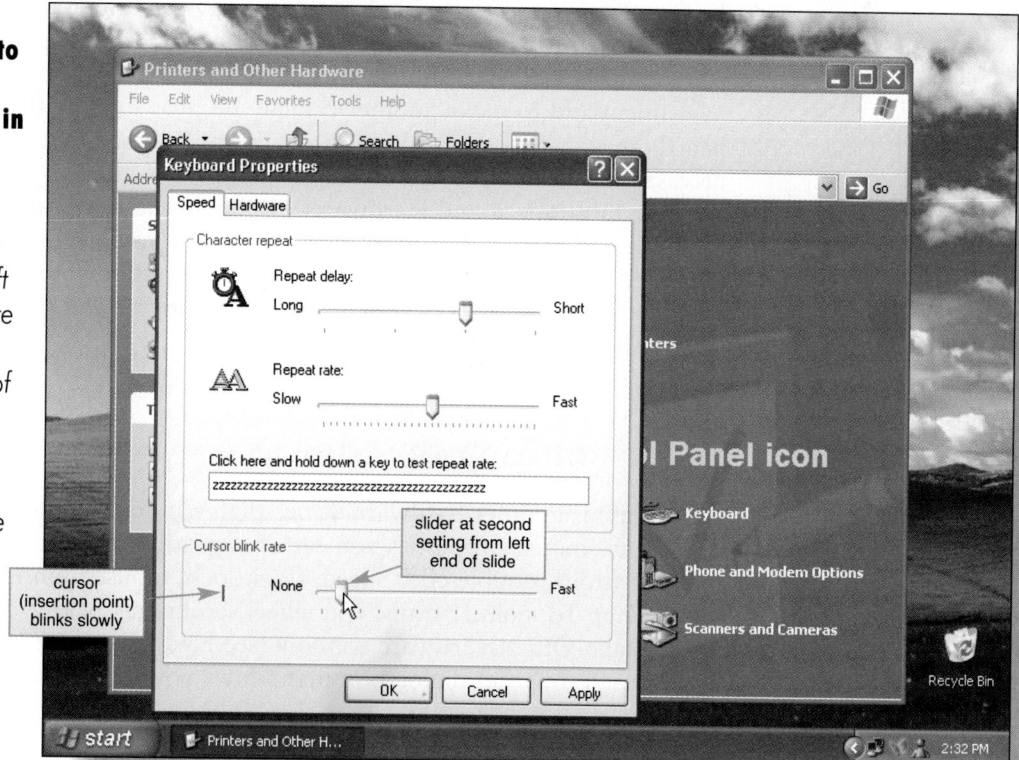

FIGURE 5-12

3 Drag the Cursor blink rate slider to the right end of the slide.

The slider is located at the right end of the Cursor blink rate slide (Figure 5-13). The cursor to the left of the Cursor blink rate slide blinks rapidly.

4 Experiment with the Cursor blink rate slider until you find the best cursor blink rate for you.

5 Click the OK button in the Keyboard Properties dialog box.

The Keyboard Properties dialog box closes.

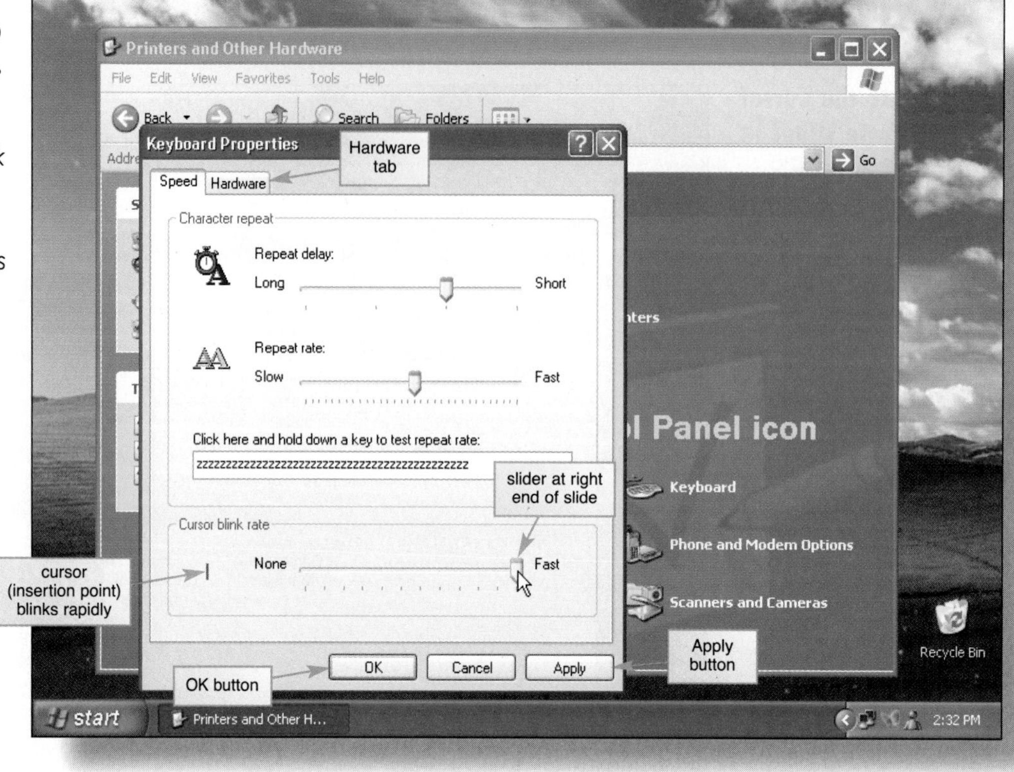

FIGURE 5-13

Other Ways

1. Click Switch to Classic View, double-click Keyboard icon, drag Cursor blink rate slider
2. Click Start button, click Help and Support, click Index button, type `keyboards`, double-click adjusting cursor blink rate, click Keyboard link, drag Cursor blink rate slider

The Keyboard Properties dialog box shown in Figure 5-13 contains the Apply button. Usually, when you click the Apply button, the requested adjustment takes place and the dialog box remains open. This allows you to see the effect of the adjustment and to make another change. Because moving the slider adjusts the keyboard repeat rate, keyboard repeat delay, and cursor blink rate immediately, it is not necessary to use the Apply button.

Two tabs (Speed and Hardware) display in the Keyboard Properties dialog box. As illustrated earlier, the **Speed sheet** allows you to change the keyboard repeat delay, keyboard repeat rate, and cursor blink rate. The **Hardware sheet** allows you to view the keyboard devices attached to the computer and their properties and to troubleshoot these devices.

Customizing the Mouse

The mouse is another hardware device that Windows XP allows you to customize. Among the mouse properties you can change are the functions of the left and right mouse buttons, double-click speed, ClickLock, mouse pointer scheme, mouse pointer speed, Snap To, pointer trails, and wheel scrolling. Clicking the Mouse icon in the Printers and Other Hardware window (see Figure 5-4 on page WIN 5.08) displays the Mouse Properties dialog box that allows you to change these properties.

Changing the Button Configuration

As mentioned in Project 1, the mouse contains a primary and a secondary mouse button. If you are right-handed, the primary mouse button typically is the left mouse button and the secondary mouse button typically is the right mouse button. This **Right-handed button configuration** assigns the mouse operations of selecting and dragging to the left mouse button and the mouse operations of right-clicking and right-dragging to the right mouse button.

If you are left-handed, you may find it more convenient to use the Left-handed button configuration. The **Left-handed button configuration** assigns the selecting and dragging operations to the right mouse button and the right-clicking and right-dragging operations to the left mouse button.

If you are using the Microsoft IntelliMouse™ (see Figures 1-4 and 1-5 on page WIN 1.11), a wheel and wheel button are positioned between the primary and secondary mouse buttons. Both the Right-handed button configuration and Left-handed button configuration are valid with the IntelliMouse. In addition, the wheel scrolling feature allows you to set the number of lines scrolled each time you move the mouse wheel one notch. The procedures that follow assume an IntelliMouse is attached to the computer. If an IntelliMouse mouse is not attached to the computer, the instructions may be slightly different.

Perform the following steps to change the button configuration to the Left-handed configuration and then change the button configuration back to the Right-handed configuration.

Steps To Change the Mouse Button Configuration

1 Click the Mouse icon in the Printers and Other Hardware window. Point to Switch primary and secondary buttons.

The Mouse Properties dialog box and Buttons sheet display (Figure 5-14). A check mark does not display in the Switch primary and secondary buttons check box and the instructions to select the check box display below the check box. The highlighted left mouse button in the mouse illustration indicates the left mouse button is the primary button and the Right-handed configuration is being used.

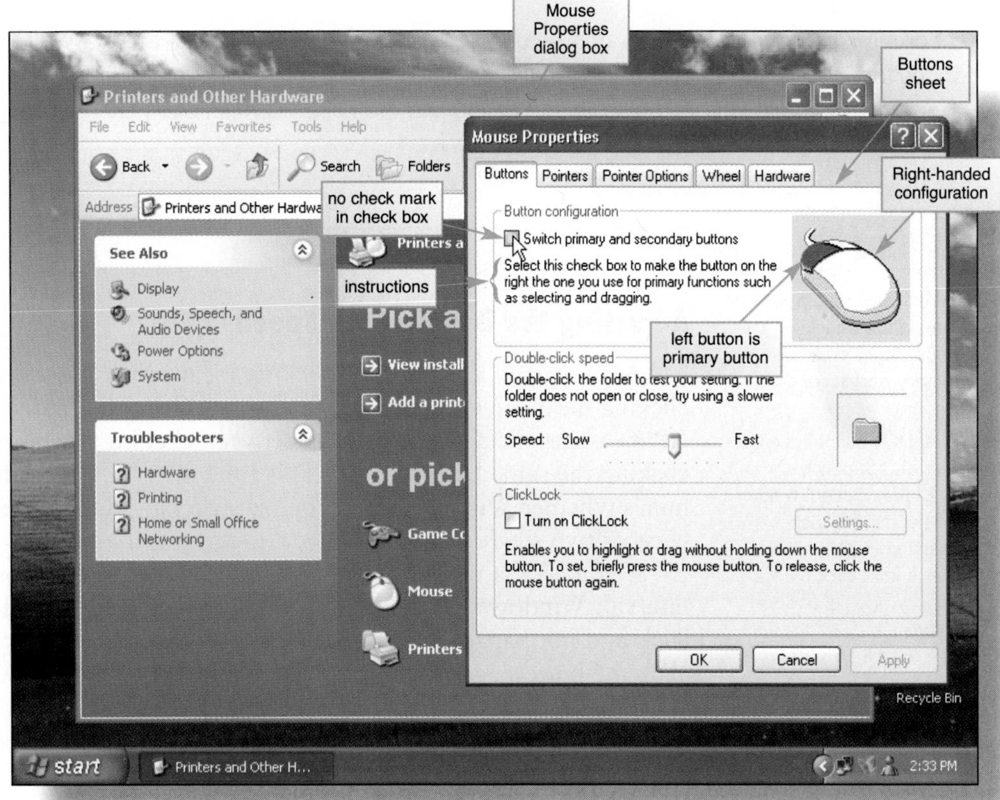

FIGURE 5-14

2 Click Switch primary and secondary buttons.

A check mark displays in the Switch primary and secondary buttons check box, the primary button in the mouse illustration changes to the right mouse button, the mouse operations associated with the left and right buttons switch, and the button configuration changes to the Left-handed configuration (Figure 5-15).

3 Experiment with the left and right mouse buttons until you are comfortable with the Left-handed configuration.

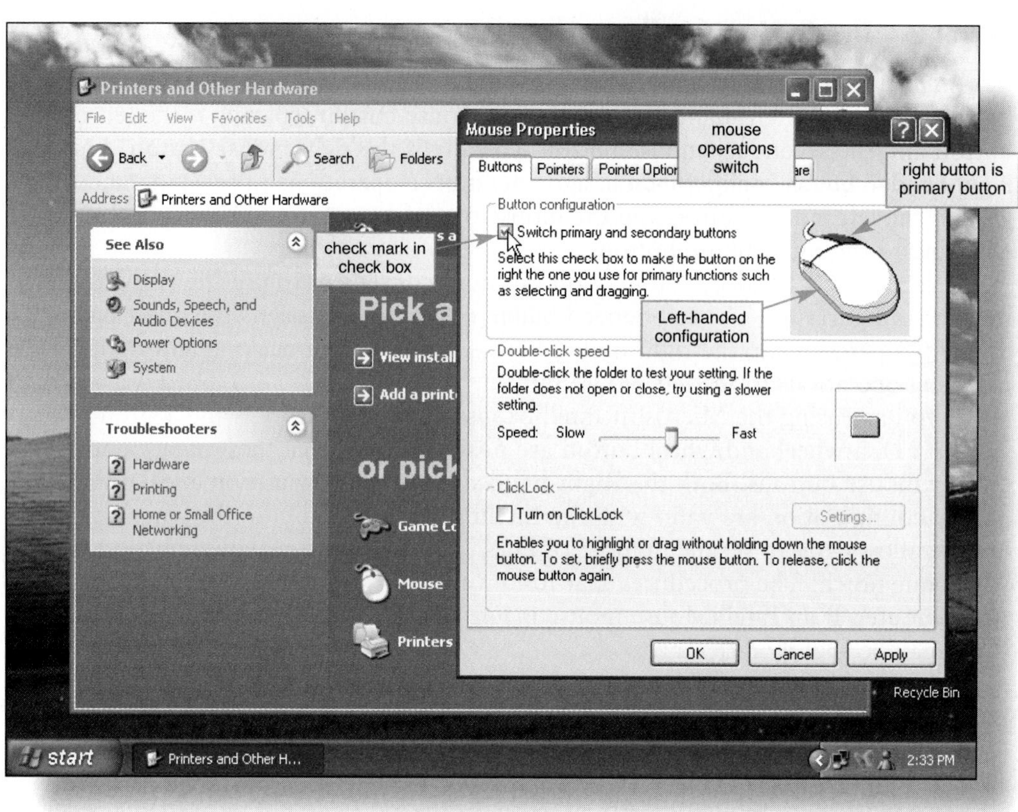

FIGURE 5-15

4 Using the right mouse button, click Switch primary and secondary buttons.

The check mark in the Switch primary and secondary buttons check box is removed, the primary button in the mouse illustration changes to the left mouse button, the mouse operations associated with the left and right buttons switch, and the button configuration changes to the Right-handed configuration.

Other Ways

1. Click Switch to Classic View, double-click Mouse icon, click Switch primary and secondary buttons
2. Click Start button, click Help and Support, click Index button, type mouse, double-click reversing buttons, click Mouse link, click Switch primary and secondary buttons

Adjusting the Double-Click Speed

As explained in Project 1, clicking means pressing a mouse button and double-clicking means quickly pressing and then releasing a mouse button twice. Windows XP measures the amount of time between clicking the mouse button once and then clicking the same button again. This time interval, called **double-click speed**, determines whether Windows XP recognizes clicking the mouse button twice as a double-click or two single clicks.

If you click a mouse button and do not click the button again within the time interval, Windows XP determines this is a single click, and another click is a second click and not part of a double-click procedure. If you click a mouse button and then click the button again within the time interval, Windows XP determines the mouse was double-clicked. To increase the double-click speed, move the Double-click speed slider to the right along the Double-click speed slide, to decrease the double-click speed, move the Double-click speed slider to the left (see Figure 5-16).

After adjusting the double-click speed, test the new speed by double-clicking the test area (see Figure 5-16). If you double-click the test area within the specified time interval, the folder icon in the test area opens to indicate that Windows XP recognizes your double-click. If the folder does not open, your double-click is not recognized, and the double-click speed is set too fast and should be reduced. Double-clicking within the specified time interval when the folder is open will close the folder.

Perform the following steps to adjust and test the double-click speed.

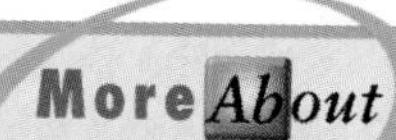

Double-Click Speed

Setting the double-click speed to its fastest speed may make it impossible to double-click an object. If this happens, open the Mouse Properties dialog box without double-clicking, use the TAB key to select the Double-click speed slide, press the LEFT ARROW key on the keyboard to reduce the speed, and then click the Apply button.

Steps To Adjust the Double-Click Speed

1 Drag the Double-click speed slider in the Double-click speed area to the right end of the slide. Double-click the test area.

The Double-click speed slider displays at the right end of the Double-click speed slide (Figure 5-16). Although the test area is double-clicked, the folder icon does not open.

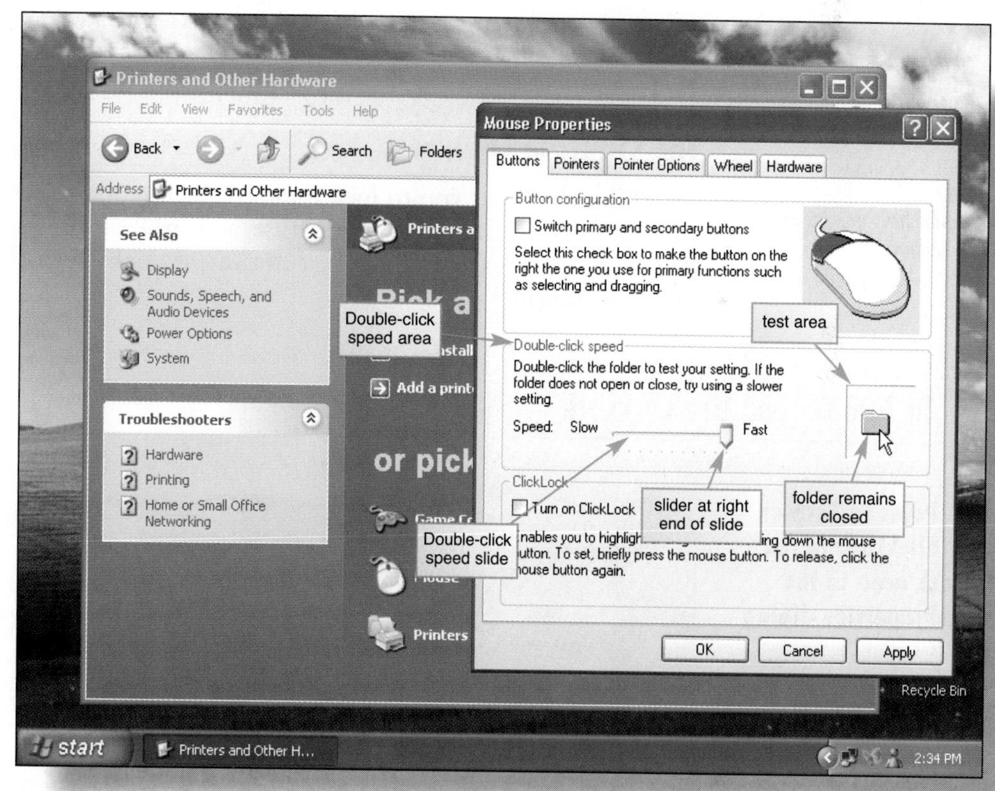

FIGURE 5-16

2 Drag the Double-click speed slider to the left along the slide until the folder opens when you double-click the test area.

Adjust the Double-click speed slider so that when you double-click the test area, the folder icon opens (Figure 5-17). This is your best double-click speed.

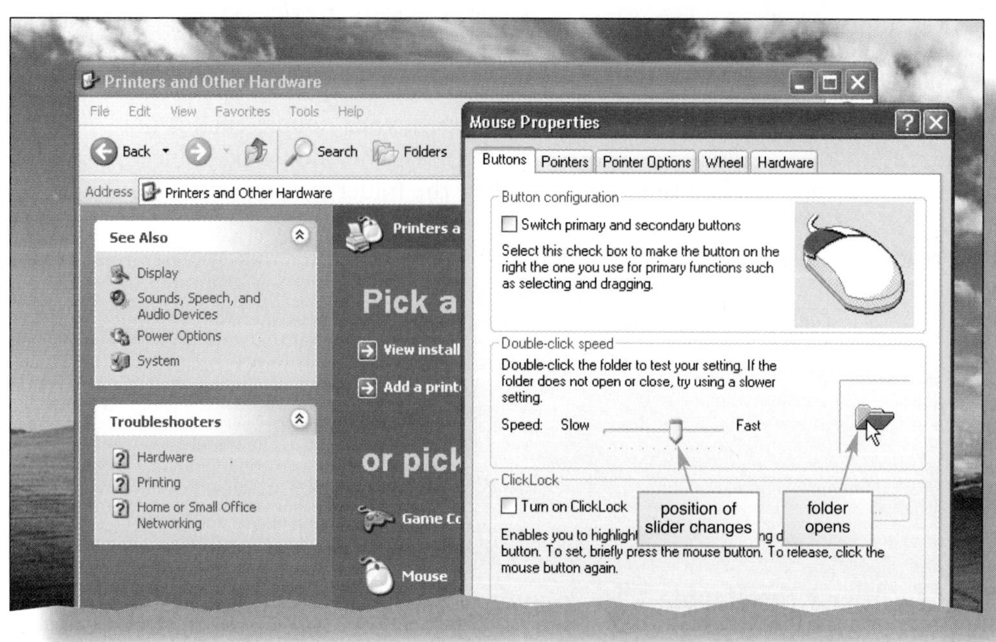

FIGURE 5-17

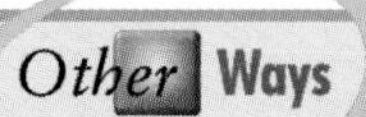

Other Ways

1. Click Switch to Classic View, double-click Mouse icon, drag Double-click speed slider
2. Click Start button, click Help and Support, click Index button, type mouse, double-click double-click speed, click Mouse link, drag Double-click speed slider

The ClickLock Feature

ClickLock allows you to lock a mouse button and select or drag text without continuously holding down the mouse button. Perform the following steps to turn on ClickLock, create a simple text document, lock the click, and then highlight text in the document.

Steps To Turn On and Use ClickLock

1 Point to Turn on ClickLock in the ClickLock area in the Mouse Properties dialog box.

A check mark does not display in the Turn on ClickLock check box and the instructions to use ClickLock display below the check box (Figure 5-18). The Settings button is dimmed.

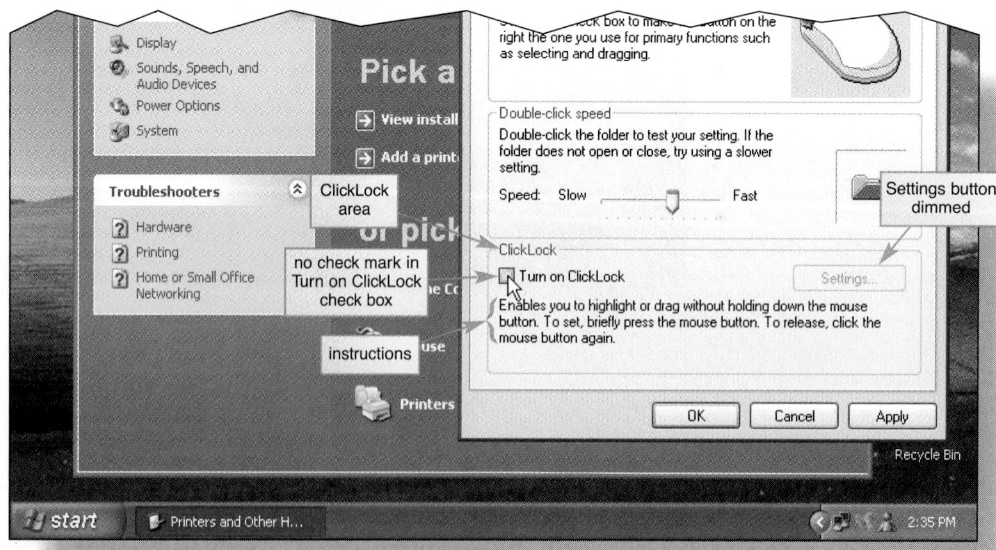

FIGURE 5-18

2 **Click Turn on ClickLock.**

A check mark displays in the Turn on ClickLock check box, ClickLock turns on, and the Settings button is no longer dimmed (Figure 5-19).

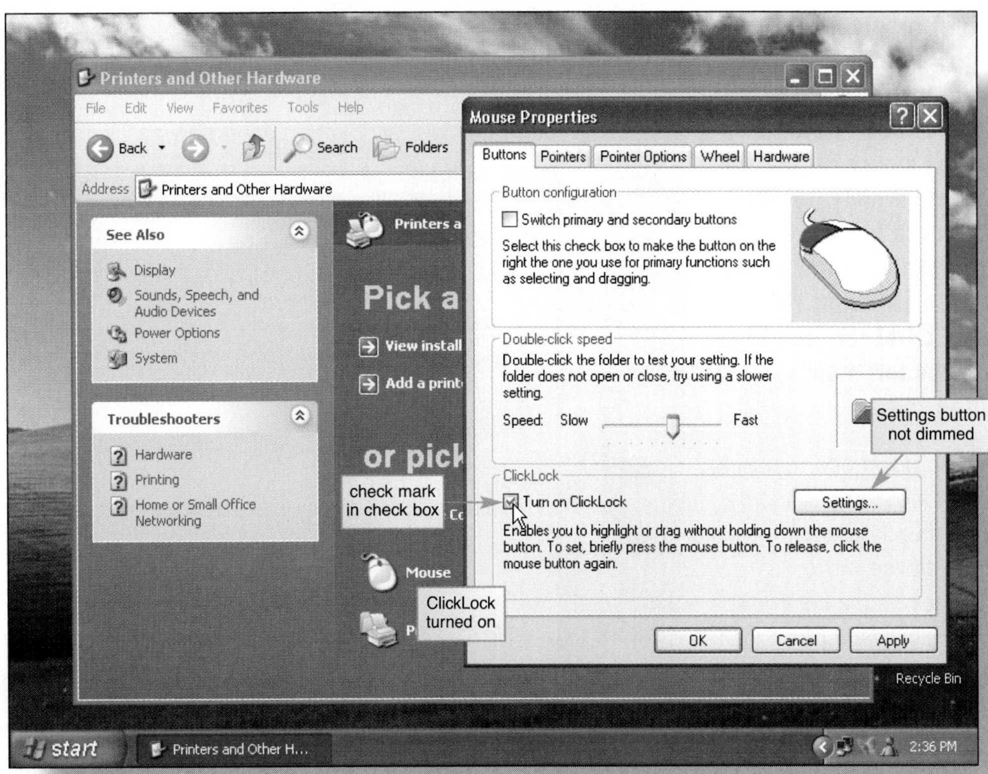

FIGURE 5-19

3 **Right-click an open area of the desktop, point to New, click Text Document, double-click the New Text Document icon on the desktop, and then type** `ClickLock allows you to lock a mouse button and select or drag text.` **in the New Text Document - Notepad window. Move the insertion point to the beginning of the text.**

The typed sentence displays in the New Text Document - Notepad window (Figure 5-20).

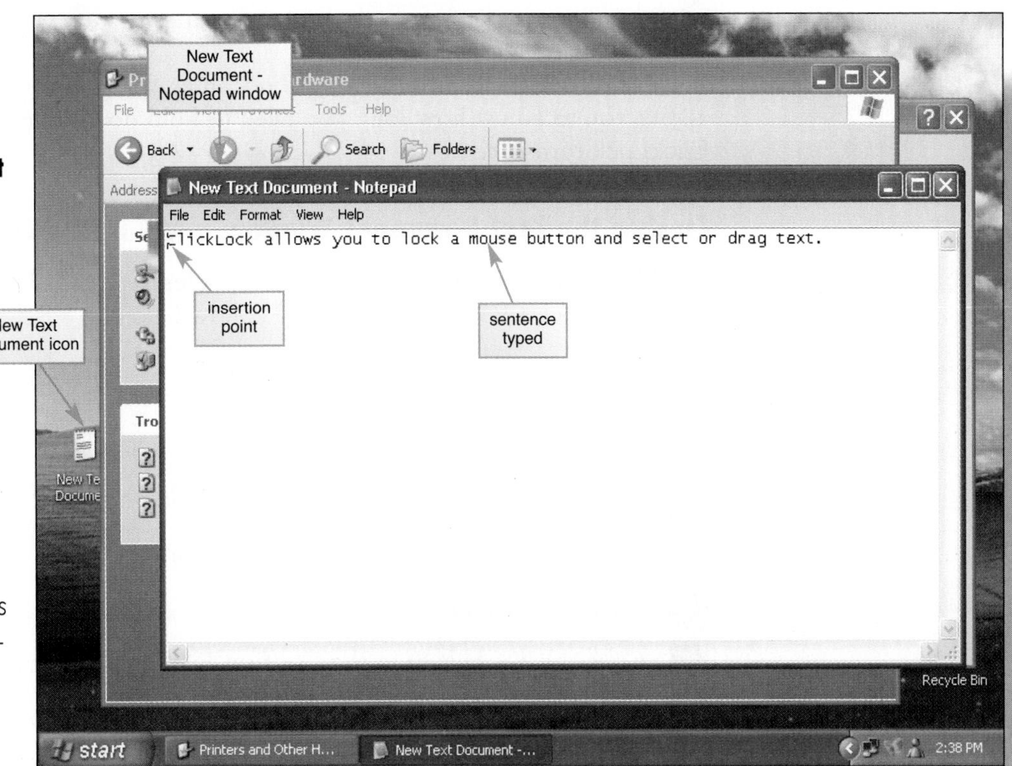

FIGURE 5-20

4 Position the mouse pointer to the left of the word, ClickLock, in the document, hold down the left mouse button for several seconds, release the mouse button, drag the insertion point to the right to highlight the word, ClickLock, and then click the left mouse button.

Holding down and releasing the left mouse button turns on ClickLock, dragging highlights the word, ClickLock, in the New Text Document - Notepad window, and clicking the left mouse turns ClickLock off (Figure 5-21).

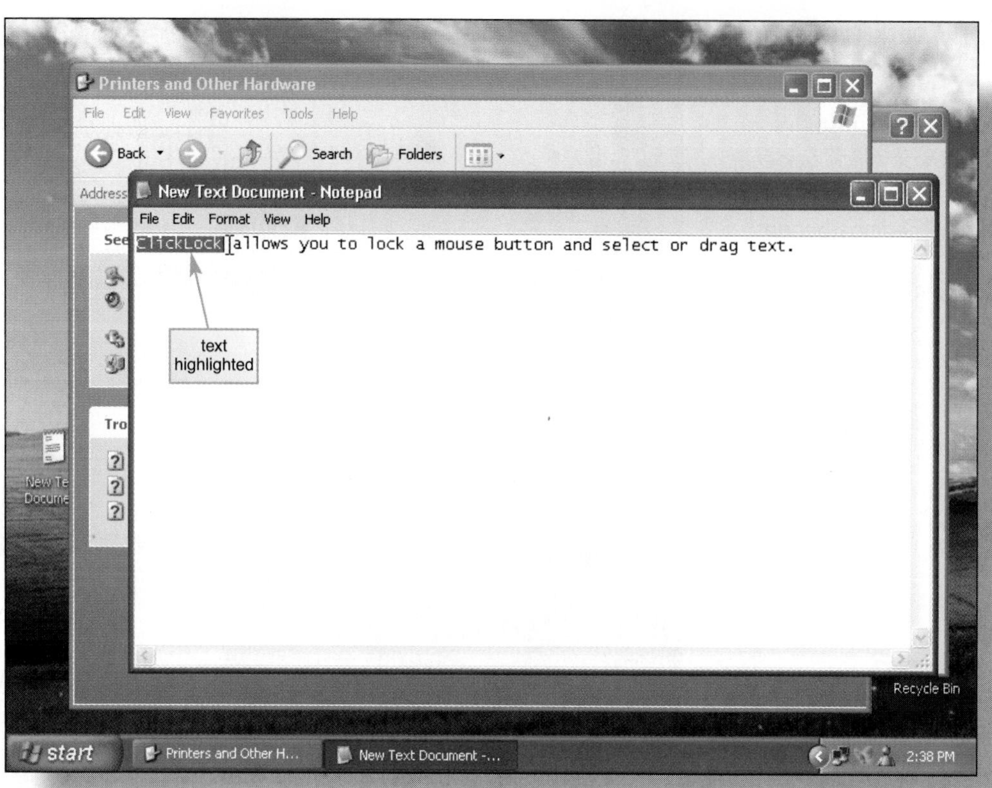

FIGURE 5-21

The Settings button in the ClickLock area in Figure 5-19 on the previous page allows you to adjust how long you need to hold down a mouse button before ClickLock turns on.

Closing the Text Document Window and Turning Off ClickLock

After turning on and using ClickLock, close the Text Document window and turn off ClickLock by performing the following steps.

TO DELETE THE TEXT DOCUMENT AND TURN OFF CLICKLOCK

1. Click the Close button in the New Text Document - Notepad window.
2. Click the No button in the Notepad dialog box.
3. Right-click the New Text Document icon.
4. Click Delete on the shortcut menu.
5. Click the Yes button in the Confirm File Delete dialog box.
6. Click the title bar of the Mouse Properties dialog box to move the dialog box on top of the Printers and Other Hardware window.
7. Click the Turn on ClickLock check box to remove the check mark.

The New Text Document is deleted and ClickLock is turned off.

Changing the Mouse Pointer Scheme

The shape of the mouse pointer when you point to an area of the desktop (block arrow), wait for an operation to be completed (hourglass), point to the border or corner of a window (two-headed arrow), enter text in a word processor (I-beam), or draw in a graphics program (pencil) is determined by the mouse pointer scheme you select. To change the mouse pointer scheme, complete the following steps.

Steps To Change the Mouse Pointer Scheme

1 Click the Pointers tab in the Mouse Properties dialog box. Write down on a piece of paper the scheme name displayed in the Scheme box so you can reset the mouse pointer scheme at a later time. Point to the Scheme box arrow.

The Pointers sheet displays (Figure 5-22). The current mouse pointer scheme, Windows Default (system scheme), is highlighted in the Scheme box in the Scheme area and a partial list of the mouse pointers that make up the scheme displays in the Customize list box. The Normal Select mouse pointer is highlighted in the list and displays in the preview box.

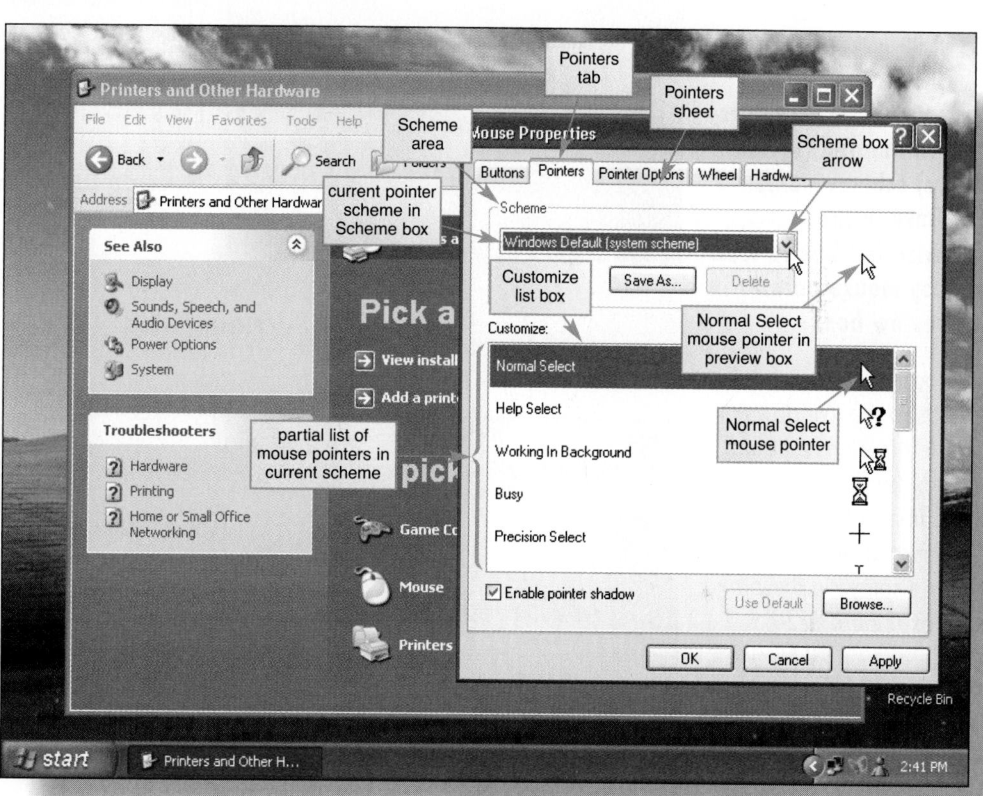

FIGURE 5-22

2 Click the Scheme box arrow. Point to the Windows Animated (system scheme) scheme name in the Scheme list.

The Scheme list box displays and the Windows Animated (system scheme) scheme name is highlighted (Figure 5-23).

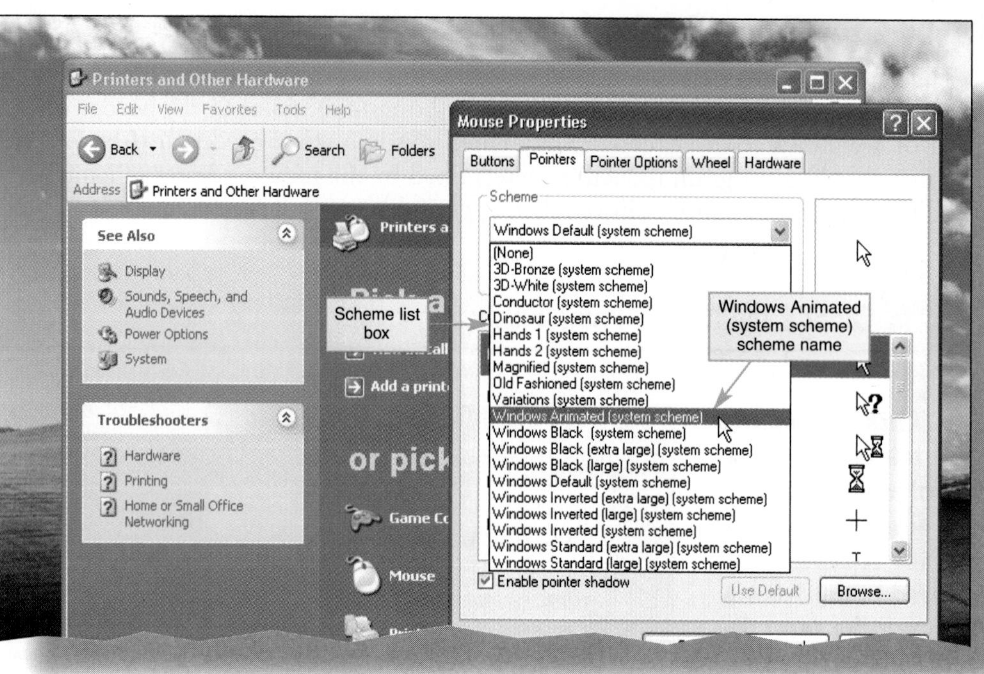

FIGURE 5-23

3 Click the Windows Animated (system scheme) scheme name. Click Busy in the Customize list box to view the Busy mouse pointer in the preview box.

The mouse pointer scheme changes to the Windows Animated (system scheme) scheme, the Busy entry is highlighted in the list, and the animated Busy mouse pointer displays in the preview box (Figure 5-24).

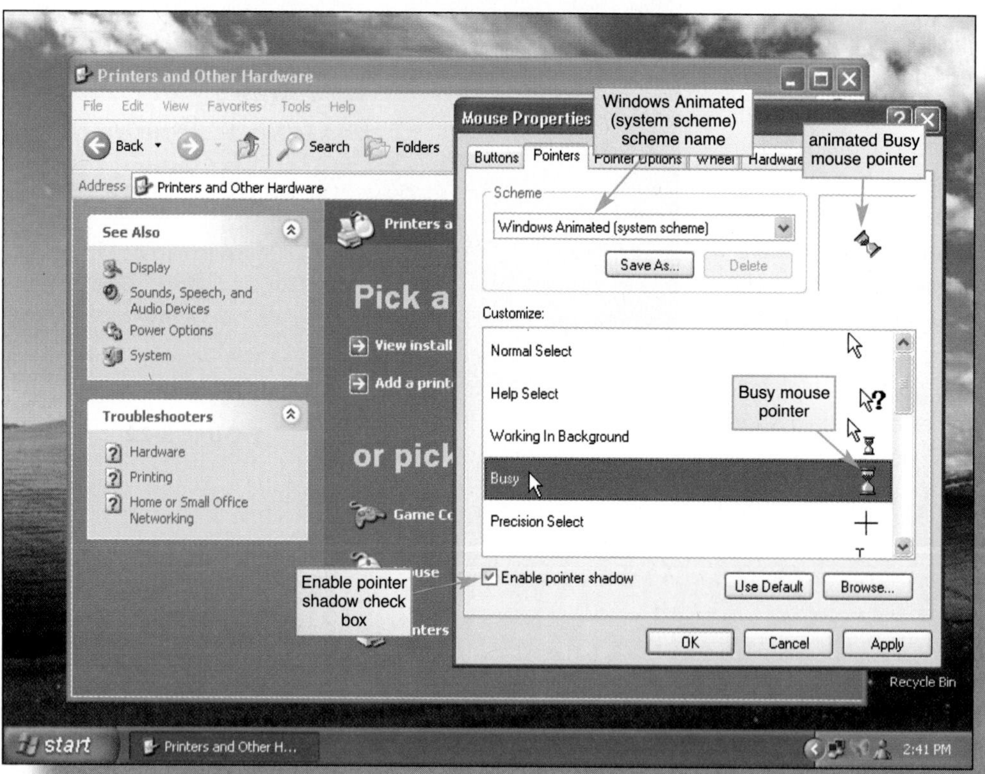

FIGURE 5-24

4 Click other entries in the list to view the different mouse pointers in the Windows Animated (system scheme) scheme.

5 Click the Scheme box arrow and then click the mouse pointer scheme name you wrote down in Step 1 to reset the mouse pointer scheme.

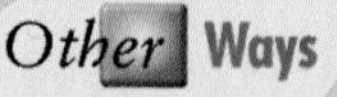

Other Ways

1. Click Switch to Classic View, double-click Mouse icon, click Pointers tab, click Scheme box arrow, click mouse scheme, click Apply button

If your display supports animation, the animated Busy mouse pointer shown in Figure 5-24 inverts itself each time the sand finishes running out of the top part of the hourglass. The Enable pointer shadow check box in the Pointers sheet allows you to turn on or turn off the drop shadow that displays behind the mouse pointer. Currently, the check box contains a check mark and the mouse pointer displays on the screen with a drop shadow. The drop shadow is not visible in the figures in this book.

Adjusting the Pointer Speed

The **pointer speed** is the speed at which the mouse pointer travels across the desktop when you move the mouse across a flat surface. Adjust the pointer speed by moving the Pointer speed slider along the Pointer speed slide. Because moving the slider adjusts the pointer speed immediately, it is not necessary to use the Apply button. Perform the following steps to adjust the pointer speed.

Steps To Adjust the Pointer Speed

1 Click the Pointer Options tab in the Mouse Properties dialog box. Drag the Pointer speed slider in the Motion area to the left end of the slide.

The Pointer Options sheet displays, the Pointer speed slider displays at the left end of the Pointer speed slide, and the adjustment to the pointer speed is made (Figure 5-25).

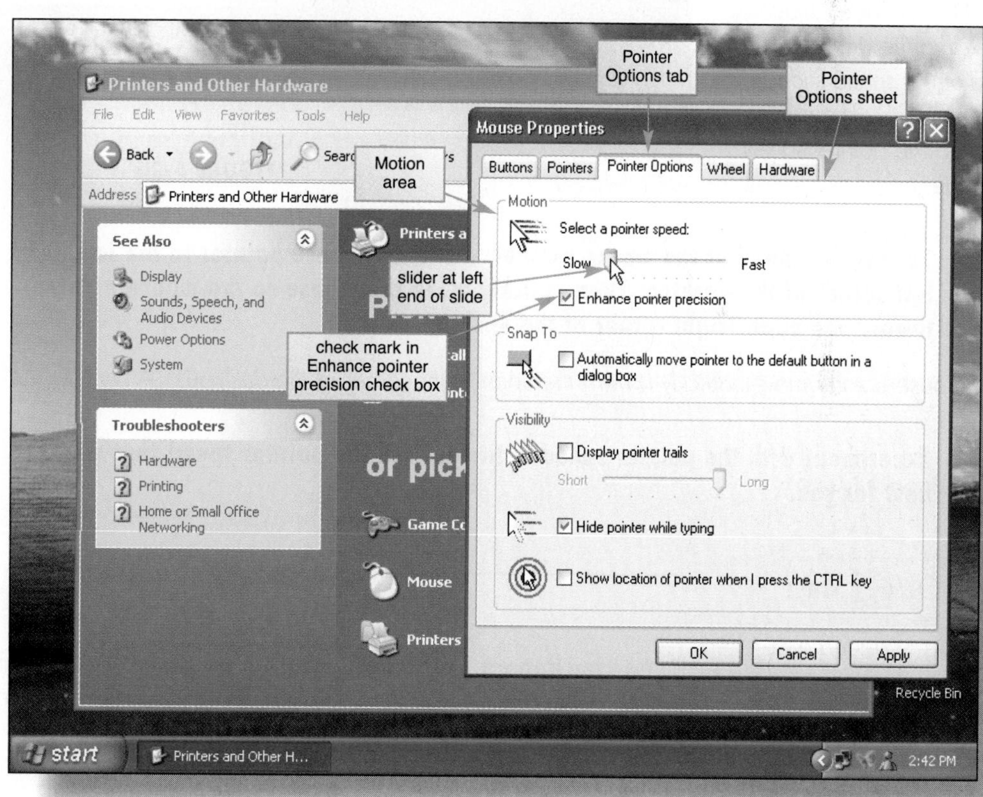

FIGURE 5-25

2 **To test the speed of the mouse pointer, move the mouse pointer to the lower-left corner of the desktop. Then, quickly move the mouse so the mouse pointer moves toward the upper-right corner of the desktop.**

The mouse pointer moves slowly toward the upper-right corner of the desktop.

3 **Drag the Pointer speed slider to the right end of the slide.**

The Pointer speed slider moves to the right end of the Pointer speed slide (Figure 5-26). The adjustment to the pointer speed is made.

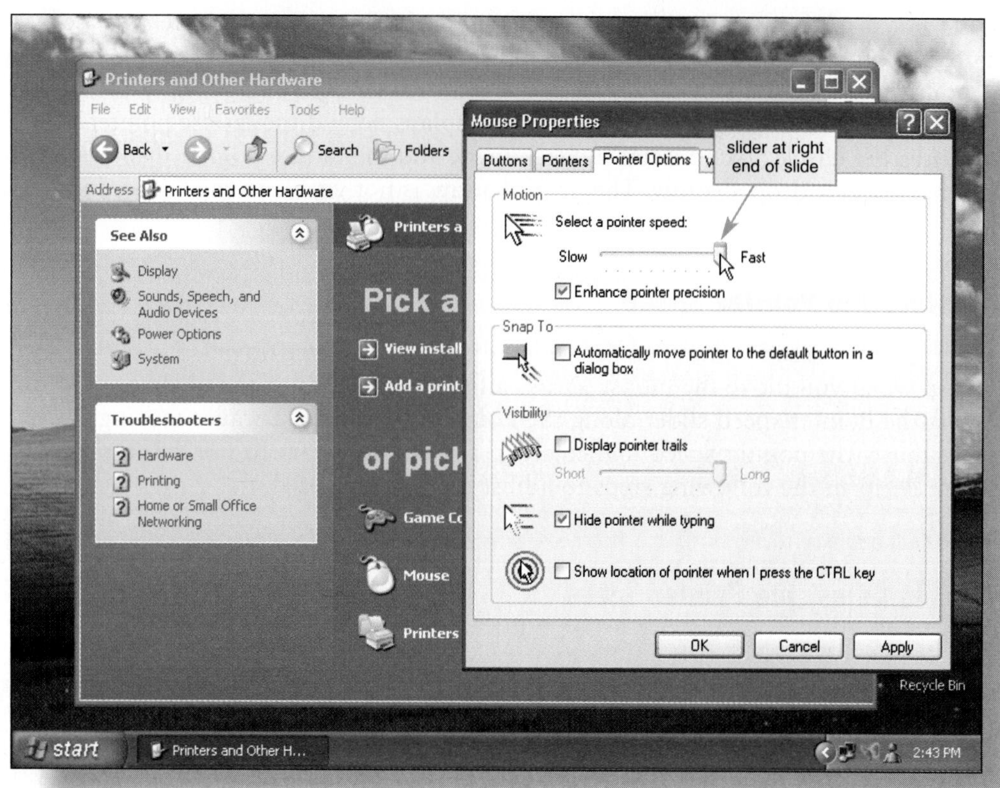

FIGURE 5-26

4 **To test the speed of the mouse pointer, move the mouse pointer to the lower-left corner of the desktop. Then, quickly move the mouse so the mouse pointer moves toward the upper-right corner of the desktop.**

The mouse pointer moves quickly toward the upper-right corner of the desktop.

5 **Experiment with the pointer speed until you find the pointer speed that works best for you.**

Other Ways

1. Click Switch to Classic View, double-click Mouse icon, click Pointer Options tab, drag Pointer speed slider, click Apply button
2. Click Start button, click Help and Support, click Index button, type `mouse pointers`, double-click speed topic, click Mouse link, click Pointer Options tab, drag Pointer speed slider, click Apply button

A check mark in the Enhance pointer precision check box in Figure 5-25 on the previous page indicates the enhanced pointer precision control feature is turned on. **Enhanced pointer precision** gives you more control over the pointer when moving small distances on the screen and provides quicker deceleration of the pointer when you slow down or stop the mouse.

The Snap To Feature

When a dialog box displays on the desktop, the mouse pointer remains in the position it occupied before the dialog box displayed. To make the mouse pointer automatically point to (snap to) the default command button in the dialog box, click the Automatically move pointer to the default button in dialog box check box in the Snap To area (see Figure 5-27). Perform the following steps to turn on Snap To and cause the mouse pointer to point to the default OK button in the Mouse Properties dialog box.

To Turn On Snap To

1 Click Automatically move pointer to the default button in a dialog box in the Snap To area. Point to the OK button in the Mouse Properties dialog box.

A check mark displays in the Automatically move pointer to the default button in a dialog box check box (Figure 5-27).

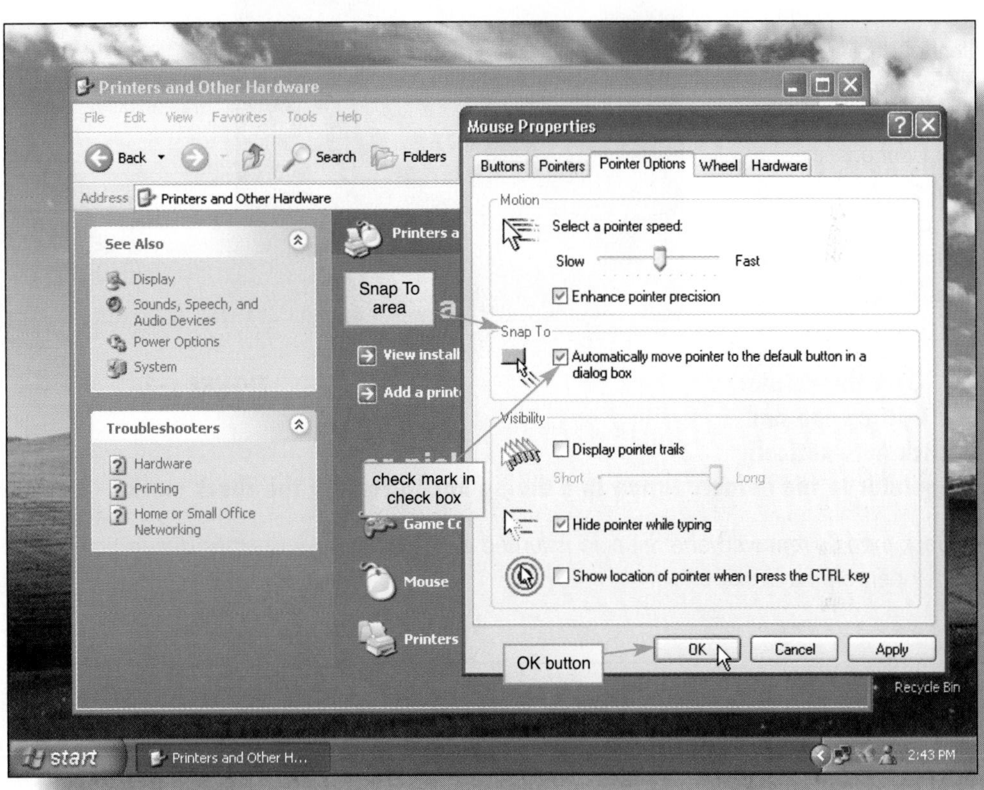

FIGURE 5-27

2 Click the OK button to close the Mouse Properties dialog box. Click the Mouse icon in the Printers and Other Hardware window.

When you click the OK button in the Mouse Properties dialog box, Snap To is turned on and the Mouse Properties dialog box closes. When you click the Mouse icon in the Printers and Other Hardware window, the Mouse Properties dialog box and Buttons sheet display, and the mouse pointer points to (snaps to) the OK button automatically (Figure 5-28).

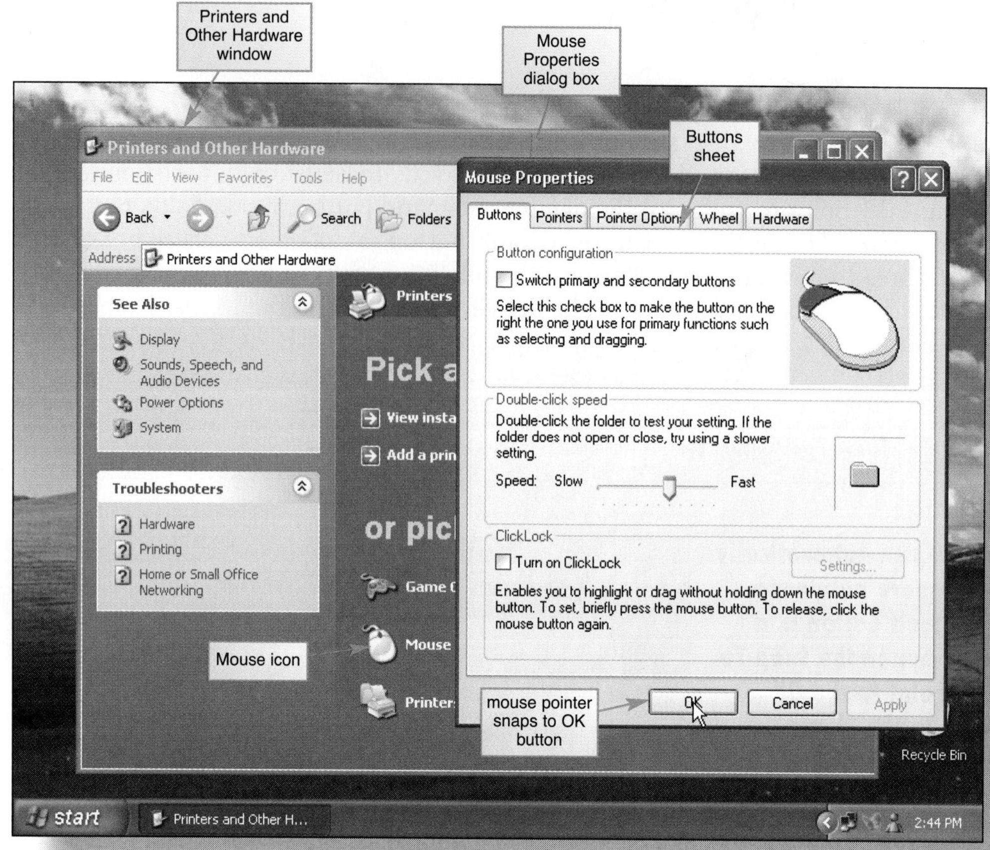

FIGURE 5-28

3 Click the Pointer Options tab and then click Automatically move pointer to the default button in a dialog box to remove the check mark.

The check mark is removed and Snap To is turned off. The Mouse Properties dialog box remains open on the desktop.

Other Ways

1. Click Switch to Classic View, double-click Mouse icon, click Power Options tab, click Automatically move pointer to the default button in a dialog box check box, click OK button
2. Click Start button, click Help and Support, click Index button, type `mouse pointers`, double-click snapping to default button topic, click Mouse link, click Automatically move pointer to the default button in a dialog box check box, click OK button

Displaying Pointer Trails

Sometimes when the mouse pointer moves across the desktop, it is difficult to see the position it occupies on the desktop. To improve the visibility of the mouse pointer, you can display a pointer trail, or trail of mouse pointers, on the desktop as you move the mouse. Perform the following steps to display a pointer trail.

To Display a Pointer Trail

1 Click Display pointer trails in the Visibility area.

The Display pointer trails check box is selected and the Pointer trails slide and slider display below the check box (Figure 5-29).

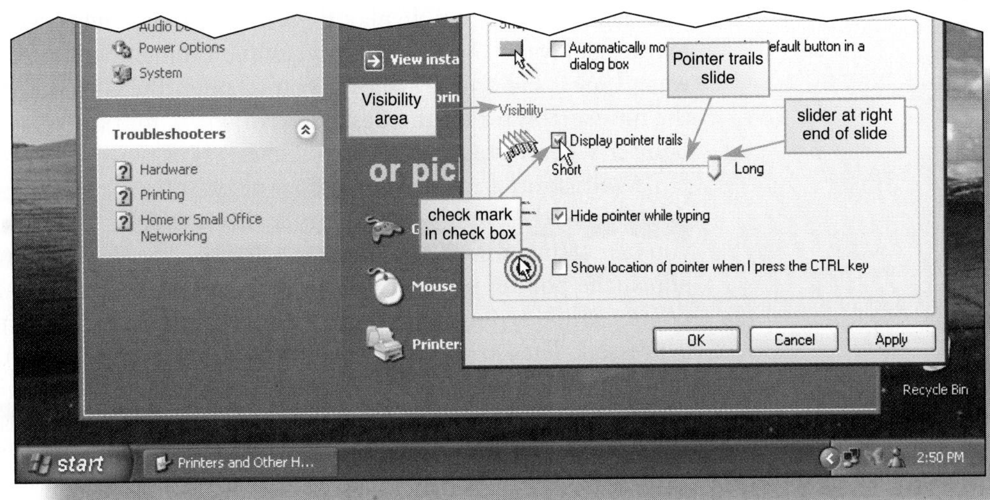

FIGURE 5-29

2 Move the mouse across a flat surface and then watch the mouse pointer as it moves across the desktop.

A series of mouse pointers displays on the desktop (Figure 5-30). The pointer trail disappears when you stop moving the mouse.

3 Experiment with the length of the pointer trail by dragging the Pointer trails slider until you find the best length for you.

4 When you have finished viewing the pointer trail, click Display pointer trails to no longer display the pointer trails. Click the OK button in the Mouse Properties dialog box.

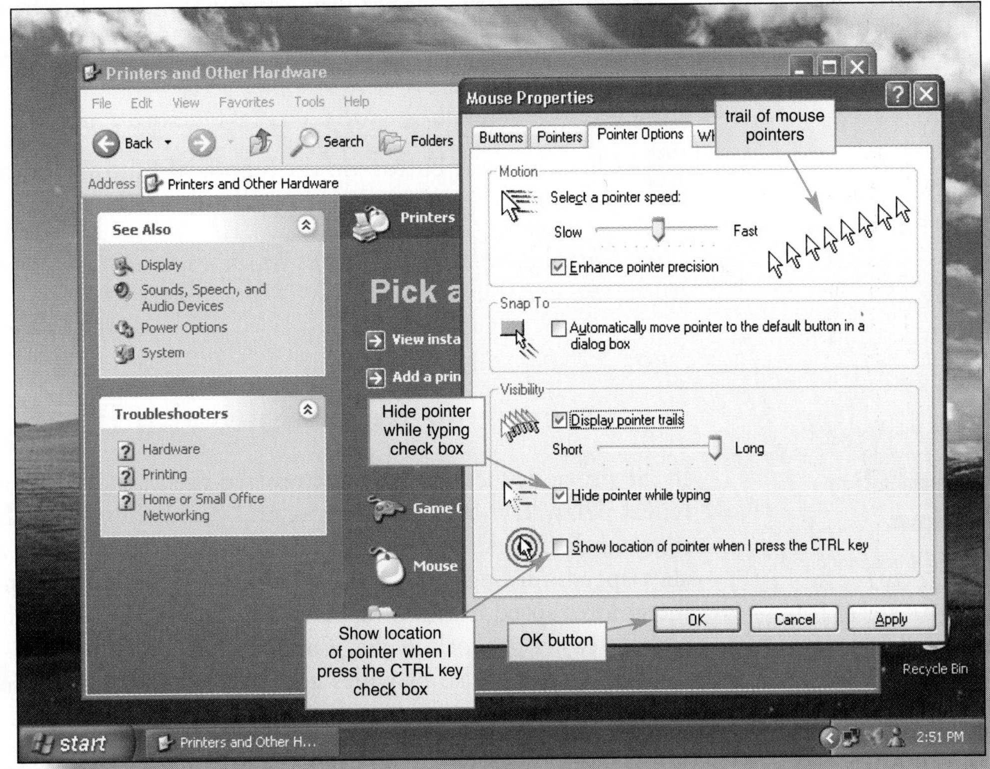

FIGURE 5-30

Other Ways

1. Click Switch to Classic View, double-click Mouse icon, click Pointer Options tab, click Display pointer trails

Two additional check boxes, Hide pointer while typing and Show location of pointer when I press the CTRL key, display in the Visibility area in Figure 5-30 on the previous page. **Hide pointer while typing** allows you to hide the mouse pointer when you begin to type and display the mouse pointer when you move the mouse. A check mark displays in the Hide pointer while typing check box. **Show location of pointer when I press the CTRL key** allows you to press the CTRL key to display the position of the mouse pointer on the desktop. No check mark displays in the Show location of pointer when I press the CTRL key check box.

As illustrated earlier, the **Buttons sheet** allows you to change the button configuration, adjust the double-click speed, and turn on ClickLock. On the **Pointers sheet**, you can change the mouse pointer scheme. The **Pointer Options sheet** permits you to adjust the pointer speed, turn on Snap To, display pointer trails, hide the mouse pointer while typing, and show the location of the mouse pointer when the CTRL key is pressed. The **Hardware sheet** allows you to view the mouse devices attached to the computer and their properties and to troubleshoot the devices. The **Wheel sheet** allows you to define how far a page scrolls each time you move the mouse wheel one notch. If your mouse does not have a mouse wheel, the Wheel tab will not display in the Mouse Properties dialog box.

Displaying the Control Panel Window

After closing the Mouse Properties dialog box and before starting the next section, display the Control Panel window.

TO DISPLAY THE CONTROL PANEL WINDOW USING THE BACK BUTTON

 Click the Back button on the Standard Buttons toolbar in the Printers and Other Hardware window.

The Control Panel window opens in the same window as the Printers and Other Hardware window displays.

Customizing for People with Physical Challenges

In the previous sections, you customized the keyboard by adjusting the keyboard repeat delay, keyboard repeat rate, and cursor blink rate. In addition, you customized the mouse by changing the button configuration, adjusting the double-click speed, turning on ClickLock, changing the mouse pointer scheme, adjusting the pointer speed, turning on Snap To, and displaying pointer trails. These changes make it easier to work in the Windows XP environment.

Windows XP also provides additional features, called **accessibility features**, which make it easier for people who are mobility, hearing, or vision impaired to use Windows XP. For example, people who have restricted movement and cannot move the mouse (**mobility impaired**) have the option of using **MouseKeys** that allow them to use the numeric keypad to move the mouse pointer, click, double-click, and drag. Clicking the Accessibility Options icon in the Control Panel window (see Figure 5-2 on page WIN 5.06) displays the Accessibility Options window that allows you to use these features.

People who are deaf or **hearing impaired** have **Sound Sentry** that generates visual warnings when the computer makes a sound and **ShowSounds** that causes an application program to display captions when a program speaks or makes sounds.

More About

Accessibility Options

For more information about accessibility options and a step-by-step guide to help you adjust options, launch the Internet Explorer browser, type www.scsite.com/winxp/more.htm in the Address box in the Microsoft Internet Explorer window, and then press the Go button.

People who have difficulty seeing the screen (**vision impaired**) have High Contrast. **High Contrast** changes the desktop color scheme to the High Contrast Black (Large) color scheme. This color scheme increases the size of text on the desktop, which improves a person's ability to read the text.

More About

MouseKeys Feature

When you turn on the MouseKeys feature, you can move the mouse pointer using the 1, 2, 3, 4, 6, 7, 8, and 9 keys on the numeric pad, click using the 5 key, double-click using the plus (+) key, and drag by pressing the INSERT key, moving the mouse pointer, and then pressing the DELETE key.

The MouseKeys Feature

To illustrate the use of an accessibility option, perform the following steps to turn on MouseKeys, and then turn off MouseKeys. When you turn on MouseKeys, you can use the numeric keys on the numeric keypad to move the mouse pointer across the desktop. Pressing the 2, 4, 6, or 8 key moves the mouse pointer down, left, right, or up, respectively. Pressing the 1, 3, 7, or 9 key moves the mouse pointer diagonally down and to the left, down and to the right, up and to the left, or up and to the right, respectively. Pressing the 5 key selects the object to which the mouse pointer points.

Steps To Turn On MouseKeys

1 Click the Accessibility Options icon in the Control Panel window. Point to the Accessibility Options icon in the Accessibility Options window.

The Accessibility Options window opens in the same window as the Control Panel window displays (Figure 5-31). The Accessibility Options icon displays in the or pick a Control Panel icon area.

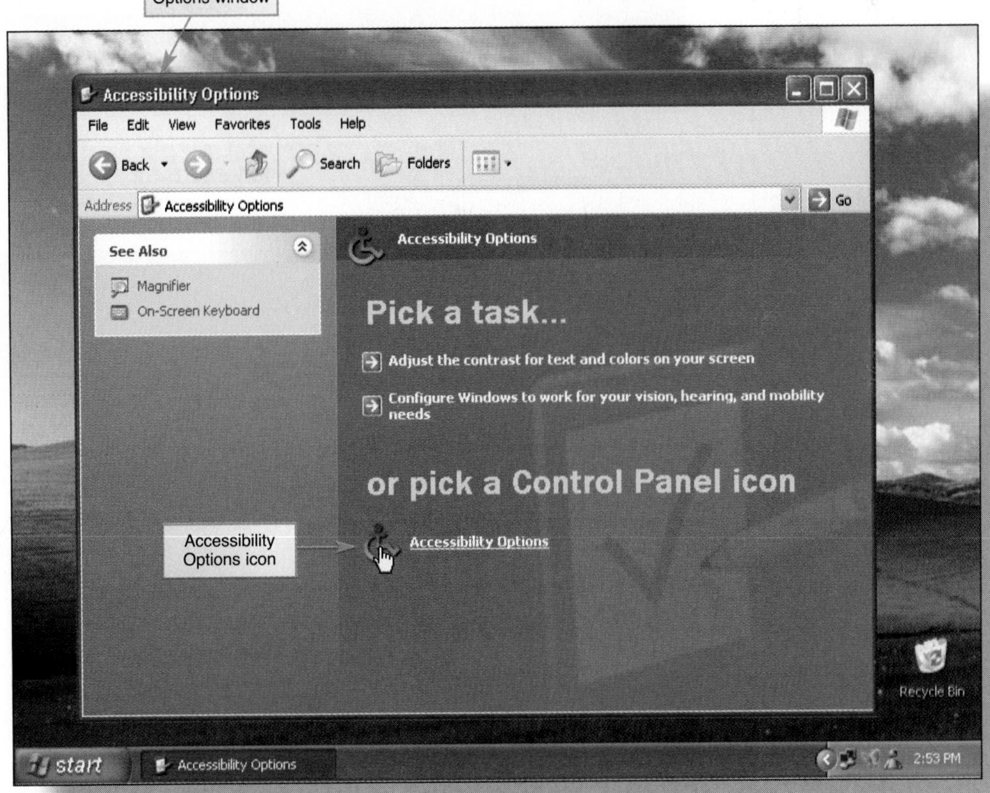

FIGURE 5-31

2 Click the Accessibility Options icon. Point to the Mouse tab.

The Accessibility Options dialog box and Keyboard sheet display (Figure 5-32). In the Keyboard sheet, you can turn on StickyKeys, FilterKeys, and ToggleKeys.

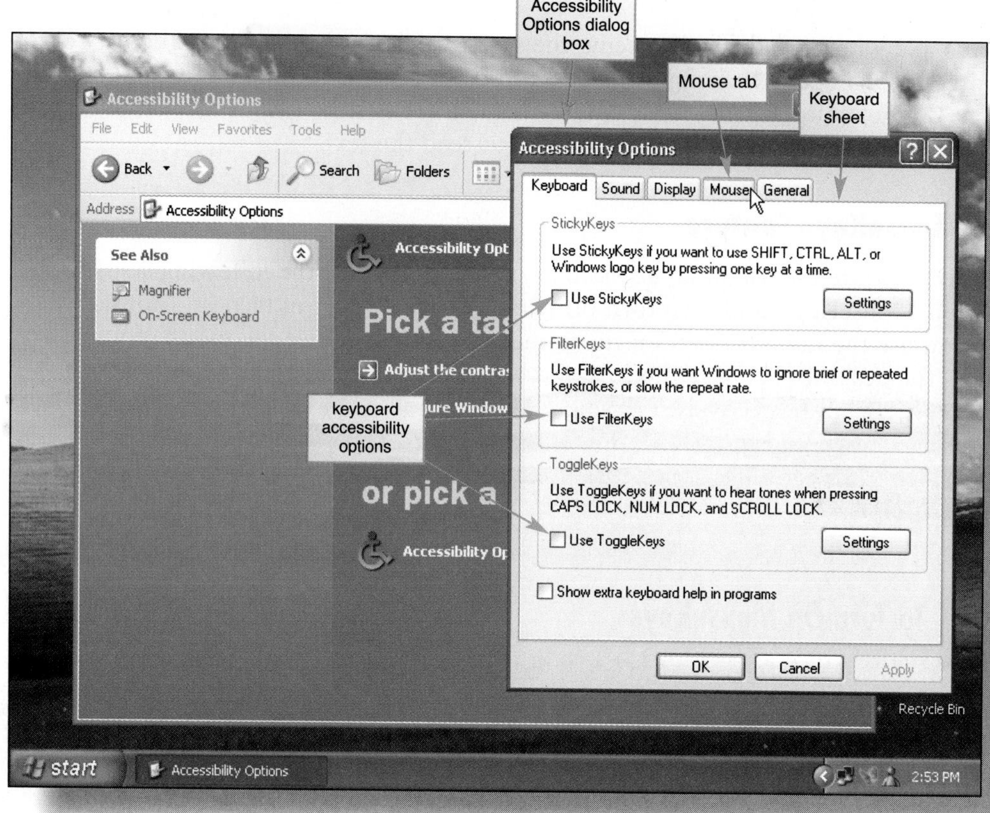

FIGURE 5-32

3 Click the Mouse tab, click Use MouseKeys, and then click the Apply button.

The Mouse sheet displays, the Use MouseKeys check box is selected in the MouseKeys area, and a mouse icon displays in the notification area on the taskbar (Figure 5-33). Clicking the Apply button turns on MouseKeys.

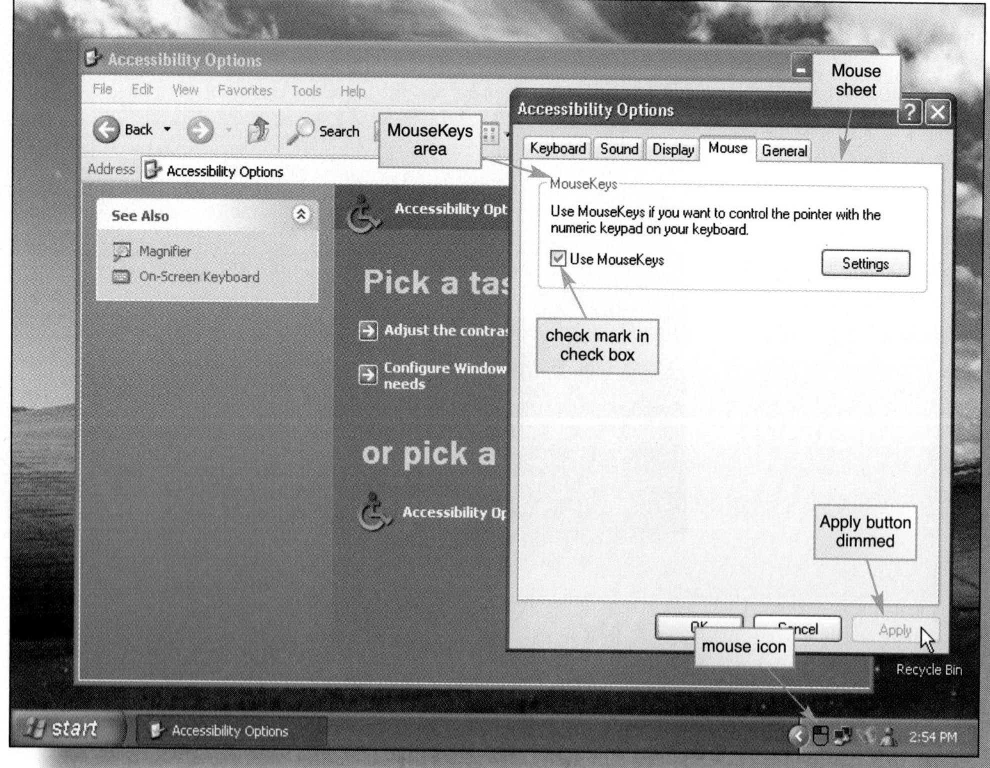

FIGURE 5-33

4 **If a circle with a slash symbol displays over the mouse icon in the notification area, press the NUM LOCK key to remove the symbol. Use the 1, 2, 3, 4, 6, 7, 8, and 9 numeric keys on the numeric keypad to move the mouse pointer to the Use MouseKeys check box and then press the 5 key to remove the check mark from the check box.**

The mouse pointer points to the Use MouseKeys check box and the check mark no longer displays in the check box (Figure 5-34).

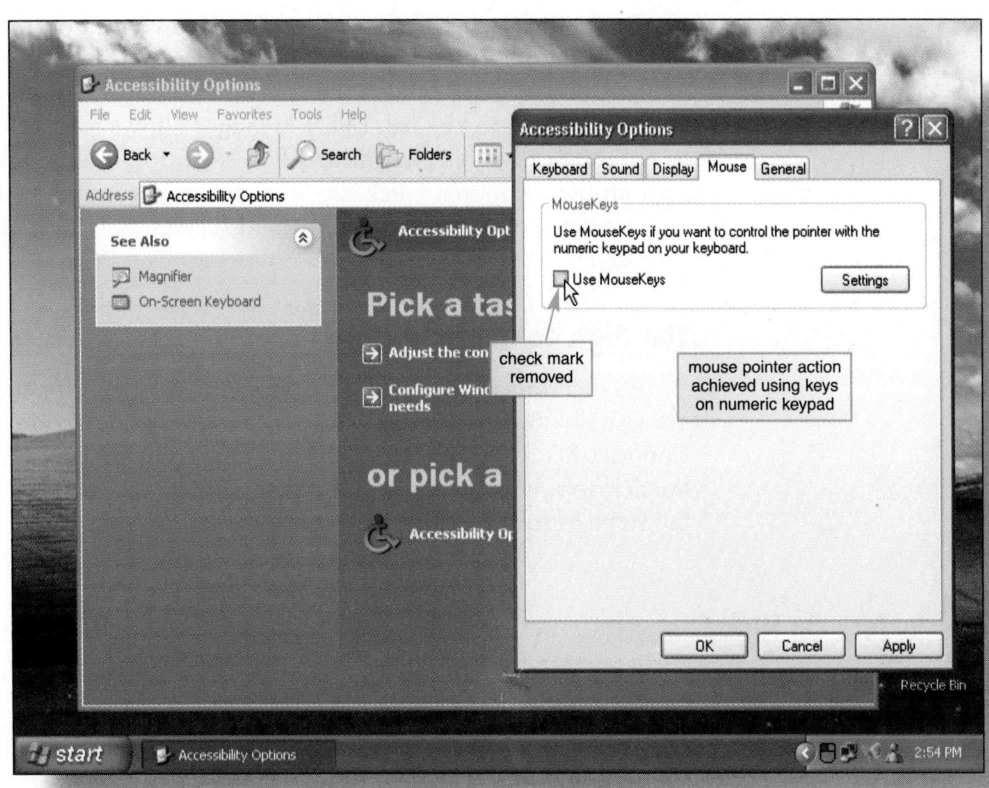

FIGURE 5-34

5 **Using the numeric keys on the numeric keypad, move the mouse pointer to the Apply button and then click the Apply button to turn off MouseKeys.**

MouseKeys turns off.

Other Ways

1. Click Switch to Classic View, double-click Accessibility Options icon, click Mouse tab, click Use MouseKeys, click Apply button
2. Click Start button, click Help and Support, click Index button, type `mousekeys`, double-click turning on and off topic, click Accessibility Options link, click Use MouseKeys, click Apply button

In addition to the accessibility options available in the Control Panel, Windows XP also includes a wizard to guide you through customizing the computer. The **Accessibility wizard** determines the smallest text you can read, allows you to select the best settings for your use (change the font size, switch to a lower screen resolution, use Microsoft Magnifier, and disable personalized menus), permits you to specify your impairment (mobility, hearing, or visual), and then turns on the appropriate options for the impairment.

Windows XP also supplies the Magnifier, Narrator, On-Screen Keyboard, and Utility Manager programs. **Magnifier** makes the screen more readable for users who have poor vision by creating a separate window that displays a magnified portion of the screen. Click the Magnifier link in the left pane of the Accessibility Options window to start Magnifier. **Narrator** is a text-to-speech program for users who are blind or have poor vision. Narrator reads out loud what displays on the screen, the contents of the active window, menu options, or text you type. Click the Start button, point to All Programs, point to Accessories, point to Accessibility, and then click Narrator to start Narrator.

On-Screen Keyboard displays a virtual keyboard on the desktop that allows users with mobility impairments to type using a pointing device or joystick. Click the On-Screen Keyboard link in the left pane of the Accessibility Options window to start On-Screen Keyboard. **Utility Manager** allows users to schedule operations such as automatically launching Magnifier, Narrator, and On-Screen Keyboard when you turn on the computer. Click the Start button, point to All Programs, point to Accessories, point to Accessibility, and then click Utility Manager to start Utility Manager.

The High Contrast Feature

As mentioned earlier, High Contrast is designed for use by individuals who are visually impaired. **High Contrast** changes the desktop color scheme to the High Contrast Black (large) color scheme. This color scheme increases the size of text on the desktop, which improves a person's ability to read the text. Perform the following steps to turn on High Contrast Black.

To Turn On High Contrast

1 Click the Display tab in the Accessibility Options dialog box. Point to Use High Contrast in the High Contrast area.

The Display sheet displays (Figure 5-35). The Use High Contrast check box displays in the High Contrast area in the Display sheet.

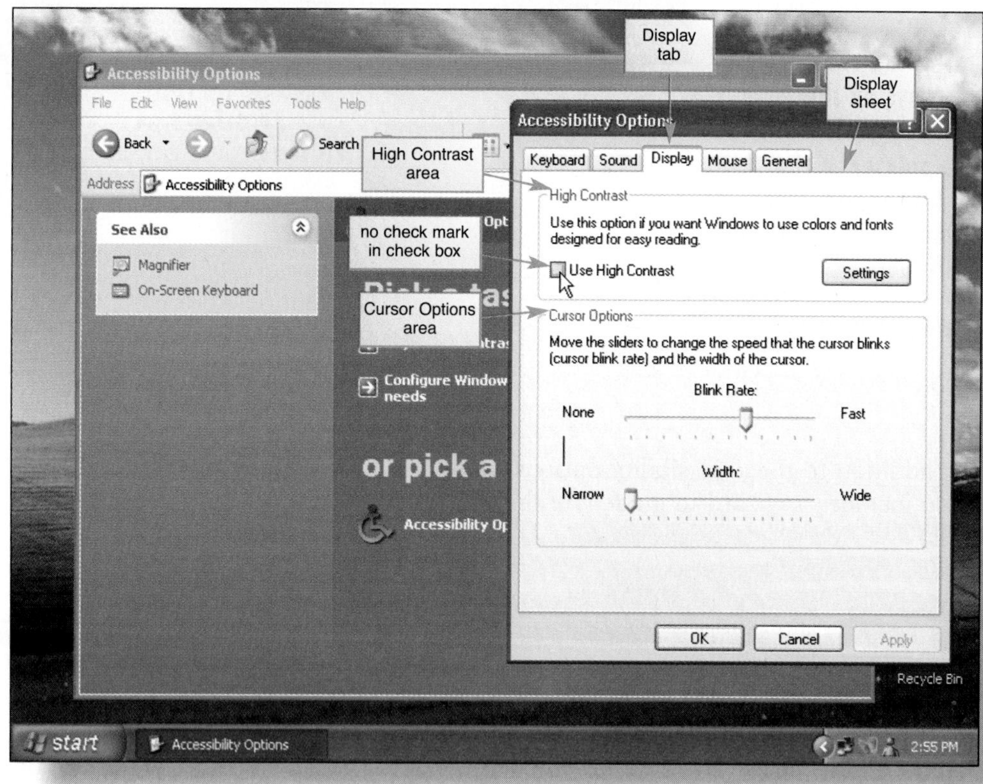

FIGURE 5-35

2 Click Use High Contrast. Click the Apply button.

Clicking High Contrast displays a check mark in the High Contrast check box. Clicking the Apply button displays the Please Wait screen momentarily while the desktop darkens and then the High Contrast Black (large) color scheme is applied to the desktop (Figure 5-36).

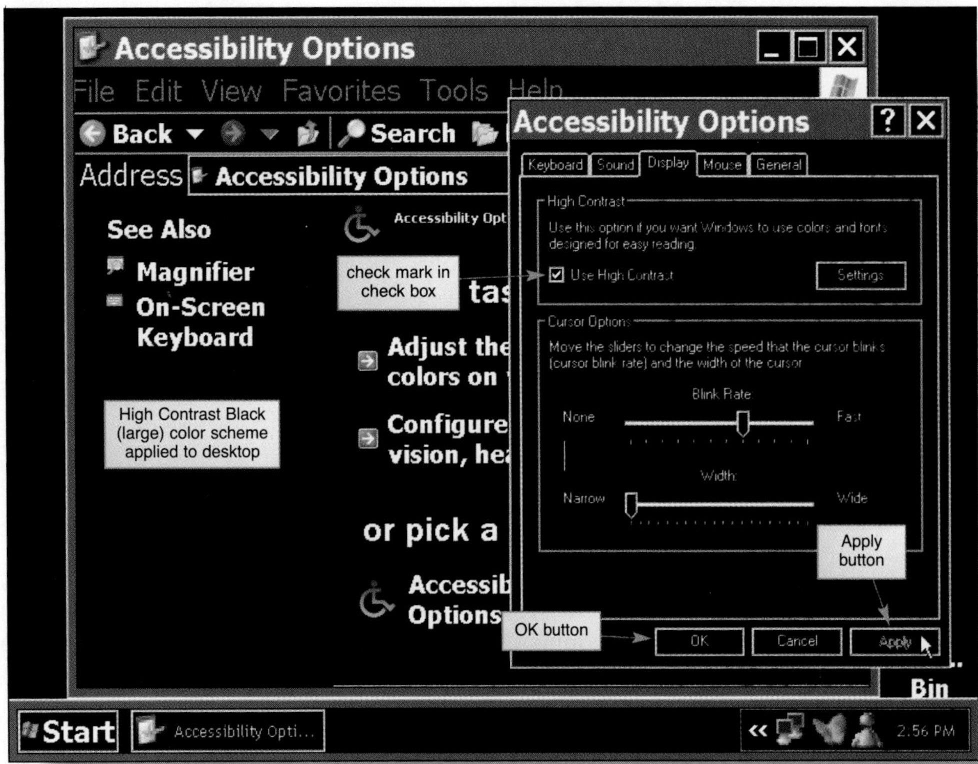

FIGURE 5-36

The Cursor Options area in Figure 5-35 allows you to adjust the speed at which the cursor blinks (cursor blink rate) and the width of the cursor.

Removing the High Contrast Black (Large) Color Scheme

After turning on High Contrast and applying the High Contrast Black (large) color scheme, remove the color scheme by turning off High Contrast. Perform the following steps to turn off High Contrast.

TO TURN OFF HIGH CONTRAST

1. Click Use High Contrast in the Accessibility Options dialog box.
2. Click the OK button in the Accessibility Options dialog box.

High Contrast is turned off and the Accessibility Options dialog box closes.

Other Ways

1. Click Switch to Classic View, double-click Accessibility Options icon, click Display tab, click Use High Contrast, click Apply button
2. Click Start button, click Help and Support, click Index button, type `high contrast tool`, double-click changing options, click Accessibility Options link, click Display tab, click Use High Contrast, click Apply button

Displaying the Control Panel Window

After closing the Accessibility Options dialog box and before starting the next section, display the Control Panel.

TO DISPLAY THE CONTROL PANEL WINDOW USING THE BACK BUTTON

1 Click the Back button on the Standard Buttons toolbar in the Accessibility Options window.

The Control Panel window opens in the same window as the Accessibility Options window displays.

User Accounts and Privileges

In Project 2, you learned that the computer administrator is responsible for assigning passwords and permissions to computer users and helping computer users with computer or networking problems. In addition, you learned that there are three types of user accounts (Administrator, Limited, and Guest) and that each user has certain privileges, or permissions, based upon the account type assigned to the user. For example, the ability of a limited user to change a password is a privilege, as is the ability of a computer administrator to create a user account. The privileges of the Administrator, Limited, and Guest user accounts are summarized in the table in Table 5-1.

Table 5-1 User Accounts and Privileges

USER ACCOUNTS	PRIVILEGES
Administrator	• Creates, changes, and deletes user accounts and groups • Installs programs • Sets folder sharing • Sets permissions • Accesses all files • Takes ownership of files • Grants rights to other user accounts and to themselves • Installs or removes hardware devices • Logs on in Safe Mode
Limited	• Changes the password, picture, and .NET Passport for their own user accounts • Uses programs that have been installed on the computer • Views permissions • Creates, changes, and deletes files in their My Document folders • Views files in shared document folders
Guest	• Same as limited account, but cannot create a password

As mentioned earlier, you will not be able to perform some tasks in this project unless you have administrative privileges. Administrative privileges are granted to all users who have an Administrator account and can be temporarily given to other users as required. In this project, each task that requires administrative privileges is noted in the paragraph above the corresponding steps. In each case, if you do not have administrative privileges, you should read the steps instead of performing them.

Viewing User Account Information

If you have administrative privileges you can view account information for all user accounts. In this case, you can change a user account, create a new user account, and change the way users log on or off. If you do not have administrative privileges, only information about your account is available. Perform the following steps to view your account information.

Steps To View Account Information

1 Click the User Accounts icon in the Control Panel window.

The User Accounts window displays (Figure 5-37). The user account type displays below the user name in the right pane of the User Accounts window. The Brad Wilson account is a limited account. As such, this user does not have administrative privileges. If the words, Administrator account, display below the user name, the user has administrative privileges.

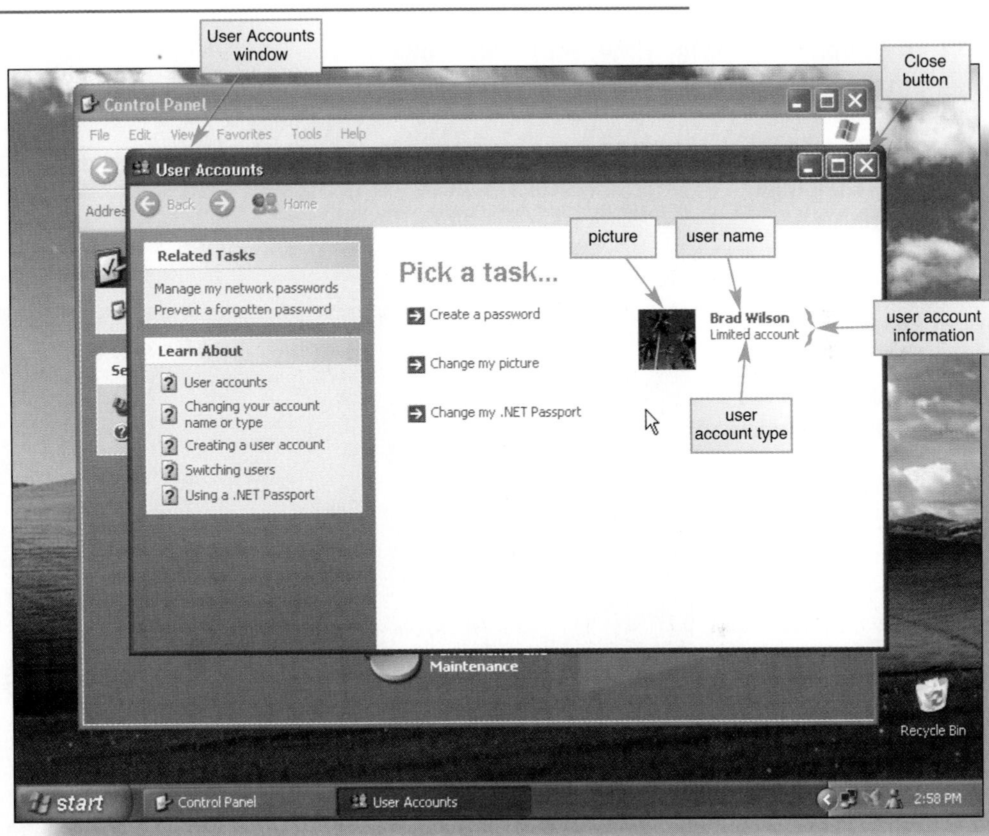

FIGURE 5-37

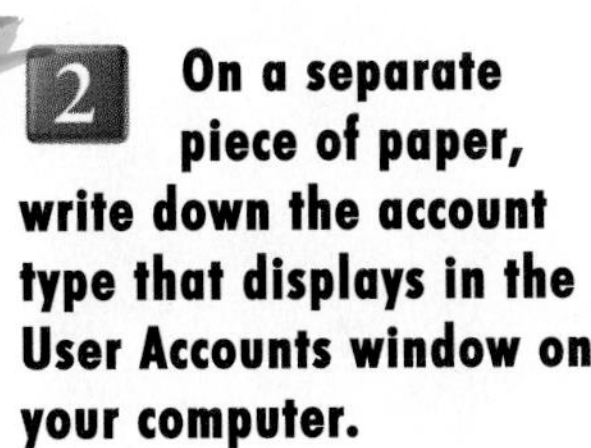

2 On a separate piece of paper, write down the account type that displays in the User Accounts window on your computer.

3 Click the Close button in the User Accounts window.

The User Accounts window closes.

Customizing the Date and Time

Previously in this project, you changed the properties of the mouse and keyboard. You also can change the properties and format of the date and time. Clicking the Date, Time, Language, and Regional Options icon in the Control Panel window (see Figure 5-2 on page WIN 5.06) allows you to change these properties.

Changes to the date, time, and time zone are made in the Date and Time Properties dialog box. After changing these settings, it is important to cancel the changes. Administrative privileges are required to change the date and time.

Changing the Date, Time, and Time Zone

Note: Administrative privileges are required to perform these steps

If you have administrative privileges, perform the following steps to change the date, time, and time zone, and then cancel the changes. If you do not have administrative privileges, read the following steps without actually performing them.

Steps To Change the Date, Time, and Time Zone

1 Click the Date, Time, Language, and Regional Options icon in the Control Panel window. Point to Change the date and time in the right pane of the window.

The Date, Time, Language, and Regional Options window opens in the same window as the Control Panel window displays (Figure 5-38). The Change the date and time task displays in the right pane.

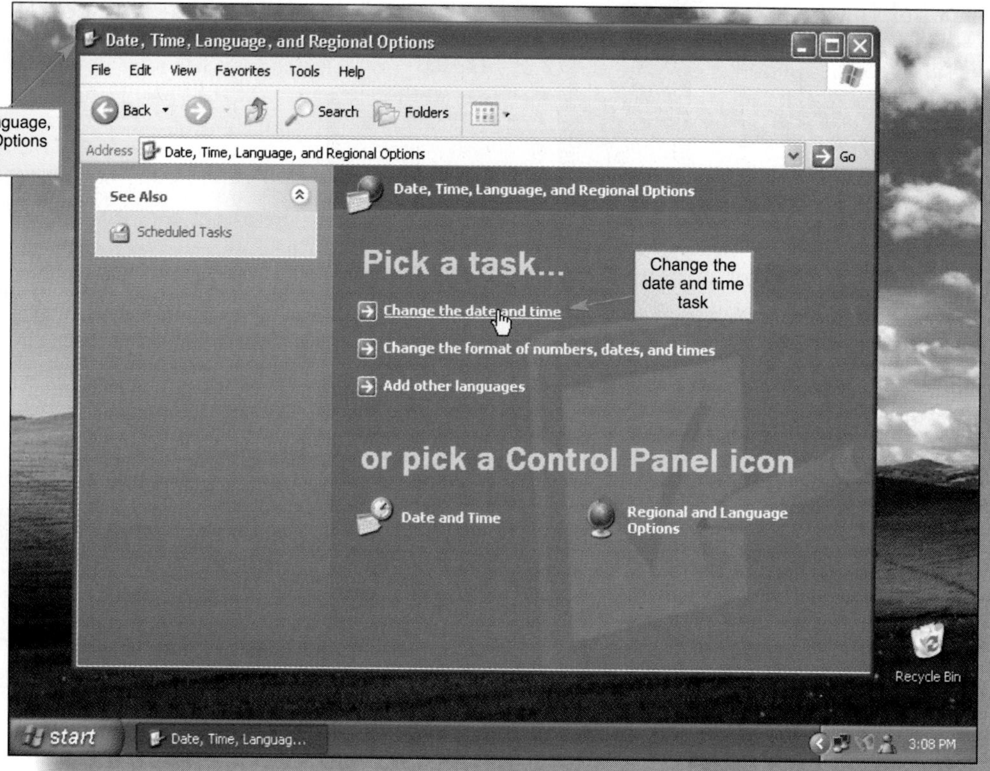

FIGURE 5-38

2 Click Change the date and time. Point to the month box arrow.

The Date and Time Properties dialog box and Date & Time sheet display (Figure 5-39). The Date area contains the month box with the current month, the year box with the current year, and a monthly calendar with the current day highlighted. The Time area contains an analog clock and the current time. The current time zone displays below the Date and Time areas. The date, time, and time zone may be different on your computer.

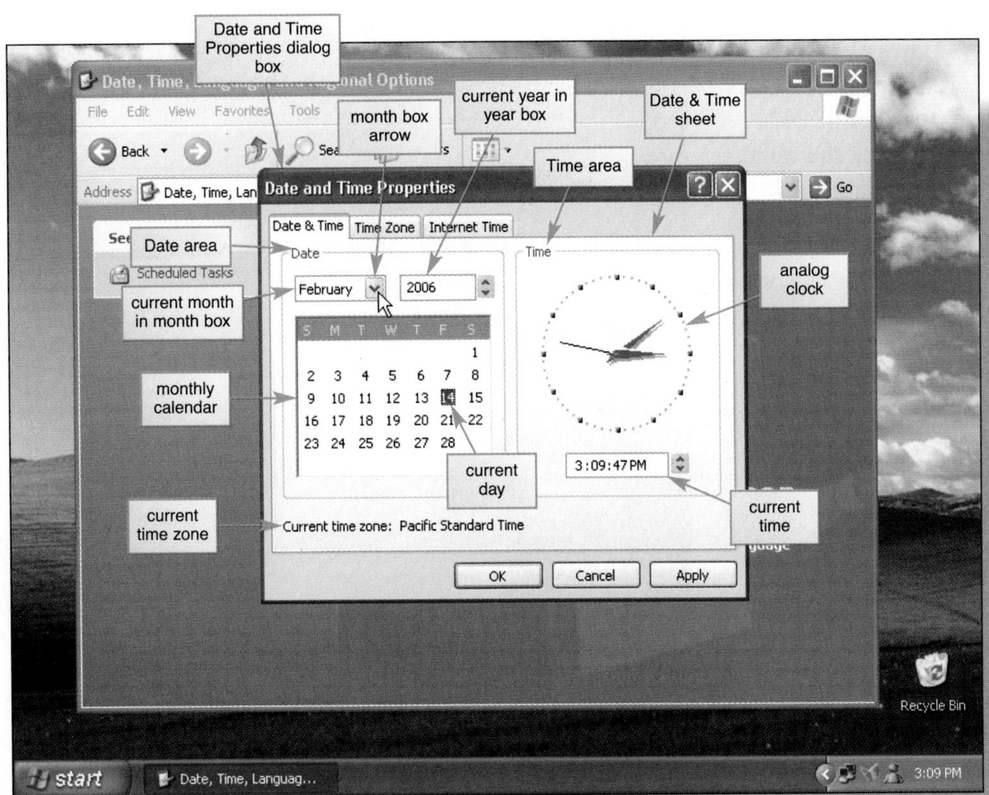

FIGURE 5-39

3 Click the month box arrow. Point to October.

The month list box, containing the highlighted October entry, displays (Figure 5-40).

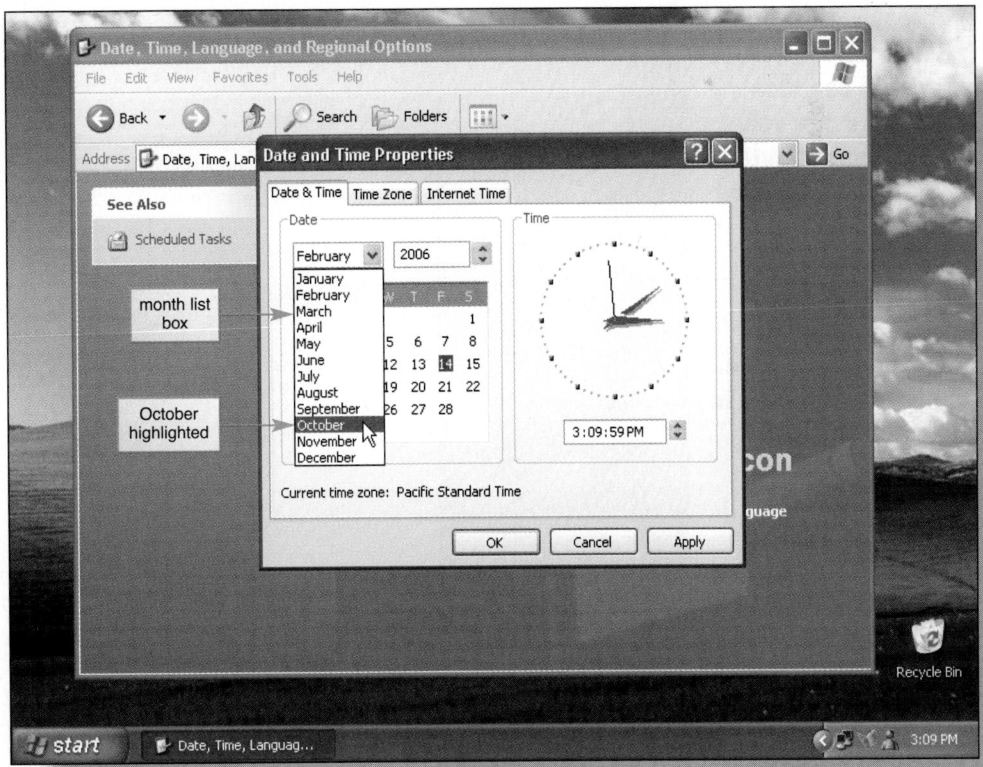

FIGURE 5-40

4 Click October. Click the year box up or down arrow until 2006 displays. Click the number 15 in the monthly calendar.

The month box contains the October entry, the year box contains the 2006 entry, and the number 15 is highlighted in the monthly calendar (Figure 5-41).

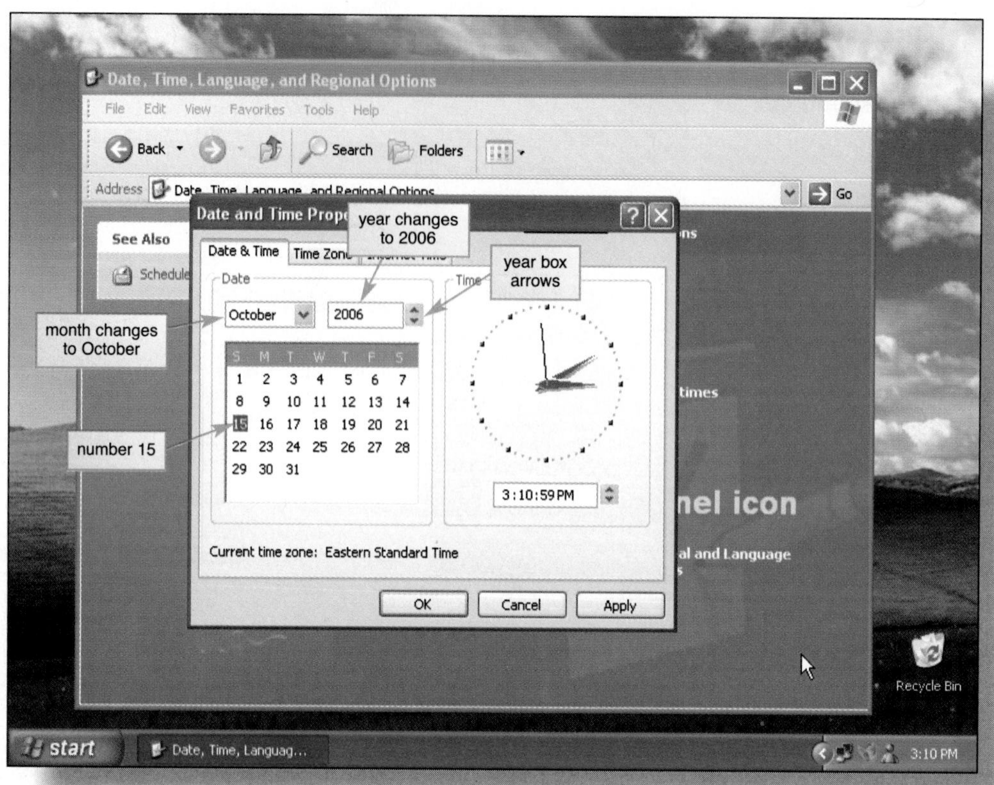

FIGURE 5-41

5 Double-click the hour value in the time text box and then type 11 as the new value. Double-click the minute value in the time text box and then type 00 as the new value. Double-click the second value in the time text box and then type 00 as the new value. If the PM entry displays in the time text box, click the PM entry and then click the up arrow to display the AM entry.

The new time (11:00:00 AM) displays in the time text box and on the analog clock (Figure 5-42).

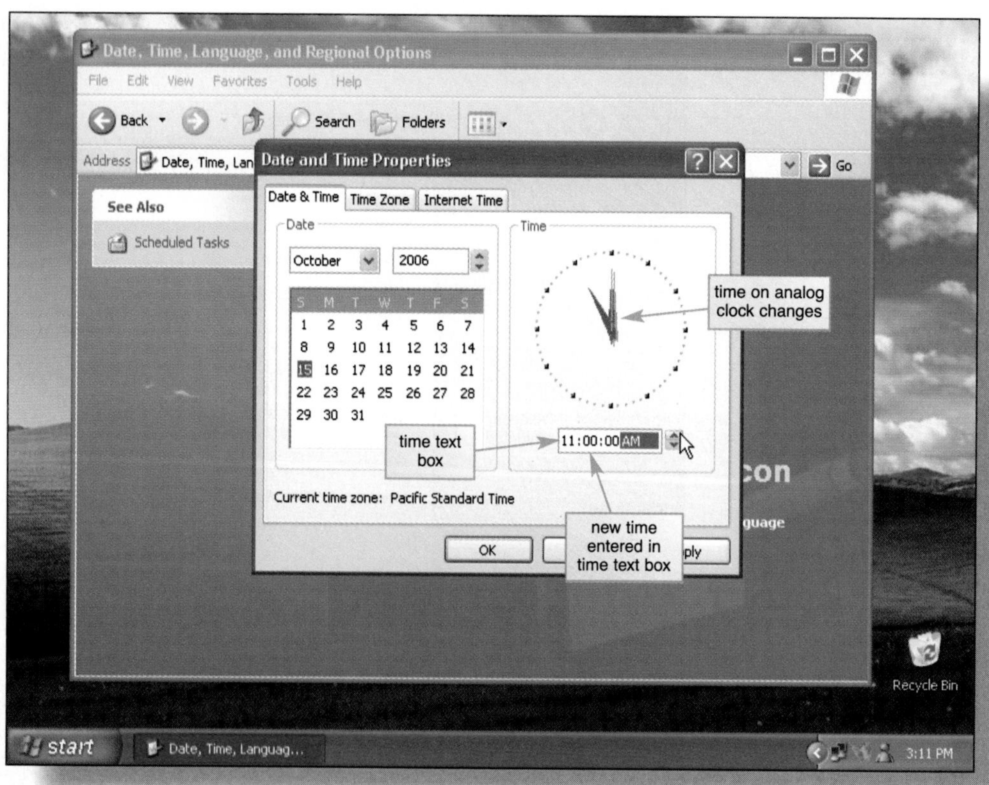

FIGURE 5-42

6 Click the Time Zone tab. Point to the Time Zone box arrow.

The Time Zone sheet displays (Figure 5-43). The Time Zone sheet contains the Time Zone box containing the current time zone, a world map, and a check mark displays in the Automatically adjust clock for daylight saving changes check box.

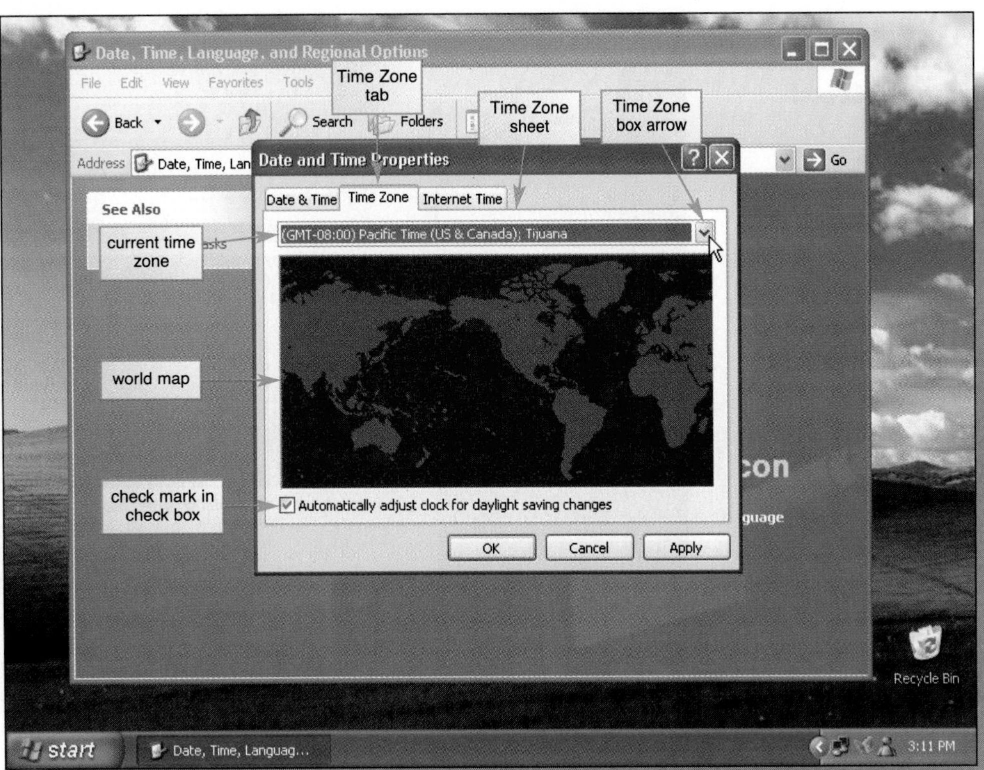

FIGURE 5-43

7 Click the Time Zone box arrow. Point to the (GMT-03:30) Newfoundland entry in the Time Zone list box.

The Time Zone list box displays (Figure 5-44). The (GMT-03:30) Newfoundland entry is highlighted in the Time Zone list.

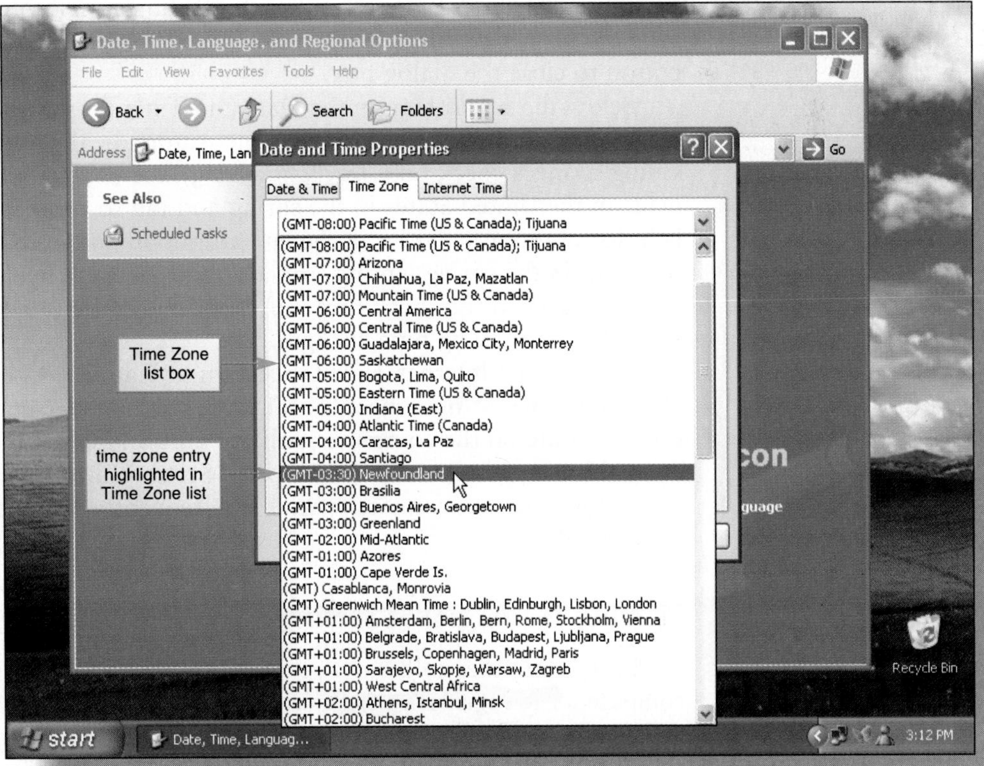

FIGURE 5-44

8 Click (GMT-03:30) Newfoundland. Point to the Cancel button.

The new time zone displays in the Time Zone box and the world map shifts to display the area of the world containing the new time zone (Figure 5-45).

9 Click the Cancel button.

Windows XP cancels the date, time, and time zone changes made and closes the Date and Time Properties dialog box.

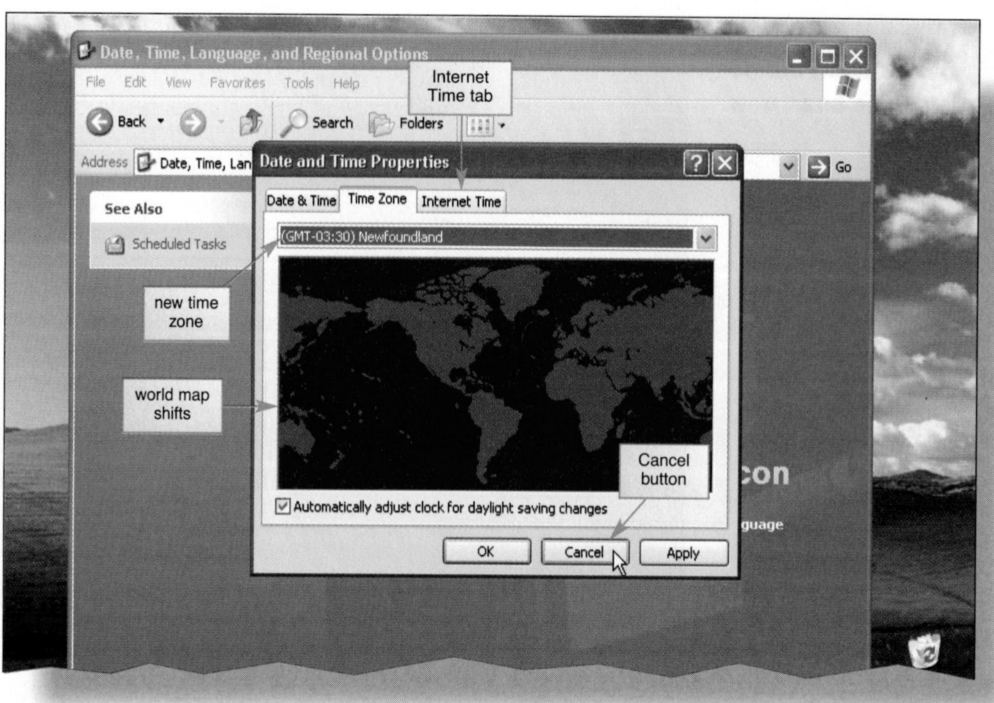

FIGURE 5-45

1. Click Switch to Classic View, double-click Date and Time icon
2. Click Date and Time icon in Date, Time, Language, and Regional Options window
3. In notification area double-click time

If you do not have administrative privileges and try to perform the previous steps, the Date and Time Properties dialog box containing the message, You do not have the proper privilege level to change the System Time, displays. Click the OK button to close the dialog box.

Below the world map in the Date and Time Properties dialog box shown in Figure 5-43 on the previous page is the Automatically adjust clock for daylight saving changes check box. **Daylight Saving Time (DST)** is a one-hour time adjustment made in the United States in the spring and fall to provide more usable hours of daylight for outdoor activities in the late afternoon and evening. Clocks are set ahead one hour in the spring (spring forward) and set back one hour in the fall (fall back). A check mark in the check box causes the computer to adjust the time automatically when daylight saving time changes.

Clicking the Internet Time tab shown in Figure 5-45 displays the Internet Time sheet. The **Internet Time sheet** contains the settings to synchronize automatically the time and date on the computer with the time and date on an Internet time server using the time.windows.com Web page. Synchronization occurs weekly if you have a continuous Internet connection and less frequently if you connect to the Internet occasionally.

Viewing the Regional Setting

Every computer sold has a regional setting preset by the manufacturer of the computer. The **regional setting** determines the manner in which numbers, currency, date, and time display on the desktop and on printed documents. For example, the default regional setting for computers manufactured and sold in the United States is the English (United States) setting. The **English (United States) setting** causes numbers, currency, date, and time to display in a format that is familiar in the United States. Computers sold in other countries have a default regional setting that is familiar in those countries.

Although each computer comes with a default regional setting, you can change the format of the numbers, currency, date, and time of a region. While you change the actual date and time using the Date and Time Properties dialog box, you change the format of the date and time using the Regional and Language Options dialog box. Perform the following steps to view the default regional settings on the computer.

Steps To View the Time and Date Formats

1 Click Change the format of numbers, dates, and times in the Date, Time, Language, and Regional Options window.

The Regional and Language Options dialog box and Regional Options sheet display (Figure 5-46). The Standards and formats area contains the default regional setting, English (United States), and a sample of the number format (123,456,789.00), currency format ($123,456,789.00), time format (3:12:36 PM), short date format (10/15/2006), and long date format (Sunday, October 15, 2006).

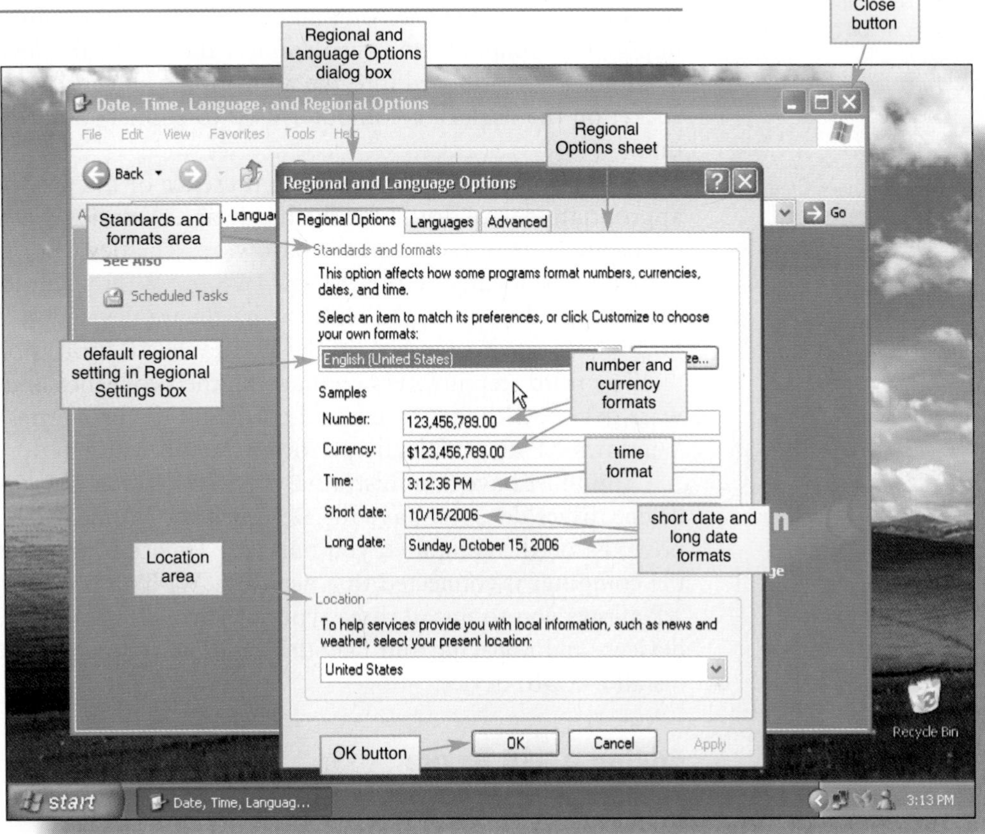

FIGURE 5-46

2 Click the OK button in the Regional and Language Options dialog box. Click the Close button in the Date, Time, Language, and Regional Options window to close the window.

The Regional and Language Options dialog box and the Date, Time, Language, and Regional Options window close.

Other Ways

1. Click Switch to Classic View, double-click Regional and Language Options icon
2. Click Regional and Language Options icon in Date, Time, Language, and Regional Options window
3. Click Start button, click Help and Support, click Index button, type `regional options`, double-click number, currency, time, and date settings, click Regional and Language Options link

Changing the default regional setting in the box in the Standards and formats area will change the format of the number, currency, time, short date, and long date to the format of the region selected.

The Location area at the bottom of the Regional and Language Options sheet contains the Location box that provides a list of countries or regions from which you can receive local content when using a Web browser. You would select a new country or region only if it is different from the default regional setting in the Regional Settings box in the Standards and formats area. For instance, if you live in United States but want to receive news, weather, and sports from the Virgin Islands when you open your Web browser, you would select Virgin Islands in the Location box.

More About

Adding New Hardware

Adding new hardware to a computer used to be a difficult task. USB devices and Plug and Play devices have made it easier by allowing a non-computer person to add hardware and thus saving the cost of having a computer professional add the hardware. Although Plug and Play devices have been around since the release of Windows 95, Windows 98 was the first operating system to allow you to install USB devices.

Adding New Hardware

When you purchase hardware for a computer, you must install the hardware physically on the computer and then set up the new hardware so that Windows XP recognizes it. Installing a new hardware device is a three-step process. The first step is to connect the hardware device to the computer. This usually involves following the hardware manufacturer's installation instructions to connect the new hardware or its components to the computer. This step may require you to shut down and unplug the computer, and then connect the hardware device to the appropriate port or insert a circuit board into the appropriate slot inside the system unit. A **port** is a socket on the back of a computer used to connect a hardware device to the system unit.

The second step is to detect the presence of the new hardware and load the appropriate device driver for the hardware. A **device driver** is a program used by the operating system to control the hardware. The device driver for a new piece of hardware may be located in the WINDOWS (or WINNT) folder on the hard disk, on a 3½" floppy disk packaged with the hardware device, on the hardware manufacturer's Web site, or located on the Windows XP Professional CD-ROM.

The third step involves configuring the properties and settings of the new hardware device. Although you could configure the properties and settings manually, Windows XP automatically performs this operation.

You must have administrative privileges to install or configure hardware if the device driver does not have the Designed for Windows logo, the device driver does not exist on the computer, you must use Device Manager to configure the device, or the computer is connected to a network. With administrative privileges, Windows XP allows you to install three types of hardware devices: USB devices, Plug and Play devices, and non-Plug and Play devices. The following section illustrates how to install a (USB) device.

More About

USB Technology

Most new computers are manufactured with one or more USB ports for connecting serial devices to your computer. The dimensions of the port are approximately 1mm by 7mm. The IEEE 1394 port, similar to the USB port, measures 1mm by 5mm and allows you to connect faster serial devices to your computer. You cannot plug a USB device into an IEEE 1394 port, and visa versa.

Adding a USB Device

Many hardware devices require you to install the hardware by shutting down Windows, removing the cover from the system unit, adding a circuit board to the computer, replacing the cover, and restarting Windows. In addition, the number of hardware devices you can add to the computer is limited by the number of spaces available inside the system unit. In most cases, you can add only two or three boards.

In response to this problem, computer hardware manufacturers built hardware devices, called **universal serial bus (USB) devices**, according to the USB specifications; computer manufacturers added one or more special ports, called the **USB ports**, to their computers; and Microsoft added support for USB devices to the Windows XP operating system. With one USB port, you can install as many as 127 USB devices without having to add a single circuit board to the computer or restart the computer. In addition, the electrical power for a USB device comes through the USB port, making an electrical power cord unnecessary.

To install a USB device, you plug the cord from the USB device into the USB port of the computer. Windows XP installs the device, finds the correct device driver for the USB device, and associates the driver with the device. If the device driver for the USB device is located on the hard drive, the device is installed automatically. If the device driver is not located on the hard disk, you may use Windows XP to search the Windows XP Professional CD-ROM, a 3½" floppy disk supplied by the device manufacturer, or the manufacturer's Web site for the device driver.

To illustrate how to add a USB hardware device, you will add the Logitech QuickCam USB device to the computer. If you have administrative privileges, perform the following steps to add the USB device. If you do not have administrative privileges, do not have a Logitech QuickCam device, or the Windows XP Professional CD-ROM, read the following steps without actually performing them.

Note: Administrative privileges are required to perform these steps

Steps To Add a USB Device

1 Connect the Logitech QuickCam USB device to a USB port on the computer.

The Logitech QuickCam USB device plugs into the USB port 2 on the computer shown in Figure 5-47.

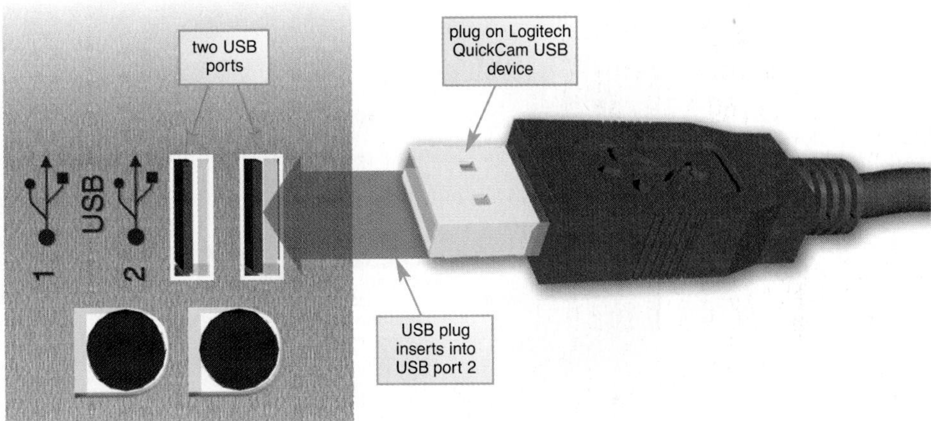

FIGURE 5-47

2 Windows XP detects the presence of a new USB hardware device.

The Add Hardware icon displays in the notification area and the Found New Hardware balloon displays above the icon (Figure 5-48). The device type, Camera, displays below the balloon title to indicate a camera is being added.

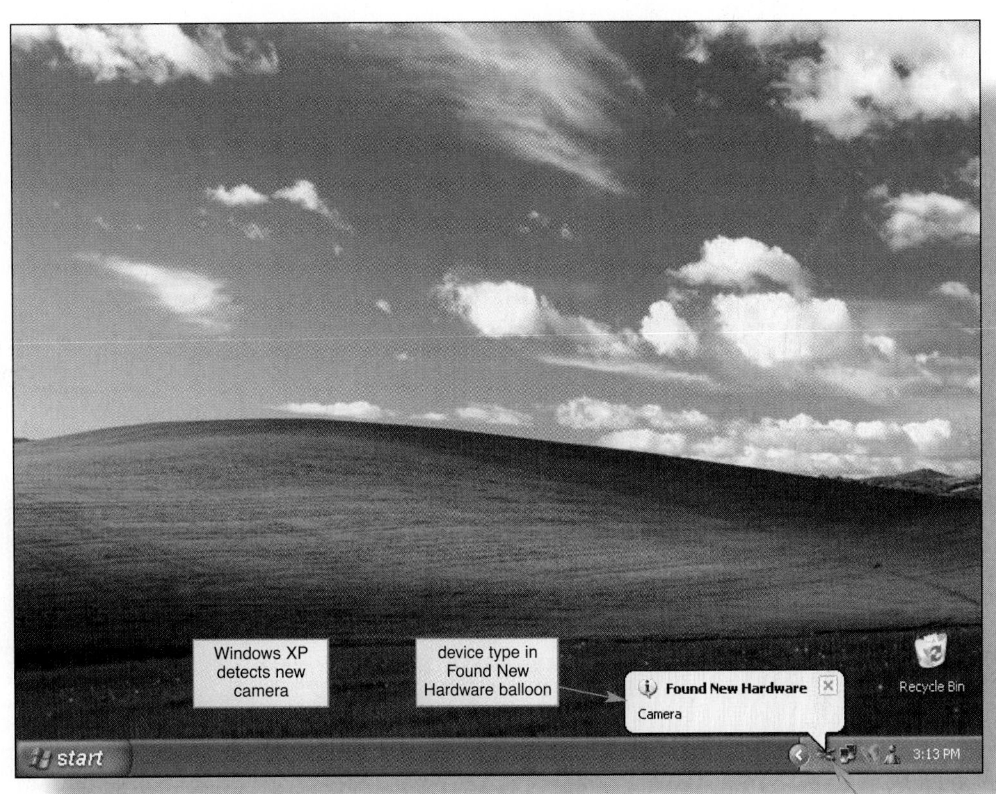

FIGURE 5-48

3 Windows XP searches for the device driver for the Logitech QuickCam USB device.

The words, Logitech QuickCam Web (0801), replace the word, Camera, in the Found New Hardware balloon to indicate the Logitech QuickCam USB device was recognized and Windows XP searched for and found the device driver for the camera (Figure 5-49).

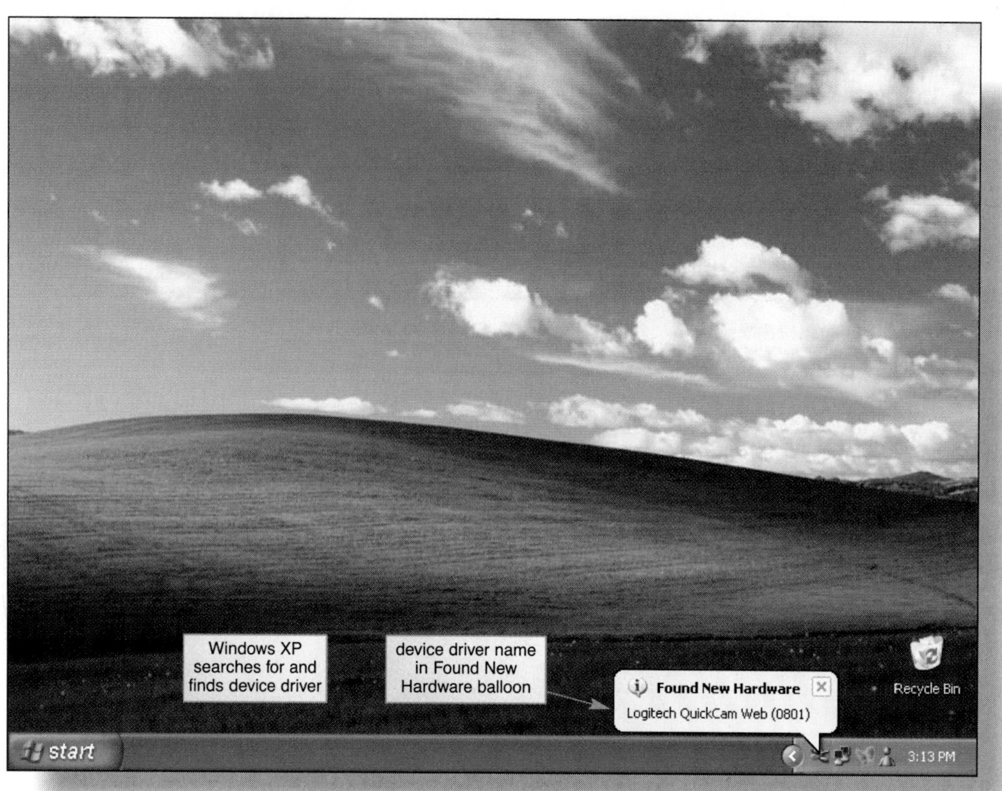

FIGURE 5-49

4 Windows XP installs the device driver for the Logitech QuickCam USB device.

The message, Your new hardware is installed and ready to use., replaces the words, Logitech QuickCam Web (0801), in the Found New Hardware balloon to indicate the Logitech QuickCam USB device is installed and ready to use.

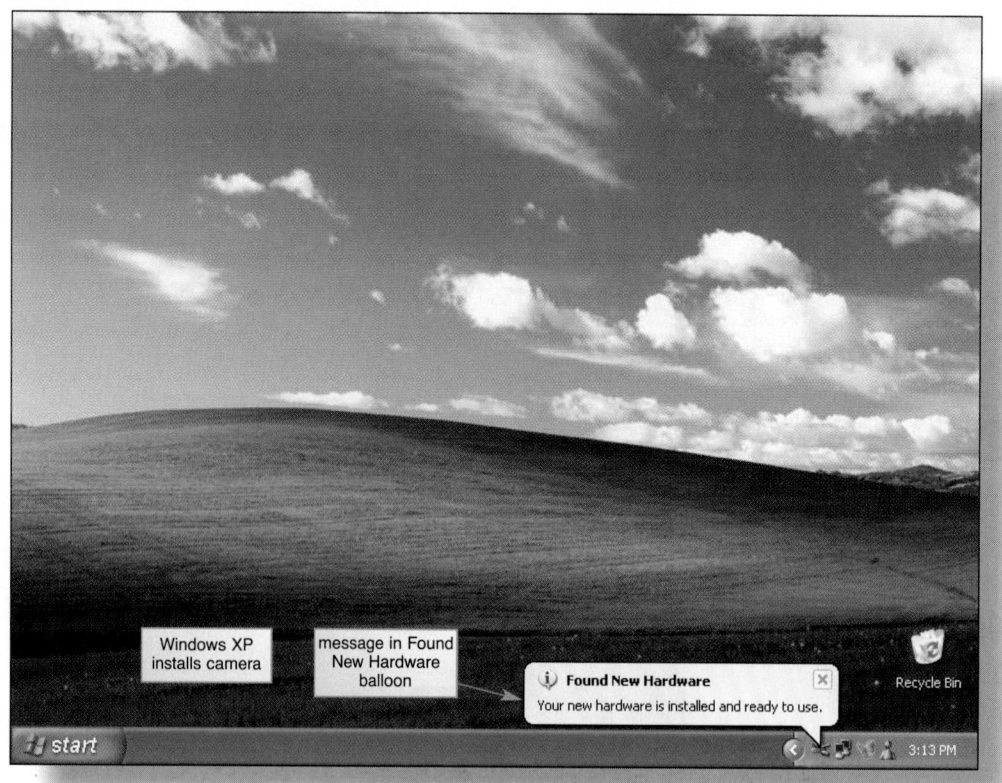

FIGURE 5-50

If you do not have administrative privileges and try to perform the previous steps, the Found New Hardware balloon containing the word, Camera, displays above the Add Hardware icon in the notification area and the Found New Hardware dialog box displays. The message, You must be a member of the Administrators group on this computer to install this hardware: Camera, and the User name box and Password text box display. With the permission of the administrator, you or the administrator can type the administrator user name and password and then click the OK button to install the USB device.

Installing a Plug and Play Device

A second type of hardware device that Windows XP allows you to install is a Plug and Play device. **Plug and Play** (**PNP**) is a design philosophy, or industry standard, developed by Intel Corporation to make it easier to add new hardware devices to a computer. Plug and Play allows the operating system to detect the presence of a new hardware device and configure the hardware automatically with little or no user intervention. If the box in which the Plug and Play hardware device is packaged identifies the device as Plug and Play and you have administrative privileges, Windows XP can use the Plug and Play technology to set up the hardware device.

When installing a Plug and Play device, turn off the power to the computer, connect the device to the computer according to the manufacturer's instructions, and then turn on the computer. Windows will detect the new Plug and Play device and install the necessary device drivers and software automatically. In some cases, you may not be required to turn off and then turn on the computer.

Installing a Non-Plug and Play Device

A third type of hardware device that Windows XP allows you to install is a non-Plug and Play device. Some devices sold today are not USB devices, and some are not manufactured according to the Plug and Play specifications. To install these devices, you must have administrative privileges and use the Add Hardware wizard. A **wizard** is a computer tool that makes a complex task easier by guiding you through the task step by step. The **Add Hardware wizard** walks you through the steps to install and configure a non-Plug and Play device.

In addition to having administrative privileges, other network policies also may prevent you from installing non-Plug and Play devices. If an administrator already has loaded the device drivers for the device, you can install the device from the computer without administrative privileges.

To install and configure a non-Plug and Play device, first you must connect the hardware to the computer according to the manufacturer's instructions. After installing the device, start the Add Hardware wizard by clicking the Start button, clicking Control Panel, clicking Printers and Other Hardware, and then clicking Add Hardware in the See Also area in the Printers and Other Hardware window. The Add Hardware wizard locates the software required to operate the device and copies the software to the correct location on the hard drive.

More *About*

Plug and Play Devices

Some hardware devices sold today still do not use the Plug and Play technology. Previous versions of the Windows operating systems allowed you to use the Add New Hardware wizard to install these devices. Information found in Windows Help and Support instructs you to use the Add New Hardware wizard only for devices that are not plug and play.

More About

Adding a Printer

When you click the Finish button shown in Figure 5-59, Windows XP may ask you to insert the Windows XP CD-ROM. If you do not have access to the disk, ask your instructor to install the printer driver for the Xerox DocuPrint N2125 printer on the hard drive of your computer.

Adding a Printer

In Project 2, you printed a document from within an application using the Print command on the File menu and then printed multiple documents from within a folder using the Print command on a shortcut menu. The procedure to add a printer to a computer depends upon whether the printer is a local printer or network printer. A **local printer** is a printer directly attached to the computer. A **network printer** is a printer attached to another computer or directly to the network. New printers generally support the Plug and Play standard, making it easier to add a printer. Older printers may not support Plug and Play.

In the following section, you will use the **Add Printer wizard** to add a local printer that supports Plug and Play. To add a local printer, you must have administrative privileges, know the port to use to connect the printer to the computer, and decide whether the printer should be the default printer. A **port** is a socket on the back of a computer used to connect a hardware device to the system unit. You typically use the **LPT1 printer port** to connect a printer to the system unit. The **default printer** is the printer to which all printed documents are sent. Most likely, a printer already is attached to the computer on which you are working and that printer is designated as the default printer. Therefore, you should not designate the printer you add to the computer in the following steps as the default printer.

The following steps add the Xerox DocuPrint N2125 printer to the computer as a local printer, use the LPT1 printer port, but does not designate the printer as the default printer. If you have administrative privileges, perform the following steps to add the Xerox DocuPrint N2125 printer even if you do not have a Xerox DocuPrint N2125 printer. If you do not have administrative privileges, read the following steps without actually performing them.

Note: Administrative privileges are required to perform these steps

Steps To Add a Printer

1 Click the Start button, click Control Panel, and then click the Printers and Other Hardware icon in the right pane of the Control Panel window. Point to Add a printer in the Pick a task area in the Printers and Other Hardware window.

The Printers and Other Hardware window opens in the same window as the Control Panel window displays (Figure 5-51). The Add a printer task displays in the Pick a task area.

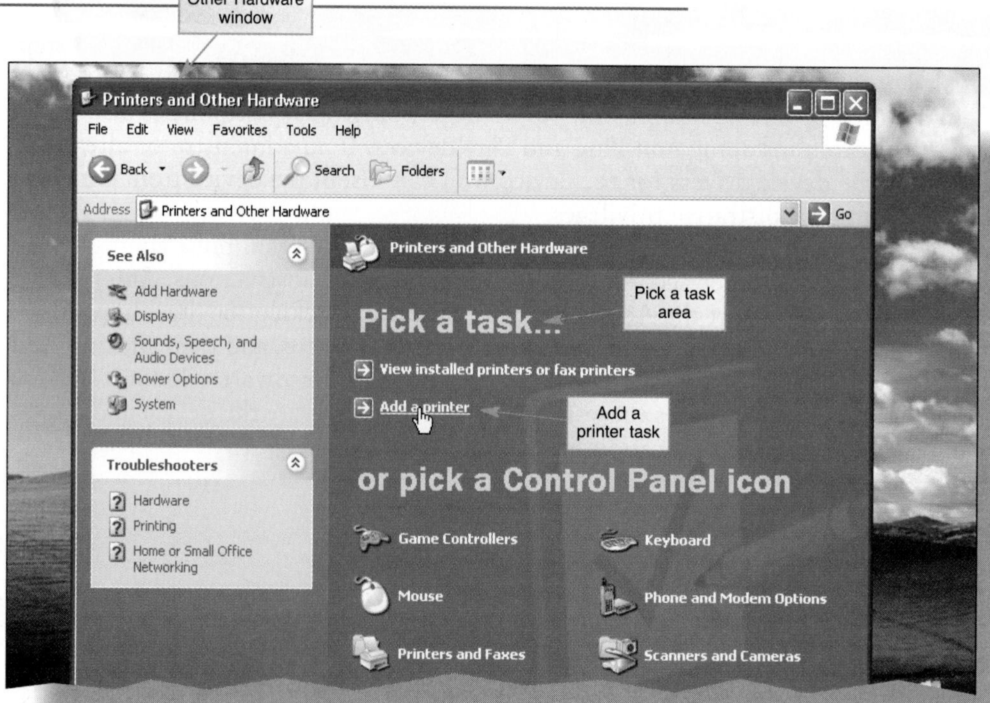

FIGURE 5-51

2 Click Add a printer. Point to the Next button.

The Printers and Faxes window opens in the same window as the Printers and Other Hardware window displays, the Add Printer wizard starts, and the Add Printer Wizard dialog box containing a title and messages displays (Figure 5-52). Although not visible, the HP LaserJet IIIP icon displays in the Printers and Faxes window. This icon represents the default printer.

FIGURE 5-52

3 Click the Next button. If necessary, click Local printer attached to this computer. Point to the Next button.

An upper and lower area display in the dialog box (Figure 5-53). The upper area contains a title and message, and the lower area contains instructions and the selected Local printer attached to this computer option button.

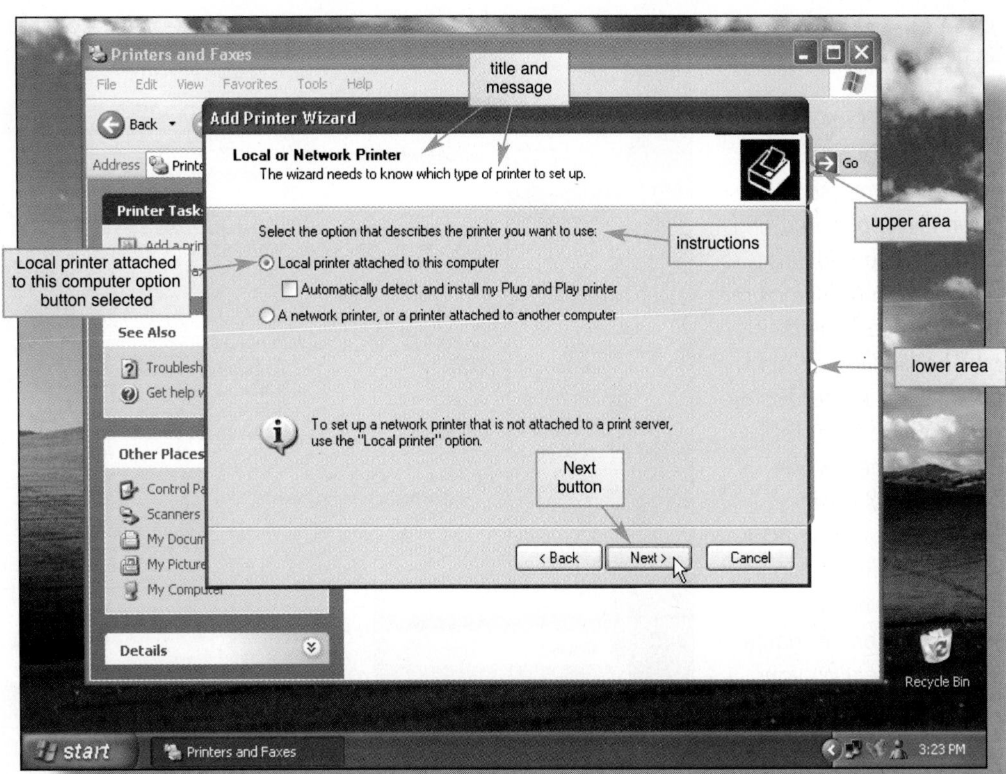

FIGURE 5-53

4 Click the Next button. Point to the Next button.

The upper and lower areas change (Figure 5-54). A new title and message display in the upper area. The lower area contains instructions, the selected Use the following port option button and box. The highlighted LPT1: (Recommended Printer Port) entry in the box indicates the new printer will use the LPT1 port.

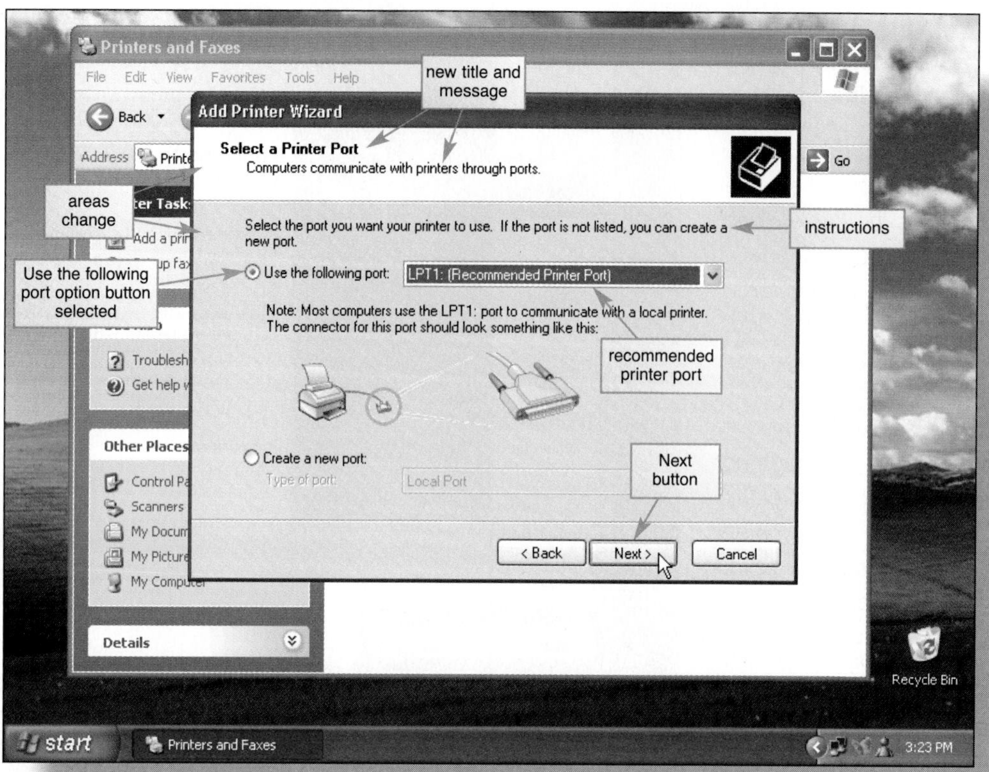

FIGURE 5-54

5 Click the Next button.

The upper and lower areas change (Figure 5-55). A new title and message display in the upper area and the lower area contains instructions, a Manufacturer list box, and a Printers list box. The highlighted Agfa manufacturer name displays in the Manufacturer list box and the dimmed AGFA-AccuSet v52.3 printer name displays in the Printers list box. The highlighted manufacturer name and dimmed printer name may be different on your computer.

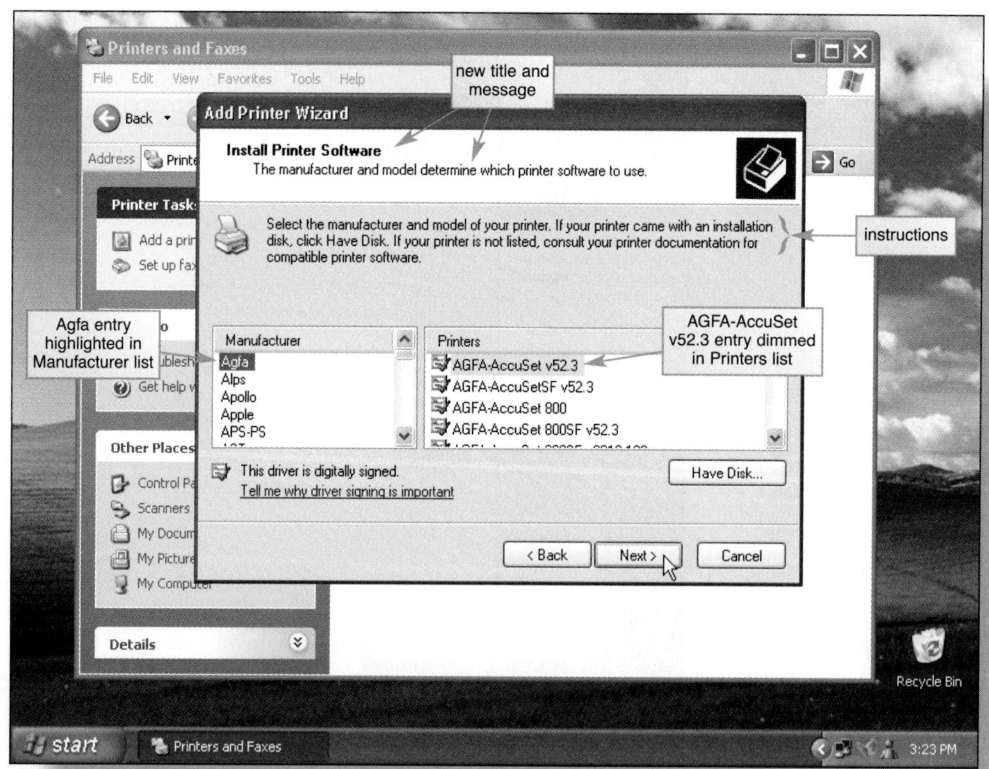

FIGURE 5-55

6 Scroll down the Manufacturer list to display Xerox and then click Xerox. Scroll down the Printers list to display Xerox DocuPrint N2125 and then click Xerox DocuPrint N2125. Point to the Next button.

The dimmed Xerox name displays in the Manufacturer list and the highlighted Xerox DocuPrint N2125 name displays in the Printers list (Figure 5-56).

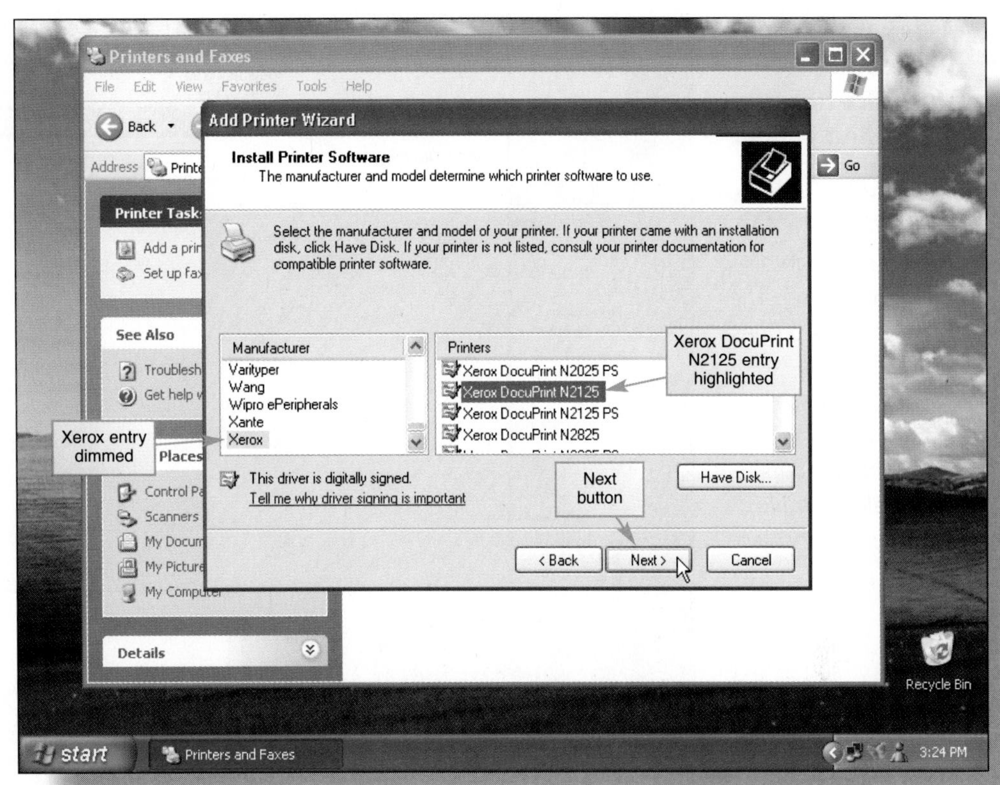

FIGURE 5-56

7 Click the Next button. If necessary, click No. Point to the Next button.

The upper and lower areas change (Figure 5-57). A new title and message display in the upper area. The lower area contains instructions, a Printer name text box containing the highlighted Xerox DocuPrint N2125 printer name, a question, and the selected No option button.

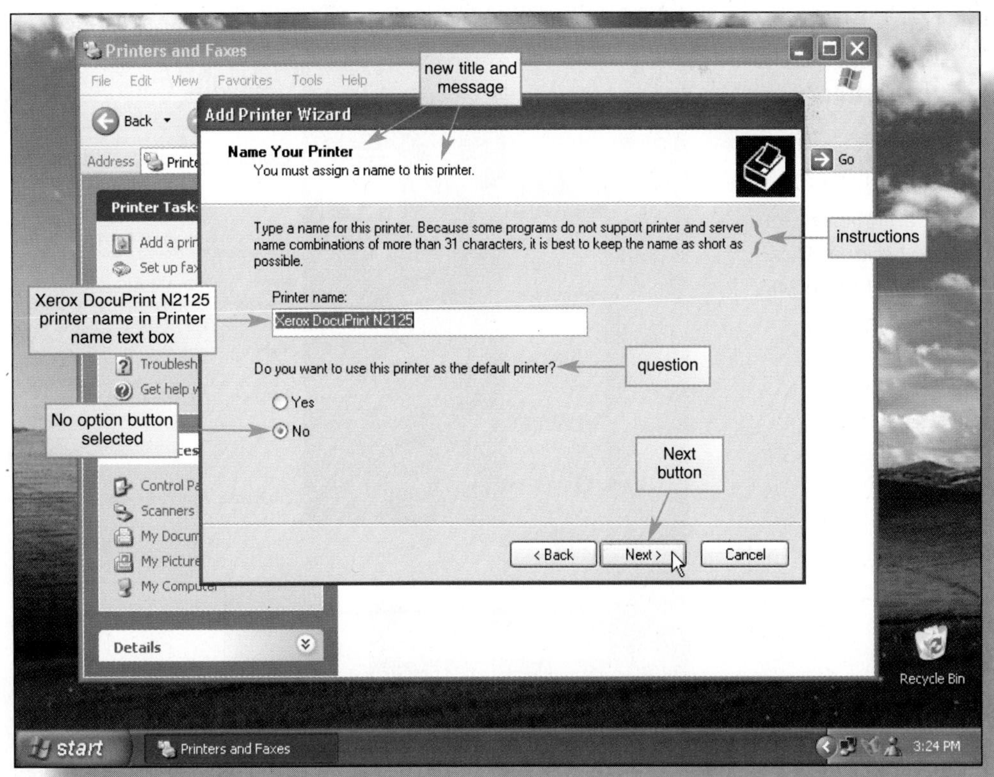

FIGURE 5-57

8 Click the Next button. If necessary, click No. Point to the Next button.

The upper and lower areas change (Figure 5-58). A new title and message display in the upper area. The lower area contains a question and the selected No option button. Because you are adding a printer without having installed the printer, you should select the No option button so that a test page will not print.

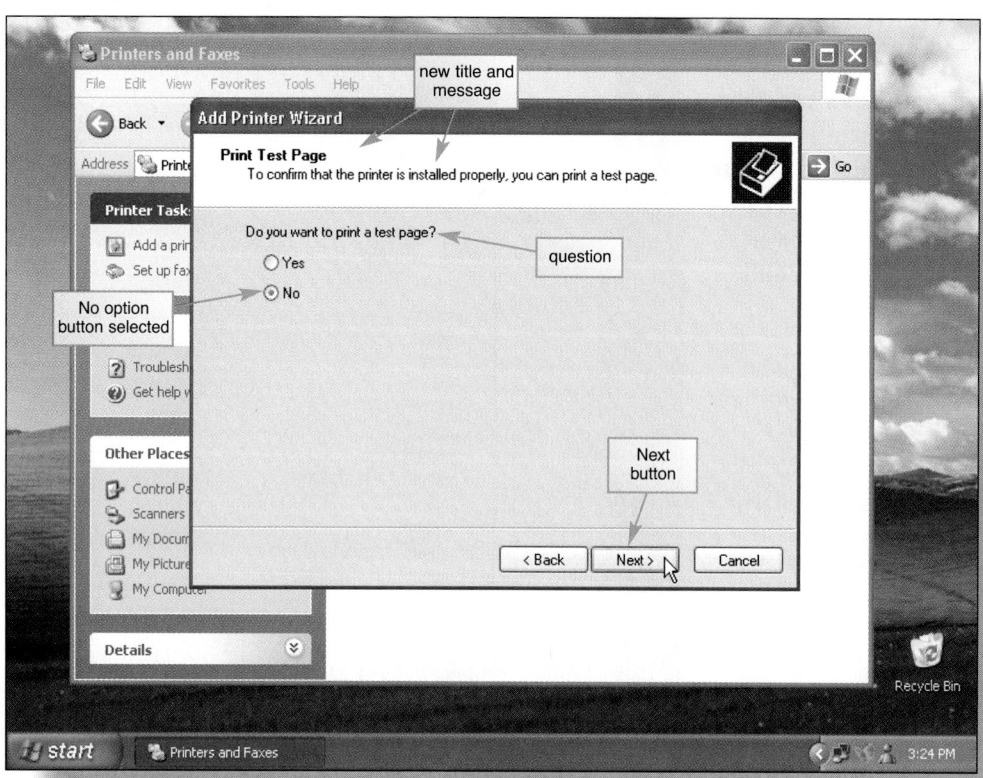

FIGURE 5-58

9 Click the Next button. Point to the Finish button.

The Completing the Add Printer Wizard title displays in the Add Printer Wizard dialog box (Figure 5-59). A summary of the printer settings displays.

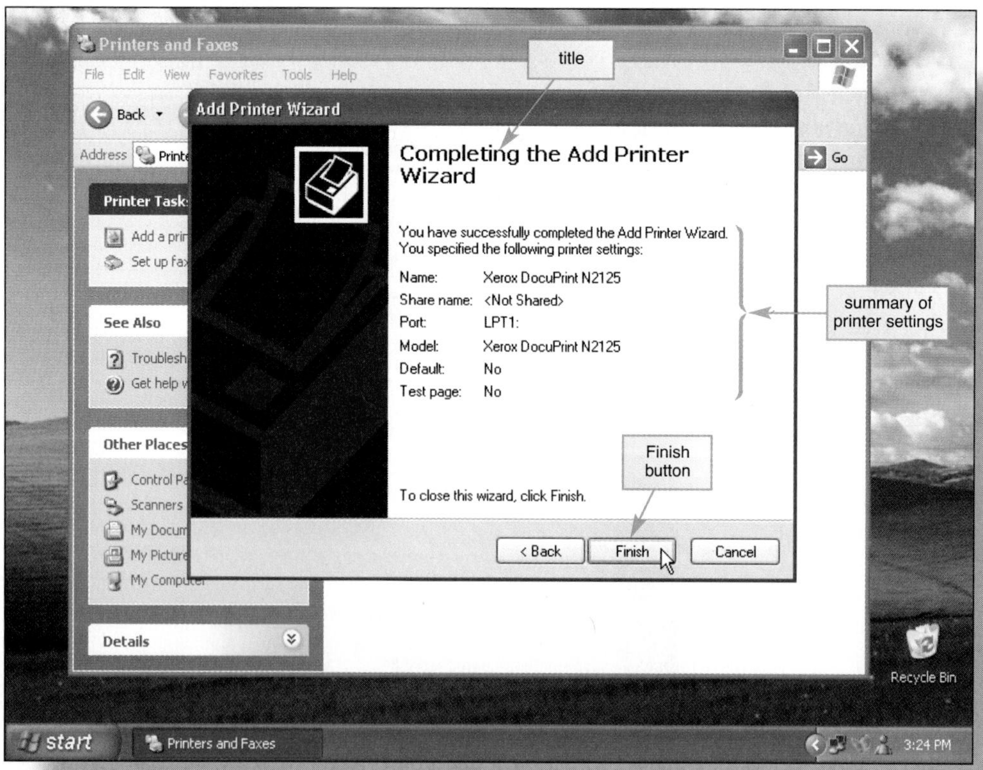

FIGURE 5-59

10 Click the Finish button.

The Copying Files dialog box may display as the printer device driver is located and copied to the WINDOWS (or WINNT) folder. Then, the Add Printer Wizard dialog box closes and the Xerox DocuPrint N2125 printer icon is added to the Printers and Faxes window (Figure 5-60). The default HP LaserJet IIIP printer icon, identified by a white check mark in a black circle, also displays in the window.

11 Click the Close button in the Printers and Faxes window.

The Printers and Faxes window closes.

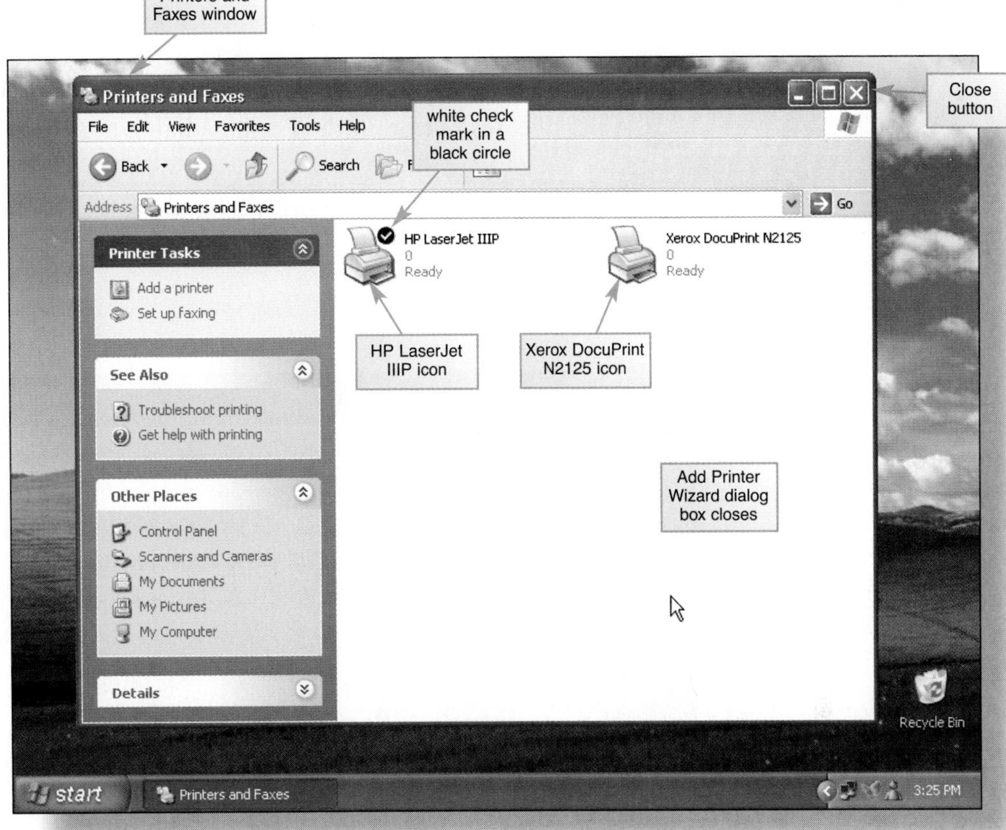

FIGURE 5-60

Other Ways

1. Click Switch to Classic View, double-click Printers and Faxes icon, click Add a printer
2. Click Start button, click Control Panel, click Printers and Other Hardware, click Printers and Faxes, click Add a Printer

Although hidden behind the Add Printer Wizard dialog box in Figure 5-52 on page WIN 5.47, the HP LaserJet IIIP icon in Figure 5-60 is visible in the Printers and Faxes window. The white check mark in a black circle on the HP LaserJet IIIP icon indicates the printer is the default printer. The HP LaserJet IIIP icon may not display on your computer.

If you do not have administrative privileges and try to perform the previous steps, Windows XP will only allow you to install a network printer or a printer attached to another computer.

Removing a Printer

After adding the Xerox DocuPrint N2125 printer to the computer, remove the Xerox DocuPrint N2125 printer from the computer and its icon from the Printers and Faxes window by performing the following steps.

TO REMOVE A PRINTER

1. Click the Start button and then click Control Panel.
2. Click the Printers and Other Hardware icon.
3. Click View installed printers or fax printers in the Pick a task area.
4. Right-click the Xerox DocuPrint N2125 printer icon in the Printers and Faxes window.

5 Click Delete on the shortcut menu.

6 Click the Yes button in the Printers dialog box.

The Xerox DocuPrint N2125 printer icon is removed from the Printers and Faxes window (Figure 5-61).

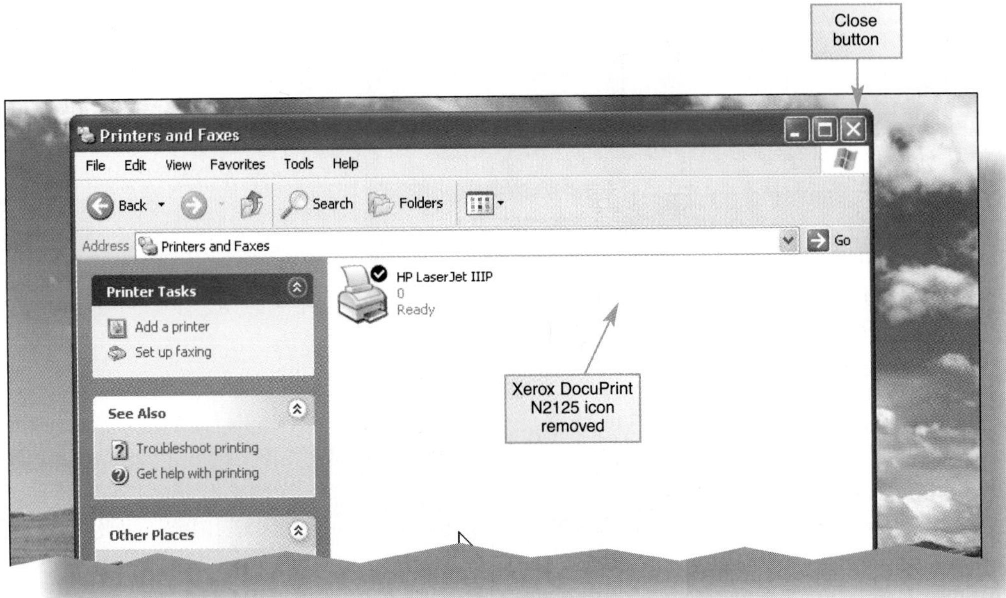

FIGURE 5-61

Closing the Printers and Faxes Window

After removing the Xerox DocuPrint N2125 printer icon from the Printers and Faxes window, close the Printers and Faxes window by performing the step below.

TO CLOSE THE PRINTERS AND FAXES WINDOW

1 Click the Close button in the Printers and Faxes window.

The Printers and Faxes window closes.

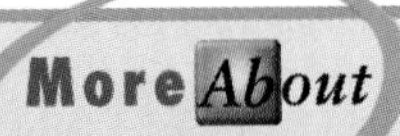

Troubleshooting

Troubleshooters allow you to investigate and solve a problem while simultaneously following a set of instructions in the Windows Help and Support window. For best results, resize the Help and Support window and move it to the right half of the desktop and use the left half of the desktop to follow the troubleshooter steps. If you must restart the computer during the process, print the troubleshooter instructions before restarting.

Solving Hardware Problems Using a Troubleshooter

A **troubleshooter** is available if you encounter problems when using Windows XP. Among the problems you can solve using a troubleshooter are problems with hardware devices (video and sound cards, hard drives and CD-ROM drives, mouse devices and keyboards, camera and scanners, and modems), networking (Internet, intranet, and dial-up connections), system setup (installing and launching Windows XP), printing, and adding new hardware.

As an example, assume you just added a set of speakers to the computer. When you insert an audio CD-ROM in the CD-ROM drive, the CD-ROM plays but no sound comes from the speaker. Because the speakers are new and you have never connected a pair of speakers to the computer before, you are unsure of the problem and would like to use the troubleshooter to investigate it. Perform the following steps to troubleshoot this sound problem.

Note: Steps may not work with Windows XP Home edition

Steps To Solve a Problem Using a Troubleshooter

1 Click the Start button and then click Help and Support. If necessary, maximize the Help and Support Center window. Point to Fixing a problem in the Pick a Help topic area.

The maximized Help and Support Center window displays (Figure 5-62). The mouse pointer changes to a hand icon when positioned on the Fixing a problem category and the category is underlined.

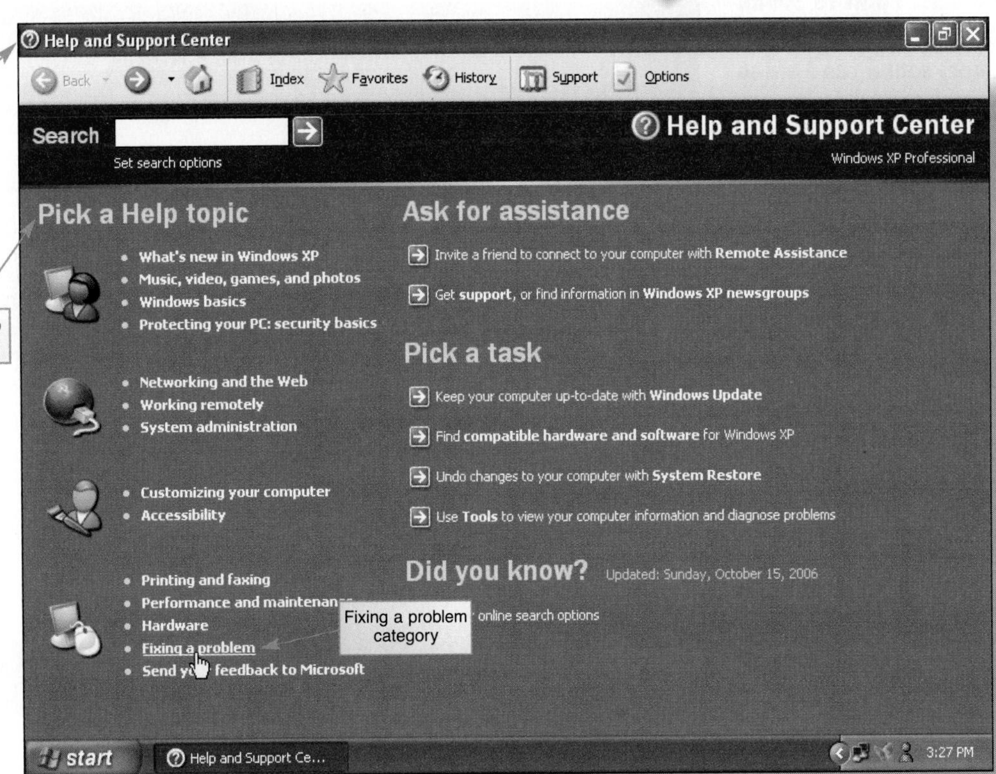

FIGURE 5-62

2 Click Fixing a problem and then point to Games, sound, and video problems.

The navigation pane and topic pane display in the Help and Support Center window (Figure 5-63). The underlined Games, sound, and video problems subcategory displays in the Fixing a problem area in the navigation pane. The Fixing a problem page in the topic pane contains information about fixing problems.

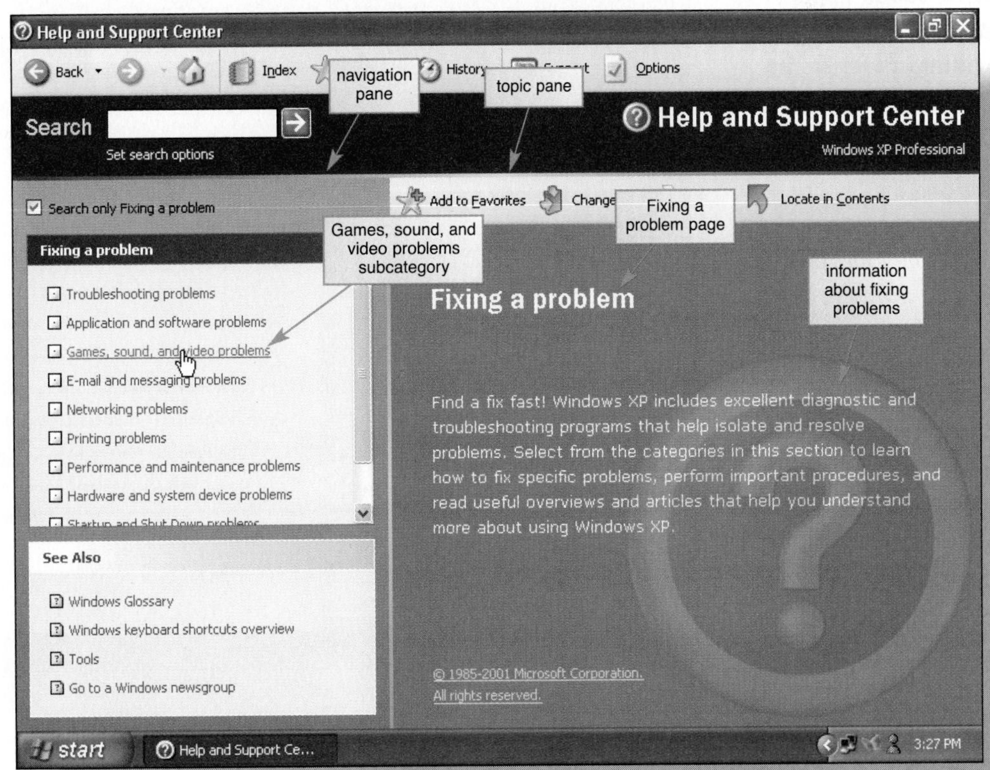

FIGURE 5-63

3 Click Games, sound, and video problems. Point to Sound Troubleshooter in the Games, sound, and video problems page.

Windows XP selects the Games, sound, and video problems subcategory in the Fixing a problem area, displays the Games, sound, and video problems page in the topic pane, and underlines the Sound Troubleshooter task (Figure 5-64).

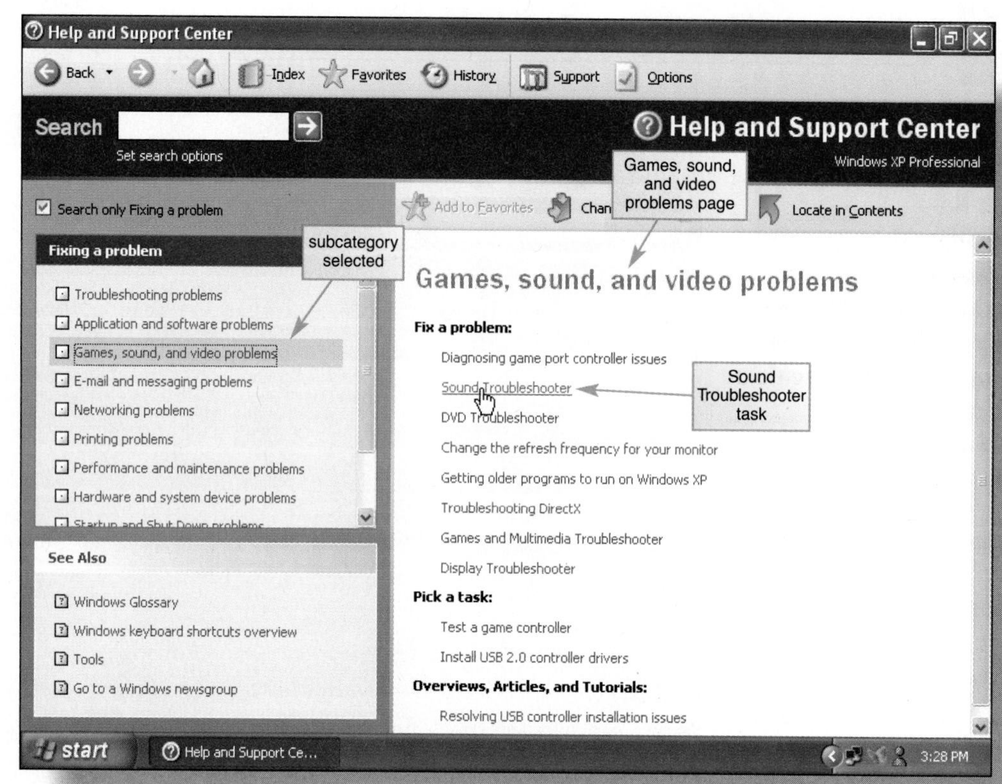

FIGURE 5-64

4 Click Sound Troubleshooter. Click A sound appears to play, but I do not hear anything. Point to the Next button.

The Sound Troubleshooter starts and the Sound Troubleshooter page displays in the topic pane (Figure 5-65). The Sound Troubleshooter page contains a question, a list of problems, and the Next button. The selected A sound appears to play, but I do not hear anything option button, is selected in the list.

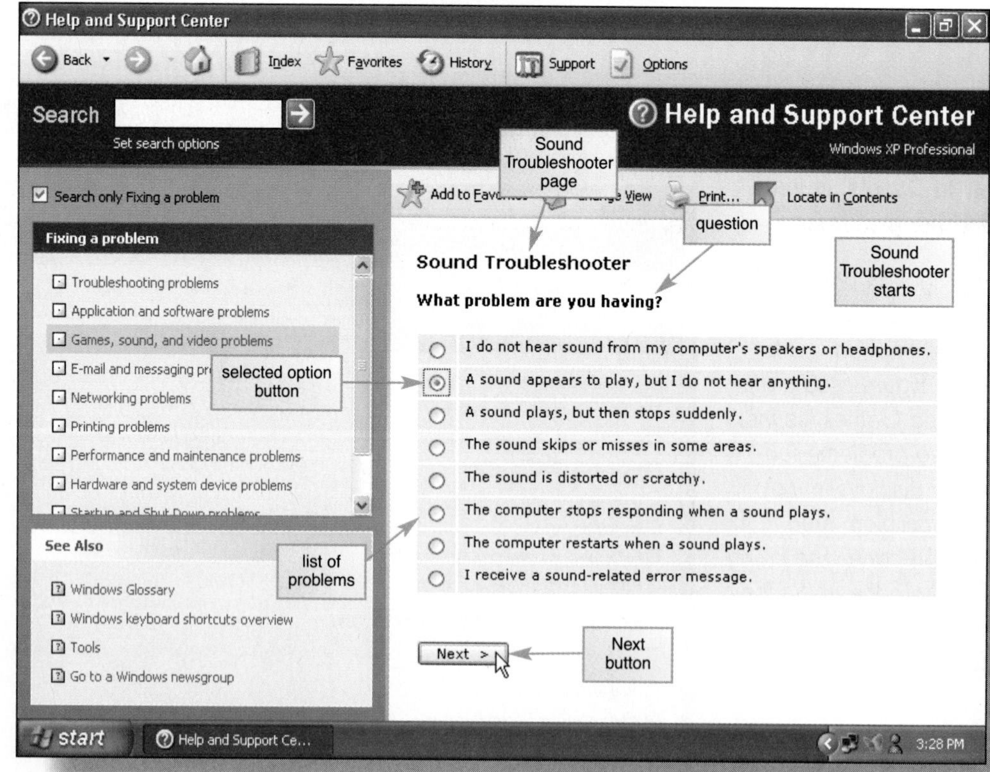

FIGURE 5-65

5 Click the Next button. Read the text in the topic pane and perform the three steps in the topic pane. In the process, you adjust the volume control and music plays through the speakers. Scroll the topic pane to display the bottom of the topic pane. Click Yes, there is sound coming from my speakers. Point to the Next button.

The problem is determined to be the volume setting. The topic pane is scrolled and the Yes, there is sound coming from my speakers option button is selected (Figure 5-66).

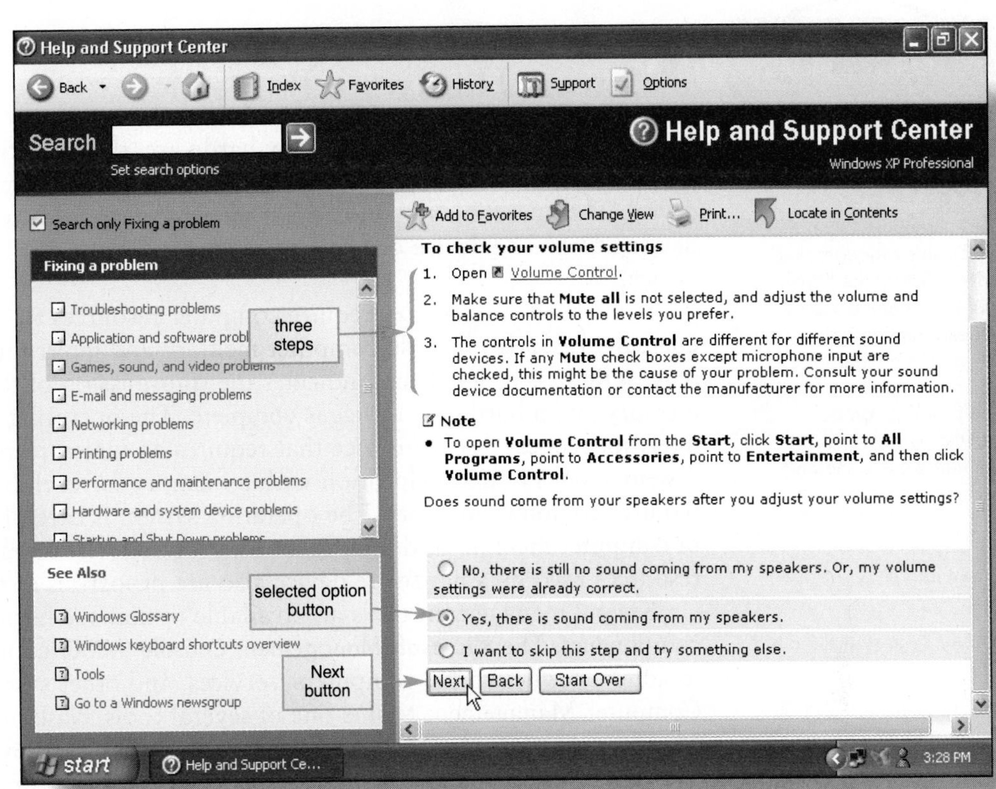

FIGURE 5-66

6 Click the Next button. Point to the Close button in the Help and Support Center window.

The topic pane changes to contain a thank you message, Back button, and Start Over button (Figure 5-67).

7 Click the Close button.

The Help and Support Center window closes.

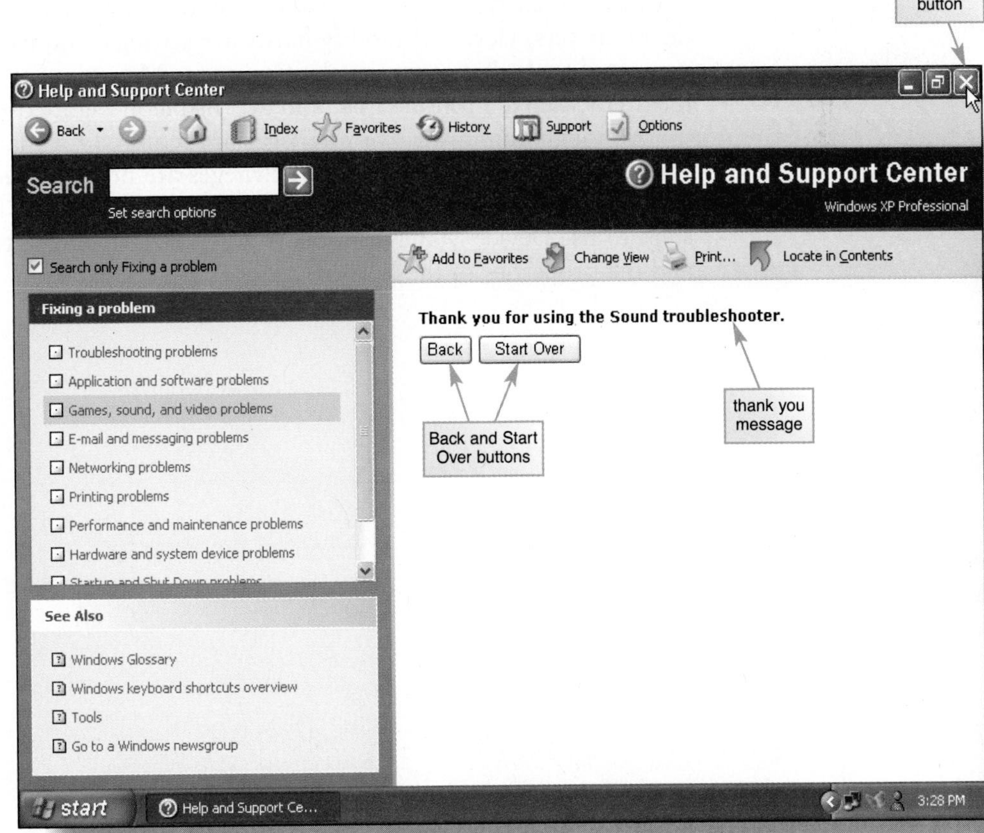

FIGURE 5-67

More About

Viewing Hardware Properties

An X through an icon in the Device Manager window indicates the hardware has been disabled. An exclamation point in a yellow circle means the hardware has a problem. The problem can be viewed by right-clicking the hardware name and clicking Properties.

Viewing Hardware Properties

During the process of setting up new hardware, the operating system detects the presence of a hardware device and associates a device driver with the hardware device. The operating system handles the hardware detection and assignment of a device driver. The device driver is one property of the newly installed hardware device.

Some hardware devices require computer resources to function properly. **Computer resources** include computer memory and interrupt requests. An **interrupt request** (**IRQ**) is a signal that indicates the transmission of data between computer memory and a hardware device is complete. The operating system assigns a unique interrupt request to each device that requires an interrupt request. The operating system assigns a unique location within memory for each hardware device that requires computer memory. The operating system is careful to assign a different area of computer memory and a different interrupt request to each device. The computer resources used by a hardware device also are properties of the device.

Several management tools are available to manage hardware and other system components. The **Microsoft Management Console (MMC)** contains tools you can use to administer networks, computers, services, and other system components. The Computer Management tool is one of several tools available in the Microsoft Management Console. The **Computer Management tool** allows you to manage local and remote computers and contains the System Tools, Storage, and Services and Applications items. The **System Tools item** contains five tools (Event Viewer, Shared Folders, Local Users and Groups, Performance Logs and Alerts, and Device Manager). The **Device Manager tool** in the System Tools item allows you to display a list of the hardware devices installed on the computer and allows you to update device drivers, view and modify hardware settings, and troubleshoot problems. The items and tools that comprise the Computer Management tool are arranged in a hierarchy, called a **console tree**, and are visible in Figure 5-69.

Although administrative privileges are required for many of the tools in the Microsoft Management Console, privileges are not required to view a list of the hardware devices on the computer using Device Manager. Perform the following steps to use Device Manager to view a list of hardware categories on the computer and the properties of the keyboard.

Steps To View Hardware Properties

1 Click the Start button, right-click the My Computer icon, and then point to Manage.

The Start menu displays and the My Computer command on the Start menu and the Manage command on the shortcut menu are highlighted (Figure 5-68).

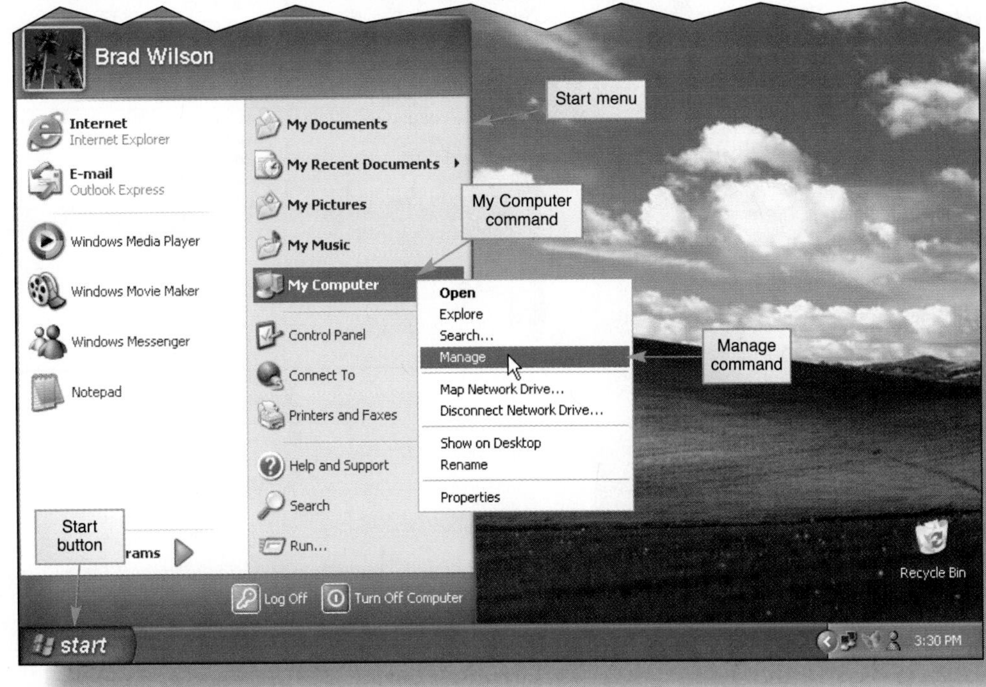

FIGURE 5-68

2 Click Manage. Point to the Device Manager icon in the left pane of the Computer Management window.

The Start menu closes and the Computer Management window displays (Figure 5-69). The Computer Management Local icon displays at the top of the console tree. The Systems Tools, Storage, and Services and Applications items display below the Computer Management Local icon and also in the right pane. The Device Manager icon displays below the System Tools icon.

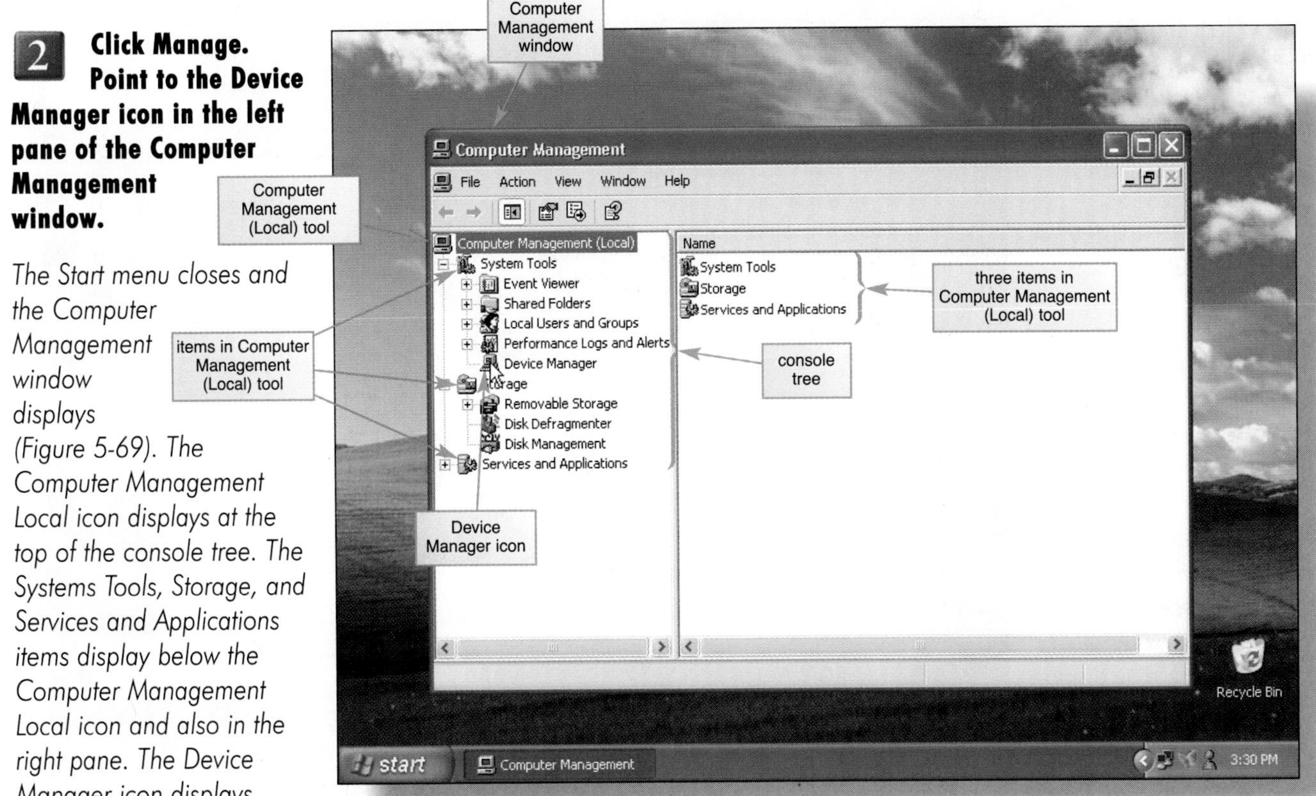

FIGURE 5-69

3 Click Device Manager. Point to the OK button in the Device Manager dialog box.

The Device Manager dialog box displays and the contents of the right pane change to contain a hierarchical structure of the hardware categories on the computer (Figure 5-70). The Device Manager dialog box does not display if you have administrative privileges.

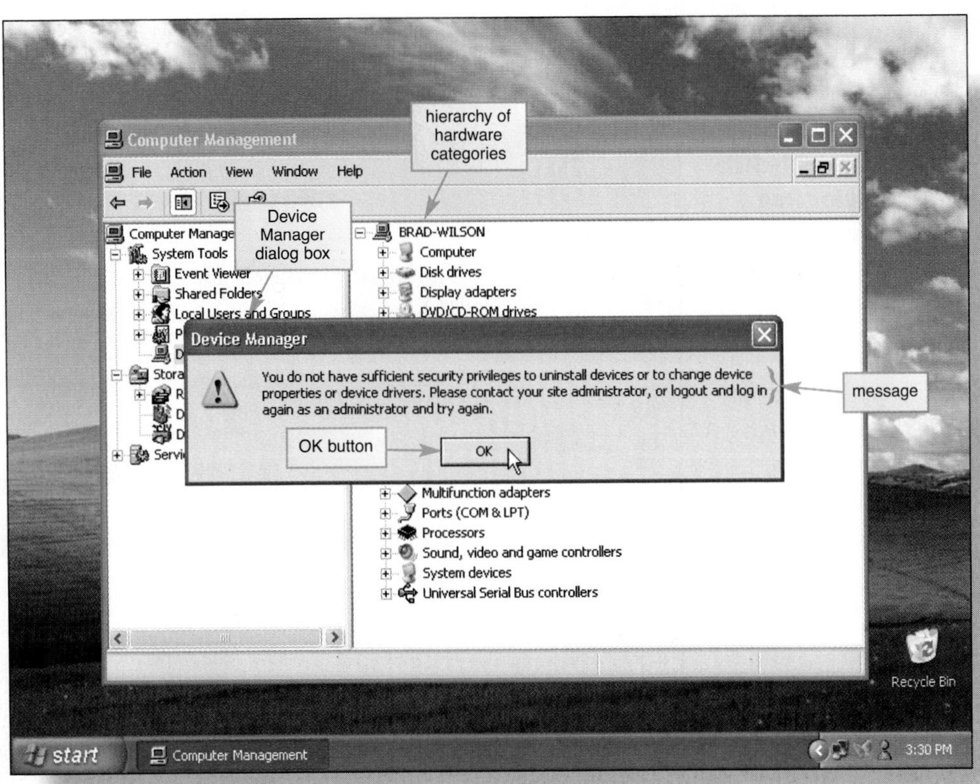

FIGURE 5-70

4 Click the OK button. Point to the plus sign in the box to the left of the Keyboards icon in the right pane.

The Device Manager dialog box closes (Figure 5-71). The hardware category names on the BRAD-WILSON computer display in the hierarchy structure. The highest level in the hierarchy is BRAD-WILSON. Connected by a dotted vertical line below BRAD-WILSON are the hardware categories preceded by a plus sign in a box. Another computer name may display on your computer.

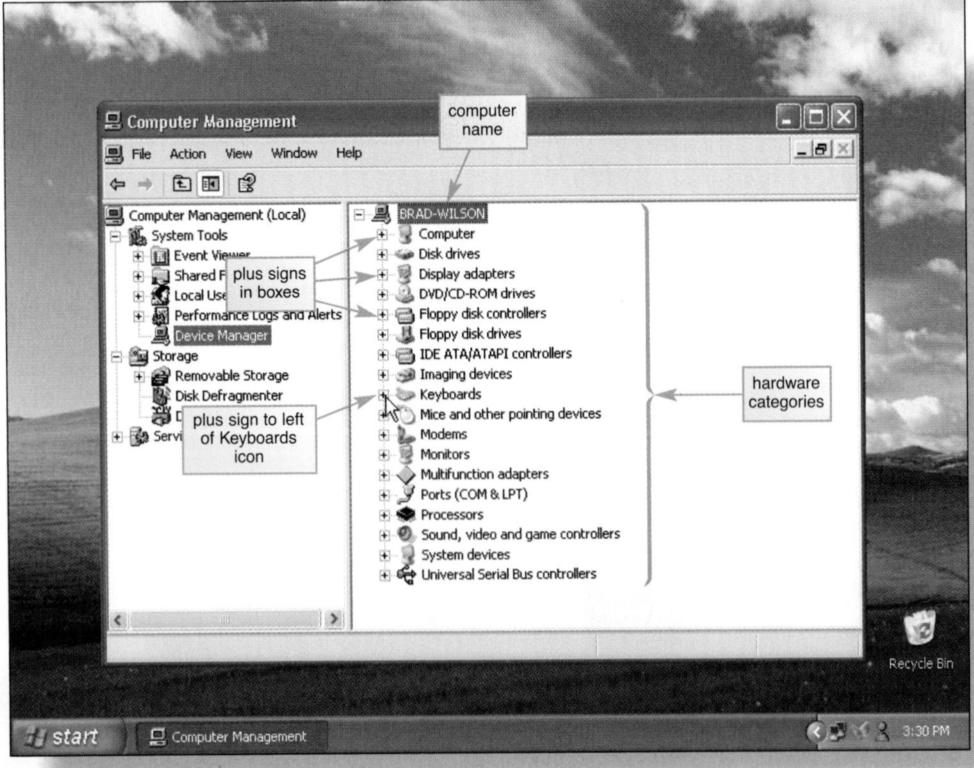

FIGURE 5-71

5 Click the plus sign and then point to the Standard 101/102-Key or Microsoft Natural PS/2 Keyboard device name. If the keyboard device name on your computer is different, point to the keyboard device name that is displayed on your computer.

The Keyboards category expands, the plus sign changes to a minus sign, and the 101/102-Key or Microsoft Natural PS/2 Keyboard device name displays (Figure 5-72). Different or additional hardware devices may display on your computer.

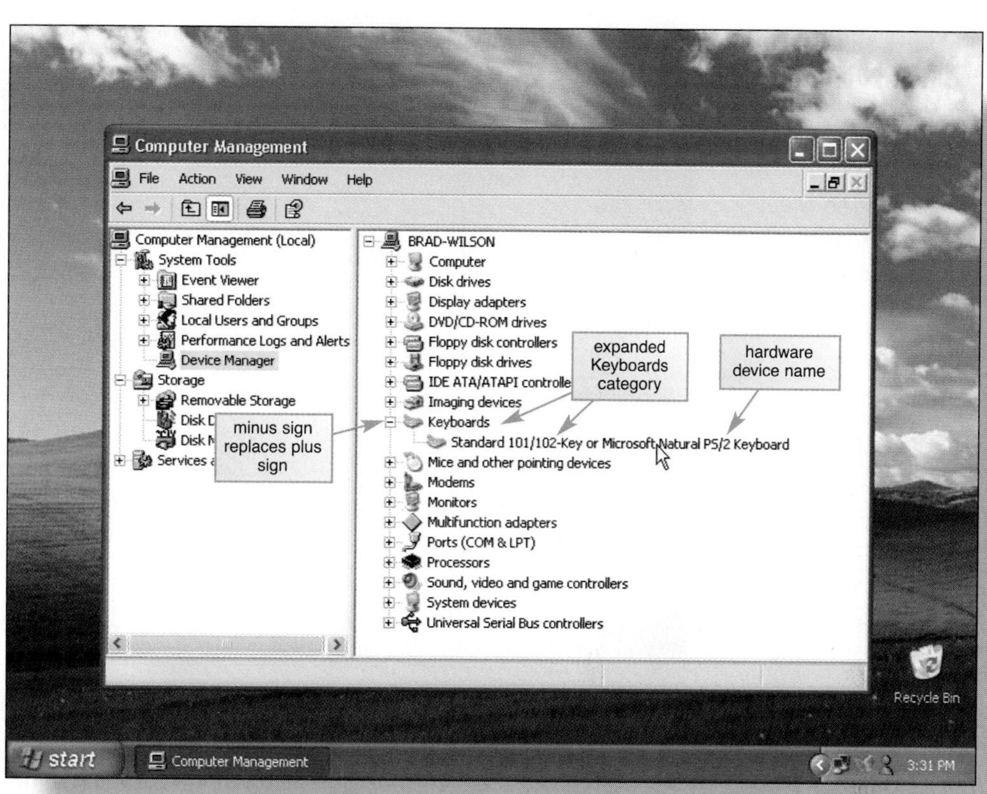

FIGURE 5-72

6 Double-click Standard 101/102-Key or Microsoft Natural PS/2 Keyboard.

The Standard 101/102-Key or Microsoft Natural PS/2 Keyboard Properties dialog box and the General sheet display (Figure 5-73). The General sheet contains information about the keyboard and its status. Depending on the keyboard available, this information may be different on your computer.

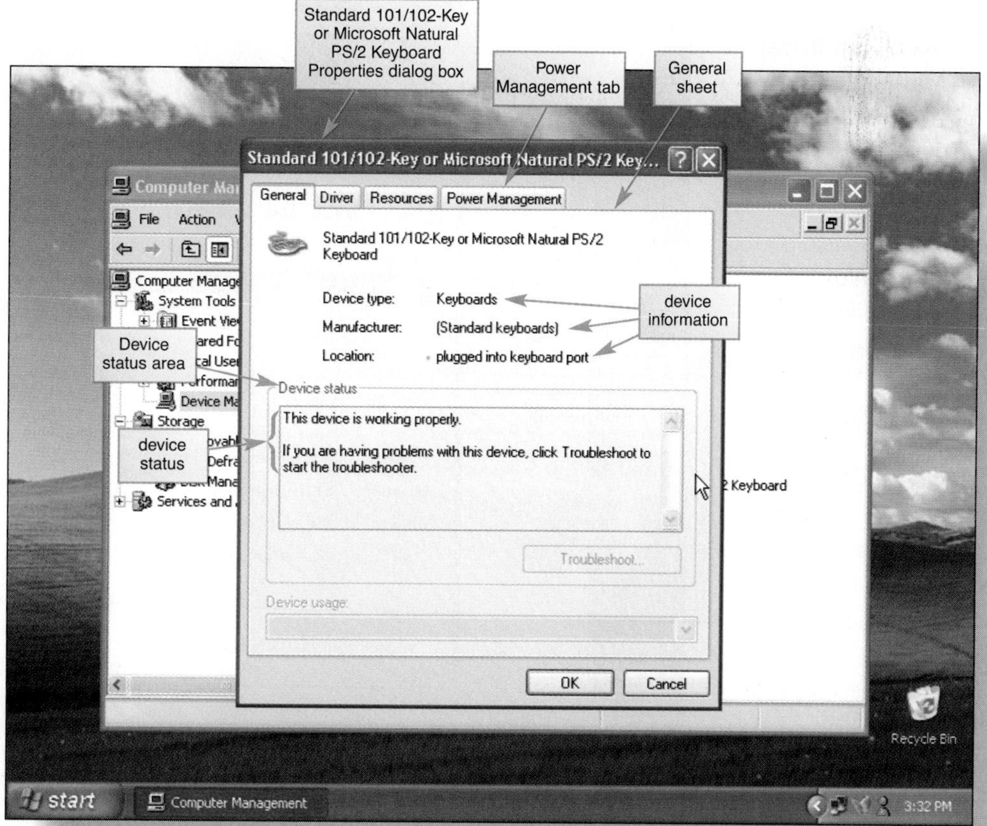

FIGURE 5-73

7 Click the Driver tab. Point to the Driver Details button.

The Driver sheet displays (Figure 5-74). The sheet contains driver information and the Driver Details button.

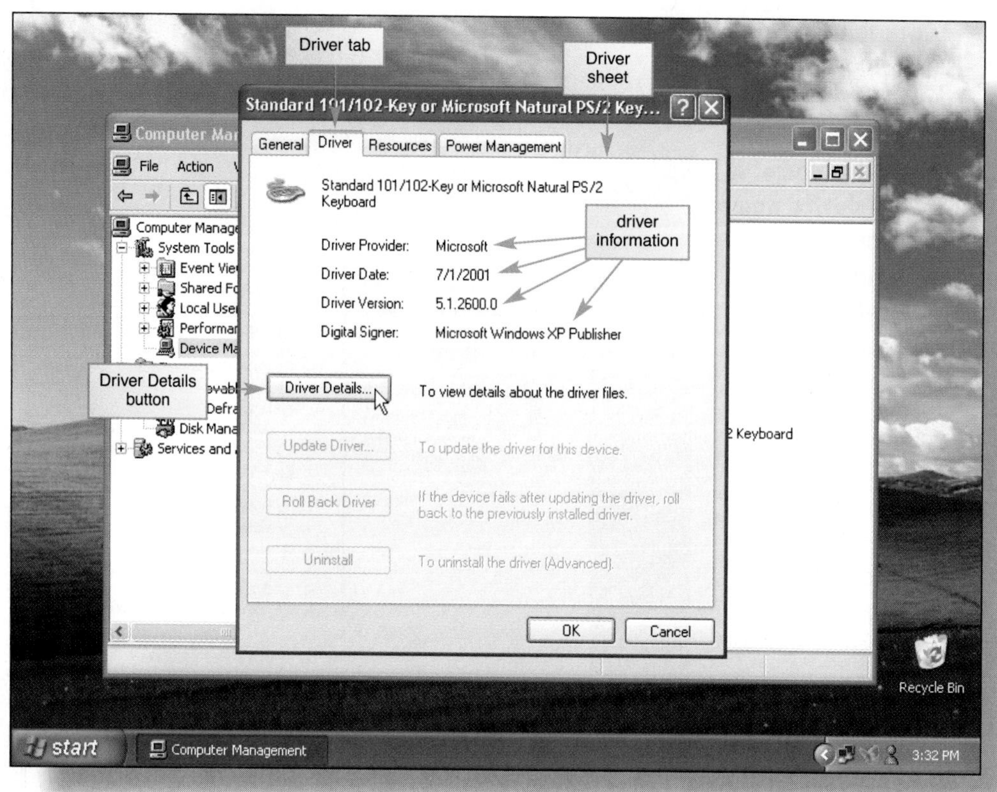

FIGURE 5-74

8 Click the Driver Details button. Point to the OK button in the Driver File Details dialog box.

The Driver File Details dialog box contains the two device driver files being used by the keyboard and file details for the highlighted device driver file (Figure 5-75).

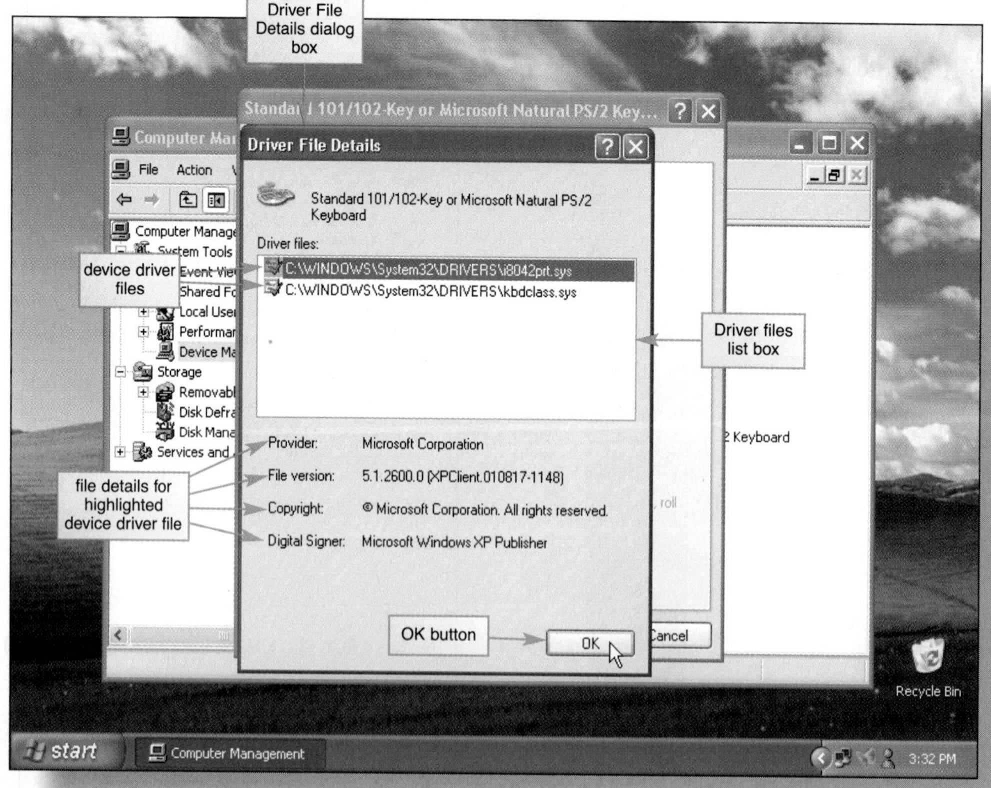

FIGURE 5-75

9 Click the OK button. Click the Resources tab. Point to the OK button.

The Resources sheet displays (Figure 5-76). The Resource settings list box contains a list of resource types and settings for the keyboard. Two input/output memory ranges (0060 - 0060 and 0064 - 0064) and an interrupt request (01) are assigned to the keyboard. The Conflicting device list box contains a message indicating there are no hardware conflicts with other hardware devices.

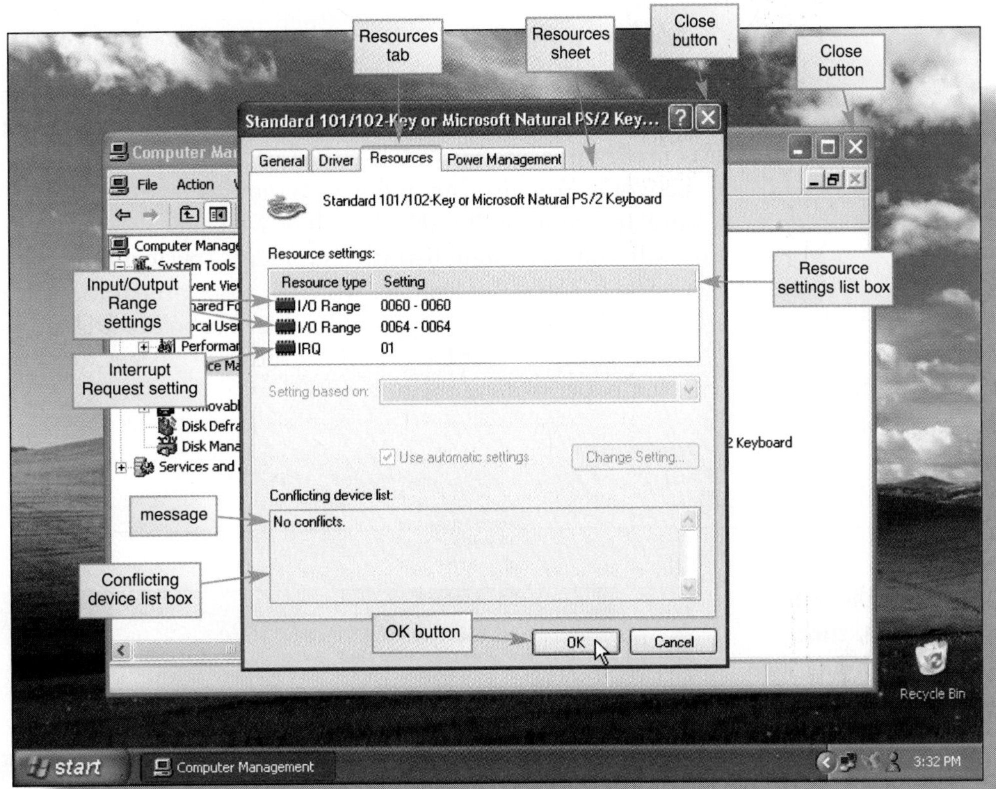

FIGURE 5-76

10 Click the OK button. Click the Close button in the Computer Management window.

The Standard 101/102-Key or Microsoft Natural PS/2 Keyboard Properties dialog box and Computer Management window close.

Other Ways

1. Click Start button, click Control Panel, click Switch to Classic View, double-click Administrative Tools, double-click Computer Management, click Device Manager, click OK button
2. Click Start button, click Control Panel, click Performance and Maintenance, click Administrative tools, double-click Computer Management, click Device Manager, click OK button

---

When you double-click a device name in the Computer Management window illustrated in Figure 5-72 on page WIN 5.59, the dialog box that displays for the hardware device may have additional tabs. For example, the Standard 101/102-Key or Microsoft Natural PS/2 Keyboard Properties dialog box has the Power Management tab to view information about the keyboard and power management (see Figure 5-73 on page WIN 5.59). The properties of a printer, which cannot be viewed using the Device Manager window, can be seen by clicking the Start button, clicking Printers and Faxes, right-clicking the printer icon, and then clicking Properties.

Adding and Removing Programs

Previously, you added a camera and printer to the computer. In addition to adding hardware, Windows XP also makes it easy to add and remove software programs.

Adding a Program

To add a program, double-click the **Add or Remove Programs icon** in the Control Panel window and then follow the steps necessary to add the program. You can add a program located on a CD-ROM or floppy disk or add a program available on the network. You also can add new Windows features, device drivers, and system updates from the Windows Update Web site.

If you have administrative privileges, perform the following steps to install Quicken TurboTax Deluxe, which is a tax preparation program, from a CD-ROM. If you do not have a copy of Quicken TurboTax Deluxe, you can install another program. If you do not have administrative privileges, read the following steps without actually performing them.

Note: Administrative privileges are required to perform these steps

Steps To Add a Program

1 Click the Start button, click Control Panel, and then point to the Add or Remove Programs icon in the Control Panel window.

The Control Panel window displays (Figure 5-77). The Add or Remove Programs category displays in the right pane.

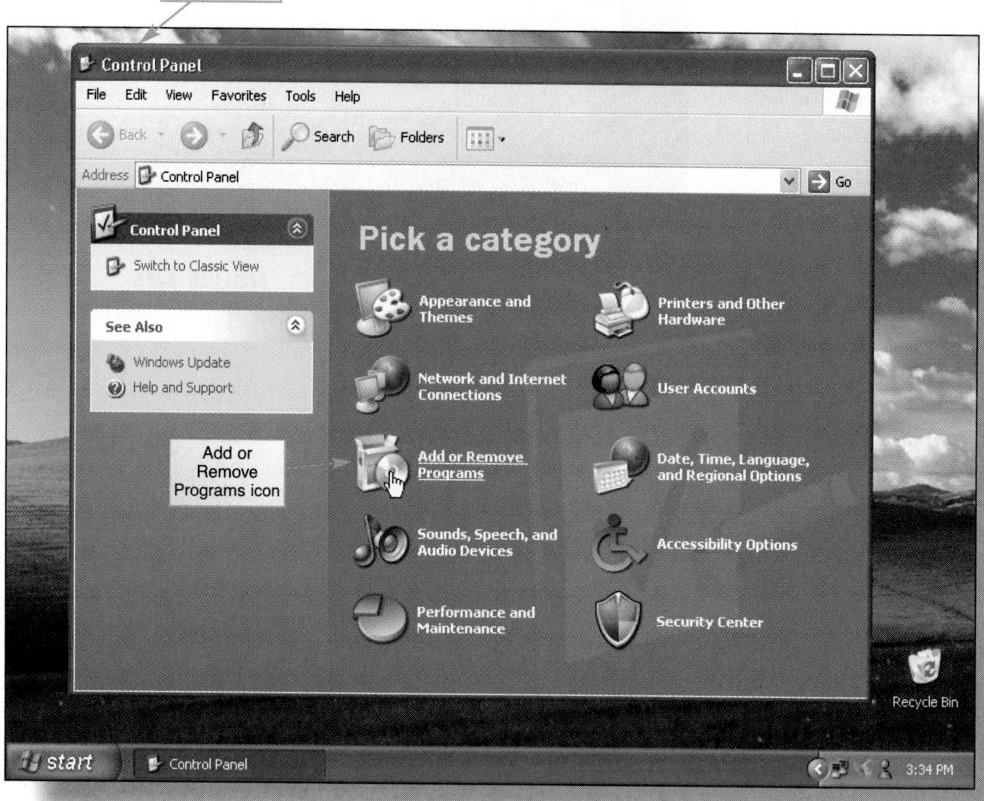

FIGURE 5-77

2 Click the Add or Remove Programs icon. Point to the Add New Programs button in the Add or Remove Programs window.

The Add or Remove Programs window contains the selected Change or Remove Programs button, the three-dimensional Add New Programs button, the Add/Remove Windows Components button, and a list box containing the currently installed programs (Figure 5-78). The only entry in the list (FullShot V6) is expanded and highlighted. Other entries may display in the lists on your computer.

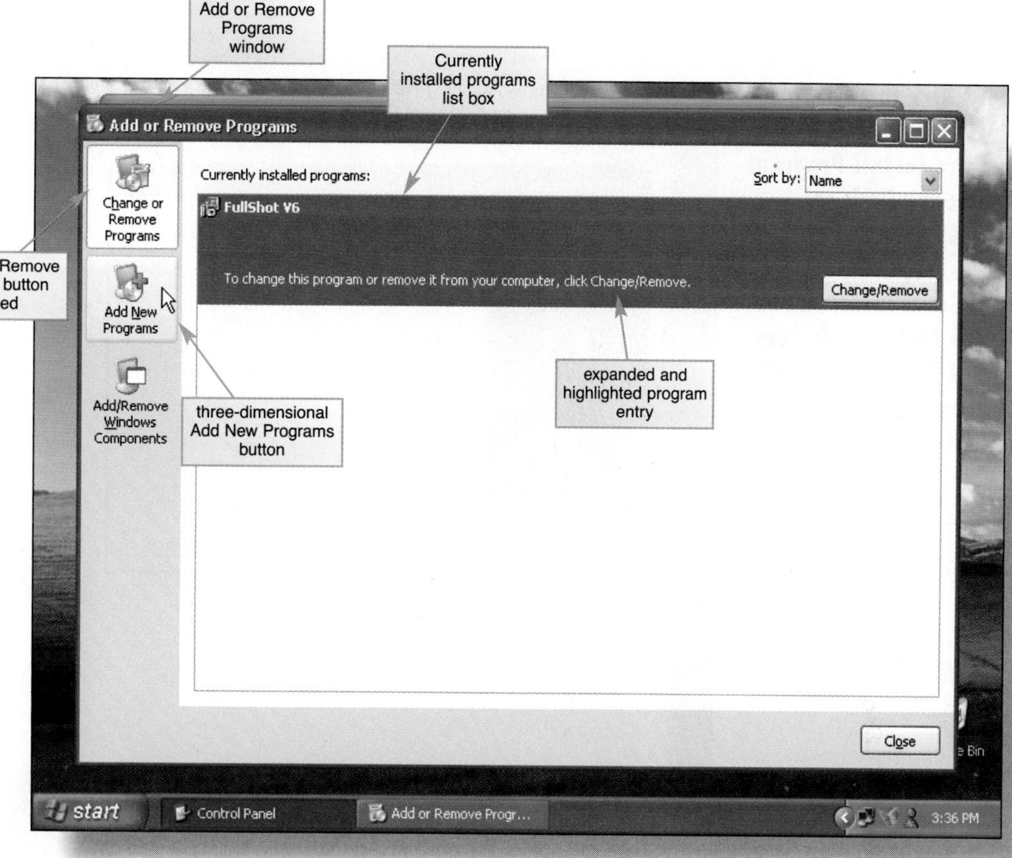

FIGURE 5-78

3 Click the Add New Programs button. Point to the CD or Floppy button.

The Change or Remove Programs button is no longer selected, the Add New Programs button is selected, and the contents of the window change (Figure 5-79). The CD or Floppy button and the Windows Update button display on the right side of the window.

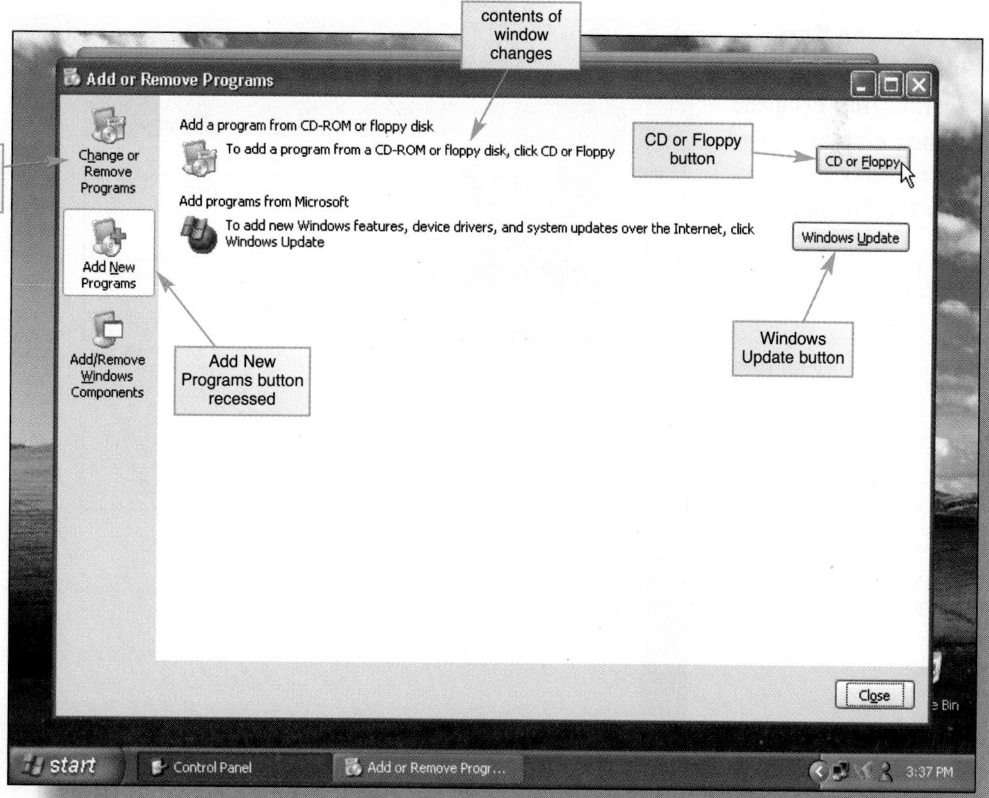

FIGURE 5-79

4 Click the CD or Floppy button. When the Install Program From Floppy Disk or CD-ROM dialog box displays, read the instructions, insert the Quicken TurboTax Deluxe CD-ROM into the CD-ROM drive, and then point to the Next button.

The Install Program From Floppy Disk or CD-ROM dialog box displays and the Quicken TurboTax Deluxe CD-ROM is inserted into the CD-ROM drive (Figure 5-80).

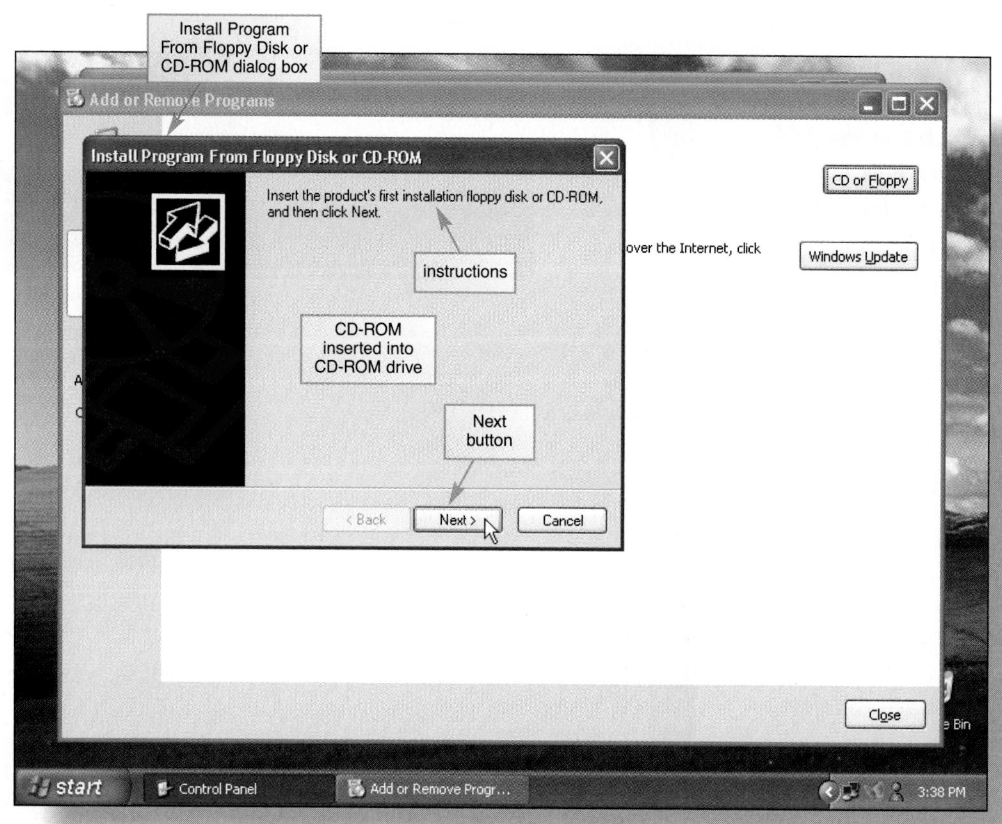

FIGURE 5-80

5 Click the Next button. When the Run Installation Program dialog box displays, read the instructions and then point to the Finish button.

The Run Installation Program dialog box displays (Figure 5-81). The dialog box contains instructions and the Open text box, which contains the path of the Quicken TurboTax Deluxe installation program (D:\SETUP.EXE). The Finish button replaces the Next button.

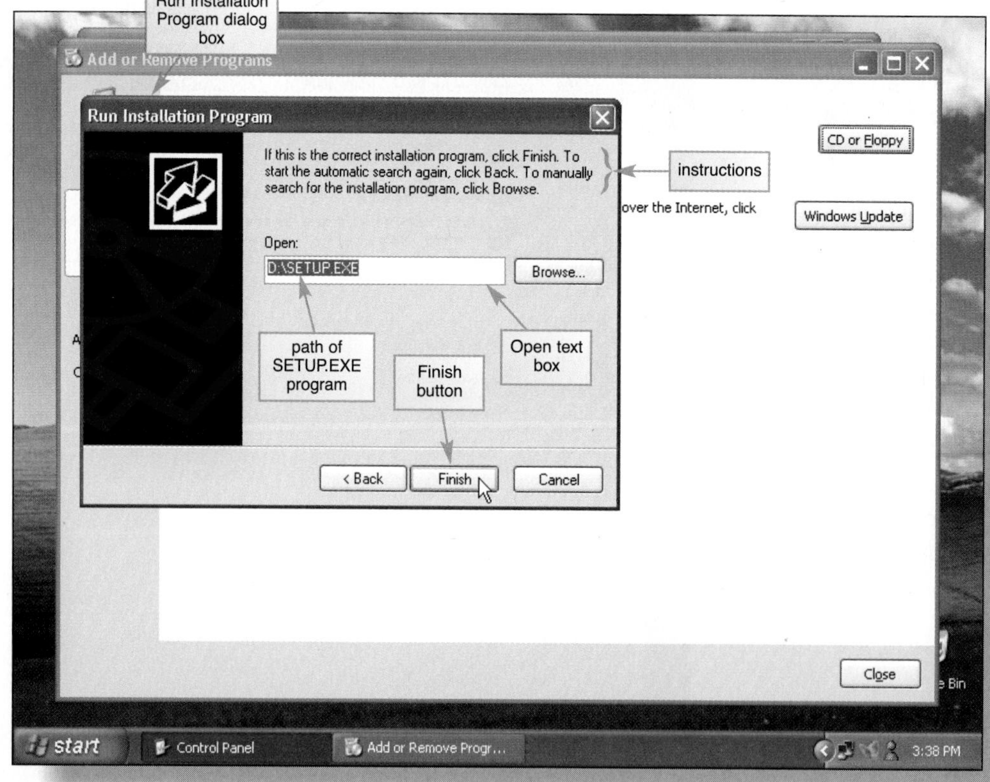

FIGURE 5-81

6 Click the Finish button. When the Welcome dialog box displays, click the Next button and then follow the instructions in the dialog box to install the Quicken TurboTax Deluxe program.

The program name and Welcome dialog box display (Figure 5-82). The Quicken TurboTax Deluxe setup program takes you through the installation of the software.

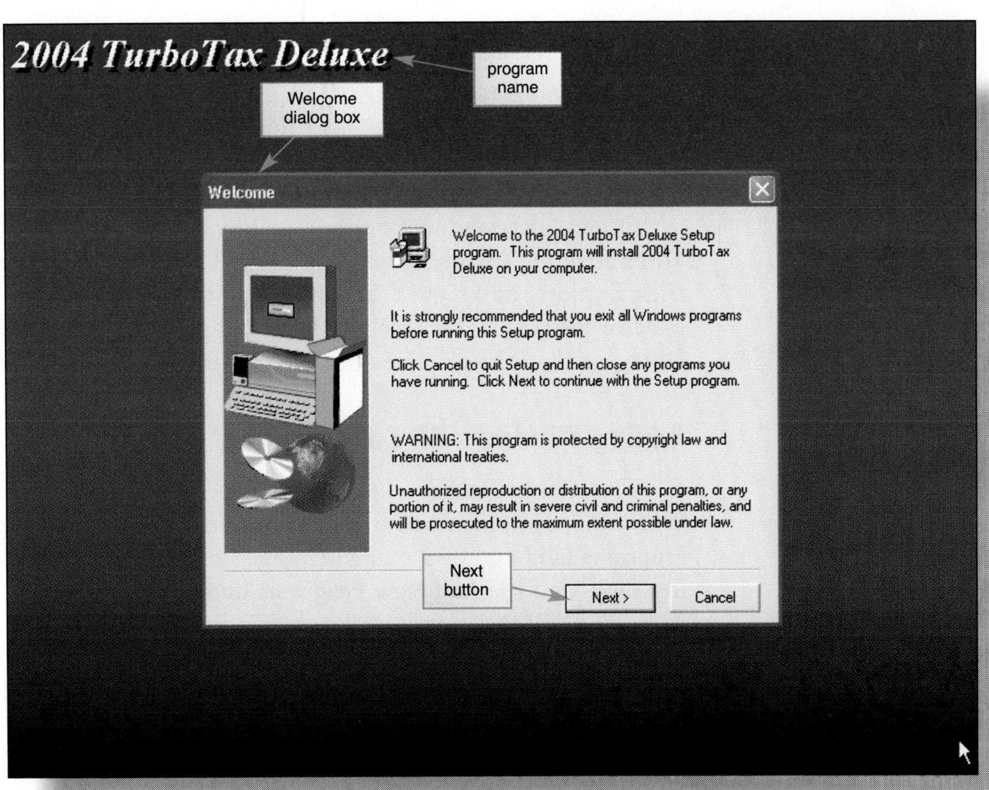

FIGURE 5-82

7 When finished, remove the Quicken TurboTax Deluxe CD-ROM from the CD-ROM drive. Click the Close button in the Add or Remove Programs window. Click the Close button in the Control Panel window.

The installation of Quicken TurboTax Deluxe is complete.

Other Ways

1. Click Start button, click Control Panel, click Switch to Classic View, double-click Add or Remove Programs icon, click Add New Programs button, click CD or Floppy button, insert CD-ROM and follow instructions
2. Insert CD-ROM into CD-ROM drive, follow instructions to install software
3. Click Start button, click Run, type `path of installation program`, click OK button

If you do not have administrative privileges and try to perform the previous steps, the Install Program As Other User dialog box displays. A message in the dialog box indicates that some programs will not install correctly if you do not have administrative privileges. With the permission of the administrator, you or the administrator can type the administrator's user name and password and then click the OK button to install the program.

Removing a Program

You may use any one of several methods to remove a program. Some software manufacturers allow you to remove their software by using an Uninstall button on the installation screen. In this case, click Add or Remove Programs in the Control Panel window, follow the instructions until the installation screen displays, click the Uninstall button, and then follow the instructions to remove the software.

Removing Programs

Only programs that were designed for Windows XP can be removed using the Add or Remove Programs Properties window. For all other programs, you should check the program's documentation to determine which files should be removed and then remove only those files.

Other software manufacturers, such as the manufacturers of Quicken TurboTax Deluxe, do not have an Uninstall button on the installation screen (see Figure 5-82 on the previous page). Instead, a menu command is available to uninstall the software. In this case, click the Start button, point to All Programs, point to Quicken TurboTax Deluxe on the All Programs submenu, click Uninstall on the TurboTax Deluxe submenu, and then follow the instructions.

Other software must be removed by deleting the files that comprise the software. To remove the software, you can click the Start button, right-click My Computer, click Explore, make the folder in which the program is stored visible in the Folders pane of the My Computer window, and then drag the folder to the Recycle Bin. Dragging the folder deletes the folder and the contents of the folder.

Adding Windows XP Components

The Add or Remove Programs Properties window shown in Figure 5-78 on page WIN 5.63 contains three buttons. As shown in this project, the **Change or Remove Programs button** allows you to change or remove programs that are currently installed, and the **Add New Programs button** allows you to install a new program from a CD-ROM, floppy disk, or Windows Update Web site. The **Add/Remove Windows Components button** allows you to add or remove Windows XP components that were not added during the initial installation of Windows XP. Components you can add or remove include the Accessories and Utilities, Fax Services, Indexing Service, Internet Explorer, Internet Information Services (IIS), Management and Monitoring Tools, Message Queuing, MSN Explorer, Networking Services, Other Network File and Print Services, and Update Root Certificates. You must have administrative privileges and the Windows XP Professional CD-ROM to add new components.

CASE PERSPECTIVE SUMMARY

Your parents are amazed at how much you have learned about your new computer. You showed them how easy it is to change the mouse and keyboard settings, how accessibility options can help physically challenged people, and then explained what a USB device is and how to install one. Your dad was surprised when you showed him your federal income tax form. He said, "Boy, I could save big bucks with that program!" Your mom wants you to buy and install a personal accounting program to balance her checkbook. You feel all the time and effort you spent to learn how to customize your computer really paid off.

Project Summary

Project 5 introduced you to the icons in the Control Panel window that allow you to customize the computer system. In this project, you used icons in the Control Panel window to customize the keyboard, mouse, and date and time. In addition, you learned how to add a new hardware device, add a software program, customize the computer for physically challenged people, add a printer, use a troubleshooter to solve a hardware problem, and view the properties of the hardware devices attached to the computer.

What You Should Know

Having completed this project, you now should be able to perform the following tasks:

- Add a Printer *(WIN 5.46)*
- Add a Program *(WIN 5.62)*
- Add a USB Device *(WIN 5.43)*
- Adjust the Cursor Blink Rate *(WIN 5.13)*
- Adjust the Double-Click Speed *(WIN 5.17)*
- Adjust the Keyboard Repeat Delay *(WIN 5.08)*
- Adjust the Keyboard Repeat Rate *(WIN 5.11)*
- Adjust the Pointer Speed *(WIN 5.23)*
- Change the Date, Time, and Time Zone *(WIN 5.36)*
- Change the Mouse Button Configuration *(WIN 5.15)*
- Change the Mouse Pointer Scheme *(WIN 5.21)*
- Close the Printers and Faxes Window *(WIN 5.52)*
- Delete the Text Document and Turn Off ClickLock *(WIN 5.20)*
- Display a Pointer Trail *(WIN 5.27)*
- Display the Control Panel Window using the Back Button *(WIN 5.28, WIN 5.34)*
- Open the Control Panel Window *(WIN 5.05)*
- Remove a Printer *(WIN 5.51)*
- Solve a Problem Using a Troubleshooter *(WIN 5.53)*
- Switch to Classic View and Back to Category View *(WIN 5.07)*
- Turn Off High Contrast *(WIN 5.33)*
- Turn On and Use ClickLock *(WIN 5.18)*
- Turn On High Contrast *(WIN 5.32)*
- Turn On MouseKeys *(WIN 5.29)*
- Turn On Snap To *(WIN 5.25)*
- View Account Information *(WIN 5.35)*
- View Hardware Properties *(WIN 5.57)*
- View the Time and Date Formats *(WIN 5.41)*

Learn It Online

Instructions: To complete the Learn It Online exercises, launch your Web browser using the steps on pages WIN 1.46 and WIN 1.47, click the Address box, enter `scsite.com/winxp/exs.htm`, and then press the ENTER key. When the Windows XP Learn It Online page displays, follow the instructions in the exercises below.

1 Project Reinforcement TF, MC, and SA

Below Windows XP Project 5, click the Project Reinforcement link. Print the quiz by clicking Print on the File menu. Answer each question. Write your first and last name at the top of each page, and then hand in the printout to your instructor.

2 Flash Cards

Below Windows XP Project 5, click the Flash Cards link. When Flash Cards displays, read the instructions. Type 20 (or a number specified by your instructor) in the Number of Playing Cards text box, type your name in the Name text box, and then click the Flip Card button. When the flash card displays, read the question and then click the Answer box arrow to select an answer. Flip through Flash Cards. Click Print on the File menu to print the last flash card if your score is 15 (75%) correct or greater and then hand it in to your instructor. If your score is less than 15 (75%) correct, then redo this exercise by clicking the Replay button.

3 Practice Test

Below Windows XP Project 5, click the Practice Test link. Answer each question, enter your first and last name at the bottom of the page, and then click the Grade Test button. When the graded practice test displays on your screen, click Print on the File menu to print a hard copy. Continue to take practice tests until you score 80% or better. Hand in a printout of the final practice test to your instructor.

4 Who Wants to Be a Computer Genius?

Below Windows XP Project 5, click the Computer Genius link. Read the instructions, enter your first and last name at the bottom of the page, and then click the Play button. Hand in a printout of your score to your instructor.

5 Wheel of Terms

Below Windows XP Project 5, click the Wheel of Terms link. Read the instructions, and then enter your first and last name and your school name. Click the Play button. Hand in a printout of your score to your instructor.

6 Crossword Puzzle Challenge

Below Windows XP Project 5, click the Crossword Puzzle Challenge link. Read the instructions, and then enter your first and last name. Click the Play button. Work the crossword puzzle. When you are finished, click the Submit button. When the crossword puzzle redisplays, click the Print button. Hand in the printout.

7 Tips and Tricks

Below Windows XP Project 5, click the Tips and Tricks link. Click a topic that pertains to Project 5. Right-click the information and then click Print on the shortcut menu. Construct a brief example of what the information relates to in Windows XP to confirm that you understand how to use the tip or trick. Hand in the example and printed information.

8 Newsgroups

Below Windows XP Project 5, click the Newsgroups link. Click a topic that pertains to Project 5. Print three comments. Hand in the comments to your instructor.

9 Expanding Your Horizons

Below Windows XP Project 5, click the Expanding Your Horizons link. Click a topic that pertains to Project 5. Print the information. Construct a brief example of what the information relates to in Windows XP to confirm that you understand the contents of the article. Hand in the example and printed information to your instructor.

10 Search Sleuth

Below Windows XP Project 5, click the Search Sleuth link. To search for a term that pertains to this project, select a term below the Project 5 title and then use the Google search engine at google.com (or any major search engine) to display and print two Web pages that present information on the term. Hand in the printouts to your instructor.

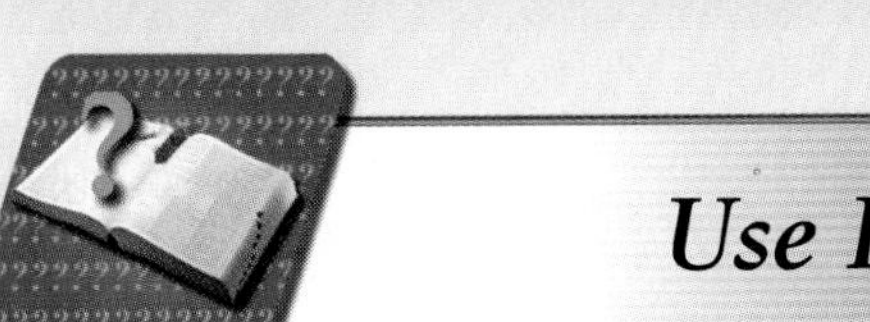

Use Help

1 Using Windows Help and Support to Troubleshoot Hardware Problems

Instructions: Use Windows XP troubleshooters to answer the following questions.

1. Click Start button, click Help and Support, type `troubleshooter list` in the Search box in the Help and Support Center window, click the Start Searching button, click List of troubleshooters to display a list of troubleshooters. Answer the questions below using the list.

   a. Your document does not print at all. What is the first question the Printing troubleshooter asks you?

   are you printing from a network printer or a local printer?

   b. Your computer restarts when a sound plays. What does the Sound troubleshooter suggest is the problem?

   Do you have a hardware device conflict?

   c. You are having trouble with the new USB keyboard you purchased. What does the Input Devices troubleshooter think might be the problem?

   are you using a USB device

   d. You are trying to set up Windows XP on your computer. Setup fails after the first time it restarts your computer. What does the System Setup troubleshooter suggest you do?

   Restart your computer and try resume setup.

   e. You are having trouble with a hard disk drive. The disk drive is not a SCSI device. What does the Drives and Network Adapters troubleshooter want you to check?

   Does Windows support your hardware

   f. A **hardware conflict** results when two hardware devices use the same computer resources (memory range or interrupt request). You are having problems with a device and need to solve a hardware conflict on your computer, so you decide to use the Hardware troubleshooter to solve the problem. You decide to remove all occurrences of a device. What five steps does the troubleshooter suggest you perform?

   Step 1: open device manager

   Step 2: click start if category for device is not expanded, double click it

   Step 3: Right click one occurance of the device then uninstal

   Step 4: Repeat step 3

   Step 5: remove all occurances and restart computer

2 Describing the Function of Other Control Panel Icons

Instructions: Use Windows XP Help and Support and the categories in the Control Panel window to determine the function of the Control Panel icons listed below. In the spaces provided, list the function of each icon.

ICON	FUNCTION
Network Connections	network connections
Phone and Modem Options	phone and modem option
Speech	assesibility
Power Options	
Game Controllers	assesibility

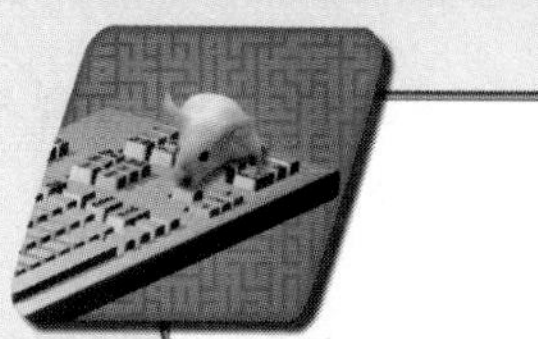

In the Lab

1 Using the Add Hardware Wizard to Add a Printer

Problem: In the past, you have added a new printer to the computer using the Add Printer wizard. A friend recently informed you that you also can use the Add Hardware wizard to add a printer. You decide to try your friend's suggestion and add an Epson AP-4000 printer using the Add Hardware wizard.

Instructions: You must have administrative privileges for this exercise. Perform the following steps to add the printer and answer several questions about the printer's properties.

Part 1: *Install the Epson AP-4000 Printer*

1. If necessary, launch Microsoft Windows XP and then log on to the computer.
2. Click the Start button and then click Control Panel.
3. Click the Printers and Other Hardware icon in Control Panel window.
4. Click Add Hardware in the See Also area in the Printers and Other Hardware window to display the Add Hardware Wizard dialog box (Figure 5-83).

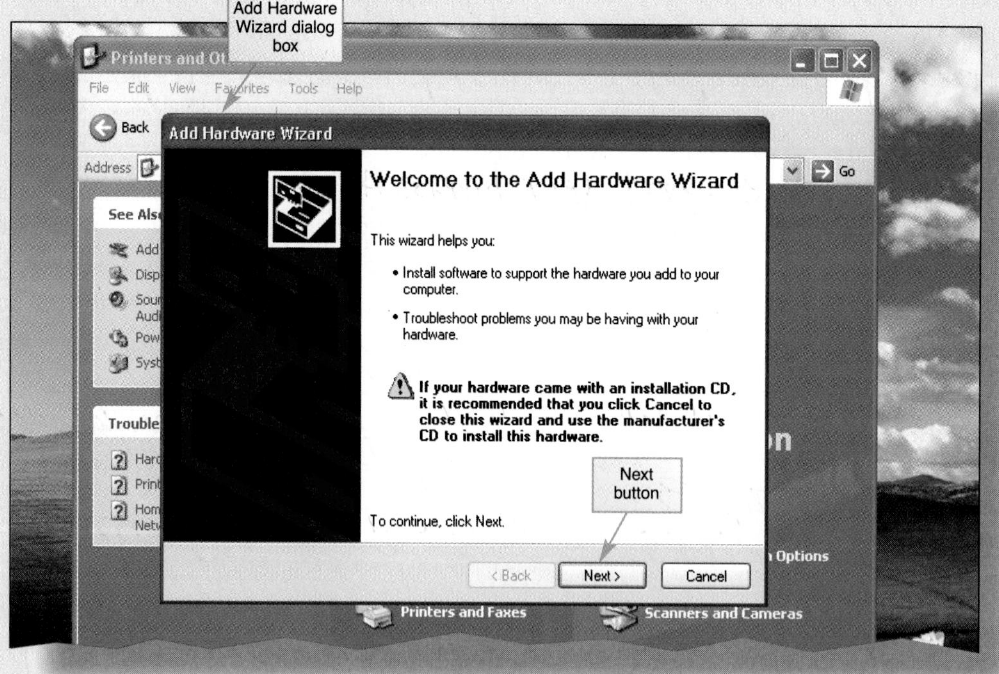

FIGURE 5-83

5. Click the Next button in the Add Hardware Wizard dialog box.
6. Even though you have not connected the printer to the computer, click Yes, I have already connected the hardware and then click the Next button.
7. Scroll the Installed hardware list box to display the Add a new hardware device entry, click Add a new hardware device, and then click the Next button.
8. Click Install the hardware that I manually select from a list (Advanced) and then click the Next button.
9. Scroll the Common hardware types list box to display Printers, click Printers, and then click the Next button.

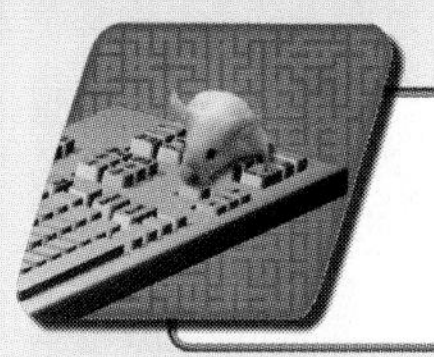

In the Lab

10. Verify the Use the following port option button is selected, the LPT1: (Recommended Printer Port) entry is highlighted in the box, and then click the Next button.
11. Scroll the Manufacturers list to make the Epson manufacturer name visible, and then click Epson. Scroll the Printers list to make the Epson AP-4000 name visible, click Epson AP-4000, and then click the Next button.
12. When the Printer name list box containing the Epson AP-4000 displays, click No, and then click the Next button.
13. If necessary, click the Do not share this printer option button and then click the Next button.
14. When the Print Test Page displays, click No, and then click the Next button.
15. When the Completing the Add Hardware Wizard page displays, click the Finish button.

Part 2:* *Printing the Contents of the Printers and Other Hardware Window

1. Maximize the Printers and Other Hardware window.
2. Click View installed printers or fax printers in the Printers and Other Hardware window.
3. Click the PRINT SCREEN key on the keyboard to place an image of the desktop on the Clipboard, which is a temporary Windows storage area.
4. Click the Start button, point to All Programs, point to Accessories, and then click Paint.
5. Maximize the Untitled – Paint window.
6. Click Edit on the menu bar and then click Paste on the Edit menu to copy the image from the Clipboard to the Paint window.
7. Click File on the menu bar, click Print on the File menu, and then click the Print button in the Print dialog box to print the Paint document.
8. Click the Close button in the Untitled – Paint window and then click the No button in the Paint dialog box to quit the Paint program.

Part 3:* *Display the Properties of the Epson AP-4000 Printer WONT WO

1. Click the Back button in the Printers and Faxes window to display the Printers and Other Hardware window.
2. Click View installed printers or fax printers in the Printers and Other Hardware window.
3. Is the Epson AP-4000 icon in the Printers and Faxes window? NO
4. Right-click the Epson AP-4000 icon and then click Properties on the shortcut menu to display the Epson AP-4000 Properties dialog box. Using the tabs in the dialog box, answer the following questions.
   a. To which port does the printer print? network port (yourown.
   b. Is the printer always available? yes
   c. What is the orientation of the paper? ready
   d. What is the page order? (1)
   e. What is the print quality? good
5. Click the OK button to close the Epson AP-4000 Properties dialog box.

Part 4:* *Delete the Epson AP-4000 Icon

1. Right-click the Epson AP-4000 icon. Click Delete on the shortcut menu.
2. Click the Yes button in the Printers dialog box to delete the Epson AP-4000 icon.
3. Click the Close button in the Printers and Faxes window.
4. Hand in the printed Paint document and the answers to the questions to your instructor.

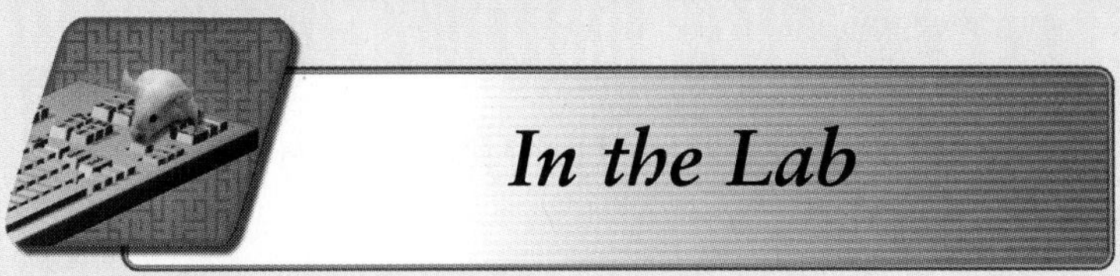

2 Developing a Control Panel Guide

Problem: Although most people like the Category view when working with Control Panel, your boss favors the Classic view. Your boss asks you to create a Control Panel guide so other employees can familiarize themselves with the Classic view and the Control Panel icons. The guide should have a title, a screen shot (a picture of the desktop) and description of the Control Panel window, and a screen shot and description of the following icons in the Control Panel window: Add Hardware, Add or Remove Programs, Printers and Faxes, Regional and Language Options, and System.

Instructions: Use **WordPad**, an application included with Windows XP, to create the document and the PRINT SCREEN key to capture the screen shots. Perform the following steps to create the Control Panel guide using WordPad and the PRINT SCREEN key.

Part 1: Launching the WordPad Application

1. If necessary, launch Microsoft Windows XP and then log on to the computer.
2. Click the Start button and then click Control Panel.
3. Click Switch to Classic View in the Control Panel window.
4. Maximize the Control Panel window and then minimize the Control Panel window. The Control Panel button displays in the taskbar button area.
5. Click the Start button, point to All Programs, point to Accessories, and then click WordPad. Maximize the Document - WordPad window (see Figure 5-84). The toolbar, Format bar, and ruler display below the menu bar in the window. The insertion point displays in the area below the ruler.

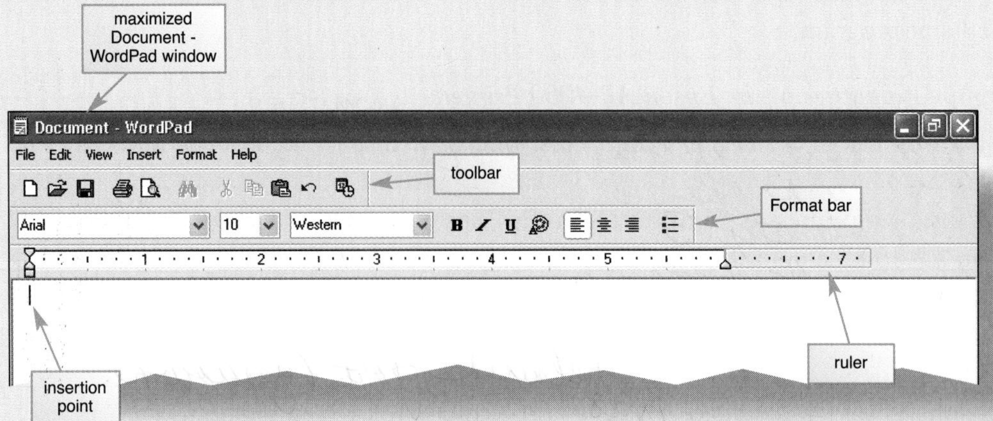

FIGURE 5-84

Part 2: Entering Text and Inserting and Resizing a Screen Shot

1. Type `The Control Panel Window (Classic View)` as the title and press the ENTER key twice.
2. Select the title that you just typed. On the Format Bar, click the Font Size box arrow, click 14 in the Font Size list, click the Bold button, and then click the Center button.
3. Move the insertion point to the bottom of the document. Type `The Control Panel window, containing thirty-one icons, displays below.` as the first sentence and then press the ENTER key twice.
4. Click the Control Panel button in the taskbar button area. Press the PRINT SCREEN key on the keyboard to take a screen shot of the desktop and copy the screen shot to the Clipboard.

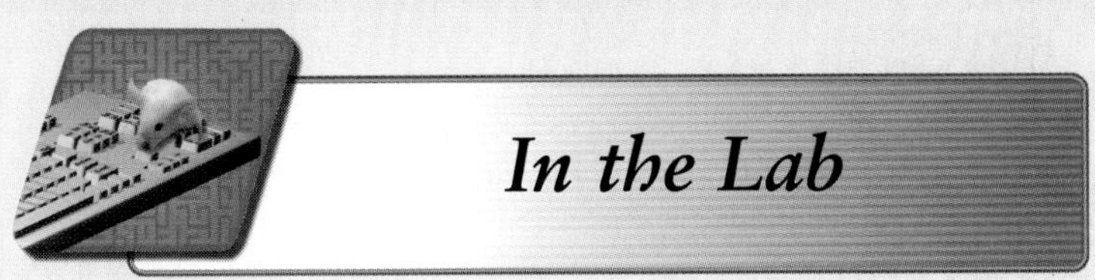

5. Click the Document - WordPad button in the taskbar button area. Right-click an open area below the insertion point in the WordPad window and then click Paste on the shortcut menu to insert a Picture box containing the screen shot in the window.
6. The entire Picture box is not visible in the WordPad window. A **selection rectangle** surrounds the box and **sizing handles**, which allow you to resize the box, display at each corner and middle location on the rectangle. Dragging a corner-sizing handle diagonally toward the center of the box reduces the size of the box proportionally. Dragging the sizing handles on the left or right sides of the box toward the center of the box reduces the size of the box disproportionately.

Part 3: *Resizing the Box Containing the Screen Shot*

1. Using the sizing handles, resize the box to resemble the box shown in Figure 5-85.
2. Press the PAGE DOWN (PgDn) key to move the insertion point to the end of the document and then press the ENTER key twice.

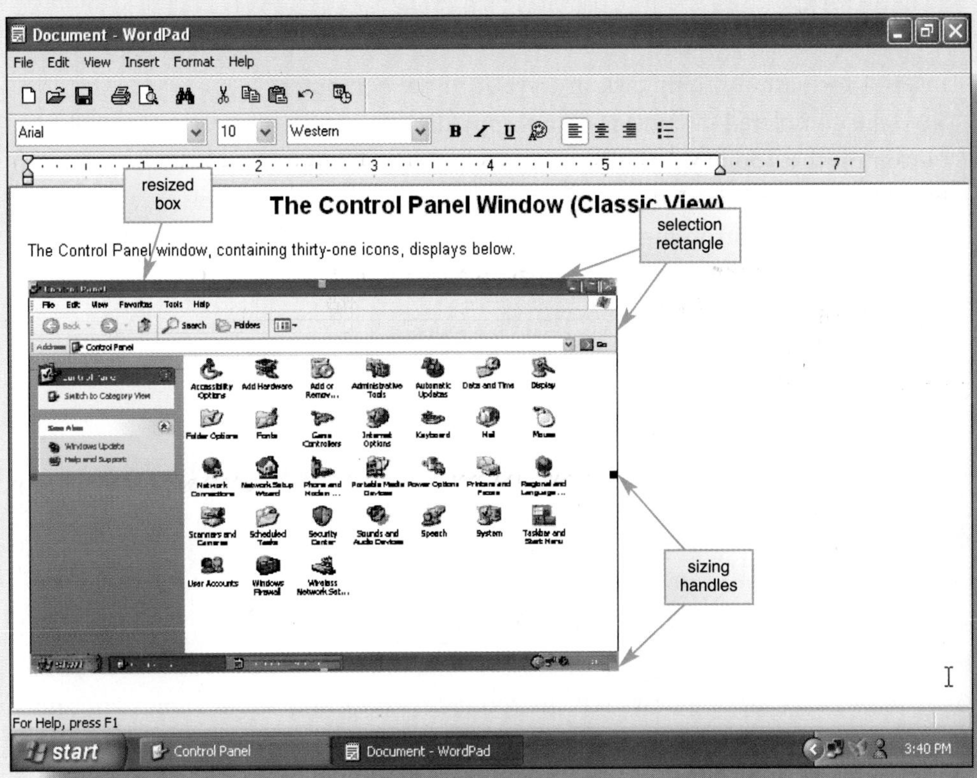

FIGURE 5-85

Part 4: *Taking a Screen Shot, Entering Text, and Inserting and Resizing a Box*

1. Click the Control Panel button in the taskbar button area. Click the Add Hardware icon to select the icon. Move the mouse pointer to the bottom of the Control Panel window.
2. Press the PRINT SCREEN key on the keyboard to take a screen shot of the desktop and copy the screen shot to the Clipboard.
3. If the status bar does not display, click View on the menu bar, and then click Status Bar. Read the information about the Add Hardware icon on the status bar.
4. Click the Document - WordPad button in the taskbar button area.
5. Summarize the information on the status bar and enter it, type `The Add Hardware icon is highlighted in the Control Panel window. The Add Hardware icon allows you to install and troubleshoot hardware.` below the summary, and then press the ENTER key twice.

(continued)

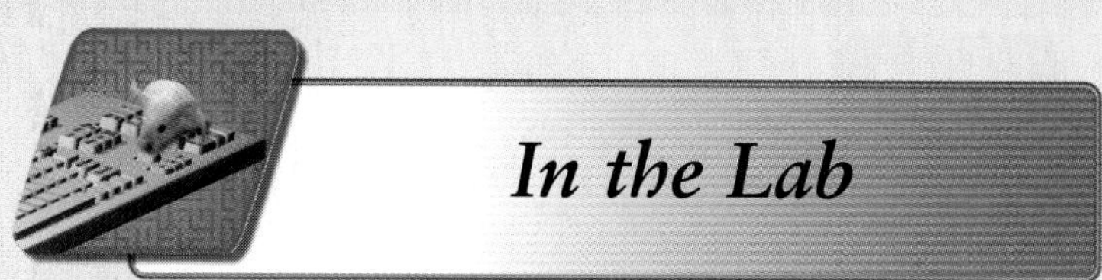

Developing a Control Panel Guide *(continued)*

6. Right-click an open area in the Document – WordPad window and then click Paste on the shortcut menu to insert the box containing the screen shot in the window.
7. Resize the box containing the screen shot using the sizing handles.
8. Press the PAGE DOWN (PgDn) key to move the insertion point to the end of the document and then press the ENTER key twice.

Part 5:* *Finishing the Control Panel Guide

1. Repeat the procedures performed in the steps in Part 4 for the Add or Remove Programs, Printers and Faxes, Regional and Language Options, and System icons.
2. If the status bar displays in the Control Panel window, click View on the menu bar, and then click Status Bar to remove the status bar.

Part 6:* *Saving and Printing the Control Panel Guide

1. Insert a formatted floppy disk in drive A of the computer.
2. Save the completed document on a floppy disk using the file name, Control Panel Guide, and the Save button on the Toolbar.
3. Print the completed document using the Print button on the Toolbar.
4. Click the Close button in the Control Panel Guide - WordPad window.
5. Click the Close button in the Control Panel window.
6. Remove the floppy disk from drive A.
7. Hand in the Control Panel Guide to your instructor.

3 Customizing the Computer Using the Accessibility Wizard

Problem: You have difficulty reading the text on the desktop, using the keyboard to type text, seeing the mouse pointer, using scroll bars, and clicking icons on the desktop. You would like the text, scroll bars, and icons to be larger, the color scheme to be black and white instead of color, and to be able to type in Notepad.

Instructions: Experiment with the Microsoft Magnifier, On-Screen Keyboard, and Accessibility wizard to make it easier to work in the Windows XP environment. Perform the following steps and answer any questions in the spaces provided.

Part 1:* *Using Microsoft Magnifier

1. If necessary, launch Microsoft Windows XP and then log on to the computer.
2. Click the Start button, point to All Programs, point to Accessories, point to Accessibility, and then click Magnifier. **Microsoft Magnifier** displays a separate window at the top of the desktop that contains the magnified text and objects that display near the mouse pointer.
3. Point to the text in the Microsoft Magnifier dialog box.
   a. What displays in the window at the top of the desktop? enlarges selected text for easier viewing
4. Point to the OK button in the Microsoft Magnifier dialog box.
   a. What displays in the window at the top of the desktop? DO NOT SHOW AGAIN
5. Click the OK button.

In the Lab

6. Click the Minimize button in the Magnifier Settings dialog box.
   a. What displays in the window at the top of the desktop? magnifier settings
7. Point to the Recycle Bin icon on the desktop, double-click the Recycle Bin icon, point to the Magnifier Settings button on the taskbar, right-click the button, and then click Close on the shortcut menu.
8. Click the Close button in the Recycle Bin window.

***Part 2:** Using On-Screen Keyboard*

1. Click the Start button, point to All Programs, point to Accessories, point to Accessibility, and then click On-Screen Keyboard. The **On-Screen Keyboard** allows you to type text in a document window using the mouse or joystick.
2. Click the OK button in the On-Screen Keyboard dialog box.
3. Drag the On-Screen Keyboard window to position the window at the bottom of the desktop.
4. Click the Start button, point to All Programs, point to Accessories, and then click Notepad.
5. Resize and position the Notepad window at the top of the desktop (Figure 5-86).
6. To type in the Untitled – Notepad window, click the key on the On-Screen Keyboard corresponding to the character you want to type in the Untitled – Notepad window. Click the SHIFT key to capitalize text. Click the SPACEBAR on the On-Screen Keyboard to insert a blank space in the Untitled – Notepad window.
7. Using the mouse pointer and On-Screen Keyboard, type the following sentence: `It is easy to type using the On-Screen Keyboard.` and then click the ENTER key twice on the On-Screen Keyboard.

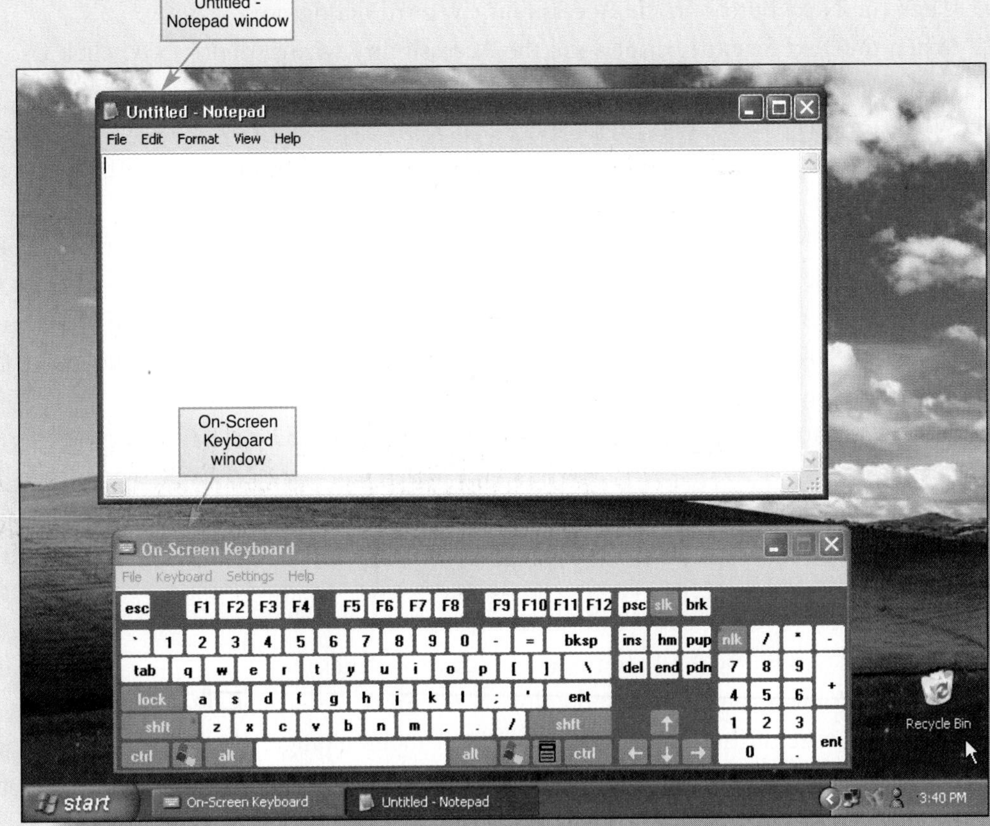

FIGURE 5-86

8. Using the mouse pointer and On-Screen Keyboard, type your first and last name and then click the ENTER key.

(continued)

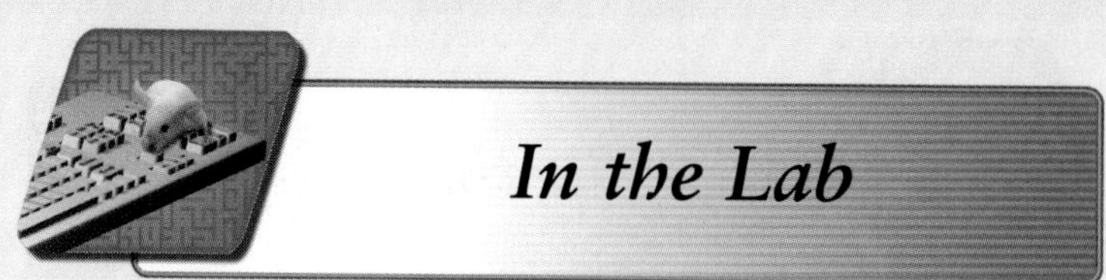

Customizing the Computer Using the Accessibility Wizard *(continued)*

9. Print the document using the Print command on the File menu in the Untitled - Notepad window.
10. Click the Close button in the On-Screen Keyboard window.
11. Click the Close button in the Untitled - Notepad window and then click the No button in the Notepad dialog box.

Part 3: ***Using the Accessibility Wizard***

1. Right-click the desktop and then click Properties to display the Display Properties dialog box.
2. On a separate piece of paper, write down the desktop theme name that displays in the Theme box on the desktop of your computer. Windows XP
3. Click the Close button in the Display Properties dialog box.
4. Click the Start button, point to All Programs, point to Accessories, point to Accessibility, and then click Accessibility Wizard to start the Accessibility wizard. The **Accessibility wizard** allows you to select the best accessibility features for your impairment.
5. Click the Next button in the Accessibility Wizard dialog box.
6. When the Text Size title displays in the Accessibility wizard dialog box, click Use large window titles and menus, and then click the Next button.
7. When the Display Settings title displays, click the Next button.
8. When the Set Wizard Options title displays, click I am blind or have difficulty seeing things on screen, and then click the Next button.
9. When the Scroll Bar and Window Border Size title displays, click the third scroll bar, and then click the Next button.
10. When the Icon Size title displays, click the Large icon, and then click the Next button.
11. When the Display Color Settings title displays, click High Contrast White in the Color schemes list, and then click the Next button.
12. When the Mouse Cursor title displays, click the mouse cursor (Large and Black), and then click the Next button.
13. When the Cursor Settings title displays, click the next button.
14. When the Completing the Accessibility Wizard page displays, click the Finish button.

Part 4: ***Working with Accessibility Settings***

1. Click the Start button and then point to Control Panel.
   a. What color is the background color on the Start menu? Black
   b. Did the size of the commands on the Start menu change? If so, how. yes, bigger
   c. Is each icon on the Start menu fully visible? yes
2. Click Control Panel. Maximize the Control Panel window.
   a. Are the icons in the Control Panel window easier to see? yes
3. Click the Close button to close the Control Panel window.

Part 5: ***Restoring the Default Settings***

1. Right-click the desktop and then click Properties to display the Display Properties dialog box.
2. Click the Theme box arrow in the Display Properties dialog box.

In the Lab

3. Click the desktop theme name in the Theme list you wrote down in Part 3, Step 2 previously.
4. Click the Appearance tab.
5. Click the Effects button.
6. Click the Use Large icons check box to remove check mark.
7. Click the OK button in the Effects dialog box.
8. Click the OK button in the Display Properties dialog box.
9. Hand in the printed Notepad document and the answers to the questions to your instructor.

4 Using the Accessibility Options to Design a Personalized Desktop

Problem: Your boss appointed you as the person to design a single Windows XP desktop for employees within the company who have both hearing and vision impaired.

Instructions: Experiment with the accessibility features until you have determined the best combination of features. Then, write down all settings so you can personalize each employee's computer to the standard. Make sure you reset the settings you changed while performing this exercise.

Cases and Places

The difficulty of these case studies varies:
▸ are the least difficult; ▸▸ are more difficult; and ▸▸▸ are the most difficult.

1 ▸ A friend of yours recently purchased a new computer. She would like to customize the mouse and keyboard. She wants to change it to look three-dimensional, add a drop shadow to the mouse pointer to make it easier to see it on the desktop, and slow down the cursor blink rate to make it easier to see the insertion point while word processing. She is left-handed and has trouble using the left mouse button. She asks if you would write down the instructions for these changes so she can make the changes herself. You agree to write the instructions using Notepad and print a copy for her.

2 ▸ You currently have a Hewlett-Packard LaserJet 6P printer to print black and white documents. The HP LaserJet 6P is set up as your default printer. You recently purchased a used Hewlett-Packard DeskJet 650C printer. You add the HP DeskJet 650C printer to the computer so you can print color documents from the same computer. Summarize in writing the procedure you must follow to print the document on the HP DeskJet 650C when the default printer is the HP LaserJet 6P.

von Eper 53   750

Cases and Places

3 ▶▶ On Thursday night, you purchase and install a new DVD-drive and video board on the computer. The process involves installing the devices and their device drivers. Friday morning, you turn on the computer and nothing happens. The Windows XP operating system will not launch. You assume it must be a problem resulting from last night's installations. Instead of calling technical support, you call a friend. Your friend suggests you investigate the problem using safe mode to launch the computer. Windows Help and Support contains information about safe mode and other features that allow you to repair a system. Write a brief report explaining these features.

4 ▶▶ Your physically challenged friend asks you to help him set up his computer and customize the keyboard to his specific needs. He is unable to hold down the ALT, CTRL, or SHIFT key while pressing another key and would prefer to use the keyboard instead of the mouse. He also would like to control the mouse pointer using the keys on the numeric keypad. List two accessibility options you can use to help your friend. Summarize each accessibility option, including how you use the keyboard with and without the option.

5 ▶▶▶ Windows XP supports the use of USB hardware devices. Using the Internet, computer magazines, or other resources, collect information about USB hardware devices. Prepare a detailed report describing how USB devices work, who developed the USB specifications, and the problems the new devices solved. Include what USB devices currently are available for sale, the cost of the devices, and where you can purchase them. If time permits, compare and contrast the USB technology to the IEEE 1394 technology.

6 ▶▶▶ Windows XP allows you to add application programs to the computer easily when you use the Add or Remove Programs feature. In addition, the same feature allows you to remove a program. Although this feature works well with application programs written for Windows XP, many computers have application programs written for previous operating systems (Windows 98, Windows 3.1, and DOS) that you cannot remove using the Add or Remove Programs feature. Several programs have been developed and marketed to remove, or uninstall, non-Windows application programs. Using the Internet, computer magazines, or visiting a computer store, obtain information about these products. Write a brief report listing the programs available and comparing and contrasting their features.

7 ▶▶▶ Many companies maintain a Standards and Procedures Manual to outline the standards for using a computer on the network. Topics often include the procedures for adding new hardware, adding and removing application programs, and customizing a company computer. Visit a small, medium, and large company in your area to find out if, and how, each company handles employee standards and procedures. Prepare a brief report summarizing the standards and procedures developed for each company. Include the procedures for adding new hardware, adding and removing application programs, and customizing the computer. In the report, make recommendations for each company based on what you found.

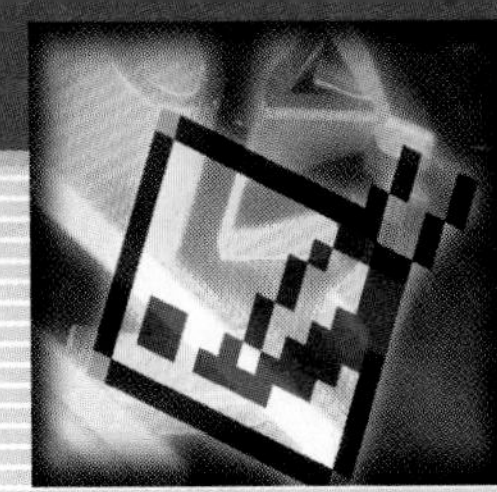

Microsoft Windows XP

PROJECT

Advanced File and Web Searching

You will have mastered the material in this project when you can:

OBJECTIVES

- Begin a new file or folder search, save a search, and find a file using a saved search
- Find a file by specifying the starting point, date, or file type, or knowing a word or series of words in the file
- Search for and display the contents of a picture file
- Search for and play a music or video file
- Search for a document file
- Search the Internet using Search Companion or Classic Internet search
- Change a search preference
- Search the Internet for Web pages, e-mail addresses, business information, and maps
- View the contents and properties of the Recycle Bin
- Restore a deleted file using the Recycle Bin
- Empty the Recycle Bin

Ready for Any Challenge

"Man is still the most extraordinary computer of all."

John Fitzgerald Kennedy (1917-1963)

It is no small wonder that the desktop workspace has donned color, icons, themes, background patterns, images, and visual styles. Combined, these elements provide a creative mix to make your desktop environment efficient and increase your productivity. The Recycle Bin icon, for example, provides access to a safety net when deleting files and folders. When you delete files to the Recycle Bin, the icon changes from empty to full. This visual caution helps you instantly recognize that you have file maintenance chores.

The assortment of icons available in Windows XP is not as extensive as the variety offered by many icon packages available for today's computer desktops, however. Some of the more popular icons from the FileWorld library are available online. Free shareware images ranging from Star Wars characters to figures from Celtic art are available for download. Some turn your blinking insertion point into any number of different animated characters or animals. They even can open your Recycle Bin to retrieve files you did not mean to discard.

The trash can icon developed an identity all its own when the Apple Macintosh computer was in the design phase during 1982. Andy Hertzfeld, an Apple programmer working to develop an innovative, user-friendly technology for the Mac, called his high school friend, Susan Kare, for assistance. Kare bought some graph paper, marked off 1,024 squares, and got to work.

She spent the next three years as Apple Computer's creative director coloring these squares to create instantly recognizable icons. Kare is credited with developing the familiar Macintosh trash can, wristwatch, paintbrush, fonts, and smiling miniature Mac. Microsoft recruited Kare in 1988 to design the icons and buttons for Windows 3.0 and most of the original solitaire cards. While developing icon ideas, she considered using a trash truck, plastic and aluminum trash cans, and fires. Samples of Kare's work are available on her Web site (kare.com).

In Project 6, you will view the contents of the Recycle Bin, restore a deleted file, empty the Recycle Bin, view the properties of the Recycle Bin, and use advanced file and Web searching techniques.

Whether you are working at a desktop computer at home, a notebook computer on the road, or using a networked computer in the office or a school lab, you will be required to perform a variety of searches. You can use Search Companion and Classic Internet search to perform a customized search that will find files and folders, digital media files, maps and addresses, and information on the World Wide Web.

With this innovative mix of searching techniques and using the Recycle Bin effectively, you can improve your productivity and Windows skills and be ready for any challenge.

Microsoft Windows XP

Advanced File and Web Searching

PROJECT

CASE PERSPECTIVE

Your organization has been using Windows XP for several months. Most people in the organization feel comfortable with simple file operations such as copying, moving, renaming, and deleting. Many people have found that being able to use Search Companion to search for a file knowing only the file name is a timesaving feature. Your boss has found, however, that most employees do not know about the additional search methods that are available to them. He wants the employees to learn these methods also.

Your goal is to learn more about advanced searching techniques so you can conduct a training seminar for the people in the organization. You decide to learn more about searching for digital media files, using Search Companion and the Classic Internet search, and searching for Web pages, mailing addresses, business information, and maps.

Introduction

In Project 3, you used Search Companion to search for files on the local hard drive knowing only the file name or partial file name of a file. In Project 4, you used the Address toolbar on the taskbar to search for Web pages on the Internet using a keyword, phrase, or Web page URL.

In addition to learning the search techniques used in previous projects, you should be familiar with the other search techniques available in Windows XP. In this project, you will search for files on the local hard drive by specifying the date or file type, or knowing a word or series of words in the file. You will learn techniques for searching the Internet for digital media files (pictures, music, and video files), document files, Web pages, mailing addresses, business information, and maps.

In addition, you will recover a deleted file from the Recycle Bin, view the properties of the Recycle Bin, and empty the Recycle Bin.

Advanced File Searching

As mentioned in Project 3, it is easy to locate files and folders on the computer. One method of searching for a file is to browse through the folders on the computer using My Computer or Windows Explorer. Another method of searching is to use Search Companion. **Search Companion** allows you to search for files and folders, digital media files, people, computers on a network, and information on the Internet.

Search Companion allows you to perform three types of searches: file search, network search, and Internet search. A **file search** allows you to search for digital media files (picture, music, and video files), document files (word processing, spreadsheet, database, and so on), and all files and folders (digital media files, document files, system files, folder files, and so on).

A **network search** allows you to search for computers and people on a network. An **Internet search** allows you to search Web pages on the Internet for information. Search Companion also has an indexing service that maintains an index of all files on the computer and makes searching faster.

Search Companion allows you to specify the search criteria to use when performing a file search. You can search for files and folders on a hard drive knowing all or part of the file name, a word or phrase within the file, the time and date the file was modified, or the file type or size. The following sections illustrate the various ways to perform a file search using Search Companion.

More About

The Search Command

Some would argue that the Search command is the handiest tool in Windows XP. If an icon for an application program does not display on the Start menu, many people use the Search command to display the icon in the Search Results window and then double-click the icon to launch the program.

Specifying the Beginning Point of a File Search

In Project 3, you used Search Companion to perform a file search to locate a file on the local hard drive knowing only the name of the file. Sometimes users forget the file name after saving a file on the local hard drive. In this case, you could use Search Companion to search for files knowing a word or series of words in the file, the file type, or the modification date. To make the search quicker, you can specify the folder in which to begin the file search. Perform the following steps to begin a file search.

To Begin a File Search

1 Click the Start button and then point to Search on the Start menu.

The Start menu and highlighted Search command display (Figure 6-1).

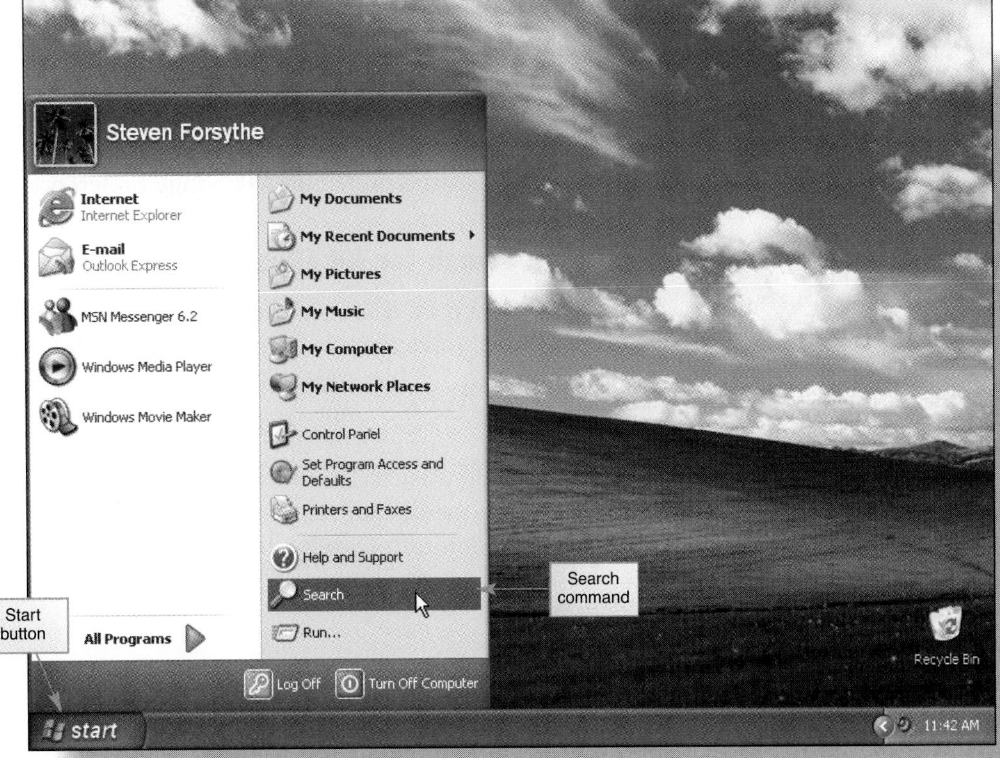

FIGURE 6-1

2 Click Search. Maximize the Search Results window.

The Search Companion pane displays in the maximized Search Results window (Figure 6-2). The pane contains the Search Companion balloon and an animated search dog named Rover. A message about starting a search displays in the right pane.

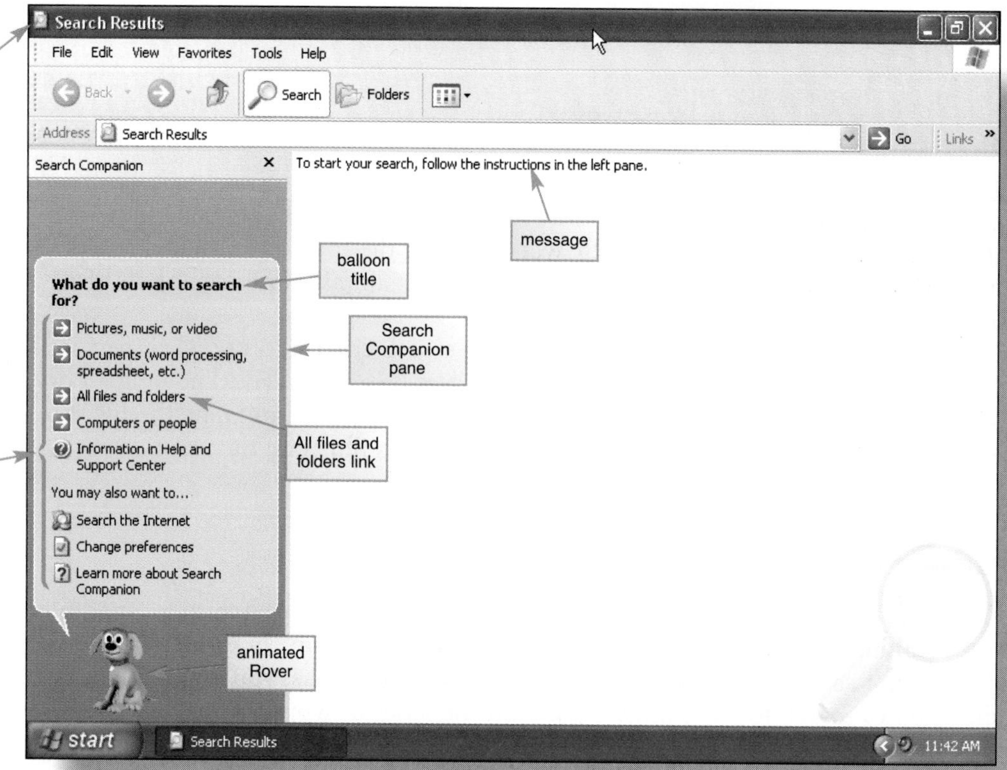

FIGURE 6-2

Other Ways

1. On Standard Buttons toolbar click Search button
2. On Start menu right-click My Documents, My Pictures, or My Computer, click Search
3. In Explorer window, press F3
4. Press CTRL+ESC, press S; or press WINDOWS+F

The first Search Companion balloon to display contains a title (What do you want to search for?) and links to search for digital media files (Pictures, music, or video), document files (Documents), all files and folders (All files and folders), computers or people (Computers or people), Help (Information in Help and Support Center), Web sites on the Internet (Search the Internet), preferences (Change preferences), and Search Companion (learn more about Search Companion). In addition, you can change the search preferences (Change preferences).

More About

Rover

If animated search dogs bother you, you can remove Rover by clicking Change Preferences and then clicking Without An Animated Screen Character. If you would prefer another animated screen character, click Change Preferences, click With A Different Character, and then use the Next or Back button to select a character.

Performing a Search for All Files and Folders

In Project 3, you used Search Companion to search all files and folders for the Soap Bubbles file on the local hard drive knowing only the name of the file (see Figures 3-72 through 3-77 on pages WIN 3.59 through WIN 3.61). In addition to searching using only the file name, you can search for all files and folders on a local hard drive knowing all or part of the file name, a word or phrase within the file, the time and date the file was last modified, and the file type or size.

Unless changed, the default search preferences for searching all files and folders cause Search Companion to search all local hard drives, all system folders, and the Recycle Bin. Perform the following step to begin a file search to search for all files and folders.

To Perform an All Files and Folders Search

1 Click All files and folders in the Search Companion balloon.

The contents of the Search Companion balloon change (Figure 6-3). The balloon title changes, an insertion point displays in the All or part of the file name text box, the A word or phrase in the file text box is empty, and the Local Hard Drives (C:) entry displays in the Look in box to indicate all local hard drives will be searched (Figure 6-3).

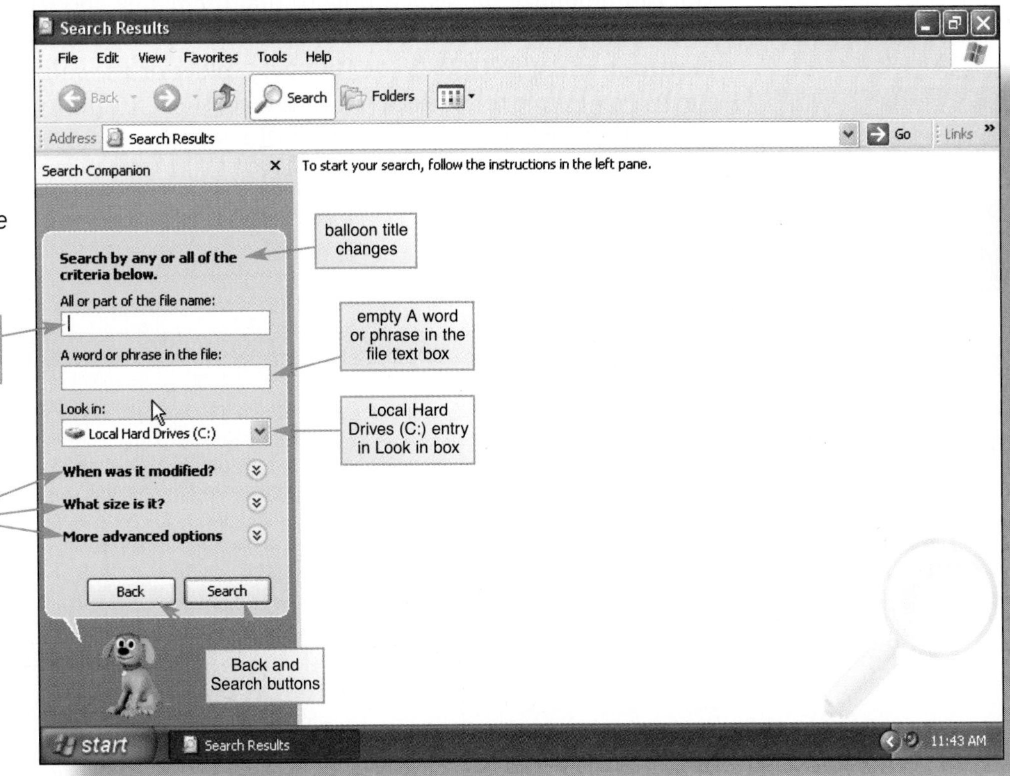

FIGURE 6-3

The All or part of the file name text box shown in Figure 6-3 allows you to type all or part of the file name or folder name you want to find and is empty to indicate no file or folder names will be examined during the search. The A word or phrase in the file text box, which allows you to search for files containing specific text, is empty to indicate the contents of the files will not be examined during the search.

The Look in box indicates the starting point of the search. The Local Hard Drives (C:) entry indicates the starting point of the search is the local hard drive and all the subfolders on the local hard drive will be searched. In addition, you can select a different starting point for a search by selecting a computer, drive, or folder in the Look in list box.

Three entries, each representing a collapsed area, display below the Look in text box and are identified by double down arrow buttons. Clicking the double down arrow button expands an area and displays additional search criteria. The When was it modified? area allows you to specify a time period within which to search for files and folders. The What size is it? area allows you to search for files and folders based on their file size. The More advanced options area allows you to select the types of files and folders to search for and whether file and folder names should be case-sensitive. A **case-sensitive search** is a search in which the capitalization of a file or folder name entered in the Search Companion balloon must match exactly the capitalization of the file or folder name on the local hard drive.

The Search button at the bottom of the Search Companion pane starts the search and the Back button displays the previously displayed balloon.

More About

Locating All Files and Folders

The Search Companion is the easiest way to locate a file or folder. Windows Explorer provides a quick way to view files and folders, My Computer provides a simpler view of folders, and My Network Places provides a view of computers, files and folders, printers, and other network resources.

Specifying the Starting Point of a Search

If you know which folder a file is stored in but do not know the name of the file, you can minimize the search time to find the file by specifying the folder in which to begin the search. Assume, for example, you want to search for a file you know is located in the WINDOWS (or WINNT) folder or the subfolders in the WINDOWS (or WINNT) folder. Perform the following steps to specify the WINDOWS (or WINNT) folder as the starting point of a search.

To Specify the Starting Point of a Search

1 Click the Look in box arrow and then point to Browse in the Look in list.

The Look in list box displays and the highlighted Browse entry displays in the Look in list (Figure 6-4).

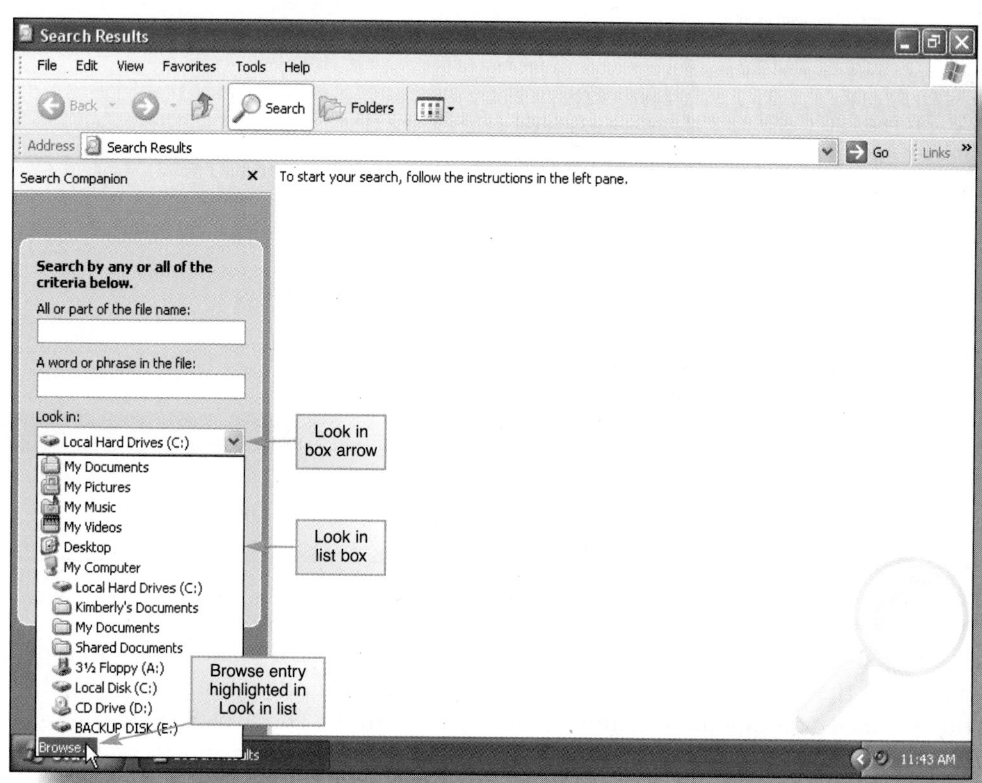

FIGURE 6-4

2 Click Browse. When the Browse For Folder dialog box displays, click the plus sign preceding the My Computer icon in the Choose directory to search list box, and then point to the plus sign preceding the LOCAL DISK (C:) icon.

The Look in list box on the balloon closes and the Browse For Folder dialog box displays (Figure 6-5). In the hierarchical structure in the Choose directory to search list box, a minus sign precedes the My Computer entry, the My Computer entry is expanded, and a plus sign precedes the indented LOCAL DISK (C:) entry.

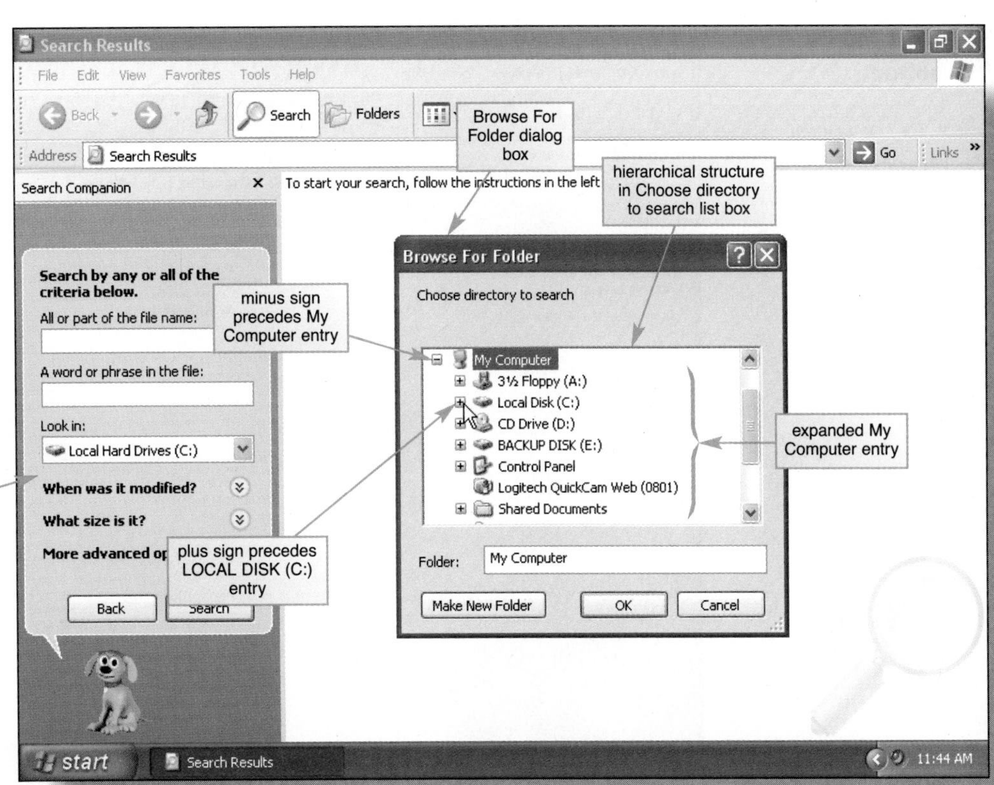

FIGURE 6-5

3 Click the plus sign. Scroll the Choose directory to search list box until the WINDOWS (or WINNT) folder name is visible and then click the folder name. Point to the OK button.

The LOCAL DISK (C:) entry expands, and the WINDOWS (or WINNT) folder name is highlighted in the list box (Figure 6-6).

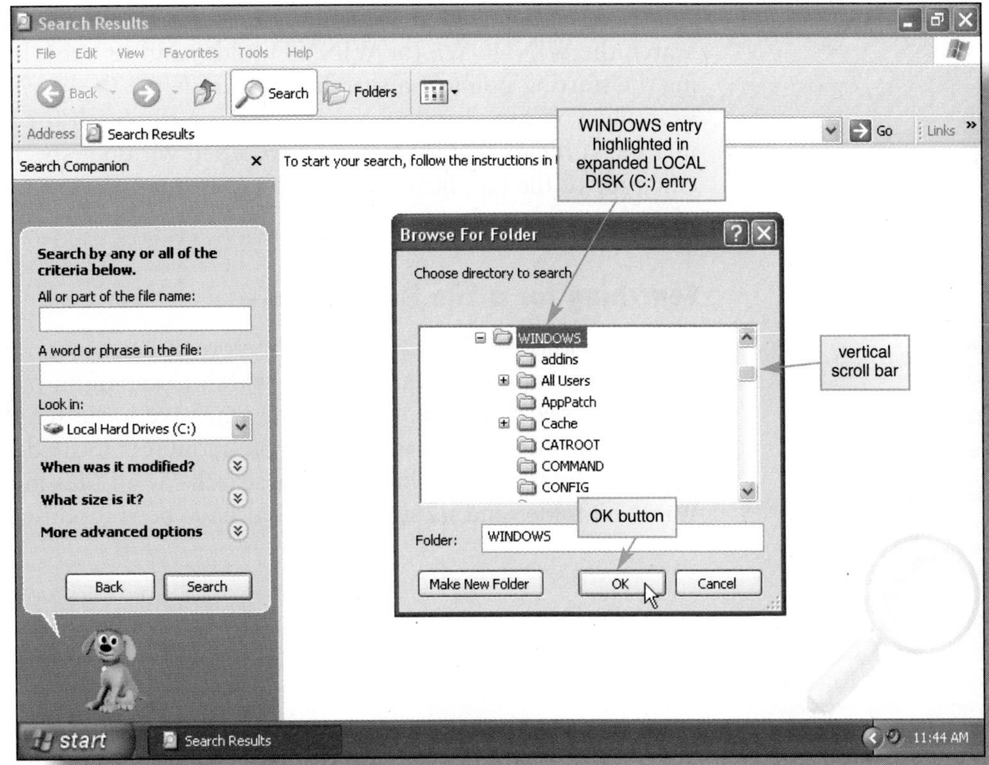

FIGURE 6-6

4 **Click the OK button.**

The Browse For Folder dialog box closes and a folder icon and WINDOWS (or WINNT) name displays in the Look in box (Figure 6-7).

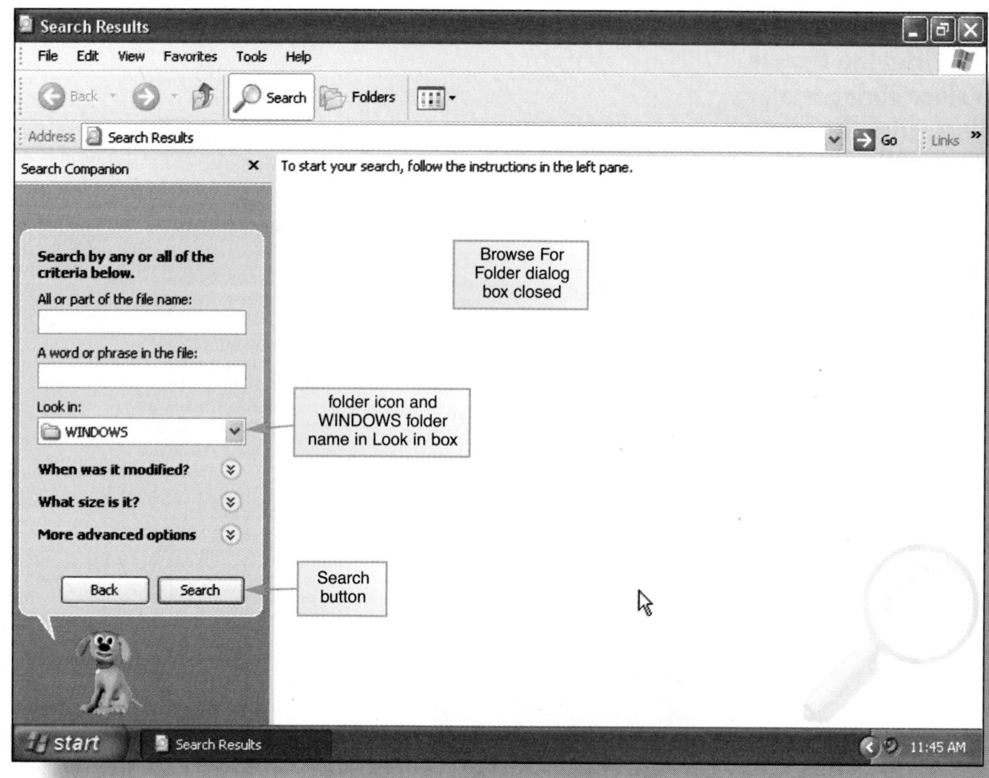

FIGURE 6-7

Other Ways

1. Click Look in box arrow, click folder name in Look in list

Unless you change the starting point of a search, clicking the Search button will search the WINDOWS (or WINNT) folder and its subfolders. In addition to specifying the starting point of a search, you can define the search criteria further. For example, you can change the search criteria to search for a word or phrase contained in a file, a file or folder created or modified within a specified period of time, a specific type of file (application file, bitmap image file, text file, and so on), or the size of a file.

Searching for a File Using a Date

If you know a file was modified before or after a certain date, you can use the When was it modified? entry in the Search Companion balloon to specify a time interval to search for the file. Assume you have forgotten the name of a file you modified within the last week, but you know it is located in the WINDOWS (or WINNT) folder. The following steps search for all files in the WINDOWS (or WINNT) folder and its subfolders that have been modified within the last week.

More About

Searching by Date

The default setting for searching by date (Don't remember) allows you to search for modified files. Clicking the Specify dates option button allows you to search for files modified within a range of days by entering a beginning date and an ending date. Only files modified in the range specified are displayed.

To Search for a File Using a Modification Date

1 Point to the When was it modified? double down arrow button in the Search Companion balloon (Figure 6-8).

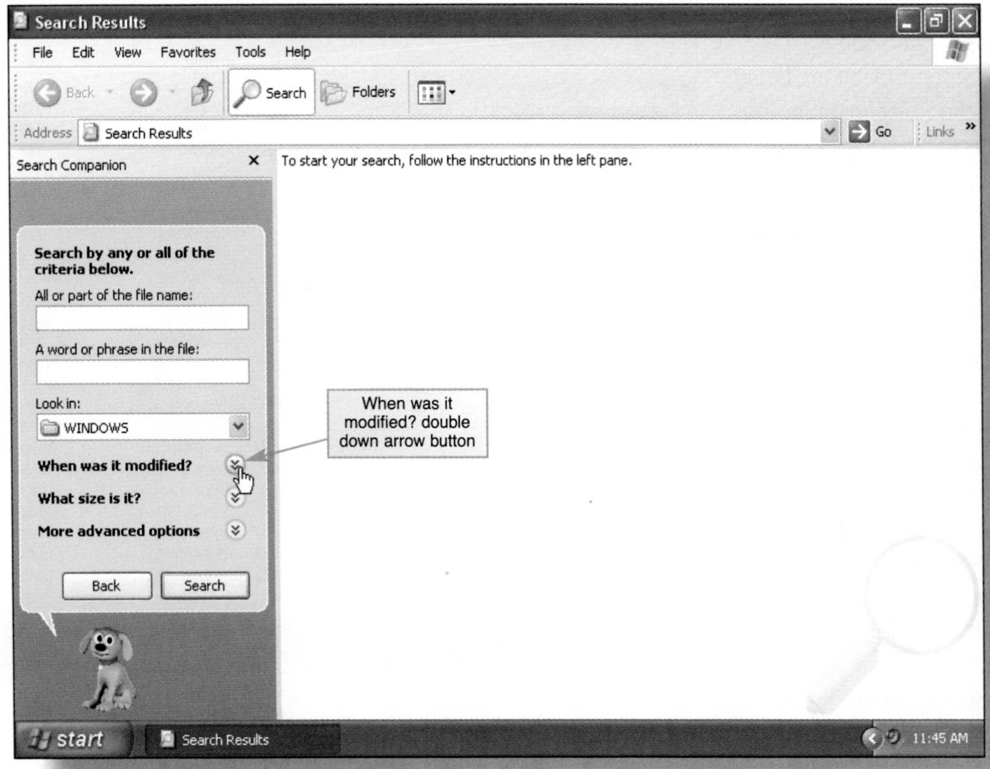

FIGURE 6-8

2 Click the When was it modified? double down arrow button. Click Within the last week. Point to the Search button.

The expanded When was it modified? area displays and the Within the last week option button is selected (Figure 6-9).

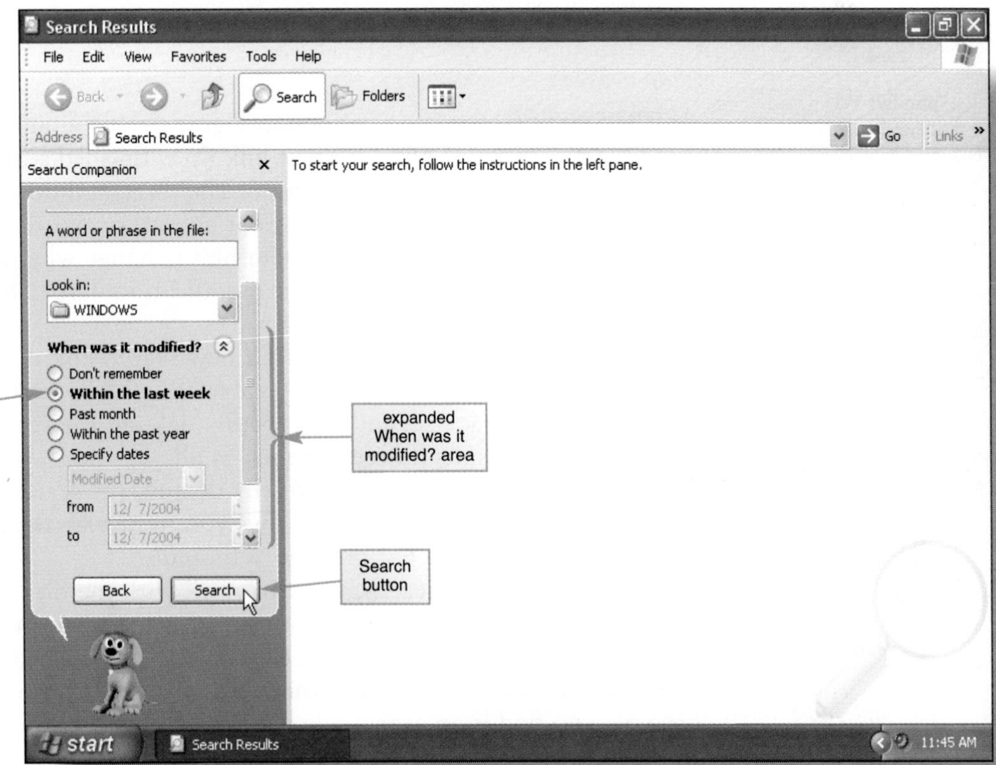

FIGURE 6-9

3 Click the Search button.

While the search progresses, the search criteria and locations being searched display in the balloon along with the path of the folder currently being searched and a progress indicator. When the search is complete, the contents of the balloon change and a partial list of the 140 files in the WINDOWS (or WINNT) folder and its subfolders modified within the last week displays in List view in the right pane (Figure 6-10). Different files may display on your computer.

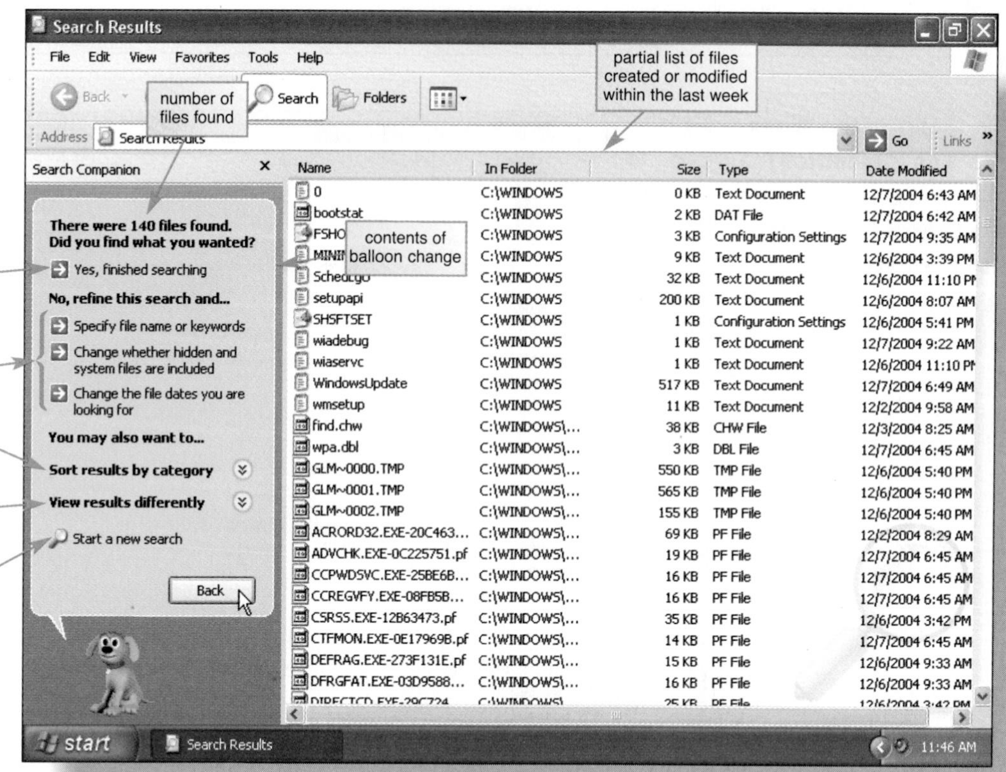

FIGURE 6-10

Other Ways

1. In expanded When was it modified? area click Past month, click Search button
2. In expanded When was it modified? area click Within the past year, click Search button
3. In expanded When was it modified? area click Specify dates, type beginning date in from text box, type ending date in to text box, click Search button

The Search Companion balloon in Figure 6-10 contains the number of files found (140) and four links. The first link (Yes, finished searching) ends the search and closes the Search Companion pane. The three additional links allow you to refine the current search by searching for a word or words in the file (Specify file name or keywords), hidden and system files (Change whether hidden and system files are included), and select another modification date (Change the file dates you are looking for).

Two collapsed areas and the Start a new search link display at the bottom of the balloon. The Sort results by category entry allows you to sort the search results by name, date modified, size, and file type. By default, the search results are sorted by name. The View results differently entry is allows you to view the search results in Details, Thumbnails, and Tiles views. By default, the search results display in Details view. The Start a new search link allows you to display the first Search Companion balloon shown in Figure 6-2 on page WIN 6.06.

After completing a search, you can work with the files you found in any manner desired. For example, if a file can be opened, you can open it by double-clicking the file icon. In addition, you can print the file, create a shortcut to the file, rename or delete the file, and copy or move the file using commands on the shortcut menu. If the file you find is an executable program file, you can launch the program by double-clicking the file icon.

Resetting the Search Criteria to Search Using a File Type

The next search to be performed examines all files in the WINDOWS (or WINNT) folder regardless of creation or modification date. In preparation for the next search, perform the following steps to remove the requirement to search for files modified within the last week and leave the WINDOWS (or WINNT) icon and folder name in the Look in text box.

To Reset the Search Criteria

1 Point to the Back button in the balloon (Figure 6-11).

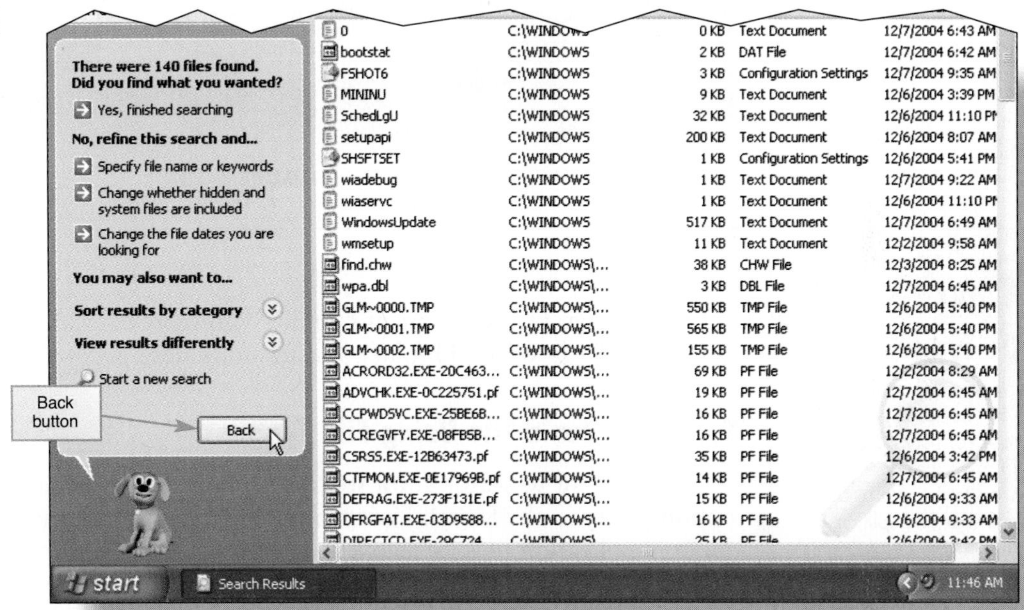

FIGURE 6-11

2 Click the Back button. Click the Don't remember button. Point to the When was it modified? double up arrow button.

The contents of the balloon change and the Don't remember option button is selected (Figure 6-12).

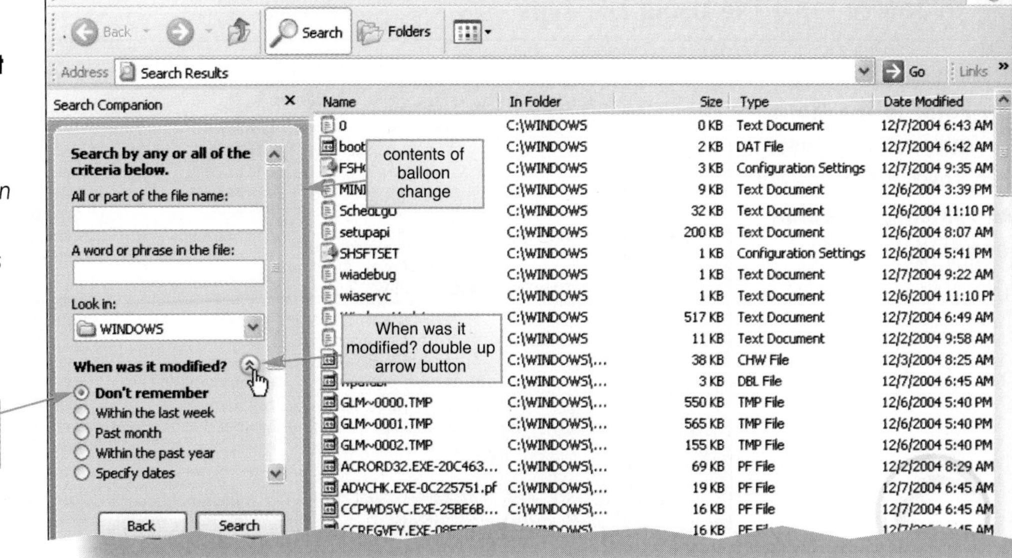

FIGURE 6-12

3 Click the When was it modified? double up arrow button.

The When was it modified area? collapses and the double down arrow button displays (Figure 6-13).

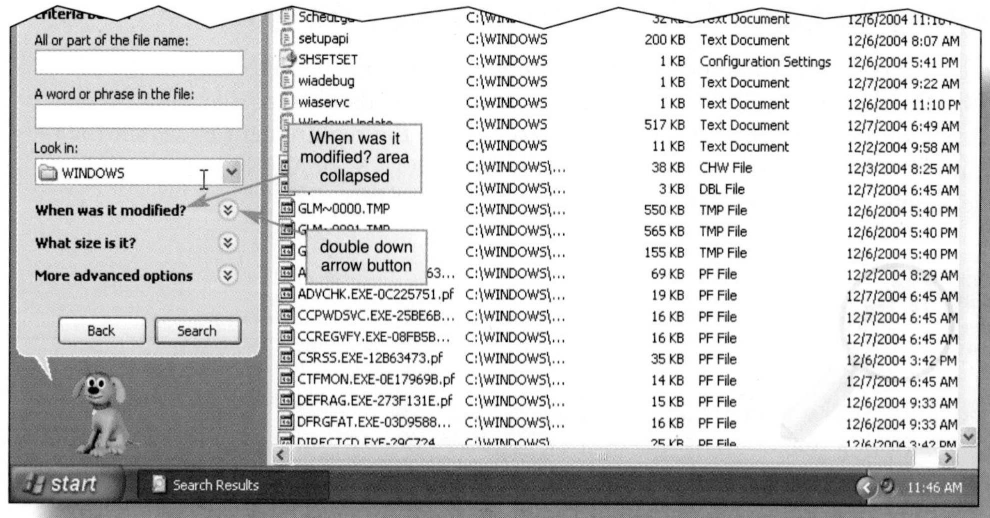

FIGURE 6-13

More About

File Types

File types are determined by file name extensions, which consist of a period and up to three characters added to the end of a file name. For example, .txt is a text document and .bmp is a bitmap image file. The Search Companion uses the file extension when searching for file types.

Unless changed, subsequent searches will search for all files and folders in the WINDOWS (or WINNT) folder and its subfolders, regardless of the date.

Searching for a File Using File Type

If you want to search for a specific type of file, you can use the More advanced options entry in the Search Companion balloon. Among the file types you can search for are application files (.exe extension), bitmap image files (.bmp extension), Help files (.hlp extension), and text document files (.txt extension). Assume, for example, that you want to find all the text document files in the WINDOWS (or WINNT) folder and its subfolders. Perform the following steps to search for only text document files in the WINDOWS (or WINNT) folder and its subfolders.

Steps To Search for a File Using File Type

1 Point to the More advanced options double down arrow button in the Search Companion balloon (Figure 6-14).

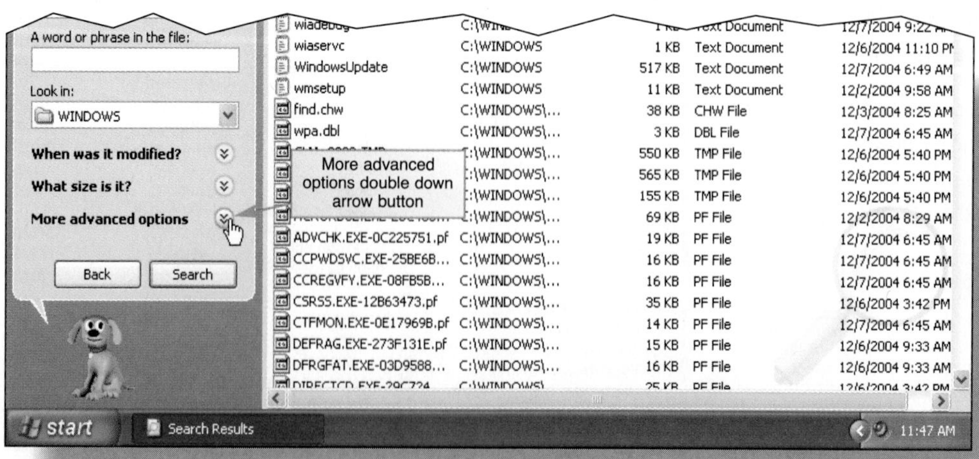

FIGURE 6-14

2 **Click the More advanced options double down arrow button. Point to the Type of file box arrow.**

The More advanced options area expands (Figure 6-15). The (All Files and Folders) entry displays in the Type of file box and five check boxes display below the box. The Search system folders and Search subfolders check boxes contain check marks.

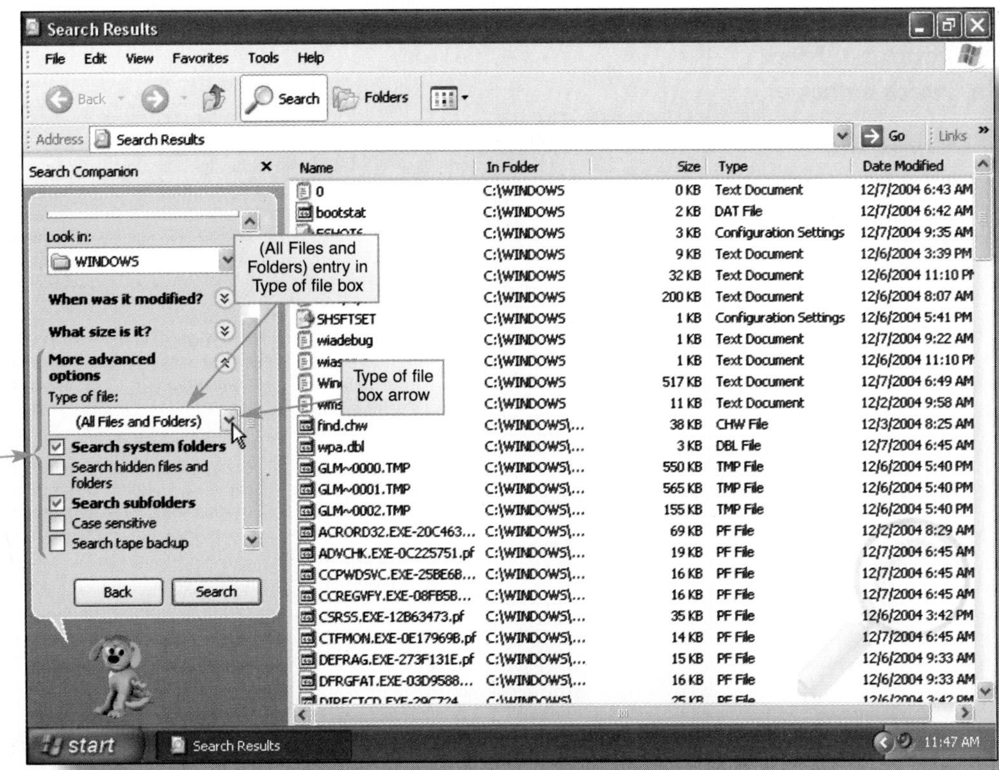

FIGURE 6-15

3 **Click the Type of file box arrow. Scroll down the Type of file list box until Text Document is visible and then point to Text Document.**

The Type of file list, containing the highlighted Text Document entry, displays in the Type of file list box (Figure 6-16).

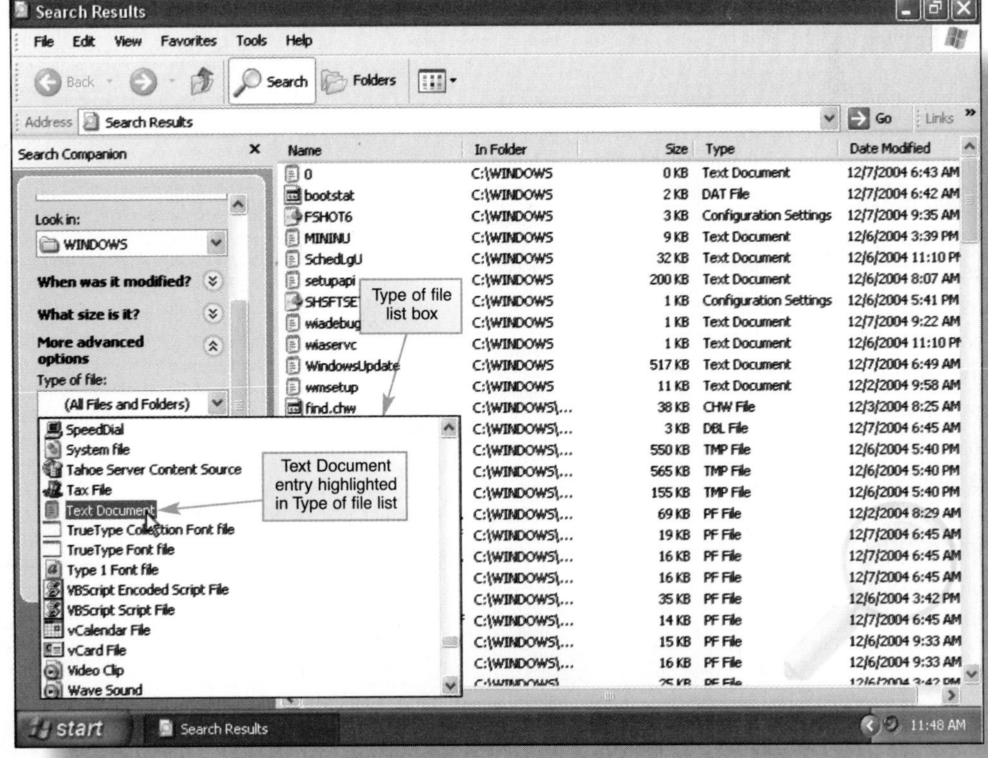

FIGURE 6-16

4 Click Text Document. Point to the Search button.

The highlighted Text Document entry displays in the Type of file box (Figure 6-17).

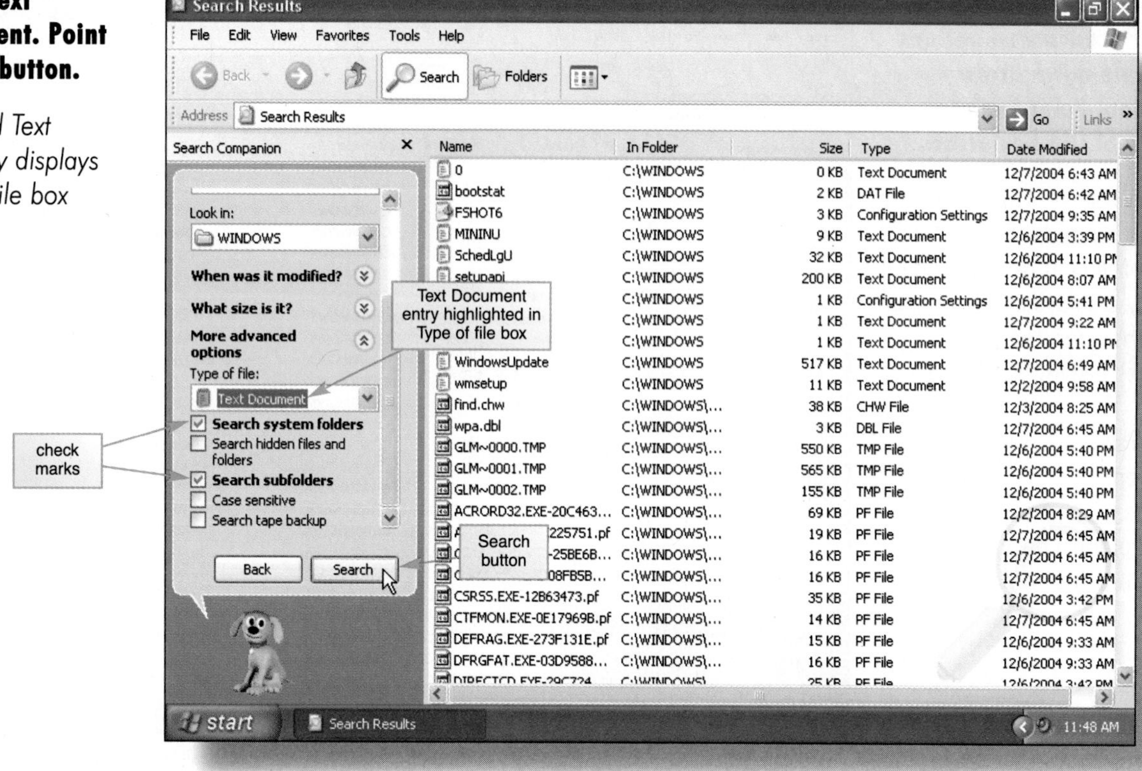

FIGURE 6-17

5 Click the Search button.

While the search progresses, the search criteria and locations being searched display in the balloon along with the path of the folder currently being searched. When the search is complete, a partial list of the 187 text document files in the WINDOWS (or WINNT) folder and its subfolders displays in the Search Results window (Figure 6-18). Different files may display on your computer.

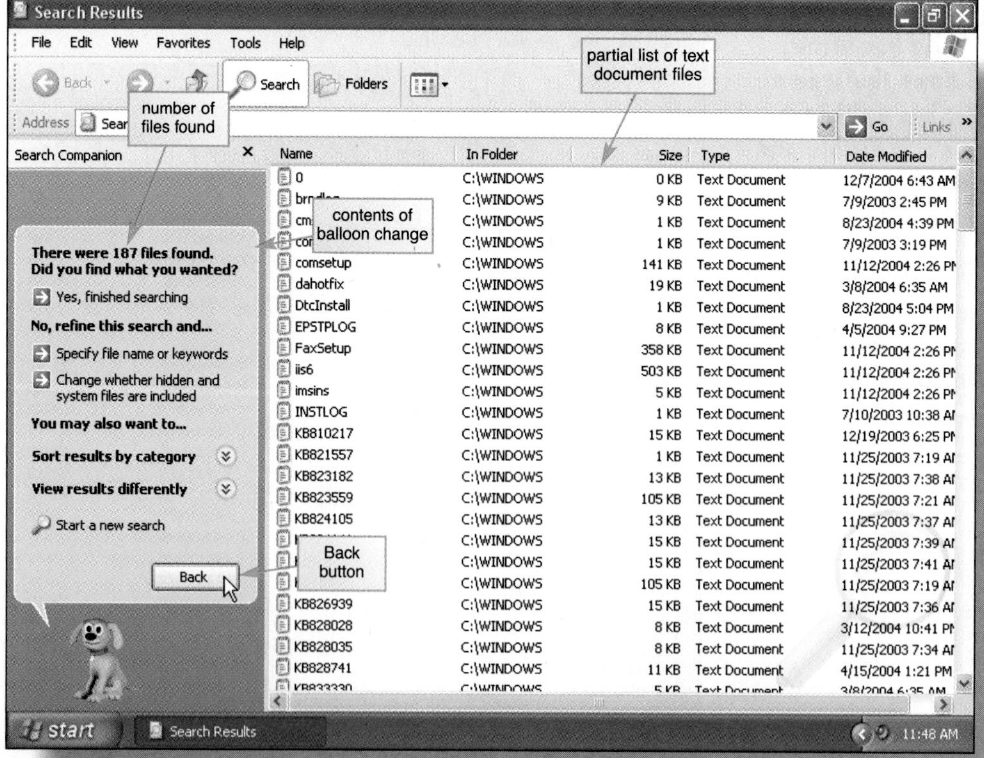

FIGURE 6-18

6 In preparation for the next search, click the Back button.

The contents of the balloon change (Figure 6-19). The text boxes ask for the information needed to begin another search.

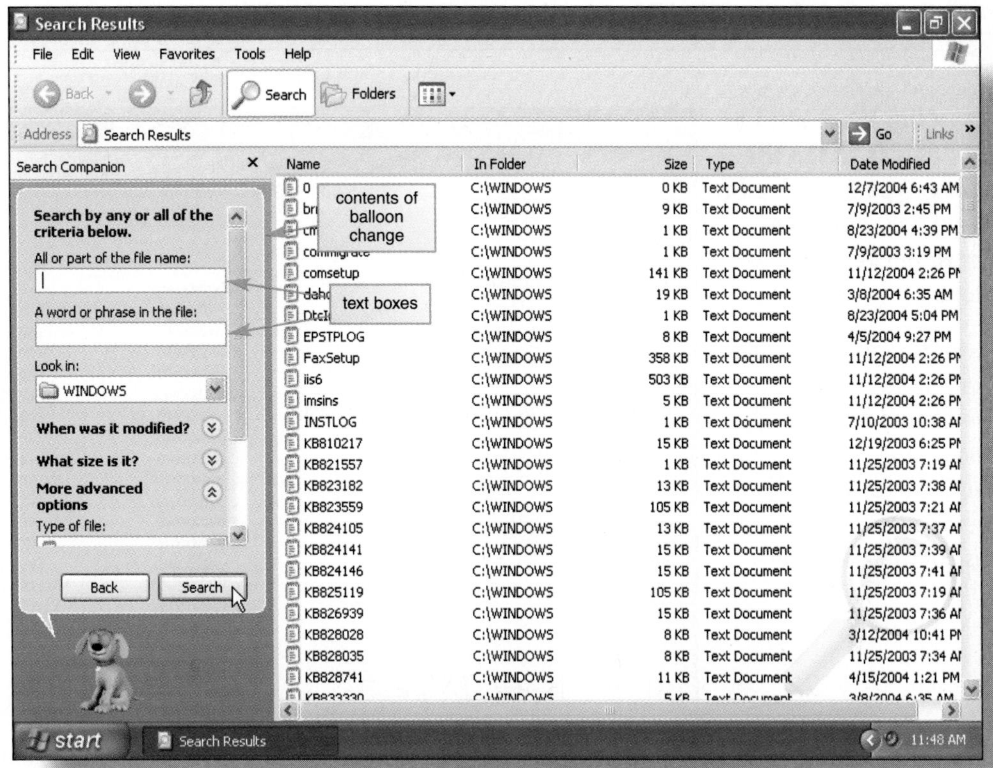

FIGURE 6-19

Other Ways

1. Click Type of file box arrow, use arrow keys to select file type, press ENTER key, click Search button

In Figure 6-15 on page WIN 6.15, the (All Files and Folders) entry in the Type of file box causes all files and folders to be searched when a search is performed. In Figure 6-17, the Text Document entry replaces the (All Files and Folders) entry in the Type of file box and causes only text documents to be found. The check mark in the Search system folders check box causes all system folders to be searched and the check mark in the Search subfolders check box causes all subfolders within the folder shown in the Look in box (WINDOWS or WINNT) to be searched.

The Search Companion balloon shown in Figure 6-18 contains the number of files found (187), three links (Yes, finished searching link, Specify file name or keywords link, and Change whether hidden and system files are included link), two collapsed areas (Sort results by category area and View results differently area), and another link (Start a new search link).

After completing a search by file type, you can double-click a file icon to view the contents of the file and right-click a file icon and click a command on the shortcut menu to perform various operations on the file.

Searching for a File Using a Word or Phrase in the File

If you want to search for a file knowing only a word or phrase in the file, you can search by typing the word or phrase in the A word or phrase in the file text box in the Search Companion balloon. Assume you want to find all Text Document files in the WINDOWS (or WINNT) folder and its subfolders containing the word, support. Perform the steps on the next page to search for all text document files containing the word, support.

To Search for a File Using a Word or Phrase in the File

1 Click the A word or phrase in the file text box, type `support` **in the text box, and then point to the Search button.**

The word, support, displays in the A word or phrase in the file text box (Figure 6-20). The WINDOWS (or WINNT) folder name continues to display in the Look in text box.

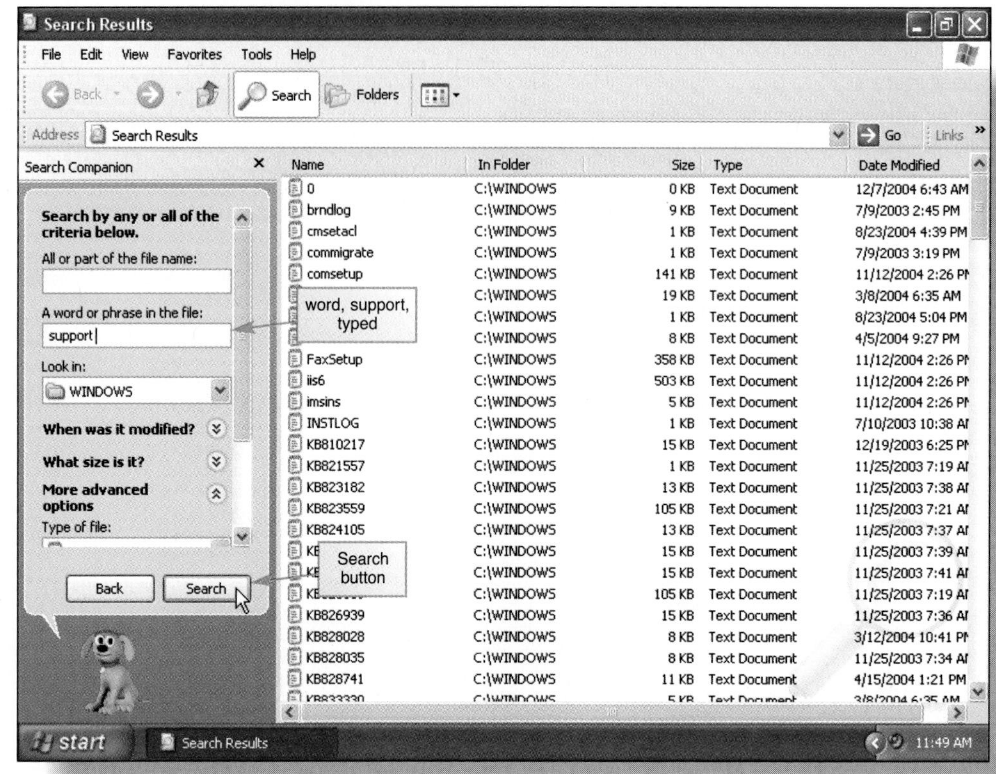

FIGURE 6-20

2 Click the Search button.

While the search progresses, the search criteria and locations being searched display in the balloon along with the path of the folder currently being searched. When the search is complete, a list of 32 text document files containing the word, support, in the WINDOWS (or WINNT) folder or its subfolders displays in the Search Results window (Figure 6-21). Different files may display on your computer.

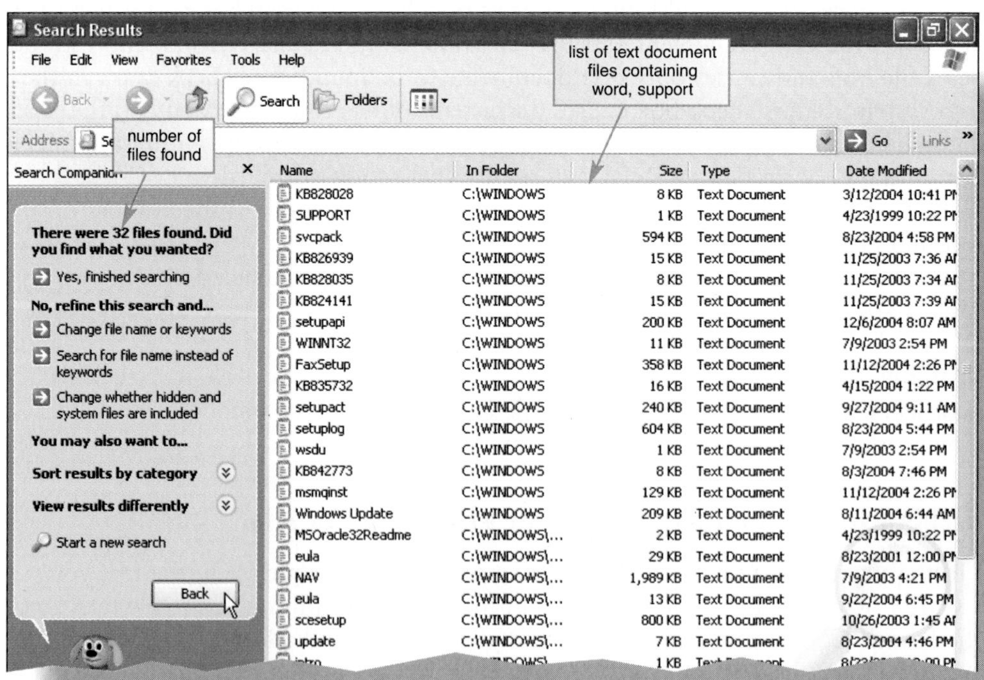

FIGURE 6-21

After completing a search, you can perform operations on the files by right-clicking a file icon and then clicking a command on the shortcut menu. In some cases, you may want to save a copy of a file in the My Documents folder.

Sending a File to the My Documents Folder

Right-clicking any object displays a shortcut menu containing commands related to that object. When you right-click a file or folder icon and point to the Send To command on the shortcut menu, the Send To menu displays. The commands on the Send To menu allow you to copy (send) a file or folder to one of several destinations (compressed folder, desktop, another person by e-mail, My Documents folder, and floppy disk). In Project 2, you used the Send To command to copy the Daily Reminders folder from the My Documents window to the floppy disk in drive A (see Figures 2-58 and 2-59 on page WIN 2.42).

Every user on the computer has a separate SendTo folder and can customize the contents of the folder by adding new destinations to the Send To menu. Perform the following steps to copy the eula file found during the last search to the My Documents folder.

To Send a File to the My Documents Folder

1 Right-click the first eula file name, point to Send To on the shortcut menu, and then point to My Documents on the Send To menu.

The highlighted eula file displays, a shortcut menu and Sent To submenu display, and the Send To and My Documents commands are highlighted (Figure 6-22).

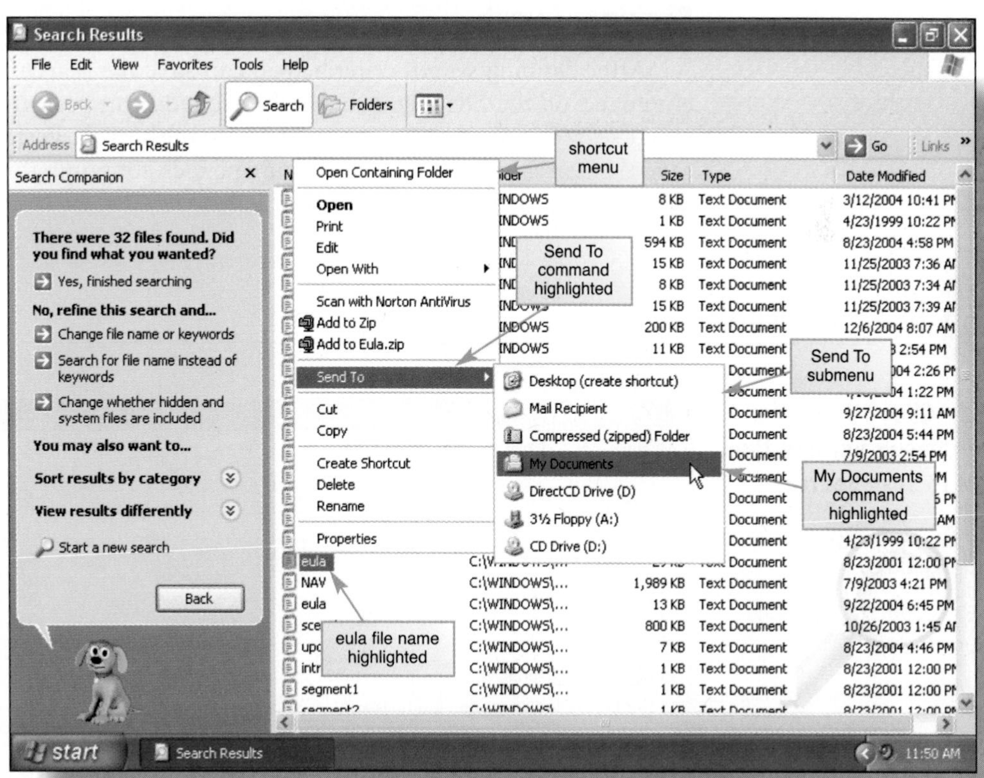

FIGURE 6-22

2 **Click My Documents.**

The eula file is copied to the My Documents folder and the Send To submenu and shortcut menu no longer display (Figure 6-23).

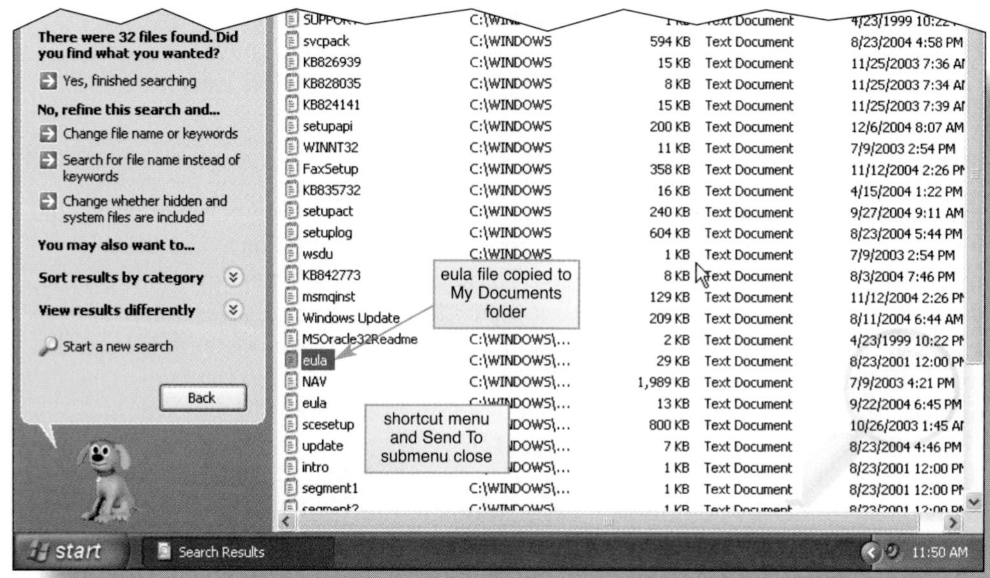

FIGURE 6-23

Saving a Search

After defining search criteria, you can save the search by using the Save Search command on the File menu. In the future, you can perform the same search using the saved search instead of having to recreate the search. Perform the following steps to save the search to find all text document files containing the word, support, in the WINDOWS (or WINNT) folders or subfolders.

Steps To Save a Search

1 **Click File on the menu bar and then point to Save Search.**

The File menu containing the highlighted Save Search command displays (Figure 6-24).

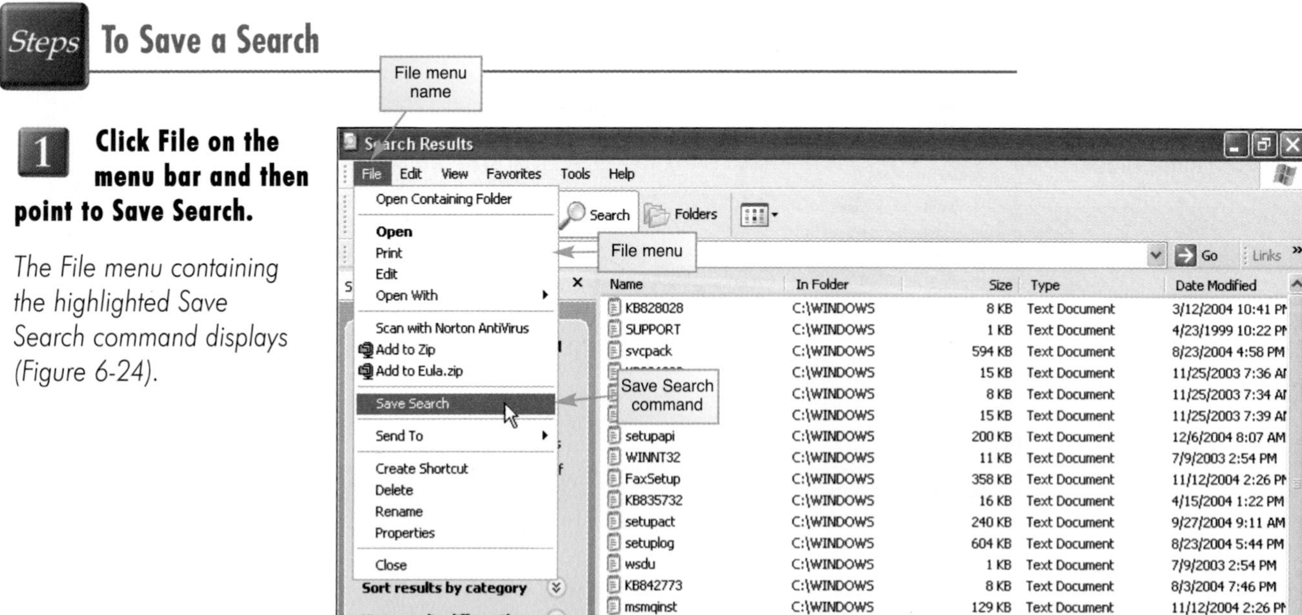

FIGURE 6-24

2 Click Save Search. Point to the Save button.

The Save Search dialog box displays (Figure 6-25). The My Documents entry in the Save in box and the selected My Documents button on the Shortcut bar indicate the file will be saved in the My Documents folder. The File name text box contains the saved search file name (Files containing text support).

3 Click the Save button. Click the Close button in the Search Results window.

Windows XP saves the Files containing text support file in the My Documents folder, closes the Save Search dialog box, and closes the Search Results window.

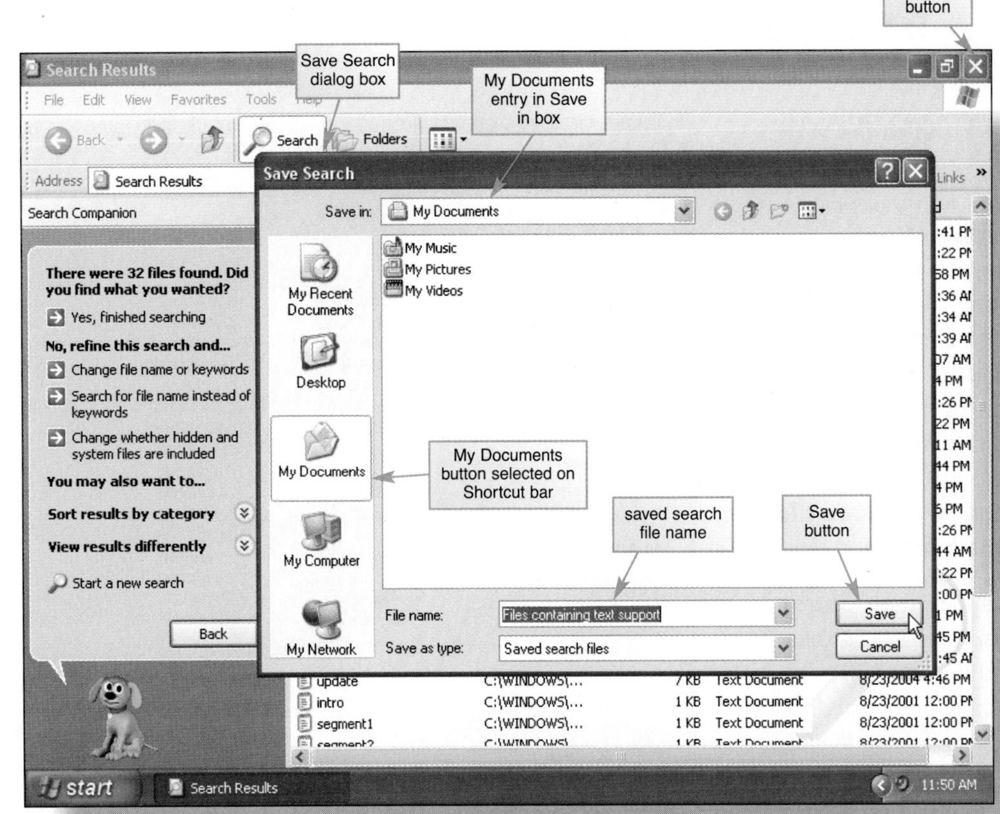

FIGURE 6-25

After saving the search, you can display the My Documents folder, double-click the Files containing text support icon to open the Search Results window, and then use the saved search to find all text documents in the WINDOWS (or WINNT) folder or its subfolders.

Using a Saved Search to Search for Files

After saving the search, perform the steps on the next page to use the saved search to find all text document files containing the word, support, in the WINDOWS (or WINNT) folder and its subfolders.

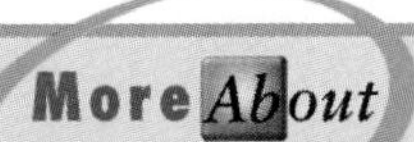

Saving a Search

The Save Search command saves the search criteria in a file on the desktop. As of the last printing of this book, the Save Search command was not working properly. Saving a search resulted in the search criteria not being saved with the saved search file. **Advice**: Verify the search criteria are saved with the file before executing a saved search.

To Search for Files Using a Saved Search

1 Click the Start button and then click My Documents on the Start menu. Double-click the Files containing text support icon in the Saved Search group. When the Search Results window displays, maximize the window and then click the Search button.

The maximized Search Results window displays and Windows XP performs a search for all text document files containing the word, support, in the WINDOWS (or WINNT) folder or its subfolders and displays a list of files in the Search Results window (Figure 6-26). The list may contain different files from those shown in Figure 6-23 on page WIN 6.20.

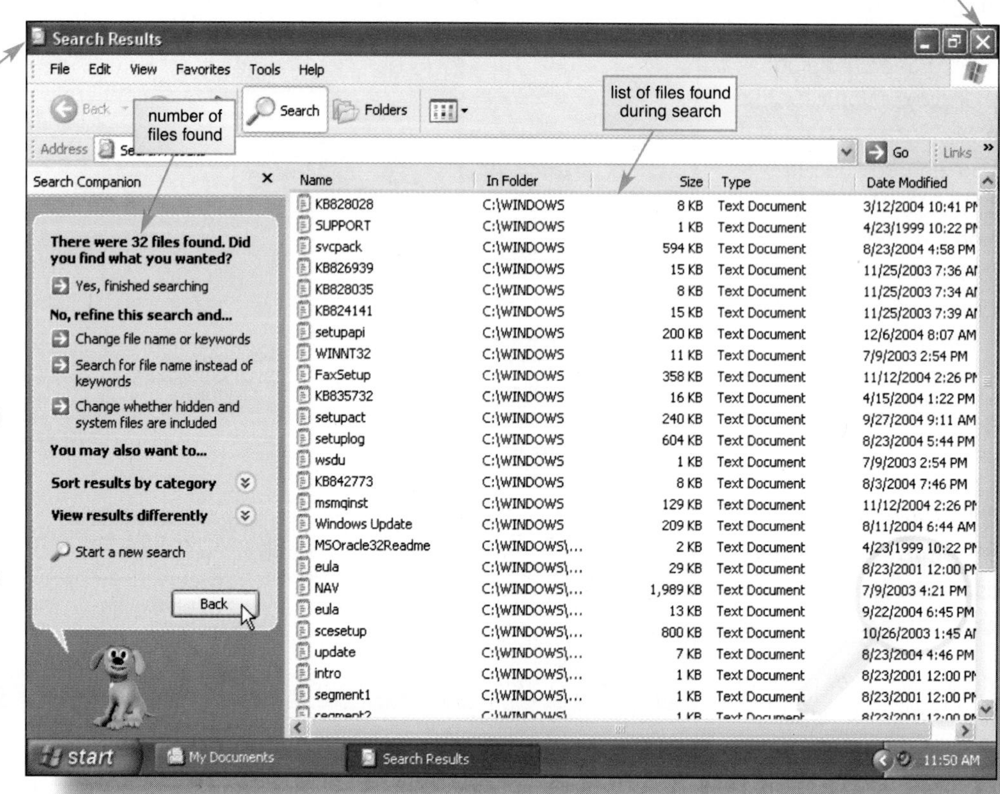

FIGURE 6-26

2 Click the Close button in the Search Results window to close the window.

The Search Results window closes.

Other Ways

1. Click Start button, click My Documents, right-click Files containing text support icon, click Open, click Search button

Deleting the Eula File and Saved Search File

After copying the eula file, saving the Files containing text support file in the My Documents folder, and using the Files containing text support file to perform a saved search, you should restore the My Documents folder to its original contents. Perform the following steps to delete the eula and Files containing text support files.

TO DELETE MULTIPLE FILES

1. Select the eula and Files containing text support files in the My Documents window.
2. Right-click either highlighted icon.
3. Click Delete on the shortcut menu.
4. Click the Yes button in the Confirm Multiple File Delete dialog box.
5. Click the Close button in the My Documents window.

The eula file and Files containing text support file are deleted and moved to the Recycle Bin.

Searching for Digital Media Files

As mentioned earlier, Search Companion allows you to perform a file search for digital media files (pictures, music, and video files), document files (word processing, spreadsheet, database, and so on), and all files and folders (media files, document files, system files, folder files, and so on). Previously in this project, file searches were performed on all the files and folders in the WINDOWS (or WINNT) folder. As a result, all files and folders including digital media files were searched. To narrow down the number of files to search and to search only for digital media files, you can choose to search for picture and photo files, music files, or video files.

Unless changed, the default search settings for searching digital media files causes Search Companion to search the digital media folders (My Music, My Pictures, and My Videos) first and then search all other files and folder on the local hard drives. Search Companion searches metadata but does not search hidden or system files. **Metadata** is identifying information about a file that is stored within the file. Typical metadata for picture and photo files includes width and height of image, resolution, and color depth. Some digital cameras will add the camera model, flash mode, f-number, and exposure time to the metadata.

When searching for digital media files, Search Companion allows you to select the type or types of files (pictures and photos files, music files, or video files) to search. The following sections explain how to search for each type of digital media file and perform operations related to the files.

More About

Searching for Digital Media Files

Many Web sites on the Internet offer media files that you can transfer and play on your computer. For more information about media files on the Internet, launch the Internet Explorer browser, type www.scsite.com/winxp/more.htm in the Address box in the Microsoft Internet Explorer window, and then press the Go button.

Searching for Picture Files

You can acquire pictures from several sources. You can search for free pictures on the Internet, purchase pictures over the Internet, copy pictures from a digital camera or scanner, or use a drawing program, such as Paint, to create a picture. In addition, you can search for pictures on the local hard drive, where four sample pictures (Blue hills, Sunset, Water lilies, and Winter) included with Windows XP, are located. Perform the steps on the next page to search for picture files on the hard drive.

To Search for Picture Files

1 Click the Start button, click Search, and then maximize the Search Results window. Point to Pictures, music, or video in the Search Companion balloon.

The maximized Search Results window displays (Figure 6-27). The Pictures, music, or video link displays in the Search Companion balloon.

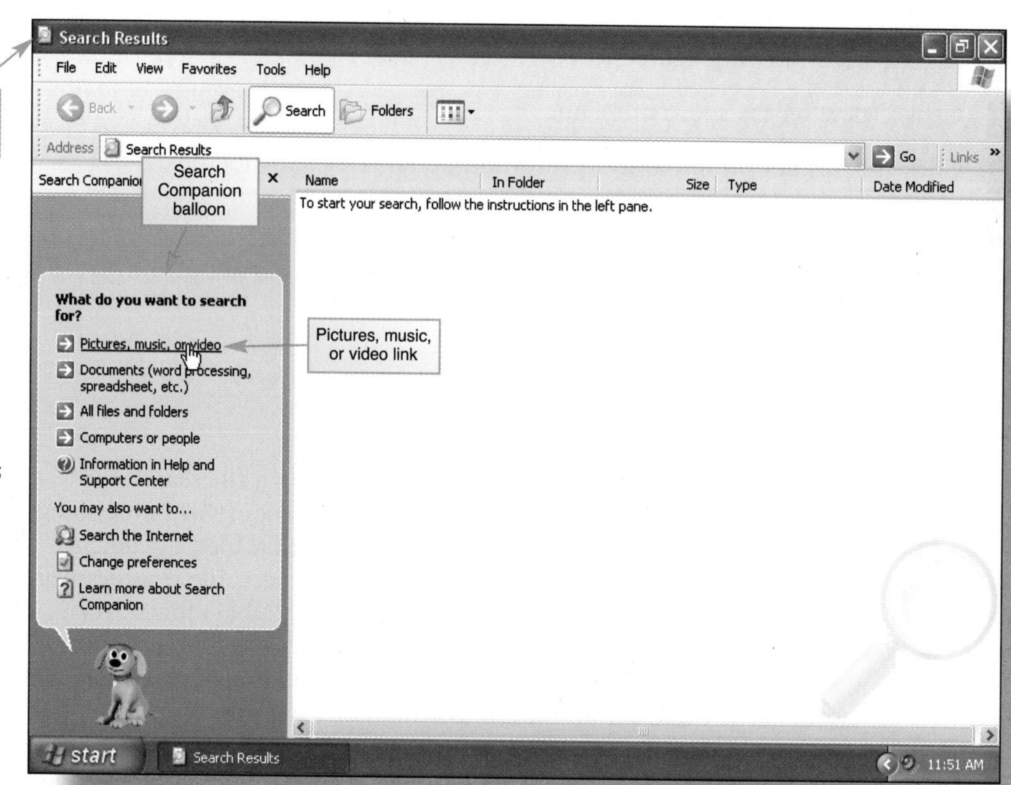

FIGURE 6-27

2 Click Pictures, music, or video. Click Pictures and Photos in the balloon. Point to the Search button.

The contents of the balloon change (Figure 6-28). The balloon contains three check boxes, the All or part of the file name text box, and the Use advanced search options link. A check mark displays in the Pictures and Photos check box.

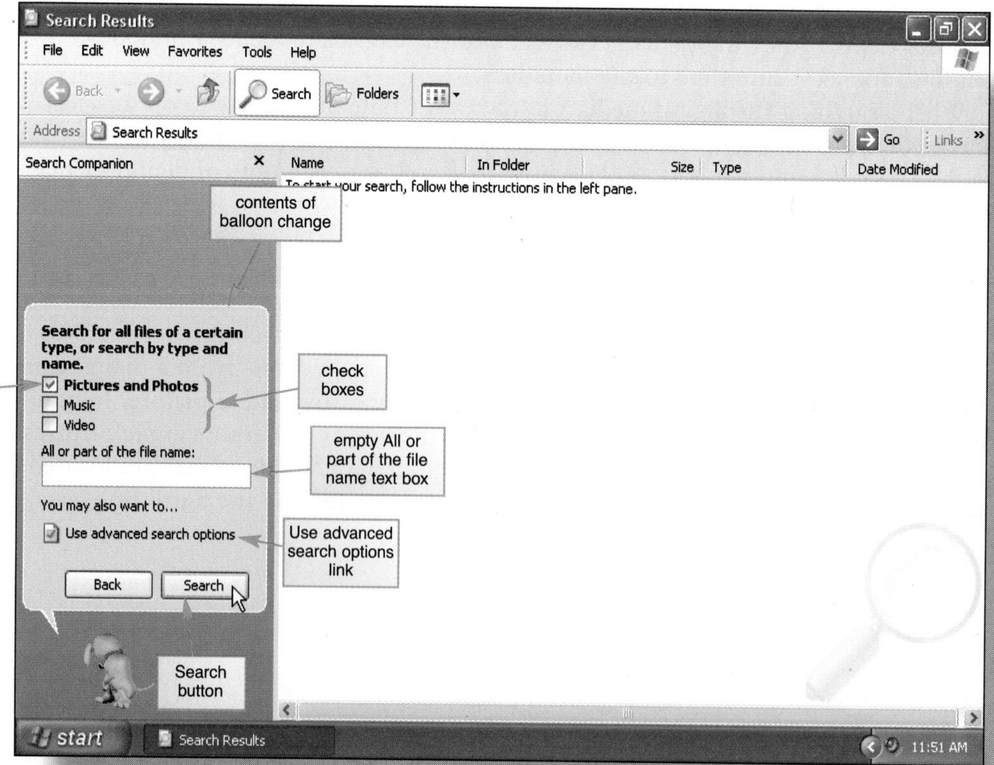

FIGURE 6-28

3 Click the Search button.

While the search progresses, the search criteria and locations being searched display in the balloon along with the path of the folder currently being searched. When the search is complete, the contents of the balloon change and a partial list of the 142 files found display in Thumbnails view in the right pane (Figure 6-29). Different files may display on your computer.

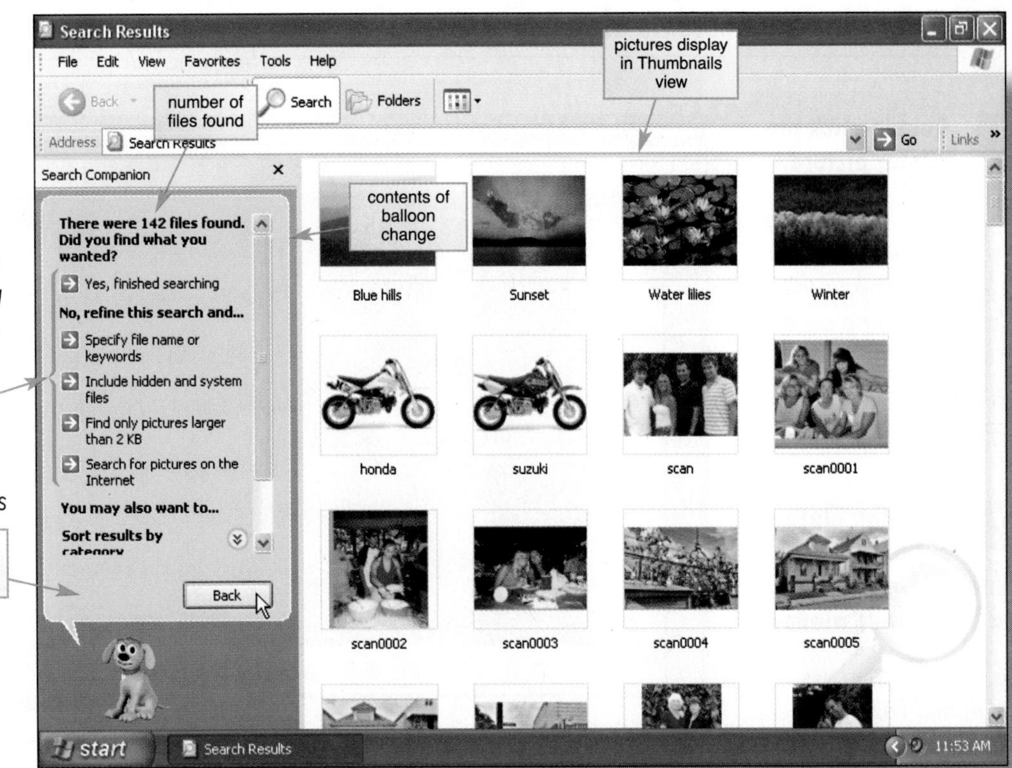

FIGURE 6-29

The All or part of the file name text box shown in Figure 6-28 allows you to type all or part of a file name you want to find and is empty to indicate no file names were examined during the search. Clicking the Use advanced search options link displays the advanced search options including the empty A word or phrase in the file box, Look in box containing the Local Hard Drives (C:) entry, and the When was it modified?, What size is it?, and More advanced options areas.

The Search Companion balloon shown in Figure 6-29 contains links that allow you to finish searching or refine a search. You can refine a search by specifying a file name or keyword(s), looking in a specific location, including hidden and system files, and finding only pictures larger than 2 KB. A thumbnail picture and file name identify each file in the Search Results window. Although not identified in the Search Results window, three types of files (JPEG images, Bitmap images, and GIF images) were found during the search. The Sort results by category area, View results differently area, and Start a new search link display at the bottom of the balloon and are not visible in Figure 6-29.

Display the Contents of a Picture File

In Figure 6-29, several pictures display in the Search Results window. Double-clicking a picture in the Search Results window launches Windows Picture and Fax Viewer (see Figures 3-12 and 3-13 on pages WIN 3.14 and WIN 3.15). Windows Picture and Fax Viewer allows you to view a picture, view other pictures in the same folder, enlarge and reduce a picture, rotate and print a picture, copy and delete a picture, and display a slide show of pictures. Perform the step on the next page to view the Winter picture in the Windows Picture and Fax Viewer.

Steps To Display the Contents of a Picture File

1 Double-click the Winter picture.

Windows XP launches the Windows Picture and Fax Viewer and displays the enlarged Winter picture in the Winter - Windows Picture and Fax Viewer window (Figure 6-30).

2 Click the Close button in the Winter - Windows Picture and Fax Viewer window.

The Winter - Windows Picture and Fax Viewer window closes.

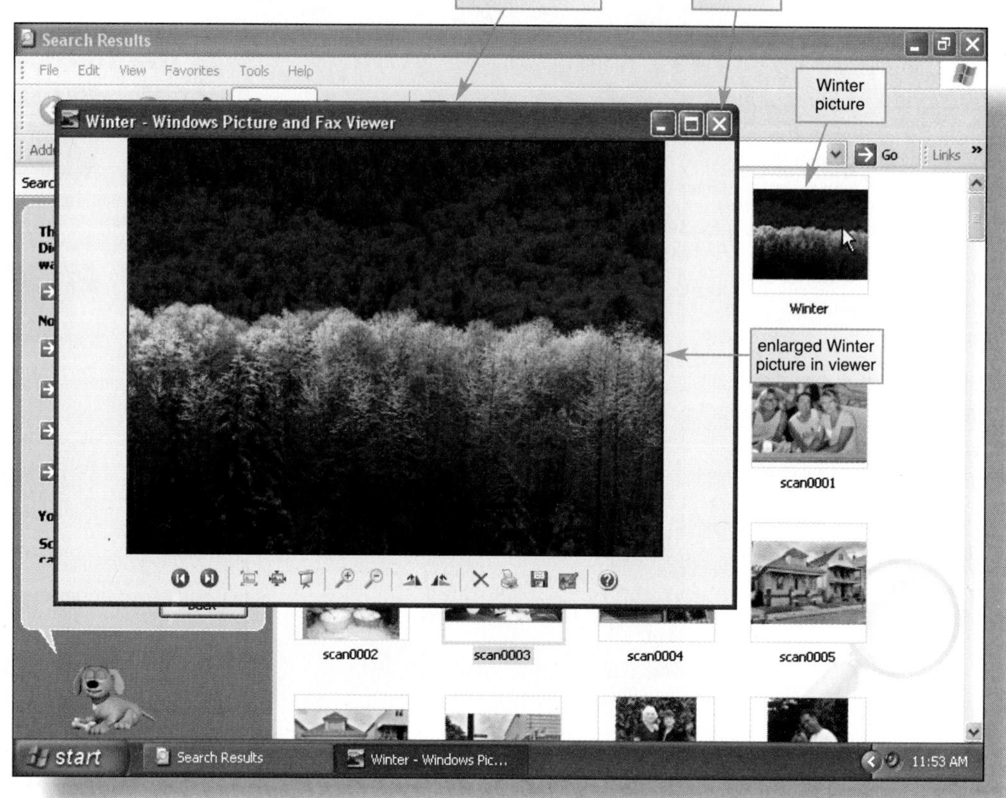

FIGURE 6-30

Resetting the Search Criteria to Search for Music Files

When you have finished searching for picture and photo files and in preparation for performing another search, you should reset the search criteria. Perform the following steps to reset the search criteria.

TO RESET THE SEARCH CRITERIA

1. Click the Back button in the Search Companion balloon.
2. Click Pictures and Photos to remove the check mark.

The contents of the Search Companion balloon change and the check mark in the Pictures and Photos check box is removed.

Searching for Music Files

There are also several sources for acquiring music files. You can search for free music files on the Internet, purchase music files over the Internet, and copy music files from a CD-ROM drive. In addition, you can search for music files on the local hard drive, where several sample music files included with Windows XP, are located. Perform the following steps to search for music files on the hard drive.

Steps To Search for Music Files

1 Click Music in the Search Companion balloon. Point to the Search button.

A check mark displays in the Music check box (Figure 6-31).

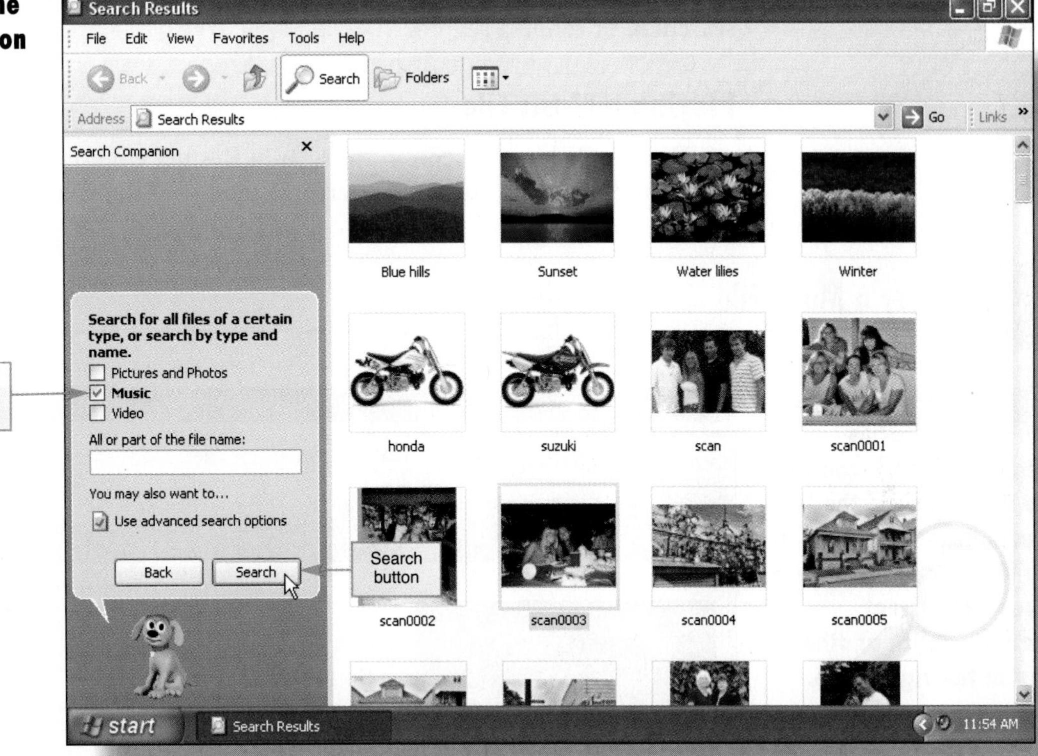

FIGURE 6-31

2 Click the Search button.

While the search progresses, the search criteria and locations being searched display in the balloon along with the path of the folder currently being searched. When the search is complete, 107 music files display in Tiles view in the right pane (Figure 6-32). Different files may display on your computer.

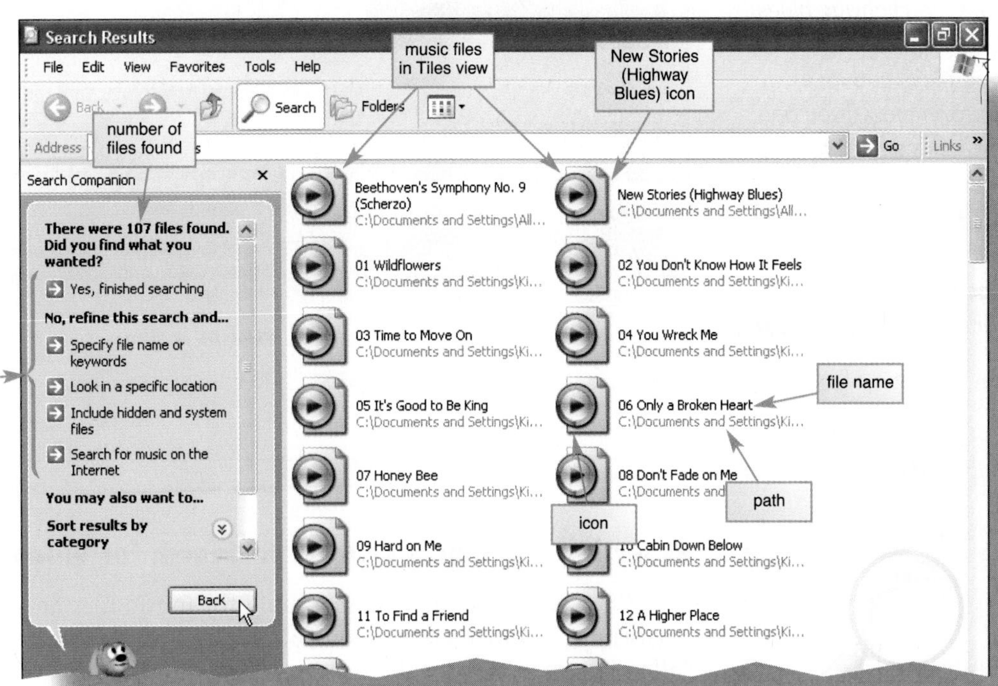

FIGURE 6-32

One-hundred-seven music files are found on the local hard drive and display in Tiles view in the right pane of the Search Results window in Figure 6-32 on the previous page. An icon, file name, and path identify each file. Double-clicking an icon plays the media file. The Search Companion balloon contains four links to end searching or refine a search.

Playing a Music File

Double-clicking an icon in the Search Results window launches Windows Media Player and plays the music file. Perform the following steps to play the music file.

Steps To Play a Music File

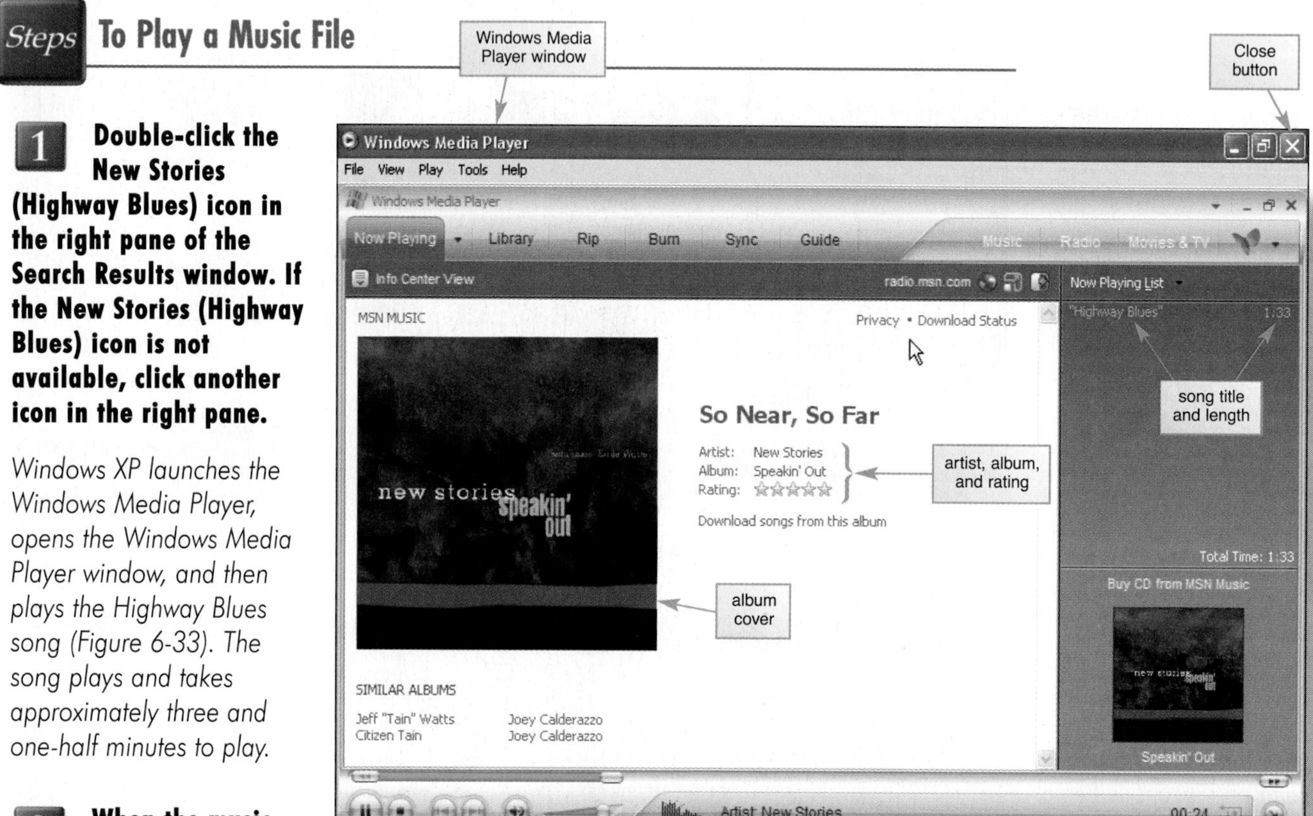

FIGURE 6-33

1 Double-click the New Stories (Highway Blues) icon in the right pane of the Search Results window. If the New Stories (Highway Blues) icon is not available, click another icon in the right pane.

Windows XP launches the Windows Media Player, opens the Windows Media Player window, and then plays the Highway Blues song (Figure 6-33). The song plays and takes approximately three and one-half minutes to play.

2 When the music stops, click the Close button in the Windows Media Player.

The Windows Media Player closes.

Other Ways

1. Right-click icon, click Play
2. Select icon, on File menu click Open

Resetting the Search Criteria to Search for Video Files

When you have finished searching for music files and in preparation for performing another search, you should reset the search criteria. Perform the following steps to reset the search criteria.

TO RESET THE SEARCH CRITERIA

1. Click the Back button in the Search Companion balloon.
2. Click Music to remove the check mark.

The contents of the Search Companion balloon change and the check mark in the Music check box is removed.

Searching for Video Files

Several sources are available for acquiring video files. You can search for free videos on the Internet, purchase videos over the Internet, and copy a video from a video camera. In addition, you can search for videos on the local hard drive, where a sample video included with Windows XP is located. Perform the following steps to search for video files on the local hard drive.

To Search for Video Files

1 Click Video in the Search Companion balloon. Point to the Search button.

A check mark displays in the Video check box (Figure 6-34).

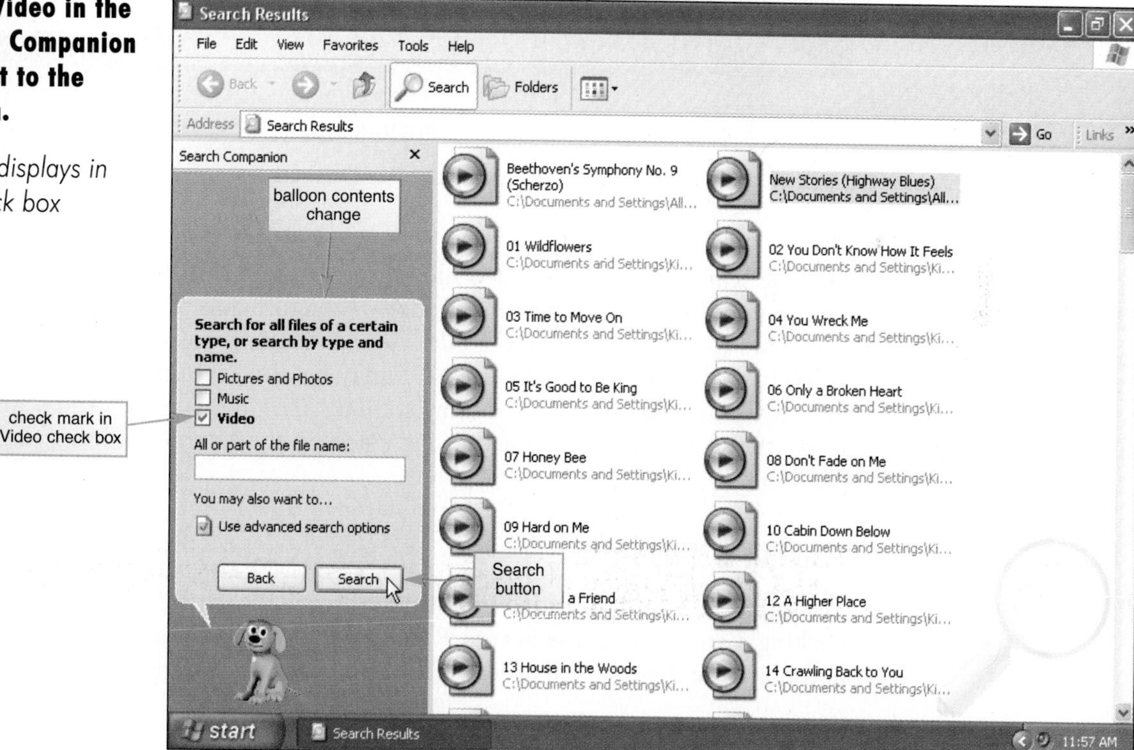

FIGURE 6-34

2 Click the Search button.

While the search progresses, the search criteria and locations being searched display in the balloon along with the path of the folder currently being searched. When the search is complete, one video file displays in Thumbnails view in the right pane (Figure 6-35). The title of the icon may be different on your computer, and different files may display on your computer.

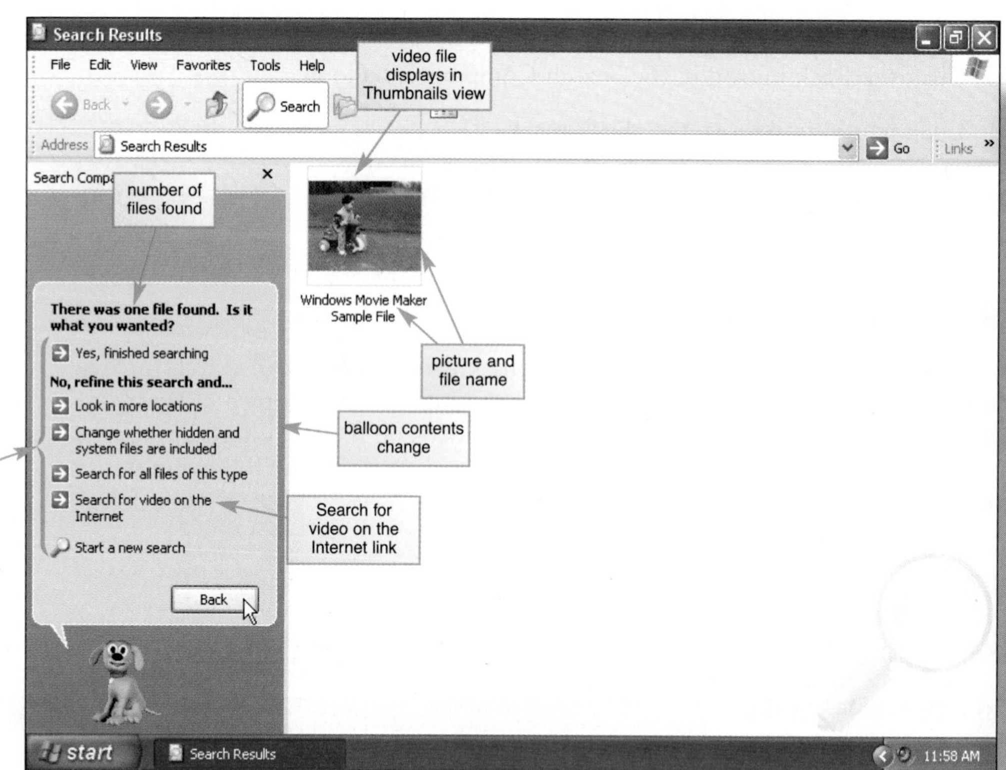

FIGURE 6-35

The search locates one video file on the local hard drive and displays it in the right pane of the Search Results window. A picture and file name identify the Windows Movie Maker Sample File. Double-clicking the icon plays the associated video file. The icon title in Figure 6-35 may be different on your computer. The Search Companion balloon contains six links that allow you to end searching or refine the search. One link (Search for video on the Internet) allows you to search for video files on the Internet.

Playing a Video File

In Figure 6-35, one video file displays in the Search Results window. Double-clicking a video file in the Search Results window launches Windows Media Player and plays the digital media file. Perform the following steps to play the video file.

Steps To Play a Video File

1 Double-click the Windows Movie Maker Sample File icon (or Sample icon).

Windows XP launches the Windows Media Player, opens the Windows Media Player window, and then plays the video file (Figure 6-36). The video file shows a child playing and takes approximately twelve seconds to play.

2 When the video file stops, click the Close button in the Windows Media Player.

The Windows Media Player closes.

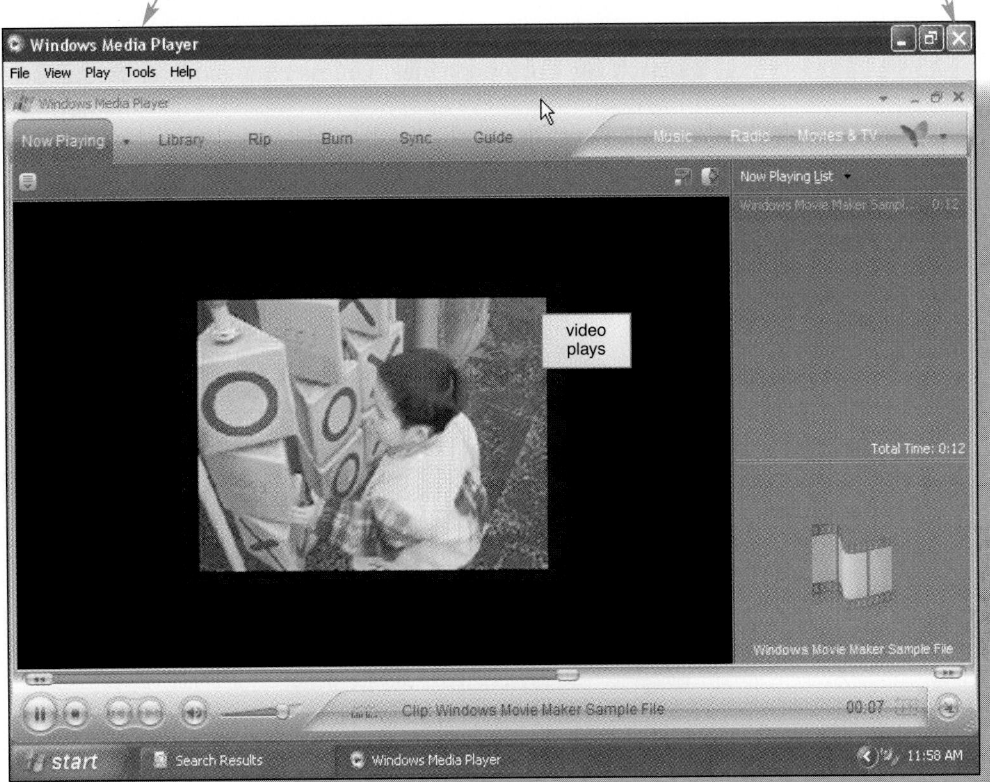

FIGURE 6-36

Other Ways

1. Right-click icon, click Play
2. Select icon, on File menu click Open

Resetting the Search Criteria to Search for Documents

When you have finished searching for video files and in preparation for performing a search for document files, you should reset the search criteria. Perform the following steps to reset the search criteria.

TO RESET THE SEARCH CRITERIA

1. Click the Back button in the Search Companion balloon.
2. Click Video to remove the check mark.
3. Click the Back button to display the Documents (word processing, spreadsheet, etc.) link.

The check mark in the Video check box is removed and the first Search Companion balloon shown in Figure 6-2 on page WIN 6.06 displays.

Searching for Document Files

In addition to searching for digital media files, Search Companion allows you to search for document files. Unless changed, the default search preferences for searching document files cause Search Companion to search the My Documents folders (My Music, My Pictures, and My Video) first and then search all other files and folders on the local hard drives, not search hidden or system files, and finally search metadata as well as file names. Among the documents Search Companion searches for are Notepad, WordPad, HTML, and Microsoft application documents.

Perform the following steps to search for all document files.

To Search for Document Files

1 Point to Documents (word processing, spreadsheet, etc.) in the Search Companion balloon (Figure 6-37).

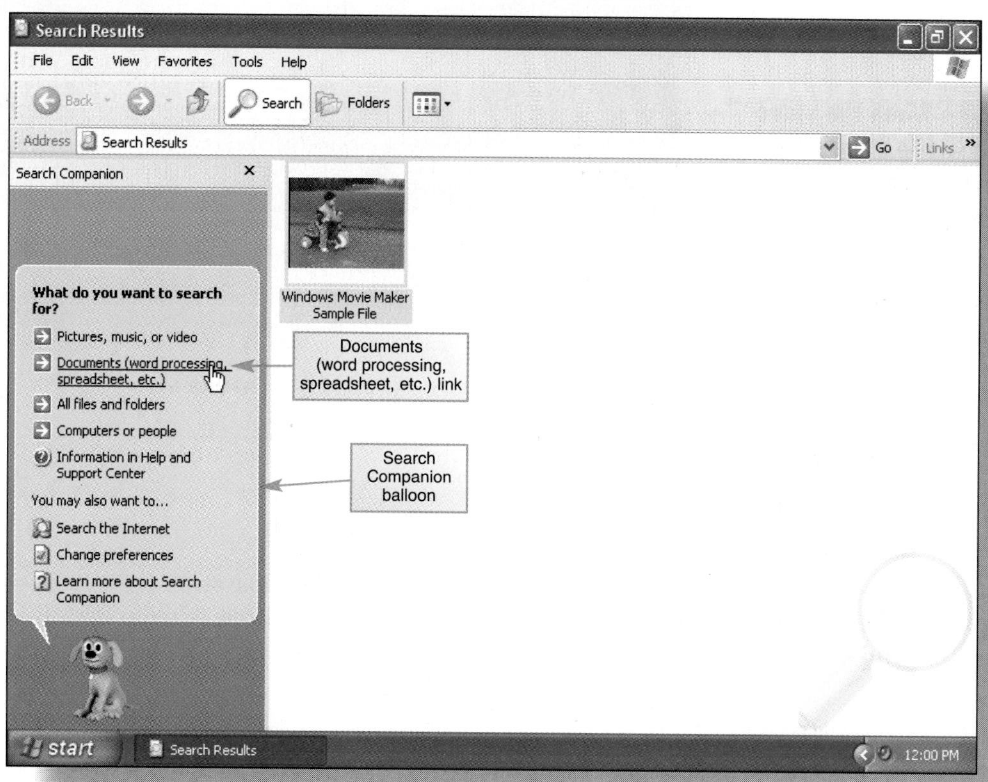

FIGURE 6-37

2 Click Documents (word processing, spreadsheet, etc.). Point to the Search button.

The contents of the balloon change (Figure 6-38). The balloon contains four option buttons, the All or part of the document name text box, and the Use advanced search options link. The Don't remember option button is selected.

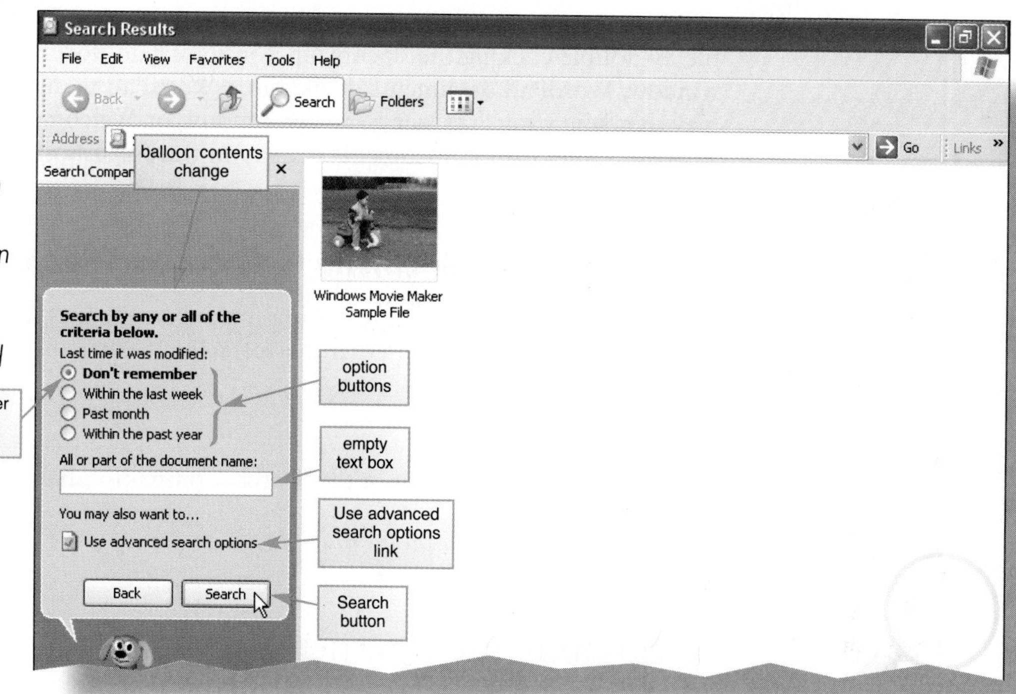

FIGURE 6-38

3 Click the Search button.

While the search progresses, the search criteria and locations being searched display in the Search Companion balloon along with the path of the folder currently being searched. When the search is complete, a partial list of the 12,948 document files found displays in Tiles view in the right pane (Figure 6-39). Different files may display on your computer.

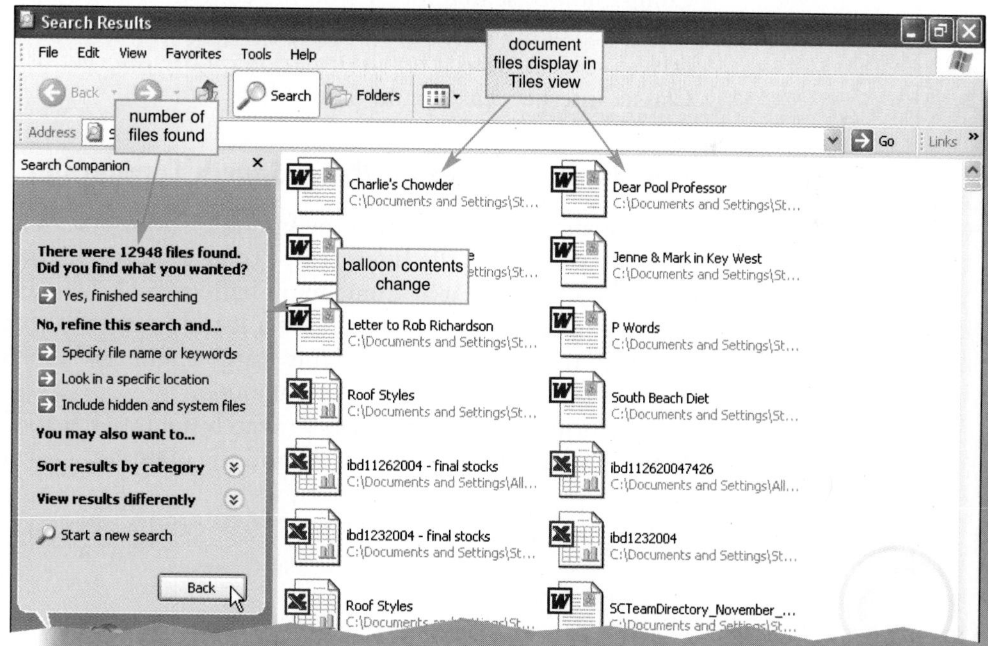

FIGURE 6-39

Other Ways

1. Click Documents (word processing, spreadsheet, etc.), click option button, click Search button
2. Click Documents (word processing, spreadsheet, etc.), type document name, click Search button

After searching for document files, you can display the contents of a document file by double-clicking the document icon. Notepad documents display in a Notepad window, WordPad documents display in a WordPad window, HTML documents display in a Microsoft Internet Explorer window or Welcome to MSN window, and Microsoft application documents display in the corresponding Microsoft application window.

Resetting the Search Criteria to Search for Files on the Internet

When you have finished searching for document files and in preparation for searching for files on the Internet, perform the following step.

TO RESET THE SEARCH CRITERIA

 Click the Back button in the Search Companion balloon two times.

The Search Companion balloon displays.

Searching the Internet

In Project 3, you used the Search command and Search Companion to search for a file on the local hard drive knowing the file name. In this project, you use the Search Companion to search for files on the computer based on date, file type, and a word or words contained in the file. In addition to searching for files on the local hard drives, you can search for information on the Internet using Search Companion, the Classic Internet search, and the Address bar.

Searching the Internet Using Search Companion

One method of searching the Internet is to use Search Companion. With this method, you search the Internet by typing a word, phrase, statement, or question in a text box in the Search Companion balloon and then click the Search button. A **search engine** retrieves and displays a list of links to Web pages based upon the keywords in the text box. The default search engine is MSN Search. The default search engine may be different on your computer.

Perform the following steps to search the Internet for links to Web pages using Search Companion, MSN Search, and the question, How do I write a resume?.

Steps To Search the Internet Using Search Companion

1 Point to Search the Internet in the Search Companion balloon.

The underlined Search the Internet link displays in the balloon (Figure 6-40).

FIGURE 6-40

2 Click Search the Internet.

The contents of the balloon change (Figure 6-41). The balloon contains a title (What are you looking for?), instructions, a text box containing highlighted instructions, a sample question and link, and the Search this computer for files, Change preferences, and Learn more about Search Companion links.

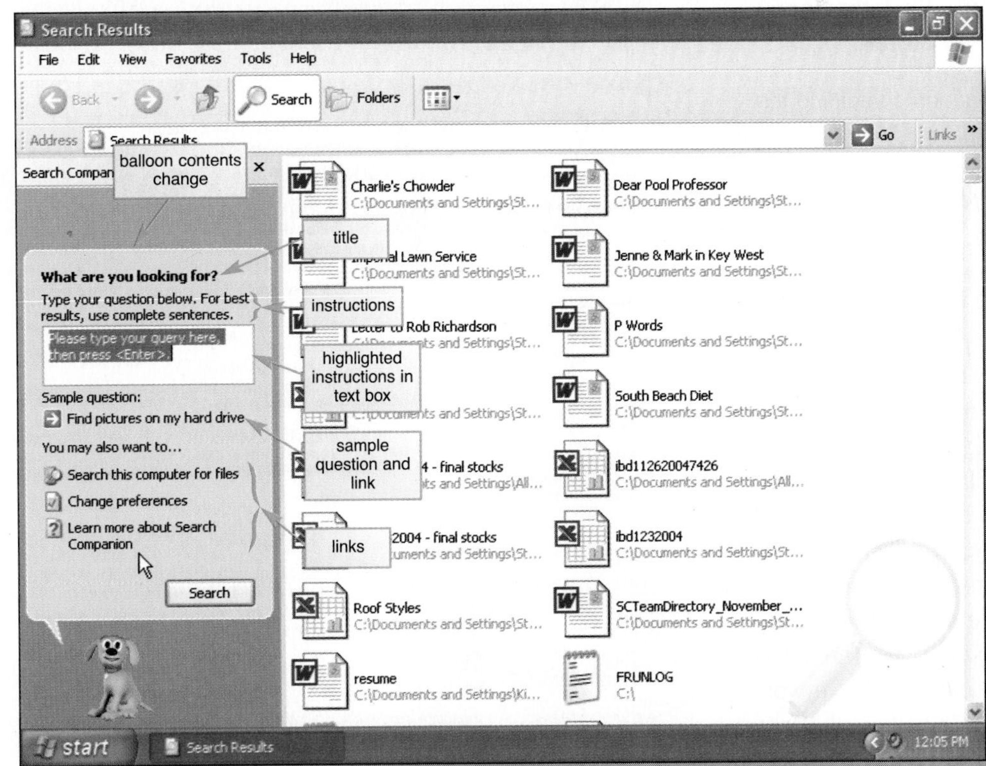

FIGURE 6-41

3 **Type** `How do I write a resume?` **in the text box. Point to the Search button.**

The question, How do I write a resume?, displays in the text box (Figure 6-42).

FIGURE 6-42

4 **Click the Search button.**

A balloon containing the words, Finding suggestions, displays momentarily while MSN Search searches for Web pages related to resumes and resume writing. When the search is complete, the contents of the Search Companion balloon change to contain additional links, the window title changes, and a partial list of Web pages displays in the MSN Search: write resume window (Figure 6-43). The window title contains the keywords used to perform the search.

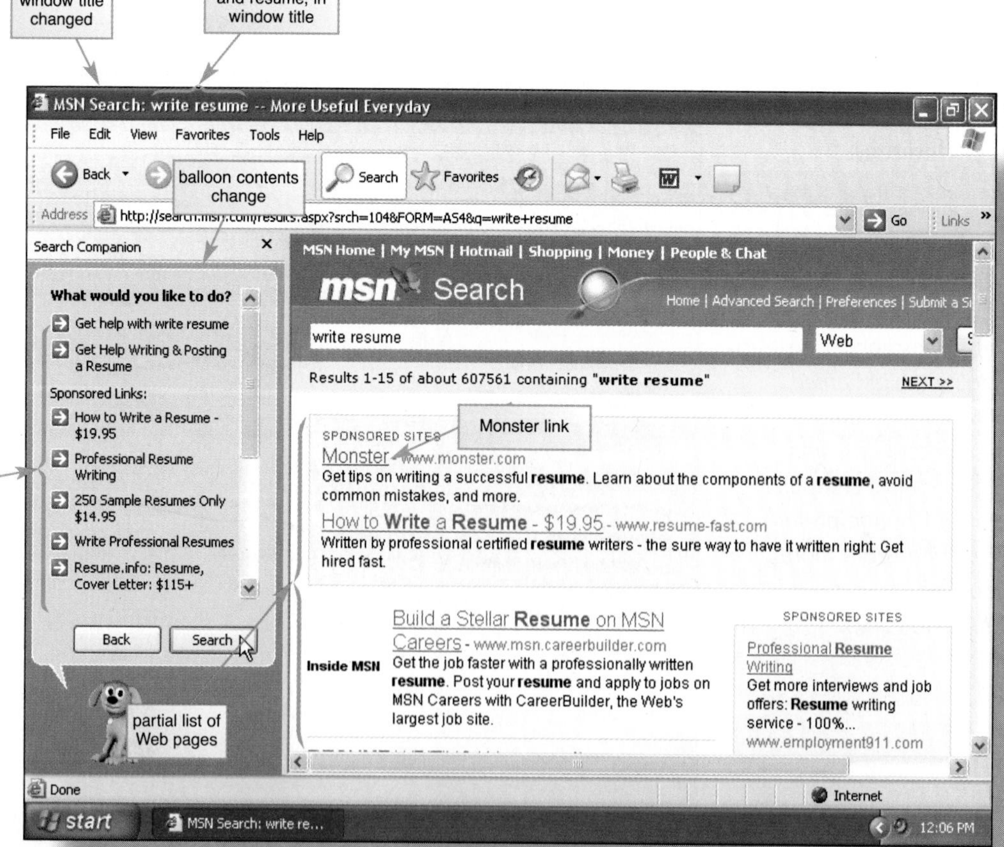

FIGURE 6-43

5 **If available, click the Monster link. If this link is not available, click another link.**

A Web page from the monster Web site displays in the Monster window (Figure 6-44). The Web page contains various links about resume writing.

6 **In preparation for changing preferences, click the Back button in the Search Companion balloon.**

The contents of the balloon change.

FIGURE 6-44

Other Ways

1. Click Start button, click Internet, type search query, click Search button
2. Click Start button, point to All Programs, click Internet Explorer, type search query, click Search button

The default MSN Search engine is one of ten search engines (MSN, AltaVista, Google, Ask Jeeves, AlltheWeb, Teoma, Excite, Overture, Yahoo, AOL Search, Lycos, and Encarta) that Search Companion uses to search for Web pages. To select another search engine as the default search engine, click the Start button, click Search on the Start menu, click Change preferences in the Search Companion balloon, click Change Internet search behavior, click another search engine name in the Select the default search engine list box, and then click the OK button.

Searching the Internet Using the Classic Internet Search

The second method of searching the Internet is to perform a Classic Internet search. The **Classic Internet search** allows you to search for Web pages, mailing or e-mail addresses, business information, maps, encyclopedia articles, and pictures. To perform a classic Internet search, you first must change a search preference. **Search preferences** include using or not using an animated screen character (Rover, Merlin, and so on), selecting a different animated screen character, using or not using the Indexing Service for faster local searches, selecting the Standard or Advanced method to search for files and folders, selecting the Search Companion or Classic Internet search behavior, show or not show balloon tips, and turn on or turn off the AutoComplete feature.

More About

Classic Internet Search

Classic Internet search allows you to use the following 12 search engines: MSN, AltaVista, Google, Ask Jeeves, AlltheWeb, Teoma, Excite, Overture, Yahoo, AOL Search, Lycos, and Encarta.

Changing a Search Preference

The default Internet search behavior for searching the Internet is the Search Companion behavior. To search the Internet using the Classic Internet search, you must select the Classic Internet search as the Internet search behavior and then close the Search Results window to make the Internet search behavior the default behavior. Perform the following steps to change a search preference by selecting the Classic Internet search.

Steps To Change a Search Preference

1 Point to Change preferences in the Search Companion balloon (Figure 6-45).

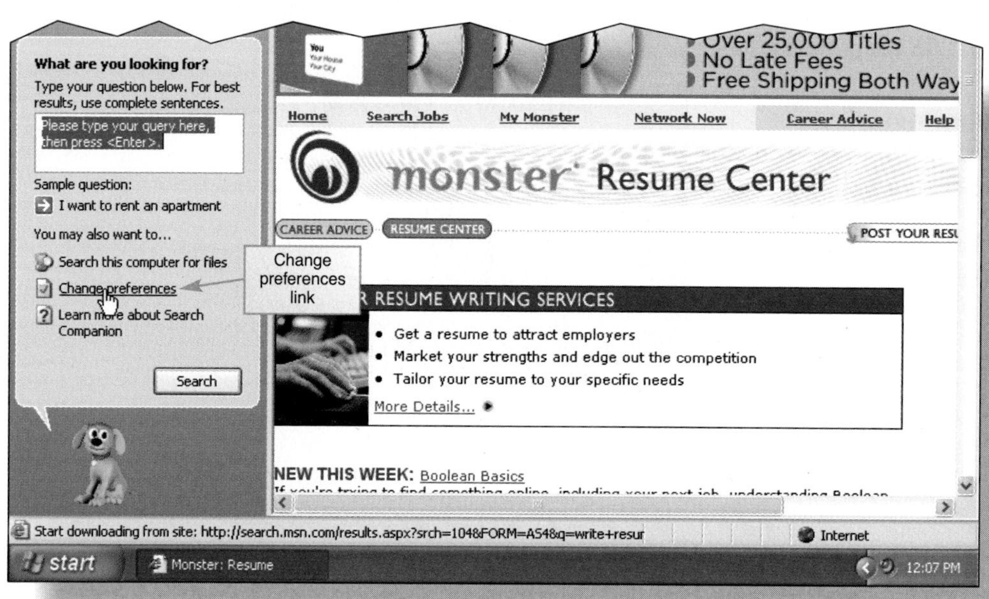

FIGURE 6-45

2 Click Change preferences. Point to Change Internet search behavior.

A title and seven preferences display in the balloon (Figure 6-46). The Change Internet search behavior is underlined.

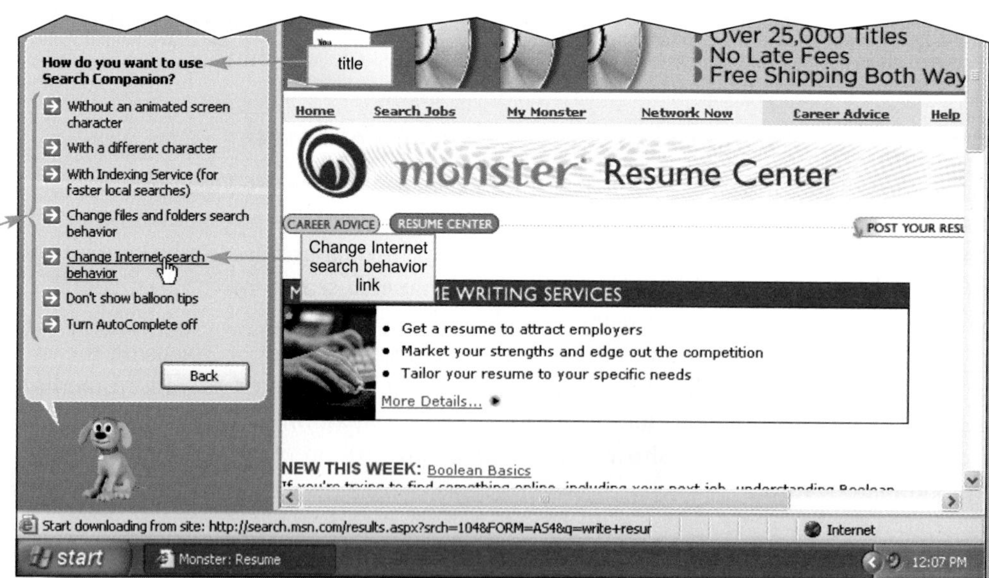

FIGURE 6-46

3 Click Change Internet search behavior. Point to the With Classic Internet search button.

The balloon contains a title, a question, two option buttons, and a list of search engine names in the Select the default search engine list box (Figure 6-47). The With Search Companion option button is selected, and the default MSN search engine name is displayed in the list box.

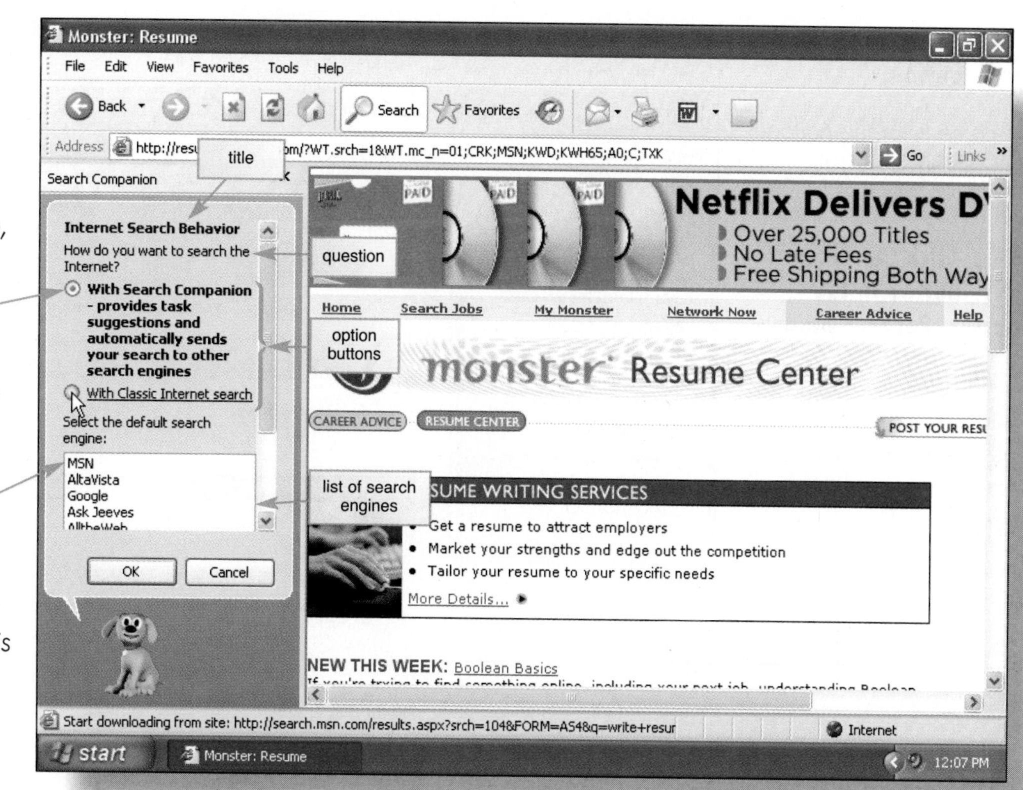

FIGURE 6-47

4 Click With Classic Internet search. Point to the OK button in the balloon.

The With Classic Internet search option button is selected (Figure 6-48).

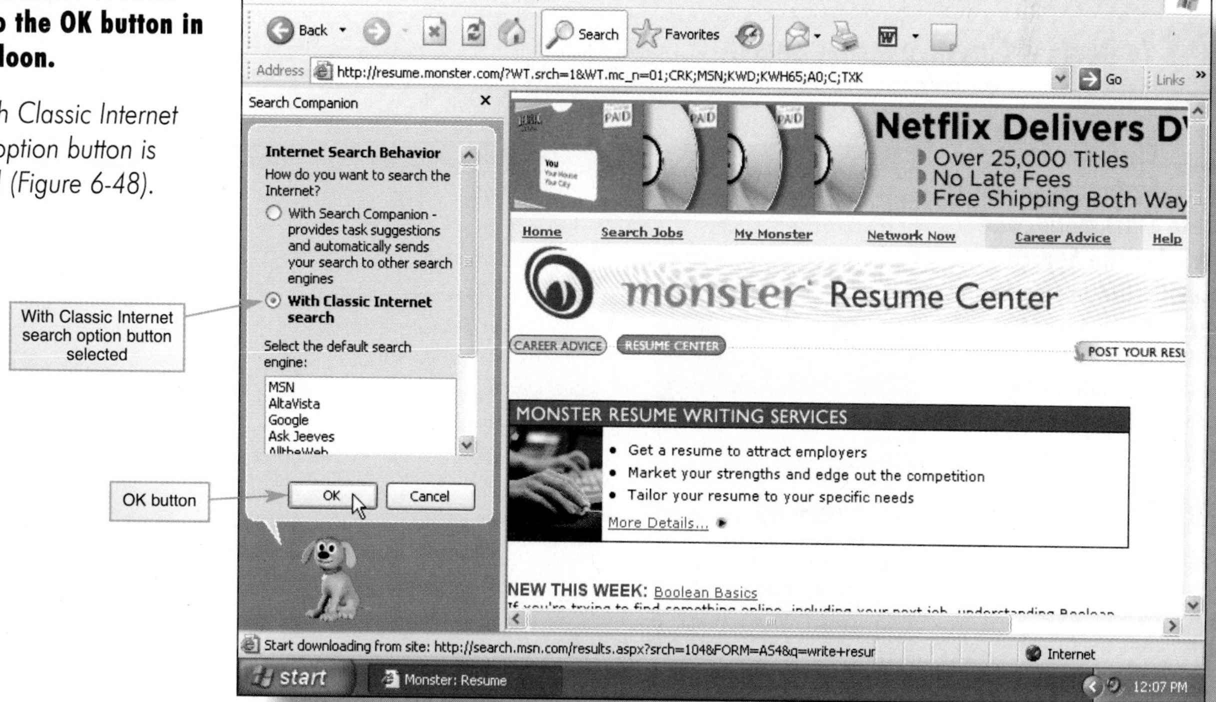

FIGURE 6-48

5 **Click the OK button.**

The contents of the balloon change (Figure 6-49).

6 **Click the Close button in the Monster: Resume window.**

The Monster: Resume window closes and the Classic Internet search becomes the default Internet search.

FIGURE 6-49

Searching Using the Classic Internet Search

After selecting the Classic Internet search as the Internet search behavior and closing the Monster: Resume window, you must open the Search Results window before you can begin searching the Internet using the Classic Internet search. Perform the following steps to begin a Classic Internet search.

Steps To Begin a Classic Internet Search

1 **Click the Start button, click Search on the Start menu, and maximize the Search Results window. Point to Search the Internet.**

The Search Companion balloon displays in the Search Results window (Figure 6-50). The Search the Internet link displays at the bottom of the balloon.

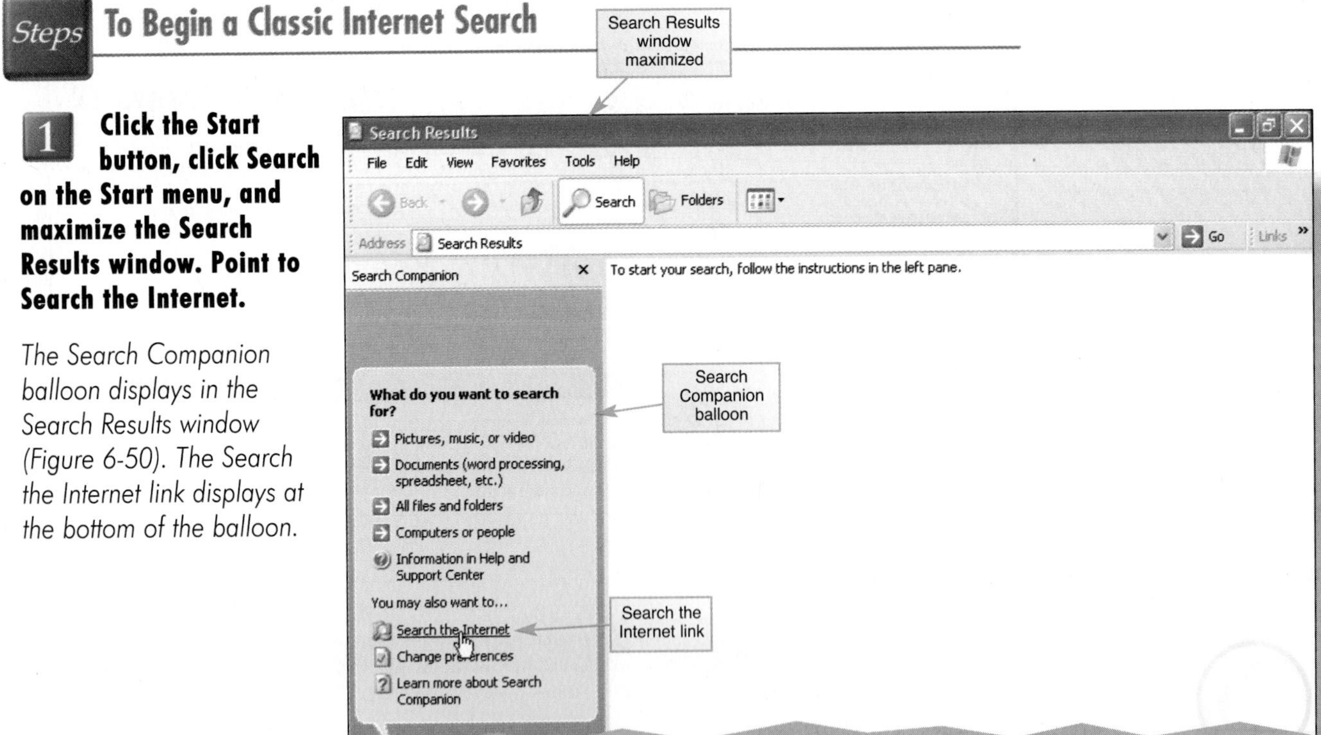

FIGURE 6-50

2 Click Search the Internet.

The Search pane displays (Figure 6-51). The Search pane contains a toolbar, seven search categories, a rectangular box, and three links. The Find a Web page button is selected and the rectangular box contains the Find a Web page containing text box, message with the default MSN Search name, and Search button. The search engine name in the message on your computer may be different.

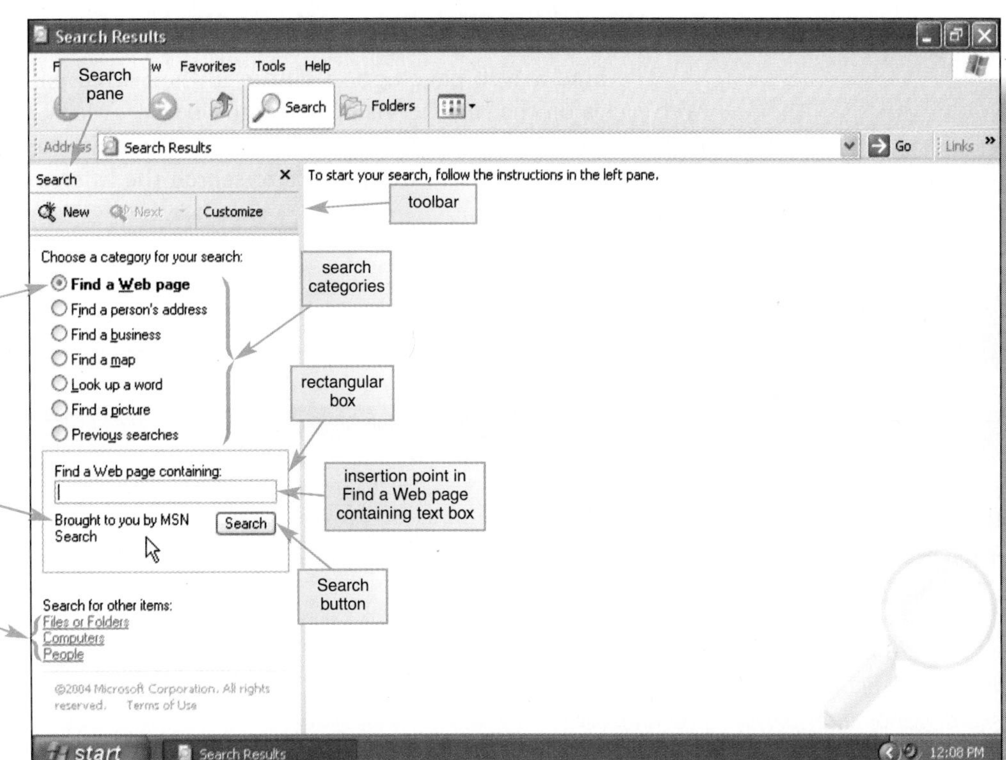

FIGURE 6-51

The seven search categories that display in the Search pane allow you to search for a Web page (Find a Web page), mailing address or e-mail address (Find a person's address), business name or category (Find a business), address or landmark (Find a map), word in an encyclopedia (Look up a word), find a picture (Find a Picture), and perform a previous search (Previous searches).

The Find a Web page button is selected and the message in the rectangular box (Brought to you by MSN Search) indicates the MSN Search service will be used to search for Web pages. A **search service** allows you to enter a keyword(s) (a word or phrase) about a topic in which you are interested, searches for the Web pages that contain the keyword(s), and then displays a list of links that you can click to display the associated Web pages. MSN Search is one of the six search services (MSN Search, Overture, AltaVista, Lycos, Excite, Yahoo!, and Euroseek) available to search for Web pages based on a keyword.

The toolbar contains three buttons. They allow you to start a new search (New), perform the previously performed search using another search service (Next), and select the search services you wish to use to search for Web pages (Customize). Three links at the bottom of the Search pane (Files or Folders, Computers, and People) allow you to search for other items.

Other Ways

1. Click Start button, click Internet, on Standard Buttons toolbar click Search button
2. Click Start button, point to All Programs, click Internet Explorer, on Standard Buttons toolbar click Search button

More About

Web Search Engines

Developers of search engines compete fiercely. Each search engine claims to have the largest index of Web resources. This competition is healthy and ensures that there are large, up-to-date indexes of Web resources.

Searching for a Web Page Using a Keyword

The Find a Web page option button in the Search pane allows you to search for Web pages on the Internet using a search service. A list of the links for the Web pages found by the search service displays in the right pane. Perform the following steps to use the MSN Search service to search the Internet for Web pages containing the keyword, genome.

To Search for a Web Page Using a Keyword

1 **If necessary, click Find a Web page. Type** genome **in the Find a Web page containing text box and then point to the Search button.**

The Find a Web page button is selected and the keyword, genome, displays in the Find a Web page containing text box (Figure 6-52).

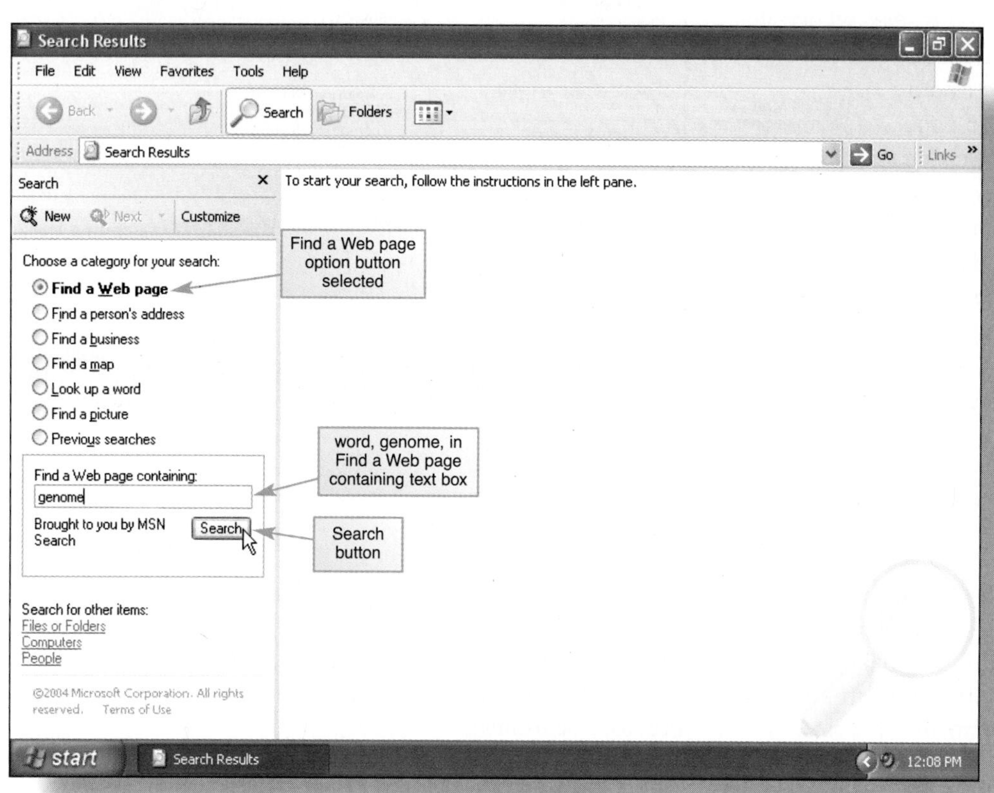

FIGURE 6-52

2 Click the Search button. If available, point to the Nat'l Human Genome Research Inst. link. Otherwise, point to the link of your choice.

The Internet Explorer icon displays on the title bar, the MSN Search form displays below the toolbar in the Search pane, and MSN Search performs the search and displays several Web sites (Figure 6-53). The groups and links on your computer may be different.

Internet Explorer icon

MSN Search form

sponsored sites

groups of links

Nat'l Human Genome Research Inst. link

FIGURE 6-53

3 Click the link.

The window title changes to genome.gov National Human Genome Research Institute and the National Human Genome Research Institute Web page displays in the right pane of the window (Figure 6-54). The URL for the Web page displays in the Address box.

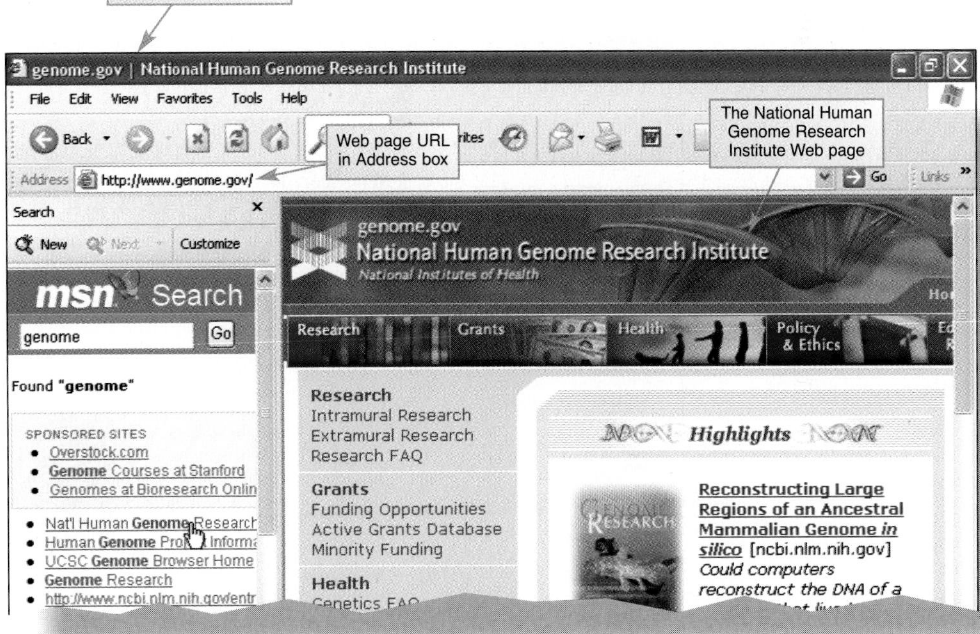

FIGURE 6-54

As you can see, it is easy to find many Web pages using a keyword-based search engine such as MSN Search.

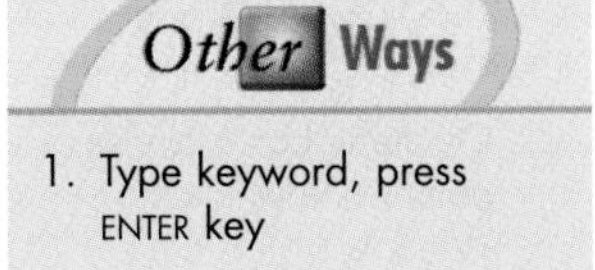

Other Ways

1. Type keyword, press ENTER key

Beginning a New Search

After performing a search for Web pages containing the keyword, genome, click the New button on the toolbar in the Search pane to begin a new search. Perform the following steps to begin a new search.

To Begin a New Search

1 Point to the New button in the Search pane (Figure 6-55).

FIGURE 6-55

2 Click the New button.

The seven search categories and a rectangular box display in the Search pane (Figure 6-56).

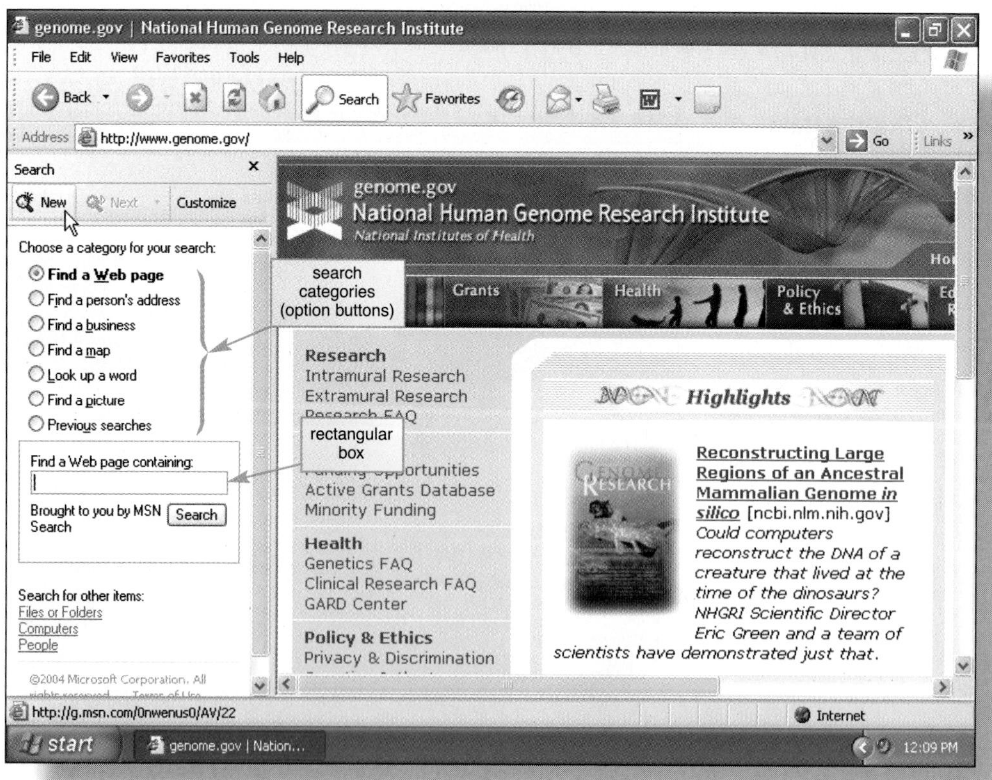

FIGURE 6-56

Other Ways

1. On menu bar click File, point to New, click Window

Searching for Mailing and E-Mail Addresses

Previously, you selected the Find a Web page option button in the Search pane, entered a keyword(s), and then MSN Search searched for Web pages containing the keyword(s) and displayed links to the Web pages in the Search pane. In addition to searching for Web pages, you can search for mailing addresses or e-mail addresses on the Internet.

When you select the Find a person's address option button in the Search pane, you are prompted to search for a mailing address or an e-mail address by entering the first and last names, city, and state/province. Clicking the Search button causes the InfoSpace search service to search a database on the InfoSpace Web site for the mailing address or e-mail address corresponding to the first and last names, city, and state/province entered. **InfoSpace** is the search service available to search for mailing and e-mail addresses.

Perform the following steps to search for the mailing address of one of the authors of this book when you know only the first and last names of the author.

To Search the Internet for a Mailing Address

1 Click Find a person's address, type Steven **in the First Name text box, type** Forsythe **in the Last Name text box, and then point to the Search button.**

The Find a person's address button is selected, the words, mailing address, display in the Search For box, the author's first name (Steven) displays in the First Name text box, and the author's last name (Forsythe) displays in the Last Name text box (Figure 6-57). The InfoSpace search service name displays to the left of the Search button on your computer.

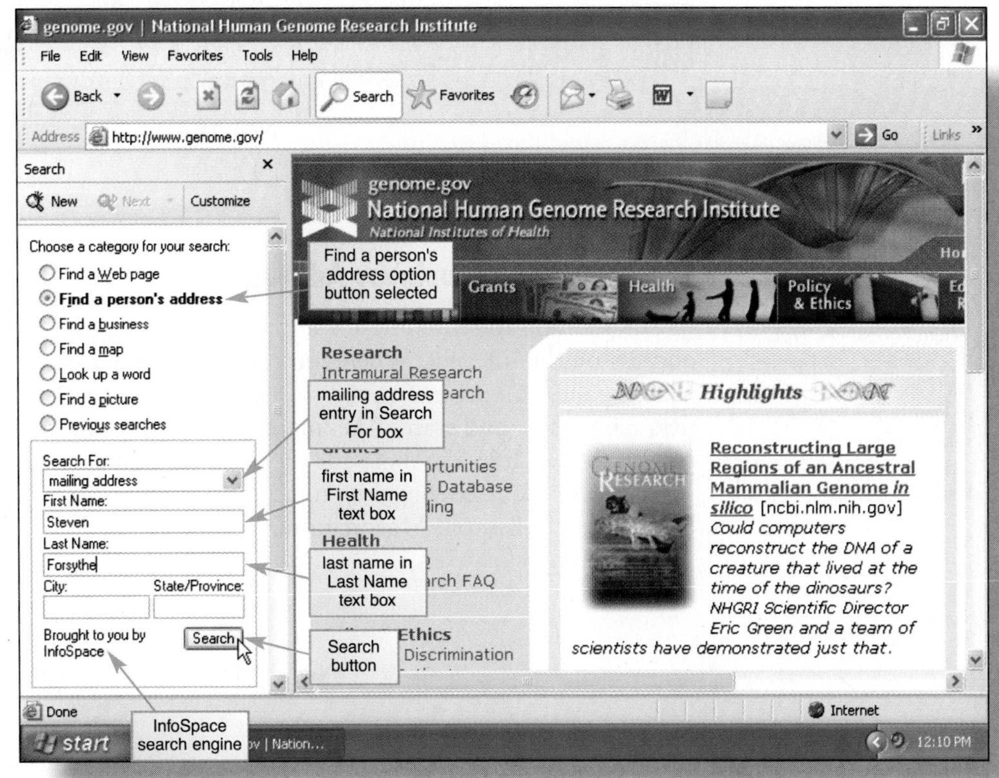

FIGURE 6-57

2 Click the Search button. Scroll the right pane to display information about the author (Steven Forsythe).

InfoSpace searches its database for the mailing address of the author, displays the InfoSpace search form containing the author's name, and displays a list of matches found during the search (Figure 6-58). The matches on your computer may be different.

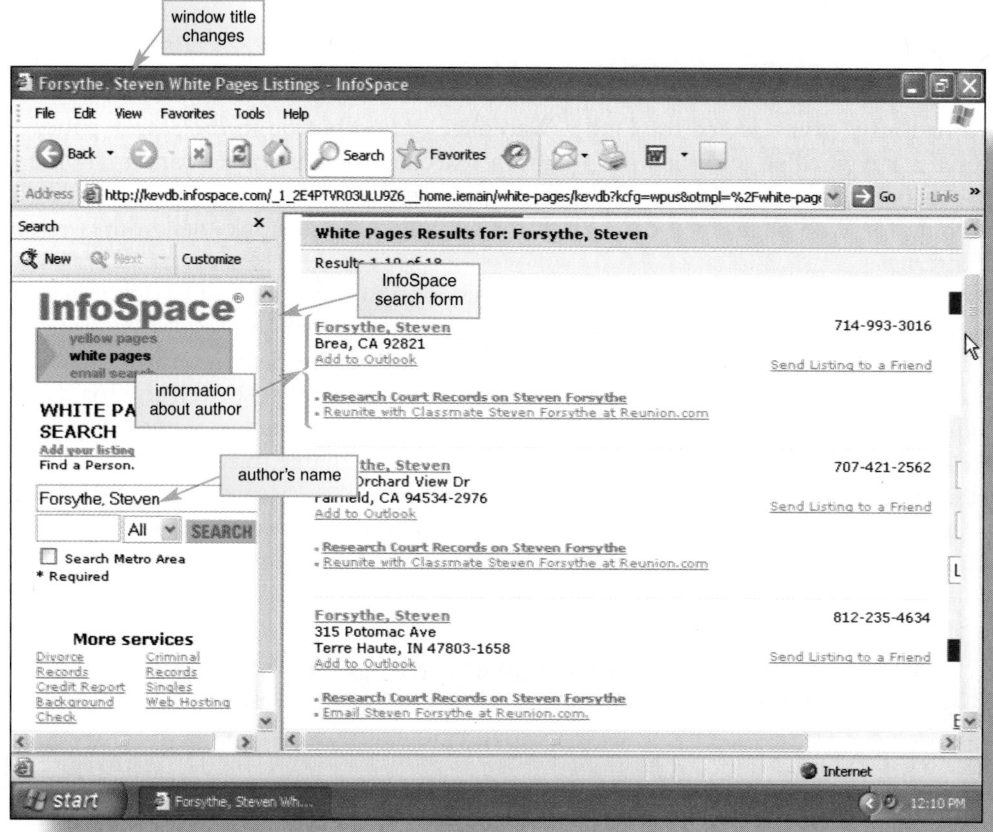

FIGURE 6-58

Other Ways

1. Type `www.infospace.com` in Address box, click Go button, click White Pages link, type last name in Last Name text box, type first name in First Name text box, select California in State/Province box, click Find button

Searching for a Business Address

In addition to searching for a mailing address, you also can search for a business address on the Internet. When you select the Find a business option button in the Search pane, you are prompted to search for a business address by entering the business name, city, and state. Clicking the Search button causes the InfoSpace search service to search its database for the business name, city, and state/province entered.

Perform the following step to search for the business address of Course Technology located in Boston, Massachusetts.

Steps To Search for a Business Address

1 Click Find a business, type `Course Technology` **in the Business text box, type** `Boston` **in the City text box, type** `MA` **in the State/Province text box, and then point to the Search button.**

The Find a business button is selected, the business name displays in the Business text box, city name displays in the City text box, and state abbreviation displays in the State/Province text box (Figure 6-59).

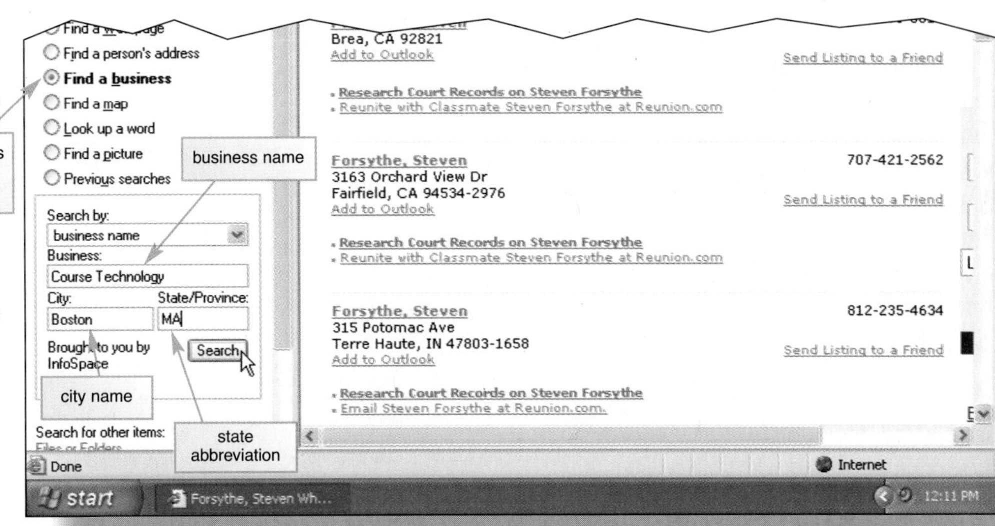

FIGURE 6-59

2 Click the Search button. Scroll the right pane to display the Course Technology name and address.

InfoSpace searches its database for business addresses, displays business name, city name, and state abbreviation in the InfoSpace search form, and displays two Course Technology names and addresses in the right pane (Figure 6-60).

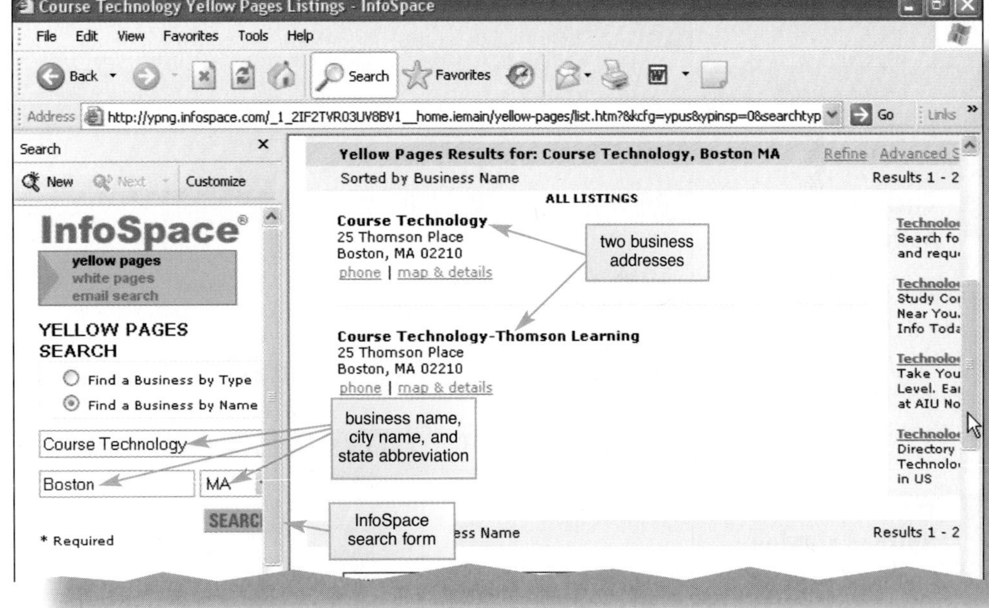

FIGURE 6-60

Searching for a Map

You also can search for maps on the Internet. When you select the Find a map button in the Search pane, Internet Explorer prompts you for an address, place, or landmark. Clicking the Search button causes the Expedia.com search service to search a database on the Expedia.com Web site for the corresponding address, place, or landmark. **Expedia.com** is one of the two search services (MapQuest and Expedia.com) available to search for maps. Perform the following steps to search for a map showing the location of the Cobo Hall (museum).

Steps To Search for a Map

1 Click the New button. Click Find a map. Click the Search For box arrow and then click Place or landmark. Click the This place or landmark text box and then type `Cobo Hall` **as the landmark. Point to the Search button.**

The Find a map option button is selected, the Search For box contains the words, Place or landmark, and the This place or landmark text box contains the words, Cobo Hall (Figure 6-61). Expedia.com is the default search engine.

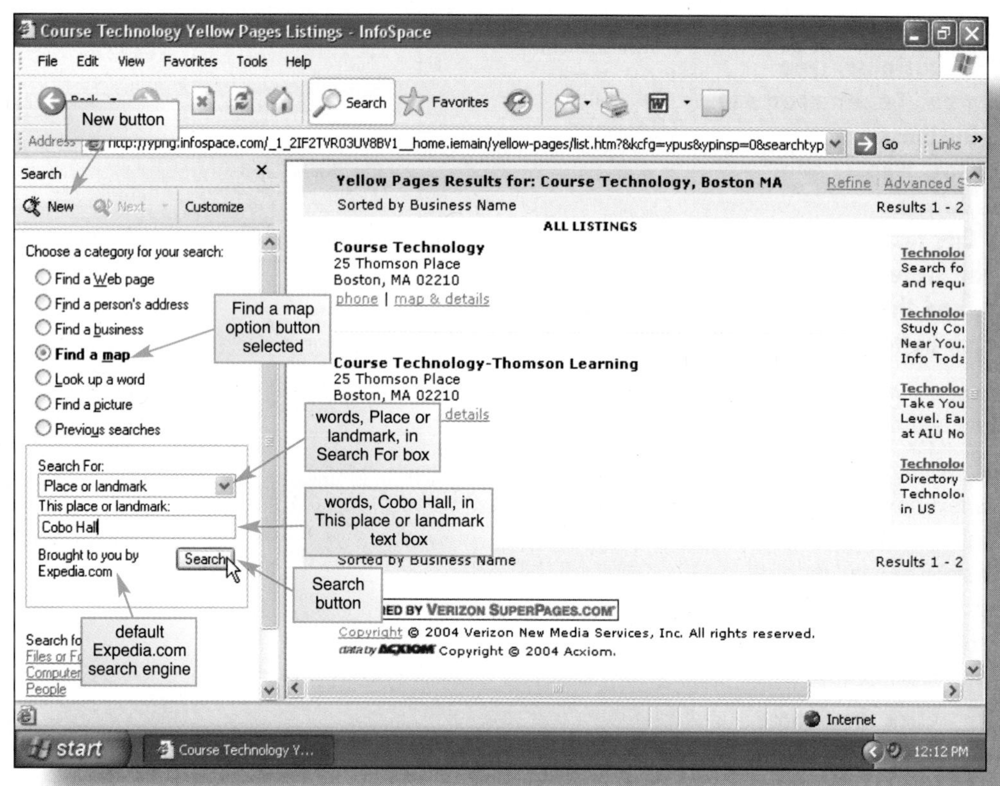

FIGURE 6-61

2 Click the Search button.

A map with the location of Cobo Hall displays in the right pane (Figure 6-62). A red dot on the map indicates the exact location.

3 When you have finished viewing the map, click the Close button in the Search results window.

The Search results window closes.

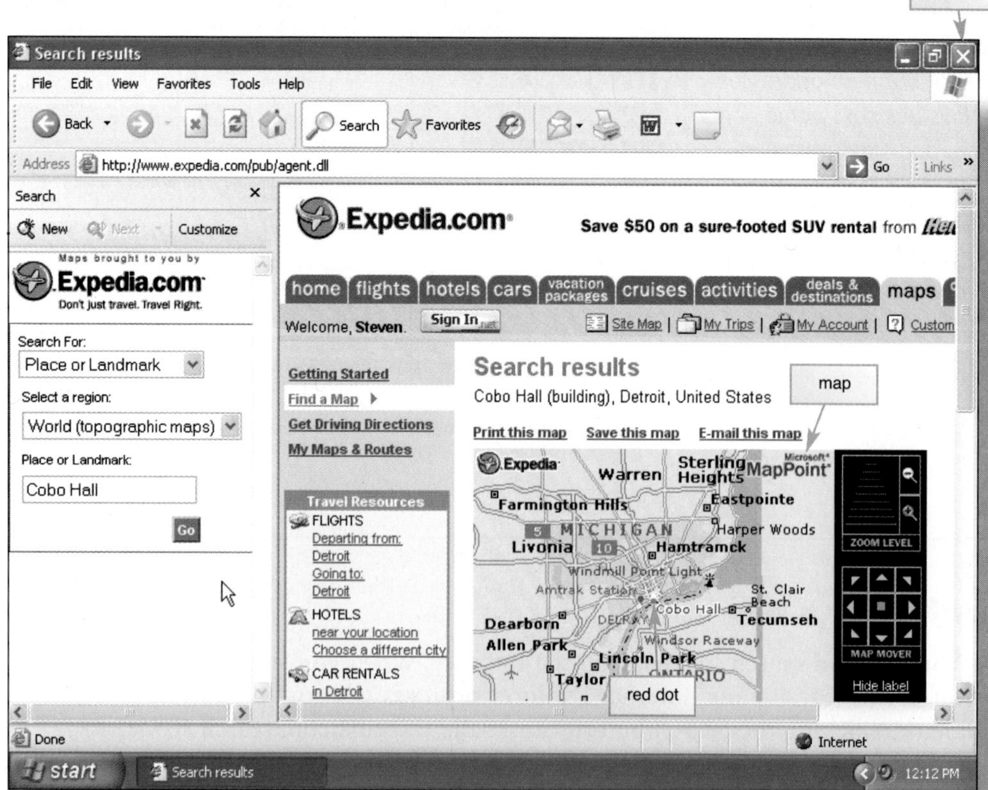

FIGURE 6-62

Other Ways

1. Type `www.expedia.com` in Address box, click Go button, click maps tab, click Find a Map, select region, enter place name, click Find a map

In this project, you used four search categories in the Search pane to search for a Web page, a mailing address, business address, and a map. In addition to these search categories, two other search categories allow you to search for a word in an encyclopedia (Look up a word) and a picture (Find a picture).

Resetting the Internet Search Behavior

After selecting the Classic Internet search, you should revert to the original search behavior by selecting the Search Companion search. Perform the following steps to reset the Internet search behavior.

TO RESET THE INTERNET SEARCH BEHAVIOR

1. Click the Start button and then click Search on the Start menu.
2. Click Change Preferences in the Search Companion balloon.
3. Click Change Internet search behavior.
4. Click With Search Companion.
5. Click the OK button in the Search Companion balloon.
6. Click the Close button in the Search Results window.

The Internet search behavior is reset by selecting the With Search Companion behavior and the Search Results window closes.

More About

Customizing Classic Internet Search

You can customize the Classic Internet search by selecting the categories that display in the Search pane, selecting which search engines to use, and then selecting the order in which the search engines display when you click the Next button. To customize, click the Customize button in the Search pane and then select the search settings in the Customize Search Settings dialog box.

The Recycle Bin

When you install Windows XP, the amount of hard drive space reserved for the Recycle Bin is set at 10 percent (10%) of the total size of the hard drive. For example, if the size of the local hard drive is 10 gigabytes (10,000 megabytes), the amount of disk space reserved for the Recycle Bin is approximately 1,000 megabytes (1,000 megabytes = 10,000 megabytes × .10). The amount of disk space reserved is a property of the Recycle Bin. You can change the amount to make more or less disk space available for the Recycle Bin. In addition to changing the size of the Recycle Bin, you can empty the contents of the Recycle Bin to make more disk space available.

Other properties of the Recycle Bin allow you to restore a file to its original location if it has been deleted mistakenly, choose to delete a file without first sending the file to the Recycle Bin, cause no confirmation dialog box to display when a file is deleted, and change the amount of disk space reserved for the Recycle Bin. Before changing the properties of the Recycle Bin, it is important to be able to view the contents of the Recycle Bin.

More About

Recycle Bin

If you are working with large files, set the space reserved for the Recycle Bin accordingly. Deleting a file that is larger than the amount of space reserved for the Recycle Bin will cause the file not to be moved to the Recycle Bin. Instead, Windows XP will permanently delete the file!

Viewing the Contents of the Recycle Bin

To view a list of the deleted files displayed in Details view, including the eula file and Files containing text support file that you deleted previously in this project, perform the step on the next page.

To View the Contents of the Recycle Bin

1 Double-click the Recycle Bin icon. Resize the Recycle Bin window to resemble the window in Figure 6-63.

The resized Recycle Bin window displays (Figure 6-63). The Recycle Bin Tasks area in the left pane contains tasks to Empty the Recycle Bin and Restore all items, and the right panel contains the eula file and Files containing text support file. File information includes the deleted file's name, file type, and file size. The file entries on your computer may be different.

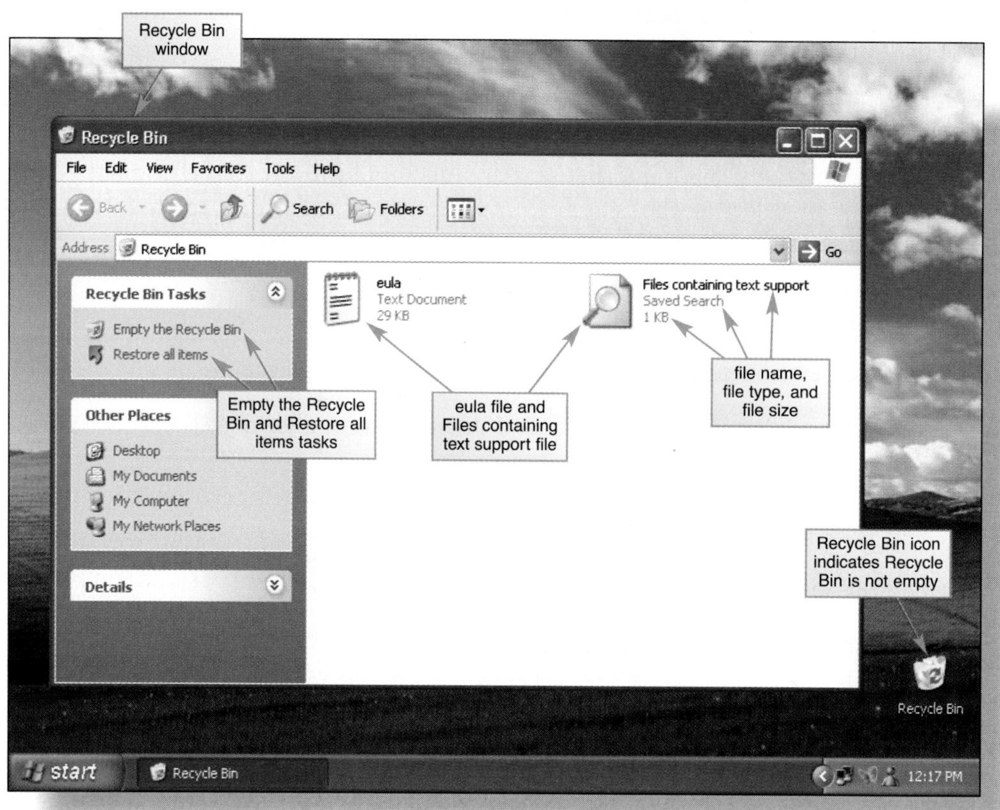

FIGURE 6-63

Other Ways

1. Right-click Recycle Bin icon, click Open on shortcut menu
2. Right-click Recycle Bin icon, click Explore on shortcut menu

In Figure 6-63, the left panel of the Recycle Bin window contains the Empty the Recycle Bin task. The Empty the Recycle Bin task permanently deletes all files, folders, and shortcuts in the Recycle Bin. After clicking the Empty the Recycle Bin task, these items are no longer available to the computer user.

As long as a file, folder, or shortcut remains in the Recycle Bin, you can **restore** the item to its original location. The Restore all items task restores all files in the Recycle Bin to their original locations on the local hard drive and returns their icons to their original locations (in a folder, on the desktop, and so on). After clicking the Restore all items task, the restored files are available for use but their entries no longer display in the right pane of the Recycle Bin window. The following section illustrates how to restore a single file that has been placed in the Recycle Bin.

Restoring a Deleted File, Folder, or Shortcut

You can recover files, folders, or shortcuts deleted in error using the Recycle Bin. When you delete an item (file, folder, or shortcut) and then restore the deleted item, the Recycle Bin restores the item to its original location. Perform the following steps to restore the Files containing text support file that you deleted previously in this project to its original location in the My Documents folder.

To Restore a Deleted File Using the Recycle Bin

1 Click the Files containing text support icon to select the icon and then point to the Restore this item in the Recycle Bin Tasks area.

The highlighted Files containing text support icon displays in the right pane (Figure 6-64).

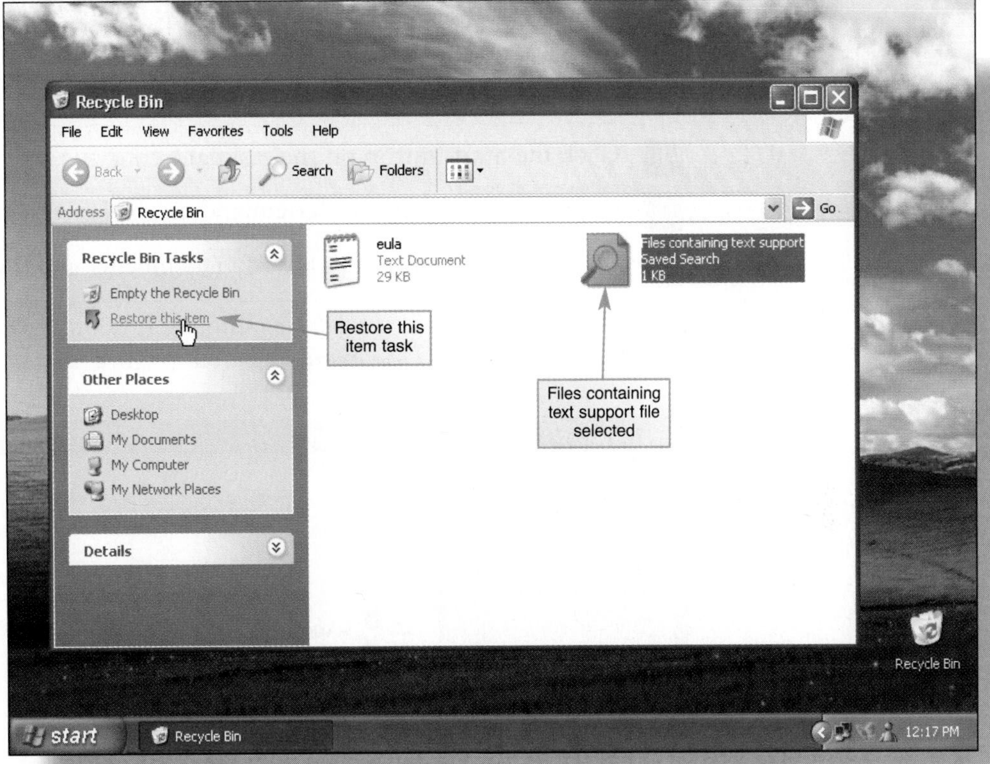

FIGURE 6-64

2 Click Restore this item.

The Files containing text support file is removed from the right pane of the Recycle Bin window, the file's icon displays in its original location in the My Documents folder, and the Restore this item changes to Restore all items in the Recycle Bin Tasks area (Figure 6-65).

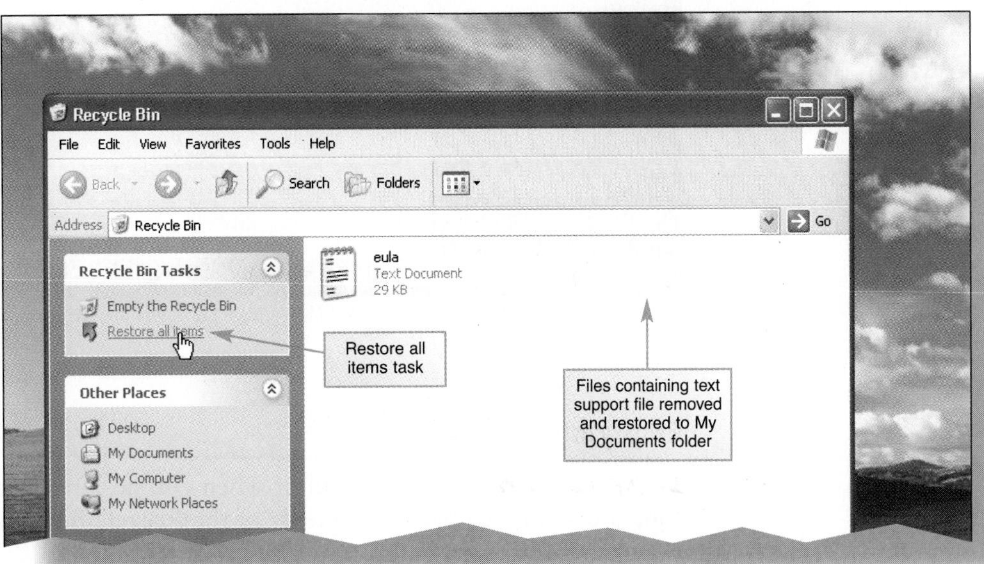

FIGURE 6-65

Other Ways

1. Click file name in Recycle Bin window, on File menu click Restore

Viewing a Restored File

After restoring the Files containing text support file, display the My Documents window to view the restored file. Perform the following steps to view the restored Files containing text support file in the My Documents window.

TO VIEW A RESTORED FILE

1. Click the Start button on the taskbar.
2. Click the My Documents command on the Start menu.
3. Click the Close button in the My Documents window.

After performing Step 2, the Files containing text support file displays in the Saved Search area in the My Documents window (Figure 6-66).

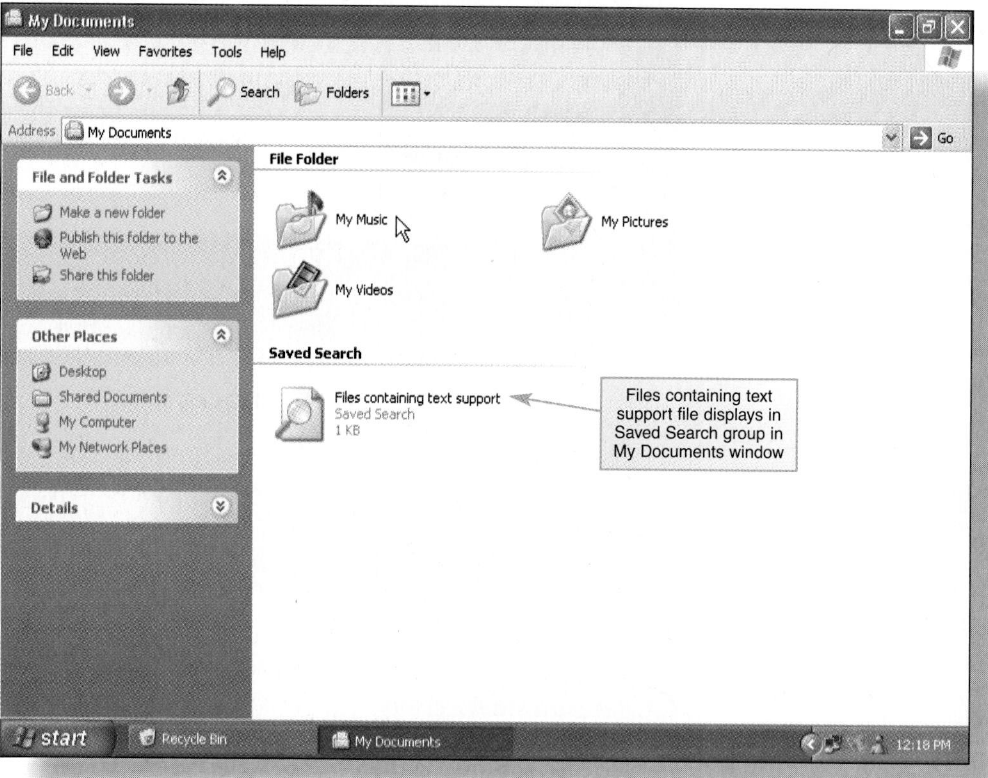

FIGURE 6-66

Emptying the Recycle Bin

When the Recycle Bin is full or when you no longer need the files in the Recycle Bin, you should empty the contents of the Recycle Bin. Perform the following steps to empty the Recycle Bin.

Steps To Empty the Recycle Bin

1 Click the Empty the Recycle Bin task in the Recycle Bin Tasks area. Point to the Yes button in the Confirm File Delete dialog box.

The Confirm File Delete dialog box displays (Figure 6-67). If the Recycle Bin contains multiple files, the Confirm Multiple File Delete dialog box displays instead of the Confirm File Delete dialog box.

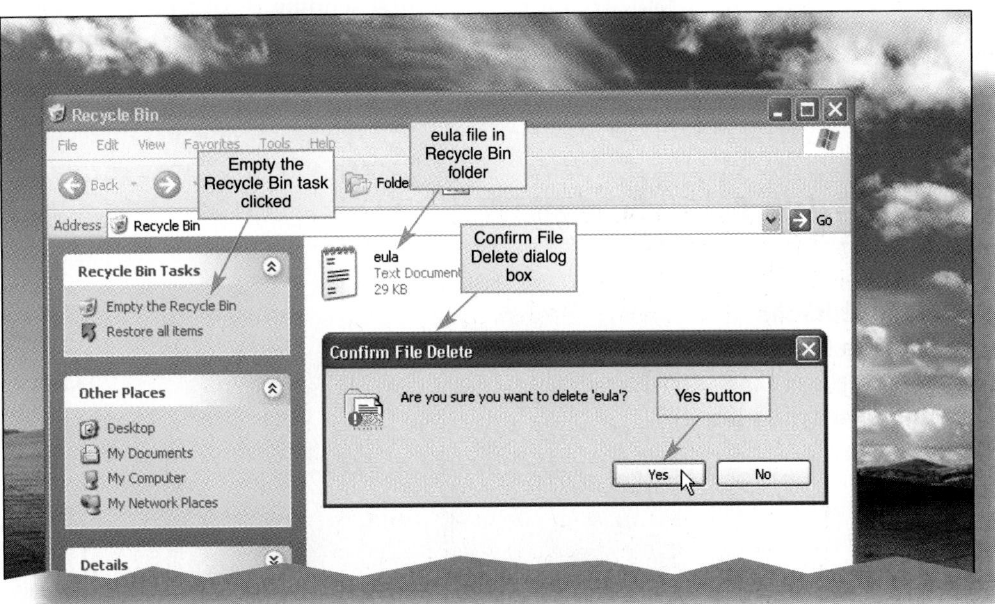

FIGURE 6-67

2 Click the Yes button.

The contents of the Recycle Bin are removed and the eula file in the right pane of the Recycle Bin window is deleted (Figure 6-68).

3 Click the Close button in the Recycle Bin window.

The Recycle Bin window closes.

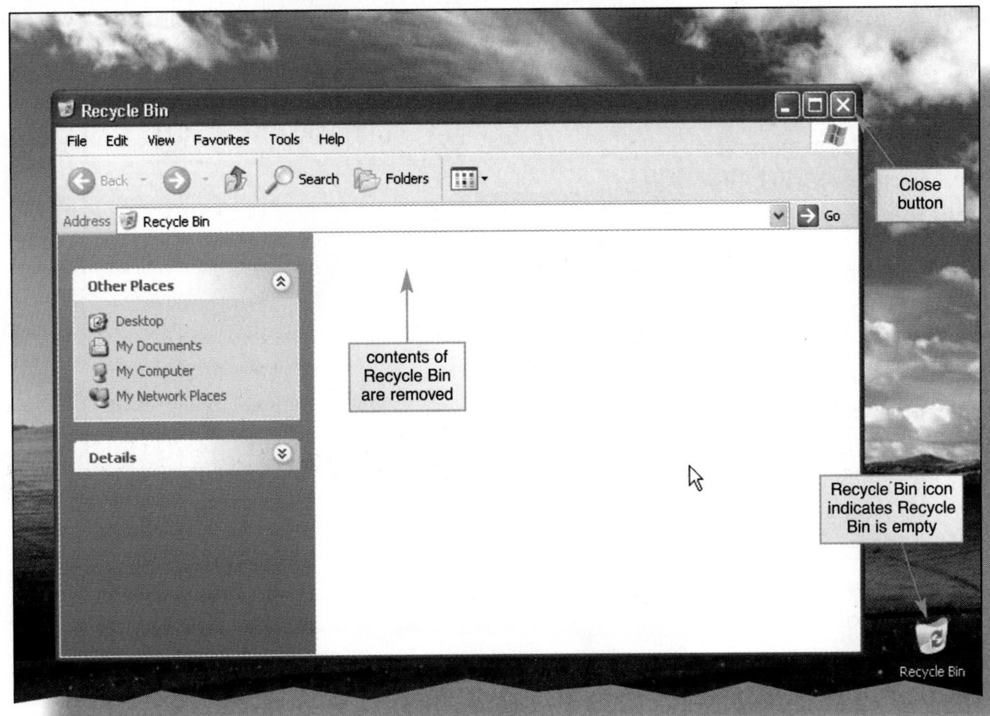

FIGURE 6-68

Other Ways

1. Right-click Recycle Bin icon on desktop, click Empty Recycle Bin, click Yes button

Viewing Recycle Bin Properties

As mentioned previously, changing the properties of the Recycle Bin allows you to delete files without first sending them to the Recycle Bin, choose to display a confirmation dialog box when a file is deleted, and change the amount of disk space reserved by the Recycle Bin. Perform the following steps to view the Recycle Bin properties.

Steps To View the Recycle Bin Properties

1 Right-click the Recycle Bin icon on the desktop and then point to Properties on the shortcut menu.

A shortcut menu, containing the highlighted Properties command, displays (Figure 6-69).

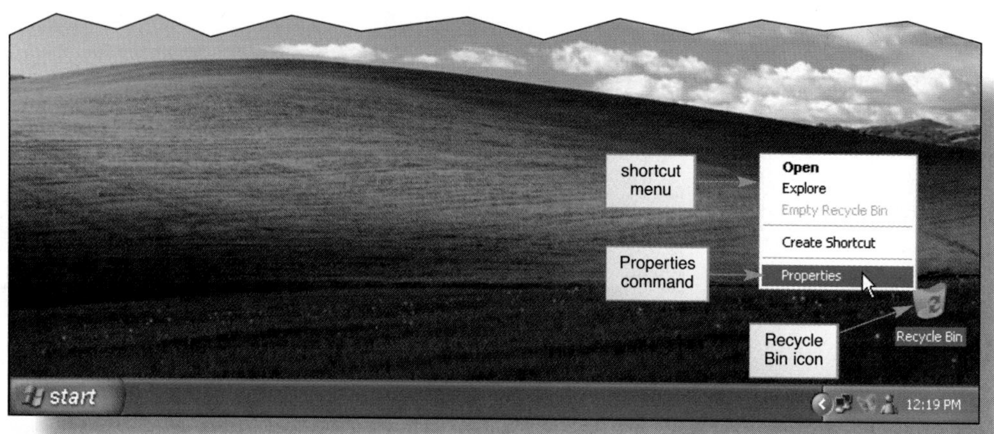

FIGURE 6-69

2 Click Properties. If necessary, click the Global tab.

The Recycle Bin Properties dialog box and Global sheet display (Figure 6-70). The Use one setting for all drives option button is selected, the maximum size of the Recycle Bin is set to 10%, a slider allows you to select the size of the Recycle Bin, the Display delete confirmation dialog check box is selected, and the Apply button is dimmed. The Recycle Bin Properties dialog box on your computer may contain additional tabbed sheets.

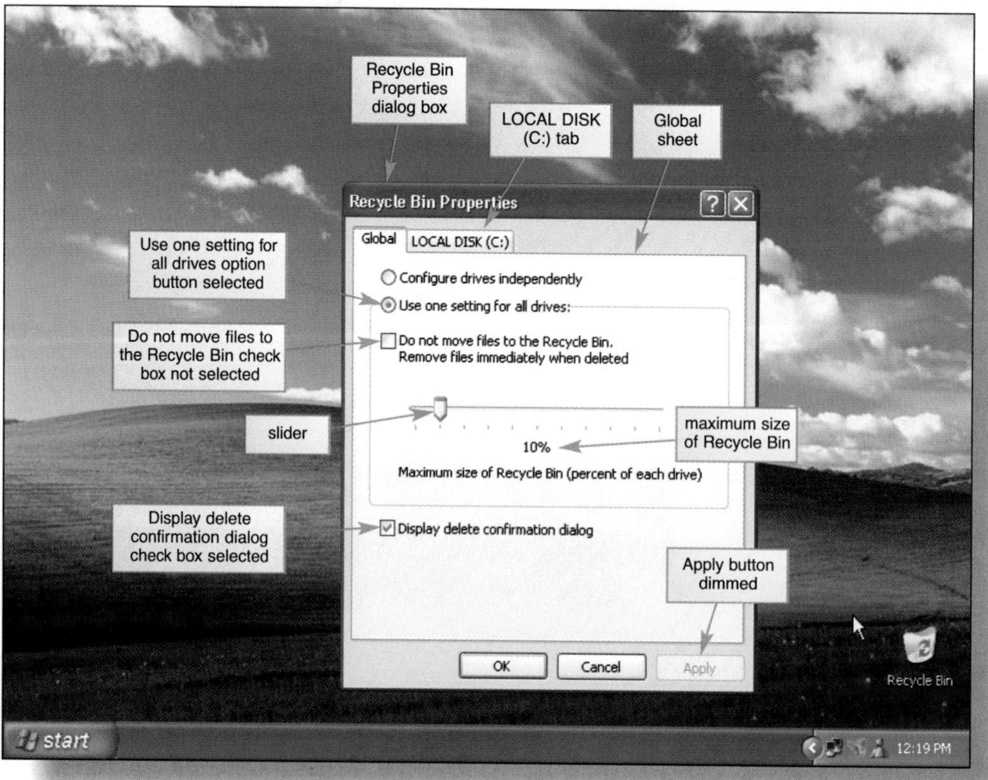

FIGURE 6-70

3 Click the LOCAL DISK (C:) tab.

The LOCAL DISK (C:) sheet indicates the size of drive C (12.6 GB) and the space reserved for the Recycle Bin (1.26 GB) (Figure 6-71). The settings on the Global sheet cause the check box and slider to display dimmed. The settings on your computer may be different.

4 Click the Close button in the Recycle Bin Properties dialog box.

The Recycle Bin Properties dialog box closes.

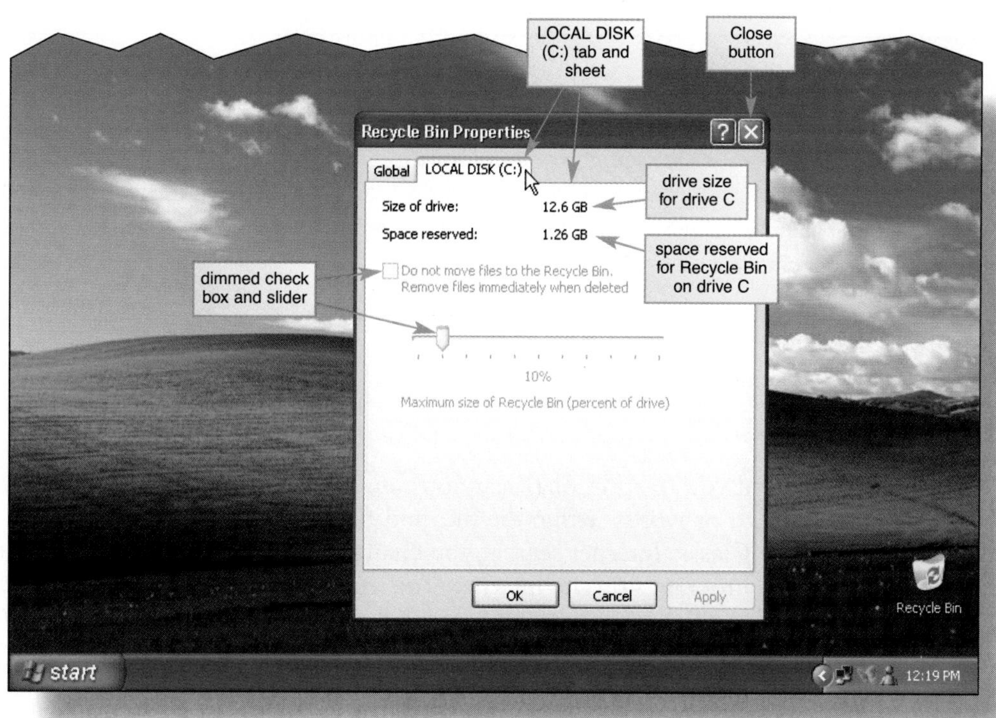

FIGURE 6-71

In Figure 6-70, the Use one setting for all drives option button is selected instead of the Configure drives independently option button because only one disk drive (drive C) is connected to the computer. The Do not move files to the Recycle Bin check box is not selected, which indicates all deleted files are sent to the Recycle Bin. The maximum size of the Recycle Bin is set at 10% of the disk drive. The Display delete confirmation dialog check box is selected, indicating that a confirmation dialog box displays when a file is deleted. To change the amount of disk space the Recycle Bin requires, you drag the slider to the left or right to achieve the desired amount and then click the Apply button.

Other Ways

1. In Recycle Bin window, right-click open area in left pane, click Properties
2. Right-click Start button, click Explore, right-click Recycle Bin icon in Folders pane, click Properties

Removing the Saved Search File

The Files containing text support icon remains in the My Documents window (see Figure 6-66 on page WIN 6.52). To restore the My Documents folder to its original configuration, remove the Files containing text support icon by performing the following steps.

TO DELETE A SAVED SEARCH FILE

1. Click the Start button and then click My Documents.
2. Right-click the Files containing text support icon, click Delete on the shortcut menu, and then click the Yes button in the Confirm File Delete dialog box.
3. Click the Close button in the My Documents window.

The Files containing text support file is removed from the My Documents folder and the My Documents window closes.

More About

Recycle Bin Properties

If you want to delete a file or folder without first placing it in the Recycle Bin, hold down the SHIFT key while dragging or right-dragging its icon to the Recycle Bin icon. Windows XP then will permanently delete the file.

CASE PERSPECTIVE SUMMARY

While focusing on learning more about searching techniques, you find several methods to refine a file search and find an array of techniques for searching for information on the Internet. You design and conduct a seminar for the employees. Your supervisor compliments you on the success of the seminar and asks you to represent the organization at the next Shelly/Cashman Institute at Purdue University. She thinks the Institute will be a good way to learn more about teaching Windows XP.

Project Summary

This project introduced you to additional search techniques. Using Search Companion, you searched for files based on a date, a word or words within the file, and file type; and then searched for digital media files and document files. Using Classic Internet search, you changed search preferences and searched for Web content, personal information, and maps on the Internet. You viewed the properties of the Recycle Bin, emptied the Recycle Bin, and used the Recycle Bin to recover a deleted file.

What You Should Know

Having completed this project, you now should be able to perform the following tasks:

- Begin a Classic Internet Search *(WIN 6.40)*
- Begin a New Search *(WIN 6.44)*
- Begin a File Search *(WIN 6.05)*
- Change a Search Preference *(WIN 6.38)*
- Delete a Saved Search File *(WIN 6.55)*
- Delete Multiple Files *(WIN 6.23)*
- Display the Contents of a Picture File *(WIN 6.26)*
- Empty the Recycle Bin *(WIN 6.53)*
- Perform an All Files and Folders Search *(WIN 6.07)*
- Play a Music File *(WIN 6.28)*
- Play a Video File *(WIN 6.31)*
- Reset the Internet Search Behavior *(WIN 6.49)*
- Reset the Search Criteria *(WIN 6.13, WIN 6.26, WIN 6.29, WIN 6.31, WIN 6.34)*
- Restore a Deleted File Using the Recycle Bin *(WIN 6.51)*
- Save a Search *(WIN 6.20)*
- Search for a File Using a Modification Date *(WIN 6.11)*
- Search for a File Using a Word or Phrase in the File *(WIN 6.18)*
- Search for a File Using File Type *(WIN 6.14)*
- Search for a Map *(WIN 6.47)*
- Search for a Web Page Using a Keyword *(WIN 6.42)*
- Search for Document Files *(WIN 6.32)*
- Search for Files Using a Saved Search *(WIN 6.22)*
- Search for Music Files *(WIN 6.27)*
- Search for Picture Files *(WIN 6.24)*
- Search for Video Files *(WIN 6.29)*
- Search the Internet for a Mailing Address *(WIN 6.45)*
- Search the Internet Using Search Companion *(WIN 6.35)*
- Send a File to the My Documents Folder *(WIN 6.19)*
- Specify the Starting Point of a Search *(WIN 6.08)*
- View a Restored File *(WIN 6.52)*
- View the Contents of the Recycle Bin *(WIN 6.50)*
- View the Recycle Bin Properties *(WIN 6.54)*

Learn It Online

Instructions: To complete the Learn It Online exercises, launch your Web browser using the steps on pages WIN 1.46 and WIN 1.47, click the Address box, enter `scsite.com/winxp/exs.htm`, and then press the ENTER key. When the Windows XP Learn It Online page displays, follow the instructions in the exercises below.

1 Project Reinforcement TF, MC, and SA

Below Windows XP Project 6, click the Project Reinforcement link. Print the quiz by clicking Print on the File menu. Answer each question. Write your first and last name at the top of each page, and then hand in the printout to your instructor.

2 Flash Cards

Below Windows XP Project 6, click the Flash Cards link. When Flash Cards displays, read the instructions. Type `20` (or a number specified by your instructor) in the Number of Playing Cards text box, type your name in the Name text box, and then click the Flip Card button. When the flash card displays, read the question and then click the Answer box arrow to select an answer. Flip through Flash Cards. Click Print on the File menu to print the last flash card if your score is 15 (75%) correct or greater and then hand it in to your instructor. If your score is less than 15 (75%) correct, then redo this exercise by clicking the Replay button.

3 Practice Test

Below Windows XP Project 6, click the Practice Test link. Answer each question, enter your first and last name at the bottom of the page, and then click the Grade Test button. When the graded practice test displays on your screen, click Print on the File menu to print a hard copy. Continue to take practice tests until you score 80% or better. Hand in a printout of the final practice test to your instructor.

4 Who Wants to Be a Computer Genius?

Below Windows XP Project 6, click the Computer Genius link. Read the instructions, enter your first and last name at the bottom of the page, and then click the Play button. Hand in a printout of your score to your instructor.

5 Wheel of Terms

Below Windows XP Project 6, click the Wheel of Terms link. Read the instructions, and then enter your first and last name and your school name. Click the Play button. Hand in a printout of your score to your instructor.

6 Crossword Puzzle Challenge

Below Windows XP Project 6, click the Crossword Puzzle Challenge link. Read the instructions, and then enter your first and last name. Click the Play button. Work the crossword puzzle. When you are finished, click the Submit button. When the crossword puzzle redisplays, click the Print button. Hand in the printout.

7 Tips and Tricks

Below Windows XP Project 6, click the Tips and Tricks link. Click a topic that pertains to Project 6. Right-click the information and then click Print on the shortcut menu. Construct a brief example of what the information relates to in Windows XP to confirm that you understand how to use the tip or trick. Hand in the example and printed information.

8 Newsgroups

Below Windows XP Project 6, click the Newsgroups link. Click a topic that pertains to Project 6. Print three comments. Hand in the comments to your instructor.

9 Expanding Your Horizons

Below Windows XP Project 6, click the Articles for Microsoft Windows XP link. Click a topic that pertains to Project 6. Print the information. Construct a brief example of what the information relates to in Windows XP to confirm that you understand the contents of the article. Hand in the example and printed information to your instructor.

10 Search Sleuth

Below Windows XP Project 6, click the Search Sleuth link. To search for a term that pertains to this project, select a term below the Project 6 title and then use the Google search engine at google.com (or any major search engine) to display and print two Web pages that present information on the term. Hand in the printouts to your instructor.

1 Using Windows Help and Support

Instructions: Use Windows Help and Support and a computer to perform the following tasks and answer the questions.

1. If necessary, launch Microsoft Windows XP and then log on to the computer.
2. Click the Start button and then click Search. Maximize the Search Results window.
3. Click Help on the menu bar and then click Help and Support Center. Maximize the window.
4. Answer the following questions by reading the Search Companion overview.
   a. What service does Search Companion have that makes it faster to search the Internet?
   ____
   b. What is an Active Directory?
   gives you everything you need to find
5. Click Search for a file or folder in the Navigation pane (left pane of Help and Support window). Answer the following questions.
   a. What should you do if you get too many results?
   Same
6. Click the Related Topics link at the bottom of the topic pane (right pane of Help and Support window) and then click Searching for files and folders. Answer the following question.
   a. List five ways to search for files or folders. ______________________________
   ____
   ____
7. Click Search the Internet in the Topic pane. Answer the following questions.
   a. What three entries can you type to find information quickly? TOOLBAR
   b. Where do you type these entries? ______________________________
   c. For more tips about using Internet Explorer, what would you click?
   ____
8. Click Search for people and groups in the Topic pane. Answer the following questions.
   a. What task does Clear All perform?
   everything
   b. What information does the Address Book contain?
   Name, phone
9. Click Search for a printer in the Topic pane. Answer the following questions.
   a. What does the method you use to search for a printer depend upon?
   where its conected
10. Click Search for a computer on the network in the Search pane. Answer the following question.
    a. How do you begin a new search?
    Clear plane
11. Click the Close button in the Help and Support Center window.
12. Click the Close button in the Search Results window.

In the Lab

1 Using Search Companion to Search for Files

Problem: You know that Search Companion is an important feature of Windows XP. You decide to use Search Companion to find the Windows XP, Zapotec, and FeatherTexture files on the local hard drive. You will store the files in the My Pictures folder, print the images, and e-mail one of them to a friend.

Instructions: Use a computer to perform the following tasks and answer the questions.

Part 1: Searching for Bitmap Image Files

1. If necessary, launch Microsoft Windows XP and then log on to the computer.
2. Click the Start button on the taskbar and then click Search on the Start menu. Maximize the Search Results window.
3. Click All files and folders in the Search Companion balloon. Type `Windows XP` in the All or part of the file name text box. Click the Search button. When the search is complete, click Yes, finished searching in the Search Companion balloon.
4. Click the Windows XP bitmap image file icon in the right pane to select the icon. Click Copy this file in the File and Folder Tasks area. Click My Documents in the Copy Items dialog box. Click My Pictures in the Copy Items dialog box. Click the Copy button to copy the image to the My Pictures folder.

Part 2: Searching for Files from Another Window

1. Click the Search button on the Standard Buttons toolbar.
2. Click All files and folders in the Search Companion balloon. Type `Zapotec` in the All or part of the file name text box. Click the Search button. When the search is complete, click Yes, finished searching in the Search Companion balloon.
3. Click the Zapotec icon in the right pane to select the icon. Click Copy this file in the File and Folder Tasks area. Click My Pictures in the Copy Items dialog box. Click the Copy button to copy the image to the My Pictures folder.

Part 3: Searching for Files by File Type — Didn't Get

1. Click the Search button on the Standard Buttons toolbar.
2. Click All files and folders in the Search Companion balloon. Remove the Zapotec entry in the All or part of the file name text box. Click the More advanced options option button in the Search Companion balloon (Figure 6-72 on the next page).
3. Click the Type of file arrow button. Click Bitmap Image in the list box. Click the Search button to search for all bitmap image files on the hard drive. Answer the following question.
   a. How many files were found? ______________________________
4. When the search is complete, click Yes, finished searching in the Search Companion balloon.
5. Click the Name button in the right pane to display the file names in alphabetical order. In the alphabetical list, click the FeatherTexture icon to select the icon.
6. Click Copy this file in the File and Folder Tasks area. Click My Pictures in the Copy Items dialog box. Click the Copy button to copy the image to the My Pictures folder.
7. Click the Close button in the Search Results window.

(continued)

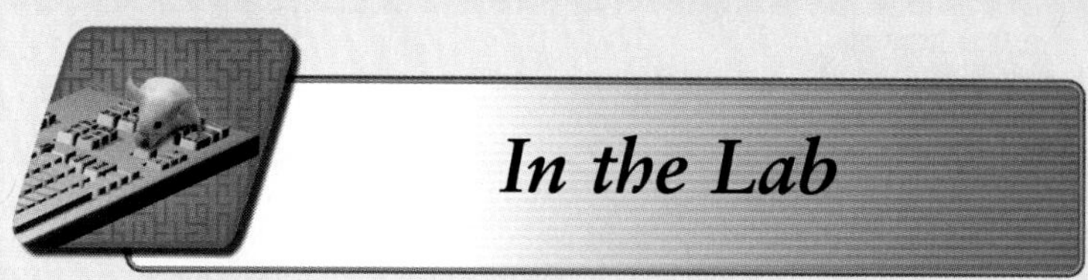

Using Search Companion to Search for Files *(continued)*

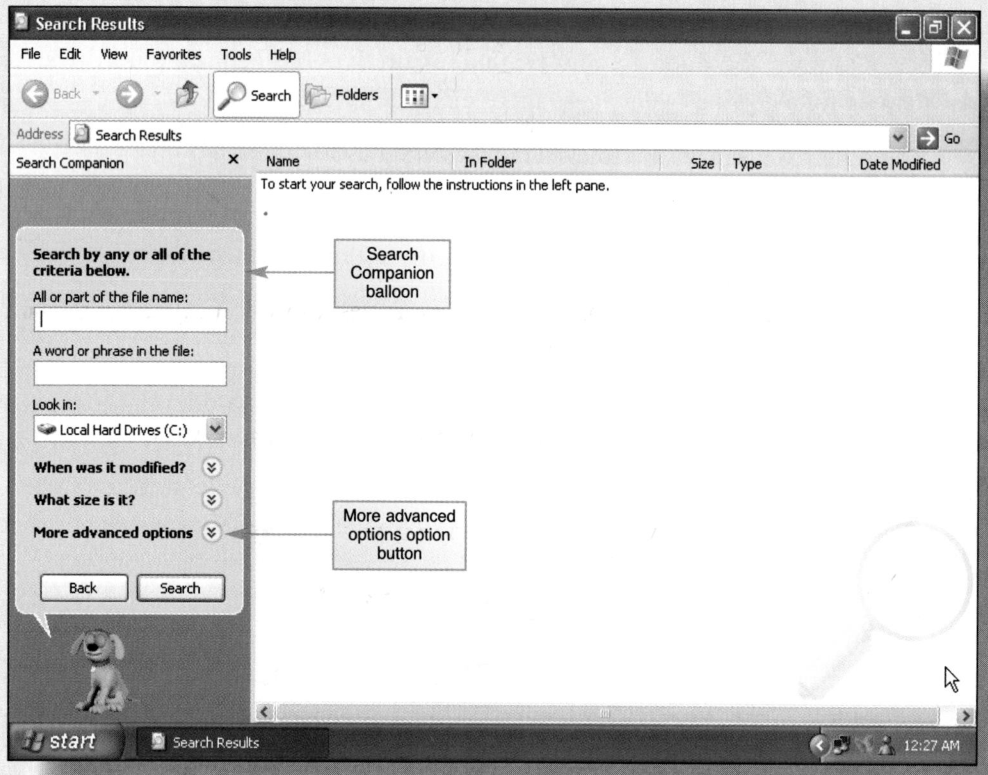

FIGURE 6-72

Part 4: *Printing the Images*

1. Click the Start menu and then click My Pictures to display the My Pictures window.
2. Select the FeatherTexture, Windows XP, and Zapotec images. Click Print the selected pictures in the Picture Tasks area to start the Photo Printing Wizard.
3. Click the Next button in the Photo Printing Wizard dialog box.
4. Verify a check mark displays in the upper-right corner of each logo. Click the Next button.
5. Verify the correct printer is being used. Click the Next button.
6. Scroll the Available layouts box to display the 3.5 x 5 in. Prints area. Click the image in the area to select the image. Click the Next button to print the images.
7. Click the Finish button in the Photo Printing Wizard dialog box.

Part 5: *E-mail the Files in the Background Images Folder*

1. Select the Windows XP icon.
2. Click E-mail this file in the File and Folder Tasks area.
3. Click the OK button in the Send Pictures via E-Mail dialog box.
4. Type `StevenForsythe@msn.com` in the To text box. Type `I just searched the Internet to find this background image. I thought you might like to see it.` in the message area.
5. Click the Send button on the toolbar.

***Part 6:* Deleting the Bitmap Images**

1. Select the FeatherTexture, Windows XP, and Zapotec icons.
2. Click Delete the selected items in the File and Folder Tasks area.
3. Click the Yes button in the Confirm Multiple File Delete dialog box.
4. Click the Close button in the My Pictures window.

2 Using Search Companion to Search for All Files and Folders

Problem: In the past, you used Search Companion to search for files knowing only their file names. A friend recently informed you that you can use Search Companion to search for files based on date, file type, content, and name. You decide to investigate the other ways to search for files using Search Companion.

Instructions: Perform the following steps to search for various files using Search Companion.

***Part 1:* Searching for Files Based on Date**

1. If necessary, launch Microsoft Windows XP and then log on to the computer.
2. Use Search Companion to search the local hard drive for all files or folders modified on 8/23/2004 (Figure 6-73). How many files or folders were found? 58 files

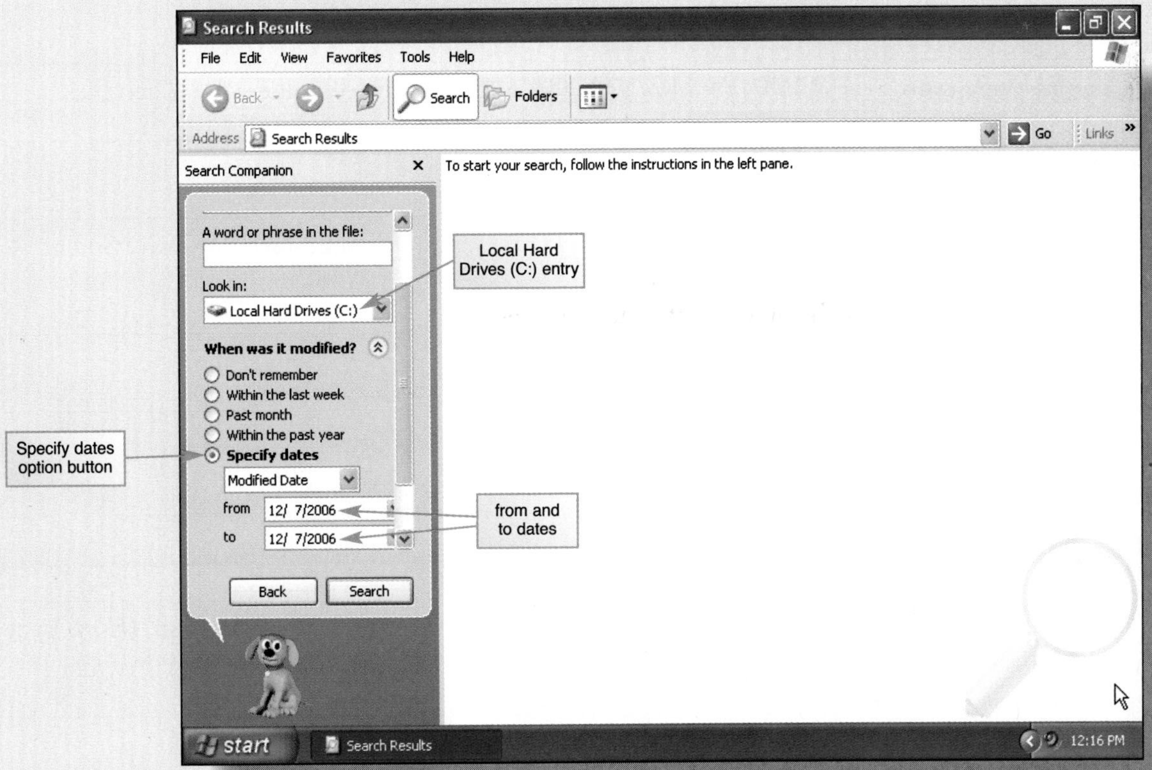

FIGURE 6-73

(continued)

In the Lab

Using Search Companion to Search for All Files and Folders *(continued)*

3. Use Search Companion to search the local hard drive for all files or folders modified on your last birthday. How many files or folders were found? 3 files
4. Use Search Companion to search the local hard drive for all files or folders modified within the past month. How many files or folders were found? 929 files

Part 2: ***Searching for Files Based on File Type***

1. Use Search Companion to search the local hard drive for JPEG files.
2. List the first three JPEG image files found during the search.
   bitmap images, christmas, jellybelly logo
3. Scroll to make the Red moon desert icon visible and then double-click the Red moon desert icon. What displays on the desktop?
   red moon background
4. Scroll to make the Windows XP icon visible and then double-click the Windows XP icon. What displays on the desktop?
   windows XP background
5. Use Search Companion to search the local hard drive for Midi Sequence files.
   a. How many files or folders were found? ________
   b. Double-click one of the files found. What do you hear?
   ____
6. Use Search Companion to search the WINDOWS (or WINNT) folder and its subfolders for Video files.
   a. How many files or folders were found? ________
   b. Double-click one of the Video file icons. What displays?
   ____
7. Use Search Companion to search the WINDOWS (or WINNT) folder and its subfolders for Wave Sound files.
   a. How many files or folders were found? ________
   b. Double-click one of the Wave Sound file icons. What do you hear?
   ____

Part 3: ***Searching for Files Based on Content or File Name***

1. Use Search Companion to search the local hard drive for all text documents containing the word, Microsoft.
   a. How many files or folders were found? ________
2. Use Search Companion to search the local hard drive for files or folders with the .bat extension. (*Hint:* Type `*.bat` in the All or part of the file name text box in the Search Companion balloon.)
   a. What type of files were found? ________
3. Close the Search Results window.

In the Lab

3 Using Search Companion to Search for Information on the Internet

Problem: While attending a one-day Internet seminar, you discover multiple methods to use Search Companion to search the Internet. You particularly like the method that allows you to search the Internet by typing a question, keyword, or statement. You decide to learn more about this method of searching the Internet.

Instructions: Perform the following steps to use Search Companion to search for information on the Internet.

***Part 1:* Searching for Information on the Internet**

1. If necessary, launch Microsoft Windows XP and then log on to the computer.
2. Design a statement for each of the topics below, type the statement into the text box in the Search Companion balloon, and then find an appropriate Web page for each statement. Print each Web page, write your name on the first printed page, and then throw away the remaining printed pages (Figure 6-74).

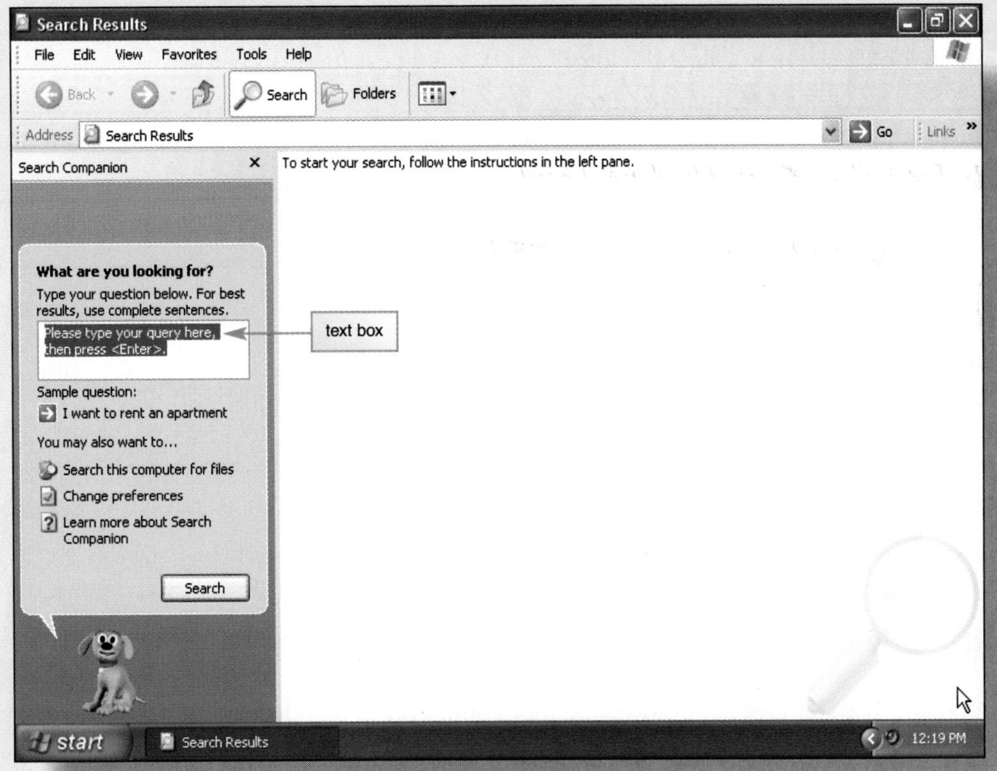

FIGURE 6-74

a. You want to look for articles that are available in the UCLA library. Write your statement on the following line.
UCLA articles last month

b. You want current temperature readings for major cities in the United States. Write your statement below.
current temps (major cities)

(continued)

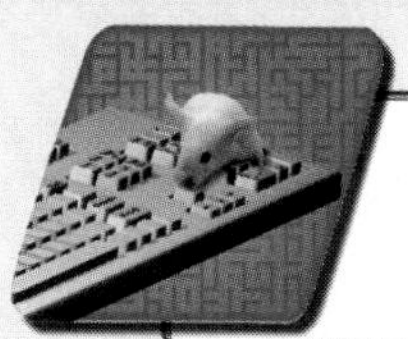

In the Lab

Using Search Companion to Search for Information on the Internet *(continued)*

c. You need information to write a report about the United States Senate. Write your statement below.

____

d. You want to shop for the best prices for a new digital camera. Write your statement below.

____

Part 2: *Searching for Information on the Internet*

1. Design a question for each of the topics below, type the question into the text box in the Search Companion balloon, and find an appropriate Web page for each question. Print each Web page, write your name on the first printed page, and then throw away the remaining printed pages.

a. You want the current winning numbers for the California Super Lotto. Write your question on the following line.

____

b. You want to look for a new General Motors car. Write your question below.

____

c. You want to know the tuition for the University of Southern California. Write your question below.

____

d. You want more information about trout fishing in Utah. Write your question below.

____

Part 3: *Searching for Information on the Internet*

1. Type the following keyword(s) into the text box in the Search Companion balloon and find an appropriate Web page for each keyword(s): aroma therapy, DNA, Niagara Falls, California flying fish.
2. Print each Web page, write your name on the first printed page, and then throw away the remaining printed pages.
3. Hand in the first printed page of each Web site to your instructor.

4 Using the Classic Internet Search to Search for Information

Problem: While reading a Help topic about the Search command in Windows XP Help and Support you discover that you also can search the Internet for Web pages, maps, and encyclopedia articles. You decide to learn more about ways to search the Internet for information.

Instructions: Perform the following steps to search for information on the Internet using the Classic Internet search.

Part 1: *Changing the Internet Search Behavior*

1. If necessary, launch Microsoft Windows XP and then log on to the computer.
2. Click the Start button and then click Search.
3. Click Change preferences in the Search Companion balloon.
4. Click Change Internet search behavior.

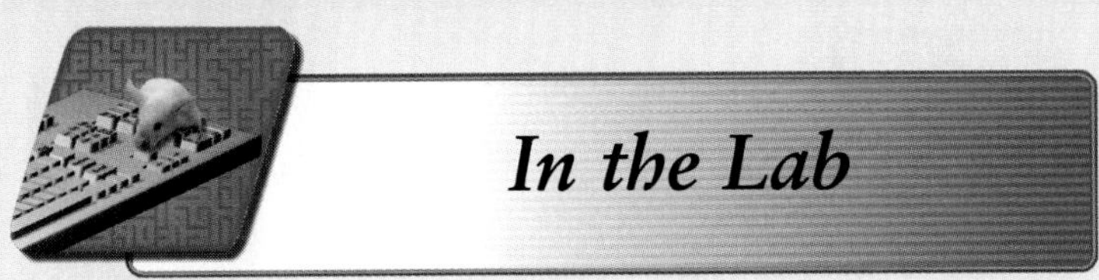

5. Click With Classic Internet search.
6. Click the OK button.
7. Click Search the Internet in the Search Companion balloon.

***Part 2:* Searching for Web Pages**

1. Find a Web page for each of the following topics: Anatomy of the Human Heart, Severe Weather, and Ocean Pollution. Click the New button after completing each search (Figure 6-75).
2. Print each Web page, write your name on the first printed page, and then throw away the remaining printed pages.

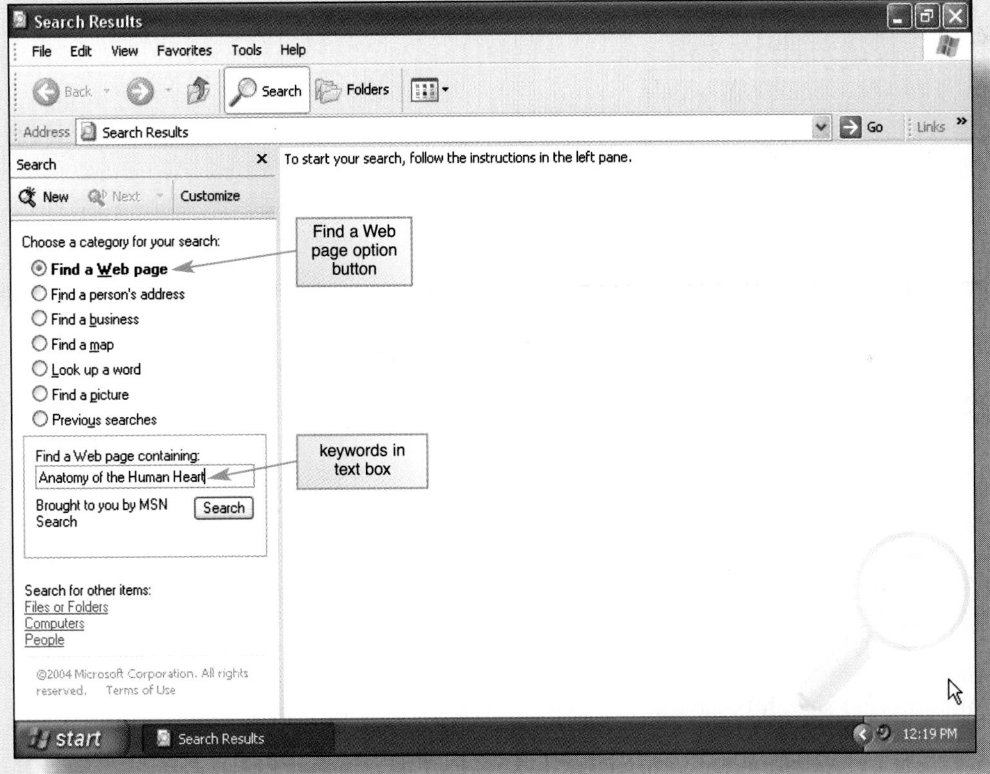

FIGURE 6-75

***Part 3:* Searching for a Business Address**

1. Search for the address and telephone number of each of the following businesses: Microsoft Corporation (Washington), Flagler Museum (Florida), and Recreational Equipment (Seattle, Washington). Click the New button after completing each search.
2. Use Notepad to create a list of business names, addresses, and telephone numbers. Include your name on the document.
3. Print out the Notepad document.

(continued)

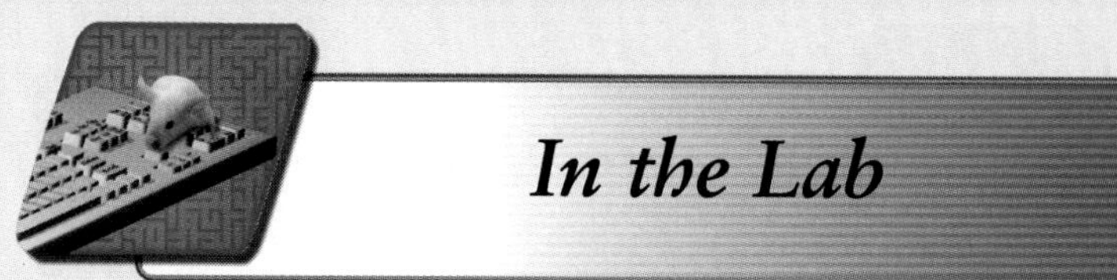

Using the Classic Internet Search to Search for Information *(continued)*

Part 4: *Searching for a Map*

1. Click the New button and then click Find a map in the Search pane.
2. Find a map for each of the following places or landmarks: Salzburg (Austria), Eiffel Tower (France), Statue of Liberty (New York), Islamorada Key (Florida), and White House (District of Columbia). Click the New button after completing each search.
3. Print each map. Circle the place or landmark on the map and write your name on each map.

Part 5: *Searching for an Encyclopedia Article*

1. Click the New button, click the More link, and then click Look up a word.
2. Find an encyclopedia article on black widow spiders. Use WordPad to create a report on black widow spiders that consists of the main article from the encyclopedia, the scientific classification, and a picture of the spider.
3. Find an encyclopedia article on blowfish (also called puffer or globefish). Use WordPad to create a report on blowfish that consists of the main article from the encyclopedia, the scientific classification, and a picture of the blowfish.
4. Find an encyclopedia article on cobra snakes. Use WordPad to create a report on cobra snakes that consists of the main article from the encyclopedia, the scientific classification, and a picture of the snake.
5. Find an encyclopedia article on killer bees (also called Africanized honey bees). Use WordPad to create a report on bees that consists of the main article from the encyclopedia, the scientific classification, and a picture of the bee.
6. Print out the WordPad documents and write your name on each report.
7. Close all open windows.

Part 6: *Resetting the Internet Search Behavior*

1. Click the Start button and then click Search.
2. Click Change preferences in the Search Companion balloon.
3. Click Change Internet search behavior.
4. Click With Search Companion.
5. Click the OK button.
6. Close the Search Results window.
7. Hand in all printouts to your instructor.

Cases and Places

The difficulty of these case studies varies:
◗ are the least difficult; ◗◗ are more difficult; and ◗◗◗ are the most difficult.

1 ◗ You help your friend Sharon buy a new computer. Late one night, she calls and is frantic because she cannot find a document on the computer. The document contains a big project for her Science class that she created using Microsoft Word and is due tomorrow. She cannot remember what file name she used to save the file but does remember the document contains her teacher's name, Ms. Lipton. To help her remember how to search for a file containing a word or series of words, write down the steps to find the file and give or e-mail her a copy.

2 ◗ You want to move music files from the My Documents folder to the My Music folder using the Send To command. To do this, you must add the My Music destination to the Send To menu. Investigate how to add a destination to the Send To menu, use the Send To menu to move the files, and then remove the destination. Using Notepad, write down the steps to add the My Music destination, copy a file from the My Documents folder to the My Music folder, and then remove the destination.

3 ◗◗ You recently graduated from college and took a job at a small investment firm. Your first job is to search for and compare the services of the major online brokers. Find five online brokers and compare their services, costs to buy and sell stocks, Web sites, and any other pertinent information. Summarize your findings in a report.

4 ◗◗ Wildcard characters often are used in a file name to locate a group of files while searching. For example, to locate all files with the Business file name regardless of the file name extension, an entry (Business.*) containing the asterisk wildcard character would be used. Using the Internet, computer magazines, or any other resources, develop a guide to using wildcards. Summarize what a wildcard character is, what are the valid wildcard characters, and give several examples to explain their use.

5 ◗◗ Windows XP is not the first operating system to contain a Recycle Bin. Apple computers have had a similar item, called the Trash Can, for years. Find an Apple computer that has the Trash Can. Have someone else show you how to use the Trash Can or experiment with the Trash Can yourself. Compare and contrast the procedures used to delete a file, restore a file, and empty the contents of the Recycle Bin with the procedures used with the Trash Can. How similar are the Recycle Bin and Trash Can?

6 ◗◗◗ A big controversy in the music industry is the practice of downloading songs from the Internet without paying royalties to songwriters, bands, and record companies. The music industry has developed software that automatically detects illegal song swapping and wants policing agencies to prosecute offenders. Others think downloading music should be legal. Analyze this problem and prepare a brief report summarizing both sides of the argument, your opinions, current developments, and possible solutions.

Cases and Places

7 ▶▶▶ The amount of information available on the Internet about an individual is amazing. Identity theft is increasingly common. Credit card fraud affects thousands monthly. Information about an individual that used to take days to find can be found in minutes with only a few mouse clicks. Should we be concerned about our privacy? Use magazine articles, personal experience, and the Internet to understand the problems. Prepare a brief report summarizing the methods used to obtain personal information, the problems arising from the use of this information, and then recommend preventive measures.

APPENDIX A

New Features of Windows XP Professional and Windows XP Home Edition

Microsoft Windows XP delivers a high standard in reliability and performance. Its many new features make it easier to use than previous versions of Windows. Windows XP is available in two editions: Microsoft Windows XP Professional and Microsoft Windows XP Home Edition. Windows XP Professional is designed for business and power users and includes advanced features for high-level performance and fast system response time. Windows XP Home Edition is intended for home computing and offers many new features that help home users work efficiently and connect faster to the Internet and with others. Table A-1 provides a list of the new features in Windows XP. The left column summarizes the major features of Windows XP Professional. The right column indicates whether the feature is available in Windows XP Home Edition.

Table A-1 Windows XP New Features and Comparison of Professional and Home Edition

WINDOWS XP PROFESSIONAL NEW FEATURES	*AVAILABLE IN WINDOWS XP HOME EDITION*
Access to all your documents and settings no matter which computer you use to log on	No
Access to files and folders on a network share when disconnected from the server	No
Advanced notebook support, including ClearType support, Dualview, and power management improvements	Yes
Allows multiple applications to run simultaneously	Yes
Automated System Recovery (ASR) assists in recovering from a major system error	No
Automatic 802.1x wireless network configuration	Yes
Automatically install, configure, repair, or remove software applications	No
CD burning lets you create CDs by dragging in Windows Explorer	Yes
Encrypting File System (EFS) allows encrypting of individual files or folders for security of files and folders on a local computer (not a network computer)	No
Faster boot and resume times	Yes
File-level access control allows an administrator with administrative privileges to limit access to some network resources (servers, directories, and files)	No
Help and Support Center lets you access Microsoft Knowledge Base on the Internet and access frequently used Help topics	Yes
Home networking	Yes
Internet Connection Firewall	Yes
Internet Information Services/Personal Web Server - IIS Web Server 5.1	No

(continued)

Table A-1 Windows XP New Features and Comparison of Professional and Home Edition *(continued)*

WINDOWS XP PROFESSIONAL NEW FEATURES	*AVAILABLE IN WINDOWS XP HOME EDITION*
Maintain control over personal information when visiting Web sites	Yes
Multi-lingual User Interface (MUI) add-on	No
Multi-processor support of up to two microprocessors	No
My Pictures and My Music folders let you organize and manipulate pictures and music	Yes
Network Setup Wizard	Yes
New user interface	Yes
Opened files grouped under one taskbar button making it easier to work with many files at the same time	Yes
Powerful management and security tools	No
Remote Desktop allows control of an office computer from home as though you are sitting in front of the office computer	No
Remote Installation Service	No
Restrict access to selected files, applications, and other resources	No
Scalable processor support	No
Scanner and Camera Wizard steps you through scanning images	Yes
Search Companion identifies the kind of help needed and retrieves relevant information	Yes
Simplifies procedures for administration of groups of users or computers	No
Single Worldwide Binary	Yes
Start menu organizes programs and frequently used tasks	Yes
System restore lets you restore computer to a previous version	Yes
Use of task panes containing commands and options in My Computer and My Documents windows	Yes
Welcome screen lets you share the same computer with others	Yes
Windows Media Player allows you to work with digital media files, watch DVD movies, and listen to radio stations	Yes
Windows Messenger lets you communicate with others	Yes

APPENDIX B

Windows XP Service Pack 2 Security Features

Periodically, Microsoft Corporation releases a free update to the Windows XP operating system. These updates, referred to as **service packs**, contain fixes and enhancements to the operating system. In August, 2004, Microsoft released Windows XP Service Pack 2 (SP2). **Windows XP Service Pack 2** contains advanced security features that protect a computer against viruses, worms, and hackers.

A **virus** is a computer program that attaches itself to another computer program or file so that it can spread from computer to computer, infecting programs and files as it spreads. Viruses can damage computer software, computer hardware, and files.

A **worm** copies itself from one computer to another using the features that transport files and information on the computer. A worm is dangerous because it has the ability to travel without supervision and replicate itself in great volume. For example, if a worm copies itself to every name in your e-mail address book and then the worm copies itself to the names of all the e-mail addresses of each of your friends' computers, the effect could result in increased Internet traffic that could slow down business networks and the Internet.

A **hacker** is an individual who uses his or her expertise to gain unauthorized access to a computer with the intention of learning more about the computer or examining the contents of the computer without the owner's permission.

The Windows Security Center

The **Windows Security Center** contains three security features: Windows Firewall, Automatic Updates, and Virus Protection. The Windows Security Center allows you to verify the status of the three security features and determines whether the security features are turned on and up to date. When a problem is detected, you receive notification of the problem and a list of steps to correct the problem. Table B-1 contains a list of the three security features and their descriptions.

Table B-1 Security Features and Descriptions

SECURITY FEATURE	*DESCRIPTION*
Windows Firewall	Windows Firewall monitors and restricts information coming from the Internet, prevents access without your permission, and protects against hackers.
Automatic Updates	Automatic Updates checks the Windows Update Web site for high-priority updates that can help protect a computer against attacks. High-priority updates include security updates, critical updates, and service packs.
Virus Protection	Installing and using antivirus software can protect a computer against virus attacks. When installed, Virus Protection reminds you to scan your computer for viruses. A list of antivirus software is available on the Microsoft Web site.

The following steps show how to display the Windows Security Center.

Steps To Display the Windows Security Center

1 Click the Start button on the Windows taskbar.

2 Click Control Panel on the Start menu.

3 If the Switch to Category View link is displayed in the Control Panel area, click the link to display the Category view in the Control Panel window.

The Control Panel window is displayed in Category view and the Switch to Classic View link is displayed in the Control Panel area (see Figure B-1). The Security Center icon is displayed in the right pane of the Control Panel window.

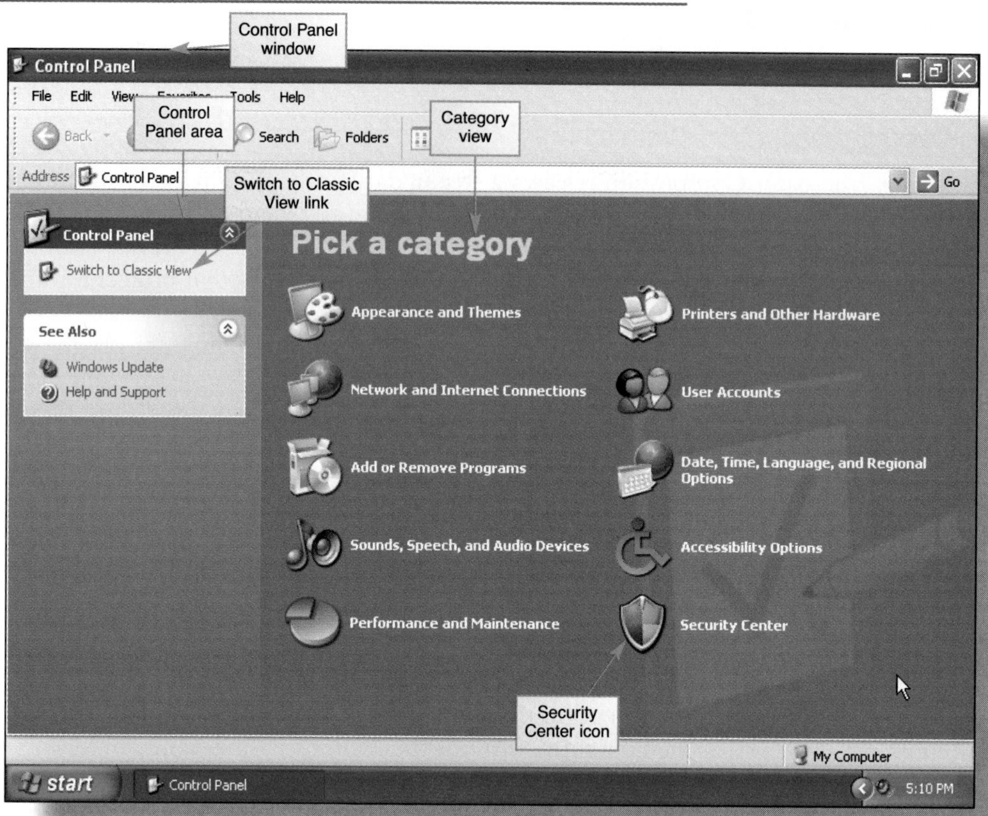

FIGURE B-1

4 Click the Security Center icon in the right pane of the Control Panel window.

5 If necessary, maximize the Windows Security Center window.

The maximized Windows Security Center window is displayed (see Figure B-2).

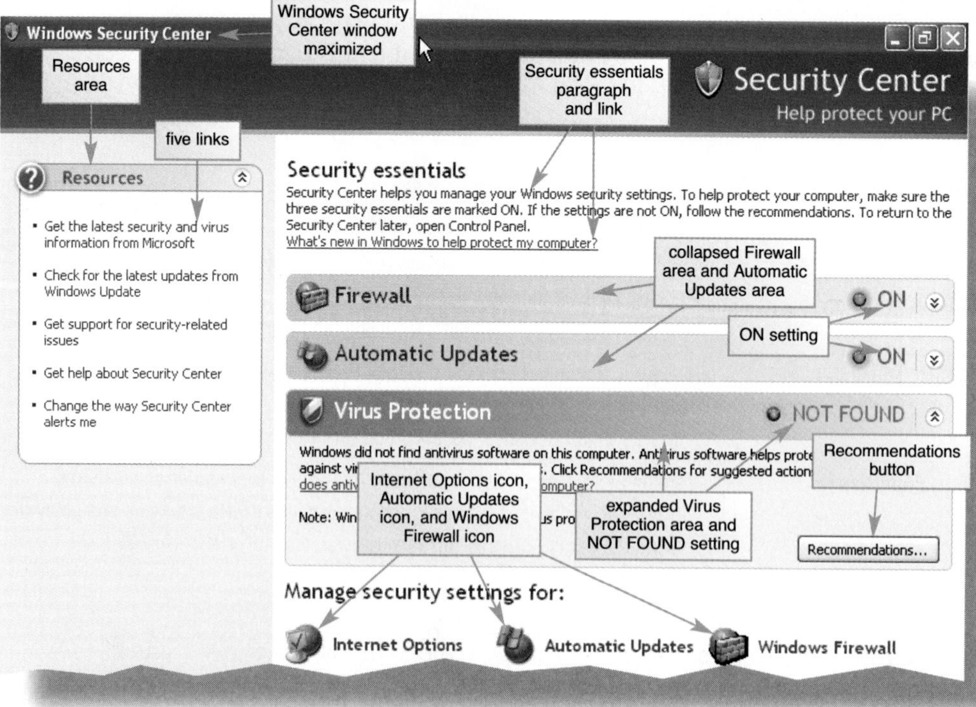

FIGURE B-2

The Resources area in the left pane of the Windows Security Center window contains five links that allow you to view the latest security and virus information from the Microsoft Security Home Page, check the latest updates from the Microsoft Windows Update Web page, get support for security-related issues from the Security Help and Support for Home Users Web site, get help about Security Center from the Help and Support Center, and change the way Security Center alerts you in the Alert Settings dialog box.

The right pane contains the Security essentials paragraph, What's new in Windows to help protect my computer? link, three panes, and the Manage security settings for area containing the Internet Options icon, Automatic Updates icon, and Windows Firewall icon.

Each of the three panes contains a title, security setting, and a double arrow. A **double down arrow** indicates that the area is collapsed, and a **double up arrow** indicates that the area is expanded. The Firewall and Automatic Updates areas are collapsed and display the ON security setting. The Virus Protection area is expanded and contains the NOT FOUND security setting and the Recommendations button. Table B-2 contains a complete list of the security settings and their descriptions.

Table B-2 Security Settings and Descriptions

SECURITY SETTING	*DESCRIPTION*
ON	Computer is protected.
NOT FOUND	Antivirus software is not installed.
NOT MONITORED	Antivirus software is installed and computer user monitors the software.
CHECK STATUS	Computer might be at risk because computer user is not monitoring the antivirus software.

Managing Windows Firewall

Windows Firewall is a software program that protects your computer against unauthorized users by monitoring and restricting information that travels between your computer and a network or the Internet. Windows Firewall also helps to block computer viruses and worms from infecting your computer. Windows Firewall is automatically turned on when Windows XP is launched. It is recommended that Windows Firewall remain on.

If someone on the Internet or on a network attempts to connect to your computer, Windows Firewall blocks the connection. For example, if you are playing a multi-player network game and another player asks to join the game, Windows Firewall displays a Windows Security Alert dialog box. The dialog box contains buttons that allow you to block or unblock the connection. If you recognize the player and choose to unblock the connection and allow the player to join the game, Windows Firewall adds an exception for the player. An **exception** is an adjustment made to the firewall settings so that the player can join the game now and in the future. To allow the new player to join the game, a program representing the player must be added to the Windows Firewall Exceptions list.

Adding a Program to the Windows Firewall Exceptions List

You can add a program to the Windows Firewall Exceptions list manually, without waiting for the program to communicate with you. Windows Firewall also may limit some programs that depend on low security settings. If you have trouble running a program with low security settings, add the program to the Exceptions list to solve the problem.

However, each time you add a program to the Exceptions list, the computer becomes easier to access and more vulnerable to attacks by hackers. The more programs you add, the more vulnerable is the firewall. To decrease the risk of security problems, only add programs that are necessary and recognizable, and promptly remove any program that is no longer required.

The following steps illustrate how to add the Hearts program to the Windows Firewall Exceptions list.

Steps To Add a Program to the Windows Firewall Exceptions List

1 Click the Windows Firewall icon in the Windows Security Center window.

The Windows Firewall dialog box, containing the General sheet, is displayed (see Figure B-3). The On (recommended) option button is selected to block all outside sources from connecting to the computer.

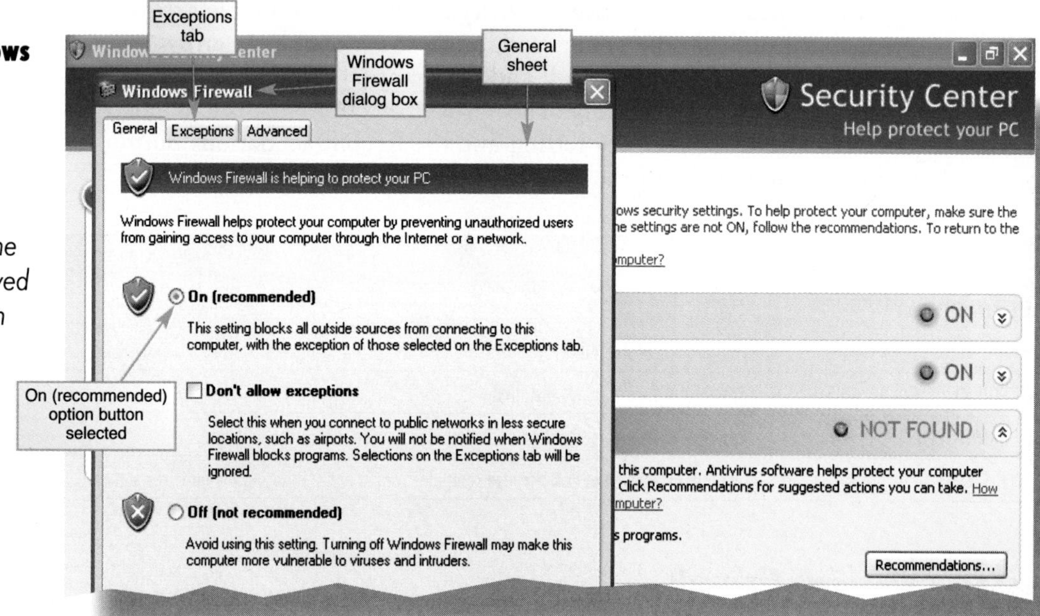

FIGURE B-3

2 Click the Exceptions tab.

The Exceptions sheet, containing the Programs and Services list box and Exceptions list, is displayed (see Figure B-4). A check mark in a check box precedes two programs (MSN Messenger 6.2 and Remote Assistance) in the Exceptions list. The Add Program button is displayed below the Exceptions list. The programs in the Exceptions list may be different on your computer.

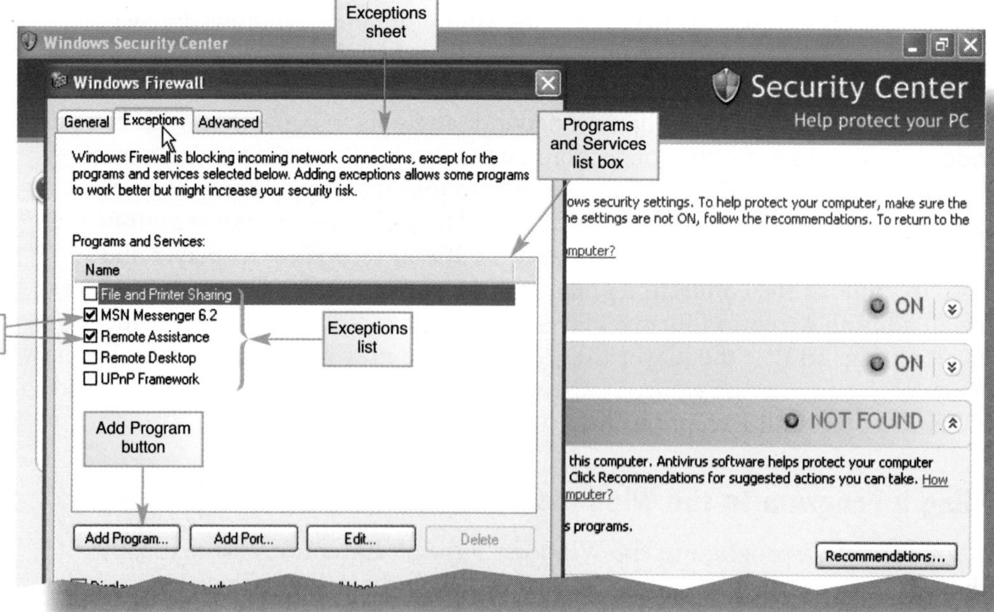

FIGURE B-4

3 Click the Add Program button. If necessary, scroll the Programs list box to view the Hearts icon.

The Add a Program dialog box, containing the Programs list box, is displayed (see Figure B-5). The first program in the list (Acrobat Reader 5.0) is selected, and the path of the selected program is displayed in the Path text box. The Hearts icon is displayed in the Programs list box. The list in the Programs list box may be different on your computer.

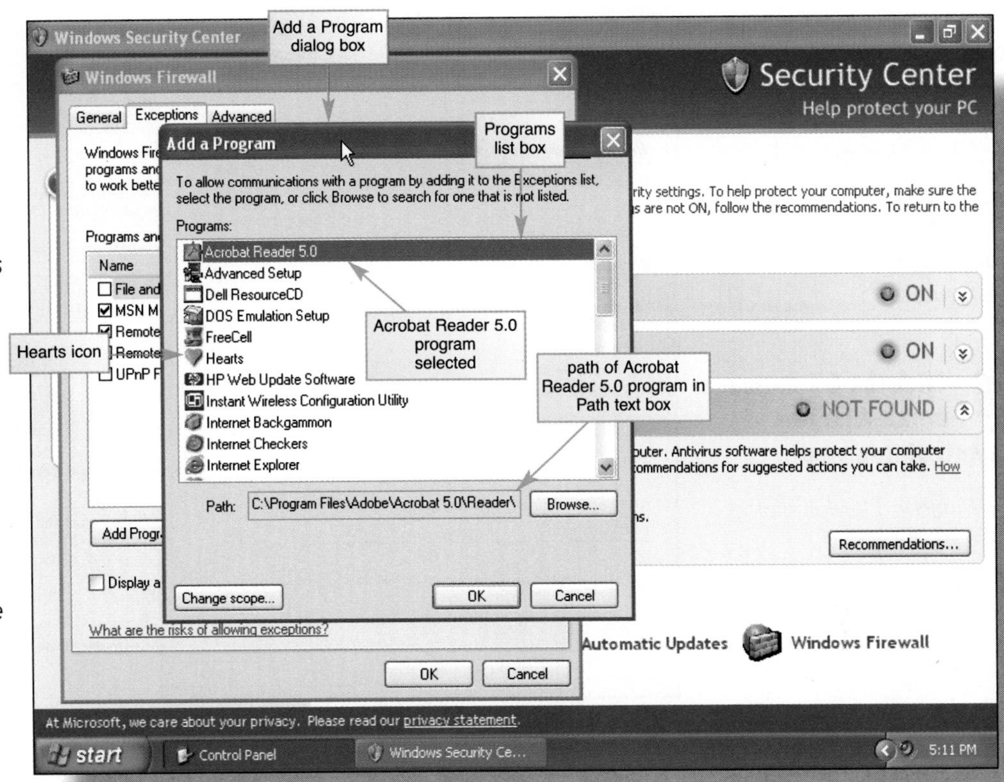

FIGURE B-5

4 Click the Hearts icon in the Programs list box.

The Hearts program is selected in the Programs list box (see Figure B-6). The path of the Hearts program is displayed in the Path text box. The Path text box may contain the WINDOWS entry instead of the WINNT entry on your computer.

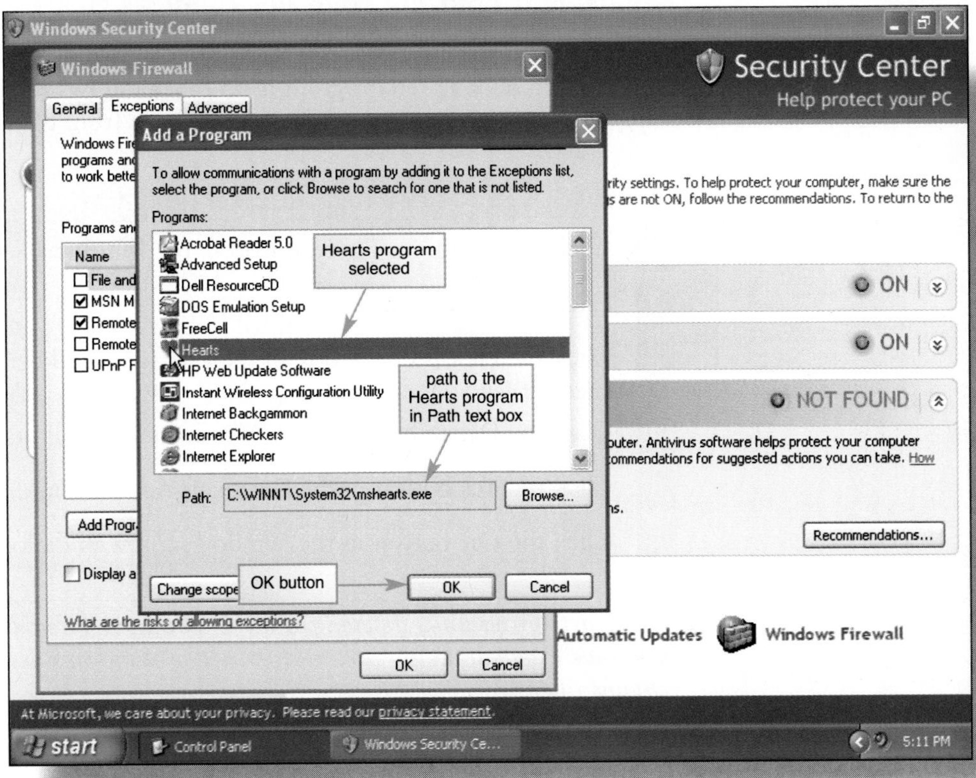

FIGURE B-6

5 Click the OK button in the Add a Program dialog box.

The Add a Program dialog box is closed, and a check mark is displayed in the Hearts check box (see Figure B-7).

6 Click the OK button in the Windows Firewall dialog box.

The Windows Firewall dialog box is closed.

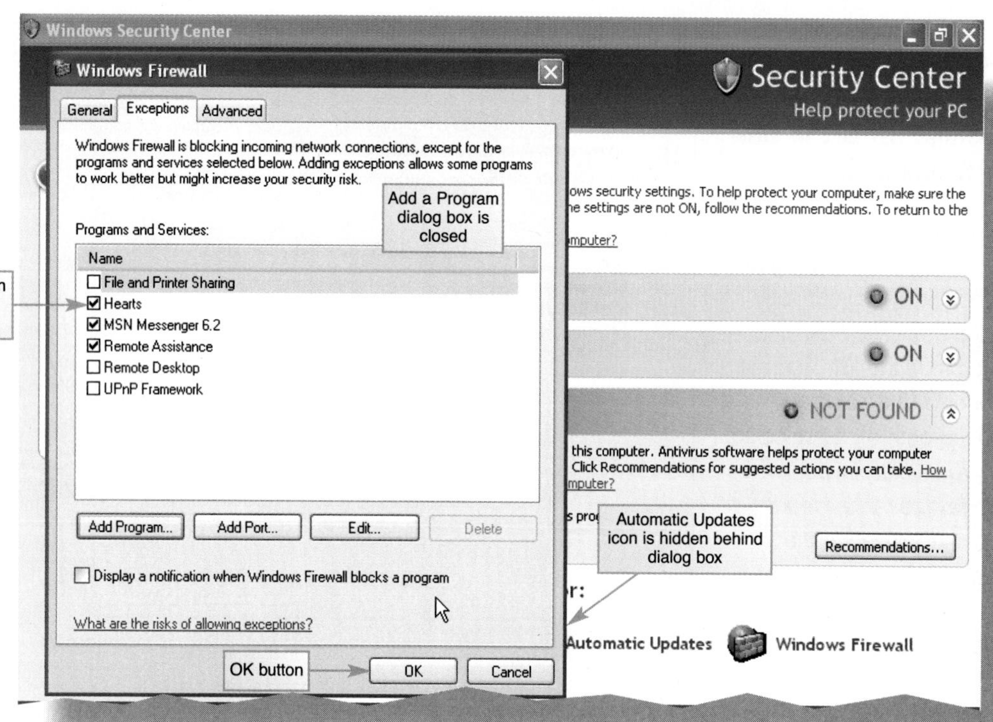

FIGURE B-7

Removing a Program from the Windows Firewall Exceptions List

After adding the Hearts program to the Windows Firewall Exceptions list, you may want to remove the program from the Windows Exceptions list. The following steps show how to remove the Hearts program from the Exceptions list.

TO REMOVE A PROGRAM FROM THE EXCEPTIONS LIST

1. Click the Windows Firewall icon in the Windows Security Center window.
2. Click the Exceptions tab.
3. Click the Hearts check box in the Programs and Services list box to remove the check mark.
4. Click the Delete button in the Windows Firewall dialog box.
5. Click the Yes button in the Delete an Application dialog box.
6. Click the OK button in the Windows Firewall dialog box.

The Hearts program is deleted from the Windows Firewall Exceptions list, and the Windows Firewall dialog box is closed. The Windows Security Center window remains open.

Automatic Updates

Automatic Updates helps to protect your computer from viruses, worms, and other security risks. When Automatic Updates is turned on and the computer is connected to the Internet, Windows XP periodically checks with the Microsoft Update

Web site to find updates and service packs, and then automatically downloads the updates and service packs. If the Internet connection is lost while downloading an update or service pack, Windows XP resumes downloading when the Internet connection is available.

The followings steps illustrate how to set an automatic update for a day (Friday) and time (6:00 AM).

Steps To Set an Automatic Update

1 Click the Automatic Updates icon in the Windows Security Center window. If necessary, click the Automatic (recommended) option button.

The Automatic Updates dialog box, containing the Automatic Updates sheet, is displayed (see Figure B-8). The dialog box contains a message and link, and four option buttons. The Automatic (recommended) option button is selected, and the day box and time box are displayed. The default day setting is Every day and the default time setting is 3:00 AM.

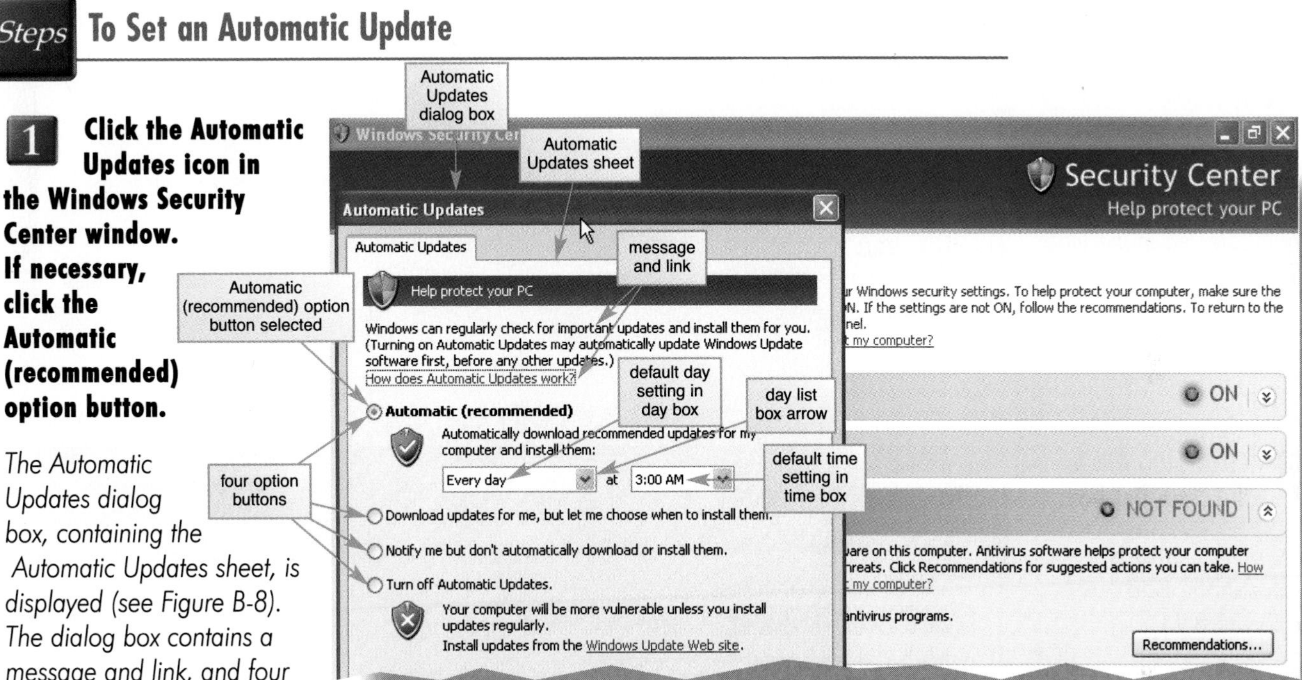

FIGURE B-8

2 Click the day list box arrow. Point to Every Friday in the day list box.

The day list box, containing the highlighted Every Friday entry, is displayed (see Figure B-9).

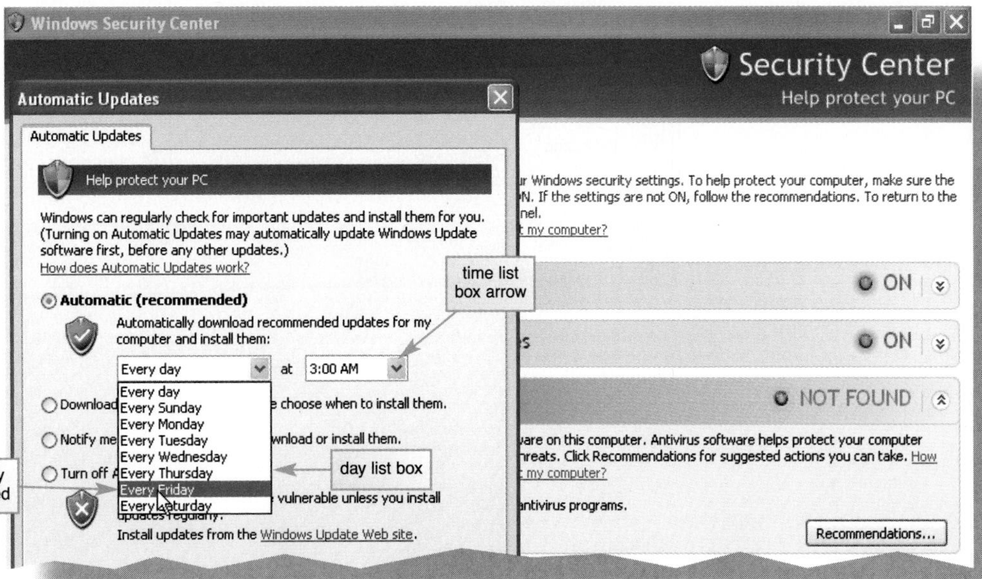

FIGURE B-9

3 **Click Every Friday in the day list box.**

4 **Click the time box arrow.**

5 **Point to 6:00 AM in the time list box.**

The Every Friday entry is displayed in the day box (see Figure B-10). The 6:00 AM entry is selected in the time list box.

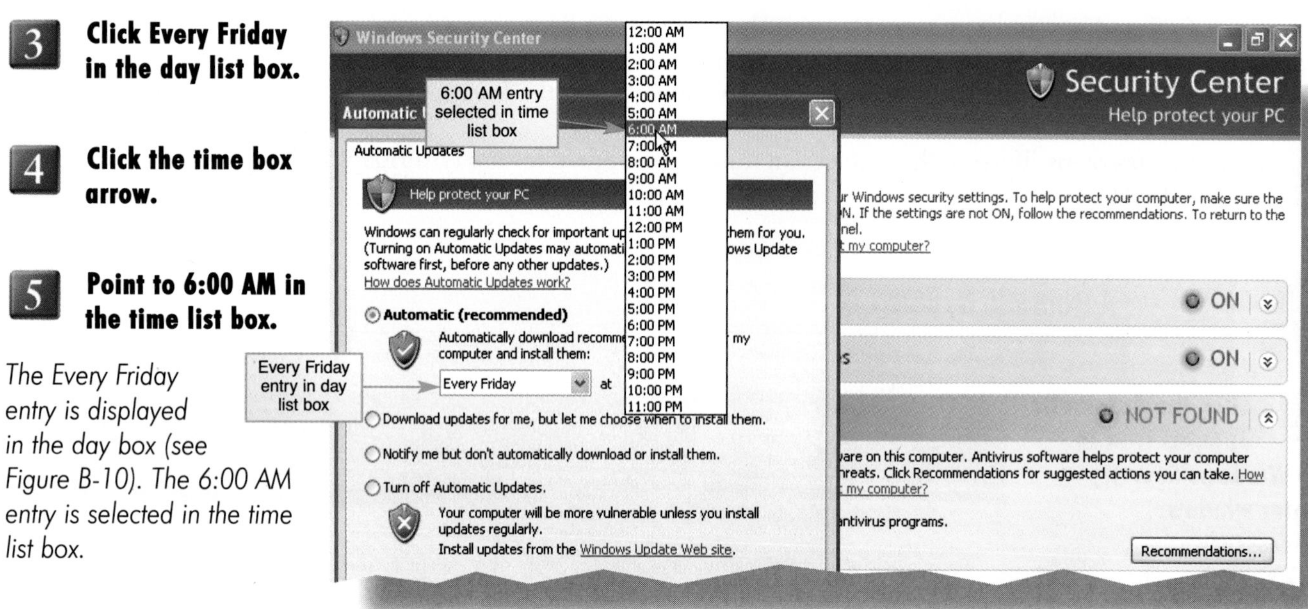

FIGURE B-10

6 **Click 6:00 AM in the time list box.**

The 6:00 AM entry is selected in the time box (see Figure B-11).

7 **Click the OK button in the Automatic Updates dialog box.**

The Automatic Updates dialog box is closed and the day (Every Friday) and time (6:00 AM) are set.

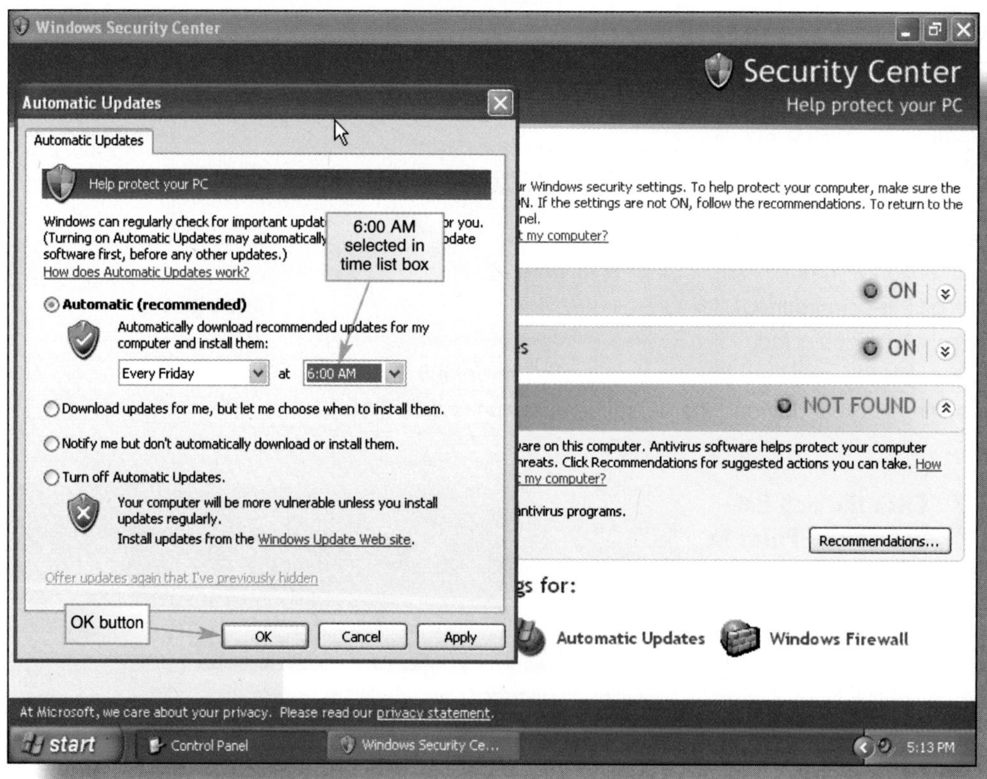

FIGURE B-11

After setting the day and time for every Friday at 6:00 AM, Windows XP checks with the Microsoft Updates Web site to find updates and service packs, and then automatically downloads any available updates and service packs.

Removing an Automatic Update

After setting an automatic update, you may want to remove the automatic update. The following steps illustrate how to remove the automatic update for Every Friday at 6:00 AM.

TO REMOVE AN AUTOMATIC UPDATE

1. Click the Automatic Updates icon in the Windows Security Center window.
2. Click the day box arrow, and then click Every day in the Day list box.
3. Click the Time box arrow, and then click 3:00 AM in the time list box.
4. Click the OK button in the Automatic Updates dialog box.

The Automatic Updates dialog box is closed, and the default day (Every day) and time (3:00 AM) are set.

Protecting Against Computer Viruses

Most computer magazines, daily newspapers, and even the nightly news channels warn us of computer virus threats. Although these threats sound alarming, a little common sense and a good antivirus program can ward off even the most malicious viruses.

A computer can be protected against viruses by following these suggestions. First, educate yourself about viruses and how they are spread. Downloading a program from the Internet, accessing an online bulletin board, or receiving an e-mail message may cause a virus to infect your computer. Second, learn the common signs of a virus. Observe any unusual messages that appear on the computer screen, monitor system performance, and watch for missing files and inaccessible hard drives. Third, programs on floppy disks may contain viruses. Scan all floppy disks before copying or opening a file on them.

Finally, Windows XP does not include an antivirus program. So, purchase and install the latest version of an antivirus program and use it regularly to check for computer viruses. Many antivirus programs run automatically and display a dialog box on the screen when a problem exists. In Figure B-12, the Norton AntiVirus dialog box contains an alert to indicate that you may not be protected against newly discovered viruses. Clicking the OK button in the dialog box initiates the process of updating the virus protection. If you do not have an antivirus program installed on your computer, use the Security Center to find an antivirus program.

In the following steps, the step to purchase and install the antivirus software is shown, but no antivirus software will be downloaded because of the complexity of purchasing and installing the antivirus software. The steps assume that the antivirus software has already been purchased and installed.

The following steps illustrate how to search for antivirus software.

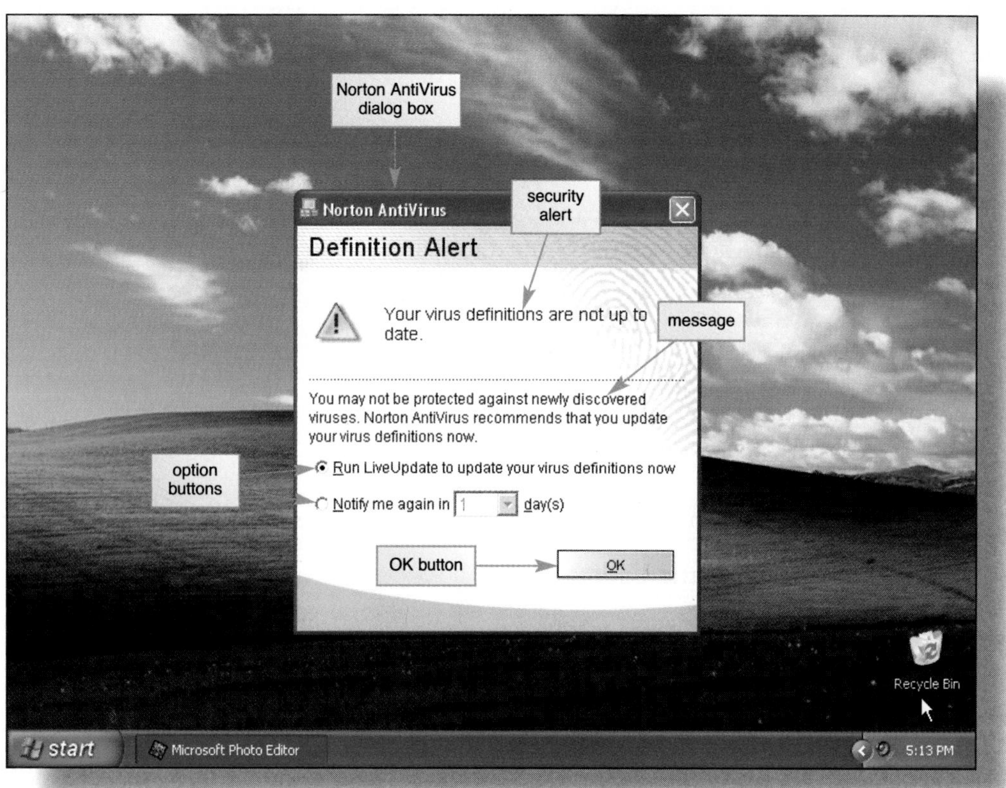

FIGURE B-12

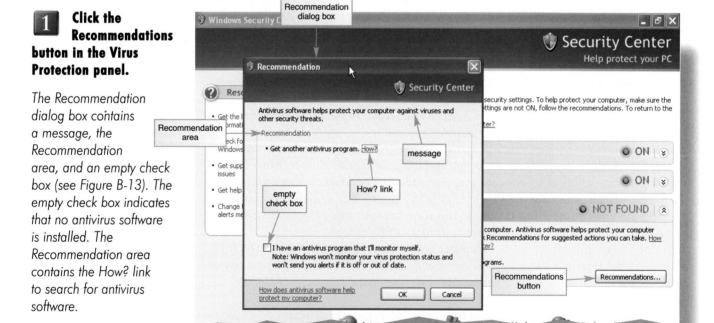

Steps To Search For Antivirus Software

1 Click the Recommendations button in the Virus Protection panel.

The Recommendation dialog box contains a message, the Recommendation area, and an empty check box (see Figure B-13). The empty check box indicates that no antivirus software is installed. The Recommendation area contains the How? link to search for antivirus software.

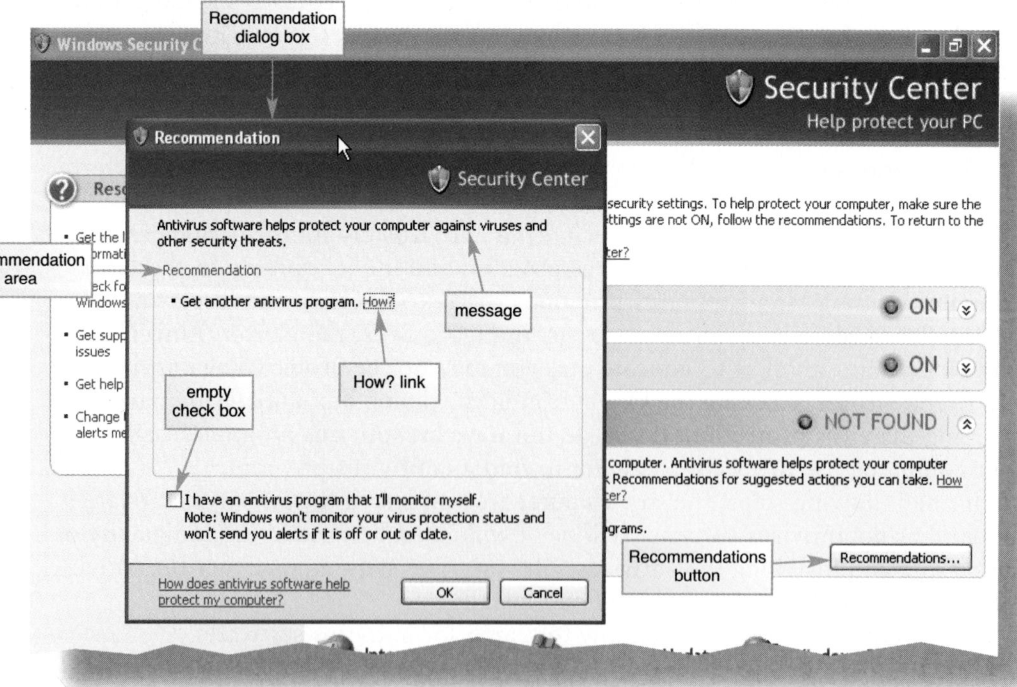

FIGURE B-13

2 Click the How? link in the Recommendation area.

3 If necessary, maximize the Microsoft Windows Security Center Antivirus Partners window.

The Microsoft Windows XP Web site is displayed in the maximized Microsoft Windows Security Center Antivirus Partners window (see Figure B-14). The Computer Associates icon is displayed in the display area. Clicking the icon initiates the process of purchasing and installing the Computer Associates antivirus software.

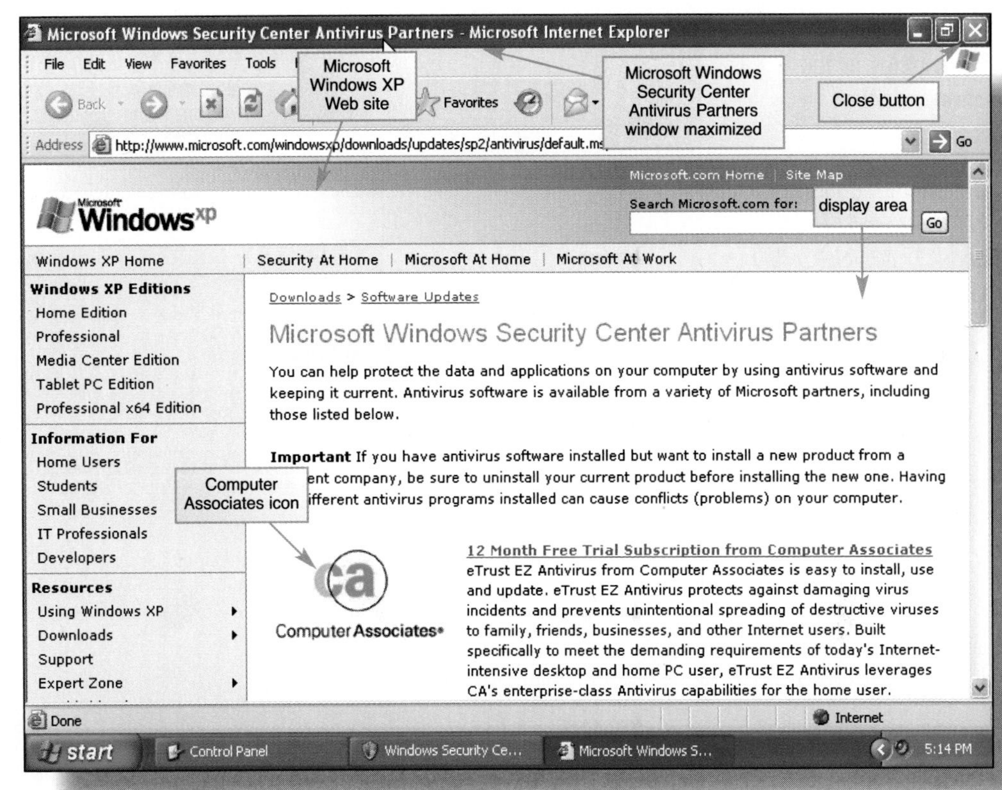

FIGURE B-14

4 Assume that the Computer Associates antivirus software is purchased and installed.

5 Click the Close button in the Microsoft Windows Security Center Antivirus Partners window.

6 Click the I have an antivirus program that I'll monitor myself check box in the Recommendation dialog box.

The Microsoft Windows Security Center Antivirus Partners window is closed, and a check mark is displayed in the I have an antivirus program that I'll monitor myself check box (see Figure B-15).

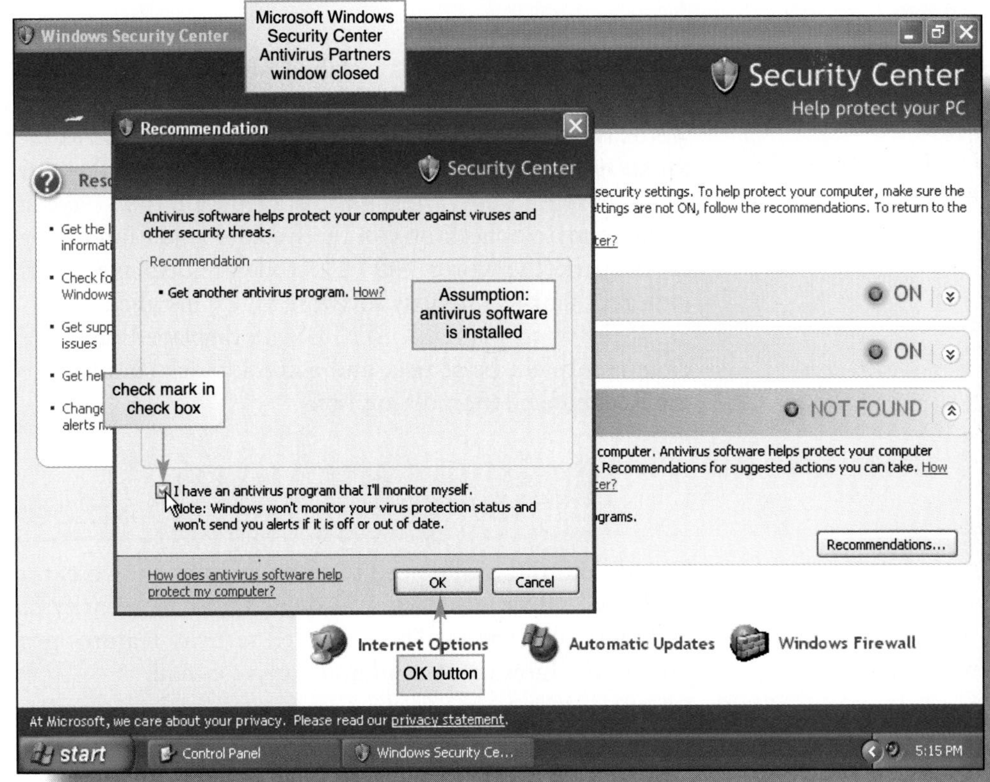

FIGURE B-15

7 Click the OK button in the Recommendation dialog box.

The Recommendation dialog box is closed. The words NOT MONITORED are displayed on the Virus Protection pane (see Figure B-16).

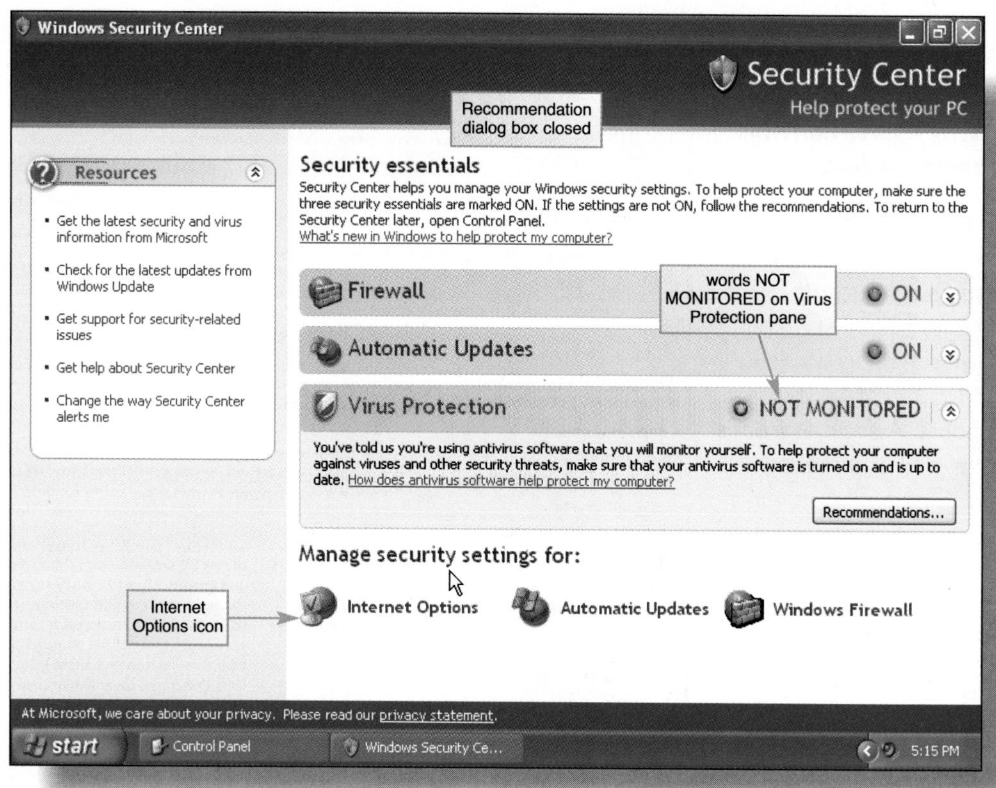

FIGURE B-16

If antivirus software is installed, and the I have an antivirus program that I'll monitor myself check box in the Recommendation dialog box contains a check mark, the words NOT MONITORED are displayed on the Virus Protection pane to indicate that the software is installed and that you will monitor the antivirus software yourself.

If antivirus software is not installed, and the I have an antivirus program that I'll monitor myself check box in the Recommendation dialog box does not contain a check mark, the words NOT FOUND are displayed on the Virus Protection pane to indicate that the antivirus software is not installed.

If the words CHECK STATUS are displayed on the Virus Protection pane, the computer might be at risk, and a check mark should be placed in the check box in the Recommendation dialog box.

Security Settings in Internet Explorer

In addition to the enhanced security features shown earlier in this appendix, Windows XP Service Pack 2 also enhances the security features in Internet Explorer and Outlook Express. The enhanced security features protect the computer while you browse the Internet or send and receive e-mail.

Internet Explorer Security Settings

The new Internet Explorer security settings protect the computer, the computer's contents, and the computer's privacy by preventing viruses and other security threats from the Internet.

One security improvement is Pop-up Blocker. **Pop-up Blocker** prevents annoying **pop-up ads** that advertise a product or service while you view a Web page. Pop-up ads can be difficult to close, often interrupt what you are doing, and can download **spyware software**, which secretly gathers information about you and your computer, and sends the information to advertisers and other individuals.

By default, Pop-up Blocker is turned on by Internet Explorer and set to a Medium setting, which blocks most pop-up ads. The setting can be adjusted to suit your needs. Pop-up Blocker also plays a sound and displays an **information bar** when a pop-up ad is blocked. The following steps illustrate how to view the pop-up ad settings in Internet Explorer.

To View Pop-Up Settings in Internet Explorer

1 Click the Internet Options icon in the Windows Security Center window.

The Internet Properties dialog box, containing the Security sheet, is displayed (see Figure B-17). The Security sheet contains a list box for the four Web content zones, highlighted Internet zone, summary of the Internet zone, and security level of Internet zone in the Security level for this zone area.

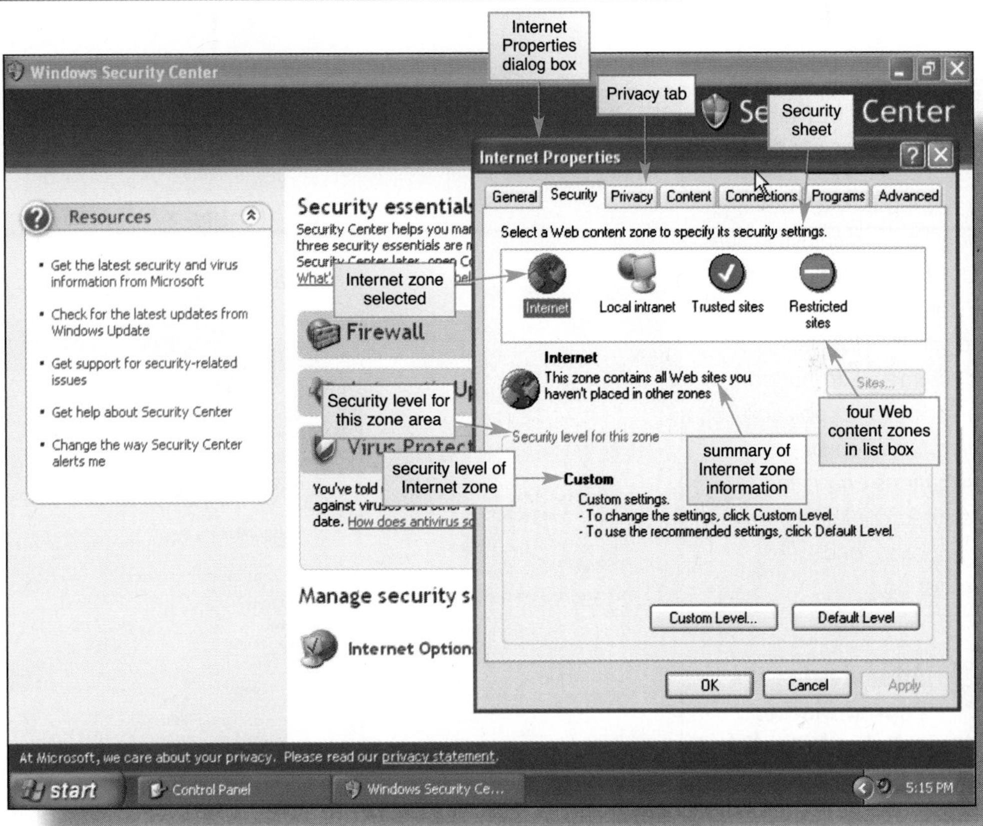

FIGURE B-17

2 **Click the Privacy tab in the Internet Properties dialog box.**

The Privacy sheet, containing the Settings area and Pop-up Blocker area, is displayed (see Figure B-18). The Settings area contains the Settings slide and slider. The default privacy setting is Medium. The Block pop-ups check box and Settings button are displayed in the Pop-up Blocker area. A check mark is displayed in the Block pop-ups check box.

3 **Click the Settings button in the Pop-up Blocker area.**

The Pop-up Blocker Settings dialog box is displayed (see Figure B-19). The dialog box contains the Address of Web site to allow text box and dimmed Add button, Allowed sites list box containing two Web sites, Notifications and Filter Level area containing two check boxes, and Filter Level list box.

4 **After viewing the Pop-up Blocker Settings dialog box, click the Close button in the Pop-up Blocker Settings dialog box.**

5 **Click the OK button in the Internet Properties dialog box.**

The Pop-up Blocker Settings dialog box and Internet Properties dialog box are closed.

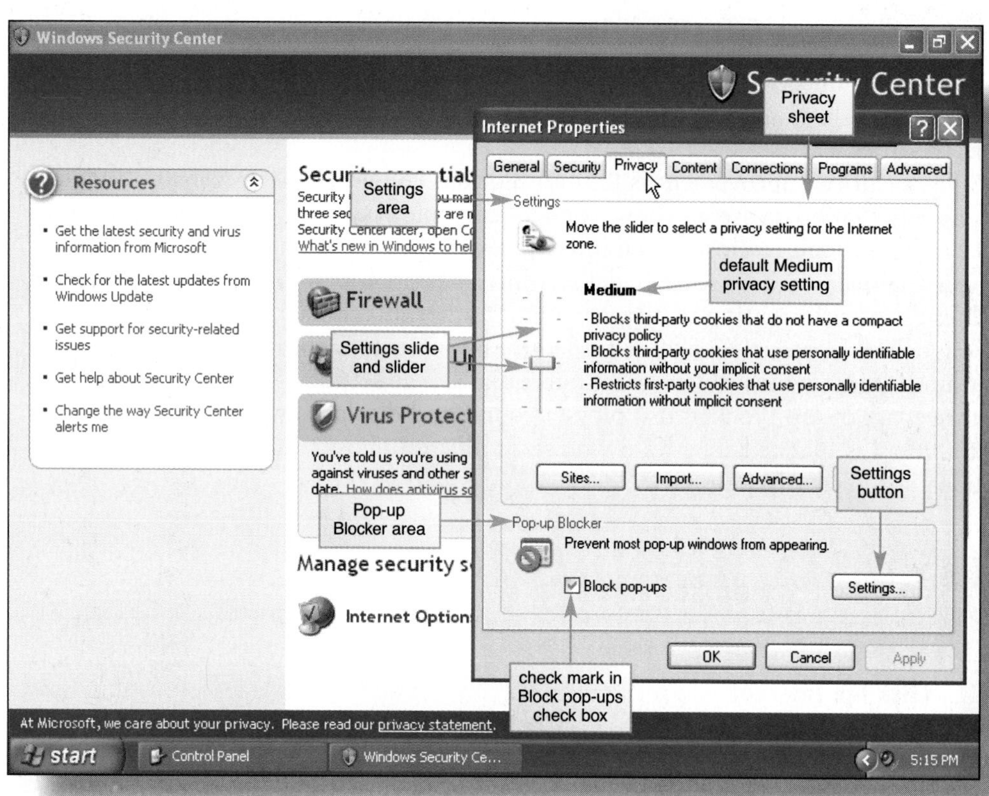

FIGURE B-18

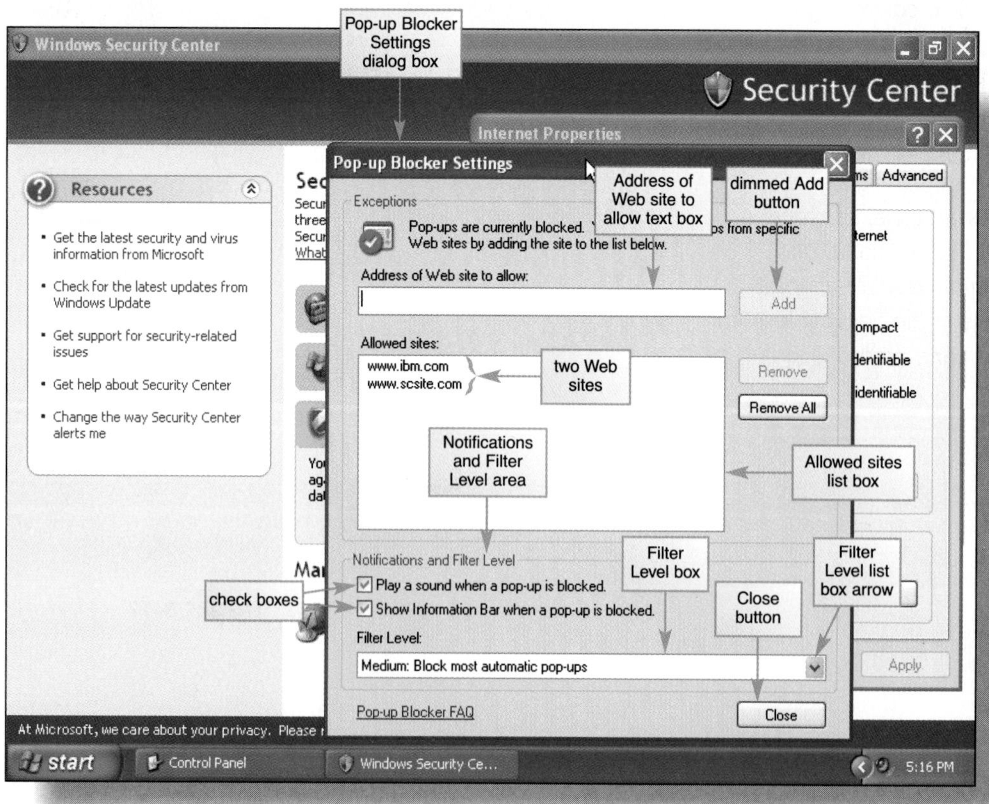

FIGURE B-19

In Figure B-18, the Settings area contains the Settings slide and slider. The position of the slider indicates that the privacy setting is set to Medium, which is the default privacy setting for the Internet zone. Sliding the Settings slider along the Settings slide changes the privacy setting for the Internet zone.

In Figure B-19, if you want to allow certain Web sites to display pop-up ads when you visit the site, type the Web site address in the Address of Web site to allow text box, and then click the Add button. Internet Explorer adds the Web site to the Allowed sites list. If you want to block all pop-ups, click the Filter Level list box arrow, and then click High: Block all pop-ups (Ctrl to override) in the Filter Level list box. If you want to allow more pop-up ads, click the Filter Level box arrow, and then click Low: Allow pop-ups from secure sites in the Filter Level list box.

Internet Explorer Add-Ons

Internet Explorer **add-ons** add functionality to Internet Explorer by allowing different toolbars, animated mouse pointers, and stock tickers. Although some add-ons are included with Windows XP, thousands are available from Web sites on the Internet. Most Web site add-ons require permission from a Web site before downloading the add-on, others are downloaded without your knowledge, and some add-ons do not need permission at all.

Add-ons are usually safe to use, but some may slow down your computer or shut down Internet Explorer unexpectedly. This usually happens when an add-on was poorly built or created for an earlier version of Internet Explorer. In some cases, spyware is included with an add-on and may track your Web surfing habits. **Internet Explorer Add-on Manager**, included with Windows XP Service Pack 2, can make add-ons function properly and get rid of the add-ons that do not function properly.

Steps To View Internet Explorer Add-On Settings

1 Click the Internet Options icon in the Windows Security Center window.

2 Click the Programs tab in the Internet Properties dialog box.

The Internet Properties dialog box, containing the Programs sheet, is displayed (see Figure B-20). The Programs sheet contains the Manage Add-ons button to allow you to enable or disable an add-on.

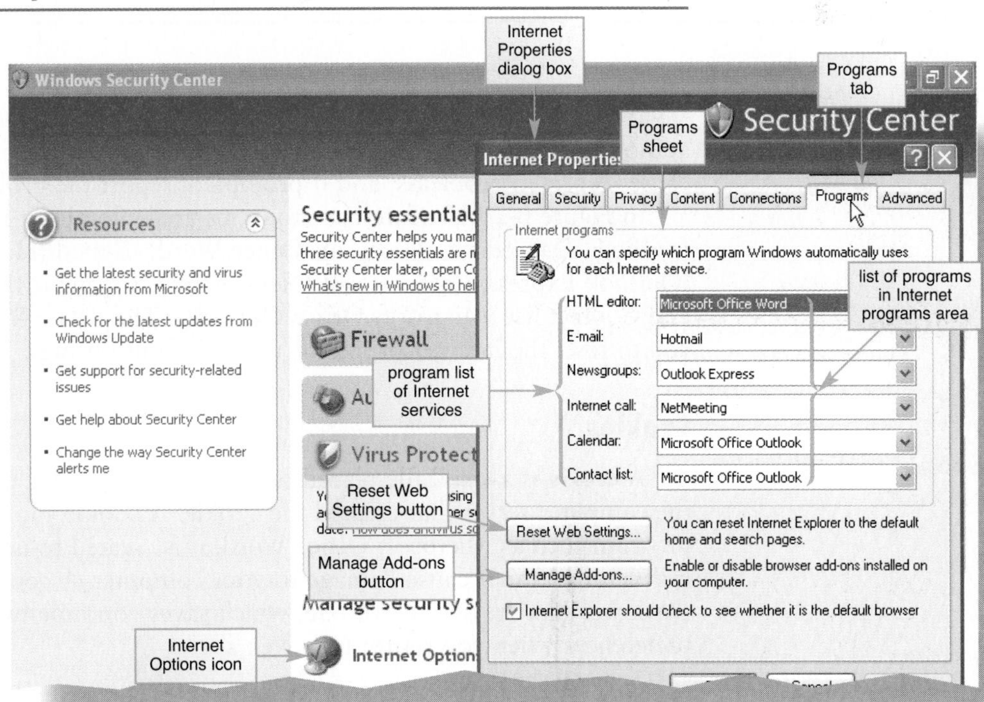

FIGURE B-20

3 Click the Manage Add-ons button in the Programs sheet to view a list of add-ons.

The Manage Add-ons dialog box is displayed (see Figure B-21). The phrase Add-ons that have been used by Internet Explorer is displayed in the Show box, and a list of add-ons is displayed in the Show list.

4 When finished viewing the add-ons, click the OK button in the Manage Add-ons dialog box.

5 Click the OK button in the Internet Properties dialog box.

The Manage Add-ons dialog box and Internet Properties dialog box are closed.

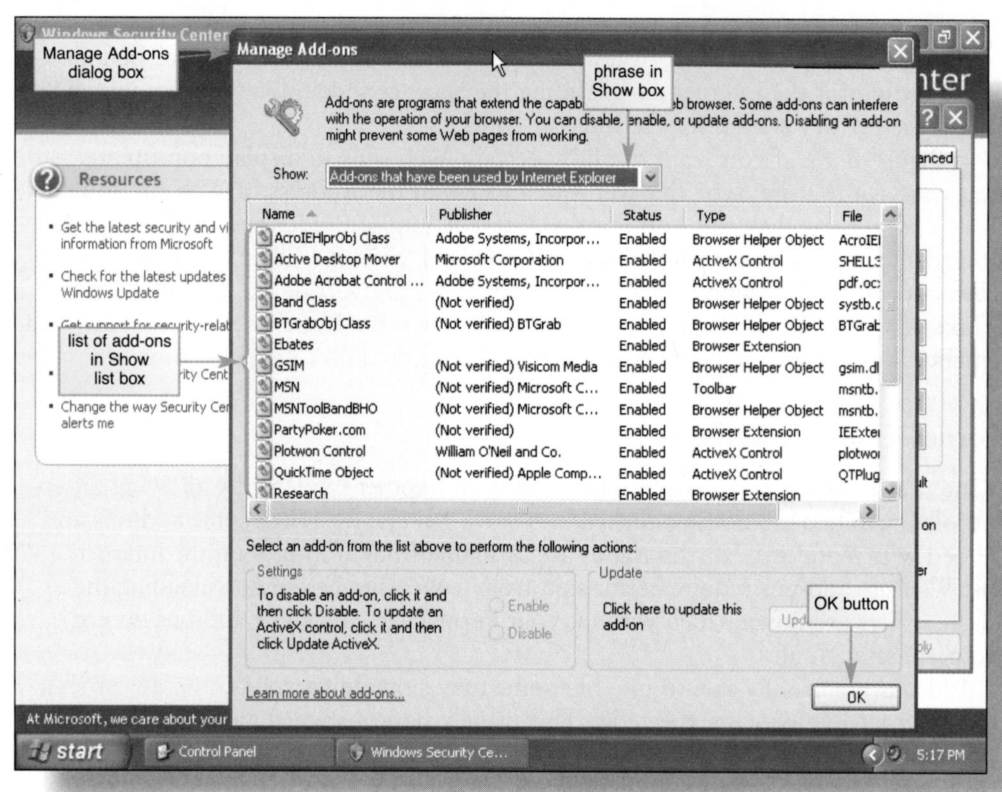

FIGURE B-21

If an add-on causes Internet Explorer to shut down unexpectedly, update the add-on if the add-on is an ActiveX component, disable the add-on if the add-on causes repeated problems, and if prompted, report the problem to Microsoft.

In Figure B-20, the Internet programs area contains a list of the programs used for the HTML editor (Microsoft Office Word), E-mail (Hotmail), Newsgroups (Outlook Express), Internet call (NetMeeting), Calendar (Microsoft Office Outlook), and Contact list (Microsoft Office Outlook). The Reset Web Settings button allows you to reset the Internet programs to the default settings.

Cookies

A **cookie** is a small file placed on the hard drive by a Web site to identify you to the computer server that created the cookie. A cookie cannot be executed like a program such as Microsoft Office Word, it is created to uniquely identify you, and it generally cannot cause damage to your computer. A cookie only can be read by the server that created the cookie, which saves you time by already knowing your preferences when you return to a Web site.

Although cookies can store **personally identifiable information**, which is information that can be used to identify or contact you (name, e-mail address, telephone number, and so on), a Web site only has access to the information you provide. However, a cookie could pose a security risk if a hacker searches for and finds a cookie that contains information such as your passwords.

The Windows Security Center window specifies privacy settings that allow or prevent Web sites from saving cookies on your computer. The following steps illustrate how to view privacy settings for cookies.

Steps To View Privacy Settings for Cookies

1. **Click Internet Options in the Windows Security Center window.**

2. **Click the Privacy tab in the Internet Properties dialog box.**

The Internet Properties dialog box, containing the Privacy sheet, is displayed (see Figure B-22). The Settings area contains the default privacy setting (Medium) and the Settings slide and slider. The settings include Accept All Cookies, Low, Medium, Medium High, High, and Block All Cookies. The privacy setting on your computer may be different.

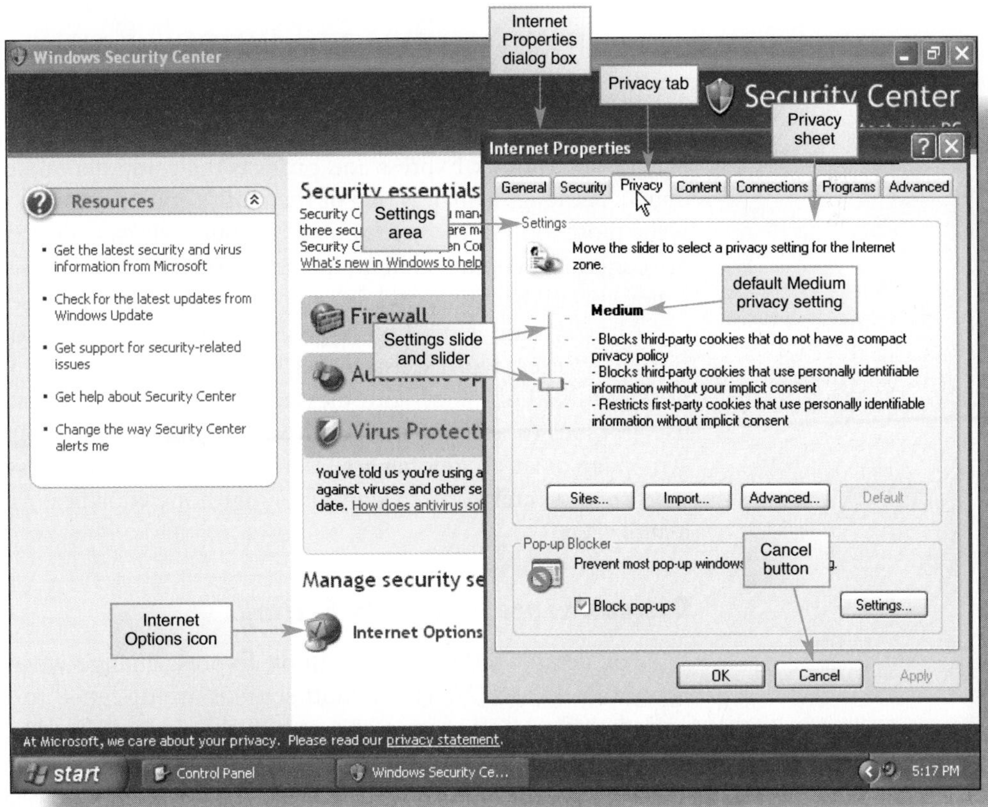

FIGURE B-22

3. **Experiment by dragging the slider up for a higher level of security and down for a lower level of security.**

4. **When finished, click the Cancel button in the Internet Properties dialog box.**

5 **Click the Close button in the Windows Security Center window.**

6 **Click the Close button in the Control Panel window.**

The Internet Properties dialog box, Windows Security Center window, and Control Panel window are closed.

Security Settings in Outlook Express

Windows XP Service Pack 2 also enhances the security features in Outlook Express. **Outlook Express** is the e-mail program included with Windows XP. The enhanced security extends to Outlook Express and protects the computer while you send and receive e-mail. Although e-mail is one of the most popular activities on the Internet, e-mail also is the most common way to spread computer viruses. Viruses and other security threats are commonly contained in attachments to an e-mail. E-mail attachments with the extensions of .bat, .exe, and .js can contain dangerous viruses and worms.

Although any e-mail message can carry a virus, Outlook Express has settings to prevent viruses, worms, and other security risks. For example, Outlook Express does not download graphics with messages sent in HTML format because spammers often use graphics to access e-mail addresses. **HTML** is a programming language used for Web page creation. **Spammers** take advantage of weaknesses in your computer to send **spam e-mail** to other computers without your permission, a practice known as **e-mail relay**.

Outlook Express Security Settings

The default settings for Outlook Express change when you install Windows XP Service Pack 2 (SP2). The default settings are designed to protect your computer against viruses and worms and reduce the amount of spam e-mail you receive. In addition, the new settings allow less offensive content in an e-mail, reduce the amount of junk mail, and lessen the risk of receiving dangerous content from an e-mail. Microsoft recommends maintaining the new default settings to help protect your computer and personal information.

The following steps illustrate how to view the Outlook Express settings.

To View Security Settings in Outlook Express

1 Click the Start button on the Windows taskbar.

2 Point to Outlook Express in the pinned items list on the Start menu.

The Start menu is displayed, and the Outlook Express command on the pinned items list is selected (see Figure B-23).

3 Click Outlook Express on the Start menu.

FIGURE B-23

4 Click Tools on the menu bar. Point to Options on the Tools menu.

The Tools menu is displayed, and the Options command is selected on the Tools menu (see Figure B-24).

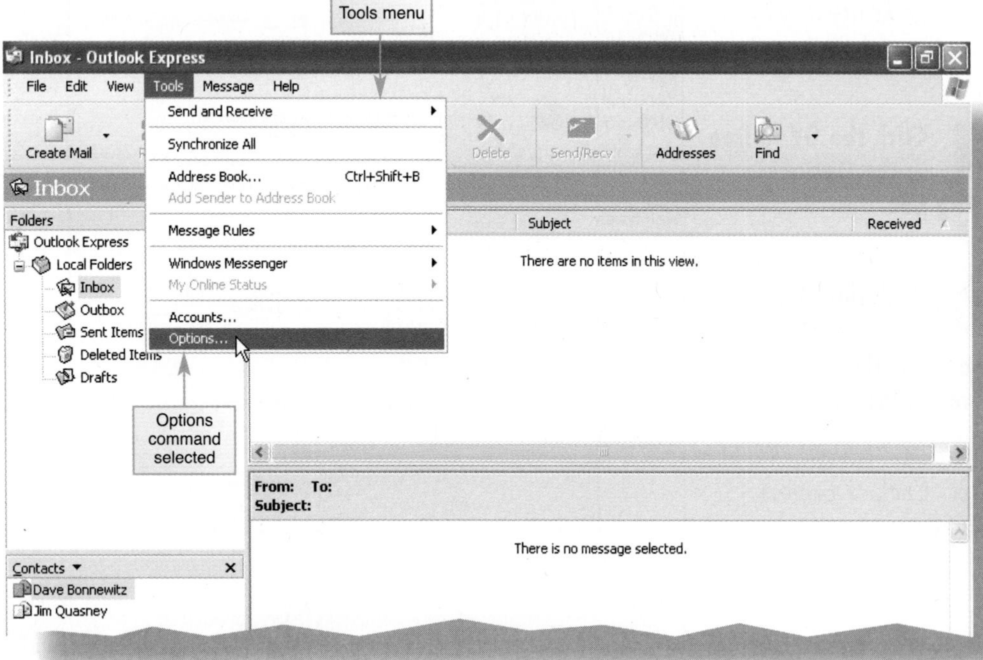

FIGURE B-24

5 **Click Options on the Tools menu.**

The Options dialog box, containing the Security tab and General sheet, is displayed (see Figure B-25).

6 **Click the Security tab in the Options dialog box.**

7 **Verify that check marks are displayed in the Warn me when other applications try to send mail as me check box, Do not allow attachments to be saved or opened that could potentially be a virus check box, and Block images and other external content in HTML e-mail check box.**

The Security sheet is displayed (see Figure B-26). Check marks are displayed in the three check boxes.

8 **Click the OK button in the Options dialog box.**

9 **Click the Close button in the Inbox – Outlook Express window.**

The Option dialog box and Inbox - Outlook Express window are closed.

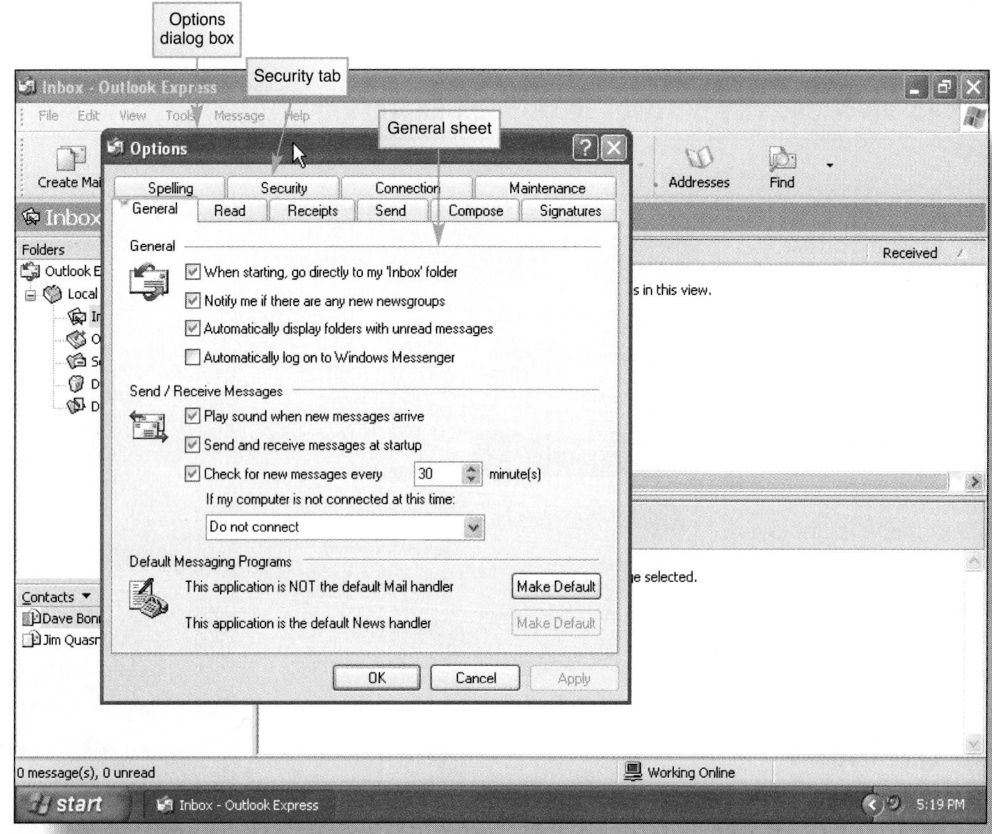

FIGURE B-25

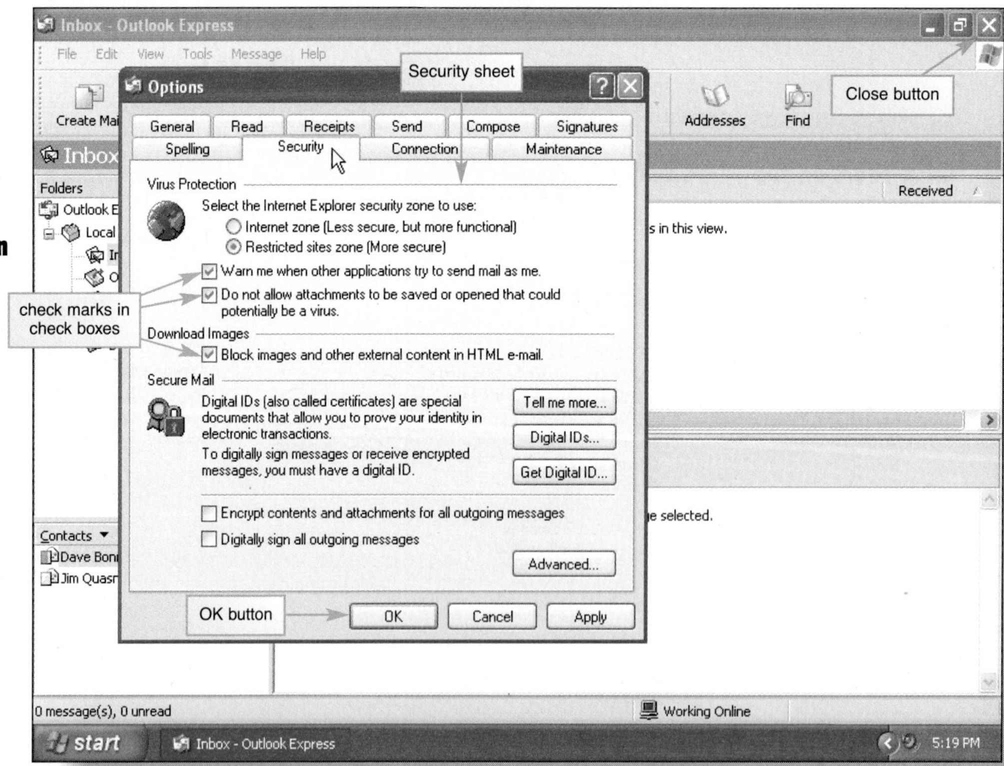

FIGURE B-26

Index

A few of the exercises in this book require that you begin by opening a data file from a Data Disk. Choose one of the following to obtain a copy of the Data Disk.

Instructors

- A copy of the Data Disk is on the Instructor Resources CD-ROM below the category Data Files for Students, which you can copy to your school's network for student use.
- Download the Data Disk via the World Wide Web by following the instructions below.
- Contact us via e-mail at reply@course.com.
- Call Course Technology's Customer Service department for fast and efficient delivery of the Data Disk.

Students

- Check with your instructor to determine the best way to obtain a copy of the Data Disk.
- Download the Data Disk via the World Wide Web by following the instructions below.

Instructions for Downloading the Data Disk from the World Wide Web

1. Insert your removable media (USB flash drive, floppy disk, or Zip disk) into your computer.
2. Start your browser. Enter the URL scsite.com in the Address box.
3. When the scsite.com Web page displays, scroll down to the Browse by Subject area and click the category to which your book belongs (for example, Office Suites).
4. When the category list expands, click the title of your textbook (for example, Microsoft Office 2003: Introductory Concepts and Techniques).
5. When the Textbook page displays, scroll down to the Data Files for Students area and click the appropriate link.
6. If Windows displays a File Download - Security Warning dialog box, click the Run button. If Windows displays an Internet Explorer - Security Warning dialog box, click the Run button.
7. When Windows displays the WinZip Self-Extractor dialog box, type in the Unzip to folder box the portable storage media drive letter followed a colon, backslash, and a sub-folder name of your choice (for example, f:/Office 2003).
8. Click the Unzip button.
9. When Windows displays the WinZip Self-Extractor dialog box, click the OK button.
10. Click the Close button on the right side of the title bar in the WinZip Self-Extractor dialog box.
11. Start Windows Explorer and display the contents of the folder to which you unzipped the Data Disk files in Step 7 to view the results.

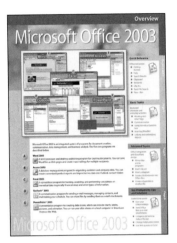